D1300174

GOD'S WORD FOR GIRLS

Larry Richards

General Editor

Illustrations by Craig Phillips

BakerBooks

a division of Baker Publishing Group
Grand Rapids, Michigan

A portion of the purchase price of your new Bible has been provided to God's
Word to the Nations. This mission society is being used by the Holy Spirit to promote and support a movement among God's people to be active participants
in his mission "to seek and to save people who are lost" (Luke 19:10).

GOD'S WORD for Girls
© 1996 by Baker Publishing Group
Illustrations © 2009 by Craig Phillips

GOD'S WORD®
© 1995 by God's Word to the Nations

Published 2008 by Baker Books
A division of Baker Publishing Group
P.O. Box 6287, Grand Rapids, MI 49516-6287

Printed in China

All rights reserved. No part of this publication may be reproduced, stored in a retrieval system, or trans-
mitted in any form or by any means—for example, electronic, photocopy, recording—without prior
written permission of the publisher. The only exception is brief quotations in printed reviews.

Up to 500 Scripture verses may be quoted in any form (printed, written, visual, electronic, or audio)
without written permission, provided that no more than half of any one book of the Bible is quoted, and
the verses quoted do not amount to 25 percent of the text of the product in which they are quoted.

If the quotation is used in a product that is not for sale, the designation (GOD'S WORD®) must always
appear following each quotation.

If the quotation is used in a product that is for sale, the following notice must be used: "Scripture is taken
from GOD'S WORD®. Copyright 1995 by God's Word to the Nations. Used by permission."

For quotations over 500 verses and/or questions about these policies, please write to Baker Publishing
Group, P.O. Box 6287, Grand Rapids, Michigan, 49516. You may also contact them through their web
site: www.bakerpublishinggroup.com.

09   10   11   12   13   14   15   7 6 5 4 3 2 1

Library of Congress Cataloging-in-Publication Data is available upon request.

Contents

The Books of the Old and New Testaments
in Alphabetical Order

Introduction

This is a special book. It's special because it's filled with romance, mystery, and miracles. It's filled with stories of heroes and villains. But most important of all, it's the story of girls and boys, women and men who discovered that God loves them. And that's what you'll discover as you read—*God loves you, too!*

This is a special book because God's word was written *for you*. God loves you and cares about you. That's why he wanted you to have this book. He wants you to read it and follow the instructions in it, so you'll discover his love and learn how to become the girl he wants you to be.

All through this Bible you'll find interesting colorful notes written just for girls. These notes will help you understand how God's message applies to you. Each one will bring you a little closer to God.

As you read, you'll see five types of notes:

Book Introductions
You'll find these pages before each book of the Bible. They'll show you what's important and exciting about each book. Many introductions have fun activities for you, as well as lessons for your life.

Women's World
These boxes will tell you what life was like for people who lived in Bible times. You'll see how women and men worked together to build families and communities. (And you'll even find some ways that life hasn't changed much!)

Be All You Can Be
These notes will help you become a godly woman. They'll help you develop a good attitude toward your parents, friends, boys, chores, and school. They'll help you live like a Christian everywhere you go.

Good Morning, God
Did you know that God can be your best friend? It's important for you to spend time with your friends—especially God. Reading these notes is a perfect way to spend time with him each day. Read one of these notes and the verse that's with it each day. Then talk to God about what you read, how you feel, and how glad you are to be his child. You'll find a list of all the *Good Morning, God* notes on page 1714.

Heroes and Heroines
These people are good role models for you. Each woman and man has qualities you can copy. Imitating these people will help you grow wise, loving, strong, and committed to God.

Enjoy this special book. It was written just for you because God doesn't want you to grow up alone—he wants to be with you as you grow!

Contributors

General Editor
Larry Richards

Senior Editors
Sue Richards

Associate Editors
Shari TeSlaa
Christopher D. Hudson

Project Editors
Donald R. Brown
Amy J. Cox
Betsy Rossen Elliot
Mary Ann Lackland
Carolyn Nystrom
Heather Stroobosscher

Artist
Paul Richards

Graphic Designer
Gary Gnidovic

Color Illustrations
Craig Phillips

Cover Design
JMK & Associates

Preface

GOD'S WORD® Is New

The twentieth century produced more Bible translations than any other. This includes English as well as foreign language translations. GOD'S WORD®, produced by God's Word to the Nations, fills a need that has remained unmet by English Bibles: to communicate in clear, natural English to God's people today without compromising the Bible's saving, life-changing message. This translation is an exceptional literary work that consciously combines scholarly fidelity with natural English.

Traditionally, the Scriptures have been translated into English by teams of Bible scholars serving part-time. This translation employed full-time Bible scholars and full-time English editorial reviewers. GOD'S WORD® is the first English Bible in which English reviewers have been actively involved with scholars at every stage of the translation process.

Because of the involvement of English reviewers, GOD'S WORD looks and reads like contemporary English literature. It uses natural grammar, follows standard punctuation and capitalization rules, and is printed in a single column. Because of the involvement of scholars, GOD'S WORD is an accurate, trustworthy translation.

GOD'S WORD® Is for Everyone

One of the goals of GOD'S WORD® is to communicate the saving, life-changing Good News about Jesus. GOD'S WORD is intended to be read by those who are well-versed in Scripture as well as first-time Bible readers, Christians as well as non-Christians, adults as well as children.

GOD'S WORD® Is a Translation

Of course, the Word of God didn't originally come to us in the English language. Since many people have wanted to read the Scriptures in their own language, scholars have found it necessary to translate the Bible from the Hebrew, Aramaic, and Greek languages in which it was written. Like many Bibles published before it, GOD'S WORD® has been translated directly from those original languages. Unlike Bibles before it, however, the translation theory used to produce GOD'S WORD® is different because the theory and practice of translation has advanced through the years.

The oldest translation theory is form-equivalent translation (often inaccurately called literal translation). In this type of translation, the translator chooses one of a limited number of meanings assigned to each Hebrew, Aramaic, or Greek word. The translator fills in the words that belong in the sentence but follows the word arrangement and grammar that is characteristic of the original language. Such a translation is often viewed as accurate. However, it can result in awkward, misleading, incomprehensible, or even amusing sentences. For instance, a form-equivalent translation of 1 Samuel 9:2 could read: "From his shoulders upward Saul was taller than any of the people." In English this implies that Saul had a misshapen head and neck. Translations using this theory have made the Bible more difficult to read and understand in English than it was in the original languages.

A newer translation theory is function-equivalent translation (often inaccurately called paraphrasing). In this type of translation, the translator tries to make the English function the same way the original language functioned for the original readers. However, in trying to make the translation easy to read, the translator can omit concepts from the original text that don't seem to have corresponding modern English equivalents. Such a translation can produce a readable text, but that text can convey the wrong meaning or not enough meaning. Furthermore, function-equivalent translations attempt to make some books readable on levels at which they were not intended. For instance, Song of Songs was not written for children. Paul's letter to the Ephesians is very sophisticated and not intended for novices.

The theory followed by God's Word to the Nations is closest natural equivalent translation. The first consideration for the translators of GOD'S WORD® was to find equivalent English ways of expressing the meaning of the Hebrew, Aramaic, or Greek text. This procedure ensures that the translation is faithful to the meaning intended by the original writer. The next consideration was readability. The meaning is expressed in natural English by using common English punctuation, capitalization, grammar, and word choice. The third consideration was to choose the natural equivalent that most closely reflects the style of the Hebrew, Aramaic, or Greek text. This translation theory is designed to avoid the awkwardness and inaccuracy associated with form-equivalent translation, and it avoids the loss of meaning and oversimplification associated with function-equivalent translation.

Features of GOD'S WORD

Layout

The features that distinguish GOD'S WORD® from other Bible translations are designed to aid readers. The most obvious of these is the open, single-column format. This invites readers into the page. The single column takes the Bible out of the reference book category and presents it as the literary work that God intended it to be.

In prose GOD'S WORD looks like other works of literature. It contains frequent paragraphing. Whenever a different speaker's words are quoted, a new paragraph begins. Lists, genealogies, and long prayers are formatted to help readers recognize the thought pattern of the text. The prose style of GOD'S WORD favors concise, clear sentences. While avoiding very long, complicated sentences, which characterize many English Bible translations, GOD'S WORD strives to vary the word arrangement in a natural way. Doing this brings the Scriptures to life.

Poetry in GOD'S WORD is instantly recognized by its format. The single-column format enables readers to recognize parallel thoughts in parallel lines of poetry. In a single-column, across-the-page layout, a variety of indentations are possible. The mission society's translators have used indentation to indicate the relationship of one line to others in the same context. This enables a person reading the Bible in English to appreciate the Bible's poetry in much the same way a person reading the Bible in the original languages of Hebrew, Aramaic or Greek would appreciate it.

Punctuation, Capitalization

In English, meaning is conveyed not only by words but also by punctuation. However, no punctuation existed in ancient Hebrew and Greek writing, and words were used where English grammar would prefer punctuation marks. GOD'S WORD® strives to use standard English punctuation wherever possible. At times this means that a punctuation mark or paragraph break represents the meaning that could only be expressed in words in Hebrew or Greek.

Italics are also used as they would be in other printed English texts: for foreign words or to indicate that a word is used as a word. (GOD'S WORD never uses italics to indicate emphasis.)

Wherever possible, GOD'S WORD has supplied information in headings or half-brackets to identify the speaker in quoted material. To minimize the confusion produced by quotations within quotations, quotation marks are used sparingly. For instance, they are not used after formulaic statements such as "This is what the LORD says: ..."

Contractions can fit comfortably into many English sentences. Certainly, "Don't you care that we're going to die" is less stiff than, "Do you not care that we are going to die?" GOD'S WORD achieves a warmer style by using contractions where appropriate. However, uncontracted words are used in contexts that require special emphasis.

GOD'S WORD capitalizes the first letter in proper nouns and sentences and all the letters in the word Lord when it represents Yahweh, the name of God in the Old Testament. Some religious literature chooses to capitalize pronouns that refer to the deity. As in the original languages, GOD'S WORD does not capitalize any pronouns (unless they begin sentences). In some cases scholars are uncertain whether pronouns in the ancient texts refer to God or someone else. In these cases the presence of capitalized pronouns would be misleading. However, when the Hebrew or Greek pronouns are not ambiguous, but an English pronoun would be, GOD'S WORD uses the appropriate proper noun in its place.

Gender References

The Scriptures contain many passages that apply to all people. Therefore, GOD'S WORD® strives to use gender-neutral language in these passages so that all readers will apply these passages to themselves. For example, traditionally, Psalm 1:1 has been translated, "Blessed is the man who does not follow the advice of the wicked ..." As a result, many readers will understand this verse to mean that only adult males, not women or children, can receive a blessing. However, in GOD'S WORD the first Psalm begins "Blessed is the person who does not follow the advice of the wicked ..."

However, if a passage focuses upon an individual, GOD'S WORD does not use plural nouns and pronouns to avoid the gender-specific pronouns *he, him*, and *his*. In these cases the translators considered the text's focus upon an individual more important than an artificial use of plural pronouns. In addition, gender-specific language is preserved in passages that apply specifically to men or specifically to women.

Word Choice

Many Bible translations contain theological terms that have little, if any, meaning for most nontheologically-trained readers. GOD'S WORD® avoids using these terms and substitutes words that carry the same meaning in common English. In some cases traditional theological words are contained in footnotes the first time they occur in a chapter. Examples of these theological terms include *covenant, grace, justify, repent*, and *righteousness*.

While all these features make GOD'S WORD® a uniquely readable and understandable Bible, the ultimate goal of the mission society is to bring the readers of GOD'S WORD into a new or closer relationship with Jesus. The translation team and support staff of God's Word to the Nations pray that your reading of GOD'S WORD makes the words of our great God and Savior, as revealed through his prophets and his apostles, come to life for you.

For more details on the translation process and the unique features that enable GOD'S WORD® to accurately and clearly communicate God's saving, life-changing, message contact—

God's Word to the Nations
P.O. Box 400
Orange Park, Florida 32067-0400

Notes on the Text of GOD'S WORD

Brackets

Proper names or foreign words whose meaning is significant for understanding a particular Bible passage are translated in brackets ([ ]) following the name or phrase. When reading aloud a bracketed word may be treated as "that is."

Half-brackets (⌞ ⌟) enclose words that the translation team supplied because the context contains meaning that is not explicitly stated in the original language.

Footnotes

Five types of footnotes are used in GOD'S WORD:

1. Explanatory footnotes clarify historical, cultural, and geographical details from the ancient world to make the text more understandable to modern readers. These footnotes also identify word play in Hebrew or Greek that would otherwise be lost to the English reader.

2. Alternate translation footnotes offer other plausible translations. They are introduced by the word *or*.

3. Footnotes that state "English equivalent difficult" mark passages where a Hebrew or Greek expression cannot be adequately translated into modern English without resorting to a long, inappropriate paraphrase.

4. Footnotes that state "Hebrew meaning uncertain" or "Greek meaning uncertain" mark passages where scholars are not sure what a Hebrew or Greek expression means.

5. Textual footnotes are included wherever GOD'S WORD translates the meaning of some text other than the Masoretic Text printed in *Biblia Hebraica Stuttgartensia* or its footnotes (Old Testament) or the Greek text printed in the twenty-seventh edition of *Novum Testamentum Graece* (New Testament).

Terms Used in Footnotes

Aramaic	one of the languages of the Old Testament, related to Hebrew
Dead Sea Scrolls	one or more of the Qumran manuscripts
Egyptian	one or more of the ancient translations of the Bible into the ancient Egyptian or Ethiopic languages
Greek	in the Old Testament: one or more of the ancient Greek translations of the Old Testament in the New Testament: the Greek language, the language of the New Testament
Hebrew	the primary language of the Old Testament
Latin	one or more of the ancient Latin translations of the Bible
Masoretic Text	the traditional Hebrew text of the Old Testament
manuscript	an ancient, handwritten copy of a text
Samaritan Pentateuch	Samaritan Hebrew version of the first five books of the Bible
Syriac	the ancient Syriac translation of the Bible
Targum	one of the ancient Aramaic translations of the Old Testament

Old Testament

AN INTRODUCTION TO
Genesis

The word "Genesis" means "beginnings." This book tells the story of the creation of the universe. It tells where human beings came from and how each of us is special to God. Genesis is a good place to begin reading the Bible.

Headlines

God Made It All
Genesis 1, page 5

Special? Who, Me?
Genesis 2, page 6

Adam Falls for Eve
Genesis 3, page 7

Water, Water Everywhere
Genesis 7, page 12

Promises, Promises
Genesis 12, page 17

Esau's in a Stew
Genesis 25, page 36

Ex-con Rules Egypt
Genesis 41, page 59

This map shows where the action in Genesis took place. Most believe Eden was near the area marked by the flower. Noah's ark landed on Mount Ararat in what is now Turkey [see boat symbol]. Abraham left his home in Ur [camel] to go to Canaan [tent]. Joseph rose from slave to ruler in Egypt [pyramid].

Creation Ideas. Who's Right?

When Moses wrote Genesis, the Greeks believed that the sun, moon, and stars existed before their gods came into being. The Egyptians had five ideas, all different from the Bible. In the part of the world Abraham came from, people thought that Earth was the body of a dead god called Tiamat. People came from drops of the dead god's blood.

Today many people think the universe just happened. Living things just happened, too. That's not much of an explanation.

What if someone tells you to mix together all the parts lying in all the junkyards of the world together, and stir them up for four billion years? He tells you that if you do that, you'll get a Cadillac and a Jeep and a Ford truck. Would you believe him?

Living things are a lot more complicated than cars. It took God to design the world and living things. That's the Bible's explanation. It beats all those other ideas. And it's true.

Who Goofed?

"Rain? Why, it's not going to rain."

Everybody but Noah.
(See Genesis 6.)

BIG IDEAS
IN GENESIS

GOD Powerful enough to create. Wise enough to design. Loving enough to care. Trustworthy enough to keep promises. Righteous enough to hate sin. Merciful enough to forgive. Someone worth knowing!

CREATION God designed and made all things. Evolution can't explain all the different forms of life on Earth. It can't explain you!

PEOPLE God made people in his image and likeness. Like God, we can think, feel, imagine, remember, and make choices. You're a lot more special than any monkey's nephew!

SIN Sin isn't just wrong. Sin is harmful. One big reason God tells us not to sin is that he doesn't want us hurt by doing wrong.

JUDGMENT People who choose to do wrong have to suffer the consequences. The story of the great flood in Genesis 6–8 reminds us that God will punish those who keep on doing wrong.

PROMISES God makes binding promises. We can count on God to do what he says he will.

"OK, Uncle Abram. I'll take Sodom."

Lot. (See Genesis 13 and 19.)

"So let's sell our brother as a slave. He'll never be able to get back at us."

Joseph's brothers, Genesis 37. (See Genesis 42!)

Discovery

Here's a list of beginnings in Genesis 1–11. When you read about one of these beginnings, write the verses here.

Heavens and earth _____

Animal life _____

Human beings _____

Marriage _____

Sin _____

Death _____

Punishment of sin _____

Languages _____

Life Hard?

Some of us have hard lives. Joseph did. He had jealous brothers. They sold him as a slave. His master's wife lied about Joseph, and he was put in prison. After many years, Joseph was able to explain the king of Egypt's dreams and was made the second most powerful person in Egypt. When life is hard, we can remember how Joseph trusted God and follow his example.

People in Genesis

Adam [AD-uhm] "human being"
Eve [EEV] "life giver"
Abram [AY-brum] "exalted father"
Abraham [AY-bruh-ham] "father of a multitude"
Sarah [SAIR-uh] "princess"
Noah [NOH-uh] "rest" or "comfort"
Lot [LAHT] "covering"
Isaac [I-zik] "laughter"
Jacob [JAY-kub] "deceiver"
Israel [IZ-ruh-el] "he struggles with God"
Joseph [JOH-suhf] "may God add"

A Big Question?

Moses wasn't around when God created the universe. So how did Moses know that God was the one who created all things? The book of Exodus tells us God spoke with Moses for 40 days on Mount Sinai (Exodus 24:18). And God was there at the beginning of time. That's a good thing to remember. Scientists and teachers who insist evolution is a fact weren't there either. Only God was there. And the Bible is God's word.

Genesis

The Creation

¹In the beginning God created heaven and earth.

²The earth was formless and empty, and darkness covered the deep water. The Spirit of God was hovering over the water.

³Then God said, "Let there be light!" So there was light. ⁴God saw the light was good. So God separated the light from the darkness. ⁵God named the light *day*, and the darkness he named *night*. There was evening, then morning—the first day.

⁶Then God said, "Let there be a horizon in the middle of the water in order to separate the water." ⁷So God made the horizon and separated the water above and below the horizon. And so it was. ⁸God named what was above the horizon *sky*. There was evening, then morning—a second day.

⁹Then God said, "Let the water under the sky come together in one area, and let the dry land appear." And so it was. ¹⁰God named the dry land *earth*. The water which came together he named *sea*. God saw that it was good. ¹¹Then God said, "Let the earth produce vegetation: plants bearing seeds, each according to its own type, and fruit trees bearing fruit with seeds, each according to its own type." And so it was. ¹²The earth produced vegetation: plants bearing seeds, each according to its own type, and trees bearing fruit with seeds, each according to its own type. God saw that they were good. ¹³There was evening, then morning—a third day.

¹⁴Then God said, "Let there be lights in the sky to separate the day from the night. They will be signs and will mark religious festivals, days, and years. ¹⁵They will be lights in the sky to shine on the earth." And so it was. ¹⁶God made the two bright lights: the larger light to rule the day and the smaller light to rule the night. He also made the stars. ¹⁷God put them in the sky to give light to the earth, ¹⁸to dominate the day and the night, and to separate the light from the darkness. God saw that it was good. ¹⁹There was evening, then morning—a fourth day.

²⁰Then God said, "Let the water swarm with swimming creatures, and let birds fly through the sky over the earth." ²¹So God created the large sea creatures, every type of creature that swims around in the water and every type of flying bird. God saw that they were good. ²²God blessed them and said, "Be fertile, increase in number,

You're Special

Genesis 1:26-27

Each person is unique on the outside. You may not like something about the way you look just now. But look inside. God made people in his image. Inside, we look like God. He gave us bright minds. He gave us the ability to love. He gave us a sense of humor. Look inside, and you can feel very special indeed.

be all you can be

fill the sea, and let there be many birds on the earth." ²³There was evening, then morning—a fifth day.

²⁴Then God said, "Let the earth produce every type of living creature: every type of domestic animal, crawling animal, and wild animal." And so it was. ²⁵God made every type of wild animal, every type of domestic animal, and every type of creature that crawls on the ground. God saw that they were good.

²⁶Then God said, "Let us make humans in our image, in our likeness. Let them rule the fish in the sea, the birds in the sky, the domestic animals all over the earth, and all the animals that crawl on the earth."

²⁷   So God created humans in his image.
        In the image of God he created them.
        He created them male and female.

²⁸God blessed them and said, "Be fertile, increase in number, fill the earth, and be its master. Rule the fish in the sea, the birds in the sky, and all the animals that crawl on the earth."

²⁹God said, "I have given you every plant with seeds on the face of the earth and every tree that has fruit with seeds. This will be your food. ³⁰I have given all green plants as food to every land animal, every bird in the sky, and every animal that crawls on the earth—every living, breathing animal." And so it was.

³¹And God saw everything that he had made and that it was very good. There was evening, then morning—the sixth day.

¹Heaven and earth and everything in them were finished. ²By the seventh day God had finished the work he had been doing. On the seventh day he stopped the work he had been doing. ³Then God blessed the seventh day and set it apart as holy, because on that day he stopped all his work of creation.

The Creation of Man and Woman

⁴This is the account of heaven and earth when they were created, at the time when the Lord God made earth and heaven.

⁵Wild bushes and plants were not on the earth yet because the Lord God hadn't sent rain on the earth. Also, there was no one to farm the land. ⁶Instead, underground water would come up from the earth and water the entire surface of the ground.

⁷Then the Lord God formed the man from the dust of the earth[a] and blew the breath of life into his nostrils. The man became a living being.

Men and Women
Genesis 2:20-23

Men and women are different. But they are the same in many ways, too. The first time Adam saw Eve, he said, "This is now bone of my bones and flesh of my flesh." Adam knew that *different* didn't mean inferior. Adam was happy to have a partner who was his equal and like him in many important ways.

be all you can be

---

[a] 2:7 There is a play on words here between Hebrew *'adam* (man) and *'adamah* (earth).

⁸The Lᴏʀᴅ God planted a garden in Eden, in the east. That's where he put the man whom he had formed. ⁹The Lᴏʀᴅ God made all the trees grow out of the ground. These trees were nice to look at, and their fruit was good to eat. The tree of life and the tree of the knowledge of good and evil grew in the middle of the garden.

¹⁰A river flowed from Eden to water the garden. Outside the garden it divided into four rivers. ¹¹The name of the first river is Pishon. This is the one that winds throughout Havilah, where there is gold. ¹²(The gold of that land is pure. Bdellium*ᵇ* and onyx are also found there.) ¹³The name of the second river is Gihon. This is the one that winds throughout Sudan. ¹⁴The name of the third river is Tigris. This is the one that flows east of Assyria. The fourth river is the Euphrates.

¹⁵Then the Lᴏʀᴅ God took the man and put him in the Garden of Eden to farm the land and to take care of it. ¹⁶The Lᴏʀᴅ God commanded the man. He said, "You are free to eat from any tree in the garden. ¹⁷But you must never eat from the tree of the knowledge of good and evil because when you eat from it, you will certainly die."

¹⁸Then the Lᴏʀᴅ God said, "It is not good for the man to be alone. I will make a helper who is right for him."

¹⁹The Lᴏʀᴅ God had formed all the wild animals and all the birds out of the ground. Then he brought them to the man to see what he would call them. Whatever the man called each creature became its name. ²⁰So the man named all the domestic animals, all the birds, and all the wild animals.

But the man found no helper who was right for him. ²¹So the Lᴏʀᴅ God caused him to fall into a deep sleep. While the man was sleeping, the Lᴏʀᴅ God took out one of the man's ribs and closed up the flesh at that place. ²²Then the Lᴏʀᴅ God formed a woman from the rib that he had taken from the man. He brought her to the man.

²³The man said,

> "This is now bone of my bones and flesh of my flesh.
>   She will be named *woman*
>   because she was taken from man."

²⁴That is why a man will leave his father and mother and will be united with his wife, and they will become one flesh. ²⁵The man and his wife were both naked, but they weren't ashamed of it.

The First Sin and the First Promise

¹The snake was more clever than all the wild animals the Lᴏʀᴅ God had made. He asked the woman, "Did God really say, 'You must never eat the fruit of any tree in the garden'?"

²The woman answered the snake, "We're allowed to eat the fruit from any tree in the garden ³except the tree in the middle of the garden. God said, 'You must never eat it or touch it. If you do, you will die!' "

⁴"You certainly won't die!" the snake told the woman. ⁵"God knows that when you eat it your eyes will be opened. You'll be like God, knowing good and evil."

⁶The woman saw that the tree had fruit that was good to eat, nice to look at, and desirable for making someone wise. So she took some of the fruit and ate it. She also gave some to her husband, who was with her, and he ate it.

⁷Then their eyes were opened, and they both realized that they were naked. They sewed fig leaves together and made clothes for themselves.

⁸In the cool of the evening, the man and his wife heard the Lᴏʀᴅ God walking

---

*ᵇ*2:12 Hebrew meaning uncertain.

around in the garden. So they hid from the Lord God among the trees in the garden. [9]The Lord God called to the man and asked him, "Where are you?"

[10]He answered, "I heard you in the garden. I was afraid because I was naked, so I hid."

[11]God asked, "Who told you that you were naked? Did you eat fruit from the tree I commanded you not to eat from?"

[12]The man answered, "That woman, the one you gave me, gave me some fruit from the tree, and I ate it."

[13]Then the Lord God asked the woman, "What have you done?"

"The snake deceived me, and I ate," the woman answered.

[14]So the Lord God said to the snake, "Because you have done this,

> You are cursed more than all the wild or domestic animals.
> You will crawl on your belly.
> You will be the lowest of animals as long as you live.
> [15] I will make you and the woman hostile toward each other.
> I will make your descendants
>   and her descendant hostile toward each other.
> He will crush your head,
>   and you will bruise his heel."

[16]He said to the woman,

> "I will increase your pain and your labor
>   when you give birth to children.
> Yet, you will long for your husband,
>   and he will rule you."

[17]Then he said to the man, "You listened to your wife and ate fruit from the tree, although I commanded you, 'You must never eat its fruit.'

> The ground is cursed because of you.
>   Through hard work you will eat food that comes from it
>   every day of your life.
> [18] The ground will grow thorns and thistles for you,
>   and you will eat wild plants.
> [19] By the sweat of your brow, you will produce food to eat
>   until you return to the ground,
>   because you were taken from it.
> You are dust, and you will return to dust."

[20]Adam named his wife Eve [Life] because she became the mother of every living person.

[21]The Lord God made clothes from animal skins for the man and his wife and dressed them.

[22]Then the Lord God said, "The man has become like one of us, since he knows good and evil. He must not reach out and take the fruit from the tree of life and eat. Then he would live forever." [23]So the Lord God sent the man out of the Garden of Eden to farm the ground from which the man had been formed. [24]After he sent the man out, God placed angels[a] and a flaming sword that turned in all directions east of the Garden of Eden. He placed them there to guard the way to the tree of life.

---

[a] 3:24 Or "cherubim."

Cain Murders Abel

4 ¹Adam made love to his wife Eve. She became pregnant and gave birth to Cain. She said, "I have gotten the man that the Lord promised." ²Then she gave birth to another child, Abel, Cain's brother. Abel was a shepherd, and Cain was a farmer.

³Later Cain brought some crops from the land as an offering to the Lord. ⁴Abel also brought some choice parts of the firstborn animals from his flock. The Lord approved of Abel and his offering, ⁵but he didn't approve of Cain and his offering. So Cain became very angry and was disappointed. ⁶Then the Lord asked Cain, "Why are you angry, and why do you look disappointed? ⁷If you do well, won't you be accepted? But if you don't do well, sin is lying outside your door ready to attack. It wants to control you, but you must master it."

⁸Cain talked to his brother Abel. Later, when they were in the fields, Cain attacked his brother Abel and killed him.

⁹The Lord asked Cain, "Where is your brother Abel?"

"I don't know," he answered. "Am I supposed to take care of my brother?"

¹⁰The Lord asked, "What have you done? Your brother's blood is crying out to me from the ground. ¹¹So now you are cursed from the ground, which has received the blood of your brother whom you killed. ¹²When you farm the ground, it will no longer yield its best for you. You will be a fugitive, a wanderer on the earth."

¹³But Cain said to the Lord, "My punishment is more than I can stand! ¹⁴You have forced me off this land today. I have to hide from you and become a fugitive, a wanderer on the earth. Now anyone who finds me will kill me!"

¹⁵So the Lord said to him, "Not so! Anyone who kills Cain will suffer vengeance seven times over." The Lord gave Cain a sign so that anyone meeting him would not kill him.

¹⁶Then Cain left the Lord's presence and lived in Nod [The Land of Wandering], east of Eden.

Anger
Genesis 4:3-11

It's easy to feel angry . . . angry enough to want to hurt others. Cain let his anger control him. Cain murdered his brother Abel, and God punished Cain. Feeling angry doesn't excuse you when you do wrong. Ask God to help you master your anger and to help you show love. God will help you, so you won't have to be sorry later.

Cain's Ten Descendants—Cain to Lamech

¹⁷Cain made love to his wife. She became pregnant and gave birth to Enoch. Cain was building a city, and he named it Enoch after his son. ¹⁸To Enoch was born Irad. Irad was the father of Mehujael. Mehujael was the father of Methushael. And Methushael was the father of Lamech.

¹⁹Lamech married two women, one named Adah and the other Zillah. ²⁰Adah gave birth to Jabal. He was the first person to live in tents and have livestock. ²¹His brother's

name was Jubal. He was the first person to play the harp and the flute. ²²Zillah also had a son, Tubalcain, who made bronze and iron tools. Tubalcain's sister was Naamah.

²³Lamech said to his wives,

> "Adah and Zillah, listen to me!
> Wives of Lamech, hear what I say!
> I killed a man for bruising me,
>   a young man for wounding me.
> ²⁴ If Cain is avenged 7 times,
>   then Lamech, 77 times."

Adam's Godly Descendants—Adam to Enosh

²⁵Adam made love to his wife again. She gave birth to a son and named him Seth, because she said, "God has given*ᵃ* me another child in place of Abel, since Cain killed him."

²⁶A son was also born to Seth, and he named him Enosh. At that time people began to worship the LORD.

Adam's Ten Descendants—Adam to Noah—
I Chronicles 1:1-3

¹This is the written account of Adam and his descendants.

> When God created humans,
>   he made them in the likeness of God.
> ²   He created them male and female.
>   He blessed them and called them humans
> when he created them.

³When Adam was 130 years old, he became the father of a son in his own likeness, in his own image. He named him Seth. ⁴After Adam became the father of Seth, he lived 800 years and had other sons and daughters. ⁵Adam lived a total of 930 years; then he died.

⁶When Seth was 105 years old, he became the father of Enosh. ⁷After he became the father of Enosh, Seth lived 807 years and had other sons and daughters. ⁸Seth lived a total of 912 years; then he died.

⁹When Enosh was 90 years old, he became the father of Kenan. ¹⁰After he became the father of Kenan, Enosh lived 815 years and had other sons and daughters. ¹¹Enosh lived a total of 905 years; then he died.

¹²When Kenan was 70 years old, he became the father of Mahalalel. ¹³After he became the father of Mahalalel, Kenan lived 840 years and had other sons and daughters. ¹⁴Kenan lived a total of 910 years; then he died.

¹⁵When Mahalalel was 65 years old, he became the father of Jared. ¹⁶After he became the father of Jared, Mahalalel lived 830 years and had other sons and daughters. ¹⁷Mahalalel lived a total of 895 years; then he died.

¹⁸When Jared was 162 years old, he became the father of Enoch. ¹⁹After he became the father of Jared, Jared lived 800 years and had other sons and daughters. ²⁰Jared lived a total of 962 years; then he died.

²¹When Enoch was 65 years old, he became the father of Methuselah. ²²After he became the father of Methuselah, Enoch walked with God for 300 years and had other

---

ᵃ 4:25 There is a play on words here between Hebrew *sheth* (Seth) and *shath* (given).

sons and daughters. [23]Enoch lived a total of 365 years. [24]Enoch walked with God; then he was gone because God took him.

[25]When Methuselah was 187 years old, he became the father of Lamech. [26]After he became the father of Lamech, Methuselah lived 782 years and had other sons and daughters. [27]Methuselah lived a total of 969 years; then he died.

[28]When Lamech was 182 years old, he became the father of a son. [29]He named him Noah [Relief], and said, "This child will bring us relief from the work and painful labor of our hands since the LORD has cursed the ground." [30]After Lamech became the father of Noah, he lived 595 years and had other sons and daughters. [31]Lamech lived a total of 777 years; then he died.

[32]When Noah was 500 years old, he became the father of Shem, Ham, and Japheth.

Evil Increases on the Earth

[1]The number of people increased all over the earth, and daughters were born to them. [2]The sons of God saw that the daughters of other humans were beautiful. So they married any woman they chose.

[3]Then the LORD said, "My Spirit will not struggle with humans forever, because they are flesh and blood. They will live 120 years."

[4]The Nephilim were on the earth in those days, as well as later, when the sons of God slept with the daughters of other humans and had children by them. These children were famous long ago.

[5]The LORD saw how evil humans had become on the earth. All day long their deepest thoughts were nothing but evil. [6]The LORD was sorry that he had made humans on the earth, and he was heartbroken. [7]So he said, "I will wipe off the face of the earth these humans that I created. I will wipe out not only humans, but also domestic animals, crawling animals, and birds. I'm sorry that I made them." [8]But the LORD was pleased with Noah.

Noah's Family and the Ship

[9]This is the account of Noah and his descendants.

Noah had God's approval and was a man of integrity among the people of his time. He walked with God. [10]He had three sons: Shem, Ham, and Japheth.

[11]The world was corrupt in God's sight and full of violence. [12]God saw the world and how corrupt it was because all people on earth lived evil lives.

[13]God said to Noah, "I have decided to put an end to all people because the earth is full of their violence. Now I'm going to destroy them along with the earth. [14]Make yourself a ship of cypress wood.[a] Make rooms in the ship and coat it inside and out with tar. [15]This is how you should build it: the ship is to be 450 feet long, 75 feet wide, and 45 feet high. [16]Make a roof for the ship, and leave an 18-inch-high opening at the top.[b] Put a door in the side of the ship. Build the ship with lower, middle, and upper decks. [17]I'm about to send a flood on the earth to destroy all people under the sky— every living, breathing human. Everything on earth will die.

[18]"But I will make my promise[c] to you. You, your sons, your wife, and your sons' wives will go into the ship. [19]Bring two of every living creature into the ship in order to keep them alive with you. They must be male and female. [20]Two of every type of bird, every type of domestic animal, and every type of creature that crawls on the ground will come to you to be kept alive. [21]Take every kind of food that can be eaten and store it. It will be food for you and the animals."

[22]Noah did this. He did everything that God had commanded him.

---

[a]6:14 Or "teakwood." [b]6:16 Hebrew meaning uncertain. [c]6:18 Or "covenant."

The Flood

7 [1]The Lord said to Noah, "Go into the ship with your whole family because I have seen that you alone are righteous among the people of today. [2]Take with you seven pairs of every kind of clean animal (a male and a female of each) and one pair of every kind of unclean[a] animal (a male and a female). [3]Also, take seven pairs of every kind of bird (a male and a female of each) to preserve animal life all over the earth after the flood. [4]In seven days I will send rain to the earth for 40 days and 40 nights. I will wipe off the face of the earth every living creature that I have made."

[5]So Noah did everything that the Lord commanded him.

[6]Noah was 600 years old when the flood came to the earth. [7]Noah, his sons, his wife, and his sons' wives went into the ship to escape the floodwaters. [8]Clean and unclean animals, birds, and creatures that crawl on the ground [9]came to Noah to go into the ship in pairs (a male and female of each) as God had commanded Noah.

[10]Seven days later the flood came on the earth. [11]On the seventeenth day of the second month of the six hundredth year of Noah's life, all the deep springs burst open. The sky opened, [12]and rain came pouring down on the earth for 40 days and 40 nights.

[13]On that same day Noah and his sons Shem, Ham, and Japheth, as well as Noah's wife and his three daughters-in-law went into the ship. [14]They had with them every type of wild animal, every type of domestic animal, every type of creature that crawls on the earth, and every type of bird (every creature with wings). [15]A pair of every living, breathing animal came to Noah to go into the ship. [16]A male and a female of every animal went in as God had commanded Noah. Then the Lord closed the door behind them.

[17]The flood continued for 40 days on the earth. The water increased and lifted the ship so that it rose high above the ground. [18]As the water rose and became very deep, the ship floated on top of the water. [19]The water rose very high above the earth. It covered all the high mountains everywhere under the sky. [20]It rose 23 feet above the mountaintops.

[21]Every creature that crawls on the earth died, including birds, domestic and wild animals, and everything that swarms over the earth, along with every human. [22]Everything on dry land (every living, breathing creature) died. [23]Every living creature on the face of the earth was wiped out. Humans, domestic animals, crawling creatures, and birds were wiped off the earth. Only Noah and those with him in the ship were left.

[24]The floodwaters were on the earth for 150 days.

God Remembers Noah

8 [1]God remembered Noah and all the wild and domestic animals with him in the ship. So God made a wind blow over the earth, and the water started to go down. [2]The deep springs and the sky had been shut, and the rain had stopped pouring. [3]The water began to recede from the land. At the end of 150 days the water had decreased. [4]On the seventeenth day of the seventh month, the ship came to rest in the mountains of Ararat. [5]The water kept decreasing until the tenth month. On the first day of the tenth month, the tops of the mountains appeared.

[6]After 40 more days Noah opened the window he had made in the ship [7]and sent out a raven. It kept flying back and forth until the water on the land had dried up. [8]Next, he sent out a dove to see if the water was gone from the surface of the ground. [9]The dove couldn't find a place to land because the water was still all over the earth. So it came back to Noah in the ship. He reached out and brought the dove back into

---

[a] 7:2 "Clean" refers to anything that is presentable to God. "Unclean" refers to anything that is not presentable to God.

the ship. [10]He waited seven more days and again sent the dove out of the ship. [11]The dove came to him in the evening, and in its beak was a freshly plucked olive leaf. Then Noah knew that the water was gone from the earth. [12]He waited seven more days and sent out the dove again, but it never came back to him.

[13]By the first day of the first month of Noah's six hundred and first year, the water on the land had dried up. Noah opened the top of the ship, looked out, and saw the surface of the ground. [14]By the twenty-seventh day of the second month the land was dry.

[15]Then God spoke to Noah, [16]"Come out of the ship with your wife, your sons, and your sons' wives. [17]Bring out every animal that's with you: birds, domestic animals, and every creature that crawls on the earth. Be fertile, increase in number, and spread over the earth."

[18]So Noah came out with his sons, his wife, and his sons' wives. [19]Every animal, crawling creature, and bird—everything that moves on the earth—came out of the ship, one kind after another.

[20]Noah built an altar to the LORD. On it he made a burnt offering of each type of clean[a] animal and clean bird. [21]The LORD smelled the soothing aroma. He said to himself, "I will never again curse the ground because of humans, even though from birth their hearts are set on nothing but evil. I will never again kill every living creature as I have just done.

[22]   As long as the earth exists,
            planting and harvesting,
            cold and heat,
            summer and winter,
            day and night
                will never stop."

God Blesses Noah and His Sons

[1]God blessed Noah and his sons and said to them, "Be fertile, increase in number, and fill the earth. [2]All the wild animals and all the birds will fear you and be terrified of you. Every creature that crawls on the ground and all the fish in the sea have been put under your control. [3]Everything that lives and moves will be your food. I gave you green plants as food; I now give you everything else.

[4]"But you are not to eat meat with blood in it. (Blood is life.) [5]In addition, I will demand your blood for your life. I will demand it from any animal or from any person. I will demand the life of any person who kills another person.

[6]   Whoever sheds human blood,
            by humans his blood will be shed,
                because in the image of God, God made humans.

[7]Be fertile, and increase in number. Spread over the earth, and increase."

God's Promise—The Sign of the Rainbow

[8]God also said to Noah and his sons, [9]"I am going to make my promise[a] to you, your descendants, [10]and every living being that is with you—birds, domestic animals, and all the wild animals, all those that came out of the ship—every living thing on earth. [11]I am making my promise to you. Never again will all life be killed by floodwaters. Never again will there be a flood that destroys the earth."

---

[a]8:20 "Clean" refers to anything that is presentable to God.   [a]9:9 Or "covenant."

¹²God said, "This is the sign of the promise I am giving to you and every living being that is with you for generations to come. ¹³I will put my rainbow in the clouds to be a sign of my promise to the earth. ¹⁴Whenever I form clouds over the earth, a rainbow will appear in the clouds. ¹⁵Then I will remember my promise to you and every living animal. Never again will water become a flood to destroy all life. ¹⁶Whenever the rainbow appears in the clouds, I will see it and remember my everlasting promise to every living animal on earth."

¹⁷So God said to Noah, "This is the sign of the promise I am making to all life on earth."

Noah Curses Canaan but Blesses Shem and Japheth

¹⁸Noah's sons, who came out of the ship, were Shem, Ham, and Japheth. ¹⁹These were Noah's three sons. From them the whole earth was populated. Ham was the father of Canaan.ᵇ

²⁰Noah, a farmer, was the first person to plant a vineyard. ²¹He drank some wine, got drunk, and lay naked inside his tent. ²²Ham, father of Canaan, saw his father naked. So he went outside and told his two brothers.

²³Shem and Japheth took a blanket and laid it over their shoulders. Then they walked in backwards and covered their father's naked body. They turned their faces away so that they didn't see their father naked.

²⁴When Noah sobered up, he found out what his youngest son had done to him. ²⁵So he said,

> "Canaan is cursed!
>   He will be the lowest slave to his brothers.
> 26 Praise the Lord, the God of Shem!
>   Canaan will be his slave.
> 27 May God expand the territory of Japheth.ᶜ
>   May he live in the tents of Shem.
>   Canaan will be his slave."

²⁸Noah lived 350 years after the flood. ²⁹Noah lived a total of 950 years; then he died.

The 14 Descendants of Japheth—
1 Chronicles 1:4-7

¹This is the account of Noah's sons Shem, Ham, and Japheth, and their descendants. Shem, Ham, and Japheth had children after the flood.

²Japheth's descendants were
    Gomer, Magog, Madai, Javan, Tubal, Meshech, and Tiras.
³Gomer's descendants were
    Ashkenaz, Riphath, and Togarmah.
⁴Javan's descendants were
    the people from Elishah, Tarshish, Cyprus, and Rhodes.ᵃ
⁵From these descendants the people of the coastlands spread into their own countries. Each nation had its own language and families.

ᵇ9:19 The second part of verse 18 (in Hebrew) has been placed just after verse 19 to express the complex Hebrew sentence structure more clearly in English. ᶜ9:27 There is a play on words here between the Hebrew *yapht* (May God expand) and *yepheth* (Japheth). ᵃ10:4 1 Chronicles 1:7, Samaritan Pentateuch, Greek; Masoretic Text "the Dodanim."

The 30 Descendants of Ham—
I Chronicles 1:8-16

⁶Ham's descendants were
    Cush, Egypt, Put, and Canaan.
⁷Cush's descendants were
    Seba, Havilah, Sabtah, Raamah, and Sabteca.
    Raamah's descendants were
    Sheba and Dedan.
⁸Cush was the father of Nimrod, the first mighty warrior on the earth. ⁹He was a mighty hunter whom the LORD blessed. That's why people used to say, "He's, like Nimrod, a mighty hunter whom the LORD blessed." ¹⁰The first cities in his kingdom were Babylon, Erech, Accad, and Calneh in Shinar [Babylonia]. ¹¹He went from that land to Assyria and built Nineveh, Rehoboth Ir, Calah, ¹²and Resen, the great city between Nineveh and Calah.
¹³Egypt was the ancestor of
    the Ludites, Anamites, Lehabites, Naphtuhites, ¹⁴Pathrusites, Casluhites (from
    whom the Philistines came), and the Caphtorites.
¹⁵Canaan was the father of
    Sidon his firstborn, then Heth, ¹⁶also the Jebusites, the Amorites, the Girgash-
    ites, ¹⁷the Hivites, the Arkites, the Sinites, ¹⁸the Arvadites, the Zemarites, and
    the Hamathites.
    Later the Canaanite families scattered. ¹⁹The border of the Canaanites extended from Sidon toward Gerar as far as Gaza and then toward Sodom, Gomorrah, Admah, and Zeboiim as far as Lasha.
²⁰These were Ham's descendants by families and languages within their countries and nations.

The 26 Descendants of Shem—
I Chronicles 1:17-23

²¹Shem, Japheth's older brother, also had children. Shem was, the ancestor of all the sons of Eber.
²²Shem's descendants were
    Elam, Asshur, Arpachshad, Lud, and Aram.
²³Aram's descendants were
    Uz, Hul, Gether, and Mash.
²⁴Arpachshad was the father of Shelah,
    and Shelah was the father of Eber.
²⁵Two sons were born to Eber.
    The name of the one was Peleg [Division], because in his day the earth was divided.
    His brother's name was Joktan.
²⁶Joktan was the father of Almodad, Sheleph, Hazarmaveth, Jerah, ²⁷Hadoram, Uzal, Diklah, ²⁸Obal, Abimael, Sheba, ²⁹Ophir, Havilah, and Jobab. These were Joktan's sons. ³⁰The region where they lived extended from Mesha toward Sephar in the eastern mountains.
³¹These were Shem's descendants by families and languages within their countries according to their nations.
³²These were the families of Noah's sons listed by their genealogies, nation by nation. From these descendants, the nations spread over the earth after the flood.

The Tower of Babel

11 ¹The whole world had one language with a common vocabulary. ²As people moved toward the east,ᵃ they found a plain in Shinar [Babylonia] and settled there.

³They said to one another, "Let's make bricks and bake them thoroughly." They used bricks as stones and tarᵇ as mortar.

⁴Then they said, "Let's build a city for ourselves and a tower with its top in the sky. Let's make a name for ourselves so that we won't become scattered all over the face of the earth."

⁵The LORD came down to see the city and the tower that the descendants of Adam were building. ⁶The LORD said, "They are one people with one language. This is only the beginning of what they will do! Now nothing they plan to do will be too difficult for them. ⁷Let us go down there and mix up their language so that they won't understand each other."

⁸So the LORD scattered them all over the face of the earth, and they stopped building the city. ⁹This is why it was named Babel, because there the LORD turned the language of the whole earth into babble. From that place the LORD scattered them all over the face of the earth.

The Ten Descendants of Shem—Shem to Terah—
I Chronicles 1:17-23

¹⁰This is the account of Shem and his descendants. Two years after the flood when Shem was 100 years old, he became the father of Arpachshad. ¹¹After he became the father of Arpachshad, Shem lived 500 years and had other sons and daughters.

¹²Arpachshad was 35 years old when he became the father of Shelah. ¹³After he became the father of Shelah, Arpachshad lived 403 years and had other sons and daughters.

¹⁴Shelah was 30 years old when he became the father of Eber. ¹⁵After he became the father of Eber, Shelah lived 403 years and had other sons and daughters.

¹⁶Eber was 34 years old when he became the father of Peleg. ¹⁷After he became the father of Peleg, Eber lived 430 years and had other sons and daughters.

¹⁸Peleg was 30 years old when he became the father of Reu. ¹⁹After he became the father of Reu, Peleg lived 209 years and had other sons and daughters.

²⁰Reu was 32 years old when he became the father of Serug. ²¹After he became the father of Serug, Reu lived 207 years and had other sons and daughters.

²²Serug was 30 years old when he became the father of Nahor. ²³After he became the father of Nahor, Serug lived 200 years and had other sons and daughters.

²⁴Nahor was 29 years old when he became the father of Terah. ²⁵After he became the father of Terah, Nahor lived 119 years and had other sons and daughters.

²⁶Terah was 70 years old when he became the father of Abram, Nahor, and Haran.

Terah Moves to Haran

²⁷This is the account of Terah and his descendants. Terah was the father of Abram, Nahor, and Haran. Haran was the father of Lot. ²⁸While his father Terah was still alive, Haran died in Ur of the Chaldeans, his native land. ²⁹Both Abram and Nahor married. The name of Abram's wife was Sarai, and the name of Nahor's wife was Milcah, daughter of Haran. (Haran was the father of Milcah and Iscah.) ³⁰Sarai was not able to have children.

ᵃ11:2 Or "from the east."   ᵇ11:3 Or "bitumen."

³¹Terah took his son Abram, his grandson Lot (son of Haran), and his daughter-in-law Sarai, wife of his son Abram. They set out together from Ur of the Chaldeans to go to Canaan. When they came as far as Haran, they stayed there. ³²Terah lived 205 years and died in Haran.

The LORD's First Promise to Abram

¹The LORD said to Abram,

> "Leave your land,
>   your relatives,
>   and your father's home.
>   Go to the land that I will show you.
> ² I will make you a great nation,
>   I will bless you.
>   I will make your name great,
>   and you will be a blessing.
> ³ I will bless those who bless you,
>   and whoever curses you, I will curse.
>   Through you every family on earth will be blessed."

The LORD's Second Promise to Abram

⁴So Abram left, as the LORD had told him, and Lot went with him. Abram was 75 years old when he left Haran. ⁵Abram set out for Canaan. He took along his wife Sarai, his nephew Lot, and all the possessions they had accumulated and the servants they had acquired in Haran.

⁶They arrived in Canaan,ᵃ and Abram traveled through the land to the oak tree belonging to Moreh at Shechem. At that time the Canaanites were in the land. ⁷Then the LORD appeared to Abram and said, "I'm going to give this land to your descendants." So he built an altar there to the LORD, who had appeared to him.

⁸He moved on to the hills east of Bethel, and he put up his tent—with Bethel on the west and Ai on the east. He also built an altar to the LORD there and worshiped the LORD. ⁹Abram kept moving toward the Negev.

Abram Deceives Pharaoh

¹⁰There was a famine in the land. Abram went to Egypt to stay awhile because the famine was severe. ¹¹When he was about to enter Egypt, Abram said to his wife Sarai, "I know that you're a beautiful woman. ¹²When the Egyptians see you, they'll say, 'This is his wife!' Then they'll kill me but let you live. ¹³Please say that you're my sister. Then everything will be alright for me, and because of you I will live."

¹⁴When Abram arrived in Egypt, the Egyptians saw how very beautiful his wife was. ¹⁵When Pharaoh's officials saw her, they raved about her to Pharaoh, so Sarai was taken to Pharaoh's palace. ¹⁶Everything went well for Abram because of her, and he was given sheep, cattle, donkeys, male and female slaves, and camels.

¹⁷However, the LORD struck Pharaoh and his household with terrible plagues because of Sarai, Abram's wife. ¹⁸Then Pharaoh called for Abram. "What have you done to me?" he asked. "Why didn't you tell me that she's your wife? ¹⁹Why did you say, 'She's my sister' and allow me to take her for my wife? Here's your wife! Take her and go!" ²⁰Pharaoh gave his men orders concerning Abram. They sent Abram away with his wife and everything that he had.

ᵃ 12:6 English equivalent difficult.

Abraham

Abraham left home when God said, "Go."

Abraham had it made. He was wealthy. He lived in a big city called Ur. He had everything he needed to be happy. Then God told Abraham (also called Abram) to leave his country, his people, and his friends.

It must have been hard for Abraham to leave everything, but he did. Abraham sold his house and bought animals to take along on his journey. He also bought tents to sleep in as he traveled. Abraham prepared for a long journey because he didn't know where God would lead him.

When God said, "Go," Abraham did what God told him to do.

Abraham made a wise choice when he decided to obey God. Because he was obedient, God gave Abraham many wonderful promises, and God kept every one. Throughout the Bible, Abraham is honored for his wise obedience and his great faith in God's promises.

Getting to Know Abraham

* Why was it hard for Abraham to obey God and leave Ur?
* Why would anyone choose to obey God if it meant doing something hard?
* Would we know about Abraham if he hadn't obeyed God and had just stayed in Ur?

* What friend do you know who obeys God, even when it's hard?

Abraham lived around 2100 B.C.

Abraham received his special name from God.

God made Abraham special promises.

Both Jews and Arabs descended from Abraham.

Abraham is remembered for believing God would do what he promised.

People in the land where Abraham grew up worshiped idols like these.

Ur's houses even had a kind of air conditioning! They were designed so the air circulated through them when the wind blew.

Abraham lived in a tent when he traveled. Husbands and wives had separate tents.

Abram and Lot Separate

13 ¹Abram left Egypt with his wife and everything he had and went to the Negev. Lot was with him. ²Abram was very rich because he had livestock, silver, and gold. ³He traveled from place to place. He went from the Negev as far as Bethel, to the area between Bethel and Ai where his tent had been originally, ⁴where he had first made an altar. There Abram worshiped the LORD.

⁵Lot, who had been traveling with Abram, also had his own sheep, cattle, and tents. ⁶There wasn't enough pastureland for both of them. They had so many possessions that they were unable to remain together. ⁷Quarrels broke out between Abram's herders and Lot's herders. (Canaanites and Perizzites were also living in that area.)

⁸Abram said to Lot, "Please, let's not have any more quarrels between us or between our herders. After all, we're relatives. ⁹Isn't all this land yours also? Let's separate. If you go to the left, I'll go to the right, and if you go to the right, I'll go to the left." ¹⁰Then Lot looked in the direction of Zoar as far as he could see. He saw that the whole Jordan Plain was well-watered like the LORD's garden or like Egypt. (This was before the LORD destroyed Sodom and Gomorrah.)

¹¹Lot chose the whole Jordan Plain for himself. He moved toward the east. They each went their own way. ¹²Abram lived in Canaan, while Lot lived among the cities of the plain, moving his tents as far as Sodom. ¹³(The people who lived in Sodom were very wicked. They committed terrible sins against the LORD.)

The LORD's Third Promise to Abram

¹⁴After Lot left, the LORD said to Abram, "Look north, south, east, and west of where you are. ¹⁵I will give all the land you see to you and to your descendants for an indefinite period of time. ¹⁶I will also give you as many descendants as the dust of the earth. If anyone could count the dust of the earth, then he could also count your descendants. ¹⁷Go! Walk back and forth across the entire land because I will give it to you." ¹⁸So Abram moved his tents and went to live by the oak trees belonging to Mamre at Hebron. There he built an altar for the LORD.

Getting Along

Genesis 13:1-13

be all you can be

The land couldn't support the herds of both Abram and Lot. Their workers fought over pasture and water. Who deserved first choice of the land? Abram was the oldest. In those days that meant he had the right to choose first. But Abram let Lot choose. How can you follow Abram's example and be a peacemaker this week?

Abram Rescues Lot

14 ¹At that time four kings —King Amraphel of Shinar, King Arioch of Ellasar, King Chedorlaomer of Elam, and King Tidal of Goiim— ²went to war against five kings —King Bera of Sodom, King Birsha of Gomorrah, King Shinab of Admah, King Shemeber of Zeboiim, and the king of Bela (that is, Zoar). ³The five kings joined forces and met in the valley of Siddim (that is, the Dead Sea). [4]For 12 years they had been subject to Chedorlaomer, but in the thirteenth year they rebelled. [5]In the fourteenth year Chedorlaomer and his allies came and defeated the Rephaim at Ashteroth Karnaim, the Zuzim at Ham, the Emim at Shaveh Kiriathaim, [6]and the Horites in the hill country of Seir, going as far as El Paran on the edge of the desert. [7]On their way back, they came to En Mishpat (that is, Kadesh), and they conquered the whole territory of the Amalekites and also the Amorites who were living at Hazazon Tamar.

[8]Then the kings of Sodom, Gomorrah, Admah, Zeboiim, and Bela (that is, Zoar) marched out and prepared for battle in the valley of Siddim. [9]They fought against King Chedorlaomer of Elam, King Tidal of Goiim, King Amraphel of Shinar, and King Arioch of Ellasar—four kings against five. [10]The valley of Siddim was full of tar pits. As the kings of Sodom and Gomorrah fled, they fell because of the tar pits, but the other kings fled to the hills. [11]So the four kings took all the possessions of Sodom and Gomorrah, as well as all their food, and left. [12]They also took Abram's nephew Lot and his possessions since he was living in Sodom.

[13]Then a soldier who had escaped came and told Abram the Hebrew what had happened. He was living next to the oak trees belonging to Mamre the Amorite, a brother of Eshcol and Aner. (These men were Abram's allies.)

[14]When Abram heard that his nephew had been captured, he armed[a] his 318 trained men, born in his own household, and pursued the four kings all the way to Dan. [15]He split up his men to attack them at night. He defeated them, pursuing them all the way to Hobah, which is north of Damascus. [16]He brought back everything they had, including women and soldiers. He also brought back his relative Lot and his possessions.

Melchizedek Blesses Abram

[17]After Abram came back from defeating Chedorlaomer and his allies, the king of Sodom came out to meet him in the Shaveh Valley (that is, the King's Valley). [18]Then King Melchizedek of Salem brought out bread and wine. He was a priest of God Most High. [19]He blessed Abram, and said,

"Blessed is Abram by God Most High,
   maker[b] of heaven and earth.
[20]   Blessed is God Most High,
   who has handed your enemies over to you."

Then Abram gave him a tenth of everything.

[21]The king of Sodom said to Abram, "Give me the people, and keep everything else for yourself."

[22]But Abram said to the king of Sodom, "I now raise my hand and solemnly swear to the LORD God Most High, maker of heaven and earth, [23]that I won't take a thread or a sandal strap. I won't take anything that is yours so that you will never be able to say, 'I made Abram rich.' [24]I won't take one single thing except what my men have eaten. But let my allies Aner, Eshcol, and Mamre take their share."

The LORD's Fourth Promise to Abram

[1]Later the LORD spoke his word to Abram in a vision. He said,

"Abram, don't be afraid.
I am your shield.
Your reward will be very great."[a]

---

²Abram asked, "Almighty Lord, what will you give me? Since I'm going to die without children, Eliezer of Damascus will inherit[b] my household. ³You have given me no children, so this member of my household will be my heir."

⁴Suddenly, the Lord spoke his word to Abram again. He said, "This man will not be your heir. Your own son will be your heir." ⁵He took Abram outside and said, "Now look up at the sky and count the stars, if you are able to count them." He also said to him, "That's how many descendants you will have!" ⁶Then Abram believed the Lord, and the Lord regarded that faith to be his approval of Abram. ⁷Then the Lord said to him, "I am the Lord, who brought you out of Ur of the Chaldeans to give you this land so that you will take possession of it."

⁸Abram asked, "Almighty Lord, how can I be certain that I will take possession of it?"

⁹He answered Abram, "Bring me a three-year-old heifer, a three-year-old female goat, a three-year-old ram, a mourning dove, and a pigeon." ¹⁰So Abram brought all these animals to him. He cut each of them in half and laid each half opposite the other. However, he did not cut the birds in half.

¹¹When birds of prey came down upon the carcasses, Abram drove them away. ¹²As the sun was just about to set, a deep sleep—a dreadful, deep darkness—came over Abram.

¹³God said to Abram, "You can know for sure that your descendants will live in a land that is not their own, where they will be slaves, and they will be oppressed for 400 years. ¹⁴But I will punish the nation they serve, and after that they will come out with many possessions. ¹⁵But you will die in peace and be buried at a very old age. ¹⁶In the fourth generation your descendants will come back here, because the sin of the Amorites will not have run its course until then."

¹⁷The sun had gone down, and it was dark. Suddenly a smoking oven and a flaming torch passed between the animal pieces. ¹⁸At that time the Lord made a promise[c] to Abram. He said, "I will give this land to your descendants. This is the land from the river of Egypt to the great river, the Euphrates. ¹⁹It is the land of the Kenites, the Kenizzites, the Kadmonites, ²⁰the Hittites, the Perizzites, the Rephaim, ²¹the Amorites, the Canaanites, the Girgashites, and the Jebusites."

Abram and Hagar

16 ¹Sarai, Abram's wife, was not able to have children. She owned an Egyptian slave named Hagar. ²So Sarai said to Abram, "The Lord has kept me from

Good Morning, God
Genesis 15:2-5

Who can you trust to keep a promise? God promised Abraham that one day Abraham would have a child. Even though Abraham was getting old, he believed God's promise. Soon, Abraham was able to hold his promised child in his arms. God's promise to Abraham seemed impossible. But God kept his word. And he will keep his word to each of us, too!

Father, thank you for always keeping your word.

---

*b*15:2 Hebrew meaning uncertain.   *c*15:18 Or "covenant."

having children. Why don't you sleep with my slave? Maybe I can build a family through her." Abram agreed with Sarai.

³After Abram had lived in Canaan for ten years, Abram's wife Sarai took her Egyptian slave Hagar and gave her to her husband Abram to be his wife. ⁴He slept with Hagar, and she became pregnant. When Hagar realized that she was pregnant, she began to be disrespectful to Sarai, her owner.

⁵So Sarai complained to Abram, "I'm being treated unfairly! And it's your fault! I know that I gave my slave to you, but now that she's pregnant, she's being disrespectful to me. May the LORD decide who is right—you or me."

⁶Abram answered Sarai, "Here, she's your slave. Do what you like with her." Then Sarai mistreated Hagar so much that she ran away.

⁷The Messenger of the LORD found her by a spring in the desert, the spring on the way to Shur. ⁸He said, "Hagar, Sarai's slave, where have you come from, and where are you going?"

She answered, "I'm running away from my owner Sarai." ⁹The Messenger of the LORD said to her, "Go back to your owner, and place yourself under her authority." ¹⁰The Messenger of the LORD also said to her, "I will give you many descendants. No one will be able to count them because there will be so many." ¹¹Then the Messenger of the LORD said to her,

> "You are pregnant,
>   and you will give birth to a son.
> You will name him Ishmael [God Hears],
>   because the LORD has heard your cry of distress.
> ¹²   He will be as free and wild as an untamed donkey.
> He will fight with everyone, and everyone will fight with him.
> He will have conflicts with all his relatives."ᵃ

¹³Hagar named the LORD, who had been speaking to her, "You Are the God Who Watches Over Me." She said, "This is the place where I watched the one who watches over me." ¹⁴This is why the well is named Beer Lahai Roi [Well of the Living One Who Watches Over Me]. It is still there between Kadesh and Bered.

¹⁵Hagar gave birth to Abram's son. Abram named him Ishmael. ¹⁶Abram was 86 years old when Hagar gave birth to Ishmael.

The LORD's Fifth Promise to Abraham

¹When Abram was 99 years old, the Lord appeared to him. He said to Abram, "I am God Almighty. Live in my presence with integrity. ²I will give you my promise,ᵃ and I will give you very many descendants." ³Immediately, Abram bowed with his face touching the ground, and again God spoke to him, ⁴"My promise is still with you. You will become the father of many nations. ⁵So your name will no longer be Abram [Exalted Father], but Abraham [Father of Many] because I have made you a father of many nations. ⁶I will give you many descendants. Many nations and kings will come from you. ⁷I will make my promise to you and your descendants for generations to come as an everlasting promise. I will be your God and the God of your descendants. ⁸I am also giving this land where you are living—all of Canaan—to you and your descendants as your permanent possession. And I will be your God."

⁹God also said to Abraham, "You and your descendants in generations to come are to be faithful to my promise. ¹⁰This is how you are to be faithful to my promise: Every male among you is to be circumcised. ¹¹All of you must be circumcised. That

---

ᵃ16:12 Hebrew meaning uncertain. ᵃ17:2 Or "covenant."

will be the sign of the promise from me to you. ¹²For generations to come every male child who is eight days old must be circumcised, whether he is born in your household or bought with money from a foreigner who's not related to you. ¹³Every male born in your household or bought with your money is to be circumcised without exception. So my promise will be a sign on your flesh, an everlasting promise. ¹⁴Any uncircumcised male must be excluded from his people because he has rejected my promise."

¹⁵God said to Abraham, "Don't call your wife by the name Sarai anymore. Instead, her name is Sarah [Princess]. ¹⁶I will bless her, and I will also give you a son by her. I will bless her, and she will become a mother of nations, and kings will come from her." ¹⁷Immediately, Abraham bowed with his face touching the ground. He laughed as he thought to himself, "Can a son be born to a hundred-year-old man? Can Sarah, a ninety-year-old woman, have a child?" ¹⁸Then Abraham said to God, "Why not let Ishmael be my heir?"

¹⁹God replied, "No! Your wife Sarah will give you a son, and you will name him Isaac [He Laughs]. I will make an everlasting promise to him and his descendants. ²⁰I have heard your request about Ishmael. Yes, I will bless him, make him fertile, and increase the number of his descendants. He will be the father of 12 princes, and I will make him a great nation. ²¹But I will make my promise to Isaac. Sarah will give birth to him at this time next year." ²²When God finished speaking with Abraham, he left him.

Abraham's Household Circumcised

²³So Abraham took his son Ishmael, everyone born in his household, and everyone bought with money—every male in his household—and circumcised them that day, as God had told him. ²⁴Abraham was 99 years old when he was circumcised. ²⁵His son Ishmael was 13 years old when he was circumcised. ²⁶That same day Abraham and his son Ishmael were circumcised. ²⁷All the men of his household, whether born in the household or bought with money from a foreigner, were circumcised with him.

The LORD's Sixth Promise to Abraham

18 ¹The LORD appeared to Abraham by the oak trees belonging to Mamre as he was sitting at the entrance of his tent during the hottest part of the day. ²Abraham looked up, and suddenly he saw three men standing near him. When he saw them, he ran to meet them, and he bowed with his face touching the ground.

³"Please, sir," Abraham said, "stop by to visit me for a while. ⁴Why don't we let someone bring a little water? After you wash your feet, you can stretch out and rest under the tree. ⁵Let me bring some bread so that you can regain your strength. After that you can leave, since this is why you stopped by to visit me."

They answered, "That's fine. Do as you say."

⁶So Abraham hurried into the tent to find Sarah. "Quick," he said, "get three measures of flour, knead it, and make bread."

⁷Then Abraham ran to the herd and took one of his best calves. He gave it to his servant, who prepared it quickly. ⁸Abraham took cheese and milk, as well as the meat, and set these in front of them. Then he stood by them under the tree as they ate.

⁹They asked him, "Where is your wife Sarah?"

He answered, "Over there, in the tent."

¹⁰The LORD said, "I promise I'll come back to you next year at this time, and your wife Sarah will have a son."

Sarah happened to be listening at the entrance of the tent, which was behind him.

¹¹Abraham and Sarah were old. Sarah was past the age of childbearing. ¹²And so Sarah laughed to herself, thinking, "Now that I've become old, will I enjoy myself again? What's more, my husband is old!"

¹³The LORD asked Abraham, "Why did Sarah laugh and say, 'Can I really have a child now that I'm old?' ¹⁴Is anything too hard for the LORD? I will come back to you next year at this time, and Sarah will have a son."

¹⁵Because she was afraid, Sarah denied that she had laughed.

But the LORD said, "Yes, you did laugh."

The LORD Tells Abraham About His Plan

¹⁶Then the men got up to leave. As Abraham was walking with them to see them off, they looked toward Sodom. ¹⁷The LORD said, "I shouldn't hide what I am going to do from Abraham. ¹⁸After all, Abraham is going to become a great and mighty nation and through him all the nations of the earth will be blessed. ¹⁹I have chosen him so that he will direct his children and his family after him to keep the way of the LORD by doing what is right and just. In this way I, the LORD, will do what I have promised Abraham."

²⁰The LORD also said, "Sodom and Gomorrah have many complaints against them, and their sin is very serious. ²¹I must go down and see whether these complaints are true. If not, I will know it."

²²From there the men turned and went on toward Sodom, but Abraham remained standing in front of the LORD. ²³Abraham came closer and asked, "Are you really going to sweep away the innocent with the guilty? ²⁴What if there are 50 innocent people in the city? Are you really going to sweep them away? Won't you spare that place for the sake of the 50 innocent people who are in it? ²⁵It would be unthinkable for you to do such a thing, to treat the innocent and the guilty alike and to kill the innocent with the guilty. That would be unthinkable! Won't the judge of the whole earth do what is fair?"

²⁶The LORD said, "If I find 50 innocent people inside the city of Sodom, I will spare the whole place for their sake."

²⁷Abraham asked, "Consider now, if I may be so bold as to ask you, although I'm only dust and ashes, ²⁸what if there are 45 innocent people? Will you destroy the whole city because of 5 fewer people?"

Good Morning, God
Genesis 18:25-33

Bad news was on the way to Sodom and Gomorrah. The Lord was going to destroy the two cities because they were full of evil people. But Abraham was worried that there might be some good people living there, too. So he prayed to the Lord—not once, but five times! God listened to Abraham and sent angels to save the few good people who lived in Sodom and Gomorrah. Abraham's story is proof that prayer makes a difference. God hears your prayers, too!

Dear Lord, thank you for listening to my prayers and answering each one.

The Lord answered, "I will not destroy it if I find 45 there."

²⁹Abraham asked him again, "What if 40 are found there?"

He answered, "For the sake of the 40 I will not do it."

³⁰"Please don't be angry if I speak again," Abraham said. "What if 30 are found there?"

He answered, "If I find 30 there, I will not do it."

³¹"Look now, if I may be so bold as to ask you," Abraham said. "What if 20 are found there?"

He answered, "I will not destroy it for the sake of the 20."

³²"Please don't be angry if I speak only one more time," Abraham said. "What if 10 are found there?"

He answered, "I will not destroy it for the sake of the 10." ³³When the Lord finished speaking to Abraham, he left. Abraham returned home.

Lot's Guests Are Assaulted

¹The two angels came to Sodom in the evening as Lot was sitting in the gateway. When Lot saw them, he got up to meet them and bowed with his face touching the ground. ²He said, "Please, gentlemen, why don't you come to my home and spend the night? You can wash your feet there. Then early tomorrow morning you can continue your journey."

"No," they answered, "we'd rather spend the night in the city square."

³But he insisted so strongly that they came with him and went into his home. He prepared a special dinner for them, baked some unleavened bread, and they ate. ⁴Before they had gone to bed, all the young and old male citizens of Sodom surrounded the house. ⁵They called to Lot, "Where are the men who came to stay with you tonight? Bring them out to us so that we can have sex with them."

⁶Then Lot went outside and shut the door behind him. ⁷"Please, my friends, don't be so wicked," he said. ⁸"Look, I have two daughters who have never had sex. Why don't you let me bring them out to you? Do whatever you like with them. But don't do anything to these men, since I'm responsible for them."

⁹But the men yelled, "Get out of the way! This man came here to stay awhile. Now he wants to be our judge! We're going to treat you worse than those men." They pushed hard against Lot and lunged forward to break down the door. ¹⁰The men inside reached out, pulled Lot into the house with them, and shut the door. ¹¹Then they struck all the men who were in the doorway of the house, young and old alike, with blindness so that they gave up trying to find the door.

Lot Leaves Sodom, and the Cities Are Destroyed

¹²Then the men asked Lot, "Do you have anyone else here—any in-laws, sons, daughters, or any other relatives in the city? Get them out of here ¹³because we're going to destroy this place. The complaints to the Lord against its people are so loud that the Lord has sent us to destroy it."

¹⁴So Lot went out and spoke to the men engaged to his daughters. He said, "Hurry! Get out of this place, because the Lord is going to destroy the city." But they thought he was joking.

¹⁵As soon as it was dawn, the angels urged Lot by saying, "Quick! Take your wife and your two daughters who are here, or you'll be swept away when the city is punished." ¹⁶When he hesitated, the men grabbed him, his wife, and his two daughters by their hands, because the Lord wanted to spare Lot. They brought them safely outside the city. ¹⁷As soon as they were outside, one of the angels said, "Run for your

lives! Don't look behind you, and don't stop on the plain. Run for the hills, or you'll be swept away!"

¹⁸Lot answered, "Oh no! ¹⁹Even though you've been so good to me and though you've been very kind to me by saving my life, I can't run as far as the hills. This disaster will overtake me, and I'll die. ²⁰Look, there's a city near enough to flee to, and it's small. Why don't you let me run there? Isn't it small? Then my life will be saved."

²¹The angel said to him, "Alright, I will grant you this request too. I will not destroy the city you're talking about. ²²Run there quickly, because I can't do anything until you get there." (The city is named Zoar [Small].)

²³The sun had just risen over the land as Lot came to Zoar. ²⁴Then the LORD made burning sulfur and fire rain out of heaven on Sodom and Gomorrah. ²⁵He destroyed those cities, the whole plain, all who lived in the cities, and whatever grew on the ground. ²⁶Lot's wife looked back and turned into a column of salt.

²⁷Early the next morning Abraham came to the place where he had stood in front of the LORD. ²⁸When he looked toward Sodom and Gomorrah and all the land in the plain, he saw smoke rising from the land like the thick smoke of a furnace.

²⁹When God destroyed the cities on the plain, he remembered Abraham. Lot was allowed to escape from the destruction that came to the cities where he was living.

Lot's Daughters Have Sons by Their Father

³⁰Lot left Zoar because he was afraid to stay there. He and his two daughters settled in the mountains where they lived in a cave. ³¹The older daughter said to the younger one, "Our father is old. No men are here. We can't get married as other people do. ³²Let's give our father wine to drink. Then we'll go to bed with him so that we'll be able to preserve our family line through our father." ³³That night they gave their father wine to drink. Then the older one went to bed with her father. He didn't know when she came to bed or when she got up. ³⁴The next day the older daughter said to the younger one, "I did it! Last night I went to bed with my father. Let's give him wine to drink again tonight. Then you go to bed with him so that we'll be able to preserve our family line through our father." ³⁵That night they gave their father wine to drink again. Then the younger one went to bed with him. He didn't know when she came to bed or when she got up. ³⁶So Lot's two daughters became pregnant by their father. ³⁷The older one gave birth to a son and named him Moab. He is the ancestor of the Moabites of today. ³⁸The younger daughter also gave birth to a son and named him Ben Ammi. He is the ancestor of the Ammonites of today.

Abraham Deceives Abimelech

20 ¹Abraham moved to the Negev and settled between Kadesh and Shur. While he was living in Gerar, ²Abraham told everyone that his wife Sarah was his sister. So King Abimelech of Gerar sent men to take Sarah. ³God came to Abimelech in a dream one night and said to him, "You're going to die because of the woman that you've taken! She's a married woman!" ⁴Abimelech hadn't come near her, so he asked, "Lord, will you destroy a nation even if it's innocent? ⁵Didn't he tell me himself, 'She's my sister,' and didn't she even say, 'He's my brother'? I did this in all innocence and with a clear conscience."

⁶"Yes, I know that you did this with a clear conscience," God said to him in the dream. "In fact, I kept you from sinning against me. That's why I didn't let you touch her. ⁷Give the man's wife back to him now, because he's a prophet. He will pray for

you, and you will live. But if you don't give her back, you and all who belong to you are doomed to die."

⁸Early in the morning Abimelech called together all his officials. He told them about all of this, and they were terrified. ⁹Then Abimelech called for Abraham and asked him, "What have you done to us? How have I sinned against you that you would bring such a serious sin on me and my kingdom? You shouldn't have done this to me." ¹⁰Abimelech also asked Abraham, "What were you thinking when you did this?"

¹¹Abraham said, "I thought that because there are no God-fearing people in this place, I'd be killed because of my wife. ¹²Besides, she is my sister—my father's daughter but not my mother's. She is also my wife. ¹³When God had me leave my father's home and travel around, I said to her, 'Do me a favor: Wherever we go, say that I'm your brother.' "

¹⁴Then Abimelech took sheep, cattle, and male and female slaves and gave them to Abraham. He also gave his wife Sarah back to him. ¹⁵Abimelech said, "Look, here's my land. Live anywhere you like." ¹⁶He said to Sarah, "Don't forget, I've given your brother 25 pounds of silver. This is to silence any criticism against you from everyone with you. You're completely cleared."

¹⁷Abraham prayed to God, and God healed Abimelech, his wife, and his female slaves so that they could have children. ¹⁸(The Lord had made it impossible for any woman in Abimelech's household to have children because of Abraham's wife Sarah.)

God Provides for Hagar and Ishmael

¹The Lord came to help Sarah and did for her what he had promised. ²So she became pregnant, and at the exact time God had promised, she gave birth to a son for Abraham in his old age. ³Abraham named his newborn son Isaac. ⁴When Isaac was eight days old, Abraham circumcised him as God had commanded. ⁵Abraham was 100 years old when his son Isaac was born.

⁶Sarah said, "God has brought me laughter, and everyone who hears about this will laugh with me. ⁷Who would have predicted to Abraham that Sarah would nurse children? Yet, I have given him a son in his old age."

⁸The child grew and was weaned. On the day Isaac was weaned, Abraham held a big feast. ⁹Sarah saw that Abraham's son by Hagar the Egyptian was laughing at Isaac. ¹⁰She said to Abraham, "Get rid of this slave and her son, because this slave's son must never share the inheritance with my son Isaac." ¹¹Abraham was upset by this because of his son Ishmael. ¹²But God said to Abraham, "Don't be upset about the boy and your slave. Listen to what Sarah says because through Isaac your descendants will carry on your name. ¹³Besides, I will make the slave's son into a nation also, because he is your child."

¹⁴Early the next morning Abraham took bread and a container of water and gave them to Hagar, putting them on her shoulder. He also gave her the boy and sent her on her way. So she left and wandered around in the desert near Beersheba. ¹⁵When the water in the container was gone, she put the boy under one of the bushes. ¹⁶Then she went about as far away as an arrow can be shot and sat down. She said to herself, "I don't want to watch the boy die." So she sat down and sobbed loudly.

¹⁷God heard the boy crying, and the Messenger of God called to Hagar from heaven. "What's the matter, Hagar?" he asked her. "Don't be afraid! God has heard the boy crying from the bushes. ¹⁸Come on, help the boy up! Take him by the hand, because I'm going to make him into a great nation."

¹⁹God opened her eyes. Then she saw a well. She filled the container with water and gave the boy a drink.

²⁰God was with the boy as he grew up. He lived in the desert and became a skilled archer. ²¹He lived in the desert of Paran, and his mother got him a wife from Egypt.

Abraham's Agreement With Abimelech

²²At that time Abimelech, accompanied by Phicol, the commander of his army, said to Abraham, "God is with you in everything you do. ²³Now, swear an oath to me here in front of God that you will never cheat me, my children, or my descendants. Show me and the land where you've been living the same kindness that I have shown you."

²⁴Abraham said, "I so swear."

²⁵Then Abraham complained to Abimelech about a well which Abimelech's servants had seized. ²⁶Abimelech replied, "I don't know who did this. You didn't tell me, and I didn't hear about it until today."

²⁷Abraham took some sheep and cattle and gave them to Abimelech, and the two of them made an agreement. ²⁸Then Abraham set apart seven female lambs from the flock. ²⁹Abimelech asked him, "What is the meaning of these seven female lambs you have set apart?"

³⁰Abraham answered, "Accept these lambs from me so that they may be proof *ᵃ* that I dug this well." ³¹This is why that place is called Beersheba,*ᵇ* because both of them swore an oath there.

³²After they made the treaty at Beersheba, Abimelech and Phicol, the commander of his army, left and went back to the land of the Philistines. ³³Abraham planted a tamarisk tree at Beersheba and worshiped the LORD, the Everlasting God, there. ³⁴Abraham lived a long time in the land of the Philistines.

God Tests Abraham

¹Later God tested Abraham and called to him, "Abraham!"

"Yes, here I am!" he answered.

²God said, "Take your son, your only son Isaac, whom you love, and go to Moriah. Sacrifice him there as a burnt offering on one of the mountains that I will show you."

³Early the next morning Abraham saddled his donkey. He took with him two of his servants and his son Isaac. When he had cut the wood for the burnt offering, he set out for the place that God had told him about. ⁴Two days later Abraham saw the place in the distance. ⁵Then Abraham said to his servants, "You stay here with the donkey while the boy and I go over there. We'll worship. After that we'll come back to you."

⁶Then Abraham took the wood for the burnt offering and gave it to his son Isaac. Abraham carried the burning coals and the knife. The two of them went on together.

⁷Isaac spoke up and said, "Father?"

"Yes, Son?" Abraham answered.

Isaac asked, "We have the burning coals and the wood, but where is the lamb for the burnt offering?"

⁸Abraham answered, "God will provide a lamb for the burnt offering, Son."

The two of them went on together. ⁹When they came to the place that God had told him about, Abraham built the altar and arranged the wood on it. Then he tied up his son Isaac and laid him on top of the wood on the altar. ¹⁰Next, Abraham picked up the knife and took it in his hand to sacrifice his son. ¹¹But the Messenger of the LORD called to him from heaven and said, "Abraham! Abraham!"

ᵃ 21:30 Or "a witness." *ᵇ* 21:31 *Beersheba* can mean either "Well of the Seven" or "Well of the Oath."

"Yes?" he answered.

¹²"Do not lay a hand on the boy," he said. "Do not do anything to him. Now I know that you fear God, because you did not refuse to give me your son, your only son."

¹³When Abraham looked around, he saw a ram behind him caught by its horns in a bush. So Abraham took the ram and sacrificed it as a burnt offering in place of his son. ¹⁴Abraham named that place The LORD Will Provide. It is still said today, "On the mountain of the LORD it will be provided."

The LORD's Seventh Promise to Abraham

¹⁵Then the Messenger of the LORD called to Abraham from heaven a second time ¹⁶and said, "I am taking an oath on my own name, declares the LORD, that because you have done this and have not refused to give me your son, your only son, ¹⁷I will certainly bless you and make your descendants as numerous as the stars in the sky and the grains of sand on the seashore. Your descendants will take possession of their enemies' cities. ¹⁸Through your descendant all the nations of the earth will be blessed, because you have obeyed me."

¹⁹Then Abraham returned to his servants, and together they left for Beersheba. Abraham remained in Beersheba.

Abraham Learns of Nahor's Descendants

²⁰Later Abraham was told, "Milcah has given birth to these children of your brother Nahor: ²¹Uz (the firstborn), Buz (his brother), Kemuel (father of Aram), ²²Kesed, Hazo, Pildash, Jidlaph, and Bethuel. ²³Bethuel is the father of Rebekah. Milcah had these eight sons by Abraham's brother Nahor. ²⁴Nahor's concubine,ᵃ whose name was Reumah, had the following children: Tebah, Gaham, Tahash, and Maacah."

Sarah's Death

23 ¹Sarah lived to be 127 years old. This was the length of her life. ²She died in Kiriath Arba (that is, Hebron) in Canaan. Abraham went to mourn for Sarah and to cry about her death.

³Then Abraham left the side of his dead wife and spoke to the Hittites, ⁴"I'm a stranger with no permanent home. Let me have some of your property for a tomb so that I can bury my dead wife."

⁵The Hittites answered Abraham, ⁶"Listen to us, sir. You are a mighty leader among us. Bury your dead in one of our best tombs. Not one of us will withhold from you his tomb for burying your dead."

⁷Abraham got up in front of the Hittites, the people of that region, and bowed with his face touching the ground. ⁸He said to them, "If you are willing to let me bury my wife, listen to me. Encourage Ephron, son of Zohar, ⁹to let me have the cave of Machpelah that he owns at the end of his field. He should sell it to me for its full price as my property to be used as a tomb among you."

¹⁰Ephron was sitting among the Hittites. He answered Abraham so that everyone who was entering the city gate could hear him. He said, ¹¹"No, sir, listen to me. I'm giving you the field together with the cave that is in it. My people are witnesses that I'm giving it to you. Bury your wife!"

¹²Abraham bowed down again in front of the people of that region. ¹³He spoke to Ephron so that the people of that region could hear him. He said, "If you would only listen to me. I will pay you the price of the field. Take it from me so that I can bury my wife there."

ᵃ 22:24 A concubine is considered a wife except she has fewer rights under the law.

[14]Ephron answered Abraham, [15]"Sir, listen to me. The land is worth ten pounds of silver. What is that between us? Bury your wife!"

[16]Abraham agreed to Ephron's terms. So he weighed out for Ephron the amount stated in front of the Hittites: ten pounds of silver at the current merchants' exchange rate.

[17]So Ephron's field at Machpelah, east of Mamre, was sold [18]to Abraham. His property included the field with the cave in it as well as all the trees inside the boundaries of the field.[a] The Hittites together with all who had entered the city gate were the official witnesses for the agreement.

[19]After this, Abraham buried his wife Sarah in the cave in the field of Machpelah, east of Mamre (that is, Hebron). [20]So the field and its cave were sold by the Hittites to Abraham as his property to be used as a tomb.

Abraham Instructs His Servant

[1]By now Abraham was old, and the LORD had blessed him in every way. [2]So Abraham said to the senior servant of his household who was in charge of all that he owned, "Take a solemn oath. [3]I want you to swear by the LORD God of heaven and earth that you will not get my son a wife from the daughters of the Canaanites among whom I'm living. [4]Instead, you will go to the land of my relatives and get a wife for my son Isaac."

[5]The servant asked him, "What if the woman doesn't want to come back to this land with me? Should I take your son all the way back to the land you came from?"

[6]"Make sure that you do not take my son back there," Abraham said to him. [7]"The LORD God of heaven took me from my father's home and the land of my family. He spoke to me and swore this oath: 'I will give this land to your descendants.'

"God will send his angel ahead of you, and you will get my son a wife from there. [8]If the woman doesn't want to come back with you, then you'll be free from this oath that you swear to me. But don't take my son back there." [9]So the servant did as his master Abraham commanded and swore the oath to him concerning this.

[10]Then the servant took ten of his master's camels and left, taking with him all of his master's best things. He traveled to Aram Naharaim, Nahor's city.

Good Morning, God

Genesis 24:1-4, 17-27

Abraham wanted his son Isaac to marry a woman who would love God and love others. Abraham's servant was in charge of returning to Abraham's relatives to find such a person. The servant asked God to help him find a wife for Isaac. He didn't look for the prettiest or most popular woman in town. The servant looked for a woman who was kind to strangers and helped others. Rebekah had those qualities, and she was the one God chose for Isaac.

God, help me to choose friends based on who they are on the inside.

---

[a]23:18 The last part of verse 17 (in Hebrew) has been placed in verse 18 to express the complex Hebrew sentence structure more clearly in English.

Rebekah

Genesis 24

Rebekah's kindness impressed Abraham's servant.

Rebekah was a daughter of Abraham's nephew, Lot. Abraham had sent a servant to these distant relatives in order to find a bride for his son, Isaac. The servant prayed that God would lead him to the right young woman by giving him a sign.

The servant's prayer was answered when Rebekah gladly drew water for the visitor and volunteered to draw water for his camels, too.

Showing hospitality was an important virtue in Bible times. Rebekah welcomed the visitor into her house, and there Abraham's servant explained the reason for his visit.

When Rebekah's family heard how the Lord had answered the servant's prayer, they decided to let Rebekah go. And when Rebekah was asked if she wanted to be Isaac's wife, she said, "Yes, I'll go!"

Rebekah became Isaac's wife, and the Bible says, "He loved her."

Getting to Know Rebekah

✳ What good qualities did the servant see in Rebekah when she drew water for him and his camels?

Rebekah was born around 2050 B.C.

Rebekah's father was a nephew of Abraham.

Rebekah married Isaac, the son of Abraham.

Rebekah had two sons, Jacob and Esau.

Rebekah's son Jacob was renamed Israel. His 12 sons became the heads of the 12 tribes of the Jewish people.

✳ Why would these qualities make her a good wife for Isaac?

✳ What good qualities should you look for in a husband or boyfriend?

✳ Why did Rebekah make the difficult decision to leave her family?

✳ Whom do you know who is like Rebekah?

The women of the village usually gathered at the well or spring each morning to fill jars with water for washing, cooking, and drinking. It was a good time to talk with friends. Women carried the full jars home by balancing them on their heads.

When Rebekah agreed to become Isaac's bride, she was given gold jewelry that may have looked like this.

Abraham's Servant Finds a Wife for Isaac

[11]The servant had the camels kneel down outside the city by the well. It was evening, when the women would go out to draw water. [12]Then he prayed, "Lord, God of my master Abraham, make me successful today. Show your kindness to Abraham. [13]Here I am standing by the spring, and the girls of the city are coming out to draw water. [14]I will ask a girl, 'May I please have a drink from your jar?' If she answers, 'Have a drink, and I'll also water your camels,' let her be the one you have chosen for your servant Isaac. This way I'll know that you've shown your kindness to my master."

[15]Before he had finished praying, Rebekah came with her jar on her shoulder. She was the daughter of Bethuel, son of Milcah, who was the wife of Abraham's brother Nahor. [16]The girl was a very attractive virgin. No man had ever had sexual intercourse with her. She went down to the spring, filled her jar, and came back.

[17]The servant ran to meet her and said, "Please give me a drink of water."

[18]"Drink, sir," she said. She quickly lowered her jar to her hand and gave him a drink. [19]When she had finished giving him a drink, she said, "I'll also keep drawing water for your camels until they've had enough to drink." [20]So she quickly emptied her jar into the water trough, ran back to the well to draw more water, and drew enough for all his camels. [21]The man was silently watching her to see whether or not the Lord had made his trip successful.

[22]When the camels had finished drinking, the man took out a gold nose ring weighing a fifth of an ounce and two gold bracelets weighing four ounces. [23]He asked, "Whose daughter are you? Please tell me whether there is room in your father's house for us to spend the night."

[24]She answered him, "I'm the daughter of Bethuel, son of Milcah and Nahor. [25]We have plenty of straw and feed for your camels, and room for you to spend the night."

[26]The man knelt, bowing to the Lord with his face touching the ground. [27]He said, "Praise the Lord, the God of my master Abraham. The Lord hasn't failed to be kind and faithful to my master. The Lord has led me on this trip to the home of my master's relatives."

[28]The girl ran and told her mother's household about these things. [29]Rebekah had a brother whose name was Laban. [30]He saw the nose ring and the bracelets on his sister's wrists and heard her tell what the man had said to her. Immediately, Laban ran out to the man by the spring.[a] He came to the man, who was standing with the camels by the spring. [31]He said, "Come in, you whom the Lord has blessed. Why are you standing out here? I have straightened up the house and made a place for the camels."

[32]So the man went into the house. The camels were unloaded and given straw and feed. Then water was brought for him and his men to wash their feet. [33]When the food was put in front of him, he said, "I won't eat until I've said what I have to say."

"Speak up," Laban said.

[34]"I am Abraham's servant," he said. [35]"The Lord has blessed my master, and he has become wealthy. The Lord has given him sheep and cattle, silver and gold, male and female slaves, camels and donkeys. [36]My master's wife Sarah gave him a son in her old age, and my master has given that son everything he has. [37]My master made me swear this oath: 'Don't get a wife for my son from the daughters of the Canaanites, in whose land I'm living. [38]Instead, go to my father's home and to my relatives, and get my son a wife.'

---

[a]24:30 The last part of verse 29 (in Hebrew) has been placed in verse 30 to express the complex Hebrew sentence structure more clearly in English.

[39]"I asked my master, 'What if the woman won't come back with me?'

[40]"He answered me, 'I have been living the way the LORD wants me to. The LORD will send his angel with you to make your trip successful. You will get my son a wife from my relatives and from my father's family. [41]Then you will be free from your oath to me. You will also be free of your oath to me if my relatives are not willing to do this when you go to them.'

[42]"When I came to the spring today, I prayed, 'LORD God of my master Abraham, please make my trip successful. [43]I'm standing by the spring. I'll say to the young woman who comes out to draw water, "Please give me a drink of water." [44]If she says to me, "Not only may you have a drink, but I will also draw water for your camels," let her be the woman the LORD has chosen for my master's son.'

[45]"Before I had finished praying, Rebekah came with her jar on her shoulder. She went down to the spring and drew water.

"So I asked her, 'May I have a drink?' [46]She quickly lowered her jar and said, 'Have a drink, and I'll water your camels too.' So I drank, and she also watered the camels.

[47]"Then I asked her, 'Whose daughter are you?'

"She answered, 'The daughter of Bethuel, son of Nahor and Milcah.'

"I put the ring in her nose and the bracelets on her wrists. [48]I knelt, bowing down to the LORD. I praised the LORD, the God of my master Abraham. The LORD led me in the right direction to get the daughter of my master's relative for his son. [49]Tell me whether or not you're going to show my master true kindness so that I will know what to do."

[50]Laban and Bethuel answered, "This is from the LORD. We can't say anything to you one way or another. [51]Here's Rebekah! Take her and go! She will become the wife of your master's son, as the LORD has said."

[52]When Abraham's servant heard their answer, he bowed down to the LORD. [53]The servant took out gold and silver jewelry and clothes and gave them to Rebekah. He also gave expensive presents to her brother and mother. [54]Then he and the men who were with him ate and drank and spent the night. When they got up in the morning, he said, "Let me go back to my master."

[55]Her brother and mother replied, "Let the girl stay with us ten days or so. After that she may go."

[56]He said to them, "Don't delay me now that the LORD has made my trip successful. Let me go back to my master."

[57]So they said, "We'll call the girl and ask her."

[58]They called for Rebekah and asked her, "Will you go with this man?"

She said, "Yes, I'll go."

[59]So they let their sister Rebekah and her nurse go with Abraham's servant and his men. [60]They gave Rebekah a blessing:

"May you, our sister, become the mother of many thousands of children.
May your descendants take possession of their enemies' cities."

[61]Then Rebekah and her maids left. Riding on camels, they followed the man. The servant took Rebekah and left.

Isaac and Rebekah Are Married

[62]Isaac had just come back from Beer Lahai Roi, since he was living in the Negev. [63]Toward evening Isaac went out into the field to meditate.[b] When he looked up, he

---

[b]24:63 Greek; Hebrew meaning uncertain.

saw camels coming. [64]When Rebekah saw Isaac, she got down from her camel. [65]She asked the servant, "Who is that man over there coming through the field to meet us?"

"That is my master," the servant answered. Then she took her veil and covered herself. [66]The servant reported to Isaac everything he had done. [67]Isaac took her into his mother Sarah's tent. He married Rebekah. She became his wife, and he loved her. So Isaac was comforted after his mother's death.

Abraham's Second Marriage and His Death—
1 Chronicles 1:32-33

[1]Abraham married again, and his wife's name was Keturah. [2]Keturah gave birth to these sons of Abraham: Zimran, Jokshan, Medan, Midian, Ishbak, and Shuah. [3]Jokshan was the father of Sheba and Dedan. Dedan's descendants were the Assyrians, the Letushites, and the Leummites. [4]The sons of Midian were Ephah, Epher, Hanoch, Abida, and Eldaah. These were the descendants of Keturah.

[5]Abraham left everything he had to Isaac. [6]But while he was still living, Abraham had given gifts to the sons of his concubines.[a] He sent them away from his son Isaac to a land in the east.

[7]Abraham lived 175 years. [8]Then he took his last breath, and died at a very old age. After a long and full life, he joined his ancestors in death. [9]His sons Isaac and Ishmael buried him in the cave of Machpelah in the field of Ephron, son of Zohar the Hittite. The cave is east of Mamre. [10]This was the field that Abraham had bought from the Hittites. There Abraham was buried with his wife Sarah. [11]After Abraham died, God blessed his son Isaac, who settled near Beer Lahai Roi.

The 12 Tribes of Ishmael—
1 Chronicles 1:29-31

[12]This is the account of the descendants of Abraham's son Ishmael. He was the son of Sarah's Egyptian slave Hagar and Abraham. [13]These are the names of the sons of Ishmael listed in the order of their birth: Nebaioth (Ishmael's firstborn), Kedar, Adbeel, Mibsam, [14]Mishma, Dumah, Massa, [15]Hadad, Tema, Jetur, Naphish, and Kedemah. [16]These are the sons of Ishmael and their names listed by their settlements and camps—12 leaders of their tribes.

[17]Ishmael lived 137 years. Then he took his last breath and died. He joined his ancestors in death. [18]His descendants lived as nomads from the region of Havilah to Shur, which is near Egypt, in the direction of Assyria. They all fought with each other.

Esau and Jacob

[19]This is the account of Abraham's son Isaac and his descendants. Abraham was the father of Isaac. [20]Isaac was 40 years old when he married Rebekah, daughter of Bethuel the Aramean from Paddan Aram and sister of Laban the Aramean. [21]Isaac prayed to the LORD for his wife because she was childless. The LORD answered his prayer, and his wife Rebekah became pregnant. [22]When the children inside her were struggling with each other, she said, "If it's like this now, what will become of me?"[b] So she went to ask the LORD.

[23]The LORD said to her,

"Two countries are in your womb.
Two nations will go their separate ways from birth.

[a]25:6 A concubine is considered a wife except she has fewer rights under the law. [b] 25:22 Hebrew meaning of this sentence uncertain.

One nation will be stronger than the other,
and the older will serve the younger."

²⁴When the time came for her to give birth, she had twins. ²⁵The first one born was red. His whole body was covered with hair, so they named him Esau [Hairy]. ²⁶Afterwards, his brother was born with his hand holding on to Esau's heel, and so he was named Jacob [Heel]. Isaac was 60 years old when they were born.

²⁷They grew up. Esau became an expert hunter, an outdoorsman. Jacob remained a quiet man, staying around the tents. ²⁸Because Isaac liked to eat the meat of wild animals, he loved Esau. However, Rebekah loved Jacob.

²⁹Once, Jacob was preparing a meal when Esau, exhausted, came in from outdoors. ³⁰So Esau said to Jacob, "Let me have the whole pot of red stuff to eat—that red stuff—I'm exhausted." This is why he was called Edom.ᶜ

³¹Jacob responded, "First, sell me your rights as firstborn."

³²"I'm about to die." Esau said. "What good is my inheritance to me?"

³³"First, swear an oath," Jacob said. So Esau swore an oath to him and sold him his rights as firstborn. ³⁴Then Jacob gave Esau a meal of bread and lentils. He ate and drank, and then he got up and left.

This is how Esau showed his contempt for his rights as firstborn.

The LORD's First Promise to Isaac

26 ¹There was a famine in the land in addition to the earlier one during Abraham's time. So Isaac went to King Abimelech of the Philistines in Gerar.

²The LORD appeared to Isaac and said, "Don't go to Egypt. Stay where I tell you. ³Live here in this land for a while, and I will be with you and bless you. I will give all these lands to you and your descendants. I will keep the oath that I swore to your father Abraham. ⁴I will make your descendants as numerous as the stars in the sky and give all these lands to your descendants. Through your descendant all the nations of the earth will be blessed. ⁵I will bless you because Abraham obeyed me and completed the duties, commands, laws, and instructions I gave him." ⁶So Isaac lived in Gerar.

Isaac and Rebekah at Gerar

⁷When the men of that place asked about his wife, Isaac answered, "She's my sister." He was afraid to say "my wife." He thought that the men of that place would kill him to get Rebekah, because she was an attractive woman. ⁸When he had been there a long time, King Abimelech of the Philistines looked out of his window and saw Isaac caressing his wife Rebekah.

⁹Abimelech called for Isaac and said, "So she's really your wife! How could you say, 'She's my sister'?"

Isaac answered him, "I thought I would be killed because of her."

¹⁰Then Abimelech said, "What have you done to us! One of the people might have easily gone to bed with your wife, and then you would have made us guilty of sin." ¹¹So Abimelech ordered his people, "Anyone who touches this man or his wife will be put to death."

¹²Isaac planted ⌐crops⌐ in that land. In that same year he harvested a hundred times as much as he had planted because the LORD had blessed him. ¹³He continued to be successful, becoming very rich. ¹⁴Because he owned so many flocks, herds, and

---

ᶜ 25:30 There is a play on words here between Hebrew *'adom* (red stuff) and Edom.

servants, the Philistines became jealous of him. [15]So the Philistines filled in all the wells that his father's servants had dug during his father Abraham's lifetime.

[16]Finally, Abimelech said to Isaac, "Go away from us! You've become more powerful than we are."

[17]So Isaac moved away. He set up his tents in the Gerar Valley and lived there. [18]He dug out the wells that had been dug during his father Abraham's lifetime. The Philistines had filled them in after Abraham's death. He gave them the same names that his father had given them.

[19]Isaac's servants dug in the valley and found a spring-fed well. [20]The herders from Gerar quarreled with Isaac's herders, claiming, "This water is ours!" So Isaac named the well Esek [Argument], because they had argued with him. [21]Then they dug another well, and they quarreled over that one too. So Isaac named it Sitnah [Accusation]. [22]He moved on from there and dug another well. They didn't quarrel over this one. So he named it Rehoboth [Roomy] and said, "Now the Lord has made room for us, and we will prosper in this land."

The Lord's Second Promise to Isaac

[23]He went from there to Beersheba. [24]That night the Lord appeared to Isaac, and said, "I am the God of your father Abraham. Don't be afraid, because I am with you. I will bless you and increase the number of your descendants for my servant Abraham's sake." [25]So Isaac built an altar there and worshiped the Lord. He also pitched his tent in that place, and his servants dug a well there.

Isaac's Agreement With Abimelech

[26]Abimelech, his friend Ahuzzath, and Phicol, the commander of his army, came from Gerar to see Isaac. [27]Isaac asked them, "Why have you come to me, since you hate me and sent me away from you?"

[28]They answered, "We have seen that the Lord is with you. So we thought, 'There should be a solemn agreement between us.' We'd like to make an agreement with you [29]that you will not harm us, since we have not touched you. We have done only good to you and let you go in peace. Now you are blessed by the Lord."

[30]Isaac prepared a special dinner for them, and they ate and drank. [31]Early the next morning they exchanged oaths. Then Isaac sent them on their way, and they left peacefully.

[32]That same day Isaac's servants came and told him about a well they had dug. They said to him, "We've found water." [33]So he named it Shibah [Oath]. That is why the name of the city is still Beersheba today.

Esau's Marriages

[34]When Esau was 40 years old, he married Judith, daughter of Beeri the Hittite. He also married Basemath, daughter of Elon the Hittite. [35]These women brought Isaac and Rebekah a lot of grief.

Jacob Gets Isaac's Blessing

27 [1]When Isaac was old and going blind, he called his older son Esau and said to him, "Son!"

Esau answered, "Here I am."

[2]Isaac said, "I'm old. I don't know when I'm going to die. [3]Now take your hunting equipment, your quiver and bow, and go out into the open country and hunt some wild game for me. [4]Prepare a good-tasting meal for me, just the way I like it. Bring it to me to eat so that I will bless you before I die."

⁵Rebekah was listening while Isaac was speaking to his son Esau. When Esau went into the open country to hunt for some wild game to bring back, ⁶Rebekah said to her son Jacob, "I've just heard your father speaking to your brother Esau. ⁷He said, 'Bring me some wild game, and prepare a good-tasting meal for me to eat so that I will bless you in the presence of the LORD before I die.' ⁸Now listen to me, Son, and do what I tell you. ⁹Go to the flock, and get me two good young goats. I'll prepare them as a good-tasting meal for your father, just the way he likes it. ¹⁰Then take it to your father to eat so that he will bless you before he dies."

¹¹Jacob said to his mother Rebekah, "My brother Esau is a hairy man, and my skin is smooth.ᵃ ¹²My father will feel ˌmy skinˌ and think I'm mocking him. Then I'll bring a curse on myself instead of a blessing."

¹³His mother responded, "Let any curse on you fall on me, Son. Just obey me and go! Get me ˌthe young goatsˌ."

¹⁴He went and got them and brought them to his mother. She prepared a good-tasting meal, just the way his father liked it. ¹⁵Then Rebekah took her older son Esau's good clothes, which she had in the house, and put them on her younger son Jacob. ¹⁶She put the skins from the young goats on his hands and on the back of his neck. ¹⁷Then she gave her son Jacob the good-tasting meal and the bread she had prepared.

¹⁸He went to his father and said, "Father?"

"Yes?" he answered. "Who are you, Son?"

¹⁹Jacob answered his father, "I'm Esau, your firstborn. I've done what you told me. Sit up and eat this meat I've hunted for you so that you may bless me."

²⁰Isaac asked his son, "How did you find it so quickly, Son?"

"The LORD your God brought it to me," he answered.

²¹Then Isaac said to Jacob, "Come over here so that I can feel your skin, Son, ˌto find outˌ whether or not you really are my son Esau." ²²So Jacob went over to his father. Isaac felt ˌhis skinˌ. "The voice is Jacob's," he said, "but the hands are Esau's." ²³He didn't recognize Jacob, because his hands were hairy like his brother Esau's hands. So he blessed him. ²⁴"Are you really my son Esau?" he asked him.

"I am," Jacob answered.

²⁵Isaac said, "Bring me some of the game, and I will eat it, Son, so that I will bless you." Jacob brought it to Isaac, and he ate it. Jacob also brought him wine, and he drank it.

²⁶Then his father Isaac said to him, "Come here and give me a kiss, Son." ²⁷He went over and gave him a kiss. When Isaac smelled his clothes, he blessed him and said,

> "The smell of my son
>   is like the smell of open country
>   that the LORD has blessed.
> ²⁸ May God give you dew from the sky,
>   fertile fields on the earth,
>   and plenty of fresh grain and new wine.
> ²⁹ May nations serve you.
> May people bow down to you.
>   Be the master of your brothers,
>   and may the sons of your mother bow down to you.
> May those who curse you be cursed.
> May those who bless you be blessed."

ᵃ27:11 Or "but I am a smooth man."

³⁰Isaac finished blessing Jacob. Jacob had barely left when his brother Esau came in from hunting. ³¹He, too, prepared a good-tasting meal and brought it to his father. Then he said to his father, "Please, Father, eat some of the meat I've hunted for you so that you will bless me."

³²"Who are you?" his father Isaac asked him.

"I'm your firstborn son Esau," he answered.

³³Trembling violently all over, Isaac asked, "Who hunted game and brought it to me? I ate it before you came in. I blessed him, and he will stay blessed."

³⁴When Esau heard these words from his father, he shouted out a very loud and bitter cry and said to his father, "Bless me too, Father!"

³⁵Isaac said, "Your brother came and deceived me and has taken away your blessing."

³⁶Esau said, "Isn't that why he's named Jacob? He's cheated me twice already: He took my rights as firstborn, and now he's taken my blessing." So he asked, "Haven't you saved a blessing for me?"

³⁷Isaac answered Esau, "I have made him your master, and I have made all his brothers serve him. I've provided fresh grain and new wine for him. What is left for me to do for you, Son?"

³⁸Esau asked, "Do you have only one blessing, Father? Bless me too, Father!" And Esau sobbed loudly.

³⁹His father Isaac answered him,

> "The place where you live will lack the fertile fields of the earth
>> and the dew from the sky above.
> ⁴⁰ You will use your sword to live,
>> and you will serve your brother.
>> But eventually you will gain your freedom*ᵇ*
>> and break his yoke*ᶜ* off your neck."

⁴¹So Esau hated Jacob because of the blessing that his father had given him. Esau said to himself, "The time to mourn for my father is near. Then I'll kill my brother Jacob."

⁴²When Rebekah was told what her older son Esau had said, she sent for her younger son Jacob and said to him, "Watch out! Your brother Esau is comforting himself by planning to kill you.*ᵈ* ⁴³So now, Son, obey me. Quick! Run away to my brother Laban in Haran. ⁴⁴Stay with him awhile, until your brother's anger cools down. ⁴⁵When your brother's anger is gone and he has forgotten what you did to him, I'll send for you and get you back. Why should I lose both of you in one day?"

⁴⁶Rebekah said to Isaac, "I can't stand Hittite women! If Jacob marries a Hittite woman like one of those from around here, I might as well die."

Isaac Sends Jacob Away

28 ¹Isaac called for Jacob and blessed him. Then he commanded him, "You are not to marry any of the Canaanite women. ²Quick! Go to Paddan Aram. Go to the home of Bethuel, your mother's father, and get yourself a wife from there from the daughters of your uncle Laban. ³May God Almighty bless you, make you fertile, and increase the number of your descendants so that you will become a community of people. ⁴May he give to you and your descendants the blessing of Abraham so that

---

ᵇ 27:40 Hebrew meaning uncertain.   *ᶜ* 27:40 A yoke is a wooden bar placed over the necks of work animals so that they can pull plows or carts. *ᵈ* 27:42 English equivalent difficult.

you may take possession of the land where you are now living, the land that God gave to Abraham."

⁵Isaac sent Jacob to Paddan Aram. Jacob went to live with Laban, son of Bethuel the Aramean and brother of Rebekah. She was the mother of Jacob and Esau.

⁶Esau learned that Isaac had blessed Jacob and had sent him away to Paddan Aram to get a wife from there. He learned that Isaac had blessed Jacob and had commanded him not to marry any of the Canaanite women. ⁷He also learned that Jacob had obeyed his father and mother and had left for Paddan Aram. ⁸Esau realized that his father Isaac disapproved of Canaanite women. ⁹So he went to Ishmael and married Mahalath, daughter of Abraham's son Ishmael and sister of Nebaioth, in addition to the wives he had.

Jacob's First Encounter With God

¹⁰Jacob left Beersheba and traveled toward Haran. ¹¹When he came to a certain place, he stopped for the night because the sun had gone down. He took one of the stones from that place, put it under his head, and lay down there. ¹²He had a dream in which he saw a stairway set up on the earth with its top reaching up to heaven. He saw the angels of God going up and coming down on it. ¹³The LORD was standing above it, saying, "I am the LORD, the God of your grandfather Abraham and the God of Isaac. I will give the land on which you are lying to you and your descendants. ¹⁴Your descendants will be like the dust on the earth. You will spread out to the west and to the east, to the north and to the south. Through you and through your descendant every family on earth will be blessed. ¹⁵Remember, I am with you and will watch over you wherever you go. I will also bring you back to this land because I will not leave you until I do what I've promised you."

¹⁶Then Jacob woke up from his sleep and exclaimed, "Certainly, the LORD is in this place, and I didn't know it!" ¹⁷Filled with awe, he said, "How awe-inspiring this place is! Certainly, this is the house of God and the gateway to heaven!"

¹⁸Early the next morning Jacob took the stone he had put under his head. He set it up as a marker and poured olive oil on top of it. ¹⁹He named that place Bethel [House of God]. Previously, the name of the city was Luz.

²⁰Then Jacob made a vow: "If God will be with me and will watch over me on my trip and give me food to eat and clothes to wear, ²¹and if I return safely to my father's home, then the LORD will be my God. ²²This stone that I have set up as a marker will be the house of God, and I will surely give you a tenth of everything you give me."

Jacob's Arrival in Haran

¹Jacob continued on his trip and came to the land in the east. ²He looked around, and out in a field he saw a well with a large stone over the opening. Three flocks of sheep were lying down near it, because the flocks were watered from that well. ³When all the flocks were gathered there, the stone would be rolled off the opening of the well so that the sheep could be watered. Then the stone would be put back in place over the opening of the well.

⁴Jacob asked some people, "My friends, where are you from?"

"We're from Haran," they replied.

⁵He asked them, "Do you know Laban, Nahor's grandson?"

They answered, "We do."

⁶"How is he doing?" Jacob asked them.

"He's fine," they answered. "Here comes his daughter Rachel with the sheep."

⁷"It's still the middle of the day," he said. "It isn't time yet to gather the livestock. Water the sheep. Then let them graze."

Leah

Leah named one of her children Judah, which means "Praise."

Leah, Laban's older daughter, was rather plain. She had a younger sister, Rachel, who was very beautiful. Their relative, Jacob, worked for seven years to earn the right to marry Rachel. But Laban tricked Jacob and gave him his daughter Leah instead. At that time, men sometimes had more than one wife, and after negotiating with Laban, a week later, Jacob also married Rachel.

Leah knew Jacob loved her sister and not her. She wanted her husband to love her as well. Leah's desire for Jacob's love continued through the births of her first three sons. The names of her sons show that she hoped the children would bring Jacob closer to her and give a glimpse of Leah's misery in feeling unloved by her husband. Leah named her sons Reuben (meaning "here's my son"), Simeon ("the Lord has heard me"), and Levi ("attached").

Leah began to have a change of heart with the births of her last three sons. Leah named her fourth son Judah ("praise") because she praised God for his birth. Her next son she named Issachar ("reward"). Her last son she named Zebulun ("honor").

At first Leah felt jealous of Rachel because Rachel was beautiful and Jacob loved her so much. Later, Leah began to look at what the Lord had given her instead of at what she didn't have. She felt joy because God had rewarded her with many children. Through her six sons, Leah became the mother of half the tribes of Israel!

Leah was born around 1950 B.C.

The name Leah is thought to mean "wild cow."

Leah was Jacob's first wife.

Leah had six sons and one daughter.

Getting to Know Leah

✳ Why was Leah so jealous of Rachel?
✳ How did God reward Leah for her love and faithfulness to her husband?
✳ Who have you compared yourself to or been jealous of? Why?
✳ What has God given you for which you are thankful?

Women who lived during Leah's time wore veils when they were married. Because Leah was wearing a veil, Jacob did not recognize her. He thought that he was marrying her sister, Rachel.

⁸They replied, "We can't until all the flocks are gathered. When the stone is rolled off the opening of the well, we can water the sheep."

⁹While he was still talking to them, Rachel arrived with her father's sheep, because she was a shepherd. ¹⁰Jacob saw Rachel, daughter of his uncle Laban, with his uncle Laban's sheep. He came forward and rolled the stone off the opening of the well and watered his uncle Laban's sheep. ¹¹Then Jacob kissed Rachel and sobbed loudly. ¹²When Jacob told Rachel that he was her father's nephew and that he was Rebekah's son, she ran and told her father.

¹³As soon as Laban heard the news about his sister's son Jacob, he ran to meet him. He hugged and kissed him and brought him into his home. Then Jacob told Laban all that had happened. ¹⁴Laban said to him, "You are my own flesh and blood."

Jacob Obtains Wives

Jacob stayed with him for a whole month. ¹⁵Then Laban said to him, "Just because you're my relative doesn't mean that you should work for nothing. Tell me what your wages should be."

¹⁶Laban had two daughters. The name of the older one was Leah, and the name of the younger one was Rachel. ¹⁷Leah had attractive eyes,ᵃ but Rachel had a beautiful figure and beautiful features. ¹⁸Jacob loved Rachel. So he offered, "I'll work seven years in return for your younger daughter Rachel."

¹⁹Laban responded, "It's better that I give her to you than to any other man. Stay with me." ²⁰Jacob worked seven years in return for Rachel, but the years seemed like only a few days to him because he loved her.

²¹At the end of the seven years, Jacob said to Laban, "The time is up; give me my wife! I want to sleep with her." ²²So Laban invited all the people of that place and gave a wedding feast. ²³In the evening he took his daughter Leah and brought her to Jacob. Jacob slept with her. When morning came, he realized it was Leah.ᵇ²⁴(Laban had given his slave Zilpah to his daughter Leah as her slave.)

²⁵"What have you done to me?" Jacob asked Laban. "Didn't I work for you in return for Rachel? Why did you cheat me?"

²⁶Laban answered, "It's not our custom to give the younger daughter in marriage before the older one. ²⁷Finish the week of wedding festivities with this daughter. Then we will give you the other one too. But you'll have to work for me another seven years."

²⁸That's what Jacob did. He finished the week with Leah. Then Laban gave his daughter Rachel to him as his wife. ²⁹(Laban had given his slave Bilhah to his daughter Rachel as her slave.) ³⁰Jacob slept with Rachel too. He loved Rachel more than Leah. So he worked for Laban another seven years.

Leah and Rachel Compete for Jacob's Love

³¹When the Lord saw Leah was unloved, he made it possible for her to have children, but Rachel had none. ³²Leah became pregnant and gave birth to a son. She named him Reuben [Here's My Son], because she said, "Certainly, the Lord has seen my misery; now my husband will love me!" ³³She became pregnant again and gave birth to another son. She said, "Certainly, the Lord has heard that I'm unloved, and he also has given me this son." So she named him Simeon [Hearing]. ³⁴She became pregnant again and gave birth to another son. She said, "Now at last my husband will become attached to me because I've given him three sons." So she named him Levi

---

ᵃ29:17 Or "had no sparkle in her eyes."   ᵇ29:23 The first part of verse 25 (in Hebrew) has been placed in verse 23 to express the complex Hebrew paragraph structure more clearly in English.

[Attached]. [35]She became pregnant again and gave birth to another son. She said, "This time I will praise the LORD." So she named him Judah [Praise]. Then she stopped having children.

[1]Rachel saw that she could not have children for Jacob, and she became jealous of her sister. She said to Jacob, "Give me children, or I'll die!"

[2]Jacob became angry with Rachel and asked, "Can I take the place of God, who has kept you from having children?"

[3]She said, "Here's my servant Bilhah. Sleep with her. She can have children for me, and I can build a family for myself through her." [4]So she gave him her slave Bilhah as his wife, and Jacob slept with her. [5]Bilhah became pregnant, and she gave birth to a son for Jacob. [6]Rachel said, "Now God has judged in my favor. He has heard my prayer and has given me a son." So she named him Dan [He Judges].

[7]Rachel's slave Bilhah became pregnant again and gave birth to a second son for Jacob. [8]Rachel said, "I have had a great struggle[a] with my sister, and I have won!" So she named him Naphtali [My Struggle].

[9]When Leah saw that she had stopped having children, she took her slave Zilpah and gave her to Jacob as his wife. [10]Leah's slave Zilpah gave birth to a son for Jacob. [11]Leah said, "I've been lucky!" So she called him Gad [Luck].

[12]Leah's slave Zilpah gave birth to her second son for Jacob. [13]Leah said, "I've been blessed! Women will call me blessed." So she named him Asher [Blessing].

[14]During the wheat harvest Reuben went out into the fields and found some mandrakes.[b] He brought them to his mother Leah. Rachel said to Leah, "Please give me some of your son's mandrakes."

[15]Leah replied, "Isn't it enough that you took my husband? Are you also going to take my son's mandrakes?"

Rachel said, "Very well, Jacob can go to bed with you tonight in return for your son's mandrakes."

[16]As Jacob was coming in from the fields that evening, Leah went out to meet him. "You are to sleep with me," she said. "You are my reward for my son's mandrakes." So he went to bed with her that night. [17]God answered Leah's prayer. She became pregnant and gave birth to her fifth son for Jacob. [18]Leah said, "God has given me my reward because I gave my slave to my husband." So she named him Issachar [Reward].

[19]She became pregnant again and gave birth to her sixth son for Jacob. [20]Leah said, "God has presented me with a beautiful present. This time my husband will honor me because I have given him six sons." So she named him Zebulun [Honor].

[21]Later she gave birth to a daughter and named her Dinah.

[22]Then God remembered Rachel. God answered her prayer and made it possible for her to have children. [23]So she became pregnant and gave birth to a son. Then she said, "God has taken away my disgrace." [24]She named him Joseph [May He Give Another] and said, "May the LORD give me another son."

Jacob's Flocks Prosper

[25]After Rachel gave birth to Joseph, Jacob said to Laban, "Let me go home to my own country. [26]Give me my wives and my children for whom I've worked, and let me go. You know how much work I've done for you."

[27]Laban replied, "Listen to me. I've learned from the signs I've seen that the LORD has blessed me because of you." [28]So he offered, "Name your wages, and I'll pay them."

[29]Jacob responded, "You know how much work I've done for you and what has

---

[a] 30:8 Or "I have struggled the struggles of God."   [b] 30:14 Mandrakes were considered a source of fertility for women.

happened to your livestock under my care. ³⁰The little that you had before I came has grown to a large amount. The LORD has blessed you wherever I've been. When can I do something for my own family?"

³¹Laban asked, "What should I give you?"

"Don't give me anything," Jacob answered. "Instead, do something for me, then I'll go back to taking care of and watching your flocks again. ³²Let me go through all of your flocks today and take every speckled or spotted sheep, every black lamb, and every spotted or speckled goat. They will be my wages. ³³My honesty will speak for itself whenever you come to check on my wages. Any goat I have that isn't speckled or spotted or any lamb that isn't black will be considered stolen."

³⁴Laban answered, "Agreed. We'll do as you've said." ³⁵However, that same day Laban took out the striped and spotted male goats, all the speckled and spotted female goats (every one with white on it), and every black lamb. He had his sons take charge of them. ³⁶He traveled three days away from Jacob. Jacob continued to take care of the rest of Laban's flocks.

³⁷Then Jacob took fresh-cut branches of poplar, almond, and plane trees and peeled the bark on them in strips of white, uncovering the white which was on the branches.ᶜ ³⁸He placed the peeled branches in the troughs directly in front of the flocks, at the watering places where the flocks came to drink. When they were in heat and came to drink, ³⁹they mated in front of the branches. Then they gave birth to young that were striped, speckled, or spotted.

⁴⁰Jacob separated the rams from the flock and made the rest of the sheep face any that were striped or black in Laban's flocks. So he made separate herds for himself and did not add them to Laban's flocks. ⁴¹Whenever the stronger of the flocks were in heat, Jacob would lay the branches in the troughs in front of them so that they would mate by the branches. ⁴²But when the flocks in heat were weak, he didn't lay down the branches. So the weaker ones belonged to Laban and the stronger ones to Jacob. ⁴³As a result, Jacob became very wealthy. He had large flocks, male and female slaves, camels, and donkeys.

Jacob's Second and Third Encounters With God

31 ¹Jacob heard that Laban's sons were saying, "Jacob has taken everything that belonged to our father and has gained all his wealth from him." ²He also noticed that Laban did not appear as friendly to him as before.

³Then the LORD said to Jacob, "Go back to the land of your ancestors and to your relatives, and I will be with you."

⁴So Jacob sent a message to Rachel and Leah to come out to the open country where his flocks were. ⁵He said to them, "I have seen that your father isn't as friendly to me as he was before, but the God of my father has been with me. ⁶You know that I have worked as hard as I could for your father. ⁷Your father has cheated me. He has changed my wages ten times. But God hasn't let him harm me. ⁸Whenever he said, 'The speckled ones will be your wages,' all the flocks gave birth to speckled young. And whenever he said, 'The striped ones will be your wages,' all the flocks gave birth to striped young. ⁹So God has taken away your father's livestock and has given them to me.

¹⁰"During the mating season I had a dream: I looked up and saw that the male goats which were mating were striped, speckled, or spotted. ¹¹In the dream the Messenger of God called to me, 'Jacob!' And I answered, 'Yes, here I am.' ¹²He said, 'Look up

and see that all the male goats which are mating are striped, speckled, or spotted, because I have seen everything that Laban is doing to you. ¹³I am the God who appeared to you at Bethel,ᵃ where you poured olive oil on a stone marker for a holy purpose and where you made a vow to me. Now leave this land, and go back to the land of your relatives.' "

¹⁴Rachel and Leah answered him, "Is there anything left in our father's household for us to inherit? ¹⁵Doesn't he think of us as foreigners? Not only did he sell us, but he has used up the money that was paid for us. ¹⁶Certainly, all the wealth that God took away from our father belongs to us and our children. Now do whatever God has told you."

Laban and Jacob Make Peace

¹⁷Then Jacob put his children and his wives on camels. ¹⁸He drove all his livestock ahead of him and took all the possessions that he had accumulated. He took his own livestock that he had accumulated in Paddan Aram and went back to his father Isaac in Canaan.

¹⁹When Laban went to shear his sheep, Rachel stole her father's idols. ²⁰Jacob also tricked Laban the Aramean by not telling him he was leaving. ²¹So he left in a hurry with all that belonged to him. He crossed the Euphrates River and went toward the mountains of Gilead.

²²Two days later Laban was told that Jacob had left in a hurry. ²³He and his relatives pursued Jacob for seven days. Laban caught up with him in the mountains of Gilead.

²⁴God came to Laban the Aramean in a dream at night and said to him, "Be careful not to say anything at all to Jacob."

²⁵When Laban finally caught up with Jacob, Jacob had put up his tents in the mountains. So Laban and his relatives put up their tents in the mountains of Gilead. ²⁶Then Laban asked Jacob, "What have you done by tricking me? You've carried off my daughters like prisoners of war. ²⁷Why did you leave secretly and trick me? You didn't even tell me you were leaving. I would have sent you on your way rejoicing, with songs accompanied by tambourines and lyres. ²⁸You didn't even let me kiss my grandchildren and my daughters. You've done a foolish thing. ²⁹I have the power to harm you. Last night the God of your father said to me, 'Be careful not to say anything at all to Jacob.' ³⁰Now you have left for your father's home because you were so homesick. But why did you steal my gods?"

³¹Jacob answered Laban, "I left because I was afraid. I thought you would take your daughters away from me by force. ³²If you find your gods, the one who has them will not be allowed to live. In the presence of our relatives, search as much as you want through what I have, and take what is yours." (Jacob didn't know that Rachel had stolen the gods.)

³³So Laban went into Jacob's tent, into Leah's tent, and into the tent of the two slaves. But he found nothing. He came out of Leah's tent and went into Rachel's tent. ³⁴Rachel had taken the idols and had put them in her camel's saddle-bag and was sitting on them. Laban rummaged through the whole tent but found nothing.

³⁵Rachel said to her father, "Don't be angry, Father, but I can't get up to greet you; I'm having my period." So even though Laban had made a thorough search, he didn't find the idols.

³⁶Then Jacob became angry and confronted Laban. "What is my crime?" Jacob demanded of Laban. "What is my offense that you have come chasing after me? ³⁷Now

---

ᵃ31:13 Greek; Masoretic Text "the God at Bethel."

that you've rummaged through all my things, did you find anything from your house? Put it here in front of all our relatives. Let them decide which one of us is right.

³⁸"I've been with you for 20 years. Your sheep and goats never miscarried, and I never ate any rams from your flocks. ³⁹I never brought you any of the flock that was killed by wild animals. I paid for the loss myself. That's what you demanded of me when any of the flock was stolen during the day or at night. ⁴⁰The scorching heat during the day and the cold at night wore me down, and I lost a lot of sleep. ⁴¹I've been with your household 20 years now. I worked for you 14 years for your two daughters and 6 years for your flocks, and you changed my wages ten times. ⁴²If the God of my father, the God of Abraham and the Fear of Isaac,ᵇ had not been with me, you would have sent me away empty-handed by now. God has seen my misery and hard work, and last night he made it right."

⁴³Then Laban answered Jacob, "These are my daughters, my grandchildren, and my flocks. Everything you see is mine! Yet, what can I do today for my daughters or for their children? ⁴⁴Now, let's make an agreement and let it stand as a witness between you and me."

⁴⁵Jacob took a stone and set it up as a marker. ⁴⁶Then Jacob said to his relatives, "Gather some stones." They took stones, put them into a pile, and ate there by the pile of stones. ⁴⁷In his language, Laban called it Jegar Sahadutha [Witness Pile], but Jacob called it Galeed.ᶜ

⁴⁸Laban said, "This pile of stones stands as a witness between you and me today." This is why it was named Galeed ⁴⁹and also Mizpah [Watchtower], because he said, "May the Lᴏʀᴅ watch between you and me when we're unable to see each other. ⁵⁰If you mistreat my daughters or marry other women behind my back, remember that God stands as a witness between you and me."

⁵¹Laban said to Jacob, "Here is the pile of stones, and here is the marker that I have set up between you and me. ⁵²This pile of stones and this marker stand as witnesses that I will not go past the pile of stones to harm you, and that you will not go past the pile of stones or marker to harm me. ⁵³May the God of Abraham and Nahor—the God of their father—judge between us."

So Jacob swore this oath by the Fear of his father Isaac ⁵⁴and offered a sacrifice on the mountain. He invited his relatives to eat the meal with him. They ate with him and spent the night on the mountain.ᵈ

⁵⁵Early the next morning Laban kissed his grandchildren and his daughters and blessed them. Then Laban left and went back home.

Jacob Sends Messages and Gifts to Esau

ᵃ¹As Jacob went on his way, God's angels met him. ²When he saw them, Jacob said, "This is God's camp!" He named that place Mahanaim [Two Camps].

³Jacob sent messengers ahead of him to his brother Esau in Seir, the country of Edom. ⁴He commanded them to give this message to Esau, "Sir, this is what Jacob has to say, 'I've been living with Laban and have stayed until now. ⁵I have cattle and donkeys, sheep and goats, and male and female slaves. I've sent these messengers to tell you this news, in order to win your favor.' "

⁶When the messengers came back to Jacob, they said, "We went to your brother Esau. He is coming to meet you with 400 men."

⁷Jacob was terrified and distressed. So he divided the people, the sheep and goats,

ᵇ31:42 Or "Protection of Isaac." ᶜ31:47 *Galeed* is the Hebrew equivalent of the Aramaic words *Jegar Sahadutha*. ᵈ31:54 Genesis 31:55 in English Bibles is Genesis 32:1 in the Hebrew Bible. ᵃ 32:1 Genesis 32:1-32 in English Bibles is Genesis 32:2-33 in the Hebrew Bible.

the cattle, and the camels into two camps. [8]He thought, "If Esau attacks the one camp, then the other camp will be able to escape."

[9]Then Jacob prayed, "God of my grandfather Abraham and God of my father Isaac! LORD, you said to me, 'Go back to your land and to your relatives, and I will make you prosperous.' [10]I'm not worthy of all the love and faithfulness you have shown me. I only had a shepherd's staff when I crossed the Jordan River, but now I have two camps. [11]Please save me from my brother Esau, because I'm afraid of him. I'm afraid that he'll come and attack me and the mothers and children too. [12]But you did say, 'I will make sure that you are prosperous and that your descendants will be as many as the grains of sand on the seashore. No one will be able to count them because there are so many.' "

[13]He stayed there that night. Then he prepared a gift for his brother Esau from what he had brought with him: [14]200 female goats and 20 male goats, 200 female sheep and 20 male sheep, [15]30 female camels with their young, 40 cows and 10 bulls, 20 female donkeys and 10 male donkeys.

[16]He placed servants in charge of each herd. Then he said to his servants, "Go ahead of me, and keep a distance between the herds." [17]He commanded the first servant, "When my brother Esau meets you and asks you, 'To whom do you belong, and where are you going, and whose animals are these ahead of you?' [18]then say, 'Sir, they belong to your servant Jacob. This is a gift sent to you. Jacob is right behind us.' " [19]He also commanded the second servant, the third, and all the others who followed the herds. He said, "Say the same thing to Esau when you find him. [20]And be sure to add, 'Jacob is right behind us, sir.' " He thought, "I'll make peace with him by giving him this gift that I'm sending ahead of me. After that I will see him, and he'll welcome me back." [21]So Jacob sent the gift ahead of him while he stayed in the camp that night.

Jacob's Fourth Encounter With God— He Wrestles With God

[22]During that night he got up and gathered his two wives, his two slaves and his eleven children and crossed at the shallow part of the Jabbok River. [23]After he sent them across the stream, he sent everything else across. [24]So Jacob was left alone. Then a man wrestled with him until dawn. [25]When the man saw that he could not win against Jacob, he touched the socket of Jacob's hip so that it was dislocated as they wrestled. [26]Then the man said, "Let me go; it's almost dawn."

But Jacob answered, "I won't let you go until you bless me."

[27]So the man asked him, "What's your name?"

"Jacob," he answered.

[28]The man said, "Your name will no longer be Jacob but Israel [He Struggles With God], because you have struggled with God and with men—and you have won."

[29]Jacob said, "Please tell me your name."

The man answered, "Why do you ask for my name?" Then he blessed Jacob there. [30]So Jacob named that place Peniel [Face of God], because he said, "I have seen God face to face, but my life was saved." [31]The sun rose as he passed Penuel.[b] He was limping because of his hip. [32](Therefore, even today the people of Israel do not eat the muscle of the thigh attached to the hip socket because God touched the socket of Jacob's hip at the muscle of the thigh.)

---

[b]32:31 Another name for Peniel.

Jacob Meets Esau

33 ¹Jacob saw Esau coming with 400 men. So he divided the children among Leah, Rachel, and the two slaves. ²He put the slaves and their children in front, Leah and her children after them, and Rachel and Joseph last. ³He went on ahead of them and bowed seven times with his face touching the ground as he came near his brother.

⁴Then Esau ran to meet Jacob. Esau hugged him, threw his arms around him, and kissed him. They both cried. ⁵When he saw the women and children, Esau asked, "Who are these people here with you?"

"The children God has graciously given me, sir," Jacob answered.

⁶Then the slaves and their children came forward and bowed down. ⁷Likewise, Leah and her children came forward and bowed down. Finally, Joseph and Rachel came forward and bowed down.

⁸Then Esau asked, "Why did you send this whole group of people and animals I met?"

He answered, "To win your favor, sir."

⁹Esau said, "I have enough. Keep what you have, Brother."

¹⁰Jacob said, "No, please take the gift I'm giving you, because I've seen your face as if I were seeing the face of God, and yet you welcomed me so warmly. ¹¹Please take the present I've brought you, because God has been gracious to me and has given me all that I need." So Esau took it because Jacob insisted.

¹²Then Esau said, "Let's get ready to go, and I'll go with you."

¹³Jacob said to him, "Sir, you know that the children are frail and that I have to take care of the flocks and cattle that are nursing their young. If they're driven too hard for even one day, all the flocks will die. ¹⁴Go ahead of me, sir. I will slowly and gently guide the herds that are in front of me at their pace and at the children's pace until I come to you in Seir."

¹⁵Esau said, "Then let me leave some of my men with you."

"Why do that?" Jacob asked. "I only want to win your favor, sir."

¹⁶That day Esau started back to Seir. ¹⁷But Jacob moved on to Succoth, where he built a house for himself and made shelters for his livestock. That is why the place is named Succoth [Shelters].

¹⁸So having come from Paddan Aram, Jacob came safely to the city of Shechem in Canaan. He camped within sight of the city. ¹⁹Then he bought the piece of land on which he had put up his tents. He bought it from the sons of Hamor, father of Shechem, for 100 pieces of silver. ²⁰He set up an altar there and named it God Is the God of Israel.

Dinah Is Raped

34 ¹Dinah, daughter of Leah and Jacob, went out to visit some of the Canaanite women. ²When Shechem, son of the local ruler Hamor the Hivite, saw her, he took her and raped her. ³He became very fond of Jacob's daughter Dinah. He loved the girl and spoke tenderly to her.

⁴So Shechem said to his father Hamor, "Get me this girl for my wife."

⁵Jacob heard that Shechem had dishonored his daughter Dinah. His sons were with his livestock out in the open country, so Jacob kept quiet until they came home.

⁶So Shechem's father Hamor came to Jacob to speak with him. ⁷Jacob's sons came in from the open country as soon as they heard the news. The men felt outraged and very angry because Shechem had committed such a godless act against Israel's family by raping Jacob's daughter. This shouldn't have happened.

⁸Hamor told them. "My son Shechem has his heart set on your daughter. Please let her marry him. ⁹Intermarry with us; give your daughters to us, and take ours for

yourselves. [10]You can live with us, and the land will be yours. Live here, move about freely in this area, and acquire property here."

[11]Then Shechem said to Dinah's father and her brothers, "Do me this favor. I'll give you whatever you ask. [12]Set the price I must pay for the bride and the gift I must give her as high as you want. I'll pay exactly what you tell me. Give me the girl as my wife."

[13]Then Jacob's sons gave Shechem and his father Hamor a misleading answer because he had dishonored their sister Dinah. [14]They said, "We can't do this. We can't give our sister to a man who is uncircumcised. That would be a disgrace to us! [15]We will give our consent to you only on one condition: Every male must be circumcised as we are. [16]Then we'll give our daughters to you and take yours for ourselves, and we'll live with you and become one people. [17]If you won't agree to be circumcised, we'll take our daughter and go."

[18]Their proposal seemed good to Hamor and his son Shechem. [19]The young man didn't waste any time in doing what they said because he took such pleasure in Jacob's daughter. He was the most honored person in all his father's family.

[20]So Hamor and his son Shechem went to their city gate to speak to the men of their city. They said, [21]"These people are friendly toward us, so let them live in our land and move about freely in the area. Look, there's plenty of room in this land for them. We can marry their daughters and let them marry ours. [22]These people will consent to live with us and become one nation on one condition: Every male must be circumcised as they are. [23]Won't their livestock, their personal property, and all their animals be ours? We only need to agree to do this for them. Then they'll live with us."

[24]All the men who had come out to the city gate agreed with Hamor and his son Shechem. So they were all circumcised at the city gate.

[25]Two days later, while the men were still in pain, two of Jacob's sons, Simeon and Levi, Dinah's brothers, took their swords and boldly attacked the city. They killed every man [26]including Hamor and his son Shechem. They took Dinah from Shechem's home and left. [27]Then Jacob's sons stripped the corpses and looted the city where their sister had been dishonored. [28]They took the sheep and goats, cattle, donkeys, and whatever else was in the city or out in the fields. [29]They carried off all the wealth and all the women and children and looted everything in the houses.

[30]Then Jacob said to Simeon and Levi, "You have caused me a lot of trouble! You've made the people living in the area, the Canaanites and the Perizzites, hate me. There are only a few of us. If they join forces against me and attack me, my family and I will be wiped out."

[31]Simeon and Levi asked, "Should Shechem have been allowed to treat our sister like a prostitute?"

Jacob's Fifth Encounter With God

[1]Then God said to Jacob, "Go to Bethel and live there. Make an altar there. I am the God who appeared to you when you were fleeing from your brother Esau."

[2]So Jacob said to his family and those who were with him, "Get rid of the foreign gods which you have, wash yourselves until you are ritually clean,[a] and change your clothes. [3]Then let's go to Bethel. I will make an altar there to God, who answered me when I was troubled and who has been with me wherever I've gone." [4]So they gave Jacob all the foreign gods that they had in their possession as well as the earrings that they had on. Jacob buried these things under the oak tree near Shechem.

---

[a] 35:2 "Clean" refers to anything that is presentable to God.

⁵As they moved on, God made the people of the cities that were all around them terrified so that no one pursued them. ⁶Jacob and all the people who were with him came to Luz (that is, Bethel) in the land of Canaan. ⁷He built an altar there and called that place El Bethel [God of the House of God]. That's where God had revealed himself to Jacob when he was fleeing from his brother. ⁸Rebekah's nurse Deborah died and was buried under the oak tree outside Bethel. So Jacob called it the Tree of Crying.

Jacob's Sixth Encounter With God— His Name Changed to Israel

⁹Then God appeared once more to Jacob after he came back from Paddan Aram, and he blessed him. ¹⁰God said to him, "Your name is Jacob. You will no longer be called Jacob, but your name will be Israel." So he named him Israel.

¹¹God also said to him, "I am God Almighty. Be fertile, and increase in number. A nation and a community of nations will come from you, and kings will come from you. ¹²I will give you the land that I gave to Abraham and Isaac. I will also give this land to your descendants." ¹³Then God went up from him at the place where he had spoken with him. ¹⁴So Jacob set up a memorial, a stone marker, to mark the place where God had spoken with him. He poured a wine offering and olive oil on it. ¹⁵Jacob named the place where God had spoken with him Bethel [House of God].

Jacob's [Israel's] Sons— 1 Chronicles 2:1-2

¹⁶Then they moved on from Bethel. When they were still some distance from Ephrath, Rachel went into labor and was having severe labor pains. ¹⁷During one of her pains, the midwife said to her, "Don't be afraid! You're having another son!" ¹⁸Rachel was dying. As she took her last breath, she named her son Benoni [Son of My Sorrow], but his father named him Benjamin [Son of My Right Hand].

¹⁹Rachel died and was buried on the way to Ephrath (that is, Bethlehem). ²⁰Then Jacob set up a stone as a marker for her grave. The same marker is at Rachel's grave today.

²¹Israel moved on again and put up his tent beyond Migdal Eder. ²²While Israel was living in that region, Reuben went to bed with his father's concubine*b* Bilhah, and Israel heard about it.

Jacob had 12 sons.
²³The sons of **Leah** were
  Jacob's firstborn Reuben, then Simeon, Levi, Judah, Issachar, and Zebulun.
²⁴The sons of **Rachel** were
  Joseph and Benjamin.
²⁵The sons of Rachel's slave **Bilhah** were
  Dan and Naphtali.
²⁶The sons of Leah's slave **Zilpah** were
  Gad and Asher.
  These were Jacob's sons, who were born in Paddan Aram.

²⁷Jacob came home to his father Isaac to Mamre's city, Kiriath Arba (that is, Hebron). Abraham and Isaac had lived there for a while. ²⁸Isaac was 180 years old ²⁹when he took his last breath and died. He joined his ancestors in death at a very old age. His sons Esau and Jacob buried him.

---

*b*35:22 A concubine is considered a wife except she has fewer rights under the law.

The Origin of Edom—
I Chronicles I:35-54

¹This is the account of Esau (that is, Edom) and his descendants. ²Esau chose his wives from the women of Canaan: Adah, daughter of Elon the Hittite; Oholibamah, daughter of Anah and granddaughter of Zibeon the Hivite; ³also Basemath, daughter of Ishmael and sister of Nebaioth. ⁴Adah gave birth to Eliphaz for Esau, and Basemath gave birth to Reuel. ⁵Oholibamah gave birth to Jeush, Jalam, and Korah. These were the sons of Esau who were born in Canaan.

⁶Esau took his wives, his sons, his daughters, all the members of his household, his possessions, all his cattle, and everything he had accumulated in Canaan and went to another land away from his brother Jacob. ⁷He did this because they had too many possessions to live together. There wasn't enough pastureland for all of their livestock. ⁸So Esau, who was also known as Edom, lived in the mountains of Seir.

⁹This is the account of Esau and his descendants. He was the father of the people of Edom in the mountains of Seir.

¹⁰These were the names of Esau's sons:

Eliphaz, son of Esau's wife Adah, and Reuel, son of Esau's wife Basemath.
¹¹The sons of Eliphaz were

Teman, Omar, Zepho, Gatam, and Kenaz. ¹²Timna was a concubine*ᵃ* of Esau's son Eliphaz. She gave birth to Amalek for Eliphaz. These were the grandsons of Esau's wife Adah.
¹³These were Reuel's sons:

Nahath, Zerah, Shammah, and Mizzah. These were the grandsons of Esau's wife Basemath.
¹⁴These were the sons of Esau's wife Oholibamah, daughter of Anah and granddaughter of Zibeon. She gave birth to Jeush, Jalam, and Korah for Esau.

¹⁵These were the tribal leaders among Esau's descendants:

The sons of Eliphaz, Esau's firstborn, were

Teman, Omar, Zepho, Kenaz, ¹⁶Korah, Gatam, and Amalek. These were the tribal leaders descended from Eliphaz in Edom. They were the grandsons of Adah.
¹⁷These were the tribal leaders among the descendants of Esau's son Reuel:

Nahath, Zerah, Shammah, and Mizzah. These were the tribal leaders descended from Reuel in Edom. They were the grandsons of Esau's wife Basemath.
¹⁸These were the tribal leaders among the descendants of Esau's wife Oholibamah:

Jeush, Jalam, and Korah. These were the tribal leaders descended from Esau's wife Oholibamah, Anah's daughter.
¹⁹These were the descendants of Esau (that is, Edom), who were tribal leaders.

²⁰These were the sons of Seir the Horite, the people living in that land:

Lotan, Shobal, Zibeon, Anah, ²¹Dishon, Ezer, and Dishan. These Horite tribal leaders were the sons of Seir in Edom.
²²The sons of Lotan were

Hori and Hemam. Lotan's sister was Timna.
²³These were the sons of Shobal:

Alvan, Manahath, Ebal, Shepho, and Onam.

ᵃ36:12 A concubine is considered a wife except she has fewer rights under the law.

²⁴These were the sons of Zibeon:

Aiah and Anah. (Anah found the hot springs*ᵇ* in the desert while he was taking care of the donkeys that belonged to his father Zibeon.)

²⁵These were the children of Anah:

Dishon and Oholibamah, daughter of Anah.

²⁶These were the sons of Dishon:

Hemdan, Eshban, Ithran, and Cheran.

²⁷These were the sons of Ezer:

Bilhan, Zaavan, and Akan.

²⁸These were the sons of Dishan:

Uz and Aran.

²⁹These were the Horite tribal leaders:

Lotan, Shobal, Zibeon, Anah, ³⁰Dishon, Ezer, and Dishan. These were the Horite tribal leaders in the land of Seir.

³¹These were the kings who ruled Edom before any king ruled the people of Israel: ³²Bela, son of Beor, ruled Edom. The name of his capital city was Dinhabah. ³³After Bela died, Jobab, son of Zerah from Bozrah, succeeded him as king. ³⁴After Jobab died, Husham from the land of the Temanites succeeded him as king. ³⁵After Husham died, Hadad, son of Bedad succeeded him as king. Hadad defeated the Midianites in the country of Moab. The name of his capital city was Avith. ³⁶After Hadad died, Samlah from Masrekah succeeded him as king. ³⁷After Samlah died, Shaul from Rehoboth on the river succeeded him as king. ³⁸After Shaul died, Baal Hanan, son of Achbor, succeeded him as king. ³⁹After Baal Hanan, son of Achbor, died, Hadar succeeded him as king, and the name of his capital city was Pau. His wife's name was Mehetabel, daughter of Matred and granddaughter of Mezahab.

⁴⁰These were the names of the tribal leaders descended from Esau, by family, place, and name:

Timna, Alvah, Jetheth, ⁴¹Oholibamah, Elah, Pinon, ⁴²Kenaz, Teman, Mibzar, ⁴³Magdiel, and Iram.

These were the tribal leaders of Edom listed by the places where they lived and the property they owned.

Esau was the father of the people of Edom.

Joseph's Brothers Sell Him Into Slavery

37 ¹Jacob continued to live in the land of Canaan, where his father had lived.
²This is the account of Jacob and his descendants.

Joseph was a seventeen-year-old young man. He took care of the flocks with the sons of Bilhah and Zilpah, his father's wives. Joseph told his father about the bad things his brothers were doing.

³Israel loved Joseph more than all his sons because Joseph had been born in Israel's old age. So he made Joseph a special robe with long sleeves. ⁴Joseph's brothers saw that their father loved him more than any of them. They hated Joseph and couldn't speak to him on friendly terms.

⁵Joseph had a dream and when he told his brothers, they hated him even more. ⁶He said to them, "Please listen to the dream I had. ⁷We were tying grain into bundles

---

*ᵇ*36:24 Latin; Hebrew meaning uncertain.

out in the field, and suddenly mine stood up. It remained standing while your bundles gathered around my bundle and bowed down to it."

⁸Then his brothers asked him, "Are you going to be our king or rule us?" They hated him even more for his dreams and his words.

⁹Then he had another dream, and he told it to his brothers. "Listen," he said, "I had another dream: I saw the sun, the moon, and 11 stars bowing down to me."

¹⁰When he told his father and his brothers, his father criticized him by asking, "What's this dream you had? Will your mother and I and your brothers come and bow down in front of you?" ¹¹So his brothers were jealous of him, but his father kept thinking about these things.

¹²His brothers had gone to take care of their father's flocks at Shechem. ¹³Israel then said to Joseph, "Your brothers are taking care of the flocks at Shechem. I'm going to send you to them."

Joseph responded, "I'll go."

¹⁴So Israel said, "See how your brothers and the flocks are doing, and bring some news back to me." Then he sent Joseph away from the Hebron Valley.

When Joseph came to Shechem, ¹⁵a man found him wandering around in the open country. "What are you looking for?" the man asked.

¹⁶Joseph replied, "I'm looking for my brothers. Please tell me where they're taking care of their flocks."

¹⁷The man said, "They moved on from here. I heard them say, 'Let's go to Dothan.'" So Joseph went after his brothers and found them at Dothan.

¹⁸They saw him from a distance. Before he reached them, they plotted to kill him. ¹⁹They said to each other, "Look, here comes that master dreamer! ²⁰Let's kill him, throw him into one of the cisterns, and say that a wild animal has eaten him. Then we'll see what happens to his dreams."

²¹When Reuben heard this, he tried to save Joseph from their plot. "Let's not kill him," he said. ²²"Let's not have any bloodshed. Put him into that cistern that's out in the desert, but don't hurt him." Reuben wanted to rescue Joseph from them and bring him back to his father.

²³So when Joseph reached his brothers, they stripped him of his special robe with long sleeves. ²⁴Then they took him and put him into an empty cistern. It had no water in it.

²⁵As they sat down to eat, they saw a caravan of Ishmaelites coming from Gilead. Their camels were carrying the materials for cosmetics, medicine, and embalming. They were on their way to take them to Egypt.

Jealousy

Genesis 37:1-11

Sometimes it seems like a brother or sister is your parent's favorite. She gets more new clothes. He gets to stay up later. Being envious won't help. Telling Mom or Dad how you feel may help. Sometimes your brother or sister may think you're the favorite. If that happens, talk to your parents about it, and be kind to your brother or sister.

all you can be

²⁶Judah asked his brothers, "What will we gain by killing our brother and covering up his death? ²⁷Let's sell him to the Ishmaelites. Let's not hurt him, because he is our brother, our own flesh and blood." His brothers agreed.

²⁸As the Midianite merchants were passing by, the brothers pulled Joseph out of the cistern. They sold him to the Ishmaelites for eight ounces of silver. The Ishmaelites took him to Egypt.

²⁹When Reuben came back to the cistern and saw that Joseph was no longer there, he tore his clothes in grief. ³⁰He went back to his brothers and said, "The boy isn't there! What am I going to do?"

³¹So they took Joseph's robe, killed a goat, and dipped the robe in the blood. ³²Then they brought the special robe with long sleeves to their father and said, "We found this. You better examine it to see whether it's your son's robe or not."

³³He recognized it and said, "It is my son's robe! A wild animal has eaten him! Joseph must have been torn to pieces!" ³⁴Then, to show his grief, Jacob tore his clothes, put sackcloth around his waist, and mourned for his son a long time. ³⁵All his other sons and daughters came to comfort him, but he refused to be comforted. He said, "No, I will mourn for my son until I die." This is how Joseph's father cried over him.

³⁶Meanwhile, in Egypt the Midianites sold Joseph to Potiphar, one of Pharaoh's officials and captain of the guard.

Judah's Sin With Tamar

38 ¹About that time Judah left his brothers and went to stay with a man from Adullam whose name was Hirah. ²There Judah met the daughter of a Canaanite man whose name was Shua. He married her and slept with her. ³She became pregnant and gave birth to a son named*ᵈ* Er. ⁴She became pregnant again and gave birth to another son, whom she named Onan. ⁵Then she became pregnant again and gave birth to another son, whom she named Shelah. He was born at Kezib.

⁶Judah chose a wife for his firstborn son Er. Her name was Tamar. ⁷Er angered the Lord. So the Lord took away his life. ⁸Then Judah said to Onan, "Go sleep with your brother's widow. Do your duty for her as a brother-in-law, and produce a descendant for your brother." ⁹But Onan knew that the descendant wouldn't belong to him, so whenever he slept with his brother's widow, he wasted his semen on the ground to avoid giving his brother a descendant. ¹⁰What Onan did angered the Lord so much that the Lord took away Onan's life too.

¹¹Then Judah said to his daughter-in-law Tamar, "Return to your father's home. Live as a widow until my son Shelah grows up." He thought that this son, too, might die like his brothers. So Tamar went to live in her father's home.

¹²After a long time Judah's wife, the daughter of Shua, died. When Judah had finished mourning, he and his friend Hirah from Adullam went to Timnah where the men were shearing Judah's sheep. ¹³As soon as Tamar was told that her father-in-law was on his way to Timnah to shear his sheep, ¹⁴she took off her widow's clothes, covered her face with a veil, and disguised herself. Then she sat down at the entrance to Enaim, which is on the road to Timnah. (She did this because she realized that Shelah was grown up now, and she hadn't been given to him in marriage.)

¹⁵When Judah saw her, he thought she was a prostitute because she had covered her face. ¹⁶Since he didn't know she was his daughter-in-law, he approached her by the roadside and said, "Come on, let's sleep together!"

ᵈ 38:3 Some Hebrew manuscripts "son, whom he named"; other Hebrew manuscripts, Samaritan Pentateuch, and Targum "son, whom she named."

She asked, "What will you pay to sleep with me?"

¹⁷"I'll send you a young goat from the flock," he answered.

She said, "First give me something as a deposit until you send it."

¹⁸"What should I give you as a deposit?" he asked.

"Your signet ring, its cord, and the shepherd's staff that's in your hand," she answered.

So he gave them to her. Then he slept with her, and she became pregnant. ¹⁹After she got up and left, she took off her veil and put her widow's clothes back on.

²⁰Judah sent his friend Hirah to deliver the young goat so that he could get back his deposit from the woman, but his friend couldn't find her. ²¹He asked the men of that area, "Where's that prostitute who was beside the road at Enaim?"

"There's no prostitute here," they answered.

²²So he went back to Judah and said, "I couldn't find her. Even the men of that area said, 'There's no prostitute here.' "

²³Then Judah said, "Let her keep what I gave her, or we'll become a laughingstock. After all, I did send her this young goat, but you couldn't find her."

²⁴About three months later Judah was told, "Your daughter-in-law Tamar has been acting like a prostitute. What's more, because of it she's pregnant."

Judah ordered, "Bring her out to be burned."

²⁵As she was brought out, she sent a message to her father-in-law, "I'm pregnant by the man who owns these things. See if you recognize whose signet ring, cord, and shepherd's staff these are."

²⁶Judah recognized them and said, "She's not guilty. I am! She did this because I haven't given her my son Shelah." Judah never made love to her again.

²⁷The time came for Tamar to give birth, and she had twin boys. ²⁸When she was giving birth, one of them put out his hand. The midwife took a piece of red yarn, tied it on his wrist, and said, "This one came out first." ²⁹As he pulled back his hand, his brother was born. So she said, "Is this how you burst into the world!" He was named Perez [Bursting Into]. ³⁰After that his brother was born with the red yarn on his hand. He was named Zerah [Sunrise].

Joseph in Potiphar's House

39 ¹Joseph had been taken to Egypt. Potiphar, one of Pharaoh's Egyptian officials and captain of the guard, bought him from the Ishmaelites who had taken him there.

²The Lord was with Joseph, so he became a successful man. He worked in the house of his Egyptian master. ³Joseph's master saw that the Lord was with him and that the Lord made everything he did successful. ⁴Potiphar liked Joseph so much that he made him his trusted servant. He put him in charge of his household and everything he owned. ⁵From that time on the Lord blessed the Egyptian's household because of Joseph. Therefore, the Lord's blessing was on everything Potiphar owned in his house and in his fields. ⁶So he left all that he owned in Joseph's care. He wasn't concerned about anything except the food he ate.

Joseph was well-built and handsome. ⁷After a while his master's wife began to desire Joseph, so she said, "Come to bed with me."

⁸But Joseph refused and said to her, "My master doesn't concern himself with anything in the house. He trusts me with everything he owns. ⁹No one in this house is greater than I. He's kept nothing back from me except you, because you're his wife. How could I do such a wicked thing and sin against God?" ¹⁰Although she kept asking Joseph day after day, he refused to go to bed with her or be with her.

¹¹One day he went into the house to do his work, and none of the household servants were there. ¹²She grabbed him by his clothes and said, "Come to bed with me!" But he ran outside and left his clothes in her hand.

¹³When she realized that he had gone but had left his clothes behind, ¹⁴she called her household servants and said to them, "Look! My husband brought this Hebrew here to fool around with us. He came in and tried to go to bed with me, but I screamed as loud as I could. ¹⁵As soon as he heard me scream, he ran outside and left his clothes with me."

¹⁶She kept Joseph's clothes with her until his master came home. ¹⁷Then she told him the same story: "The Hebrew slave you brought here came in and tried to fool around with me. ¹⁸But when I screamed, he ran outside and left his clothes with me."

¹⁹When Potiphar heard his wife's story, especially when she said, "This is what your slave did to me," he became very angry. ²⁰So Joseph's master arrested him and put him in the same prison where the king's prisoners were kept.

While Joseph was in prison, ²¹the Lord was with him. The Lord reached out to him with his unchanging love and gave him protection. The Lord also put Joseph on good terms with the warden. ²²So the warden placed Joseph in charge of all the prisoners who were in that prison. Joseph became responsible for everything that they were doing. ²³The warden paid no attention to anything under Joseph's care because the Lord was with Joseph and made whatever he did successful.

Joseph in Prison

40 ¹Later the king's cupbearer[a] and his baker offended their master, the king of Egypt. ²Pharaoh was angry with his chief cupbearer and his chief baker. ³He put them in the prison of the captain of the guard, the same place where Joseph was a prisoner. ⁴The captain of the guard assigned them to Joseph, and he took care of them.

After they had been confined for some time, ⁵both prisoners—the cupbearer and the baker for the king of Egypt—had dreams one night. Each man had a dream with its own special meaning.

⁶When Joseph came to them in the morning, he saw that they were upset. ⁷So he asked these officials of Pharaoh who were with him in his master's prison, "Why do you look so unhappy today?"

⁸"We both had dreams," they answered him, "but there's no one to tell us what they mean."

"Isn't God the only one who can tell what they mean?" Joseph asked them. "Why don't you tell me all about them."

⁹So the chief cupbearer told Joseph his dream. He said "In my dream a grapevine with three branches appeared in front of me. ¹⁰Soon after it sprouted it blossomed. Then its clusters ripened into grapes. ¹¹Pharaoh's cup was in my hand, so I took the grapes and squeezed them into it. I put the cup in Pharaoh's hand."

¹²"This is what it means," Joseph said to him. "The three branches are three days. ¹³In the next three days Pharaoh will release you and restore you to your position. You will put Pharaoh's cup in his hand as you used to do when you were his cupbearer. ¹⁴Remember me when things go well for you, and please do me a favor. Mention me to Pharaoh, and get me out of this prison. ¹⁵I was kidnapped from the land of the Hebrews, and even here I've done nothing to deserve being put in this dungeon."

¹⁶The chief baker saw that the meaning Joseph had given to the cupbearer's dream was good. So he said to Joseph, "I had a dream too. In my dream three baskets of white

---

[a] 40:1 A cupbearer was a trusted royal official who ensured that the king's drink was not poisoned.

baked goods were on my head. ¹⁷The top basket contained all kinds of baked goods for Pharaoh, but the birds were eating them out of the basket on my head."

¹⁸"This is what it means," Joseph replied. "The three baskets are three days. ¹⁹In the next three days Pharaoh will cut off your head and hang your dead body on a pole. The birds will eat the flesh from your bones."

²⁰Two days later, on his birthday, Pharaoh had a special dinner prepared for all his servants. Of all his servants he gave special attention to the chief cupbearer and the chief baker. ²¹He restored the chief cupbearer to his position. So the cupbearer put the cup in Pharaoh's hand. ²²But he hung the chief baker just as Joseph had said in his interpretation.

²³Nevertheless, the chief cupbearer didn't remember Joseph. He forgot all about him.

Joseph Interprets Pharaoh's Dreams

¹After two full years Pharaoh had a dream. He dreamed he was standing by the Nile River. ²Suddenly, seven nice-looking, well-fed cows came up from the river and began to graze among the reeds. ³Seven other cows came up from the river behind them. These cows were sickly and skinny. They stood behind the first seven cows on the riverbank. ⁴The cows that were sickly and skinny ate the seven nice-looking, well-fed cows. Then Pharaoh woke up.

⁵He fell asleep again and had a second dream. Seven good, healthy heads of grain were growing on a single stalk. ⁶Seven other heads of grain, thin and scorched by the east wind, sprouted behind them. ⁷The thin heads of grain swallowed the seven full, healthy heads. Then Pharaoh woke up. It was only a dream.

⁸In the morning he was so upset that he sent for all the magicians and wise men of Egypt. Pharaoh told them his dreams, but no one could tell him what they meant.

⁹Then the chief cupbearer[a] spoke to Pharaoh, "I remember a promise I failed to keep.[b] ¹⁰Some time ago when Pharaoh was angry with his servants, he confined me and the chief baker to the captain of the guard's prison. ¹¹We both had dreams the same night. Each dream had its own meaning. ¹²A young Hebrew, a slave of the captain of the guard, was with us. We told him our dreams, and he told each of us what they meant. ¹³What he told us happened: Pharaoh restored me to my position, but he hung the baker on a pole."

¹⁴Then Pharaoh sent for Joseph, and immediately he was brought from the dungeon. After he had shaved and changed his clothes, he came in front of Pharaoh.

¹⁵Pharaoh said to Joseph, "I had a dream, and no one can tell me what it means. I heard that when you are told a dream, you can say what it means."

¹⁶Joseph answered Pharaoh, "I can't, but God can give Pharaoh the answer that he needs."

¹⁷Then Pharaoh said to Joseph, "In my dream I was standing on the bank of the Nile. ¹⁸Suddenly, seven nice-looking, well-fed cows came up from the river and began to graze among the reeds. ¹⁹Seven other cows came up behind them. These cows were scrawny, very sick, and thin. I've never seen such sickly cows in all of Egypt! ²⁰The thin, sickly cows ate up the seven well-fed ones. ²¹Even though they had eaten them, no one could tell they had eaten them. They looked just as sick as before. Then I woke up.

²²"In my second dream I saw seven good, full heads of grain growing on a single stalk. ²³Seven other heads of grain, withered, thin, and scorched by the east wind,

ᵃ41:9 A cupbearer was a trusted royal official who ensured that the king's drink was not poisoned. ᵇ41:9 English equivalent difficult.

Joseph

Pharaoh put Joseph in charge of Egypt.

Joseph's jealous brothers sold him to slave traders when he was a teenager. In Egypt his master's wife lied about him, sending Joseph to prison for many years.

Joseph might have become bitter. He might have been angry at God. Instead, Joseph trusted God and worked hard. Eventually, God helped Joseph explain a confusing dream to Pharaoh, and Pharaoh put Joseph in charge of all Egypt.

Later, Joseph told his brothers, "Even though you planned evil against me, God planned good to come out of it" (Genesis 50:20).

Getting to Know Joseph

✳ Why is it hard to keep doing right when you are treated unfairly?

✳ Joseph forgave his brothers for what they did. Why is it hard to forgive?

✳ Why would you want to marry a person like Joseph?

Important people in Egypt rode in golden chariots. People ran in front to announce who was coming.

Joseph lived around 1900 B.C.

Joseph's jealous brothers sold him as a slave.

Joseph became the second most powerful person in Egypt.

Joseph saved the lives of his brothers when a famine threatened to starve them.

When Joseph lived in Egypt, the Great Pyramid of Cheops was already over 700 years old. It still stands today. It is 450 feet high. The king's burial chamber is 137 feet up from the base, as high as a 13-story building!

sprouted behind them. ²⁴The thin heads of grain swallowed the seven good heads. I told this to the magicians, but no one could tell me what it meant."

²⁵Then Joseph said to Pharaoh, "Pharaoh had the same dream twice. God has told Pharaoh what he's going to do. ²⁶The seven good cows are seven years, and the seven good heads of grain are seven years. It's all the same dream. ²⁷The seven thin, sickly cows that came up behind them are seven years. The seven empty heads of grain scorched by the east wind are also seven years. Seven years of famine are coming.

²⁸"It's just as I said to Pharaoh. God has shown Pharaoh what he's going to do. ²⁹Seven years are coming when there will be plenty of food in Egypt. ³⁰After them will come seven years of famine. People will forget that there was plenty of food in Egypt, and the famine will ruin the land. ³¹People won't remember that there once was plenty of food in the land, because the coming famine will be so severe. ³²The reason Pharaoh has had a recurring dream is because the matter has been definitely decided by God, and he will do it very soon.

Joseph Advises Pharaoh

³³"Pharaoh should look for a wise and intelligent man and put him in charge of Egypt. ³⁴Make arrangements to appoint supervisors over the land to take a fifth of Egypt's harvest during the seven good years. ³⁵Have them collect all the food during these good years and store up grain under Pharaoh's control, to be kept for food in the cities. ³⁶This food will be a reserve supply for our country during the seven years of famine that will happen in Egypt. Then the land will not be ruined by the famine."

³⁷Pharaoh and all his servants liked the idea. ³⁸So Pharaoh asked his servants, "Can we find anyone like this—a man who has God's Spirit in him?"

³⁹Then Pharaoh said to Joseph, "Because God has let you know all this, there is no one as wise and intelligent as you. ⁴⁰You will be in charge of my palace, and all my people will do*ᶜ* what you say. I will be more important than you, only because I'm Pharaoh."

⁴¹Then Pharaoh said to Joseph, "I now put you in charge of Egypt." ⁴²Then Pharaoh took off his signet ring and put it on Joseph's finger. He had Joseph dressed in robes of fine linen and put a gold chain around his neck. ⁴³He had him ride in the chariot of the second-in-command. Men ran ahead of him and shouted, "Make way!"*ᵈ* Pharaoh put Joseph in charge of Egypt.

⁴⁴He also said to Joseph, "Even though I am Pharaoh, no one anywhere in Egypt will do anything without your permission." ⁴⁵Pharaoh named Joseph Zaphenathpaneah and gave him Asenath as his wife. She was the daughter of Potiphera, priest from the city of On. Joseph traveled around Egypt.

Joseph Serves Pharaoh

⁴⁶Joseph was 30 years old when he entered the service of Pharaoh (the king of Egypt). He left Pharaoh and traveled all around Egypt. ⁴⁷During the seven good years the land produced large harvests. ⁴⁸Joseph collected all the food grown in Egypt during those seven years and put this food in the cities. In each city he put the food from the fields around it. ⁴⁹Joseph stored up grain in huge quantities like the sand on the seashore. He had so much that he finally gave up keeping any records because he couldn't measure it all.

⁵⁰Before the years of famine came, Joseph had two sons by Asenath, daughter of Potiphera, priest from the city of On. ⁵¹Joseph named his firstborn son Manasseh [He

---

ᶜ41:40 Greek; Hebrew meaning uncertain. ᵈ41:43 Hebrew meaning uncertain.

Helps Me Forget], because God helped him forget all his troubles and all about his father's family. [52]He named the second son Ephraim [Blessed Twice With Children], because God gave him children in the land where he had suffered.

[53]The seven years when there was plenty of food in Egypt came to an end. [54]Then the seven years of famine began as Joseph had said they would. All the other countries were experiencing famine. Yet, there was food in Egypt. [55]When everyone in Egypt began to feel the effects of the famine, the people cried to Pharaoh for food. But Pharaoh said to all the Egyptians, "Go to Joseph! Do what he tells you!"

[56]When the famine had spread all over the country, Joseph opened all the storehouses[e] and sold grain to the Egyptians. He did this because the famine was severe in Egypt. [57]The whole world came to Joseph in Egypt to buy grain, since the famine was so severe all over the world.

Jacob [Israel] Sends Ten Sons to Egypt

42 [1]When Jacob found out that grain was for sale in Egypt, he said to his sons, "Why do you keep looking at each other? [2]I've heard there's grain for sale in Egypt. Go there and buy some for us so that we won't starve to death."

[3]Ten of Joseph's brothers went to buy grain in Egypt. [4]Jacob wouldn't send Joseph's brother Benjamin with the other brothers, because he was afraid that something would happen to him. [5]Israel's sons left with the others who were going to buy grain, because there was also famine in Canaan.

Joseph Sends Nine of His Brothers Back to Canaan

[6]As governor of the country, Joseph was selling grain to everyone. So when Joseph's brothers arrived, they bowed in front of him with their faces touching the ground. [7]As soon as Joseph saw his brothers, he recognized them. But he acted as if he didn't know them and spoke harshly to them. "Where did you come from?" he asked them.

"From Canaan, to buy food," they answered.

[8]Even though Joseph recognized his brothers, they didn't recognize him. [9]Then he remembered the dreams he once had about them. "You're spies!" he said to them, "And you've come to find out where our country is unprotected."

[10]"No, sir!" they answered him. "We've come to buy food. [11]We're all sons of one man. We're honest men, not spies."

[12]He said to them, "No! You've come to find out where our country is unprotected."

[13]They answered him, "We were 12 brothers, sons of one man in Canaan. The youngest brother stayed with our father, and the other one is no longer with us."

[14]"It's just as I told you," Joseph said to them. "You're spies! [15]This is how you'll be tested: I solemnly swear, as surely as Pharaoh lives, that you won't leave this place unless your youngest brother comes here. [16]One of you must be sent to get your brother while the rest of you stay in prison. We'll see if you're telling the truth. If not, I solemnly swear, as surely as Pharaoh lives, you are spies!" [17]Then he put them in jail for three days.

[18]On the third day Joseph said to them, "Do this, and you will live. I, too, fear God. [19]If you are honest men, you will let one of your brothers stay here in prison. The rest of you will go and take grain back to your starving families. [20]But you must bring me your youngest brother. This will show that you've been telling the truth. Then you won't die." So they agreed.

---

[e] 41:56 Greek, Syriac; Masoretic Text "all that was in them."

²¹They said to each other, "We're surely being punished for what we did to our brother. We saw how troubled he was when he pleaded with us for mercy, but we wouldn't listen. That's why we're in trouble now."

²²Reuben said to them, "Didn't I tell you not to sin against the boy? But you wouldn't listen. Now we must pay for this bloodshed."

²³They didn't know that Joseph could understand them, because he was speaking through an interpreter. ²⁴He stepped away from them to cry. When he could speak to them again, he came back. Then he picked Simeon and had him arrested right in front of their eyes.

²⁵Joseph gave orders to fill their bags with grain. He put each man's money back into his sack and gave them supplies for their trip. After their bags were filled, ²⁶they loaded their grain on their donkeys and left.

²⁷At the place where they stopped for the night, one of them opened his sack to feed his donkey. His money was right inside his sack. ²⁸He said to his brothers, "My money has been put back! It's right here in my sack!"

They wanted to die. They trembled and turned to each other and asked, "What has God done to us?"

Jacob's [Israel's] Sons Report to Him

²⁹When they came to their father Jacob in Canaan, they told him all that had happened to them. They said, ³⁰"The governor of that land spoke harshly to us and treated us like spies. ³¹But we said to him, 'We're honest men, not spies. ³²We were 12 brothers, sons of the same father. One is no longer with us. The youngest brother stayed with our father in Canaan.'

³³"Then the governor of that land said to us, 'This is how I'll know that you're honest men: Leave one of your brothers with me. Take food for your starving families and go. ³⁴But bring me your youngest brother. Then I'll know that you're not spies but honest men. I'll give your brother back to you, and you'll be able to move about freely in this country.' "

³⁵As they were emptying their sacks, each man found his bag of money in his sack. When they and their father saw the bags of money, they were frightened. ³⁶Their father Jacob said to them, "You're going to make me lose all my children! Joseph is no longer with us, Simeon is no longer with us, and now you want to take Benjamin. Everything's against me!"

³⁷So Reuben said to his father, "You may put my two sons to death if I don't bring him back to you. Let me take care of him, and I'll bring him back to you."

³⁸Jacob replied, "My son will not go with you. His brother is dead, and he's the only one left. If any harm comes to him on the trip you're taking, the grief would drive this gray-haired old man to his grave!"

Jacob [Israel] Sends Ten Sons Back to Egypt

43 ¹The famine was severe in the land. ²When they finished eating the grain they had brought from Egypt, Israel said to his sons, "Go back and buy us a little more food."

³Judah said to him, "The man gave us a severe warning: 'You won't be allowed to see me again unless your brother is with you.' ⁴If you let our brother go with us, we'll go and buy food for you. ⁵If you won't let him go, we won't go. The man said to us, 'You won't be allowed to see me again unless your brother is with you.' "

⁶Israel asked, "Why have you made trouble for me by telling the man you had another brother?"

⁷They answered, "The man kept asking about us and our family: 'Is your father still alive? Do you have another brother?' We simply answered his questions. How could we possibly know he would say, 'Bring your brother here'?"

⁸Then Judah said to his father Israel, "Send the boy along with me. Let's get going so that we won't starve to death. ⁹I guarantee that he will come back. You can hold me responsible for him. If I don't bring him back to you and place him here in front of you, you can blame me the rest of my life. ¹⁰If we hadn't waited so long, we could have made this trip twice by now."

¹¹Then their father Israel said to them, "If that's the way it has to be, then take the man a gift. Put some of the best products of the land in your bags. Take a little balm, a little honey, gum, myrrh, pistachio nuts, and almonds. ¹²Take twice as much money with you. You must return the money that was put back in your sacks. Maybe it was a mistake. ¹³Take your brother, and go back to the man. ¹⁴May God Almighty make him merciful to you so that he will send your other brother and Benjamin home with you. If I lose my children, I lose my children."

¹⁵The men took the gifts, twice as much money, and Benjamin. They went to Egypt, where they presented themselves to Joseph.

The Banquet at Joseph's House

¹⁶When Joseph saw Benjamin with them, he said to the man in charge of his house, "Take these men to my house. Butcher an animal, and prepare a meal, because they are going to eat with me at noon."

¹⁷So the man did as Joseph said and took them to Joseph's house. ¹⁸The men were frightened, because they had been brought to Joseph's house. They thought, "We've been brought here because of the money that was put back into our sacks the first time. They're going to attack us, overpower us, take our donkeys, and make us slaves."

¹⁹So they came to the man in charge of Joseph's house and spoke to him at the door. ²⁰"Please, sir," they said, "we came here to buy food once before. ²¹When we stopped for the night, we opened our sacks, and each man found all of his money inside. So we brought it back with us. ²²We also brought more money to buy food. We have no idea who put our money back in our sacks."

²³"It's alright," he said. "Don't be afraid! Your God, the God of your father, must have given you treasure in your sacks. I received your money." Then he brought Simeon out to them.

²⁴The man took the brothers into Joseph's house. He gave them water to wash their feet and feed for their donkeys. ²⁵They got their gifts ready for Joseph's return at noon, because they had heard they were going to eat there.

²⁶When Joseph came home, they gave him the gifts they had brought to the house. Then they bowed to him with their faces touching the ground. ²⁷He asked them how they were. Then he said, "You told me about your elderly father. How is he? Is he still alive?"

²⁸They answered, "Yes, sir. Our father is alive and well." Then they knelt, bowing down.

²⁹As Joseph looked around, he saw his brother Benjamin, his mother's son. "Is this your youngest brother, the one you told me about?" he asked. "God be gracious to you, my son," he said. ³⁰Deeply moved at the sight of his brother, he hurried away, looking for a place to cry. He went into his private room and cried there.

³¹Then he washed his face and came out. He was in control of his emotions when he said, "Serve the food."

³²He was served separately from his brothers. The Egyptians who were there with him were also served separately, because they found it offensive to eat with Hebrews.

[33]The brothers were seated facing him according to their ages—from the oldest to the youngest. They looked at each other in amazement.

[34]Joseph had portions of food brought to them from his table, but Benjamin's portion was five times more than any of the others. So they ate and drank with Joseph until they were drunk.

Joseph's Plan to Trap His Brothers

[1]Joseph commanded the man in charge of his house, "Fill the men's sacks with as much food as they can carry. Put each man's money in his sack. [2]Then put my silver cup in the youngest brother's sack along with the money for his grain." He did what Joseph told him.

[3]At dawn the men were sent on their way with their donkeys. [4]They had not gone far from the city when Joseph said to the man in charge of his house, "Go after those men at once, and when you catch up with them, say to them, 'Why have you paid me back with evil when I was good to you? [5]Isn't this the cup that my master drinks from and that he uses for telling the future? What you have done is evil!' "

[6]When he caught up with them, he repeated these words to them. [7]They answered him, "Sir, how can you say such things? We would never think of doing anything like that! [8]We brought the money we found in our sacks back from Canaan. So why would we steal any silver or gold from your master's house? [9]If one of us has it, he will die, and the rest of us will become your slaves."

[10]"I agree," he said. "We'll do what you've said. The man who has the cup will be my slave, and the rest of you can go free."

[11]Each one quickly lowered his sack to the ground and opened it. [12]Then the man made a thorough search. He began with the oldest and ended with the youngest. The cup was found in Benjamin's sack. [13]When they saw this, they tore their clothes in grief. Then each one loaded his donkey and went back into the city.

[14]Judah and his brothers arrived at Joseph's house while Joseph was still there. Immediately, they bowed with their faces touching the ground. [15]Joseph asked them, "What have you done? Don't you know that a man like me can find things out because he knows the future?"

[16]"Sir, what can we say to you?" Judah asked. "How else can we explain it? How can we prove we're innocent? God has uncovered our guilt. Now all of us are your slaves, including the one who had the cup."

[17]But Joseph said, "I would never think of doing that! Only the man who had the cup will be my slave. The rest of you can go back to your father in peace."

Judah Defends Benjamin

[18]Then Judah went up to Joseph and said, "Please, sir, let me speak openly with you. Don't be angry with me, although you are equal to Pharaoh. [19]Sir, you asked us, 'Do you have a father or a brother?' [20]We answered, 'We have a father who is old and a younger brother born to him when he was already old. The boy's brother is dead, so he's the only one of his mother's sons left, and his father loves him.'

[21]"Then you said to us, 'Bring him here to me so that I can see him myself.' [22]We replied, 'The boy can't leave his father. If the boy leaves him, his father will die.' [23]Then you told us, 'If your youngest brother doesn't come here with you, you will never be allowed to see me again.' [24]When we went back to our father, we told him what you had said.

[25]"Then our father said, 'Go back and buy us a little more food.' [26]We answered, 'We can't go back. We can only go back if our youngest brother is with us. The man won't see us unless our youngest brother is with us.'

[27]"Then our father said to us, 'You know that my wife ⌊Rachel⌋ gave me two sons. [28]One is gone, and I said, "He must have been torn to pieces!" I haven't seen him since. [29]If you take this one away from me too and anything happens to him, you'll drive this gray-haired old man to his grave.'

[30]"Our father's life is wrapped up with the boy's life. If I come ⌊home⌋ without the boy [31]and he sees that the boy isn't ⌊with me⌋, he'll die. The grief would drive our gray-haired old father to his grave.

[32]"I guaranteed my father that the boy would come back. I said, 'If I don't bring him back to you, then you can blame me the rest of my life, Father.'[33]Sir, please let me stay and be your slave in the boy's place, and let the boy go back with his brothers. [34]How could I go back to my father if the boy isn't with me? I couldn't bear to see my father's misery!"

Joseph Reveals His Identity

[1]Joseph could no longer control his emotions in front of everyone who was standing around him, so he cried out, "Have everyone leave me!" No one else was there when Joseph told his brothers who he was. [2]He cried so loudly that the Egyptians heard him, and Pharaoh's household heard about it.

[3]Joseph said to his brothers, "I am Joseph! Is my father still alive?" His brothers could not answer him because they were afraid of him.

[4]"Please come closer to me," Joseph said to his brothers. When they did so, he said, "I am Joseph, the brother you sold into slavery in Egypt! [5]Now, don't be sad or angry with yourselves that you sold me. God sent me ahead of you to save lives. [6]The famine has been in the land for two years. There will be five more years without plowing or harvesting. [7]God sent me ahead of you to make sure that you would have descendants on the earth and to save your lives in an amazing way. [8]It wasn't you who sent me here, but God. He has made me ⌊like⌋ a father to Pharaoh, lord over his entire household, and ruler of Egypt.

[9]"Hurry back to my father, and say to him, 'This is what your son Joseph says, "God has made me lord of Egypt. Come here to me right away! [10]Live in the land of Goshen, where you will be near me. Live there with your children and your grandchildren, as well as your flocks, your herds, and everything you have. [11]I will provide for you in Egypt, since there will be five more years of famine. Then you, your family, and all who belong to you won't lose everything.' "

[12]"You and my brother Benjamin can see for yourselves that I am the one who is speaking to you. [13]Tell my father how greatly honored I am in Egypt and about everything you have seen. Hurry and bring my father here!"

[14]He threw his arms around his brother Benjamin and cried with Benjamin, who was crying on his shoulder. [15]He kissed all his brothers and cried with them. After that his brothers talked with him.

Pharaoh Invites Jacob's [Israel's] Family to Live in Egypt

[16]When Pharaoh's household heard the news that Joseph's brothers had come, Pharaoh and his officials were pleased. [17]So Pharaoh said to Joseph, "Say to your brothers, 'Load up your animals, and go back to Canaan. [18]Take your father and your families, and come to me. I will give you the best land in Egypt. Then you can enjoy the best food in the land.'

[19]"Give them this order: 'Take wagons with you from Egypt for your children and your wives. Bring your father, and come back. [20]Don't worry about your belongings because the best of everything in Egypt is yours.' "

²¹Israel's sons did as they were told. Joseph gave them wagons and supplies for their trip as Pharaoh had ordered. ²²He gave each of them a change of clothes, but he gave Benjamin three hundred pieces of silver and five changes of clothes. ²³He sent his father ten male donkeys carrying Egypt's best products and ten female donkeys carrying grain, bread, and food for his father's trip. ²⁴So Joseph sent his brothers on their way. As they were leaving, he said to them, "Don't quarrel on your way back!"

²⁵So they left Egypt and came to their father Jacob in Canaan. ²⁶They told him, "Joseph is still alive! Yes, he is ruler of Egypt." Jacob was stunned and didn't believe them. ²⁷Yet, when they told their father everything Joseph had said to them and he saw the wagons Joseph had sent to bring him back, his spirits were lifted.

²⁸"You have convinced me!" Israel said. "My son Joseph is still alive. I will go and see him before I die."

Jacob's [Israel's] Seventh Encounter With God

46 ¹Israel moved with all he had. When he came to Beersheba, he offered sacrifices to the God of his father Isaac.

²God spoke to Israel in a vision that night and said, "Jacob, Jacob!"

"Here I am," he answered.

³"I am God, the God of your father," he said. "Don't be afraid to go to Egypt, because I will make you a great nation there. ⁴I will go with you to Egypt, and I will make sure you come back again. Joseph will close your eyes when you die,."

⁵So Jacob left Beersheba. Israel's sons put their father Jacob, their children, and their wives in the wagons Pharaoh had sent to bring him back. ⁶They also took their livestock and the possessions they had accumulated in Canaan.

Jacob and all his family arrived in Egypt. ⁷He had brought his sons, his grandsons, his daughters, and his granddaughters—his entire family.

Jacob's [Israel's] Descendants—
Exodus 6:14-16; I Chronicles 2:3-5

⁸These are the names of Israel's descendants (Jacob and his descendants) who arrived in Egypt.

Reuben was Jacob's firstborn.

⁹The sons of **Reuben** were

Hanoch, Pallu, Hezron, and Carmi.

¹⁰The sons of **Simeon** were

Jemuel, Jamin, Ohad, Jakin, Zohar, and Shaul, the son of a Canaanite woman.

¹¹The sons of **Levi** were

Gershon, Kohath, and Merari.

¹²The sons of **Judah** were

Er, Onan, Shelah, Perez, and Zerah. (Er and Onan had died in Canaan.)

The sons of Perez were

Hezron and Hamul.

¹³The sons of **Issachar** were

Tola, Puvah, Iob, and Shimron.

¹⁴The sons of **Zebulun** were

Sered, Elon, and Jahleel.

¹⁵These were the descendants of the sons Leah gave to Jacob in Paddan Aram, in addition to his daughter Dinah. The total number of these sons and daughters was 33.

¹⁶The sons of **Gad** were
  Ziphion, Haggi, Shuni, Ezbon, Eri, Arodi, and Areli.
¹⁷The sons of **Asher** were
  Imnah, Ishvah, Ishvi, and Beriah. Their sister was Serah.
  The sons of Beriah were
    Heber and Malchiel.
¹⁸These were the descendants of Zilpah, whom Laban gave to his daughter Leah.
  She gave birth to these children for Jacob. The total was 16.

¹⁹The sons of Jacob's wife Rachel were
  Joseph and Benjamin.
²⁰ In Egypt, Manasseh and Ephraim were born to **Joseph** by Asenath, daugh-
    ter of Potiphera, priest from the city of On.
²¹ The sons of **Benjamin** were
    Bela, Beker, Ashbel, Gera, Naaman, Ehi, Rosh, Muppim, Huppim, and Ard.
²²These were the descendants of Rachel who were born to Jacob. The total was 14.

²³The son of **Dan** was
  Hushim.
²⁴The sons of **Naphtali** were
  Jahzeel, Guni, Jezer, and Shillem.
²⁵These were the descendants of Bilhah, whom Laban gave to his daughter Rachel.
  She gave birth to these sons for Jacob. The total was 7.

²⁶The total number of Jacob's direct descendants who went with him to Egypt was
  66. This didn't include the wives of Jacob's sons. ²⁷Joseph had two sons who
  were born in Egypt. The grand total of people in Jacob's household who went
  to Egypt was 70.

Joseph and Jacob [Israel] Reunited

²⁸Israel sent Judah ahead of him to Joseph to get directions to Goshen. When
Israel's family arrived in the region of Goshen, ²⁹Joseph prepared his chariot and went
to meet his father Israel. As soon as he saw his father, he threw his arms around him
and cried on his shoulder a long time.
³⁰Israel said to Joseph, "Now that I've seen for myself that you're still alive, I'm
ready to die."
³¹Then Joseph said to his brothers and his father's family, "I'm going to Pharaoh
to tell him, 'My brothers and my father's family, who were in Canaan, have come to
me. ³²The men are shepherds. They take care of livestock. They've brought their
flocks and herds and everything they own.' ³³Now, when Pharaoh calls for you and
asks, 'What kind of work do you do?' ³⁴you must answer, 'We have taken care of herds
all our lives, as our ancestors have done.' You must say this, so that you may live in
the region of Goshen, because all shepherds are disgusting to Egyptians."

Jacob [Israel] Meets Pharaoh

¹Joseph went and told Pharaoh, "My father and my brothers have arrived from
Canaan with their flocks, herds, and everything they have. Now they are in
Goshen." ²Since he had taken five of his brothers with him, he presented them to
Pharaoh.
³Pharaoh asked the brothers, "What kind of work do you do?"
  They answered Pharaoh, "We are shepherds, as were our ancestors. ⁴We have

come to live in this land for a while. The famine is so severe in Canaan that there's no pasture for our flocks. So please let us live in Goshen."

[5]Then Pharaoh said to Joseph, "Your father and your brothers have come to you. [6]All of Egypt is available to you. Have your father and your brothers live in the best part of the land. Let them live in Goshen. If they are qualified, put them in charge of my livestock."

[7]Then Joseph brought his father Jacob and had him stand in front of Pharaoh. Jacob blessed Pharaoh. [8]Pharaoh asked him, "How old are you?"

[9]Jacob answered Pharaoh, "The length of my stay on earth has been 130 years. The years of my life have been few and difficult, fewer than my ancestors' years." [10]Then Jacob blessed Pharaoh and left.

[11]As Pharaoh had ordered, Joseph had his father and his brothers live in the best part of Egypt, the region of Rameses. He gave them property there. [12]Joseph also provided his father, his brothers, and all his father's family with food based on the number of children they had.

Joseph Acquires All the Land in Egypt for Pharaoh

[13]The famine was so severe that there was no food anywhere. Neither Egypt nor Canaan were producing crops because of the famine. [14]Joseph collected all the money that could be found in Egypt and in Canaan as payment for the grain people bought. Then he took it to Pharaoh's palace. [15]When the money in Egypt and Canaan was gone, all the Egyptians came to Joseph. "Give us food," they said. "Do you want us to die right in front of you? We don't have any more money!"

[16]Joseph replied, "If you don't have any more money, give me your livestock, and I'll give you food[a] in exchange." [17]So they brought their livestock to Joseph, and he gave them food in exchange for their horses, sheep, goats, cattle, and donkeys. During that year he supplied them with food in exchange for all their livestock.

[18]When that year was over, they came to him the next year. "Sir," they said to him, "you know that our money is gone, and you have all our livestock. There's nothing left to bring you except our bodies and our land. [19]Do you want us to die right in front of you? Do you want the land to be ruined? Take us and our land in exchange for food. Then we will be Pharaoh's slaves and our land will be his property. But give us seed so that we won't starve to death and the ground won't become a desert."

[20]Joseph bought all the land in Egypt for Pharaoh. Every Egyptian sold his fields because the famine was so severe. The land became Pharaoh's. [21]All over Egypt Joseph moved the people to the cities. [22]But he didn't buy the priests' land because the priests received an income from Pharaoh, and they lived on that income. That's why they didn't sell their land.

[23]Joseph said to the people, "Now that I have bought you and your land for Pharaoh, here is seed for you. Plant crops in the land. [24]Every time you harvest, give one-fifth of the produce to Pharaoh. Four-fifths will be yours to use as seed for your fields and as food for your households."

[25]"You have saved our lives," they said. "Please, sir, we are willing to be Pharaoh's slaves."

[26]Joseph made a law concerning the land in Egypt which is still in force today: One-fifth of the produce belongs to Pharaoh. Only the land of the priests didn't belong to Pharaoh.   •

---

[a]47:16 Samaritan Pentateuch, Greek, Targum; Masoretic Text "I'll give to you."

Jacob's [Israel's] Last Days in Egypt

[27]So the Israelites settled in Egypt in the region of Goshen. They acquired property there and had many children.

[28]Jacob lived in Egypt 17 years, so he lived a total of 147 years. [29]Israel was about to die. He called for his son Joseph and said to him, "I want you to swear that you love me and are faithful to me. Please don't bury me here. [30]I want to rest with my ancestors. Take me out of Egypt, and bury me in their tomb."

"I will do as you say," Joseph answered.

[31]"Swear to me," he said. So Joseph swore to him. Then Israel bowed down in prayer with his face at the head of his bed.

Jacob [Israel] Blesses Joseph's Two Sons

48 [1]Later Joseph was told, "Your father is ill." So he took his two sons Manasseh and Ephraim to see Jacob. [2]When Jacob was told, "Your son Joseph is here to see you," Israel gathered his strength and sat up in bed.

[3]Jacob said to Joseph, "God Almighty appeared to me at Luz in Canaan and blessed me. [4]He said to me, 'I will make you fertile and increase the number of your descendants so that you will become a community of people. I will give this land to your descendants as a permanent possession.'

[5]"So your two sons, who were born in Egypt before I came here, are my sons. Ephraim and Manasseh will be mine just as Reuben and Simeon are. [6]Any other children you have after them will be yours. They will inherit the land listed under their brothers' names. [7]As I was coming back from Paddan, Rachel died in Canaan when we were still some distance from Ephrath. So I buried her there on the way to Ephrath" (that is, Bethlehem).

[8]When Israel saw Joseph's sons, he asked, "Who are they?"

[9]"They are my sons, whom God has given me here in Egypt," Joseph answered his father.

Then Israel said, "Please bring them to me so that I may bless them."

[10]Israel's eyesight was failing because of old age, and he could hardly see. So Joseph brought his sons close to his father, and Israel hugged them and kissed them.

[11]Israel said to Joseph, "I never expected to see you again, and now God has even let me see your sons."

[12]Joseph took them off his father's lap and bowed with his face touching the ground. [13]Then Joseph took both of them, Ephraim on his right, facing Israel's left, and Manasseh on his left, facing Israel's right, and brought them close to him. [14]But Israel crossed his hands and reached out. He put his right hand on Ephraim's head, although Ephraim was the younger son. He put his left hand on Manasseh's head, although Manasseh was older.

[15]Then Jacob blessed Joseph,

> "May God, in whose presence my grandfather Abraham
>   and my father Isaac walked,
> may God, who has been my shepherd all my life to this very day,
> [16] may the Messenger, who has rescued me from all evil,
>   bless these boys.
> May they be called by my name
>   and by the names of my grandfather Abraham and my father Isaac.
> May they have many children on the earth."

¹⁷When Joseph saw that his father had put his right hand on Ephraim's head, he didn't like it. So he took his father's hand in order to move it from Ephraim's head to Manasseh's. ¹⁸Then he said to his father, "That's not right, Father! This is the first-born. Put your right hand on his head."

¹⁹His father refused and said, "I know, Son, I know! Manasseh, too, will become a nation, and he, too, will be important. Nevertheless, his younger brother will be more important than he, and his descendants will become many nations." ²⁰That day he blessed them. He said,

> "Because of you, Israel will speak this blessing,
>   'May God make you like Ephraim and Manasseh!'"

In this way Israel put Ephraim ahead of Manasseh.

²¹Then Israel said to Joseph, "Now I'm about to die, but God will be with you. He will bring you back to the land of your fathers. ²²I'm giving you one more mountain ridge than your brothers. I took it from the Amorites with my own sword and bow."

Jacob [Israel] Blesses His 12 Sons

49 ¹Jacob called for his sons and said, "Come here, and let me tell you what will happen to you in the days to come.

²   "Gather around and listen, sons of Jacob.
         Listen to your father Israel.

³   "**Reuben**, you are my firstborn,
         my strength, the very first son I had,
             first in majesty and first in power.
⁴   You will no longer be first
         because you were out of control like a flood
             and you climbed into your father's bed.
                 Then you dishonored it.
         He climbed up on my couch.

⁵   "**Simeon** and **Levi** are brothers.
         Their swordsᵃ are weapons of violence.
⁶   Do not let me attend their secret meetings.
     Do not let me join their assembly.
         In their anger they murdered men.
         At their whim they crippled cattle.
⁷   May their anger be cursed because it's so fierce.
     May their fury be cursed because it's so cruel.
         I will divide them among the sons of Jacob
             and scatter them among the tribes of Israel.

⁸   "**Judah**, your brothers will praise you.
         Your hand will be on the neck of your enemies.
     Your father's sons will bow down to you.
⁹   Judah, you are a lion cub.
         You have come back from the kill, my son.

ᵃ 49:5 Hebrew meaning uncertain.

He lies down and rests like a lion.
He is like a lioness. Who dares to disturb him?

10 A scepter will never depart from Judah
      nor a ruler's staff from between his feet
          until Shiloh comes
              and the people obey him.

11 He will tie his donkey to a grapevine,
      his colt to the best vine.
   He will wash his clothes in wine,
      his garments in the blood of grapes.

12 His eyes are darker than wine.
   His teeth are whiter than milk.

13 "**Zebulun** will live by the coast.
   He will have ships by the coast.
      His border will go as far as Sidon.

14 "**Issachar** is a strong donkey,
      lying down between the saddlebags.

15 When he sees that his resting place is good
      and that the land is pleasant,
          he will bend his back to the burden
              and will become a slave laborer.

16 "**Dan** will hand down decisions*b* for his people
      as one of the tribes of Israel.

17 Dan will be a snake on a road,
      a viper on a path,
          that bites a horse's heels
              so that its rider falls off backwards.

18 "I wait with hope for you to rescue me, O LORD.

19 "**Gad** will be attacked by a band of raiders,
      but he will strike back at their heels.

20 "**Asher**'s food will be rich.
   He will provide delicacies fit for a king.

21 "**Naphtali** is a doe set free
      that has beautiful fawns.

22 "**Joseph** is a fruitful tree,
      a fruitful tree by a spring,
          with branches climbing over a wall.

23 Archers provoked him,
      shot at him,
          and attacked him.

24 But his bow stayed steady, and his arms remained limber
      because of the help of the Mighty One of Jacob,
      because of the name of the Shepherd, the Rock of Israel,
25 because of the God of your father who helps you,

---

b 49:16 There is a play on words here between Hebrew *Dan* and *yadin* (he will hand down decisions).

because of the Almighty who gives you
    blessings from the heavens above,
    blessings from the deep springs below the ground,
    blessings from breasts and womb.
26   The blessings of your father are greater than
    the blessings of the oldest mountains
    and the riches of the ancient hills.
May these blessings rest on the head of Joseph,
    on the crown of the prince among his brothers.

27   "**Benjamin** is a ravenous wolf.
    In the morning he devours his prey.
    In the evening he divides the plunder."

²⁸These are the 12 tribes of Israel and what their father said to them when he gave each of them his special blessing.

²⁹Then he gave them these instructions, "I am about to join my ancestors in death. Bury me with my ancestors in the cave in the field of Ephron the Hittite. ³⁰Abraham bought the cave that is in the field of Machpelah, east of Mamre in Canaan, from Ephron the Hittite to use as a tomb. ³¹Abraham and his wife Sarah are buried there. Isaac and his wife Rebekah are buried there. I also buried Leah there. ³²The field and the cave in it were bought from the Hittites."

³³When Jacob finished giving these instructions to his sons, he pulled his feet into his bed. He took his last breath and joined his ancestors in death.

Joseph Buries His Father

50 ¹Joseph threw himself on his father, cried over him, and kissed him. ²Then Joseph ordered the doctors in his service to embalm his father. So the doctors embalmed Israel. ³The embalming was completed in the usual time—40 days. The Egyptians mourned for him 70 days.

⁴When the time of mourning for Jacob was over, Joseph spoke to Pharaoh's palace staff. He said, "Please speak directly to Pharaoh. Tell him, ⁵'My father made me swear an oath. He said, "I'm about to die. Bury me in the tomb I bought for myself in Canaan." Please let me go there and bury my father; then I'll come back.'"

⁶Pharaoh replied, "Go and bury your father, as you have promised him."

⁷So Joseph left to bury his father. All Pharaoh's officials, the leaders in his palace staff, and all the leaders of Egypt went with him. ⁸Joseph's household, his brothers, and his father's household also went with him. (Only their children, their flocks, and their cattle were left in Goshen.) ⁹Chariots and horsemen went with him. It was a very large group.

¹⁰When they came to the threshing floor*ᵃ* of Atad, which is on the east side of the Jordan River, they began a great and solemn ceremony to mourn Jacob's death. Joseph took seven days to mourn his father's death. ¹¹When the Canaanites living there saw the funeral ceremonies at the threshing floor of Atad, they said, "These funeral ceremonies are taken very seriously by the Egyptians." That's why that place on the east side of the Jordan was named Abel Mizraim [Egyptian Funeral Ceremonies].

¹²Jacob's sons did for him what he had told them to do. ¹³They carried him back to Canaan and buried him in the cave in the field of Machpelah, east of Mamre. Abraham had bought this tomb from Ephron the Hittite.

ᵃ50:10 A threshing floor is an outdoor area where grain is separated from its husks.

[14]After Joseph had buried his father, he went back to Egypt along with his brothers and everyone who had gone there with him to bury his father.

Joseph Forgives His Brothers

[15]Joseph's brothers realized what their father's death could mean. So they thought, "What if Joseph holds a grudge against us? What if he decides to pay us back for all the evil we did to him?" [16]They sent a messenger to Joseph to say, "Before your father died, he commanded us, [17]'This is what you should say to Joseph, "I'm begging you to forgive the crime and the sin your brothers committed against you. What they did to you was very evil." ' So now, please forgive our crime, because we are servants of your father's God." Joseph cried when he got their message.

[18]Then his brothers also came and immediately bowed down in front of him. "We are your slaves!" they said.

[19]Joseph said to them, "Don't be afraid! I can't take God's place. [20]Even though you planned evil against me, God planned good to come out of it. This was to keep many people alive, as he is doing now. [21]Don't be afraid! I will provide for you and your children." In this way he reassured them, setting their minds at ease.

[22]Joseph and his father's family stayed in Egypt. Joseph lived to be 110 years old. [23]He saw his grandchildren, Ephraim's children. Even the children of Machir, son of Manasseh, were adopted by Joseph at birth.

[24]At last Joseph said to his brothers, "I'm about to die. God will definitely take care of you and take you out of this land to the land he swore with an oath to give to Abraham, Isaac, and Jacob." [25]Joseph made Israel's sons swear an oath. He said, "God will definitely take care of you. So be sure to carry my bones back with you."

[26]Joseph died when he was 110 years old. His body was embalmed and placed in a coffin in Egypt.

Good Morning, God

Genesis 50:15-21

Joseph's life seemed to go from bad to worse. He was rescued from a pit only to be thrown into prison. Yet God was watching over Joseph. He arranged for Joseph to become one of the most important men in Egypt so he could save his family from starvation. Joseph believed God could turn anything bad that happened to him into even greater good. Do you have an attitude like Joseph's? You can trust God even when things appear bad.

Father, help me remember that you can use bad things for my good.

Exodus

We can call Exodus "the Great Escape!" The Israelites were slaves in Egypt. But God had promised to give the Israelites the land of Canaan. To keep his promise, God performed miracles in order to force Egypt's king to free the people. Then God led them across a desert to Mount Sinai. There God gave the Israelites rules for living good and happy lives and taught them how to worship him.

Headlines

Miriam, the Bible's first song leader, praises God for victory. See Exodus 15.

Scavenger Hunt!

Challenge your family to identify these things in Exodus. Have each person write down the objects and how long it takes to find them. Add each person's times together and use the chart below to rank one another.
(Hint: Check chapters 2, 7, 17, 26, 28, 32, and 39.)

Object / Time

1. A water-proof cradle _____

2. A cannibal reptile _____

3. A stone fountain _____

4. Furry drapes _____

5. Headgear with a message _____

6. A fool's gold god _____

7. Holy armor _____

TOTAL _____

Add the times.
1-5 minutes: Expert
6-10 minutes: Master
11-15 minutes: Apprentice

What's In It For Me?

Exodus shows me . . .

GOD USES HIS POWER TO HELP PEOPLE.

GOD TEACHES ME HOW TO LIVE RIGHT.

GOD PROVIDES FOR ALL MY NEEDS.

GOD LIKES ME TO WORSHIP HIM.

Ten Commandments Dangerous?

Your mom and dad may have seen the ten commandments posted on classroom walls when they were kids in school. But if you go to a public school today, you won't see the ten commandments anywhere.

Public schools are not allowed to post the ten commandments today. Why not? Are the ten commandments dangerous? Of course not! Actually, they protect people from danger.

God gave Moses the ten commandments. When you follow God's rules, you not only do what's right, you do what's good for you. The ten commandments teach people not to lie, steal, or hurt each other. They teach people to love each other.

Today, schools have hate, crime, drugs, violence, guns, and not much love. They don't have the ten commandments either. Wouldn't school be a great place if everyone followed the ten commandments? There would be a lot less hate and a lot more love.

Even though public schools won't post the ten commandments in classrooms, school is a good place to follow these guidelines. If you follow the ten commandments, you'll be doing what's right. And you'll help make school a better place to be.

What Good Are Rules?

What if you didn't have any rules? What if you never had to brush your teeth? (Yuck! Mouth rot!) Or if you never had to clean your room? (Bug heaven!) If you think about it, you can probably come up with good reasons for most of your mom and dad's rules.

No wonder God gave the Israelites rules to live by! Without rules, life gets bad—fast! And just think, nobody knows better than God what's good for you! You'll be much happier if you obey God's rules!

Knock, knock.

Who's there?

Manna.

Manna who?

Manna, would you look at all this food!

Riddle:

Who broke the most commandments?

And how many did he break?

(Exodus 32:19)

She: Gee, Moses must have been ugly.

He: Why do you say that?

She: Because he had to wear a veil over his face (Exodus 34:33).

1. Love God above everything.
2. Worship only God.
3. Use God's name with respect.
4. Rest and worship one day each week.
5. Respect parents.
6. Protect life.
7. Respect boys.
8. Respect others' property.
9. Protect others' reputations.
10. Be satisfied with what you have.

Exodus

Israel Comes to Egypt

¹These are the names of the sons of Israel (that is, Jacob) who came with him to Egypt with their families: ²Reuben, Simeon, Levi, and Judah; ³Issachar, Zebulun, and Benjamin; ⁴Dan and Naphtali; Gad and Asher. ⁵Joseph was already in Egypt. The total number of Jacob's descendants was 70.

⁶Eventually, Joseph, all his brothers, and that entire generation died. ⁷But the descendants of Israel had many children. They became so numerous and strong that the land was filled with them.

The Israelites Become Slaves

⁸Then a new king, who knew nothing about Joseph, began to rule in Egypt. ⁹He said to his people, "There are too many Israelites, and they are stronger then we are. ¹⁰We have to outsmart them, or they'll increase in number. Then, if war breaks out, they will join our enemies, fight against us, and leave the country."

¹¹So the Egyptians put slave drivers in charge of them in order to oppress them through forced labor. They built Pithom and Rameses as supply cities for Pharaoh. ¹²But the more the Israelites were oppressed, the more they increased in number and spread out. The Egyptians couldn't stand them ˌany longerˌ. ¹³So they forced the Israelites to work hard as slaves. ¹⁴They made their lives bitter with back-breaking work in mortar and bricks and every kind of work in the fields. All the jobs the Egyptians gave them were brutally hard.

Pharaoh Tells the Midwives to Kill All Hebrew Baby Boys

¹⁵Then the king of Egypt told the Hebrew midwives, whose names were Shiphrah and Puah, ¹⁶"When you help the Hebrew women in childbirth, look at the child when you deliver it. If it's a boy, kill it, but if it's a girl, let it live."

¹⁷However, the midwives feared God and didn't obey the king of Egypt's orders. They let the boys live. ¹⁸So the king of Egypt called for the midwives. He asked them, "Why have you done this? Why have you let the boys live?"

¹⁹The midwives answered Pharaoh, "Hebrew women are not like Egyptian women. They are so healthy that they have their babies before a midwife arrives."

²⁰God was good to the midwives. So the people increased in number and became very strong. ²¹Because the midwives feared God, he gave them families of their own.

²²Then Pharaoh commanded all his people to throw into the Nile every ˌHebrewˌ boy that was born, but to let every girl live.

Pharaoh's Daughter Adopts Moses

¹A man from Levi's family married a Levite woman. ²The woman became pregnant and had a son. She saw how beautiful he was and hid him for three months. ³When she couldn't hide him any longer, she took a basket made of papyrus plants and coated it with tar and pitch. She put the baby in it and set it among the papyrus plants near the bank of the Nile River. ⁴The baby's sister stood at a distance to see what would happen to him.

⁵While Pharaoh's daughter came to the Nile to take a bath, her servants walked along the bank of the river. She saw the basket among the papyrus plants and sent her slave girl to get it. ⁶Pharaoh's daughter opened the basket, looked at the baby, and saw it was a boy. He was crying, and she felt sorry for him. She said, "This is one of the Hebrew children."

⁷Then the baby's sister asked Pharaoh's daughter, "Should I go and get one of the Hebrew women to nurse the baby for you?"

⁸She answered, "Yes!" So the girl brought the baby's mother.

⁹Pharaoh's daughter said to the woman, "Take this child, nurse him for me, and I will pay you."

She took the child and nursed him. ¹⁰When the child was old enough, she brought him to Pharaoh's daughter, and he became her son. Pharaoh's daughter named him Moses [Pulled Out] and said, "I pulled him out of the water."

Moses Commits Murder and Flees to Midian

¹¹In the course of time Moses grew up. Then he went to see his own people and watched them suffering under forced labor. He saw a Hebrew, one of his own people, being beaten by an Egyptian. ¹²He looked all around, and when he didn't see anyone, he beat the Egyptian to death and hid the body in the sand.

¹³When Moses went there the next day, he saw two Hebrew men fighting. He asked the one who started the fight, "Why are you beating another Hebrew?"

¹⁴The man asked, "Who made you our ruler and judge? Are you going to kill me as you killed the Egyptian?" Then Moses was afraid and thought that everyone knew what he had done.

¹⁵When Pharaoh heard what Moses had done, he tried to have him killed. But Moses fled from Pharaoh and settled in the land of Midian.

Moses Marries Zipporah

One day, while Moses was sitting by a well, ¹⁶seven daughters of the priest of Midian came. They drew water and filled the troughs to water their father's sheep. ¹⁷But some shepherds came and chased them away. So Moses got up, came to their defense, and then watered their sheep.

¹⁸When they came back to their father Reuel, he asked them, "Why have you come home so early today?"

¹⁹They answered, "An Egyptian rescued us from some shepherds. He even drew water for us and watered the sheep."

²⁰Reuel asked his daughters, "Where is he? Why did you leave the man there? Go, invite him to supper."

²¹Moses decided to stay with the man. So Reuel gave his daughter Zipporah to Moses as his wife. ²²She gave birth to a son. Moses named him Gershom [Foreigner], because he said, "I was a foreigner living in another country."

The Israelites Pray to God During Their Suffering

²³After a long time passed, the king of Egypt died. The Israelites still groaned because they were slaves. So they cried out, and their cries for help went up to God. ²⁴God heard their groaning, and he remembered his promise[a] to Abraham, Isaac, and Jacob. ²⁵God saw the Israelites being oppressed, and was concerned about them.

ᵃ2:24 Or "covenant."

Moses at the Burning Bush

¹Moses was taking care of the sheep of his father-in-law Jethro, the priest of Midian. As he led the sheep to the far side of the desert, he came to Horeb, the mountain of God.

²The Messenger of the Lord appeared to him there as flames of fire coming out of a bush. Moses looked, and although the bush was on fire, it was not burning up. ³So he thought, "Why isn't this bush burning up? I must go over there and see this strange sight."

⁴When the Lord saw that Moses had come over to see it, God called to him from the bush, "Moses, Moses!"

Moses answered, "Here I am!"

⁵God said, "Don't come any closer! Take off your sandals because this place where you are standing is holy ground. ⁶I am the God of your ancestors,ᵃ the God of Abraham, Isaac, and Jacob." Moses hid his face because he was afraid to look at God.

⁷The Lord said, "I have seen the misery of my people in Egypt, and I have heard them crying out because of the slave drivers. I know how much they're suffering. ⁸I have come to rescue them from the power of the Egyptians and to bring them from that land to a good land with plenty of room for everyone. It is a land flowing with milk and honey where the Canaanites, Hittites, Amorites, Perizzites, Hivites, and Jebusites live. ⁹I have heard the cry of the people of Israel. I have seen how the Egyptians are oppressing them. ¹⁰Now, go! I am sending you to Pharaoh so that you can bring my people Israel out of Egypt."

¹¹But Moses said to God, "Who am I that I should go to Pharaoh and bring the people of Israel out of Egypt?"

¹²God answered, "I will be with you. And this will be the proof that I sent you: When you bring the people out of Egypt, all of you will worship God on this mountain."

¹³Then Moses replied to God, "Suppose I go to the people of Israel and say to them, 'The God of your ancestors has sent me to you,' and they ask me, 'What is his name?' What should I tell them?"

¹⁴God answered Moses, "I Am Who I Am. This is what you must say to the people of Israel: 'I Am has sent me to you.'"

¹⁵Again God said to Moses, "This is what you must say to the people of Israel: The Lord God of your ancestors, the God of Abraham, Isaac, and Jacob, has sent me to you. This is my name forever. This is my title throughout every generation.

¹⁶"Go, assemble the leaders of Israel. Say to them, 'The Lord God of your ancestors, the God of Abraham, Isaac, and Jacob, appeared to me. He said, "I have paid close attention to you and have seen what has been done to you in Egypt. ¹⁷I promise I will take you away from your misery in Egypt to the land of the Canaanites, Hittites, Amorites, Perizzites, Hivites, and Jebusites, a land flowing with milk and honey."'

¹⁸"The leaders of Israel will listen to you. Then you and the leaders must go to the king of Egypt and say to him, 'The Lord God of the Hebrews has met with us. Please let us travel three days into the desert to offer sacrifices to the Lord our God.' ¹⁹I know that the king of Egypt will not let you go, even if he is forced to. ²⁰So I will use my power to strike Egypt. After all the miracles that I will do there, he will let you go. ²¹I will make the Egyptians kind to the people of Israel so that, when you leave, you will not leave empty-handed.

²²"Every Hebrew woman should ask her Egyptian neighbor and any woman living

---

ᵃ 3:6 Samaritan Pentateuch, Greek, Acts 7:32; Masoretic Text "ancestor."

in her home for silver and gold jewelry and for clothes. Put them on your sons and daughters. This way you will strip Egypt of its wealth."

¹"They will never believe me or listen to me!" Moses protested. "They will say, 'The Lord didn't appear to you.' "

²Then the Lord asked him, "What's that in your hand?"

He answered, "A shepherd's staff."

³The Lord said, "Throw it on the ground."

When Moses threw it on the ground, it became a snake, and he ran away from it. ⁴Then the Lord said to Moses, "Reach out and grab the snake by its tail." He reached out and grabbed it, and it turned back into a staff as he held it. ⁵The Lord explained, "This is to convince the people that the Lord God of their ancestors, the God of Abraham, Isaac, and Jacob, appeared to you."

⁶The Lord said to him, "Put your hand inside your shirt." So Moses did this, and when he took his hand out, it had a skin disease. It looked as flaky as snow. ⁷"Now put your hand back inside your shirt," the Lord said. Moses put it back, and when he took it out this time, it was healthy again like the rest of his body.

⁸Then the Lord said, "If they won't believe you or pay attention to the first miraculous sign, they may believe the second. ⁹But if they won't believe these two miraculous signs or listen to you, take some water from the Nile River and pour it on the ground. The water you take from the Nile will turn into blood on the ground."

¹⁰Moses said to the Lord, "Please, Lord, I'm not a good speaker. I've never been a good speaker, and I'm not now, even though you've spoken to me. I speak slowly, and I become tongue-tied easily."

¹¹The Lord asked him, "Who gave humans their mouths? Who makes humans unable to talk or hear? Who gives them sight or makes them blind? It is I, the Lord! ¹²Now go, and I will help you speak and will teach you what to say."

¹³But Moses said, "Please, Lord, send someone else."

¹⁴Then the Lord became angry with Moses and asked, "What about your brother Aaron the Levite? I know he can speak well. He's already on his way to meet you, and he will be very glad to see you. ¹⁵You will speak to him and tell him what to say. I will help both of you speak, and I will teach you both what to do. ¹⁶Aaron will speak to the people for you. He will be your spokesman, and you will be like God. ¹⁷Take that shepherd's staff with you, and use it to do the miraculous signs."

Moses Returns to Egypt

¹⁸Then Moses went back to his father-in-law Jethro. Moses said to him, "Please let me go back to my own people in Egypt. I would like to see if they're still alive."

Jethro said to Moses, "You may go."

¹⁹Now, the Lord had said to Moses in Midian, "Go back to Egypt, because all the men who wanted to kill you are dead."

²⁰So Moses took his wife and sons, put them on a donkey, and started out for Egypt. He also brought with him the staff God had told him to take.

²¹The Lord said to Moses, "When you get back to Egypt, see that you show Pharaoh all the amazing things that I have given you the power to do. But I will make him stubborn so that he will not let the people go. ²²Then tell Pharaoh, 'This is what the Lord says: Israel is my firstborn son. ²³I told you to let my son go so that he may worship me. But you refused to let him go. So now I'm going to kill your firstborn son.' "

²⁴Along the way they stopped for the night. The Lord met Moses and tried to kill him. ²⁵Then Zipporah took a flint knife, cut off her son's foreskin, and touched Moses'

The LORD Divides the Red Sea

The LORD Divides the Red Sea

Exodus 14:21–28

21 Then Moses stretched out his hand over the sea. All that night the LORD pushed back the sea with a strong east wind and turned the sea into dry ground. The water divided, **22** and the Israelites went through the middle of the sea on dry ground. The water stood like a wall on their right and on their left.

23 The Egyptians pursued them, and all Pharaoh's horses, chariots, and cavalry followed them into the sea. **24** Just before dawn, the LORD looked down from the column of fire and smoke and threw the Egyptian camp into a panic. **25** He made the wheels of their chariots come off so that they could hardly move. Then the Egyptians shouted, "Let's get out of here! The LORD is fighting for Israel! He's against us!"

26 Then the LORD said to Moses, "Stretch out your hand over the sea so that the water will flow back over the Egyptians, their chariots, and their cavalry."

27 Moses stretched his hand over the sea, and at daybreak the water returned to its usual place. The Egyptians tried to escape, but the LORD swept them into the sea. **28** The water flowed back and covered Pharaoh's entire army, as well as the chariots and the cavalry that had followed Israel into the sea. Not one of them survived.

feet with it. She said, "You are a bridegroom of blood to me!" ²⁶So the LORD let him alone. It was because of the circumcision that she said at that time, "You are a bridegroom of blood!"

Moses and Aaron Tell the People What the LORD Said

²⁷Meanwhile, the LORD had told Aaron to meet Moses in the desert.

When Aaron met Moses at the mountain of God, he kissed him. ²⁸Moses told Aaron everything the LORD had sent him to say and all the miraculous signs the LORD had commanded him to do.

²⁹Then Moses and Aaron went to Egypt and assembled all the leaders of the people of Israel. ³⁰Aaron told them everything the LORD had said to Moses. He also did the miraculous signs for the people, ³¹and the people believed them. When they heard that the LORD was concerned about the people of Israel and that he had seen their misery, they knelt, bowing with their faces touching the ground.

Moses and Aaron Confront Pharaoh

¹Later Moses and Aaron went to Pharaoh and said, "This is what the LORD God of Israel says: Let my people go into the desert to celebrate a festival in my honor."

²Pharaoh asked, "Who is the LORD? Why should I obey him and let Israel go? I don't know the LORD, and I won't let Israel go."

³They replied, "The God of the Hebrews has met with us. Please let us travel three days into the desert to offer sacrifices to the LORD our God. If we don't go, he may kill us with a plague or a war."

⁴The king of Egypt said to them, "Moses and Aaron, why are you distracting the people from their work? Get back to work!" ⁵Then Pharaoh added, "Look how many people there are in the land! Do you want them to quit working?"

Pharaoh Increases the Israelites' Labor

⁶That same day Pharaoh gave these orders to the slave drivers and foremen: ⁷"Don't give the people any more straw to make bricks as you have been doing. Let them gather their own straw, ⁸but insist that they make the same number of bricks they were making before. Making fewer bricks will not be acceptable. They're lazy! That's why they're crying, 'Let us go offer sacrifices to our God.' ⁹Make the work harder for these people so that they will be too busy to listen to lies."

¹⁰The slave drivers and foreman went out and said to them, "This is what Pharaoh says: I'm no longer giving you straw.

Unfairness
Exodus 5:1–6:1

Adults aren't always fair. A teacher can punish you when you don't deserve it. Maybe your teacher lost your assignment and thought you didn't turn it in. If that happens, tell the teacher your side. Even if the teacher doesn't change your punishment, you will know you've done right. And God will know, too.

be you can be all

¹¹Get your own straw wherever you can find it, but your work load will not be reduced one bit."

¹²So the people scattered all over Egypt to gather stubble for straw. ¹³The slave drivers kept hurrying them. They said, "Finish the same amount of work each day, just as when you had straw."

¹⁴Pharaoh's slave drivers had placed Israelite foremen in charge of the people. The slave drivers beat the foremen and said, "You didn't finish all the bricks you were ordered to make yesterday or today. Why didn't you make as many as you used to?"

¹⁵Then the Israelite foremen complained to Pharaoh. They asked, "Why are you treating us this way? ¹⁶We're given no straw, and yet we're told to make bricks. We're being beaten, but your men are at fault."

¹⁷"You're lazy! ¸Just plain¸ lazy!" Pharaoh answered. "That's why you keep saying, 'Let us go offer sacrifices to the LORD.' ¹⁸Now get back to work! You won't be given any straw, but you must still make the same number of bricks."

¹⁹The Israelite foremen realized they were in trouble when they were told, "Don't make fewer bricks each day than you're supposed to."

²⁰As they left Pharaoh, they found Moses and Aaron waiting for them. ²¹So they said, "May the LORD see what you have done and judge you! You have made Pharaoh and his officials hate us. You have given them an excuse to kill us."

²²Moses went back to the LORD and asked, "Why have you brought this trouble on your people? Why did you send me? ²³Ever since I went to Pharaoh to speak for you, he has treated your people cruelly, and you have done nothing at all to rescue your people."

¹Then the LORD said to Moses, "Now you will see what I will do to Pharaoh. I will show him my power, and he will let my people go. I will show him my power, and he will throw them out of his country."

The LORD Tells Moses to Speak to Pharaoh Again

²God spoke to Moses, "I am the LORD. ³I appeared to Abraham, Isaac, and Jacob as God Almighty, but I didn't make myself known to them by my name, the LORD. ⁴I even made a promise*ᵃ* to give them Canaan, the land where they lived as foreigners. ⁵Now I have heard the groaning of the Israelites, whom the Egyptians hold in slavery, and I have remembered my promise.

⁶"Tell the Israelites, 'I am the LORD. I will bring you out from under the oppression of the Egyptians, and I will free you from slavery. I will rescue you with my powerful arm and with mighty acts of judgment. ⁷Then I will make you my people, and I will be your God. You will know that I am the LORD your God, who brought you out from under the forced labor of the Egyptians. ⁸I will bring you to the land I solemnly swore to give to Abraham, Isaac, and Jacob. I will give it to you as your own possession. I am the LORD.' "

⁹Moses reported this to the Israelites. But they would not listen to him because they were so discouraged by their back-breaking work.

¹⁰Then the LORD spoke to Moses, ¹¹"Go tell Pharaoh (the king of Egypt) to let the Israelites leave his country."

¹²But Moses protested to the LORD, "The Israelites wouldn't listen to me. Why would Pharaoh listen to me? I'm such a poor speaker."

¹³The LORD spoke to Moses and Aaron about the Israelites and Pharaoh (the king of Egypt). He commanded them to bring the Israelites out of Egypt.

ᵃ6:4 Or "covenant."

Aaron and Moses' Ancestry—
Genesis 46:9-11

[14]These were the heads of the families:

The sons of **Reuben**, Israel's firstborn, were Hanoch, Pallu, Hezron, and Carmi. These were the families descended from Reuben.

[15]The sons of **Simeon** were Jemuel, Jamin, Ohad, Jachin, Zohar, and Shaul, the son of a Canaanite woman. These were the families descended from Simeon.

[16]These are the names of the sons of **Levi** listed in birth order: Gershon, Kohath, and Merari. Levi lived 137 years.

[17]The sons of Gershon listed by their families were Libni and Shimei.

[18]The sons of Kohath were Amram, Izhar, Hebron, and Uzziel. Kohath lived 133 years.

[19]The sons of Merari were Mahli and Mushi.

These were the families descended from Levi listed in birth order.

[20]Amram married his father's sister Jochebed. She gave birth to Aaron and Moses. Amram lived 137 years.

[21]The sons of Izhar were Korah, Nepheg, and Zichri.

[22]The sons of Uzziel were Mishael, Elzaphan, and Sithri.

[23]Aaron married Elisheba, daughter of Amminadab and sister of Nahshon. She gave birth to Nadab, Abihu, Eleazar, and Ithamar.

[24]The sons of Korah were Assir, Elkanah, and Abiasaph.

These were the families descended from Korah.

[25]Eleazar, son of Aaron, married one of the daughters of Putiel. She gave birth to Phinehas.

These were the heads of Levite households listed by their families.

[26]This was the same Aaron and Moses to whom the LORD said, "Bring the Israelites out of Egypt in organized family groups." [27]They—this same Moses and Aaron— told Pharaoh (the king of Egypt) to let the Israelites leave Egypt.

Aaron's Staff Becomes a Snake

[28]At that time the LORD spoke to Moses in Egypt. [29]He said to Moses, "I am the LORD. Tell Pharaoh (the king of Egypt) everything I tell you."

[30]But Moses said to the LORD, "Why would Pharaoh listen to me?"

[1]The LORD answered Moses, "I have made you a god to Pharaoh, and your brother Aaron is your prophet. [2]Tell your brother Aaron everything I command you, and he must tell Pharaoh to let the Israelites leave the country. [3]But I will make Pharaoh stubborn. Even though I will do many miraculous signs and amazing things in Egypt, [4]Pharaoh will not listen to you. Then I will use my power to punish Egypt severely, and I will bring my people, the Israelites, out of Egypt in organized family groups. [5]The Egyptians will know that I am the LORD when I use my power against Egypt and bring the Israelites out of there."

[6]Moses and Aaron did as the LORD had commanded them. [7]Moses was 80 years old and Aaron was 83 when they talked to Pharaoh.

[8]The LORD said to Moses and Aaron, [9]"When Pharaoh says to you, 'Give me a sign to prove that God has sent you,' tell Aaron, 'Take your shepherd's staff and throw it down in front of Pharaoh,' and it will become a large snake."

[10]Moses and Aaron went to Pharaoh and did as the LORD had commanded. Aaron threw his staff down in front of Pharaoh and his officials, and it became a large snake. [11]Then Pharaoh sent for his wise men and sorcerers. These Egyptian magicians did the same thing using their magic spells. [12]Each of them threw his

staff down, and they all became large snakes. But Aaron's staff swallowed theirs. [13]Yet, Pharaoh continued to be stubborn and would not listen to them, as the Lord had predicted.

The First Plague—The Nile River Turns Into Blood

[14]Then the Lord said to Moses, "Pharaoh is being stubborn. He refuses to let my people go. [15]In the morning meet Pharaoh when he's on his way to the Nile. Wait for him on the bank of the river. Take along the staff that turned into a snake. [16]Say to him, 'The Lord God of the Hebrews sent me to tell you, "Let my people go to worship me in the desert." So far you have not listened. [17]Here is what the Lord says: This is the way you will recognize that I am the Lord: With this staff in my hand, I'm going to strike the Nile, and the water will turn into blood. [18]The fish in the Nile will die, and the river will stink. The Egyptians will not be able to drink any water from the Nile.' "

[19]The Lord said to Moses, "Tell Aaron, 'Take your staff and stretch out your hand over the waters of Egypt—its rivers, canals, ponds, and all its reservoirs—so that they turn into blood. There will be blood everywhere in Egypt, even in the wooden and stone containers.' "

[20]Moses and Aaron did as the Lord had commanded. In front of Pharaoh and his officials, Aaron raised his staff and struck the Nile. All the water in the river turned into blood. [21]The fish in the Nile died, and it smelled so bad that the Egyptians couldn't drink any water from the river. There was blood everywhere in Egypt.

[22]But the Egyptian magicians did the same thing using their magic spells. So Pharaoh continued to be stubborn and would not listen to Moses and Aaron, as the Lord had predicted. [23]Pharaoh turned and went back to his palace. He dismissed the entire matter from his mind.

[24]All the Egyptians dug along the Nile for water to drink because they couldn't drink any of the water from the river.

[25]Seven days passed after the Lord struck the Nile.

The Second Plague—Frogs

[a][1]Then the Lord said to Moses, "Go to Pharaoh, and tell him, 'This is what the Lord says: Let my people go to worship me. [2]If you refuse to let them go, I will bring a plague of frogs on your whole country. [3]The Nile River will swarm with frogs. They will come into your palace, into your bedroom, on your bed, into the houses of your officials, on your people, into your ovens and into your mixing bowls. [4]The frogs will jump on you, on your people, and on all your officials.' "

[5]Then the Lord said to Moses, "Tell Aaron, 'Hold your staff over the rivers, canals, and ponds. This will bring frogs onto the land.' "

[6]So Aaron held his staff over the waters of Egypt. The frogs came up and covered the land of Egypt. [7]But the magicians did the same thing using their magic spells and brought frogs onto the land.

[8]Pharaoh sent for Moses and Aaron and said, "Pray that the Lord will take the frogs away from me and my people. Then I will let your people go to offer sacrifices to the Lord."

[9]Moses answered Pharaoh, "You may have the honor of choosing when I should pray for you, your officials, and your people. Then the frogs will leave you and your homes. The only ones left will be those in the Nile."

---

[a] 8:1 Exodus 8:1–32 in English Bibles is Exodus 7:26–8:28 in the Hebrew Bible.

¹⁰"Pray for me tomorrow," Pharaoh said.

Moses replied, "It will be as you say so that you will know that there is no one like the LORD our God. ¹¹The frogs will leave you, your homes, your officials, and your people. The only frogs left will be those in the Nile."

¹²After Moses and Aaron left Pharaoh, Moses prayed to the LORD about the frogs he had brought on Pharaoh. ¹³The LORD did what Moses asked. The frogs died in the houses, in the yards, and in the fields. ¹⁴They were piled into countless heaps, and the land began to stink because of them.

¹⁵When Pharaoh saw that the plague was over, he became stubborn and would not listen to Moses and Aaron, as the LORD had predicted.

The Third Plague—Gnats

¹⁶Then the LORD said to Moses, "Tell Aaron, 'Hold out your staff and strike the dust on the ground. All over Egypt the dust will turn into gnats.' "

¹⁷When Moses told him, Aaron held out the staff in his hand and struck the dust on the ground. It turned into gnats that bit people and animals. All the dust on the ground everywhere in Egypt turned into gnats.

¹⁸The magicians also tried to produce gnats using their magic spells, but they couldn't do it. The gnats bit people and animals. ¹⁹So the magicians said to Pharaoh, "This is the hand of God!"

Yet, Pharaoh continued to be stubborn and would not listen to Moses and Aaron, as the LORD had predicted.

The Fourth Plague—Flies

²⁰Then the LORD said to Moses, "Early in the morning, stand in Pharaoh's way when he's going to the Nile. Say to him, 'This is what the LORD says: Let my people go to worship me. ²¹If you will not let my people go, I will send swarms of flies on you, your officials, your people, and your houses. The homes of the Egyptians will be filled with flies, and even the ground outside will be covered with them. ²²But on that day I will treat the region of Goshen differently. That is where my people live. There won't be any flies there. This way you will know that I, the LORD, am here in this land. ²³I will distinguish between my people and yours. This miraculous sign will happen tomorrow.' "

²⁴The LORD did what he said. Dense swarms of flies came into Pharaoh's palace and into the houses of his officials. All over Egypt the flies were ruining everything. ²⁵Pharaoh called for Moses and Aaron and said, "Go, sacrifice to your God here in this country."

²⁶Moses replied, "It wouldn't be right to do that. The sacrifices we offer to the LORD our God are disgusting to Egyptians. If they see us offer sacrifices that they consider disgusting, won't they stone us to death? ²⁷We need to travel three days into the desert to offer sacrifices to the LORD our God, as he told us to do."

²⁸Pharaoh said, "I will let you go, but don't go very far. You may offer sacrifices to the LORD your God in the desert and pray for me."

²⁹Moses answered, "As soon as I leave you, I will pray to the LORD. Tomorrow the swarms of flies will go away from you, your officials, and your people. But you must stop tricking us by not letting the people go to offer sacrifices to the LORD."

³⁰Moses left Pharaoh and prayed to the LORD. ³¹The LORD did what Moses asked. The swarms of flies left Pharaoh, his officials, and his people. Not one fly was left. ³²Yet, this time, too, Pharaoh was stubborn and did not let the people go.

The Fifth Plague—Death of Livestock

¹Then the LORD said to Moses, "Go to Pharaoh, and tell him, 'This is what the LORD God of the Hebrews says: Let my people go to worship me. ²If you refuse to let them go and continue to hold them in slavery, ³the LORD will bring a terrible plague on your livestock, including your horses, donkeys, camels, cattle, sheep, and goats. ⁴But the LORD will distinguish between Israel's livestock and the livestock of the Egyptians. No animals belonging to the Israelites will die.' " ⁵The LORD set a definite time. He said, "Tomorrow I will do this."

⁶The next day the LORD did as he said. All the livestock of the Egyptians died, but none of the Israelites' animals died. ⁷Pharaoh found out that not one of the Israelites' animals had died. Yet, Pharaoh continued to be stubborn and would not let the people go.

The Sixth Plague—Boils

⁸Then the LORD said to Moses and Aaron, "Take a handful of ashes from a kiln, and have Moses throw them up in the air as Pharaoh watches. ⁹They will become a fine dust throughout Egypt. The dust will cause boils to break into open sores on people and animals throughout Egypt."

¹⁰They took ashes from a kiln and stood in front of Pharaoh. Moses threw the ashes up in the air, and they caused boils to break into open sores on people and animals. ¹¹The magicians couldn't compete with Moses because they had boils like all the other Egyptians.

¹²But the LORD made Pharaoh stubborn, so he wouldn't listen to Moses and Aaron, as the LORD had predicted to Moses.

The Seventh Plague—Hail

¹³Then the LORD said to Moses, "Early in the morning, go to Pharaoh and say to him, 'This is what the LORD God of the Hebrews says: Let my people go to worship me. ¹⁴Now I will send plagues that will affect you personally as well as your officials and people. This is how you will know that there is no one like me anywhere on earth. ¹⁵By now I could have used my power to kill you and your people with a plague that would have wiped you off the earth. ¹⁶But I have spared you for this reason. I want to show you my power and make my name famous throughout the earth. ¹⁷You are still blocking my people from leaving. ¹⁸So, at this time tomorrow I will send the worst hailstorm that has ever happened in Egypt since the beginning of its history. ¹⁹Now, send servants to bring your livestock and everything else you have indoors. All people and animals still outside and not brought in will die when the hail falls on them.' "

²⁰Those members of Pharaoh's court who listened to the LORD's warning brought their servants and cattle indoors quickly. ²¹But those who didn't take the LORD's warning seriously left their servants and animals out in the open.

²²Then the LORD said to Moses, "Lift your hand toward the sky, and hail will fall on people, animals, and every plant in the fields of Egypt."

²³When Moses lifted his staff toward the sky, the LORD sent thunder and hail, and lightning struck the earth. So the LORD made it hail on Egypt. ²⁴It hailed, and lightning flashed while it hailed. This was the worst storm in all the land of Egypt since it had become a nation. ²⁵All over Egypt the hail knocked down everything that was out in the open. It struck down people, animals, and every plant in the fields and destroyed every tree in the fields. ²⁶The only place it didn't hail was the region of Goshen, where the Israelites lived.

²⁷Then Pharaoh sent for Moses and Aaron. "This time I have sinned," he told them. "The LORD is right, and my people and I are wrong. ²⁸Pray to the LORD. We've had enough of God's thunder and hail. I'll let you go; you don't have to stay here any longer."

²⁹Moses replied, "As soon as I'm out of the city, I'll spread out my hands to the LORD in prayer. The thunder will stop, and there will be no more hail. This is how you will know that the earth belongs to the LORD. ³⁰But I know that you and your officials still don't fear the LORD God."

³¹(The flax and the barley were ruined, because the barley had formed heads and the flax was in bloom. ³²Neither the wheat nor the wild grain was damaged, because they ripen later.)

³³As soon as he left Pharaoh and went out of the city, Moses spread out his hands to the LORD in prayer. The thunder and the hail stopped, and no more rain came pouring down on the ground.

³⁴When Pharaoh saw that the rain, the hail, and the thunder had stopped, he sinned again. He and his officials continued to be stubborn. ³⁵Pharaoh was stubborn and would not let the Israelites go, as the LORD had predicted through Moses.

The Eighth Plague—Locusts

¹Then the LORD said to Moses, "Go to Pharaoh. I have made him and his officials stubborn so that I can do these miraculous signs among them. ²You will be able to tell your children and grandchildren exactly how I treated the Egyptians and what miraculous signs I did among them. This is how you will all know that I am the LORD."

³So Moses and Aaron went to Pharaoh and said to him, "This is what the LORD God of the Hebrews says: How long will you refuse to humble yourself in my presence? Let my people go to worship me. ⁴If you refuse to let my people go, tomorrow I will bring locusts into your country. ⁵They will cover the land so that the ground can't be seen. They will eat everything left by the hail, including every tree still standing in the fields. ⁶They will fill your houses and the houses of all your officials and those of all the Egyptians. Your parents and ancestors never saw anything like this from the time they first came here until now." Moses turned and left Pharaoh.

⁷Then Pharaoh's officials asked him, "How long will this man hold us in his grip? Let the Israelite men go to worship the LORD their God. When will you realize that Egypt is ruined?"

⁸So Moses and Aaron were brought back to Pharaoh. "Go, worship the LORD your God," he said to them. "But exactly who will be going?"

⁹Moses answered, "Everyone! We'll be taking our young and old, our sons and daughters, our flocks and herds with us. For us it's a pilgrimage festival in the LORD's honor."

¹⁰Pharaoh said to them, "The LORD would have to be with you if I would ever let you take your women and children along. I know you're up to no good! ¹¹No! Only the men may go to worship the LORD, since that's what you've been asking for." Then Moses and Aaron were thrown out of Pharaoh's palace.

¹²The LORD said to Moses, "Stretch out your hand over Egypt to bring locusts. They will invade Egypt and eat up every plant in the land—everything left by the hail."

¹³Moses held his staff over the land of Egypt, and the LORD made a wind from the east blow over the land all that day and all that night. By morning the east wind had brought the locusts. ¹⁴They invaded all of Egypt and landed all over the country in great swarms. Never before had there been so many locusts like this, nor would there

ever be that many again. ¹⁵They covered all the ground until it was black with them. They ate all the plants and all the fruit on the trees that the hail had left. Nothing green was left on any tree or plant anywhere in Egypt.

¹⁶Then Pharaoh quickly called for Moses and Aaron and said, "I have sinned against the LORD your God and against you. ¹⁷Please forgive my sin one more time. Pray to the LORD your God to take this deadly plague away from me."

¹⁸Moses left Pharaoh and prayed to the LORD. ¹⁹Then the LORD changed the wind to a very strong west wind. It picked up the locusts and blew them into the Red Sea. Not one locust was left anywhere in Egypt.

²⁰But the LORD made Pharaoh stubborn, so he did not let the Israelites go.

The Ninth Plague—Darkness

²¹Then the LORD said to Moses, "Lift your hand toward the sky, and a darkness so thick that it can be felt will come over Egypt." ²²Moses lifted his hand toward the sky, and throughout Egypt there was total darkness for three days. ²³People couldn't see each other, and no one went anywhere for three days. But all the Israelites had light where they were living.

²⁴Then Pharaoh called for Moses and said, "Go, worship the LORD! Even your women and children may go with you, but your flocks and herds must stay behind."

²⁵But Moses said, "You must allow us to take our animals for the sacrifices and burnt offerings we have to make to the LORD our God. ²⁶All our livestock must go with us. Not one animal must be left behind. We'll have to use some of them for worshiping the LORD our God, and we won't know what we'll need until we get there."

²⁷But the LORD made Pharaoh stubborn, so he refused to let them go. ²⁸Pharaoh said to Moses, "Get out of my sight! Don't ever let me see your face again. The day I do, you will die."

²⁹"You're right!" Moses answered. "You'll never see my face again."

The Tenth Plague—The Death of the Firstborn

11 ¹Then the LORD said to Moses, "I will bring one more plague on Pharaoh and Egypt. After that he will let you go. When he does, he will be certain to force all of you out of here. ²Now announce to the people of Israel that each man and woman must ask the Egyptians for silver and gold jewelry."

³The LORD made the Egyptians kind to the people. And Moses was highly respected by Pharaoh's officials and all the Egyptians.

⁴Moses said, "This is what the LORD says: About midnight I will go out among the Egyptians. ⁵Every firstborn son in Egypt will die, from the firstborn of Pharaoh who rules the land, to the firstborn children of female slaves who use their handmills, including every firstborn domestic animal. ⁶There will be loud crying throughout Egypt, such as there has never been or ever will be again. ⁷But where the Israelites are, not even a dog will be startled by any person or animal. This is how you will see that the LORD shows the distinction between Egypt and Israel. ⁸Then all these officials of yours will come, bow down to me, and say, 'You and all the people who follow you, get out!' After that I will leave." Burning with anger, Moses left Pharaoh.

⁹The LORD had said to Moses, "Pharaoh will not listen to you. This is why I will do more amazing things in Egypt." ¹⁰Moses and Aaron showed Pharaoh all these amazing things. Yet, the LORD made Pharaoh stubborn, so he wouldn't let the Israelites leave his country.

Passover / *Exodus 12*

For almost 3,500 years, Jewish families have celebrated Passover. A week before the celebration, the girls and women search their home and throw out every speck of yeast. They do this because God told the Jewish people to be very careful to get rid of the yeast in their homes (see Exodus 12:15). The highlight of the Passover is a special meal the family eats together. Exodus 12 answers some interesting questions about Passover. How long is the Passover celebration? What can't the family eat during this holiday? What do families eat at the Passover meal? How are they dressed? What do they thank God for at Passover?

Passover

¹The LORD said to Moses and Aaron in Egypt, ²"This month will be the very first month of the year for you. ³Tell the whole community of Israel: On the tenth day of this month each man must take a lamb or a young goat for his family—one animal per household. ⁴A household may be too small to eat a whole animal. That household and the one next door can share one animal. Choose your animal based on the number of people and what each person can eat. ⁵Your animal must be a one-year-old male that has no defects. You may choose a lamb or a young goat. ⁶Take care of it until the fourteenth day of this month.

"Then at dusk, all the assembled people from the community of Israel must slaughter their animals. ⁷They must take some of the blood and put it on the sides and tops of the doorframes of the houses where they will eat the animals. ⁸The meat must be eaten that same night. It must be roasted over a fire and eaten with bitter herbs and unleavened bread. ⁹Don't eat any of it raw or boiled but roast the whole animal over a fire. ¹⁰Don't leave any of it until morning. Anything left over in the morning must be burned up. ¹¹This is how you should be dressed when you eat it: with your belt on, your sandals on your feet, and your shepherd's staff in your hand. You must eat it in a hurry. It is the LORD's Passover.

¹²"On that same night I will go throughout Egypt and kill every firstborn male, both human and animal. I will severely punish all the gods of Egypt, because I am the LORD. ¹³But the blood on your houses will be a sign for your protection. When I see the blood, I will pass over you. Nothing will touch or destroy you when I strike Egypt.

¹⁴"This day will be one for you to remember. This is a permanent law for generations to come: You will celebrate this day as a pilgrimage festival in the LORD's honor. ¹⁵For seven days you must eat unleavened bread. On the very first day you must

remove any yeast that you have in your houses. Whoever eats anything with yeast in it from the first day through the seventh day must be excluded from Israel. [16]You must have a holy assembly on the first day and another one on the seventh. You must not work on these days except to prepare your own meals. That's all you may do.

[17]You must celebrate the Festival of Unleavened Bread because it was on this very day that I brought you out of Egypt in organized family groups. This is a permanent law for future generations: You must celebrate this day. [18]From the evening of the fourteenth day of the first month until the evening of the twenty-first day you must eat unleavened bread. [19]There should be no yeast in your houses for seven days. Whoever eats anything with yeast in it must be excluded from the community of Israel, whether he is an Israelite or not. [20]Eat nothing made with yeast. Wherever you live, you must eat only unleavened bread."

[21]Then Moses called for all the leaders of Israel. He said to them, "Pick out a lamb or a young goat for your families, and kill the Passover animal. [22]Take the branch of a hyssop plant, dip it in the blood which is in a bowl, and put some of the blood on the top and sides of the doorframes of your houses. No one may leave the house until morning. [23]The Lord will go throughout Egypt to kill the Egyptians. When he sees the blood on the top and sides of the doorframe, he will pass over that doorway, and he will not let the destroyer come into your home to kill you.

[24]"You must follow these instructions. They are a permanent law for you and your children. [25]When you enter the land that the Lord will give you as he promised, observe this ceremony. [26]When your children ask you what this ceremony means to you, [27]you must answer, 'It's the Passover sacrifice in the Lord's honor. The Lord passed over the houses of the Israelites in Egypt and spared our homes when he killed the Egyptians.' "

Then the people knelt, bowing with their faces touching the ground. [28]The Israelites did as the Lord had commanded Moses and Aaron.

[29]At midnight the Lord killed every firstborn male in Egypt from the firstborn son of Pharaoh who ruled the land to the firstborn son of the prisoner in jail, and also every firstborn animal. [30]Pharaoh, all his officials, and all the other Egyptians got up during the night. There was loud crying throughout Egypt because in every house someone had died.

Pharaoh Allows the Israelites to Leave Egypt

[31]Pharaoh called for Moses and Aaron during the night. He said, "You and the Israelites must leave my people at once. Go, worship the Lord as you asked. [32]Take your flocks and herds, too, as you asked. Just go! And bless me, too!"

[33]The Egyptians begged the people to leave the country quickly. They said, "Soon we'll all be dead!" [34]So the people picked up their bread dough before it had risen and carried it on their shoulders in bowls, wrapped up in their clothes.

[35]The Israelites did what Moses had told them and asked the Egyptians for gold and silver jewelry and for clothes. [36]The Lord made the Egyptians generous to the people, and they gave them what they asked for. So the Israelites stripped Egypt of its wealth.

The Israelites Leave Egypt

[37]The Israelites left Rameses to go to Succoth. There were about six hundred thousand men on foot, plus all the women and children. [38]Many other people also went with them, along with large numbers of sheep, goats, and cattle.

[39]With the dough they had brought from Egypt, they baked round, flat bread. The

dough hadn't risen because they'd been thrown out of Egypt and had no time to prepare food for the trip. ⁴⁰The Israelites had been living in Egypt for 430 years. ⁴¹After exactly 430 years all the LORD's people left Egypt in organized family groups. ⁴²That night the LORD kept watch to take them out of Egypt. (All Israelites in future generations must keep watch on this night, since it is dedicated to the LORD.)

Rules for the Passover

⁴³The LORD said to Moses and Aaron, "These are the rules for the Passover:

"No foreigner may eat the Passover meal.

⁴⁴"Any male slave you have bought may eat it after you have circumcised him.

⁴⁵"No foreigner visiting you may eat it.

"No hired worker may eat it.

⁴⁶"The meal must be eaten inside one house. Never take any of the meat outside the house.

"Never break any of the bones.

⁴⁷"The whole community of Israel must celebrate the Passover.

⁴⁸"Foreigners may want to celebrate the LORD's Passover. First, every male in the household must be circumcised. Then they may celebrate the Passover like nativeborn Israelites. But no uncircumcised males may ever eat the Passover meal. ⁴⁹The same instructions apply to native-born Israelites as well as foreigners."

⁵⁰All the Israelites did as the LORD had commanded Moses and Aaron. ⁵¹That very day the LORD brought all the Israelites out of Egypt in organized family groups.

¹The LORD spoke to Moses, ²"Set apart every firstborn male for me. Every first born male offspring among the Israelites is mine, whether human or animal."

³Then Moses said to the people, "Remember this day—the day when you left Egypt, the land of slavery. The LORD used his mighty hand to bring you out of there. Don't eat anything made with yeast. ⁴Today, in the month of Abib, you are leaving Egypt. ⁵The LORD swore to your ancestors that he would give you the land of the Canaanites, Hittites, Amorites, Hivites, and Jebusites. When he brings you into that land flowing with milk and honey, you must observe this ceremony in this month.

⁶"For seven days you must eat unleavened bread. The seventh day will be a pilgrimage festival in the LORD's honor. ⁷Only unleavened bread should be eaten during these seven days. No sourdough or yeast should be seen anywhere in your territory. ⁸On that day tell your children, 'We do this because of what the LORD did for us when we left Egypt.' ⁹This festival will be like a mark on your hand or a reminder on your forehead that the teachings of the LORD are always to be a part of your conversation. Because the LORD used his mighty hand to bring you out of Egypt, ¹⁰you must follow these rules every year at this time.

Rules Concerning the Firstborn Child

¹¹"When the LORD brings you to the land of the Canaanites and gives it to you, as he swore to you and your ancestors, ¹²sacrifice every firstborn male offspring to the LORD. The firstborn male offspring of each of your animals belongs to the LORD. ¹³It will cost you a sheep or a goat to buy any firstborn donkey back from the LORD. If you don't buy it back, then you must break the donkey's neck. You must also buy every firstborn son back from the LORD.

¹⁴"In the future when your children ask you what this means, tell them, 'The LORD used his mighty hand to bring us out of slavery in Egypt. ¹⁵When Pharaoh was too

stubborn to let us go, the LORD killed every firstborn male in Egypt—human and animal. This is why we sacrifice every firstborn male to the LORD and buy every first-born son back from the LORD.' ¹⁶So this festival will be like a mark on your hand and like a band on your forehead, because the LORD used his mighty hand to bring us out of Egypt."

God Leads the People out of Egypt

¹⁷When Pharaoh let the people go, God didn't lead them on the road through Phil-istine territory, although that was the shortest route. God said, "If they see that they have to fight a war, they may change their minds and go back to Egypt." ¹⁸So God led the people around the other way, on the road through the desert toward the Red Sea. The Israelites were ready for battle when they left Egypt.

¹⁹Moses took the bones of Joseph with him, because Joseph had made the Israel-ites solemnly swear to do this. Joseph had said, "God will definitely come to help you. When he does, take my bones with you."

²⁰They moved from Succoth and camped at Etham, on the edge of the desert. ²¹By day the LORD went ahead of them in a column of smoke to lead them on their way. By night he went ahead of them in a column of fire to give them light so that they could travel by day or by night. ²²The column of smoke was always in front of the people during the day. The column of fire was always there at night.

Pharaoh Pursues Israel

14 ¹Then the LORD said to Moses, ²"Tell the Israelites to go back and set up their camp facing Pi Hahiroth, between Migdol and the sea. Set up your camp fac-ing north—by the sea. ³Pharaoh will think, 'The Israelites are just wandering around. The desert is blocking their escape.' ⁴I will make Pharaoh so stubborn that he will pursue them. Then, because of what I do to Pharaoh and his entire army, I will re-ceive honor, and the Egyptians will know that I am the LORD." So that is what the Israelites did.

⁵When Pharaoh (the king of Egypt) was told that the people had fled, he and his officials changed their minds about them. They said, "What have we done? We've lost our slaves because we've let Israel go." ⁶So Pharaoh prepared his chariot and took his army with him. ⁷He took 600 of his best chariots as well as all the other chariots in Egypt, placing an officer in each of them. ⁸The LORD made Pharaoh (the king of Egypt) so stubborn that he pursued the Israelites, who were boldly leaving Egypt. ⁹The Egyptians pursued the Israelites. Pharaoh's army, including all his horse-drawn chariots and cavalry, caught up with them as they were setting up their camp by the sea at Pi Hahiroth facing north.

¹⁰As Pharaoh approached, the Israelites looked up and saw that the Egyptians were coming after them. Terrified, the Israelites cried out to the LORD. ¹¹They said to Moses, "Did you bring us out into the desert to die because there were no graves in Egypt? Look what you've done by bringing us out of Egypt! ¹²Didn't we tell you in Egypt, 'Leave us alone! Let us go on serving the Egyptians'? It would have been better for us to serve the Egyptians than to die in the desert!"

The LORD Divides the Red Sea

¹³Moses answered the people, "Don't be afraid! Stand still, and see what the LORD will do to save you today. You will never see these Egyptians again. ¹⁴The LORD is fighting for you! So be still!"

¹⁵Then the LORD said to Moses, "Why are you crying out to me? Tell the Israelites

to start moving. ¹⁶Raise your staff, stretch out your hand over the sea, and divide the water. Then the Israelites will go through the sea on dry ground. ¹⁷I am making the Egyptians so stubborn that they will follow the Israelites. I will receive honor because of what I will do to Pharaoh, his entire army, his chariots, and cavalry. ¹⁸The Egyptians will know that I am the LORD when I am honored for what I did to Pharaoh, his chariots, and his cavalry."

¹⁹The Messenger of God, who had been in front of the Israelites, moved behind them. So the column of smoke moved from in front of the Israelites and stood behind them ²⁰between the Egyptian camp and the Israelite camp. The column of smoke was there when darkness came, and it lit up the night. Neither side came near the other all night long.

²¹Then Moses stretched out his hand over the sea. All that night the LORD pushed back the sea with a strong east wind and turned the sea into dry ground. The water divided, ²²and the Israelites went through the middle of the sea on dry ground. The water stood like a wall on their right and on their left.

²³The Egyptians pursued them, and all Pharaoh's horses, chariots, and cavalry followed them into the sea. ²⁴Just before dawn, the LORD looked down from the column of fire and smoke and threw the Egyptian camp into a panic. ²⁵He made the wheels of their chariots come off so that they could hardly move. Then the Egyptians shouted, "Let's get out of here! The LORD is fighting for Israel! He's against us!"

²⁶Then the LORD said to Moses, "Stretch out your hand over the sea so that the water will flow back over the Egyptians, their chariots, and their cavalry."

²⁷Moses stretched his hand over the sea, and at daybreak the water returned to its usual place. The Egyptians tried to escape, but the LORD swept them into the sea. ²⁸The water flowed back and covered Pharaoh's entire army, as well as the chariots and the cavalry that had followed Israel into the sea. Not one of them survived.

²⁹Meanwhile, the Israelites had gone through the sea on dry ground while the water stood like a wall on their right and on their left. ³⁰That day the LORD saved Israel from the Egyptians, and Israel saw the Egyptians lying dead on the seashore. ³¹When the Israelites saw the great power the LORD had used against the Egyptians, they feared the LORD and believed in him and in his servant Moses.

The Song of Moses

15 ¹Then Moses and the Israelites sang this song to the LORD:

"I will sing to the LORD.
    He has won a glorious victory.
    He has thrown horses and their riders into the sea.
2   The LORD is my strength and my song.
    He is my Savior.
        This is my God, and I will praise him,
            my father's God, and I will honor him.
3   The LORD is a warrior!
    The LORD is his name.
4   He has thrown Pharaoh's chariots and army into the sea.
        Pharaoh's best officers were drowned in the Red Sea.
5   The deep water covered them.
        They sank to the bottom like a rock.
6   Your right hand, O LORD, wins glory because it is strong.
    Your right hand, O LORD, smashes your enemies.

⁷ With your unlimited majesty, you destroyed those who attacked you.
    You sent out your burning anger.
       It burned them up like straw.
⁸ With a blast from your nostrils, the water piled up.
    The waves stood up like a dam.
       The deep water thickened in the middle of the sea.

⁹ "The enemy said, 'I'll pursue them!
    I'll catch up with them!
      I'll divide the loot!
        I'll take all I want!
          I'll use my sword!
            I'll take all they have!'
¹⁰ Your breath blew the sea over them.
    They sank like lead in the raging water.

¹¹ "Who is like you among the gods, O Lᴏʀᴅ?
Who is like you?
    You are glorious because of your holiness
      and awe-inspiring because of your splendor.
    You perform miracles.
¹² You stretched out your right hand.
    The earth swallowed them.

¹³ "Lovingly, you will lead the people you have saved.
Powerfully, you will guide them to your holy dwelling.
¹⁴   People will hear of it and tremble.
      The people of Philistia will be in anguish.
¹⁵   The tribal leaders of Edom will be terrified.
      The powerful men of Moab will tremble.
      The people of Canaan will be deathly afraid.
¹⁶   Terror and dread will fall on them.
Because of the power of your arm, they will be petrified
    until your people pass by, O Lᴏʀᴅ,
    until the people you purchased pass by.
¹⁷ You will bring them and plant them on your own mountain,
    the place where you live, O Lᴏʀᴅ,
    the holy place that you built with your own hands, O Lord.
¹⁸ The Lᴏʀᴅ will rule as king forever and ever."

¹⁹When Pharaoh's horses, chariots, and cavalry went into the sea, the Lᴏʀᴅ made the water of the sea flow back over them. However, the Israelites had gone through the sea on dry ground.

The Song of Miriam

²⁰Then the prophet Miriam, Aaron's sister, took a tambourine in her hand. All the women, dancing with tambourines, followed her. ²¹Miriam sang to them:

    "Sing to the Lᴏʀᴅ.
      He has won a glorious victory.
      He has thrown horses and their riders into the sea."

Miriam

**Miriam grew jealous of Moses,
but God forgave her sin.**

Miriam proved she was special and reliable even as a child. It was
probably Miriam who watched over her baby brother, Moses, as he floated in
the Nile River.

Pharaoh had ordered all the Hebrew baby boys two years and under to be killed.
Moses' mother came up with a plan to save her son. She hid Moses in a
basket, and Miriam kept watch over him. Pharaoh's daughter saw the basket
floating in the river and had it brought to her. She adopted Moses and kept him safe.

Moses grew up to become the leader of his people. Moses led God's people out of slavery and into the promised land. And when he did, his brother Aaron and sister Miriam helped him carry out God's will. Both Aaron and Miriam had special jobs to do in leading the people. Even when they later criticized Moses, God forgave Aaron and Miriam and allowed them to continue doing their special jobs.

When Miriam was struck with a skin disease, she was sent outside the camp. But God healed her and allowed her to return.

"Please, God, heal her!"

Miriam was born around 1450 B.C.

Miriam means "loved by the Lord" or "plump."

Miriam was the sister of Moses and Aaron.

Miriam was a prophet.

Miriam was one of the leaders of the people when God led them out of Egypt.

Getting to Know Miriam

✳ What important jobs did God give Miriam?
✳ Why do you think Miriam criticized Moses?
✳ How do you help your brothers and sisters?
✳ How do you criticize your brothers and sisters?
✳ What important jobs has God given you?

God Provides Water for the Israelites

[22]Moses led Israel away from the Red Sea into the desert of Shur. For three days they traveled in the desert without finding water. [23]When they came to Marah, they couldn't drink the water because it tasted bitter. That's why the place was called Marah [Bitter Place]. [24]The people complained about Moses by asking, "What are we supposed to drink?"

[25]Moses cried out to the Lord, and the Lord showed[a] him a piece of wood. He threw it into the water, and the water became sweet.

There the Lord set down laws and rules for them to live by, and there he tested them. [26]He said, "If you will listen carefully to the Lord your God and do what he considers right, if you pay attention to his commands and obey all his laws, I will never make you suffer any of the diseases I made the Egyptians suffer, because I am the Lord, who heals you."

[27]Next, they went to Elim, where there were 12 springs and 70 palm trees. They camped there by the water.

The Lord Provides Manna and Quails for the Israelites to Eat

[1]The whole community of Israelites moved from Elim and came to the desert of Sin, which is between Elim and Sinai. This was on the fifteenth day of the second month after they had left Egypt. [2]In the desert the whole community complained about Moses and Aaron. [3]The Israelites said to them, "If only the Lord had let us die in Egypt! There we sat by our pots of meat and ate all the food we wanted! You brought us out into this desert to let us all starve to death!"

[4]The Lord said to Moses, "I'm going to send you food from heaven like rain. Each day the people should go out and gather only what they need for that day. In this way I will test them to see whether or not they will follow my instructions. [5]But on the sixth day when they prepare what they bring home, it should be twice as much as they gather on other days."

[6]So Moses and Aaron said to all the Israelites, "In the evening you will know that it was the Lord who brought you out of Egypt. [7]In the morning you will see the glory of the Lord, because he has heard you complaining about him. Why are you complaining about us?" [8]Moses also said, "The Lord will give you meat to eat in the evening and all the food you want in the morning. The Lord has heard you complaining about him. Who are we? You're not complaining about us but about the Lord."

[9]Moses said to Aaron, "Tell the whole community of Israelites, 'Come into the Lord's presence. He has heard you complaining.' "

[10]While Aaron was speaking to the whole community of Israelites, they looked toward the desert. Suddenly, they saw the glory of the Lord in the column of smoke.

[11]The Lord said to Moses, [12]"I've heard the Israelites complaining. Tell them, 'At dusk you will eat meat, and in the morning you will eat all the food you want. Then you will know that I am the Lord your God.' "

[13]That evening quails came and covered the camp, and in the morning there was a layer of dew around the camp. [14]When the dew was gone, the ground was covered with a thin layer of flakes like frost on the ground. [15]When the Israelites saw it, they asked each other, "What is this?" because they didn't know what it was.

Moses said to them, "It's the food the Lord has given you to eat. [16]This is what the Lord has commanded: Each of you should gather as much as you can eat. Take two quarts for each person in your tent."

---

[a]15:25 Samaritan Pentateuch, Syriac, Targum, Latin; Masoretic Text "taught."

¹⁷So that is what the Israelites did. Some gathered more, some less. ¹⁸They measured it into two-quart containers. Those who had gathered more didn't have too much. Those who had gathered less didn't have too little. They gathered as much as they could eat.

¹⁹Then Moses said to them, "No one may keep any of it until morning."

²⁰But some of them didn't listen to Moses. They kept part of it until morning, and it was full of worms and smelled bad. So Moses was angry with them.

²¹Each morning they gathered as much food as they could eat. When the sun was hot, it melted away. ²²But on the sixth day they gathered twice as much food, four quarts per person. All the leaders of the community came to Moses and told him about it.

²³He said to them, "This is what the LORD said: Tomorrow is a day of worship, a holy day of worship dedicated to the LORD. Bake what you want to bake, and boil what you want to boil. Save all that's left over, and keep it until tomorrow morning."

²⁴So they saved it until the next morning as Moses had commanded, but it didn't smell or have worms in it. ²⁵"Eat it today," Moses said, "because today is a day of worship dedicated to the LORD. You won't find anything on the ground today. ²⁶You can gather food on six days, but on the seventh day, the day of worship, you won't find any."

²⁷On the seventh day some people went out to gather food, but they didn't find any. ²⁸The LORD said to Moses, "How long will you refuse to do what I have commanded and instructed you to do? ²⁹Remember: The LORD has given you this day of worship. That's why he gives you enough food on the sixth day for two days. On the seventh day you may not leave. Everyone, stay where you are." ³⁰So the people never worked on the seventh day of the week.

³¹The Israelites called the food *manna*. It was like coriander seeds. It was white and tasted like wafers made with honey.

³²Moses said, "This is what the LORD has commanded: Take two quarts of manna to be kept for your descendants. This way they will see the food that I gave you to eat in the desert when I brought you out of Egypt."

³³Moses said to Aaron, "Take a jar, put two quarts of manna in it, and put it in the LORD's presence to be kept for your descendants." ³⁴Aaron put the jar of manna in front of the words of God's promise to be kept there, as the LORD commanded Moses.

³⁵The Israelites ate manna for 40 years until they came to a place to settle. They ate manna until they came to the border of Canaan.

³⁶(Now, the standard dry measure at that time held 20 quarts.)

The LORD Provides Water for the Israelites From a Rock

¹The whole community of Israelites left the desert of Sin and traveled from place to place as the LORD commanded them. They camped at Rephidim, but there was no water for the people to drink. ²So they complained to Moses by saying, "Give us water to drink!"

Moses said to them, "Why are you complaining to me? Why are you testing the LORD?"

³But the people were thirsty for water there. They complained to Moses and asked, "Why did you bring us out of Egypt? Was it to make us, our children, and our livestock die of thirst?"

⁴So Moses cried out to the LORD, "What should I do with these people? They're almost ready to stone me!"

⁵The LORD answered Moses, "Bring some of the leaders of Israel with you, and

go to where the people can see you. Take the staff you used to strike the Nile River. ⁶I'll be standing in front of you there by a rock at Mount Horeb. Strike the rock, and water will come out of it for the people to drink."

Moses did this while the leaders of Israel watched him.

⁷He named that place Massah [Testing] and Meribah [Complaining] because the Israelites complained and because they tested the LORD, asking, "Is the LORD with us or not?"

God Defeats the Amalekites

⁸The Amalekites fought Israel at Rephidim. ⁹Moses said to Joshua, "Choose some of our men. Then fight the Amalekites. Tomorrow I will stand on top of the hill. I will hold in my hand the staff God told me to take along."

¹⁰Joshua did as Moses told him and fought the Amalekites, while Moses, Aaron, and Hur went to the top of the hill. ¹¹As long as Moses held up his hands, Israel would win, but as soon as he put his hands down, the Amalekites would start to win. ¹²Eventually, Moses' hands felt heavy. So Aaron and Hur took a rock, put it under him, and he sat on it. Aaron held up one hand, and Hur held up the other. His hands remained steady until sunset. ¹³So Joshua defeated the Amalekite army in battle.

¹⁴The LORD said to Moses, "Write this reminder on a scroll, and make sure that Joshua hears it, too: I will completely erase any memory of the Amalekites from the earth."

¹⁵Moses built an altar and called it The LORD Is My Banner. ¹⁶He said, "Because a hand was lifted against the LORD's throne,ᵃ he will be at war against the Amalekites from one generation to the next."

Moses' Father-in-law Visits Israel's Camp

18 ¹Moses' father-in-law Jethro, the priest of Midian, heard about everything God had done for Moses and his people Israel and how the LORD had brought Israel out of Egypt. ²When Moses had sent away his wife Zipporah, his father-in-law Jethro had taken her in, ³along with her two sons. The one son was named Gershom [Foreigner], because Moses said, "I was a foreigner living in another country." ⁴The name

Good Morning, God
Exodus 18:13-26

Every time the Israelites had a disagreement or needed advice, they went to Moses. Imagine one man trying to help close to two million people! Talk about stress! Jethro talked to Moses about Moses' workload, and they worked out a solution together. Don't let your problems overwhelm you. Ask God for a good friend like Jethro who can help you when you feel overwhelmed. Then later you can help your friend when she needs help.

Father, give me friends I can talk to about my problems.

ᵃ 17:16 Hebrew meaning uncertain.

of the other was Eliezer [My God Is a Helper], because he said, "My father's God was my helper. He saved me from Pharaoh's death sentence."

⁵Moses' father-in-law Jethro brought Moses' sons and wife to Moses in the desert where he was camped near the mountain of God. ⁶Jethro had sent word to Moses, "I'm coming to visit you, and I'm bringing your wife and her two sons."

⁷So Moses went out to meet his father-in-law. Moses bowed with his face touching the ground and kissed Jethro. After they asked each other how they were, they went into the tent. ⁸Moses told his father-in-law everything the LORD had done to Pharaoh and the Egyptians for Israel, all the hardships they had had on the way, and how the LORD had saved them.

⁹Jethro was delighted to hear about all the good things the LORD had done for Israel in rescuing them from the Egyptians. ¹⁰He said, "Thank the LORD! He rescued you from the Egyptians and their Pharaoh and rescued these people from the control of the Egyptians, ¹¹who treated Israel with contempt. Now I know that the LORD is greater than all other gods."

¹²Then Jethro, Moses' father-in-law, brought a burnt offering and other sacrifices to God. Aaron and all the leaders of Israel came to eat the meal with Moses' father-in-law in God's presence.

¹³The next day Moses was settling disagreements among the people. The people stood around Moses from morning until evening. ¹⁴When Moses' father-in-law saw everything Moses was doing for the people, he asked, "Why are you doing this for the people? Why do you sit here alone, while all the people stand around you from morning until evening?"

¹⁵Moses answered his father-in-law, "Because the people come to me to find out God's will. ¹⁶Whenever they have a disagreement and bring it to me, I decide which person is right, and I tell them God's laws and instructions."

¹⁷Moses' father-in-law replied, "What you're doing is not good. ¹⁸You and your people will wear yourselves out. This is too much work for you. You can't do it alone! ¹⁹Now listen to me, and I'll give you some advice. May God be with you! You must be the people's representative to God and bring their disagreements to him. ²⁰You must instruct them in the laws and the teachings, show them how to live, and tell them what to do.

²¹"But choose capable men from all the people, men who fear God, men you can trust, men who hate corruption. Put them in charge of groups of 1,000, or 100, or 50, or 10 people. ²²Let them be the ones who usually settle disagreements among the people. They should bring all important cases to you, but they should settle all minor cases themselves. Make it easier for yourself by letting them help you. ²³If God commands you, and you do this, you will be able to continue your work, and all these people will have their disagreements settled so that they can go home."

²⁴Moses listened to his father-in-law and did everything he said. ²⁵Moses chose capable men from all the Israelites and put them in charge of groups of 1,000, or 100, or 50, or 10 people. ²⁶These men were the ones who usually settled disagreements among the people. They would bring difficult cases to Moses, but they settled all minor ones themselves.

²⁷Moses sent his father-in-law on his way. So Jethro went back to his own country.

Israel at Mount Sinai

19 ¹Two months after the Israelites left Egypt, they came to the desert of Sinai. ²Israel had moved from Rephidim and had come into the desert of Sinai. They had set up camp there in front of the mountain.

³Then Moses went up the mountain to God, and the LORD called to him from the mountain, "This is what you must say to the descendants of Jacob. Tell the Israelites, ⁴'You have seen for yourselves what I did to Egypt and how I carried you on eagles' wings and brought you to my mountain. ⁵If you carefully obey me and are faithful to the terms of my promise,ᵃ then out of all the nations you will be my own special possession, even though the whole world is mine. ⁶You will be my kingdom of priests and my holy nation.' These are the words you must speak to the Israelites."

⁷So Moses went down and called for the leaders of the people. He repeated to them all the words that the LORD had commanded him. ⁸All the people answered together, "We will do everything the LORD has said." So Moses brought their answer back to the LORD.

⁹The LORD said to Moses, "I am coming to you in a storm cloud so that the people will hear me speaking with you and will always believe you." Moses told the LORD what the people had said.

¹⁰So the LORD said to Moses, "Go to the people, and tell them they have two days to get ready. They must set themselves apart as holy. Have them wash their clothes ¹¹and be ready by the day after tomorrow. On that day the LORD will come down on Mount Sinai as all the people watch. ¹²Mark off a boundary around the mountain for the people, and tell them not to go up the mountain or even touch it. Those who touch the mountain must be put to death. ¹³No one should touch them. They must be stoned or shot with arrows. No matter whether it's an animal or a person, it must not live. The people may go up the mountain only, when the ram's horn sounds a long blast."

¹⁴After Moses went down the mountain to the people, he had them get ready, and they washed their clothes. ¹⁵Then Moses said to the people, "Be ready two days from now. Don't disqualify yourselves by having sexual intercourse."

¹⁶On the morning of the second day, there was thunder and lightning with a heavy cloud over the mountain, and a very loud blast from a ram's horn was heard. All the people in the camp shook with fear. ¹⁷Then Moses led the people out of the camp to meet with God, and they stood at the foot of the mountain. ¹⁸All of Mount Sinai was covered with smoke because the LORD had come down on it in fire. Smoke rose from the mountain like the smoke from a kiln, and the whole mountain shook violently. ¹⁹As the sound of the horn grew louder and louder, Moses was speaking, and the voice of God answered him.

²⁰The LORD came down on top of Mount Sinai and called Moses to the top of the mountain. So Moses went up. ²¹The LORD said to him, "Go down and warn the people not to force their way through the boundary, to see the LORD, or many of them will die. ²²Even the priests who are allowed to come near the LORD must set themselves apart as holy, or the LORD will violently kill them."

²³Moses said to the LORD, "The people can't come up Mount Sinai, because you warned us yourself to mark off a boundary around the mountain and consider it holy."

²⁴The LORD said to him, "Go down, and bring Aaron back with you. But the priests and the people must not force their way through the boundary to come up to the LORD, or he will violently kill them."

²⁵So Moses went down to the people and told them.

ᵃ 19:5 Or "terms of my covenant."

Ten Commandments

Exodus 20

1. **"Never have any other god"** (20:3)
   Encourages you to love God more than anything else.
2. **"Never make your own carved idols"** (20:4)
   Encourages you to worship only God.
3. **"Never use the name of the Lᴏʀᴅ your God carelessly"** (20:7)
   Encourages you to use God's name with respect.
4. **"Remember the day of worship . . . as a holy day"** (20:8)
   Encourages you to rest and worship one day each week.
5. **"Honor your father and your mother"** (20:12)
   Encourages you to show respect for your parents.
6. **"Never murder"** (20:13)
   Encourages you to protect life.
7. **"Never commit adultery"** (20:14)
   Encourages you to show respect for boys.
8. **"Never steal"** (20:15)
   Encourages you to respect others' property.
9. **"Never lie when you testify"** (20:16)
   Encourages you to protect others' reputations.
10. **"Never desire . . . your neighbor's household"** (20:17)
   Encourages you to be satisfied with what you have.

The Ten Commandments—
Deuteronomy 5:6-21

20 ¹Then God spoke all these words:

²"I am the Lᴏʀᴅ your God, who brought you out of slavery in Egypt.

³"Never have any other god. ⁴Never make your own carved idols or statues that represent any creature in the sky, on the earth, or in the water. ⁵Never worship them or serve them, because I, the Lᴏʀᴅ your God, am a God who does not tolerate rivals. I punish children for their parents' sins to the third and fourth generation of those who hate me. ⁶But I show mercy to thousands of generations of those who love me and obey my commandments.

⁷"Never use the name of the Lᴏʀᴅ your God carelessly. The Lᴏʀᴅ will make sure that anyone who carelessly uses his name will be punished.

⁸"Remember the day of worship by observing it as a holy day. ⁹You have six days to do all your work. ¹⁰The seventh day is the day of worship dedicated to the Lᴏʀᴅ your God. You, your sons, your daughters, your male and female slaves, your cattle, and the foreigners living in your city must never do any work ˌon that dayˌ. ¹¹In six

days the Lord made heaven, earth, and the sea, along with everything in them. He didn't work on the seventh day. That's why the Lord blessed the day he stopped his work and set this day apart as holy.

¹²"Honor your father and your mother, so that you may live for a long time in the land the Lord your God is giving you.

¹³"Never murder.

¹⁴"Never commit adultery.

¹⁵"Never steal.

¹⁶"Never lie when you testify about your neighbor.

¹⁷"Never desire to take your neighbor's household away from him.

"Never desire to take your neighbor's wife, his male or female slave, his ox, his donkey, or anything else that belongs to him."

The People's Reaction

¹⁸All the people heard the thunder and saw the lightning. They heard the blast of the ram's horn and saw the mountain covered with smoke. So they shook with fear and stood at a distance. ¹⁹Then they said to Moses, "You speak to us, and we'll listen. But don't let God speak to us, or we'll die!"

²⁰Moses answered the people, "Don't be afraid! God has come only to test you, so that you will be in awe of him and won't sin."

²¹The people kept their distance while Moses went closer to the dark cloud where God was.

General Rules for Worship

²²The Lord said to Moses, "This is what you must say to the Israelites: You've seen for yourselves that I have spoken to you from heaven. ²³Never make any gods of silver or gold for yourselves. Never worship them.

²⁴"You must build an altar for me made out of dirt. Sacrifice your burnt offerings and your fellowship offerings, your sheep, goats, and cattle on it. Wherever I choose to have my name remembered, I will come to you and bless you. ²⁵If you build an altar for me made out of stones, never make it with cut stone blocks. If you use a chisel on it, you will make it unacceptable to me. ²⁶Never use stairs to go up to my altar. Otherwise, people will be able to see under your clothes."

Laws Concerning the Treatment of Slaves

¹The Lord continued, "Here are the legal decisions to be used by the Israelites:

²"Whenever you buy a Hebrew slave, he will be your slave for six years. In the seventh year he may leave as a free man, without paying for his freedom. ³If he comes to you by himself, he must leave by himself. If he comes as a married man, his wife may leave with him. ⁴If his master gives him a wife and she gives birth to sons or daughters, the wife and her children belong to the master, and the slave must leave by himself. ⁵But if he makes this statement: 'I hereby declare my love for my master, my wife, and my children. I don't want to leave as a free man,' ⁶then his master must bring him to God. The master must bring him to the door or the doorframe and pierce his ear with an awl. Then he will be his slave for life.

⁷"Whenever a man sells his daughter into slavery, she will not go free the way male slaves do. ⁸If she doesn't please the master who has chosen her as a wife,ᵃ he must let her be bought back by one of her close relatives. He has no right to sell her to foreigners, since he has treated her unfairly. ⁹But if he has chosen her for his son,

---

ᵃ21:8 Or "master so that he does not choose her as a wife."

he must treat her like a daughter. ¹⁰If that son marries another woman, he must not deprive the first wife of food, clothes, or sex. ¹¹If he doesn't give her these three things, she can go free, without paying any money for her freedom.

Laws Concerning Injury to People

¹²"Whoever strikes someone and kills him must be put to death. ¹³If it wasn't done intentionally, but God let it happen, the killer should flee to a place I will set aside for you. ¹⁴But whenever someone becomes so angry that he plans to kill his neighbor, you must take him away from my altar and put him to death.

¹⁵"Whoever hits his father or mother must be put to death.

¹⁶"Whoever kidnaps another person must be put to death, whether he has sold the kidnapped person or still has him.

¹⁷"Whoever curses his father or mother must be put to death.

¹⁸"This is what you must do whenever men quarrel and one hits the other with a rock or with his fist and injures him so that he has to stay in bed. ¹⁹If the injured man can get up again and walk around outside with a cane, the one who hit him must not be punished. He must pay the injured man for the loss of his time and for all his medical expenses.

²⁰"Whenever an owner hits his male or female slave with a stick so that the slave dies from the beating, the owner must be punished. ²¹But if the slave gets up in a day or two, the owner must not be punished. The slave is his property.

²²"This is what you must do whenever men fight and injure a pregnant woman so that she gives birth prematurely. If there are no other injuries, the offender must pay whatever fine the court allows the woman's husband to demand. ²³If anyone is injured, the offender must pay a life for a life, ²⁴an eye for an eye, a tooth for a tooth, a hand for a hand, a foot for a foot, ²⁵a burn for a burn, a bruise for a bruise, a wound for a wound.

²⁶"Whenever an owner hits his male or female slave in the eye and the slave is blinded, he must let the slave go free to make up for the loss of the eye. ²⁷If the owner knocks out the tooth of his male or female slave, he must let the slave go free to make up for the loss of the tooth.

²⁸"Whenever a bull gores a man or a woman to death, the bull must be stoned to death, and its meat may not be eaten. The bull's owner is free from any liability. ²⁹But if the bull has had the habit of goring, and the owner has been warned but has not kept it confined, and it kills a man or a woman, then the bull must be stoned and its owner must be put to death, too. ³⁰However, if only a cash settlement is demanded from the owner, the bull's owner may save his life by paying whatever price is demanded of him. ³¹If the bull gores someone's son or daughter, this same ruling applies. ³²If the bull gores a male or female slave, its owner must pay 12 ounces of silver to the slave's master, and the bull must be stoned.

Laws Concerning Property

³³"Whenever someone opens up a cistern or digs a new one and doesn't cover it and a bull or a donkey falls into it, ³⁴the owner of the cistern must make up for the loss. He must pay money to the animal's owner, and then the dead animal will be his.

³⁵"Whenever one person's bull kills another person's bull, they must sell the live bull and divide the money between them. They must divide the dead bull, too. ³⁶However, if it was known that the bull had the habit of goring, and its owner didn't keep it confined, the owner must make up for the loss—bull for bull—and then the dead bull will be his."

22 ^a¹The LORD continued, "Whenever someone steals a bull or a sheep and butchers it or sells it, he must make up for the loss with five head of cattle to replace the bull or four sheep to replace the sheep.

²"If anyone catches a thief breaking in and hits him so that he dies, he is not guilty of murder. ³But if it happens after sunrise, he is guilty of murder.

"A thief must make up for what he has stolen. If he is unable to do so, he must be sold as a slave to pay for what he stole. ⁴But if the stolen animal is found alive in his possession, whether it's a bull, donkey, or a sheep, he must make up for the loss with double the amount.

⁵"Whenever someone lets his livestock graze in a field or a vineyard, and they stray and graze in another person's field, he must make up for what the damaged field was expected to produce. But if he lets them ruin the whole field with their grazing,^b he must make up from his own field for the loss with the best from his field and vineyard.

⁶"Whenever a fire starts and spreads into the underbrush so that it burns up stacked or standing grain or ruins a field, the person who started the fire must make up for the loss.

⁷"This is what you must do whenever someone gives his neighbor silver or other valuables to keep for him, and they are stolen from that person's house: If the thief is caught, he must make up for the loss with double the amount. ⁸If the thief is not caught, the owner of the house must be brought to God to find out whether or not he took his neighbor's valuables. ⁹If there is a dispute over the ownership of a bull, a donkey, a sheep, an article of clothing, or any other lost property which two people claim as their own, both people must bring their case to God. The one whom God declares guilty must make up for his neighbor's loss with double the amount.

¹⁰"This is what you must do whenever someone gives his neighbor a donkey, a bull, a sheep, or any other kind of animal to keep for him, and it dies, is injured, or is captured in war, and there are no witnesses. ¹¹The case between them must be settled by swearing an oath to the LORD that the neighbor did not take the other person's animal. The owner must accept the oath. The neighbor doesn't have to make up for the loss. ¹²But if the animal was stolen from the neighbor, he must make up for the owner's loss. ¹³If it was killed by a wild animal, he must bring in the dead body as evidence. He doesn't have to make up for an animal that has been killed.

¹⁴"Whenever someone borrows an animal from his neighbor, and it is injured or dies while the owner is not present, the borrower must make up for the loss. ¹⁵If the owner is with the animal, the borrower doesn't have to make up for the loss. If it is rented, the rental fee covers the loss.

Laws for Living as God's Holy People

¹⁶"Whenever a man seduces a virgin who is not engaged to anyone and has sexual intercourse with her, he must pay the bride-price and marry her. ¹⁷If her father absolutely refuses to give her to him, he must pay an amount of money equal to the bride-price for virgins.

¹⁸"Never let a witch live.

¹⁹"Whoever has sexual intercourse with an animal must be put to death.

²⁰"Whoever sacrifices to any god except the LORD must be condemned and destroyed.

²¹"Never mistreat or oppress foreigners, because you were foreigners living in Egypt.

---

^a22:1 Exodus 22:1-31 in English Bibles is Exodus 21:37—22:30 in the Hebrew Bible.   ^b22:5 "he must make . . . grazing" Greek, Samaritan Pentateuch, Dead Sea Scrolls; Masoretic Text omits these words.

²²"Never take advantage of any widow or orphan. ²³If you do and they cry out to me, you can be sure that I will hear their cry. ²⁴I will become angry and have you killed in combat. Then your wives and children will become widows and orphans.

²⁵"If you lend money to my people—to any poor person among you—never act like a moneylender. Charge no interest. ²⁶If you take any of your neighbor's clothes as collateral, give it back to him by sunset. ²⁷It may be the only clothes he has to cover his body. What else will he sleep in? When he cries out to me, I will listen because I am compassionate.

²⁸"Never show disrespect for God or curse a leader of your people.

²⁹"Never withhold your best wine*c* from me.

"You must give me your firstborn son. ³⁰You must do the same with your cattle and your sheep. They will stay with their mothers seven days, but on the eighth day you must give them to me.

³¹"You must be my holy people. Never eat the meat of an animal that has been killed by wild animals out in the countryside. Throw it to the dogs."

23 ¹The Lord continued, "Never spread false rumors. Don't join forces with wicked people by giving false testimony. ²Never follow a crowd in doing wrong. When you testify in court, don't side with the majority to pervert justice. ³Never give special favors to poor people in court.

⁴"Whenever you come across your enemy's ox or donkey wandering loose, be sure to take it back to him. ⁵Whenever you see that the donkey of someone who hates you has collapsed under its load, don't leave it there. Be sure to help him with his animal.

⁶"Never deny justice to poor people in court. ⁷Avoid telling lies. Don't kill innocent or honest people, because I will never declare guilty people innocent. ⁸Never take a bribe, because bribes blind those who can see and deny justice to those who are in the right.

⁹"Never oppress foreigners. You know what it's like to be foreigners because you were foreigners living in Egypt.

¹⁰"For six years you may plant crops in your fields and harvest them, ¹¹but in the seventh year you must leave the land unplowed and unused. In that way the poor among your people will have food to eat, and wild animals may eat what the poor people leave. You must do the same with your vineyards and olive groves.

¹²"For six days you will do your work, but on the seventh day you must not work. Then your ox and donkey can rest. The slaves born in your household and foreigners will also be refreshed.

¹³"Be careful to do everything I told you.

"Never mention the names of other gods or let them be heard on your lips.

Laws for Three Festivals

¹⁴"Three times a year you must celebrate a pilgrimage festival in my honor.

¹⁵"Celebrate the Festival of Unleavened Bread: For seven days you must eat unleavened bread, as I commanded you. Do this at the appointed time in the month of Abib, because that was when you left Egypt. No one may come into my presence without an offering.

¹⁶"Celebrate the Festival of the Harvest with the first produce harvested from whatever you plant in your fields.

"Celebrate the Festival of the Final Harvest at the end of the year when you harvest your crops from the fields.

---

*c*22:29 Hebrew meaning of "your best wine" uncertain.

¹⁷"These are the three times each year that all your men must come into the presence of the Master, the LORD.

¹⁸"Never offer the blood of a sacrifice to me at the same time you offer anything containing yeast. The fat sacrificed at my festivals should never be left over in the morning.

¹⁹"You must bring the best of the first produce harvested from your soil to the house of the LORD your God.

"Never cook a young goat in its mother's milk.

Laws About God's Messenger, Who Will Bring Israel to the Promised Land

²⁰"I'm going to send a Messenger in front of you to protect you on your trip and bring you to the place I have prepared. ²¹Pay attention to him, and listen to him. Don't defy him, because he will not forgive your disobedience. He is acting on my authority. ²²But if you will listen to him and do everything I say, then I will be an enemy to your enemies and an opponent to your opponents.

²³"My Messenger will go ahead of you and will bring you to the land of the Amorites, Hittites, Perizzites, Canaanites, Hivites, and Jebusites. I will wipe them out. ²⁴Never worship or serve their gods or follow their practices. Instead, you must destroy their gods and crush their sacred stones. ²⁵You must serve the LORD your God, and he will bless your food and water. I will take away all sickness from among you. ²⁶No woman in your land will miscarry or be unable to have children. I will let you live a normal life span.

²⁷"I will send my terror ahead of you and throw any nation you meet into a panic. I will make all your enemies flee from you. ²⁸I will spread panic ahead of you to force the Hivites, Canaanites, and Hittites out of your way. ²⁹I will not force them out of your way in one year. Otherwise, the land would be deserted, and wild animals would take over. ³⁰Little by little I will force them out of your way until you have increased enough in number to take possession of the land.

³¹"I will establish your borders from the Red Sea to the Mediterranean Sea and from the Sinai Desert to the Euphrates River. I will put the people living in the land under your control, and you will force them out of your way. ³²Never make a treaty with them and their gods. ³³Never let them live in your land, or they will make you sin against me and trap you into serving their gods."

The Promise Sealed With Blood

24 ¹The LORD said to Moses, "You and Aaron, Nadab, Abihu, and 70 of Israel's leaders come up the mountain to me and worship at a distance. ²Moses may come near the LORD, but the others may not. The people must not come along with Moses."

³Moses went and told the people all the LORD's words and legal decisions. Then all the people answered with one voice, "We will do everything the LORD has told us to do." ⁴So Moses wrote down all the LORD's words.

Early the next morning he built an altar at the foot of the mountain and set up 12 sacred stones for the 12 tribes of Israel. ⁵Then he sent young Israelite men, and they sacrificed bulls as burnt offerings and fellowship offerings to the LORD. ⁶Moses took half of the blood and put it into bowls, and he threw the other half against the altar. ⁷Then he took the Book of the LORD's Promise*ᵃ* and read it while the people listened. They said, "We will obey and do everything the LORD has said."

ᵃ 24:7 Or "Covenant."

[8]Moses took the blood and sprinkled it on the people and said, "Here is the blood which seals the promise that the Lord has made to you based on everything you have just heard."

[9]Moses went up with Aaron, Nadab, Abihu, and 70 of Israel's leaders. [10]They saw the God of Israel. Under his feet was something like a pavement made out of sapphire as clear and blue as the sky itself. [11]God didn't harm these leaders of the Israelites. So they saw God, and then they ate and drank.

Moses Goes up the Mountain to Receive God's Words Written on Stone

[12]The Lord said to Moses, "Come up to me on the mountain. Stay there, and I will give you the stone tablets with the teachings and the commandments I have written for the people's instruction."

[13]Moses set out with his assistant Joshua, and Moses went up on the mountain of God. [14]He said to the leaders, "Wait here for us until we come back to you. Aaron and Hur are here with you. Take all your disagreements to them."

[15]So Moses went up on the mountain, and the cloud covered it. [16]The glory of the Lord settled on Mount Sinai. For six days the cloud covered it, and on the seventh day the Lord called to Moses from inside the cloud. [17]To the Israelites, the glory of the Lord looked like a raging fire on top of the mountain. [18]Moses entered the cloud as he went up the mountain. He stayed on the mountain 40 days and 40 nights.

Gifts for Use in the Tent of Meeting—
Exodus 35:4-9

[1]The Lord said to Moses, [2]"Tell the Israelites to choose something to give me as a special contribution. You must accept whatever contribution each person freely gives. [3]This is the kind of contribution you will accept from them: gold, silver, and bronze, [4]violet, purple, and bright red yarn, fine linen, goats' hair, [5]rams' skins dyed red, fine leather,*a* acacia wood, [6]olive oil for the lamps, spices for the anointing oil and for the sweet-smelling incense, [7]onyx stones, and other precious stones to be set in the chief priest's ephod*b* and his breastplate.

[8]"Then have them make a holy place for me, and I will live among them. [9]Make the tent and all its furnishings exactly like the plans I am showing you.

The Ark—
Exodus 37:1-9

[10]"Make an ark of acacia wood 45 inches long, 27 inches wide, and 27 inches high. [11]Cover it with pure gold inside and out, and put a gold molding around it. [12]Cast four gold rings for it, and fasten them to its four feet, two rings on each side. [13]Make poles of acacia wood, and cover them with gold. [14]Put the poles through the rings on the sides of the ark in order to carry it. [15]The poles must stay in the rings of the ark. Never remove them. [16]Then you will put into the ark the words of my promise which I will give you.

[17]"Make a throne of mercy to cover the ark out of pure gold 45 inches long and 27 inches wide. [18]Make two angels*c* out of hammered gold for the two ends of the throne of mercy, [19]one on each end. Form the angels and the throne of mercy out of one piece of gold. [20]The angels should have their wings spread above the throne of mercy, overshadowing it. They should face each other, looking at the throne of mercy. [21]After you

---

*a*25:5 Hebrew meaning uncertain. *b*25:7 *Ephod* is a technical term for a part of the priest's clothes. Its exact usage and shape are unknown. *c*25:18 Or "cherubim."

put into the ark the words of my promise which I will give you, place the throne of mercy on top. ²²I will be above the throne of mercy between the angels whenever I meet with you and give you all my commands for the Israelites.

The Table—
Exodus 37:10-16

²³"Make a table of acacia wood 36 inches long, 18 inches wide, and 27 inches high. ²⁴Cover it with pure gold, and put a gold molding around it. ²⁵Make a rim three inches wide around it, and put a gold molding around the rim. ²⁶Make four gold rings for it, and fasten them to the four corners, where the four legs are. ²⁷The rings are to be close to the rim. They are to hold the poles for carrying the table. ²⁸Make the poles out of acacia wood, cover them with gold, and use them to carry the table. ²⁹Make plates and dishes for the table out of pure gold, as well as pitchers and bowls to be used for pouring wine offerings. ³⁰Put the bread of the presence on this table so that it will be in front of me all the time.

The Lamp Stand—
Exodus 37:17-24

³¹"Make a lamp stand out of pure gold. The lamp stand, its base, and its shaft, as well as the flower cups, buds, and petals must be hammered out of one piece of gold. ³²Six branches are to come out of the sides, three branches on one side and three on the other. ³³Each of the six branches coming out of the lamp stand is to have three flower cups shaped like almond blossoms, with buds and petals. ³⁴The lamp stand itself is to have four flower cups shaped like almond blossoms, with buds and petals. ³⁵There should be a bud under each of the three pairs of branches coming out of the lamp stand. ³⁶The buds and branches should also be hammered out of the same piece of pure gold as the lamp stand.

³⁷"Make seven lamps, and set them on the lamp stand so that they light up the area in front of it. ³⁸The tongs and incense burners must be made of pure gold. ³⁹Use 75 pounds of pure gold to make the lamp stand and all the utensils. ⁴⁰Be sure to make them according to the plans you were shown on the mountain."

The Tent—
Exodus 36:8-38

26 ¹The Lord continued, "Make the inner tent with ten sheets made from fine linen yarn. Take violet, purple, and bright red yarn, and creatively work an angel^a design into the fabric. ²Each sheet will be 42 feet long and 6 feet wide—all the same size. ³Five of the sheets must be sewn together, and the other five must also be sewn together. ⁴Make 50 violet loops along the edge of the end sheet in each set, ⁵placing the loops opposite each other. ⁶Make 50 gold fasteners. Use them to link the two sets of sheets together so that the tent is a single unit.

⁷"Make 11 sheets of goats' hair to form an outer tent over the inner tent. ⁸Each of the 11 sheets will be 45 feet long and 6 feet wide. ⁹Sew five of the sheets together into one set and the remaining six into another set. Fold the sixth sheet in half to hang in front of the tent. ¹⁰Make 50 loops along the edge of the end sheet in each set. ¹¹Make 50 bronze fasteners, and put them through the loops to link the inner tent together as a single unit. ¹²The remaining half-sheet should hang over the back of the inner tent. ¹³There will be 18 inches left over on each side because of the length

---

of the outer tent's sheets. That part should hang over each side in order to cover the inner tent. ¹⁴Make a cover of rams' skins that have been dyed red for the outer tent. Over that put a cover made of fine leather.*ᵇ*

¹⁵"Make a framework out of acacia wood for the inner tent. ¹⁶Each frame is to be 15 feet long and 27 inches wide, ¹⁷with two identical pegs. Make all the frames for the inner tent the same way. ¹⁸Make 20 frames for the south side of the inner tent. ¹⁹Then make 40 silver sockets at the bottom of the 20 frames, two sockets at the bottom of each frame for the two pegs. ²⁰For the north side of the inner tent make 20 frames ²¹and 40 silver sockets, two at the bottom of each frame. ²²Make six frames for the far end, the west side. ²³Make two frames for each of the corners at the far end of the inner tent. ²⁴These will be held together at the bottom and held tightly at the top by a single ring.*ᶜ* Both corner frames will be made this way. ²⁵There will be eight frames with 16 silver sockets, two at the bottom of each frame.

²⁶"Make crossbars out of acacia wood: five for the frames on one side of the inner tent, ²⁷five for those on the other side, and five for the frames on the far end of the inner tent, the west side. ²⁸The middle crossbar will run from one end to the other, halfway up the frames. ²⁹Cover the frames with gold, make gold rings to hold the crossbars, and cover the crossbars with gold.

³⁰"Set up the inner tent according to the plans you were shown on the mountain.

³¹"Make a canopy of violet, purple, and bright red yarn. Creatively work an angel design into fine linen yarn. ³²Use gold hooks to hang it on four posts of acacia wood covered with gold, standing in four silver sockets. ³³Hang the canopy from the fasteners in the ceiling, and put the ark containing the words of my promise under it. The canopy will mark off the most holy place from the holy place. ³⁴Put the throne of mercy that is on the ark in the most holy place.

³⁵"Place the table outside the canopy on the north side of the inner tent, and put the lamp stand opposite the table on the south side.

³⁶"For the entrance of the outer tent, make a screen out of fine linen yarn, embroidered with violet, purple, and bright red yarn. ³⁷Make five posts of acacia wood for the screen and cover them with gold. Make gold hooks for this screen. Cast five bronze bases for the posts."

The Altar—
Exodus 38:1-7

27 ¹The Lord continued, "Make an altar out of acacia wood. It should be 7½ feet square, and 4½ feet high. ²Make a horn at each of its four corners. The four horns and the altar must be made out of one piece of wood, covered with bronze.

³"Make all the utensils for it out of bronze: pots for taking away the altar's ashes, also shovels, bowls, forks, and incense burners.

⁴"Make a grate for it out of bronze mesh, and make a bronze ring for each of the four corners of the grate. ⁵Put the grate under the ledge of the altar so that it comes halfway up the altar.

⁶"Make poles out of acacia wood for the altar, and cover them with bronze. ⁷The poles should be put through the rings on both sides of the altar to carry it.

⁸"Make the altar out of boards so that it's hollow inside. It must be made just as you were shown on the mountain.

---

*ᵇ*26:14 Hebrew meaning uncertain.   *ᶜ*26:24 Or "These are to be separated at the bottom but held together at the top by a single ring."

The Courtyard—
Exodus 38:9-20

⁹"Make a courtyard for the tent. The south side of the courtyard should be 150 feet long and have curtains made out of fine linen yarn, ¹⁰hung on 20 posts set in 20 bronze bases. The hooks and bands on the posts should be made of silver. ¹¹The north side should be the same: 150 feet long, with curtains on 20 posts set in 20 bronze bases. The hooks and bands on the posts should be made of silver.

¹²"The courtyard on the west end should be 75 feet wide and have curtains hung on ten posts set in ten bases. ¹³On the east end, facing the rising sun, the courtyard should also be 75 feet wide. ¹⁴⁻¹⁵Each side of the entrance will be 22½ feet wide with curtains hung on three posts set in three bases.

¹⁶"The entrance to the courtyard must have a 30-foot screen made from fine linen yarn, embroidered with violet, purple, and bright red yarn, hung on four posts set in four bases. ¹⁷All the posts around the courtyard should have silver bands, silver hooks, and bronze bases. ¹⁸The courtyard should be 150 feet long, 75 feet wide, and 7½ feet high, with curtains made of fine linen yarn and with bronze bases.

¹⁹"All the things for the tent, no matter how they're used, including all the pegs for the tent and the courtyard, must be made of bronze.

Lamps in the Tent—
Leviticus 24:1-4

²⁰"For the lighting, you must command the Israelites to bring you pure, virgin olive oil so that the lamps won't go out. ²¹In the tent of meeting outside the canopy where the words of my promise are, Aaron and his descendants must keep the lamps lit in the LORD's presence from evening until morning. This is a permanent law among the Israelites for generations to come."

The Holy Clothes—
Exodus 39:1

28 ¹The LORD continued, "Out of all the Israelites, bring your brother Aaron and his sons Nadab, Abihu, Eleazar, and Ithamar to you. They will serve me as priests. ²Make holy clothes for your brother Aaron to give him dignity and honor.

³"Tell all those who have the skill—those to whom I have given this ability—to make Aaron's clothes. These clothes will set him apart as holy when he serves me as priest. ⁴These are the clothes they will make: a breastplate, an ephod and the robe

Good Morning, God
Exodus 28:3-5

You have something no one else has. God gives everyone special talents and abilities so people can serve him in different ways. God gave a few of the Israelites a special talent for sewing the decorative clothes worn by the priest. What unique abilities has God given to you? How can you use your abilities and gifts for God?

Thank you, Lord, for giving me special abilities. Show me ways I can use them to serve you.

that is worn with it, another specially woven linen robe, the chief priest's turban, and a cloth belt. They will make these holy clothes for your brother Aaron and his sons so that they can serve me as priests. ⁵They must use gold, violet, purple, and bright red yarn, and fine linen.

The Ephod—
Exodus 39:2-7

⁶"Make the ephod out of fine linen yarn. Creatively work gold, violet, purple, and bright red yarn into the fabric. ⁷It will have two shoulder straps attached at the top corners so that it can be fastened. ⁸Make the belt that is attached to the ephod out of the same fabric. ⁹Take two onyx stones, and engrave on them the names of the sons of Israel ¹⁰in birth order—six of their names on one stone and the remaining six on the other. ¹¹Engrave the names of the sons of Israel on the two stones the same way a jeweler engraves a signet ring. Mount them in gold settings, ¹²and fasten them on the shoulder straps of the ephod as reminders of who the Israelites are. In this way Aaron will carry their names on his shoulders as a reminder in the Lord's presence. ¹³Make gold settings ¹⁴and two chains of pure gold, twisted like ropes, and fasten these chains to the settings.

The Breastplate—
Exodus 39:8-21

¹⁵"Make the breastplate for decision-making as creatively as you make the ephod. Make it out of gold, violet, purple, and bright red yarn and out of fine linen yarn. ¹⁶Fold it in half so that it's 9 inches square. ¹⁷Fasten four rows of precious stones on it. In the first row put red quartz, topaz, and emerald. ¹⁸In the second row put turquoise, sapphire, and crystal. ¹⁹In the third row put jacinth, agate, and amethyst. ²⁰In the fourth row put beryl, onyx, and gray quartz. Mount them in gold settings. ²¹The stones correspond to the 12 sons of Israel, by name, each stone engraved (like a signet ring) with the name of one of the 12 tribes.

²²"For the breastplate make chains out of pure gold, twisted like ropes. ²³Make two gold rings for the breastplate. Attach them to the two top corners of the breastplate. ²⁴Then fasten the two gold ropes to the rings at the top corners of the breastplate. ²⁵Fasten the other ends of the ropes to the two settings on the shoulder straps of the ephod so that the breastplate hangs in front of it. ²⁶Make two gold rings, and fasten them to the other two corners of the breastplate on the inside edge next to the ephod. ²⁷Make two more gold rings, and fasten them to the bottom of the shoulder straps on the front of the ephod. This will be close to the seam just above the belt of the ephod. ²⁸Then the breastplate should be fastened by its rings to the rings of the ephod with a violet cord. This will attach it just above the belt of the ephod and will hold the breastplate in place.

²⁹"Whenever Aaron goes into the holy place, he will be carrying the names of the sons of Israel over his heart as a constant reminder in the Lord's presence. He must do this by wearing the breastplate for decision-making. ³⁰Put the Urim and Thummim[a] into the breastplate for decision-making. They, too, will be over Aaron's heart when he comes into the Lord's presence. In this way whenever he's in the Lord's presence, Aaron will always be carrying over his heart the means for determining the Lord's decisions for the Israelites.

---

[a]28:30 The Urim and Thummim were used by the chief priest to determine God's answer to questions.

Other Clothes for Aaron and His Sons—
Exodus 39:22-31

[31]"Make the robe that is worn with the ephod entirely of violet material. [32]Make an opening for the head in the center with a reinforced edge (like a leather collar*[b]*) all around it to keep it from tearing. [33]All around the hem of the robe make pomegranates of violet, purple, and bright red yarn with gold bells in between— [34]a gold bell alternating with a pomegranate all around the hem of the robe. [35]Aaron must wear it when he serves as priest. The sound of the bells must be heard when he comes into and goes out of the LORD's presence in the holy place so that he won't die.

[36]"Make a flower-shaped medallion out of pure gold, and engrave on it (as on a signet ring): Holy to the LORD. [37]Fasten a violet cord to it, and tie it so that it's on the front of the turban. [38]It will be on Aaron's forehead. He's the one to be blamed for anything done wrong when the Israelites bring their holy offerings—whatever their gifts may be. The medallion must always be on Aaron's forehead so that the LORD will accept their offerings.

[39]"Make the specially woven inner robe of fine linen. Make the turban of fine linen, but the belt should be embroidered with colored yarn.

[40]"Also make linen robes, belts, and turbans for Aaron's sons. These clothes will give them dignity and honor. [41]Put these clothes on your brother Aaron and his sons, anoint them, ordain them, and set them apart to serve me as priests.

[42]"Make linen undergarments to cover them down to their thighs. [43]Aaron and his sons must wear them when they go into the tent of meeting or when they come near the altar to serve as priests in the holy place. Then they will be blameless and won't die.

"This is a permanent law for him and his descendants."

Make Aaron and His Sons Priests—
Leviticus 8:1-36

[1]The LORD continued, "Now, this is what you must do in order to set Aaron and his sons apart to serve me as priests: "Take a young bull that has no defects and two rams that have no defects. [2]Use the finest wheat flour, but no yeast, and bake some loaves of bread, some rings of bread made with olive oil, and some wafers brushed with olive oil. [3]Put the bread in a basket, and bring the basket along with the young bull and the two rams.

[4]"Then bring Aaron and his sons to the entrance of the tent of meeting, and wash them. [5]Take the clothes, and put them on Aaron—the linen robe, the ephod and the robe that is worn with it, and the breastplate. Use the belt to tie it on him tightly. [6]Put his turban on him, and fasten the holy crown to it. [7]Take the anointing oil, pour it on his head, and anoint him.

[8]"Have his sons come forward. Dress them in their linen robes, [9]and put turbans on them. Tie belts around the waists of Aaron and his sons. They alone are to be priests; this is a permanent law. In this way you will ordain Aaron and his sons.

[10]"Then bring the young bull to the front of the tent of meeting. Aaron and his sons will place their hands on its head. [11]Slaughter the bull in the LORD's presence at the entrance to the tent of meeting. [12]Take some of the bull's blood, and put it on the horns of the altar with your finger. Pour the rest of it out at the bottom of the altar.

[13]"Then take all the fat that covers the internal organs, the lobe of the liver, and

---

[b]28:32 Hebrew meaning of "a leather collar" uncertain.

the two kidneys with the fat on them, and burn them on the altar. [14]But burn the bull's meat, skin, and excrement outside the camp. It is an offering for sin.

[15]"Take one of the rams. Then Aaron and his sons will place their hands on its head. [16]Slaughter it, take the blood, and throw it against the altar on all sides. [17]Cut the ram into pieces, wash the internal organs and legs, and put them with the other pieces and the head. [18]Then burn the whole ram on the altar. It's a burnt offering, a soothing aroma, an offering by fire to the Lord.

[19]"Take the other ram. Then Aaron and his sons will place their hands on its head. [20]Slaughter it, take some of the blood, and put it on the right ear lobes of Aaron and his sons, on their right thumbs, and on the big toes of their right feet. Throw the rest of the blood against the altar on all sides. [21]Take some of the blood that is on the altar and some of the anointing oil, and sprinkle it on Aaron and his clothes and on his sons and their clothes. In this way Aaron, his sons, and their clothes will be holy.

[22]"From this same ram take the fat, the fat from the tail, the fat that covers the internal organs, the lobe of the liver, the two kidneys with the fat on them, and the right thigh. (This is the ram for the ordination.) [23]From the basket of unleavened bread which is in the Lord's presence, take a round loaf of bread, a ring of bread made with olive oil, and a wafer. [24]Put all of these in the hands of Aaron and his sons, who will offer them to the Lord. [25]Then take them from their hands, and burn them on the altar on top of the burnt offering. It's a soothing aroma in the Lord's presence, an offering by fire to the Lord.

[26]"Take the breast from the ram used for Aaron's ordination, and present it to the Lord. This will be your share. [27]Set apart as holy the breast that is offered to the Lord and the thigh that is the contribution. Both will come from the ram used for the ordination. They both belong to Aaron and his sons. [28]It is a permanent law that the Israelites give this portion to Aaron and his sons as a contribution. This will also be their contribution to the Lord from the fellowship offerings.

[29]"Aaron's holy clothes will belong to his descendants so that they can be anointed and ordained in them. [30]The son who succeeds him as priest—the one who goes into the tent of meeting to serve in the holy place—will wear them for seven days.

[31]"Take the ram used for the ordination, and boil its meat in a holy place. [32]At the entrance to the tent of meeting, Aaron and his sons will eat the meat of the ram and the bread left in the basket. [33]They will eat those offerings through which they made peace with the Lord at their ordination and installation. No one else may eat them because the offerings are holy. [34]If any meat or bread from the ordination is left over until morning, burn it up. It must not be eaten because it is holy.

[35]"Do this with Aaron and his sons exactly as I have commanded you. Take seven days to ordain them. [36]Each day sacrifice a young bull as an offering to make peace with the Lord. Sacrifice this offering for sin on the altar in order to pay for its sins. Then anoint it with olive oil in order to dedicate it. [37]For seven days at the altar make peace with the Lord and set the altar apart for its holy purpose. Then the altar will be most holy. Anything that touches the altar will become holy.

[38]"This is what you are to offer on the altar regularly every day: two one-year-old lambs. [39]Offer one in the morning and the other at dusk. [40]With the first lamb make an offering of eight cups of flour mixed with one quart of virgin olive oil. Make a wine offering of one quart of wine. [41]Offer the other lamb at dusk, and with it make the same grain offering and wine offering as in the morning. This is a soothing aroma, an offering by fire to the Lord.

[42]"For generations to come this will be the daily burnt offering made in the Lord's presence at the entrance to the tent of meeting. There I will meet with you to speak

to you. ⁴³I will also meet with the Israelites there, and my glory will make this place holy. ⁴⁴I will dedicate the tent of meeting and the altar for their holy purposes. I will set Aaron and his sons apart for their holy duties of serving me as priests.

⁴⁵"Then I will live among the Israelites and be their God. ⁴⁶They will know that I am the LORD their God. I brought them out of Egypt so that I might live among them. I am the LORD their God."

The Altar for Incense—
Exodus 37:25-29

¹The LORD continued, "Build an altar out of acacia wood for burning incense. ²Make it 18 inches square and 36 inches high. The horns and altar must be made out of one piece of wood. ³Cover all of it with pure gold—the top, the sides, and the horns. Put a gold molding around it. ⁴Make two gold rings, and put them below the molding on opposite sides to hold the poles for carrying it. ⁵Make the poles out of acacia wood, and cover them with gold. ⁶Put the altar in front of the canopy which hangs over the ark containing the words of my promise. I will meet with you there in front of the throne of mercy that is on the ark.

⁷"Aaron must burn sweet-smelling incense on this altar every morning when he takes care of the lamps. ⁸Also, when Aaron lights the lamps at dusk, he must burn incense. For generations to come an incense offering must burn constantly in the LORD's presence.

⁹"Never burn any unauthorized incense on this altar or any burnt offerings or grain offerings. Never pour a wine offering on it. ¹⁰Once a year Aaron must make peace with the LORD by putting blood on its horns. Once a year—for generations to come—blood from the offering must be placed on the altar to make peace with the LORD. It is most holy to the LORD."

Counting the Israelites

¹¹Then the LORD said to Moses, ¹²"When you take a census of the Israelites, each person must pay the LORD a ransom for his life when he is counted. Then no plague will happen to them when they are counted. ¹³As each person is counted, he must give one-fifth of an ounce of silver using the standard weight of the holy place.ᵃ This one-fifth of an ounce of silver is a contribution to the LORD. ¹⁴Everyone counted who is at least 20 years old must give this contribution to the LORD. ¹⁵The rich must not give more than one-fifth of an ounce of silver, and the poor must not give less. This contribution is given to make peace with the LORD and make your lives acceptable to the LORD. ¹⁶Take the money the Israelites give to make peace with the LORD, and use it to pay the expenses of the tent of meeting. It will be a reminder for the Israelites in the LORD's presence that the sins in their lives are removed."

The Bronze Basin—
Exodus 38:8

¹⁷The LORD said to Moses, ¹⁸"Make a bronze basin with a bronze stand for washing. Put it between the tent of meeting and the altar, and fill it with water. ¹⁹Aaron and his sons will use it for washing their hands and feet. ²⁰Before they go into the tent of meeting, they must wash so that they will not die. Before they come near the altar to serve as priests and burn an offering by fire to the LORD, ²¹they will wash their hands and feet so that they will not die. This will be a permanent law for him and his descendants for generations to come."

ᵃ30:13 Hebrew adds, "There are 20 gerahs to the standard shekel."

The Oil for Anointing

²²The LORD said to Moses, ²³"Take the finest spices: 12½ pounds of powdered*ᵇ* myrrh; half as much, that is, 6¼ pounds of fragrant cinnamon; 6¼ pounds of fragrant cane; ²⁴12½ pounds of cassia—all weighed using the standard weight of the holy place—and 4 quarts of olive oil. ²⁵Have a perfumer make these into a holy oil, a fragrant mixture, used only for anointing. This will be the holy oil used for anointing.

²⁶"Use it to anoint the tent of meeting, the ark containing the words of my promise, ²⁷the table and all the dishes, the lamp stand and all the utensils, the altar for incense, ²⁸the altar for burnt offerings and all its accessories, and the basin with its stand. ²⁹In this way you will dedicate them for their holy purpose. Then they will be most holy, and anything that touches them will become holy. ³⁰Anoint Aaron and his sons as well. In this way you will set them apart for their holy duties of serving me as priests.

³¹"Say to the Israelites, 'For generations to come, this will be my holy oil used only for anointing. ³²It must never be poured on the bodies of other people. Never make any perfumed oil using this formula. It is holy, and you must treat it as holy. ³³Whoever prepares a perfume like this or puts it on anyone who is not a priest must be excluded from the people.' "

The Incense for Use in the Tent

³⁴The LORD said to Moses, "Take one part fragrant spices (two kinds of gum resin and aromatic mollusk shells), and mix them with one part pure frankincense. ³⁵Have a perfumer make it into fragrant incense, seasoned with salt, pure and holy. ³⁶Grind some of it into a fine powder, and put it in front of the ark containing the words of my promise in the tent of meeting, where I will meet with you. You must treat it as most holy. ³⁷Never make any incense for yourselves using this formula. Treat it as holy to the LORD. ³⁸Whoever prepares anything like it for his own enjoyment must be excluded from his people."

The Craftsmen for the Tent—
Exodus 35:30-35

31 ¹The LORD said to Moses, ²"I have chosen Bezalel, son of Uri and grandson of Hur, from the tribe of Judah. ³I have filled Bezalel with the Spirit of God, making him highly skilled, resourceful, and knowledgeable in all trades. ⁴He's a master artist familiar with gold, silver, and bronze. ⁵He knows how to cut and set stones and how to work with wood. He's an expert in all trades. ⁶Also, I have appointed Oholiab, son of Ahisamach, from the tribe of Dan, to help him. I have given every craftsman the skill necessary to make everything I have commanded you: ⁷the tent of meeting, the ark containing the words of my promise with the throne of mercy on it, and all the other furnishings for the tent, ⁸the table and the dishes, the pure gold lamp stand and all its utensils, the altar for incense, ⁹the altar for burnt offerings and all its accessories, the basin with its stand, ¹⁰the special*ᵃ* clothes—the holy clothes for the priest Aaron and the clothes for his sons when they serve as priests, ¹¹the anointing oil, and the sweet-smelling incense for the holy place. They will make all these things as I commanded you."

---

*ᵇ*30:23 Or "liquid."   *ᵃ*31:10 Greek, Syriac, Targum; Hebrew meaning uncertain.

The Sign Between the LORD and His People

¹²The LORD said to Moses, ¹³"Say to the Israelites, 'Be sure to observe my days of worship. This will be a sign between me and you for generations to come so that you will know that I am the LORD who makes you holy.

¹⁴" 'Observe the day of worship because it is holy to you. Whoever treats it like any other day must be put to death. Whoever works on that day must be excluded from the people. ¹⁵You may work for six days, but the seventh day is a day of worship, a day when you don't work. It is holy to the LORD. Whoever works on that day must be put to death. ¹⁶The Israelites must observe this day of worship, celebrating it for generations to come as a permanent reminder of my promise.ᵇ ¹⁷It will be a permanent sign between me and the Israelites, because the LORD made heaven and earth in six days, and on the seventh day he stopped working and was refreshed.' "

¹⁸The LORD finished speaking to Moses on Mount Sinai. Then he gave him the two tablets with his words on them, stone tablets inscribed by God himself.

The Gold Calf

32 ¹When the people saw that Moses delayed coming down from the mountain, they gathered around Aaron. They said to him, "We don't know what has happened to this Moses, who led us out of Egypt. Make gods who will lead us."

²Aaron said to them, "Have your wives, sons, and daughters take off the gold earrings they are wearing, and bring them to me."

³So all the people took off their gold earrings and handed them to Aaron. ⁴After he had worked on the gold with a tool,ᵃ he made it into a statue of a calf.

Then they said, "Israel, here are your gods who brought you out of Egypt."

⁵When Aaron saw this, he built an altar in front of it and announced, "Tomorrow there will be a festival in the LORD's honor."

⁶Early the next day the people sacrificed burnt offerings and brought fellowship offerings. Afterward, they sat down to a feast, which turned into an orgy.

⁷The LORD said to Moses, "Go back down there. Your people whom you brought out of Egypt have ruined ⌊everything⌋. ⁸They've already turned from the way I commanded them to live. They've made a statue of a calf for themselves. They've bowed down to it and offered sacrifices to it. They've said, 'Israel, here are your gods who brought you out of Egypt.' "

⁹The LORD added, "I've seen these people, and they are impossible to deal with. ¹⁰Now leave me alone. I'm so angry with them I am going to destroy them. Then I'll make you into a great nation."

¹¹But Moses pleaded with the LORD his God. "LORD," he said, "why are you so angry with your people whom you brought out of Egypt using your great power and mighty hand? ¹²Don't let the Egyptians say, 'He was planning all along to kill them in the mountains and wipe them off the face of the earth. That's why he brought them out ⌊of our land⌋.' Don't be so angry. Reconsider your decision to bring this disaster on your people. ¹³Remember your servants Abraham, Isaac, and Israel. You took an oath, swearing on yourself. You told them, 'I will make your descendants as numerous as the stars in the sky. I will give to your descendants all the land I spoke of. It will be their permanent possession.' "

¹⁴So the LORD reconsidered his threat to destroy his people.

¹⁵Moses turned and went down the mountain carrying the two tablets with God's

---

ᵇ31:16 Or "covenant."   ᵃ32:4 Hebrew meaning uncertain.

words. They were written on both sides, front and back. [16]The tablets were the work of God, and the writing was God's writing inscribed on the tablets.

[17]Then Joshua heard the noise of the people shouting. He said to Moses, "It's the sound of war in the camp!"

[18]Moses replied,

> "It's not the sound of winners shouting.
> It's not the sound of losers crying.
> It's the sound of a wild celebration[b] that I hear."

[19]When he came near the camp, he saw the calf and the dancing. In a burst of anger Moses threw down the tablets and smashed them at the foot of the mountain. [20]Then he took the calf they had made, burned it, ground it into powder, scattered it on the water, and made the Israelites drink it.

[21]Moses asked Aaron, "What did these people do to you that you encouraged them to commit such a serious sin?"

[22]"Don't be angry, sir," Aaron answered. "You know that these people are evil. [23]They said to me, 'We don't know what's happened to this Moses who brought us out of Egypt. Make gods for us. They will lead us.' [24]So I told them to take off any gold they were wearing. They gave it to me. I threw it into the fire, and out came this calf!"

[25]Aaron had let the people get out of control, and they became an object of ridicule to their enemies. When Moses saw this, [26]he stood at the entrance to the camp and said, "If you're on the LORD's side, come over here to me!" Then all the Levites gathered around him.

[27]He said to them, "This is what the LORD God of Israel says: Each of you put on your sword. Go back and forth from one end of the camp to the other, and kill your relatives, friends, and neighbors."

[28]The Levites did what Moses told them, and that day about 3,000 people died.

[29]Moses said, "Today you are ordained as the LORD's priests. God gave you a blessing today because each of you fought with your own sons and brothers."[c]

Moses Begs the LORD to Spare the People

[30]The next day Moses said to the people, "You have committed a serious sin. Now I will go up the mountain to the LORD. Maybe I will be able to make a payment for your sin and make peace with the LORD for your sin."

[31]So Moses went back to the LORD and said, "These people have committed such a serious sin! They made gods out of gold for themselves. [32]But will you forgive their sin? If not, please wipe me out of the book you have written."

[33]The LORD answered Moses, "I will wipe out of my book whoever sins against me. [34]Now, go! Lead the people to the place I told you about. My Messenger will go ahead of you. But when I punish, I will punish them for their sin."

[35]So the LORD killed people because they had Aaron make the calf.

The LORD Assures Moses That He Will Have Mercy on Israel

33 [1]Then the LORD said to Moses, "You and the people you brought out of Egypt must leave this place. Go to the land I promised to Abraham, Isaac, and Jacob with an oath, saying, 'I will give it to your descendants.' [2]I will send a Messenger ahead

---

[b]32:18 Hebrew meaning of "wild celebration" uncertain.   [c]32:29 Or "God gave you a blessing today at the cost of your own sons and brothers."

of you, and I will force out the Canaanites, Amorites, Hittites, Perizzites, Hivites, and Jebusites. ³Go to that land flowing with milk and honey. But I will not be with you, because you are impossible to deal with, and I would destroy you on the way."

⁴When the people heard this bad news, they acted as if someone had died. No one wore any jewelry. ⁵The Lord had said to Moses, "Tell the Israelites, 'You are impossible to deal with. If I were with you, I might destroy you at any time. Now take off your jewelry, and I'll decide what to do with you.' " ⁶After they left Mount Horeb, the Israelites no longer wore their jewelry.

⁷Now, Moses used to take a tent and set it up far outside the camp. He called it the tent of meeting. Anyone who was seeking the Lord's will used to go outside the camp to the tent of meeting. ⁸Whenever Moses went out to the tent, all the people would rise and stand at the entrances to their tents and watch Moses until he went in. ⁹As soon as Moses went into the tent, the column of smoke would come down and stay at the entrance to the tent while the Lord spoke with Moses. ¹⁰When all the people saw the column of smoke standing at the entrance to the tent, they would all bow with their faces touching the ground at the entrance to their own tents. ¹¹The Lord would speak to Moses personally, as a man speaks to his friend. Then Moses would come back to the camp, but his assistant, Joshua, son of Nun, stayed inside the tent.

¹²Moses said to the Lord, "You've been telling me to lead these people, but you haven't let me know whom you're sending with me. You've also said, 'I know you by name, and I'm pleased with you.' ¹³If you really are pleased with me, show me your ways so that I can know you and so that you will continue to be pleased with me. Remember: This nation is your people."

¹⁴The Lord answered, "My presence will go ⌐with you,⌐ and I will give you peace."

¹⁵Then Moses said to him, "If your presence is not going ⌐with us⌐, don't make us leave this place. ¹⁶How will anyone ever know you're pleased with your people and me unless you go with us? Then we will be different from all other people on the face of the earth."

¹⁷The Lord answered Moses, "I will do what you have asked, because I am pleased with you, and I know you by name."

¹⁸Then Moses said, "Please let me see your glory."

¹⁹The Lord said, "I will let all my goodness pass in front of you, and there I will call out my name 'the Lord.' I will be kind to anyone I want to. I will be merciful to anyone I want to. ²⁰But you can't see my face, because no one may see me and live."

²¹Then the Lord said, "Look, there's a place near me. Stand by this rocky cliff. ²²When my glory passes by, I will put you in a crevice in the cliff and cover you with my hand until I have passed by. ²³Then I will take my hand away, and you'll see my back, but my face must not be seen."

The Lord Meets With Moses on the Mountain

34 ¹The Lord said to Moses, "Cut two ⌐more⌐ stone tablets like the first ones, and I will write on them the words that were on the first tablets which you smashed. ²Be ready in the morning. Then come up on Mount Sinai, and stand in my presence on the top of the mountain. ³No one may come with you or even be seen anywhere on the mountain. Even the flocks and herds may not graze in front of this mountain."

⁴So Moses cut two ⌐more⌐ stone tablets like the first ones. Early the next morning he went up on Mount Sinai, as the Lord had commanded him, carrying the two stone tablets.

⁵The Lord came down in a cloud and stood there with him and called out his name "the Lord."

⁶Then he passed in front of Moses, calling out, "The Lord, the Lord, a compassionate and merciful God, patient, always faithful and ready to forgive. ⁷He continues to show his love to thousands of generations, forgiving wrongdoing, disobedience, and sin. He never lets the guilty go unpunished, punishing children and grandchildren for their parents' sins to the third and fourth generation."

⁸Immediately, Moses knelt, bowing with his face touching the ground. ⁹Then he said, "Lord, please go with us! Even though we are impossible to deal with, forgive our sin and the wrong we have done, and accept us as your own people."

The Lord Makes His Promise With Israel Again

¹⁰The Lord said, "I'm making my promise*ᵃ* again. In front of all your people I will perform miracles that have never been done in any other nation in all the world. All the people around you will see how awesome these miracles are that I will perform for you. ¹¹Do everything that I command today. Then I will force the Amorites, Canaanites, Hittites, Perizzites, Hivites, and Jebusites out of your way. ¹²Be careful not to make a treaty with those who live in the land where you're going. This will prove to be a trap to you. ¹³But tear down their altars, crush their sacred stones, and cut down their poles dedicated to the goddess Asherah. ¹⁴(Never worship any other god, because the Lord is a God who does not tolerate rivals. In fact, he is known for not tolerating rivals.) ¹⁵Be careful not to make a treaty with those who live in that land. When they chase after their gods as though they were prostitutes and sacrifice to them, they may invite you to eat the meat from their sacrifices with them. ¹⁶Then your sons will end up marrying their daughters. When their daughters chase after their gods as though they were prostitutes, they'll lead your sons to do the same thing.

¹⁷"Never make an idol.

¹⁸"You must celebrate the Festival of Unleavened Bread. As I commanded you, you must eat unleavened bread for seven days at the appointed time in the month of Abib, because in that month you came out of Egypt.

¹⁹"Every first male offspring is mine, even the firstborn males*ᵇ* of all your livestock, whether cattle, sheep, or goats. ²⁰It will cost you a sheep or a goat to buy back the firstborn donkey. If you don't buy it back, then you must break the donkey's neck. You must buy back every firstborn of your sons.

"No one may come into my presence without an offering.

²¹"You may work six days, but on the seventh day you must not work. Even during the time of plowing or harvesting you must not work ⎣on this day⎦.

²²"You must celebrate the Festival of Weeks with the first grain from your wheat harvest, and the Festival of the Final Harvest at the end of the season.

²³"Three times a year all your men must come into the presence of the Master, the Lord God of Israel. ²⁴I will force nations out of your way and will expand ⎣your country's⎦ borders. No one will want to take away your land while you're gone three times a year to the Lord's festivals.

²⁵"Never offer the blood of a sacrifice to me at the same time you offer anything containing yeast. No part of the sacrifice at the Passover festival should be left over in the morning.

²⁶"You must bring the first and best of the produce harvested from your soil to the house of the Lord your God.

"Never cook a young goat in its mother's milk."

²⁷Then the Lord said to Moses, "Write down these words, because on the basis of these words I'm making a promise to Israel and to you."

---

*ᵃ*34:10 Or "covenant." *ᵇ*34:19 Greek, Latin; Hebrew meaning of the Masoretic Text uncertain.

²⁸Moses was there with the Lᴏʀᴅ 40 days and 40 nights without food or water. He wrote on the tablets the words of the promise, the ten commandments.

Moses Returns to the People

²⁹Moses came down from Mount Sinai, carrying the two tablets with God's words on them. His face was shining from speaking with the Lᴏʀᴅ, but he didn't know it.

³⁰When Aaron and all the Israelites looked at Moses and saw his face shining, they were afraid to come near him. ³¹Moses called to them, so Aaron and all the leaders of the community came back to him. Then Moses spoke to them. ³²After that, all the other Israelites came near him, and he commanded them to do everything the Lᴏʀᴅ told him on Mount Sinai. ³³When Moses finished speaking to them, he put a veil over his face. ³⁴But whenever Moses went into the Lᴏʀᴅ's presence to speak with him, he took off the veil until he came out. Whenever he came out and told the Israelites what he had been commanded, ³⁵they would see that Moses' face was shining. Then Moses would put the veil back on until he went in again to speak with the Lᴏʀᴅ.

Rules About the Day of Worship

¹Moses assembled the whole Israelite community and said to them, "These are the things the Lᴏʀᴅ has commanded you to do: ²You may work for six days, but the seventh day is a holy day of worship, a day when you don't work. It is dedicated to the Lᴏʀᴅ. Whoever does any work on this day should be put to death. ³Never light a fire in any of your homes on this day of worship."

The People Contribute Their Wealth—
Exodus 25:1-7

⁴Then Moses said to the whole Israelite community, "This is what the Lᴏʀᴅ has commanded: ⁵Choose something of your own to give as a special contribution to the Lᴏʀᴅ. Let everyone who is willing bring this kind of contribution to the Lᴏʀᴅ: gold, silver, and bronze, ⁶violet, purple, and bright red yarn, fine linen, goats' hair, ⁷rams' skins dyed red, fine leather,ᵃ acacia wood, ⁸olive oil for the lamps, spices for the anointing oil and for the sweet-smelling incense, ⁹onyx stones, and other precious stones to be set in the ⸤chief priest's⸥ ephodᵇ and breastplate.

The Craftsmen for the Tent—
Exodus 31:2-6

¹⁰"Have all the skilled craftsmen among you come and make everything the Lᴏʀᴅ has commanded: ¹¹the inner tent, the outer tent, and cover, along with the fasteners, frames, crossbars, posts, and sockets, ¹²the ark with its poles, the throne of mercy and the canopy over it, ¹³the table with its poles, all the dishes, the bread of the presence, ¹⁴the lamp stand used for the light with its utensils, its lamps and the olive oil for the lamps, ¹⁵the altar for incense with its poles, the anointing oil, the sweet-smelling incense, the screen for the entrance to the tent, ¹⁶the altar for burnt offerings with its bronze grate, its poles, and all its accessories, the basin with its stand, ¹⁷the curtains for the courtyard, the posts, bases, and the screen for the entrance to the courtyard, ¹⁸the pegs for the tent and the courtyard with their ropes, ¹⁹the special clothesᶜ worn for official duties in the holy place—both the holy clothes for Aaron the priest and the clothes for his sons when they serve as priests."

ᵃ 35:7 Hebrew meaning uncertain.   ᵇ 35:9 *Ephod* is a technical term for a part of the priest's clothes. Its exact usage and shape are unknown.   ᶜ 35:19 Hebrew meaning uncertain.

²⁰Then the whole Israelite community left Moses. ²¹Those who were willing and whose hearts moved them came and brought their contributions to the Lᴏʀᴅ. The gifts were used to construct the tent of meeting, to pay other expenses, and to make the holy clothes. ²²All who were willing—men and women alike—came and brought all kinds of gold jewelry: pins,ᵈ earrings, signet rings, and pendants. They took these gifts of gold and offered them to the Lᴏʀᴅ. ²³Those who had violet, purple, or bright red yarn, fine linen, goats' hair, rams' skins dyed red, or fine leather brought them. ²⁴Those who could give silver or bronze brought it as their contribution to the Lᴏʀᴅ. Those who had acacia wood that could be used in the construction brought it. ²⁵All the women who were skilled in spinning yarn brought violet, purple, and bright red yarn, and fine linen, which they had made by hand. ²⁶All the women who were willing and had the skill spun the goats' hair. ²⁷The leaders brought onyx stones and other precious stones to be set in the ⌐chief priest's⌐ ephod and breastplate. ²⁸They also brought the spices and the olive oil for the lamps, the anointing oil, and the sweet-smelling incense. ²⁹Every Israelite man and woman who was willing brought all these items to the Lᴏʀᴅ as a freewill offering. They brought these items to be used to make everything the Lᴏʀᴅ had commanded through Moses.

³⁰Then Moses said to the Israelites, "The Lᴏʀᴅ has chosen Bezalel, son of Uri and grandson of Hur, from the tribe of Judah. ³¹The Lᴏʀᴅ has filled Bezalel with the Spirit of God, making him highly skilled, resourceful, and knowledgeable in all trades. ³²He's a master artist familiar with gold, silver, and bronze. ³³He knows how to cut and set stones and how to work with wood. He's an expert in all trades. ³⁴Also, the Lᴏʀᴅ has given Bezalel and Oholiab, son of Ahisamach, from the tribe of Dan the ability to teach others. ³⁵The Lᴏʀᴅ has made these men highly skilled in all trades. They can do the work of jewelers, carpenters, and designers. They know how to embroider violet, purple and bright red yarn on fine linen. They know how to weave yarn on a loom. They can do all kinds of trades. They are master artists."

36 ¹Moses continued, ⌐"So Bezalel and Oholiab will do the work as the Lᴏʀᴅ has commanded. They will do this with the help of every other craftsman to whom the Lᴏʀᴅ has given the necessary skills and talents. They will know how to do all the work for constructing the holy place."

²Moses called Bezalel and Oholiab and

Gifts and Talents
Exodus 35:30-35

People who preach and sing aren't the only ones with gifts. The ability to make useful and beautiful things is a gift, too. Perhaps God has given you the gift of being a "master artist." Or a builder. Or a craft-maker. Do your best always, and you'll find the gifts that God has given you.

be
all you
can
be

ᵈ35:22 Hebrew meaning uncertain.

every other craftsman to whom the LORD had given these skills and who was willing to come and do the work.

Excess Contributions

[3]Moses turned over to them all the contributions the Israelites had brought for the work of constructing the holy place. But the people still kept bringing him free-will offerings every morning. [4]Finally, all the skilled craftsmen who were working on the holy place stopped what they were doing. They all came to Moses. [5]They said, "The people are bringing much more than we need for doing the work the LORD commanded us to do."

[6]So Moses gave instructions to have the following message announced all over camp: "No man or woman needs to make anything more to give as their special contribution to the holy place." Then the people stopped bringing gifts. [7]The material they had was more than enough to do the job.

The Tent—
Exodus 26:1-37

[8]All the skilled craftsmen among the workers made the inner tent with ten sheets made from fine linen yarn and violet, purple, and bright red yarn. An angel[a] design was creatively worked into the fabric. [9]Each sheet was 42 feet long and 6 feet wide—all the same size. [10]Five of the sheets were sewn together, and the other five were also sewn together. [11]Then they made 50 violet loops along the edge of the end sheet in each set, [12]placing the loops opposite each other. [13]They also made 50 gold fasteners. They used them to link the two sets of sheets together so that the inner tent was a single unit.

[14]They made 11 sheets of goats' hair to form an outer tent over the inner tent. [15]Each of the 11 sheets was 45 feet long and 6 feet wide. [16]Five of the sheets were sewn together into one set, and the remaining six into another set. [17]Then they made 50 loops along the edge of the end sheet in each set. [18]They also made 50 bronze fasteners to link the inner tent together as a single unit. [19]They made a cover out of rams' skins that had been dyed red for the outer tent, and over that they put a cover made of fine leather.[b]

[20]They made a framework out of acacia wood for the inner tent. [21]Each frame was 15 feet long and 27 inches wide, [22]with two identical pegs. They made all the frames for the inner tent this same way. [23]They made 20 frames for the south side of the inner tent. [24]Then they made 40 silver sockets at the bottom of the 20 frames, two sockets at the bottom of each frame for the two pegs. [25]For the north side of the inner tent they made 20 frames [26]and 40 silver sockets, two at the bottom of each frame. [27]They made six frames for the far end, the west side. [28]They made two frames for each of the corners at the far end of the inner tent. [29]They were held together at the bottom and held tightly at the top by a single ring.[c] Both corner frames were made this way. [30]There were eight frames with 16 silver sockets, two at the bottom of each frame.

[31]They also made crossbars out of acacia wood. Five were for the frames on one side of the inner tent, [32]five were for those on the other side, and five were for the frames on the far side of the inner tent, the west side. [33]They made the middle crossbar so that it ran from one end to the other, halfway up the frames. [34]They covered the frames with gold and made gold rings to hold the crossbars. They also covered the crossbars with gold.

---

[a] 36:8 Or "A cherubim."   [b] 36:19 Hebrew meaning uncertain.   [c] 36:29 Or "These were separated at the bottom but held together at the top by a single ring."

[35]They made the canopy out of violet, purple, and bright red yarn and fine linen yarn. An angel design was creatively worked into the fabric. [36]They made four posts of acacia wood for it and covered them with gold. They made gold hooks for the posts, and they cast four silver bases for them.

[37]They made a screen out of fine linen yarn for the entrance to the outer tent. It was embroidered with violet, purple, and bright red yarn. [38]They also made five posts with hooks for hanging the screen. They covered the tops of the posts and the bands with gold, but the five bases for the posts were made of bronze.

The Ark—
Exodus 25:10-20

[1]Bezalel made the ark out of acacia wood 45 inches long, 27 inches wide, and 27 inches high. [2]He covered it with pure gold inside and out and put a gold molding around it. [3]He cast four gold rings for its four feet, two rings on each side. [4]Then he made poles out of acacia wood and covered them with gold. [5]He put them through the rings on the sides of the ark in order to carry it.

[6]He made the throne of mercy out of pure gold 45 inches long and 27 inches wide. [7]Then he made two angels[a] out of hammered gold for the two ends of the throne of mercy, [8]one on each end. He formed the angels and the throne of mercy out of one piece of gold. [9]The angels had their wings spread above the throne of mercy, overshadowing it. They faced each other, looking at the throne of mercy.

The Table—
Exodus 25:23-30

[10]He made the table out of acacia wood 36 inches long, 18 inches wide, and 27 inches high. [11]He covered it with pure gold and put a gold molding around it. [12]He made a rim 3 inches wide around it and put a gold molding around the rim. [13]He cast four gold rings for it and fastened the rings to the four corners, where the four legs were. [14]The rings were put close to the rim to hold the poles for carrying the table. [15]These poles were made out of acacia wood and were covered with gold. [16]For the table he made plates, dishes, bowls, and pitchers to be used for pouring wine offerings. All of them were made out of pure gold.

The Lamp Stand—
Exodus 25:31-39

[17]He made the lamp stand out of pure gold. The lamp stand, its base, and its shaft, as well as the flower cups, buds, and petals were hammered out of one piece of gold. [18]Six branches came out of its sides, three branches on one side and three on the other. [19]Each of the six branches coming out of the lamp stand had three flower cups shaped like almond blossoms, with buds and petals. [20]The lamp stand itself had four flower cups shaped like almond blossoms, each with a bud and petals. [21]There was a bud under each of the three pairs of branches coming out of the lamp stand. [22]The buds and branches were hammered out of the same piece of pure gold as the lamp stand.

[23]He made the seven lamps, the tongs, and the incense burners out of pure gold. [24]The lamp stand and all the utensils were made out of 75 pounds of pure gold.

---

[a] 37:7 Or "cherubim."

The Altar for Incense—
Exodus 30:1-5

[25]He made an altar out of acacia wood for burning incense. It was 18 inches square and 36 inches high. The horns and altar were made out of one piece of wood. [26]He covered all of it with pure gold—the top, the sides, and the horns—and he put a gold molding around it. [27]He made two gold rings and put them below the molding on opposite sides to hold the poles for carrying it. [28]He made the poles out of acacia wood and covered them with gold.

[29]He also had a perfumer make the holy oil to be used for anointing and for the pure, sweet-smelling incense.

The Altar for Burnt Offerings—
Exodus 27:1-8

[1]He made the altar for burnt offerings out of acacia wood 7½ feet square and 4½ feet high. [2]He made a horn at each of its four corners. He made the four horns and the altar out of one piece of wood covered with bronze.

[3]He made all the utensils out of bronze: pots, shovels, bowls, forks, and incense burners.

[4]He made a grate for the altar out of bronze mesh, and put it under the ledge, halfway up the altar. [5]He cast four rings to hold the poles (one for each of the four corners of the bronze grate). [6]He made the poles out of acacia wood and covered them with bronze. [7]He put the poles through the rings on the sides of the altar to carry it. He made the altar out of boards so that it was hollow inside.

The Bronze Basin—
Exodus 30:17-21

[8]He made the basin and stand out of the bronze mirrors given by the women who served at the entrance to the tent of meeting.

The Courtyard—
Exodus 27:9-19

[9]He also made the courtyard. The south side of the courtyard was 150 feet long and had curtains made out of fine linen yarn, [10]hung on 20 posts set in 20 bronze bases. The hooks and bands on the posts were made of silver. [11]The north side was also 150 feet long with 20 posts and 20 bronze bases. The hooks and bands on the posts were made of silver.

[12]The west side was 75 feet long and had curtains hung on 10 posts set in 10 bases. The hooks and bands on the posts were made of silver. [13]The east side, facing the rising sun, was 75 feet wide. [14-15]Each side of the entrance to the courtyard was 22½ feet wide with curtains hung on three posts set in three bases [16]All the curtains around the courtyard were made out of fine linen yarn. [17]The bases for the posts were made of bronze. The hooks and bands on the posts were made of silver. The tops of the posts were covered with silver. And the bands on all the posts of the courtyard were made of silver.

[18]The screen for the entrance to the courtyard was made of violet, purple, and bright red yarn embroidered on fabric made from fine linen yarn. It was 30 feet long and 7½ feet high, just like the curtains of the courtyard. [19]It was hung on four posts set in four bronze bases. The hooks and bands on the posts were made of silver. The tops of the posts were covered with silver.

[20]All the pegs for the tent and the surrounding courtyard were made of bronze.

Tent of Meeting
Exodus 38:21-31

Everyone was excited when Moses said they could build a place to worship God. The women brought gold jewelry and other expensive materials to the Lord. Skilled workers used the gifts to make a tent of meeting for God. The portable tent reminded the people that God was always with them.

How many pounds of gold and silver did it take to make this worship center? What expensive materials were used for each of the different parts of the tent church? You can find out by reading Exodus 38:21-31.

The Amount of Gold, Silver, and Bronze Used

²¹This is the amount of material that was used for the tent (the tent of the words of God's promise). An inventory was ordered by Moses and carried out by the Levites under the direction of Ithamar, son of the priest Aaron.

²²Now Bezalel, son of Uri and grandson of Hur, from the tribe of Judah, made everything the Lord had commanded Moses. ²³He was a jeweler, carpenter, designer, and he knew how to embroider violet, purple, and bright red yarn on fine linen. His assistant was Oholiab, son of Ahisamach, from the tribe of Dan.

²⁴The total amount of gold from the offerings presented to the Lord used in building the holy place weighed over 2,193 pounds using the standard weight of the holy place.

²⁵The silver collected when the census of the community was taken weighed 7,544 pounds using the standard weight of the holy place. ²⁶This came to one-fifth of an ounce per person, for everyone counted who was at least 20 years old: 603,550 people. ²⁷He used 7,500 pounds of silver to cast the 100 bases for the holy place and the canopy. This was 75 pounds per base. ²⁸He used 44 pounds of silver to make the hooks and bands for the posts and the coverings for the tops of the posts.

²⁹The bronze from the offerings presented to the Lord weighed 5,310 pounds. ³⁰With this he made the bases for the entrance to the tent of meeting, the bronze altar with its bronze grate and all its accessories, ³¹the bases all around the courtyard, the bases for the entrance to the courtyard, all the pegs for the tent, and all the pegs for the surrounding courtyard.

The Holy Clothes—
Exodus 28:1-5

39 ¹From the violet, purple, and bright red yarn they made special clothes worn for official duties in the holy place. They also made the holy clothes for Aaron. They followed the Lord's instructions to Moses.

The Ephod—
Exodus 28:6-14

²They made the ephod out of fine linen yarn and gold, violet, purple, and bright red yarn. ³They hammered the gold into thin sheets and cut them up. They twisted the gold into threads, which they creatively worked into each strand of the violet, purple, and bright red yarn, and throughout the fine linen. ⁴They made two shoulder straps attached at the ,top, corners so that the ephod could be fastened. ⁵They made the belt that is attached to the ephod out of the same fabric. They followed the LORD's instructions to Moses. ⁶They mounted the onyx stones in gold settings, and engraved on them the names of the sons of Israel. ⁷Then they fastened them on the shoulder straps of the ephod as a reminder of who the Israelites are. They followed the LORD's instructions to Moses.

The Breastplate—
Exodus 28:15-28

⁸They made the breastplate as creatively as they made the ephod. It was made out of gold, violet, purple, and bright red yarn, and of fine linen yarn. ⁹It was folded in half and was 9 inches square. ¹⁰They fastened four rows of precious stones on it. In the first row they put red quartz, topaz, and emerald. ¹¹In the second row they put turquoise, sapphire, and crystal. ¹²In the third row they put jacinth, agate, and amethyst. ¹³In the fourth row they put beryl, onyx, and gray quartz. The stones were mounted in gold settings. ¹⁴They corresponded to the 12 sons of Israel, by name, each stone engraved (like a signet ring) with the name of one of the 12 tribes.

¹⁵For the breastplate they made chains out of pure gold, twisted like ropes. ¹⁶They made two gold settings and two gold rings and attached the two rings to the ,top, two corners of the breastplate. ¹⁷They fastened the two gold ropes to the rings at the ,top, corners of the breastplate. ¹⁸They fastened the other ends of the ropes to the two set-

Giving
Exodus 38:21-31

Everyone was happy to give gold and silver to make the tent where God was worshiped. Today Christians also give money to pay for churches. The money also helps support missionaries and buy Sunday school materials. Ask how the money is used at your church. How much do *you* want to give each Sunday?

be all you can be

tings on the shoulder straps of the ephod ,so that the breastplate hung, in front of it. ¹⁹They made two gold rings and fastened them to the other two corners of the breastplate on the inside edge next to the ephod. ²⁰They made two ,more, gold rings and fastened them to the bottom of the shoulder straps on the front of the ephod. This was close to the seam just above the belt of the ephod. ²¹Then they fastened the breastplate by its rings to the rings of the ephod with a violet cord. So the breastplate was attached just above the belt of the ephod and was held in place. They followed the LORD's instructions to Moses.

Other Clothes for Aaron and His Sons—
Exodus 28:31-43

²²They made the robe that is worn with the ephod, woven entirely of violet yarn. ²³The opening in the center of the robe had a finished edge (like a leather collar*) all around it to keep it from tearing. ²⁴On the hem of the robe they made pomegranates of violet, purple, and bright red yarn, and fine yarn. ²⁵They made bells out of pure gold and fastened them in between the pomegranates all around the hem of the robe. ²⁶A gold bell alternated with a pomegranate all around the hem of the robe that is worn by Aaron when he serves as priest. They followed the LORD's instructions to Moses.

²⁷They wove inner robes out of fine linen for Aaron and his sons. ²⁸They also made the chief priest's turban and the other beautiful turbans out of fine linen. They made the undergarments and belt out of fine linen yarn. ²⁹The belt was embroidered with violet, purple, and bright red yarn. They followed the LORD's instructions to Moses.

³⁰They made the flower-shaped medallion (the holy crown) out of pure gold and engraved on it (as on a signet ring): Holy to the LORD. ³¹They fastened a violet cord to it and tied it on top of the turban. They followed the LORD's instructions to Moses.

The Tent Is Brought to Moses

³²So all the work on the inner tent (the tent of meeting) was now done. The Israelites followed all the LORD's instructions to Moses. ³³Then they brought everything to Moses—the inner tent, the outer tent and all its furnishings, the fasteners, frames, crossbars, posts, sockets, ³⁴the cover made of rams' skins dyed red, the cover made of fine leather,ᵇ the canopy over ˏthe arkˎ, ³⁵the ark containing the words of God's promise with its poles and the throne of mercy, ³⁶the table with all the dishes, the bread of the presence, ³⁷the pure ˏgoldˎ lamp stand with its lamps in a row and all its utensils, the olive oil for the lamps, ³⁸the gold altar, the anointing oil, the sweet-smelling incense, the screen for the entrance to the tent, ³⁹the bronze altar with its bronze grate, its poles, and all its accessories, the basin with its stand, ⁴⁰the curtains for the courtyard, the posts, bases, and screen for the entrance to the courtyard, the ropes and pegs—all the equipment needed for the service of the inner tent (the tent of meeting)— ⁴¹the special clothes worn when serving as priests in the holy place—both the holy clothes for the priest Aaron and the clothes for his sons when serving as priests. ⁴²The Israelites had done all the work following the LORD's instructions to Moses.

⁴³Moses inspected all the work and saw that they had followed the LORD's instructions. So Moses blessed them.

Instructions for Setting Up the Tent

40 ¹Then the LORD said to Moses, ²"Set up the tent (the tent of meeting) on the first day of the first month of the year. ³Place the ark containing the words of my promise inside it, and hang the canopy over the ark. ⁴Bring in the table, and arrange everything on it. Bring in the lamp stand, and set up the lamps. ⁵Put the gold altar for incense in front of the ark. Put up the screen at the entrance to the tent.

⁶"Put the altar for burnt offerings in front of the entrance to the tent of meeting. ⁷Put the basin between the tent of meeting and the altar, and put water in it. ⁸Set up

---

ᵃ39:23 Hebrew meaning of "a leather collar" uncertain.　ᵇ39:34 Hebrew meaning uncertain.

the surrounding courtyard, and put up the screen at the entrance to the courtyard. [9]Take the anointing oil, and anoint the tent and everything in it. In this way you will dedicate it and all its furnishings. Then it will be holy. [10]Anoint the altar for burnt offerings and all the utensils. In this way you will dedicate the altar, and it will be most holy. [11]Anoint the basin and stand, and they will be dedicated.

[12]"Bring Aaron and his sons to the entrance of the tent of meeting, and wash them. [13]Then dress Aaron in the holy clothes, and anoint him. In this way you will dedicate him to serve me as priest. [14]Have his sons come forward, and dress them in their linen robes. [15]Anoint them to serve me as priests, as you anointed their father. Their anointing will begin a permanent priesthood for them for generations to come."

Moses Sets Up the Tent

[16]Moses did everything as the LORD commanded him. [17]So the tent was set up on the first day of the first month of the second year after the Israelites had left Egypt. [18]When Moses set up the tent, he put the sockets in place, put up the frames, inserted the crossbars, and set up the posts. [19]He spread the outer tent over the inner tent and put the cover on top. Moses followed the LORD's instructions.

[20]He took the words of God's promise and put them in the ark. He put the poles on the ark and placed the throne of mercy on top of the ark. [21]Then he brought the ark into the tent and hung the canopy over it to mark off where the ark was. Moses followed the LORD's instructions.

[22]Moses put the table in the tent of meeting on the north side of the tent outside the canopy. [23]He arranged the bread on the table in the LORD's presence, following the LORD's instructions. [24]He placed the lamp stand in the tent of meeting opposite the table, on the south side of the tent. [25]He set up the lamps in the LORD's presence, following the LORD's instructions.

[26]Moses put the gold altar in the tent of meeting in front of the canopy. [27]He burned sweet-smelling incense on it, following the LORD's instructions. [28]Then he put up the screen at the entrance to the tent.

[29]He put the altar for burnt offerings at the entrance to the tent (the tent of meeting). He sacrificed burnt offerings and grain offerings on it. Moses followed the LORD's instructions.

[30]He put the basin between the tent of meeting and the altar and put water in it for washing. [31]Moses, Aaron, and his sons used this water to wash their hands and feet. [32]They would wash whenever they went into the tent of meeting or whenever they approached the altar. Moses followed the LORD's instructions.

[33]He set up the courtyard around the tent and the altar and put up the screen at the entrance to the courtyard. Finally, Moses finished the work.

The LORD Comes to the Tent

[34]Then the column of smoke covered the tent of meeting, and the glory of the LORD filled the tent. [35]Moses couldn't go into the tent of meeting, because the smoke settled on it and the glory of the LORD filled the tent.

[36]In all their travels, whenever the column of smoke moved from the tent, the Israelites would break camp. [37]But if the column didn't move, they wouldn't break camp. [38]So the LORD's column stayed over the tent during the day, and there was fire in the smoke at night. In this way all the Israelites could see the column throughout their travels.

Leviticus

The Israelites might have thought they had all the rules they needed when God gave them the ten commandments. But they were wrong! God knew the Israelites needed to know how to be holy and how to worship him.

Leviticus gives more rules for the Israelites, both for priests and for other people.

In Old Testament times, animals were sacrificed for the sins of men and women. See Leviticus 17:11.

Cruelty to Animals?

Why did God tell Moses to sacrifice lambs and other animals? What did the animals ever do to deserve being killed? They were innocent!

God put human beings in charge of his creation. People are supposed to help take care of the fish, birds, and animals God made. But it was God who told Moses to sacrifice animals!

When a person sinned, he or she brought an animal to the priest. The person put his or her hands on the animal's head while the priest killed the animal and sprinkled its blood on God's altar. Then the person who sinned was forgiven. This sacrifice showed everyone that sin is so bad that it must be punished by death.

Each animal sacrifice was also an example of the future when Jesus would die on the cross. Jesus was innocent, too. But he was killed for the sins of people. Because Jesus died and paid for sins, all people can be forgiven.

God didn't tell people to make sacrifices to be mean to animals. God wanted people to realize that because we sin, Jesus needed to sacrifice his life to save ours.

God wanted the Israelites to remember that they were special, even when they ate their meals. That's why God called some animals "unclean" (don't eat!) and others "clean" (help yourself!). Which animals were unclean? Check Leviticus 11.

What's In It For Me?

How can I be holy? . . .

BY OBEYING GOD.
BY WORSHIPING ONLY GOD.
BY GIVING TO THE POOR.
BY ASKING GOD TO FORGIVE MY SINS.
BY SERVING GOD.

REVERSED RULES

These commands are backward—in two ways. Can you set them right again?

rehtona eno evieced 11:91 sucitiveL
ytilaitrap wohs 51:91 sucitiveL
rehtorb ruoy etah 71:91 sucitiveL
egnever kees 81:91 sucitiveL

Leviticus

1 ¹The Lord called Moses and spoke to him from the tent of meeting. He said, ²"Tell the Israelites: If any of you bring a sacrifice to the Lord, you must offer an animal from your cattle, sheep, or goats.

Burnt Offerings of Cattle

³"If you bring a burnt offering from your cattle, you must offer a male that has no defects. Offer it at the entrance to the tent of meeting so that the Lord will accept you. ⁴Place your hand on the animal's head. The burnt offering will be accepted to make peace with the Lord. ⁵Then slaughter the bull in the Lord's presence. Aaron's sons, the priests, will offer the blood. They will throw it against all sides of the altar that is at the entrance to the tent of meeting. ⁶Skin the burnt offering, and cut it into pieces. ⁷Then the sons of the priest Aaron will start a fire on the altar and lay the wood on the fire. ⁸Aaron's sons, the priests, will also lay the pieces, the head, and the fat on top of the wood burning on the altar. ⁹Wash the internal organs and legs. Then the priest will burn all of it on the altar. It is a burnt offering, an offering by fire, a soothing aroma to the Lord.

Burnt Offerings of Sheep or Goats

¹⁰"If your offering is a sheep or goat, you must bring a male that has no defects. ¹¹Slaughter it in the Lord's presence on the north side of the altar. Aaron's sons, the priests, will throw the blood against the altar on all sides. ¹²Then cut it into pieces. The priest will lay the head and the fat on the wood burning on the altar. ¹³Wash the internal organs and legs. Then the priest will burn all of it on the altar. It is a burnt offering, an offering by fire, a soothing aroma to the Lord.

Burnt Offerings of Birds

¹⁴"If your offering to the Lord is a bird, you must sacrifice a mourning dove or pigeon. ¹⁵The priest must bring it to the altar. He will break its neck and burn the bird on the altar. First, he will drain the blood against the side of the altar. ¹⁶Remove the gizzard with its filth and throw it on the east side of the altar on the place for the ashes. ¹⁷Then pull on the bird's wings to tear the bird open, but don't pull the wings off. Then the priest will lay the bird on the wood burning on the altar. It is a burnt offering, an offering by fire, a soothing aroma to the Lord."

Uncooked Grain Offerings

2 ¹The Lord continued, "Now, if any of you bring a grain offering to the Lord, your offering must be flour. Pour olive oil on it, and put incense on it. ²Then bring it to Aaron's sons, the priests. Take from this a handful of flour with olive oil, and all the incense. The priest will burn it on the altar as a reminder. It is an offering by fire, a soothing aroma to the Lord. ³The rest of the grain offering will belong to Aaron and his sons. It is very holy, set apart from the Lord's offering by fire.

Cooked Grain Offerings

⁴"If you bring a grain offering which has been baked in an oven, it must be rings of unleavened bread made of flour mixed with olive oil or wafers of unleavened bread

brushed with olive oil. ⁵If your grain offering is prepared in a frying pan, it, too, will be unleavened bread made of flour mixed with olive oil. ⁶Break it into pieces and pour olive oil over it. It is a grain offering. ⁷If your grain offering is prepared in a skillet, it will be made of flour with olive oil.

⁸"Bring the Lord the grain offering prepared in any of these ways. Offer it to the priest who will bring it to the altar. ⁹The priest will remove part of the grain offering and burn it as a reminder on the altar. It is an offering by fire, a soothing aroma to the Lord. ¹⁰The rest of the grain offering belongs to Aaron and his sons. It is very holy, set apart from the Lord's offering by fire.

Other Ingredients

¹¹"Every grain offering that you bring to the Lord must be prepared without yeast. Never burn yeast or honey as an offering to the Lord. ¹²You may bring them to the Lord as offerings of your first products. But they must never be placed on the altar to make a soothing aroma. ¹³Also put salt on each of your grain offerings. The salt of God's promise* must never be left out of your grain offerings. Put salt on all your offerings.

Offering the First Grain Harvested

¹⁴"If you bring a grain offering to the Lord from the first grain you harvest, roast the cracked grain over fire. ¹⁵Put olive oil on it, and place incense on it. It is a grain offering. ¹⁶The priest will burn the flour, olive oil, and all the incense as a reminder. It is an offering by fire to the Lord."

Fellowship Offerings of Cattle

¹The Lord continued, "If your sacrifice is a fellowship offering of cattle in the Lord's presence, it must be a male or female animal that has no defects. ²Place your hand on the animal's head. Then slaughter it at the entrance to the tent of meeting. Then Aaron's sons, the priests, will throw the blood against the altar on all sides. ³From your offering remove the fat that covers the internal organs ⁴and the two kidneys with the fat on them and offer them by fire to the Lord. Also cut off the lobe of the liver along with the kidneys. ⁵Then Aaron's sons will lay them on top of the burnt offering on the burning wood. It is an offering by fire, a soothing aroma to the Lord.

Fellowship Offerings of Sheep

⁶"If your sacrifice is a fellowship offering of sheep to the Lord, you must bring a male or female animal that has no defects. ⁷If your offering is a lamb, you must bring it to the Lord. ⁸Place your hand on the animal's head. Slaughter it in front of the tent of meeting. Then Aaron's sons will throw the blood against the altar on all sides. ⁹Then take the fat from the fellowship offering and offer it by fire to the Lord. Remove all the fat from the tail and the fat that covers the internal organs. ¹⁰Also remove the two kidneys with the fat on them along with the lobe of the liver. ¹¹Then the priest will burn the fellowship offering on the altar. It is food, an offering by fire to the Lord.

Fellowship Offerings of Goats

¹²"If your offering is a goat, you must bring it to the Lord. ¹³Place your hand on its head. Slaughter it in front of the tent of meeting. Then Aaron's sons will throw the blood against the altar on all sides. ¹⁴Then bring the fat that covers the internal organs

---

*2:13 Or "covenant."

¹⁵and the two kidneys with the fat on them as an offering by fire to the Lord. Also remove the lobe of the liver along with the kidneys. ¹⁶Then the priest will burn them on the altar. It is food, an offering by fire to the Lord. It is a soothing aroma. All the fat belongs to the Lord. ¹⁷This is a permanent law for generations to come wherever you live: Never eat any fat or blood."

Offerings for Unintentional Wrongdoing

4 ¹The Lord spoke to Moses, ²"Tell the Israelites: If a person unintentionally does something wrong—even one thing that is forbidden by any of the Lord's commands—this is what he must do.

Offerings for Wrongdoing by the Chief Priest

³"If the anointed priest does something wrong and brings guilt on the people, he must bring a bull that has no defects as an offering for sin to the Lord. ⁴He must bring the bull into the Lord's presence at the entrance to the tent of meeting. He will place his hand on the bull's head. He will then slaughter the bull in the Lord's presence. ⁵Then the anointed priest will take some of the bull's blood and bring it into the tent of meeting. ⁶The priest will dip his finger in it and sprinkle some of the blood seven times in the Lord's presence facing the canopy in the holy place. ⁷Then the priest will put some of the blood on the horns of the altar for sweet-smelling incense in the Lord's presence in the tent of meeting. He will pour the rest of the bull's blood at the bottom of the altar for burnt offerings at the entrance to the tent of meeting. ⁸He will remove all of the fat from the bull that is the offering for sin, the fat that covers the internal organs, ⁹and the two kidneys with the fat on them. He will also remove the lobe of the liver and the kidneys ¹⁰the same way they were removed from the bull used for the fellowship offering. The priest will lay them on the altar for burnt offerings. ¹¹Then he will take the entire bull (the skin, meat, head, legs, internal organs, and excrement) ¹²to a clean*ᵃ* place outside the camp where the ashes are dumped. He will burn it there on a wood fire.

Offerings for Wrongdoing by the Whole Congregation

¹³"If the whole congregation of Israel unintentionally does something wrong, without the assembly being aware of it, if they do even one thing that is forbidden by any of the Lord's commands, they will be guilty. ¹⁴When the wrong they have done becomes known, the congregation must sacrifice a bull as an offering for sin. They must bring it in front of the tent of meeting. ¹⁵The leaders of the congregation will place their hands on the bull's head in the Lord's presence. One of them will slaughter it in the Lord's presence. ¹⁶Then the anointed priest will bring some of the bull's blood into the tent of meeting. ¹⁷The priest will dip his finger in some of the blood and sprinkle it seven times in the Lord's presence facing the canopy. ¹⁸He will also put some blood on the horns of the altar in the Lord's presence in the tent of meeting. He will pour the rest of the blood at the bottom of the altar for burnt offerings at the entrance to the tent of meeting. ¹⁹He will remove all the fat and burn it on the altar. ²⁰He will do the same thing with this bull that he did with the bull used as the offering for sin. So the priest will make peace with the Lord for the people, and they will be forgiven. ²¹Then he will take the bull outside the camp and will burn it the same way he burned the first bull. It is an offering for sin for the community.

---

*ᵃ*4:12 "Clean" refers to anything that is presentable to God.

Offerings for Wrongdoing by a Leader

²²"When a leader unintentionally does something wrong—even one thing that is forbidden by any of the commands of the Lord his God—he will be guilty. ²³When he is told about what he has done wrong, he must bring a male goat that has no defects as his offering. ²⁴He will place his hand on the goat's head and slaughter it in the Lord's presence where he slaughters animals for burnt offerings. It is an offering for sin. ²⁵Then the priest will take some of the blood of the offering for sin with his finger and put it on the horns of the altar for burnt offerings. He will pour the rest of the blood at the bottom of the altar for burnt offerings. ²⁶He will burn all the fat on the altar the same way the fat of the fellowship offering is burned. So the priest will make peace with the Lord for what the leader did wrong, and the leader will be forgiven.

Offerings for Wrongdoing by a Common Person—Goats

²⁷"If a common person unintentionally does something wrong—even one thing forbidden by the Lord's commands—he will be guilty. ²⁸When he is told about what he has done wrong, he must bring a female goat that has no defects as his offering for what he has done wrong. ²⁹He will place his hand on the animal's head and slaughter it where animals for burnt offerings are slaughtered. ³⁰The priest will take some of the blood with his finger and put it on the horns of the altar for burnt offerings. He will pour the rest of the blood at the bottom of the altar. ³¹He will remove all the fat the same way it is removed from the fellowship offering. The priest will burn it on the altar for a soothing aroma to the Lord. So the priest will make peace with the Lord for that person, and that person will be forgiven.

Offerings for Wrongdoing by a Common Person—Lambs

³²"If someone brings a lamb as his offering for sin, he must bring a female that has no defects. ³³He will place his hand on the animal's head and slaughter it where he slaughters animals for burnt offerings. ³⁴Then the priest will take some of the blood from the offering for sin with his finger and put it on the horns of the altar for burnt offerings. He will pour the rest of the blood at the bottom of the altar. ³⁵He will remove all the fat the same way the fat of the lamb is removed from the fellowship offerings. Then the priest will burn it on the altar with the offering by fire to the Lord. So the priest will make peace with the Lord for what that person did wrong, and that person will be forgiven."

Sins Which Require an Offering for Sin

¹ The Lord continued, "Now, if you are a witness under oath and won't tell what you saw or what you know, you are sinning and will be punished.
²"If you touch anything unclean*—the unclean dead body of a wild or tame animal or the body of an unclean, swarming creature—and then ignore what you did, you are unclean and will be guilty.
³"If you become unclean by touching human uncleanness of any kind and then ignore it (although you know what you did), you will be guilty.
⁴"If you hastily take a vow about what you will or will not do (as some people do) and then ignore it (although you know what you said), you will be guilty.
⁵"So if you are guilty of any of these sins, you must confess it. ⁶Bring your guilt offering to the Lord for the sin you committed. It must be a female sheep or goat as an offering for sin. Then the priest will make peace with the Lord for what you did wrong.

*5:2 "Unclean" refers to anything that is not presentable to God.

If You Cannot Afford a Sheep

[7]"Now, if you cannot afford a sheep, you must bring to the LORD two mourning doves or two pigeons as a guilt offering for the sin you committed. One will be an offering for sin, the other a burnt offering. [8]Bring them to the priest, and he will sacrifice the offering for sin first. He will break the bird's neck without pulling its head off. [9]He will sprinkle some of the blood from the offering for sin on the side of the altar, and the rest of the blood will be drained at the bottom of the altar. It is an offering for sin. [10]Then, following the proper procedures, he will sacrifice the second bird as a burnt offering. So the priest will make peace with the LORD for what you did wrong.

If You Cannot Afford Two Mourning Doves

[11]"But if you cannot afford two mourning doves or two pigeons, then bring eight cups of flour as an offering for the sin you committed. Never put olive oil on it or add incense to it, because it is an offering for sin. [12]Bring it to the priest. The priest will take a handful of it. He will burn it as a reminder on top of the offering by fire to the LORD on the altar. It is an offering for sin. [13]So the priest will make peace with the LORD for what you did wrong, and you will be forgiven. The offering will belong to the priest like the grain offering."

For Unintentional Wrongdoing Against the LORD's Property

Honesty
Leviticus 5:1

If you saw a friend break a window, would you tell on her to the police? What if you saw a fight at school, and the principal asked you to tell what really happened? No one wants to tattle on friends. But it is important to tell the truth when you are asked.

[14]The LORD spoke to Moses, [15]"If any of you fail to do your duty by unintentionally doing something wrong with any of the LORD's holy things, bring a guilt offering to the LORD. It must be a ram that has no defects or its value in silver weighed according to the official standards of the holy place. [16]Pay for whatever holy things you used plus one-fifth more. Give it to the priest. So the priest will use the ram sacrificed for the guilt offering to make peace with the LORD for what you did wrong, and you will be forgiven.

For Unintentionally Disobeying the LORD's Commands

[17]"If any of you do wrong—even one thing forbidden by any of the LORD's commands, but you didn't know it—when you realize your guilt, you must be punished. [18]You must bring the priest a ram that has no defects from the flock or its value in money for a guilt offering. The priest will make peace with the LORD for the wrong you did unintentionally (although you didn't know what you did), and you will be

forgiven. [19]It is a guilt offering because you are certainly guilty as far as the LORD is concerned."

For Sins Against the LORD's People

[a1]The LORD spoke to Moses, [2]"If any of you sin against the LORD by failing to do your duty, if you lie to your neighbor about something you were supposed to take care of or if you lie about something stolen or seized from your neighbor, you are sinning and will be guilty. [3]If you find something that someone lost and lie about it under oath, or commit any other sin like this, [4]you are sinning and will be guilty. Return what you stole or seized, what you were supposed to take care of, the lost item you found, [5]or whatever it was that you swore falsely about. Pay it back in full plus one-fifth more. Give it back to its owner on the day you bring your guilt offering. [6]Then bring the LORD your guilt offering, a ram that has no defects or its value in money. Bring it to the priest. [7]So the priest will make peace with the LORD. Then you will be forgiven for whatever you did that made you guilty."

Instructions for Taking Care of the Fire

[8]The LORD spoke to Moses, [9]"Command Aaron and his sons: These are the instructions for the burnt offering that stays on the altar overnight while the altar fire is kept burning.

[10]"The priest must put on his linen clothes, including his linen undergarments. Then he will remove the ashes left on the altar from the fire that consumed the burnt offering and will put them next to the altar. [11]Then he will take off these clothes and put on some others. He will take the ashes to a clean place outside the camp. [12]The fire must always be burning on the altar. It must never go out. The priest will burn wood on it every morning. He will lay the burnt offering on the fire and burn the fat of the fellowship offering. [13]The fire must always be burning on the altar. It must never go out.

The Grain Offering From the People

[14]"These are the instructions for the grain offering. Aaron's sons must bring it into the LORD's presence in front of the altar. [15]One of them will remove a handful of flour from the grain offering, together with the olive oil and all the incense. He will burn it on the altar as a reminder. It is a soothing aroma to the LORD. [16]Aaron and his sons will eat the rest of it. They will eat unleavened bread in a holy place, in the courtyard of the tent of meeting. [17]Don't use yeast in baking the bread. I have given it to them as their share from the offerings by fire made to me. It is very holy like the offering for sin and the guilt offering. [18]Every male descendant of Aaron may eat it. It is a permanent law for generations to come regarding the offering by fire to the LORD. Everyone who touches it will become holy."

Special Grain Offerings From the Priests

[19]The LORD spoke to Moses, [20]"This is the offering that Aaron and his sons must bring to the LORD on the day he is anointed—eight cups of flour. They must do this every day. He must offer half of it in the morning and half in the evening. [21]Prepare it in a frying pan with olive oil, mixing it well. Offer baked pieces of the grain offering as a soothing aroma to the LORD. [22]Aaron's son who is anointed to take his place as priest will prepare it. This is a permanent law of the LORD: It must be completely

[a]6:1 Leviticus 6:1-30 in English Bibles is Leviticus 5:20–6:23 in the Hebrew Bible.

burned. [23]Every grain offering made by a priest must be completely burned. It must not be eaten."

Instructions for the Offering for Sin

[24]The Lord spoke to Moses, [25]"Tell Aaron and his sons: These are the instructions for the offering for sin. The offering for sin must be slaughtered in the Lord's presence in the same place where the burnt offering is slaughtered. It is very holy. [26]The priest who makes the offering for sin will eat it in a holy place, in the courtyard of the tent of meeting. [27]Anything that touches its meat will be holy. If blood gets on someone's clothes, he must wash them in a holy place. [28]Any piece of pottery in which the offering for sin is cooked must be broken into pieces. Any copper kettle in which the offering for sin is cooked must be scoured and rinsed with water. [29]Any male among the priests may eat the offering for sin. It is very holy. [30]Any offering for sin must not be eaten if some of the blood was brought into the holy place in the tent of meeting to make peace with the Lord. It must be burned."

Instructions for the Guilt Offering

[1]The Lord continued, "These are the instructions for the guilt offering. It is very holy. [2]It must be slaughtered in the same place where the burnt offering is slaughtered. A priest will throw the blood against the altar on all sides. [3]He will offer all the fat, the fat from the tail, the fat covering the internal organs, [4]and the two kidneys with the fat on them. He will also remove the lobe of the liver along with the kidneys. [5]The priest will burn them on the altar. It is a guilt offering by fire to the Lord. [6]Any male among the priests may eat it. It will be eaten in a holy place. It is very holy.

[7]"The same instructions apply to the offering for sin and the guilt offering. Both offerings belong to the priest to make peace with the Lord. [8]The skin of the burnt offering belongs to the priest who sacrifices it. [9]Every grain offering, whether baked in an oven or prepared in a skillet or a frying pan, belongs to the priest who offers it. [10]Every grain offering, whether mixed with olive oil or dry, will be shared equally by all of Aaron's sons.

Instructions for the Fellowship Offering of Thanksgiving

[11]"These are the instructions for the fellowship offering that you must bring to the Lord. [12]If you offer it as a thank offering, you must also bring rings of unleavened bread mixed with olive oil, wafers of unleavened bread brushed with olive oil, and loaves made from flour mixed well with olive oil. [13]In addition to these rings of bread, you must bring bread with yeast along with your fellowship offering of thanksgiving. [14]From every offering you must bring one loaf to the Lord as a special contribution. It will belong to the priest who throws the blood of the fellowship offering.

[15]"The meat from your fellowship offering of thanksgiving must be eaten on the day it is offered. Never leave any of it until morning.

Instructions for Other Fellowship Offerings

[16]"If your sacrificial offering is something you vowed or a freewill offering, it must be eaten the day you offer it or the next day. [17]However, on the third day any meat left over from the sacrifice must be burned. [18]You will not be accepted if any meat from the fellowship offering is eaten on the third day. You will not receive credit for it. It is repulsive to God. The person who eats any of it must be punished.

[19]"Meat that touches anything unclean must not be eaten. It must be burned.

Anyone who is clean may eat from these sacrifices. [20]Those who eat meat from the LORD's fellowship offering while unclean must be excluded from the people. [21]Those who touch anything unclean, human or animal, or any other disgusting uncleanness and still eat the LORD's fellowship offering must be excluded from the people."

No Fat or Blood May Be Eaten

[22]The LORD spoke to Moses, [23]"Tell the Israelites: Never eat any fat from bulls, sheep, or goats. [24]The fat from an animal that dies naturally or is killed by wild animals you may use for any other purpose, but you must never eat it. [25]Those who eat the fat from an animal which they sacrificed by fire to the LORD must be excluded from the people.

[26]"Never eat the blood of any bird or animal no matter where you live. [27]Those who eat any blood must be excluded from the people."

Dividing the Fellowship Offering Between the People and the Priests

[28]The LORD spoke to Moses, [29]"Tell the Israelites: Anyone who offers the LORD a fellowship offering must bring a part of that sacrifice as a gift to the LORD. [30]Bring the sacrifices by fire made to the LORD yourself. Bring the fat with the breast. Take the breast and present it to the LORD.

[31]"The priest will burn the fat on the altar. However, the breast will belong to Aaron and his sons. [32]You will also give the priest the right thigh as a contribution. [33]When any of Aaron's sons offer the blood and fat of the fellowship offering, the right thigh will belong to him as his share. [34]From the fellowship offerings of the Israelites, I have taken the breast that was presented to me, and the thigh from the contribution offering. I have given them to the priest Aaron and his sons. This is a permanent law for generations to come.

[35]"This is the share for Aaron and his sons from the sacrifices by fire made to the LORD. It was given to them on the day Moses ordained them to serve the LORD as priests. [36]The LORD commanded the Israelites to give it to them on the day he anointed them. This is a permanent law for generations to come."

Summary of Offerings

[37]These are the instructions for the burnt offering, the grain offering, the offering for sin, the guilt offering, the ordination offering, and the fellowship offering. [38]On Mount Sinai the LORD gave Moses commands about these offerings at the same time that he commanded the Israelites to bring their offerings to him in the Sinai Desert.

Aaron and His Sons Made Priests—
Exodus 29:1-45

[1]The LORD spoke to Moses, [2]"Take Aaron and his sons, the priests' clothes, the anointing oil, the bull that will be the offering for sin, the two rams, and the basket of unleavened bread. [3]Gather the whole congregation at the entrance to the tent of meeting."

[4]Moses did as the LORD commanded him, and the congregation gathered at the entrance to the tent of meeting. [5]Moses told the congregation, "The LORD has commanded that this is what you must do."

[6]Moses had Aaron and his sons come forward, and he washed them. [7]He put the linen robe on Aaron and fastened the belt around him. He also dressed him in the

robe that is worn with the ephod.[a] He fastened the ephod to it. [8]Then he put the breastplate on him, and into it he placed the Urim and Thummim.[b] [9]He put the turban on him and fastened the gold medallion (the holy crown) to the front of the turban as the Lord had commanded Moses.

[10]Moses took the anointing oil to anoint the tent and everything in it and dedicate them. [11]He sprinkled some of the oil on the altar seven times and anointed the altar, all the utensils, and the basin with its stand to dedicate them.

[12]He also poured some of the anointing oil on Aaron's head and anointed him to set him apart for his holy duties.

[13]Moses had Aaron's sons come forward. He put linen robes on them, fastened their belts around them, and put turbans on them as the Lord had commanded Moses.

[14]He brought the bull that was the offering for sin. Aaron and his sons placed their hands on its head. [15]When it was slaughtered, Moses took the blood and put it on the horns of the altar all around with his finger and cleansed the altar from sins. He poured the rest of the blood at the bottom of the altar and declared it holy so that priests could use it to make peace with the Lord. [16]Moses took all the fat that was on the internal organs, the lobe of the liver, and the two kidneys with their fat, and he burned them on the altar. [17]He burned the rest of the bull, its skin, meat, and excrement outside the camp, as the Lord commanded him.

[18]He brought forward the ram for the burnt offering. Aaron and his sons placed their hands on the ram's head. [19]Moses slaughtered it and threw the blood against the altar on all sides. [20]When the ram was cut into pieces, Moses burned the head with the other pieces and the fat. [21]He washed the internal organs and the legs. Then Moses burned the whole ram on the altar as the Lord commanded him. It was a burnt offering, a soothing aroma, an offering by fire to the Lord.

[22]He brought forward the second ram for the ordination offering. Aaron and his sons placed their hands on the ram's head. [23]Moses slaughtered it, took some of the blood, and put it on Aaron's right ear lobe, on his right thumb, and on the big toe of his right foot. [24]Moses also brought Aaron's sons forward. He put some of the blood on their right ear lobes, on their right thumbs, and on the big toes of their right feet. Moses threw the rest of the blood against all the sides of the altar. [25]He took the fat, the fat from the tail, all the fat on the internal organs, the lobe of the liver, the two kidneys with their fat, and the right thigh. [26]He took a loaf of unleavened bread, a ring of bread made with olive oil, and a wafer from the basket of unleavened bread which was in the Lord's presence. He put them on the fat and the right thigh. [27]Then he placed all these things in the hands of Aaron and his sons. Moses presented all these things to the Lord as an offering. [28]Then he took them from their hands and burned them on top of the burnt offering on the altar. These were ordination offerings, offerings by fire, a soothing aroma to the Lord. [29]Moses also took the breast from the ram of the ordination offering and presented it to the Lord. It was Moses' share, as the Lord had commanded.

[30]Moses took some of the anointing oil and some of the blood that was on the altar, sprinkled it on Aaron and his clothes and on his sons and their clothes. In this way he dedicated Aaron, his clothes, his sons, and their clothes.

[31]Moses told Aaron and his sons: "Cook the meat at the entrance to the tent of meeting. Take the meat and the bread in the basket of the ordination offering. Eat them there as I commanded when I said, 'Aaron and his sons will eat it.' [32]You must burn any meat or bread that is left over. [33]You will not leave the entrance to the tent

---

[a]8:7 *Ephod* is a technical term for part of the priest's clothes. Its exact usage and shape are unknown. [b]8:8 The Urim and Thummim were used by the chief priest to determine God's answer to questions.

of meeting for seven days, not until the last day of your ordination is over. It will take seven days to ordain you. ³⁴I did today what the LORD commanded me to make peace with the LORD for you. ³⁵You will stay at the entrance to the tent of meeting day and night for seven days and serve as the LORD tells you. Then you will not die. This is what I was commanded."

³⁶So Aaron and his sons did everything the LORD commanded through Moses.

Aaron's First Sacrifices

9 ¹On the eighth day Moses summoned Aaron and his sons and the leaders of Israel. ²He told Aaron, "Take a calf that has no defects for yourself as an offering for sin and a ram that has no defects as a burnt offering. Sacrifice them in the LORD's presence. ³Also tell the Israelites: 'Take a male goat as an offering for sin, a calf and a lamb (each one year old and without defects) as a burnt offering, ⁴a bull and a ram as a fellowship offering, and a grain offering mixed with olive oil to sacrifice in the LORD's presence. The LORD will appear to you today.' "

⁵So they took the things Moses commanded and brought them in front of the tent of meeting. The whole congregation came and stood in the LORD's presence. ⁶Moses said, "The LORD has commanded you to offer these sacrifices so that you may see the LORD's glory." ⁷Moses told Aaron, "Come to the altar and sacrifice an offering for sin and a burnt offering to make peace with the LORD for your sins and the sins of the people. Also make an offering for the people, to make peace with the LORD for them as the LORD commanded."

⁸Aaron came to the altar and slaughtered the calf as his own offering for sin. ⁹Aaron's sons brought him the blood. He dipped his finger in the blood and put it on the horns of the altar. Then he poured out the blood at the bottom of the altar. ¹⁰On the altar he burned the fat, kidneys, and lobe of the liver from the offering for sin as the LORD had commanded Moses. ¹¹He burned the meat and the skin outside the camp.

¹²He slaughtered the animal for the burnt offering. Aaron's sons gave him the blood, and he threw it against the altar on all sides. ¹³They also gave him the burnt offering, which was cut in pieces and included the head. He burned it on the altar. ¹⁴He washed the internal organs and the legs and laid them on top of the burnt offering on the altar.

¹⁵He brought the people's offerings. He took the male goat for the people's offering for sin and slaughtered it. He sacrificed it to take away sins as he had done before. ¹⁶Following the proper procedures, he brought forward the burnt offering and sacrificed it. ¹⁷He also brought the grain offering. He took a handful of grain and burned it on the altar in addition to the morning burnt offering. ¹⁸He slaughtered the bull and the ram for the people's fellowship offering. Aaron's sons gave him the blood, which he threw against the altar on all sides. ¹⁹However, the fat from the bull and the ram (the fat from the tail, the layer of fat, the kidneys, and the lobe of the liver) ²⁰they placed on the breasts. Aaron burned them all on the altar. ²¹However, he first took the breasts and the right thighs and presented them to the LORD as Moses commanded.

²²Then Aaron raised his hands toward the people and blessed them. He sacrificed the offering for sin, the burnt offering, and the fellowship offering. Then he came down from the altar. ²³Moses and Aaron went into the tent of meeting. When they came out, they blessed the people. Then the LORD's glory appeared to all the people. ²⁴Fire came out from the LORD's presence and consumed the burnt offering and the pieces of fat on the altar. When all the people saw this, they shouted and bowed with their faces touching the ground.

Improper Conduct for Priests

¹Aaron's sons Nadab and Abihu each took an incense burner and put burning coals and incense in it. Then in the LORD's presence they offered this unauthorized fire. ²A fire flashed from the LORD and burned them, and they died in the presence of the LORD.

³Moses said to Aaron, "This is exactly what the LORD said:

'I will show my holiness among those who come to me.
I will show my glory to all the people.' "

Aaron was speechless.

⁴Moses called Mishael and Elzaphan, the sons of Aaron's uncle, Uzziel. He told them, "Come and take your relatives away from in front of the holy place. Take them outside the camp." ⁵So they came and took them away to a place outside the camp, as Moses told them. The dead men were still in their linen robes.

⁶Moses told Aaron and his sons Eleazar and Ithamar: "Do not mourn by leaving your hair uncombed or tearing your clothes. If you do, you will die and the LORD will become angry with the whole congregation. All the other Israelites may cry over the fire the LORD sent, but you may not. ⁷You must not leave the entrance to the tent of meeting or else you, too, will die, because the LORD has anointed you with his oil." They obeyed Moses.

Proper Conduct for Priests

⁸The LORD spoke to Aaron, ⁹"You and your sons must not drink any wine or liquor when you go into the tent of meeting, or you will die. This is a permanent law for generations to come. ¹⁰Teach them the difference between what is holy and what is unholy, what is clean and what is unclean.ᵃ ¹¹Also teach the Israelites all the laws that I gave them through Moses."

¹²Moses told Aaron and his surviving sons Eleazar and Ithamar, "Take the grain offering left over from the offering by fire to the LORD. Make unleavened bread, and eat it next to the altar because it is very holy. ¹³Eat it in a holy place because it is the part of the offering by fire to the LORD that belongs to you and your children. That is the command I received. ¹⁴Also eat the breast presented to the LORD and the thigh that was given as a contribution. You and your sons and daughters may eat them in a clean place because they are your part of the fellowship offerings from the Israelites. ¹⁵They will bring the thigh given as a contribution, the breast presented to the LORD, and the fat that is to be burned and present them to the LORD. These parts will belong to you and your children. This will be a permanent law, as the LORD has commanded."

Eleazar and Ithamar Sacrifice the Offering for Sin

¹⁶Moses tried to find out what had happened to the male goat that was supposed to be the offering for sin. To his surprise, it had already been burned. So he became angry with Eleazar and Ithamar, Aaron's surviving sons. ¹⁷He asked them, "Why didn't you eat the offering for sin in the holy place? It is very holy and was given to you to take away the sins of the congregation and to make peace with the LORD for them. ¹⁸Since its blood was not brought inside the holy place, you certainly should have eaten it there, as I commanded."

¹⁹Aaron answered Moses, "Today they sacrificed their offering for sin and their

---

ᵃ 10:10 "Clean" refers to anything that is presentable to God. "Unclean" refers to anything that is not presentable to God.

Clean and Unclean Animals
Leviticus 11

Which of these animals wouldn't an Israelite woman cook? Leviticus 11 explains God's rules for eating animals. Some creatures were "unclean," and the people of Israel were not allowed to eat them. The animals weren't dirty or bad; God just wanted his people to remember that he was interested in their health and how they lived their daily lives. When you or your parents pray at meals, thank God for caring about your daily life, too.

burnt offering in the LORD's presence, and look what happened to me. If I had eaten the offering for sin today, would the LORD have approved?"

²⁰When Moses heard this, he was satisfied.

Laws About Animals the Israelites May and May Not Eat—
Deuteronomy 14:3-20

¹The LORD spoke to Moses and Aaron, ²"Tell the Israelites: Here are the kinds of land animals you may eat: ³all animals that have completely divided hoofs and that also chew their cud. ⁴However, from those that either chew their cud or have divided hoofs, these are the kinds you must never eat: You must never eat camels. (Camels are unclean because they chew their cud but do not have divided hoofs.) ⁵You must never eat rock badgers. (Rock badgers are unclean because they chew their cud but do not have divided hoofs.) ⁶You must never eat rabbits. (Rabbits are unclean because they chew their cud but do not have divided hoofs.) ⁷You must never eat pigs. (Because pigs have completely divided hoofs but do not chew their cud, they are also unclean.) ⁸Never eat the meat of these animals or touch their dead bodies. They are unclean for you.

⁹"Here are the kinds of creatures that live in the water which you may eat—anything in the seas and streams that has fins and scales. ¹⁰However, you must consider all swarming creatures living in the seas or the streams that have no fins or scales disgusting. ¹¹They must remain disgusting to you. Never eat their meat. Consider their dead bodies disgusting. ¹²Every creature in the water without fins or scales is disgusting to you.

¹³"Here are the kinds of birds you must consider disgusting and must not eat. They are eagles, bearded vultures, black vultures, ¹⁴kites, all types of buzzards, ¹⁵all types of crows, ¹⁶ostriches, nighthawks, seagulls, all types of falcons, ¹⁷little owls,

cormorants, great owls, [18]barn owls, pelicans, ospreys, [19]storks, all types of herons, hoopoes, and bats.

[20]"Every swarming, winged insect that walks across the ground like a four-legged animal is disgusting to you. [21]However, you may eat winged insects that swarm if they use their legs to hop on the ground. [22]You may eat any kind of locust, cricket, katydid, or grasshopper. [23]Every kind of winged insect that walks across the ground like a four-legged animal is disgusting to you.

[24]"Regarding the creatures mentioned above, this is how you would become unclean: Whoever touches their dead bodies will be unclean until evening. [25]Whoever carries any part of their dead bodies must wash his clothes. He will be unclean until evening. [26]All animals whose hoofs are not completely divided or that don't chew their cud are unclean for you. Whoever touches them is unclean. [27]All four-legged animals that walk on their paws are unclean for you. Whoever touches their dead bodies will be unclean until evening. [28]Those who carry the dead body of any of these animals must wash their clothes and will be unclean until evening. These animals are unclean for you.

[29]"The following swarming creatures that move on the ground are unclean for you—moles, mice, and all types of lizards: [30]geckos, monitors, lizards, skinks, and chameleons. [31]Among all the swarming creatures that move on the ground, these are unclean for you. Whoever touches their dead bodies will be unclean until evening. [32]When the dead body of one of these creatures falls on something, that thing will be unclean. It may be a wooden article, clothing, leather, a sack, or anything used for any purpose. It should be put in water and will be unclean until evening. Then it will be clean again.

[33]"If any of these creatures falls into a piece of pottery, break the pottery because everything in it is unclean. [34]If water from that pottery touches any food, the food is unclean. Any liquid that you drink from that pottery is unclean. [35]Anything on which their dead bodies fall is unclean. If it is an oven or a stove, smash it. It is unclean and will remain unclean for you. [36]However, a spring or a cistern holding water will remain clean. But anyone who touches their dead bodies will be unclean. [37]If their dead bodies fall on seed that is to be planted, the seed is clean. [38]But if water is poured on the seed and their dead bodies fall on it, the seed is unclean for you.

[39]"When any animal that you are allowed to eat dies, whoever touches its dead body will be unclean until evening. [40]Those who eat any of its dead body must wash their clothes and will be unclean until evening. Those who carry its dead body away will wash their clothes and will be unclean until evening.

[41]"Any creature that swarms on the ground is disgusting and must not be eaten. [42]Don't eat any creature with many legs that goes on its belly or on the ground like a four-legged animal, or any creature that swarms on the ground. Consider them disgusting. [43]Don't become disgusting by eating anything that swarms on the ground. Never allow yourselves to become unclean because of them.

[44]"Here is the reason: I am the LORD your God. You must live holy lives. Be holy because I am holy. Never become unclean by touching anything that swarms or crawls on the ground. [45]Here is the reason again: I am the LORD. I brought you out of Egypt to be your God. Be holy because I am holy.

[46]"These are the instructions about animals, birds, and every living creature that swims in the water and every creature that swarms on the ground. [47]These instructions help you distinguish between clean and unclean, the animals you may eat and those you may not eat."

Instructions for Women After Childbirth

¹The LORD spoke to Moses, ²"Tell the Israelites: When a woman gives birth to a boy, she will be unclean for seven days. This is the same number of days she is unclean for her monthly period. ³The boy must be circumcised when he is eight days old. ⁴Then she must stay at home for 33 days in order to be made clean from her bleeding. She must not touch anything holy or go into the holy place until the days needed to make her clean are over.

⁵"When a woman gives birth to a girl, she will be unclean as in her monthly period. However, she will be unclean for two weeks. Then she must stay at home for 66 days in order to be made clean from her bleeding.

⁶"When the days needed to make her clean are over, she must bring a one-year-old lamb for a burnt offering and a pigeon or a mourning dove as an offering for sin. She must bring them to the priest at the entrance to the tent of meeting. ⁷The priest will offer them in the LORD's presence to make peace with the LORD for her. Then she will be clean from her flow of blood.

"These are the instructions for the woman who gives birth to a boy or a girl. ⁸If she cannot afford a lamb, she must use two mourning doves or two pigeons. One will be the burnt offering and the other the offering for sin. So the priest will make peace with the LORD for her, and she will be clean."

Skin Diseases

¹The LORD spoke to Moses and Aaron, ²"If anyone has a sore, a rash, or an irritated area on his skin that turns into an infectious skin disease, he must be taken to the priest Aaron or to one of his sons who are also priests. ³The priest will examine the disease. If the hair in the diseased area has turned white, and the diseased area looks deeper than the rest of his skin, it is an infectious skin disease. When the priest has examined him, he must declare him unclean. ⁴But if the irritated area is white and does not look deeper than the rest of the skin, and the hair has not turned white, the priest must put him in isolation for seven days. ⁵On the seventh day the priest will examine him again. If the disease looks the same and has not spread, the priest must put him in isolation for another seven days. ⁶On the seventh day the priest will examine him again. If the diseased area has faded and not spread, the priest must declare him clean. It is only a rash. The person must wash his clothes and will be clean. ⁷But if the rash has spread after he has shown himself to the priest to be declared clean, he must show himself to the priest again. ⁸The priest will examine him one more time, and if the rash has spread, the priest must declare him unclean. It is an infectious skin disease.

⁹"If anyone has an infectious skin disease, he must be taken to the priest. ¹⁰The priest will examine him. If there is a white sore that has turned the hair white, and if there is raw flesh in the sore, ¹¹he has a chronic skin disease. Without putting him in isolation, the priest must declare him unclean because he is unclean. ¹²If skin disease develops and covers the whole person from head to foot (so far as the priest can see), ¹³the priest will examine him. If the disease does cover his whole body, the priest must declare the diseased person clean. His body has turned white. The person is clean. ¹⁴But if raw flesh appears, he will be unclean. ¹⁵The priest will examine the raw flesh and declare him unclean. The raw flesh is unclean. It is an infectious skin disease. ¹⁶But if the raw flesh turns white again, he must go to the priest. ¹⁷The priest will examine him again, and if the diseased area has turned white, the priest must declare the diseased person clean. He is clean.

¹⁸"If a boil on the skin has healed ¹⁹and in its place there is a white sore or a pink

area, it must be shown to the priest. ²⁰The priest will examine it. If it looks deeper than the rest of the skin and its hair has turned white, the priest must declare the person unclean. An infectious skin disease has developed in the boil. ²¹But if the priest examines the affected area and the hair in it is not white or the affected area is not deeper than the rest of the skin but has faded, the priest must put him in isolation for seven days. ²²If the area has spread, the priest must declare him unclean. It is a skin disease. ²³But if the irritated area has not spread, it is a scar caused by the boil. The priest must declare him clean.

²⁴"If anyone has a burn on his skin and the raw flesh of the burn turns into a pink or bright white area, ²⁵the priest will examine it. If the hair on the affected area has turned white and the affected area looks deeper than the rest of the skin, an infectious skin disease has developed in the burn. The priest must declare him unclean. It is an infectious skin disease. ²⁶But if the priest examines it and the hair in it is not white and the affected area is not deeper than the rest of the skin but has faded, the priest must put him in isolation for seven days. ²⁷On the seventh day the priest will examine him again. If the area has spread, the priest must declare him unclean. It is an infectious skin disease. ²⁸If the irritated area does not spread but has faded, it is only a sore caused by the burn. The priest must declare him clean, because it is a scar caused by the burn.

²⁹"If a man or a woman has some disease on the head or chin, ³⁰the priest will examine the disease. If it looks deeper than the rest of the skin and there is thin yellow hair on it, the priest must declare the person unclean. It is a scab, a disease on the head or the chin. ³¹But if the priest examines the scabby disease and it does not look deeper than the rest of the skin and there is no black hair in it, the priest must put the person with the scabby disease in isolation for seven days. ³²On the seventh day the priest will examine the disease. If the scab has not spread, there is no yellow hair on it, and the scab does not look deeper than the rest of the skin, ³³the person will shave everything except the scab. The priest will put the person with the scab in isolation for another seven days. ³⁴On the seventh day the priest will examine the scab again. If the scab has not spread on the skin and does not look deeper than the rest of the skin, the priest must declare him clean. When he has washed his clothes, he will be clean. ³⁵But if the scab spreads after the person has been declared clean, ³⁶the priest will make another examination. If the scab has spread on the skin, the priest does not have to look for yellow hair. The person is unclean. ³⁷But if he sees that the scab hasn't spread and black hair grows on it, the scab is healed. The person is clean, so the priest must declare him clean.

³⁸"If a man or a woman has white irritated areas of skin, ³⁹the priest will make an examination. If the irritated areas on the skin are pale white, a rash has developed on the skin. The person is clean.

⁴⁰"If a man loses his hair, he is clean, even though he is bald. ⁴¹If he loses the hair on the front of his head, he is clean, even though he is bald on the forehead. ⁴²But if there is a pink patch on the bald places in back or in front, a skin disease is developing in those places. ⁴³The priest will examine him. If the sore from the disease in the bald places in back or in front is pink like a skin disease somewhere else on the body, ⁴⁴the man has come down with an infectious skin disease. He is unclean. The priest must declare him unclean because of the skin disease on his head.

⁴⁵"People who come down with a skin disease must wear torn clothes and leave their hair uncombed. They must cover their upper lips and call out, 'Unclean, unclean!' ⁴⁶As long as they have the skin disease, they are unclean. They must live outside the camp.

Mildew in Clothing or Leather Articles

⁴⁷"Now about clothing—if there is a green or red area on a piece of clothing ⁴⁸that is woven or knitted from linen or wool or on any leather article, ⁴⁹it is mildew. It must be shown to the priest. ⁵⁰The priest will examine the mildew and will put the clothing in a separate place for seven days. ⁵¹On the seventh day he will examine the area again. If the spot is spreading, it is unclean. ⁵²He must burn the piece of clothing or the leather article because the mildew is growing. ⁵³But if the priest sees that the area has not spread, ⁵⁴he must order the area to be washed and put the clothing in a separate place for seven more days. ⁵⁵The priest will examine the area again after it is washed. If it doesn't look any different and the mildew has not spread, it is still unclean. It must be burned, whether the area is on the outside or the inside. ⁵⁶If the priest sees that the area is pale after washing, he will tear it out of the clothing or the leather. ⁵⁷However, if it shows up again, you must burn the clothing or the leather article. ⁵⁸But if the area disappears from the woven or knitted clothing or any leather article when it is washed, wash it again, and it will be clean.

⁵⁹"These are the instructions for deciding whether mildew in clothing that is woven or knitted from linen or wool or in any leather article is clean or unclean."

¹The Lord spoke to Moses, ²"These are the instructions for making a person clean after a skin disease. He must be taken to the priest. ³The priest will go outside the camp and examine him. If the person is healed, ⁴the priest will order someone to get two living, clean birds, some cedar wood, red yarn, and a hyssop sprig to use for the cleansing. ⁵Then the priest will order someone to kill one bird over a clay bowl containing fresh water. ⁶The priest will take the living bird, the cedar wood, the red yarn, and the hyssop sprig and dip them and the living bird in the blood of the bird that was killed over the fresh water. ⁷He will sprinkle the blood seven times on the one to be cleansed and will declare that person clean. Then he will let the living bird fly away into the open country.

⁸"The one to be cleansed must wash his clothes, shave off all his hair, and wash. Then he will be clean. After that he may go into the camp. However, for seven days he will live outside his tent. ⁹On the seventh day he must shave off all the hair on his head, his beard, and his eyebrows, and he must wash his clothes and body. Then he will be clean.

¹⁰"On the eighth day he must take two male lambs that have no defects and a one-year-old female lamb that has no defects. He must also take eight cups of flour mixed with olive oil for a grain offering along with a quart of olive oil. ¹¹The priest who will declare him clean must bring the person and his offerings into the Lord's presence at the entrance to the tent of meeting. ¹²The priest will take one of the male lambs and the quart of olive oil and present them to the Lord as a guilt offering. ¹³He will slaughter the lamb in the holy place where he slaughters the offering for sin and the burnt offering. He will do this because the guilt offering, like the offering for sin, belongs to the priest. It is very holy. ¹⁴Then the priest will take some of the blood from the guilt offering and put it on the right ear lobe, on the right thumb, and on the big toe of the right foot of the one to be cleansed. ¹⁵The priest will also take some of the olive oil and pour it into his own left hand. ¹⁶He will dip his right finger in the oil in his left hand, and with his finger sprinkle some of the oil seven times in the Lord's presence. ¹⁷The priest will put some of the oil that is still in his hand on the right ear lobe, on the right thumb, and on the big toe of the right foot of the one to be cleansed. These are the same places he had put the blood of the guilt offering. ¹⁸The priest will put

the rest of the oil in his hand on the head of the one to be cleansed. So he will make peace with the LORD for that person in the LORD's presence. [19]The priest will also sacrifice the offering for sin to make peace with the LORD for the one who is being cleansed from his impurity. After that, he will slaughter the burnt offering. [20]The priest will sacrifice the burnt offering and the grain offering on the altar. So the priest will make peace with the LORD for that person, and the person who had the skin disease will be clean.

Cleansing for a Poor Person After a Skin Disease

[21]"But if the one to be cleansed is poor and cannot afford that much, he must take one male lamb, present it to make peace with the LORD for himself, and use it for his guilt offering. He will take only eight cups of flour mixed with olive oil as a grain offering, a quart of olive oil, [22]and two mourning doves or two pigeons (whatever he can afford). The one will be an offering for sin and the other a burnt offering. [23]On the eighth day he will take them to the priest for his cleansing at the entrance to the tent of meeting in the LORD's presence. [24]The priest will take the lamb for the guilt offering and the quart of olive oil and present them to the LORD. [25]He will slaughter the lamb as a guilt offering. Then the priest will take some of the blood of the guilt offering and put it on the right ear lobe, on the right thumb, and on the big toe of the right foot of the one to be cleansed. [26]The priest will pour some of the olive oil into his own left hand. [27]With his right finger he will sprinkle some of the oil seven times in the LORD's presence. [28]The priest will put some of the oil that is in his hand on the right ear lobe, on the right thumb, and on the big toe of the right foot of the one to be cleansed. These are the same places he had put the blood of the guilt offering. [29]In the LORD's presence, the priest will pour the rest of the oil in his hand on the head of the one to be cleansed in order to make a payment for him. [30]Then the one to be cleansed must take one of the mourning doves or pigeons (whichever he can afford),[a] [31]and sacrifice it as an offering for sin. He will take the other and sacrifice it as a burnt offering together with the grain offering. So in the LORD's presence the priest will make peace with the LORD for the one who is being cleansed. [32]These are the instructions for one who has an infectious skin disease but cannot afford what is needed for his cleansing."

Mildew in Houses

[33]The LORD spoke to Moses and Aaron, [34]"When you come to Canaan that I am going to give to you, mildew may appear in a house. [35]The owner of that house must come and tell the priest that there is something that looks like mildew in his house.

[36]"Before the priest examines the house, he will order everything taken out of it so that nothing in the house will become unclean. Then the priest will go inside to examine the house. [37]He will examine the mildew area on the walls. If it is green and red in sunken areas that are deeper than the rest of the wall, [38]the priest will go out to the door of the house and close up the house for seven days. [39]On the seventh day the priest will go back and examine it again. If the mildew in the walls of the house has spread, [40]the priest must order the stones that have the mildew to be torn out and thrown outside the city in an unclean place. [41]He must have the entire inside of the house scraped. The plaster dust scraped off the walls must be dumped in an unclean place outside the city. [42]The stones must be replaced, and the house must be plastered again. [43]If the mildew develops again in the house after all this, [44]the priest

<hr>

[a]14:30 Greek, Syriac; Masoretic Text repeats "whichever he can afford."

will examine it one more time. If it is a spreading type of mildew, the house is unclean. ⁴⁵The house—stones, wood, and all the plaster—must be torn down and taken to an unclean place outside the city. ⁴⁶Whoever goes into the house any time it is closed up will be unclean until evening. ⁴⁷Whoever sleeps or eats in the house must wash his clothes. ⁴⁸But if the priest comes and makes an examination and the mildew has not spread in the house after it is plastered again, the priest must declare the house clean. The mildew is gone.

⁴⁹"The priest must take two birds, cedar wood, red yarn, and a hyssop sprig and use them to make the house clean. ⁵⁰He must kill the one bird over a clay bowl containing fresh water. ⁵¹He must take the cedar wood, the hyssop sprig, the red yarn, and the living bird and dip them in the fresh water containing the blood of the bird that was killed. He must sprinkle the house seven times. ⁵²So he must use the bird's blood, the fresh water, the living bird, the cedar wood, the hyssop, and the red yarn to make the house clean. ⁵³Then he will let the living bird fly from the city into the open country. He will make peace with the Lord for the house, and it will be clean.

⁵⁴"These are the instructions for any kind of mildew or fungus ⁵⁵that infects clothing or houses ⁵⁶and for skin diseases where there is a sore, a rash, or an irritated area. ⁵⁷These instructions for skin diseases and mildew help you distinguish between what is clean and what is unclean."

Bodily Discharges From Men

¹The Lord spoke to Moses and Aaron, ²"Tell the Israelites: If a man has a discharge from his penis, his discharge is unclean. ³He is unclean because of the discharge from his penis. Whether it is chronic or not makes no difference; he is still unclean.

⁴"The man who has a discharge makes everything he lies on or sits on unclean. ⁵Those who touch his bed must wash their clothes and their bodies. They will be unclean until evening. ⁶Those who sit on anything he sat on must wash their clothes and their bodies. They will be unclean until evening. ⁷Those who touch a man who has a discharge must wash their clothes and their bodies. They will be unclean until evening. ⁸If a man who has a discharge spits on anyone who is clean, the person he spits on must wash his clothes and his body. He will be unclean until evening. ⁹When a man who has a discharge sits on a saddle, it becomes unclean. ¹⁰Those who carry such things must wash their clothes and their bodies. They will be unclean until evening. ¹¹If a man who has a discharge touches anyone without first rinsing his hands, the person he touched must wash his clothes and his body. He will be unclean until evening. ¹²When a man who has a discharge touches pottery, it must be broken, and any wooden bucket he touches must be rinsed.

¹³"When a man's discharge stops, he must wait seven days to be cleansed. He must wash his clothes and his body in fresh water. Then he will be clean. ¹⁴On the eighth day he must take two mourning doves or two pigeons and come into the Lord's presence at the entrance to the tent of meeting. He will give these birds to the priest. ¹⁵The priest will sacrifice one as an offering for sin and the other as a burnt offering. So in the Lord's presence, the priest will make peace with the Lord for the man who had a discharge.

¹⁶"If a man has an emission of semen, he must bathe his whole body. He will be unclean until evening. ¹⁷Any clothes or any leather with semen on it must be washed. It will be unclean until evening.

¹⁸"When a man has sexual intercourse with a woman and has an emission of semen, they must wash themselves. They will be unclean until evening.

Bodily Discharges From Women

[19]"When a woman has her monthly period, she will be unclean for seven days. Those who touch her will be unclean until evening. [20]Everything she lies on or sits on during her period will be unclean. [21]Those who touch her bed must wash their clothes and their bodies. They will be unclean until evening. [22]Those who touch anything she sits on must wash their clothes and their bodies. They will be unclean until evening. [23]If her blood touches anything on the bed or anything she sits on, it will be unclean until evening. [24]If a man has sexual intercourse with her while she has her period, he will be unclean for seven days. Any bed he lies on will become unclean.

[25]"If a woman has a discharge of blood for many days other than her monthly period, she is unclean. If her period lasts longer than usual, she will be unclean as long as she has a discharge. It is like her period. [26]As long as she has a discharge, any bed she lies on or anything she sits on is unclean. It is like her period. [27]Those who touch these things are unclean and must wash their clothes and their bodies. They will be unclean until evening.

[28]"When her discharge stops, she must wait seven days. After that, she will be clean. [29]On the eighth day she must take two mourning doves or two pigeons and bring them to the priest at the entrance to the tent of meeting. [30]The priest will offer one as an offering for sin and the other as a burnt offering. So in the LORD's presence the priest will make peace with the LORD for the woman who had an unclean discharge.

[31]"You must separate the Israelites from anything that keeps them from being presentable to me. Otherwise, they will die because they make my tent, which is among them, unclean.

[32]"These are the instructions for any man who has a discharge or an emission of semen that makes him unclean, [33]for any woman who has her period, for any man or woman who has a discharge, or for any man who has sexual intercourse with a woman when she is unclean."

The Day for Making Peace With the LORD

[1]The LORD spoke to Moses after Aaron's two sons had come into the LORD's presence and died. [2]The LORD said, "Tell your brother Aaron that he cannot go into the holy place whenever he wants to. If he goes up to the canopy and stands in front of the throne of mercy on the ark, he will die, because I appear in the smoke above the throne of mercy.

[3]"This is what Aaron must do in order to come into the holy place: He must take a bull as an offering for sin and a ram as a burnt offering. [4]He must put on a holy linen robe and wear linen undergarments. He must wear a linen belt and turban. These are holy clothes. He must wash his body and put them on. [5]He will take two male goats from the congregation of Israel as an offering for sin and a ram as a burnt offering.

[6]"Aaron must sacrifice the bull as his own offering for sin. By doing this, he will make peace with the LORD for himself and his family. [7]He must take the two male goats and bring them into the LORD's presence at the entrance to the tent of meeting. [8]Then Aaron must throw lots for the two goats. One lot will be for the LORD and the other for Azazel.[a] [9]Aaron must sacrifice the goat chosen by lot for the LORD as an offering for sin. [10]But he must bring the goat chosen by lot for Azazel into the LORD's presence. He will release it in the desert to Azazel in order to make peace with the LORD for himself and his family.

[11]"Aaron will bring the bull. He will then slaughter it as his own offering for sin.

---

[a] 16:8 Unknown Hebrew term.

Day for Making Peace
Leviticus 16

Once a year, the high priest brought the blood of a sacrifice into the tent of meeting. He sprinkled the blood on the lid of the ark, called the "throne of mercy" (Leviticus 16:2). The blood paid for all the sins of the Israelites and made peace with God for another year. This special sacrifice reminds us of the sacrifice Jesus would later make when he died on the cross. Jesus' sacrifice ensures peace with God and paid once and for all for the sins of everyone who trusts him as Savior.

By doing this he will make peace with the Lord for himself and his family. [12]He will take an incense burner full of burning coals from the altar, which is in the Lord's presence, and two handfuls of finely ground, sweet-smelling incense. He will bring them up to the canopy. [13]Then he will put the incense on the fire in the Lord's presence. The cloud of incense will cover the throne of mercy, which is over the words of God's promise, so that he will not die. [14]He will take some of the bull's blood and sprinkle it with his finger on the east side of the throne of mercy. Then he will sprinkle some of the blood with his finger seven times in front of the throne of mercy.

[15]"Next, Aaron will slaughter the goat for the people's offering for sin. He will take the blood inside, go up to the canopy, and sprinkle it on the throne of mercy and in front of it, as he did with the bull's blood. [16]So he will make peace with the Lord for all the sins the Israelites committed against the holy place. These sins happened because the Israelites were unclean and because they committed rebellious acts. He will do the same for the tent of meeting which is among an unclean people. [17]No one may be in the tent of meeting from the time Aaron enters the holy place to do this until he comes out. Aaron will make peace with the Lord for his own sins, his family's sins, and the sins of the entire assembly of Israel. [18]Then he will go out to the altar that is in the Lord's presence and make peace with the Lord there for the sins committed. He will take some of the blood from the bull and some of the goat's blood and put it all around the horns of the altar. [19]With his finger he will sprinkle some of the blood on it seven times. Because the Israelites made it unclean, he will cleanse it and declare it holy.

[20]"When he finishes making peace with the Lord at the holy place, the tent of meeting, and the altar, he will bring the living goat forward. [21]Aaron will place both hands on its head. He will confess over it all the sins, all the rebellious acts, and all the things the Israelites did wrong. He will transfer them to the goat's head. A man will be appointed to release the goat in the desert. [22]The goat will take all their sins away to a deserted place. The man must release the goat in the desert.

²³"Then Aaron will go to the tent of meeting, take off the linen clothes he had put on to go into the holy place, and leave them there. ²⁴He will wash his body in the holy place and put on his other clothes. Then he will come out and sacrifice the burnt offering for himself and for the people to make peace with the Lord for his own sins and the sins of the people. ²⁵He will burn the fat of the offering for sin on the altar.

²⁶"The man who released the goat to Azazel must wash his clothes and his body. Then he may return to the camp. ²⁷He must take the bull and the goat outside the camp. These animals were the offering for sin whose blood was brought into the holy place to make peace with the Lord for sins. The skin, meat, and excrement from the animals must be burned. ²⁸Whoever burns them must wash his clothes and his body. Then he may return to the camp.

²⁹"This will be a permanent law for you: On the tenth day of the seventh month both native Israelites and foreigners must humble themselves. They must do no work. ³⁰On this day Aaron will make peace with the Lord to make you clean. Then you will be clean from all your sins in the Lord's presence. ³¹This is the most important worship festival there is for you. You will humble yourselves. It is a permanent law. ³²The priest who is anointed and ordained to serve as chief priest in his father's place will pay for sins. He will put on the holy linen clothes ³³and will make peace with the Lord at the holy place, the tent of meeting, and the altar. He will make peace with the Lord for the priests and all the worshipers.

³⁴"This permanent law tells you how to make peace with the Lord once a year for all the sins the Israelites committed."

Aaron did as the Lord had commanded Moses.

Eating Sacrifices

¹The Lord spoke to Moses, ²"Tell Aaron, his sons, and all the Israelites that this is what the Lord has commanded: ³Any Israelite who slaughters a bull, sheep, or goat inside or outside the camp ⁴is guilty of bloodshed. He has shed blood and must be excluded from the people. Bring the animal to the entrance of the tent of meeting. Offer it to the Lord in front of the Lord's tent. ⁵This means that the people of Israel must take the sacrifices they have been making in the open fields and bring them to the Lord. They must bring them to the priest at the entrance to the tent of meeting. The people will sacrifice them as fellowship offerings to the Lord. ⁶The priest will pour the blood against the Lord's altar at the entrance to the tent of meeting. He will burn the fat as a soothing aroma to the Lord. ⁷The people must stop sacrificing to goat idols and chasing after them as though they were prostitutes. This is a permanent law for the people and for future generations.

⁸"Tell them: If Israelites or foreigners make burnt offerings or sacrifices ⁹but do not bring them to the entrance of the tent of meeting to offer them to the Lord, they must be excluded from the people.

Eating Blood

¹⁰"If Israelites or foreigners eat any blood, I will condemn them and exclude them from the people, ¹¹because blood contains life. I have given this blood to you to make peace with me on the altar. Blood is needed to make peace with me. ¹²That is why I have said to the people of Israel: Neither you nor foreigners should ever eat blood.

¹³"If Israelites or foreigners hunt any animal or bird that may be eaten, they must pour out the animal's blood and cover it with dirt. ¹⁴This is because the life of any creature is in its blood. So I have said to the people of Israel: Never eat any blood,

because the life of any creature is in its blood. Whoever eats blood must be excluded from the people.

¹⁵"Native Israelites or foreigners who eat the body of an animal that dies naturally or is killed by another animal must wash their clothes and their bodies. They will be unclean until evening. Then they will be clean. ¹⁶If they don't wash their clothes and their bodies, they will be guilty of sin."

Forbidden Sexual Practices

18 ¹The LORD spoke to Moses, ²"Tell the Israelites: I am the LORD your God. ³You used to live in Egypt. Don't live the way the Egyptians do. I am bringing you to Canaan. Don't live the way the Canaanites do. Never live by their standards. ⁴Follow my rules, and live by my standards. I am the LORD your God. ⁵Live by my standards, and obey my rules. You will have life through them. I am the LORD.

⁶"Never have sexual intercourse with anyone related to you by blood. I am the LORD.

⁷"Never have sexual intercourse with your mother. She is your own mother. Never have sexual intercourse with her. ⁸Never have sexual intercourse with your stepmother. She is related to you through your father. ⁹Never have sexual intercourse with your stepsister, whether she is your father's daughter or your mother's daughter. It makes no difference whether or not she was born in your house. ¹⁰Never have sexual intercourse with your granddaughter, whether she is your son's daughter or your daughter's daughter, because she is related to you. ¹¹Never have sexual intercourse with a daughter of your father and his wife. She is your own sister. ¹²Never have sexual intercourse with your father's sister. She is your paternal aunt. ¹³Never have sexual intercourse with your mother's sister. She is your maternal aunt. ¹⁴Never have sexual intercourse with the wife of your father's brother. She, too, is your aunt. ¹⁵Never have sexual intercourse with your daughter-in-law. She is your son's wife. Never have sexual intercourse with her. ¹⁶Never have sexual intercourse with your sister-in-law. She is your brother's wife. ¹⁷Never have sexual intercourse with a woman and her daughter or a woman and her granddaughter. They are related. Doing this is perverted. ¹⁸While your wife is living, never marry her sister as a rival wife and have sexual intercourse with her.

¹⁹"Never have sexual intercourse with a woman while she is unclean during her

Abuse
Leviticus 18:6-9

What should you do if an adult touches you in inappropriate ways? What if he or she threatens to hurt you or someone else if you tell? First, ask God to help you to think of an adult you trust. Then tell that adult what happened. Tell that adult if you are afraid. Let the adult help you decide what to do next.

be all you can be

monthly period. [20]Never have sexual intercourse with your neighbor's wife and become unclean with her. [21]Never give your children as sacrifices to the god Molech by burning them alive. If you do, you are dishonoring the name of your God. I am the LORD. [22]Never have sexual intercourse with a man as with a woman. It is disgusting. [23]Never have sexual intercourse with any animal and become unclean with it. A woman must never offer herself to an animal for sexual intercourse. It is unnatural.

Punishment for Sexual Sins

[24]"Do not become unclean in any of these ways. By these practices all the nations which I am forcing out of your way have become unclean. [25]The land has become unclean. I will punish it for its sins. The land will vomit out those who live in it. [26]Live by my standards, and obey my rules. Neither you nor any foreigner should ever do any of these disgusting things. [27]The people of the land who were there before you did all these disgusting things. As a result, the land has become unclean. [28]If you make the land unclean, it will vomit you out as it has vomited out the people who were there before you. [29]Whoever does any of these disgusting things must be excluded from the people. [30]So you must follow my instructions. Don't live by the standards of the people who lived there before you. What they do is disgusting. Never become unclean that way. I am the LORD your God."

Duties of the People Toward God

19 [1]The LORD spoke to Moses, [2]"Tell the whole congregation of Israel: Be holy because I, the LORD your God, am holy.

[3]"Respect your mother and father. Observe my days of worship. I am the LORD your God.

[4]"Don't turn to worthless gods or cast metal idols. Never make any gods for yourselves. I am the LORD your God.

[5]"When you bring a fellowship offering to the LORD, sacrifice it properly so that you will be accepted. [6]Eat your sacrifice on the day you bring it and on the next day. On the third day burn whatever is left over. [7]If you eat any of it on the third day, it is repulsive and will not be accepted. [8]Those who eat it will be punished because they have dishonored what is holy to the LORD. They must be excluded from the people.

Duties of the People Toward Each Other

[9]"When you harvest the grain in your land, don't harvest the grain in the corners of your fields or gather what is left after you're finished. [10]Don't harvest your vineyard a second time or pick up fallen grapes. Leave them for poor people and foreigners. I am the LORD your God.

[11]"Never steal, lie, or deceive your neighbor.

[12]"Never swear by my name in order to deceive anyone. This dishonors the name of your God. I am the LORD.

[13]"Never oppress or rob your neighbor. Never keep the pay you owe a hired worker overnight. [14]Never curse deaf people or put anything in the way of blind people to make them stumble. Instead, fear your God. I am the LORD.

[15]"Don't be corrupt when administering justice. Never give special favors to poor people, and never show preference to important people. Judge your neighbor fairly. [16]Never gossip. Never endanger your neighbor's life. I am the LORD.

[17]"Never hate another Israelite. Be sure to correct your neighbor so that you will not be guilty of sinning along with him. [18]Never get revenge. Never hold a grudge

against any of your people. Instead, love your neighbor as you love yourself. I am the LORD.

Other Duties

¹⁹"Obey my laws. Never crossbreed different kinds of animals. Never plant two kinds of crops in your field. Never wear clothes made from two kinds of material.

²⁰"If a man has sexual intercourse with a female slave who is engaged to another man and if her freedom was never bought or given to her, they should not be put to death. He will only pay a fine because she is a slave. ²¹He must bring a ram for his guilt offering to the LORD at the entrance to the tent of meeting. ²²In the LORD's presence the priest will use them to make peace with the LORD for this sin. The man will be forgiven for this sin.

²³"When you come into the land and plant all kinds of fruit trees, you must not eat the fruit for the first three years. ²⁴In the fourth year all the fruit will be a holy offering of praise to the LORD. ²⁵In the fifth year you may eat the fruit. Do this to make the trees produce more for you. I am the LORD your God.

²⁶"Never eat any meat with blood still in it.

"Never cast evil spells, and never consult fortunetellers.

²⁷"Never shave the hair on your foreheads, and never cut the edges of your beard. ²⁸Never slash your body to mourn the dead, and never get a tattoo. I am the LORD.

²⁹"Never dishonor your daughter by making her a prostitute, or the country will turn to prostitution and be filled with people who are perverted.

³⁰"Observe my days of worship and respect my holy tent. I am the LORD.

³¹"Don't turn to psychics or mediums to get help. That will make you unclean. I am the LORD your God.

³²"Show respect to the elderly, and honor older people. In this way you show respect for your God. I am the LORD.

³³"Never mistreat a foreigner living in your land. ³⁴Foreigners living among you will be like your own people. Love them as you love yourself, because you were foreigners living in Egypt. I am the LORD your God.

³⁵"Don't be corrupt when administering justice concerning length, weight, or measuring liquid. ³⁶Use honest scales, honest weights, and honest measures. I am the LORD your God who brought you out of Egypt.

³⁷"Obey all my laws and all my rules, and live by them. I am the LORD."

Punishment for Serious Crimes

¹The LORD spoke to Moses, ²"Tell the Israelites: If Israelites or foreigners living among you give one of their children as a sacrifice to the god Molech, they must be put to death. The common people must stone them to death. ³I will condemn them and exclude them from the people. They gave one of their children to Molech, made my holy tent unclean, and dishonored my holy name. ⁴If the common people ignore those who give their children to Molech and do not put them to death, ⁵I will condemn them and their families. I will exclude them from the people. I will exclude from the people everyone who chases after Molech as if he were a prostitute.

⁶"I will condemn people who turn to mediums and psychics and chase after them as though they were prostitutes. I will exclude them from the people.

⁷"Live holy lives. Be holy because I am the LORD your God. ⁸Obey my laws, and live by them. I am the LORD who sets you apart as holy.

⁹"Whoever curses his father or mother must be put to death. He has cursed his father or mother and deserves to die.

¹⁰"If a man commits adultery with another man's wife or with his neighbor's wife, both he and the woman must be put to death for their adultery. ¹¹Whoever has sexual intercourse with his father's wife has violated his father's marriage. Both he and his father's wife must be put to death. They deserve to die. ¹²If a man has sexual intercourse with his daughter-in-law, both of them must be put to death. They have done a disgusting thing and deserve to die. ¹³When a man has sexual intercourse with another man as with a woman, both men are doing something disgusting and must be put to death. They deserve to die. ¹⁴When a man marries a woman and her mother, they have done a perverted thing. The man and the two women must be burned. Never do this perverted thing. ¹⁵A man who has sexual intercourse with an animal must be put to death. You must kill the animal, too. ¹⁶When a woman offers herself sexually to any animal, you must kill both the woman and the animal. They must be put to death. They deserve to die. ¹⁷Whoever takes his sister, his father's daughter, or his mother's daughter and has sexual intercourse does a shameful thing. They both must be publicly excluded from the people. He has had sexual intercourse with his sister and must be punished. ¹⁸If a man has sexual intercourse with a woman while she has her monthly period, both of them have had sexual intercourse in blood. They must be excluded from the people. ¹⁹Never have sexual intercourse with your mother's sister or your father's sister. Whoever has sexual intercourse with a close relative must be punished. ²⁰Whoever has sexual intercourse with his uncle's wife violates his uncle's marriage. That man and woman are guilty of sin. They will die without children. ²¹Whoever marries his brother's wife violates his brother's marriage and does an unclean thing. That man and woman will have no children.

²²"If you carefully obey all my laws and my rules, the land I am bringing you to live in will not vomit you out. ²³Never follow the practices of the people I am forcing out of your way. I cannot stand them because they did all these things. ²⁴I have told you that you will take their land. I will give it to you as your own. It is a land flowing with milk and honey. I am the Lord your God who separated you from other people. ²⁵Separate clean and unclean* animals and birds. Never become disgusting by eating any animal or bird or anything that crawls on the ground. I have separated you from every unclean thing. ²⁶Be my holy people because I, the Lord, am holy. I have separated you from other people to be my very own.

²⁷"Every man or woman who is a medium or a psychic must be put to death. They must be stoned to death because they deserve to die."

Holiness for All the Priests

¹The Lord spoke to Moses, "Tell the priests, Aaron's sons: None of you should become unclean by touching one of your relatives who has died. ²However, you are allowed to become unclean when one of your nearest relatives dies. These relatives include your mother, father, son, daughter, or brother, ³and especially an unmarried virgin sister who is still close to you. ⁴As the head of your people, you should never become unclean. That would make you unholy.

⁵"You should never mourn by shaving bald spots on your heads, shaving the edges of your beards, or slashing your bodies.

⁶"Be God's holy men, and don't dishonor the name of your God. Be holy because you bring sacrifices by fire to the Lord. It is the food of your God. ⁷You should never marry prostitutes, those who have lost their virginity, or divorced women because a priest is God's holy man. ⁸Be holy because you offer the food of your God. Be holy

---

*20:25 "Clean" refers to anything that is presentable to God. "Unclean" refers to anything that is not presentable to God.

because I, the Lord, am holy. I set you apart as holy. [9]When a priest's daughter dishonors herself by becoming a prostitute, she dishonors her father. She must be burned.

Holiness for the Chief Priest

[10]"The priest who is anointed with oil and wears the chief priest's clothes is chief over his brothers. He must never mourn by leaving his hair uncombed or by tearing his clothes. [11]He must never go near any dead bodies or become unclean, even for his father or mother. [12]He must not leave the holy tent of his God. If he does, he will be dishonoring it, because he is dedicated with the anointing oil of his God. I am the Lord.

[13]"The anointed priest must marry a virgin. [14]He must never marry a widow, a divorced woman, a woman who has lost her virginity, or a prostitute. He may only marry a virgin from his own people. [15]He must not dishonor his children among his people because I, the Lord, set him apart as holy."

[16]The Lord spoke to Moses, [17]"Tell Aaron: If any of your descendants (now or in future generations) has a physical defect, he must never bring food to offer to God. [18]Indeed, no one who has a physical defect may ever come near the altar . That means anyone who is blind or lame, who has a disfigured face, a deformity, [19]or a crippled hand or foot, [20]who is a hunchback or dwarf, who has defective sight, skin diseases, or crushed testicles. [21]If a descendant of the priest Aaron has a physical defect, he must never bring sacrifices by fire to the Lord. He has a defect. He must never bring food to offer to God. [22]He may eat the food of his God—what is holy and what is very holy. [23]However, he must never come up to the canopy or to the altar, since he has a physical defect. He must never dishonor the holy places because I, the Lord, set them apart as holy."

[24]So Moses spoke to Aaron and his sons and to all the Israelites.

Eating the Priests' Share of the Sacrifice

22 [1]The Lord spoke to Moses, [2]"Tell Aaron and his sons that they must respect the holy offerings which the Israelites set apart for me. In this way they will not dishonor my holy name. I am the Lord.

[3]"Tell them: In future generations if any of your descendants, while unclean, comes near the holy offerings the Israelites set apart for the Lord, that person must be excluded from my presence. I am the Lord.

[4]"No descendant of Aaron who has a skin disease or a discharge may eat any of the holy offerings until he is clean. Any person who has an emission of semen or touches a dead body, [5]an unclean swarming creature, or an unclean person [6]will be unclean until evening. He must not eat any of the holy offerings unless he has washed himself. [7]When the sun has set, he will be clean. Then he may eat the holy offerings because they are his food. [8]He must never eat the meat of an animal that dies naturally or is killed by wild animals. It will make him unclean. I am the Lord. [9]The priests must do what I order, or their sin will bring them death because they dishonored a holy offering. I am the Lord, who sets them apart as holy.

[10]"Laypeople must never eat any holy offering, even if they are visiting a priest or are working for him. [11]But if a priest buys a slave, the slave and anyone born in his household may eat the priest's food. [12]However, if a priest's daughter marries a layman, she must never eat the food taken from the holy contributions. [13]If a priest's daughter is widowed or divorced, doesn't have any children, and comes back to live in her father's home, she may eat her father's food. But a layperson must never eat it.

[14]"Those who eat a holy offering by mistake must give another holy offering to

the priest and add one-fifth more to it. ¹⁵Priests must not dishonor the holy offerings that the Israelites contribute to the LORD. ¹⁶They must make those people pay the penalty for their guilt because they have eaten the priests' holy offerings. I am the LORD, who sets them apart as holy."

Animals Accepted for Sacrifice

¹⁷The LORD spoke to Moses, ¹⁸"Tell Aaron, his sons, and all the Israelites: Israelites or foreigners may bring burnt offerings to the LORD for anything they vowed or as freewill offerings. ¹⁹The offering must be a male that has no defects from your cattle, sheep, or goats in order to be accepted. ²⁰Never bring any animal with a physical defect, because it will not be accepted on your behalf. ²¹A person may bring the LORD a fellowship offering to fulfill a vow or for a freewill offering. Whether it is from the cattle, sheep, or goats, it must be an animal that has no defects in order to be accepted. It must never be an animal that has defects. ²²Never bring the LORD an animal that is blind, has broken bones, cuts, warts, scabs, or ringworm. Never give the LORD any of these in a sacrifice by fire on the altar. ²³You may use a bull or a sheep with a deformity or one that is stunted in growth as a freewill offering. However, it will not be accepted for a vow. ²⁴Never bring the LORD an animal that has bruised, crushed, torn out, or cut out testicles. Never do any of these things to an animal in your land. ²⁵Never bring any kind of castrated animal received from a foreigner as a food offering for your God. A castrated animal will not be accepted on your behalf because castration is a physical defect."

²⁶The LORD spoke to Moses, ²⁷"When a calf, a lamb, or a goat is born, it must stay with its mother for seven days. From the eighth day on it may be accepted as a sacrifice by fire to the LORD. ²⁸Never slaughter a cow or a sheep and its young the same day.

²⁹"When you sacrifice a thank offering to the LORD, do it in the proper way. ³⁰Eat it the same day. Never leave any of it until morning. I am the LORD.

³¹"Carefully obey my commands. I am the LORD. ³²Never dishonor my holy name. I will show my holiness among the Israelites. I am the LORD, who sets you apart as holy. ³³I brought you out of Egypt to be your God. I am the LORD."

The Day of Worship

¹The LORD spoke to Moses, ²"Tell the Israelites: These are the appointed festivals with the LORD, which you must announce as holy assemblies. ³You may work for six days. But the seventh day is a day of worship, a day when you don't work, a holy assembly. Don't do any work. It is the LORD's day of worship wherever you live.

⁴"The following are the LORD's appointed festivals with holy assemblies, which you must announce at their appointed times.

The Spring Festivals

⁵"The fourteenth day of the first month, in the evening, is the LORD's Passover. ⁶The fifteenth day of this same month is the LORD's Festival of Unleavened Bread. For seven days you must eat unleavened bread. ⁷On the first day there will be a holy assembly. Don't do any regular work. ⁸Bring the LORD a sacrifice by fire for seven days. On the seventh day there will be a holy assembly. Don't do any regular work."

⁹The LORD spoke to Moses, ¹⁰"Tell the Israelites: When you come to the land I am going to give you and you harvest grain, bring the priest a bundle of the first grain you harvest. ¹¹He will present it to the LORD so that you will be accepted. He will

present it on the day after Passover. ¹²On the day you present the bundle, you must sacrifice a one-year-old male lamb that has no defects as a burnt offering to the LORD. ¹³Bring a grain offering of four quarts of flour mixed with olive oil with it. This will be a sacrifice by fire made to the LORD, a soothing aroma. Use one quart of wine for the wine offering. ¹⁴Don't eat bread, roasted grain, or fresh grain until this same day, when you bring the offering to your God. It is a permanent law for generations to come wherever you live.

¹⁵"Count seven full weeks from the day after Passover (the day you bring the bundle of grain as an offering presented to the LORD) ¹⁶until the day after the seventh week. This is a total of fifty days. Then bring a new grain offering to the LORD. ¹⁷Bring two loaves of bread from your homes to present to the LORD. Bake them with four quarts of flour. They are the first harvested grain for the LORD. ¹⁸With the bread bring seven one-year-old lambs that have no defects, one bull, and two rams. They will be a burnt offering to the LORD. With these offerings also bring grain and wine offerings. They will be a sacrifice by fire, a soothing aroma to the LORD. ¹⁹Also sacrifice one male goat as an offering for sin and two one-year-old lambs as a fellowship offering. ²⁰The priest must present them along with the bread of the first harvested grain as an offering to the LORD. All this, along with the two lambs, will be holy and will belong to the LORD's priests. ²¹Make an announcement that there will be a holy assembly on that same day. Don't do any regular work. It is a permanent law for generations to come wherever you live.

²²"When you harvest the grain in your land, don't harvest the grain in the corners of your fields or gather what is left after you're finished. Leave it for poor people and foreigners. I am the LORD your God."

The Fall Festivals

²³The LORD spoke to Moses, ²⁴"Tell the Israelites: On the first day of the seventh month hold a worship festival. It will be a memorial day, a holy assembly announced by the blowing of rams' horns. ²⁵Don't do any regular work. Bring a sacrifice by fire to the LORD."

²⁶The LORD spoke to Moses, ²⁷"In addition, the tenth day of this seventh month is a special day for the payment for sins. There will be a holy assembly. Humble yourselves, and bring the LORD a sacrifice by fire. ²⁸Don't do any work that day. It is a special day for the payment for sins. It is a time when you make peace with the LORD your

Good Morning, God
Leviticus 23:4

God told the Israelites to celebrate festivals on certain days like we celebrate Christmas and Easter. These occasions were more than just special days on the calendar. They were reminders of God's goodness to his people. How do holidays like Christmas and Easter remind you of God's blessings? Remember, you don't have to worship only on Sundays or special holidays. Jesus Christ is a reason to celebrate every day!

Father, thank you for special days when I can celebrate your goodness to me, and thank you for giving me a reason to celebrate every day—Jesus!

God. [29]Those who do not humble themselves on that day will be excluded from the people. [30]I will kill those who do any work on that day. [31]Don't do any work. It is a permanent law for generations to come wherever you live. [32]It is a day of worship, a day when you don't work. Humble yourselves starting on the evening of the ninth day of the month. From that evening to the next, observe the day of worship."

[33]The LORD spoke to Moses, [34]"Tell the Israelites: The fifteenth day of this seventh month is the Festival of Booths to the LORD. It will last seven days. [35]On the first day there will be a holy assembly. Don't do any regular work. [36]For seven consecutive days bring a sacrifice by fire to the LORD. On the eighth day there will be a holy assembly. Bring the LORD a sacrifice by fire. This is the last festival of the year. Don't do any regular work.

[37]"These are the LORD's appointed festivals. Announce them as holy assemblies for bringing sacrifices by fire to the LORD. Bring burnt offerings, grain offerings, other sacrifices, and wine offerings—each one on its special day. [38]This is in addition to the LORD's days of worship, your gifts, all your vows, and your freewill offerings to the LORD.

[39]"However, on the fifteenth day of the seventh month, when you have gathered what the land produces, celebrate the LORD's festival for seven days. The first and the eighth days will be worship festivals. [40]On the first day take the best fruits, palm branches, and the branches of leafy trees and poplars, and celebrate in the presence of the LORD your God for seven days. [41]It is the LORD's festival. Celebrate it for seven days each year. This is a permanent law for generations to come. Celebrate this festival in the seventh month. [42]Live in booths for seven days. Everyone born in Israel must live in booths [43]so that generations to come may learn how I made the people of Israel live in booths when I brought them out of Egypt. I am the LORD your God."

[44]So Moses told the Israelites about the LORD's appointed festivals.

Duties in the Tent of Meeting—
Exodus 27:20-21

[1]The LORD spoke to Moses, [2]"Command the Israelites to bring you pure, virgin olive oil for the lamp stand so that the lamps won't go out. [3]In the tent of meeting, outside the canopy where the words of my promise are, Aaron must keep the lamps lit in the LORD's presence from evening until morning. It is a permanent law for generations to come. [4]Aaron must keep the lamps on the pure gold lamp stand lit in the LORD's presence.

[5]"Also take flour and bake twelve rings of bread. Each ring will contain four quarts of flour. [6]Put them in two stacks of six each on the gold table in the LORD's presence. [7]Lay pure incense on top of each stack. The incense on the bread will be a reminder, an offering by fire to the LORD. [8]Every day of worship a priest must arrange the bread in the LORD's presence. It is a continual reminder of my promise[a] to the Israelites. [9]The bread will belong to Aaron and his sons. They will eat it in a holy place. It is very holy, set apart from the LORD's offering by fire. This is a permanent law."

The Man Who Cursed the LORD's Name

[10]A man, whose mother was Shelomith (daughter of Dibri, from the tribe of Dan in Israel) and whose father was from Egypt, got into a quarrel with an Israelite in the camp. [11]The Israelite woman's son began cursing the LORD's name and treating it with contempt. So they brought him to Moses.[b] [12]They kept him in custody until the LORD told them what to do.

---

[a]24:8 Or "covenant." [b]24:11 Part of verse 11 (in Hebrew) has been placed in verse 10 to express the complex Hebrew paragraph structure more clearly in English.

¹³The LORD spoke to Moses, ¹⁴"The man who cursed ˌmy nameˌ must be taken outside the camp. All who heard him curse ˌmy nameˌ must lay their hands on his head. Then the whole congregation must stone him to death.

¹⁵"Also tell the Israelites: Those who treat their God with contempt will be punished for their sin. ¹⁶But those who curse the LORD's name must be put to death. The whole congregation must stone them to death. It makes no difference whether they are Israelites or foreigners. Whoever curses the LORD's name must die.

¹⁷"Whoever kills another person must be put to death. ¹⁸Whoever kills an animal must replace it, life for life. ¹⁹Whoever injures a neighbor must receive the same injury in return— ²⁰a broken bone for a broken bone, an eye for an eye, a tooth for a tooth. Whoever injures another person must receive the same injury in return. ²¹Whoever kills an animal must replace it. Whoever kills a person must be put to death. ²²The same rule applies to every one of you. It makes no difference whether you are a foreigner or an Israelite, because I am the LORD your God."

²³Moses spoke to the people of Israel. So the man who had cursed the LORD's name was taken outside the camp. There they stoned him to death as the LORD commanded Moses. The Israelites did as the LORD commanded Moses.

The Year to Honor the LORD

¹The LORD spoke to Moses on Mount Sinai, ²"Tell the Israelites: When you come into the land I'm giving you, the land will celebrate a year to honor the LORD. ³Then, for six years you may plant crops in your fields, prune your vineyards, and gather what they produce. ⁴However, the seventh year will be a festival year for the land. It will be a year to honor the LORD. Don't plant crops in your fields or prune your vineyards. ⁵Don't harvest what grows by itself or harvest grapes from your vines. That year will be a festival for the land. ⁶Whatever the land produces during that year is for all of you to eat—for you, your male and female slaves, your hired workers, foreigners among you, ⁷your animals, and the wild animals in your land. Everything the land produces will be yours to eat.

The Jubilee for the Land

⁸"Count seven of these years seven times for a total of 49 years. ⁹On the tenth day of the seventh month, the special day for the payment for sin, sound rams' horns throughout the country. ¹⁰Set apart the fiftieth year as holy, and proclaim liberty to everyone living in the land. This is your jubilee year. Every slave will be freed in order to return to his property and to his family. ¹¹That fiftieth year will be your jubilee year. Don't plant or harvest what grows by itself or pick grapes from the vines in the land. ¹²The jubilee ˌyearˌ will be holy to you. You will eat what the field itself produces.

¹³"In this jubilee year every slave will be freed in order to return to his property. ¹⁴If you sell anything to your neighbor or buy anything from him, don't take advantage of him. ¹⁵When you buy property from your neighbor, take into account the number of years since the jubilee. Your neighbor must sell it to you taking into account the number of crops ˌuntil the next jubileeˌ. ¹⁶If there are still many years ˌuntil the jubileeˌ, you will pay more for it. If there are only a few years ˌuntil the jubileeˌ, you will pay less for it because he is selling you only the number of crops. ¹⁷Never take advantage of each other. Fear your God, because I am the LORD your God.

¹⁸"Obey my laws, and carefully follow my rules. Then you will live securely in the land. ¹⁹The land will give you its products, and you will eat all you want and live there securely. ²⁰You may ask, 'What will we eat in the seventh year if we do not plant or bring in our crops?' ²¹I will give you my blessing in the sixth year so that the land will

Women's World

Agriculture / *Leviticus 25*

Most people in ancient Israel lived on farms. These farms produced most of the food a family needed. A typical farm lay on a hillside. Stone walls kept the earth from washing away and created "terraces," a series of raised platforms of earth. Springs watered some of these terraces; other farms had ponds carved in the rock and plastered to hold rainwater. Vegetables grew on the irrigated terraces. Grain, grapes, figs, and olives grew on others.

The women worked hard all year. They helped with the olive harvest in September and October, the grain harvest in April and May, and the grape harvest in June and July. The women dried the grapes to make raisins and prepared all the family food. They made thread from wool or flax, wove the thread into cloth, and used the cloth to make all the family clothing. Women were partners with their husbands in running the farm and providing for their families.

---

produce enough for three years. ²²You will plant ⌐again⌐ in the eighth year but live on what the land already produced. You will eat it, even in the ninth year, until the land produces more.

²³"Land must never be sold permanently, because the land is mine. To me you are strangers without permanent homes. ²⁴People must always have the right to buy their property back. ²⁵If your brother becomes poor and sells some of his property, then the one who can assume responsibility, his nearest relative, must buy back what he sold. ²⁶If a man doesn't have anyone to buy it back for him, but if he prospers and earns enough to buy it back himself, ²⁷he must count the years from its sale. Then he will pay what is left to the man to whom he sold it, and it will be his property again. ²⁸However, if he cannot earn enough to buy it back, what he sold stays in the hands of the buyer until the year of jubilee. In the jubilee it will be released, and he will own it again.

²⁹"If anyone sells a home in a walled city, for one year after selling it he has the right to buy it back. He may buy it back only within that time. ³⁰If he does not buy it back during that year, the house in the city belongs to the buyer for generations to come. It will not be released in the jubilee. ³¹However, houses in villages without walls

are regarded as belonging to the fields of the land. They can be bought back. They will be released in the jubilee.

³²"The Levites always have the right to buy back their property in the cities they own. ³³If any Levite buys back a house, in the jubilee the purchased house in the city will be released, because the houses in the Levite cities are their property among the Israelites. ³⁴But a field that belongs to their cities must not be sold, because it is their permanent property.

The Jubilee for the People

³⁵"If an Israelite becomes poor and cannot support himself, help him. He must live with you as a stranger without a permanent home. ³⁶Don't collect interest or make any profit from him. Fear your God by respecting other Israelites' lives. ³⁷Never collect any kind of interest on your money or on the food you give them. ³⁸I am the LORD your God, who brought you out of Egypt to give you Canaan and to be your God.

³⁹"If an Israelite becomes poor and sells himself to you, don't work him like a slave. ⁴⁰He will be like a hired worker or a visitor to you. He may work with you until the year of jubilee. ⁴¹Then you will release him and his children to go back to their family and the property of their ancestors. ⁴²They are my servants. I brought them out of Egypt. They must never be sold as slaves. ⁴³Do not treat them harshly. Fear your God.

⁴⁴"You may have male and female slaves, but buy them from the nations around you. ⁴⁵You may also buy them from the foreigners living among you and from their families born in your country. They will be your property. ⁴⁶You may acquire them for yourselves and for your descendants as permanent property. You may work them as slaves. However, do not treat the Israelites harshly. They are your relatives.

⁴⁷"Someone who is a foreigner without a permanent home among you may become rich, and your relative living with him may be poor. The poor Israelite may sell himself to that foreigner or a member of his family. ⁴⁸After he has sold himself, he has the right to be bought back. One of his brothers may buy him back. ⁴⁹His uncle, his cousin, or some other relative could also buy him back. If he becomes rich, he could buy his own freedom. ⁵⁰Then he and his buyer must take into account the number of years from the year he was bought until the year of jubilee. His sale price will be adjusted based on the number of years he was with his buyer, like the wages of a hired worker. ⁵¹If there are many years left, he must refund from his purchase price an amount equal to those years. ⁵²If there are only a few years left until the year of jubilee, he must take them into account. He must refund from his purchase price an amount equal to those years. ⁵³During those years he should serve his buyer as a hired worker. His buyer should not treat him harshly. ⁵⁴If he cannot buy his freedom in these ways, he and his children will be released in the year of jubilee.

⁵⁵"The Israelites belong to me as servants. They are my servants. I brought them out of Egypt. I am the LORD your God."

God's Promises for Those Who Keep His Laws

26 ¹The LORD continued, "Never make worthless idols or set up a carved statue or a sacred stone for yourselves. Never cut figures in stone to worship them in your country, because I am the LORD your God. ²Observe my days of worship and respect my holy tent. I am the LORD.

³"This is what I will do if you will live by my laws and carefully obey my commands: ⁴"I will give you rain at the right time. The land will produce its crops, and the trees in the field will produce their fruit. ⁵Threshing*ᵃ* time will last until grape

---

ᵃ26:5 Threshing is the process of beating stalks to separate them from the grain.

gathering, and grape gathering will last until planting. You will eat all you want and live securely in your land.

⁶"I will bring peace to your land. You will lie down with no one to scare you. I will remove dangerous animals, and there will be no war in your land. ⁷You will chase your enemies, and you will defeat them. ⁸Five of you will chase a hundred of them, and a hundred of you will chase ten thousand of them. You will defeat your enemies, ⁹and I will be pleased with you. Your families will be large, and I will keep my promise*ᵇ* to you. ¹⁰You will clear out old food supplies to make room for new ones.

¹¹"I will put my tent among you, and I will never look at you with disgust. ¹²So I will live among you and be your God, and you will be my people. ¹³I am the Lord your God. I brought you out of Egypt so that you are no longer slaves of the Egyptians. I have broken their power over you and made you live as a free people.

God's Curses for Those Who Break His Laws

¹⁴"If you will not listen to me and obey all these commands, ¹⁵if you reject my laws and look at my rules with disgust, if you reject my promise by disobeying my commands, ¹⁶then this is what I will do to you: I will terrorize you with disease and fever. You will suffer from eye problems and depression. You will plant your crops and get nothing because your enemies will eat them. ¹⁷I will condemn you so that you will go down in defeat in front of your enemies. Those who hate you will be your rulers. You will run away even when no one is chasing you.

¹⁸"If you still will not listen to me, I will discipline you seven times for your sins. ¹⁹I will crush your arrogance. You will have no rain, and your land will be as hard as cement. ²⁰You will work hard for nothing because your land will produce no crops and the trees will produce no fruit.

²¹"If you resist and don't listen to me, I will increase the punishment for your sins seven times. ²²I will send wild animals among you. They will rob you of your children, destroy your cattle, and make you so few that your roads will be deserted.

²³"If this discipline does not help and you still resist, ²⁴then I, too, will resist you. I will punish you seven times for your sins. ²⁵I will bring war on you to get revenge for my promise that you rejected. When you gather in your cities, I will send plagues on you and you will fall under the control of your enemy. ²⁶I will destroy your food supply. Ten women will need only one oven to prepare your food. You will eat and go away hungry.

²⁷"If in spite of this you do not listen to me and still resist me, ²⁸I will fiercely resist you. I will discipline you seven times for your sins. ²⁹You will eat the bodies of your sons and daughters. ³⁰I will destroy your worship sites, cut down your incense altars, and pile your dead bodies on top of your dead idols. I will look at you with disgust. ³¹I will make your cities deserted and ruin your sacred places. I will no longer accept the soothing aroma from your sacrifices. ³²I will make your land so deserted that your enemies will be shocked as they settle in it. ³³I will scatter you among the nations. War will follow you. Your country will be in ruins. Your cities will be deserted.

³⁴"Then the land will enjoy its time to honor the Lord, while it lies deserted and you are in your enemies' land. Then the land will joyfully celebrate its time to honor the Lord. ³⁵All the days it lies deserted, it will celebrate the time to honor the Lord, it never celebrated while you lived there. ³⁶I will fill with despair those who are left in the land of their enemies. The sound of a windblown leaf will make them run. They will run away and fall, but no one will be chasing them. ³⁷They will stumble over each

---

ᵇ26:9 Or "covenant."

other, but no one will be after them. They will not be able to stand up to their enemies. ³⁸They will be destroyed among the nations. The land of their enemies will devour them. ³⁹Those who are left will waste away in the lands of their enemies because of their sins and the sins of their ancestors.

God Will Remember His Promise

⁴⁰"But if they confess their sins and the sins of their ancestors—the treacherous things they did to oppose me— ⁴¹I will oppose them and bring them into the lands of their enemies. Then, if they humble their uncircumcised hearts and accept their guilt, ⁴²I will remember my promise to Jacob, Isaac, and Abraham. I will also remember the land. ⁴³The land, abandoned by them, will enjoy its time to honor the LORD while it lies deserted without them. They must accept their guilt because they rejected my rules and looked at my laws with disgust. ⁴⁴Even when they are in the land of their enemies, I will not reject them or look at them with disgust. I will not reject or cancel my promise to them, because I am the LORD their God. ⁴⁵But for their sake, I will remember the promise to their ancestors. I brought them out of Egypt to be their God while nations looked on. I am the LORD."

⁴⁶These are the laws, rules, and instructions that the LORD gave to the Israelites through Moses on Mount Sinai.

Special Vows

27 ¹The LORD spoke to Moses, ²"Tell the Israelites: If any of you makes a special vow to give a person to the LORD, you may give money instead of the person. ³The amount you must give for a man from 20 to 60 years old is 20 ounces of silver. Use the standard weight of the holy place. ⁴If it is a woman, give 12 ounces. ⁵For a boy from 5 to 20 years old, give 8 ounces and for a girl give 4 ounces. ⁶For a boy from one month to five years old, give 2 ounces of silver and for a girl give about one ounce. ⁷For a man 60 years or over, give 6 ounces and for a woman give 4 ounces. ⁸But the person who is too poor to pay the required amount must stand in front of the priest. The priest will determine the amount based on what the person can afford.

⁹"If the vow is to give the kind of animal that people offer to the LORD, it will be considered holy. ¹⁰Don't exchange or substitute animals, a good one for a bad one or a bad one for a good one. If you do exchange one animal for another, then both animals will be holy. ¹¹If it is an unclean animal that cannot be brought to the LORD as an offering, bring it in front of the priest. ¹²The priest will determine what its value is. The value will be whatever the priest decides. ¹³If you want to buy it back, you must pay its full value plus one-fifth more.

¹⁴"If you give your house to the LORD as something holy, the priest will determine what its value is. The value will be whatever the priest decides. ¹⁵If you want to buy it back, you must pay its full value plus one-fifth more.

¹⁶"If a person gives part of a field to the LORD as something holy, its value will be based on the seed planted on it. Ground planted with 2 quarts of barley will be worth 20 ounces of silver. ¹⁷If you give your field in the jubilee year, it will have its full value. ¹⁸But if you give the field after the jubilee year, the priest will estimate its value based on the number of years left until the next jubilee year. ¹⁹If you want to buy it back, you must pay its full value plus one-fifth more. ²⁰But if you don't buy it back and it is sold to someone else, you cannot buy it back. ²¹When the field is released in the jubilee year, it will be holy like a field claimed by the LORD. It will become the property of the priest. ²²You may give a field you bought (not one that was a part of your family property) to the LORD as something holy. ²³The priest must figure out the field's value

until the jubilee year. You will pay its value on that day as something holy, belonging to the LORD. [24]In the jubilee year the field will go back to the person from whom it was bought, to whom it belongs as family property.

[25]"All values will be set using the standard weight of the holy place.[a]

[26]"A firstborn animal already belongs to the LORD because it was born first. Therefore, it cannot be set apart as holy. Whether it is a bull or a sheep, it belongs to the LORD. [27]But if it is an unclean animal, it must be bought back. The payment will be its full value plus one-fifth more. If it is not bought back, it must be sold at the value given it.

[28]"However, everything dedicated to the LORD for destruction—a person, an animal, or a field that belongs to you—must not be sold or bought back. Everything dedicated in that way is very holy. It belongs to the LORD. [29]People dedicated this way cannot be bought back. They must be put to death.

[30]"One-tenth of what comes from the land, whether grain or fruit, is holy and belongs to the LORD. [31]If you buy back any part of it, you must add one-fifth more to it. [32]Every tenth head of cattle or sheep that you counted is holy and belongs to the LORD. [33]You must not look to see if it is good or bad or exchange it. But if you do exchange it, both the first animal and its substitute will be holy. They cannot be bought back."

[34]These are the commands the LORD gave Moses on Mount Sinai for the Israelites.

---

[a]27:25 Hebrew adds "There are 20 gerahs to the standard shekel."

Numbers

This book gets its name from the two times that the Israelites were counted, or "numbered." The people were first counted right before they journeyed to the edge of Canaan, the land God had promised them. God wanted the people to enter the land and conquer it, but they were too afraid. So God made the people wander in the wilderness for 40 years. During those long years, the children of the people who disobeyed God learned to trust God. At the end of this book, after another numbering, the children were grown-up and ready to conquer Canaan.

Why was opposing Moses like opposing God? See Numbers 12.

Headlines

Women and Children Aren't Counted
Numbers 1, page 171

Women Promise to Eat No Raisins
Numbers 6, page 178

Moses Gets Under Miriam's Skin
Numbers 12, page 187

Spies See Giants!
Numbers 13, page 188

New Laws for Women to Inherit Land
Numbers 36, page 221

Be Glad to Be YOU

Miriam was a prophet who was really special. But she was jealous of her brother, Moses. Miriam wondered: *Why is Moses the leader?* God had chosen Moses to lead, and when Miriam rebelled, God confronted her. You can learn a lesson from Miriam. Instead of being jealous of what God gives others, be thankful and proud of the special gifts God has given you.

mind numb-ers

Why was the tent of meeting ill?

It smoked all day. (See Numbers 9:15.)

What bugged the spies who entered Canaan?

The Canaanites made them feel like grasshoppers. (See Numbers 13:33.)

What's got four legs, long ears, and is smarter than a pagan prophet?

Balaam's donkey. (See Numbers 22:33.)

Does God Favor Men?

When Miriam and Aaron criticized Moses, God gave Miriam a skin disease (Numbers 12:1-16). But God didn't give Aaron that disease. Did God favor Aaron because he was a man? The answer is "no." The only reason Aaron wasn't given a skin disease was because it would have stopped him from being high priest (see Leviticus 21:16-23). God healed Miriam, and she was able to continue being a prophet. God also let Aaron continue to be high priest. God forgave both and let each one continue being important. That's not favoring men at all.

What's In It For Me?

Numbers teaches me . . .

GOD BELONGS AT THE CENTER OF MY LIFE.

GOD INVITES ME TO ASK QUESTIONS—BUT NOT TO COMPLAIN.

WHEN I DISOBEY, THERE WILL BE CONSEQUENCES.

TRUST IN GOD GIVES ME COURAGE.

I CAN BE HAPPY WITH WHO I AM.

Numbers

Moses Takes a Census of Israel

1 ¹The Lord spoke to Moses in the tent of meeting in the Desert of Sinai. It was the first day of the second month in the second year after leaving Egypt. He said, ²"Take a census of the whole community of Israel by families and households. List every man by name ³who is at least 20 years old. You and Aaron must register everyone in Israel who is eligible for military duty. List them by divisions. ⁴One man from each tribe will help you. Each of these men must be the head of a household.

⁵"Here are the names of the men who will help you:
Elizur, son of Shedeur, from the tribe of Reuben;
⁶Shelumiel, son of Zurishaddai, from the tribe of Simeon;
⁷Nahshon, son of Amminadab, from the tribe of Judah;
⁸Nethanel, son of Zuar, from the tribe of Issachar;
⁹Eliab, son of Helon, from the tribe of Zebulun;
¹⁰Elishama, son of Ammihud, from the tribe of Ephraim;
Gamaliel, son of Pedahzur, from the tribe of Manasseh;
(Ephraim and Manasseh are Joseph's descendants.)
¹¹Abidan, son of Gideoni, from the tribe of Benjamin;
¹²Ahiezer, son of Ammishaddai, from the tribe of Dan;
¹³Pagiel, son of Ochran, from the tribe of Asher;
¹⁴Eliasaph, son of Deuel, from the tribe of Gad;
¹⁵Ahira, son of Enan, from the tribe of Naphtali."

¹⁶These were the men chosen from the community, the leaders of their ancestors' tribes, and heads of the divisions of Israel.

¹⁷Moses and Aaron took the men who had been named ¹⁸and assembled the whole community on the first day of the second month. Each man at least 20 years old provided his genealogy by family and household. Then his name was listed. ¹⁹So Moses registered the men of Israel in the Desert of Sinai as the LORD had commanded him.

²⁰The roster of families and households for the descendants of **Reuben**, Israel's firstborn son, listed every man by name who was at least 20 years old and eligible for military duty. ²¹The total for the tribe of Reuben was 46,500.

²²The roster of families and households for the descendants of **Simeon** registered and listed every man by name who was at least 20 years old and eligible for military duty. ²³The total for the tribe of Simeon was 59,300.

²⁴The roster of families and households for the descendants of **Gad** listed the men by name who were at least 20 years old and eligible for military duty. ²⁵The total for the tribe of Gad was 45,650.

²⁶The roster of families and households for the descendants of **Judah** listed the men by name who were at least 20 years old and eligible for military duty. ²⁷The total for the tribe of Judah was 74,600.

²⁸The roster of families and households for the descendants of **Issachar** listed the men by name who were at least 20 years old and eligible for military duty. ²⁹The total for the tribe of Issachar was 54,400.

³⁰The roster of families and households for the descendants of **Zebulun** listed the

men by name who were at least 20 years old and eligible for military duty. ³¹The total for the tribe of Zebulun was 57,400.

³²The roster of families and households for the descendants of **Joseph**—those from **Ephraim**—listed the men by name who were at least 20 years old and eligible for military duty. ³³The total for the tribe of Ephraim was 40,500.

³⁴The roster of families and households for the descendants of **Manasseh** listed the men by name who were at least 20 years old and eligible for military duty. ³⁵The total for the tribe of Manasseh was 32,200.

³⁶The roster of families and households for the descendants of **Benjamin** listed the men by name who were at least 20 years old and eligible for military duty. ³⁷The total for the tribe of Benjamin was 35,400.

³⁸The roster of families and households for the descendants of **Dan** listed the men by name who were at least 20 years old and eligible for military duty. ³⁹The total for the tribe of Dan was 62,700.

⁴⁰The roster of families and households for the descendants of **Asher** listed the men by name who were at least 20 years old and eligible for military duty. ⁴¹The total for the tribe of Asher was 41,500.

⁴²The roster of families and households for the descendants of **Naphtali** listed the men by name who were at least 20 years old and eligible for military duty. ⁴³The total for the tribe of Naphtali was 53,400.

⁴⁴Moses, Aaron, and the 12 leaders of Israel, each representing his own family, added up these totals. ⁴⁵So the Israelites were registered by households. The grand total of men who were at least 20 years old and eligible for military duty ⁴⁶was 603,550.

⁴⁷But the households from the tribe of **Levi** were not registered along with the other Israelites. ⁴⁸The LORD had said to Moses, ⁴⁹"Don't register the tribe of Levi or include them in the census with the other Israelites. ⁵⁰Put the Levites in charge of the tent of God's words, including the equipment for the tent and everything else having to do with the tent. The Levites will carry the tent and all its equipment. They will take care of the tent and camp around it. ⁵¹When the tent has to be moved, the Levites will take it down. When we camp, they will set it up. Anyone else who comes near the tent will be put to death.

⁵²"The other Israelites will camp with each family in its own area under its own flag. ⁵³The Levites will camp all around the tent of God's words. In this way the LORD won't be angry with the community of Israel. So the Levites will be in charge of the tent of God's words."

⁵⁴The Israelites did everything as the LORD commanded Moses.

The Arrangement of Israel's Camp

¹The LORD spoke to Moses and Aaron, ²"The Israelites will put up their tents with each family under the flag that symbolizes its household. They will put their tents around the tent of meeting, facing it.

³"On the east side, facing the rising sun, the armies led by **Judah** will camp under their flag. The leader for the people of Judah is Nahshon, son of Amminadab. ⁴The total number of men in his army is 74,600.

⁵"Next to them will be the tribe of **Issachar**. The leader for the people of Issachar is Nethanel, son of Zuar. ⁶The total number of men in his army is 54,400.

⁷"Then will be the tribe of **Zebulun**. The leader for the people of Zebulun is Eliab, son of Helon. ⁸The total number of men in his army is 57,400.

⁹"The grand total of all the troops in Judah's camp is 186,400. They will be the first group to move out.

¹⁰"On the south side the armies led by **Reuben** will camp under their flag. The leader for the people of Reuben is Elizur, son of Shedeur. ¹¹The total number of men in his army is 46,500.

¹²"Next to them will be the tribe of **Simeon**. The leader for the people of Simeon is Shelumiel, son of Zurishaddai. ¹³The total number of men in his army is 59,300.

¹⁴"Then will be, the tribe of **Gad**. The leader for the people of Gad is Eliasaph, son of Deuel. ¹⁵The total number of men in his army is 45,650.

¹⁶"The grand total of all the troops in Reuben's camp is 151,450. They will be the second group to move out.

¹⁷"When the tent of meeting is moved, the **Levites** will stay in the middle of the groups. The tribes will move out in the same order as they are in the camp, everyone in place under his own flag.

¹⁸"On the west side the armies led by **Ephraim** will camp under their flag. The leader for the people of Ephraim is Elishama, son of Ammihud. ¹⁹The total number of men in his army is 40,500.

²⁰"Next to them will be the tribe of **Manasseh**. The leader for the people of Manasseh is Gamaliel, son of Pedahzur. ²¹The total number of men in his army is 32,200.

²²"Then will be, the tribe of **Benjamin**. The leader for the people of Benjamin is Abidan, son of Gideoni. ²³The total number of men in his army is 35,400.

²⁴"The grand total of all the troops in Ephraim's camp is 108,100. They will be the third group to move out.

²⁵"On the north side the armies led by **Dan** will camp under their flag. The leader for the people of Dan is Ahiezer, son of Ammishaddai. ²⁶The total number of men in his army is 62,700.

²⁷"Next to them will be the tribe of **Asher**. The leader for the people of Asher is Pagiel, son of Ochran. ²⁸The total number of men in his army is 41,500.

²⁹"Then will be, the tribe of **Naphtali**. The leader for the people of Naphtali is Ahira, son of Enan. ³⁰The total number of men in his army is 53,400.

³¹"The grand total of all the men in Dan's camp is 157,600. They will be the last group to move out. They will travel under their own flag."

³²This is the total number of Israelites, counted by households. The grand total of all the troops in the camps was 603,550. ³³As the LORD had commanded Moses, the Levites were not registered along with the other Israelites.

³⁴So the Israelites did everything as the LORD had commanded Moses. They set up camp under their flags, and each person traveled with his own family and household.

Responsibility
Numbers 2:1-14

be all you can be

Everything was a mess. The Israelites were scattered all over the desert. God told Moses to help them get organized. Moses made a flag for each tribe to show where the people should camp.

In our world, sometimes bedrooms get messy. Why not try Moses' solution? Make flag labels to show where things go. And then put things where they belong.

The Tribe of Levi Is Registered and Assigned Duties

3 ¹This is the list of Aaron and Moses' descendants at the time when the LORD spoke to Moses on Mount Sinai. ²The names of Aaron's sons are Nadab (the firstborn), Abihu, Eleazar, and Ithamar. ³These are the names of Aaron's sons, the anointed priests, who were ordained to serve as priests. ⁴Nadab and Abihu died in the LORD's presence because they offered unauthorized fire in his presence in the Desert of Sinai. They had no children. So only Eleazar and Ithamar served as priests during the lifetime of their father Aaron.

⁵The LORD said to Moses, ⁶"Bring the tribe of Levi, and have them stand in front of the priest Aaron to assist him. ⁷They will work for him and the whole community in front of the tent of meeting, doing what needs to be done for the inner tent. ⁸They will take care of all the furnishings in the tent of meeting and work for the Israelites, doing what needs to be done for the inner tent. ⁹Give the Levites to Aaron and his sons. The Levites will be the only Israelites given to them. ¹⁰Appoint Aaron and his sons to serve as priests. Anyone else who tries to do the priests' duties must be put to death."

¹¹The LORD said to Moses, ¹²"Out of all the Israelites, I have taken the Levites to be substitutes for every firstborn male offspring among them. The Levites are mine, ¹³because every firstborn is mine. The day I killed every firstborn male in Egypt, I set apart as holy every firstborn in Israel, whether human or animal. They will be mine. I am the LORD."

¹⁴The LORD said to Moses in the Desert of Sinai, ¹⁵"Count the Levites by households and families. Count every male who is at least one month old." ¹⁶So Moses did what the LORD said and registered them as he had been commanded.

¹⁷Gershon, Kohath, and Merari were the sons of Levi.

¹⁸Libni and Shimei were the sons of Gershon. Their families were named after them.

¹⁹Amram, Izhar, Hebron, and Uzziel were the sons of Kohath. Their families were named after them.

²⁰Mahli and Mushi were the sons of Merari. Their families were named after them. These were the households of Levite families.

²¹To **Gershon** belonged the families descended from Libni and Shimei. These were the families descended from Gershon. ²²The total number of all the males at least one month old was 7,500. ²³The families descended from Gershon put up their tents on the west side behind the tent of meeting. ²⁴The leader of the Gershonite households was Eliasaph, son of Lael. ²⁵At the tent of meeting the Gershonites were in charge of the inner tent, the outer tent and cover, the screen for the entrance to the tent of meeting, ²⁶the curtains for the courtyard, the screen for the entrance to the courtyard that surrounds the inner tent and the altar, and the ropes. They took care of all these things.

²⁷To **Kohath** belonged the families descended from Amram, Izhar, Hebron, and Uzziel. These were the families descended from Kohath. ²⁸The number of all the males at least one month old was 8,600. They were in charge of the holy place. ²⁹The families descended from Kohath put up their tents on the south side of the tent of meeting. ³⁰The leader of the Kohathite families and households was Elizaphan, son of Uzziel. ³¹They were in charge of the ark, the table, the lamp stand, the altars, the utensils used in the holy place, and the screen. They took care of all these things.

³²The chief leader of the Levites was Eleazar, son of the priest Aaron. It was Eleazar's duty to supervise those who were in charge of the holy place.

³³To **Merari** belonged the families descended from Mahli and Mushi. These were

the families descended from Merari. [34]The total number of all the males at least one month old was 6,200. [35]The leader of the Merarite families and households was Zuriel, son of Abihail. They put up their tents on the north side of the tent of meeting. [36]It was the duty of the Merarites to be in charge of the framework of the inner tent, the crossbars, posts, sockets, and all the equipment. They took care of all these things. [37]They also took care of the posts for the surrounding courtyard, the bases, pegs, and ropes.

[38]Moses, Aaron, and his sons put up their tents on the east side in front of the tent of meeting. They were in charge of the holy place on behalf of the Israelites. Anyone else who tried to do the Levites' duties had to be put to death.

[39]The grand total of Levites that Moses and Aaron counted at the LORD's command, by families, every male who was at least one month old, was 22,000.

[40]The LORD said to Moses, "Register every firstborn male of the Israelites who is at least one month old, and make a list of their names. [41]I am the LORD. Take the Levites for me to be substitutes for all firstborn Israelites. Also take the animals of the Levites to be substitutes for all firstborn animals of the Israelites."

[42]So Moses registered all the firstborn Israelites as the LORD commanded him. [43]The total of all the firstborn males at least one month old was 22,273. They were listed by name.

[44]The LORD said to Moses, [45]"Take the Levites to be substitutes for all the firstborn Israelites and the animals of the Levites to be substitutes for their animals. The Levites will be mine. I am the LORD. [46]There are 273 more firstborn male Israelites than there are Levites. [47]It will cost you two ounces of silver per person (using the standard weight of the holy place) to buy them back. [48]Give the silver to Aaron and his sons. It will buy back those Israelites who outnumber the Levites."

[49]So Moses took this ransom money from the Israelites who outnumbered the Levites. [50]The silver Moses collected for the firstborn Israelites weighed 34 pounds using the standard weight of the holy place. [51]Then Moses did what the LORD said and gave Aaron and his sons this ransom money as he had been commanded.

The Duties of the Families Descended From Levi's Sons

[1]The LORD said to Moses and Aaron, [2]"Take a census of the Levites who are descended from Kohath. List them by families and households. [3]Register all the men between the ages of 30 and 50 who are qualified to work at the tent of meeting.

[4]"This is the work the Kohathites will do in the tent of meeting: They will take care of the most holy things. [5]When the camp is supposed to move, Aaron and his sons will go in and take down the canopy that hangs over the ark containing the words of God's promise. First they will cover the ark with the canopy. [6]Over this they will put a covering of fine leather.[a] On top of that they will spread a cloth made entirely of violet material. Then they will put the poles in place.

[7]"They will spread a violet cloth over the table of the presence and put on it the plates, dishes, bowls, and pitchers for the wine offerings. The bread that is always in the LORD's presence will also be on it. [8]They will spread a bright red cloth over everything on the table. They will cover all this with fine leather. Then they will put the poles in place.

[9]"They will take a violet cloth and cover the lamp stand, as well as the lamps, tongs, trays, and all the containers for the olive oil used in the lamps. [10]Then they will put the lamp stand and all its utensils under a covering of fine leather and put them on a frame to carry them.

---

[a] 4:6 Hebrew meaning uncertain.

¹¹"They will spread a violet cloth over the gold altar and cover the cloth with fine leather. Then they will put the poles in place. ¹²"They will take all the articles that are used in the holy place, put them in a violet cloth, cover that with fine leather, and put them on a frame to carry them.

¹³"After they take the ashes away, they will spread a purple cloth over the altar. ¹⁴Next, they will put all the accessories used at the altar on it. These are the trays, forks, shovels, and bowls—all the altar's accessories. They will spread a covering of fine leather over all this. Then they will put the poles in place.

¹⁵"When Aaron and his sons have finished covering the holy things and the camp is ready to move, the Kohathites will come to carry all the holy articles. They must never touch the holy things, or they will die. The Kohathites will carry all the things from the tent of meeting.

¹⁶"Eleazar, son of the priest Aaron, will be in charge of the oil for the lamps, the sweet-smelling incense, the daily grain offering, and the anointing oil. He is in charge of the whole tent and everything in it, the holy place and its contents."

¹⁷The LORD said to Moses and Aaron, ¹⁸"Don't let the Kohathite families from Levi's tribe be destroyed. ¹⁹This is what you must do so that they won't die when they come near the most holy things: Aaron and his sons will go into the holy place and tell each man what he will do and what he will carry. ²⁰But the Kohathites must not go in to look at the holy things, even for a moment, or they will die."

²¹The LORD said to Moses, ²²"Also take a census of the Gershonites. List them by households and families. ²³Register all the men between the ages of 30 and 50 who are qualified to serve at the tent of meeting.

²⁴"This is what the Gershonite families will do and what they will carry: ²⁵They will carry the sheets that are part of the inner tent and the tent of meeting. They will also carry the inner cover for the tent of meeting, the outer cover of fine leather that goes over it, the screen for the entrance to the tent of meeting, ²⁶the curtains for the courtyard around the tent and the altar, the screen for the entrance to the courtyard, the ropes, and all the equipment used to set up the curtains. The Gershonites will do everything that needs to be done with these things. ²⁷All their work, whatever they carry and all their duties, will be done under the direction of Aaron and his sons. You are in charge of telling them everything they're supposed to carry. ²⁸This is the work of the Gershonite families in the tent of meeting. Ithamar, son of the priest Aaron, will be in charge of them.

²⁹"Register the Merarites by families and households. ³⁰Register all the men between the ages of 30 and 50 who are qualified to serve at the tent of meeting. ³¹These are their duties as they work at the tent of meeting: They will carry the framework for the inner tent, the crossbars, posts, and sockets, ³²the posts for the surrounding courtyard, the bases, pegs, and ropes. They must take care of all this equipment. Tell each man by name the things he will carry. ³³This is what the Merarite families will do as they work at the tent of meeting. Ithamar, son of the priest Aaron, will be in charge of them."

³⁴Moses, Aaron, and the leaders of the community registered the Kohathites by their families and households. ³⁵They registered all the men between the ages of 30 and 50 who were qualified to work at the tent of meeting. ³⁶The total of those who were registered was 2,750. They were listed by families. ³⁷This was the total of all those in the Kohathite families who served at the tent of meeting. Moses and Aaron did as the LORD had commanded Moses and registered the Kohathites.

³⁸The Gershonites were registered by families and households. ³⁹All the men between the ages of 30 and 50 who were qualified to serve at the tent of meeting were

registered. [40]The total of those who were registered was 2,630. They were listed by families and households. [41]This was the total of all those in the Gershonite families who worked at the tent of meeting. Moses and Aaron did as the LORD had commanded Moses and registered the Gershonites.

[42]The Merarites were registered by families and households. [43]All the men between the ages of 30 and 50 who were qualified to serve at the tent of meeting were registered. [44]The total of all those who were registered was 3,200. They were listed by families. [45]This was the total of those registered in the Merarite families. Moses and Aaron did as the LORD had commanded Moses and registered the Merarites.

[46]The grand total of all the Levites whom Moses, Aaron, and the leaders of Israel registered was 8,580. They were listed by families and households. [47]These were the men between the ages of 30 and 50 who were qualified to do the work of serving and who carried the tent of meeting.[b] [49]At the LORD's command through Moses each man was registered and told what to do and what to carry.

So they were registered as the LORD commanded Moses.

Removing Unclean People From the Camp

[1]The LORD said to Moses, [2]"Command the Israelites to send outside the camp anyone who has a serious skin disease or a discharge or anyone who is unclean[a] from touching a dead body. [3]Send all of these unclean men and women outside the camp. They must not make this camp where I live among you unclean." [4]So the Israelites did as the LORD had told Moses. They sent these unclean people outside the camp.

Confessing and Paying for Sins

[5]The LORD said to Moses, [6]"Tell the Israelites: If you do something wrong to another person, you have been unfaithful to the LORD. When you realize your guilt, [7]you must confess your sin, pay in full for what you did wrong, add one-fifth to it, and give it to the person who was wronged. [8]But there may be no heir to whom the payment can be made. In that case, the payment for what you did wrong must be given to the LORD for the priest to use. This payment is in addition to the ram which makes peace with the LORD.

[9]"Any contribution over and above the holy offerings that the Israelites bring to the priest will belong to the priest. [10]Each person's holy offerings will belong to that person, but whatever is given to the priest will belong to the priest."

When a Husband Suspects That His Wife Has Been Unfaithful

[11]The LORD said to Moses: [12]"Speak to the Israelites and tell them: A man's wife may have been unfaithful to him [13]and may have had sexual intercourse with another man without her husband's knowledge. She may have kept it secret if there were no witnesses to accuse her and she wasn't caught in the act.

[14]"A husband may have a fit of jealousy and suspect his wife, whether she was actually unfaithful or not. [15]He must then take his wife to the priest along with eight cups of barley flour as an offering for her. He must not pour olive oil on the flour or put frankincense on it, since it is a grain offering brought because of the husband's jealousy, an offering used for a confession—to remind someone of a sin that was committed.

---

[b]4:47 Verse 48 (in Hebrew) has been placed in verse 46 to express the complex Hebrew sentence structure more clearly in English.   [a]5:2 "Unclean" refers to anything that is not presentable to God.

[16]"The priest will have the woman come forward and stand in the LORD's presence. [17]Then the priest will take holy water in a piece of pottery and put some dust from the floor of the tent into the water. [18]The priest will bring the woman into the LORD's presence and loosen her hair. In her hands he will put the offering used for a confession (that is, the grain offering brought because of the husband's jealousy). The priest will hold in his hands the bitter water that can bring a curse.[b]

[19]"Then the priest will say to her, 'If no other man has had sexual intercourse with you and you haven't been unfaithful to your husband, you're not guilty. This bitter water that can bring a curse will not harm you. [20]If, in fact, you have been unfaithful and have had sexual intercourse with another man, [21]may the LORD make you an example for your people to see what happens when the curse of this oath comes true: The LORD will make your uterus drop and your stomach swell.'[c]

"Then the priest will administer the oath and the curse by saying: [22]'May this water that can bring a curse go into your body and make your stomach swell and your uterus drop!'

"Then the woman will say, 'Amen, amen!'

[23]"The priest will write these curses on a scroll and wash them off into the bitter water. [24]Then he will have the woman drink the bitter water that can bring the curse. This water will go into her and become bitter. [25]The priest will take the grain offering she was holding, present it to the LORD, and bring it to the altar. [26]The priest will take a handful of the grain offering as a memorial portion and burn it on the altar. Then he will have the woman drink the water. [27]If she has become unclean by being unfaithful to her husband, the water that can bring the curse will go into her and become bitter. Her stomach will swell, her uterus will drop, and she will become cursed among her people. [28]But if the woman is not unclean and is pure, she is not guilty and will be able to have children.

[29]"These are the instructions for how to deal with jealousy. They tell you what to do when a woman is unfaithful to her husband and becomes unclean. [30]They also tell you what to do when a husband has a fit of jealousy and is suspicious of his wife. He will make his wife stand in the LORD's presence, and the priest will do everything these instructions tell him to do. [31]The husband isn't guilty of doing anything wrong, but the woman will suffer the consequences of her sin."

Taking a Special Vow

[1]The LORD said to Moses, [2]"Speak to the Israelites and tell them: A man or a woman may make a special vow to live as a Nazirite dedicated to the LORD. [3]Nazirites must never drink wine, liquor, vinegar made from wine or liquor, or any kind of grape juice, and they must never eat fresh grapes or raisins. [4]As long as they are Nazirites, they must never eat anything that comes from a grapevine, not even grape seeds or skins.

[5]"As long as they are under the Nazirite vow, no razor may touch their heads. During the entire time that they are dedicated to the LORD as Nazirites, they will be holy. They must let their hair grow long. [6]While they are dedicated to the LORD as Nazirites, they must never go near a dead body. [7]Even if their own father, mother, brother, or sister dies, they must not make themselves unclean[a] by going near them. Nazirites show their vow to God with their long hair. [8]As long as they are Nazirites, they will be holy to the LORD.

---

[b]5:18 In this verse and the following verses there is a play on words between the Hebrew words *hammarîm* (bitter) and *hame 'araîm* (that can bring a curse). [c]5:21 Or "make you have miscarriages and become sterile." [a]6:7 "Unclean" refers to anything that is not presentable to God.

⁹"Someone might suddenly drop dead next to a Nazirite and make the Nazirite's hair unclean. Seven days later he must shave his head in order to be declared clean.ᵇ ¹⁰On the eighth day he must bring two mourning doves or two young pigeons to the priest at the entrance to the tent of meeting. ¹¹The priest will sacrifice one as an offering for sin and the other one as a burnt offering. The priest will make peace with the LORD for the person who touched the dead body. That same day the person must dedicate his head again. ¹²Once again he will dedicate himself to the LORD as a Nazirite for the same length of time as before. He must bring a one-year-old male lamb as an offering for guilt. The first time period won't count. He has to start over from when he became unclean.

¹³"These are the instructions for Nazirites who complete their vows: They must come to the entrance of the tent of meeting. ¹⁴They must bring these offerings to the LORD: a one-year-old male lamb as a burnt offering, a one-year-old female lamb as an offering for sin, and a ram as a fellowship offering. All of these animals must have no defects. ¹⁵They must also bring a basket of unleavened bread containing some rings of bread made with olive oil and wafers of unleavened bread brushed with olive oil, along with other grain offerings and wine offerings.

¹⁶"The priest will bring these offerings to the LORD and make the offering for sin and the burnt offering. ¹⁷He will sacrifice the ram as a fellowship offering to the LORD, offer the basket of unleavened bread along with it, and make the grain offerings and wine offerings.

¹⁸"Then the Nazirites will shave their heads at the entrance to the tent of meeting, take the hair as proof that they had made this vow, and put it on the fire under the fellowship offering.

¹⁹"Then the priest will take one of the shoulders from a boiled ram, one ring of unleavened bread from the basket, and one wafer of unleavened bread and hand them to the Nazirites after they have shaved off their hair. ²⁰The priest will present them as an offering to the LORD. They are holy and belong to the priest, along with the ram's breast that is presented and the thigh that is given. After that, the Nazirites may drink wine.

²¹"These are the instructions for those who have vowed to bring their offerings to the LORD because they were Nazirites. They must bring these offerings in addition to anything else they can afford. They must fulfill the requirements of these instructions for Nazirites and finish whatever they vowed to do."

How Aaron and His Sons Will Bless the Israelites

²²The LORD said to Moses, ²³"Tell Aaron and his sons, 'This is how you will bless the Israelites. Say to them:

²⁴   The LORD will bless you and watch over you.
²⁵   The LORD will smile on you and be kind to you.
²⁶   The LORD will look on you with favor and give you peace.'

²⁷"So whenever they use my name to bless the Israelites, I will bless them."

Offerings for the Dedication of the Altar

¹When Moses finished setting up the tent, he anointed it and dedicated it and all the furnishings. He also anointed and dedicated the altar and all the utensils. ²Then the leaders of Israel, the heads of the households—those tribal leaders who helped

---

ᵇ 6:9 "Clean" refers to anything that is presentable to God.

in the census—came to give their offerings. ³They brought these gifts to the LORD:
six freight wagons and twelve oxen, one wagon from every two leaders and one ox
from each leader. They brought them in front of the tent.

⁴The LORD said to Moses, ⁵"Accept these gifts from them to use in the work done
for the tent of meeting. Give them to the Levites to use wherever they need these
gifts for their work." ⁶Moses took the wagons and the oxen and gave them to the
Levites. ⁷He gave two wagons and four oxen to the Gershonites for the work they
had to do. ⁸He gave four wagons and eight oxen to the Merarites for the work they
had to do under the direction of Ithamar, son of the priest Aaron. ⁹But Moses gave
none of these gifts to the Kohathites, because they took care of the holy things. They
had to carry the holy things on their own shoulders.

¹⁰The leaders also brought offerings for the dedication of the altar when it was
anointed. They presented their gifts in front of the altar. ¹¹The LORD said to Moses,
"Each day a different leader will bring his gift for the dedication of the altar."

¹²The one who brought his gifts on the first day was Nahshon, son of Amminadab,
from the tribe of **Judah**. ¹³He brought a silver plate that weighed 3¼ pounds and a
silver bowl that weighed 1¾ pounds using the standard weight of the holy place. Each
dish was filled with flour mixed with olive oil as a grain offering. ¹⁴He also brought a
gold dish that weighed 4 ounces, filled with incense; ¹⁵a young bull, a ram, and a one-
year-old male lamb as a burnt offering; ¹⁶a male goat as an offering for sin; ¹⁷and two
bulls, five rams, five male goats, and five one-year-old male lambs as a fellowship
offering. These were the gifts from Nahshon, son of Amminadab.

¹⁸On the second day Nethanel, son of Zuar, the leader from the tribe of **Issachar**,
brought his gifts. ¹⁹He brought a silver plate that weighed 3¼ pounds and a silver bowl
that weighed 1¾ pounds using the standard weight of the holy place. Each dish was
filled with flour mixed with olive oil as a grain offering. ²⁰He also brought a gold dish
that weighed 4 ounces, filled with incense; ²¹a young bull, a ram, and a one-year-old
male lamb as a burnt offering; ²²a male goat as an offering for sin; ²³and two bulls, five
rams, five male goats, and five one-year-old male lambs as a fellowship offering. These
were the gifts from Nethanel, son of Zuar.

²⁴On the third day the leader of the descendants of **Zebulun**, Eliab, son of Helon,
²⁵brought his gifts: a silver plate that weighed 3¼ pounds and a silver bowl that
weighed 1¾ pounds using the standard weight of the holy place. Each dish was filled
with flour mixed with olive oil as a grain offering. ²⁶He also brought a gold dish that
weighed 4 ounces, filled with incense; ²⁷a young bull, a ram, and a one-year-old male
lamb as a burnt offering; ²⁸a male goat as an offering for sin; ²⁹and two bulls, five rams,
five male goats, and five one-year-old male lambs as a fellowship offering. These were
the gifts from Eliab, son of Helon.

³⁰On the fourth day the leader of the descendants of **Reuben**, Elizur, son of Shedeur,
³¹brought his gifts: a silver plate that weighed 3¼ pounds and a silver bowl that
weighed 1¾ pounds using the standard weight of the holy place. Each dish was filled
with flour mixed with olive oil as a grain offering. ³²He also brought a gold dish that
weighed 4 ounces, filled with incense; ³³a young bull, a ram, and a one-year-old male
lamb as a burnt offering; ³⁴a male goat as an offering for sin; ³⁵and two bulls, five rams,
five male goats, and five one-year-old male lambs as a fellowship offering. These were
the gifts from Elizur, son of Shedeur.

³⁶On the fifth day the leader of the descendants of **Simeon**, Shelumiel, son of
Zurishaddai, ³⁷brought his gifts: a silver plate that weighed 3¼ pounds and a silver
bowl that weighed 1¾ pounds using the standard weight of the holy place. Each dish
was filled with flour mixed with olive oil as a grain offering. ³⁸He also brought a gold

dish that weighed 4 ounces, filled with incense; [39]a young bull, a ram, and a one-year-old male lamb as a burnt offering; [40]a male goat as an offering for sin; [41]and two bulls, five rams, five male goats, and five one-year-old male lambs as a fellowship offering. These were the gifts from Shelumiel, son of Zurishaddai.

[42]On the sixth day the leader of the descendants of **Gad**, Eliasaph, son of Deuel, [43]brought his gifts: a silver plate that weighed 3¼ pounds and a silver bowl that weighed 1¾ pounds using the standard weight of the holy place. Each dish was filled with flour mixed with olive oil as a grain offering. [44]He also brought a gold dish that weighed 4 ounces, filled with incense; [45]a young bull, a ram, and a one-year-old male lamb as a burnt offering; [46]a male goat as an offering for sin; [47]and two bulls, five rams, five male goats, and five one-year-old male lambs as a fellowship offering. These were the gifts from Eliasaph, son of Deuel.

[48]On the seventh day the leader of the descendants of **Ephraim**, Elishama, son of Ammihud, [49]brought his gifts: a silver plate that weighed 3¼ pounds and a silver bowl that weighed 1¾ pounds using the standard weight of the holy place. Each dish was filled with flour mixed with olive oil as a grain offering. [50]He also brought a gold dish that weighed 4 ounces, filled with incense; [51]a young bull, a ram, and a one-year-old male lamb as a burnt offering; [52]a male goat as an offering for sin; [53]and two bulls, five rams, five male goats, and five one-year-old male lambs as a fellowship offering. These were the gifts from Elishama, son of Ammihud.

[54]On the eighth day the leader of the descendants of **Manasseh**, Gamaliel, son of Pedahzur, [55]brought his gifts: a silver plate that weighed 3¼ pounds and a silver bowl that weighed 1¾ pounds using the standard weight of the holy place. Each dish was filled with flour mixed with olive oil as a grain offering. [56]He also brought a gold dish that weighed 4 ounces, filled with incense; [57]a young bull, a ram, and a one-year-old male lamb as a burnt offering; [58]a male goat as an offering for sin; [59]and two bulls, five rams, five male goats, and five one-year-old male lambs as a fellowship offering. These were the gifts from Gamaliel, son of Pedahzur.

[60]On the ninth day the leader of the descendants of **Benjamin**, Abidan, son of Gideoni, [61]brought his gifts: a silver plate that weighed 3¼ pounds and a silver bowl that weighed 1¾ pounds using the standard weight of the holy place. Each dish was filled with flour mixed with olive oil as a grain offering. [62]He also brought a gold dish that weighed 4 ounces, filled with incense; [63]a young bull, a ram, and a one-year-old male lamb as a burnt offering; [64]a male goat as an offering for sin; [65]and two bulls, five rams, five male goats, and five one-year-old male lambs as a fellowship offering. These were the gifts from Abidan, son of Gideoni.

[66]On the tenth day the leader of the descendants of **Dan**, Ahiezer, son of Amishaddai, [67]brought his gifts: a silver plate that weighed 3¼ pounds and a silver bowl that weighed 1¾ pounds using the standard weight of the holy place. Each dish was filled with flour mixed with olive oil as a grain offering. [68]He also brought a gold dish that weighed 4 ounces, filled with incense; [69]a young bull, a ram, and a one-year-old male lamb as a burnt offering; [70]a male goat as an offering for sin; [71]and two bulls, five rams, five male goats, and five one-year-old male lambs as a fellowship offering. These were the gifts from Ahiezer, son of Amishaddai.

[72]On the eleventh day the leader of the descendants of **Asher**, Pagiel, son of Ochran, [73]brought his gifts: a silver plate that weighed 3¼ pounds and a silver bowl that weighed 1¾ pounds using the standard weight of the holy place. Each dish was filled with flour mixed with olive oil as a grain offering. [74]He also brought a gold dish that weighed 4 ounces, filled with incense; [75]a young bull, a ram, and a one-year-old male lamb as a burnt offering; [76]a male goat as an offering for sin; [77]and two bulls, five rams,

five male goats, and five one-year-old male lambs as a fellowship offering. These were the gifts from Pagiel, son of Ochran.

⁷⁸On the twelfth day the leader of the descendants of **Naphtali**, Ahira, son of Enan, ⁷⁹brought his gifts: a silver plate that weighed 3¼ pounds and a silver bowl that weighed 1¾ pounds using the standard weight of the holy place. Each dish was filled with flour mixed with olive oil as a grain offering. ⁸⁰He also brought a gold dish that weighed 4 ounces, filled with incense; ⁸¹a young bull, a ram, and a one-year-old male lamb as a burnt offering; ⁸²a male goat as an offering for sin; ⁸³and two bulls, five rams, five male goats, and five one-year-old male lambs as a fellowship offering. These were the gifts from Ahira, son of Enan.

⁸⁴These were the gifts from the leaders of Israel for the dedication of the altar when it was anointed: 12 silver plates, 12 silver bowls, and 12 gold dishes. ⁸⁵Each silver plate weighed 3¼ pounds, and each bowl weighed 1¾ pounds. Together all the silver dishes weighed 60 pounds using the standard weight of the holy place. ⁸⁶The 12 gold dishes filled with incense weighed 4 ounces each using the standard weight of the holy place. Together all the gold dishes weighed about 3 pounds. ⁸⁷The total number of animals for the burnt offerings was 12 young bulls, 12 rams, 12 one-year-old male lambs, along with their grain offerings. Twelve male goats were used as offerings for sin. ⁸⁸The total number of animals for fellowship offerings was 24 bulls, 60 rams, 60 male goats, and 60 one-year-old male lambs. These were the gifts for the dedication of the altar after it was anointed.

⁸⁹Whenever Moses went into the tent of meeting to speak with the Lᴏʀᴅ, he heard the voice speaking to him from above the throne of mercy on the ark containing the words of God's promise, from between the two angels.ᵃ This is how the Lᴏʀᴅ spoke with Moses.

The Lamp Stand in the Tent

¹The Lᴏʀᴅ said to Moses, ²"Speak to Aaron and tell him: When you set up the seven lamps on the lamp stand, they should light up the area in front of it."

³So Aaron set up the lamps on the lamp stand to light up the area in front of it, as the Lᴏʀᴅ commanded Moses.

⁴This is how the lamp stand was made: The whole lamp stand, from top to bottom, was hammered out of gold. It was made exactly like the one the Lᴏʀᴅ had shown Moses.

The Levites Are Made Ready to Do the Lᴏʀᴅ's Work

⁵The Lᴏʀᴅ said to Moses, ⁶"Separate the Levites from the rest of the Israelites, and make them clean.ᵃ ⁷This is what you must do to make them clean: Sprinkle them with water to take away their sins. Make them shave their whole bodies and wash their clothes. Then they will be clean. ⁸Next, they must take a young bull and the grain offering of flour mixed with olive oil that is offered with it. You must take a second young bull as an offering for sin. ⁹Bring the Levites to the front of the tent of meeting, and assemble the whole community of Israel. ¹⁰Then bring the Levites into the Lᴏʀᴅ's presence, and the Israelites will place their hands on them. ¹¹Aaron will present the Levites to the Lᴏʀᴅ as an offering from the Israelites. Then they will be ready to do the Lᴏʀᴅ's work.

¹²"The Levites will place their hands on the heads of the young bulls. Sacrifice one of them as an offering for sin and the other one as a burnt offering to the Lᴏʀᴅ.

ᵃ 7:89 Or "cherubim." ᵃ 8:6 "Clean" refers to anything that is presentable to God.

These sacrifices will make peace with the Lord for the Levites. ¹³Make the Levites stand in front of Aaron and his sons, and present them as an offering to the Lord. ¹⁴In this way you will separate the Levites from the other Israelites, and the Levites will be mine.

¹⁵"Once you have made them clean and presented them as an offering, the Levites may come and do their work at the tent of meeting. ¹⁶They will be the only Israelites given to me. I have taken them to be mine as substitutes for every firstborn male offspring of the Israelites. ¹⁷Every firstborn in Israel, whether human or animal, is mine. The day I killed every firstborn male in Egypt, I set them apart as holy to me. ¹⁸So I have taken the Levites as substitutes for all the firstborn sons of the Israelites. ¹⁹The Levites will be the only Israelites I give to Aaron and his sons. They will work for the Israelites at the tent of meeting. They will make peace with the Lord for the Israelites. Then no plague will strike the Israelites when they come near the holy place."

²⁰Moses, Aaron, and the whole community of Israel did what the Lord commanded Moses to do to the Levites. ²¹The Levites performed the ceremonies to take away their sins and washed their clothes. Aaron presented them as an offering to the Lord and made peace with the Lord for them in order to make them clean. ²²After that, the Levites came and did their work at the tent of meeting in the presence of Aaron and his sons. They did as the Lord had commanded Moses.

²³The Lord said to Moses, ²⁴"These are the instructions for the Levites: Men 25 years old or older are eligible to serve at the tent of meeting. ²⁵But when they're 50 years old, they must retire from active service and not work anymore. ²⁶They may assist the other Levites in their duties at the tent of meeting, but they may not do any regular work. This is how you will handle the Levites' duties."

The Second Passover

¹In the first month of the second year after the Israelites left Egypt, the Lord spoke to Moses in the Desert of Sinai. He said, ²"The Israelites must celebrate the Passover at the same time every year. ³You must celebrate it on the fourteenth day of this month at dusk. Follow all the rules and regulations for the celebration of the Passover."

⁴So Moses told the Israelites to celebrate the Passover, ⁵and they celebrated it on the fourteenth day of the first month at dusk while they were in the Desert of Sinai. The Israelites did everything as the Lord had commanded Moses.

⁶But there were some men who had become unclean*ᵃ* from touching a dead body, and they couldn't celebrate the Passover that day. They came to Moses and Aaron ⁷and said, "We are unclean because we touched a dead body. Why won't you let us bring our offerings to the Lord at the same time the rest of the Israelites bring their offerings?"

⁸Moses answered them, "Wait here until I find out what the Lord commands you to do."

⁹Then the Lord said to Moses, "Tell the Israelites: ¹⁰Suppose you or any of your descendants is unclean from touching a dead body or is away on a long trip. You may still celebrate the Passover. ¹¹You will celebrate it on the fourteenth day of the second month at dusk. You must eat the Passover animal along with unleavened bread and bitter herbs. ¹²You must never leave any of the meat until morning or break any of the animal's bones. You must follow all the rules for the Passover when you celebrate

---

ᵃ 9:6 "Unclean" refers to anything that is not presentable to God.

it. [13]But if you are clean[b] and not on a trip and yet don't bother to celebrate the Passover, you must be excluded from the people. You didn't bring your offering to the LORD at the right time. You must suffer the consequences for your sin.

[14]"Foreigners living with you may want to celebrate the LORD's Passover. They must follow these same rules and regulations. The same rules will apply to foreigners and native-born Israelites."

The Column of Smoke Leads Israel Through the Desert

[15]On the day the tent of the words of God's promise was set up, the column of smoke covered it. From evening until morning, the smoke over the tent glowed like fire. [16]The smoke always glowed this way. At night the smoke covering the tent glowed like fire. [17]Whenever the smoke moved from the tent, the Israelites would break camp, and wherever it stopped, the Israelites would set up camp. [18]At the LORD's command the Israelites would break camp, and at his command they would set up camp. As long as the column of smoke stayed over the tent, they would stay in the same place. [19]When the smoke stayed over the tent for a long time, the Israelites obeyed the LORD's command and wouldn't break camp. [20]The same thing happened when the smoke stayed only a few days over the tent: At the LORD's command they would set up camp, and at his command they would break camp. [21]Sometimes the column of smoke stayed only from evening until morning. When the smoke moved in the morning, they broke camp. Day or night, when the smoke moved, they broke camp. [22]Whether it was two days, a month, or a year, as long as the column of smoke stayed over the tent, the Israelites would stay in the same place and not break camp. But when the smoke moved, they would break camp. [23]At the LORD's command they set up camp, and at his command they broke camp. They obeyed the command that the LORD had given through Moses.

Two Silver Signal Trumpets

[1]The LORD said to Moses, [2]"Make two trumpets out of hammered silver. Use them to call the community together and as a signal to break camp. [3]When you blow both trumpets, the whole community will meet with you at the entrance to the tent of meeting. [4]If only one trumpet blows, the leaders, the heads of the divisions of Israel, will meet with you. [5]When they hear the trumpet fanfare, the tribes that are camped on the east side will break camp first. [6]When the trumpets sound a second fanfare, the tribes that are camped on the south will break camp. The fanfare is the signal to break camp. [7]But when you gather the assembly, the trumpets will blow without sounding a fanfare. [8]The sons of Aaron, the priests, will blow the trumpets. This will be a permanent law for you and your descendants.

[9]"When you go to war in your own country against an enemy who is oppressing you, the trumpets will sound a fanfare. Then the LORD your God will remember you and rescue you from your enemies. [10]Also, on your festival days and on the first day of the month, blow the trumpets when you sacrifice your burnt offerings and fellowship offerings. The trumpets will be a reminder for you in God's presence. I am the LORD your God."

Israel Leaves Mount Sinai

[11]On the twentieth day of the second month of the second year, the column of smoke left the tent of the words of God's promise. [12]So the Israelites moved from the

---

[b]9:13 "Clean" refers to anything that is presentable to God.

Desert of Sinai and traveled from place to place until the column of smoke stopped in the Desert of Paran.

¹³This was the first time they moved, following the command that the LORD had given through Moses. ¹⁴With their flag in front, the armies led by Judah's descendants broke camp first. Nahshon, son of Amminadab, was in command. ¹⁵Nethanel, son of Zuar, commanded the army of Issachar. ¹⁶Eliab, son of Helon, commanded the army of Zebulun. ¹⁷Then the tent of meeting was taken down, and the Gershonites and Merarites, who carried it, broke camp.

¹⁸With their flag in front, the armies led by Reuben's descendants broke camp next. Elizur, son of Shedeur, was in command. ¹⁹Shelumiel, son of Zurishaddai, commanded the army of Simeon. ²⁰Eliasaph, son of Deuel, commanded the army of Gad. ²¹Then the Kohathites, who carried the holy things, broke camp. By the time they arrived, the tent of meeting would already be set up.

²²With their flag in front, the armies led by Ephraim's descendants broke camp next. Elisha, son of Ammihud, was in command. ²³Gamaliel, son of Pedahzur, commanded the army of Manasseh. ²⁴Abidan, son of Gideoni, commanded the army of Benjamin.

²⁵As a rear guard for the whole camp, the armies led by Dan's descendants broke camp last with their flag in front. Ahiezer, son of Ammishaddai, was in command. ²⁶Pagiel, son of Ochran, commanded the army of Asher. ²⁷Ahira, son of Enan, commanded the army of Naphtali.

²⁸This was the order in which the Israelite armies broke camp when they went from place to place.

²⁹Moses said to his brother-in-law Hobab, son of Reuel the Midianite, "We are going to the place the LORD promised to give us. Come with us. We will be good to you, because the LORD has promised good things to Israel."

³⁰Hobab answered, "No, I won't go. I want to go back to my own country where my relatives are."

³¹But Moses said, "Please don't leave us. You know where we can set up camp in the desert, and you could be our guide. ³²If you come with us, we will share with you all the good things the LORD gives us."

³³So they left the mountain of the LORD and traveled for three days. The ark of the LORD's promise went ahead of them a distance of three days' journey to find them a place to rest. ³⁴The LORD's column of smoke was over them by day when they moved the camp.

³⁵Whenever the ark started to move, Moses would say,

> "Arise, O LORD!
>   Scatter your enemies!
>   Make those who hate you run away from you!"

³⁶And whenever it stopped, he would say,

> "Return, O LORD, to the countless thousands of Israel!"

The People of Israel Demand Meat to Eat

¹The people began complaining out loud to the LORD about their troubles. When the LORD heard them, he became angry, and fire from the LORD began to burn among them. It destroyed some people on the outskirts of the camp. ²The people cried out to Moses, Moses prayed to the LORD, and the fire died down. ³That place was called Taberah [Fire] because fire from the LORD burned among them there.

⁴Some foreigners among the Israelites had a strong craving for other kinds of food. Even the Israelites started crying again and said, "If only we had meat to eat! ⁵Remember all the free fish we ate in Egypt and the cucumbers, watermelons, leeks, onions, and garlic we had? ⁶But now we've lost our appetite! Everywhere we look there's nothing but manna!"

⁷(Manna was small, like coriander seeds and looked like resin. ⁸The people would go around and gather it, then grind it in a handmill or crush it in a mortar. They would cook it in a pot or make round loaves of bread out of it. It tasted like rich pastry made with olive oil. ⁹When dew fell on the camp at night, manna fell with it.)

¹⁰Moses heard people from every family crying at the entrance to their tents. The Lord became very angry, and Moses didn't like it either. ¹¹So he asked, "Lord, why have you brought me this trouble? How have I displeased you that you put the burden of all these people on me? ¹²Am I their mother? Did I give birth to them? Are you really asking me to carry them in my arms—as a nurse carries a baby—all the way to the land you promised their ancestors with an oath? ¹³Where can I get meat for all these people? They keep crying for me to give them meat to eat. ¹⁴I can't take care of all these people by myself. This is too much work for me! ¹⁵If this is how you're going to treat me, why don't you just kill me? I can't face this trouble anymore."

¹⁶The Lord answered Moses, "Bring me 70 Israelite men who you know are leaders and officers of the people. Take them to the tent of meeting, and have them stand with you. ¹⁷I'll come down and speak with you there. I'll take some of the Spirit that is on you and put it on them. They will help you take care of the people. You won't have to take care of the people alone. ¹⁸Tell the people to get ready for tomorrow. They must be set apart as holy. Then they will eat meat. I, the Lord, heard them crying and saying, 'If only we had meat to eat! We were better off in Egypt!' So I will give them meat. ¹⁹They won't eat it just for one or two days, or five, or ten, or twenty days, ²⁰but for a whole month, until it comes out of their ears and they're sick of it. This is because they rejected the Lord who is here among them and cried in front of him, asking, 'Why did we ever leave Egypt?' "

²¹But Moses said, "Here I am with 600,000 foot soldiers around me. Yet, you say, 'I will give them meat to eat for a whole month!' ²²Would they have enough if all the flocks and herds were butchered for them? Would they have enough if all the fish in the sea were caught for them?"

²³The Lord asked Moses, "Is there a limit to the Lord's power? Now you will see whether or not my words come true."

²⁴Moses went out and told the people what the Lord said. He gathered 70 of the leaders of the people and had them stand around the tent. ²⁵Then the Lord came down in the column of smoke and spoke with him. He took some of the Spirit that was on Moses and put it on the 70 leaders. When the Spirit came to rest on them, they prophesied, but they never prophesied again.

²⁶Two men, named Eldad and Medad, had stayed in the camp. They were on the list with the other leaders but hadn't gone with them to the tent. The Spirit came to rest on them, too, and they prophesied in the camp.

²⁷Then a young man ran and told Moses, "Eldad and Medad are prophesying in the camp." ²⁸So Joshua, son of Nun, who had been Moses' assistant ever since he was a young man, spoke up and said, "Stop them, sir!"

²⁹But Moses asked him, "Do you think you need to stand up for me? I wish all the Lord's people were prophets and that the Lord would put his Spirit on them."

³⁰Then Moses and the leaders went back to the camp.

³¹The Lord sent a wind from the sea that brought quails and dropped them all

around the camp. There were quails on the ground about three feet deep as far as you could walk in a day in any direction.

³²All that day and night and all the next day the people went out and gathered the quails. No one gathered less than 60 bushels. Then they spread the quails out all around the camp.

³³While the meat was still in their mouths—before they had even had a chance to chew it—the Lord became angry with the people and struck them with a severe plague. ³⁴That place was called Kibroth Hattaavah [Graves of Those Who Craved Meat] because there they buried the people who had a strong craving for meat.

³⁵From Kibroth Hattaavah the people moved to Hazeroth, and they stayed there.

Miriam and Aaron Oppose Moses

¹Miriam and Aaron began to criticize Moses because he was married to a woman from Sudan. ²They asked, "Did the Lord speak only through Moses? Didn't he also speak through us?" The Lord heard their complaint.

³(Moses was a very humble man, more humble than anyone else on earth.)

⁴Suddenly, the Lord said to Moses, Aaron, and Miriam, "All three of you come to the tent of meeting." So all three of them came. ⁵Then the Lord came down in the column of smoke and stood at the entrance to the tent. He called to Aaron and Miriam, and they both came forward.

⁶He said, "Listen to my words: When there are prophets of the Lord among you, I make myself known to them in visions or speak to them in dreams. ⁷But this is not the way I treat my servant Moses. He is the most faithful person in my household.ᵃ ⁸I speak with him face to face, plainly and not in riddles. He even sees the form of the Lord. Why weren't you afraid to criticize my servant Moses?"

⁹The Lord was angry with them, so he left.

¹⁰When the smoke left the tent, Miriam was covered with an infectious skin disease. She was as white as snow. Aaron turned to her and saw she was covered with the disease. ¹¹So he said to Moses, "Please, sir, don't punish us for this foolish sin we committed. ¹²Don't let her be like a stillborn baby that's not completely developed."

¹³So Moses cried to the Lord, "Please, God, heal her!"

¹⁴The Lord replied to Moses, "If her own father had spit in her face, wouldn't she

Good Morning, God
Numbers 12:4-5

The Lord led the people of Israel through the desert with a column of smoke. They followed the smoke wherever it went. When Moses needed to know what to do next, God appeared to him in a column of smoke. The smoke reminded the Israelites that God was with them.

God is with us and will lead us, too. He shows us in his word what we should do. Are you feeling lost or confused? Get out your "guide"— read God's word!

Thank you, Lord, for guiding me through your word.

ᵃ12:7 Or "He is in charge of my entire household."

be excluded from the community for seven days? She must be put in isolation outside the camp for seven days. Then she can be brought back." ¹⁵So Miriam was put in isolation outside the camp for seven days. The people didn't break camp until she was brought back.

¹⁶After that, the people moved from Hazeroth and set up camp in the Desert of Paran.

Moses Sends Out 12 Spies

13 ¹The Lᴏʀᴅ said to Moses, ²"Send men to explore Canaan, which I'm giving to the Israelites. Send one leader from each of their ancestors' tribes."

³So at the Lᴏʀᴅ's command, Moses sent these men from the Desert of Paran. All of them were leaders of the Israelites.

⁴These are their names:

Shammua, son of Zaccur, from the tribe of Reuben;
⁵Shaphat, son of Hori, from the tribe of Simeon;
⁶Caleb, son of Jephunneh, from the tribe of Judah;
⁷Igal, son of Joseph, from the tribe of Issachar;
⁸Hoshea, son of Nun, from the tribe of Ephraim;
⁹Palti, son of Raphu, from the tribe of Benjamin;
¹⁰Gaddiel, son of Sodi, from the tribe of Zebulun;
¹¹Gaddi, son of Susi, from the tribe of Joseph (that is, the tribe of Manasseh);
¹²Ammiel, son of Gemalli, from the tribe of Dan;
¹³Sethur, son of Michael, from the tribe of Asher;
¹⁴Nahbi, son of Vophsi, from the tribe of Naphtali;
¹⁵Geuel, son of Machi, from the tribe of Gad.

¹⁶These are the names of the men Moses sent to explore the land. But Moses gave Hoshea, son of Nun, the name Joshua.

¹⁷When Moses sent them to explore Canaan, he told them, "Go through the Negev and then into the mountain region. ¹⁸See what the land is like and whether the people living there are strong or weak, few or many. ¹⁹Is the land they live in good or bad? Do their cities have walls around them or not? ²⁰Is the soil rich or poor? Does the land have trees or not? Do your best to bring back some fruit from the land." (It was the season when grapes were beginning to ripen.)

²¹So the men explored the land from the Desert of Zin to the border of Hamath. ²²They went through the Negev and came to Hebron, where Ahiman, Sheshai, and Talmai lived. They are descendants of Anak. (Hebron was built seven years before Zoan in Egypt.) ²³When they came to the Eshcol Valley, they cut off a branch with only one bunch of grapes on it. They carried it on a pole between two of them. They also brought some pomegranates and figs. ²⁴So they called that valley Eshcol [Bunch of Grapes] because of the bunch of grapes the Israelites cut off there.

²⁵Forty days later, they came back from exploring the land. ²⁶They came back to Moses, Aaron, and the whole community of Israel at Kadesh in the Desert of Paran. They gave their report and showed them the fruit from the land.

²⁷This is what they reported to Moses: "We went to the land where you sent us. It really is a land flowing with milk and honey. Here's some of its fruit. ²⁸But the people who live there are strong, and the cities have walls and are very large. We even saw the descendants of Anak there. ²⁹The Amalekites live in the Negev. The Hittites, Jebusites, and Amorites live in the mountain region. And the Canaanites live along the coast of the Mediterranean Sea and all along the Jordan River."

³⁰Caleb told the people to be quiet and listen to Moses. Caleb said, "Let's go now and take possession of the land. We should be more than able to conquer it."

³¹But the men who had gone with him said, "We can't attack those people! They're too strong for us!" ³²So they began to spread lies among the Israelites about the land they had explored. They said, "The land we explored is one that devours those who live there. All the people we saw there are very tall. ³³We saw Nephilim there. (The descendants of Anak are Nephilim.) We felt as small as grasshoppers, and that's how we must have looked to them."

The People Rebel Against the LORD

¹Then all the people in the Israelite community raised their voices and cried out loud all that night. ²They complained to Moses and Aaron, "If only we had died in Egypt or this desert! ³Why is the LORD bringing us to this land—just to have us die in battle? Our wives and children will be taken as prisoners of war! Wouldn't it be better for us to go back to Egypt?" ⁴They said to each other, "Let's choose a leader and go back to Egypt."

⁵Immediately, Moses and Aaron bowed with their faces touching the ground in front of the whole community of Israel assembled there. ⁶At the same time, two of those who had explored the land, Joshua (son of Nun) and Caleb (son of Jephunneh), tore their clothes in despair. ⁷They said to the whole community of Israel, "The land we explored is very good. ⁸If the LORD is pleased with us, he will bring us into this land and give it to us. This is a land flowing with milk and honey! ⁹Don't rebel against the LORD, and don't be afraid of the people of the land. We will devour them like bread. They have no protection, and the LORD is with us. So don't be afraid of them."

¹⁰But when the whole community of Israel talked about stoning Moses and Aaron to death, they all saw the glory of the LORD shining at the tent of meeting. ¹¹The LORD said to Moses, "How long will these people treat me with contempt? How long will they refuse to trust me in spite of all the miraculous signs I have done among them? ¹²I'll strike them with a plague, I'll destroy them,ᵃ and I'll make you into a nation larger and stronger than they are."

"I'm Sorry"

Numbers 14:19

It can be hard to admit when you do something wrong and then say, "I'm sorry." It can be hard for Mom or Dad to forgive you, especially if you do the same bad things over and over. It's good to know that God keeps on forgiving us. We never have to be afraid to tell God, "I'm sorry."

be you can be all

¹³But Moses said to the LORD, "What if the Egyptians hear about it? (You used your power to take these people away from them.) ¹⁴What if the Egyptians tell the people

---

ᵃ 14:12 Or "I'll take away the land I promised them."

who live in this land? Lord, they have already heard that you are with these people, that they have seen you with their own eyes, that your column of smoke stays over them, and that you go ahead of them in a column of smoke by day and in a column of fire by night. [15]But if you kill all these people at the same time, then the nations who have heard these reports about you will say, [16]'The Lord wasn't able to bring these people into the land he promised them, so he slaughtered them in the desert.'

[17]"Lord, let your power be as great as when you said, [18]'The Lord . . . patient, forever loving. . . . He forgives wrongdoing and disobedience. . . . He never lets the guilty go unpunished, punishing children . . . for their parents' sins to the third and fourth generation. . . .' [19]By your great love, please forgive these people's sins, as you have been forgiving them from the time they left Egypt until now."

[20]The Lord said, "I forgive them, as you have asked. [21]But as I live and as the glory of the Lord fills the whole earth, I solemnly swear that [22]none of the people who saw my glory and the miraculous signs I did in Egypt and in the desert will see the land which I promised their ancestors. They have tested me now ten times and refused to obey me.[b] [23]None of those who treat me with contempt will see it! [24]But because my servant Caleb has a different attitude and has wholeheartedly followed me, I'll bring him to the land he already explored. His descendants will possess it. [25](The Amalekites and Canaanites are living in the valleys.) Tomorrow you must turn around, go back into the desert, and follow the road that goes to the Red Sea."

[26]Then the Lord said to Moses and Aaron, [27]"How long must I put up with this wicked community that keeps complaining about me? I've heard the complaints the Israelites are making about me. [28]So tell them, 'As I live, declares the Lord, I solemnly swear I will do everything to you that you said I would do. [29]Your bodies will drop dead in this desert. All of you who are at least 20 years old, who were registered and listed, and who complained about me will die. [30]I raised my hand and swore an oath to give you this land to live in. But none of you will enter it except Caleb (son of Jephunneh) and Joshua (son of Nun). [31]You said your children would be taken as prisoners of war. Instead, I will bring them into the land you rejected, and they will enjoy it. [32]However, your bodies will drop dead in this desert. [33]Your children will be shepherds in the desert for 40 years. They will suffer for your unfaithfulness until the last of your bodies lies dead in the desert. [34]For 40 days you explored the land. So for 40 years—one year for each day—you will suffer for your sins and know what it means for me to be against you.' [35]I, the Lord, have spoken. I swear I will do these things to all the people in this whole wicked community who have joined forces against me. They will meet their end in this desert. Here they will die!"

[36]So the men Moses sent to explore the land died in front of the Lord from a plague. [37]They died because they had returned and made the whole community complain about Moses by spreading lies about the land.[c] [38]Of all the men who went to explore the land, only Joshua (son of Nun) and Caleb (son of Jephunneh) survived.

The Amalekites and Canaanites Defeat Israel

[39]When Moses told these things to all the Israelites, the people mourned bitterly, as if someone had died. [40]Early the next morning they headed into the mountain region. They said, "We have sinned. Now we'll go to the place the Lord promised."

[41]But Moses asked, "Why are you disobeying the Lord's command? Your plan won't work! [42]Don't go! You will be defeated by your enemies because the Lord is not with

---

[b]14:22 Part of verse 23 (in Hebrew) has been placed in verse 22 to express the complex Hebrew sentence structure more clearly in English. [c]14:37 Part of verse 37 (in Hebrew) has been placed at the end of verse 36 to express the complex Hebrew sentence structure more clearly in English.

you. ⁴³The Amalekites and Canaanites are there, and you will die in battle. Now that you have turned away from the LORD, the LORD will not be with you."

⁴⁴But they headed into the mountain region anyway, even though the ark of the LORD's promise and Moses stayed in the camp. ⁴⁵The Amalekites and Canaanites who lived there came down from those mountains, attacked the Israelites, and defeated them at Hormah.*ᵈ*

Grain and Wine Made Part of the Sacrifices to the LORD

¹The LORD said to Moses, ²"Speak to the Israelites and tell them: Once you're settled in the land I'm giving you, ³you may bring offerings by fire to the LORD. They may be burnt offerings or any other kind of sacrifice. They may be offered to fulfill a vow, as a freewill offering, or as one of your festival offerings. They may be cattle, sheep, or goats—offerings that are a soothing aroma to the LORD. ⁴Whoever brings the offering must also give the LORD a grain offering of eight cups of flour mixed with one quart of olive oil. ⁵With each sheep or goat for the burnt offering or any other sacrifice, also give an offering of one quart of wine.

⁶"With a ram, give a grain offering of 16 cups of flour mixed with 1¼ quarts of oil ⁷and an offering of 1¼ quarts of wine. Offer them as a soothing aroma to the LORD.

⁸"Suppose you sacrifice a young bull as a burnt offering to the LORD or make any other kind of sacrifice—to keep a vow or as a fellowship offering. ⁹Offer with the young bull a grain offering of 24 cups of flour mixed with two quarts of olive oil. ¹⁰Also give an offering of two quarts of wine. It is an offering by fire, a soothing aroma to the LORD. ¹¹Do this for each bull, each ram, and each sheep or goat. ¹²Do it for each animal, however many you sacrifice. ¹³All native-born Israelites must do it this way when they bring an offering by fire, a soothing aroma to the LORD.

¹⁴"Suppose foreigners are visiting you or living among you in future generations. If they bring an offering by fire, a soothing aroma to the LORD, they must do as you do. ¹⁵There is one law for the whole assembly: for you and foreigners who are living with you. It is a permanent law for future generations. As far as the LORD is concerned, you and foreigners are the same. ¹⁶The instructions and rules are the same for you as well as foreigners who are living with you."

Offering the First Bread Dough to the LORD

¹⁷The LORD said to Moses, ¹⁸"Speak to the Israelites and tell them: When you enter the land where I'm taking you ¹⁹and eat any of the food from the land, give some of it as a contribution to the LORD. ²⁰Shape one part of your dough into a ring the same way you do with the contribution you make from the threshing floor.*ᵃ* ²¹For generations to come, you must give one part of your dough as a contribution to the LORD.

What Is to Be Done About Unintentional and Intentional Wrongdoings

²²"Suppose you unintentionally do something wrong by not obeying all these commands the LORD gave Moses. ²³(Everything the LORD commanded you through Moses holds as true for generations to come as it did the day the LORD gave the commands.) ²⁴If it was unintentional and no one else knows about it, the whole community must sacrifice a young bull as a burnt offering, a soothing aroma to the LORD, along with the proper grain and wine offerings, and a male goat as an offering for sin. ²⁵The priest will make peace with the LORD for the whole community of Israel. Then they will be

---

ᵈ14:45 Or "and defeated them, chasing them all the way to Hormah." ᵃ15:20 A threshing floor is an outdoor area where grain is separated from its husks.

forgiven because the wrongdoing was unintentional and they brought these two offerings to the LORD for their sin: an offering by fire and an offering for sin. ²⁶So the whole community of Israel will be forgiven, including foreigners who are living among them, since all the people were involved in the unintentional wrongdoing.

²⁷"If one person unintentionally does something wrong, a one-year-old female goat must be sacrificed as an offering for sin. ²⁸The priest will offer the sacrifice to make peace with the LORD for that person, and that person will be forgiven. ²⁹You must give the same instructions to everyone who does something wrong unintentionally, whether they are native-born Israelites or not.

³⁰"But any native-born Israelite or foreigner who deliberately does something wrong insults the LORD and must be excluded from the people. ³¹That person has despised the word of the LORD and broken the LORD's command. He must be excluded completely. He remains guilty."

A Man Breaks the Rules for the Day of Worship

³²While the Israelites were in the desert, they found a man gathering wood on the day of worship. ³³Those who found him gathering wood brought him to Moses and Aaron and the whole community. ³⁴They kept him in custody until they decided what to do with him. ³⁵Then the LORD said to Moses, "This man must be put to death. The whole community must take him outside the camp and stone him." ³⁶So the whole community took him outside the camp and stoned him to death, as the LORD commanded Moses.

Family
Numbers 15:37-41

al be you can be

The tassels on the Israelites' clothes meant that they belonged to God. Ask your mom or dad to buy paint and plain tee shirts at a fabric shop. Create your own design and make tee shirts for your family. What can you put on the shirts to show that you belong to God, too?

The Israelites Are Commanded to Wear Tassels

³⁷The LORD said to Moses, ³⁸"Speak to the Israelites and tell them: For generations to come they must wear tassels on the corners of their clothes with violet threads in each tassel. ³⁹Whenever you look at the threads in the tassel, you will remember all the LORD's commands and obey them. Then you won't do whatever you want and go after whatever you see, as if you were chasing after prostitutes. ⁴⁰You will remember to obey all my commands, and you will be holy to your God. ⁴¹I am the LORD your God, who brought you out of Egypt to be your God. I am the LORD your God."

Korah's Rebellion

16 ¹Korah (son of Izhar), Dathan and Abiram (sons of Eliab), and On (son of Peleth) dared to challenge Moses.ᵃ (Korah was a descendant of Kohath and Levi.

ᵃ 16:1 The beginning of verse 2 (in Hebrew) has been placed in verse 1 to express the complex Hebrew sentence structure more clearly in English.

Dathan, Abiram, and On were descendants of Reuben.) ²These four men were joined by 250 Israelite men, well-known leaders of the community, chosen by the assembly. ³They came together to confront Moses and Aaron and said to them, "You've gone far enough! Everyone in the whole community is holy, and the LORD is among them. Why do you set yourselves above the LORD's assembly?"

⁴As soon as Moses heard this, he bowed with his face touching the ground. ⁵Then he said to Korah and all his followers, "In the morning the LORD will show who belongs to him, who is holy, and who it is that he will allow to come near him. Only the person the LORD chooses will be allowed to come near him. ⁶Korah, you and all your followers must do this tomorrow: Take incense burners, ⁷and put burning coals and incense in them in the LORD's presence. Then the LORD will choose the man who is holy. You've gone far enough!"

⁸Moses also said to Korah, "Listen, you Levites! ⁹Isn't it enough for you that the God of Israel has separated you from the rest of the community of Israel? The LORD has brought you near himself to do the work for his tent and stand in front of the community to serve them. ¹⁰He has brought you and all the other Levites near himself, but now you demand to be priests. ¹¹So you and all your followers have joined forces against the LORD! Who is Aaron that you should complain about him?"

¹²Then Moses sent for Dathan and Abiram, sons of Eliab. But they said, "We won't come! ¹³Isn't it enough that you brought us out of a land flowing with milk and honey only to kill us in the desert? Do you also have to order us around? ¹⁴Certainly you haven't brought us into a land flowing with milk and honey or given us any fields and vineyards to own. Do you think you can still pull the wool over our eyes? We won't come."

¹⁵Moses became angry and said to the LORD, "Don't accept their offering. I haven't taken anything from them, not even a donkey. And I haven't mistreated any of them."

¹⁶Moses said to Korah, "Tomorrow you and all your followers must come into the LORD's presence. Aaron will also be there with you. ¹⁷Each man will take his incense burner and put incense in it. They will offer all 250 incense burners to the LORD. Then you and Aaron offer your incense burners."

¹⁸So each man took his incense burner, put burning coals and incense in it, and stood with Moses and Aaron at the entrance to the tent of meeting. ¹⁹When Korah had gathered all his followers—those who opposed Moses and Aaron—at the entrance to the tent of meeting, the glory of the LORD appeared to the whole group.

²⁰The LORD said to Moses and Aaron, ²¹"Move away from these men, and I'll destroy them in an instant." ²²Immediately, they bowed with their faces touching the ground and said, "O God, you are the God who gives the breath of life to everyone! If one man sins, will you be angry with the whole community?"

²³Then the LORD said to Moses, ²⁴"Tell the community: Move away from the tents of Korah, Dathan, and Abiram."

²⁵Moses got up and went to Dathan and Abiram, and the leaders of Israel followed him. ²⁶He said to the community, "Move away from the tents of these wicked men. Don't touch anything that belongs to them, or you'll be swept away because of all their sins." ²⁷So they moved away from the tents of Korah, Dathan, and Abiram. Dathan and Abiram had come out and were standing at the entrances to their tents with their wives and children.

²⁸Moses said, "This is how you will know that the LORD sent me to do all these things and that it wasn't my idea: ²⁹If these men die like all other people—if they die a natural death—then the LORD hasn't sent me. ³⁰But if the LORD does something totally new—if the ground opens up, swallows them and everything that belongs to them,

and they go down alive to their graves—then you'll know that these men have treated the Lord with contempt."

³¹As soon as he had finished saying all this, the ground under them split, ³²and the earth opened up to swallow them, their families, the followers of Korah, and all their property. ³³They went down alive to their graves with everything that belonged to them. The ground covered them, and so they disappeared from the assembly. ³⁴All the Israelites around them ran away when they heard their screams. They thought the ground would swallow them, too.

³⁵Fire came from the Lord and consumed the 250 men who were offering incense.ᵇ

³⁶Then the Lord said to Moses, ³⁷"Tell Eleazar, son of the priest Aaron, to take the incense burners out of the fire and scatter the coals and incense somewhere else, because the incense burners have become holy. ³⁸The incense burners of these men who sinned and lost their lives are holy, because they were offered to the Lord. Hammer them into thin metal sheets to cover the altar. This will be a sign to the Israelites."

³⁹So the priest Eleazar took the bronze incense burners which had been brought by those who had been burned to death. The incense burners were then hammered into thin metal sheets to cover the altar, ⁴⁰following the command that the Lord had given through Moses. The bronze-covered altar will remind Israel that no one but a descendant of Aaron can come near to burn incense to the Lord. Everyone else will die like Korah and his followers.

⁴¹The next day the whole community of Israel complained to Moses and Aaron. They said, "You have killed the Lord's people." ⁴²The community came together to confront Moses and Aaron. When they turned toward the tent of meeting, they saw the smoke covering it, and the glory of the Lord appeared.

⁴³Then Moses and Aaron went to the front of the tent of meeting. ⁴⁴The Lord said to Moses, ⁴⁵"Get away from these people, and let me destroy them in an instant!" Immediately, they bowed with their faces touching the ground.

⁴⁶Moses said to Aaron, "Take your incense burner, put burning coals from the altar and incense in it, and go quickly into the community to make peace with the Lord for the people. The Lord is showing his anger; a plague has started."

⁴⁷Aaron took his incense burner, as Moses told him, and ran into the middle of the assembly, because the plague had already begun among the people. He put incense on the incense burner to make peace with the Lord for the people. ⁴⁸He stood between those who had died and those who were still alive, and the plague stopped. ⁴⁹Still, 14,700 died from the plague in addition to those who had died because of Korah. ⁵⁰By the time Aaron came back to Moses at the entrance to the tent of meeting, the plague had stopped.

Aaron's Staff Grows

17 ᵃ¹The Lord said to Moses, ²"Speak to the Israelites, and get 12 staffs from them, one from the leader of each of their tribes.ᵇ Write each man's name on his staff. ³Write Aaron's name on the staff for Levi because there must be one staff for the head of each tribe. ⁴Put them in the tent of meeting where I meet with you, in front of the words of my promise. ⁵The staff from the man I choose will begin to grow. In this way I will silence the frequent complaints the Israelites make against you and Aaron."

⁶So Moses spoke to the Israelites. Their leaders gave him 12 staffs, one from the

---

ᵇ16:35 Numbers 16:36-50 in English Bibles is Numbers 17:1-15 in the Hebrew Bible.   ᵃ17:1 Numbers 17:1-13 in English Bibles is Numbers 17:16-28 in the Hebrew Bible.   ᵇ17:2 There is a play on words here. Hebrew *matteh* can mean "staff" or "tribe."

leader of each of their tribes. Aaron's staff was among them. ⁷Moses put the staffs in the Lᴏʀᴅ's presence in the tent of the words of God's promise.

⁸The next day Moses went into the tent. He found that Aaron's staff for the tribe of Levi had not only begun to grow, but it had also blossomed and produced ripe almonds. ⁹Moses brought out the staffs from the Lᴏʀᴅ's presence and showed them to all the Israelites. They looked at them, and each man took his staff.

¹⁰The Lᴏʀᴅ said to Moses, "Put Aaron's staff back in front of the words of my promise, and keep it there as a sign to warn any other rebels. Then you will stop their complaints about me, and they won't die."

¹¹Moses did exactly what the Lᴏʀᴅ commanded him to do.

¹²The Israelites said to Moses, "Now we're going to die! We're lost! We're all lost! ¹³Anyone who comes near the Lᴏʀᴅ's tent will die! Are we all going to die?"

The Duties of the Levites and Priests

18 ¹The Lᴏʀᴅ said to Aaron, "You, your sons, and your family will be responsible for any sins against the holy place. You and your sons will also be responsible for any sins you commit when you work as priests. ²Bring the other Levites from your ancestor's tribe to join you and help you and your sons serve in front of the tent of the words of my promise. ³They will work for you, doing whatever work is necessary for the whole tent. But they must not come near the altar or the furnishings in the holy place, or they will die, and you will die, too. ⁴They will join you and do whatever work is necessary for the tent of meeting, including all the maintenance work for the tent. But no one else may come near you.

⁵"You must be in charge of the work done at the holy place and at the altar. Then I won't show my anger against the Israelites again. ⁶I have chosen the other Levites from among the Israelites to help you. They are a gift given to the Lᴏʀᴅ to do whatever work is necessary at the tent of meeting. ⁷Only you and your sons may do the work of priests—everything done at the altar and under the canopy. This is my gift to you: You may serve me as priests. Anyone else who comes near the holy place to do this work must die."

Contributions for the Levites and Priests

⁸The Lᴏʀᴅ said to Aaron, "I am putting you in charge of all the contributions given to me. I am giving you and your descendants all the holy gifts from the Israelites as your share. These contributions will always be yours. ⁹That part of the most holy offerings which is not burned belongs to you. It may come from a grain offering, an offering for sin, or a guilt offering. Whatever is brought to me as a most holy offering will belong to you and your sons. ¹⁰Eat it in a most holy place. Any male may eat it. You must consider it holy.

¹¹"The contributions that come as gifts taken from the offerings presented by the Israelites are also yours. I am giving these to you, your sons, and your daughters. They will always be yours. Anyone in your household who is clean*ᵃ* may eat them.

¹²"I am also giving you the first of the produce they give the Lᴏʀᴅ: the best of all the olive oil and the best of the new wine and fresh grain. ¹³The first of all produce harvested in their land that they bring to the Lᴏʀᴅ is yours. Anyone in your household who is clean may eat it.

¹⁴"Anything in Israel that is claimed by the Lᴏʀᴅ is yours. ¹⁵Every firstborn male, human or animal, that is brought to the Lᴏʀᴅ is yours. But you must buy back every

---

*ᵃ*18:11 "Clean" refers to anything that is presentable to God.

firstborn son and the firstborn male of any unclean animal. [16]When they are one month old, you must buy them back at the fixed price of two ounces of silver using the standard weight of the holy place.

[17]"But you must never buy back a firstborn ox, sheep, or goat. They are holy. Throw the blood from these animals against the altar, and burn the fat as an offering by fire, a soothing aroma to the Lord. [18]But the meat is yours, like the breast and the right thigh that are presented. [19]I am giving you, your sons, and your daughters all the holy contributions the Israelites bring to the Lord. These contributions will always be yours. It is an everlasting promise of salt in the Lord's presence for you and your descendants."

[20]The Lord said to Aaron, "You will have no land or property of your own as the other Israelites will have. I am your possession and your property among the Israelites.

[21]"I am giving the Levites one-tenth of every Israelite's income. This is in return for the work they do at the tent of meeting. [22]The other Israelites must never again come near the tent of meeting. Otherwise, they'll suffer the consequences of their sin and die. [23]Only the Levites will do the work at the tent of meeting. They will be responsible for their own sins. This is a permanent law for future generations. They will own no property as the other Israelites will. [24]Instead, I will give the Levites what the Israelites contribute to the Lord—one-tenth of the Israelites' income. This is why I said about them, 'They will own no property as the other Israelites do.' "

[25]The Lord said to Moses, [26]"Speak to the Levites and say to them: You will take one-tenth of the Israelites' income which I'm giving you as your property. When you do, you must contribute one-tenth of that income as your contribution to the Lord. [27]Your contribution will be considered to be grain from the threshing floor[b] or juice from the winepress. [28]So you, too, will contribute one-tenth of your income to the Lord out of all that you receive from the Israelites' income. You will give the Lord's contribution to the priest Aaron. [29]Out of all the gifts you receive, you must contribute the best and holiest parts to the Lord.

[30]"Also tell them: When you contribute the best part, your contribution will be considered to be produce from the threshing floor or winepress. [31]So you and your households may eat it anywhere, because it's the wages you receive for your work at the tent of meeting. [32]When you contribute the best part, you won't suffer the consequences of any sin. You won't be dishonoring the holy offerings given by the Israelites, and you won't die."

Water That Makes Israel Clean After Someone Dies

19 [1]The Lord said to Moses and Aaron, [2]"This is what the Lord's teachings have commanded: Tell the Israelites to bring you a red cow that is perfect, with no defects. Also, it must never have worn a yoke.[a] [3]Give it to the priest Eleazar. It must be taken outside the camp and slaughtered in his presence. [4]The priest Eleazar will take some of the blood with his finger and sprinkle it seven times toward the front of the tent of meeting. [5]Then the entire cow (the skin, meat, blood, and excrement) will be burned while he watches. [6]The priest will take some cedar wood, a hyssop sprig, and some red yarn and throw them onto the burning cow. [7]The priest must then wash his clothes and his body. After that, he may go into the camp. But he will be unclean[b] until evening. [8]The person who burned the calf must also wash his clothes and his body. He, too, will be unclean until evening.

---

[b]18:27 A threshing floor is an outdoor area where grain is separated from its husks.   [a]19:2 A yoke is a wooden bar placed over the necks of work animals so that they can pull plows or carts.   [b]19:7 "Unclean" refers to anything that is not presentable to God.

⁹"A man who is clean*ᶜ* will collect the ashes from the cow and put them in a clean place outside the camp. They will be kept by the community of Israel and used in the water that takes away uncleanness. The cow is an offering for sin. ¹⁰The person who collected the ashes from the cow must also wash his clothes. He will be unclean until evening. This will be a permanent law for the Israelites and for the foreigners who live with them.

¹¹"Whoever touches the dead body of any human being will be unclean for seven days. ¹²The unclean person must use this water on the third day and the seventh day to take away his sin. Then he will be clean. But if he doesn't use this water on the third day and the seventh day, he will not be clean. ¹³Whoever touches the dead body of a human being and doesn't use this water to take away his sin makes the Lord's tent unclean. That person must be excluded from Israel, because the water that takes away uncleanness wasn't sprinkled on him. He is unclean; his uncleanness stays with him.

¹⁴"These are your instructions for when a person dies in a tent: Everyone who goes into the tent and everyone who is in the tent will be unclean for seven days. ¹⁵Every container without a lid fastened on it is unclean.

¹⁶"Whoever is outdoors and touches someone who was killed or has died naturally or anyone who touches a human bone or a grave will be unclean for seven days.

¹⁷"This is what you must do for people who become unclean from touching a dead body. Put some of the ashes from the red cow that was burned as an offering for sin into a container. Then pour fresh water on them. ¹⁸A person who is clean will take a sprig of hyssop, dip it in the water, and sprinkle the tent, all the furnishings, and all the people who were in the tent with the dead body. He must also sprinkle any person who has touched a human bone or a grave and any person who has touched someone who has been killed or who has died naturally. ¹⁹A person who is clean will sprinkle these types of unclean people on the third day and the seventh day. On the seventh day the clean person will finish taking away their sins. Then they must wash their clothes and bodies, and in the evening they will be clean. ²⁰But if the person who becomes unclean doesn't have his sin taken away, that person must be excluded from the assembly. He has made the holy place of the Lord unclean. The water to take away uncleanness wasn't sprinkled on him. He is unclean. ²¹This will be a permanent law for them.

"Whoever sprinkles the water to take away uncleanness must wash his clothes. And whoever touches this water will be unclean until evening. ²²Anything that an unclean person touches becomes unclean, and the person who touches it will be unclean until evening."

Water From the Rock

20 ¹In the first month the whole community of Israel came into the Desert of Zin, and they stayed at Kadesh. Miriam died and was buried there.

²Since the community was without water, they came together to confront Moses and Aaron. ³The people complained to Moses and said, "If only we had died when the other Israelites died in the Lord's presence! ⁴Did you bring the Lord's assembly into this desert just to have us and our animals die here? ⁵Why did you make us leave Egypt and bring us into this terrible place? This is no place to plant crops. Even figs, grapes, and pomegranates won't grow here. And there's no water to drink!"

⁶Moses and Aaron went from the assembly to the entrance of the tent of meeting.

ᶜ19:9 "Clean" refers to anything that is presentable to God.

Immediately, they bowed with their faces touching the ground, and the glory of the LORD appeared to them.

⁷The LORD said to Moses, ⁸"Take your staff, then you and your brother Aaron gather the community. Right before their eyes, tell the rock to give up its water. In this way you will give the community water from the rock for them and their animals to drink."

⁹Moses took his staff out of the tent in the LORD's presence as he had been commanded. ¹⁰Then Moses and Aaron assembled the community in front of the rock and said to them, "Listen, you rebels, must we bring water out of this rock for you?" ¹¹Moses raised his hand and hit the rock twice with the staff. Water came pouring out, and all the people and their animals drank.

¹²But the LORD said to Moses and Aaron, "You didn't trust me! You didn't show the Israelites how holy I am! So you will not bring this congregation into the land I'm giving them."

¹³This was the oasis of Meribah [Complaining], where the Israelites complained about the LORD and where he showed them he was holy.

Edom Refuses to Allow Israel to Pass Through Its Territory

¹⁴Moses sent messengers from Kadesh to the king of Edom. He said, "This is what your brother Israel says: You know all the hardships we've had. ¹⁵Our ancestors went to Egypt, and we lived there for many years. The Egyptians mistreated us and our ancestors. ¹⁶When we cried out to the LORD, he heard us, sent a messenger, and brought us out of Egypt.

"Now we're here in Kadesh, a city on the edge of your territory. ¹⁷Please let us go through your country. We won't go through any of your fields or vineyards, or drink any of the water from your wells. We'll stay on the king's highway and never leave it until we've passed through your territory."

¹⁸But the Edomites answered, "You may not pass through our country. If you try, we'll come out and attack you."

¹⁹The Israelites replied, "We'll stay on the main road, and if we or our livestock drink any of your water, we'll pay for it. We want to pass through on foot. That's all."

²⁰But the Edomites said, "You may not pass through." Then they came out and attacked with many well-armed troops. ²¹Since the Edomites refused to let Israel go through their territory, the Israelites turned around and went a different way.

Good Morning, God
Numbers 20:2-5

When was a time when you felt like giving up? The Israelites almost quit when they had no water in the desert. Although God had helped them through many trials, they began to wish they were dead. They became discouraged and didn't think about how God had helped them.

When you're ready to quit, think back on how far you've come. God has helped you through tough times before, and he will help you again.

Father, when I'm ready to give up, help me to keep going.

Aaron's Death

²²The whole community of Israel left Kadesh and came to Mount Hor. ²³At Mount Hor, near the border of Edom, the LORD said to Moses and Aaron, ²⁴"Aaron must now join his ancestors in death, since he cannot enter the land I'm giving the Israelites. This is because you both rebelled against my command at the oasis of Meribah. ²⁵Bring Aaron and his son Eleazar up on Mount Hor. ²⁶Take off Aaron's priestly clothes, and put them on his son Eleazar. Then Aaron will die there and join his ancestors."

²⁷Moses did as the LORD commanded. The whole community saw them go up on Mount Hor. ²⁸Moses took off Aaron's priestly clothes and put them on his son Eleazar. Aaron died there on top of the mountain. Then Moses and Eleazar came down from the mountain. ²⁹The whole community saw that Aaron had died, and all the Israelites mourned for Aaron 30 days.

The King of Arad Is Defeated

¹When the Canaanite king of Arad, who lived in the Negev, heard that the Israelites were coming on the road to Atharim, he fought them and took some of them as prisoners. ²Then the Israelites made this vow to the LORD: "If you will hand these people over to us, we'll destroy their cities because you've claimed them." ³The LORD listened to the Israelites and handed the Canaanites over to them. They destroyed the Canaanites and their cities. So they called the place Hormah [Claimed for Destruction].

The Bronze Snake

⁴Then they moved from Mount Hor, following the road that goes to the Red Sea, in order to get around Edom. The people became impatient on the trip ⁵and criticized God and Moses. They said, "Why did you make us leave Egypt—just to let us die in the desert? There's no bread or water, and we can't stand this awful food!"

⁶So the LORD sent poisonous snakes among the people. They bit the people, and many of the Israelites died. ⁷The people came to Moses and said, "We sinned when we criticized the LORD and you. Pray to the LORD so that he will take the snakes away from us." So Moses prayed for the people.

⁸The LORD said to Moses, "Make a snake, and put it on a pole. Anyone who is bitten can look at it and live." ⁹So Moses made a bronze snake and put it on a pole. People looked at the bronze snake after they were bitten, and they lived.ᵃ

Israel Travels Past Edom to Moab

¹⁰The Israelites moved and set up camp at Oboth. ¹¹Next they moved from Oboth and set up camp at Iye Abarim in the desert west of Moab. ¹²From there they moved and set up camp at the Zered River. ¹³They moved from there and set up camp on the other side of the Arnon Valley in the desert that extends into Amorite territory. (The Arnon Valley is the border between Moab and the Amorites.) ¹⁴This is how it's described in the Book of the Wars of the LORD:

> ". . . Waheb in Suphah and the valleys,
> ¹⁵ Arnon and the slopes of the valleys
>   that go down to the site of Ar
>   and lie along the border of Moab. . . ."

ᵃ21:9 There is a play on words here between Hebrew *nachash* (snake) and *nechosheth* (bronze).

[16] From there they went to Beer [Well]. This is the well where the Lord said to Moses, "Gather the people, and I will give them water." [17] Then Israel sang this song about the well:

> "Make your water spring up!
>   Sing to the well,
> [18]   the well dug by princes,
>   dug out by the nobles of the people
>   with their scepters and staffs."

From the desert they went to Mattanah, [19] and from Mattanah to Nahaliel, and from Nahaliel to Bamoth, [20] and from Bamoth to the valley in Moab where Mount Pisgah overlooks Jeshimon.

Sihon and Og Defeated

[21] Then Israel sent messengers to say to King Sihon of the Amorites, [22] "Let us go through your country. We won't go through any of your fields or vineyards or drink any of the water from your wells. We'll stay on the king's highway until we've passed through your territory."

[23] Sihon wouldn't let Israel pass through his territory. Sihon gathered all his troops and came out into the desert to attack Israel. When Sihon's troops came to Jahaz, they fought against Israel. [24] But Israel defeated them in battle and took possession of their land from the Arnon Valley to the Jabbok River. They stopped at the border of the Ammon because it was fortified. [25] Israel took all those Amorite cities, including Heshbon and all its villages, and lived in them. [26] Heshbon was the city of King Sihon of the Amorites. He had fought the former king of Moab and had taken all his land up to the Arnon Valley.

[27] This is why the poets say:

> "Come to Heshbon! Rebuild it!
>   Restore Sihon's city!
> [28] Fire came out of Heshbon,
>   flames from Sihon's city.
>   They destroyed Ar of Moab,
>   the rulers of Arnon's worship sites.[b]
> [29] How horrible it is for you, Moab!
> You are destroyed, you people of the god Chemosh.
>   Chemosh let his sons become refugees
>   and he let his daughters become prisoners
>   of King Sihon of the Amorites.
> [30] But we shot the Amorites full of arrows.
>   From Heshbon to Dibon they all died.
>   We destroyed everyone and everything
>   between Nophah and Medeba."

[31] So Israel settled in the land of the Amorites. [32] After Moses sent spies to Jazer, the Israelites captured its cities and villages and forced out the Amorites who were there. [33] Then they turned and followed the road that goes to Bashan. King Og of Bashan and all his troops came out to fight the Israelites at Edrei. [34] The Lord said to Moses, "Don't be afraid of him. I'll hand him, all his troops, and

---

[b] 21:28 Masoretic Text; Greek "it consumed Arnon's worship sites."

his land over to you. Do to him what you did to King Sihon of the Amorites, who ruled in Heshbon." ³⁵The Israelites defeated him, his sons, and all his troops, leaving no survivors. And they took possession of his land.

Balaam Is Hired to Curse Israel

22 ¹Then the Israelites moved and set up camp across from Jericho, on the plains of Moab east of the Jordan River.

²Balak, son of Zippor, saw all that Israel had done to the Amorites. ³The Moabites were very afraid because there were so many Israelites. Besides, the Moabites couldn't stand these people.

⁴So the Moabites said to the leaders of Midian, "All those people will eventually eat up everything around us the same way an ox eats up the grass in a field."

At that time Balak, son of Zippor, was king of Moab. ⁵He sent messengers to summon Balaam, son of Beor, who was at Pethor, on the Euphrates River, in the land where his people lived. Balak's message was, "A nation has just come here from Egypt. They've spread out all over the countryside and are setting up their camp here in front of me. ⁶Please come and curse these people for me, because they are too strong for me. Maybe then I'll be able to defeat them and force them out of the country. I know that whomever you bless is blessed and whomever you curse is cursed."

⁷The leaders of Moab and Midian left, taking money with them to pay for Balaam's services. They came to Balaam and told him what Balak had said.

⁸"Spend the night here," Balaam said to them, "and I'll report to you what the LORD tells me." So the princes of Moab stayed with Balaam.

⁹God came to Balaam and asked, "Who are these men with you?"

¹⁰Balaam answered, "Balak, son of King Zippor of Moab, sent them with this message: ¹¹'Some people have just come from Egypt and are spreading out all over the countryside. Now come and curse them for me. Maybe I'll be able to fight them and force them out.' "

¹²But God said to Balaam, "Don't go with them! Don't curse these people, because they are blessed."

¹³When Balaam got up in the morning, he said to Balak's princes, "Go back to your own country, because the LORD has refused to let me go with you."

¹⁴So the Moabite princes went back to Balak and said, "Balaam refused to come with us."

¹⁵Balak sent a larger group of more highly respected princes. ¹⁶When they came to Balaam, they said to him, "This is what Balak, son of Zippor, says: Don't let anything keep you from coming to me. ¹⁷I will make sure you are richly rewarded, and I will do whatever you ask. Please, come and curse these people for me."

¹⁸But Balaam answered Balak's servants, "Even if Balak gave me his palace filled with silver and gold, I couldn't disobey the command of the LORD my God no matter whether the request was important or not. ¹⁹Now, why don't you stay here tonight, as the others did, and I'll find out what else the LORD may have to tell me."

²⁰That night God came to Balaam and said, "If these men have come to summon you, go with them, but do only what I tell you."

Balaam's Journey to Moab

²¹When Balaam got up in the morning, he saddled his donkey and left with the Moabite princes.

²²God became angry that he was going. So the Messenger of the LORD stood in the road to stop him. Balaam was riding on his donkey, accompanied by his two

servants. ²³When the donkey saw the Messenger of the L ord standing in the road with his sword drawn, the donkey turned off the road into a field. Balaam hit the donkey to get it back on the road.

²⁴Where the road went through the vineyards, it was narrow, with stone walls on both sides. Now the Messenger of the L ord stood there. ²⁵When the donkey saw the Messenger of the L ord, it moved over and pinned Balaam's foot against the wall. So Balaam hit the donkey again.

²⁶Then the Messenger of the L ord moved ahead and stood in a narrower place where there was no room to turn to the right or the left. ²⁷When the donkey saw the Messenger of the L ord, it lay down under Balaam. Balaam became so angry he hit the donkey with his stick. ²⁸Then the L ord made the donkey speak, and it asked Balaam, "What have I done to make you hit me three times?"

²⁹Balaam answered, "You've made a fool of me! If I had a sword in my hand, I'd kill you right now."

³⁰The donkey said to Balaam, "I'm your own donkey. You've always ridden me. Have I ever done this to you before?"

"No," he answered.

³¹Then the L ord let Balaam see the Messenger of the L ord who was standing in the road with his sword drawn. So Balaam knelt, bowing with his face touching the ground.

³²The Messenger of the L ord asked him, "Why have you hit your donkey three times like this? I've come here to stop you because the trip you're taking is evil." [a] ³³The donkey saw me and turned away from me these three times. If it had not turned away from me, I would certainly have killed you by now but spared the donkey."

³⁴Balaam said to the Messenger of the L ord, "I've sinned. I didn't know you were standing there in the road to stop me. If you still think this trip is evil, I'll go back."

³⁵The Messenger of the L ord said to Balaam, "Go with the men, but say only what I tell you." So Balaam went with Balak's princes.

³⁶When Balak heard that Balaam had come, he went out to meet him at Ir Moab, in the region of the Arnon Valley, right on the border of Moab. ³⁷Balak said to Balaam, "Why didn't you come when I summoned you? You knew I'd be able to reward you."

³⁸Balaam replied, "Well, I've come to you now. But I can't say whatever I want to. I can only say what God tells me to say."

³⁹Balaam went with Balak to Kiriath Huzoth. ⁴⁰Balak sacrificed cattle, sheep, and goats, and sent some of the meat to Balaam and the princes who were with him.

⁴¹The next morning Balak took Balaam up to Bamoth Baal. From there he could see the outskirts of the Israelites' camp.

Balaam's First Prophecy

23 ¹Balaam said to Balak, "Build seven altars here, and prepare seven bulls and seven rams for me." ²Balak did what Balaam told him, and the two of them offered a bull and a ram on each altar.

³Balaam said to Balak, "Stay here beside your burnt offering while I'm gone. Maybe the L ord will come and meet with me. I will tell you whatever he reveals to me." Then Balaam went off to a higher place where there were no trees.

⁴God came to him, and Balaam said, "I have set up seven altars, and I offered a bull and a ram on each altar."

⁵The L ord told Balaam, "Go back to Balak, and give him my message."

---

a 22:32 Greek; Hebrew meaning of "because . . . evil" uncertain.

⁶So he went back to Balak and found him standing beside his burnt offering with all the princes of Moab. ⁷Then Balaam delivered this message:

> "Balak brought me from Aram.
> The king of Moab summoned me from the eastern mountains.
> > 'Come, curse Jacob for me,' he said.
> > 'Come, condemn Israel.'
> 8 How can I curse those whom God hasn't cursed?
> How can I condemn those whom the LORD hasn't condemned?
> 9 I see them from the top of rocky cliffs,
> I look at them from the hills.
> > I see a nation that lives by itself,
> > > people who do not consider themselves
> > > > to be like other nations.
> 10 The descendants of Jacob are like specks of dust.
> > Who can count them
> > > or number even one-fourth of the people of Israel?
> Let me die the death of innocent people.
> Let my end be like theirs."

¹¹Balak said to Balaam, "What have you done to me? I brought you here to curse my enemies, but all you've done is bless them!"

¹²Balaam answered, "I must say what the LORD tells me to say."

Balaam's Second Prophecy

¹³Then Balak said to him, "Please come with me to another place, where you can see the Israelites. You will see only some of them, not all of them. Curse them for me from there."

¹⁴So he took him to the Field of Zophim[a] on top of Mount Pisgah, where he built seven altars. He offered a bull and a ram on each altar. ¹⁵Then Balaam said to Balak, "Stay here beside your burnt offering while I meet with God over there."

¹⁶The LORD came to Balaam and told him, "Go back to Balak, and give him my message."

¹⁷He came to Balak and found him standing beside his burnt offering with the princes of Moab. Balak asked him, "What did the LORD say?" ¹⁸Then Balaam delivered this message:

> "Stand up, Balak, and listen!
> Hear me, son of Zippor!
> 19 God is not like people. He tells no lies.
> He is not like humans. He doesn't change his mind.
> > When he says something, he does it.
> > When he makes a promise, he keeps it.
> 20 I have received a command to bless.
> He has blessed, and I can't change it.
> 21 He doesn't want any trouble for the descendants of Jacob.
> He sees no misfortune for the people of Israel.
> The LORD their God is with them,
> > praised as their king.

ᵃ23:14 Or "to a lookout point."

22   The God who brought them out of Egypt
           has the strength of a wild bull.
23   No spell can curse the descendants of Jacob.
               No magic can harm the people of Israel.
       Now it will be said of Jacob and Israel:
           'See what God has done!'
24   Here is a nation that attacks like a lioness
           and is as ferocious as a lion.
               It doesn't lie down until it eats its prey
                   and drinks the blood of its victim.''

²⁵Balak said to Balaam, "If you won't curse them, then at least don't bless them!"
²⁶Balaam answered, "Didn't I tell you that I must do whatever the LORD says?"

²⁷Balak said to Balaam, "Come, let me take you to another place. Maybe God wants
you to curse them for me from there." ²⁸So Balak took Balaam to the top of Mount
Peor, which overlooks Jeshimon.

²⁹Balaam said to Balak, "Build seven altars here, and prepare seven bulls and seven
rams for me." ³⁰Balak did what Balaam told him, and he offered a bull and a ram on
each altar.

Balaam's Third Prophecy

24 ¹When Balaam saw that the LORD wanted to bless Israel, he didn't look for
omens as he had done before. He turned toward the desert, ²looked up, and
saw Israel's camp grouped by tribes. The Spirit of God entered him, ³and he delivered this message:

       "This is the message of Balaam, son of Beor.
       This is the message of the man whose eyesight is clear.ᵃ
4   This is the message of the one who hears the words of God,
           has a vision from the Almighty,
               and falls into a trance with his eyes open:
5   How beautiful are your tents, Jacob,
           and the places where you live, Israel.
6   Your tents spread out like rivers,
           like gardens by a river,
               like aloes planted by the LORD,
               like cedars by the water.
7   Water will flow from their buckets,
           and their crops will have plenty of water.
       Their king will be greater than Agag,
           and their kingdom will be considered the best.
8   The God who brought them out of Egypt
           has the strength of a wild bull.
       He will devour nations that are his enemies,
           crush their bones,
               and pierce them with arrows.
9   His people lie down and rest like a lion.
       They are like a lioness. Who dares to disturb them?
       Those who bless you will be blessed!
       Those who curse you will be cursed!"

ᵃ24:3 Greek, Targum; Hebrew meaning uncertain.

Balaam's Fourth Prophecy

¹⁰Balak became angry with Balaam. He clapped his hands and said, "I summoned you to curse my enemies, and now you have blessed them three times. ¹¹Get out of here! Go home! I said I'd reward you richly, but the LORD has made you lose your reward."

¹²Balaam answered Balak, "I told the messengers you sent me, ¹³'Even if Balak would give me his palace filled with silver and gold, I couldn't disobey the LORD's command no matter how good or bad the request might seem to me. I must say only what the LORD says.' ¹⁴Even though I'm going back to my people, I'll give you some advice. I'll tell you what these people will do to your people in the days to come."

¹⁵Then Balaam delivered this message:

"This is the message of Balaam, son of Beor.
This is the message of the man whose eyesight is clear.

16 This is the message of the one who hears the words of God,
        receives knowledge from the Most High,
            has a vision from the Almighty,
                and falls into a trance, with his eyes open:

17 I see someone who is not here now.
    I look at someone who is not nearby.
    A star will come from Jacob.
    A scepter will rise from Israel.
        He will crush the heads of the Moabites
        and destroy all the people of Sheth.ᵇ

18 Edom will be conquered,
        and Seir, his enemy, will be conquered.
        So Israel will become wealthy.

19 He will rule from Jacob
        and destroy whoever is left in their cities."

²⁰Then Balaam saw the Amalekites and delivered this message:

"Amalek was first among the nations,
    but in the end it will be destroyed."

²¹Then he saw the Kenites and delivered this message:

"You have a permanent place to live.
Your nest is built in a rock.

22 But it is destined to be burned, you descendants of Cain,
        when Assyria takes you as prisoners of war."ᶜ

²³He delivered this message:

"Oh no! Who will live when God decides to do this?

24 Ships will come from the shores of Cyprus.
        They will conquer Assyria and Eber.
        But they, too, will be totally destroyed."

²⁵Then Balaam got up and went back home, and Balak also went on his way.

ᵇ24:17 Or "all the descendants of Seth."   ᶜ24:21-22 There is a play on words here among Hebrew *qeyniy* (Kenite), *qinneka* (your nest), and *qayin* (Cain).

Israel Commits Idolatry

25 [1]While Israel was staying at Shittim, the men began to have sex with Moabite women [2]who invited the people to the sacrifices offered to their gods. The people ate the meat from the sacrifices and worshiped these gods. [3]Since the Israelites joined in worshiping the god Baal of Peor, the LORD became angry with Israel.

[4]The LORD said to Moses, "Take all the leaders of the people, and execute them in broad daylight in the LORD's presence. This will turn the LORD's anger away from Israel."

[5]So Moses said to the judges of Israel, "Each of you must kill the men who have joined in worshiping the god Baal of Peor."

[6]One of the Israelite men brought a Midianite woman to his brothers. He did this right in front of Moses and the whole community of Israel while they were crying at the entrance to the tent of meeting. [7]Phinehas, son of Eleazar and grandson of the priest Aaron, saw this. So he left the assembly, took a spear in his hand, [8]and went into the tent after the Israelite man. He drove the spear through the man and into the woman's body. Because of this, the plague that the Israelites were experiencing stopped. [9]However, 24,000 people died from that plague.

[10]Then the LORD said to Moses, [11]"Phinehas, son of Eleazar and grandson of the priest Aaron, turned my fury away from the Israelites. Since he stood up for me, I didn't have to stand up for myself and destroy them. [12]So tell Phinehas that I'm making a promise of peace to him. [13]My promise is that he and his descendants will be priests permanently because he stood up for his God and he made peace with the LORD for the Israelites."

[14]The name of the Israelite man who was killed with the Midianite woman was Zimri, son of Salu. (Salu was the leader of a family from Simeon.) [15]The name of the Midianite woman who was killed was Cozbi, daughter of Zur. (Zur was the head of a family from the Midianite tribes.)

[16]The LORD said to Moses, [17]"Treat the Midianites as your enemies, and kill them [18]because they treated you as enemies. They plotted to trick you in the incident that took place at Peor. They used their sister Cozbi, daughter of a Midianite leader, who was killed on the day of the plague caused by the incident at Peor."

Moses Takes Another Census of Israel

26 [1]After the plague the LORD said to Moses and Eleazar, son of the priest Aaron, [2]"Take a census of the whole community of Israel by households. List those who are at least 20 years old and eligible for military duty."

[3]So Moses and the priest Eleazar spoke to the Israelites on the plains of Moab near the Jordan River across from Jericho. They said, [4]"Take a census of those at least 20 years old, as the LORD commanded Moses."

These are the Israelites who came from Egypt:

[5]**Reuben** was Israel's firstborn. The descendants of Reuben were the family of Hanoch, the family of Pallu, [6]the family of Hezron, and the family of Carmi.

[7]These were the families of Reuben. The total number of men was 43,730.

[8]Eliab was the son[a] of Pallu, [9]and Nemuel, Dathan, and Abiram were the sons of Eliab. (It was Dathan and Abiram, men chosen by the community, who defied Moses and Aaron's authority. They joined Korah's followers when they defied the LORD's authority. [10]The ground opened up and swallowed them along with Korah. They and

---

[a]26:8 Ancient scribal tradition; Masoretic Text "sons."

their followers died when the fire consumed the 250 men. This was a warning. [11]But the descendants of Korah didn't die.)

[12]The families descended from **Simeon** were the family of Nemuel, the family of Jamin, the family of Jakin, [13]the family of Zerah, and the family of Shaul. [14]These were the families of Simeon. The total number of men was 22,200.

[15]The families descended from **Gad** were the family of Zephon, the family of Haggi, the family of Shuni, [16]the family of Ozni, the family of Eri, [17]the family of Arodi,[b] and the family of Areli. [18]These were the families of Gad's descendants. The total number of men was 40,500.

[19]Er and Onan were sons of Judah, but they died in Canaan. [20]The families descended from **Judah** were the family of Shelah, the family of Perez, and the family of Zerah. [21]The descendants of Perez were the family of Hezron and the family of Hamul. [22]These were the families of Judah. The total number of men was 76,500.

[23]The families descended from **Issachar** were the family of Tola, the family of Puah,[c] [24]the family of Jashub, and the family of Shimron. [25]These were the families of Issachar. The total number of men was 64,300.

[26]The families descended from **Zebulun** were the family of Sered, the family of Elon, and the family of Jahleel. [27]These were the families of Zebulun. The total number of men was 60,500.

[28]The families descended from **Joseph** through Manasseh and Ephraim were [29](from Manasseh) the family of Machir (Machir was the father of Gilead) and the family of Gilead. [30]The descendants of Gilead were the family of Iezer, the family of Helek, [31]the family of Asriel, the family of Shechem, [32]the family of Shemida, and the family of Hepher. [33](Zelophehad, son of Hepher, had no sons—only daughters. Their names were Mahlah, Noah, Hoglah, Milcah, and Tirzah.) [34]These were the families of Manasseh. The total number of men was 52,700.

[35]The families descended from Ephraim were the family of Shuthelah, the family of Beker, and the family of Tahan. [36]The descendants of Shuthelah were the family of Eran. [37]These were the families of Ephraim's descendants. The total number of men was 32,500.

These were the families descended from Joseph.

[38]The families descended from **Benjamin** were the family of Bela, the family of Ashbel, the family of Ahiram, [39]the family of Shupham,[d] and the family of Hupham. [40]The descendants of Bela (through Ard and Naaman) were the family of Ard and the family of Naaman. [41]These were the families descended from Benjamin. The total number of men was 45,600.

[42]The family descended from **Dan** was the family of Shuham.

This was the family descended from Dan. [43]The total number of men in all the family of Shuham was 64,400.

---

[b]26:17 Genesis 46:16, Samaritan Pentateuch, Greek, Syriac; Masoretic Text "Arod." [c]26:23 Samaritan Pentateuch, Greek, Syriac, Latin; Masoretic Text "Puvah." [d]26:39 A few Hebrew manuscripts, Samaritan Pentateuch, Greek, Syriac, Targum, Latin; Masoretic Text "Shephupham."

⁴⁴The families descended from **Asher** were the family of Imnah, the family of Ishvi, and the family of Beriah.

⁴⁵The descendants of Beriah were the family of Heber and the family of Malchiel. ⁴⁶(Asher had a daughter named Serah.)

⁴⁷These were the families of Asher's descendants. The total number of men was 53,400.

⁴⁸The families descended from **Naphtali** were the family of Jahzeel, the family of Guni, ⁴⁹the family of Jezer, and the family of Shillem.

⁵⁰These were the families of Naphtali. The total number of men was 45,400.

⁵¹The total number of Israelite men was 601,730.

⁵²Then the LORD said to Moses, ⁵³"The land these people will possess must be divided using the list of names from the census. ⁵⁴Give more land to larger tribes and less land to smaller ones. Use the totals from the census in giving land to each tribe. ⁵⁵But the land must be divided by drawing lots. The tribes will receive their land based on the names of their ancestors. ⁵⁶Whether the tribes are large or small, the land must be divided by drawing lots."

⁵⁷The families descended from **Levi** were listed as the family of Gershon, the family of Kohath, and the family of Merari.

⁵⁸These were the families of Levi: the Libnite family, the Hebronite family, the Mahlite family, the Mushite family, and the Korahite family.

Kohath was the ancestor of Amram. ⁵⁹The name of Amram's wife was Jochebed, a descendant of Levi, who was born in Egypt. She gave birth to Amram's children: Aaron, Moses, and their sister Miriam. ⁶⁰Aaron was the father of Nadab, Abihu, Eleazar, and Ithamar. ⁶¹But Nadab and Abihu had died because they offered unauthorized fire in the LORD's presence.

⁶²The total number of all the Levite males at least one month old was 23,000. They were not counted along with the other Israelites, because they were given no land of their own.

⁶³Moses and the priest Eleazar added up the total number of Israelites on the plains of Moab near the Jordan River across from Jericho. ⁶⁴Among them there wasn't a single one of the Israelites Moses and the priest Aaron had counted in the Desert of Sinai. ⁶⁵The LORD had said, "They must all die in the desert." The only ones left were Caleb (son of Jephunneh) and Joshua (son of Nun).

A Request From Zelophehad's Daughters

27 ¹The daughters of Zelophehad, son of Hepher, grandson of Gilead, descendant of Machir, whose father was Manasseh, belonged to the families of Manasseh, son of Joseph. Their names were Mahlah, Noah, Hoglah, Milcah, and Tirzah. They came ²to Moses and stood in front of him, the priest Eleazar, the leaders, and the whole community at the entrance to the tent of meeting. They said, ³"Our father died in the desert. He was not a part of Korah's followers who joined forces against the LORD. He died for his own sin and left no sons. ⁴Why should our father's name be allowed to die out in his family because he had no son? Give us property among our father's relatives."

⁵So Moses brought their case to the LORD, ⁶and the LORD said to him, ⁷"Zelophehad's daughters are right. You must give them property of their own among their father's relatives. Turn their father's property over to them.

⁸"Tell the Israelites: If a man dies and leaves no sons, turn his property over to his daughters. ⁹If he has no daughters, give his property to his brothers. ¹⁰If he has

no brothers, give his property to his uncles on his father's side of the family. ¹¹If he has no uncles, give his property to the nearest relative in his family, and that relative will take possession of it. This will be a rule for the Israelites, as the LORD commanded Moses."

The LORD Appoints Joshua to Succeed Moses

¹²The LORD said to Moses, "Go up into the Abarim Mountains, and take a look at the land I will give the Israelites. ¹³After you see it, you, too, will join your ancestors in death, as your brother Aaron did. ¹⁴You both rebelled against my command in the Desert of Zin. You didn't show the people how holy I am when they were complaining at the oasis." (This was the oasis of Meribah at Kadesh in the Desert of Zin.)

¹⁵Moses said to the LORD, ¹⁶"LORD, you are the God who gives the breath of life to everyone. Please appoint someone over the community ¹⁷who will lead them in and out of battle, so that the LORD's community will not be like sheep without a shepherd."

¹⁸So the LORD said to Moses, "Take Joshua, son of Nun, a man who has the Spirit, and place your hand on him. ¹⁹Make him stand in front of the priest Eleazar and the whole community, and give him his instructions in their presence. ²⁰Give him some of your authority so that the whole community of Israel will obey him. ²¹He will stand in front of the priest Eleazar, who will use the Urim[a] to make decisions in the LORD's presence. At his command Joshua and the whole community of Israel will go into battle. And at his command they will return."

²²Moses did as the LORD commanded him. He took Joshua and made him stand in front of the priest Eleazar and the whole community. ²³Moses placed his hands on Joshua and gave him his instructions as the LORD had told him.

Daily Sacrifices

28 ¹The LORD said to Moses, ²"Give this command to the Israelites: Be sure to bring me my offerings at the right times. They are my food. They are offerings by fire, a soothing aroma. ³These are the offerings by fire that you must bring to the LORD. Every day you must bring as a daily burnt offering two one-year-old lambs that have no defects. ⁴Offer one in the morning and the other at dusk. ⁵With each of them, also bring a grain offering of eight cups of flour mixed with one quart of virgin olive oil. ⁶This is the daily burnt offering which was established on Mount Sinai. This offering is a soothing aroma, an offering by fire to the LORD. ⁷Also bring a wine offering of one quart of wine for each lamb. Pour it out to the LORD in a holy place. ⁸Offer the other lamb at dusk along with the same grain offering and wine offering as you brought in the morning. This is an offering by fire, a soothing aroma to the LORD.

Weekly Sacrifices

⁹"On the day of worship offer two one-year-old lambs that have no defects, a grain offering of 16 cups of flour mixed with olive oil, and the wine offering that goes with it. ¹⁰This burnt offering is for every day of worship in addition to the daily burnt offerings and the wine offerings that go with them.

Monthly Sacrifices

¹¹"On the first of every month bring the LORD a burnt offering of two young bulls, one ram, and seven one-year-old lambs that have no defects. ¹²With each bull there will be a grain offering of 24 cups of flour mixed with olive oil, with each ram a grain

---

[a] 27:21 The Urim and Thummim were used by the chief priest to determine God's answer to questions.

Daughters of Zelophehad

Numbers 27

"Our father died in the desert and left no sons. Give us property among our father's relatives."

Daughters of Zelophehad were great examples of how people can stand up for their rights. These women were not powerful or wealthy, but they were intelligent and respectful.

The Hebrew law of inheritance said that a man's property passed on to his sons when he died. If there were no sons, the property was given to someone outside the family. When Zelophehad died, his daughters went to the top leaders in the community. They asked for their father's property because they thought it should be theirs.

Moses and Eleazar were wise and fair. They didn't make an immediate decision or try to change God's law. They asked God what to do.

The Lord agreed that what the women asked for was fair. He told Moses to give them their father's land. He also told Moses to change the law of inheritance.

Mahlah means "weak and sickly."

Noah means "rest or comfort."

Hoglah means "partridge."

Milcah means "counsel."

Tirzah's meaning is unknown.

These sisters were born around 1400 B.C.

They gained rights from God for Hebrew women.

Getting to Know the Five Daughters of Zelophehad

✷ How does God treat the women in this story?

✷ How can you speak up for your rights while still being respectful and Christlike?

✷ How can you stick up for someone else's rights?

offering of 16 cups of flour mixed with olive oil, ¹³and with each one-year-old lamb a grain offering of 8 cups of flour mixed with olive oil. This is a burnt offering, a soothing aroma, an offering by fire to the LORD. ¹⁴The wine offering that goes with each bull will be 2 quarts of wine, with each ram 1½ quarts of wine, and with each lamb 1 quart of wine. This will be the monthly burnt offering for every month of the year. ¹⁵In addition to the daily burnt offering with its wine offering, one male goat must be offered to the LORD as an offering for sin.

Annual Sacrifices

¹⁶"The fourteenth day of the first month is the LORD's Passover. ¹⁷The fifteenth of this same month is a pilgrimage festival. For seven days you must eat only unleavened bread. ¹⁸On the first day there will be a holy assembly. Don't do any regular work. ¹⁹Instead, bring the LORD an offering by fire, a burnt offering of two young bulls, one ram, and seven one-year-old lambs, all of them without defects. ²⁰Along with them bring grain offerings of flour mixed with olive oil. Bring 24 cups for each bull, 16 cups for each ram, ²¹and 8 cups for each of the seven lambs. ²²Also bring one male goat as an offering for sin to make peace with the LORD. ²³Offer these in addition to the morning burnt offering. ²⁴Bring all these offerings on each of the seven days. They are food. They are offerings by fire, a soothing aroma to the LORD. They will be offered in addition to the daily burnt offering and the wine offering that goes with it. ²⁵On the seventh day you must have a holy assembly. You must not do any regular work.

²⁶"During the Festival of Weeks, you must have a holy assembly. On that day you must not do any regular work. Bring the LORD your new grain offering, the first produce harvested from your fields. ²⁷Bring a burnt offering as a soothing aroma to the LORD—two young bulls, one ram, and seven one-year-old lambs. ²⁸Along with them bring grain offerings of flour mixed with olive oil. Bring 24 cups for each bull, 16 cups for each ram, ²⁹and 8 cups for each of the seven lambs. ³⁰Also bring one male goat to make peace with the LORD. ³¹Offer these animals that have no defects along with their wine offerings, in addition to the daily burnt offerings and their grain offerings."

29 ¹The LORD continued, "On the first day of the seventh month you must have a holy assembly. You must not do any regular work. It is a day for the trumpets to sound a fanfare. ²As a burnt offering, a soothing aroma to the LORD, bring one young bull, one ram, and seven one-year-old lambs that have no defects. ³Along with them bring grain offerings of flour mixed with olive oil. Bring 24 cups for each bull, 16 cups for each ram, ⁴and 8 cups for each of the seven lambs. ⁵Also bring one male goat as an offering for sin to make peace with the LORD. ⁶Offer these in addition to the monthly burnt offering with its grain offering, and the daily burnt offerings with their proper grain offerings and wine offerings. They are a soothing aroma, an offering by fire to the LORD.

⁷"On the tenth day of the seventh month you must have a holy assembly. You must humble yourselves. You must not do any work. ⁸As a burnt offering, a soothing aroma, bring one young bull, one ram, and seven one-year-old lambs, all of them without defects. ⁹Along with them bring grain offerings of flour mixed with olive oil. Bring 24 cups for each bull, 16 cups for each ram, ¹⁰and 8 cups for each of the seven lambs. ¹¹Also bring one male goat as an offering for sin (in addition to the other offering for sin to make peace with the LORD) and the daily burnt offerings with their grain offerings and wine offerings.

¹²"On the fifteenth day of the seventh month you must have a holy assembly. You must not do any regular work. Instead, celebrate a festival to the LORD for seven days. ¹³As a burnt offering, an offering by fire, a soothing aroma to the LORD, bring 13 young

bulls, 2 rams, and 14 one-year-old lambs, all of them without defects. [14]Along with them bring grain offerings of flour mixed with olive oil. Bring 24 cups for each of the 13 bulls, 16 cups for each of the 2 rams, [15]and 8 cups for each of the 14 one-year-old lambs. [16]Also bring one male goat as an offering for sin in addition to the daily burnt offerings with their grain offerings and wine offerings.

[17]"On the second day bring 12 young bulls, 2 rams, and 14 one-year-old lambs that have no defects. [18]Along with them bring the proper amount of grain offerings and wine offerings for each of the bulls, rams, and lambs. [19]Also bring one male goat as an offering for sin in addition to the daily burnt offerings with their grain offerings and wine offerings.

[20]"On the third day bring 11 bulls, 2 rams, and 14 one-year-old lambs that have no defects. [21]Along with them bring the proper amount of grain offerings and wine offerings for each of the bulls, rams, and lambs. [22]Also bring one male goat as an offering for sin in addition to the daily burnt offerings with their grain offerings and wine offerings.

[23]"On the fourth day bring 10 bulls, 2 rams, and 14 one-year-old lambs that have no defects. [24]Along with them bring the proper amount of grain offerings and wine offerings for each of the bulls, rams, and lambs. [25]Also bring one male goat as an offering for sin in addition to the daily burnt offerings with their grain offerings and wine offerings.

[26]"On the fifth day bring 9 bulls, 2 rams, and 14 one-year-old lambs that have no defects. [27]Along with them bring the proper amount of grain offerings and wine offerings for each of the bulls, rams, and lambs. [28]Also bring one male goat as an offering for sin in addition to the daily burnt offerings with their grain offerings and wine offerings.

[29]"On the sixth day bring 8 bulls, 2 rams, and 14 one-year-old lambs that have no defects. [30]Along with them bring the proper amount of grain offerings and wine offerings for each of the bulls, rams, and lambs. [31]Also bring one male goat as an offering for sin in addition to the daily burnt offerings with their grain offerings and wine offerings.

[32]"On the seventh day bring 7 bulls, 2 rams, and 14 one-year-old lambs that have no defects. [33]Along with them bring the proper amount of grain offerings and wine offerings for each of the bulls, rams, and lambs. [34]Also bring one male goat as an offering for sin in addition to the daily burnt offerings with their grain offerings and wine offerings.

[35]"On the eighth day you must hold a religious assembly. You must not do any daily work. [36]As a burnt offering, an offering by fire, a soothing aroma to the LORD, bring one bull, one ram, and seven one-year-old lambs that have no defects. [37]Along with them bring the proper amount of grain offerings and wine offerings for the bull, the ram, and the lambs. [38]Also bring one male goat as an offering for sin in addition to the daily burnt offerings with their grain offerings and wine offerings.

[39]"These are the offerings you must bring to the LORD at your festivals. They are the offerings you must bring in addition to the offerings for anything you vowed to give to the LORD, your freewill offerings, your burnt offerings, your grain offerings, your wine offerings, and your fellowship offerings."[a]

[40]Moses told the Israelites everything the LORD had commanded him.

---

[a]29:39 Numbers 29:40 in English Bibles is Numbers 30:1 in the Hebrew Bible.

Teachings About Vows

30 [a]1Moses said to the heads of the tribes of Israel, "This is what the LORD has commanded about vows : 2If a man makes a vow to the LORD that he will do something or swears an oath that he won't do something, he must not break his word. He must do everything he said he would do.

3"A young girl, who still lives in her father's house, might make a vow to the LORD that she will do something or swear an oath that she won't do something. 4If her father says nothing to her when he hears about it, her vow or oath must be kept. 5But if her father objects when he hears about it, her vow or oath doesn't have to be kept. The LORD will free her from this vow or oath because her father objected.

6"An unmarried woman might make a vow that she will do something or carelessly promise that she won't do something. When she marries, 7her husband may hear about it but say nothing to her. Then her vow or oath must be kept. 8But if her husband objects when he hears about it, he can cancel the vow or promise she made. The LORD will free her from this vow or promise.

9"But a widow or a divorced woman must keep her vow or her promise.

10"A married woman might make a vow that she will do something or swear an oath that she won't do something. 11Her husband may hear about it but may say nothing and not object. Then her vow or oath must be kept. 12But if her husband cancels it when he hears about it, nothing she said in her vow or oath has to be kept. Her husband has canceled it, and the LORD will free her from this vow or oath.

13"A husband decides whether or not his wife has to keep any vow to do something or any oath to do without something. 14If he says nothing to her about it day after day, this means he's decided that she must keep her vow or oath. She must keep it because he said nothing to her when he heard about it. 15But if he cancels it later, he will suffer the consequences."

16These are the laws the LORD gave Moses for husbands and wives, and for fathers with young daughters still living at home.

The LORD Commands Israel to Defeat Midian

31 1The LORD said to Moses, 2"Get even with the Midianites for what they did to the Israelites. After that you will join your ancestors in death ."

3Moses said to the people, "Some of your men must get ready to go to war against the Midianites. The LORD will use them to get even with Midian. 4Send 1,000 men from each of the tribes of Israel."

5So 1,000 men from each tribe were supplied from the divisions of Israel—12,000 men ready for war. 6Then Moses sent them off to war, 1,000 men from each tribe along with Phinehas, son of the priest Eleazar. Phinehas took with him the holy articles and the trumpets for the fanfare.

7They went to war against Midian, as the LORD commanded Moses, and killed every man. 8Among those killed were the five kings of Midian—Evi, Rekem, Zur, Hur, and Reba. They also killed Balaam, son of Beor, in battle. 9The Israelites took the Midianite women and children as prisoners of war. They also took all their animals, their livestock, and their valuables as loot. 10They burned all the cities where the Midianites lived and all their settlements. 11Then they took everything as loot, including all the people and animals, 12and brought the prisoners of war, the loot, and everything to Moses, the priest Eleazar, and the community of Israel at the camp on the plains of Moab near the Jordan River across from Jericho.

---

[a] 30:1 Numbers 30:1-16 in English Bibles is Numbers 30:2-17 in the Hebrew Bible.

¹³Moses, the priest Eleazar, and all the leaders of the community went outside the camp to meet them. ¹⁴Moses was angry with the officers of the army, the commanders of the companies and battalions, who were returning from battle.

¹⁵"Why did you let all the women live?" he asked them. ¹⁶"Remember, they were the ones who followed Balaam's advice and caused[a] the Israelites to be unfaithful to the Lord in the incident that took place at Peor. The Lord's community experienced a plague at that time. ¹⁷So kill all the Midianite boys and every Midianite woman who has gone to bed with a man. ¹⁸But save for yourselves every girl who has never gone to bed with a man.

¹⁹"Everyone who killed a person or touched a dead body must stay outside the camp seven days. You and your prisoners of war must use the ritual water on the third and seventh days in order to take away your sin. ²⁰Do the same for all the clothes and everything made of leather, goats' hair, or wood."

²¹Then the priest Eleazar said to the soldiers who had gone into battle, "This is what the Lord's teachings told Moses to do: ²²Any gold, silver, bronze, iron, tin, or lead— ²³anything that won't burn—must be put through fire in order to make it clean.[b] Then it must also be put through the ritual water in order to take away its sin. Whatever might burn must only be put through the ritual water. ²⁴On the seventh day wash your clothes, and you will be clean. Then you may come into the camp."

²⁵The Lord said to Moses, ²⁶"You, the priest Eleazar, and the heads of the families of the community need to count all the loot, including the people and animals you captured. ²⁷Divide the loot between the soldiers who served in the war and the rest of the community. ²⁸Collect a tax for the Lord. From the soldiers who served in the war collect one out of every 500 things. This includes people, cattle, donkeys, sheep, and goats. ²⁹Collect all these things from the soldiers' half of the loot, and give them to the priest Eleazar as a contribution to the Lord. ³⁰From the Israelites' half of the loot, collect one out of every 50 things. This includes people, cattle, donkeys, sheep, goats, and every other kind of animal. Give them to the Levites who are in charge of the work done at the Lord's tent." ³¹Moses and the priest Eleazar did as the Lord commanded Moses.

³²This is the loot that was left from everything that the troops took: 675,000 sheep and goats, ³³72,000 cattle, ³⁴61,000 donkeys, and ³⁵32,000 women who had never gone to bed with a man.

³⁶Half of it went to the soldiers who served in the war. Of the 337,500 sheep and goats they received, ³⁷675 went to the Lord as taxes. ³⁸Of the 36,000 cattle they received, 72 went to the Lord as taxes. ³⁹Of the 30,500 donkeys they received, 61 went to the Lord as taxes. ⁴⁰Of the 16,000 people they received, 32 went to the Lord as taxes.

⁴¹Moses gave the Lord's taxes to the priest Eleazar, as the Lord had commanded him.

⁴²Moses took the Israelites' half of the loot from the soldiers. ⁴³The community received 337,500 sheep and goats, ⁴⁴36,000 cattle, ⁴⁵30,500 donkeys, ⁴⁶and 16,000 people.

⁴⁷From the Israelites' half Moses collected one out of every 50 things, including people and animals, as the Lord commanded him. Then he gave all this to the Levites who were in charge of the work done at the Lord's tent.

⁴⁸Then the officers from the military divisions, the commanders of the companies and battalions of men, came to Moses. ⁴⁹They said to him, "Sir, we have counted all the soldiers under our command, and not one of them is missing. ⁵⁰So we have brought

---

[a] 31:16 Targum; Hebrew meaning of "caused" uncertain.   [b] 31:23 "Clean" refers to anything that is presentable to God.

as gifts to the LORD the gold jewelry that each of us found—arm bands, bracelets, signet rings, earrings, and pendants. We offer them to make peace with the LORD."

⁵¹Moses and the priest Eleazar took all the hand-crafted gold articles from them. ⁵²All the gold contributed to the LORD by the commanders weighed about 420 pounds. ⁵³Each soldier kept his own loot. ⁵⁴Moses and the priest Eleazar took the gold from the commanders and brought it into the LORD's presence at the tent of meeting as a reminder to the Israelites.

The Tribes of Reuben and Gad Request Land East of the Jordan River

32 ¹The tribes of Reuben and Gad had a large number of livestock. They saw that the regions of Jazer and Gilead were a good place for livestock. ²So they came to Moses, the priest Eleazar, and the leaders of the community, and said to them, ³"Ataroth, Dibon, Jazer, Nimrah, Heshbon, Elealeh, Sebam, Nebo, and Beon, ⁴the land that the LORD won for the community of Israel, is a good place for livestock. Gentlemen, we have livestock. ⁵Please give us this land as our property. Don't make us cross the Jordan River."

⁶Moses asked the tribes of Gad and Reuben, "Are you going to stay here while the rest of the Israelites go to war? ⁷That might discourage them from entering the land the LORD has given them. ⁸That's what your ancestors did when I sent them from Kadesh Barnea to take a look at the land. ⁹They went as far as the Eshcol Valley and saw the land. But then they discouraged the rest of the Israelites from entering the land that the LORD had given them. ¹⁰That day the LORD became angry and swore this oath, ¹¹'None of the people 20 years old or older, who came from Egypt, will see the land I promised Abraham, Isaac, and Jacob with an oath. This is because they didn't wholeheartedly follow me.' ¹²Only Caleb (son of Jephunneh the Kenizzite) and Joshua (son of Nun) will get to see the land. This is because they wholeheartedly followed the LORD. ¹³Since the LORD was angry with the Israelites, he made them wander in the desert for 40 years until the whole generation of those who had done evil in the LORD's presence was gone.

¹⁴"You're just like your parents! You're a bunch of sinners trying to make the LORD angry with Israel again. ¹⁵If you turn away from him, he will abandon all these people in the desert. You would be responsible for their destruction."

¹⁶Then the tribes of Gad and Reuben came up to Moses and said, "Allow us to build stone fences for our livestock and cities for our families here. ¹⁷Then we'll be ready to march in battle formation*ª* ahead of the other Israelites until we have brought them to their land. Meanwhile our families will live in walled cities, safe from the other people who live here. ¹⁸We will not return to our homes until every Israelite has received his own land. ¹⁹We won't take possession of any land on the other side of the Jordan River, to the west and beyond. We already have our land here, east of the Jordan."

²⁰Moses answered, "Do what you have said. In the LORD's presence have all your armed men get ready for battle. ²¹Have them cross the Jordan, and fight until the LORD forces out his enemies ²²and the land is conquered. Then you may come back. You will have fulfilled your military duty to the LORD and Israel. This land will be your own property in the LORD's presence.

²³"If you don't do all these things, you will be sinning against the LORD. You can be sure that you will be punished for your sin. ²⁴Build cities for your families and stone fences for your flocks, but do what you have promised."

ª 32:17 Greek, Latin; Masoretic Text "ready to march ahead quickly."

²⁵Then the tribes of Gad and Reuben said to Moses, "Sir, we will do as you command. ²⁶Our children, our wives, our livestock, and all our other animals will stay here in the cities of Gilead. ²⁷But in the LORD's presence we will all get ready for battle and go with you, as you have said."

²⁸So Moses gave orders about them to the priest Eleazar, Joshua (son of Nun), and the family heads of the tribes of Israel. ²⁹Moses told them, "If the tribes of Gad and Reuben get ready for battle in the LORD's presence and cross the Jordan River with you and you conquer the land, give them Gilead as their own property. ³⁰If they don't get ready for battle and go with you, the land they will take possession of must be in Canaan with yours."

³¹The tribes of Gad and Reuben answered, "Sir, we will do as the LORD has said. ³²We will enter Canaan as armed troops in the LORD's presence, but the land we will take possession of is here, east of the Jordan."

³³So Moses gave the tribes of Gad, Reuben, and half of the tribe of Manasseh, son of Joseph, the kingdoms of King Sihon of the Amorites and King Og of Bashan—the whole land with its cities and its surrounding territory.

³⁴The tribe of Gad rebuilt the cities of Dibon, Ataroth, Aroer, ³⁵Atroth Shophan, Jazer, Jogbehah, ³⁶Beth Nimrah, and Beth Haran as walled cities. They also built stone fences for their flocks.

³⁷The tribe of Reuben rebuilt the cities of Heshbon, Elealeh, Kiriathaim, ³⁸Nebo, Baal Meon (whose names were changed), and Sibmah. These are the names they gave the cities they rebuilt.

³⁹The descendants of Machir, son of Manasseh, went to Gilead, captured it, and forced out the Amorites who were there. ⁴⁰So Moses gave Gilead to the people of Machir (the descendants of Manasseh), and they lived there. ⁴¹Then Jair, a descendant of Manasseh, captured the settlements in Gilead. He called them Havvoth Jair [Settlements of Jair]. ⁴²Nobah captured Kenath and its villages. He named it Nobah after himself.

A Summary of Israel's Journeys After Leaving Egypt

33 ¹This is a list of all the places where the Israelites set up camp after they left Egypt in organized groups under the leadership of Moses and Aaron. ²At the LORD's command Moses wrote down the places where they went as they traveled. This is the list:

³They moved from Rameses on the fifteenth day of the first month, the day after the Passover. The Israelites boldly left in full view of all the Egyptians. ⁴The Egyptians were burying all their firstborn sons, whom the LORD had killed in a mighty act of judgment on their gods.

⁵The Israelites moved from Rameses and set up camp at Succoth.

⁶They moved from Succoth and set up camp at Etham, on the edge of the desert.

⁷They moved from Etham and turned back to Pi Hahiroth, east of Baal Zephon, and set up camp near Migdol.

⁸They moved from Pi Hahiroth*ᵃ* and went through the middle of the sea into the desert. After they traveled for three days in the Desert of Etham, they set up camp at Marah.

⁹They moved from Marah and came to Elim. Elim had 12 springs and 70 palm trees, so they set up camp there.

¹⁰They moved from Elim and set up camp by the Red Sea.

ᵃ33:8 Most Hebrew manuscripts, Samaritan Pentateuch, Syriac, Latin; some Hebrew manuscripts "moved from in front of Hahiroth."

¹¹They moved from the Red Sea and set up camp in the Desert of Sin.

¹²They moved from the Desert of Sin and set up camp at Dophkah.

¹³They moved from Dophkah and set up camp at Alush.

¹⁴They moved from Alush and set up camp at Rephidim, where there was no water for the people to drink.

¹⁵They moved from Rephidim and set up camp in the Desert of Sinai.

¹⁶They moved from the Desert of Sinai and set up camp at Kibroth Hattaavah.

¹⁷They moved from Kibroth Hattaavah and set up camp at Hazeroth.

¹⁸They moved from Hazeroth and set up camp at Rithmah.

¹⁹They moved from Rithmah and set up camp at Rimmon Perez.

²⁰They moved from Rimmon Perez and set up camp at Libnah.

²¹They moved from Libnah and set up camp at Rissah.

²²They moved from Rissah and set up camp at Kehelathah.

²³They moved from Kehelathah and set up camp at Mount Shepher.

²⁴They moved from Mount Shepher and set up camp at Haradah.

²⁵They moved from Haradah and set up camp at Makheloth.

²⁶They moved from Makheloth and set up camp at Tahath.

²⁷They moved from Tahath and set up camp at Terah.

²⁸They moved from Terah and set up camp at Mithcah.

²⁹They moved from Mithcah and set up camp at Hashmonah.

³⁰They moved from Hashmonah and set up camp at Moseroth.

³¹They moved from Moseroth and set up camp at Bene Jaakan.

³²They moved from Bene Jaakan and set up camp at Hor Haggidgad.

³³They moved from Hor Haggidgad and set up camp at Jotbathah.

³⁴They moved from Jotbathah and set up camp at Abronah.

³⁵They moved from Abronah and set up camp at Ezion Geber.

³⁶They moved from Ezion Geber and set up camp at Kadesh in the Desert of Zin.

³⁷They moved from Kadesh and set up camp at Mount Hor on the border of Edom.

³⁸At the Lᴏʀᴅ's command the priest Aaron went up on Mount Hor. He died there on the first day of the fifth month in the fortieth year after the Israelites had left Egypt. ³⁹Aaron was 123 years old when he died on Mount Hor.

⁴⁰(The Canaanite king of Arad, who lived in the Negev, which was in Canaan, heard that the Israelites were coming.)

⁴¹They moved from Mount Hor and set up camp at Zalmonah.

⁴²They moved from Zalmonah and set up camp at Punon.

⁴³They moved from Punon and set up camp at Oboth.

⁴⁴They moved from Oboth and set up camp at Iye Abarim on the border of Moab.

⁴⁵They moved from Iyim*ᵇ* and set up camp at Dibon Gad.

⁴⁶They moved from Dibon Gad and set up camp at Almon Diblathaim.

⁴⁷They moved from Almon Diblathaim and set up camp in the Abarim Mountains east of Nebo.

⁴⁸They moved from the Abarim Mountains and set up camp on the plains of Moab near the Jordan River across from Jericho. ⁴⁹They set up camp on the plains of Moab along the Jordan. Their camp extended from Beth Jeshimoth to Abel Shittim.

The Canaanites Must Be Forced Out

⁵⁰The Lᴏʀᴅ said to Moses on the plains of Moab near the Jordan River across from Jericho, ⁵¹"Tell the Israelites, 'You will be crossing the Jordan River and entering

---

ᵇ 33:45 Or "Iye Abarim."

Canaan. ⁵²As you advance, force out all the people who live there. Get rid of all their stone and metal idols, and destroy all their places of worship. ⁵³Take possession of the land and live there, because I will give it to you for your own. ⁵⁴Divide the land among your families by drawing lots. Give more land to larger families and less land to smaller ones. The land must be given to each family by drawing lots. Divide it among your ancestors' tribes.

⁵⁵" 'But if you do not force out those who live in the land, they will be like splinters in your eyes and thorns in your sides. They will constantly fight with you over the land you live in. ⁵⁶Then I will do to you what I planned to do to them.' "

The Boundaries of Israel's Land

34 ¹The LORD said to Moses, ²"Give the Israelites these instructions. When you enter Canaan, the land that will be given to you as your inheritance has these borders:

³"The southern side includes part of the Desert of Zin along the border of Edom. In the east the southern border starts from the end of the Dead Sea ⁴and turns south of the Akrabbim Pass. It then goes past Zin and ends at Kadesh Barnea. From there it goes to Hazar Addar and on to Azmon. ⁵From Azmon it turns toward the River of Egypt so that the border ends at the Mediterranean Sea.

⁶"The western border is the coastline of the Mediterranean Sea.

⁷"The northern border extends from the Mediterranean Sea to Mount Hor, ⁸and from Mount Hor to the border of Hamath so that it ends at Zedad. ⁹From there the border goes to Ziphron and ends at Hazar Enan.

¹⁰"The eastern border extends from Hazar Enan to Shepham. ¹¹From Shepham the border goes down to Riblah, east of Ain, and continues along the eastern slope of the Sea of Galilee. ¹²Then the border goes along the Jordan River so that it ends at the Dead Sea.

"This will be your land and the borders around it."

¹³Moses commanded the Israelites, "This is the land you will divide by drawing lots. The LORD has commanded that this land will be given to the nine-and-a-half tribes. ¹⁴The households from the tribes of Reuben, Gad, and half of the tribe of Manasseh have already received their land. ¹⁵Those two-and-a-half tribes received land east of the Jordan River across from Jericho."

Men Are Appointed to Divide the Land

¹⁶The LORD said to Moses, ¹⁷"These are the names of the men who will divide the land for you: the priest Eleazar and Joshua, son of Nun. ¹⁸You must also take one leader from each tribe to divide the land. ¹⁹These are their names:

Caleb, son of Jephunneh, from the tribe of Judah;
²⁰Shemuel, son of Ammihud, from the tribe of Simeon;
²¹Elidad, son of Kislon, from the tribe of Benjamin;
²²Bukki, son of Jogli, the leader of the tribe of Dan;
²³Hanniel, son of Ephod, the leader of the tribe of Manasseh;
²⁴Kemuel, son of Shiphtan, the leader of the tribe of Ephraim;
(Manasseh and Ephraim are Joseph's descendants.)ª
²⁵Elizaphan, son of Parnach, the leader of the tribe of Zebulun;
²⁶Paltiel, son of Azzan, the leader of the tribe of Issachar;
²⁷Ahihud, son of Shelomi, the leader of the tribe of Asher;

ª34:24 This sentence has been moved from verse 23 in order to express the complex Hebrew sentence structure more clearly in English.

²⁸Pedahel, son of Ammihud, the leader of the tribe of Naphtali."

²⁹These are the men the LORD commanded to divide Canaan for the Israelites.

Cities for the Levites

35 ¹The LORD spoke to Moses on the plains of Moab near the Jordan River across from Jericho. He said, ²"Tell the Israelites to give the Levites some cities from their own property. They must also give the Levites the pastureland around those cities. ³Then the Levites will have cities to live in and pastureland for their cattle, the flocks they own, and any other animals they have.

⁴"The land around the cities that you give the Levites will extend 1,500 feet from the city wall. ⁵Outside the city measure off 3,000 feet on the east side, 3,000 feet on the south side, 3,000 feet on the west side, and 3,000 feet on the north side, with the city in the center. This will be their pastureland around the city.

⁶"Six of the cities you give the Levites will be cities of refuge. You must allow murderers to escape to these cities. In addition, you must also give the Levites 42 other cities. ⁷So you will give a total of 48 cities with pastureland to the Levites. ⁸The cities you give the Levites from the property of the other Israelites must be given based on the amount of land each tribe owns. Take more cities from larger tribes and fewer from smaller tribes."

Cities of Refuge

⁹The LORD said to Moses, ¹⁰"Tell the Israelites: When you cross the Jordan River and enter Canaan, ¹¹select certain cities to be places of refuge. Anyone who unintentionally kills another person may run to them. ¹²These cities will be places of refuge from any relative who can avenge the death. So anyone accused of murder will not have to die until he has had a trial in front of the community. ¹³There will be six cities you select as places of refuge, ¹⁴three on the east side of the Jordan River and three in Canaan. ¹⁵These six cities will be places of refuge for Israelites, foreigners, and strangers among you. Anyone who unintentionally kills another person may flee to these cities.

Privacy

Numbers 35:9-15

Everyone needs a safe place now and then. God even provided a safe place for people who killed someone by accident. Do you have a safe, private place where you can go when you want to be alone? If you don't, ask your parents to help you pick one. And ask them to tell your brothers and sisters to leave you alone when you go there.

---

¹⁶"But if any of you uses an iron weapon to kill another person, you are a murderer. Murderers must be put to death. ¹⁷If any of you picks up a stone as a weapon and uses it to kill another person, you are a murderer. Murderers must be put to death. ¹⁸Or if any of you picks up a piece of wood as a weapon and uses it to kill another person, you are a murderer. Murderers must be put to death. ¹⁹The relative who can avenge the death must make sure a murderer is put to death. When he catches up

with the murderer, he must kill him. ²⁰If any of you kills someone you hate by shoving him or by deliberately throwing something at him, ²¹or if you beat your enemy to death with your bare hands, you must be put to death. You are a murderer. The relative who can avenge the death must kill you when he catches up with you, because you are a murderer.

²²"But suppose you accidentally kill someone who wasn't your enemy. Maybe you shoved him or threw something at him but didn't mean to kill him. ²³Or suppose you drop a big stone, and someone is killed. However, you didn't know the person was there, he wasn't your enemy, and you weren't trying to harm him. ²⁴Then the community must use these rules in order to decide if you are innocent, or if the dead person's relative can avenge the death. ²⁵If you are innocent, the community must protect you from that relative. They must take you back to the city of refuge you fled to. You must live there until the death of the chief priest who was anointed with the holy oil.

²⁶"But don't go outside the city of refuge you fled to. ²⁷If the relative who can avenge the death finds you outside the city of refuge and kills you, the relative is not guilty of murder. ²⁸Accused murderers must stay in their city of refuge until the death of the chief priest. They may go back to their own property only after his death.

²⁹"These will be the rules for future generations wherever you live.

³⁰"Whoever kills another person will be put to death as a murderer only on the testimony of more than one witness. No one can be put to death on the testimony of only one witness.

³¹"Never accept a cash payment in exchange for the life of a convicted murderer who has been given the death penalty. Murderers must be put to death.

³²"An accused murderer who has fled to a city of refuge must never go back and live on his own land before the death of the chief priest. Don't accept a cash payment to allow him to do this.

³³"You must not pollute the land where you live. Murder is what pollutes the land. The land where a murder was committed can never make peace with the LORD except through the death of the murderer. ³⁴Never make the land where you and I live unclean.ᵃ I, the LORD, live among the Israelites."

The Rights of Women to Inherit Land

36 ¹The heads of the households whose families were descended from Gilead, son of Machir and grandson of Manasseh (families of Joseph's descendants), came and spoke to Moses and the leaders of the other Israelite households. ²They said, "Sir, the LORD commanded you to give the Israelites their land by drawing lots. The LORD also commanded you to give the land of our relative Zelophehad to his daughters. ³Suppose they marry men from the other tribes of Israel. Their land will be taken away from that of our ancestors and added to the land of the tribe they marry into. Then we will have lost part of our land. ⁴When the Israelites' jubilee year comes, their land will be added to that of the tribe they married into. Then part of the land of our ancestor's tribe will be gone."

⁵So Moses gave the Israelites a command from the LORD. "The tribe of Joseph's descendants is right. ⁶This is what the LORD commands for Zelophehad's daughters: They may marry anyone they want to, but only within a family of their ancestor's tribe. ⁷In this way no land of the Israelites will pass from one tribe to another. Every Israelite must keep the tribal land inherited from his ancestors. ⁸A woman who inherits

---

ᵃ 35:34 "Unclean" refers to anything that is not presentable to God.

land in any of the tribes of Israel may marry a man from any family in her ancestor's tribe. In this way every Israelite keeps the land inherited from his ancestors. [9]No land may pass from one tribe to another. Each Israelite tribe must keep the land it inherits."

[10]Zelophehad's daughters did as the Lord commanded Moses. [11]Mahlah, Tirzah, Hoglah, Milcah, and Noah married their cousins on their father's side of the family. [12]They married within the families of the descendants of Manasseh, son of Joseph. So their land stayed in the tribe of their father's family.

[13]These are the commands and rules the Lord gave the Israelites through Moses on the plains of Moab near the Jordan River across from Jericho.

AN INTRODUCTION TO
Deuteronomy

After 40 years of wandering in the wilderness, the new generation of Israelites needed a reminder of who they were and how God wanted them to live. So Moses gave them a history lesson and reviewed God's law. The name of this book means "second law." Deuteronomy repeats the ten commandments and other rules for living good and happy lives. It also reminds us that God gave Israel his law because God loves his people.

Headlines

Women, Children Settle Towns
Deuteronomy 3, page 229

Respectful Children Live Longer
Deuteronomy 5, page 232

God Fights for Israel
Deuteronomy 9, page 237

People Don't Have to Pay Debts!
Deuteronomy 15, page 243

Watch Out for Widows
Deuteronomy 24, page 253

Moses' Grave Is Lost!
Deuteronomy 34, page 269

Israelite women wore clothes like these while they wandered in the wilderness.

Scrambled Laws

These laws are mixed up. Draw a line from the first part of the law to the second part. To check yourself, look up the chapter and verse in Deuteronomy.

14:3   Never eat anything   but justice.

16:20   Strive for nothing   when it's threshing grain.

22:8   When you build a new home   that is disgusting to the LORD.

25:4   Never muzzle an ox   put a railing around the edge of the roof.

What's In It For Me?

God's law . . .

PROTECTS WOMEN.
PROVIDES FOR THE POOR.
PROMOTES JUSTICE.
OFFERS MERCY.
LEADS TO PROSPERITY.
WILL LAST FOREVER.

Who Should Support the Poor?

In the United States, many poor people are on welfare. The government gives them money that is collected from other people through taxes. Today some say welfare doesn't always help poor people.

The Bible tells us to care for the poor. But what is the best way to help people in need? One Old Testament law says people should loan money to the poor and not charge interest. Another Old Testament law says farmers should leave some crops in their fields so the poor can gather their own food. Another law says that a person who is really poor can agree to work seven years for someone who has money. During the time the poor person is working, he or she will learn how to do different jobs. After the seven years are up, the richer person is supposed to give the poor person enough money to start his or her own business.

God expects us to care about people who need our help. But God also expects people who need help to try to help themselves. To learn more about the Bible's approach to welfare, see Exodus 23:10-11; Deuteronomy 14:28-29; Deuteronomy 15:12-18; and Deuteronomy 24:17-22.

You Be
the Judge

Deuteronomy records laws to help judges decide cases. If you were a judge, how would you decide the cases below? After you decide, look up the verse and see what God's law says.

Case #1: Your best friend asks you to lie so she doesn't get in trouble. What should you do? (Deuteronomy 5:20)

Case #2: Your bike was stolen! A month later you find it in the park, broken. A girl named Kris says she saw Jill take it. Jill says she didn't. Is Jill guilty? (Deuteronomy 17:6)

Case #3: A friend wants you to play with a Oiuja board and communicate with the spirit world. It's just a game, so is it OK? (Deuteronomy 18:9-13)

Case #4: Someone tells you she lost a hat. Later you find it. Should you return it, or is it "finders keepers"? (Deuteronomy 22:1-3)

Case #5: On your way home from school, you pass an apple orchard. Is it all right to fill a basket with apples and take them home? (Deuteronomy 23:24)

Law = Love

God gave the Israelites the law because he loved them. The law was part of a special agreement that God made with his people. By keeping the law, people showed God that they loved him. God loves you, too. If you do right, you can show your love for God, also.

**ISRAEL'S
OBEDIENCE BROUGHT:**
health
many children
victory over enemies
plenty of food and wealth
respect from other nations
(see Deuteronomy 28:1-14)

**ISRAEL'S
DISOBEDIENCE BROUGHT:**
disease
few children
defeat by enemies
lack of food and shelter
cruel treatment from other nations
(see Deuteronomy 28:15-68)

Deuteronomy

Moses Speaks to the People 40 Years After Leaving Egypt

[1] ¹This is the speech Moses gave in the desert east of the Jordan River, on the plains, near Suph, between Paran and Tophel, and near Laban, Hazeroth, and Di Zahab. He spoke to all the Israelites. ²(It takes 11 days to go from Mount Horeb to Kadesh Barnea by way of Mount Seir.)

³On the first day of the eleventh month in the fortieth year after they had left Egypt, Moses told the Israelites everything the LORD had commanded him to tell them. ⁴This was after he had defeated King Sihon of the Amorites, who ruled in Heshbon, and King Og of Bashan, who ruled in Ashtaroth and* in Edrei. ⁵The Israelites were east of the Jordan River in Moab when Moses began to review God's teachings.

Moses Reminds Israel of the Events at Mount Horeb

This is what he said:

⁶At Mount Horeb the LORD our God said to us, "You have stayed at this mountain long enough. ⁷Break camp, and get ready! Go to the mountain region of the Amorites, and go to everyone living on the plains, in the mountains, in the foothills, in the Negev, on the whole Mediterranean coast (the land of the Canaanites), and into Lebanon as far as the Euphrates River. ⁸I'm giving you this land. Enter, and take possession of the land the LORD swore to give to your ancestors Abraham, Isaac, and Jacob, and to you, their descendants."

⁹At that time I said to you, "I'm not able to take care of you by myself. ¹⁰The LORD your God has made your population increase so that you are now as numerous as the stars in the sky. ¹¹May the LORD God of your ancestors make you a thousand times more numerous, and may he bless you as he has promised. ¹²How can I take care of your problems, your troubles, and your disagreements all by myself? ¹³From each of your tribes, choose some men who are wise, intelligent, and experienced, and I'll appoint them to be your leaders."

¹⁴You agreed that this was a good idea.

¹⁵So I took the heads of your tribes who were wise and experienced men and made them officers for each of your tribes. I put them in charge of groups of 1,000, or 100, or 50, or 10 people. ¹⁶Also at that time I gave these instructions to your judges: "Hear the cases that your people bring. Judge each case fairly, no matter whether it is a dispute between two Israelites or a dispute between an Israelite and a non-Israelite. ¹⁷Be impartial in your decisions. Listen to the least important people the same way you listen to the most important people. Never be afraid of anyone, since your decisions come from God. You may bring me any case that's too hard for you, and I will hear it." ¹⁸So I told you how to handle these situations.

Moses Reminds Israel of the Events at Kadesh Barnea

¹⁹So we left Mount Horeb, as the LORD our God had commanded. We traveled through all that vast and dangerous desert you saw on the way to the mountain region of the Amorites. At last we came to Kadesh Barnea. ²⁰Then I said to you, "We

---

*1:4 One Hebrew manuscript, Greek, Syriac, Latin; Masoretic Text omits "and."

have come to the mountain region of the Amorites, which the LORD our God is giving us. ²¹The LORD your God is giving you this land. Go ahead! Take possession of it, as the LORD God of your ancestors told you. Don't be afraid or terrified."

²²All of you came to me and said, "Let's send men ahead of us to gather information about the land for us. Have them report to us about the route we should take and the cities we'll come to."

²³It seemed like a good idea to me. So I chose 12 of your men, one from each tribe. ²⁴They left and went into the mountains. When they came to the Eshcol Valley, they explored it. ²⁵They took some of the region's fruit with them and brought it back to us. They reported, "The land that the LORD our God is giving us is good."

²⁶But you rebelled against the command of the LORD your God and refused to go. ²⁷You complained in your tents and said, "The LORD hates us! That's why he brought us out of Egypt. He wanted to hand us over to the Amorites so that they could destroy us! ²⁸Where are we going anyway? Our own men have discouraged us by saying, 'The people there are taller and stronger than we are. The cities are big with sky-high walls! We even saw the people of Anak there.' "

²⁹Then I said to you, "Don't tremble. Don't be afraid of them. ³⁰The LORD your God, who is going ahead of you, will fight for you as you saw him fight for you in Egypt ³¹and in the desert." There you saw how the LORD your God carried you, as parents carry their children. He carried you wherever you went until you came to this place.

³²In spite of this, you didn't trust the LORD your God, ³³who went ahead of you to find places for you to camp. He appeared in a column of fire at night and in a column of smoke during the day to show you which route to take.

³⁴When the LORD heard what you said, he was angry and took this oath: ³⁵"Not one of these evil people will ever see the good land that I swore to give to your ancestors, ³⁶except Caleb, son of Jephunneh. He will see it, and I will give the land that he set his feet on to him and his descendants, because he wholeheartedly followed the LORD."

³⁷The LORD became angry with me because of you. He said, "You won't go there either. ³⁸But your assistant Joshua, son of Nun, will go there. Encourage him, because he will help Israel take possession of the land. ³⁹Although you thought the little children would be captured in war, your children, who are still too young to know the difference between good and evil, will enter that land. I will give it to them, and they will take possession of it. ⁴⁰Turn around, go back into the desert, and follow the road that goes to the Red Sea."

⁴¹You responded, "We have sinned against the LORD. We'll go and fight, as the LORD our God commanded us to do." Each of you armed yourself for war, thinking you could easily invade the mountain region.

⁴²But the LORD said to me, "Tell them, 'Don't go and fight, because I won't be with you. You will be defeated by your enemies.' "

⁴³I told you, but you wouldn't listen. You defied the LORD's command and invaded the mountain region. ⁴⁴The Amorites who lived there came out and attacked you and chased you like a swarm of bees. They defeated you, chasing you from Seir all the way to Hormah. ⁴⁵When you came back, you cried to the LORD, but the LORD didn't listen to you or hear you. ⁴⁶That's why you stayed in Kadesh as long as you did.

Moses Reminds Israel of the Events at Mount Seir

¹We went back into the desert, following the road that goes to the Red Sea as the LORD had told me. For a long time we traveled around the region of Mount Seir.

²The LORD said to me, ³"You've traveled around this region long enough. Now go north. ⁴Give the people these instructions: 'You're going to pass through the territory

of your relatives, the descendants of Esau, who live in Seir. They'll be afraid of you, but be very careful. ⁵Don't start a fight with them, because I'm not giving you any of their land—not even enough to stand on. I've given Esau's descendants the region of Mount Seir as their property. ⁶You must pay them in silver for the food you eat and the water you drink.' "

⁷The LORD your God has blessed you in everything you have done. He has watched over you as you traveled through this vast desert. For 40 years now the LORD your God has been with you, and you haven't needed a thing.

⁸So we passed by our relatives, the descendants of Esau, who lived in Seir. We turned off the road that goes through the plains to Elath and Ezion Geber and took the road that goes through the desert of Moab.

⁹The LORD said to me, "Don't bother the people of Moab or start a war with them. I'm not giving you any of Ar as your property. I have given it to the descendants of Lot."

¹⁰The Emites used to live there. These people were as strong, as numerous, and as tall as the people of Anak. ¹¹They were thought to be Rephaim, like the people of Anak, but the Moabites called them Emites. ¹²The Horites used to live in Seir, but the descendants of Esau claimed their land, wiped them out, and took their place, as Israel did in the land that the LORD gave them.

¹³Then the LORD said, "Now cross the Zered River."

So we crossed the Zered River. ¹⁴Thirty-eight years passed from the time we left Kadesh Barnea until we crossed the Zered River. During that time all our soldiers from that generation died, as the LORD had sworn they would. ¹⁵In fact, it was the LORD himself who got rid of all of them until none were left in the camp.

Moses Reminds Israel About Ammon

¹⁶When the last of these soldiers had died, ¹⁷the LORD said to me, ¹⁸"Today you are going to pass by the border of Moab at Ar. ¹⁹When you come near the Ammonites, don't bother them or start a fight with them. I'm not giving you any of the land that I have already given to the descendants of Lot as their property."

²⁰This land was thought of as the land of the Rephaim who used to live there, but the Ammonites called them Zamzummim. ²¹These people were as strong, as numerous, and as tall as the people of Anak. But the LORD wiped them out before the Ammonites came so that the Ammonites claimed their land and took their place. ²²The LORD did the same thing for the descendants of Esau, who lived in Seir. Before the descendants of Esau came, he wiped out the Horites so that Esau's descendants claimed their land and took their place. Esau's descendants are still there today. ²³The same thing happened to the Avvites who lived in villages as far away as Gaza. The Caphtorites, who came from Crete, wiped them out and took their place.

Moses Reminds Israel About King Og and King Sihon

²⁴The LORD continued, "Now break camp. Cross the Arnon Valley. I'm going to hand King Sihon of Heshbon, the Amorite, over to you. Fight him, and take possession of his country. ²⁵Today I will start to make all the people under heaven terrified of you. When they hear about you, they will tremble and shake because of you."

²⁶From the desert of Kedemoth, I sent messengers to King Sihon of Heshbon with the following offer of peace: ²⁷"If you allow us to travel through your country, we'll go straight through and won't ever leave the road. ²⁸We'll pay you in silver for the food we eat and the water we drink. Please let us go through, ²⁹as the descendants of Esau, who live in Seir, and the Moabites, who live in Ar, did for us. We'll keep going until we cross the Jordan River into the land the LORD our God is giving us."

³⁰But King Sihon of Heshbon wouldn't allow us to pass through. The LORD your God made him stubborn and overconfident in order to hand him over to you, as he has now done. ³¹The LORD said to me, "I have begun to give you Sihon and his country. Go ahead! Take possession of his land."

³²Sihon and all his troops came out to meet us in battle at Jahaz. ³³The LORD our God gave Sihon to us, and we defeated him, his sons, and all his troops. ³⁴At that time we captured all his cities and claimed them for God by destroying men, women, and children. There were no survivors. ³⁵However, we did loot the cities that we captured, taking the cattle and goods. ³⁶From Aroer on the edge of the Arnon Valley and the city in that valley as far as Gilead, no city had walls that could keep us out. The LORD our God gave us all of them. ³⁷But the LORD our God had forbidden you to go anywhere near the land of the Ammonites. So you didn't enter the land along the bank of the Jabbok River or capture the cities in the mountains.

Moses Reminds Israel of How They Defeated King Og of Bashan

¹Next we turned and followed the road that goes to Bashan. King Og of Bashan and all his troops came to fight us at Edrei. ²The LORD said to me, "Don't be afraid of him. I'll hand him, all his troops, and his land over to you. Do to him what you did to King Sihon of the Amorites, who ruled in Heshbon."

³So the LORD our God also handed King Og of Bashan and all his troops over to us. We defeated him, leaving no survivors. ⁴At that time we captured all of his cities. There wasn't a city we didn't take. We captured a total of 60 cities—the whole territory of Argob, the kingdom of Og in Bashan. ⁵All of these cities were fortified with high walls and double-door gates with bars across the gates. We also captured a large number of unwalled villages. ⁶We claimed them all for God, destroying every city, including men, women, and children—as we did to King Sihon of Heshbon. ⁷However, we did loot the cities, taking all of the cattle and goods.

⁸We took the land of the two Amorite kings east of the Jordan River, from the Arnon Valley to Mount Hermon. ⁹(The Sidonians call Mount Hermon by the name Sirion, and the Amorites call it Senir.) ¹⁰We took all of the cities of the plateau, all of Gilead, and all of Bashan as far as Salcah and Edrei, cities of Og's kingdom in Bashan. ¹¹(Of the Rephaim only King Og of Bashan was left. His bed was made of iron and was more than 13 feet long and 6 feet wide. It is still in the Ammonite city of Rabbah.)

¹²At that time we took possession of this land. I gave the tribes of Reuben and Gad the land north of Aroer near the Arnon Valley and half of the mountain region of Gilead with its cities. ¹³I gave the rest of Gilead and all of Bashan ruled by Og to half of the tribe of Manasseh. (The whole territory of Argob in Bashan used to be called the land of the Rephaim. ¹⁴Jair, a descendant of Manasseh, took the whole territory of Argob as far as the border of the Geshurites and the Maacathites. The settlements in Bashan he named Havvoth Jair after himself. This is still their name today.) ¹⁵I gave Gilead to Machir. ¹⁶I gave the tribes of Reuben and Gad some of Gilead from the Arnon Valley (the middle of the valley is the border) to the Jabbok River, which is the border of Ammon. ¹⁷Their land included the plains around the Jordan River. The western border was the river, from the Sea of Galilee to the Sea of the Plains (the Dead Sea), which is near Mount Pisgah on the east.

¹⁸I gave the tribes of Reuben and Gad and half of the tribe of Manasseh this command: "The LORD your God has given you this land so that you can take possession of it. All your soldiers must be ready for battle when they cross the Jordan River ahead of the other Israelites. ¹⁹I know you have a lot of livestock. Your wives, children, and

livestock must stay here in the cities that I gave you. ²⁰Your soldiers will go with the other Israelites until they take possession of the land the LORD your God is giving them on the other side of the Jordan River. Then they will have a place to rest as you have. After that each of you may go back to the land I gave you."

²¹I also gave Joshua this command: "You have seen with your own eyes everything that the LORD your God has done to these two kings. The LORD will do the same to all of the kingdoms on the other side of the Jordan River, where you're going. ²²Don't be afraid of them, because the LORD your God himself will fight for you."

Moses Reminds Israel Why He Will Not Enter Canaan

²³Then I pleaded with the LORD: ²⁴"Almighty LORD, you have only begun to show me how great and powerful you are. What kind of god is there in heaven or on earth who can do the deeds and the mighty acts you have done? ²⁵Please let me go over and see the beautiful land on the other side of the Jordan River—those beautiful mountains in Lebanon."

²⁶The LORD was angry with me because of you, so he wouldn't listen to me. He said, "That's enough out of you! Don't talk to me anymore about this. ²⁷Go to the top of Mount Pisgah, and look west, north, south, and east. You may look at the land, but you will never cross the Jordan River. ²⁸Give instructions to Joshua. Encourage and strengthen him, because he will lead these people across the Jordan River, and he will help them take possession of the land you see."

²⁹So we stayed in the valley near Beth Peor.

Moses Reminds Israel to Be Loyal to the LORD

¹Israel, listen to the laws and rules I am about to teach you. Obey them so that you will live and be able to enter and take possession of the land that the LORD God of your ancestors is giving you. ²Never add anything to what I command you, or take anything away from it. Then you will be able to obey the commands of the LORD your God that I give you.

³With your own eyes you saw what the LORD did at Baal Peor. The LORD your God destroyed everyone among you who worshiped the god Baal while you were at Peor. ⁴But you were loyal to the LORD your God and are still alive today.

⁵I have taught you laws and rules as the LORD my God commanded me. You must obey them when you've entered the land and taken possession of it. ⁶Faithfully obey these laws. This will show the people of the world your wisdom and insight. When they hear about all these laws, they will say, "What wise and insightful people there are in this great nation!"

⁷What great nation ever had their gods as near to them as the LORD our God is near to us whenever we pray to him? ⁸Or what other great nation has such fair laws and rules as all these teachings I am giving you today?

⁹However, be careful, and watch yourselves closely so that you don't forget the things which you have seen with your own eyes. Don't let them fade from your memory as long as you live. Teach them to your children and grandchildren. ¹⁰Never forget the day you stood in front of the LORD your God at Mount Horeb. The LORD had said to me, "Assemble the people in front of me, and I will let them hear my words. Then they will learn to fear me as long as they live on earth, and they will teach their children the same thing."

¹¹So you came and stood at the foot of the mountain, which was on fire with flames shooting into the sky. It was dark, cloudy, and gloomy. ¹²The LORD spoke to you from

the fire. You heard a voice speaking but saw no one. There was only a voice. [13]The LORD told you about the terms of his promise, the ten commandments, which he commanded you to do. Then he wrote them on two stone tablets. [14]The LORD also commanded me to teach you the laws and rules you must obey after you cross the Jordan River, and take possession of the land.

[15]You didn't see the LORD the day he spoke to you from the fire at Mount Horeb. So be very careful [16]that you don't become corrupt and make your own carved idols. Don't make statues that represent men or women, [17]any animal on earth, any creature with wings that flies, [18]any creature that crawls on the ground, or any fish in the water. [19]Don't let yourselves be tempted to worship and serve what you see in the sky—the sun, the moon, the stars, or anything else. The LORD your God has given them to all people everywhere. [20]But you are the people the LORD brought out of Egypt, the iron smelter, in order to make you his own people as you still are today.

[21]The LORD was angry with me because of you. So the LORD your God took an oath that I wouldn't cross the Jordan River and enter the good land he is giving you as your property. [22]I'm going to die in this land and not cross the Jordan River, but you're going to go across and take possession of that good land. [23]Be careful that you don't forget the promise[a] that the LORD your God made to you. Don't make your own carved idols or statues that represent anything the LORD your God has forbidden. [24]The LORD your God is a raging fire, a God who does not tolerate rivals.

[25]Even when you have children and grandchildren and have grown old in that land, don't become corrupt and make carved idols or statues that represent anything. I call heaven and earth as witnesses against you today:[b] If you do this thing that the LORD your God considers evil, making him furious, [26]you will quickly disappear from the land you're going to possess on the other side of the Jordan River. You won't live very long there. You'll be completely wiped out. [27]The LORD will scatter you among the people of the world, and only a few of you will be left among the nations where the LORD will force you to live. [28]There you will worship wooden and stone gods made by human hands. These gods can't see, hear, eat, or smell.

[29]But if you look for the LORD your God when you are among those nations, you will find him whenever you search for him with all your heart and with all your soul. [30]When you're in distress and all these things happen to you, then you will finally come back to the LORD your God and obey him. [31]The LORD your God is a merciful God. He

Good Morning, God

Deuteronomy 4:23-24

Some people may try to tell you that all religions are right. But the Bible makes it clear that there is only one true God. This is why God forbids us to worship any other person or thing. God is the only one worthy of our praise. Aren't you glad you know the one and only God?

God, thank you that you alone are worth worshiping.

---

[a]4:23 Or "covenant." [b]4:25 The first part of verse 26 (in Hebrew) has been placed in verse 25 to express the complex Hebrew sentence structure more clearly in English.

will not abandon you, destroy you, or forget the promise to your ancestors that he swore he would keep.

³²Search the distant past, long before your time. Start from the very day God created people on earth. Search from one end of heaven to the other. Has anything as great as this ever happened before, or has anything like it ever been heard of? ³³Have any other people ever heard God speak from a fire and lived? You did! ³⁴Or has any god ever tried to come and take one nation away from another for himself? The LORD your God used his mighty hand and powerful arm to do this for you in Egypt. He did this using plagues, miraculous signs, amazing things, and war. He did his great and awe-inspiring deeds in front of you.

³⁵You were shown these things so that you would know that the LORD is God. There is no other god. ³⁶He let you hear his voice from heaven so that he could instruct you. He showed you his great fire on earth, and you heard him speak from the column of fire. ³⁷Because he loved your ancestors and chose their descendants, he was with you as he brought you out of Egypt by his great power. ³⁸He forced nations greater and stronger than you out of your way to bring you into their land and give it to you. This land is your own possession today.

³⁹Remember today, and never forget that the LORD is God in heaven above and here on earth. There is no other god. ⁴⁰Obey his laws and commands which I'm giving you today. Then things will go well for you and your descendants. You will live for a long time in the land. The LORD your God is giving you the land for as long as you live.

Three Cities of Refuge East of the Jordan River

⁴¹Then Moses set aside three cities on the east side of the Jordan River. ⁴²Those who unintentionally killed someone whom they had never hated could flee to one of these cities and save their lives. ⁴³The cities were Bezer on the desert plateau for the tribe of Reuben, Ramoth in Gilead for the tribe of Gad, and Golan in Bashan for the tribe of Manasseh.

Introduction to Moses' Teachings

⁴⁴This is what Moses taught the people of Israel. ⁴⁵These are the commandments, laws, and rules Moses gave the Israelites after they had left Egypt. ⁴⁶He gave these to the people when they were east of the Jordan River in the valley near Beth Peor, in the land of King Sihon of the Amorites, who ruled in Heshbon. Moses and Israel defeated him after they left Egypt. ⁴⁷They took possession of his land and the land of King Og of Bashan, the two kings of the Amorites who were east of the Jordan River. ⁴⁸This land went from Aroer on the edge of the Arnon Valley to Mount Siyon (that is, Mount Hermon). ⁴⁹It included all the plains on the east side of the Jordan River as far as the Dead Sea at the foot of the slopes of Mount Pisgah.

The Ten Commandments—
Exodus 20:1-21

⁵¹Moses summoned all Israel and said to them: Israel, listen to the laws and rules I'm telling you today. Learn them and faithfully obey them.

²The LORD our God made a promise*ᵃ* to us at Mount Horeb. ³He didn't make this promise to our ancestors, but to all of us who are alive here today. ⁴The LORD spoke to you face to face from the fire on the mountain. ⁵I stood between the LORD and you to tell you the word of the LORD, because you were afraid of the fire and didn't go up on the mountain. The LORD said:

---
*ᵃ*5:2 Or "covenant."

⁶"I am the LORD your God, who brought you out of slavery in Egypt.

⁷"Never have any other gods. ⁸Never make your own carved idols or statues that represent any creature in the sky, on the earth, or in the water. ⁹Never worship them or serve them, because I, the LORD your God, am a God who does not tolerate rivals. I punish children for their parents' sins to the third and fourth generation of those who hate me. ¹⁰But I show mercy to thousands of generations of those who love me and obey my commandments.

¹¹"Never use the name of the LORD your God carelessly. The LORD will make sure that anyone who uses his name carelessly will be punished.

¹²"Observe the day of worship as a holy day. This is what the LORD your God has commanded you. ¹³You have six days to do all your work. ¹⁴The seventh day is the day of worship dedicated to the LORD your God. You, your sons, your daughters, your male and female slaves, your oxen, your donkeys—all of your animals—even the foreigners living in your city must never do any work ͺon that dayͺ. In this way your male and female slaves can rest as you do. ¹⁵Remember that you were slaves in Egypt and that the LORD your God used his mighty hand and powerful arm to bring you out of there. This is why the LORD your God has commanded you to observe the day of worship.

¹⁶"Honor your father and your mother as the LORD your God has commanded you. Then you will live for a long time, and things will go well for you in the land the LORD your God is giving you.

¹⁷"Never murder.

¹⁸"Never commit adultery.

¹⁹"Never steal.

²⁰"Never avoid the truth when you testify about your neighbor.*ᵇ*

²¹"Never desire to take your neighbor's wife away from him.

"Never long for your neighbor's household, his field, his male or female slave, his ox, his donkey, or anything else that belongs to him."

²²These are the commandments the LORD spoke to your whole assembly on the mountain. He spoke in a loud voice from the fire, the cloud, and the gloomy darkness. Then he stopped speaking. He wrote the commandments on two stone tablets and gave them to me.

²³But when you heard the voice coming from the darkness and saw the mountain blazing with fire, all the leaders and heads of your tribes came to me. ²⁴You said, "The LORD our God has let us see how great and glorious he is. We've heard his voice come from the fire. Today we've seen that people can live even if God speaks to them. ²⁵Why should we die? This great fire will consume us! If we continue to hear the voice of the LORD our God, we'll die! ²⁶Who has ever heard the voice of the living God speak from a fire, as we did, and lived? ²⁷ͺMoses,ͺ go and listen to everything that the LORD our God says. Then tell us whatever the LORD our God tells you. We'll listen and obey."

²⁸When the LORD heard the words that you spoke to me, he said, "I have heard what these people said to you. Everything they said was good. ²⁹If only they would fear me and obey all my commandments as long as they live! Then things would go well for them and their children forever.

³⁰"Tell the people to go back to their tents. ³¹But you stay here with me. I will give you all the commands, laws, and rules that you must teach them to obey in the land which I'm giving them to possess."

³²So be careful to do what the LORD your God has commanded you. Never stop living this way. ³³Follow all the directions the LORD your God has given you. Then

---

*ᵇ*5:20 Deuteronomy 5:21-33 in English Bibles is Deuteronomy 5:17-30 in some Hebrew Bibles.

Education / *Deuteronomy 6*

Homeschooling isn't a new idea. Girls who lived in ancient Israel were homeschooled, too. They didn't learn about science, math, or spelling. Instead, they worked beside their mothers and learned how to run a home. They learned how to garden, how to sew, and how to cook. All of these jobs were very difficult without power tools, sewing machines, or gas ovens. Girls also learned about God's law and what they needed to do to obey it (Deuteronomy 6:4-6).

you will continue to live, life will go well for you, and you will live for a long time in the land that you are going to possess.

Love the LORD

⁶ ¹These are the commands, laws, and rules the LORD your God commanded me to teach you. Obey them after you enter the land and take possession of it. ²As long as you live, you, your children, and your grandchildren must fear the LORD your God. All of you must obey all his laws and commands that I'm giving you, and you will live a long time. ³Listen, Israel, and be careful to obey these laws. Then things will go well for you and your population will increase in a land flowing with milk and honey, as the LORD God of your ancestors promised you.

⁴Listen, Israel: The LORD is our God. The LORD is the only God. ⁵Love the LORD your God with all your heart, with all your soul, and with all your strength. ⁶Take to heart these words that I give you today. ⁷Repeat them to your children. Talk about them when you're at home or away, when you lie down or get up. ⁸Write them down, and tie them around your wrist, and wear them as headbands as a reminder. ⁹Write them on the doorframes of your houses and on your gates.

¹⁰The LORD your God will bring you into the land and give it to you, as he swore to your ancestors Abraham, Isaac, and Jacob. This land will have large, prosperous cities that you didn't build. ¹¹Your houses will be filled with all kinds of things that you didn't put there. You will have cisterns that you didn't dig and vineyards and olive trees that you didn't plant. After you have eaten all that you want, ¹²be careful that you don't forget the LORD, who brought you out of slavery in Egypt. ¹³You must fear the LORD your God, serve him, and take your oaths only in his name. ¹⁴Never worship any of the gods worshiped by the people around you. ¹⁵If you do, the LORD your God will become very angry with you and will wipe you off the face of the earth, because the LORD your God, who is with you, is a God who does not tolerate rivals.

¹⁶Never test the LORD your God as you did at Massah. ¹⁷Be sure to obey the commands of the LORD your God and the regulations and laws he has given you. ¹⁸Do what the LORD considers right and good. Then things will go well for you, and you will enter

and take possession of that good land which the Lord promised to your ancestors with an oath. ¹⁹You will see the Lord expel your enemies as he said he would.

²⁰In the future your children will ask you, "What do these regulations, laws, and rules which the Lord our God commanded you mean to you?" ²¹Tell them, "We were Pharaoh's slaves in Egypt, but the Lord used his mighty hand to bring us out of there. ²²Right before our eyes the Lord did miraculous signs and amazing things that were spectacular but terrible for Egypt, Pharaoh, and his whole family. ²³The Lord led us out of there to bring us here and give us this land he promised to our ancestors with an oath. ²⁴The Lord our God commanded us to obey all these laws and to fear him. These laws are for our own good as long as we live so that he will preserve our lives. It's still true today. ²⁵This is how we'll have the Lord's approval: If we faithfully obey all these laws in the presence of the Lord our God, as he has commanded us."

Israel Is Commanded to Destroy the Caananites and Their Idols

7 ¹The Lord your God will bring you to the land you're about to enter and take possession of. He will force many nations out of your way: the Hittites, Girgashites, Amorites, Canaanites, Perizzites, Hivites, and Jebusites—seven nations larger and more powerful than you. ²When the Lord your God gives them to you and you defeat them, destroy every one of them because they have been claimed by the Lord. Don't make any treaties with them or show them any mercy. ³Never marry any of them. Never let your daughters marry their sons or your sons marry their daughters. ⁴These people will turn your children away from me to worship other gods. Then the Lord will get very angry with you and will quickly destroy you.

⁵But this is what you must do to these people: Tear down their altars, smash their sacred stones, cut down their poles dedicated to the goddess Asherah, and burn their idols. ⁶You are a holy people, who belong to the Lord your God. He chose you to be his own special possession out of all the nations on earth.

⁷The Lord set his heart on you and chose you, even though you didn't outnumber all the other people. You were the smallest of all nations. ⁸You were chosen because the Lord loved you and kept the oath he swore to your ancestors. So he used his mighty hand to bring you out. He freed you from slavery under Pharaoh (the king of Egypt). ⁹Keep in mind that the Lord your God is the only God. He is a faithful God, who keeps his promise[a] and is merciful to thousands of generations of those who love him and obey his commands. ¹⁰But he sends destruction to pay back everyone who hates him. He never takes long to pay back anyone who hates him.

¹¹So obey the commands, laws, and rules I'm giving you today.

¹²If you listen to these rules and faithfully obey them, the Lord your God will keep his promise to you and be merciful to you, as he swore to your ancestors. ¹³He will love you, bless you, and increase the number of your descendants. He will bless you with children. He will bless your land with produce: grain, new wine, and olive oil. He will bless your herds with calves, and your flocks with lambs and kids. This will all happen in the land the Lord will give you, as he swore to your ancestors. ¹⁴You will be blessed more than any other people. Your men and women will be able to have children, and your animals will be able to have offspring. ¹⁵The Lord will keep you from having any kind of illness. He will not strike you with any of the terrible diseases you experienced in Egypt. Instead, he will strike all those who hate you. ¹⁶You must destroy all the people the Lord your God hands over to you. Have no pity on them, and never worship their gods, because they will be a trap for you.

ª7:9 Or "covenant."

¹⁷You may say to yourselves, "These nations outnumber us. How can we force them out?" ¹⁸Don't be afraid of them. Remember what the Lord your God did to Pharaoh and all of Egypt. ¹⁹You saw with your own eyes the terrible plagues, the miraculous signs, and the amazing things the Lord did. He used his mighty hand and powerful arm to bring you out. He will do the same thing to all the people you're afraid of. ²⁰The Lord your God will spread panic among them until they all die. There will be no one left—not even those who were hiding from you. ²¹Don't be afraid of them, because the Lord your God is with you. He is a great and awe-inspiring God. ²²Little by little he will force these nations out of your way. You won't be able to wipe them out quickly. Otherwise, you would be overrun with wild animals. ²³The Lord your God will hand these people over to you and will throw them into a great panic until they're destroyed. ²⁴He will hand their kings over to you, and no one on earth will even remember their names. No one will be able to stop you. You will destroy them all. ²⁵Burn their idols. Don't ever long for the silver and gold on these idols or take any of it for yourselves. It might be a trap for you. Besides, these idols are disgusting to the Lord your God. ²⁶Never bring a disgusting idol into your house. If you do, you and the idol will be destroyed. Consider it detestable and disgusting. It must be destroyed."

Israel Told Never to Forget God

8 ¹Be careful to obey every command I give you today. Then you will live, and your population will increase. You will enter and take possession of the land that the Lord promised to your ancestors with an oath.

²Remember that for 40 years the Lord your God led you on your journey in the desert. He did this in order to humble you and test you. He wanted to know whether or not you would wholeheartedly obey his commands. ³So he made you suffer from hunger and then fed you with manna, which neither you nor your ancestors had seen before. He did this to teach you that a person cannot live on bread alone but on every word that the Lord speaks. ⁴Your clothes didn't wear out, and your feet didn't swell these past 40 years. ⁵Learn this lesson by heart: The Lord your God was disciplining you as parents discipline their children. ⁶Obey the commands of the Lord your God. Follow his directions, and fear him.

⁷The Lord your God is bringing you into a good land. It is a land with rivers that don't dry up. There are springs and underground streams flowing through the valleys and hills. ⁸The land has wheat and barley, grapevines, fig trees, and pomegranates. The land has honey and olive trees for olive oil. ⁹The land will have enough food for you, and you will have everything you need. The land has rocks with iron ore, and you will be able to mine copper ore in the hills. ¹⁰When you have eaten all you want, thank the Lord your God for the good land he has given you.

¹¹Be careful that you don't forget the Lord your God. Don't fail to obey his commands, rules, and laws that I'm giving you today. ¹²You will eat all you want. You will build nice houses and live in them. ¹³Your herds and flocks, silver and gold, and everything else you have will increase. ¹⁴When this happens, be careful that you don't become arrogant and forget the Lord your God, who brought you out of slavery in Egypt. ¹⁵He was the one who led you through that vast and dangerous desert—a thirsty and arid land, with poisonous snakes and scorpions. He was the one who made water come out of solid rock for you. ¹⁶He was the one who fed you in the desert with manna, which your ancestors had never seen. He did this in order to humble you and test you. But he also did this so that things would go well for you in the end. ¹⁷You may say to yourselves, "I became wealthy because of my own ability and strength." ¹⁸But

remember the LORD your God is the one who makes you wealthy. He's confirming the promise*ᵃ* which he swore to your ancestors. It's still in effect today.

¹⁹I warn you today that if you forget the LORD your God and follow other gods, and if you serve them and bow down to them, you will certainly be destroyed. ²⁰The LORD is going to destroy other nations as you enter the land. You will be destroyed like them if you don't obey the LORD your God.

Israel Has Been Given Canaan Because of God's Mercy

¹Listen, Israel, you're about to cross the Jordan River. You'll be forcing out nations that are larger and stronger than you, with big cities that have sky-high walls. ²Their people are tall and strong. They're descendants of Anak. You know all about them. You've also heard it said, "Who can oppose the descendants of Anak?" ³Realize today that the LORD your God is the one who is going ahead of you like a raging fire. He will wipe them out and will use you to crush their power. You will take possession of their land and will quickly destroy them as the LORD promised you.

⁴When the LORD your God expels these people in front of you, don't say to yourselves, "Because we've been living right, the LORD brought us here to take possession of this land." No, it's because these nations are so wicked that the LORD is forcing them out of your way. ⁵It's not because you've been living right or because you're so honest that you're entering to take possession of their land. It's because these people are so wicked that the LORD your God is forcing them out of your way. It's also because the LORD wants to confirm the promise he swore to your ancestors Abraham, Isaac, and Jacob. ⁶So understand this: It's not because you've been living right that the LORD your God is giving you this good land to possess. You are impossible to deal with!

⁷Never forget how you made the LORD your God angry in the desert. You've rebelled against the LORD from the day you left Egypt until you came here. ⁸Even at Mount Horeb you made the LORD so angry that he wanted to destroy you. ⁹When I went up on the mountain to get the stone tablets, the tablets of the promise that the LORD made to you, I stayed on the mountain 40 days and 40 nights without food or water. ¹⁰Then the LORD gave me the two stone tablets inscribed by God himself. On them were written all the words that the LORD spoke to you from the fire on the mountain on the day of the assembly.

¹¹At the end of the 40 days and 40 nights, the LORD gave me the two stone tablets with his promise on them. ¹²He told me, "Leave right away. Your people whom you brought out of Egypt have ruined everything. They've quickly turned from the way I commanded them to live. They've made an idol for themselves."

¹³The LORD also said to me, "I've seen these people, and they are impossible to deal with. ¹⁴Leave me alone! I'll destroy them and wipe their name off the earth. Then I'll make you into a nation larger and stronger than they are."

¹⁵So I turned and went down the mountain while it was still burning with fire. I was carrying the two tablets with the promise on them. ¹⁶Then I saw that you had sinned against the LORD your God. You had made a statue of a calf for yourselves. You had quickly turned from the way the LORD commanded you to live. ¹⁷I took the two tablets, threw them down, and smashed them in front of you.

¹⁸Once again I threw myself down in front of the LORD. I went without food and water for 40 days and 40 nights because of the sin you committed. You did what the LORD considered evil and made him furious. ¹⁹I was terrified of the LORD's anger and fury. He was so angry he wanted to destroy you. But once more the LORD listened to me.

ᵃ 8:18 Or "covenant."

²⁰The Lord also became very angry with Aaron and wanted to destroy him. But at that time I prayed for Aaron, too.

²¹I took that sinful calf you made and burned it. I crushed it, grinding it thoroughly until it was as fine as powder. Then I threw the powder into the river that flowed down the mountain.

²²You also made the Lord angry at Taberah, Massah, and Kibroth Hattaavah.

²³When the Lord sent you from Kadesh Barnea, he said, "Go and take possession of the land I'm giving you." But you rebelled against the word of the Lord your God. You didn't believe him or obey him. ²⁴You've rebelled against the Lord as long as I've known you.

²⁵I threw myself down in front of the Lord for 40 days and 40 nights because the Lord said he would destroy you. ²⁶I prayed to the Lord and said, "Almighty Lord, don't destroy your people. They belong to you. You saved them by your great power and used your mighty hand to bring them out of Egypt. ²⁷Remember your servants Abraham, Isaac, and Jacob. Disregard the stubbornness, wickedness, and sin of these people. ²⁸Otherwise, the country we left will say, "The Lord wasn't able to bring them to the land he promised them. He hated them. That's why he brought them out—to let them die in the desert." ²⁹They are your people. They belong to you. You used your great strength and powerful arm to bring them out of Egypt.

¹At that time the Lord said to me, "Cut two more stone tablets like the first ones, and come up to me on the mountain. Also make an ark out of wood. ²I will write on the tablets the same words that were on the first tablets, which you smashed. Then you will put them in the ark."

³I made an ark out of acacia wood. I cut two more stone tablets like the first ones. I carried the two tablets up the mountain. ⁴The Lord wrote on these tablets the same words as before, the ten commandments. He had spoken these words to you from the fire on the mountain on the day of the assembly. Then the Lord gave them to me. ⁵I came back down the mountain and put the tablets in the ark I had made. They are still there, where the Lord commanded me to put them.

⁶The Israelites moved from the wells of the Jaakanites to Moserah. Aaron died there and was buried, and his son Eleazar succeeded him as priest. ⁷They moved from there to Gudgodah, and from Gudgodah to Jotbathah, a land with rivers that don't dry up. ⁸At that time the Lord set apart the tribe of Levi to carry the ark of the Lord's promise, to stand in the Lord's presence when they serve him as priests, and to praise his name, as they still do today. ⁹This is why the tribe of Levi has no land of their own as the other tribes have. The Lord your God is their only possession, as he promised them.

Playing Favorites
Deuteronomy 10:12-22

Imagine that a poor child came to your school or to your Sunday school class. Would you be friendly to that person? Sometimes we worry, What will others think if I have a friend who is different? But God doesn't play favorites. He loves everyone. Follow God's example and make friends with everyone.

¹⁰I stayed on the mountain 40 days and 40 nights as I did the first time. Once again the Lord listened to me and agreed not to destroy you. ¹¹The Lord said to me, "Lead the people on their journey. They will enter and take possession of the land I will give them, as I swore to their ancestors."

Israel Encouraged to Follow God's Guidance

¹²Israel, what does the Lord your God want you to do? He wants you to fear him, follow all his directions, love him, and worship him with all your heart and with all your soul. ¹³The Lord wants you to obey his commands and laws that I'm giving you today for your own good. ¹⁴Remember that the sky, the highest heaven, the earth and everything it contains belong to the Lord your God. ¹⁵The Lord set his heart on your ancestors and loved them. Because of this, today he chooses you, their descendants, out of all the people of the world.

¹⁶So circumcise your uncircumcised hearts, and don't be impossible to deal with any longer. ¹⁷The Lord your God is God of gods and Lord of lords, the great, powerful, and awe-inspiring God. He never plays favorites and never takes a bribe. ¹⁸He makes sure orphans and widows receive justice. He loves foreigners and gives them food and clothes. ¹⁹So you should love foreigners, because you were foreigners living in Egypt. ²⁰Fear the Lord your God, worship him, be loyal to him, and take your oaths in his name. ²¹He is your glory. He is your God, who did for you these spectacular and awe-inspiring deeds you saw with your own eyes. ²²When your ancestors went to Egypt, there were 70 of them. Now the Lord your God has made you as numerous as the stars in the sky.

11 ¹Love the Lord your God, and do what he wants you to do. Always obey his laws, rules, and commands. ²Remember today the discipline you learned from the Lord your God. (I'm not talking to your children. They didn't see or experience any of this.) You saw and experienced his great power—his mighty hand and powerful arm. ³You saw the miraculous signs and deeds he did in Egypt to Pharaoh (the king of Egypt) and to his whole country. ⁴You saw what he did to the Egyptian army, its horses and chariots. He drowned them in the Red Sea when they pursued you. So the Lord destroyed them forever. ⁵You saw what he did for you in the desert until you came here. ⁶You also saw what he did to Dathan and Abiram, the sons of Eliab, from the tribe of Reuben. In the middle of all the Israelites the ground opened up and swallowed them, their families, their tents, and every living creature with them. ⁷You saw with your own eyes all these spectacular things that the Lord did.

⁸Obey all the commands I'm giving you today. Then you will have the strength to enter and take possession of the land once you've crossed the Jordan River. ⁹Then you will also live for a long time in the land the Lord swore to give your ancestors and their descendants—a land flowing with milk and honey.

¹⁰The land you're about to enter and take possession of isn't like the land you left in Egypt. There you used to plant your seed, and you had to water it like a vegetable garden. ¹¹The land you're about to enter is a land with hills and valleys, watered by rain from the sky. ¹²It is a land the Lord your God cares about. He watches over it all year long.

¹³If you faithfully obey the commands that I'm giving you today, love the Lord your God, and serve him with all your heart and with all your soul, ¹⁴I will send rain on your land at the right time, both in the fall and in the spring. Then you will gather your own grain, new wine, and olive oil. ¹⁵I will provide grass in the fields for your animals, and you will be able to eat all you want.

¹⁶Be careful, or you'll be tempted to turn away and worship other gods and bow

down to them. [17]The Lord will become angry with you. He'll shut the sky so that there'll be no rain. Then the ground won't grow any crops, and you'll quickly disappear from this good land the Lord is giving you.

[18]Take these words of mine to heart and keep them in mind. Write them down, tie them around your wrist, and wear them as headbands as a reminder. [19]Teach them to your children, and talk about them when you're at home or away, when you lie down or get up. [20]Write them on the doorframes of your houses and on your gates. [21]Then you and your children will live for a long time in this land that the Lord swore to give to your ancestors—as long as there's a sky above the earth.

[22]Faithfully obey all these commands I'm giving you. Love the Lord your God, follow all his directions, and be loyal to him. [23]Then the Lord will force all these people out of your way. Then you will take possession of the land belonging to people taller and stronger than you. [24]I will give you every place on which you set foot. Your borders will be from the desert to Lebanon, from the Euphrates River to the Mediterranean Sea. [25]No one will be able to stop you. As the Lord your God promised, he will make people terrified of you wherever you go in this land.

Choose the Blessing or the Curse

[26]Today I'm giving you the choice of a blessing or a curse. [27]You'll be blessed if you obey the commands of the Lord your God that I'm giving you today. [28]You'll be cursed if you disobey the commands of the Lord your God, if you turn from the way I'm commanding you to live today, and if you worship other gods you never knew. [29]When the Lord your God brings you into the land you're about to enter, recite the blessing from Mount Gerizim and the curse from Mount Ebal. [30](These mountains are on the west side of the Jordan, beyond the road that goes west, in the region of the Canaanites who live on the plains facing Gilgal, next to the oak trees of Moreh.) [31]You're about to cross the Jordan River to enter and take possession of the land the Lord your God is giving you. When you take possession of it and live there, [32]be careful to obey all the laws and rules I'm giving you today.

The Proper Place to Worship

12 [1]Here are the laws and rules you must faithfully obey in the land that the Lord God of your ancestors is giving you as your own. You must obey them as long as you live in the land.

[2]Completely destroy all the worship sites on the high mountains, on the hills, and under every large tree. The people you're forcing out worship their gods in these places. [3]Tear down their altars, crush their sacred stones, burn their poles dedicated to the goddess Asherah, cut down their idols, and wipe out the names of their gods from those places.

[4]Never worship the Lord your God in the way they worship their gods. [5]The Lord your God will choose a place out of all your tribes to live and put his name. Go there and worship him. [6]Bring him your burnt offerings, your sacrifices, one-tenth of your income, your contributions, the offerings you vow to bring, your freewill offerings, and the firstborn of your cattle, sheep, and goats. [7]There, in the presence of the Lord your God, you and your families will eat and enjoy everything you've worked for, because the Lord your God has blessed you.

[8]Never worship in the way that it's being done here today, where everyone does whatever he considers right. [9]Up until now you haven't come to your place of rest, the property the Lord your God is giving you. [10]But you will cross the Jordan River and settle in the land the Lord your God is giving you as your own property. He will

give you peace from all your enemies around you so that you will live securely. ¹¹Then the LORD your God will choose a place where his name will live. You must bring everything I command you to that place. Bring your burnt offerings, your sacrifices, one-tenth of your income, your contributions, and all the best offerings you vow to bring to the LORD. ¹²Enjoy yourselves in the presence of the LORD your God along with your sons, daughters, male and female slaves, and the Levites. (The Levites live in your cities because they have no land of their own as you have.) ¹³Be careful that you don't sacrifice your burnt offerings wherever you want. ¹⁴Instead, sacrifice them only at the place that the LORD will choose in one of your tribes. There you must do everything I command you.

¹⁵In whatever city you live, you may slaughter and eat as much meat as you want from what the LORD your God has blessed you with. Clean and unclean*ᵃ* people may eat it as if they were eating a gazelle or a deer. ¹⁶But never eat the blood. Pour it on the ground like water. ¹⁷You may not eat the LORD's offerings in your cities. Those offerings are: one-tenth of your grain, new wine, and olive oil; the firstborn of your cattle, sheep, or goats; the offerings you vow to bring; your freewill offerings; and your contributions. ¹⁸Instead, you, your sons and daughters, male and female slaves, and the Levites who live in your cities must eat these in the presence of the LORD your God at the place he will choose. There in the presence of the LORD your God enjoy everything you've worked for. ¹⁹Don't forget to take care of the Levites as long as you live in your land.

²⁰The LORD your God will expand your country's borders as he promised. You will say, "I'm hungry for meat." Then eat as much meat as you want. ²¹If the place the LORD your God chooses to put his name is too far away from you, you may slaughter an animal from the herds or flocks that the LORD has given you. Eat as much as you want in your city. I have commanded you to do this. ²²Eat it as you would eat a gazelle or a deer: Clean and unclean people may eat it together. ²³However, be sure you never eat blood, because blood contains life. Never eat the life with the meat. ²⁴Never eat blood. Pour it on the ground like water. ²⁵If you don't eat blood, things will go well for you and your descendants. You will be doing what the LORD considers right.

²⁶Take the holy things and the offerings you have vowed to bring, and go to the place the LORD will choose. ²⁷Sacrifice the meat and the blood of your burnt offerings on the altar of the LORD your God. The blood of your sacrifices is to be poured out beside the altar of the LORD your God, but you may eat the meat. ²⁸Be sure you obey all these instructions I'm giving you. Then things will always go well for you and your descendants because you will be doing what the LORD your God considers good and right.

²⁹The LORD your God will destroy the nations where you're going and force them out of your way. You will take possession of their land and live there. ³⁰After they've been destroyed, be careful you aren't tempted to follow their customs. Don't even ask about their gods and say, "How did these people worship their gods? We want to do what they did." ³¹Never worship the LORD your God in the way they worship their gods, because everything they do for their gods is disgusting to the LORD. He hates it! They even burn their sons and daughters as sacrifices to their gods.*ᵇ*

³²Be sure to do everything I command you. Never add anything to it or take anything away from it.

---

*ᵃ*12:15 "Clean" refers to anything that is presentable to God. "Unclean" refers to anything that is not presentable to God.   *ᵇ*12:31 Deuteronomy 12:32 in English Bibles is Deuteronomy 13:1 in the Hebrew Bible.

How Israel Is to Deal With False Prophets

13 [a]1One of your people, claiming to be a prophet or to have prophetic dreams, may predict a miraculous sign or an amazing thing. 2What he predicts may even take place. But don't listen to that prophet or dreamer [b] if he says, "Let's worship and serve other gods." (Those gods may be gods you've never heard of.) 3The LORD your God is testing you to find out if you really love him with all your heart and with all your soul. 4Worship the LORD your God, fear him, obey his commands, listen to what he says, serve him, and be loyal to him. 5That prophet or dreamer must be put to death because he preached rebellion against the LORD your God, who brought you out of Egypt and freed you from slavery. He was trying to lead you away from following the directions the LORD your God gave you. You must get rid of this evil.

6Your own brother, son, or daughter, the wife you love, or your best friend may secretly tempt you, saying, "Let's go worship other gods." (Those gods may be gods that you and your ancestors never knew. 7They may be the gods of the people around you, who live near or far, from one end of the land to the other.) 8Don't be influenced by any of these people or listen to them. Have no pity on them. Don't feel sorry for them or protect them. 9You must put them to death. You must start the execution. Then all the other people will join you in putting them to death. 10Stone them to death because they were trying to lead you away from the LORD your God, who brought you out of slavery in Egypt. 11All Israel will hear about it and be afraid. Then no one among you will ever do such a wicked thing again.

12You may hear that the residents in one of the cities which the LORD your God is giving you to live in 13have been led away from the LORD your God by worthless people. You may hear that these people have been saying, "Let's worship other gods." (Those gods may be gods you've never heard of.) 14Then make a thorough investigation. If it is true, and you can prove that this disgusting thing has been done among you, 15you must kill the residents of that city with swords and destroy that city and everyone in it, including the animals, because they are claimed by God. 16Gather their goods into the middle of the city square. Then burn their city and all their goods as a burnt offering to the LORD your God. It must remain a mound of ruins and never be rebuilt. 17Don't ever take any of the things claimed for destruction. Then the LORD will stop being angry and will show you mercy. In his mercy he will make your population increase, as he swore to your ancestors. 18The LORD your God will do this if you listen to him, obey all the commands that I'm giving you today, and do what he considers right.

Religious Practices—
Leviticus 11:1-23

14 1You are the children of the LORD your God. So when someone dies, don't mourn by cutting yourselves or shaving bald spots on your head. 2You are people who are holy to the LORD your God. Out of all the people who live on earth, the LORD has chosen you to be his own special possession.

3Never eat anything that is disgusting to the LORD. 4Here are the kinds of animals you may eat: oxen, sheep, goats, 5deer, gazelles, fallow deer,[c] wild goats, mountain goats, antelope, and mountain sheep. 6You may eat all animals that have completely divided hoofs and that also chew their cud. 7But some animals chew their cud, while others have completely divided hoofs. You may not eat these kinds of animals. They include camels, rabbits, and rock badgers. (Although they chew their cud, they don't

---

[a]13:1 Deuteronomy 13:1-18 in English Bibles is Deuteronomy 13:2-19 in the Hebrew Bible. [b]13:2 The first part of verse 3 (in Hebrew) has been placed in verse 2 to express the complex Hebrew paragraph structure more clearly in English. [c]14:5 A specific species of deer.

have divided hoofs. They are unclean[b] for you.) [8]Also, you may not eat pigs. (Although their hoofs are divided, they don't chew their cud.) Never eat their meat or touch their dead bodies.

[9]Here's what you may eat of every creature that lives in the water: You may eat any creature that has fins and scales. [10]But never eat anything that doesn't have fins and scales. It is unclean for you.

[11]You may eat any clean bird. [12]But here are the birds that you should never eat: eagles, bearded vultures, black vultures, [13]buzzards, all types of kites, [14]all types of crows, [15]ostriches, nighthawks, seagulls, all types of falcons, [16]little owls, great owls, barn owls, [17]pelicans, ospreys, cormorants, [18]storks, all types of herons, hoopoes, and bats.

[19]Every swarming, winged insect is also unclean for you. They must never be eaten. [20]However, you may eat any other kind of flying creature that is clean.

[21]Never eat any creature that dies naturally. You may give it to the foreigners who live in your cities, and they may eat it. You may also sell it to foreigners who are visiting. But you are people who are holy to the LORD your God.

Never cook a young goat in its mother's milk.

Giving God One-Tenth of Everything

[22]Every year be sure to save a tenth of the crops harvested from whatever you plant in your fields. [23]Eat the tenth of your grain, new wine, and olive oil, and eat the firstborn of your cattle, sheep, and goats in the presence of the LORD your God in the place he will choose to put his name. Then you will learn to fear the LORD your God as long as you live.

[24]But the place the LORD your God will choose to put his name may be too far away. He may bless you with so much that you can't carry a tenth of your income that far. [25]If so, exchange the tenth part of your income for silver. Take the silver with you, and go to the place the LORD your God will choose. [26]Use the silver to buy whatever you want: cattle, sheep, goats, wine, liquor—whatever you choose. Then you and your family will eat and enjoy yourselves there in the presence of the LORD your God. [27]Never forget to take care of the Levites who live in your cities. They have no land of their own as you have.

[28]At the end of every third year bring a tenth of that year's crop, and store it in your cities. [29]Foreigners, orphans, and widows who live in your cities may come to eat all they want. The Levites may also come because they have no land of their own as you have. Then the LORD your God will bless you in whatever work you do.

The Seventh-Year Celebration

[1]At the end of every seven years, you must cancel debts. [2]This is what you will do: If you've made a loan, don't collect payment on the debt your neighbor still owes you. Don't demand that your neighbor or relative pay you, because the time for suspending payments on debts has been proclaimed in the LORD's honor. [3]You may demand that a foreigner pay, but don't collect payment on the debt another Israelite still owes you. [4]In any case, there shouldn't be any poor people among you, because the LORD your God will certainly bless you in the land he is giving you as your own possession. [5]He will bless you only if you listen carefully to the LORD your God and faithfully obey all these commands I'm giving you today. [6]The LORD your God will bless you, as he promised. You will make loans to many nations, but you will not have

---

[b]14:7 "Unclean" refers to anything that is not presentable to God.

to borrow from any of them. You will rule many nations, but no nation will ever rule you.

[7]This is what you must do whenever there are poor Israelites in one of your cities in the land that the LORD your God is giving you. [8]Be generous to these poor people, and freely lend them as much as they need. Never be hard-hearted and tight-fisted with them.[a]

[9]When the seventh year—the year when payments on debts are canceled—is near, you might be stingy toward poor Israelites and give them nothing. Be careful not to think these worthless thoughts. The poor will complain to the LORD about you, and you will be condemned for your sin. [10]Be sure to give to them without any hesitation. When you do this, the LORD your God will bless you in everything you work for and set out to do. [11]There will always be poor people in the land. That's why I command you to be generous to other Israelites who are poor and needy.

[12]Whenever Hebrew men or women are sold to you as slaves, they will be your slaves for six years. In the seventh year you must let them go free. [13]But when you let them go, don't send them away empty-handed. [14]Generously give them provisions—sheep from your flocks, grain from your threshing floor,[b] and wine from your winepress. Be as generous to them as the LORD your God has been to you. [15]Remember that you were slaves in Egypt and the LORD your God freed you. That's why I'm giving you this command today.

[16]But suppose a male slave says to you, "I don't want to leave you," because he loves you and your family and is happy with you. [17]Then take an awl and pierce it through his ear lobe into a door, and he will be your slave for life. Do the same to a female slave if she doesn't want to leave.

[18]If you have to let your slave go free, it won't be a hardship for you. It would have cost you twice as much to hire someone to do the same work for those six years. Besides, the LORD your God will bless you in everything you do.

Setting Aside Firstborn Males for God

[19]You must dedicate every firstborn male from your herds and flocks to the LORD your God. Never use a firstborn ox for work, and never shear a firstborn sheep. [20]Every year you and your family must eat these animals in the presence of the LORD your God in the place the LORD will choose. [21]But if an animal is lame or blind or has any other serious defect—never sacrifice it to the LORD your God. [22]Eat it in your city. Clean and unclean[c] people may eat them together as if they were eating a gazelle or a deer. [23]But never eat the blood. Pour it on the ground like water.

Three Major Festivals

16 [1]Honor the LORD your God by celebrating Passover in the month of Abib. In the month of Abib the LORD your God brought you out of Egypt at night. [2]Slaughter an animal from your flock or herd as the Passover sacrifice to the LORD your God. Do this at the place where the LORD will choose for his name to live. [3]Never eat leavened bread with the meat from this sacrifice. Instead, for seven days you must eat unleavened bread at this festival. (It is the bread of misery because you left Egypt in a hurry.) Eat this bread so that, as long as you live, you will remember the day you left Egypt. [4]There should be no yeast anywhere in your land for seven days. Never leave until morning any of the meat you slaughter on the evening of the first day.

---

[a]15:8 This sentence has been moved from verse 7 to express the complex Hebrew sentence structure more clearly in English. [b]15:14 A threshing floor is an outdoor area where grain is separated from its husks. [c]15:22 "Clean" refers to anything that is presentable to God. "Unclean" refers to anything that is not presentable to God.

⁵You're not allowed to slaughter the animals for Passover in any of the cities the LORD your God is giving you. ⁶Instead, slaughter your animals for Passover in the place where the LORD your God will choose for his name to live. Do this in the evening as the sun goes down. This is the same time you did it when you left Egypt. ⁷Cook the meat, and eat it at the place the LORD your God will choose. In the morning you may go back to your tents. ⁸For six days eat unleavened bread, and on the seventh day hold a religious assembly dedicated to the LORD your God. Don't do any work that day.

⁹Count seven weeks from the time you start harvesting grain. ¹⁰Then celebrate the Festival of Weeks to the LORD your God. Bring a freewill offering in proportion to the blessings the LORD your God has given you. ¹¹Enjoy yourselves in the presence of the LORD your God along with your sons, daughters, male and female slaves, the Levites who live in your cities, the foreigners, orphans, and widows who live among you. Enjoy yourselves at the place the LORD your God will choose for his name to live. ¹²Remember that you were slaves in Egypt, and obey these laws carefully.

¹³After you have gathered the grain from your threshing floor *ᵃ* and made your wine, celebrate the Festival of Booths for seven days. ¹⁴Enjoy yourselves at the festival along with your sons, daughters, male and female slaves, the Levites, foreigners, orphans, and widows who live in your cities. ¹⁵For seven days you will celebrate this festival dedicated to the LORD your God in the place he will choose. You will enjoy yourselves, because the LORD your God will bless all your harvest and all your work.

¹⁶Three times a year all your men must come into the presence of the LORD your God at the place he will choose: at the Festival of Unleavened Bread, the Festival of Weeks, and the Festival of Booths. But no one may come into the presence of the LORD without an offering. ¹⁷Each man must bring a gift in proportion to the blessings the LORD your God has given him.

Administering Justice

¹⁸Appoint judges and officers for your tribes in every city that the LORD your God is giving you. They are to judge the people fairly. ¹⁹Never pervert justice. Instead, be impartial. Never take a bribe, because bribes blind wise people and deny justice to those who are in the right. ²⁰Strive for nothing but justice so that you will live and take possession of the land that the LORD your God is giving you.

²¹When you build the altar for the LORD your God, never plant beside it any tree dedicated to the goddess Asherah. ²²Never set up a sacred stone. These are things the LORD your God hates.

17 ¹Never offer an ox or a sheep that has a defect or anything seriously wrong with it as a sacrifice to the LORD your God. That would be disgusting to him.

²In one of the cities the LORD your God is giving you, there may be a man or woman among you who is doing what the LORD considers evil. This person may be disregarding the conditions of the LORD's promise *ᵃ* ³by worshiping and bowing down to other gods, the sun, the moon, or the whole army of heaven. I have forbidden this. ⁴When you are told about it, investigate it thoroughly. If it's true and it can be proven that this disgusting thing has been done in Israel, ⁵then bring the man or woman who did this evil thing to the gates of your city, and stone that person to death. ⁶The person can only be sentenced to death on the testimony of two or three witnesses, but no one should ever be sentenced to death on the testimony of only one witness. ⁷The witnesses must start the execution, then all the other people will join them in putting the person to death. You must get rid of this evil.

---

*ᵃ*16:13 A threshing floor is an outdoor area where grain is separated from its husks.   *ᵃ*17:2 Or "covenant."

[8]There may be a case that is too hard for you to decide. It may involve murder, assault, or a dispute—any case which may be brought to court in your cities. Take this case to the place that the LORD your God will choose. [9]Go to the Levitical priests and the judge who is serving at that time. Ask for their opinion, and they will give you their verdict [10]at the place that the LORD will choose. Do what they tell you. Follow all their instructions carefully, [11]and do what they tell you to do in their verdict. Do exactly what they tell you to do in their decision. [12]If anyone deliberately disobeys the priest (who serves the LORD your God) or the judge, that person must die. You must get rid of this evil in Israel. [13]When all the people hear about it, they will be afraid and will never defy God's law again.

[14]You will enter the land that the LORD your God is giving you. You will take possession of it and live there. You will say, "Let's have our own king like all the other nations around us." [15]Be sure to appoint the king the LORD your God will choose. He must be one of your own people. Never let a foreigner be king, because he's not one of your own people.

[16]The king must never own a large number of horses or make the people return to Egypt to get more horses. The LORD has told you, "You will never go back there again." [17]The king must never have a large number of wives, or he will turn away from God. And he must never own a lot of gold and silver.

[18]When he becomes king, he should have the Levitical priests make him a copy of these teachings on a scroll. [19]He must keep it with him and read it his entire life. He will learn to fear the LORD his God and faithfully obey everything found in these teachings and laws. [20]Then he won't think he's better than the rest of his people, and he won't disobey these commands in any way. So he and his sons will rule for a long time in Israel.

Laws for the Levites

18 [1]The Levitical priests—in fact, the whole tribe of Levi—will receive no land or property of their own like the rest of the Israelites. They will eat what has been sacrificed to the LORD. These sacrifices will be what they receive.[a] [2]So the Levites will have no land of their own like the other Israelites. The LORD will be their inheritance, as he promised them.

[3]This is what the people owe the priests whenever they sacrifice an ox, a sheep, or a goat: the shoulder, jaws, and stomach. [4]Also, give them the first produce harvested: grain, new wine, olive oil, and the first wool you shear from your sheep. [5]Out of all your tribes, the LORD your God has chosen the Levites and their descendants to do the work of serving in the name of the LORD forever.

[6]A Levite from any of your cities in Israel may come from where he has been living to the place the LORD will choose. He may come as often as he wants [7]and may serve in the name of the LORD his God like all the other Levites who do their work in the LORD's presence. [8]If he does, he'll get the same amount of food as they do, in addition to what he gets from selling his family's goods.[b]

Laws About Prophets

[9]When you come to the land that the LORD your God is giving you, never learn the disgusting practices of those nations. [10]You must never sacrifice your sons or daughters by burning them alive, practice black magic, be a fortuneteller, witch, or sorcerer, [11]cast spells, ask ghosts or spirits for help, or consult the dead. [12]Whoever

---

[a] 18:1 Or "They are to eat the sacrifices offered by fire to the LORD or any of the other sacrifices to the LORD."
[b] 18:8 Hebrew meaning of "what he gets from selling his family's goods" uncertain.

does these things is disgusting to the LORD. The LORD your God is forcing these nations out of your way because of their disgusting practices. ¹³You must have integrity in dealing with the LORD your God. ¹⁴These nations you are forcing out listen to fortunetellers and to those who practice black magic. But the LORD your God won't let you do anything like that.

¹⁵The LORD your God will send you a prophet, an Israelite like me. You must listen to him. ¹⁶This is what you asked the LORD your God to give you on the day of the assembly at Mount Horeb. You said, "We never want to hear the voice of the LORD our God or see this raging fire again. If we do, we'll die!"

¹⁷The LORD told me, "What they've said is good. ¹⁸So I will send them a prophet, an Israelite like you. I will put my words in his mouth. He will tell them everything I command him. ¹⁹Whoever refuses to listen to the words that prophet speaks in my name will answer to me. ²⁰But any prophet who dares to say something in my name that I didn't command him to say or who speaks in the name of other gods must die."

²¹You may be wondering, "How can we recognize that the LORD didn't speak this message?" ²²If a prophet speaks in the LORD's name and what he says doesn't happen or come true, then it didn't come from the LORD. That prophet has spoken on his own authority. Never be afraid of him.

Criminal Laws

¹The LORD your God will destroy all the nations that are living in the land that he's giving you. You will force them out and live in their cities and houses. ²When all this is done, set aside three cities in the land that the LORD your God is giving you. ³Provide a route to each of these cities and divide the land that the LORD your God is giving you into three regions. Whoever kills someone may run to one of these cities.

Fortune Tellers
Deuteronomy 18:9-14

Can people really tell your fortune? Should you make decisions by reading your horoscope in the newspaper or by playing with a Ouija board? God says these types of things are wrong. God wants you to ask

him to help you make good decisions. He doesn't want you to ask some astrologer for advice. After all, who's smarter? A palm reader or God?

⁴A person who unintentionally kills someone he never hated in the past may run to one of these cities to save his life. ⁵Suppose two people go into the woods to cut wood. As one of them swings the ax to cut down a tree, the head flies off the handle, hits, and kills the other person. The one who accidentally killed the other person may run to one of these cities and save his life. ⁶Otherwise, in a rage the relative who has the authority to avenge the death will pursue him. If the place is too far away, the relative may catch up with him and take his life even though he didn't deserve the death penalty, because in the past he never hated the person he killed. ⁷This is why I'm commanding you to set aside three cities for yourselves.

⁸The LORD your God may expand your country's borders as he promised your

ancestors with an oath. He may give you the whole land he promised to give them. [9]He may do this because you faithfully obey all these commands I am now giving you— to love the LORD your God and follow his directions as long as you live. If this happens, you may add three more cities of refuge to these three. [10]That way, innocent people won't be killed in the land that the LORD your God is giving you, and you won't be guilty of murder.

[11]Suppose someone hates another person, waits in ambush for him, attacks him, takes his life, and runs to one of these cities. [12]If someone does this, the leaders of your city must send for that person. They must take him from that city and hand him over to the relative who has the authority to avenge the death. He must die. [13]They must have no pity on him. The guilt of murdering an innocent person must be removed from Israel. Then things will go well for Israel.

[14]Never move your neighbor's original boundary marker on any property in the land that the LORD your God is giving you.

[15]One witness is never enough to convict someone of a crime, offense, or sin he may have committed. Cases must be settled based on the testimony of two or three witnesses.

[16]This is what you must do whenever a witness takes the stand to accuse a person falsely of a crime. [17]The two people involved must stand in the LORD's presence, in front of the priests and judges who are serving at that time. [18]The judges must make a thorough investigation. If it is found that the witness lied when he testified against the other Israelite, [19]then do to him what he planned to do to the other person. You must get rid of this evil. [20]When the rest of the people hear about this, they will be afraid. Never again will such an evil thing be done among you. [21]Have no pity on him: Take a life for a life, an eye for an eye, a tooth for a tooth, a hand for a hand, and a foot for a foot.

Laws for Warfare

20 [1]When you go to war against your enemies, you may see horses, chariots, and armies larger than yours. Don't be afraid of them, because the LORD your God, who brought you out of Egypt, will be with you. [2]Before the battle starts, a priest must come and speak to the troops. [3]He should tell them, "Listen, Israel, today you're going into battle against your enemies. Don't lose your courage! Don't be afraid or alarmed or tremble because of them. [4]The LORD your God is going with you. He will fight for you against your enemies and give you victory."

[5]The officers should tell the troops, "If you have built a new house but not

---

Friendship

Deuteronomy 19:15

be you can be

Someone tells you that your best friend said something mean about you. Before you get mad, stop and think. The Bible says, "One witness is never enough to convict someone." Maybe the person who told the story made a mistake. Maybe that person didn't tell the truth. If you feel upset, ask your best friend about it. But don't accuse her until you know the truth.

dedicated it, you may go home. Otherwise, you might die in battle, and someone else will dedicate it. ⁶If you have planted a vineyard and not enjoyed the grapes, you may go home. Otherwise, you might die in battle, and someone else will enjoy the grapes. ⁷If you are engaged to a woman but have not married her, you may go home. Otherwise, you might die in battle, and someone else will marry her."

⁸The officers should also tell the troops, "If you are afraid or have lost your courage, you may go home. Then you won't ruin the morale of the other Israelites." ⁹When the officers finish speaking to the troops, they should appoint commanders to lead them.

¹⁰When you approach a city to attack it, offer its people a peaceful way to surrender. ¹¹If they accept it and open their gates to you, then all the people there will be made to do forced labor and serve you. ¹²If they won't accept your offer of peace but declare war on you, set up a blockade around the city. ¹³When the LORD your God hands the city over to you, kill every man in that city with your swords. ¹⁴But take the women and children, the cattle and everything else in the city, including all its goods, as your loot. You may enjoy your enemies' goods that the LORD your God has given you. ¹⁵This is what you must do to all the cities that are far away which don't belong to the nations nearby.

¹⁶However, you must not spare anyone's life in the cities of these nations that the LORD your God is giving you as your property. ¹⁷You must claim the Hittites, Amorites, Canaanites, Perizzites, Hivites, and Jebusites for the LORD and completely destroy them, as the LORD your God has commanded you. ¹⁸Otherwise, they will teach you to do all the disgusting things they do for their gods, and you will sin against the LORD your God.

¹⁹This is what you must do whenever you blockade a city for a long time in order to capture it in war. Don't harm any of its fruit trees with an ax. You can eat the fruit. Never cut those trees down, because the trees of the field are not people you have come to blockade. ²⁰You may destroy trees that you know are not fruit trees. You may cut them down and use them in your blockade until you capture the city.

When a Murder Is Committed, but the Murderer Can't Be Found

21 ¹This is what you must do if you find a murder victim lying in a field in the land that the LORD your God is giving you. If no one knows who committed the murder, ²your leaders and judges must go and measure the distance from the body to each of the neighboring cities. ³When it has been determined which city is nearest the body, the leaders from that city must choose a heifer that has never been put to work and never worn a yoke.ᵃ ⁴The leaders of that city will bring the heifer down to a river, to a location where the land hasn't been plowed or planted. At the river they must break the heifer's neck. ⁵The priests, the descendants of Levi, must come forward. The LORD your God has chosen them to serve him as priests and to bless people in the LORD's name. Their decision is final in all cases involving a disagreement or an assault. ⁶All the leaders from the city which was nearest the murder victim must wash their hands over the dead heifer. ⁷Then they must make this formal statement: "We didn't commit this murder, and we didn't witness it. ⁸LORD, make peace with your people Israel, whom you freed. Don't let the guilt of this unsolved murder remain among your people Israel." Then there will be peace with the LORD despite the murder. ⁹This is how you will get rid of the guilt of an unsolved murder by doing what the LORD considers right.

ᵃ21:3 A yoke is a wooden bar placed over the necks of work animals so that they can pull plows or carts.

Laws About Marriage and Family

[10]When you go to war with your enemies and the LORD your God hands them over to you, you may take them captive. [11]If you see a beautiful woman among the captives and have your heart set on her, you may marry her. [12]Bring her into your home. She must shave her head, cut her nails, [13]and no longer wear the clothes she was wearing when you captured her. Then she may live in your house and mourn the loss of her father and mother for one month. After that, you may sleep with her. Then you will become husband and wife.

[14]But if it happens that you are no longer pleased with her, let her go wherever she wants. You must never sell her or mistreat her as if she were a slave,[b] since you've already had sex with her.

[15]A man might have two wives and love one but not the other. Both wives might have children, and the firstborn son might belong to the wife that the man doesn't love. [16]When the day comes for the father to give his sons their inheritance, he can't treat the son of the wife he loves as if that son were the firstborn. This would show a total disregard for the real firstborn (the son of the wife he doesn't love). [17]Instead, he must recognize the son of the wife he doesn't love as the firstborn. He must give that son a double portion of whatever he owns. That son is the very first son he had. The rights of the firstborn son are his.

[18]Parents might have a stubborn and rebellious son who doesn't obey them. Even though they punish him, he still won't listen to them. [19]His father and mother must take him to the leaders of the city at the city gate. [20]They will say to the leaders of the city, "This son of ours is stubborn and rebellious. He won't obey us. He eats too much and is a drunk." [21]All the men of the city should stone him to death. You must get rid of this evil. When all Israel hears about it, they will be afraid.

Various Laws

[22]When a convicted person is put to death, [23]never leave his dead body hung on a pole overnight. Be sure to bury him that same day, because anyone whose body is hung on a pole is cursed by God. The land that the LORD your God is giving you must never become unclean.[c]

22 [1]If you see another Israelite's ox or sheep out where it doesn't belong, don't pretend that you don't see it. Make sure you take it back. [2]If the owner doesn't live near you or you don't know who owns it, take the animal home with you. Keep it until the owner comes looking for it. Then give it back. [3]Do the same if you find a donkey, some clothes, or anything else that another Israelite may have lost. Don't pretend that you don't know what to do.

[4]If you see another Israelite's donkey or ox lying on the road, don't pretend that you don't see it. Make sure you help him get it back on its feet.

[5]A woman must never wear anything men would wear, and a man must never wear women's clothes. Whoever does this is disgusting to the LORD your God.

[6]Whenever you're traveling and find a nest containing chicks or eggs, this is what you must do. If the mother bird is sitting on the nest, never take her with the chicks. [7]You may take the chicks, but make sure you let the mother go. Then things will go well for you, and you will live for a long time.

[8]Whenever you build a new house, put a railing around the edge of the roof. Then you won't be responsible for a death at your home if someone falls off the roof.

---

[b]21:14 Hebrew meaning of "mistreat her as if she were a slave" uncertain.   [c]21:23 "Unclean" refers to anything that is not presentable to God.

Women's World — Clothing / *Deuteronomy 22:5*

What did well-dressed men wear in Bible times? Most men wore a knee-length undershirt. Over this was a lined, long-sleeved tunic that came below the knees. The man wrapped a sash around his waist and folded it to make pockets. A loose coat or robe topped everything when it was cold or on special occasions. Important men wore decorated coats that showed their occupation or high office. For protection from the sun, men wore turbans or a square of cloth held by a headband. Sandals were strapped to the feet.

Women's clothing looked very similar, except their tunics came to their feet, the headdress was different, and women's sleeves were usually pointed. The most common material for any clothing was wool. It came in natural colors and could be easily dyed.

Deuteronomy 22:5 says men and women should never wear each other's clothing. God made each sex special and important, so we can be proud to be women, and boys can be proud to be men.

⁹Never plant anything between the rows in your vineyard. Otherwise, you will have to give everything that grows there to the holy place. This includes the crop you planted and the grapes from the vineyard.

¹⁰Never plow with an ox and a donkey harnessed together.

¹¹Never wear clothes made of wool and linen woven together.

¹²Make tassels on the four corners of the shawl you wear over your clothes.

Laws About Sex and Marriage

¹³A man might marry a woman, sleep with her, and decide he doesn't like her. ¹⁴Then he might make up charges against her and ruin her reputation by saying, "I married this woman. But when I slept with her, I found out she wasn't a virgin." ¹⁵The girl's father and mother must go to the city gate where the leaders of the city are and submit the evidence that their daughter was a virgin. ¹⁶The girl's father will tell the leaders, "I gave my daughter in marriage to this man, but he doesn't like her. ¹⁷Now he has made up charges against her. He says he found out that my daughter wasn't a virgin. But here's the evidence!" Then the girl's parents must spread out the cloth in front of the leaders of the city. ¹⁸The leaders of that city must take the man and punish

him. ¹⁹They will fine him 2¼ pounds of silver and give it to the girl's father. The husband ruined the reputation of an Israelite virgin. She will continue to be his wife, and he can never divorce her as long as he lives.

²⁰But if the charge is true, and no evidence that the girl was a virgin can be found, ²¹they must take the girl to the entrance of her father's house. The men of her city must stone her to death because she has committed such a godless act in Israel: She had sex before marriage, while she was still living in her father's house. You must get rid of this evil.

²²If a man is caught having sexual intercourse with a married woman, both that man and the woman must die. You must get rid of this evil in Israel.

²³This is what you must do when a man has sexual intercourse with a virgin who is engaged to another man. If this happens in a city, ²⁴take them to the gate of the city and stone them to death. The girl must die because she was in a city and didn't scream for help. The man must die because he had sex with another man's wife. You must get rid of this evil.

²⁵But if a man rapes an engaged girl out in the country, then only the man must die. ²⁶Don't do anything to the girl. She has not committed a sin for which she deserves to die. This is like the case of someone who attacks and murders another person. ²⁷The man found the girl out in the country. She may have screamed for help, but no one was there to rescue her.

²⁸This is what you must do when a man rapes a virgin who isn't engaged. When the crime is discovered, ²⁹the man who had sexual intercourse with her must give the girl's father 1¼ pounds of silver, and she will become his wife. Since he raped her, he can never divorce her as long as he lives.ᵃ

³⁰A man must never marry his father's wife because this would disgrace his father.

Various Laws

23 ᵃ¹A man whose testicles are crushed or whose penis is cut off may never join the assembly of the LORD.

²A man born from an illicit union may not join the assembly of the LORD. No descendant of his may join the assembly of the LORD for ten generations.

³Ammonites or Moabites may not join the assembly of the LORD. Not one descendant of theirs may join the assembly of the LORD for ten generations. ⁴They cannot join because they didn't greet you with food and water on your trip from Egypt. They even hired Balaam, son of Beor, from Pethor in Aram Naharaim, to curse you. ⁵But the LORD your God refused to listen to Balaam. Instead, he turned Balaam's curse into a blessing for you because the LORD your God loves you. ⁶Never offer them peace or friendship as long as you live.

⁷Never consider the Edomites disgusting. They're your relatives. Never consider the Egyptians disgusting. You once were foreigners living in their country. ⁸Their grandchildren may join the assembly of the LORD.

⁹When you're at war and have set up camp to fight your enemies, stay away from anything that will make you unclean.ᵇ ¹⁰If one of your men becomes unclean from a nocturnal emission, he must go outside the camp and stay there. ¹¹Toward evening he must wash, and at sunset he may come back to camp.

¹²Choose a place outside the camp where you can go ⌊to relieve yourself⌋. ¹³You must carry a pointed stick as part of your equipment. When you go outside to squat,

---

ᵃ22:29 Deuteronomy 22:30 in English Bibles is Deuteronomy 23:1 in the Hebrew Bible.   ᵃ23:1 Deuteronomy 23:1-25 in English Bibles is Deuteronomy 23:2-26 in the Hebrew Bible.   ᵇ23:9 "Unclean" refers to anything that is not presentable to God.

dig a hole with it. When you're done, cover up your excrement. [14]The LORD your God moves around in your camp to protect you and hand your enemies over to you. So your camp must always be holy. This way, the LORD will never see anything offensive among you and turn away from you.

[15]If a slave escapes from his master and comes to you, don't return him to his master. [16]Let him stay with you and live among your people wherever he chooses, in any of your cities that seems best to him. Never mistreat him.

[17]No Israelite man or woman should ever become a temple prostitute. [18]Never bring gifts or money earned by prostitution into the house of the LORD your God as an offering you vowed to give. These earnings are disgusting to the LORD your God.

[19]Never charge another Israelite any interest on money, food, or anything else that is borrowed. [20]You may charge a foreigner interest, but not an Israelite. Then the LORD your God will bless you in everything you do once you've entered the land and taken possession of it.

[21]If you make a vow to the LORD your God, don't avoid keeping it. The LORD your God expects you to keep it. You would be guilty of a sin if you didn't. [22]If you didn't make a vow, you would not be guilty. [23]Make sure you do what you said you would do in your vow. You freely chose to make your vow to the LORD your God.

[24]If you go into your neighbor's vineyard, you may eat as many grapes as you like until you're full. But never put any in your basket. [25]If you go into your neighbor's grain field, you may pick grain by hand. But never use a sickle to cut your neighbor's grain.

Various Laws

[1]This is what you must do if a husband writes out a certificate of divorce, gives it to his wife, and makes her leave his house. (He divorced her because he found out something indecent about her and she no longer pleased him.) [2]She might marry another man after she leaves his house. [3]If her second husband doesn't love her and divorces her, or if he dies, [4]her first husband is not allowed to marry her again. She has become unclean.[a] This would be disgusting in the LORD's presence. Don't pollute with sin the land that the LORD your God is giving you as your property.

[5]A man who has recently been married will be free from military duty or any other public service. For one year he is free to stay at home and make his new wife happy.

[6]Never let a family's handmill for grinding flour—or even part of a handmill—be taken to guarantee a loan. The family wouldn't be able to prepare food in order to stay alive.

[7]Whoever kidnaps another Israelite must die. The kidnapper must die, whether he treated the other person like a slave[b] or sold him. You must get rid of this evil.

[8]Guard against outbreaks of serious skin diseases. Be very careful to do exactly as the Levitical priests instruct you. Make sure you do what I commanded them. [9]Remember what the LORD your God did to Miriam on your trip from Egypt.

[10]When you make a loan to your neighbor, don't go into his house to take a security deposit. [11]Wait outside, and the person to whom you're making the loan will bring the deposit out to you. [12]If the person is poor, don't keep the coat you took as a deposit overnight. [13]Make sure you bring it back to him at sunset. When he wears his coat to bed that night, he'll bless you. You will have done the right thing in the presence of the LORD your God.

[14]Don't withhold pay from hired workers who are poor and needy, whether they

---

[a]24:4 "Unclean" refers to anything that is not presentable to God.   [b]24:7 Hebrew meaning of "treated like a slave" uncertain.

are Israelites or foreigners living in one of your cities. ¹⁵Pay them each day before sunset because they are poor and need their pay. Otherwise, they will complain to the Lord about you, and you will be condemned for your sin.

¹⁶Parents must never be put to death for the crimes of their children, and children must never be put to death for the crimes of their parents. Each person must be put to death for his own crime.

¹⁷Never deprive foreigners and orphans of justice. And never take widows' clothes to guarantee a loan. ¹⁸Remember that you were slaves in Egypt and the Lord your God freed you from slavery. So I'm commanding you to do this.

¹⁹This is what you must do when you're harvesting wheat in your field. If you forget to bring in one of the bundles of wheat, don't go back to get it. Leave it there for foreigners, orphans, and widows. Then the Lord your God will bless you in everything you do.

²⁰When you harvest olives from your trees, never knock down all of them. Leave some for foreigners, orphans, and widows.

²¹When you pick the grapes in your vineyard, don't pick all of them. Leave some for foreigners, orphans, and widows. ²²Remember that you were slaves in Egypt. So I'm commanding you to do this.

Various Laws

¹This is what you must do whenever two people have a disagreement that is brought into court. The judges will hear the case and decide who's right and who's wrong. ²If the person who's in the wrong deserves to be beaten, the judge will order him to lie down. Then the judge will have him beaten with as many lashes as the crime deserves. ³Forty lashes may be given, but no more. If an Israelite were given more than that, he would be publicly humiliated.

⁴Never muzzle an ox when it's threshing* grain.

⁵When brothers live together and one of them dies without having a son, his widow must not marry outside the family. Her husband's brother must marry her and sleep with her. He must do his duty as her brother-in-law. ⁶Then the first son she has will carry the dead brother's name so that his name won't die out in Israel.

⁷But if the man doesn't want to marry his brother's widow, she must go to the leaders of the city at the city gate. She must say, "My brother-in-law refuses to let his brother's name continue in Israel. He doesn't want to do his duty as my brother-in-law." ⁸Then the leaders of the city must summon him and talk to him. If he persists in saying that he doesn't want to marry her, ⁹his brother's widow must go up to him in the presence of the leaders. She must take off one of his sandals and spit in his face. She must make this formal statement: "This is what happens to a man who refuses to continue his brother's family line." ¹⁰Then in Israel his family will be called the Family of the Man Without a Sandal.

¹¹This is what you must do when two men are fighting and the wife of one of them comes to rescue her husband from the man who is beating him. If she tries to stop the fight by grabbing the other man's genitals, ¹²cut off her hand. Have no pity on her.

¹³Never carry two sets of weights, a heavier one and a lighter one. ¹⁴Never have two kinds of measures in your house, a larger one and a smaller one. ¹⁵Use accurate and honest weights and measures. Then you will live for a long time in the land that the Lord your God is giving you. ¹⁶Everyone who uses dishonest weights and measures is disgusting to the Lord.

---

*25:4 Threshing is the process of beating stalks to separate them from the grain.

[17]Remember what the Amalekites did to you on your trip from Egypt. [18]They attacked you when you were tired and exhausted and killed all those who were lagging behind. They weren't afraid of God. [19]So when the LORD your God gives you peace from all your enemies around you in the land that he is giving you as your own property, don't forget to erase every memory of the Amalekites from the earth.

A Reminder to Keep God's Laws

26 [1]Soon you will enter and take possession of the land that the LORD your God is giving you as your property. When you have settled there, [2]take some of the first produce harvested from the fields in the land that the LORD your God is giving you, and put it in a basket. Then go to the place where the LORD your God will choose for his name to live. [3]Go to the priest who is serving at that time, and tell him, "I declare today to the LORD your God that I have come to the land that the LORD is giving us, as he swore to our ancestors." [4]Then the priest will take the basket from you and set it down in front of the altar of the LORD your God. [5]You will make this formal statement in the presence of the LORD your God: "My ancestors were wandering Arameans. There were only a few of them when they went to Egypt and lived as foreigners. But then they became a great, powerful, and large nation. [6]So the Egyptians treated us cruelly, oppressed us, and made us do back-breaking work for them. [7]We cried out to the LORD God of our ancestors, and he heard us. He saw our misery, suffering, and oppression. [8]Then the LORD used his mighty hand and powerful arm to bring us out of Egypt. He used spectacular and awe-inspiring deeds, miraculous signs, and amazing things. [9]He brought us to this place and gave us this land flowing with milk and honey. [10]So now I've brought the first produce harvested from the fields you gave me, LORD."

You will place the basket in the presence of the LORD your God and bow down in front of him. [11]Then you, the Levites, and the foreigners who live among you can enjoy all the good things which the LORD your God has given you and your family.

[12]Every third year is the year when you will store a tenth of that year's crops in your houses. During that year distribute what you have stored to the Levites, foreigners, orphans, and widows in your cities, and they may eat all they want. [13]When you have distributed all that was stored, say to the LORD your God, "Nothing is left of the holy offering stored in my house. I distributed it to the Levites, foreigners, orphans, and widows as you commanded me. I disobeyed none of your

Needy People
Deuteronomy 26:12-15

Does your church or school have food or clothing drives for the poor? God cares about people who are hungry. He wants his people to care, too. Maybe you can donate food to the next food drive or give away some clothes you don't wear anymore. Learning to care about people in need is an important part of being a Christian.

commands, and I didn't forget to do what you commanded. [14]I didn't eat any of this holy offering while I was in mourning. I didn't distribute any of it while I was unclean.[ᵃ] I didn't offer any of it to the dead. I have obeyed the Lord my God. I have done everything you commanded me. [15]Look down from your holy place in heaven. Bless your people Israel and the land flowing with milk and honey that you have given us, as you promised with an oath to our ancestors."

[16]Today the Lord your God is commanding you to obey these laws and rules. You must faithfully obey them with all your heart and with all your soul. [17]Today you have declared that the Lord is your God and that you will follow his directions, obey his laws, commands, and rules, and listen to him. [18]Today the Lord has declared that you are his people, his own special possession, as he told you. But you must be sure to obey his commands. [19]Then he will place you high above all the other nations he has made. He will give you praise, fame, and honor, and you will be a people holy to the Lord your God, as he promised.

Write the Law on Stones

27 [1]Moses and the leaders of Israel told the people, "Obey every command I'm giving you today.

[2]The day you cross the Jordan River and enter the land that the Lord your God is giving you, set up some large stones and cover them with plaster. [3]The Lord God of your ancestors is giving you a land flowing with milk and honey, as he promised you. After you're in that land, write all the words of these teachings on the stones. [4]After you cross the Jordan River, set up these stones on Mount Ebal, and cover them with plaster, following the command I'm giving you today. [5]Build an altar of stones there dedicated to the Lord your God. Don't use an iron chisel on the stones. [6]You must use uncut stones to build the altar of the Lord your God. Sacrifice burnt offerings on it to the Lord your God. [7]Sacrifice fellowship offerings, eat them there, and enjoy yourselves in the presence of the Lord your God. [8]Write clearly and carefully all the words of these teachings on the stones you set up."

[9]Then Moses and the Levitical priests said to all Israel, "Be quiet and listen, Israel. Today you have become the people of the Lord your God. [10]Obey the Lord your God and follow his commands and laws which I'm giving you today."

Curses Which Are to Be Recited

[11]That same day Moses gave the people this command: [12]After you cross the Jordan River, these are the tribes that will stand on Mount Gerizim to bless the people: Simeon, Levi, Judah, Issachar, Joseph, and Benjamin. [13]These are the tribes that will stand on Mount Ebal to announce the curses: Reuben, Gad, Asher, Zebulun, Dan, and Naphtali.

[14]The Levites will declare to all the people of Israel in a loud voice:

[15]"Whoever has a carved or metal statue, anything disgusting to the Lord that was made by a craftsman, and sets it up in secret will be cursed." Then all the people will say amen.

[16]"Whoever curses his father or mother will himself be cursed." Then all the people will say amen.

[17]"Whoever moves his neighbor's boundary marker will be cursed." Then all the people will say amen.

[18]"Whoever leads blind people in the wrong direction will be cursed." Then all the people will say amen.

ᵃ26:14 "Unclean" refers to anything that is not presentable to God.

¹⁹"Whoever deprives foreigners, orphans, or widows of justice will be cursed." Then all the people will say amen.

²⁰"Whoever has sexual intercourse with his father's wife will be cursed. He has disgraced his father." Then all the people will say amen.

²¹"Whoever has sexual intercourse with any animal will be cursed." Then all the people will say amen.

²²"Whoever has sexual intercourse with his sister, his father's daughter, or his mother's daughter will be cursed." Then all the people will say amen.

²³"Whoever has sexual intercourse with his mother-in-law will be cursed." Then all the people will say amen.

²⁴"Whoever kills another person secretly will be cursed." Then all the people will say amen.

²⁵"Whoever accepts money to kill an innocent person will be cursed." Then all the people will say amen.

²⁶"Whoever doesn't obey every word of these teachings will be cursed." Then all the people will say amen.

Blessings From the LORD

28 ¹Carefully obey the LORD your God, and faithfully follow all his commands that I'm giving you today. If you do, the LORD your God will place you high above all the other nations in the world. ²These are all the blessings that will come to you and stay close to you because you obey the LORD your God:

³You will be blessed in the city and blessed in the country.

⁴You will be blessed. You will have children. Your land will have crops. Your animals will have offspring. Your cattle will have calves, and your flocks will have lambs and kids.

⁵The grain you harvest and the bread you bake will be blessed.

⁶You will be blessed when you come and blessed when you go.

⁷The LORD will defeat your enemies when they attack you. They will attack you from one direction but run away from you in seven directions.

⁸The LORD will bless your barns and everything you do. The LORD your God will bless you in the land that he is giving you.

⁹You will be the LORD's holy people, as he promised you with an oath. He will do this if you obey the commands of the LORD your God and follow his directions. ¹⁰Then all the people in the world will see that you are the LORD's people, and they will be afraid of you. ¹¹The LORD will give you plenty of blessings: You will have many children. Your animals will have many offspring. Your soil will produce many crops in the land the LORD will give you, as he swore to your ancestors.

¹²The LORD will open the heavens, his rich storehouse, for you. He will send rain on your land at the right time and bless everything you do. You will be able to make loans to many nations but won't need to borrow from any. ¹³The LORD will make you the head, not the tail. You will always be at the top, never at the bottom, if you faithfully obey the commands of the LORD your God that I am giving you today. ¹⁴Do everything I'm commanding you today. Never worship other gods or serve them.

Curses From the LORD

¹⁵Obey the LORD your God, and faithfully follow all his commands and laws that I am giving you today. If you don't, all these curses will come to you and stay close to you:

¹⁶You will be cursed in the city and cursed in the country.

¹⁷The grain you harvest and the bread you bake will be cursed.
¹⁸You will be cursed. You will have few children. Your land will have few crops. Your cattle will be cursed with few calves, and your flocks will have few lambs and kids.
¹⁹You will be cursed when you come and cursed when you go.
²⁰The LORD will send you curses, panic, and frustration in everything you do until you're destroyed and quickly disappear for the evil you will do by abandoning the LORD. ²¹The LORD will send one plague after another on you until he wipes you out of the land you're about to enter and take possession of. ²²The LORD will strike you with disease, fever, and inflammation; heat waves,ᵃ drought,ᵇ scorching winds,ᶜ and ruined crops. They will pursue you until you die. ²³The sky above will look like bronze, and the ground below will be as hard as iron. ²⁴The LORD will send dust storms and sandstorms on you from the sky until you're destroyed.
²⁵The LORD will let your enemies defeat you. You will attack them from one direction but run away from them in seven directions. You will become a thing of horror to all the kingdoms in the world. ²⁶Your dead bodies will be food for all the birds and wild animals. There will be no one to scare them away. ²⁷The LORD will strike you with the same boils that plagued the Egyptians. He will strike you with hemorrhoids,ᵈ sores,ᵉ and itchingᶠ that won't go away. ²⁸The LORD will strike you with madness, blindness, and panic. ²⁹You will grope in broad daylight as blind people grope in their blindness. You won't be successful in anything you do.ᵍ As long as you live, you will be oppressed and robbed with no one to rescue you.
³⁰You will be engaged to a woman, but another man will have sex with her. You will build a house, but you won't live in it. You will plant a vineyard, but you won't enjoy the grapes. ³¹Your ox will be butchered as you watch, but you won't eat any of its meat. You will watch as your donkey is stolen from you, but you'll never get it back. Your flock will be given to your enemies, and no one will rescue it. ³²You will watch with your own eyes as your sons and daughters are given to another nation. You will strain your eyes looking for them all day long, but there will be nothing you can do. ³³People you never knew will eat what your land and your hard work have produced. As long as you live, you will know nothing but oppression and abuse. ³⁴The things you see will drive you mad. ³⁵The LORD will afflict your knees and legs with severe boils that can't be cured. The boils will cover your whole body from the soles of your feet to the top of your head.
³⁶The LORD will lead you and the king you choose to a nation that you and your ancestors never knew. There you will worship gods made of wood and stone. ³⁷You will become a thing of horror. All the nations where the LORD will send you will make an example of you and ridicule you.
³⁸You will plant many crops in your fields, but harvest little because locusts will destroy your crops. ³⁹You will plant vineyards and take care of them, but you won't drink any wine or gather any grapes, because worms will eat them. ⁴⁰You will have olive trees everywhere in your country but no olive oil to rub on your skin, because the olives will fall off the trees. ⁴¹You will have sons and daughters, but you won't be able to keep them because they will be taken as prisoners of war. ⁴²Crickets will swarm all over your trees and the crops in your fields.
⁴³The standard of living for the foreigners who live among you will rise higher and higher, while your standard of living will sink lower and lower. ⁴⁴They will be

ᵃ28:22 Or "uncontrolled fever." ᵇ28:22 Latin; Masoretic Text "warfare." ᶜ28:22 Or "blight." ᵈ28:27 Or "boils."
ᵉ28:27 Or "scurvy." ᶠ28:27 Hebrew meaning uncertain. ᵍ28:29 Or "darkness, but you won't be able to find your way."

able to make loans to you, but you won't be able to make loans to them. They will be the head, and you will be the tail.

⁴⁵All these curses will come to you. They will pursue you and stay close to you until you're destroyed, because you didn't obey the Lord your God or follow his commands and laws, which I'm giving you. ⁴⁶These curses will be a sign and an amazing thing to warn you and your descendants forever. ⁴⁷You didn't serve the Lord your God with a joyful and happy heart when you had so much. ⁴⁸So you will serve your enemies, whom the Lord will send against you. You will serve them even though you are already hungry, thirsty, naked, and in need of everything. The Lord will put a heavy burden of hard work on you until he destroys you.

⁴⁹The Lord will bring against you a nation from far away, from the ends of the earth. The nation will swoop down on you like an eagle. It will be a nation whose language you won't understand. ⁵⁰Its people will be fierce-looking. They will show no respect for the old and no pity for the young. ⁵¹They'll eat the offspring of your animals and the crops from your fields until you're destroyed. They'll leave you no grain, no new wine, no olive oil, no calves from your herds, and no lambs or kids from your flocks. They'll continue to do this until they've completely ruined you. ⁵²They will blockade all your cities until the high, fortified walls in which you trust come down everywhere in your land. They'll blockade all the cities everywhere in the land that the Lord your God is giving you.

⁵³Because of the hardships your enemies will make you suffer during the blockade, you will eat the flesh of your own children, the sons and daughters, whom the Lord your God has given you. ⁵⁴Even the most tender and sensitive man among you will become stingy toward his brother, the wife he loves, and the children he still has left. ⁵⁵He will give none of them any of the flesh of his children that he is eating. It will be all that he has left, because of the hardships your enemies will make you suffer during the blockade of all your cities. ⁵⁶The most tender and sensitive woman among you—so sensitive and tender that she wouldn't even step on an ant—will become stingy toward the husband she loves or toward her own son or daughter. ⁵⁷She won't share with them the afterbirth from her body and the children she gives birth to. She will secretly eat them out of dire necessity, because of the hardships your enemies will make you suffer during the blockade of your cities.

⁵⁸You might not faithfully obey every word of the teachings that are written in this book. You might not fear this glorious and awe-inspiring name: the Lord your God. ⁵⁹If so, the Lord will strike you and your descendants with unimaginable plagues. They will be terrible and continuing plagues and severe and lingering diseases. ⁶⁰He will again bring all the diseases of Egypt that you dreaded, and they will cling to you. ⁶¹The Lord will also bring you every kind of sickness and plague not written in this Book of Teachings. They will continue until you're dead. ⁶²At one time you were as numerous as the stars in the sky. But only a few of you will be left, because you didn't obey the Lord your God. ⁶³At one time the Lord was more than glad to make you prosperous and numerous. Now the Lord will be more than glad to destroy you and wipe you out. You will be torn out of the land you're about to enter and take possession of.

⁶⁴Then the Lord will scatter you among all the people of the world, from one end of the earth to the other. There you will serve gods made of wood and stone that neither you nor your ancestors ever knew. ⁶⁵Among those nations you will find no peace, no place to call your own. There the Lord will give you an unsettled mind, failing eyesight, and despair. ⁶⁶Your life will always be hanging by a thread. You will live in terror day and night. You will never feel sure of your life. ⁶⁷In the morning you'll say, "If only it were evening!" And in the evening you'll say, "If only it were morning!"

You'll talk this way because of the things that will terrify you and because of the things you'll see. [68]The Lord will bring you back to Egypt in ships[h] on a journey that I said you would never take again. There you will try to sell yourselves as slaves to your enemies, but no one will buy you.

Israel's Past, Present, and Future

29 [1]These are the terms of the promise[b] that the Lord commanded Moses to give to the Israelites in Moab. This was in addition to the promise the Lord gave them at Mount Horeb.

[2]Moses summoned all the people of Israel and said to them:

You've seen with your own eyes everything that the Lord did in Egypt to Pharaoh, to all his officials, and to his whole country. [3]You also saw those terrible plagues, those miraculous signs, and those spectacular, amazing things. [4]But to this day the Lord hasn't given you a mind that understands, eyes that see, or ears that hear. [5]For 40 years I led you through the desert. During that time your clothes and shoes never wore out. [6]You ate no bread and drank no wine or liquor. I did this so that you would know that I am the Lord your God.

[7]When you came to this place, King Sihon of Heshbon and King Og of Bashan came out to fight us, but we defeated them. [8]We took their land and gave it to the tribes of Reuben, Gad, and half of the tribe of Manasseh as their property. [9]Faithfully obey the terms of this promise. Then you will be successful in everything you do.

[10]All of you are standing here today in the presence of the Lord your God. The heads of your tribes,[c] your leaders, your officers, and all the men of Israel are here. [11]Your children, your wives, and the foreigners who cut wood and carry water in your camp are also here. [12]You are ready to accept the terms and conditions of the promise that the Lord your God is giving you today. [13]With this promise the Lord will confirm today that you are his people and that he is your God. This is what he told you, and this is what he promised your ancestors Abraham, Isaac, and Jacob with an oath. [14]You aren't the only people to receive this promise and its conditions. [15]It is for those of you who are standing here with us today in the presence of the Lord our God and also for those who are not here today.

Good Morning, God

Deuteronomy 29:2-9

The Israelites often complained about their harsh conditions in the desert. Moses tried to remind them of the miracles they had experienced together, so they would be hopeful instead of unhappy. The next time you are tempted to complain, think back. How has God been good to you? Remembering the ways he has come through in the past makes it easier to face problems in the future.

Dear Lord, help me to see all that you do for me.

---

[h]28:68 Or "in sorrow." [a]29:1 Deuteronomy 29:1-29 in English Bibles is Deuteronomy 28:69–29:28 in the Hebrew Bible. [b]29:1 Or "covenant." [c]29:10 Syriac, Greek, Targum; Masoretic Text "your heads, your tribes."

¹⁶You know how we lived in Egypt and how we passed through other countries on our way here. ¹⁷You saw their disgusting gods and idols made of wood, stone, silver, and gold. ¹⁸Make sure there is no man, woman, family, or tribe among you today who turns from the Lord our God to worship the gods of those nations. Make sure that no one among you is the source of this kind of bitter poison.

¹⁹Someone may hear the conditions of this promise. He may think that he is so blessed that he can say, "I'll be safe even if I go my own stubborn way. After all, the Lord would never, sweep away well-watered ground along with dry*ᵈ* ground." ²⁰The Lord will never be willing to forgive that person, because the Lord's burning anger will smolder against him. All the curses described in this book will happen to him. The Lord will erase ,every memory of, that person's name from the earth. ²¹And the Lord will single him out from all the tribes of Israel for disaster based on all the conditions of the promise written in this Book of the Teachings.

²²Then the next generation of your children and foreigners who come from distant countries will see the plagues that have happened in this land and the diseases the Lord sent here. ²³They will see all the soil poisoned with sulfur and salt. Nothing will be planted. Nothing will be growing. There will be no plants in sight. It will be as desolate as Sodom, Gomorrah, Admah, and Zeboiim, cities the Lord destroyed in fierce anger. ²⁴Then all the other nations in the world will ask, "Why has the Lord done this to their land? Why is he so angry?"

²⁵The answer will be, "Because they abandoned the promise of the Lord God of their ancestors. He made this promise to them when he brought them out of Egypt. ²⁶They worshiped other gods and bowed down to them. These were gods they never heard of, gods the Lord didn't permit them to have. ²⁷So the Lord became angry with this land and brought on it all the curses described in this book. ²⁸In his fierce anger and fury the Lord uprooted these people from their land and deported them to another country, where they still are today."

²⁹Some things are hidden. They belong to the Lord our God. But the things that have been revealed in these teachings belong to us and to our children forever. We must obey every word of these teachings.

30 ¹All these blessings and curses I have spoken about will happen to you. Take them to heart when you are among all the nations where the Lord your God will scatter you. ²If you and your children return to the Lord your God and obey him with all your heart and with all your soul, doing everything I command you today, ³he will restore your fortunes. He will have mercy on you and gather you from all the nations of the world where he will scatter you. ⁴Even if you are scattered to the most distant country in the world, the Lord your God will gather you and bring you back from there. ⁵The Lord your God will bring you to the land your ancestors owned. You will take possession of it, and the Lord will make you more prosperous and numerous than your ancestors were.

⁶The Lord your God will circumcise your hearts and the hearts of your descendants. You will love the Lord your God with all your heart and with all your soul, and you will live. ⁷Then the Lord your God will put all these curses on your enemies, those who hate you and persecute you. ⁸You will again obey the Lord and follow all his commands that I'm giving you today. ⁹The Lord your God will give you many blessings in everything you do: You will have many children. Your animals will have many offspring. Your soil will produce many crops. The Lord will again delight in making you as prosperous as he made your ancestors. ¹⁰He will do this if you obey him and

---

ᵈ29:19 Hebrew meaning of "After all . . . dry" uncertain.

follow his commands and laws that are written in this Book of Teachings and return to the LORD your God with all your heart and with all your soul. ¹¹This command I'm giving you today isn't too hard for you or beyond your reach. ¹²It's not in heaven. You don't have to ask, "Who will go to heaven to get this command for us so that we can hear it and obey it?" ¹³This command isn't on the other side of the sea. You don't have to ask, "Who will cross the sea to get it for us so that we can hear it and obey it?" ¹⁴No, these words are very near you. They're in your mouth and in your heart so that you will obey them.

Choose Between Life and Death

¹⁵Today I offer you life and prosperity or death and destruction. ¹⁶This is what I'm commanding you today: Love the LORD your God, follow his directions, and obey his commands, laws, and rules. Then you will live, your population will increase, and the LORD your God will bless you in the land that you're about to enter and take possession of.

¹⁷But your hearts might turn away, and you might not listen. You might be tempted to bow down to other gods and worship them. ¹⁸If you do, I tell you today that you will certainly be destroyed. You will not live for a long time in the land that you're going to take possession of when you cross the Jordan River.

¹⁹I call on heaven and earth as witnesses today that I have offered you life or death, blessings or curses. Choose life so that you and your descendants will live. ²⁰Love the LORD your God, obey him, and be loyal to him. This will be your way of life, and it will mean a long life for you*ᵃ* in the land that the LORD swore to give to your ancestors Abraham, Isaac, and Jacob.

Joshua Becomes Israel's Leader to Replace Moses

31 ¹Moses continued to speak to all the Israelites:

²"I'm 120 years old now, and I'm not able to lead you anymore. Besides, the LORD has told me that I cannot cross the Jordan River. ³The LORD your God is the one who will cross the river ahead of you. He will destroy those nations as you arrive, and you will take possession of their land. Joshua will also cross the river ahead of you, as the LORD told you. ⁴The LORD will do to those nations what he did to King Sihon and King Og of the Amorites and to their lands when he destroyed them. ⁵The LORD will hand them over to you, and you must do to them everything that I commanded you. ⁶Be strong and courageous. Don't tremble! Don't be afraid of them! The LORD your God is the one who is going with you. He won't abandon you or leave you."

⁷Then Moses called for Joshua and said to him in the presence of all Israel, "Be strong and courageous. You will go with these people into the land that the LORD will give them, as he swore to their ancestors. You will help them take possession of the land.*ᵇ* ⁸The LORD is the one who is going ahead of you. He will be with you. He won't abandon you or leave you. So don't be afraid or terrified."

⁹Moses wrote down these teachings and gave them to the Levitical priests who carried the ark of the LORD's promise and to all the leaders of Israel. ¹⁰Then Moses commanded them, "At the end of every seventh year you must cancel debts. At that time, during the Festival of Booths, ¹¹all the Israelites will come into the presence of the LORD your God at the place he will choose. Read these teachings so that they can hear them. ¹²Assemble the men, women, and children, as well as the foreigners who live in your cities. Have them listen and learn to fear the LORD your God and faithfully

---

ᵃ30:20 Or "He is your life, and he will let you live for a long time."   ᵇ31:7 Or "And you will distribute the land to them."

obey every word of these teachings. [13]Their children, who don't know these teachings, must hear them and learn to fear the Lord your God as long as you live in the land that you are going to take possession of when you cross the Jordan River."

[14]The Lord said to Moses, "The time of your death is coming soon. Call for Joshua. Both of you come to the tent of meeting, and I will give him his instructions." Moses and Joshua came to the tent of meeting. [15]Then the Lord appeared in a column of smoke at the entrance to the tent.

[16]The Lord said to Moses, "Soon you are going to lie down in death with your ancestors. When these people enter the land and are living among the foreigners there, they will chase after foreign gods as though they were prostitutes. They will abandon me and reject the promise[b] I made to them. [17]On that day I will become angry with them. I will abandon them and turn away from them. They will be destroyed, and many terrible disasters will happen to them. On that day they will ask, 'Haven't these disasters happened to us because our God isn't with us?' [18]On that day I will certainly turn away from them because of all the evil they've done in turning to other gods.

[19]"Write down this song, teach it to the Israelites, and have them sing it. This song will be a witness for me against the Israelites. [20]I will bring them into the land that I swore to give to their ancestors, a land flowing with milk and honey. When they have eaten all they want and have become fat,[c] they will turn to other gods and worship them. They will despise me and reject my promise. [21]When many terrible disasters happen to them, this song will testify against them, because it will never be forgotten by their descendants. I know what their hearts are set on doing, even now before I bring them into the land that I swore to give them." [22]That day Moses wrote down this song and taught it to the Israelites.

[23]The Lord gave this command to Joshua, son of Nun: "Be strong and courageous, because you will bring the Israelites into the land that I swore to give them, and I will be with you."

[24]Finally, Moses finished writing all the words of these teachings in a book. [25]He gave this command to the Levites who carried the ark of the Lord's promise: [26]"Take this Book of Teachings, and put it next to the ark of the promise of the Lord your God, where it will be a witness against you. [27]I know how rebellious you are. You are impossible to deal with. While I am alive and still with you, you are rebelling against the Lord. How much more rebellious will you be after I die? [28]Assemble all the leaders of your tribes and your officers in front of me. As they listen, I will speak these words and call on heaven and earth to testify against them. [29]I know that after I die you will become thoroughly corrupt and turn from the way I have commanded you to live. In the days to come disasters will happen to you because you will make the Lord furious by doing what he considers evil."

The Song of Moses

[30]Then, as the whole congregation of Israel listened, Moses recited all the words of this song:

32
    [1] Listen, heaven, and I will speak.
        Earth, hear the words from my mouth.

    [2] Let my teachings come down like raindrops.
        Let my words drip like dew,
            like gentle rain on grass,
            like showers on green plants.

---

[b]31:16 Or "covenant."   [c]31:20 Or "prosperous."

3   I will proclaim the name of the LORD.
    Give our God the greatness he deserves!
4   He is a rock.
            What he does is perfect.
                All his ways are fair.
        He is a faithful God, who does no wrong.
            He is honorable and reliable.

5   He recognizes that his people are corrupt.
    To their shame they are no longer his children.
    They are devious and scheming.
6   Is this how you repay the LORD,
        you foolish and silly people?
    Isn't he your Father and Owner,
        who made you and formed you?

7   Remember a time long ago.
        Think about all the past generations.
            Ask your fathers to remind you,
                and your leaders to tell you.
8   When the Most High gave nations their land,
        when he divided the descendants of Adam,
            he set up borders for the tribes
                corresponding to the number of the sons of Israel.

9   But the LORD's people were his property.
        Jacob was his own possession.
10   He found his people in a desert land,
                in a barren place where animals howl.
            He guarded them, took care of them,
                and protected them because they were helpless.
11 Like an eagle that stirs up its nest,
        hovers over its young,
            spreads its wings to catch them,
                and carries them on its feathers,
12 so the LORD alone led his people.
        No foreign god was with him.
13   He made them ride on the heights of the earth
                and fed them with the produce of the fields.
            He gave them honey from rocks
                and olive oil from solid rock.
14   They ate cheese from cows
                and drank milk from sheep and goats.
            He gave them fat from lambs,
                rams from the stock of Bashan,
                    male goats, and the best wheat.
            They drank the blood-red wine of grapes.

15 Jeshurun[a] got fat and disrespectful.
        (You got fat! You were stuffed! You were gorged!)

---

[a]32:15 "Jeshurun" is another name for Israel.

They abandoned the God who made them
 and treated the rock of their salvation like a fool.
16 They made him furious because they worshiped foreign gods
 and angered him because they worshiped worthless idols.
17 They sacrificed to demons that are not God,
 to gods they never heard of.
  These were new gods, who came from nearby,
   gods your ancestors never worshiped.
18 (You ignored the rock who fathered you
 and forgot the God who gave you life.)

19 The Lord saw this and rejected them,
 because his own sons and daughters had made him angry.
20 He said, "I will turn away from them
 and find out what will happen to them.
  They are devious people,
   children who can't be trusted.
21 They made him furious because they worshiped foreign gods
 and angered him because they worshiped worthless idols.
So I will use those who are not my people to make them jealous
 and a nation of godless fools to make them angry.
22 My anger has started a fire
 that will burn to the depths of hell.
  It will consume the earth and its crops
   and set the foundations of the mountains on fire.
23 I will bring one disaster after another on them.
I will use up all my arrows on them.
24 They will be starved by famines
 and ravaged by pestilence and deadly epidemics.
I will send vicious animals against them
 along with poisonous animals that crawl on the ground.
25 Foreign wars will kill off their children,
 and even at home there will be horrors.
  Young men and young women alike will die
   as well as nursing babies and gray-haired men.
26 I said that I would cut them in pieces*b*
 and erase everyone's memory of them.
27 But I didn't want their enemies to make me angry.
 I didn't want their opponents to misunderstand and say,
  'We won this victory!
   It wasn't the Lord who did all this!' "

28 My people have lost their good sense.
 They are not able to understand.
29 If only they were wise enough to understand this
 and realize what will happen to them!
30 How could one person chase a thousand
 or two people make ten thousand flee?
Their rock used these people to defeat them

---

*b*32:26 Hebrew meaning of "cut them in pieces" uncertain.

and the Lord gave them no help.
31 Their rock isn't like our rock.
Even our enemies will agree with this.
32 Their grapevines come from the vineyards of Sodom
and from the fields of Gomorrah.
Their grapes are poisonous,
and their clusters are bitter.
33 Their wine is snake venom,
the deadly poison of cobras.

34 Isn't this what I've stored
under lock and key in my storehouses?
35 I will take revenge and be satisfied.
In due time their foot will slip,
because their day of disaster is near.
Their doom is coming quickly.
36 The Lord will judge his people
and have compassion on his servants
when he sees that their strength is gone
and that no one is left, neither slaves nor free people.
37 Then he will ask, "Where are their gods?
Where is the rock they took refuge in?
38 Where are the gods who ate the fat from their sacrifices
and drank the wine from their wine offerings?
Let them come to help you!
Let them be your refuge!"

39 See, I am the only God.
There are no others.
I kill, and I make alive.
I wound, and I heal,
and no one can rescue you from my power.
40 I raise my hand toward heaven and solemnly swear:
As surely as I live forever,
41 I will sharpen my flashing sword
and take justice into my own hands.
Then I will take revenge on my enemies
and pay back those who hate me.
42 My arrows will drip with blood
from those who were killed and taken captive.
My sword will cut off the heads
of the enemy who vowed to fight.

43 Joyfully sing with the Lord's people, you nations,
because he will take revenge for the death of his servants.
He will get even with his enemies
and make peace for his people's land.*c*

---

*c*32:43 Dead Sea Scrolls, Samaritan Pentateuch, Greek, Latin; Masoretic Text "his land ,and, his people."

Moses Is Allowed to See Canaan

⁴⁴Moses came with Hoshea,*ᵈ* son of Nun, and recited all the words of this song as the people listened. ⁴⁵When Moses had finished reciting all these words to Israel, ⁴⁶he said to them, "Pay attention to all these warnings I've given you today. Then you will command your children to faithfully obey every word of these teachings. ⁴⁷Don't think these words are idle talk. They are your life! By these words you will be able to live for a long time in the land that you are going to take possession of when you cross the Jordan River."

⁴⁸That same day the LORD said to Moses, ⁴⁹"Go into the Abarim Mountains, to Mount Nebo in Moab, across from Jericho. Take a look at the land of Canaan that I'm giving the Israelites as their own property. ⁵⁰On this mountain where you're going, you will die and join your ancestors in death, as your brother Aaron died on Mount Hor. ⁵¹This is because both of you were unfaithful to me at the oasis of Meribah at Kadesh in the Desert of Zin. You didn't show the Israelites how holy I am. ⁵²You may see the land from a distance, but you may not enter the land I'm giving the Israelites."

Moses Blesses the Twelve Tribes

¹Moses, the man of God, blessed the Israelites with this blessing before he died. ²He said,

"The LORD came from Sinai.
  For his people he rose from Seir like the sun.
  He appeared like sunshine from Mount Paran.
He came with tens of thousands of holy ones.
  On his right was a raging fire for them.*ᵃ*
3 You certainly love your people.
  All your holy ones are in your hands.
    They bow at your feet
      to receive your instructions.*ᵇ*
4   Moses gave us these teachings.
      They belong to the assembly of Jacob.
5 The LORD was king of Jeshurun*ᶜ*
    when the leaders of the people assembled
      together with all the tribes of Israel.

6 "May the tribe of **Reuben** live and not die out,
    though their people are few in number."

⁷This is what he said about the tribe of **Judah**:

"Hear the cry of Judah, O LORD,
  and bring them to their people.
They must defend themselves.
  Help them against their enemies."

⁸About the tribe of **Levi** he said,

"Your Thummim and Urim*ᵈ* belong to your faithful people.
You tested your people at Massah.
You quarreled with them at the oasis of Meribah.

---

*ᵈ*32:44 "Hoshea" is another name for Joshua.   *ᵃ*33:2 Hebrew meaning of "a raging fire" uncertain.   *ᵇ*33:3 Hebrew meaning of "They bow . . . your instructions" uncertain.   *ᶜ*33:5 "Jeshurun" is another name for Israel.   *ᵈ*33:8 The Urim and Thummim were used by the chief priest to determine God's answer to questions.

9   They said that they didn't know their father and mother.
They didn't recognize their own brothers.
They didn't acknowledge their own children.
>But they obeyed your word
>>and were faithful to the terms of your promise.*

10   They teach Jacob your rules
>and give Israel your teachings.
They burn incense for you to smell
>and sacrifice burnt offerings on your altar.

11   LORD, bless them with strength
>and be pleased with the work they do.
Break the backs of those who attack them and hate them
>so that they can never get up again."

12About the tribe of **Benjamin** he said,

>"The LORD's beloved people will live securely with him.
>The LORD will shelter them all day long,
>>since he, too, lives on the mountain slopes."

13About the tribes of **Joseph** he said,

>"May the LORD bless their land with water,
>>the best gift heaven can send,
>>with dew and deep springs below the ground.

14   May the LORD bless their land with crops,
>the best gift the sun can give,
>>the best produce of each month,

15   the finest fruits from the oldest mountains,
>the best from the ancient hills,

16   and the most plentiful crops of the earth.
May the LORD bless their land with the favor
>of the one who was in the burning bush.
May these blessings come to the tribes of Joseph.
May they crown the people who are like princes in Israel.

17   They will be as majestic as a firstborn bull.
Their horns will be like the horns of a wild ox.
They will use them to push away nations
>including those at the ends of the earth.
The tens of thousands from the tribe of Ephraim
>and the thousands from the tribe of Manasseh will be like this."

18About the tribe of **Zebulun** he said,

>"People of Zebulun, enjoy yourselves when you go to war,
>>and you people of **Issachar**, enjoy yourselves when you stay at home.

19   They will invite nations to their mountain,
>and there they will offer the proper sacrifices.
They will be nourished by the abundance from the seas
>and the treasures hidden in the sand."

---

*33:9 Or "covenant."

20About the tribe of **Gad** he said,

> "Blessed is the one who gives the people of Gad more land.
>> They wait there like a lion.
>> They can tear off an arm or a head.

21   They chose the best land for themselves.
>> Indeed, a commander's piece of land was reserved for them.
> They were leaders of the people
>> and did for Israel what the LORD considers fair and honorable."*

22About the tribe of **Dan** he said,

> "The people of Dan are a lion cub.
> Out of Bashan they pounce on their enemies."

23About the tribe of **Naphtali** he said,

> "The people of Naphtali enjoy the LORD's favor
> and are filled with the LORD's blessings.
> They will take possession of the lake and the land south of it."

24About the tribe of **Asher** he said,

> "The people of Asher are the most blessed of the sons of Israel.
>> May they be the Israelites' favorite tribe
>> and wash their feet in olive oil.

25   May the locks and bolts of your gates be made of iron and copper.
> May your strength last as long as you live.

26   "There's no one like your God, Jeshurun!
>> He rides through the heavens to help you.
>> In majesty he rides through the clouds.

27   The eternal God is your shelter,
>> and his everlasting arms support you.
> He will force your enemies out of your way
>> and tell you to destroy them.

28   So Israel will live securely.
>> Jacob's spring will be left alone
>> in a land of grain and new wine.
> Dew will drip from Israel's skies.

29   You are blessed, Israel!
> Who is like you,
>> a nation saved by the LORD?
> He is a shield that helps you
>> and a sword that wins your victories.
> Your enemies will come crawling to you,
>> and you will stomp on their backs."

Moses' Death and Burial

34 1Then Moses went up on Mount Nebo from the plains of Moab. He went to the top of Pisgah, across from Jericho. The LORD showed him the whole land. He could see Gilead as far as Dan, 2all of Naphtali, the territory of Ephraim and

---

*33:21 Hebrew meaning of this sentence uncertain.

Manasseh, all the territory of Judah as far as the Mediterranean Sea, ³the Negev, and the Jordan Plain—the valley of Jericho (the City of Palms)—as far as Zoar.

⁴Then the LORD said to him, "This is the land I promised with an oath to Abraham, Isaac, and Jacob. I said I would give it to their descendants. I have let you see it with your own eyes, but you may not go there."

⁵As the LORD had predicted, the LORD's servant Moses died in Moab. ⁶He was buried in a valley in Moab, near Beth Peor. Even today no one knows where his grave is.

⁷Moses was 120 years old when he died. His eyesight never became poor, and he never lost his physical strength. ⁸The Israelites mourned for Moses in the plains of Moab for 30 days. Then the time of mourning for him was over.

⁹Joshua, son of Nun, was filled with the Spirit of wisdom, because Moses had laid his hands on him. The Israelites obeyed him and did what the LORD had commanded through Moses.

¹⁰There has never been another prophet in Israel like Moses, whom the LORD dealt with face to face. ¹¹He was the one the LORD sent to do all the miraculous signs and amazing things in Egypt to Pharaoh, to all his officials, and to his whole country. ¹²Moses used his mighty hand to do all the spectacular and awe-inspiring deeds that were seen by all the Israelites.

Death

Deuteronomy 34:5-8

When Moses died, everyone was sad. All the Israelites would miss their leader. It's all right to be sad when someone you love dies. You will miss that special person. But you have happy memories about him or her, too. Best of all, when people are Christians, they'll meet in heaven and be together always.

Joshua

Joshua was the general of the Israelite army while Moses was alive. When Moses died, General Joshua took Moses' place as the leader of the people. Then Joshua led Israel's army to victory in Canaan. In great battles, the Israelites defeated the powerful Canaanites and conquered their walled cities. Afterward, Joshua gave each of Israel's 12 tribes its own part of the land God promised to them.

Headlines

Woman Saves Spies

People Cross Wet River Dry!

Shout Tumbles Stone Walls

History's Longest Day!

Springtime for Caleb's Daughter!

The Israelites conquered powerful nations. What was their secret weapon? See Joshua 10:42.

Why did the Israelites suffer one defeat?

They were Achan to lose.
(See Joshua 7.)

What did the soldiers find when they looked for the spies in Jericho?

The flax and nothing but the flax.
(See Joshua 2:6.)

Why was Joshua tired at Gibeon?

He'd had a really long day.
(See Joshua 10:12-14.)

What's In It For Me?

Trusting God gives me . . .

THE COURAGE OF JOSHUA.
THE FAITH OF RAHAB.
THE CONFIDENCE OF CALEB.
THE WISDOM TO AVOID ACHAN'S SIN.
VICTORY WHEN I OBEY GOD.

Is War Ever Right?

Just about everybody agrees that war is bad. In war, people are killed and homes are destroyed. So why did God tell the Israelites to go to war against the Canaanites? Why did God tell Joshua to kill all the Canaanites? How could a loving God do such a thing? Wasn't this cruel?

The Canaanites had an evil religion. Their religion involved prostitution and witchcraft. Some Canaanites even burned their own children alive as sacrifices to their gods. They thought their gods liked the smell of human blood.

God had given the people of Canaan a long time to stop doing evil, but they kept on worshiping their own gods. God knew it was time to punish the sins of the Canaanites. He also had to protect his own people. If the Canaanites remained in the land, they would lead the Israelites into their own wicked ways (see Deuteronomy 20:16-18).

Actually, not all of the Canaanites were killed, and eventually they did teach the Israelites their immoral ways—just as God had warned. When that happened, God had to punish the Israelites, too.

War is terrible. And God doesn't like war or killing. But when the Israelites entered Canaan, God used war to stop the wicked ways of many evil people.

Rahab **Rescues** Spies

While soldiers searched throughout Jericho, Rahab hid the Israelite spies under a pile of flax plants drying on her roof (Joshua 2). Why did Rahab risk her life to help enemy spies?

All the people of Jericho had heard how God helped Israel. But only Rahab decided to trust God instead of the great stone walls of Jericho. Because she trusted God, Rahab and her family were saved when Jericho fell. It's good to know about God. But we need to follow Rahab's example. We need to put our trust in him.

What Makes a Great Leader?

God knew Joshua would make a good leader. He was a brilliant general; his military plan was to divide the land of Canaan in half and attack the southern cities first, then the northern cities. Joshua's plan is still studied in military colleges today. Joshua also used clever tactics like night marches and ambushes to overcome the powerful Canaanites. But most important, Joshua trusted God and obeyed him. By listening to God, Joshua was able to lead the Israelites to victory.

God's Secret Weapons

On the line above the verse, write each secret weapon that helped the Israelites defeat the people of Canaan.

Canaanite Weapons	Israelite Weapons
Bows	_____
Arrows	Joshua 1:16-17
Swords	_____
Spears	Joshua 10:11
Chariots	_____
Stone walls	Joshua 10:13
	_____
	Joshua 24:12

Joshua

The LORD Instructs Joshua

¹After the death of the LORD's servant Moses, the LORD said to Moses' assistant Joshua, son of Nun, ²"My servant Moses is dead. Now you and all these people must cross the Jordan River into the land that I am going to give the people of Israel. ³I will give you every place on which you set foot, as I promised Moses. ⁴Your borders will be the desert on the south, nearby Lebanon to the Euphrates River (the country of the Hittites) on the north, and the Mediterranean Sea on the west. ⁵No one will be able to oppose you successfully as long as you live. I will be with you as I was with Moses. I will never neglect you or abandon you. ⁶Be strong and courageous, because you will help these people take possession of the land I swore to give their ancestors.

⁷"Only be strong and very courageous, faithfully doing everything in the teachings that my servant Moses commanded you. Don't turn away from them. Then you will succeed wherever you go. ⁸Never stop reciting these teachings. You must think about them night and day so that you will faithfully do everything written in them. Only then will you prosper and succeed.

⁹"I have commanded you, 'Be strong and courageous! Don't tremble or be terrified, because the LORD your God is with you wherever you go.'"

The People Promise to Obey Joshua

¹⁰Then Joshua ordered the officers of the people, ¹¹"Go through the camp. Tell the people, 'Get your supplies ready. In three days you will cross the Jordan River to take possession of the land the LORD your God is going to give you.'"

¹²Next, Joshua said to the tribes of Reuben and Gad and half of the tribe of Manasseh, ¹³"Remember what the LORD's servant Moses commanded you. Moses said, 'The LORD your God will give you this land—a place to rest.' ¹⁴Your wives, children, and livestock may stay in the land that Moses gave you east of the Jordan River. However, all your best soldiers must march in battle formation ahead of your relatives. You must help your relatives ¹⁵take possession of the land the Lord your God is going to give them. Then they will have a place to rest like you do. After that, you may go back and take possession of the land east of the Jordan River which the Lord's servant Moses gave you."

¹⁶The people responded to Joshua, "We'll do everything you tell us and go wherever you send us. ¹⁷We will obey you as we obeyed Moses. May the Lord your God be with you as he was with Moses. ¹⁸Whoever rebels against your authority or does not obey your orders will be put to death. Just be strong and courageous!"

Joshua Sends Spies to Jericho

¹From Shittim Joshua, son of Nun, secretly sent out two men as spies. He told them, "Go, look at that country, especially the city of Jericho." So they went to Jericho and entered the house of a prostitute named Rahab to spend the night there.

²The king of Jericho was told, "Some Israelites have entered the city tonight. They came to gather information about our land." ³So the king of Jericho sent messengers to Rahab, who told her, "Bring out the men who came to your house. They came here to gather information about the entire land."

⁴But the woman had already taken the two men inside and hidden them. So she

Jericho Is Destroyed

Jericho Is Destroyed

Joshua 6:12–20

12 Joshua got up early in the morning. The priests carried the LORD's ark. **13** The seven priests carrying the seven rams' horns were ahead of it. The priests blew their horns as they went. The armed men were ahead of them, and the rear guard followed the LORD's ark while the horns blew continually. **14** They went around the city once on the second day and returned to the camp. They did this for six days.

15 On the seventh day they got up at dawn. They marched around the city seven times the same way they had done it before. That was the only day they marched around it seven times. **16** When they went around the seventh time, the priests blew their rams' horns.

Joshua said to the troops, "Shout, because the LORD has given you the city! **17** The city has been claimed by the LORD. Everything in it belongs to the LORD. Only the prostitute Rahab and all who are in the house with her will live because she hid the messengers we sent. **18** But stay away from what has been claimed by the LORD for destruction, or you, too, will be destroyed by the LORD. If you take anything that is claimed by the LORD, you will bring destruction and disaster on the camp of Israel. **19** All the silver and gold and everything made of bronze and iron are holy and belong to the LORD. They must go into the LORD's treasury."

20 So the troops shouted very loudly when they heard the blast of the rams' horns, and the wall collapsed. The troops charged straight ahead and captured the city.

said, "Yes, the men did come here. But I didn't know where they had come from. ⁵When it was dark and the gate was just about to close, they left. I don't know where they went. If you hurry, you'll catch up with them." ⁶(She had taken them up to the roof and covered them with the flax which she had laid up there.)

⁷The king's men pursued them on the road leading to a shallow place to cross the Jordan River. As soon as the king's men had left, the gate was closed.

⁸Before the spies fell asleep, Rahab went up to them on the roof. ⁹She said to them, "I know the Lord will give you this land. Your presence terrifies us. All the people in this country are deathly afraid of you. ¹⁰We've heard how the Lord dried up the water of the Red Sea in front of you when you left Egypt. We've also heard what you did to Sihon and Og, the two kings of the Amorites, who ruled east of the Jordan River. We've heard how you destroyed them for the Lord. ¹¹When we heard about it, we lost heart. There was no courage left in any of us because of you. The Lord your God is the God of heaven and earth. ¹²Please swear by the Lord that you'll be as kind to my father's family as I've been to you. Also give me some proof ¹³that you'll protect my father, mother, brothers, sisters, and their households, and that you'll save us from death."

¹⁴The men promised her, "We pledge our lives for your lives. If you don't tell anyone what we're doing here, we'll treat you kindly and honestly when the Lord gives us this land."

¹⁵So she let them down by a rope from her window since her house was built into the city wall. (She lived in the city wall.) ¹⁶She told them, "Go to the mountains so that the men who are pursuing you will not find you. Hide there for three days until they return to Jericho. Then you can go on your way."

¹⁷The men told her, "We will be free from the oath which you made us swear, if you tell anyone what we're doing here. ¹⁸When we invade your land, tie this red cord in the window through which you let us down. Also, gather your father, mother, brothers, and all your father's family into your house. ¹⁹Whoever leaves your house will be responsible for his own life. We will be free from that responsibility. But we will take responsibility if anyone inside your house is harmed. ²⁰If you tell anyone what we're doing here, we will be free from the oath which you made us swear."

²¹"I agree," she said. So she let them go and tied the red cord in the window.

²²The men went to the mountains and stayed there for three days until the king's men returned to Jericho. The king's men had searched for them all along the road but had not found them. ²³Then the two spies came down out of the mountains, crossed the Jordan River, and returned to Joshua, son of Nun. They told him everything that had happened to them. ²⁴They told Joshua, "The Lord has given us the whole country. The people who live there are deathly afraid of us."

Crossing the Jordan River

3 ¹Joshua got up early the next morning. He and all the Israelites left Shittim. They came to the Jordan River, where they camped before crossing.

²Three days later the officers went through the camp. ³They told the people, "As soon as you see the ark of the promise of the Lord your God and the Levitical priests who carry it, break camp and follow them. ⁴However, stay about half a mile behind them. Don't come any closer to them so that you will know which way to go because you have not gone this way before."

⁵Joshua told the people, "Perform the ceremonies to make yourselves holy because tomorrow the Lord will do miracles among you."

⁶Joshua also told the priests, "Take the ark of the promise, and go ahead of the people." They did as they were told.

[7]Then the Lord said to Joshua, "Today I will begin to honor you in front of all the people of Israel. I will do this to let them know that I am with you just as I was with Moses. [8]Order the priests who carry the ark of the promise, 'When you step into the water of the Jordan River, stand there.' "

[9]So Joshua said to the people of Israel, "Come here, and listen to the words of the Lord your God." [10]Joshua continued, "This is how you will know that the living God is among you and that he will certainly force the Canaanites, Hittites, Hivites, Perizzites, Girgashites, Amorites, and Jebusites out of your way. [11]Watch the ark of the promise of the Lord of the whole earth as it goes ahead of you into the Jordan River. [12]Choose one man from each of the 12 tribes of Israel. [13]The priests who carry the ark of the Lord, the Lord of the whole earth, will stand in the water of the Jordan. Then the water flowing from upstream will stop and stand up like a dam."

[14]So they broke camp to cross the Jordan River. The priests who carried the ark of the promise went ahead of the people. [15](The Jordan overflows all its banks during the harvest season.)[a] When the priests who were carrying the ark came to the edge of the Jordan River and set foot in [16]the water, the water stopped flowing from upstream. The water rose up like a dam as far away as the city of Adam near Zarethan. The water flowing down toward the Sea of the Plains (the Dead Sea) was completely cut off. Then the people crossed from the east side of the Jordan River, directly opposite Jericho. [17]The priests who carried the ark of the Lord's promise stood firmly on dry ground in the middle of the Jordan until the whole nation of Israel had crossed the Jordan River on dry ground.

A Reminder of the Crossing

[1]The whole nation finished crossing the Jordan River. The Lord had told Joshua, [2]"Choose one man from each of the 12 tribes. [3]Order them to pick up 12 stones from the middle of the Jordan, where the priests' feet stood firmly. Take the stones along with you, and set them down where you will camp tonight."

[4]Joshua called the 12 men whom he had selected (one from each tribe). [5]He said

Good Morning, God

Joshua 4:1-3

The Lord told Joshua to have the Israelites pick up 12 stones from the Jordan River—one for each of the 12 tribes. These stones would be a reminder to everyone of the miracle God performed for the Israelites. How are you keeping track of God's blessings to you? Just for fun, you could begin your own "rock collection" by collecting some small stones each time you receive a gift from God. When curious friends and neighbors ask, you can tell them about God's answers to prayer.

God, I thank you for answered prayers and for blessings. Help me keep a record of these, so I don't forget your goodness.

---

[a]3:15 This sentence has been moved from verse 16 to express the complex Hebrew paragraph structure more clearly in English.

to them, "Go to the middle of the Jordan River in front of the ark of the LORD your God. Each man must take a stone on his shoulder, one for each tribe of Israel. [6]This will be a sign for you. In the future your children will ask, 'What do these stones mean to you?' [7]You should answer, 'The water of the Jordan River was cut off in front of the ark of the LORD's promise. When the ark crossed the Jordan, the river stopped flowing. These stones are a permanent reminder for the people of Israel.' "

[8]The people of Israel did as Joshua had ordered. They took 12 stones, one for each of the tribes of Israel. They took them from the middle of the Jordan as the LORD had told Joshua. They carried them to the camp and set them down there.

[9]Joshua also set 12 stones in the middle of the Jordan River, where the priests who carried the ark of the promise had stood. The stones are still there today.

[10]The priests who carried the ark remained standing in the middle of the Jordan. They stood there until everything the LORD had ordered Joshua to tell the people had been carried out. This was as Moses had told Joshua. The people hurried to the other side. [11]As soon as everyone had crossed, the priests with the LORD's ark crossed and went ahead of them.

[12]The men of Reuben, Gad, and half of the tribe of Manasseh did as Moses had told them. They marched across in battle formation ahead of the people of Israel. [13]About 40,000 armed men crossed the river in front of the LORD to the plains of Jericho for battle.

[14]On that day the LORD honored Joshua in the presence of all the Israelites. As long as Joshua lived, the Israelites respected him in the same way they had respected Moses.

[15]The LORD said to Joshua, [16]"Order the priests who carry the ark of the testimony to come out of the Jordan River."

[17]So Joshua ordered the priests, "Come out of the Jordan."

[18]The priests who carried the ark of the LORD's promise came out of the middle of the Jordan. When their feet stepped onto dry land, the water of the Jordan returned to its seasonal flood level.

[19]On the tenth day of the first month, the people came out of the Jordan River. They made their camp at Gilgal, just east of Jericho. [20]At Gilgal Joshua set up the 12 stones they had taken from the Jordan. [21]He said to the people of Israel, "In the future when children ask their parents, 'What do these stones mean?' [22]the children should be told that Israel crossed the Jordan River on dry ground. [23]The LORD your God dried up the Jordan ahead of you until you had crossed, as he did to the Red Sea until we had crossed. [24]The LORD did this so that everyone in the world would know his mighty power and that you would fear the LORD your God every day of your life."

Preparations for the First Passover in Canaan

[1]All the Amorite kings west of the Jordan River and all the Canaanite kings along the Mediterranean Sea heard that the LORD had dried up the Jordan River so that the Israelites could cross. So they lost heart and had no courage left to face the people of Israel.

[2]At that time the LORD spoke to Joshua, "Make flint knives, and circumcise the men of Israel." [3]So Joshua made flint knives and circumcised the men of Israel at the Hill of Circumcision.[a]

[4]This is the reason Joshua circumcised them: All the soldiers had died on the way through the desert after they left Egypt. [5]The men who left Egypt had been circumcised. However, the men born later, on the way through the desert, were

---

[a] 5:3 Or "Hill of Foreskins."

not circumcised. ⁶For 40 years the Israelites wandered through the desert until all their soldiers who left Egypt died. They died because they disobeyed the Lord. The Lord swore that he would not let them see this land flowing with milk and honey which he had sworn to give our ancestors.

⁷The sons who took their place had not been circumcised on the way. So Joshua circumcised them. ⁸When all the men had been circumcised, they remained in the camp until they recovered.

⁹The Lord said to Joshua, "Today I have removed the disgrace of Egypt from you." So Joshua named the place Gilgal,ᵇ the name it still has today.

¹⁰The people of Israel camped at Gilgal in the Jericho plain. There they celebrated the Passover on the evening of the fourteenth day of the month. ¹¹On the day after the Passover, they ate some of the produce of the land, unleavened bread and roasted grain. ¹²The day after that, the manna stopped. The people of Israel never had manna again. That year they began to eat the crops that grew in Canaan.

The Commander of the LORD's Army Speaks With Joshua

¹³When Joshua was near Jericho, he looked up and saw a man standing in front of him with a sword in his hand. Joshua went up to him and asked, "Are you one of us or one of our enemies?" ¹⁴He answered, "Neither one! I am here as the commander of the Lord's army." Immediately, Joshua bowed with his face touching the ground and worshiped. He asked, "Sir, what do you want to tell me?" ¹⁵The commander of the Lord's army said to Joshua, "Take off your sandals because this place where you are standing is holy." So Joshua did as he was told.

Jericho Is Destroyed

¹Jericho was bolted and barred shut because the people were afraid of the Israelites. No one could enter or leave.

²The Lord said to Joshua, "I am about to hand Jericho, its king, and its warriors over to you. ³All the soldiers will march around the city once a day for six days. ⁴Seven priests will carry rams' horns ahead of the ark. But on the seventh day you must march around the city seven times while the priests blow their horns. ⁵When you hear a long blast on the horn, all the troops must shout very loudly. The wall around the city will collapse. Then the troops must charge straight ahead into the city."

⁶Joshua, son of Nun, summoned the priests. He said to them, "Pick up the ark of the promise, and have seven priests carry seven rams' horns ahead of the Lord's ark."

⁷He told the troops, "March around the city. Let the armed men march ahead of the Lord's ark."

⁸After Joshua had given orders to the troops, the seven priests carrying the seven rams' horns ahead of the Lord marched off as they blew their horns. The ark of the Lord's promise followed them. ⁹The armed men went ahead of the priests, who blew their horns. The rear guard followed the ark while the priests continued to blow their horns.

¹⁰Joshua ordered the troops, "Don't shout, make any noise, or let one word come out of your mouth until I tell you to shout. Then shout!" ¹¹So the Lord's ark went around the city once. Then they went back to the camp and stayed there for the night.

¹²Joshua got up early in the morning. The priests carried the Lord's ark. ¹³The seven priests carrying the seven rams' horns were ahead of it. The priests blew their horns as they went. The armed men were ahead of them, and the rear guard followed

---

ᵇ5:9 There is a play on words here between Hebrew *gilgal* (rolled) and *gallothi* (roll away/remove).

the LORD's ark while the horns blew continually. ¹⁴They went around the city once on the second day and returned to the camp. They did this for six days.

¹⁵On the seventh day they got up at dawn. They marched around the city seven times the same way they had done it before. That was the only day they marched around it seven times. ¹⁶When they went around the seventh time, the priests blew their rams' horns.

Joshua said to the troops, "Shout, because the LORD has given you the city! ¹⁷The city has been claimed by the LORD. Everything in it belongs to the LORD. Only the prostitute Rahab and all who are in the house with her will live because she hid the messengers we sent. ¹⁸But stay away from what has been claimed by the LORD for destruction, or you, too, will be destroyed by the LORD. If you take anything that is claimed by the LORD, you will bring destruction and disaster on the camp of Israel. ¹⁹All the silver and gold and everything made of bronze and iron are holy and belong to the LORD. They must go into the LORD's treasury."

²⁰So the troops shouted very loudly when they heard the blast of the rams' horns, and the wall collapsed. The troops charged straight ahead and captured the city. ²¹They claimed everything in it for the LORD. With their swords they killed men and women, young and old, as well as cattle, sheep, and donkeys.

Obedience

Joshua 6

Why do you have to go to bed so early, especially when you're not sleepy? Mom or Dad has probably told you why. But chances are you still don't really understand. The Israelites didn't understand why God told them to walk around Jericho for seven days.

But they obeyed— and an amazing thing happened. We, too, need to obey even when we don't understand why.

²²But Joshua said to the two spies, "Go to the prostitute's house. Bring the woman out, along with everything she has, as you swore you would do for her."

²³The spies went and brought out Rahab, her father, mother, brothers, everything she had, and even all of her relatives. They gave them a place outside the camp of Israel. ²⁴Then Israel burned the city and everything in it. But they put the silver and gold and everything made of bronze and iron into the LORD's treasury. ²⁵Joshua spared the prostitute Rahab, her father's family, and everything she had. She still lives in Israel today because she hid the messengers Joshua had sent to look at Jericho.

²⁶At that time Joshua pronounced this curse:

"The LORD will curse
        whoever comes to rebuild the city of Jericho.
    It will cost him his firstborn son
        to lay the foundation.
    It will cost him his youngest son
        to set up the city doors."

²⁷So the LORD was with Joshua, and his fame spread throughout the land.

Achan's Sin and Its Consequences

¹The people of Israel proved to be disloyal about the things claimed by the LORD. Achan, son of Carmi, grandson of Zabdi, great-grandson of Zerah, and a member of the tribe of Judah, took something that had been claimed by the LORD. So the LORD became angry with the people of Israel.

²Joshua sent men from Jericho to Ai. Ai is near Beth Aven, east of Bethel. He said to them, "Go, look at that country." So the men went and looked at Ai. ³They came back to Joshua and told him, "You don't need to send all the troops. Only about two or three thousand men are needed to destroy Ai. Don't tire the troops out by sending all of them. There are only a few troops in Ai."

⁴So about three thousand men were sent. However, they fled from the men of Ai. ⁵The men of Ai killed about thirty-six of them, chasing them from the city gate to the slope of the stone quarries. Israel's troops lost heart and were scared stiff.

⁶Joshua and the leaders of Israel tore their clothes in grief. They put dust on their heads and bowed down to the ground in front of the LORD's ark. They stayed there until evening. ⁷Joshua said, "Almighty LORD, why did you bring these people across the Jordan River? Was it to hand us over to the Amorites so that they could destroy us? I wish we had been content to live on the other side of the Jordan! ⁸Lord, what else can I say after Israel ran away from its enemy? ⁹When the Canaanites and everyone who lives in the land hears about it, they will surround us and remove every memory of us from the earth. What will you do then so that your great name will be remembered?"

¹⁰The LORD said to Joshua, "Get up! What are you doing bowing on the ground? ¹¹Israel has sinned. They have ignored the requirements[a] that I have placed on them. They have taken what I claimed for myself and put it among their own goods. They have not only stolen, but they have also lied.

¹²"The people of Israel will not be able to defend themselves against their enemies. They will run away from their enemies because the people of Israel are now claimed for destruction. I will not be with you anymore unless you destroy what I have claimed for myself.

¹³"Get up! Tell the people, 'Get ready for tomorrow by performing the ceremonies to make yourselves holy. This is what the LORD God of Israel says: You have what I claimed for myself, Israel. You will not be able to defend yourselves against your enemies until you get rid of what I have claimed. ¹⁴In the morning come forward by tribes to the tent of meeting. The tribe the LORD selects will come forward by families. Then the family the LORD selects will come forward by households, and the household the LORD selects will come forward man by man. ¹⁵The man who is selected, along with everything he has, must be burned because he has stolen what the LORD has claimed. He has ignored the LORD's requirements and done a godless thing in Israel.'"

¹⁶Joshua got up early in the morning. He had Israel come forward by tribes. The tribe of Judah was selected. ¹⁷Then he had the families of Judah come forward, and the family of Zerah was selected. Then he had the family of Zerah come forward man by man, and Zabdi was selected. ¹⁸Then he had Zabdi's household come forward man by man, and Achan was selected. Achan from the tribe of Judah was the son of Carmi, grandson of Zabdi, and great-grandson of Zerah.

¹⁹Joshua said to Achan, "Son, give honor and praise to the LORD God of Israel! Tell me what you have done. Don't hide anything from me."

ᵃ7:11 Or "covenant."

²⁰Then Achan answered Joshua, "It's true. I have sinned against the Lord God of Israel. This is what I did: ²¹I saw a fine robe from Babylonia, five pounds of silver, and a bar of gold weighing about one pound among the loot. I wanted them, so I took them. You will find them buried inside my tent with the silver beneath them."

²²Joshua sent messengers, and they ran to the tent. The loot was buried inside with the silver beneath it. ²³They took the loot from the tent and brought it to Joshua and all the people of Israel. Then they laid it out in the presence of the Lord.

²⁴Joshua and all Israel took Achan (son of Zerah), the silver, the robe, the bar of gold, his sons and daughters, his cattle, his donkeys, his sheep, and his tent—everything he had—and brought them to the valley of Achor [Disaster].

²⁵Then Joshua said, "Why did you bring this disaster on us? The Lord will bring disaster on you today!" And all Israel stoned Achan and his family to death. Then they burned the bodies and piled stones over them. ²⁶They made such a large pile of stones over Achan that it is still there today. Then the Lord withdrew his burning anger. For this reason that place is still called the valley of Achor today.

Israel's Victory at Ai

¹The Lord said to Joshua, "Don't be terrified or afraid. Take all the troops with you, and march against Ai. I am about to hand the king of Ai, his people, city, and land over to you. ²You will do the same thing to Ai and its king that you did to Jericho and its king. However, you may take its loot and livestock for yourselves. Set an ambush behind the city."

³So Joshua and all the soldiers started to march against Ai. Joshua picked 30,000 of his best soldiers and sent them out at night ⁴with these orders: "Set an ambush behind the city. Don't go very far away from the city. Everyone must be ready. ⁵I'll approach the city with the rest of the troops. When they come out to attack us as they did the first time, we will run away from them. ⁶They'll come out after us, and we will lure them away from the city. They'll say, 'They're running away from us just like the first time.' As we run away from them, ⁷you come out of hiding and capture the city. The Lord your God will hand it over to you. ⁸When you have captured the city, set it on fire. Do what the Lord says. These are your orders."

⁹So Joshua sent them out, and they hid. They took their position west of Ai, between Bethel and Ai. Joshua spent the night with the troops.

¹⁰Joshua got up early in the morning and assembled the troops. Then he and the leaders of Israel led the army to Ai. ¹¹All the troops with him marched until they were near the city. They camped north of Ai with the ravine between them and Ai.

¹²Joshua had taken about five thousand men and had them hide between Bethel and Ai, west of the city. ¹³All the troops were positioned. The main camp was north of the city, and the other troops were hiding west of the city. That night Joshua went down into the middle of the valley.

¹⁴When the king of Ai saw the main camp, he and all his troops got up early in the morning. They rushed out toward the plains to meet Israel for battle, just where Joshua expected. However, the king didn't know there were troops behind the city waiting to attack him.

¹⁵Joshua and all Israel pretended to be defeated. They ran away toward the desert. ¹⁶All the troops in the city were called out to chase them. As they chased Joshua, they were lured away from the city. ¹⁷Not one man was left in Ai or Bethel; they all went after Israel. So the city was left unprotected as they chased Israel.

¹⁸Then the Lord said to Joshua, "Hold out the spear in your hand toward the city, because I am handing Ai over to you." So Joshua held out his spear. ¹⁹The men who

were hiding got up as soon as he stretched out his hand. They entered the city, captured it, and quickly set it on fire. [20]When the men of Ai looked back, they could see the city going up in smoke. They had no place to go, since the Israelites, who had been running toward the desert, had now turned back on them. [21]When Joshua and all Israel saw that the men who had been hiding had captured the city and that it was going up in smoke, they turned and attacked the men of Ai. [22]The men who had captured the city also came out and attacked them. The men of Ai were caught between the battle lines of Israel. So Israel attacked them on both sides. None of them survived or escaped. [23]But they captured the king of Ai alive and brought him to Joshua.

[24]Israel had finished killing all the inhabitants of Ai in the fields and in the desert where they had been pursued. They put them all to death; not one person survived. Then the Israelites went back to Ai and killed everyone left there. [25]Twelve thousand men and women from Ai died that day. [26]Joshua did not lower his hand holding the spear until he had completely destroyed all the inhabitants of Ai. [27]Israel took the loot and the livestock of that city for themselves, as the LORD had commanded Joshua. [28]So Joshua burned Ai and made it a deserted mound of ruins.[a] It is still in ruins today.

[29]Joshua hung the king of Ai's dead body on a pole and left him there until evening. When the sun went down, Joshua gave the order to take his body down. They threw it in the entrance of the city and made a large pile of stones over it. That pile is still there today.

The LORD Renews His Promise With Israel

[30]At that time Joshua built an altar on Mount Ebal to the LORD God of Israel. [31]He built an altar with uncut stones on which no iron chisels had been used. This was as the LORD's servant Moses had commanded the people of Israel in the Book of Moses' Teachings. They made burnt offerings to the LORD and sacrificed fellowship offerings on the altar. [32]There in front of the people of Israel he wrote on stone slabs a copy of the Teachings which Moses had written down.

[33]All the people of Israel, whether foreigners or native Israelites, the leaders, officers, and judges were standing on opposite sides of the ark. They faced the Levitical priests who carried the ark of the LORD's promise. Half of the people were in front of Mount Gerizim and the other half in front of Mount Ebal. Right from the beginning, the LORD's servant Moses had commanded the priests to bless the people of Israel this way. [34]Afterwards, Joshua read all the Teachings—the blessings and curses—as they had all been written down by Moses. [35]Joshua read Moses' Teachings in front of the whole assembly of Israel, including women, children, and foreigners living among them. He did not leave out one word from everything Moses had commanded.

The People From Gibeon Deceive Joshua

9 [1]When all the kings west of the Jordan River heard about these events, [2]they joined together to fight Joshua and Israel. (They were the kings in the mountains, the foothills, and along the whole Mediterranean coast as far as Lebanon, the kings of the Hittites, Amorites, Canaanites, Perizzites, Hivites, and Jebusites.)[a]

[3]When the people living in Gibeon heard what Joshua had done to Jericho and Ai, [4]they devised a scheme. They posed as messengers. They took worn-out sacks on their donkeys. Their wineskins were old, split, and patched. [5]Their sandals were worn-out and repaired, and their clothes were tattered. All their bread was dried out and

---

[a]8:28 Ai means "ruins." [a]9:2 Part of verse 1 (in Hebrew) has been placed in verse 2 to express the complex Hebrew paragraph structure more clearly in English.

crumbling. ⁶They came to Joshua in the camp at Gilgal. They told Joshua and the men of Israel, "We have come from a distant country. Make a treaty with us right now."

⁷The men of Israel said to the Hivites, "What if you're living in this area? We wouldn't be able to make a treaty with you."

⁸They responded to Joshua, "We're at your mercy."

Joshua asked them, "Who are you, and where did you come from?"

⁹They answered him, "We came from a country very far away because the LORD your God has become famous. We heard stories about him and everything he did in Egypt. ¹⁰We also heard everything he did to the two kings of the Amorites east of the Jordan, King Sihon of Heshbon and King Og of Bashan in Ashtaroth. ¹¹Our leaders and everyone who lives in our country told us, 'Take what you need for the trip, and go meet them. Tell them, "We're at your mercy. Make a treaty with us right now."' "

¹²Our bread was warm when we left home to meet with you. Look at it now! It's dry and crumbling. ¹³These were new wine-skins when we filled them. Look at them now! See how they are splitting! Our clothes and sandals are also worn-out because we have come such a long way."

¹⁴The men believed the evidence they were shown, but they did not ask the LORD about it. ¹⁵So Joshua made peace with them by making a treaty which allowed them to live. The leaders of the congregation swore to it with an oath.

¹⁶But three days after the treaty was made, the Israelites heard that these people were their neighbors and lived with them. ¹⁷The Israelites broke camp. They came to the cities of Gibeon, Chephirah, Beeroth, and Kiriath Jearim two days later. ¹⁸The Israelites didn't destroy these other people, because the leaders of the congregation had sworn an oath about them to the LORD God of Israel. The whole congregation complained about the leaders. ¹⁹But all the leaders said to them, "We have sworn an oath about them to the LORD God of Israel, so we cannot touch them now. ²⁰We must let them live to avoid the LORD's anger because of the oath we swore." ²¹The leaders said that they should be allowed to live. So they became woodcutters and water carriers for the whole congregation, as the leaders had said.

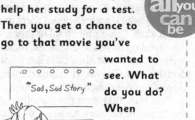

Promises

Joshua 9:3-21

You've told a friend you'll help her study for a test. Then you get a chance to go to that movie you've

wanted to see. What do you do? When Joshua learned he had been tricked into making a promise, he still kept his word. Be the kind of person who keeps promises— even when it's hard.

²²Joshua sent for the people of Gibeon and asked, "Why did you deceive us by saying, 'We live very far away from you,' when you live here with us? ²³You are under a curse now. You will always be servants. You will be woodcutters and water carriers for the house of my God."

²⁴They answered Joshua, "We were told that the LORD your God commanded his servant Moses to give you the whole land and destroy all who live there. We deceived

you because we feared for our lives. ²⁵Now we're at your mercy. Do to us what you think is good and right."

²⁶So Joshua rescued them and did not let the people of Israel kill them. ²⁷But that day Joshua made them woodcutters and water carriers for the congregation. They served the LORD's altar, wherever he chose to put it. They still serve today.

The Day the Sun Stood Still

10 ¹King Adoni Zedek of Jerusalem heard that Joshua had captured Ai and claimed it for the LORD the same way he had destroyed Jericho and its king. He also heard that the people of Gibeon had made peace with the people of Israel and were living with them. ²He and his people were terribly afraid because Gibeon was a large city. It was like one of the royal cities, larger than Ai. All its men were warriors. ³So King Adoni Zedek of Jerusalem sent this message to King Hoham of Hebron, King Piram of Jarmuth, King Japhia of Lachish, and King Debir of Eglon: ⁴"Come, help me destroy Gibeon because it has made peace with Joshua and the people of Israel." ⁵So the five Amorite kings of Jerusalem, Hebron, Jarmuth, Lachish, and Eglon combined their armies. They marched to Gibeon, camped there, and attacked it.

⁶The men of Gibeon sent this message to Joshua at the camp in Gilgal: "Don't abandon us! Come quickly, and save us. Help us because all the Amorite kings who live in the mountains have united against us."

⁷So Joshua, with all his soldiers and best warriors, set out from Gilgal. ⁸The LORD told Joshua, "Don't be afraid of them. I have handed them over to you. None of them can stand up to you." ⁹So Joshua marched all night from Gilgal and took them by surprise. ¹⁰The LORD threw the enemy into disorder in front of Israel and defeated them decisively at Gibeon. He chased them along the road that goes to the slope of Beth Horon and continued to defeat them all the way to Azekah and Makkedah.

¹¹As they fled from the Israelites down the slope of Beth Horon toward Azekah, the LORD threw huge hailstones on them. More died from the hailstones than from Israelite swords.

¹²The day the LORD handed the Amorites over to the people of Israel, Joshua spoke to the LORD while Israel was watching,

> "Sun, stand still over Gibeon,
>   and moon, stand still over the valley of Aijalon!"
> ¹³ The sun stood still,
>   and the moon stopped
>   until a nation got revenge on its enemies.

Isn't this recorded in the Book of Jashar? The sun stopped in the middle of the sky, and for nearly a day the sun was in no hurry to set. ¹⁴Never before or after this day was there anything like it. The LORD did what a man told him to do, because the LORD fought for Israel.

¹⁵Then Joshua and all Israel returned to the camp at Gilgal.

¹⁶The five kings ran away and hid in the cave at Makkedah. ¹⁷Someone told Joshua, "The five kings have been found. They are hiding in the cave at Makkedah."

¹⁸Joshua replied, "Roll large stones against the mouth of the cave, and post a guard there. ¹⁹But don't stop. Chase your enemies! Cut off their rear guard. Don't let them get back into their own cities, because the LORD your God has handed them over to you."

²⁰Joshua and the Israelites defeated them decisively, almost destroying them. But some who survived got back into the fortified cities. ²¹Then the whole army returned

safely to Joshua in the camp at Makkedah. Not a single person dared to speak against any of the Israelites.

²²Joshua said, "Open the cave, and bring me the five kings!" ²³So they brought him the kings of Jerusalem, Hebron, Jarmuth, Lachish, and Eglon.

²⁴When they brought them to Joshua, he called for all the men of Israel. He told the officers who had gone with him, "Come forward and put your feet on the necks of these kings." So that's what they did. ²⁵Joshua told them, "Don't be afraid or terrified! Be strong and courageous, because this is what the Lord will do to all the enemies you're fighting against."

²⁶After this, Joshua put them to death and hung their bodies on five poles until evening. ²⁷When the sun went down, Joshua gave the order to take them down from the poles. Then they threw them into the cave where they had been hiding and put large stones over the mouth of the cave. These stones are still there today.

Joshua Defeats the Southern Kings

²⁸That same day Joshua captured Makkedah, and the Israelites killed its people and king with swords. He claimed them for the Lord by destroying them. There were no survivors. He did the same thing to the king of Makkedah that he had done to the king of Jericho.

²⁹Joshua and all Israel marched from Makkedah to Libnah and attacked it. ³⁰The Lord also handed Libnah and its king over to Israel. He killed all the people. There were no survivors. He did the same thing to the king of Libnah that he had done to the king of Jericho.

³¹Joshua and all Israel marched from Libnah to Lachish, camped there, and attacked it. ³²The Lord handed Lachish over to Israel. He captured it on the next day and killed all the people, the same way he had captured Libnah. ³³At that time King Horam of Gezer had come to help Lachish. But Joshua killed him and his troops. There were no survivors.

³⁴Joshua and all Israel marched from Lachish to Eglon, camped there, and attacked it. ³⁵They captured it that day and killed everyone in it. He claimed it for the Lord by destroying it the same way he had destroyed Lachish.

³⁶Then Joshua and all Israel marched from Eglon to Hebron and attacked it. ³⁷They captured it and its neighboring villages and killed its king and all the people. There were no survivors, the same as at Eglon. He claimed the city and all its people for the Lord by destroying them.

³⁸Then Joshua and all Israel went back to Debir and attacked it. ³⁹He captured it and its king and all its neighboring villages and killed everyone. So they claimed them all for the Lord by destroying them. There were no survivors. He did the same thing to Debir and its king that he had done to Hebron and Libnah and their kings.

⁴⁰So Joshua captured the whole land—the mountains, the Negev, the foothills, and the slopes. There were no survivors. He claimed every living creature for the Lord by destroying it, as the Lord God of Israel had commanded. ⁴¹So Joshua defeated the people from Kadesh Barnea to Gaza and from all the country of Goshen as far as Gibeon. ⁴²Joshua captured all these kings and their territories in one campaign because the Lord God of Israel fought for Israel. ⁴³Then Joshua and all Israel returned to the camp at Gilgal.

Joshua Defeats the Northern Kings

11 ¹King Jabin of Hazor heard what had happened. So he sent messengers to King Jobab of Madon and to the kings of Shimron and Achshaph. ²He also sent messengers to the northern kings in the mountains, the plains south of Chinneroth, the foothills, and Naphoth Dor in the west, ³the Canaanites from east and west, the Amorites, Hittites, Perizzites, the Jebusites in the mountains, and the Hivites at the foot of Mount Hermon in Mizpah. ⁴They came out with all their armies. Their troops were as numerous as the grains of sand on the seashore. They also had horses and chariots. ⁵All these kings camped together by the Springs of Merom in order to fight Israel.

⁶The Lord told Joshua, "Don't be afraid of them because I am going to give them to Israel. About this time tomorrow they will all be dead. You must disable their horses so that they cannot be used in battle. You must burn their chariots." ⁷Joshua and all his troops arrived suddenly at the Springs of Merom and attacked the Canaanite armies. ⁸The Lord handed them over to Israel, and the Israelites defeated them. The Israelites chased them as far as Great Sidon, Misrephoth Maim, and the valley of Mizpah in the east. There were no survivors. ⁹Joshua disabled their horses and burned their chariots, as the Lord had told him.

¹⁰Then Joshua turned back and captured Hazor. He killed its king with a sword. (Hazor was formerly the head of all these kingdoms.) ¹¹They claimed everyone for the Lord by destroying them with swords. Not one person survived. Joshua also burned Hazor.

¹²So Joshua captured all these cities and their kings. He claimed them for the Lord by destroying them, as the Lord's servant Moses had commanded him. ¹³Israel did not burn cities built on mounds. However, Joshua made an exception and burned Hazor. ¹⁴The people of Israel took all the loot and livestock from these cities. But they put everyone to death until they were all destroyed. Not one person survived. ¹⁵So Joshua carried out what the Lord had commanded his servant Moses and what Moses had commanded him. He did not leave out anything the Lord had commanded Moses.

¹⁶Joshua took all this land, the mountains, all the Negev, all the land of Goshen, the foothills, the plains, and the mountains and foothills of Israel. ¹⁷The land extended from Mount Halak which ascends to Seir as far as Baal Gad in the Lebanon Valley at the foot of Mount Hermon. He captured all their kings and killed them. ¹⁸Joshua waged war with all these kings for a long time. ¹⁹Not one city had made a peace treaty with the people of Israel except Gibeon, where the Hivites lived. Israel captured everything in battle. ²⁰The Lord made their enemies stubborn enough to continue fighting against Israel so that he could claim them all for destruction without mercy, as he had commanded Moses.

²¹At that time Joshua also wiped out the people of Anak in the mountains, in Hebron, Debir, and Anab, and in all the hills of Judah and Israel. Joshua claimed them for the Lord by destroying them and their cities. ²²None of the people of Anak remained in Israel. Some of them were left in Gaza, Gath, and Ashdod. ²³Joshua captured the whole land as the Lord had promised Moses. He gave it to Israel as a possession, dividing it among the tribes. So the land had peace.

Kings East of the Jordan River Defeated by Moses

12 ¹These are the kings of the land east of the Jordan River that the people of Israel defeated. Israel also took possession of their lands from the Arnon Valley to Mount Hermon, and all the eastern plains.

²Sihon was the Amorite king who lived in Heshbon. His rule extended from Aroer on the edge of the Arnon Valley to the Jabbok River, which is the border of Ammon. This included the middle of the valley and half of Gilead. ³It included the eastern plains from the Sea of Galilee to the Sea of the Plains (the Dead Sea) and the road that goes south from Beth Jeshimoth to the foot of the slopes of Pisgah.

⁴The territory of King Og of Bashan who lived in Ashtaroth and Edrei was captured. He was the last of the Rephaim. ⁵He ruled Mount Hermon, Salecah, all of Bashan to the border of Geshur and Maacath, and half of Gilead to the border of King Sihon of Heshbon.

⁶The Lord's servant Moses and the people of Israel defeated them. Then he gave their land as a possession to the tribes of Reuben and Gad and half of the tribe of Manasseh.

Kings West of the Jordan River Defeated by Joshua

⁷These are the kings of the land west of the Jordan River that Joshua and the people of Israel defeated. Their lands extended from Baal Gad in the valley of Lebanon to Mount Halak which rises toward Seir. Joshua gave it as a possession to Israel, dividing it among the tribes. ⁸It included the mountains, foothills, plains, slopes, desert, and the Negev that the Hittites, Amorites, Canaanites, Perizzites, Hivites, and Jebusites had possessed.

The kings were
⁹the king of Jericho, the king of Ai (near Bethel),
¹⁰the king of Jerusalem, the king of Hebron,
¹¹the king of Jarmuth, the king of Lachish,
¹²the king of Eglon, the king of Gezer,
¹³the king of Debir, the king of Geder,
¹⁴the king of Hormah, the king of Arad,
¹⁵the king of Libnah, the king of Adullam,
¹⁶the king of Makkedah, the king of Bethel,
¹⁷the king of Tappuah, the king of Hepher,
¹⁸the king of Aphek, the king of Sharon,ᵃ
¹⁹the king of Madon, the king of Hazor,
²⁰the king of Shimron Meron, the king of Achshaph,
²¹the king of Taanach, the king of Megiddo,
²²the king of Kedesh, the king of Jokneam in Carmel,
²³the king of Dor in Naphoth Dor, the king of Goiim in Gilgal,ᵇ
²⁴the king of Tirzah.
The total was 31 kings.

Land Yet to Be Conquered

¹Joshua was old, near the end of his life. So the Lord said to him, "You are old, near the end of your life, and there is a lot of land left to be conquered. ²The land that is left includes all the districts that belong to the Philistines and Geshur. ³It extends from the Shihor River, east of Egypt, northward as far as the border of Ekron. This is considered to be Canaanite territory, even though there are five Philistine rulers over Gaza, Ashdod, Ashkelon, Gath, and Ekron, as well as the Avvim people ⁴in the south. This territory includes all the land of the Canaanites as well as Mearah which belongs to Sidon as far as Aphek, the Amorite border. ⁵It also includes the land of the people of Gebal, all Lebanon eastward from Baal Gad at the foot of Mount Hermon to the border of Hamath. ⁶I will force out of the way of the people of Israel everyone who lives in the mountains from Lebanon to Misrephoth Maim and all the people of Sidon. However, you must distribute the land as an inheritance to Israel by drawing lots, as I commanded you. ⁷So divide this land. It will be an inheritance for the nine tribes and half of the tribe of Manasseh."

ᵃ 12:18 Or "Lasharon."   ᵇ 12:23 Or "Galilee."

Tribes That Received Land East of the Jordan River

⁸The tribes of Reuben and Gad with half of the tribe of Manasseh had received their inheritance east of the Jordan River, since the Lord's servant Moses had already given it to them. ⁹The border extended from Aroer on the edge of the Arnon Valley, including the city in the middle of the valley, and the whole plateau from Medeba to Dibon. ¹⁰It included all the cities of King Sihon of the Amorites up to the border of Ammon. Sihon's capital was Heshbon. ¹¹It also included Gilead, the territory of the people of Geshur and Maacath, all of Mount Hermon, and all of Bashan as far as Salecah ¹²(the whole kingdom of Og in Bashan). Og ruled in Ashtaroth and Edrei. He was the last of the Rephaim. Moses had defeated them and forced them out. ¹³But the Israelites did not force out the people of Geshur and Maacath. So they still live in Israel today.

¹⁴Moses did not give any land as an inheritance to the tribe of Levi. The sacrifices offered to the Lord God of Israel are what the Levites inherited, as the Lord had promised them.

¹⁵Moses gave some land as an inheritance to the tribe of Reuben for their families. ¹⁶Their territory extended from Aroer on the edge of the Arnon Valley, including the city in the middle of the valley and the whole plateau near Medeba. ¹⁷It included Heshbon and all its cities on the plateau, Dibon, Bamoth Baal, Beth Baal Meon, ¹⁸Jahaz, Kedemoth, Mephaath, ¹⁹Kiriathaim, Sibmah, Zereth Shahar on the mountain in the valley, ²⁰Beth Peor, the slopes of Pisgah, and Beth Jeshimoth. ²¹It also included all the cities of the plateau, the whole kingdom of King Sihon of the Amorites, who ruled in Heshbon. Moses defeated him and Midian's leaders—Evi, Rekem, Zur, Hur, and Reba. They were princes of Sihon, who lived in that country. ²²Along with these leaders, the people of Israel also killed Balaam, son of Beor, who used black magic. ²³The border of Reuben's territory was the Jordan River. This was Reuben's inheritance for its families. It included cities with their villages.

²⁴Moses gave some land as an inheritance to the tribe of Gad for its families. ²⁵Their territory included Jazer, all the cities of Gilead, and half of Ammon as far as Aroer, which is by Rabbah. ²⁶It extended from Heshbon to Ramath Mizpeh and Betonim, and from Mahanaim as far as the border of Lidbir. ²⁷In the Jordan Valley it included Beth Haram, Beth Nimrah, Succoth, and Zaphon, the rest of the kingdom of King Sihon of Heshbon. The Jordan River served as its western border, extending to the end of the Sea of Galilee. ²⁸This was Gad's inheritance for its families. It included cities with their villages.

²⁹Moses gave some land as an inheritance to half of the tribe of Manasseh. It was only for the families of that half of the tribe. ³⁰Their territory extended from Mahanaim and included all of Bashan (the whole kingdom of King Og of Bashan) and all 60 settlements of Jair that were in Bashan. ³¹It also included half of Gilead with Ashtaroth and Edrei, the royal cities of Og in Bashan. They were given to half the families of Machir, son of Manasseh, for their inheritance.

³²This is the land that Moses distributed on Moab's plains, east of the Jordan River near Jericho. ³³Moses did not give any land as an inheritance to the tribe of Levi. The Lord God of Israel is what they inherited, as he had promised them.

The First Stage in Dividing the Land

14 ¹This is the land that the people of Israel inherited in Canaan. The priest Eleazar, Joshua (son of Nun), and the heads of Israel's tribes distributed it to the people. ²The land inherited by the nine-and-a-half tribes was determined by drawing lots as the Lord had commanded through Moses. ³Moses had given the two-and-a-half tribes their inheritance east of the Jordan River. He did not give any land as an inheritance to Levi's tribe, ⁴because Joseph's descendants, Manasseh and Ephraim, formed two tribes. The Levites were not given a share of the land. Joseph's descendants gave the Levites cities to live in with pasturelands for their cattle and everything they had. ⁵So the people of Israel divided the land as the Lord had commanded Moses.

Special Land for Caleb

⁶Then the people of Judah came to Joshua at Gilgal. Caleb, son of Jephunneh and grandson of Kenaz, said to him, "You know what the Lord said to Moses, the man of God, at Kadesh Barnea about you and me. ⁷I was 40 years old when the Lord's servant Moses sent me from Kadesh Barnea to explore the land. I reported to him exactly what I thought. ⁸But my companions discouraged the people. However, I was completely loyal to the Lord my God. ⁹On that day Moses swore this oath: 'The land your feet walked on will be a permanent inheritance for you and your descendants because you were completely loyal to the Lord my God.'

¹⁰"So look at me. The Lord has kept me alive as he promised. It's been 45 years since Israel wandered in the desert when the Lord made this promise to Moses. So now look at me today. I'm 85 years old. ¹¹I'm still as fit to go to war now as I was when Moses sent me out. ¹²Now give me this mountain region which the Lord spoke of that day. You heard that the people of Anak are still there and that they have large, fortified cities. If the Lord is with me, I can force them out, as he promised."

¹³So Joshua blessed Caleb, son of Jephunneh, and gave him Hebron as his inheritance. ¹⁴Hebron is still the inheritance of Caleb, son of Jephunneh and grandson of Kenaz, because Caleb was completely loyal to the Lord God of Israel. ¹⁵In the past Hebron was called Kiriath Arba. Arba was the greatest man among the people of Anak. So the land had peace.

Judah's Land

15 ¹The lot was drawn for the families of the tribe of Judah. Their territory extends as far south as the territory of Edom and the desert of Zin. ²The southern border starts from the south end of the Dead Sea ³and goes south of the Akrabbim Pass. It then passes Zin and goes up south of Kadesh Barnea. From there it goes to Hezron, up to Addar, around to Karka, ⁴and on to Azmon. It comes out at the River of Egypt so that the border ends at the Mediterranean Sea. This is the southern border.

Good Morning, God

Joshua 14:6-9

When the spies returned from scouting out the promised land, most of them were too afraid to attack the giants living there. But not Caleb! He encouraged the Israelites to be courageous and fight. When those around you seem ready to give in and do wrong, you can inspire them to have faith. Courage is contagious!

Lord, give me strength like Caleb's to do what is right and not give in to the crowd.

⁵The eastern border is the Dead Sea as far north as the mouth of the Jordan River. The northern border starts from the north end of the Dead Sea at the mouth of the Jordan ⁶and goes up to Beth Hoglah. It then passes north to Beth Arabah and goes up to the Rock of Bohan, son of Reuben. ⁷From the valley of Achor, the border goes up to Debir and turns north to the region that faces the Adummim Pass, south of the valley. Then the border passes the Springs of En Shemesh and ends at En Rogel. ⁸It continues up the valley of Ben Hinnom to the south slope of the Jebusite city Jerusalem. It then goes to the top of the mountain that overlooks the valley of Hinnom to the west at the north end of the valley of Rephaim. ⁹From the top of that mountain the border goes around to the spring of Nephtoah. From there it goes to the cities of Mount Ephron and around to Baalah (now called Kiriath Jearim). ¹⁰From Baalah the border turns west to Mount Seir and over to the north slope of Mount Jearim (now called Chesalon). Then it goes down to Beth Shemesh and on to Timnah. ¹¹From there the border goes on the north side of Ekron and turns to Shikkeron, on to Mount Baalah, and comes out at Jabneel. The border ends at the Mediterranean Sea. ¹²The western border is the coastline of the Mediterranean Sea. These are the borders around Judah that belong to their families.

¹³Joshua gave Caleb, son of Jephunneh, a share of land among the people of Judah as the LORD had told them. It was Kiriath Arba (now called Hebron). Arba was the father of Anak. ¹⁴Caleb forced out Sheshai, Ahiman, and Talmai, three descendants of Anak from Hebron. ¹⁵From there he marched against the people living in Debir. (In the past Debir was called Kiriath Sepher.)

¹⁶Caleb said, "I will give my daughter Achsah as a wife to anyone who attacks Kiriath Sepher and captures it." ¹⁷Then Othniel, son of Caleb's brother Kenaz, captured it. So Caleb gave him his daughter Achsah as a wife. ¹⁸When she came to Othniel, she persuaded him to ask her father for a field. When she got down from her donkey, Caleb asked her, "What do you want?"

¹⁹She answered, "Give me a blessing. Since you've given me some dry land, also give me some springs." So Caleb gave her the upper and lower springs.

²⁰This is the land inherited by the families of the tribe of Judah.

²¹On the farthest edge of the Negev, on the border of Edom, they gave the tribe of Judah 29 cities with their villages: Kabzeel, Eder, Jagur, ²²Kinah, Dimonah, Adadah, ²³Kedesh, Hazor, Ithnan, ²⁴Ziph, Telem, Bealoth, ²⁵Hazor Hadattah, Kerioth Hezron (now called Hazor), ²⁶Amam, Shema, Moladah, ²⁷Hazar Gaddah, Heshmon, Beth Pelet, ²⁸Hazar Shual, Beersheba, Biziothiah, ²⁹Baalah, Iim, Ezem, ³⁰Eltolad, Chesil, Hormah, ³¹Ziklag, Madmannah, Sansannah, ³²Lebaoth, Shilhim, Ain, and Rimmon.

³³In the foothills they gave Judah 14 cities with their villages: Eshtaol, Zorah, Ashnah, ³⁴Zanoah, En Gannim, Tappuah, Enam, ³⁵Jarmuth, Adullam, Socoh, Azekah, ³⁶Shaaraim, Adithaim, Gederah, and Gederothaim.

³⁷They also gave Judah 16 other cities with their villages: Zenan, Hadashah, Migdalgad, ³⁸Dilean, Mizpah, Joktheel, ³⁹Lachish, Bozkath, Eglon, ⁴⁰Cabbon, Lahmas, Chitlish, ⁴¹Gederoth, Beth Dagon, Naamah, and Makkedah.

⁴²An additional nine cities with their villages were given to Judah: Libnah, Ether, Ashan, ⁴³Iphtah, Ashnah, Nezib, ⁴⁴Keilah, Achzib, and Mareshah.

⁴⁵Judah also received Ekron with its cities and villages. ⁴⁶This included all the cities with their villages between Ekron and the Mediterranean Sea and alongside Ashdod. ⁴⁷Added to this were Ashdod and Gaza with their cities and villages as far as the River of Egypt and the coast of the Mediterranean Sea.

⁴⁸In the mountains they gave Judah 11 cities with their villages: Shamir, Jattir,

Socoh, [49]Dannah, Kiriath Sannah (now called Debir), [50]Anab, Eshtemoh, Anim, [51]Goshen, Holon, and Giloh.

[52]They also gave Judah nine other cities with their villages: Arab, Dumah, Eshan, [53]Janim, Beth Tappuah, Aphekah, [54]Humtah, Kiriath Arba (now called Hebron), and Zior.

[55]They also received another ten cities with their villages: Maon, Carmel, Ziph, Juttah, [56]Jezreel, Jokdeam, Zanoah, [57]Kain, Gibeah, and Timnah.

[58]Halhul, Bethzur, Gedor, [59]Maarath, Bethanoth, and Eltekon were six other cities with their villages that were given to Judah.[a]

[60]The two cities of Kiriath Baal (now called Kiriath Jearim) and Rabbah with their villages were given to Judah.

[61]In the desert Judah was given six cities with their villages: Beth Arabah, Middin, Secacah, [62]Nibshan, Ir Hamelah, and En Gedi.

[63]However, Judah was not able to force out the people of Jebus who lived in Jerusalem. So they still live with Judah in Jerusalem today.

Land for Joseph's Sons

[1]The lot was drawn for Joseph. The border of Joseph's territory goes from the Jordan River at Jericho to the springs of Jericho on the east, through the desert that goes up from Jericho, and through the mountains to Bethel. [2]From Bethel the border goes to Luz and over to Ataroth at the border of the Archites. [3]Then it descends west to the border of Japhlet and Lower Beth Horon, on to Gezer, and ends at the Mediterranean Sea. [4]So Joseph's sons, Manasseh and Ephraim, received this land as their inheritance.

Ephraim's Land

[5]This is the territory for the families descended from Ephraim. The eastern border of the land they inherited is from Ataroth Addar to Upper Beth Horon. [6]From there the border goes west, with Michmethath on the north. The border then turns east to Taanath Shiloh and passes east to Janoah. [7]From Janoah it descends to Ataroth and Naarah, touches Jericho, and ends at the Jordan River. [8]At Tappuah the border goes west along the Kanah River and ends at the Mediterranean Sea. This is the land given as an inheritance to the families of the tribe of Ephraim [9]with all the cities and their villages selected for Ephraim in Manasseh's territory. [10]However, they did not force out the Canaanites who lived in Gezer. So the Canaanites still live in Ephraim today, but they are required to do forced labor.

Manasseh's Land

[1]The lot was drawn for the tribe of Manasseh, because Manasseh was Joseph's firstborn. Machir, Manasseh's firstborn, the ancestor of the people living in Gilead, had received Gilead and Bashan because he was a soldier. [2]The land was given to the rest of the families descended from Manasseh, to the descendants of Abiezer, Helek, Asriel, Shechem, Hepher, and Shemida. These were the male descendants of Joseph's son Manasseh listed by their families.

[3]Zelophehad, son of Hepher, grandson of Gilead, and great-grandson of Machir, whose father was Manasseh, had no sons—only daughters. Their names were Mahlah, Noah, Hoglah, Milcah, and Tirzah. [4]They came to the priest Eleazar, Joshua (son of Nun), and the leaders. They said, "The Lord commanded Moses to give us some land

---

[a] 15:59 Greek adds, "They also gave them 11 cities with their villages: Tekoa, Ephrathah (now called Bethlehem), Peor, Etam, Dulon, Tatam, Sores, Carem, Gallim, Bether, and Manach."

as an inheritance among our male relatives." So they gave them an inheritance among their father's relatives as the LORD had required. ⁵Ten portions of land went to Manasseh, besides the land of Gilead and Bashan east of the Jordan River. ⁶These portions were distributed because Manasseh's daughters were given an inheritance along with his sons, while Gilead belonged to Manasseh's other descendants.

⁷Manasseh's border extends from Asher to Michmethath, which faces Shechem. Then the border goes south toward the people who live in En Tappuah. ⁸(The land of Tappuah belongs to Manasseh, but Tappuah itself, on the border of Manasseh, belongs to Ephraim.) ⁹The border then descends southward to the Kanah River. These cities belong to Ephraim, although they are among Manasseh's cities. Manasseh's southern border is the river, which ends at the Mediterranean Sea. ¹⁰What is south of the river belongs to Ephraim, and what is north of it belongs to Manasseh. So the Mediterranean Sea is its western border, Asher its northern border, and Issachar its eastern border. ¹¹In Issachar and Asher, Manasseh possessed Beth Shean and Ibleam with their villages and the people living in Dor, En Dor, Taanach, and Megiddo and their villages. The last three are on mountain ridges.ᵃ

¹²But Manasseh was not able to take possession of these cities since the Canaanites were determined to stay in this land. ¹³When the Israelites became strong enough, they made the Canaanites do forced labor, since they didn't force all of them out.

¹⁴Joseph's descendants asked Joshua, "Why did you give us only one region for an inheritance? We have a lot of people because the LORD has blessed us."

¹⁵Joshua replied, "If there are so many of you, go into the forest! Clear ground for yourselves there in the land of the Perizzites and Rephaim if the mountains of Ephraim are too confining for you."

¹⁶Joseph's descendants responded, "The mountains are not enough for us either. Besides, all the Canaanites living in the valley, in Beth Shean and its villages, and in the valley of Jezreel have chariots made of iron."

¹⁷Then Joshua said to the descendants of Joseph, the tribes of Ephraim and Manasseh, "You are an important and very powerful people. One region is really not enough for you. ¹⁸The mountain region will be yours as well. It is a forest, so you will have to clear it. All of it will be yours. But you must force out the Canaanites, even though they are strong and have chariots made of iron."

The Second Stage in Dividing the Land

18 ¹The whole congregation of Israel gathered at Shiloh and set up the tent of meeting there. The land was under their control.

²There were still seven tribes in Israel who had not yet received any land as their inheritance. ³So Joshua asked the Israelites, "How long are you going to waste time conquering the land which the LORD God of your ancestors has given you? ⁴Choose three men from each tribe, and I will send them out. They will survey the land and write a description of it which shows the borders of their inheritance. Then they will come back to me. ⁵They will divide the land into seven parts. Judah will stay within its territory in the south, and Joseph's descendants will stay within their territory in the north. ⁶You must describe the seven parts of the land and report to me here. I will draw lots for you here in the presence of the LORD our God. ⁷Levi's tribe has no separate region among you, because their inheritance is to serve the LORD as priests. The tribes of Gad and Reuben and half of the tribe of Manasseh have received the inheritance that the LORD's servant Moses gave them on the east side of the Jordan River."

ᵃ17:11 Hebrew meaning uncertain.

⁸As the men got ready to go, Joshua ordered them to write a description of the land. He said, "Go survey the land. Write a description of it, and return to me. Then I will draw lots for you in the presence of the Lord here in Shiloh."
⁹The men surveyed the land. They described it in a book. The land was divided into seven parts according to its cities. Then they returned to Joshua at the camp at Shiloh. ¹⁰So Joshua drew lots for them in the presence of the Lord in Shiloh. There Joshua divided the land among the tribes of Israel.

Benjamin's Land

¹¹The lot was drawn for the families of the tribe of Benjamin. Their territory lies between Judah's and Joseph's. ¹²Their northern border starts at the Jordan, goes up the slope north of Jericho, west through the mountains, and ends at the desert of Beth Aven. ¹³From there the border goes to the south slope of Luz (now called Bethel). Then the border goes down to Ataroth Addar over the mountains south of Lower Beth Horon. ¹⁴The border turns and goes around on the west side, south of the mountain that faces Beth Horon, and ends at Kiriath Baal (now called Kiriath Jearim), a city of Judah. ¹⁵The southern border begins just outside Kiriath Jearim and goes west, to the springs of Nephtoah. ¹⁶Then the border descends to the foot of the mountain that overlooks the valley of Ben Hinnom, in the north end of the valley of Rephaim. It descends to the valley of Hinnom, to the south slope of the city of Jebus, and down to En Rogel. ¹⁷Then it turns north and goes to En Shemesh and from there to the region opposite the Adummim Pass. It descends to the Rock of Bohan, son of Reuben. ¹⁸Then it continues on to the north side of the slope facing the plains and down into the plains. ¹⁹The border continues to the north slope of Beth Hoglah and ends at the northern bay of the Dead Sea at the south end of the Jordan River. This is its southern border. ²⁰The Jordan River is its eastern border. These are the borders surrounding the inheritance given to Benjamin for its families.

²¹These are the 12 cities with their villages that belong to the tribe of Benjamin for its families: Jericho, Beth Hoglah, Emek Keziz, ²²Beth Arabah, Zemaraim, Bethel, ²³Avvim, Parah, Ophrah, ²⁴Chephar Ammoni, Ophni, and Geba. ²⁵There were 14 other cities with their villages: Gibeon, Ramah, Beeroth, ²⁶Mizpeh, Chephirah, Mozah, ²⁷Rekem, Ir Peel, Taralah, ²⁸Zela, Eleph, Jebus (now called Jerusalem), Gibeath, and Kiriath. This is Benjamin's inheritance for its families.

Simeon's Land

19 ¹The second lot was drawn for the families of the tribe of Simeon. Their inheritance was within Judah. ²In their inheritance they received 13 cities and their villages: Beersheba (Sheba), Moladah, ³Hazar Shual, Balah, Ezem, ⁴Eltolad Bethul, Hormah, ⁵Ziklag, Beth Marcaboth, Hazar Susah, ⁶Beth Lebaoth, and Sharuhen. ⁷There were four other cities with their villages: Ain, Rimmon, Ether, and Ashan. ⁸All the villages around these cities as far as Baalath Beer and Ramath Negev were also included. This is the inheritance of the tribe of Simeon for its families. ⁹Simeon's inheritance was a part of Judah's because Judah had more land than it needed. So Simeon received its inheritance inside Judah's borders.

Zebulun's Land

¹⁰The third lot was drawn for the families descended from Zebulun. The border of their inheritance goes as far as Sarid. ¹¹Toward the west the border ascends to Maralah and touches Dabbesheth and the river near Jokneam. ¹²But from Sarid it turns directly east toward the border of Chisloth Tabor, on to Daberath, and then ascends toward

Japhia. [13]From there it goes directly east to Gath Hepher, Eth Kazin, and Rimmon, where it turns to Neah. [14]There the border turns north to Hannathon and ends at the valley of Iphtah El. [15]This also includes Kattath, Nahalal, Shimron, Idalah, and Bethlehem. There were 12 cities with their villages. [16]These cities with their villages are the inheritance given to the families descended from Zebulun.

Issachar's Land

[17]The fourth lot was drawn for the families descended from Issachar. [18]Their territory included Jezreel, Chesulloth, Shunem, [19]Hapharaim, Shion, Anaharath, [20]Rabbith, Kishion, Ebez, [21]Remeth, En Gannim, En Haddah, and Beth Pazzez. [22]The border touches Tabor, Shahazimah, and Beth Shemesh and ends at the Jordan River. There were 16 cities with their villages. [23]These cities with their villages are the inheritance for the families of the tribe of Issachar.

Asher's Land

[24]The fifth lot was drawn for the families of the tribe of Asher. [25]Their territory included Helkath, Hali, Beten, Achshaph, [26]Allammelech, Amad, and Mishal. The border touches Carmel and Shihor Libnath in the west. [27]Then it turns east to Beth Dagon and touches Zebulun and the valley of Iphtah El in the north and goes to Beth Emek and Neiel. From there it goes northward to Cabul, [28]Abdon,[a] Rehob, Hammon, Kanah, and as far as Great Sidon. [29]Then it turns at Ramah and goes on to the fortified city of Tyre. The border then turns to Hosah and ends at the Mediterranean Sea. The territory includes Meheleb, Achzib, [30]Umma, Acco, Aphek, and Rehob. There were 22 cities with their villages. [31]These cities with their villages are the inheritance for the families of the tribe of Asher.

Naphtali's Land

[32]The sixth lot was drawn for the families descended from the tribe of Naphtali. [33]Their border starts from Heleph at the oak tree at Zaanannim. It continues to Adami Nekeb, Jabneel, to Lakkum, and ends at the Jordan River. [34]The border turns west to Aznoth Tabor, and from there to Hukok. It touches Zebulun in the south, Asher in the west, and Judah in the east at the Jordan. [35]The fortified cities were Ziddim, Zer, Hammath, Rakkath, Chinnereth, [36]Adamah, Ramah, Hazor, [37]Kedesh, Edrei, En Hazor, [38]Yiron, Migdal El, Horem, Beth Anath, and Beth Shemeth. There were 19 cities with their villages. [39]These cities with their villages are the inheritance for the families of the tribe of Naphtali.

Dan's Land

[40]The seventh lot was drawn for the families of the tribe of Dan. [41]The territory of their inheritance included Zorah, Eshtaol, Ir Shemesh, [42]Shaalabbin, Aijalon, Ithlah, [43]Elon, Timnah, Ekron, [44]Eltekeh, Gibbethon, Baalath, [45]Jehud, Bene Berak, Gath Rimmon, [46]Me Jarkon, and Rakkon, with the border passing in front of Joppa. [47]The border of Dan extended beyond them. Dan's descendants went up and attacked Leshem, captured it, and killed everyone there. They took it, settled there, and renamed the city Dan after their ancestor Dan. [48]These cities with their villages are the inheritance for the families of the tribe of Dan.

---

[a] 19:28 Some Hebrew manuscripts, Joshua 21:30, 1 Chronicles 6:59; other Hebrew manuscripts "Ebron."

Roods / *Joshua 20*

In Old Testament times, Israel had no cement or asphalt roads. Most roads were just narrow paths leading from town to town, although major trade routes became wider with use. It took about three days to travel the 60 miles from Nazareth to Jerusalem.

But did you know that no one in Israel was more than a day's travel from one of six special "cities of refuge"? God commanded the routes to these cities to be kept open always (see Deuteronomy 19:2-3). God wanted to make sure anyone who killed a person accidentally could hurry to one of these cities to be safe from any relative who wanted to take revenge. Can you find on a Bible map some of the six cities of refuge listed in Joshua 20:7-8?

Special Land for Joshua

⁴⁹When they all had finally received the land they were to inherit, the people of Israel also gave land within their territory as an inheritance to Joshua, son of Nun. ⁵⁰They gave him the city he asked for, as the LORD had instructed them to do. It was Timnath Serah in the mountains of Ephraim. He rebuilt the city and lived there.

⁵¹This is the land that the tribes of Israel drew by lot. The priest Eleazar, Joshua son of Nun, and the leaders of the families divided the land by drawing lots. They did this in Shiloh in the presence of the LORD at the entrance of the tent of meeting. So they finished dividing the land.

Six Cities of Refuge

20 ¹The LORD said to Joshua, ²"Tell the people of Israel, 'Now choose for yourselves the cities of refuge about which I spoke to you through Moses. ³Choose them so that anyone who unintentionally kills someone may run to them. They will be a place of refuge from any relative who can avenge the death.

⁴" 'A person who kills someone accidentally can run to one of these cities. There he will stand at the entrance to the city, where court is held, and present his case to the leaders of that city. Then they will take him into their city and give him a place to live with them.

⁵" 'If the relative who can avenge the death pursues him, the leaders must not hand him over to the relative because he didn't intend to kill the other person. He didn't even hate the person he killed. ⁶The accused person may remain in that city

until he can stand trial in front of the congregation or until whoever is chief priest at that time dies. Then he may go back to his home in the city from which he ran away.' "

⁷Kedesh in Galilee in the mountains of Naphtali, Shechem in the mountains of Ephraim, and Kiriath Arba (now called Hebron) in the mountains of Judah were chosen as cities of refuge. ⁸Bezer on the desert plateau from the tribe of Reuben, Ramoth in Gilead from the tribe of Gad, and Golan in Bashan from the tribe of Manasseh were chosen as cities of refuge on the east side of the Jordan River, east of Jericho.

⁹These are the cities chosen as cities of refuge for all Israelites, including the foreigners living among them. Anyone who accidentally kills someone may escape to these cities. Then he will not be handed over to the relative who can avenge a death before he stands trial in front of the congregation.

Cities for the Tribe of Levi

21 ¹Then the leaders of the families of Levi came to the priest Eleazar, to Joshua (son of Nun), and to the leaders of the families of the other Israelite tribes ²at Shiloh in Canaan. They said to them, "The LORD commanded through Moses that we should receive cities to live in and pasturelands for our livestock." ³So, as the LORD had instructed, Levi's descendants were given the following cities with pasturelands from the Israelites' inheritance.

⁴These are the cities for the families of Kohath that were chosen by drawing lots. These descendants of the priest Aaron the Levite received 13 cities from the tribes of Judah, Simeon, and Benjamin. ⁵The rest of Kohath's descendants received 10 cities from the families of the tribes of Ephraim and Dan and half of the tribe of Manasseh.

⁶Gershon's descendants received 13 cities from the families of the tribes of Issachar, Asher, Naphtali, and half of the tribe of Manasseh in Bashan.

⁷Merari's descendants received 12 cities for their families from the tribes of Reuben, Gad, and Zebulun. ⁸The Israelites gave these cities with pasturelands to Levi's descendants by drawing lots, as the LORD had commanded through Moses.

Cities for Kohath's Descendants

⁹These are the names of the cities from the tribes of Judah and Simeon ¹⁰that they gave Aaron's descendants who were from the families of Kohath in the tribe of Levi. Their lot was the first one drawn. ¹¹They gave them Kiriath Arba (Arba was Anak's father) and the pastureland around it. This is the city of Hebron located in the mountains of Judah. ¹²But they gave its fields and villages to Caleb, son of Jephunneh, as his possession. ¹³So they gave the following cities with pasturelands to the descendants of Aaron, the priest. The nine cities from those two tribes were Hebron (a city of refuge for murderers), Libnah, ¹⁴Jattir, Eshtemoa, ¹⁵Holon, Debir, ¹⁶Ain, Juttah, and Beth Shemesh. ¹⁷The tribe of Benjamin also gave them four cities: Gibeon, Geba, ¹⁸Anathoth, and Almon. ¹⁹In all, 13 cities with pasturelands were given to the priests, the descendants of Aaron.

²⁰Cities were chosen by lot from the tribe of Ephraim to give to the rest of Levi's descendants who were from the families of Kohath. ²¹These four cities with pasturelands were Shechem (a city of refuge for murderers) in the mountains of Ephraim, Gezer, ²²Kibzaim, and Beth Horon. ²³The tribe of Dan gave them four cities: Eltekeh, Gibbethon, ²⁴Aijalon, and Gath Rimmon. ²⁵Half of the tribe of Manasseh gave them two cities with pasturelands: Taanach and Gath Rimmon. ²⁶In all, ten cities with pasturelands were given to the rest of the families of Kohath.

Cities for Gershon's Descendants

²⁷They gave the families of Gershon's descendants, who were in the tribe of Levi, two cities with pasturelands from half of the tribe of Manasseh: Golan in Bashan (a city of refuge for murderers) and Ashtaroth. ²⁸Four cities with pasturelands were also given to them from the tribe of Issachar: Kishion, Daberath, ²⁹Jarmuth, and En Gannim. ³⁰Another four cities with pasturelands were given to them from the tribe of Asher: Mishal, Abdon, ³¹Helkath, and Rehob. ³²Also three cities with pasturelands were given to them from the tribe of Naphtali: Kedesh in Galilee (a city of refuge for murderers), Hammoth Dor, and Kartan. ³³In all, 13 cities with pasturelands were given to Gershon's families.

Cities for Merari's Descendants

³⁴To the families of Merari, who were from the tribe of Levi, the tribe of Zebulun gave four cities with pasturelands: Jokneam, Kartah, ³⁵Dimnah, and Nahalal. ³⁶The tribe of Reuben also gave them four cities with pasturelands: Bezer, Jahaz, ³⁷Kedemoth, and Mephaath. ³⁸The tribe of Gad also gave them four cities with pasturelands: Ramoth in Gilead (a city of refuge for murderers), Mahanaim, ³⁹Heshbon, and Jazer. ⁴⁰All these cities belonged to the families of Merari. They were the last of the families of Levi. These 12 cities were chosen by lot.

⁴¹Within the territory owned by the Israelites there were 48 cities in all for Levi's descendants. ⁴²Each of these cities had its own pastureland around it.

⁴³So the LORD gave Israel the whole land he had sworn to give their ancestors. They took possession of it and settled there. ⁴⁴The LORD allowed them to have peace on every side, as he had sworn with an oath to their ancestors. Not one of their enemies stood up to them. The LORD handed all their enemies over to them. ⁴⁵Every single good promise that the LORD had given the nation of Israel came true.

Joshua Blesses the Tribes That Live East of the Jordan River

22 ¹Joshua summoned the tribes of Reuben and Gad and half of the tribe of Manasseh. ²He said to them, "You have done everything the LORD's servant Moses commanded you. You have also obeyed me in everything I commanded you. ³All this time, to this day, you have never deserted your relatives. You have carefully kept the commands of the LORD your God.

⁴"Now the LORD your God has given your relatives peace, as he promised them. So return home, to the land that is your own possession. It is the land that the LORD's servant Moses gave you east of the Jordan River. ⁵Carefully follow the commands and teachings that the LORD's servant Moses gave you. Love the LORD your God, follow his directions, and keep his commands. Be loyal to him, and serve him with all your heart and soul." ⁶Then Joshua blessed them. He sent them on their way, and they went to their homes.

⁷Moses had given land in Bashan as an inheritance to half of Manasseh, and Joshua had given the other half of the tribe their land with their relatives west of the Jordan. When Joshua sent them home, he blessed them. ⁸He also said to them, "Return to your homes with your vast wealth, large herds of livestock, silver, gold, bronze, iron, and loads of clothing. Divide the loot from your enemies with your relatives."

An Altar for the LORD Is Built East of the Jordan River

⁹So the tribes of Reuben and Gad and half of the tribe of Manasseh left the rest of the Israelites at Shiloh in Canaan. They returned to Gilead. This was their own

possession which they had captured as the LORD had instructed them through Moses.
¹⁰Reuben, Gad, and half of the tribe of Manasseh came to the region of the Jordan that was still in Canaan. They built an altar by the Jordan River. The altar was very large and highly visible. ¹¹The rest of the Israelites heard about it and said, "See there! Reuben, Gad, and half of the tribe of Manasseh have built an altar at the border of Canaan. It's in the region near the Jordan River on Israel's side." ¹²When the people of Israel heard about it, the whole congregation of Israel gathered at Shiloh. They intended to wage war against them.

¹³The Israelites sent Phinehas, son of the priest Eleazar, to the tribes of Reuben and Gad and half of the tribe of Manasseh in Gilead. ¹⁴Ten leaders, one from each tribe in Israel, went with him. Each man was a leader of a household and head of a family division in Israel. ¹⁵When they arrived these leaders said to the people of Gilead, ¹⁶"All of the LORD's congregation is asking, 'What is this faithless act you have committed against the God of Israel?' Today you have turned away from following the LORD by building an altar for yourselves. Today you have rebelled against the LORD! ¹⁷Does the sin we committed at Peor mean nothing to us anymore? Didn't we cleanse ourselves from it? Because of that sin there was a plague on the LORD's congregation! ¹⁸You have turned away from following the LORD! Today you rebel against the LORD, and tomorrow he will be angry with the whole congregation of Israel. ¹⁹If your land is unclean,ᵃ come over here to the LORD's land. The LORD's tent is standing here. Take some property for yourselves among us. Don't rebel against the LORD or against us by building an altar for yourselves in addition to the altar of the LORD our God. ²⁰Didn't Achan, son of Zerah, act faithlessly with the things claimed by the LORD? Didn't the LORD become angry with the whole congregation of Israel? Achan wasn't the only one who died because of his sin."

²¹Then the tribes of Reuben and Gad and half of the tribe of Manasseh answered the heads of the divisions of Israel. ²²They said, "The LORD is ˏthe only trueˏ God! The LORD is ˏthe only trueˏ God! He knows, so let Israel know! If our act is rebellious or unfaithful to the LORD, ²³don't spare us today. If we built an altar with the intention of

Good Morning, God
Joshua 22:30-34

What a misunderstanding! The 12 tribes lived on both sides of the Jordan River. Those on one side thought the others were disobeying God. But before their argument turned into a war, each side sent some leaders to talk things over. What originally seemed like cause for war was really a big misunderstanding. It's easy to start yelling, hitting, and name-calling when you don't have all the facts straight. Talking about your problems with someone who is neutral can help you see the issues clearly and help you decide how to resolve the conflict fairly.

Lord, thank you for showing me how to solve problems with others when I'm upset.

ᵃ22:19 "Unclean" refers to anything that Moses' Teachings say is not presentable to God.

no longer following him, and if we built it for making burnt offerings, grain offerings, or fellowship offerings, let the LORD punish us. ²⁴"We were worried because of the situation we're in. We thought sometime in the future your children might say to our children, 'What relationship do you have with the LORD God of Israel? ²⁵The LORD has made the Jordan River a dividing line between us and you, the descendants of Reuben and Gad. You have no connection with the LORD!' So your descendants would stop our descendants from worshiping the LORD. ²⁶Then we said, 'Let's build an altar for ourselves. It will not be for burnt offerings or sacrifices, ²⁷but it will stand as a witness between us for generations to come. It will stand as a witness that we may worship in the presence of the LORD with our burnt offerings, sacrifices, and fellowship offerings.' Then your descendants cannot say to our descendants, 'You have no connection with the LORD!' ²⁸So we thought, if this statement is made to us or to our descendants in the future, we will answer, 'Look at the model of the LORD's altar our ancestors made. They didn't make it for burnt offerings or sacrifices but to stand as a witness between us.' ²⁹It would be unthinkable for us to rebel against the LORD or to turn back today from following the LORD by building an altar for burnt offerings, grain offerings, or sacrifices in addition to the altar of the LORD our God that is in front of his tent."

³⁰When the priest Phinehas, the leaders of the congregation, and the heads of the divisions of Israel heard what the tribes of Reuben, Gad, and Manasseh said, they were satisfied. ³¹Then Phinehas, son of the priest Eleazar, said to the tribes of Reuben, Gad, and Manasseh, "Today we know the LORD is among us, because you did not commit an unfaithful act against the LORD. Now you have rescued the people of Israel from the LORD's punishment."

³²Then Phinehas (son of the priest Eleazar) and the leaders returned from Reuben and Gad in Gilead to Israel in Canaan and gave them the report. ³³The people of Israel were satisfied with the report. So they praised God and didn't talk anymore about going to war against Reuben and Gad and destroying the land where they were living.

³⁴The tribes of Reuben and Gad gave the altar a name: Witness Between Us That the LORD Is the Only True God.

A Reminder to Follow Moses' Teachings

¹A long time afterward, the LORD gave the Israelites peace with all their enemies around them. Joshua was old, near the end of his life. ²So he called all the leaders, chiefs, judges, and officers of Israel together. He said to them, "I am old, near the end of my life. ³You have seen for yourselves everything the LORD your God did to all those nations. The LORD your God fought for you! ⁴I have given you the territory of the nations that still remain as an inheritance for your tribes. This includes the territory of all the nations I have already destroyed from the Jordan River westward to the Mediterranean Sea. ⁵The LORD your God will expel them right in front of your eyes and force them out of your way. You will take their land as the LORD your God told you. ⁶Now you must be very strong to keep and to do everything written in the Book of Moses' Teachings. Don't turn away from them. ⁷Don't get mixed up with the nations left in your territory. Don't ever mention the names of their gods or swear an oath to them. Don't ever serve their gods or bow down to them. ⁸But you must be loyal to the LORD your God, as you have been until now. ⁹The LORD has forced important and powerful nations out of your way. Not one person has ever been able to stand up to you. ¹⁰One of you used to chase a thousand. That was because the LORD your God was fighting for you, as he had promised you. ¹¹Be very careful to love the LORD your God.

¹²"But if you turn away and go along with the other nations within your ⌞borders⌟, if you intermarry with them or associate with them, ¹³then you should know that the LORD your God will never again force these people out of your way. Instead, they will be a snare and a trap for you, a whip laid to your sides, and thorns in your eyes until none of you are left in this good land that the LORD your God has given you.

¹⁴"Pay attention, because I will soon die like everyone else. You know with all your heart and soul that not one single promise which the LORD your God has given you has ever failed to come true. Every single word has come true.

¹⁵"Every good word the LORD your God has promised you has come true for you. In the same way the LORD will bring about every evil curse until he has destroyed you from this good land that he has given you. ¹⁶When you ignore the conditions*placed on you by the LORD your God and follow other gods, serve them and bow down to them, the LORD will be angry with you. Then you will quickly disappear from the good land he has given you."

Joshua Adds an Agreement to the Book of God's Teachings

24 ¹Joshua gathered all the tribes of Israel together at Shechem. He called together Israel's leaders, chiefs, judges, and officers, and they presented themselves to God.

²Joshua said to all the people, "This is what the LORD God of Israel says: Long ago your ancestors, Terah and his sons Abraham and Nahor, lived on the other side of the Euphrates River and served other gods. ³But I took your ancestor Abraham from the other side of the Euphrates River. I led him through all of Canaan and gave him many descendants. I also gave him Isaac. ⁴To Isaac I gave Jacob and Esau. I gave Esau the mountains in Seir as his own. However, Jacob and his sons went to Egypt.

⁵"Then I sent Moses and Aaron, and I struck Egypt with plagues. Later I led you out. ⁶When I led your ancestors out of Egypt, you came to the sea. The Egyptians with their chariots and horsemen chased your ancestors to the Red Sea. ⁷When your ancestors cried out to the LORD, he put darkness between you and the Egyptians. He made the sea flow back and cover them. You saw for yourselves what I did to Egypt. Then you lived in the desert for a long time.

⁸"After that I brought you to the land of the Amorites who lived on the east side of the Jordan River. They fought you. However, I handed them over to you. So you took their land, and I destroyed them in front of you. ⁹Then Balak, son of King Zippor of Moab, fought Israel. He summoned Balaam, son of Beor, to curse you. ¹⁰But I refused to listen to Balaam. All he could do was bless you. So I saved you from his power.

¹¹"Then you crossed the Jordan River and came to Jericho. The citizens of Jericho, the Amorites, Perizzites, Canaanites, Hittites, Girgashites, Hivites, and Jebusites fought you. But I handed them over to you. ¹²I sent hornets ahead of you to force out the two kings of the Amorites ahead of you. These things didn't happen because of your battle skills or fighting ability. ¹³So I gave you a land that you hadn't farmed, cities to live in that you hadn't built, vineyards and olive groves that you hadn't planted. So you ate all you wanted!

¹⁴"Fear the LORD, and serve him with integrity and faithfulness. Get rid of the gods your ancestors served on the other side of the Euphrates River and in Egypt, and serve only the LORD. ¹⁵But if you don't want to serve the LORD, then choose today

ᵃ23:16 Or "covenant."

whom you will serve. Even if you choose the gods your ancestors served on the other side of the Euphrates or the gods of the Amorites in whose land you live, my family and I will still serve the LORD."

¹⁶The people responded, "It would be unthinkable for us to abandon the LORD to serve other gods. ¹⁷The LORD our God brought us and our ancestors out of slavery in Egypt. He did these spectacular signs right before our eyes. He guarded us wherever we went, especially as we passed through other nations. ¹⁸The LORD forced out all the people ahead of us, including the Amorites who lived in this land. We, too, will serve the LORD, because he is our God."

¹⁹But Joshua answered the people, "Since the LORD is a holy God, you can't possibly serve him. He is a God who does not tolerate rivals. He will not forgive your rebellious acts and sins. ²⁰If you abandon the LORD and serve foreign gods, he will turn and bring disaster on you. He will destroy you, although he has been so good to you."

²¹The people answered Joshua, "No! We will only serve the LORD!"

²²Joshua said to the people, "You have testified that you have chosen to serve the LORD."

They answered, "Yes, we have!"

²³"Get rid of the foreign gods that are among you. Turn yourselves entirely over to the LORD God of Israel."

²⁴The people replied to Joshua, "We will serve the LORD our God and obey him."

²⁵That day Joshua made an agreement for the people and set up laws and rules for them at Shechem. ²⁶Joshua wrote these things in the Book of God's Teachings. Then he took a large stone and set it up under the oak tree at the LORD's holy place. ²⁷Joshua told all the people, "This stone will stand as a witness for us. It has heard all the words which the LORD spoke to us. It will stand as a witness for you. You cannot deceive your God." ²⁸Then Joshua sent the people away, each to his own property.

The Deaths of Joshua and Eleazar

²⁹After these events, the LORD's servant Joshua, son of Nun, died. He was 110 years old. ³⁰He was buried on his own land at Timnath Serah in the mountains of Ephraim north of Mount Gaash.

³¹Israel served the LORD as long as Joshua and the older leaders, who outlived him and who knew everything the LORD had done for Israel, were alive.

³²Joseph's bones, which the people of Israel had brought from Egypt, were buried at Shechem. They were placed in the plot of ground Jacob had bought from the sons of Hamor, father of Shechem, for 100 pieces of silver. The plot was inherited by Joseph's descendants.

³³Aaron's son Eleazar also died. He was buried on the hill that had been given to his son Phinehas in the mountains of Ephraim.

AN INTRODUCTION TO

Judges

After Joshua died, the people of Israel began to
disobey God. They forgot God and worshiped
idols. So God allowed enemies to defeat the people of
Israel. But when the Israelites turned back to God for
help, the Lord gave them leaders to save
them. These leaders were called
"judges." This book tells how the
Israelites disobeyed again and
again. But God also helped them
again and again when they
turned back to him.

Headlines

**Woman Leads
the Nation**
Judges 4, page 308

Jael Has Sisera Pegged
Judges 4, page 308

Say It Right, or Die!
Judges 12, page 321

**Samson Brings Down
the House**
Judges 16, page 326

Stolen Wives Wed
Judges 21, page 333

How did Jael end a war between
Israel and the Canaanites? See
Judges 4.

What's In It For Me?

Judges reminds me that . . .

GOD GIVES PEACE TO THOSE WHO OBEY HIM.

GOD GIVES VICTORY TO THOSE WHO SERVE HIM.

GOD PUNISHES THOSE WHO REJECT HIM.

GOD FORGIVES THOSE WHO TURN BACK TO HIM.

GOD RESCUES THOSE WHO CRY OUT TO HIM.

Who Makes a Good Boyfriend?

What should you look for in a boyfriend? Many girls look for a guy who is strong, handsome, and athletic.

Nobody was stronger than Samson. Nobody was a better athlete. One time he tore a lion apart with his bare hands! So does that mean that Samson was the perfect boyfriend?

Samson wasn't even close! Samson was a strong man, but he wasn't always a good man. When tricked, he became violently angry. When he was angry, Samson looked for revenge.

Samson also failed to obey God in his relationships with women. He refused to marry a woman who believed in God, as his parents wanted. He went to prostitutes, even though he knew it was wrong. Samson might have looked good. But any girl who fell for Samson was sure to have her heart broken.

It's not the size of the muscles, but the strength of a guy's love for God that makes him a good choice for a girl.

Real Strength

Samson was physically strong but morally weak. When tempted to do something wrong, he often gave in. Because he was spiritually weak, Samson never freed his people from Philistine rule. As a judge, Samson was a failure.

Deborah was physically much weaker than Samson. But she had inner strength. Unlike Samson, Deborah obeyed God's call and led Israel to victory over its enemies.

Samson:	Deborah:
Followed selfish desires	Obeyed God
Acted rashly	Acted wisely
Sinned repeatedly	Was a righteous prophet
Was abandoned by God	Aided by God
Failed to free Israel of oppressors	Freed Israel from oppressors
Led Israel for 20 years	Gave Israel 40 years of peace

Judges

Israel Fails to Force Out the Canaanites

1 ¹After Joshua's death the Israelites asked the LORD, "Who will go first to fight the Canaanites for us?"

²The LORD answered, "Judah's troops will go first. I am about to hand the Canaanites over to you."

³The tribe of Judah said to the tribe of Simeon, "Come with us into the territory given to us when we drew lots, and together we will fight the people of Canaan. Then we'll go with you into your territory." So the tribe of Simeon went along with Judah.

Judah Attempts to Force Out the Canaanites

⁴Judah's troops went into battle, and the LORD handed the Canaanites and Perizzites over to them. They defeated 10,000 men at Bezek. ⁵At Bezek they also caught up with Adoni Bezek. They fought him and defeated the Canaanites and Perizzites. ⁶Adoni Bezek fled. Judah's troops chased him, caught him, and cut off his thumbs and big toes. ⁷Adoni Bezek said, "Seventy kings who had their thumbs and big toes cut off used to pick up food under my table. God has paid me back for what I did to them." Judah's troops brought Adoni Bezek to Jerusalem, where he died.

⁸The men of Judah attacked Jerusalem and captured it. They killed everyone there and set the city on fire. ⁹After that, the men of Judah went to fight the Canaanites who lived in the mountains, the Negev, and the foothills. ¹⁰Then they went to fight the Canaanites who lived at Hebron. (In the past Hebron was called Kiriath Arba.) There they killed Sheshai, Ahiman, and Talmai.

¹¹From there Judah's troops went to fight the people living at Debir. (In the past Debir was called Kiriath Sepher.) ¹²Caleb said, "I will give my daughter Achsah as a wife to whoever defeats Kiriath Sepher and captures it." ¹³Then Othniel, son of Caleb's younger brother Kenaz, captured it. So Caleb gave him his daughter Achsah as a wife. ¹⁴When she came to Othniel, she persuaded him to ask her father for a field. When she got down from her donkey, Caleb asked her, "What do you want?"

¹⁵She answered, "Give me a blessing. Since you've given me some dry land, also give me some springs." So Caleb gave her the upper and lower springs.

¹⁶The descendants of Moses' father-in-law, the Kenite, went with the people of Judah from the City of Palms into the desert of Judah. There they lived with the people of Judah in the Negev near Arad.

¹⁷The tribe of Judah went to fight along with the tribe of Simeon, their close relatives. They defeated the Canaanites who lived in Zephath and claimed it for the LORD by destroying it. So the city was called Hormah [Claimed for Destruction]. ¹⁸Judah also captured Gaza, Ashkelon, and Ekron with their territories. ¹⁹The Lord was with the men of Judah so that they were able to take possession of the mountains. But they could not force out the people living in the valley who had chariots made of iron. ²⁰As Moses had promised, Hebron was given to Caleb, who forced out the three sons of Anak.

²¹The men of Benjamin did not force out the Jebusites who lived in Jerusalem. The Jebusites still live with the tribe of Benjamin in Jerusalem today.

²²The descendants of Joseph also went into battle against Bethel, and the Lord

was with them. ²³They sent men to spy on Bethel. (In the past the city was called Luz.) ²⁴The spies saw a man coming out of the city. They told him, "Show us how we can get into the city, and we'll treat you kindly." ²⁵He showed them. So they got into the city and killed everyone there. But they let that man and his whole family go free. ²⁶The man went to the land of the Hittites. There he built a city and called it Luz. The city still has that name today.

²⁷Now, the tribe of Manasseh did not force out the people of Beth Shean, Taanach, Dor, Ibleam, and Megiddo or their villages. The Canaanites were determined to live in this land. ²⁸When the Israelites were strong enough, they made the Canaanites do forced labor. But they did not force all of them out.

²⁹The tribe of Ephraim did not force out the Canaanites who lived in Gezer. So the Canaanites continued to live with them in Gezer.

³⁰The tribe of Zebulun did not force out those who lived at Kitron or Nahalol. So the Canaanites continued to live with them and were made to do forced labor.

³¹The tribe of Asher did not force out those who lived at Acco or Sidon, Ahlab, Achzib, Helbah, Aphek, or Rehob. ³²So the tribe of Asher continued to live with the Canaanites because they did not force them out.

³³The tribe of Naphtali did not force out those who lived at Beth Shemesh or Beth Anath. So they continued to live with the Canaanites. But the people of Beth Shemesh and Beth Anath were made to do forced labor.

³⁴The Amorites forced the tribe of Dan into the mountains and would not let them come down into the valley.

³⁵The Amorites were determined to live at Har Heres, Aijalon, and Shaalbim. But when the tribes of Joseph became stronger, they made the Amorites do forced labor. ³⁶The territory of the Amorites extended from the Akrabbim Pass—from Selah northward.

The Messenger of the LORD Reacts to Israel's Failure

2 ¹The Messenger of the Lord went from Gilgal to Bochim. He said, "I brought you out of Egypt into the land that I swore to give to your ancestors. I said, 'I will never break my promise*ᵃ* to you. ²You must never make a treaty with the people who live in this land. You must tear down their altars.' But you didn't obey me. What do you think you're doing? ³So I have this to say, 'I will not force them out of your way. They will be like thorns in your sides, and their gods will become a trap for you.' "

⁴While the Messenger of the LORD was saying this to all the people of Israel, they began to cry loudly. ⁵So they called that place Bochim [Those Who Cry]. They offered sacrifices there to the LORD.

The Death of Joshua

⁶Now, Joshua sent the people of Israel home. So each family went to take possession of the territory they had inherited. ⁷The people served the LORD throughout Joshua's lifetime and throughout the lifetimes of the leaders who had outlived him and who had seen all the spectacular works the LORD had done for Israel. ⁸The LORD's servant Joshua, son of Nun, died at the age of 110. ⁹He was buried at Timnath Heres within the territory he had inherited. This was in the mountains of Ephraim north of Mount Gaash. ¹⁰That whole generation had joined their ancestors in death. So another generation grew up after them. They had no personal experience with the LORD or with what he had done for Israel.

ᵃ2:1 Or "covenant."

The Sin of the Next Generation

[11]The people of Israel did what the LORD considered evil. They began to serve other gods—the Baals. [12]The Israelites abandoned the LORD God of their ancestors, the God who brought them out of Egypt. They followed the other gods of the people around them. They worshiped these gods, and that made the LORD angry. [13]They abandoned the LORD to serve the god Baal and the goddess Astarte. [14]So the LORD became angry with the people of Israel. He handed them over to people who robbed them. He also used their enemies around them to defeat them. They could no longer stand up against their enemies. [15]Whenever the Israelites went to war, the power of the LORD brought disaster on them. This was what the LORD said he would do in an oath. So he made them suffer a great deal.

[16]Then the LORD would send judges[b] to rescue them from those who robbed them. [17]But the people wouldn't listen to the judges. The Israelites chased after other gods as though they were prostitutes and worshiped them. They quickly turned from the ways of their ancestors who had obeyed the LORD's commands. They refused to be like their ancestors. [18]But when the LORD appointed judges for the Israelites, he was with each judge. The LORD rescued them from their enemies as long as that judge was alive. The LORD was moved by the groaning of those who were tormented and oppressed. [19]But after each judge died, the people went back to their old ways and acted more corruptly than their parents. They followed, served, and worshiped other gods. They never gave up their evil practices and stubborn ways.

The LORD Allows the Nations to Stay in Order to Test His People

[20]The LORD became angry with Israel. He said, "Because the people of this nation have rejected the promise I gave their ancestors and have not obeyed me, [21]I will no longer force out the nations Joshua left behind when he died. [22]I will test the people of Israel with these nations to see whether or not they will carefully follow the LORD's ways as their ancestors did." [23]So the LORD let these nations stay. He had not handed them over to Joshua or forced them out quickly.

[1]These are the nations the LORD left behind to test all the Israelites who had not experienced any war in Canaan. [2]The LORD left them to teach Israel's descendants about war, at least those who had known nothing about it in the past. [3]He left the five rulers of the Philistines, all the Canaanites, the Sidonians, and the Hivites who lived on Mount Lebanon from Mount Baal Hermon to the border of Hamath. [4]These nations were left to test the Israelites, to find out if they would obey the commands the LORD had given their ancestors through Moses.

The People Fail the Test

[5]So the people of Israel lived among the Canaanites, Hittites, Amorites, Perizzites, Hivites, and Jebusites. [6]The Israelites allowed their sons and daughters to marry these people. Israel also served their gods.

Othniel Defeats Cushan Rishathaim

[7]The people of Israel did what the LORD considered evil. They forgot the LORD their God and served other gods and goddesses—the Baals and the Asherahs. [8]The LORD became angry with the people of Israel. He used King Cushan Rishathaim of Aram Naharaim to defeat them. So Israel served Cushan Rishathaim for eight years.

---

[b]2:16 The judges served as God-appointed political/religious leaders of Israel.

[9]Then the people of Israel cried out to the LORD for help. The LORD sent a savior to rescue them. It was Othniel, son of Caleb's younger brother Kenaz. [10]When the LORD's Spirit came over him, he became the judge of Israel. He went out to war. The LORD handed King Cushan Rishathaim of Aram Naharaim over to him, and Othniel overpowered him. [11]So there was finally peace in the land for 40 years. Then Othniel, son of Kenaz, died.

Ehud Defeats Moab

[12]Once again, the people of Israel did what the LORD considered evil. So the LORD made King Eglon of Moab stronger than Israel, because Israel did what the LORD considered evil. [13]Eglon got the Ammonites and the Amalekites to help him, and they defeated the Israelites and occupied the City of Palms. [14]The Israelites served King Eglon of Moab for 18 years.

[15]Then the people of Israel cried out to the LORD for help. The LORD sent a savior to rescue them. It was Ehud, a left-handed man from the tribe of Benjamin. (Ehud was the son of Gera.)

The people sent him with their tax payment to King Eglon of Moab. [16]Ehud made a two-edged dagger for himself. He fastened it to his right side under his clothes. [17]Then he brought the tax payment to King Eglon. (Eglon was a very fat man.) [18]When Ehud had finished delivering the payment, he sent back the men who had carried it. [19]However, Ehud turned around at the stone idols near Gilgal and returned to Eglon. He said, "Your Majesty, I have a secret message for you."

The king replied, "Keep quiet!" Then all his advisers left the room.

[20]Ehud came up to him as he sat alone in his room on the roof. He said to the king, "I have a message from God for you." As the king rose from his throne, [21]Ehud reached with his left hand, took the dagger from his right side, and plunged it into Eglon's belly. [22]Even the handle went in after the blade. Eglon's fat covered the blade because Ehud didn't pull the dagger out. The blade stuck out in back.[a] [23]Ehud left the room.[b] (He had closed and locked the doors of the room before he left.)

[24]After Ehud went out, Eglon's advisers came in. They were surprised that the doors were locked. "He must be using the toilet," they said. [25]They waited and waited, but Eglon didn't open the doors. So they took the key and opened the door. They were shocked to see their ruler lying on the floor, dead.

[26]While they had been waiting, Ehud escaped. He went past the stone idols and escaped to Seirah. [27]When he arrived there, he blew a ram's horn in the mountains of Ephraim to summon the troops. So the troops of Israel came down from the mountains with him, and he led them. [28]He told them, "Follow me! The LORD will hand your enemy Moab over to you."

They followed him and captured the shallow crossings of the Jordan River that led to Moab and refused to let anyone cross. [29]At that time they killed about ten thousand of Moab's best fighting men. Not one of them escaped. [30]The power of Moab was crushed by Israel that day. So there was finally peace in the land for 80 years.

Shamgar Defeats the Philistines

[31]After Ehud came Shamgar, son of Anath. He killed 600 Philistines with a sharp stick used for herding oxen. So he, too, rescued Israel.

---

[a]3:22 Hebrew meaning uncertain.   [b]3:23 Hebrew meaning uncertain.

The LORD Calls Barak Through Deborah

4 ¹After Ehud died, the people of Israel again did what the LORD considered evil. ²So the LORD used King Jabin of Canaan, who ruled at Hazor, to defeat them. The commander of King Jabin's army was Sisera, who lived at Harosheth Haggoyim. ³The people of Israel cried out to the LORD for help. King Jabin had 900 chariots made of iron and had cruelly oppressed Israel for 20 years.

⁴Deborah, wife of Lappidoth, was a prophet. She was the judge in Israel at that time. ⁵She used to sit under the Palm Tree of Deborah between Ramah and Bethel in the mountains of Ephraim. The people of Israel would come to her for legal decisions.

⁶Deborah summoned Barak, son of Abinoam, from Kedesh in Naphtali. She told him, "The LORD God of Israel has given you this order: 'Gather troops on Mount Tabor. Take 10,000 men from Naphtali and Zebulun with you. ⁷I will lead Sisera (the commander of Jabin's army), his chariots, and troops to you at the Kishon River. I will hand him over to you.'"

⁸Barak said to her, "If you go with me, I'll go. But if you don't go with me, I won't go."

⁹Deborah replied, "Certainly, I'll go with you. But you won't win any honors for the way you're going about this, because the LORD will use a woman to defeat Sisera."

Barak Defeats Jabin

So Deborah started out for Kedesh with Barak. ¹⁰Barak called the tribes of Zebulun and Naphtali together at Kedesh. Ten thousand men went to fight under his command. Deborah also went along with him.

¹¹Heber the Kenite had separated from the other Kenites (the descendants of Hobab, Moses' father-in-law). Heber went as far away as the oak tree at Zaanannim near Kedesh and set up his tent.

¹²The report reached Sisera that Barak, son of Abinoam, had come to fight at Mount Tabor. ¹³So Sisera summoned all his chariots (900 chariots made of iron) and all his troops from Harosheth Haggoyim to come to the Kishon River.

¹⁴Then Deborah said to Barak, "Attack! This is the day the LORD will hand Sisera over to you. The LORD will go ahead of you."

So Barak came down from Mount Tabor with 10,000 men behind him. ¹⁵The LORD threw Sisera, all his chariots, and his whole army into a panic in front of Barak's deadly assault. Sisera got down from his chariot and fled on foot. ¹⁶Barak pursued the chariots and the army to Harosheth Haggoyim. So Sisera's whole army was killed in combat. Not one man survived.

¹⁷Meanwhile, Sisera fled on foot toward the tent of Jael, the wife of Heber the Kenite. Sisera did this because King Jabin of Hazor and Heber's family were on peaceful terms. ¹⁸When Jael came out of her tent, she met Sisera. She told him, "Sir, come in here! Come into my tent. Don't be afraid." So he went into her tent, and she hid him under a tent curtain.

¹⁹Sisera said to her, "Please give me a little water to drink. I'm thirsty." But instead she gave him milk to drink and covered him up again.

²⁰He said to her, "Stand at the door of the tent. If anyone comes and asks if there has been a man around here, tell them no."

²¹When Sisera had fallen sound asleep from exhaustion, Jael, Heber's wife, took a tent peg and walked quietly toward him with a hammer in her hand. She hammered the tent peg through his temples into the ground. So Sisera died.

²²Barak was still pursuing Sisera. When Jael came out of her tent, she met him. She said to him, "Come in! I have something to show you—the man you've been

looking for." So Barak went into her tent. He saw Sisera lying there dead with the tent peg through his temples.

²³So on that day, God used the people of Israel to crush the power of King Jabin of Canaan. ²⁴The Israelites became stronger and stronger until they destroyed him.

The Victory Song of Deborah and Barak

5 ¹On that day Deborah and Barak, son of Abinoam, sang this song:

² Praise the LORD!
Men in Israel vowed to fight,
and people volunteered for service.

³ Listen, you kings!
Open your ears, you princes!
I will sing a song to the LORD.
I will make music to the LORD God of Israel.

⁴ O LORD,
when you went out from Seir,
when you marched from the country of Edom,
the earth quaked,
the sky poured,
the clouds burst,
⁵ and the mountains shook
in the presence of the LORD God of Sinai,
in the presence of the LORD God of Israel.

⁶ In the days of Shamgar, son of Anath,
in the days of Jael,
roads were deserted.
Those who traveled took back roads.
⁷ Villages in Israel were deserted—
deserted until I, Deborah, took a stand—
took a stand as a mother of Israel.
⁸ When the people chose new gods,
war broke out inside the city gates.
Not a weapon was seen among 40,000 in Israel.

⁹ My heart goes out to Israel's commanders,
to those people who volunteered.
Praise the LORD!
¹⁰ You people who ride on brown donkeys,
who sit on saddle blankets,
and who walk on the road—think.
¹¹ Listen to the voices of those singing at the wells.*
Over and over again they repeat
the victories of the LORD,
the victories for his villages in Israel.
Then the LORD's people went down to the city gates.

¹² Get up! Get up, Deborah!
Get up! Get up and create a song!

---

*5:11 Hebrew meaning of this line uncertain.

Barak, attack! Take your prisoners, son of Abinoam.
13   Then those mighty men who were left came down.
The LORD's people went into battle for me against the mighty soldiers.
14   Those who had settled in Amalek's country
            came down from Ephraim.
         Benjamin came with its troops
            after Ephraim.
         Commanders from Machir went into battle.
         The officers from Zebulun also went.
15   Issachar's commanders were with Deborah.
            They were also with Barak,
               sent into the valley under his command.

         Among Reuben's divisions important men had second thoughts.
16   Why did you sit between the saddlebags?
Was it to listen to the shepherds playing their flutes?
         Reuben's divisions of important men had second thoughts.
17   Gilead remained east of the Jordan River.
         And Dan . . . Why did he stay by the ships?
         Asher sat on the seashore and remained along the inlets.
18   But Zebulun mocked death,
               and Naphtali risked his life on the battlefield.

19   Kings came and fought.
Then the kings of Canaan fought.
         They fought at Taanach by the waters of Megiddo.
            But they didn't carry off any rich loot.
20   The stars fought from heaven.
         They fought against Sisera from their heavenly paths.
21   The Kishon River swept them away—
         that old river, the Kishon.

I must march on with strength!

22   Then the horses' hoofs pounded.
         The mighty war horses galloped on and on.
23   "Curse Meroz!" said the Messenger of the LORD.
"Bitterly curse those who live there!
         They did not come to help the LORD,
            to help the LORD and his heroes."
24   Jael, wife of Heber the Kenite,
         should be the most blessed woman,
         the most blessed woman living in a tent.
25   Sisera asked for water.
         She gave him milk.
         She offered him buttermilk in a royal bowl.
26   She reached for a tent peg with one hand,
            for a workman's hammer with the other.
         She struck Sisera.
            She crushed his head.
               She shattered and pierced his temples.

²⁷ He sank.
    He fell.
        He lay between her feet!
He sank.
    He fell between her feet.
    Where he sank, he fell dead.

²⁸ Sisera's mother looked through her window
    and cried as she peered through the lattice.
"Why is his chariot taking so long?
Why don't I hear the clatter of his chariots?"
²⁹   Her wisest servants gave her an answer.
But she kept repeating to herself,
³⁰   "They're really finding and dividing the loot:
    A girl or two for each soldier,
        colorful clothes for Sisera,
          colorful, embroidered clothes,
            and two pieces of colorful, embroidered cloth
              for the neck of the looter."

³¹ May all your enemies die like that, O Lord.
But may those who love the Lord
    be like the sun when it rises in all its brightness.

So the land had peace for 40 years.

Israel Sins Again

¹The people of Israel did what the Lord considered evil. So the Lord handed them over to Midian for seven years. ²Midian's power was too strong for Israel. The Israelites made hiding places in the mountains, caves, and mountain strongholds to protect themselves from Midian. ³Whenever Israel planted crops, Midian, Amalek, and Kedem came and damaged the crops. ⁴The enemy used to camp on the land and destroy the crops all the way to Gaza. They left nothing for Israel to live on—not one sheep, cow, or donkey. ⁵Like swarms of locusts, they came with their livestock and their tents. They and their camels could not be counted. They came into the land only to ruin it. ⁶So the Israelites became very poor because of Midian and cried out to the Lord for help.

⁷When the people of Israel cried out to the Lord for help because of what the Midianites had done to them, ⁸the Lord sent a prophet to them. He said, "This is what the Lord God of Israel says:

I brought you out of Egypt.
I took you away from slavery.
⁹   I rescued you from the power of the Egyptians
    and from the power of those who oppressed you.
I forced people out of your way.
I gave you their land.
¹⁰   I said to you, 'I am the Lord your God.
    You must never fear the gods of the Amorites
        in whose land you will live.'
        But you have not obeyed me."

Gideon Is Chosen to Be a Judge

¹¹The Messenger of the LORD came and sat under the oak tree in Ophrah that belonged to Joash from Abiezer's family. Joash's son Gideon was beating out wheat in a winepress to hide it from the Midianites. ¹²The Messenger of the LORD appeared to Gideon and said, "The LORD is with you, brave man."

¹³Gideon responded, "Excuse me, sir! But if the LORD is with us, why has all this happened to us? Where are all the miracles our ancestors have told us about? Didn't they say, 'The LORD brought us out of Egypt?' But now the LORD has abandoned us and has handed us over to Midian."

¹⁴The LORD turned to him and said, "You will rescue Israel from Midian with the strength you have. I am sending you."

¹⁵Gideon said to him, "Excuse me, sir! How can I rescue Israel? Look at my whole family. It's the weakest one in Manasseh. And me? I'm the least important member of my family."

¹⁶The LORD replied, "I will be with you. You will defeat Midian as if it were only one man."

¹⁷Gideon said to him, "If you find me acceptable, give me a sign that it is really you speaking to me. ¹⁸Don't leave until I come back. I want to bring my gift and set it in front of you."

"I will stay until you come back," he said.

¹⁹Then Gideon went into his house and prepared a young goat and unleavened bread made with 18 quarts of flour. He put the meat in a basket and the broth in a pot. Then he went out and presented them to the messenger of the LORD under the oak tree.

²⁰The Messenger of the LORD told him, "Take the meat and the unleavened bread, put them on this rock, and pour the broth over them." Gideon did so. ²¹Then the Messenger of the LORD touched the meat and the bread with the tip of the staff that was in his hand. Fire flared up from the rock and burned the meat and the bread. Then the Messenger of the LORD disappeared. ²²That's when Gideon realized that this had been the Messenger of the LORD. So he said, "LORD God! I have seen the Messenger of the LORD face to face."

²³The LORD said to him, "Calm down! Don't be afraid. You will not die." ²⁴So Gideon built an altar there to the LORD. He called it The LORD Calms. To this day it is still in Ophrah, which belongs to Abiezer's family.

Good Morning, God

Judges 6:14-16

When the Lord's messenger told Gideon to lead an army against Israel's enemies, Gideon gave excuses: His family was the weakest in town, and he was the least important member. But because the Lord was with him, Gideon defeated the huge enemy army with only 300 men. Don't make excuses for not courageously following God.

Thank you, God, for giving me the strength I need to do what you want me to.

Gideon Destroys an Altar Dedicated to Baal

²⁵That same night the Lord said to Gideon, "Take a bull from your father's herd, a bull that is seven years old. Tear down your father's altar dedicated to the god Baal and cut down the pole dedicated to the goddess Asherah that is next to it. ²⁶Then, in the proper way, build an altar to the Lord your God on top of this fortified place. Take this second bull and sacrifice it as a burnt offering on the wood from the Asherah pole that you have cut down."

²⁷Gideon took ten of his servants and did what the Lord had told him to do. However, he didn't do anything during the day. He was too afraid of his father's family and the men of the city, so he did it at night. ²⁸When the men of the city got up early in the morning, they saw that the Baal altar had been torn down. The Asherah pole next to it had also been cut down. They saw that the second bull had been sacrificed as a burnt offering on the altar that had been built. ²⁹They asked each other, "Who did this?" While they were investigating the matter, someone said, "Gideon, son of Joash, did this."

³⁰Then the men of the city told Joash, "Bring your son out. He must die. He has torn down the Baal altar and cut down the Asherah pole that was beside it."

³¹But Joash said to everyone standing around him, "You're not going to defend Baal, are you? Do you think you should save him? Whoever defends him will be put to death in the morning. If he's a god, let him defend himself when someone tears down his altar." ³²So that day they nicknamed Gideon "Jerubbaal" [Let Baal Defend Himself], because they said, "When someone tears down Baal's altar, let Baal defend himself."

Gideon Summons an Army

³³All of Midian, Amalek, and Kedem combined their armies, crossed the Jordan River, and camped in the valley of Jezreel. ³⁴Then the Lord's Spirit gave Gideon strength. So Gideon blew the ram's horn to summon Abiezer's family to follow him. ³⁵He also sent messengers throughout Manasseh to summon the people to follow him. The tribes of Asher, Zebulun, and Naphtali were also summoned to follow him, and they went to meet the enemy in battle.

³⁶Then Gideon said to God, "You said that you would rescue Israel through me. ³⁷I'll place some wool on the threshing floor.^a If there is dew on the wool while all the ground is dry, then I'll know that you will rescue Israel through me, as you said." ³⁸And that is what happened. The next morning Gideon got up early. He squeezed out a bowl full of water from the wool.

³⁹Then Gideon said to God, "Don't be angry with me. But let me ask one more thing. Let me make one more test with the wool. Let the wool be dry while all the ground is covered with dew." ⁴⁰During the night, God did what Gideon asked. The wool was dry, but all the ground was covered with dew.

Gideon Defeats Midian

7 ¹Jerubbaal (that is, Gideon) and all the troops with him got up early and camped above En Harod. Midian's camp was north of him at the hill of Moreh in the valley.

²The Lord said to Gideon, "You have too many men with you for me to hand Midian over to you. Israel might brag and say, 'We saved ourselves.' ³Announce to the troops, 'Whoever is scared or frightened should leave Mount Gilead and go back home.' " So 22,000 men went back home, and 10,000 were left.

⁴The Lord said to Gideon, "There are still too many men. Bring them down to

---

^a6:37 A threshing floor is an outdoor area where grain is separated from its husks.

the water, and I will test them for you there. If I say to you, 'This one will go with you,' he must go with you. And if I say to you, 'This one won't go with you,' he must not go."

⁵So Gideon took the men down to the water. The LORD said to him, "Separate those who lap water with their tongues like dogs from those who kneel down to drink." ⁶Three hundred men lapped water with their hands to their mouths. All the rest of the men knelt down to drink water. ⁷Then the LORD said to Gideon, "With the 300 men who lapped water I will save you and hand Midian over to you. All the other men should go home." ⁸So Gideon sent the other men of Israel home, but the 300 men who stayed kept all the supplies and rams' horns.

The camp of Midian was below him in the valley.

⁹That night the LORD said to Gideon, "Attack! Go into the camp! I will hand it over to you. ¹⁰But if you're afraid to go, take your servant Purah to the camp with you. ¹¹Listen to what people are saying. After that, you will have the courage to go into the camp and attack it."

So Gideon and his servant Purah went to the edge of the camp. ¹²Midian, Amalek, and all of Kedem were spread out in the valley like a swarm of locusts. There were so many camels that they could not be counted. They were as numerous as the grains of sand on the seashore.

¹³When Gideon got there, he heard a man telling his friend a dream. The man said, "I had a strange dream. There was a loaf of barley bread rolling around in the camp of Midian. When it got to the command post, the loaf of bread hit that tent so hard that the tent collapsed, turned upside down, and fell flat."

¹⁴His friend replied, "That can only be the sword of Gideon, son of Joash, from Israel. God is going to hand Midian and the whole camp over to him."

¹⁵When Gideon heard the dream and its interpretation, he worshiped the LORD. Then he went back to the camp of Israel and said, "Attack! The LORD will hand Midian's camp over to you."

¹⁶Gideon divided the 300 men into three companies. He gave them each rams' horns and jars with torches inside. ¹⁷He said to them, "Watch me, and do what I do. When I come to the edge of the camp, do exactly as I do. ¹⁸When I and those with me blow our rams' horns, then the rest of you around the camp do the same and shout, 'For the LORD and for Gideon!' "

¹⁹Gideon and his 100 men came to the edge of the camp. It was the beginning of the midnight watch just at the change of the guards. They blew their rams' horns and smashed the jars they were holding in their hands. ²⁰The three companies also blew their rams' horns and broke their jars. They held the torches in their left hands and the rams' horns in their right hands so that they could blow them. They shouted, "A sword for the LORD and for Gideon!" ²¹While each man kept his position around the camp, everyone in the Midianite camp began to run away, screaming as they fled. ²²The 300 men kept on blowing their rams' horns, and the LORD caused the whole camp of Midian to fight among themselves. They fled as far as Beth Shittah, toward Zererah, and as far as the bank of the stream at Abel Meholah near Tabbath.

²³The men of Israel were summoned from Naphtali, Asher, and all Manasseh to help pursue the troops of Midian. ²⁴Gideon also sent messengers to the whole mountain region of Ephraim with this message, "Go into battle against Midian. Capture the watering holes as far as Beth Barah and the Jordan River." All the men of Ephraim were also summoned to help. They captured the watering holes as far as Beth Barah and the Jordan River. ²⁵They also captured Oreb and Zeeb, the two Midianite commanders. They killed Oreb at the Rock of Oreb and Zeeb at the Winepress of Zeeb

and kept on pursuing Midian. Then they brought the severed heads of Oreb and Zeeb to Gideon on the other side of the Jordan River.

¹The men from Ephraim strongly protested Gideon's actions. They said, "Why did you do this to us? You didn't invite us to go fight Midian with you."

²Gideon replied, "I haven't done anything compared with what you have done. Aren't the grapes that Ephraim picked after the harvest better than all the grapes in Abiezer's entire harvest? ³God handed Oreb and Zeeb, Midian's commanders, over to you. What have I done compared with that?" When they heard what Gideon said, they weren't angry with him anymore.

⁴Gideon and his 300 men headed toward the Jordan River. They were exhausted when they crossed it, but they kept pursuing the enemy. ⁵So Gideon said to the men of Succoth, "Please give me some food for the men under my command. They're exhausted, and I'm pursuing King Zebah and King Zalmunna of Midian."

⁶The generals at Succoth replied, "We shouldn't give your army food. You haven't captured Zebah and Zalmunna yet."

⁷Gideon responded, "Alright, then. When the Lord hands Zebah and Zalmunna over to me, I'll whip your bodies with thorns and thistles from the desert."

⁸Then Gideon went to Penuel and asked the people there for the same help. But they gave him the same reply that the men of Succoth gave. ⁹So he told them, "When I come back after my victory, I'll tear down this tower."

¹⁰Zebah and Zalmunna were in Karkor with an army of about 15,000 men. This was all that was left of Kedem's entire army. In the battle, 120,000 soldiers died. ¹¹So Gideon went up Tent Dwellers Road, east of Nobah and Jogbehah, and defeated the unsuspecting Midianite army. ¹²Zebah and Zalmunna fled as Gideon pursued them. He captured King Zebah and King Zalmunna of Midian, and the whole Midianite army panicked.

¹³Gideon, son of Joash, returned from the battle through the Heres Pass ¹⁴and captured a young man from Succoth. He questioned him, and the young man wrote down for him the names of the 77 officials and leaders of Succoth. ¹⁵Gideon went to the men of Succoth and said, "Here are Zebah and Zalmunna! You insulted me when you said, 'We shouldn't give your exhausted men food before you've captured Zebah and Zalmunna.'" ¹⁶So Gideon took the leaders of the city and taught them a lesson using thorns and thistles from the desert. ¹⁷Then he tore down the tower of Penuel and killed the men of that city.

¹⁸He asked Zebah and Zalmunna, "What kind of men did you kill at Tabor?"

They answered, "They were like you. Each one looked like a king's son."

¹⁹Gideon replied, "They were my brothers, my mother's sons. I solemnly swear, as the Lord lives, if you had let them live, I would not have to kill you now." ²⁰Then he told Jether, his firstborn son, "Get up and kill them!" But Jether didn't draw his sword. He was afraid because he was only a young man.

²¹Zebah and Zalmunna said, "Get up and do it yourself! It's a man's job!" So Gideon got up and killed them. Then he took the half-moon ornaments that were on their camels' necks.

Gideon Makes a Gold Idol

²²The men of Israel said to Gideon, "You, then your son, and then your grandson, must rule us. You rescued us from Midian."

²³Gideon replied, "I will not rule you nor will my son. The Lord will rule you." ²⁴Then Gideon said to them, "Do me a favor. Each of you give me the earrings from your loot." (Their enemies, the Ishmaelites, wore gold earrings.)

²⁵The men of Israel answered, "Yes, we'll give them to you." So they spread out a coat. Each man took the earrings from his loot and dropped them on it. ²⁶The gold earrings Gideon had asked for weighed 40 pounds. This did not include the half-moon ornaments, the earrings, the purple clothes worn by the kings of Midian, and the chains from their camels' necks. ²⁷Then Gideon used the gold to make an idol*ᵃ* and placed it in his hometown, Ophrah. All Israel chased after it there as though it were a prostitute. It became a trap for Gideon and his family.

²⁸The power of Midian was crushed by the people of Israel, and Midian never again became a threat. So the land had peace for 40 years during Gideon's life.

²⁹Jerubbaal, son of Joash, went home to live. ³⁰Gideon had 70 sons because he had many wives. ³¹His concubine*ᵇ* at Shechem also gave birth to a son. That son was named Abimelech.

³²Gideon, son of Joash, died at a very old age. He was buried in the tomb of his father Joash at Ophrah, the city belonging to Abiezer's family.

³³As soon as Gideon died, the people of Israel chased after other gods—the Baals—as though they were prostitutes. They made Baal Berith their god. ³⁴The Israelites did not remember the Lᴏʀᴅ their God, who had rescued them from all the enemies around them. ³⁵And they were not kind to the family of Jerubbaal (that is, Gideon) despite all the good he had done for Israel.

Abimelech Kills His Brothers

¹Abimelech, son of Jerubbaal [Gideon], went to Shechem to see the uncles on his mother's side of the family. He spoke to them and his mother's whole family. ²He said, "Please ask all citizens of Shechem, 'What seems best to you? Do you really want all of Jerubbaal's 70 sons to rule you or just one man? Remember, I'm your own flesh and blood.' "

³His uncles repeated everything he said to all citizens of Shechem. They were persuaded to follow Abimelech because he was their relative. ⁴So they gave him 70 pieces of silver from the temple of Baal Berith. With the silver, Abimelech hired worthless and reckless men to follow him. ⁵Then he went to his father's home in Ophrah. There he executed his 70 brothers, Jerubbaal's sons. But Jotham, Jerubbaal's youngest son, survived because he hid. ⁶All the citizens from Shechem and Beth Millo united. They went to the oak tree that was still standing in Shechem and proclaimed Abimelech king.

Jotham's Story

⁷When Jotham was told about this, he went to a high spot on Mount Gerizim. He shouted to them, "Listen to me, you citizens of Shechem, so that God might listen to you.

8   "The trees went to anoint someone to be king over them.
            They said to the olive tree,
                'Be our king!'
9   But the olive tree responded,
                'Should I stop producing oil,
                    which people use to honor gods and humans,
                        in order to rule the trees?'
10   Then the trees said to the fig tree,

ᵃ8:27 Or "ephod," a technical term for a part of the priest's clothes. Its exact usage and shape are unknown.
ᵇ8:31 A concubine is considered a wife except she has fewer rights under the law.

'You come and be our king!'
11 But the fig tree responded,
   'Should I stop producing my good, sweet fruit
       in order to rule the trees?'
12 Then the trees said to the grapevine,
   'You come and be our king!'
13 But the grapevine responded,
   'Should I stop producing my wine,
       which makes gods and humans happy,
       in order to rule the trees?'
14 Then all the trees said to the thornbush,
   'You come and be our king!'
15 But the thornbush responded to the trees,
   'If you really want to anoint me to be your king,
       then come and take shelter in my shade.
   But if not, fire will come out of the thornbush
       and burn up the cedars of Lebanon.'

16"If you acted with sincerity and integrity when you made Abimelech king, be happy. If you treated Jerubbaal and his family well, if you treated him as he deserved, be happy. 17My father fought for you. He risked his life and rescued you from Midian. 18But today you have attacked my father's family. You have executed his 70 sons. You have made Abimelech, who is the son of my father's slave girl, king over the citizens of Shechem just because he's your brother. 19So if you are now acting with sincerity and integrity toward Jerubbaal and his family, then be happy with Abimelech and let Abimelech be happy with you. 20But if that's not the case, let fire come out of Abimelech and burn up citizens of Shechem and Beth Millo. Also let fire come out of citizens of Shechem and Beth Millo and burn up Abimelech."

21Then Jotham ran away quickly. He went to Beerah and lived there to avoid his brother Abimelech.

Abimelech's Battles

22Abimelech ruled Israel for three years. 23Then God sent an evil spirit to cause problems between Abimelech and citizens of Shechem. So citizens of Shechem turned against Abimelech. 24God did this so that the bloody violence committed against Jerubbaal's 70 sons would happen to Abimelech and citizens of Shechem. Citizens of Shechem had helped Abimelech execute his brothers.

25So citizens of Shechem set ambushes for Abimelech on top of the mountains. They also robbed everyone who passed by them on the road. This was reported to Abimelech.

26Then Gaal (son of Ebed) and his brothers moved into Shechem. Citizens of Shechem trusted him. 27They went into the country and harvested grapes in the vineyards to make wine. Then they made an offering of praise in the temple of their gods. They ate, drank, and cursed Abimelech. 28Gaal (son of Ebed) said, "Who's Abimelech, and who are we, the people of Shechem, that we should serve him? Isn't he Jerubbaal's son, and isn't Zebul his officer? Serve the descendants of Hamor, Shechem's father! Why should we serve Abimelech? 29How I wish I controlled these people! Then I'd get rid of Abimelech. I would tell him,ᵃ 'Get yourself a big army and come out.' "

ᵃ9:29 Greek; Masoretic Text "So he said to Abimelech."

³⁰Zebul, Shechem's ruler, heard what Gaal (son of Ebed) had said, and he became angry. ³¹He secretly sent messengers to Abimelech. "Watch out! Gaal (son of Ebed) and his brothers have come to Shechem. They have turned the city against you. ³²You and your men must start out tonight. Set an ambush for them in the fields around Shechem. ³³In the morning, when the sun rises, get up quickly and raid the city. When Gaal and his men come out to attack you, do whatever you want to him."

³⁴Abimelech and all his troops started out at night. He used four companies to set ambushes around Shechem. ³⁵Gaal (son of Ebed) went out and stood at the entrance to the city. Then Abimelech and his troops rose from their ambush. ³⁶When Gaal saw the troops, he said to Zebul, "Look, troops are coming down from the mountaintops!"

Zebul replied, "The shadows of the mountains look like men to you."

³⁷Gaal spoke again, "No, there are troops coming down from Tabbur Haares. One company is coming along the road by the Fortunetellers' Tree."

³⁸Then Zebul said to him, "Where is your big mouth now? You were the one who said, 'Who's Abimelech that we should serve him?' Aren't these the troops whose ruler you despised? Now go out and fight him."

³⁹Then Gaal led citizens of Shechem out to fight Abimelech. ⁴⁰Abimelech chased Gaal so that he ran away from him. Many were killed at the entrance of the city. ⁴¹Abimelech continued to live at Arumah. Zebul threw Gaal and his brothers out and would not let them live in Shechem.

⁴²The next day the people of Shechem went into the fields. Abimelech was told about it. ⁴³So he took his troops, divided them into three companies, and set an ambush in the fields. He watched and saw the people coming out of the city. Then he began to attack them. ⁴⁴Abimelech and his company charged the city and captured its entrance. The other two companies charged at everyone in the fields and attacked them. ⁴⁵Abimelech attacked the city all day long. He captured the city and killed the people in it. He also tore down the city and scattered salt all over the land.

⁴⁶All the citizens of Shechem's Tower heard about it and went into the basement of the temple of El Berith. ⁴⁷When Abimelech was told that they had gathered there, ⁴⁸he and all his men went to Mount Zalmon. Abimelech took an ax, cut some brushwood, and carried it on his shoulder. He told his men, "Hurry and do what you've seen me do!" ⁴⁹So all his troops also cut brushwood and followed Abimelech. They piled the brushwood on top of the basement and set it on fire with the people inside. So all the people in Shechem's Tower died too. There were about a thousand men and women.

⁵⁰Then Abimelech went to Thebez, camped there, and captured it. ⁵¹Now, there was a strong tower inside the town. All the men, women, and leaders of the town fled to it. They locked the door behind them and went up on the roof of the tower. ⁵²Abimelech came to the tower. He began to fight against it and went near the entrance of the tower to burn it down. ⁵³Then a woman threw a small millstone that hit Abimelech on the head and cracked his skull. ⁵⁴He quickly called his armorbearer. He told him, "Take your sword and kill me! I don't want anyone to say, 'A woman killed Abimelech.' " His armorbearer did as he said, so Abimelech died. ⁵⁵When the people of Israel saw that Abimelech was dead, they all went home.

⁵⁶So God paid back Abimelech for the evil he had done to his father when he killed his 70 brothers. ⁵⁷God also paid back the men of Shechem for all their evil. So the curse of Jotham, son of Jerubbaal, came true.

Tola Serves as Judge

¹After Abimelech, Tola, who was the son of Puah and grandson of Dodo, came to rescue Israel. Tola was from Issachar and lived in Shamir in the mountains of Ephraim. ²He judged Israel for 23 years. Tola died and was buried in Shamir.

Jair Serves as Judge

³After Tola, Jair from Gilead became a judge. He judged Israel for 22 years. ⁴Jair had 30 sons who rode on 30 donkeys. He also had 30 towns that are still called Havvoth Jair to this day. They are in the region of Gilead. ⁵Jair died and was buried in Kamon.

Israel Sins Again

⁶The people of Israel again did what the LORD considered evil. They began to serve other gods and goddesses—the Baals and the Astartes—and the gods of Aram, Sidon, Moab, Ammon, and the gods of the Philistines. They abandoned the LORD and did not serve him.

⁷The LORD became angry with the people of Israel. So he used the Philistines and Ammonites to defeat them. ⁸They oppressed and crushed the people of Israel that year. For 18 years they oppressed all who lived east of the Jordan River in the land of the Amorites in Gilead. ⁹Ammon also crossed the Jordan River to fight the tribes of Judah, Benjamin, and Ephraim. So Israel suffered a great deal.

¹⁰Then the people of Israel cried out to the LORD for help. They said, "We have sinned against you. We have abandoned our God and served other gods—the Baals."

¹¹The LORD said to the people of Israel, "When the Egyptians, the Amorites, the Ammonites, the Philistines, ¹²the Sidonians, the Amalekites, and the Maonites oppressed you, you cried out to me for help. Didn't I rescue you from them? ¹³But you still abandoned me and served other gods. That's why I won't rescue you again. ¹⁴Cry out for help to the gods you chose. Let them rescue you when you're in trouble."

¹⁵The people of Israel said to the LORD, "We have sinned. Do to us whatever you think is right. But please rescue us today!" ¹⁶Then they got rid of the foreign gods they had and served the LORD. So the LORD could not bear to have Israel suffer any longer.

¹⁷The troops of Ammon were summoned to fight, and they camped at Gilead. The people of Israel also gathered together and camped at Mizpah. ¹⁸The leaders of the people of Gilead said to each other, "Whoever starts the fight against Ammon will rule everyone who lives in Gilead."

Jephthah Called to Be Judge

¹Jephthah was a soldier from the region of Gilead. Jephthah's father was named Gilead. His mother was a prostitute. ²Gilead's wife also gave birth to sons. When his wife's sons grew up, they threw Jephthah out. They told him, "You'll get no inheritance from our father. You're the son of that other woman." ³Jephthah fled from his brothers. He went to live in the land of Tob. Worthless men gathered around Jephthah and went out on raids with him.

⁴Later, Ammon waged war with Israel. ⁵When the Ammonites attacked Israel, Gilead's leaders went to get Jephthah from the land of Tob. ⁶They said to Jephthah, "Come and be our commander so that we can wage war against Ammon."

⁷But Jephthah replied to Gilead's leaders, "Don't you hate me? Didn't you throw me out of my father's house? So why are you coming to me now when you're in trouble?"

⁸Gilead's leaders answered Jephthah, "The reason we've turned to you now is that we want you to go with us and wage war against Ammon. You will be the ruler of everyone who lives in Gilead."

⁹Jephthah told them, "If you take me back to fight against Ammonites and the LORD gives them to me, I will be your leader."

¹⁰Gilead's leaders said to Jephthah, "The LORD is a witness between us. We will certainly do what you say." ¹¹Jephthah went with them, and the people made him their leader and commander. So Jephthah went to Mizpah and repeated all these things in the presence of the LORD.

The King of Ammon Refuses to Deal With Jephthah

¹²Jephthah sent messengers to the king of Ammon. They asked the king, "Why did you invade my land and wage war against me?"

¹³The king of Ammon answered Jephthah's messengers, "When the people of Israel left Egypt, they took my land. It stretched from the Arnon River to the Jabbok River and the Jordan River. Now give it back peacefully."

¹⁴Jephthah again sent messengers to the king of Ammon. ¹⁵They said, "This is what Jephthah says: The people of Israel didn't take away the land belonging to Moab or Ammon. ¹⁶When the people of Israel left Egypt, they went through the desert to the Red Sea and came to Kadesh. ¹⁷The people of Israel sent messengers to the king of Edom. They said, 'Please let us go through your country.' But the king of Edom wouldn't listen to them. They also sent messengers to the king of Moab. But he wouldn't allow it, either. So the people of Israel remained at Kadesh.

¹⁸"Then they went through the desert, by-passing Edom and Moab. They camped east of Moab—east of the Arnon River. They did not cross the Arnon River because it was Moab's border.

¹⁹"Then the people of Israel sent messengers to King Sihon of the Amorites. Sihon ruled from Heshbon. The people of Israel said to him, 'Please let us go through your land to our own.' ²⁰But Sihon did not trust the Israelites enough to let them go through his territory. Sihon assembled all his troops. He camped at Jahaz and attacked Israel. ²¹But the LORD God of Israel handed Sihon and all his people over to Israel. Israel defeated them and took possession of all the land of the Amorites who lived there. ²²Israel took all the Amorite territory from the Arnon River to the Jabbok River and from the desert to the Jordan River.

Good Morning, God

Judges 11:4-9

The people closest to Jephthah hurt him the most. In fact, his family was so hateful that they drove Jephthah out of town. But when an enemy army invaded the town, Jephthah's family begged him to come back and defend them. Jephthah wanted to obey God, so he forgave his family and saved their town. What would you have done if you were Jephthah? Remember his forgiving response the next time someone you love hurts you.

Father, help me to forgive those who hurt me.

²³"The LORD God of Israel forced the Amorites out of the way of his people Israel. So what right do you have to take it back? ²⁴Shouldn't you take possession of what your god Chemosh took for you? Shouldn't we take everything the LORD our God took for us? ²⁵You're not any better than Balak, son of King Zippor of Moab, are you? Did he ever have a case against Israel? Or did he ever fight against Israel? ²⁶Israel has now lived in Heshbon, Aroer, all their villages, and in all the cities along the Arnon River for 300 years. Why didn't you recapture these cities during that time? ²⁷I haven't sinned against you. But you have done wrong by waging war against me. The LORD is the judge who will decide today whether Israel or Ammon is right."

²⁸But the king of Ammon didn't listen to the message Jephthah sent him.

Jephthah's Vow

²⁹Then the LORD's Spirit came over Jephthah. Jephthah went through Gilead, Manasseh, and Mizpah in Gilead to gather an army. From Mizpah in Gilead Jephthah went to attack Ammon.

³⁰Jephthah made a vow to the LORD. He said, "If you will really hand Ammon over to me, ³¹then whatever comes out of the doors of my house to meet me when I return safely from Ammon will belong to the LORD. I will sacrifice it as a burnt offering."

³²So Jephthah went to fight against Ammon. The LORD handed the people of Ammon over to him. ³³He defeated them from Aroer to Minnith and on to Abel Keramim, 20 cities in all. It was a decisive defeat. So the Ammonites were crushed by the people of Israel.

³⁴When Jephthah went to his home in Mizpah, he saw his daughter coming out to meet him. She was dancing with tambourines in her hands. She was his only child. Jephthah had no other sons or daughters. ³⁵When he saw her, he tore his clothes in grief and said, "Oh no, Daughter! You've brought me to my knees! What disaster you've brought me! I made a foolish promise to the LORD. Now I can't break it."

³⁶She said to him, "Father, you made a promise to the LORD. Do to me whatever you promised since the LORD has punished your enemy Ammon." ³⁷Then she said to her father, "Do me a favor. Give me two months for my friends and me to walk in the mountains and mourn that I will never have an opportunity to get married."

³⁸"Go!" he said, and he sent her off for two months. She and her friends went to the mountains, and she cried about never being able to get married. ³⁹At the end of those two months she came back to her father. He did to her what he had vowed, and she never had a husband. So the custom began in Israel ⁴⁰that for four days every year the girls in Israel would go out to sing the praises of the daughter of Jephthah, the man from Gilead.

Ephraim's Jealousy

12 ¹The men of Ephraim were summoned to fight. They crossed the Jordan River to Zaphon. They said to Jephthah, "Why did you fight against Ammon without inviting us to go with you? Now we're going to burn your house down with you in it."

²Jephthah answered, "My people and I were involved in a legal dispute with Ammon. I asked you for help, but you didn't rescue me from them. ³When I saw that you would not rescue me, I risked my life and went to fight the people of Ammon. The LORD handed them over to me. So why did you come to fight against me today?"

⁴Then Jephthah gathered all the men of Gilead and fought Ephraim. The men of Gilead defeated Ephraim. They did this because Ephraim had said, "You people from Gilead are nothing but fugitives from Ephraim and Manasseh."

⁵The men of Gilead captured the shallow crossings of the Jordan River leading

back to Ephraim. Whenever a fugitive from Ephraim said, "Let me cross," the men of Gilead would ask, "Are you from Ephraim?" If he answered, "No," ⁶they would tell him, "Say the word *shibboleth*." If the fugitive would say *sibboleth*, because he couldn't pronounce the word correctly, they would grab him and kill him at the shallow crossings of the Jordan River. At that time 42,000 men from Ephraim died.

⁷Jephthah judged Israel for six years. Then Jephthah of Gilead died and was buried in one of the cities of Gilead.

Ibzan Serves as Judge

⁸After Jephthah, Ibzan from Bethlehem judged Israel. ⁹He had 30 sons and 30 daughters. His sons and daughters married people from outside their own families. He judged Israel for seven years. ¹⁰When Ibzan died, he was buried in Bethlehem.

Elon Serves as Judge

¹¹After Ibzan, Elon from the tribe of Zebulun judged Israel. He judged Israel for ten years. ¹²When Elon died, he was buried in Aijalon in the territory of Zebulun.

Abdon Serves as Judge

¹³After Elon, Abdon, son of Hillel, from Pirathon judged Israel. ¹⁴He had 40 sons and 30 grandsons who rode on 70 donkeys. He judged Israel for eight years. ¹⁵When Abdon died, he was buried in Pirathon, in the territory of Ephraim, in the mountains of Amalek.

The Messenger of the LORD Appears to Samson's Parents

¹The people of Israel again did what the LORD considered evil. So the LORD handed them over to the Philistines for 40 years.

²There was a man from Zorah named Manoah. Manoah was from the family of Dan. His wife was not able to have children. ³The Messenger of the LORD appeared to her and said, "You've never been able to have a child, but now you will become pregnant and have a son. ⁴Now you must be careful. Don't drink any wine or liquor or eat any unclean*ᵃ* food. ⁵You're going to become pregnant and have a son. You must never cut his hair because the boy will be a Nazirite dedicated to God from birth. He will begin to rescue Israel from the power of the Philistines."

⁶The woman went to tell her husband. She said, "A man of God came to me. He had a very frightening appearance like the Messenger of God. So I didn't ask him where he came from, and he didn't tell me his name. ⁷He told me, 'You're going to become pregnant and have a son. So don't drink any wine or liquor or eat any unclean food because the boy will be a Nazirite dedicated to God from the time he is born until he dies.' "

⁸Then Manoah pleaded with the LORD, "Please, Lord, let the man of God you sent come back to us. Let him teach us what we must do for the boy who will be born."

⁹God did what Manoah asked. The Messenger of God came back to his wife while she was sitting out in the fields. But her husband Manoah was not with her. ¹⁰The woman ran quickly to tell her husband. She said, "The man who came to me the other day has just appeared to me again."

¹¹Manoah immediately followed his wife. When he came to the man, he asked him, "Are you the man who spoke to my wife?"

"Yes," he answered.

ᵃ 13:4 "Unclean" refers to anything that Moses' Teachings say is not presentable to God.

¹²Then Manoah asked, "When your words come true, how should the boy live and what should he do?"

¹³The Messenger of the LORD answered Manoah, "Your wife must be careful to do everything I told her to do. ¹⁴She must not eat anything that comes from the grapevines, drink any wine or liquor, or eat any unclean food. She must be careful to do everything I commanded."

¹⁵Manoah said to the Messenger of the LORD, "Please stay while we prepare a young goat for you to eat."

¹⁶But the Messenger of the LORD responded, "If I stay here, I will not eat any of your food. But if you make a burnt offering, sacrifice it to the LORD." (Manoah did not realize that it was the Messenger of the LORD.)

¹⁷Then Manoah asked the Messenger of the LORD, "What is your name? When your words come true, we will honor you."

¹⁸The Messenger of the LORD asked him, "Why do you ask for my name? It's a name that works miracles."

¹⁹So Manoah took a young goat and a grain offering and sacrificed them to the LORD on a rock he used as an altar. While Manoah and his wife watched, the LORD did something miraculous. ²⁰As the flame went up toward heaven from the altar, the Messenger of the LORD went up in the flame. When Manoah and his wife saw this, they immediately bowed down with their faces touching the ground.

²¹The Messenger of the LORD didn't appear again to Manoah and his wife. Then Manoah knew that this had been the Messenger of the LORD. ²²So Manoah said to his wife, "We will certainly die because we have seen God."

²³But Manoah's wife replied, "If the LORD wanted to kill us, he would not have accepted our burnt offering and grain offering. He would not have let us see or hear all these things just now."

²⁴So the woman had a son and named him Samson. The boy grew up, and the LORD blessed him. ²⁵The LORD's Spirit began to stir in him while he was at Mahaneh Dan, between Zorah and Eshtaol.

Samson Marries a Philistine

14 ¹When Samson went to Timnah, he saw a young Philistine woman. ²He went home and told his father and mother, "I've seen a Philistine woman at Timnah. Now get her for me so that I can marry her."

³His father and mother asked him, "Aren't there any women among our relatives or all our people? Do you have to marry a woman from those godless Philistines?"

But Samson told his father, "Get her for me! She's the one I want!" ⁴His father and mother didn't know that the LORD was behind this. The LORD was looking for an opportunity to do something to the Philistines. (At that time the Philistines were ruling Israel.)

⁵Samson went with his father and mother to Timnah. When they were coming to the vineyards of Timnah, a young roaring lion met Samson. ⁶The LORD's Spirit came over him. With his bare hands, he tore the lion apart as if it were a young goat. He didn't tell his parents what he had done.

⁷Then he went to talk to the young woman. She was the one he wanted. ⁸Later he went back to marry her. On his way, he left the road to look at the lion he had killed. He saw a swarm of bees and some honey in the lion's dead body. ⁹He scraped the honey into his hands and ate it as he walked along. When he came to his father and mother, he gave them some of the honey to eat. He didn't tell them he had scraped it out of the lion's dead body.

Women's World

Marriage / *Judges 14*

In Bible times, weddings were times of happiness and joy. Friends and relatives came from miles around, and the celebration might last a whole week. During this happy time, the bride and groom were dressed and treated like a queen and a king. The people ate and danced and sang.

Today, people think of love as something that leads to marriage. In Bible times, people thought of love as something that grew after marriage, although there are cases in the Bible where a person fell in love and then married. Usually in ancient times, the parents of the groom chose their son's future wife. The man's parents then spoke with the parents of the bride to arrange the marriage.

The groom gave the woman's father a "bride price." He wasn't "buying" his wife; the bride price showed that the groom valued his bride and wanted to make up for the loss to her father. The bride's father gave the bride a gift, called a dowry. The dowry allowed the bride to come into the marriage bringing property of value. Women were not "sold." Both the groom's gifts to the father and the father's gifts to the bride show how important women really were in Bible times.

¹⁰After his father went to see the woman, Samson threw a party. (This is what young men used to do.) ¹¹When ˌher familyˌ saw him, they chose 30 of their friends to be with him.

¹²Then Samson said to them, "Let me tell you a riddle. If you solve it during the seven days of the party, I'll give you 30 linen shirts and 30 changes of clothes. ¹³But if you can't solve it, you will give me the same things."

They responded, "Tell us your riddle! Let's hear it!"

¹⁴So Samson said to them,

> "From the eater
>   came something to eat.
> From the strong one
>   came something sweet."

For three days they couldn't solve the riddle. ¹⁵On the fourth day they said to Samson's wife, "Trick your husband into solving the riddle for us. If you don't, we'll burn you and your family to death. Did the two of you invite us ˌjust to make us poorˌ?"

[16]So Samson's wife cried on his shoulder. She said, "You hate me! You don't really love me! You gave my friends a riddle and didn't tell me the answer."

Samson replied, "I haven't even told my father and mother, so why should I tell you?"

[17]But she cried on his shoulder for the rest of the seven days of the party. Finally, on the seventh day he told her the answer because she made his life miserable. Then she told her friends the answer to the riddle.

[18]So before sundown on the seventh day, the men of the city said to him,

"What is sweeter than honey?
What is stronger than a lion?"

Samson replied,

"If you hadn't used my cow to plow,
you wouldn't know my riddle now."

[19]When the LORD's Spirit came over him, he went to Ashkelon and killed 30 men there. He took their clothes and gave them to the men who solved the riddle. He was angry, and he went to his father's house. [20]Samson's wife was given to his best man.

Samson Serves as Judge

[1]Later, during the wheat harvest, Samson went to visit his wife. He took a young goat along for her. He said, "I'm going to sleep with my wife in her bedroom."

But her father would not let him go in. [2]Her father said, "I thought you hated her. So I gave her to your best man. Isn't her younger sister better looking? Marry her instead!"

[3]Samson said to him, "This time I won't be guilty when I get even with the Philistines, even though I'm going to do something terrible to them." [4]So Samson caught 300 foxes. He tied them together in pairs by their tails. Then he fastened a torch between their tails. [5]He set the torches on fire and released the foxes in the Philistines' grain fields. So he set fire to all their grain, whether it was stacked or in the fields. Their olive orchards also caught on fire.

[6]Some Philistines asked, "Who did this?"

They were told, "Samson! He's the son-in-law of the man at Timnah. Samson did it because the man at Timnah took Samson's wife and gave her to his best man." So the Philistines burned Samson's wife and her father to death.

[7]Samson said to them, "If that's how you're going to act, I'll get even with you before I stop." [8]So he attacked them violently and slaughtered them. Then he went to live in a cave in the cliff at Etam.

[9]The Philistines came, camped in Judah, and overran Lehi. [10]The men of Judah asked, "Why did you come to fight us?"

The Philistines answered, "We've come to tie up Samson and do to him what he did to us."

[11]So 3,000 men from Judah went to the cave in the cliff at Etam. They said to Samson, "Don't you know that the Philistines rule us? Why have you done this to us?"

Samson replied, "I did to them what they did to me."

[12]So the men from Judah told him, "We've come to tie you up and hand you over to the Philistines."

Samson said to them, "Swear to me that you won't harm me yourselves."

[13]They told him, "We promise we'll only tie you up and hand you over to them. We

certainly won't kill you." So they tied him up with two new ropes and brought him back from the cliff.

¹⁴When he came to Lehi, the Philistines met him with shouts of triumph. But the LORD's Spirit came over him. The ropes on his arms became like strings burned in a fire, and those on his hands snapped.

¹⁵Samson found the jawbone from a donkey that had just died. He picked it up and killed 1,000 men with it. ¹⁶Then Samson said,

> "With a jawbone from a donkey,
>   I've made two piles of them.
> With a jawbone from a donkey,
>   I've killed a thousand men."

¹⁷When he finished saying this, he threw the jawbone away. He called that place Ramath Lehi [Jawbone Hill].

¹⁸Samson was very thirsty. So he called out to the LORD and said, "You have given me this great victory. But now I'll die from thirst and fall into the power of godless men."

¹⁹So God split open the hollow place at Lehi, and water gushed out. Samson drank some water. Then he was refreshed and revived. So he called the place En Hakkore [Spring of the One Who Calls Out]. It is still there at Lehi today.

²⁰Samson judged Israel for 20 years during the time of the Philistines.

16 ¹Samson went to Gaza. There he saw a prostitute and slept with her. ²The people of Gaza were told, "Samson's here!" So they surrounded the place and waited all night at the city gate to ambush him. They were quiet all night. They thought, "We'll kill him at dawn."

³But Samson was in bed ⌊with the prostitute⌋ only until midnight. Then he got up, took hold of the doors, door posts, and bar of the city gate and pulled them out. He carried them on his shoulders to the top of the hill facing Hebron.

Samson and Delilah

⁴After ⌊leaving Gaza⌋, he fell in love with a woman in the Sorek Valley. Her name was Delilah. ⁵The Philistine rulers came to her and said, "Trick him, and find out what makes him so strong. Find out how we can overpower him. We want to tie him up in order to torture him. Each of us will give you 1,100 pieces of silver."

Good Morning, God
Judges 16:4-6

Samson knew how Delilah looked on the outside. But he did not pay any attention to the kind of person she was on the inside. She wanted to ruin Samson by revealing to his enemies the secret of his strength. A person may make a great first impression. But look deeper! Is she really the kind of friend God wants you to have? Choose your friends wisely. Like Samson, you could be sorry for making a bad choice!

Thank you, Lord, for helping me look for the right kind of friends.

⁶So Delilah said to Samson, "Please tell me what makes you so strong. How can you be tied up so that someone could torture you?"

⁷Samson told her, "If someone ties me up with seven new bowstrings that are not dried out, I will be like any other man."

⁸The Philistine rulers brought her seven new bowstrings that were not dried out. She tied Samson up with them. ⁹Some men were hiding in the bedroom waiting for her to tie him up. Then she said to him, "Samson, the Philistines are attacking!" Samson snapped the bowstrings as a thread snaps when it touches fire. So no one found out why he was so strong.

¹⁰Delilah told Samson, "Look, you're making fun of me by telling me lies. Now, tell me how you can be tied up."

¹¹Samson told her, "If someone ties me up tightly with new ropes that have never been used, I will be like any other man."

¹²So Delilah took some new ropes and tied him up with them. Then she said to him, "Samson, the Philistines are attacking!" Some men were in her bedroom waiting to ambush him. But Samson tore the ropes off his arms as though they were strings.

¹³Delilah told Samson, "You're still making fun of me by telling me lies. Tell me how you can be tied up."

Samson replied, "Just weave the seven braids of my hair with the other threads in the loom."

¹⁴So Delilah tied his braids to the loom shuttle. Then she said to him, "Samson, the Philistines are attacking!" But Samson woke up and tore his braids and the threads out of the loom shuttle.

¹⁵Delilah said to Samson, "How can you say that you love me when your heart isn't mine? You've made fun of me three times now, but you still haven't told me what makes you so strong."

¹⁶Every day she made his life miserable with her questions. She pestered him until he wished he were dead. ¹⁷Finally, he told her the truth. He told her, "Because I'm a Nazirite, no one has ever cut the hair on my head. I was dedicated to God before I was born. If my hair is ever shaved off, my strength will leave me. Then I'll be like any other man."

¹⁸When Delilah realized that he had told her everything, she sent a message to the Philistine rulers, "Come here once more." (She did this because Samson had told her everything.) So the Philistine rulers arrived with the money in their hands.

¹⁹Delilah put Samson to sleep on her lap. She called for a man to shave off his seven braids. Then she began to torture him because his strength had left him. ²⁰She said, "Samson, the Philistines are attacking!" Samson woke up. He thought, "I'll get out of this as usual and shake myself free." (He didn't realize that the Lord had left him.) ²¹The Philistines grabbed him. They poked out his eyes and took him to the prison in Gaza. They tied him up with double chains and made him grind grain in the mill there.

²²But his hair started to grow back as soon as it was shaved off.

²³Now, the Philistine rulers gathered together to offer a great sacrifice to their god Dagon and to celebrate. They said, "Our god handed Samson, our enemy, over to us." ²⁴When the people saw him, they praised their god. They said,

> "Our god gave our enemy,
>   destroyer of our land
>   and killer of so many,
>   into our very hand!"

²⁵When all the Philistines were enjoying themselves, they said, "Call Samson in to entertain us."

Samson was called from the prison, and he made them laugh. They made him stand between two columns. ²⁶Samson told the young man who was leading him by the hand, "Let me rest. Let me touch the columns on which the building stands so that I can lean against them." ²⁷The building was filled with people. All the Philistine rulers were there. On the roof there were about three thousand men and women who watched Samson entertain them.

²⁸Then Samson called to the LORD, "Almighty LORD, please remember me! God, give me strength just one more time! Let me get even with the Philistines for at least one of my two eyes." ²⁹Samson felt the two middle columns on which the building stood. With his right hand on one column and his left on the other, he pushed hard against them. ³⁰"Let me die with the Philistines," he said. With that, he pushed with all his might, and the building fell on the rulers and everyone in it. So he killed more Philistines when he died than he had when he was alive.

³¹Then his relatives and his father's whole family went to Gaza. They took Samson and buried him between Zorah and Eshtaol in the tomb of his father Manoah.

Samson had judged Israel for 20 years.

Micah's Idolatry

¹There was a man named Micah from the mountain region of Ephraim. ²He told his mother, "You were upset about the 1,100 pieces of silver that were taken from you. I even heard you put a curse on them. Here's the silver. I took it!"

His mother said, "The LORD bless you, my son!"

³So Micah gave the 1,100 pieces of silver back to his mother. Then his mother said, "I dedicate this silver to the LORD for my son's benefit. I want to make a carved idol and a metal idol. So now I'm giving the silver back to you."

⁴When Micah returned the silver to his mother, she took 200 pieces of the silver and gave it to a silversmith. He made a carved idol and a metal idol. Both were placed in Micah's home. ⁵Micah owned a shrine. He also made an ephodᵃ and household idols. He ordained one of his sons to be his priest. ⁶In those days Israel didn't have a king. Everyone did whatever he considered right.

⁷There was a young man from Bethlehem in Judah. (Bethlehem belongs to the family of Judah.) He was a Levite but was living in Bethlehem. ⁸This man left Bethlehem in Judah to live wherever he could find a place. He came to Micah's house in the mountains of Ephraim to carry on his work.

⁹Micah asked him, "Where do you come from?"

The man told him, "I'm a Levite from Bethlehem in Judah. I'm going to live wherever I can find a place."

¹⁰Micah told him, "Stay with me! Be a father and a priest to me. I'll give you ten pieces of silver a year, a set of clothes, and your room and board."

The Levite accepted the offer ¹¹and agreed to live with Micah. The young man became like one of Micah's sons. ¹²Micah ordained the Levite. So the young man became his priest and a part of his family.

¹³Then Micah said, "Now I know that the LORD will be good to me. I have a Levite for my priest."

ᵃ17:5 *Ephod* is a technical term for a part of the priest's clothes. Its exact usage and shape are unknown.

Micah Brings Idolatry to the Tribe of Dan

18 ¹In those days Israel didn't have a king. And in those days the tribe of Dan was looking for a place to live. Up to that time they had not received land as an inheritance among the tribes of Israel as they should have. ²So all the families of Dan sent out five qualified men from Zorah and Eshtaol. They were sent to spy throughout the land and explore it. They were told, "Go and explore the land!"

They came to Micah's house in the mountains of Ephraim. They spent the night there. ³While they were at Micah's house, they recognized the young Levite's voice. So they stopped to ask him, "Who brought you here? What are you doing here? Why are you here?"

⁴The Levite told them what Micah had done for him and added, "Micah hired me, so I became his priest."

⁵They said to him, "Please find out from God if our journey will be successful."

⁶The priest told them, "Go in peace. The LORD approves of your journey."

⁷The five men left there and came to the city of Laish. They saw that the people there lived without a care. These people were like the people of Sidon. They were peaceful and secure. There was no one around who threatened to take away their property by force. They were far from the people of Sidon and totally independent.

⁸The men went back to their relatives in Zorah and Eshtaol. Their relatives asked them, "What did you find?"

⁹They replied, "Get up, let's attack Laish. We saw the land. It's very good!

"Don't just sit there! Go at once and take the land. ¹⁰When you get there, you will come to a secure people. The land is wide open to you. God will hand it over to you. It's a place where you will have everything you could want."

¹¹So 600 men from the tribe of Dan left Zorah and Eshtaol armed for war. ¹²They camped at Kiriath Jearim in Judah. This is why the place just west of Kiriath Jearim is still called Mahaneh Dan [The Camp of Dan] today. ¹³From there they marched to the mountains of Ephraim as far as Micah's house. ¹⁴Then the five men who had gone to spy throughout the land around Laish spoke up. They said to the other men of Dan, "Do you know that there's an ephod, a carved idol, a metal idol, and household idols in these houses? What do you think we should do?"

¹⁵So they stopped and entered Micah's house and greeted the young Levite. ¹⁶The 600 armed men from Dan stood at the entrance to the city. ¹⁷The five men who had gone to spy throughout the land went inside. They took the carved idol, the ephod, the household idols, and the metal idol. The priest stood at the entrance to the city with the 600 armed men. ¹⁸When these men entered Micah's house and took the carved idol, the ephod, the household idols, and the metal idol, the priest asked them, "What are you doing?"

¹⁹They told him, "Keep quiet! Don't say a word! Come with us and be our father and priest. Is it better for you to be a priest for one man's house or for a tribe in Israel and its families?"

²⁰The priest was content. He took the ephod, the household idols, and the carved idol and went with the people. ²¹When they left, they put their children, livestock, and property in front of them.

²²When they had already gone some distance from Micah's house, Micah's neighbors were called together to help him catch up to the people of Dan. ²³They shouted at them. But the people of Dan turned around and said to Micah, "What's your problem? Why did you call your neighbors together to attack us?"

²⁴Micah answered, "You've taken away the gods I made as well as my priest. What do I have left? How can you say to me, 'What's your problem?' "

²⁵The people of Dan replied, "Don't make another sound, or some violent men will attack you. Then you and your family will lose your lives." ²⁶The people of Dan went on their way. Micah saw they were stronger than he was, so he turned around and went home.

²⁷The people of Dan took what Micah had made and the man who had become his priest and went to the city of Laish. They attacked a peaceful and secure people, killed them all with swords, and burned their city. ²⁸There was no one to rescue them because their city was far from Sidon and totally independent. The city was in the valley that belonged to Beth Rehob. The people of Dan rebuilt the city and lived in it. ²⁹They named the city Dan in honor of their ancestor Dan, Israel's son. Originally, the city was called Laish.

³⁰The people of Dan set up the carved idol for themselves. Jonathan (son of Gershom and grandson of Moses) and his descendants were priests for Dan's tribe until the people living in that land were taken captive. ³¹So they set up for themselves the carved idol Micah had made. It stayed there the whole time the house of God was at Shiloh.

Sexual Immorality

¹In those days when Israel didn't have a king, there was a Levite who lived in a remote area in the mountains of Ephraim. He took a woman from Bethlehem in Judah to be his concubine.ᵃ ²But she was unfaithful to him. She left him and went to her father's home, to Bethlehem in Judah. When she had been there four months, ³her husband went to persuade her to come back home. He took along his servant and two donkeys.

She took her husband into her father's house. Her father was thrilled to see him. ⁴He made the Levite stay there with him, celebrating for three days.

⁵On the fourth day they got up early in the morning to leave, but the woman's father told his son-in-law, "Eat something to keep up your strength and then you can go." ⁶So they both sat down and ate and drank together. The woman's father said to his son-in-law, "Why don't you spend the night and enjoy yourself?" ⁷When the Levite started to leave, his father-in-law urged him to stay another night, so he did.

⁸On the morning of the fifth day, the Levite got up early to leave. The woman's father said, "Eat something to keep up your strength!" So they spent the time eating until late afternoon. ⁹The Levite started to leave with his concubine and his servant. But his father-in-law said to him, "It's already evening. Please stay another night. It's too late to leave now. Stay here, and enjoy yourself. Tomorrow you can start out early to go home." ¹⁰But the Levite refused to spend another night.

He left and traveled as far as Jebus (now called Jerusalem). He had with him two saddled donkeys and his concubine. ¹¹By the time they were near Jebus, it was very late in the day. The Levite's servant said to him, "Let's go spend the night in Jebus." ¹²The Levite told him, "We'll never go into a city of foreigners. They're not Israelites. We'll go on to Gibeah." ¹³He told his servant, "Let's go someplace else. We'll spend the night either at Gibeah or Ramah."

¹⁴So they went on. It was sunset by the time they arrived at Gibeah. (Gibeah belonged to the tribe of Benjamin.) ¹⁵They went to spend the night there. The Levite entered Gibeah and sat down in the city square, because no one offered to take them home for the night.

¹⁶That evening an old man came into the city from his work in the fields. He was

---

ᵃ 19:1 A concubine is considered a wife except she has fewer rights under the law.

from the mountain region of Ephraim but lived in Gibeah. The other people who lived there were from the tribe of Benjamin. ¹⁷He saw the traveler in the city square. So the old man asked, "Where do you come from? And where are you going?"

¹⁸The Levite replied, "We're on our way from Bethlehem in Judah to a remote area in the mountains of Ephraim. That's where I'm from. I had gone to Bethlehem in Judah. Now I'm going to the LORD's house, but no one has offered to take me into his home. ¹⁹We have straw and fodder for our donkeys. I even have bread and wine for myself, the woman, and my servant. We have everything we need."

²⁰Then the old man said, "Welcome! Let me take care of your needs. Just don't spend the night in the city square." ²¹So he took the Levite to his house and fed the donkeys. After they washed, they ate and drank.

²²While they were enjoying themselves, some worthless men from the city surrounded the house and pounded on the door. They told the old man, the owner of the house, "Bring out the man who came to your house so that we can have sex with him."

²³The owner went out to them. He told them, "No, my friends! Please don't do anything so evil! This man is a guest in my home. Don't do such a godless thing! ²⁴Here, let me bring out my virgin daughter and this man's concubine. Rape them, and do with them whatever you want. Just don't do such a godless thing to this man."

²⁵But the men refused to listen to him. So the Levite grabbed his concubine and forced her outside. They had sex with her and abused her all night until morning. They let her go when the sun was coming up. ²⁶At daybreak, the woman came to the door of the house where her husband was and collapsed. She was still there when it became light.

²⁷Her husband got up in the morning, opened the doors of the house, and was about to leave. His wife (that is, his concubine) was lying at the door of the house with her hands on the doorstep. ²⁸The Levite said to her, "Get up! Let's go!" But she did not answer. So he put her on the donkey and left for home.

²⁹When he arrived home, he got a knife. He took his concubine and cut her limb from limb into 12 pieces. Then he sent the pieces throughout the territories of Israel. ³⁰Everyone who saw it said, "Never has such a thing happened or been seen from the time the people of Israel came out of Egypt until today. Think about it! Form a plan, and speak out!"

Israel Slaughters the Tribe of Benjamin

20 ¹All the people of Israel from Dan to Beersheba and from Gilead came to Mizpah. The congregation stood united in the presence of the LORD. ²The leaders of all Israel's tribes took their places in the congregation of God's people. There were 400,000 foot soldiers with swords. ³The people of Benjamin heard that Israel had come to Mizpah.

The people of Israel said, "Tell us how such an evil thing could happen."

⁴The Levite, the husband of the murdered woman, answered, "My concubine *ᵃ* and I went to Gibeah in Benjamin to spend the night. ⁵The citizens of Gibeah came to attack me. They surrounded the house where I was staying that night. They intended to kill me, but instead, they raped my concubine until she died. ⁶So I took my concubine and cut her into pieces. Then I sent the pieces throughout the territory of Israel. I did this because the citizens of Gibeah did this perverted and godless thing in Israel. ⁷All you people of Israel, tell me what you think. Give me your advice right now!"

⁸All the people stood united, saying, "None of us will go to his tent or return to

---

ᵃ20:4 A concubine is considered a wife except she has fewer rights under the law.

his house. ⁹This is what we'll do to Gibeah. We'll decide by lot who should attack it.ᵇ ¹⁰We'll take one-tenthᶜ of all the men from the tribes of Israel to get supplies for the troops. When the troops go to Gibeah in the territory of Benjamin they can punish the citizens of Gibeah for the godless thing they did in Israel." ¹¹So all the men of Israel assembled. They stood united against the city.

¹²The tribes of Israel sent men throughout the tribe of Benjamin. They asked, "How could such an evil thing happen among you? ¹³Now hand over those worthless men in Gibeah. We must put them to death to rid ourselves of this kind of evil in Israel."

But the men of Benjamin refused to listen to the men of Israel. ¹⁴So the men of Benjamin went from their towns and assembled at Gibeah to go to war with the men of Israel. ¹⁵That day 26,000 men armed with swords came from Benjamin's cities and organized for battle along with 700 of Gibeah's best men. ¹⁶Out of all these troops, the best 700 were left-handed. Each could sling a stone at a hair and not miss.

¹⁷The men of Israel (Benjamin not included) totaled 400,000 soldiers armed with swords.

¹⁸The men of Israel went to Bethel. They asked God, "Who will go first to fight Benjamin?"

The Lord answered, "Judah will go first."

¹⁹The Israelites got up early in the morning and camped at Gibeah. ²⁰So the men of Israel went to war with the men of Benjamin. The Israelites formed their battle line facing Gibeah. ²¹That day the men of Benjamin came out from Gibeah. They slaughtered 22,000 of Israel's men.

²²But Israel's troops got reinforcements. They formed their battle line where they had formed it on the first day. ²³The Israelites went and cried in the presence of the Lord until evening. They asked the Lord, "Should we continue to wage war against our close relatives, the men of Benjamin?"

The Lord answered, "Go fight them!"

²⁴On the second day the Israelite troops advanced against Benjamin. ²⁵Benjamin went out from Gibeah to meet them. This time they slaughtered 18,000 men from Israel who were armed with swords. ²⁶Then all the men of Israel and all the troops went to Bethel. They sat there and cried in the presence of the Lord and fasted that day until evening. Then they sacrificed burnt offerings and fellowship offerings to the Lord.

²⁷In those days the ark of God's promise was at Bethel. ²⁸(Phinehas, son of Eleazar and grandson of Aaron, served in front of it.) So the people of Israel asked the Lord, "Should we continue to wage war against our close relatives, the men of Benjamin? Or should we stop?"

The Lord answered, "Go! Tomorrow I will hand them over to you."

²⁹Then Israel placed troops in ambush around Gibeah. ³⁰On the third day the men of Israel went to fight the men of Benjamin. They formed their battle line facing Gibeah as they did before. ³¹The men of Benjamin went out to attack Israel's troops and were led away from the city. They started to inflict casualties as before. They killed about 30 men from Israel in the open country and on the roads to Bethel and Gibeah. ³²The men of Benjamin shouted, "They're defeated as before!"

But the men of Israel had said, "Let's flee in order to lead them from the city to the roads." ³³So the men of Israel left their positions. They formed their battle line at Baal Tamar. Meanwhile, those waiting in ambush rushed from their position to the west of Gibeah. ³⁴Then 10,000 of Israel's best men attacked Gibeah. The battle was

---

ᵇ20:9 Hebrew meaning uncertain.   ᶜ20:10 Or "10 out of every battalion, 100 out of every regiment, and 1,000 out of every company."

fierce. But Benjamin's men didn't realize their own evil was about to overtake them. [35]So the LORD defeated them in front of Israel. On that day the Israelites slaughtered 25,100 men from Benjamin who were armed with swords. [36]Then the men of Benjamin realized they were defeated.

The Israelites had allowed the men of Benjamin to take back some ground. The Israelites relied on those waiting in ambush near Gibeah. [37]The men in ambush quickly charged toward Gibeah. They spread out in the city and killed everyone. [38]The men of Israel had arranged with those waiting in ambush that they would make a big column of smoke rise from the city as a signal. [39]Then the men of Israel would turn around in the battle.

The men of Benjamin had already killed about 30 men of Israel. They even said, "Israel is completely defeated, just like in the first battle."

[40]But when the column of smoke started to rise from the city, the men of Benjamin turned around and saw the whole city going up in smoke. [41]Then the men of Israel turned around, and the men of Benjamin panicked. They realized that their evil had overtaken them. [42]They turned in front of Israel toward the road to the desert. But the battle caught up with the men of Benjamin. Israel slaughtered whoever came out of the cities on the road to the desert. [43]They closed in on the men of Benjamin and pursued them without stopping. They overtook them east of Gibeah. [44]There were 18,000 experienced men from Benjamin who died in battle. [45]The others turned and fled into the desert to Rimmon Rock. But the men of Israel killed 5,000 more on the roads. They caught up with another 2,000 and killed them near Gidom. [46]In all, 25,000 men from Benjamin who were armed with swords were killed that day. They were all experienced men.

[47]But 600 men turned and fled into the desert to Rimmon Rock. They stayed at Rimmon Rock for four months.

[48]Then the men of Israel went back to attack the rest of the territory of Benjamin. They killed all the people and cattle they found in every city. They also burned down every city they came to.

Israel Provides Wives for the Surviving Men of Benjamin

21 [1]The men of Israel had taken this oath in Mizpah: "None of us will ever let our daughters marry anyone from Benjamin."

[2]The people went to Bethel and sat there in the presence of God until evening. They cried very loudly, [3]"LORD God of Israel, why has this happened among us? Why should one tribe be missing today in Israel?"

[4]The next day the people got up early. They built an altar there and sacrificed burnt offerings and fellowship offerings. [5]The people asked, "Is there any family from Israel that did not take part in the assembly in the presence of the LORD?" They had taken a solemn oath that whoever had not come into the presence of the LORD at Mizpah must be put to death.

[6]The people of Israel felt sorry for their close relatives, the men of Benjamin. They said, "Today one tribe has been excluded from Israel. [7]What will we do to provide wives for the men who are left? We swore to the LORD that we would not let any of our daughters marry them." [8]Then they asked, "Is there any family from Israel that did not come into the presence of the LORD at Mizpah?" No one from Jabesh Gilead had come to the assembly in the camp. [9]So they questioned the people, and there was no one there from Jabesh Gilead.

[10]The congregation sent 12,000 soldiers. They ordered them, "Go and kill the people of Jabesh Gilead, including the women and children. [11]These are your

directions: Claim every female who has gone to bed with a man, and claim every male. Claim them for the LORD by destroying them."

¹²Among the people of Jabesh Gilead they found 400 unmarried women who had never gone to bed with a man. They brought them to the camp at Shiloh in Canaan.

¹³Then the whole congregation sent messengers to the men of Benjamin at Rimmon Rock and offered them peace. ¹⁴So the men of Benjamin came back at that time. These men were given the women from Jabesh Gilead who had been kept alive. However, the congregation had not found enough women for all of them.

¹⁵The congregation felt sorry for the people of Benjamin because the LORD had broken the unity of the tribes of Israel. ¹⁶The leaders of the congregation asked, "What should we do to provide wives for the men who are left, since the women in Benjamin have been killed?"

¹⁷Some said, "Benjamin's men who survived must be allowed to have families. No tribe of Israel should be wiped out. ¹⁸However, we can't give them any of our daughters as wives. The people of Israel have taken an oath that whoever gives wives to the men of Benjamin is under a curse."

¹⁹Others said, "Every year the LORD's festival is held at Shiloh. Shiloh is north of Bethel, east of the highway going from Bethel to Shechem, and south of Lebonah." ²⁰So they told the men of Benjamin, "Hide in the vineyards and ²¹watch. When the young women of Shiloh come out to take part in the dances, come out of the vineyards. Each of you catch a woman from Shiloh to be your wife. Then go back to the territory of Benjamin. ²²When their fathers or brothers come to us to complain, we'll tell them, 'Have pity on them, since we didn't provide a wife for each man in the battle. You won't be guilty because you didn't give them the wives yourselves.' "

²³The men of Benjamin did just that. They captured the number of wives they needed from the women who were dancing and went home. So they rebuilt their cities and lived in them.

²⁴At that time the people of Israel left. Each man went to his tribe and family. They all went home.

²⁵In those days Israel didn't have a king. Everyone did whatever he considered right.

Ruth

When her husband died, a young Moabite woman named Ruth chose to travel to Israel with her Jewish mother-in-law, Naomi. Ruth trusted the God of her mother-in-law as the true God. Ruth took care of Naomi and attracted the attention of a good and kind man named Boaz.

Ruth saw Boaz watching her take grain from his field. Would he be kind or mean? See Ruth 2.

What's In It For Me?

Ruth's life teaches . . .

TRUE FRIENDS ARE LOYAL.

GOD ACCEPTS ANYONE WHO TRUSTS HIM.

HARD WORK LEADS TO A GOOD REPUTATION.

GOD USES PEOPLE TO BRING GOOD TO OTHERS.

GOD MAKES GOOD COME OUT OF BAD.

FAMILIES ARE IMPORTANT TO GOD.

Headlines

Love That Mother-in-Law!
Ruth 1, page 336

Work Ethic Attracts Boaz
Ruth 2, page 337

Sandal Seals Wedding Contract
Ruth 4, page 339

Great-Grandmother to a King
Ruth 4, page 339

Ruth

The Move to Moab and Tragedy

1 ¹In the days when the judges were ruling, there was a famine in the land. A man from Bethlehem in Judah went with his wife and two sons to live for a while in the country of Moab. ²The man's name was Elimelech, his wife's name was Naomi, and the names of their two sons were Mahlon and Chilion. They were descendants of Ephrathah from Bethlehem in the territory of Judah. They went to the country of Moab and lived there.

³Now, Naomi's husband Elimelech died, and she was left alone with her two sons. ⁴Each son married a woman from Moab. One son married a woman named Orpah, and the other son married a woman named Ruth. They lived there for about ten years. ⁵Then both Mahlon and Chilion died as well. So Naomi was left alone, without her two sons or her husband.

Departure From Moab

⁶Naomi and her daughters-in-law started on the way back from the country of Moab. (While they were still in Moab she heard that the Lord had come to help his people and give them food. ⁷So she left the place where she had been living, and her two daughters-in-law went with her.) They began to walk back along the road to the territory of Judah.

Naomi's Appeal to Her Daughters-in-law

⁸Then Naomi said to her two daughters-in-law, "Go back! Each of you should go back to your mother's home. May the Lord be as kind to you as you were to me and to our loved ones who have died. ⁹May the Lord repay each of you so that you may find security in a home with a husband."

When she kissed them goodbye, they began to cry loudly. ¹⁰They said to her, "We are going back with you to your people."

¹¹But Naomi said, "Go back, my daughters. Why should you go with me? Do I have any more sons in my womb who could be your husbands? ¹²Go back, my daughters. Go, because I am too old to get married again. If I said that I still have hope. . . . And if I had a husband tonight. . . . And even if I gave birth to sons, ¹³would you wait until they grew up and stay single just for them? No, my daughters. My bitterness is much worse than yours because the Lord has sent me so much trouble."

¹⁴They began to cry loudly again. Then Orpah kissed her mother-in-law goodbye, but Ruth held on to her tightly. ¹⁵Naomi said, "Look, your sister-in-law has gone back to her people and to her gods. Go back with your sister-in-law."

¹⁶But Ruth answered, "Don't force me to leave you. Don't make me turn back from following you. Wherever you go, I will go, and wherever you stay, I will stay. Your people will be my people, and your God will be my God. ¹⁷Wherever you die, I will die, and I will be buried there with you. May the Lord strike me down if anything but death separates you and me!"

¹⁸When Naomi saw that Ruth was determined to go with her, she ended the conversation.

Naomi Arrives in Bethlehem

¹⁹So both of them went on until they came to Bethlehem. When they entered Bethlehem, the whole town was excited about them. "This can't be Naomi, can it?" the women asked.

²⁰She answered them, "Don't call me Naomi [Sweet]. Call me Mara [Bitter] because the Almighty has made my life very bitter. ²¹I went away full, but the Lord has brought me back empty. Why do you call me Naomi when the Lord has tormented me and the Almighty has done evil to me?"

²²When Naomi came back from the country of Moab, Ruth, her Moabite daughter-in-law, came along with her. They happened to enter Bethlehem just when the barley harvest began.

Ruth Gathers Grain in the Field of Boaz

2 ¹Naomi had a relative. He was from Elimelech's side of the family. He was a man of outstanding character named Boaz.

²Ruth, who was from Moab, said to Naomi, "Please let me go to the field of anyone who will be kind to me. There I will gather the grain left behind by the reapers."

Naomi told her, "Go, my daughter."

³So Ruth went. She entered a field and gathered the grain left behind by the reapers. Now it happened that she ended up in the part of the field that belonged to Boaz, who was from Elimelech's family.

⁴Just then, Boaz was coming from Bethlehem, and he said to his reapers, "May the Lord be with all of you!"

They answered him, "May the Lord bless you!"

⁵Boaz asked the young man in charge of his reapers, "Who is this young woman?"

⁶The young man answered, "She's a young Moabite woman who came back with Naomi from the country of Moab. ⁷She said, 'Please let me gather grain. I will only gather among the bundles behind the reapers.' So she came here and has been on her feet from daybreak until now. She just sat down this minute in the shelter."

Boaz Speaks With Ruth

⁸Boaz said to Ruth, "Listen, my daughter. Don't go in any other field to gather grain, and don't even leave this one. Stay here with my young women. ⁹Watch where my men are reaping, and follow the young women in that field. I have ordered my young men not to touch you. When you're thirsty, go to the jars and drink some of the water that the young men have drawn."

¹⁰Ruth immediately bowed down to the ground and said to him, "Why are you so helpful? Why are you paying attention to me? I'm only a foreigner."

¹¹Boaz answered her, "People have told me about everything you have done for your mother-in-law after your husband died. They told me how you left your father and mother and the country where you were born. They also told me how you came to people that you didn't know before. ¹²May the Lord reward you for what you have done! May you receive a rich reward from the Lord God of Israel, under whose protection you have come for shelter."

¹³Ruth replied, "Sir, may your kindness to me continue. You have comforted me and reassured me, and I'm not even one of your own servants."

¹⁴When it was time to eat, Boaz told her, "Come here. Have some bread, and dip it into the sour wine." So she sat beside the reapers, and he handed her some roasted grain. She ate all she wanted and had some left over.

¹⁵When she got up to gather grain, Boaz ordered his servants, "Let her gather grain

even among the bundles. Don't give her any problems. [16]Even pull some grain out of the bundles and leave it for her to gather. Don't give her a hard time about it."

Ruth and Naomi Talk About Boaz

[17]So Ruth gathered grain in the field until evening. Then she separated the grain from its husks. She had about half a bushel of barley. [18]She picked it up and went into the town, and her mother-in-law saw what she had gathered. Ruth also took out what she had left over from lunch and gave it to Naomi.

[19]Her mother-in-law asked her, "Where did you gather grain today? Just where did you work? May the man who paid attention to you be blessed."

So Ruth told her mother-in-law about the person with whom she worked. She said, "The man I worked with today is named Boaz."

[20]Naomi said to her daughter-in-law, "May the LORD bless him. The LORD hasn't stopped being kind to people—living or dead." Then Naomi told her, "That man is a relative of ours. He is a close relative, one of those responsible for taking care of us."

[21]Ruth, who was from Moab, told her, "He also said to me, 'Stay with my younger workers until they have finished the harvest.' "

[22]Naomi told her daughter-in-law Ruth, "It's a good idea, my daughter, that you go out to the fields with his young women. If you go to someone else's field, you may be molested."

[23]So Ruth stayed with the young women who were working for Boaz. She gathered grain until both the barley harvest and the wheat harvest ended. And she continued to live with her mother-in-law.

Naomi's Plan for Ruth's Marriage

[1]Naomi, Ruth's mother-in-law, said to her, "My daughter, shouldn't I try to look for a home that would be good for you? [2]Isn't Boaz, whose young women you've been working with, our relative? He will be separating the barley from its husks on the threshing floor[a] tonight. [3]Freshen up, put on some perfume, dress up, and go down to the threshing floor. Don't let him know that you're there until he's finished eating and drinking. [4]When he lies down, notice the place where he is lying. Then uncover his feet, and lie down there. He will make it clear what you must do."

[5]Ruth answered her, "I will do whatever you say."

Ruth at the Feet of Boaz

[6]Ruth went to the threshing floor and did exactly as her mother-in-law had directed her. [7]Boaz had eaten and drunk to his heart's content, so he went and lay at the edge of a pile of grain. Then she went over to him secretly, uncovered his feet, and lay down.

[8]At midnight the man was shivering. When he turned over, he was surprised to see a woman lying at his feet. [9]"Who are you?" he asked.

She answered, "I am Ruth. Spread the corner of your garment over me because you are a close relative who can take care of me."

[10]Boaz replied, "May the LORD bless you, my daughter. This last kindness—that you didn't go after the younger men, whether rich or poor—is better than the first. [11]Don't be afraid, my daughter. I will do whatever you say. The whole town knows that you are a woman who has strength of character. [12]It is true that I am a close relative of yours, but there is a relative closer than I. [13]Stay here tonight. In the morning

---

[a]3:2 A threshing floor is an outdoor area where grain is separated from its husks.

if he will agree to take care of you, that is good. He can take care of you. But if he does not wish to take care of you, then, I solemnly swear, as the LORD lives, I will take care of you myself. Lie down until morning."

Ruth Returns to Bethlehem

¹⁴So Ruth lay at his feet until morning. Then she got up early before anyone could be recognized. At that moment Boaz thought to himself, "I hope that no one will ever know that this woman came to the threshing floor."

¹⁵Then Boaz told Ruth, "Stretch out the cape you're wearing and hold it tight." So she held it tight while he measured out six measures of barley. Then he placed it on her back, and went into the town.

¹⁶When Ruth returned, her mother-in-law Naomi asked, "How did things go, my daughter?"

Ruth told Naomi everything the man had done for her. ¹⁷She said, "He gave me these six measures of barley and told me not to come back to you empty-handed."

¹⁸Naomi replied, "Stay here, my daughter, until you know how it turns out. The man won't rest unless he settles this matter today."

Boaz Assumes Responsibility for Ruth

¹Boaz went to the city gate and sat there. Just then, the relative about whom he had spoken was passing by. Boaz said, "Please come over here and sit, my friend." So the man came over and sat down.

²Then Boaz chose ten men who were leaders of that city and said, "Sit here." So they also sat down.

³Boaz said to the man, "Naomi, who has come back from the country of Moab, is selling the field that belonged to our relative Elimelech. ⁴So I said that I would inform you. Buy it in the presence of these men sitting here and in the presence of the leaders of our people. If you wish to buy back the property, you can buy back the property. But if you do not wish to buy back the property, tell me. Then I will know that I am next in line because there is no other relative except me."

The man said, "I'll buy back the property."

⁵Boaz continued, "When you buy the field from Naomi, you will also assume responsibility for the Moabite Ruth, the dead man's widow. This keeps the inheritance in the dead man's name."

⁶The man replied, "In that case I cannot assume responsibility for her. If I did, I would ruin my inheritance. Take all my rights to buy back the property for yourself, because I cannot assume that responsibility."

⁷(This is the way it used to be in Israel concerning buying back property and exchanging goods: In order to make every matter legal, a man would take off his sandal and give it to the other man. This was the way a contract was publicly approved in Israel.) ⁸So when the man said to Boaz, "Buy it for yourself," he took off his sandal.

⁹Then Boaz said to the leaders and to all the people, "Today you are witnesses that I have bought from Naomi all that belonged to Elimelech and all that belonged to Chilion and Mahlon. ¹⁰In addition, I have bought as my wife the Moabite Ruth, Mahlon's widow, to keep the inheritance in the dead man's name. In this way the dead man's name will not be cut off from his relatives or from the public records. Today you are witnesses."

¹¹All the people who were at the gate, including the leaders, said, "We are witnesses. May the LORD make this wife, who is coming into your home, like Rachel and Leah, both of whom built our family of Israel. So show your strength of character in

Ephrathah and make a name for yourself in Bethlehem. ¹²Also, from the descendant whom the LORD will give you from this young woman, may your family become like the family of Perez, the son whom Tamar gave birth to for Judah."

Ruth Gives Birth to David's Ancestor

¹³Then Boaz took Ruth home, and she became his wife. He slept with her, and the LORD gave her the ability to become pregnant. So she gave birth to a son.

¹⁴The women said to Naomi, "Praise the LORD, who has remembered today to give you someone who will take care of you. The child's name will be famous in Israel. ¹⁵He will bring you a new life and support you in your old age. Your daughter-in-law who loves you is better to you than seven sons, because she has given birth."

¹⁶Naomi took the child, held him on her lap, and became his guardian.

¹⁷The women in the neighborhood said, "Naomi has a son." So they gave him the name Obed.

He became the father of Jesse, who was the father of David.

The Ancestry of David

¹⁸This is the account of Perez and his family.
   Perez was the father of Hezron.
¹⁹   **Hezron** was the father of Ram.
   Ram was the father of Amminadab.
²⁰   **Amminadab** was the father of Nahshon.
   Nahshon was the father of Salmon.
²¹   **Salmon** was the father of Boaz.
   Boaz was the father of Obed.
²²   **Obed** was the father of Jesse.
   Jesse was the father of **David**.

1 Samuel

This adventure book begins with the story of Israel's last judge, Samuel. During Samuel's time as judge, the people decided they wanted to be like other nations and have a king. God chose Saul to be king, but Saul disobeyed God. So God sent Samuel on a secret mission to select the next king—a boy named David.

David became famous when he killed a giant, and Saul even made David a commander in the army. But later Saul became jealous of David. As David ran from King Saul, David continued to trust God for protection.

Headlines

Michal helped her husband escape. Who wanted to kill David? See 1 Samuel 19.

Better Than Getting Even

Did you ever feel like getting even? David did. When a man whose flocks he protected insulted him, David was ready to kill! It took a wise woman, Abigail, to set David straight.

Abigail reminded David that taking revenge is wrong. She told David revenge would cause him trouble in the future. David listened to Abigail and thanked her. After Abigail's husband died, David asked Abigail to marry him. David appreciated having a brave and wise wife who could give him good advice.

What's In It For Me?

A leader worth following . . .

DOES WHAT IS RIGHT IN GOD'S EYES.

SHOWS RESPECT FOR OTHERS.

TREATS FOLLOWERS WITH KINDNESS.

PROTECTS THE HELPLESS.

LISTENS TO GOOD ADVICE.

LOOKS TO THE LORD FOR WISDOM.

Which King Would You Crown?

Check out Saul on the left and David on the right. Which one looks like he'd make the better king?

Remember the Bible stories in this book. Put an X by the things that made Saul a poor king. Circle the things that made David a great king.

Tall and strong	Shorter and younger
Great warrior	Great warrior
Doubted himself	Trusted in God's strength
Acted in fear and anger	Looked to God for direction
Jealous and cruel	Kind and respectful
Disobeyed God	Obeyed God
Rejected by God	Special to God
A DISAPPOINTING KING	**ISRAEL'S GREATEST KING**

1 Samuel

Samuel's Birth

1 ¹There was a man named Elkanah from Ramathaim Zophim in the mountains of Ephraim. He was the son of Jeroham, grandson of Elihu, great-grandson of Tohu, whose father was Zuph from the tribe of Ephraim. ²Elkanah had two wives, one named Hannah, the other Peninnah. Peninnah had children, but Hannah had none. ³Every year this man would go from his own city to worship and sacrifice to the Lord of Armies at Shiloh. Eli's two sons, Hophni and Phinehas, served there as priests of the Lord.

⁴Whenever Elkanah offered a sacrifice, he would give portions of it to his wife Peninnah and all her sons and daughters. ⁵He would also give one portion to Hannah because he loved her, even though the Lord had kept her from having children. ⁶Because the Lord had made her unable to have children, her rival Peninnah tormented her endlessly in order to make her miserable. ⁷This happened year after year. Whenever Hannah went to the Lord's house, Peninnah would make her miserable, and Hannah would cry and not eat. ⁸Her husband Elkanah would ask her, "Hannah, why are you crying? Why haven't you eaten? Why are you so downhearted? Don't I mean more to you than ten sons?"

⁹One day, after Hannah had something to eat and drink in Shiloh, she got up. (The priest Eli was sitting on a chair by the door of the Lord's temple.) ¹⁰Though she was resentful, she prayed to the Lord while she cried. ¹¹She made this vow, "Lord of Armies, if you will look at my misery, remember me, and give me a boy, then I will give him to you for as long as he lives. A razor will never be used on his head." ¹²While Hannah was praying a long time in front of the Lord, Eli was watching her mouth. ¹³She was praying silently. Her voice couldn't be heard; only her lips were moving. Eli thought she was drunk.

¹⁴"How long are you going to stay drunk?" Eli asked her. "Get rid of your wine."

¹⁵Hannah responded, "No, sir. I'm not drunk. I'm depressed. I'm pouring out my heart to the Lord. ¹⁶Don't take me to be a good-for-nothing woman. I was praying like this because I've been troubled and tormented."

¹⁷Eli replied, "Go in peace, and may the God of Israel grant your request."

¹⁸"May you continue to be kind to me," she said. Then the woman went her way and ate. She was no longer sad.[a]

¹⁹Early in the morning Elkanah and his family got up and worshiped in front of the Lord. Then they returned home to Ramah. Elkanah made love to his wife Hannah, and the Lord remembered her. ²⁰Hannah became pregnant and gave birth to a son. She named him Samuel [God Hears], because she said, "I asked the Lord for him."

Samuel's Childhood

²¹To keep his vow, Elkanah and his entire household again went to offer the annual sacrifice to the Lord. ²²But Hannah didn't go. She told her husband, "I'll wait until the boy is weaned. Then I'll bring him and present him to the Lord, and he'll stay there permanently."

²³"Do what you think is best," her husband Elkanah told her. "Wait until you've weaned him. May the Lord keep his word." The woman stayed and nursed her son until she had weaned him.

---

a 1:18 English equivalent difficult.

Hannah

God answered Hannah's prayer and gave her a son.

Hannah's husband, Elkanah, loved her. But Hannah was often sad because her husband's other wife, Peninnah, had many children and always made fun of Hannah, who had no children. Hannah cried and prayed to God, but her misery went on for many years.

One day Hannah went to the temple where she cried and prayed. Hannah's lips moved as she prayed silently. Eli the priest saw Hannah and accused her of being drunk. But Hannah said she was just very sad and was pouring out her heart to the Lord. Eli then told her that God would answer her prayer.

Hannah was born around 1095 B.C.

Hannah means "grace."

Hannah prayed to God when she was depressed, and God answered her prayer.

Hannah was the mother of Samuel, Israel's last judge.

Hannah prays for a son.

Hannah had promised God that if he would give her a son, she would dedicate him to God's work. Soon after that, Hannah became pregnant and had a son.

Getting to Know Hannah

* How did Hannah show her thanks to God for giving her a son?
* What have you prayed for that God hasn't seemed to answer?
* How have you thanked God for answering your prayers?

Peninnah tormented Hannah by constantly teasing her.

²⁴As soon as she had weaned Samuel, she took him with her. She also brought a three-year-old bull,[b] half a bushel of flour, and a full wineskin. She brought him to the Lord's house at Shiloh while the boy was still a child.

²⁵Then the parents butchered the bull and brought the child to Eli. ²⁶"Sir," Hannah said, "as sure as you live, I'm the woman who stood here next to you and prayed to the Lord. ²⁷I prayed for this child, and the Lord granted my request. ²⁸In return, I am giving him to the Lord. He will be dedicated to the Lord for his whole life."

And they worshiped the Lord there.

Hannah's Prayer

2 ¹Hannah prayed out loud,

"My heart finds joy in the Lord.
My head is lifted to the Lord.
My mouth mocks my enemies.
    I rejoice because you saved me.
² There is no one holy like the Lord.
There is no one but you, O Lord.
There is no Rock like our God.

³ "Do not boast
    or let arrogance come out of your mouth
      because the Lord is a God of knowledge,
      and he weighs our actions.

⁴ "The bows of the warriors are broken,
    but those who stumble are armed with strength.
⁵ Those who were well-fed hire themselves out for a piece of bread,
    but those who were hungry hunger no more.
Even the woman who was childless gives birth to seven children,
    but the mother of many children grieves all alone.

⁶ "The Lord kills, and he gives life.
He makes people go down to the grave, and he raises them up again.
⁷ The Lord causes poverty and grants wealth.
He humbles people; he also promotes them.
⁸ He raises the poor from the dust.
He lifts the needy from the trash heap
    in order to make them sit with nobles
    and even to make them inherit a glorious throne.

"The pillars of the earth are the Lord's.
He has set the world on them.
⁹ He safeguards the steps of his faithful ones,
    but wicked people are silenced in darkness
    because humans cannot succeed by their own strength.

¹⁰ "Those who oppose the Lord are broken into pieces.
He thunders at them from the heavens.
The Lord judges the ends of the earth.
He gives strength to his King
    and lifts the head of his Messiah."[a]

---

[b] 1:24 Dead Sea Scrolls, Greek, Latin, Syriac; Masoretic Text "three bulls." (See verse 25.)   [a] 2:10 Or "Anointed One."

¹¹Then Elkanah went home to Ramah. But the boy ⌊Samuel⌋ served the LORD under the priest Eli.

The Sins of Eli's Sons

¹²Eli's sons, ⌊Hophni and Phinehas,⌋ were good-for-nothing priests; they had no faith in the LORD. ¹³Now, this was how the priests dealt with the people who were offering sacrifices: While the meat was boiling, the priest's servant would come with a three-pronged fork in his hand. ¹⁴Then he would stick it into the pot, kettle, cauldron, or pan. Whatever the fork brought up ⌊from the pot⌋ belonged to the priest. This is what the priests did in Shiloh to all the people of Israel who came there ⌊to sacrifice⌋. ¹⁵But ⌊in the case of Eli's sons,⌋ even before the people burned the fat, their servants would come and say to the man who was sacrificing, "Give the meat to the priest to roast. He doesn't want boiled meat from you. He wants it raw."

¹⁶If the man said to the servant, "First let the fat be burned, then take as much as you want," the servant would say to him, "Give it to me now, or I'll take it by force." ¹⁷The sin of Eli's sons was a serious matter to the LORD, because these men were treating the offerings made to the LORD with contempt.

The Faithfulness of Samuel's Family

¹⁸Meanwhile, Samuel continued to serve in front of the LORD. As a boy he was ⌊already⌋ wearing a linen ephod.ᵇ ¹⁹His mother would make him a robe and bring it to him every year when she went with her husband to offer the annual sacrifice.

²⁰Eli would bless Elkanah (and his wife) and say, "May the Lord give you children from this woman in place of the one which she has given to the Lord." Then they would go home.

²¹The Lord came to Hannah. She became pregnant ⌊five times⌋ and had three sons and two daughters. Meanwhile, the boy Samuel grew up in front of the Lord.

Eli's Family Condemned

²²Now, Eli was very old, and he had heard everything that his sons were doing to all Israel and that they were sleeping with the women who served at the gate of the tent of meeting. ²³So he asked them, "Why are you doing such things? I hear about your wicked ways from all these people. ²⁴Sons, the report that I hear the people of the LORD spreading isn't good! ²⁵If one person sins against another, God will take care of him. However, when a person sins against the LORD, who will pray for him?" But they wouldn't listen to their father's warning—the LORD wanted to kill them.

²⁶The boy Samuel continued to grow and gained the favor of the LORD and the people.

²⁷Then a man of God came to Eli and said to him, "This is what the LORD says: I revealed myself to your ancestors when they were under Pharaoh's control in Egypt. ²⁸I chose ⌊one of your ancestors⌋ out of all the tribes of Israel to serve as my priest, to sacrifice burnt offerings on my altar, to burn incense, and to wear the ephod in my presence. And I gave your ancestors the right to keep portions of the sacrifices that the people of Israel burned on the altar. ²⁹Why do you show no respect for my sacrifices and grain offerings that I have commanded people to make in my dwelling place? Why do you honor your sons more than me by making yourselves fat on the best of all the sacrifices offered by my people Israel?

³⁰"Therefore, the LORD God of Israel declares: I certainly thought that your family and your father's family would always live in my presence.

ᵇ2:18 *Ephod* is a technical term for a part of the priest's clothes. Its exact usage and shape are unknown.

"But now the LORD declares: I promise that I will honor those who honor me, and those who despise me will be considered insignificant. [31]The time is coming when I will break your strength and the strength of your father's house so that no one will grow old in your family. [32]You will see distress in my dwelling place. In spite of the good that I do for Israel, no one in your family will live to an old age. [33]Any man in your family whom I do not remove from my altar will have his eyes fail, and he[c] will be heartbroken. And all your descendants will die in the prime of life. [34]What is going to happen to your two sons, Hophni and Phinehas, will be a sign to you: Both of them will die on the same day. [35]Then I will appoint a faithful priest to serve me. He will do everything I want him to do. I will give him faithful descendants, and he will always live as my anointed one. [36]Then anyone who is left from your household will bow down in front of him to get a coin or a loaf of bread and say, 'Please appoint me to one of the priestly classes so that I may eat a piece of bread.'"

The LORD Calls Samuel

3 [1]The boy Samuel was serving the LORD under Eli. In those days a prophecy from the LORD was rare; visions were infrequent. [2]One night Eli was lying down in his room. His eyesight had begun to fail so that he couldn't see well. [3]The lamp in God's temple[a] hadn't gone out yet, and Samuel was asleep in the temple of the LORD where the ark of God was kept.

[4]Then the LORD called Samuel. "Here I am," Samuel responded. [5]He ran to Eli and said, "Here I am. You called me."

"I didn't call you," Eli replied. "Go back to bed." So Samuel went back and lay down.

[6]The LORD called Samuel again. Samuel got up, went to Eli, and said, "Here I am. You called me."

"I didn't call you, son," he responded. "Go back to bed." [7]Samuel had no experience with the LORD, because the word of the LORD had not yet been revealed to him.

[8]The LORD called Samuel a third time. Samuel got up, went to Eli, and said, "Here I am. You called me."

Then Eli realized that the LORD was calling the boy. [9]"Go, lie down," Eli told Samuel. "When he calls you, say, 'Speak, LORD. I'm listening.'" So Samuel went and lay down in his room.

[10]The LORD came and stood there. He called as he had called the other times: "Samuel! Samuel!" And Samuel replied, "Speak. I'm listening."

[11]Then the LORD said to Samuel, "I am going to do something in Israel that will make the ears of everyone who hears it ring. [12]On that day I am going to do to Eli and his family everything I said from beginning to end. [13]I told him that I would hand down a permanent judgment against his household because he knew about his sons' sin— that they were cursing God[b]—but he didn't try to stop them. [14]That is why I have taken an oath concerning Eli's family line: No offering or sacrifice will ever be able to make peace for the sins that Eli's family committed."

[15]Samuel remained in bed until morning. Then he opened the doors of the LORD's house. But Samuel was afraid to tell Eli about the vision.

[16]Then Eli called Samuel. "Samuel, my son!" he said.

"Here I am," he responded.

---

*c*2:33 Dead Sea Scrolls and Greek; Masoretic Text "you." *a*3:3 According to Exodus 27:21, each night the priests were to light a lamp in the tent of meeting which was to burn from dusk to dawn. *b*3:13 Ancient scribal tradition, Greek, and Latin; Masoretic Text "cursing themselves." At times some scribes would alter the text when they thought it was disrespectful to God.

[17]"What did the LORD tell you?" he asked. "Please don't hide anything from me. May God strike you dead if you hide anything he told you from me."

[18]So Samuel told Eli everything.

Eli replied, "He is the LORD. May he do what he thinks is right."

[19]Samuel grew up. The LORD was with him and didn't let any of his words go unfulfilled. [20]All Israel from Dan to Beersheba knew Samuel was the LORD's appointed prophet. [21]The LORD continued to appear in Shiloh, since the LORD revealed himself to Samuel in Shiloh through the word of the LORD. And Samuel spoke to all Israel.[c]

The Army Sends for the Ark

4 [1]Israel went to fight against the Philistines and camped near Ebenezer while the Philistines camped at Aphek. [2]The Philistines organized their troops to meet Israel in battle. As the battle spread,[a] the Philistines defeated Israel and killed about 4,000 soldiers in the field.

[3]When the troops came back to the camp, the leaders of Israel asked, "Why has the LORD used the Philistines to defeat us today? Let's get the ark of the LORD's promise from Shiloh so that he may be with us and save us from our enemies." [4]The troops sent some men who brought back the ark of the promise of the LORD of Armies—who is enthroned over the angels.[b] Eli's two sons, Hophni and Phinehas, came along with God's ark. [5]When the LORD's ark came into the camp, all Israel shouted so loudly that the earth rang with echoes.

[6]As the Philistines heard the noise, they asked, "What's all this shouting in the Hebrew camp?" The Philistines found out that the LORD's ark had come into the camp. [7]Then they were frightened and said, "A god has come into their camp." They also said, "Oh no! Nothing like this has ever happened before. [8]We're in trouble now! Who can save us from the power of these mighty gods? These are the gods who struck the Egyptians with every kind of plague in the desert. [9]Be strong, Philistines, and act like men, or else you will serve the Hebrews as they served you. Act like men and fight."

The Ark Captured

[10]The Philistines fought and defeated Israel. Every Israelite soldier fled to his tent. It was a major defeat in which 30,000 Israelite foot soldiers died. [11]The ark of God was captured. Both of Eli's sons, Hophni and Phinehas, died.

[12]A man from the tribe of Benjamin ran from the front line of the battle. He went to Shiloh that day with his clothes torn and dirt on his head.[c] [13]When he arrived, Eli was sitting on a chair beside the road, watching. He was worried about the ark of God. The man went into the city to tell the news. The whole city cried out. [14]Hearing the cry, Eli asked, "What is this commotion?" So the man went quickly to tell Eli the news. [15](Eli was 98 years old, and his eyesight had failed so that he couldn't see.)

[16]The man told Eli, "I'm the one who came from the battle. I fled from the front line today."

"What happened, son?" Eli asked.

[17]"Israel fled from the Philistines," the messenger answered. "Our troops suffered heavy casualties. Your two sons, Hophni and Phinehas, also are dead, and the ark of God has been captured."

[18]When the messenger mentioned the ark of God, Eli fell from his chair backwards

---

[c]3:21 This sentence is the first part of 1 Samuel 4:1 in the Hebrew Bible and most English Bibles.   [a]4:2 Hebrew meaning uncertain.   [b]4:4 Or "cherubim."   [c]4:12 Tearing one's clothes and throwing dirt on one's head was a sign of mourning.

toward the gate. He broke his neck, and he died. (The man was old and heavy.) He had judged^d Israel for 40 years.

¹⁹His daughter-in-law, Phinehas' wife, was pregnant. When she heard the news that the ark of God had been captured and her father-in-law and her husband were dead, she went into labor prematurely and gave birth to a son. ²⁰As she was dying, the women helping her said, "Don't be afraid. You've given birth to a son." But she didn't answer or pay attention.

²¹She called the boy Ichabod [No Glory], saying, "Israel's glory is gone," because the ark of God had been captured and because her father-in-law and her husband died. ²²"Israel's glory is gone because the ark of God has been captured," she said.

The Ark in Philistia

¹After the Philistines had captured the ark of God, they brought it from Ebenezer to Ashdod. ²They brought it into the temple of Dagon and placed it beside Dagon. ³Early the next day the people of Ashdod saw that Dagon had fallen forward on the ground in front of the Lord's ark. So they took Dagon and put him back in his place. ⁴But the next morning they saw that Dagon had again fallen forward on the ground in front of the Lord's ark. Dagon's head and his two hands were cut off and were lying on the temple's threshold. The rest of Dagon's body was intact.^a ⁵This is why the priests of Dagon and everyone else who comes into Dagon's temple in Ashdod still don't step on the temple's threshold.

⁶The Lord dealt harshly with the people of Ashdod. He destroyed them by striking the people in the vicinity of Ashdod with tumors. ⁷When the people of Ashdod realized what was happening, they said, "The ark of the God of Israel must not stay with us, because their God is dealing harshly with us and our god Dagon." ⁸The people of Ashdod called together all the Philistine rulers. "What should we do with the ark of the God of Israel?" they asked.

"The ark of the God of Israel must be taken to Gath," the rulers said.^b So the people took the ark of the God of Israel there.

⁹But after they had moved it,^c the Lord threw the city into a great panic: He struck all the important and unimportant people in the city, and they were covered with tumors. ¹⁰So the people of Gath sent the ark of God to Ekron. But when the ark of God came to Ekron, the people of Ekron cried out, "They brought the ark of the God of Israel here to kill us." ¹¹They called together all the Philistine rulers. "Send the ark of the God of Israel away," they said. "Let it go back to its own place so that it won't kill us or our people." There was a fear of death throughout the city, where God dealt with them very harshly. ¹²The people who didn't die were struck with tumors. So the cry of the city went up to heaven.

The Ark Is Returned to Israel

¹The ark of the Lord had been in Philistine territory seven months ²when the Philistines called for priests and people skilled in explaining omens. The Philistines asked, "What should we do with the ark of the Lord? Tell us how to return it to its proper place."

³The priests answered, "If you're returning the ark of the God of Israel, don't send it away empty, but by all means return it to its proper place with a guilt offering.

---

^d4:18 Eli served as a God-appointed political/religious leader of Israel like the judges in the book of Judges.
^a5:4 Greek; Masoretic Text "Only Dagon was left." ^b5:8 Dead Sea Scrolls, Greek read "The citizens of Gath said, 'Let the ark of God be brought to us.'" ^c5:9 Dead Sea Scrolls add "to Gath."

Ark of the Lord / *1 Samuel 6*

The ark of the Lord was the holiest object in Old Testament religion. It was the symbol of God's presence with his people. But a symbol is not God, nor is it magical. To learn what happened when the Israelites trusted the ark instead of trusting God, read chapters 4–6.

Then you will be healed, and you will know why he would not turn his anger away from you."

⁴The Philistines asked, "What kind of guilt offering should we give him?"

The priests answered, "Five gold tumors and five gold mice for the five Philistine rulers because all of you and your rulers suffer from the same plague. ⁵Make models of your tumors and your mice which are destroying the country, and give glory to the God of Israel. Maybe he will no longer be so hard on you, your gods, and your country. ⁶Why should you be as stubborn as the Egyptians and their Pharaoh were? After he toyed with the Egyptians, didn't they send the Israelites on their way? ⁷Now get a new cart ready for two dairy cows that have never been yoked. Hitch the cows to the cart. Take their calves away, and leave them in their stall. ⁸Take the ark of the Lord, and put it on the cart. Put the gold objects which you're giving him as a guilt offering in a box beside the ark. Send the cart on its way, ⁹but then watch where it goes. If it goes up the road to its own country toward Beth Shemesh, then this disaster is the Lord's doing. But if not, we'll know it wasn't his hand that struck us, but what happened to us was an accident."

¹⁰The people did this. They took two dairy cows, hitched them to a cart, and shut the calves in the stall. ¹¹They put the ark of the Lord and the box containing the gold mice and the models of their hemorrhoids on the cart. ¹²The cows went straight up the road to Beth Shemesh. Continually mooing, they stayed on the road and didn't turn right or left. The rulers of the Philistines followed them to the border of Beth Shemesh.

¹³The people of Beth Shemesh were harvesting wheat in the valley. When they looked up and saw the ark, they were overjoyed. ¹⁴The cart came into the field of Joshua of Beth Shemesh and stopped there by a large rock. The people chopped up the wood of the cart and sacrificed the cows as a burnt offering to the Lord. ¹⁵(The Levites had already taken down from the cart the ark of the Lord and the box which contained the gold objects and put them on the large rock.) The people of Beth Shemesh presented burnt offerings and sacrifices to the Lord that day. ¹⁶After the five rulers of the Philistines saw this, they went back to Ekron that same day.

¹⁷The gold hemorrhoids which the Philistines sent as a guilt offering to the Lord

were for the cities of Ashdod, Gaza, Ashkelon, Gath, and Ekron. [18]And the number of gold mice was the same as the number of Philistine cities belonging to the five rulers, including walled cities and farm villages. The large rock on which they put the ark of the Lord is a witness.[a] It is still there today in the field of Joshua of Beth Shemesh.

[19]God struck down some of the people from Beth Shemesh because they looked inside the ark of the Lord. He struck down 70 people.[b] The people mourned because the Lord struck them with such a great blow. [20]The people of Beth Shemesh asked, "Who can stand before the Lord, this holy God? And to which people will he go when he leaves us?" [21]They sent messengers to the people living at Kiriath Jearim to say, "The Philistines have brought back the ark of the Lord. Come and take it back with you."

[1]The men of Kiriath Jearim came to take the Lord's ark and brought it into Abinadab's house on the hill. They gave Abinadab's son Eleazar the holy occupation of guarding the Lord's ark.

Israel Admits It Has Sinned

[2]A long time passed after the ark came to stay at Kiriath Jearim. For 20 years the entire nation of Israel mournfully sought the Lord.

[3]Samuel told the entire nation of Israel, "If you are returning to the Lord wholeheartedly, get rid of the foreign gods you have, including the statues of the goddess Astarte. Make a commitment to the Lord, and serve only him. Then he will rescue you from the Philistines."

[4]So the Israelites got rid of the statues of Baal and Astarte and served only the Lord.

[5]Then Samuel said, "Gather all the Israelites together at Mizpah, and I will pray to the Lord for you." [6]So the Israelites gathered together at Mizpah. They drew some water, poured it out in front of the Lord, and fasted that day. They confessed, "We have sinned against the Lord." So Samuel judged Israel in Mizpah.

The Philistines Defeated

[7]When the Philistines heard that the Israelites had gathered at Mizpah, the Philie rulers came to attack Israel. The Israelites heard about the Philistine plan, and were afraid of them. [8]The Israelites said to Samuel, "Don't turn a deaf ear to us! Don't stop crying to the Lord our God for us! Ask him to save us from the Philistines!"

[9]Then Samuel took a lamb, one still feeding on milk, and sacrificed it as a burnt offering to the Lord. Samuel cried to the Lord on behalf of Israel, and the Lord answered him. [10]While Samuel was sacrificing the burnt offering, the Philistines came to fight against Israel. On that day the Lord thundered loudly at the Philistines and threw them into such confusion that they were defeated by Israel. [11]Israel's soldiers left Mizpah, pursued the Philistines, and killed them as far as Beth Car.

[12]Then Samuel took a rock and set it up between Mizpah and Shen. He named it Ebenezer [Rock of Help] and said, "Until now the Lord has helped us."

[13]The power of the Philistines was crushed, so they didn't come into Israel's territory again. The Lord restrained the Philistines as long as Samuel lived. [14]The cities between Ekron and Gath which the Philistines took from Israel were returned to Israel. And Israel recovered the territory controlled by these cities from the Philistines. There was also peace between Israel and the Amorites.

[15]Samuel judged Israel as long as he lived. [16]Every year he went around to Bethel,

---

[a]6:18 Hebrew meaning uncertain.　[b]6:19 "70 people" is found in a few Hebrew manuscripts and the writings of the ancient Jewish historian Josephus. Masoretic Text and Greek read "50,070 people."

Gilgal, and Mizpah in order to judge Israel in all those places. [17]Then he would return home to Ramah. There, too, he judged Israel. And in Ramah he built an altar to the LORD.

Israel Rejects the LORD as King

8 [1]When Samuel was old, he made his sons judges over Israel. [2]The name of his firstborn son was Joel; the name of his second son was Abijah. They were judges in Beersheba. [3]The sons didn't follow their father's example but turned to dishonest ways of making money. They took bribes and denied people justice.

[4]Then all the leaders of Israel gathered together and came to Samuel at Ramah. [5]They told him, "You're old, and your sons aren't following your example. Now appoint a king to judge us so that we will be like all the other nations."

[6]But Samuel considered it wrong for them to request a king to judge them. So Samuel prayed to the LORD. [7]The LORD told Samuel, "Listen to everything the people are saying to you. They haven't rejected you; they've rejected me. [8]They're doing just what they've done since I took them out of Egypt—leaving me and serving other gods. [9]Listen to them now, but be sure to warn them and tell them about the rights of a king."

[10]Then Samuel told the people who had asked him for a king everything the LORD had said. [11]Samuel said, "These are the rights of a king:

He will draft your sons, make them serve on his chariots and horses, and make them run ahead of his chariots. [12]He will appoint them to be his officers over 1,000 or over 50 soldiers, to plow his ground and harvest his crops, and to make weapons and equipment for his chariots. [13]He will take your daughters and have them make perfumes, cook, and bake. [14]He will take the best of your fields, vineyards, and olive orchards and give them to his officials. [15]He will take a tenth of your grain and wine and give it to his aids and officials. [16]He will take your male and female slaves, your best cattle,[a] and your donkeys for his own use. [17]He will take a tenth of your flocks.

In addition, you will be his servants. [18]"When that day comes, you will cry out because of the king whom you have chosen for yourselves. The LORD will not answer you when that day comes."

[19]But the people refused to listen to Samuel. They said, "No, we want a king! [20]Then we, too, will be like all the other nations. Our king will judge us, lead us out ⌊to war⌋, and fight our battles."

[21]When Samuel heard everything the people had to say, he reported it privately to the LORD. [22]The LORD told him, "Listen to them, and give them a king."

Then Samuel told the people of Israel, "Go ⌊back⌋ to your own cities."

Saul Searches for His Father's Donkeys

9 [1]There was a man from the tribe of Benjamin whose name was Kish. He was a son of Abiel, grandson of Zeror, and great-grandson of Becorath, whose father was Aphiah, a descendant of Benjamin. Kish was a powerful man. [2]He had a son named Saul, a handsome, young man. No man in Israel was more handsome than Saul. He stood a head taller than everyone else.

[3]When some donkeys belonging to Saul's father Kish were lost, Kish told Saul, "Take one of the servants with you, and go look for the donkeys."

---

[a]8:16 Greek; Masoretic Text "best young men."

[4]They went through the mountains of Ephraim and the region of Shalisha without finding the donkeys. Then Saul and his servant went through the region of Shaalim, but the donkeys weren't there. The men went through the territory of Benjamin but still didn't find them. [5]When they came to the territory of Zuph, Saul told his servant who was with him, "Let's go back, or my father will stop worrying about the donkeys and worry about us instead."

Saul Seeks Samuel's Advice

[6]The servant responded, "There's a man of God in this city, a highly respected man. Everything he says is sure to happen. Let's go there. Maybe he'll tell us which way we should go."

[7]"If we go," Saul asked his servant, "what could we bring the man since the food in our sacks is gone? There's no present we can bring the man of God. What do we have?"

[8]The servant again answered Saul, "Look, here! I have one-tenth of an ounce of silver. I'll give it to the man of God. Then he'll tell us where to find the donkeys."

[9](Formerly in Israel, when a person went to ask God a question, he would say, "Come, let's go to the seer," because a person we now call a prophet used to be called a seer.)

[10]Saul told his servant, "That's a good idea! Come on, let's go." They went to the city where the man of God was.

[11]As they were going up the hill to the city, they met girls coming out to get water. They asked the girls, "Is the seer here?"

[12]The girls answered, "He's there ahead of you. Hurry! He just went into the city today since the people are offering a sacrifice on the worship site. [13]As you go into the city, you can find him before he goes to the worship site to eat. The people will not eat until he comes, since he blesses the sacrifice. Then those who are invited may eat. Go. You should be able to find him now."

[14]So Saul and his servant went to the city. As they entered it, Samuel was coming toward them on his way to the worship site. [15]Now, the LORD had revealed the following message to Samuel one day before Saul came: [16]"About this time tomorrow I will send you a man from the territory of Benjamin. Anoint him to be ruler of my people Israel. He will save my people from the Philistines because I've seen my people's suffering and their cry has come to me." [17]When Samuel noticed Saul, the LORD told him, "There's the man I told you about. This man will govern my people."

[18]Saul approached Samuel inside the gateway and said, "Please tell me where the seer's house is."

[19]Samuel replied, "I'm the seer. Go ahead of me to the worship site. You will eat with me today. In the morning I'll let you go after I tell you all that's on your mind. [20]Don't trouble yourself about the donkeys that were lost three days ago because they've been found. Who will have all that is desirable in Israel? Won't it be you and your father's family?"

[21]Saul replied, "I am a man from the tribe of Benjamin, the smallest tribe of Israel. My family is the most insignificant of all the families of the tribe of Benjamin. So why are you saying such things to me?"

[22]Samuel brought Saul and his servant to the banquet hall and had them sit at the head of the guests—about 30 people. [23]Samuel said to the cook, "Bring me the portion of the sacrificial meat that I gave you and told you to put aside." [24]So the cook

picked up the leg and thigh[a] and laid it in front of Saul. Samuel said, "This was kept in order to be laid in front of you. Eat it. When I invited people to the feast, I set it aside for you."[b] Saul ate with Samuel that day.

²⁵Then they left the worship site for the city. They spread blankets on the roof for Saul, and he slept there.[c]

²⁶At dawn Samuel called to Saul on the roof, "Get up! It's time for me to send you away." Saul got up, and both he and Samuel went outside. ²⁷As they were going toward the city limits, Samuel told Saul, "Have the servant go ahead of you." (He went ahead.) "But you stay here, and I will tell you God's word."

Saul Anointed by Samuel

¹Samuel took a flask of olive oil, poured it on Saul's head, kissed him, and said, "The Lord has anointed you to be ruler of his people Israel. You will rule his people and save them from all their enemies. This will be the sign that the Lord has anointed you[a] to be ruler of his people. ²When you leave me today, two men will be at Rachel's grave on the border of Benjamin at Zelzah. They'll tell you, 'We've found the donkeys you went looking for. Your father no longer cares about them. Instead, he's worried about you. He keeps asking, "What can I do to find my son?" ' ³Keep going until you come to the oak tree at Tabor. There you will find three men on their way to worship God at Bethel: One will be carrying three young goats, one will be carrying three loaves of bread, and one will be carrying a full wineskin. ⁴They will greet you and give you two loaves of bread, which you should accept from them. ⁵After that, you will come to the hill of God, where the Philistines have a military post. When you arrive at the city, you will meet a group of prophets prophesying as they come from the worship site. They will be led by men playing a harp, a tambourine, a flute, and a lyre. ⁶Then the Lord's Spirit will come over you. You will be a different person while you prophesy with them. ⁷When these signs happen to you, do what you must, because God is with you. ⁸Go ahead of me to Gilgal. Then I will come to sacrifice burnt offerings and make fellowship offerings. Wait seven days until I come to tell you what to do."

Saul's Anointing Confirmed by Signs

⁹When Saul turned around to leave Samuel, God changed Saul's attitude. That day all these signs happened. ¹⁰When Saul came to the hill, a group of prophets came to meet him, and God's Spirit came over him. He prophesied with them. ¹¹When all who had known him before saw how he prophesied with the prophets, the people asked one another, "What has happened to the son of Kish? Is Saul one of the prophets?" ¹²But a man from that place asked, "But who's the chief prophet?" So it became a proverb: "Is Saul one of the prophets?" ¹³And when he had finished prophesying, he came to the worship site.

¹⁴Saul's uncle asked him and his servant, "Where did you go?"

Saul answered, "To look for the donkeys, and when we couldn't find them, we went to Samuel."

¹⁵Saul's uncle said, "Please tell me what Samuel said to you."

¹⁶"He assured us the donkeys had been found," Saul answered his uncle. But Saul didn't tell him what Samuel said about his becoming king.

---

[a]9:24 Hebrew meaning uncertain.   [b]9:24 Hebrew meaning of this sentence uncertain.   [c]9:25 Greek; Masoretic Text reads ". . . for the city, and he spoke with Saul on the roof, and they got up early."   [a]10:1 "to be ruler of his people . . . has anointed you" Greek; Masoretic Text omits these words.

The LORD Chooses Saul

[17]Samuel called the people to come into the presence of the LORD at Mizpah. [18]He said to the Israelites, "This is what the LORD God of Israel says: I brought Israel out of Egypt and rescued you from the power of the Egyptians and all the kings who were oppressing you. [19]But now you have rejected your God, who saves you from all your troubles and distresses. You said, 'No! Place a king over us.' Now then, stand in front of the LORD by your tribes and family groups."

[20]When Samuel had all the tribes of Israel come forward, the tribe of Benjamin was chosen. [21]When he had the tribe of Benjamin come forward by families, the family of Matri was chosen. Then Saul, the son of Kish, was chosen. They looked for him but couldn't find him. [22]They asked the LORD again, "Has he arrived here yet?"

The LORD answered, "He's hiding among the baggage."

[23]They ran and got him from there. As he stood among the people, he was a head taller than everyone else. [24]Samuel asked the people, "Do you see whom the LORD has chosen? There is no one like him among all the people."

Then all the people shouted, "Long live the king!"

[25]Samuel explained the laws concerning kingship to the people. He wrote the laws on a scroll, which he placed in front of the LORD. Then Samuel sent the people back to their homes. [26]Saul also went home to Gibeah. With him went some soldiers whose hearts God had touched. [27]However, some good-for-nothing people asked, "How can this man save us?" They despised him and wouldn't bring him presents, but he didn't respond.

Saul Defeats Ammon

11 [1]King Nahash of Ammon was severely oppressing the tribes of Gad and Reuben. He would poke out everyone's right eye and allow no one to rescue Israel. There was no one among the Israelites east of the Jordan River whose right eye King Nahash of Ammon had not poked out. However, seven thousand men had escaped from the Ammonites and gone to Jabesh Gilead. About a month later[a] Nahash the Ammonite blockaded

---

Friends
1 Samuel 10:20-23

be all you can be

The Israelites liked their new king because he was tall. Is looking at someone's size the best way to pick a leader or choose a friend? Probably not. How do you pick good friends? What do you think are the most important qualities in a friend? Listening? Taking turns deciding what to do on Saturday afternoons? Helping when you need help? Not pressuring you to do wrong? Do you have friends that have good qualities? Are you this kind of friend?

---

[a]11:1 Dead Sea Scrolls and the ancient Jewish historian Josephus add this first part of verse 1 between chapters 10 and 11 (usually denoted as verse 10:27b).

Jabesh Gilead. All the men of Jabesh said to Nahash, "Make a treaty with us, and we'll serve you."

²Nahash the Ammonite responded, "I'll make a treaty with you on this one condition: I'll poke out everyone's right eye and bring disgrace on all Israel."

³The leaders of Jabesh told him, "Give us seven days so that we can send messengers throughout the territory of Israel. And if there's no one to save us, we'll surrender to you."

⁴The messengers came to Saul's town, Gibeah. When they told the people the news, the people cried loudly. ⁵Just then Saul was coming from the field behind some oxen. "Why are these people crying?" Saul asked. So they told him the news about the men of Jabesh. ⁶When he heard this news, God's Spirit came over him, and he became very angry. ⁷Saul took a pair of oxen, cut them in pieces, and sent them by messengers throughout the territory of Israel with the following message: "This is what will be done to the oxen of anyone who doesn't follow Saul and Samuel into battle." So the people became terrified by the LORD, and they came out united behind Saul. ⁸When Saul counted them at Bezek, there were 300,000 troops from Israel and 30,000 troops from Judah. ⁹They told the messengers who had come, "This is what you are to say to the men of Jabesh Gilead: 'Tomorrow, by the time the sun gets hot, you will be rescued.'" When the men of Jabesh received the message, they were overjoyed.

¹⁰They said to Nahash, "Tomorrow we'll surrender to you, and you may do to us whatever you think is right."

¹¹The next day Saul arranged the army in three divisions. They came into the Ammonite camp during the morning hours and continued to defeat the Ammonites until it got hot that day. The survivors were so scattered that no two of them were left together.

¹²Then the people asked Samuel, "Who said that Saul shouldn't rule us? Let us have them, and we'll kill them."

¹³But Saul said, "No one will be killed today, because today the LORD saved Israel."

¹⁴Samuel told the troops, "Come, let's go to Gilgal and there acknowledge Saul's kingship." ¹⁵Then all the troops went to Gilgal, and there in the LORD's presence, they confirmed Saul as their king. There they sacrificed fellowship offerings to the LORD. Saul and all of Israel's soldiers celebrated.

Samuel's Spotless Leadership

¹Then Samuel said to all Israel, "I have listened to everything you have said to me and appointed a king over you. ²And now, here is the king who will lead you. I am old and gray, but my sons are with you. I have led you from my youth until this day. ³Here I am. Testify against me in front of the LORD and in front of his anointed king. Did I take anyone's ox? Did I take anyone's donkey? Did I cheat or oppress anyone? Did I take a bribe from anyone to look the other way? If so, I will give it all back."

⁴They answered, "You didn't cheat us, oppress us, or take anything from anyone."

⁵Samuel told them, "The LORD is a witness to what you've said, and his anointed king is a witness today that you've found nothing in my hands."

"He is a witness," they answered.

⁶Samuel told the people, "The LORD appointed Moses and Aaron and brought your ancestors out of Egypt. ⁷Now, stand up while I put you on trial in front of the LORD and cite all the righteous things the LORD did for you and your ancestors. ⁸When your ancestors went with Jacob to Egypt and were oppressed, they cried out to the LORD,

who sent Moses and Aaron to bring them out of Egypt. The Lord settled them in this place. ⁹But they forgot the Lord their God. So he handed them over to Sisera, who was the commander of the army of Hazor, to the Philistines, and to the king of Moab. All of them fought against your ancestors. ¹⁰Then they cried out to the Lord and said, 'We have sinned. We have abandoned the Lord and served other gods and goddesses— the Baals and the Astartes. But rescue us from our enemies now, and we will serve you.'

¹¹"Then the Lord sent Jerubbaal, Bedan, Jephthah, and Samuel and rescued you from your enemies on every side so that you could live securely. ¹²But when you saw King Nahash of Ammon coming to attack you, you told me, 'No, a king should rule over us,' though the Lord your God was your king.

The New Kingship

¹³"Now, here is the king you have chosen, the one you asked for. See, the Lord has put a king over you. ¹⁴If you fear the Lord, serve him, obey him, and don't rebel against what he says, then you and your king will follow the Lord your God. ¹⁵But if you don't obey the Lord, if you rebel against what he says, then the Lord will be against you as he was against your ancestors. ¹⁶Now then, stand still and watch this great thing the Lord is going to do right before your eyes. ¹⁷Isn't the wheat being harvested today? I will call on the Lord, and he'll send thunder and rain. Then you will realize what a wicked thing you did in the Lord's presence when you asked for a king."

¹⁸Then Samuel called on the Lord. That day the Lord sent thunder and rain so that all the people feared the Lord and Samuel very much.

¹⁹All the people pleaded with Samuel, "Pray to the Lord your God for us so that we will not die. We have added another evil thing to all our other sins by asking for a king."

²⁰"Don't be afraid," Samuel told the people. "You did do all these evil things. But don't turn away from the Lord. Instead, serve the Lord wholeheartedly. ²¹Don't turn away to follow other gods. They can't help or rescue you, because they don't exist. ²²For the sake of his great name, the Lord will not abandon his people, because the Lord wants to make you his people. ²³It would be unthinkable for me to sin against the Lord by failing to pray for you. I will go on teaching you the way that is good and right. ²⁴Fear the Lord, and serve him sincerely. Consider the great things he did for you. ²⁵But if you go on doing what is evil, you and your king will be wiped out."

The LORD Rejects Saul as King

¹Saul was thirty years old when he became king, and he was king of Israel forty-two years.ª

²Saul chose 3,000 men from Israel; 2,000 of them were stationed with Saul at Michmash and in the mountains of Bethel, and 1,000 were stationed with Jonathan at Gibeah in Benjamin. But the rest of the people he sent home.

³Jonathan defeated the Philistine troops at Geba, and the Philistines heard about it. With the sounding of the ram's horn throughout the land, Saul announced, "Listen, Hebrews!" ⁴(So all Israel listened.) "I, Saul, have defeated the Philistine troops, and now Israel has become offensive to the Philistines!" All the troops rallied behind Saul at Gilgal.

⁵The Philistines assembled to fight against Israel. They had 30,000 chariots, 6,000

ª 13:1 The text of 1 Samuel 13:1 is problematic in all traditions. Some late Greek manuscripts state Saul was 30 years old when he became king. The ancient Jewish historian Josephus and Acts 13:21 state that Saul ruled for 40 years.

horsemen, and as many soldiers as the sand on the seashore. They camped at Michmash, east of Beth Aven. ⁶When the Israelites saw they were in trouble because the army was hard-pressed, they hid in caves, in thorny thickets, among rocks, in pits, and in cisterns. ⁷Some Hebrews crossed the Jordan River into the territory of Gad and Gilead. But Saul remained in Gilgal, and all the people who followed him trembled ⌊in fear⌋.

⁸He waited seven days, the time set by Samuel. But Samuel had not come to Gilgal, and the troops began to scatter. ⁹Then Saul said, "Bring me the animals for the burnt offering and the fellowship offerings." So he sacrificed the burnt offering. ¹⁰As he finished sacrificing the burnt offering, Samuel came, and Saul went to greet him.

¹¹Samuel asked, "What have you done?"

Saul replied, "I saw the troops were scattering. You didn't come when you said you would, and the Philistines were assembling at Michmash. ¹²So I thought, 'Now, the Philistines will come against me at Gilgal, but I haven't sought the LORD's favor.' I felt pressured into sacrificing the burnt offering."

¹³"You did a foolish thing," Samuel told Saul. "You didn't follow the command of the LORD your God. ⌊If you had,⌋ the LORD would have established your kingdom over Israel permanently. ¹⁴But now your kingdom will not last. The LORD has searched for a man after his own heart. The LORD has appointed him as ruler of his people, because you didn't follow the command of the LORD."

¹⁵Samuel left Gilgal. The rest of the people followed Saul to meet the soldiers. They went from Gilgal[b] to Gibeah in Benjamin, where Saul counted the troops who were still with him—about 600 men. ¹⁶Saul, his son Jonathan, and the troops who were with them stayed at Geba in Benjamin while the Philistines camped at Michmash.

¹⁷Raiding parties left the Philistine camp in three columns. One column turned onto the road to Ophrah to the region of Shual. ¹⁸Another column turned onto the road to Beth Horon. And one turned onto the road toward the region that overlooks the valley of Zeboim and the desert.

¹⁹No blacksmith could be found in the entire land of Israel. In this way the Philistines kept the Hebrews from making swords and spears. ²⁰Everyone in Israel had to go to the Philistines to sharpen the blade of his plow, his mattock, ax, or sickle. ²¹The price was a pim[c] for plow blades and mattocks, and one-tenth of an ounce of silver to sharpen a mattock[d] or set a metal point on a cattle-prod. ²²So on the day of battle, not one sword or spear could be found among all the troops who were with Saul and Jonathan. But Saul and his son Jonathan had them.

²³Now, Philistine troops had gone out to the pass at Michmash.

Jonathan Defeats the Philistines

¹One day Saul's son Jonathan said to his armorbearer, "Let's go to the Philistine military post on the other side." But Jonathan didn't tell his father ⌊he was going⌋.

²Saul was staying on the outskirts of Gibeah under a pomegranate tree at Migron. He had with him about 600 men ³in addition to Ahijah, the son of Ichabod's brother Ahitub, who was the son of Phinehas and the grandson of Eli, the LORD's priest at Shiloh. Ahijah was wearing the priestly ephod.[a]

The troops didn't know Jonathan had left. ⁴There was a cliff on each side of the mountain pass where Jonathan searched for a way to cross over to attack the Philistine

---

b13:15 "Samuel . . . from Gilgal" Greek; Masoretic Text omits these words.   c13:21 A pim was a measure of weight.   d13:21 Hebrew meaning of "one-tenth . . . a mattock" uncertain.   a14:3 *Ephod* is a technical term for a part of the priest's clothes. Its exact usage and shape are unknown.

military post. The name of one ˌcliffˌ was Bozez, and the name of the other was Seneh. ⁵One cliff stood like a pillar on the north facing Michmash, the other stood south facing Geba.

⁶Jonathan said to his armorbearer, "Let's go to the military post of these uncircumcised people. Maybe the LORD will act on our behalf. The LORD can win a victory with a few men as well as with many."

⁷His armorbearer answered him, "Do whatever you have in mind. Go ahead! I agree with you."

⁸Jonathan continued, "Listen, we'll cross over to the Philistines and show ourselves to them. ⁹If they say to us, 'Stay where you are until we come to you,' then we'll stay where we are and not go up to them. ¹⁰But if they say to us, 'Come up here,' then we'll go up, because that will be our sign that the LORD has handed them over to us."

¹¹So both of them showed themselves to the Philistine troops. The Philistines said, "Look, some Hebrews are coming out of the holes they were hiding in."

¹²"Come up here," the men of the military post said to Jonathan and his armorbearer. "We have something to show you."

Jonathan told his armorbearer, "Follow me up ˌto the military postˌ because the LORD has handed the troops over to Israel."

¹³Jonathan climbed up ˌthe cliffˌ and his armorbearer followed him. Jonathan struck down the Philistines. His armorbearer, who was behind him, finished killing them. ¹⁴In their first slaughter Jonathan and his armorbearer killed about twenty men within about a hundred yards. ¹⁵There was panic among the army in the field and all the troops in the military post. The raiding party also trembled ˌin fearˌ. The earth shook, and there was a panic sent from God.

¹⁶Saul's watchmen at Gibeah in Benjamin could see the crowd ˌin the Philistine campˌ dispersing in all directions.

¹⁷"Look around," Saul told the troops who were with him, "and see who has left ˌour campˌ." They looked and found that Jonathan and his armorbearer were not there.

¹⁸Then Saul said to Ahijah, "Bring the priestly ephod," because Ahijah carried the ephod in front of Israel that day.ᵇ ¹⁹While Saul was talking to the priest, the confusion in the Philistine camp grew worse and worse. Then Saul said to the priest, "Remove your hand ˌfrom the ephodˌ."ᶜ ²⁰Saul and all the troops with him assembled and went into battle. They found Philistine soldiers killing their fellow soldiers in wild confusion. ²¹The Hebrews who had been with the Philistines before this and had been stationed in the camp now joined the Israelites who were with Saul and Jonathan. ²²When all the men of Israel who had been hiding in the mountains of Ephraim heard that the Philistines were fleeing, they also pursued the Philistines in battle. ²³So the LORD saved Israel that day.

Saul's Curse

Now, the battle moved beyond Beth Aven. ²⁴Israel's soldiers were driven hard that day. Saul made the troops swear, "Cursed is anyone who eats food before the evening comes and before I've gotten revenge on my enemies." So none of his troops tasted any food. ²⁵The entire land had honeycombs,ᵈ and there was honey on the ground. ²⁶When the troops entered the woods, the honey was flowing. But no one put his hand to his mouth, because the troops were afraid of violating their oath.

ᵇ14:18 Greek; Masoretic Text problematic: "Bring the ark of God because the ark of God that day and the sons of Israel." ᶜ14:19 Hebrew meaning uncertain. ᵈ14:25 Or "The entire land came into the woods."

²⁷Jonathan hadn't heard that his father forced the troops to take an oath. So he stretched out the tip of the staff he had in his hand and dipped it in the honeycomb. When he put it to his mouth, his eyes lit up. ²⁸Then one of the soldiers told him, "Your father forced the troops to take a solemn oath: 'Cursed is anyone who eats food today.' "

Now, the army was exhausted. ²⁹Jonathan answered, "My father has brought trouble to the country. See how my eyes lit up when I tasted a little of this honey? ³⁰If only the troops had eaten some of the enemies' food, which they found today. We would have killed more Philistines."

³¹That day they struck down the Philistines from Michmash to Aijalon, but the troops were thoroughly exhausted. ³²So the troops seized the Philistines' belongings. They took sheep, cows, and calves, and butchered them on the ground. The troops ate the meat with blood still in it. ³³Some soldiers told Saul, "The troops are sinning against the Lord by eating meat with blood in it."

Saul replied, "You have been unfaithful. Roll a large rock over to me now." ³⁴Then Saul said, "Spread out through the troops, and tell them, 'Each of you, bring me your ox or your sheep, and butcher it here, and eat. But don't sin against the Lord by eating meat with blood in it.' "

So each of the soldiers brought his ox with him that night and butchered it there.

³⁵Then Saul built an altar to the Lord; it was the first time he had built an altar to the Lord.

³⁶Saul said to his men, "Let's attack the Philistines tonight and take their possessions until the light of dawn. And let's not leave any of them alive."

"Do whatever you think is best," they responded.

But the priest said, "Let's consult God first."

³⁷Then Saul asked God, "Should I attack the Philistines? Will you hand them over to Israel?" But he received no answer that day.

³⁸So Saul ordered all the leaders of the troops, "Come here! Find out what sin was committed today. ³⁹I solemnly swear, as the Lord and Savior of Israel lives, even if it is my son Jonathan who did it, he must die." But not one of the soldiers replied.

⁴⁰Saul told all Israel, "You stand on one side, and my son Jonathan and I will stand on the other side."

"Do whatever you think is best," the troops responded to Saul.

⁴¹Then Saul said to the Lord, "O God of Israel, why didn't you answer me today? If this sin is mine or my son Jonathan's, Lord God of Israel, let the priest draw Urim. But if it is in your people Israel,ᵉ let him draw Thummim." Jonathan and Saul were chosen, and the people were freed from guilt.

⁴²"Choose between me and my son Jonathan," Saul said. Then Jonathan was chosen.

⁴³"Tell me," Saul asked Jonathan. "What did you do?"

So Jonathan told him, "I tasted a little honey on the tip of the staff I had in my hand. And for that I am to die?"

⁴⁴Saul said, "May God do worse things to me than are in this curse if you do not die, Jonathan!"

⁴⁵The troops asked Saul, "Should Jonathan die after he has won this great victory in Israel? That would be unthinkable! We solemnly swear, as the Lord lives, not a single hair of his head will fall to the ground, because he has done this with God's help today." So the troops rescued Jonathan from death. ⁴⁶Then Saul stopped pursuing the Philistines. So the Philistines returned to their own land.

ᵉ14:41 "Why didn't you . . . your people Israel" Greek, Latin; Masoretic Text omits these words.

Summary of Saul's Reign

⁴⁷When Saul had taken over the kingdom of Israel, he fought against his enemies on every side—against Moab, the Ammonites, Edom, the kings of Zobah, and the Philistines. Wherever he turned, he was victorious. ⁴⁸He acted forcefully and defeated Amalek. He rescued Israel from the enemies who looted their possessions.

⁴⁹Saul's sons were Jonathan, Ishvi, and Malchishua. The names of his two daughters were Merab (the firstborn daughter) and Michal (the younger daughter). ⁵⁰The name of Saul's wife was Ahinoam, the daughter of Ahimaaz. The name of the commander of his army was Abner, the son of Saul's uncle Ner. ⁵¹Kish (Saul's father) and Ner (Abner's father) were the sons of Abiel.

⁵²There was intense warfare with the Philistines as long as Saul lived. Whenever any warrior or any skilled fighting man came to Saul's attention, Saul would enlist him in the army.

Saul Disobeys the LORD

15 ¹Samuel told Saul, "The LORD sent me to anoint you king of his people Israel. Now listen to the LORD's words. ²This is what the LORD of Armies says: I will punish Amalek for what it did to Israel. They blocked Israel's way after the Israelites came from Egypt. ³Now go and attack Amalek. Claim everything they have for God by destroying it. Don't spare them, but kill men and women, infants and children, cows and sheep, camels and donkeys."

⁴Saul organized the troops, and he counted them at Telaim: 200,000 foot soldiers and 10,000 men from Judah. ⁵Saul went to the city of Amalek and set an ambush in the valley. ⁶Then Saul said to the Kenites, "Get away from the Amalekites so that I won't destroy you with them. You were kind to all the Israelites when they came from Egypt." So the Kenites left the Amalekites.

⁷Saul attacked the Amalekites from Havilah to Shur, east of Egypt. ⁸He captured King Agag of Amalek alive. But he claimed all the people for God by destroying them. ⁹Saul and the army spared Agag and the best sheep and cows, the fattened animals, the lambs, and all the best property. The army refused to claim them for God by destroying them. But everything that was worthless and weak the army did claim for God and destroy.

The LORD Rejects Saul

¹⁰Then the LORD spoke to Samuel: ¹¹"I regret that I made Saul king. He turned away from me and did not carry out my instructions." Samuel was angry, and he prayed to the LORD all night. ¹²Early in the morning he got up to meet Saul. Samuel was told, "Saul went to Carmel to set up a monument in his honor. Then he left there and went to Gilgal."

¹³Samuel came to Saul, who said, "The LORD bless you. I carried out the LORD's instructions."

¹⁴However, Samuel asked,

> "But what is this sound of sheep in my ears
> and this sound of cows that I hear?"

¹⁵Saul answered, "The army brought them from the Amalekites. They spared the best sheep and cows to sacrifice to the LORD your God. But the rest they claimed for God and destroyed."

¹⁶"Be quiet," Samuel told Saul, "and let me tell you what the LORD told me last night."

"Speak," Saul replied.

[17]Samuel said, "Even though you don't consider yourself great, you were the head of Israel's tribes. The LORD anointed you king of Israel. [18]And the LORD sent you on a mission. He said, 'Claim those sinners, the Amalekites, for me by destroying them. Wage war against them until they're wiped out.' [19]Why didn't you obey the LORD? Why have you taken their belongings and done what the LORD considers evil?"

[20]"But I did obey the LORD," Saul told Samuel. "I went where the LORD sent me, brought back King Agag of Amalek, and claimed the Amalekites for God. [21]The army took some of their belongings—the best sheep and cows were claimed for God—in order to sacrifice to the LORD your God in Gilgal."

[22]Then Samuel said,

> "Is the LORD as delighted
> with burnt offerings
> and sacrifices
> as he would be
> with your obedience?
> To follow instructions
> is better than to sacrifice.
> To obey is better than sacrificing
> the fat of rams.
> [23] The sin of black magic
> is rebellion.
> Wickedness and idolatry
> are arrogance.
> Because you rejected
> the word of the LORD,
> he rejects you as king."

[24]Then Saul told Samuel, "I have sinned by not following the LORD's command or your instructions. I was afraid of the people and listened to them. [25]Now please forgive my sin and come back with me so that I may worship the LORD."

[26]Samuel told Saul, "I will not go back with you because you rejected what the LORD told you. So the LORD rejects you as king of Israel." [27]When Samuel turned to leave, Saul grabbed the hem of his robe, and it tore. [28]Samuel told him, "The LORD has torn the kingdom of Israel from you today. He has given it to your neighbor who is better than you. [29]In addition, the Glory of Israel does not lie or change his mind, because he is not a mortal who changes his mind."

[30]Saul replied, "I have sinned! Now please honor me in front of the leaders of my people and in front of Israel. Come back with me, and let me worship the LORD your God." [31]Then Samuel turned and followed Saul, and Saul worshiped the LORD.

[32]"Bring me King Agag of Amalek," Samuel said.

Agag came to him trembling.[a] "Surely, the bitterness of death is past,"[b] Agag said.

Earning Respect
1 Samuel 15:24-29

be all you can be

Sometimes parents don't understand. They make you do something weird, like bringing a funny-looking umbrella to school. Everyone will laugh! Maybe. But don't be so afraid of others that you do something wrong just to fit in. Saul did that, and look what happened to him. If you keep on doing right, others will respect you, not laugh at you.

---

[a] 15:32 Or "Agag came to him in shackles."   [b] 15:32 Hebrew meaning uncertain.

³³But Samuel said, "As your sword made women childless, so your mother will be made childless among women." And Samuel cut Agag in pieces in the presence of the Lord at Gilgal.

³⁴Then Samuel went to Ramah, and Saul went to his home at Gibeah. ³⁵Samuel didn't see Saul again before he died, though Samuel mourned over Saul. And the Lord regretted that he had made Saul king of Israel.

David Chosen to Be King

16 ¹The Lord asked Samuel, "How long are you going to mourn for Saul now that I have rejected him as king of Israel? Fill a flask with olive oil and go. I'm sending you to Jesse in Bethlehem because I've selected one of his sons to be king."

²"How can I go?" Samuel asked. "When Saul hears about it, he'll kill me."

The Lord said, "Take a heifer with you and say, 'I've come to sacrifice to the Lord.' ³Invite Jesse to the sacrifice. I will reveal to you what you should do, and you will anoint for me the one I point out to you."

⁴Samuel did what the Lord told him. When he came to Bethlehem, the leaders of the city, trembling with fear, greeted him and said, "May peace be with you."

⁵"Greetings," he replied, "I have come to sacrifice to the Lord. Perform the ceremonies to make yourselves holy, and come with me to the sacrifice." He performed the ceremonies for Jesse and his sons and invited them to the sacrifice. ⁶When they came, he saw Eliab and thought, "Certainly, here in the Lord's presence is his anointed king."

⁷But the Lord told Samuel, "Don't look at his appearance or how tall he is, because I have rejected him. God does not see as humans see.ª Humans look at outward appearances, but the Lord looks into the heart."

⁸Then Jesse called Abinadab and brought him to Samuel. But Samuel said, "The Lord has not chosen this one either."

⁹Then Jesse had Shammah come to Samuel. "The Lord has not chosen this one either," Samuel said. ¹⁰So Jesse brought seven more of his sons to Samuel, but Samuel told Jesse, "The Lord has not chosen any of these. ¹¹Are these all the sons you have?"

"There's still the youngest one," Jesse answered. "He's tending the sheep."

Samuel told Jesse, "Send someone to get him. We won't continue until he gets here."

¹²So Jesse sent for him. He had a healthy complexion, attractive eyes, and a handsome appearance. The Lord said, "Go ahead, anoint him. He is the one." ¹³Samuel took the flask of olive oil and anointed David in the presence of his brothers. The Lord's Spirit came over David and stayed with him from that day on. Then Samuel left for Ramah.

David Plays the Lyre for Saul

¹⁴Now, the Lord's Spirit had left Saul, and an evil spirit from the Lord tormented him. ¹⁵Saul's officials told him, "An evil spirit from God is tormenting you. ¹⁶Your Majesty, why don't you command us to look for a man who can play the lyre well? When the evil spirit from God comes to you, he'll strum a tune, and you'll feel better."

¹⁷Saul told his officials, "Please find me a man who can play well and bring him to me."

¹⁸One of the officials said, "I know one of Jesse's sons from Bethlehem who can play well. He's a courageous man and a warrior. He has a way with words, he is handsome, and the Lord is with him."

ª 16:7 Greek; Masoretic Text "Not that which humans see."

[19]Saul sent messengers to Jesse to say, "Send me your son David, who is with the sheep."

[20]Jesse took six bushels of bread, a full wineskin, and a young goat and sent them with his son David to Saul. [21]David came to Saul and served him. Saul loved him very much and made David his armorbearer. [22]Saul sent this message to Jesse, "Please let David stay with me because I have grown fond of him."

[23]Whenever God's spirit came to Saul, David took the lyre and strummed a tune. Saul got relief from his terror, and felt better, and the evil spirit left him.

David and Goliath

[1]The Philistines assembled their armies for war. They assembled at Socoh, which is in Judah, and camped between Socoh and Azekah at Ephes Dammim. [2]So Saul and the army of Israel assembled and camped in the Elah Valley. They formed a battle line to fight the Philistines. [3]The Philistines were stationed on a hill on one side, and the Israelites were stationed on a hill on the other side. There was a ravine between the two of them.

[4]The Philistine army's champion came out of their camp. His name was Goliath from Gath. He was ten feet tall.[a] [5]He had a bronze helmet on his head, and he wore a bronze coat of armor scales weighing 125 pounds. [6]On his legs he had bronze shin guards and on his back a bronze javelin. [7]The shaft of his spear was like the beam used by weavers. The head of his spear was made of 15 pounds of iron. The man who carried his shield walked ahead of him.

[8]Goliath stood and called to the Israelites, "Why do you form a battle line? Am I not a Philistine, and aren't you Saul's servants? Choose a man, and let him come down to fight me. [9]If he can fight me and kill me, then we will be your slaves. But if I overpower him and kill him, then you will be our slaves and serve us." [10]The Philistine added, "I challenge the Israelite battle line today. Send out a man so that we can fight each other." [11]When Saul and all the Israelites heard what this Philistine said, they were gripped with fear.

[12]David was a son of a man named Jesse from the region of Ephrath and the city of Bethlehem in Judah. Jesse had eight sons, and in Saul's day he was an old man.[b] [13]Jesse's three oldest sons joined Saul's army for the battle. The firstborn was Eliab, the second was Abinadab, the third was Shammah, [14]and David was the youngest. The three oldest joined Saul's army. [15]David went back and forth from Saul's camp to Bethlehem, where he tended his father's flock.

[16]Each morning and evening for 40 days, the Philistine came forward and made his challenge.

[17]Jesse told his son David, "Take this half-bushel of roasted grain and these ten loaves of bread to your brothers. Take them to your brothers in the camp right away. [18]And take these ten cheeses to the captain of the regiment. See how your brothers are doing, and bring back some news about them. [19]They, along with Saul and all the soldiers of Israel, are in the Elah Valley fighting the Philistines."

[20]David got up early in the morning and had someone else watch the sheep. He took the food and went, as Jesse ordered him. He went to the camp as the army was going out to the battle line shouting their war cry. [21]Israel and the Philistines formed their battle lines facing each other. [22]David left the supplies behind in the hands of the quartermaster, ran to the battle line, and greeted his brothers. [23]While he was talking to them, the Philistine champion, Goliath from Gath, came from the battle lines

---

[a] 17:4 Masoretic Text; Dead Sea Scrolls and Greek "seven feet tall."   [b] 17:12 Greek; Masoretic Text "he came a leader among men."

of the Philistines. He repeated his words, and David heard them. [24]When all the men of Israel saw Goliath, they fled from him because they were terrified. [25]The men of Israel said, "Did you see that man coming from the Philistine lines? He keeps coming to challenge Israel. The king will make the man who kills this Philistine very rich. He will give his daughter to that man to marry and elevate the social status of his family."[c]

[26]David asked the men who were standing near him, "What will be done for the man who kills this Philistine and gets rid of Israel's disgrace? Who is this uncircumcised Philistine that he should challenge the army of the living God?"

[27]The soldiers repeated to David how the man who kills Goliath would be treated.

[28]Eliab, David's oldest brother, heard David talking to the men. Then Eliab became angry with David. "Why did you come here," he asked him, "and with whom did you leave those few sheep in the wilderness? I know how overconfident and headstrong you are. You came here just to see the battle."

[29]"What have I done now?" David snapped at him. "Didn't I merely ask a question?" [30]He turned to face another man and asked the same question, and the other soldiers gave him the same answer.

[31]What David said was overheard and reported to Saul, who then sent for him. [32]David told Saul, "No one should be discouraged because of this. I will go and fight this Philistine."

[33]Saul responded to David, "You can't fight this Philistine. You're just a boy, but he's been a warrior since he was your age."

[34]David replied to Saul, "I am a shepherd for my father's sheep. Whenever a lion or a bear came and carried off a sheep from the flock, [35]I went after it, struck it, and rescued the sheep from its mouth. If it attacked me, I took hold of its mane, struck it, and killed it. [36]I have killed lions and bears, and this uncircumcised Philistine will be like one of them because he has challenged the army of the living God." [37]David added, "The LORD, who saved me from the lion and the bear, will save me from this Philistine."

"Go," Saul told David, "and may the LORD be with you."

[38]Saul put his battle tunic on David; he put a bronze helmet on David's head and dressed him in armor. [39]David fastened Saul's sword over his clothes and tried to walk, but he had never practiced doing this. "I can't walk in these things," David told Saul. "I've never had any practice doing this." So David took all those things off.

Good Morning, God
1 Samuel 17:34-37

Israel's army was scared of the giant Goliath—and with good reason. But when the young shepherd named David heard Goliath's threats, he bravely accepted the challenge. With God on your side, you can face anything. Because of him, you can be courageous when others are tempted to become cowards.

I praise you, God, for giving little people courage to accept mighty challenges.

---

[c]17:25 Hebrew meaning of "elevate the social status of his family" uncertain.

⁴⁰He took his stick with him, picked out five smooth stones from the riverbed, and put them in his shepherd's bag. With a sling in his hand, he approached the Philistine. ⁴¹The Philistine, preceded by the man carrying his shield, was coming closer and closer to David. ⁴²When the Philistine got a good look at David, he despised him. After all, David was a young man with a healthy complexion and good looks.

⁴³The Philistine asked David, "Am I a dog that you come to attack me with sticks?" So the Philistine called on his gods to curse David. ⁴⁴"Come on," the Philistine told David, "and I'll give your body to the birds."

⁴⁵David told the Philistine, "You come to me with sword and spear and javelin, but I come to you in the name of the Lord of Armies, the God of the army of Israel, whom you have insulted. ⁴⁶Today the Lord will hand you over to me. I will strike you down and cut off your head. And this day I will give the dead bodies of the Philistine army to the birds and the wild animals. The whole world will know that Israel has a God. ⁴⁷Then everyone gathered here will know that the Lord can save without sword or spear, because the Lord determines every battle's outcome. He will hand all of you over to us."

⁴⁸When the Philistine moved closer in order to attack, David quickly ran toward the opposing battle line to attack the Philistine. ⁴⁹Then David reached into his bag, took out a stone, hurled it from his sling, and struck the Philistine in the forehead. The stone sank into Goliath's forehead, and he fell to the ground on his face. ⁵⁰So using only a sling and a stone, David proved to be stronger than the Philistine. David struck down and killed the Philistine, even though David didn't have a sword in his hand. ⁵¹David ran and stood over the Philistine. He took Goliath's sword, pulled it out of its sheath, and made certain the Philistine was dead by cutting off his head.

When the Philistines saw their hero had been killed, they fled. ⁵²Then the soldiers of Israel and Judah rose up, shouted a battle cry, and pursued the Philistines as far as Gath and to the gates of Ekron. Wounded Philistines lay on the road to Shaaraim and all the way to Gath and Ekron. ⁵³When the Israelites came back from their pursuit of the Philistines, they looted all the goods in the Philistine camp. ⁵⁴David took the Philistine's head and brought it to Jerusalem, but he kept Goliath's armor in his tent.

⁵⁵As Saul watched David going out against the Philistine, he asked Abner, the commander of the army, "Abner, whose son is this young man?"

Abner answered, "I solemnly swear, as you live, Your Majesty, I don't know."

⁵⁶The king said, "Find out whose son this young man is."

⁵⁷When David returned from killing the Philistine, Abner brought him to Saul. David had the Philistine's head in his hand.

⁵⁸Saul asked him, "Whose son are you, young man?"

"The son of your servant Jesse of Bethlehem," David answered.

David's Love for Jonathan

18 ¹David finished talking to Saul. After that, Jonathan became David's closest friend. He loved David as much as he loved himself. ²(From that day on Saul kept David as his servant and didn't let him go back to his family.) ³So Jonathan made a pledge of mutual loyalty with David because he loved him as much as he loved himself. ⁴Jonathan took off the coat he had on and gave it to David along with his battle tunic, his sword, his bow, and his belt.

⁵David was successful wherever Saul sent him. Saul put him in charge of the fighting men. This pleased all the people, including Saul's officials.

Jonathan

1 Samuel 18

Jonathan defended his friend David when
Saul threatened to kill David.

Jonathan was Saul's son, but everyone thought David would be the next
king. Saul wanted his son Jonathan to be king. But Jonathan knew that David
was chosen by God to be the next king. Jonathan didn't get mad because David
was getting this honor. He was happy for his friend David.

Jonathan was an example of a good friend. He was loyal, stood up for David,
and helped David. He wasn't jealous when David won military victories and
was praised by others. Jonathan even helped David escape when Jonathan's
father, Saul, wanted to kill David.

> **Jonathan was a brave soldier.**
>
> **Jonathan was the son of King Saul.**
>
> **Jonathan was David's closest friend.**

Jonathan used a war bow and arrows like these to warn David to flee when King Saul planned to kill David.

Jonathan was a brave soldier. He attacked an enemy post and won a great victory (1 Samuel 14).

Getting to Know Jonathan

* Why did David need a friend?
* What did it cost Jonathan to be loyal to his friend David?
* Who is your best friend?
* How is your friend like Jonathan?
* How is she different?

David's Success Makes Saul Jealous

⁶As they arrived, David was returning from a campaign against the Philistines. Women from all of Israel's cities came to meet King Saul. They sang and danced, accompanied by tambourines, joyful music, and triangles.ᵃ ⁷The women who were celebrating sang,

"Saul has defeated thousands
  but David tens of thousands!"

⁸Saul became very angry because he considered this saying to be insulting. "To David they credit tens of thousands," he said, "but to me they credit only a few thousand. The only thing left for David is my kingdom." ⁹From that day on Saul kept an eye on David.

¹⁰The next day an evil spirit from God seized Saul. He began to prophesy in his house while David strummed a tune on the lyre as he did every day. Now, Saul had a spear in his hand. ¹¹He raised the spear and thought, "I'll nail David to the wall." But David got away from him twice.

¹²Saul was afraid of David, because the Lord was with David but had left Saul. ¹³So he kept David away. He made David captain of a regiment. David led the troops out to battle and back again. ¹⁴He was successful in everything he undertook because the Lord was with him. ¹⁵Saul noticed how very successful he was and became even more afraid of him. ¹⁶Everyone in Israel and Judah loved David, because he led them in and out of battle.

¹⁷Finally, Saul said to David, "Here is my oldest daughter Merab. I will give her to you as your wife if you prove yourself to be a warrior for me and fight the Lord's battles." (Saul thought, "I must not lay a hand on him. Let the Philistines do that.")

¹⁸"Who am I?" David asked Saul. "And how important are my relatives or my father's family in Israel that I should be the king's son-in-law?"

¹⁹But when the time came to give Saul's daughter Merab to David, she was married to Adriel from Meholah. ²⁰However, Saul's daughter Michal fell in love with David. When Saul was told about it, the news pleased him. ²¹Saul thought, "I'll give her to David. She will trap him, and the Philistines will get him." So he said to David a second time, "You will now be my son-in-law."

²²Saul ordered his officers, "Talk to David in private. Tell him, 'The king likes you, and all his officers are fond of you. Become the king's son-in-law.' "

²³When Saul's officers made it a point to say this, David asked, "Do you think it's easy to become the king's son-in-law? I am a poor and unimportant person."

²⁴When the officers told Saul what David had said, ²⁵Saul replied, "Tell David, 'The king doesn't want any payment for the bride except 100 Philistine foreskins so that he can get revenge on his enemies.' " In this way Saul planned to have David fall into the hands of the Philistines. ²⁶When his officers told David this, David concluded that it was acceptable to become the king's son-in-law. Before the time was up, ²⁷David and his men went out and struck down 200 Philistines. David brought the foreskins, and they counted them out for the king so that David could become the king's son-in-law. Then Saul gave him his daughter Michal as his wife. ²⁸Saul realized that the Lord was with David and that his daughter Michal loved David. ²⁹Then Saul was even more afraid of David, and so Saul became David's constant enemy.

³⁰The Philistine generals still went out to fight Israel. But whenever they went

---

ᵃ18:6 Hebrew meaning uncertain.

David and Goliath

David and Goliath

1 Samuel 17:38–46a

38 Saul put his battle tunic on David; he put a bronze helmet on David's head and dressed him in armor. **39** David fastened Saul's sword over his clothes and tried to walk, but he had never practiced doing this. "I can't walk in these things," David told Saul. "I've never had any practice doing this." So David took all those things off.

40 He took his stick with him, picked out five smooth stones from the riverbed, and put them in his shepherd's bag. With a sling in his hand, he approached the Philistine. **41** The Philistine, preceded by the man carrying his shield, was coming closer and closer to David. **42** When the Philistine got a good look at David, he despised him. After all, David was a young man with a healthy complexion and good looks.

43 The Philistine asked David, "Am I a dog that you come to ⌞attack⌟ me with sticks?" So the Philistine called on his gods to curse David. **44** "Come on," the Philistine told David, "and I'll give your body to the birds."

45 David told the Philistine, "You come to me with sword and spear and javelin, but I come to you in the name of the Lord of Armies, the God of the army of Israel, whom you have insulted. **46** Today the Lord will hand you over to me.

out ˌto fightˌ, David was more successful than the rest of Saul's officers. So David gained a good reputation.

Saul's Plan to Kill David

19 ¹Saul told his son Jonathan and all his officers to kill David. But Saul's son Jonathan was very fond of David, ²so he reported to David, "My father Saul is trying to kill you. Please be careful tomorrow morning. Go into hiding, and stay out of sight. ³I'll go out and stand beside my father in the field where you'll be. I'll speak with my father about you. If I find out anything, I'll tell you."

⁴So Jonathan spoke well of David to his father Saul. "You should not commit a sin against your servant David," he said. "He hasn't sinned against you. Instead, he has done some very fine things for you: ⁵He risked his life and killed the Philistine Goliath, and the LORD gave all Israel a great victory. When you saw it, you rejoiced. Why then should you sin by shedding David's innocent blood for no reason?"

⁶Saul listened to Jonathan, and he promised, "I solemnly swear, as the LORD lives, he will not be killed." ⁷Jonathan told David all of this. Then Jonathan took David to Saul. So David was returned to his former status in Saul's court.

Saul Tries to Kill David

⁸When war broke out again, David went to fight the Philistines. He defeated them so decisively that they fled from him. ⁹Then an evil spirit from the LORD came over Saul while he was sitting in his house with his spear in his hand. David was strumming a tune. ¹⁰Saul tried to nail David to the wall with his spear. But David dodged it, and Saul's spear struck the wall. David fled, escaping ˌfrom Saulˌ that night.

¹¹Saul sent messengers to watch David's house and kill him in the morning. But Michal, David's wife, advised him, "If you don't save yourself tonight, you'll be dead tomorrow!" ¹²So Michal lowered David through a window, and he ran away to escape. ¹³Then Michal took some idols, laid them in the bed, put a goat-hair blanket at its head, and covered the idols with a garment.

¹⁴When Saul sent messengers to get David, Michal said, "He's sick." ¹⁵Then Saul sent the messengers back to see David themselves. Saul told them, "Bring him here to me in his bed so that I can kill him." ¹⁶The messengers came, and there in the bed were the idols with the goat-hair blanket at its head.

¹⁷Saul asked Michal, "Why did you betray me by sending my enemy away so that he could escape?"

Michal answered, "He told me, 'Let me go! Why should I kill you?' "

¹⁸David escaped and went to Samuel at Ramah. He told Samuel everything Saul had done to him. Then he and Samuel went to the pastures and lived there.

¹⁹When it was reported to Saul that David was in the pastures at Ramah, ²⁰Saul sent messengers to get David. But when they saw a group of prophets prophesying with Samuel serving as their leader, God's Spirit came over Saul's messengers so that they also prophesied. ²¹When they told Saul ˌabout thisˌ, he sent other messengers, but they also prophesied. Saul even sent a third group of messengers, but they also prophesied. ²²Then he went to Ramah himself. He went as far as the big cistern in Secu and asked ˌthe peopleˌ, "Where are Samuel and David?"

He was told, "Over there in the pastures at Ramah." ²³As he went toward the pastures at Ramah, God's Spirit came over him too. He continued his journey, prophesying until he came to the pastures at Ramah. ²⁴He even took off his clothes as he prophesied in front of Samuel and lay there naked all day and all night. This is where the saying, "Is Saul one of the prophets?" came from.

David Makes a Promise to Jonathan

¹David fled from the pastures at Ramah, came to Jonathan, and asked, "What have I done? What crime am I guilty of? What sin have I committed against your father that he's trying to kill me?"

²Jonathan answered, "That's unthinkable! You're not going to die! My father does nothing without telling me, whether it's important or not. Why should my father hide this from me? It's just not that way."

³But David took an oath, saying, "Your father certainly knows that you support me, so he said to himself, 'Jonathan must not know about this. It will bring him distress.' But I solemnly swear, as the LORD and you live, I'm only one step away from death."

⁴Jonathan said to David, "I'll do whatever you say."

⁵David replied, "Tomorrow is the New Moon Festival, when I should sit and eat at the king's table. But let me go and hide in the countryside for two more nights. ⁶If your father really misses me, tell him, 'David repeatedly begged me to let him run to Bethlehem, his hometown, because his relatives are offering the annual sacrifice there.' ⁷If he says, 'Good!' then I will be safe. But if he gets really angry, then you'll know for sure that he has decided to harm me. ⁸Now, be kind to me. After all, you forced me into an agreement with the LORD. If I have committed any crime, kill me yourself. Why bother taking me to your father?"

⁹Jonathan answered, "That's unthinkable! If I knew for sure that my father had decided to harm you, I would have told you about it."

¹⁰Then David asked, "Who will tell me whether or not your father gives you a harsh answer?"

¹¹Jonathan said, "Let's go out into the country." So they went out into the country.

¹²"As the LORD God of Israel is my witness," Jonathan continued, "I'll find out in the next two or three days how my father feels about you. If he does feel kindly toward you, then I will send someone to tell you. ¹³If my father plans to harm you and I fail to tell you and send you away safely, may the LORD harm me even more. May the LORD be with you as he used to be with my father. ¹⁴But as long as I live, promise me that you will show me kindness because of the LORD. And even when I die, ¹⁵never stop being kind to my family. The Lord will wipe each of David's enemies off the face of the earth. ¹⁶At that time, if Jonathan's name*^a* is cut off from David's family, then may the LORD punish David's house."*^b*

¹⁷Once again Jonathan swore an oath to David because of his love for David. He loved David as much as he loved himself. ¹⁸"Tomorrow is the New Moon Festival," Jonathan told him, "and you will be missed when your seat is empty. ¹⁹The day after tomorrow you will be missed even more.*^c* So go to the place where you hid on that other occasion, and stay by the rock. ²⁰I will shoot three arrows from beside it toward a target. ²¹Then I will send out a boy and say, 'Go, find the arrows.' Now, if I tell the boy, 'Look, the arrows are next to you; get them,' then come back with me. You will be safe, and there will be no trouble. I swear it, as the LORD lives. ²²But if I tell the boy, 'The arrows are next to you,' then go, because the LORD has sent you away. ²³We have made a promise to each other, and the LORD is a witness between you and me forever."

²⁴So David hid in the countryside. When the New Moon Festival came, King Saul sat down to eat the festival meal. ²⁵He sat in his usual seat by the wall, while Jonathan

---

^a20:16 Greek; Masoretic Text omits "name." ^b20:16 Ancient scribal tradition; Masoretic Text "punish David's enemies." At times some scribes would alter the text when they thought it was disrespectful. ^c20:19 Hebrew meaning uncertain.

stood. Abner sat beside Saul, but David's place was empty. ²⁶Saul didn't say anything that day, thinking, "Something has happened to him so that he's unclean.ᵈ He must be unclean." ²⁷But on the second day of the month, David's place was still empty.

Saul asked his son Jonathan, "Why hasn't Jesse's son come to the meal either yesterday or today?"

²⁸Jonathan answered Saul, "David repeatedly begged me to let him go to Bethlehem. ²⁹David said to me 'Please let me go. Our relatives will offer a sacrifice in the city, and my brother ordered me to be there. If you will permit it, please let me go to see my brothers.' This is why he hasn't come to your banquet."

³⁰Then Saul got angry with Jonathan. "Son of a crooked and rebellious woman!" he called Jonathan. "I know you've sided with Jesse's son. You have no shame. You act as if you are your mother's son but not mine.ᵉ ³¹As long as Jesse's son lives on earth, neither you nor your right to be king is secure. Now, send some men to bring him to me. He's a dead man!"

³²Jonathan asked his father, "Why should he be killed? What has he done?"

³³Saul raised his spear to strike him. Then Jonathan knew his father was determined to kill David. ³⁴Jonathan got up from the table very angry and ate nothing that second day of the month. He was worried sick about David because Jonathan had been humiliated by his own father.

³⁵In the morning Jonathan went out to the country to the place he and David had agreed on. Jonathan had a young boy with him. ³⁶"Run," he told the boy, "please find the arrows I shoot."

The boy ran, and Jonathan shot the arrow over him. ³⁷When the boy reached the place where Jonathan's arrow had landed, Jonathan called after him, "The arrows are next to you!" ³⁸Jonathan added, "Quick! Hurry up! Don't stand there!" Jonathan's young servant gathered the arrows and came to his master. ³⁹The boy had no idea what was going on, but Jonathan and David understood. ⁴⁰Then Jonathan gave his weapons to the boy. He told the boy, "Take them back into town."

⁴¹When the boy had left, David came out from the south side of the rock, and quickly bowed down three times with his face touching the ground. Then they kissed each other and cried together, but David cried the loudest.ᶠ

⁴²"Go in peace!" Jonathan told David. "We have both taken an oath in the LORD's name, saying, 'The LORD will be a witness between me and you and between my descendants and your descendants forever.' "ᵍ

So David left, and Jonathan went into the city.

David at Nob

ᵃ¹David went to the priest Ahimelech at Nob. Ahimelech was trembling as he went to meet David. "Why are you alone?" he asked David. "Why is no one with you?"

²"The king ordered me to do something," David answered the priest Ahimelech, "and he told me, 'No one must know anything about this mission I'm sending you on and about the orders I've given you. I've stationedᵇ my young men at a certain place.' " ³David added, "Now, what do you have to eat? Give me five loaves of bread or whatever you can find."

⁴"I don't have any ordinary bread," the chief priest answered David. "But there is holy bread for the young men if they haven't had sexual intercourse today."

ᵈ20:26 "Unclean" refers to anything that Moses' Teachings say is not presentable to God.   ᵉ20:30 English equivalent difficult.   ᶠ20:41 Hebrew meaning uncertain.   ᵍ20:42 1 Samuel 20:42b in English Bibles is 1 Samuel 21:1 in the Hebrew Bible.   ᵃ21:1 1 Samuel 21:1-15 in English Bibles is 1 Samuel 21:2-16 in the Hebrew Bible.   ᵇ21:2 Dead Sea Scrolls, Greek; Masoretic Text "I've informed."

⁵David answered the priest, "Of course women have been kept away from us as usual when we go on a mission. The young men's bodies are kept holy even on ordinary campaigns. How much more then will their bodies be holy today?"

⁶So the priest gave him holy bread, because he only had the bread of the presence which had been taken from the LORD's presence and replaced with warm bread that day.

⁷That same day one of Saul's servants who was obligated to stay in the LORD's presence was there. His name was Doeg. A foreman for Saul's shepherds, he was from Edom.

⁸David asked Ahimelech, "Don't you have a spear or a sword here? I didn't take either my spear or any other weapon because the king's business was urgent."

⁹The chief priest answered, "The sword of Goliath the Philistine, whom you killed in the Elah Valley, is here. It is wrapped in a cloth behind the priestly ephod.ᶜ If you want to take it, take it. There's no other weapon here."

David said, "There's none like it. Let me have the sword."

David at Gath

¹⁰That day David left. He was still fleeing from Saul when he came to King Achish of Gath. ¹¹Achish's officers asked, "Isn't this David, the king of his country? He's the one they used to sing about in the dances:

'Saul has defeated thousands
    but David tens of thousands.' "

¹²When David realized what they had said, he was terrified of King Achish of Gath. ¹³So he changed his behavior when he was in their presence and acted insane as long as he was under their authority. He scribbled on the doors of the city gate and let his spit run down his beard.

¹⁴Achish said to his officers, "Look at him! Don't you see that he's insane? Why bring him to me? ¹⁵Do I have such a shortage of lunatics that you bring this man so that he can show me he is insane? Does this man have to come into my house?"

David in Judah and Moab

¹So David escaped from that place and fled to the cave at Adullam. When his brothers and all the rest of his family heard about it, they went to him. ²Then everyone who was in trouble, in debt, or bitter about life joined him, and he became their commander. There were about four hundred men with him.

³From there David went to Mizpah in Moab. He asked the king of Moab, "Please let my father and mother stay with you until I know what God is going to do for me." ⁴He brought them to the king of Moab, and they stayed with him as long as David was living in his fortified camp.

⁵"Don't live in your fortified camp," the prophet Gad told David. "Go to the land of Judah." So David went to the forest of Hereth.

Saul Massacres the Priests at Nob

⁶Saul heard that David and his men had been found. Saul was staying in Gibeah under the tamarisk tree at the worship siteᵈ with his spear in his hand and all his officials standing around him. ⁷He said to his officials, "Listen here, men of Benjamin! Will Jesse's son give every one of you fields and vineyards? Will he make you all

---

ᶜ21:9 *Ephod* is a technical term for a part of the priest's clothes. Its exact usage and shape are unknown.
ᵈ22:6 Greek; Masoretic Text "at Ramah."

officers over a regiment or a battalion of soldiers? ⁸All of you are plotting against me, and no one informed me when my son entered into a loyalty pledge with Jesse's son. No one felt sorry for me and informed me that my son has encouraged my servant David to ambush me, as he's doing now."

⁹Then Doeg from Edom, standing with Saul's officials, answered him, "I saw Jesse's son when he came to Ahimelech, Ahitub's son, in Nob. ¹⁰Ahimelech prayed to the Lord for David and gave him food and the sword of Goliath the Philistine."

¹¹Then the king sent for the priest Ahimelech, who was Ahitub's son, and his entire family who were the priests in Nob. All of them came to the king. ¹²Saul said, "Listen here, son of Ahitub!"

"Yes, sir?" he responded.

¹³Saul asked him, "Why did you and Jesse's son plot against me? You gave him bread and a sword and prayed to God for him so that he can rise up against me and ambush me, as he's doing now."

¹⁴Ahimelech asked the king, "But whom among all your officials can you trust like David? Your Majesty, he's your son-in-law, the commander of your bodyguard. He's honored in your own household. ¹⁵Is this the first time I have prayed to God for him? Not at all! You shouldn't blame me or anyone in my family for this. I knew nothing at all about this."

¹⁶Saul said, "Ahimelech, you and your entire family are going to die."

¹⁷"Turn and kill the Lord's priests because they support David," the king said to the runners standing around him. "When they knew David was fleeing, they didn't inform me." But the king's men refused to attack the Lord's priests.

¹⁸So the king said to Doeg, "You turn and attack the priests." Doeg from Edom turned and attacked the priests, and that day he killed 85 men wearing the linen priestly ephod.ᵇ ¹⁹He also killed the people of Nob, the city of the priests. Using his sword, he killed men and women, children and infants, cows, donkeys, and sheep.

²⁰But Ahimelech, Ahitub's son, had one son who escaped. His name was Abiathar. He fled to David. ²¹Abiathar told David that Saul had killed the Lord's priests.

²²David told Abiathar, "I knew that day when Doeg from Edom was there that he would be certain to tell Saul. I am the one responsibleᶜ for all the lives of your family. ²³Stay with me. Don't be afraid. The one who is seeking my life is also seeking your life. However, you will be under my protection."

David Saves the City of Keilah

¹David was asked, "Did you know that the Philistines are fighting against Keilah? They are robbing the threshing floors."ᵃ

²David asked the Lord, "Should I go and attack these Philistines?"

"Go," the Lord told David, "attack the Philistines, and save Keilah."

³David's men told him, "We're afraid of staying here in Judah. How much more afraid do you think we'll be if we go to Keilah against the Philistine army?"

⁴David asked the Lord again, and the Lord answered him. He said, "Go to Keilah. I'm giving you the power to defeat the Philistines."

⁵David and his men went to Keilah, fought the Philistines, drove off their livestock, and decisively defeated them. So David rescued the people who lived in Keilah.

⁶When Ahimelech's son Abiathar fled to David at Keilah, Abiathar brought a priestly ephodᵇ with him.

ᵇ22:18 *Ephod* is a technical term for a part of the priest's clothes. Its exact usage and shape are unknown.
ᶜ22:22 Greek; Masoretic Text "I turned." ᵃ23:1 A threshing floor is an outdoor area where grain is separated from its husks. ᵇ23:6 *Ephod* is a technical term for a part of the priest's clothes. Its exact usage and shape are unknown.

⁷When Saul was told that David went to Keilah, Saul said, "God has delivered him into my hands. He has trapped himself by going into a city which has a gate with a double door held shut by a bar." ⁸So Saul called together all the troops to go to war and blockade Keilah, where David and his men were.

⁹When David learned that Saul was planning to harm him, he told the priest Abiathar, "Bring the ephod." ¹⁰Then David said, "Lord God of Israel, I have actually heard that Saul is going to come to Keilah and destroy the city on account of me. ¹¹Will the citizens of Keilah hand me over to him? Will Saul come here as I have heard? Lord God of Israel, please tell me."

"He will come," the Lord answered.

¹²"Will the citizens of Keilah hand me and my men over to Saul?" David asked.

"They will hand you over," the Lord answered.

¹³So David and his men, about six hundred[c] in all, left Keilah. They went wherever they could go. Then Saul was told, "David has escaped from Keilah!" So he gave up the campaign. ¹⁴David lived in fortified camps in the desert, and he lived in fortified camps in the mountains of the desert of Ziph. Saul was always searching for him, but God didn't let him capture David.

David in the Desert of Ziph

¹⁵David was afraid because[d] Saul had come to kill him at Horesh in the desert of Ziph. ¹⁶Saul's son Jonathan came to David at Horesh. He strengthened David's faith in the Lord.[e] ¹⁷"Don't be afraid," he told David, "my father Saul won't find you. You will rule Israel, and I will be your second-in-command. Even my father Saul knows this." ¹⁸Both of them made a pledge in the Lord's presence. David stayed in Horesh, and Jonathan went home.

¹⁹Then the men of Ziph went to Saul in Gibeah. They said, "David is hiding with us in fortified camps at Horesh on the hills of Hachilah, south of Jeshimon. ²⁰Come, Your Majesty, whenever you want. We will hand him over to you."

²¹Saul responded, "The Lord bless you for feeling sorry for me! ²²Please make more plans, and watch where he goes. Who has seen him there? I'm told he's very clever. ²³Watch and learn about all the hiding places where he may be hiding, and come back to me with the facts. Then I'll go with you, and if he's in the country, I'll search for him among all the families of Judah." ²⁴They left for Ziph ahead of Saul.

David in the Desert of Maon

David and his men were in the desert of Maon, in the plains south of Jeshimon. ²⁵When Saul and his men came to look for him, David was told the news. So he went to his mountain stronghold in the desert of Maon. Saul heard about it and pursued David into the desert of Maon. ²⁶Saul went on one side of the mountain, and David and his men went on the other side of the mountain. David was hurrying to get away from Saul, and Saul and his men were going around the mountain toward David and his men, trying to capture them. ²⁷Then a messenger came to Saul and said, "Come quickly! The Philistines are raiding the country."

²⁸Saul gave up pursuing David and went to fight the Philistines. So that place was called Slippery Rock.[f] ²⁹From there David went to stay in the fortified camps of En Gedi.

---

c23:13 Masoretic Text; Greek "four hundred." d23:15 Or "David saw that." e23:16 Dead Sea Scrolls, Greek; Masoretic Text "in God." f23:28 1 Samuel 23:29 in English Bibles is 1 Samuel 24:1 in the Hebrew Bible.

David Spares Saul's Life

24 [a]1When Saul came back from ˏfightingˌ the Philistines, he was told "Now David is in the desert near En Gedi." 2Then Saul took 3,000 of the best-trained men from all Israel and went to search for David and his men on the Rocks of the Wild Goats. 3He came to some sheep pens along the road where there was a cave. Saul went into ˏitˌ to relieve himself while David and his men were sitting further back in the cave.

4David's men told him, "Today is the day the Lord referred to when he said, 'I'm going to hand your enemy over to you. You will do to him whatever you think is right.' "

David quietly got up and cut off the border of Saul's robe. 5But afterward, David's conscience bothered him because he had cut off the border of Saul's robe. 6He said to his men, "It would be unthinkable for me to raise my hand against His Majesty, the Lord's anointed king, since he is the Lord's anointed." 7So David stopped[b] his men by saying this to them and didn't let them attack Saul.

Saul left the cave and went out onto the road. 8Later, David got up, left the cave, and called to Saul, "Your Majesty!" When Saul looked back, David knelt down with his face touching the ground. 9David asked Saul, "Why do you listen to rumors that I am trying to harm you? 10Today you saw how the Lord handed you over to me in the cave. Although I was told to kill you, I spared you, saying, 'I will not raise my hand against Your Majesty because you are the Lord's anointed.' 11My master, look at this! The border of your robe is in my hand! Since I cut off the border of your robe and didn't kill you, you should know and be able to see I mean no harm or rebellion. I haven't sinned against you, but you are trying to ambush me in order to take my life. 12May the Lord decide between you and me. May the Lord take revenge on you for what you did to me. However, I will not lay a hand on you. 13It's like people used to say long ago, 'Wickedness comes from wicked people.' But I will not lay a hand on you. 14Against whom has the king of Israel come out? Whom are you pursuing? A dead dog? One flea? 15So the Lord must be the judge. He will decide between you and me. He will watch and take my side in ˏthisˌ matter and set me free from you."

16When David finished saying this, Saul asked, "Is that you speaking, my servant David?" and Saul cried loudly. 17He told David, "You are more righteous than I. You treated me well while I treated you badly. 18Today you have proved how good you've been to me. When the Lord handed me over to you, you didn't kill me. 19When a person finds an enemy, does he send him away unharmed? The Lord will repay you completely for what you did for me today. 20Now I know that you certainly will rule as king, and under your guidance the kingdom of Israel will prosper. 21Swear an oath to the Lord for me that you will not wipe out my descendants or destroy my name in my father's family."

22So David swore to Saul. Then Saul went home, and David and his men went to their fortified camp.

Samuel Dies

25 1Samuel died, and all Israel gathered to mourn for him. They buried him at his home in Ramah. Then David went to the desert of Paran.

David, Nabal, and Abigail

2Now, there was a man in Maon whose business was in Carmel. He was a very rich man. He had 3,000 sheep and 1,000 goats. And he was shearing his sheep in

---

[a]24:1 1 Samuel 24:1-22 in English Bibles is 1 Samuel 24:2-23 in the Hebrew Bible. [b]24:7 Hebrew meaning uncertain.

Carmel. ³This man's name was Nabal, and his wife's name was Abigail. She was sensible and beautiful, but he was harsh and mean. He was a descendant of Caleb.

⁴While David was in the desert, he heard that Nabal was shearing his sheep. ⁵So David sent ten young men and told them, "Go to Carmel, visit Nabal, and greet him for me. ⁶Say to him, 'May you live long! May you, your home, and all you have prosper! ⁷I hear that your sheepshearers are with you. Your shepherds have been with us, and we have not mistreated them. Nothing of theirs has been missing as long as they've been in Carmel. ⁸Ask your young men, and let them tell you. Be kind to my young men, since we have come on a special occasion. Please give us and your son David anything you can spare.'"

⁹When David's young men came to Nabal, they repeated all of this to him for David, and then they waited.

¹⁰"Who is David?" Nabal answered David's servants. "Who is Jesse's son? So many servants nowadays are leaving their masters. ¹¹Should I take my bread, my water, and my meat that I butchered for my shearers and give them to men coming from who knows where?"

¹²David's young men returned and told him all this.

¹³"Each of you put on your swords!" David told his men. And everyone, including David, put on his sword. About four hundred men went with David, while two hundred men stayed with the supplies.

¹⁴One of the young men told Abigail, Nabal's wife, "David sent messengers from the desert to greet our master, who yelled at them. ¹⁵Those men were very good to us. They didn't mistreat us, and we found that nothing was missing wherever we went with them when we were in the fields. ¹⁶They were a wall protecting us day and night as long as we were watching the sheep near them. ¹⁷Now, consider what you should do because our master and his whole household are doomed. And he's such a worthless man that it's useless to talk to him."

¹⁸So Abigail quickly took 200 loaves of bread, 2 full wineskins, 5 butchered sheep, a bushel of roasted grain, 100 bunches of raisins, and 200 fig cakes and loaded them on donkeys. ¹⁹"Go on ahead," she told her young men, "and I'll follow you." But she didn't tell her husband Nabal about it.

²⁰She was riding on her donkey down a hidden mountain path when she met David and his men coming toward her. ²¹David had thought, "I guarded this man's stuff in the desert for nothing! Not one of his possessions was missing. Yet, he has paid me back with evil when I was good to him. ²²May God punish me*ᵃ* if I leave even one of his men*ᵇ* alive in the morning."

²³When Abigail saw David, she quickly got down from her donkey. She immediately bowed down in front of David with her face touching the ground. ²⁴After she bowed at his feet, she said, "Sir, let me be held responsible for this wrong. Please let me speak with you. Please listen to my words. ²⁵You shouldn't take this worthless person Nabal seriously. He is like his name. His name is Nabal [Godless Fool], and he's foolish. But I didn't see the young men you sent.

²⁶"The Lord has kept you from spilling innocent blood and from getting a victory by your own efforts. Now, sir, I solemnly swear, as the Lord and you live, may your enemies and those who are trying to harm you end up like Nabal. ²⁷Here is a gift I am bringing to you. May it be given to the young men who are in your service. ²⁸Please forgive my offense. The Lord will certainly give you, sir, a lasting dynasty, because you are fighting the Lord's battles. May evil never be found in you as long as you

---

ᵃ25:22 Greek; Masoretic Text "To David's enemies." ᵇ25:22 Hebrew uses a coarse term for "men" here and at verse 34.

live. ²⁹Even though someone pursued you and sought your life, your life is wrapped in the bundle of life which comes from the LORD your God. But he will dispose of the lives of your enemies like stones thrown from a sling. ³⁰When the LORD does all the good he promised and makes you ruler of Israel, ³¹you shouldn't have a troubled conscience because you spilled blood for no good reason and claimed your own victory. When the LORD has given you success, remember me."

³²David said to Abigail, "Blessed be the LORD God of Israel, who sent you today to meet me. ³³May your good judgment be blessed. Also, may you be blessed for keeping me from slaughtering people today and from getting a victory by my own efforts. ³⁴But I solemnly swear—as the LORD God of Israel, who has kept me from harming you, lives—if you hadn't come to meet me quickly, Nabal certainly wouldn't have had one of his men left at dawn."

³⁵Then David accepted what she brought him and told her, "Go home in peace. I've listened to what you've said and granted your request."

³⁶When Abigail came to Nabal, he was holding a banquet in his home. It was like a king's banquet. He was in a good mood and very drunk, so she didn't tell him anything until dawn. ³⁷But in the morning, when the effects of the wine had worn off, his wife told him what had happened. Nabal's heart failed, and he could not move.ᶜ ³⁸About ten days later the LORD made him even more sick, and Nabal died.

³⁹When David heard Nabal was dead, he said, "Blessed be the LORD, who defended me against the insults of Nabal and kept me from doing wrong. The LORD has turned Nabal's own wickedness back on him."

Then David sent men on his behalf to propose marriage to Abigail. ⁴⁰When David's servants came to Abigail at Carmel, they told her, "David has sent us to you so that we can take you to him to be his wife."

⁴¹She bowed down with her face touching the ground. "I am ready to serve," she said. "I am ready to wash the feet of my master's servants." ⁴²Then Abigail quickly got up and rode on a donkey with five of her female servants following her. So she went with David's messengers and became his wife.

⁴³David also married Ahinoam of Jezreel. Both she and Abigail were his wives. ⁴⁴Saul had given his daughter Michal, David's wife, to Palti, Laish's son, who was from Gallim.

Good Morning, God
1 Samuel 25:32-34

Abigail knew that David was going to do a foolish thing. She quickly acted to stop him from harming her husband. If you know someone who needs good advice, don't be afraid to talk to that person. Follow Abigail's example: Plan ahead for what you will do and say, be humble, don't accuse, be an encourager, and trust God.

Father, give me wisdom to help others when they do wrong.

ᶜ25:37 English equivalent difficult.

Saul's Final Pursuit of David

26 ¹The people of Ziph came to Saul at Gibeah. "David is hiding at the hill of Hachilah near Jeshimon," they said.

²Saul went to the desert of Ziph, taking with him 3,000 of Israel's best-trained men to search for David. ³Saul camped by the road at the hill of Hachilah near Jeshimon, but David stayed in the desert. When he realized Saul had come to the desert for him, ⁴David sent spies to confirm that Saul had arrived.

⁵Then David went to the place where Saul had camped. David saw the place where Saul and Ner's son Abner, the commander of the army, were lying. Saul was lying in the camp, and the troops were camped around him.

⁶David asked Ahimelech the Hittite and Abishai, who was Zeruiah's son and Joab's brother, "Who will go with me to Saul in the camp?"

Abishai answered, "I'll go with you."

⁷So David and Abishai went among Saul's troops that night. Saul was lying asleep inside the camp with his spear stuck in the ground near his head. Abner and the soldiers were lying around him. ⁸Abishai said to David, "Today God has turned your enemy over to you. Please let me nail him to the ground with one stab of the spear. I won't have to do it twice!"

⁹"Don't kill him!" David told Abishai. "No one has ever attacked the Lord's anointed king and remained free of guilt. ¹⁰I solemnly swear, as the Lord lives," David added, "the Lord will strike him. Either his time will come when he'll die naturally, or he'll go into battle and be swept away. ¹¹It would be unthinkable for me to attack the Lord's anointed king. But please take that spear near his head and that jar of water, and let's go."

¹²David took the spear and the jar of water near Saul's head, and they left. All of them were asleep. No one saw them, knew about it, or woke up. The Lord had made them fall into a deep sleep.

¹³David went over to the other side and stood on top of the hill some distance away. (There was a wide space between them.) ¹⁴Then David called to the troops and to Ner's son Abner. "Won't you answer, Abner?" he asked.

"Who is calling the king?" Abner asked.

¹⁵David asked Abner, "Aren't you a man? Is there anyone like you in Israel? Then why didn't you guard your master, the king? Someone came to kill His Royal Majesty. ¹⁶What you've done isn't good. I solemnly swear, as the Lord lives, you are dead men. You didn't guard your master, the Lord's anointed king. Look at the king's spear and the jar of water that were near his head."

¹⁷Saul recognized David's voice. "Is that your voice, my servant David?" he asked.

"It is my voice, Your Royal Majesty," David answered. ¹⁸"Why are you pursuing me?" he added. "What have I done? What crime have I committed? ¹⁹Your Majesty, please listen to my words. If the Lord has turned you against me, let him be satisfied with an offering. But if mere mortals have turned you against me, let them be cursed by the Lord. They have prevented me from having a share of the Lord's inheritance. 'Go and serve other gods,' they tell me. ²⁰Don't let my blood fall to the ground, away from the Lord's presence. The king of Israel has come to search for one flea like someone hunting a partridge in the hills."

²¹"My servant David," Saul said, "I have sinned. Come back. I will not harm you again, because you valued my life today. I've acted like a fool and made a terrible mistake."

²²David responded, "Here's the king's spear. One of the young men should come over and get it. ²³The Lord will reward any person who is righteous and faithful. The

LORD handed you over to me today, but I refused to attack the LORD's anointed king. ²⁴As I placed great value on your life today, may the LORD place great value on my life and rescue me from all trouble."

²⁵Then Saul said, "Blessed are you, my servant David. You will accomplish many things and certainly will succeed."

So David went his way, while Saul returned home.

David at Ziklag

¹David said to himself, "One of these days Saul will sweep me away. The best thing for me to do is to make sure that I escape to Philistine territory. Then Saul will give up looking all over Israel for me, and I'll escape from him." ²So David went with his 600 men to King Achish of Gath, Moach's son. ³David and his men stayed with Achish in Gath. Each one had his family, and David had his two wives, Ahinoam from Jezreel and Abigail (who had been Nabal's wife) from Carmel. ⁴When Saul was told that David had fled to Gath, he didn't search for him anymore.

⁵David said to Achish, "If you will permit me, let me have a place in one of the outlying towns so that I can live there. Why should I live in the royal city with you?" ⁶So Achish immediately gave him Ziklag. (This is why Ziklag still belongs to the kings of Judah today.)

⁷David stayed in Philistine territory for one year and four months. ⁸Then David and his men went to raid the Geshurites, the Girzites, and the Amalekites. (They lived in the territory which extends from Telaim*to Shur and Egypt.) ⁹Whenever David attacked the territory, he left no man or woman alive. He also took sheep, cattle, donkeys, camels, and clothing and returned to Achish.

¹⁰Achish would ask, "Whom did you raid today?"*ᵇ

And David would answer, "the Negev in Judah," or "the portion of the Negev where the descendants of Jerahmeel live," or "the portion of the Negev where the Kenites live." ¹¹He did not bring a single man or woman back to Gath alive. He thought, "They could tell Achish what I really did." This was his practice as long as he lived in Philistine territory. ¹²And Achish believed David. Achish thought, "He has definitely made his own people in Israel despise him. He'll be my servant from now on." ¹At that time the Philistines had gathered their army to fight against Israel.

Then Achish said to David, "You need to know that you and your men will be going with me into battle."

²"Very well," David responded to Achish, "you will then know what I can do."

"Very well," Achish told David, "I will make you my bodyguard for life."

Saul's Sin—The Occult

³Meanwhile, Samuel had died, and all Israel had mourned for him and buried him in his hometown Ramah. (Saul had rid the land of mediums and psychics.)

⁴The Philistines assembled and camped in Shunem. Saul also assembled the whole Israelite army, and they camped at Gilboa. ⁵When Saul looked at the Philistine army, he was very afraid—terrified. ⁶He prayed to the LORD, but the LORD didn't answer him through dreams, the Urim,*or prophets. ⁷Saul told his officers, "Find me a woman who conjures up the dead. Then I'll go to her and ask for her services."

His officers told him, "There is a woman at Endor who conjures up the dead."

⁸After disguising himself by putting on other clothes, Saul left with two men and

---

*27:8 Greek; Masoretic Text "lived in the country for a long time." ᵇ27:10 Dead Sea Scrolls, Greek; Masoretic Text "Did you raid today?" *28:6 The Urim and Thummim were used by the chief priest to determine God's answer to questions.

came to the woman that night. He said to her, "Please consult with a dead person for me. Conjure up the person I request."

⁹The woman told him, "You know that Saul rid the land of mediums and psychics. Why are you trying to trap me and have me killed?"

¹⁰But Saul took an oath in the Lord's name, "I solemnly swear, as the Lord lives, you will not be harmed if you do this."

¹¹"Whom should I conjure up for you?" the woman asked.

"Conjure up Samuel for me," he answered.

¹²When the woman saw Samuel, she cried out loudly and asked, "Why did you deceive me? You're Saul!"

¹³"Don't be afraid," the king said to her. "What do you see?"

"I see a god rising from the ground," the woman answered.

¹⁴"In what form?" he asked her.

She answered, "An old man is coming up, and he's wearing a robe." Then Saul knew it was Samuel. Saul knelt down with his face touching the ground.

¹⁵Samuel asked Saul, "Why did you disturb me by conjuring me up?"

Saul answered, "I'm in serious trouble. The Philistines are at war with me, and God has turned against me and doesn't answer me anymore—either by the prophets or in dreams. So I've called on you to tell me what to do."

¹⁶Samuel said, "Why are you asking me when the Lord has turned against you and become your enemy? ¹⁷The Lord has done to you exactly what he spoke through me: The Lord has torn the kingship out of your hands and given it to your fellow Is-raelite David. ¹⁸The Lord is doing this to you today because you didn't listen to him or unleash his burning anger on Amalek. ¹⁹For the same reasons the Lord will hand you and Israel over to the Philistines. Tomorrow you and your sons will be with me. And then the Lord will hand Israel's army over to the Philistines."

²⁰Immediately, Saul fell flat on the ground. He was frightened by Samuel's words. He also had no strength left, because he hadn't eaten anything all day or all night. ²¹The woman came over to Saul and saw that he was terrified. "I listened to you," she told him, "and I took my life in my hands when I did what you told me to do. ²²Now please listen to me. I will serve you something to eat. Eat it so that you will have strength when you leave."

²³But he refused. "I don't want to eat," he said. Nevertheless, his officers and the woman kept urging ᵇ him until he listened to them. So he got up from the ground and sat on the bed.

²⁴The woman immediately butchered a fattened calf that she owned. She took flour, kneaded it, and baked some unleavened bread. ²⁵Then she served it to Saul and his officers. They ate and left that same night.

The Philistines Reject David

29 ¹The Philistines assembled their whole army at Aphek, and Israel camped at the spring in Jezreel. ²The Philistine leaders were marching by with their com-panies and regiments. David and his men were marching in the rear with Achish.

³The Philistine officers asked, "What are these Hebrews doing here?"

Achish asked the Philistine officers, "Isn't this David, the servant of King Saul of Israel, who has been with me now for a year or two? I've found nothing wrong with him from the day he defected until now."

⁴But the Philistine officers were angry with Achish. "Send the man back," the

---

ᵇ28:23 Greek; Masoretic Text "the woman broke through."

Philistine officers told him. "Return him to the place you assigned him. He shouldn't go with us into battle. He shouldn't be allowed to become our enemy during the battle. Is this man going to try to regain his master's favor? He'll do it with the lives of our men! ⁵Isn't this David of whom people sing in dances:

> 'Saul has defeated thousands
>   but David tens of thousands'?"

⁶Then Achish called David and told him, "I solemnly swear, as the Lord lives, you are a dependable man. I consider your campaigning with me a good thing, because I've never found anything wrong with you from the day you came to me until now. But the rulers don't approve of you. ⁷So leave peacefully without doing anything to displease the Philistine rulers."

⁸"What have I done?" David asked Achish. "What have you learned about me from the time I came to you until now? Why shouldn't I fight your enemies, Your Majesty?"

⁹Achish answered David, "I admit that in my judgment you're as good as God's Messenger. However, the Philistine officers said, 'He shouldn't go into battle with us.' ¹⁰Get up early in the morning with Saul's servants who came with you, and go to the place I have assigned to you. Don't worry about the unkind words, because I still approve of you.ᵃ Get up in the morning, and leave when it's light."

¹¹Early the next morning David and his men returned to Philistine territory, while the Philistines went to Jezreel.

David Defeats the Amalekites

30 ¹Two days later, when David and his men came to Ziklag, the Amalekites had raided the Negev, including Ziklag. They had attacked Ziklag and burned it. ²Although they captured the young and old women who were there, they killed no one. Instead, they had taken the women and other prisoners and gone away. ³By the time David and his men came to the town, it had been burned down, and their wives, sons, and daughters had been taken captive. ⁴Then David and his men cried loudly until they didn't have the strength to cry anymore. ⁵The Amalekites also captured David's two wives, Ahinoam from Jezreel and Abigail (who had been Nabal's wife) from Carmel. ⁶David was in great distress because the people in their bitterness said he should be stoned. (They were thinking of their sons and daughters. But David found strength in the Lord his God.)

⁷David told the priest Abiathar, Ahimelech's son, "Please bring me the priestly ephod."ᵃ So Abiathar brought David the ephod.

⁸Then David asked the Lord, "Should I pursue these troops? Will I catch up with them?"

"Pursue them," the Lord told him. "You will certainly catch up with them and rescue the captives."

⁹So David and his 600 men went to the Besor Valley, where some were left behind. ¹⁰David and 400 men went in pursuit, while 200 men who were too exhausted to cross the Besor Valley stayed behind.

¹¹David's men found an Egyptian in the open country and took him to David. They gave him food to eat and water to drink. ¹²They gave him a slice of fig cake and two bunches of raisins. After he had eaten, he revived. (He hadn't eaten any food or drunk any water for three whole days.) ¹³David asked him, "To whom do you belong? Where do you come from?"

ᵃ29:10 "and go . . . approve of you" Greek; Masoretic Text omits these words.   ᵃ30:7 *Ephod* is a technical term for a part of the priest's clothes. Its exact usage and shape are unknown.

"I'm an Egyptian, the slave of an Amalekite," the young man answered. "My master left me behind because I got sick three days ago. [14]We raided the portion of the Negev where the Cherethites live, the territory of Judah, the portion of the Negev where Caleb settled, and we burned down Ziklag."

[15]"Will you lead me to these troops?" David asked him.

He answered, "Take an oath in front of God that you won't kill me or hand me over to my master, and I'll lead you to these troops."

[16]The Egyptian led him to them. They were spread out all over the land, eating, and drinking. They were celebrating because they had taken so much loot from Philistine territory and from the land of Judah. [17]From dawn until evening the next day, David attacked them. No one escaped except 400 young men who rode away on camels. [18]David rescued everything the Amalekites had taken, including his two wives. [19]Nothing was missing—young or old, sons or daughters, the loot or anything else they had taken with them. David brought back everything. [20]He took all the sheep and the cattle. His men drove the animals ahead of him and said, "This is David's loot."

[21]David came to the 200 men who had been too exhausted to go with him and had stayed in the Besor Valley. They came to meet David and the people with him. As David approached the men, he greeted them. [22]Then every wicked and worthless man who had gone with David said, "Since they didn't go with us, they shouldn't be given any of the loot we recovered. Each of them should take only his wife and children and leave."

[23]But David said, "My brothers, don't do that with the things which the LORD has given us. He has protected us and handed the troops that attacked us over to us. [24]Besides, who is going to pay attention to what you have to say in this matter? Certainly, the share of those who go into battle must be like the share of those who stay with the supplies. They will all share alike." [25]From that time on he made this a rule and a custom in Israel as it is to this day.

[26]When David came to Ziklag, he sent part of the loot to his friends, the leaders of Judah. He said, "Here is a gift for you from the loot taken from the LORD's enemies." [27]There were shares for those in Bethel, Ramoth in the Negev, Jattir, [28]Aroer, Siphmoth, Eshtemoa, [29]Racal, the cities belonging to the Jerahmeelites, the cities belonging to the Kenites, [30]Hormah, Borashan, Athach, [31]Hebron, and to all the places David and his men visited from time to time.

The Death of Saul—
1 Chronicles 10:1-14

31 [1]When the Philistines were fighting against Israel, the men of Israel fled from the Philistines and were killed in battle on Mount Gilboa. [2]The Philistines caught up to Saul and his sons. They killed Jonathan, Abinadab, and Malchishua, Saul's sons. [3]The heaviest fighting was against Saul. When the archers got him in their range, he was badly wounded by them.

[4]Saul told his armorbearer, "Draw your sword! Stab me, or these godless men will come, stab me, and make fun of me." But his armorbearer refused because he was terrified. So Saul took the sword and fell on it. [5]When the armorbearer saw that Saul was dead, he also fell on his sword and died with him. [6]So Saul, his three sons, his armorbearer, and all his men died together that day.

[7]When the people of Israel on the other side of the valley and across the Jordan River saw that the men of Israel had fled and that Saul and his sons were dead, they abandoned their cities. So the Philistines came to live in these cities.

[8]The next day, when the Philistines came to strip the dead, they found Saul and his three sons lying on Mount Gilboa. [9]They cut off his head and stripped off his armor.

Then they sent men throughout Philistine territory to tell the people this good news in their idols' temples. ¹⁰They put his armor in the temple of their goddesses—the Asherahs—and fastened his corpse to the wall of Beth Shan.

¹¹When the people living in Jabesh Gilead heard what the Philistines had done to Saul, ¹²all the fighting men marched all night and took the dead bodies of Saul and his sons from the wall of Beth Shan. They came back to Jabesh and burned the bodies there. ¹³They took the bones and buried them under the tamarisk tree in Jabesh. Then they fasted seven days.

2 Samuel

David ruled Israel for 40 years. He led the Israelites into many victorious battles. He turned a scattered group of tribes into a great nation. The first part of David's reign was a complete success.

But David wasn't perfect. He took another man's wife and arranged for the man to be killed. Later, David changed the way he thought and acted and was forgiven by God. But as a result of his sin, David had many troubles in the last years of his life.

Headlines

One of David's enemies was the Philistines. These people were a warlike people who lived along the coast of Canaan.

Parents Too Tough?

Do you think it would be better if your parents never punished you? If you never got grounded?

When David's son Amnon sinned, David was angry, but he didn't do anything to punish Amnon. Later, another of David's sons, Absalom, killed Amnon. Again, David did nothing. Absalom thought his father didn't care about him. He became bitter and rebelled against David. Eventually, Absalom was killed in a battle between his troops and David's troops. David was a do-nothing dad. And that didn't help his sons one bit. If your parents are a little tough, remember that it's because they care about you.

What's In It For Me?

David's life teaches . . .

GOD KEEPS HIS PROMISES.

YOUNG PEOPLE CAN MAKE A DIFFERENCE IN THE WORLD.

EVEN GOOD PEOPLE MUST WATCH OUT FOR SIN.

GOD DISCIPLINES THOSE HE LOVES.

GOD FORGIVES THOSE WHO CONFESS THEIR SIN.

GOD IS ALWAYS WITH ME.

David's Accomplishments

Israel had many kings after David, but none as great. The Bible has more stories about David than any other person except Jesus. These are some of David's accomplishments:

- He united Israel under his leadership.
- He organized a national government.
- He conquered all of Israel's enemies.
- He increased Israel's territory tenfold.
- He organized worship at Jerusalem.
- He wrote many of the Bible's psalms.

Israel's Greatest Enemy: The Philistines

Who were they?

The Philistines were a warlike people who lived along the coast of Canaan.

Where did they come from?

The Philistines were a sea people who came from the island of Crete. During the time of the judges, they left their homes in hundreds of ships and conquered Canaanite cities.

Who was the most famous Philistine?

The greatest Philistine champion of all was the 10-foot giant Goliath. He was killed by David when David was a teenager.

What happened to the Philistines?

David defeated them. Never again did the Philistines threaten Israel.

2 Samuel

The Report of Saul's Death

¹After Saul died and David returned from defeating the Amalekites,[a] David stayed in Ziklag two days. ²On the third day a man came from Saul's camp. His clothes were torn, and he had dirt on his head. When he came to David, he immediately bowed down with his face touching the ground.

³"Where did you come from?" David asked him.

"I escaped from the camp of Israel," he answered.

⁴"What happened?" David asked him. "Please tell me."

The man answered, "The army fled from the battle, and many of the soldiers died. Saul and his son Jonathan are dead too."

⁵"How do you know Saul and his son Jonathan are dead?" David asked the young man who had brought him the news.

⁶The young man answered, "I happened to be on Mount Gilboa. Saul was there leaning on his spear, and the chariots and horsemen were catching up with him. ⁷When he looked back and saw me, he called to me, and I said, 'Yes?' "

⁸"He asked me, 'Who are you?'

"I said to him, 'I'm an Amalekite.'

⁹"He said to me, 'Please stand over me and kill me. I'm alive, but I'm suffering.'[b]

¹⁰"So I stood over him and killed him, since I knew he couldn't survive after he had been wounded. And I took the crown that was on his head and the band that was on his arm and brought them here to you, sir."

¹¹Then David grabbed his own clothes and tore them in grief. All the men with him did the same. ¹²They mourned, cried, and fasted until evening because Saul, his son Jonathan, the LORD's army, and the nation of Israel had been defeated in battle.

¹³David asked the young man who had brought him the news, "Where are you from?"

And the young man answered, "I'm an Amalekite, the son of a foreign resident."

¹⁴David asked, "Why weren't you afraid to take it upon yourself to destroy the LORD's anointed king?" ¹⁵Then David called one of his young men and told him, "Come here and attack him." David's young man executed him ¹⁶while David said, "You are responsible for spilling your own blood. You testified against yourself when you said, 'I killed the LORD's anointed king.' "

David's Lament

¹⁷David wrote this song of mourning for Saul and his son Jonathan. ¹⁸He said,

"Teach this *kesheth*[c] to the people of Judah."
(It is recorded in the Book of Jashar.)

¹⁹ "Your glory, Israel, lies dead on your hills.
   See how the mighty have fallen!
²⁰ Don't tell the news in Gath.
   Don't announce the victory in the streets of Ashkelon,
      or the daughters of the Philistines will be glad,
   and the daughters of godless men will celebrate.

---

[a] 1:1 Some Hebrew manuscripts, Syriac; other Hebrew manuscripts, Greek "Amalek."   [b] 1:9 Hebrew meaning uncertain.   [c] 1:18 Unknown musical term.

21 You mountains in Gilboa,
        may there be no dew or rain on you
    or on your slopes,[d]
        because warriors' shields were tarnished there.
        Saul's shield was never rubbed with olive oil.
22 From the blood of those killed and the fat of the warriors,
        Jonathan's bow did not turn away,
    nor did Saul's sword return unused.
23 Saul and Jonathan were loved and well-liked while they were living.
        They were not separated even when they died.
        They were swifter than eagles and stronger than lions.
24 Daughters of Israel, cry over Saul,
        who dressed you in decorated, red clothes,
        who put gold jewelry on your clothes.
25 See how the mighty have fallen in battle!
    On your hills Jonathan was killed!
26 I am heartbroken over you, my brother Jonathan.
        You were my great delight.
        Your love was more wonderful to me than the love of women.
27 See how the mighty have fallen!
    See how the weapons of war have been destroyed!"

David Becomes King of Judah

¹After this, David asked the LORD, "Should I go to one of the cities of Judah?"
"Go," the LORD answered him.
"Where should I go?" David asked.
"To Hebron," the LORD replied.

²David went there with his two wives, Ahinoam from Jezreel and Abigail (who had been Nabal's wife) from Carmel. ³David took his men and their families with him, and they settled in the towns around Hebron. ⁴Then the people of Judah came to Hebron and anointed David to be king over the tribe of Judah.

They told David, "The people of Jabesh Gilead were the ones who buried Saul."
⁵So David sent messengers to the people of Jabesh Gilead. He said to them, "May the LORD bless you because you showed kindness to your master Saul by burying him. ⁶May the LORD always show you kindness. I, too, will be good to you because you did this. ⁷Now, be strong and courageous. Because your master Saul is dead, the tribe of Judah has anointed me to be their king."

Abner Makes Ishbosheth King of Israel

⁸Ner's son Abner, commander of Saul's army, took Saul's son Ishbosheth[a] and brought him to Mahanaim. ⁹Abner made him king of Gilead, Asher,[b] Jezreel, Ephraim, and Benjamin, that is, all Israel. ¹⁰Saul's son Ishbosheth was 40 years old when he became king of Israel. He ruled for two years, but the tribe of Judah followed David. ¹¹In Hebron David was king over the tribe of Judah for seven years and six months.

Conflicts Between Abner and Joab

¹²Ner's son Abner and the officers of Saul's son Ishbosheth went from Mahanaim to Gibeon. ¹³Zeruiah's son Joab and David's officers also left Hebron. Both groups

---

[d] 1:21 Hebrew meaning uncertain.   [a] 2:8 Masoretic Text; 1 Chronicles 8:33, 9:39, Greek "Ishbaal."
[b] 2:9 Or "the Ashurites."

met at the pool of Gibeon. They sat down there, one group on one side of the pool and the other group on the other side of the pool. ¹⁴Abner said to Joab, "Let's have the young men hold a contest." Joab agreed. ¹⁵The men got up and were counted as they passed by. Twelve were from the tribe of Benjamin (representing Saul's son Ishbosheth), and twelve were from David's officers. ¹⁶Each one grabbed his opponent by the head, stuck his sword into his opponent's side, and they fell down together. Therefore, that place in Gibeon is called the Field of Enemies. ¹⁷Fierce fighting broke out that day, and David's men defeated Abner and the men of Israel.

¹⁸Zeruiah's three sons were there: Joab, Abishai, and Asahel. Asahel was as fast on his feet as a wild gazelle. ¹⁹He chased Abner and refused to leave him alone. ²⁰When Abner looked back, he asked, "Are you Asahel?"

"Yes," Asahel answered.

²¹Abner told him, "Leave me alone! Catch one of the young men, and take his weapon."ᶜ

But Asahel refused to turn away from him. ²²So Abner spoke again to Asahel. "Stop following me," he said. "Why should I kill you? How could I look your brother Joab in the face again?"

²³But Asahel refused to turn away. So Abner struck him with the butt of the spear. The spear went into his belly and came out his back. He fell down there and died on the spot. And everyone who came to the place where Asahel fell and died stopped there.

²⁴But Joab and Abishai chased Abner. When the sun went down, they came to the hill of Ammah, opposite Giah on the road from Gibeon to the desert. ²⁵The men of Benjamin rallied behind Abner, banding together and taking their position on top of a hill.

²⁶Then Abner called to Joab, "Should this slaughter go on forever? Don't you know this will end in bitterness? How long will it be before you will call off your troops from chasing their relatives?"

²⁷Joab answered, "I solemnly swear, as God lives, if you had not spoken, the men would not have stopped chasing their relatives until morning." ²⁸So Joab blew a ram's horn, and all the troops stopped. They didn't chase or fight Israel anymore.

²⁹Abner and his men marched through the plains all that night. They crossed the Jordan River and passed through the entire Bithron until they came to Mahanaim.

³⁰Joab returned from chasing Abner. When he had gathered all the troops, only 19 of David's officers and Asahel were missing. ³¹However, David's officers had killed 360 of the men of Benjamin under Abner's command. ³²They took Asahel and buried him in his father's tomb in Bethlehem. Then Joab and his men marched all night and arrived at Hebron by daybreak.

3 ¹As the war between the royal families of Saul and David dragged on, David's family became stronger and stronger, and Saul's family became weaker and weaker.

David's Sons—
I Chronicles 3:1-4

²Sons were born to David while he was in Hebron. His first son was Amnon, born to Ahinoam from Jezreel. ³The second was Chileab, born to Abigail (who had been Nabal's wife) from Carmel. The third was Absalom, whose mother was Maacah (the daughter of King Talmai) from Geshur. ⁴The fourth was Adonijah, whose mother was

---

ᶜ2:21 Hebrew meaning uncertain.

Haggith. The fifth was Shephatiah, whose mother was Abital. [5]The sixth was Ithream, born to David's wife Eglah. These sons were born to David while he was in Hebron.

Abner's Death

[6]During the war between the families of Saul and David, Abner strengthened his position in Saul's royal family. [7]Saul had a concubine[a] named Rizpah (Aiah's daughter). Ishbosheth asked Abner, "Why did you have sex with my father's concubine?" [8]Ishbosheth's question made Abner very angry. "Have I been behaving like some Judean dog?"[b] he asked. "Until now I've been faithful to your father Saul's family, to his relatives and friends, and I haven't handed you over to David. But now you charge me with a crime because of this woman. [9]May God strike me dead unless I do for David what the LORD had promised him with an oath: [10]'I, the LORD, will transfer the kingship from Saul's family and establish David's throne over Israel and Judah from Dan to Beersheba.' " [11]Ishbosheth couldn't respond to a single word, because he was afraid of Abner.

[12]Then Abner sent messengers to David to speak on his behalf. "Who owns this country?" he asked. "Make an agreement with me," he said. "I'll support you and bring all Israel to you."

[13]"Good!" David answered. "I'll make an agreement with you. But there's one condition: You can't come to see me unless you bring Michal, Saul's daughter, when you come."

[14]Then David sent messengers to Saul's son Ishbosheth to say, "Give me my wife Michal. I made a payment of 100 Philistine foreskins for her."

[15]So Ishbosheth sent men to take her from her husband Paltiel, son of Laish. [16]Her husband went with her and cried over her all the way to Bahurim. "Go home," Abner told him. So he went home.

[17]Meanwhile, Abner sent the following message to the leaders of Israel: "For some time now you've wanted to make David your king. [18]Do it now, because the LORD said about David: 'I will save my people Israel from the Philistines and all their other enemies through my servant David.' " [19]Abner also spoke specifically to the people of Benjamin.

Then Abner went directly to David in Hebron to tell him everything Israel and the entire tribe of Benjamin had approved. [20]So Abner came with 20 men to David in Hebron, and David had a feast for Abner and his men.

[21]Abner told David, "I must go now so that I can gather all Israel for you, Your Majesty. They will make a treaty with you, and you will rule everything your heart desires." Then David dismissed Abner, who left peacefully.

[22]Just then David's men and Joab were coming home from a raid with a lot of goods. Abner had been dismissed, so he was no longer with David in Hebron. [23]When Joab came back with the whole army, he was told, "Ner's son Abner came to the king, but David dismissed him, and Abner left peacefully."

[24]Then Joab went to the king and asked, "What have you done? Abner came to see you. Why did you dismiss him and let him get away? [25]Certainly you must know that Ner's son Abner came to deceive you, to find out about your movements and learn everything you're doing!"

[26]After leaving David, Joab sent messengers after Abner. They brought him back from the cistern of Sirah without David knowing about it. [27]When Abner returned to Hebron, Joab took him aside in the gateway as if to talk to him privately. There he

---

[a]3:7 A concubine is considered a wife except she has fewer rights under the law.   [b]3:8 English equivalent difficult.

stabbed Abner in the belly. Abner died because he spilled the blood of Joab's brother Asahel.

²⁸Later when David heard about it, he said, "As far as the LORD is concerned, my kingdom and I are forever innocent of spilling the blood of Ner's son Abner. ²⁹May the blame fall on the head of Joab and all of his family. May there always be members of Joab's family who have oozing sores and skin diseases, who can only work a spindle,ᶜ who die in battle, and who never have any food." ³⁰(Joab and his brother Abishai killed Abner because he had killed their brother Asahel in the battle at Gibeon.)

³¹David told Joab and all the people with him, "Tear your clothes, put on sackcloth, and mourn for Abner." King David followed the open casket. ³²They buried Abner in Hebron. The king cried loudly at Abner's grave, and all the people cried. ³³The king sang a funeral song for Abner:

> Should Abner die like a godless fool?
> ³⁴   Your hands were not tied.
>   Your feet were not chained.
> You fell as one falls in front of wicked men.

And all the people continued to cry for him.

³⁵That entire day all the people tried to get David to eat some food. But David had taken an oath: "May God strike me dead if I taste any food or anything else before the sun goes down." ³⁶Then all the people understood and approved of this, as all the people approved of everything the king did. ³⁷That day all the people of Israel knew the king wasn't responsible for killing Ner's son Abner. ³⁸The king said to his officers, "Don't you know that today a leader, a great man, has fallen in Israel? ³⁹Today I'm weak, though I'm the anointed king. These men, Zeruiah's sons, are too cruel for me. May the LORD repay this evildoer as his evil deeds deserve."

Ishbosheth Is Murdered

4 ¹When Saul's son Ishbosheth heard that Abner had died in Hebron, he lost his courage, and all Israel was alarmed. ²Saul's son had two men who were captains of raiding parties. One was named Baanah, and the other was named Rechab. They were the sons of Rimmon from Beeroth from the tribe of Benjamin.

(Beeroth was considered a part of Benjamin, ³even though the people of Beeroth had fled to Gittaim. They still live there today. ⁴In addition, Saul's son Jonathan had a son who was crippled. When the boy was five years old, the news about the death of Saul and Jonathan came from Jezreel. His nurse picked him up and fled to Gittaim. She was in a hurry when she left, and he fell from her arms and became disabled. His name was Mephibosheth.)

⁵Rechab and Baanah, the sons of Rimmon from Beeroth, came to Ishbosheth's home at the hottest time of the day. Ishbosheth was taking his midday nap ⁶when they came into the house as though they were going to get some flour. Instead, they stabbed him in the belly. Then Rechab and his brother Baanah escaped. ⁷(They had come into the house while Ishbosheth was sleeping on his bed in his bedroom. They stabbed him, killed him, and cut off his head.) They took his head and traveled all night along the road to the plains.

⁸They brought Ishbosheth's head to David at Hebron. "Here is the head of Ishbosheth, the son of your enemy Saul who tried to kill you," they told the king. "Today the LORD has given Your Royal Majesty revenge on Saul and his descendants."

ᶜ3:29 Spinning yarn and thread was normally done only by women and therefore was something only the weakest of men would do.

⁹David responded to Rechab and his brother Baanah, the sons of Rimmon from Beeroth, ¹⁰"I once seized a man who told me that Saul had died. He thought he was bringing good news. I killed him in Ziklag to reward him for his news. ¹¹How much more should I reward wicked men who kill an innocent man on his own bed in his home? The LORD has rescued me from every trouble. I solemnly swear, as the LORD lives,ᵃ I'll now seek revenge for his murder and rid the land of you." ¹²So David gave an order to his young men, who executed Rechab and Baanah, cut off their hands and feet, and hung their dead bodies by the pond in Hebron. Then they took Ishbosheth's head and buried it in Abner's tomb in Hebron.

David Anointed King of Israel—
I Chronicles 11:1-3; 3:4

¹All the tribes of Israel came to David at Hebron. "We are your own flesh and blood," they said. ²"Even in the past when Saul ruled us, you were the one who led Israel in battle. The LORD has said to you, 'You will be shepherd of my people Israel, the leader of Israel.' "

³All the leaders of Israel had come to Hebron. King David made an agreement with them at Hebron in front of the LORD. So they anointed David king of Israel. ⁴David was 30 years old when he became king, and he ruled for 40 years. ⁵In Hebron he ruled Judah for seven years and six months. In Jerusalem he ruled for 33 years over all Israel and Judah.

David Captures Jerusalem—
I Chronicles 11:4-9

⁶The king and his men went to Jerusalem to attack the Jebusites, who lived in that region. The Jebusites told David, "You will never get in here. Even the blind and the lame could turn you away" (meaning that David could never get in there). ⁷But David captured the fortress Zion (that is, the City of David). ⁸That day David said, "Whoever wants to defeat the Jebusites must reach the lame and the blind who hate me by using the water shaft." So there is a saying, "The blind and the lame will not get into the palace."ᵃ ⁹David lived in the fortress and called it the City of David. He built the city of Jerusalem around it from the Milloᵇ to the palace. ¹⁰David continued to grow more powerful because the LORD Godᶜ of Armies was with him.

David's Palace, Wives, and Children in Jerusalem—
I Chronicles 14:1-7; 3:5-9

¹¹Then King Hiram of Tyre sent messengers to David, along with cedarwood, carpenters, and stonemasons. They built a palace for David. ¹²So David realized that the LORD had established him as king of Israel and made his kingship famous for the sake of Israel, the LORD's people.

¹³David married more concubinesᵈ and wives from Jerusalem after he had come there from Hebron, and he fathered more sons and daughters. ¹⁴These are the names of the children born to him in Jerusalem: Shammua, Shobab, Nathan, Solomon, ¹⁵Ibhar, Elishua, Nepheg, Japhia, ¹⁶Elishama, Eliada, and Eliphelet.

ᵃ4:11 The last part of verse 9 (in Hebrew) has been placed in verse 11 to express the complex Hebrew paragraph structure more clearly in English. ᵃ5:8 Or "temple." ᵇ5:9 The exact place referred to as "the Millo" is unknown. ᶜ5:10 Masoretic Text; Dead Sea Scrolls, Greek, 1 Chronicles 11:9 omit "God." ᵈ5:13 A concubine is considered a wife except she has fewer rights under the law.

David Defeats the Philistines—
1 Chronicles 14:8-17

[17]When the Philistines heard that David had been anointed king of Israel, all of them came to attack David. But David heard about it and went to the fortress. [18]The Philistines had come and overrun the valley of Rephaim.

[19]David asked the LORD, "Should I attack the Philistines? Will you hand them over to me?"

The LORD answered David, "Attack! I will certainly hand the Philistines over to you."

[20]So David went to Baal Perazim and defeated the Philistines there. He said, "The LORD has overwhelmed my enemies in front of me like an overwhelming flood." That is why that place is called Baal Perazim [The Lord Overwhelms]. [21]The Philistines left their idols there, so David and his men carried the idols away.

[22]The Philistines again attacked and overran the valley of Rephaim. [23]David asked the LORD, and he answered, "Don't attack now, but circle around behind them, and come at them in front of the balsam trees. [24]When you hear the sound of marching in the tops of the balsam trees, act immediately because the LORD has gone ahead of you to defeat the Philistine army." [25]David did as the LORD ordered him and defeated the Philistines from Geba to Gezer.

David Brings the Ark to Jerusalem—
1 Chronicles 13:5-14; 15:25–16:3, 43

[1]David again assembled all the best soldiers in Israel, 30,000 men. [2]He and all the people with him left Baalah in Judah*a* to bring God's ark ⌞to Jerusalem⌟. (The ark is called by the name of the LORD of Armies, who is enthroned over the angels.*b*) [3]David and his men put God's ark on a new cart and brought it from Abinadab's home on the hill. Uzzah and Ahio, Abinadab's sons, were guiding the new cart. [4]They brought it from Abinadab's home, with Ahio walking ahead of the ark. [5]David and the entire nation of Israel were celebrating in the LORD's presence with all kinds of instruments made from cypress wood*c* and with lyres, harps, tambourines, sistrums,*d* and cymbals.

[6]But when they came to Nacon's threshing floor,*e* the oxen stumbled. So Uzzah reached out for the ark of God and grabbed it. [7]The LORD became angry with Uzzah, so God killed him there for his lack of respect. He died beside the ark of God.

[8]David was angry because the LORD had struck Uzzah so violently. (That place is still called Perez Uzzah [The Striking of Uzzah] today.) [9]David was afraid of the LORD that day. "How can the ark of the LORD come to my ⌞city⌟?" he asked. [10]So David wouldn't bring the ark of the LORD with him to the City of David. Instead, he rerouted it to the home of Obed Edom, who was from Gath. [11]The ark of the LORD stayed at the home of Obed Edom from Gath for three months, and the LORD blessed Obed Edom and his whole family.

[12]King David was told, "The LORD has blessed Obed Edom's home and everything he owns because of the ark of God." Then David joyfully went to get the ark of God from Obed Edom's house and bring it to the City of David. [13]When those who carried the ark of the LORD had gone six steps, David sacrificed a bull and a fattened calf.

[14]Wearing a linen ephod,*f* David danced in the LORD's presence with all his might. [15]He and the entire nation of Israel brought the ark of the LORD with shouts of joy and the sounding of rams' horns. [16]When the ark of the LORD came to the City of David,

---

a 6:2 Or "Baal in Judah" or "the citizens of Judah"; Dead Sea Scrolls and 1 Chronicles 13:6 "Baalah in Kiriath Jearim."
b 6:2 Or "cherubim."   *c* 6:5 Or "with all their might." See 1 Chronicles 13:8.   *d* 6:5 A type of rattle used as a musical instrument.   *e* 6:6 A threshing floor is an outdoor area where grain is separated from its husks.
f 6:14 *Ephod* is a technical term for a part of the priest's clothes. Its exact usage and shape are unknown.

Saul's daughter Michal looked out of a window and saw King David leaping and dancing in the Lord's presence, so she despised him.

¹⁷The men carrying the ark set it in its place inside the tent David had put up for it. David sacrificed burnt offerings and fellowship offerings in the Lord's presence. ¹⁸When David had finished sacrificing the burnt offerings and the fellowship offerings, he blessed the people in the name of the Lord of Armies. ¹⁹He also distributed to all the people—to the whole crowd of Israelites, both men and women—one loaf of bread, one date cake, and one raisin cake. Then all the people went home.

²⁰When David returned to bless his family, Saul's daughter Michal came out to meet him. "How dignified Israel's king was today! He was exposing himself before the eyes of the slave girls of his palace staff—like a mindless fool might expose himself!"

²¹David answered Michal, "I didn't dance in front of the slave girls but in front of the Lord. He chose me rather than your father or anyone in your father's house, and he appointed me leader of Israel, the Lord's people. I will celebrate in the Lord's presence, ²²and I will degrade myself even more than this. Even if I am humiliated in your eyes, I will be honored by these slave girls you speak about."

²³So Saul's daughter Michal was childless her entire life.

David's Wish to Build a House for God—
I Chronicles 17:1-27

¹While King David was living in his house, the Lord gave him peace with all his enemies around him. ²So the king said to the prophet Nathan, "Look, I'm living in a house made of cedar, while the ark of God remains in the tent."

³Nathan told the king, "Do everything you have in mind, because the Lord is with you."

⁴But that same night the Lord spoke his word to Nathan: ⁵"Say to my servant David, 'This is what the Lord says: Are you the one who will build me a house to live in? ⁶I haven't lived in a house from the day I took Israel out of Egypt to this day. Instead, I moved around in a tent, the tent ⌞of meeting⌟. ⁷In all the places I've moved with all the Israelites, did I ever ask any of the judges*a* of Israel whom I ordered to be shepherds of my people Israel why they didn't build me a house of cedar?'

⁸"Now this is what you will say to my servant David: 'This is what the Lord of Armies says: I took you from the pasture where you followed sheep so that you could be the leader of my people Israel. ⁹I was with you wherever you went, and I destroyed all your enemies in front of you. I will make your name famous like the names of the greatest people on earth. ¹⁰I will make a place for my people Israel and plant them there. They will live in their own place and not be troubled anymore. The wicked will no longer oppress them as they used to do ¹¹ever since I appointed judges to rule my people Israel. So I will give you peace with all your enemies. I, the Lord, tell you that I will make a house for you.

¹²" 'When the time comes for you to lie down in death with your ancestors, I will send one of your descendants, ⌞one⌟ who will come from you. I will establish his kingdom. ¹³He will build a house for my name, and I will establish the throne of his kingdom forever. ¹⁴I will be his Father, and he will be my Son. If he sins, I will punish him with a rod and with blows inflicted by people. ¹⁵But I will never stop showing him my love as I did to Saul, whom I took out of your way. ¹⁶Your royal house will remain in my presence*b* forever. Your throne will be established forever.' "

¹⁷Nathan told David all these words and everything he had seen.

¹⁸King David went into the tent and sat in front of the Lord. "Who am I, Almighty

---

*a*7:7 1 Chronicles 17:6; Masoretic Text "tribes."   *b*7:16 Some Hebrew manuscripts, Greek, Latin, Syriac; other Hebrew manuscripts "in your presence."

LORD," he asked, "and why is my house so important that you have brought me this far? ¹⁹And even this you consider to be a small act, Almighty LORD. You've also spoken about the distant future of my house. Almighty LORD, this is the teaching about the man.

²⁰"What more can I, David, say to you, Almighty LORD, since you know me so well! ²¹You've done this great thing because of your promise and your own desire. You made it known to me.

²²"That is why you are great, LORD God. There is no one like you, and there is no other god except you, as we have heard with our own ears. ²³Who is like your people Israel? It is the one nation on earth that God came to free in order to make its people his own, to make his name^c known, and to do great and wonderful things for them. You forced^d nations and their gods out of the way of your people, whom you freed from Egypt to be your own. ²⁴You created the people of Israel to be your people forever. And you, LORD, became their God.

²⁵"Now, LORD God, keep the promise you made to me and my house forever. Do as you promised. ²⁶Your name will be respected forever when ˌpeopleˎ say, 'The LORD of Armies is God over Israel.' And the house of your servant David will be established in your presence. ²⁷You, LORD of Armies, God of Israel, have revealed it especially to me, saying, 'I will build a house for you.' That is why I have found the courage to offer this prayer to you.

²⁸"Almighty LORD, you are God, and your words are trustworthy. You promised me this good thing. ²⁹Now, please bless my house so that it may continue in your presence forever. Indeed, you, Almighty LORD, have promised it. With your blessing my house will be blessed forever."

David's Successes—
1 Chronicles 18:1-17

8 ¹After this, David defeated and crushed the Philistines. He took control of the main Philistine city from them.^a

²He also defeated Moab, made the Moabites lie down on the ground, and measured them with a rope. He measured two lengths which were to be killed, and one length which was to be spared. So the Moabites became David's subjects and paid taxes ˌto himˎ.

³When David went to restore his control ˌover the territoryˎ along the Euphrates River, he defeated Zobah's King Hadadezer, son of Rehob. ⁴David took 1,700 horsemen and 20,000 foot soldiers from him. David also disabled all but 100 of their horses so that they couldn't pull chariots.

⁵When the Arameans from Damascus came to help King Hadadezer of Zobah, David killed 22,000 of them. ⁶David put troops in the Aramean kingdom of Damascus, and the Arameans became his subjects and paid taxes ˌto himˎ. Everywhere David went, the LORD gave him victories.

⁷David took the gold shields that belonged to Hadadezer's^b servants, and he brought them to Jerusalem. ⁸King David also took a large quantity of bronze from Betah and Berothai, Hadadezer's cities.

⁹When King Toi of Hamath heard that David had defeated Hadadezer's whole army, ¹⁰he sent his son Joram to greet King David and congratulate him for fighting and defeating Hadadezer. (There had often been war between Hadadezer and Toi.) Joram

---

^c7:23 Or "its name."   ^d7:23 Greek and 1 Chronicles 17:21; Masoretic Text "Your land."   ^a8:1 Or "of Metheg Ammah."
^b8:7 Most Hebrew manuscripts; some Hebrew manuscripts, 1 Chronicles 18:7, Syriac, Targum "Hadadezer's servants carried."

brought articles of gold, silver, and bronze with him. [11]King David dedicated these articles to the Lord, along with the silver and gold he had dedicated from all the nations he conquered— [12]from Edom, Moab, Ammon, the Philistines, Amalek, and from the goods taken from Zobah's King Hadadezer, son of Rehob.

[13]David made a name for himself by killing 18,000 Edomites[c] in the Dead Sea region as he returned to Jerusalem. [14]He put troops everywhere in Edom, and all the Edomites were David's subjects. Everywhere David went, the Lord gave him victories.

[15]So David ruled all Israel. He did what was fair and right for all his people. [16]Zeruiah's son Joab was in charge of the army. Ahilud's son Jehoshaphat was the royal historian. [17]Ahitub's son Zadok and Abiathar's son Ahimelech were priests. Seraiah was the royal scribe. [18]Jehoiada's son Benaiah was commander of the Cherethites and the Pelethites. And David's sons were priests.[d]

David Keeps His Promise to Jonathan

9 [1]David asked, "Is there anyone left in Saul's family to whom I can show kindness for Jonathan's sake?"

[2]Now, Saul's family had a servant whose name was Ziba. He was summoned to come to David. "Are you Ziba?" the king asked him.

"Yes, I am," he answered.

[3]David asked, "Is there someone left in Saul's family to whom I can show God's kindness?"

"Jonathan has a son who is disabled," Ziba answered.

[4]"Where is he?" the king asked.

Ziba replied, "He is at the home of Machir, Ammiel's son, in Lo Debar."

[5]So King David sent men to get him from the home of Ammiel's son Machir in Lo Debar. [6]When Mephibosheth (son of Jonathan and grandson of Saul) came to David, he quickly bowed down with his face touching the ground.

"Mephibosheth!" David said to him.

"Yes, sir," he answered.

[7]"Don't be afraid," David told him, "I will certainly show you kindness for your father Jonathan's sake. I will give back to you all the land of your grandfather Saul, and you will always eat at my table."

[8]Mephibosheth bowed down again and answered, "Who am I that you would look at a dead dog like me?"

[9]Then the king called for Ziba, Saul's servant, and said to him, "I have given your master's grandson everything that belonged to Saul and his family. [10]You, your sons, and your servants should farm the land for him and harvest the crops, so that your master's family will have food to eat. However, your master's grandson Mephibosheth will always eat at my table." (Ziba had 15 sons and 20 servants.)

[11]Ziba responded, "I will do everything you've commanded, Your Majesty." From then on, Mephibosheth ate at David's table as one of the king's sons.

[12]Mephibosheth had a young son whose name was Mica. Everyone who lived at Ziba's home became Mephibosheth's servant. [13]However, Mephibosheth, who was disabled, lived in Jerusalem. He always ate at the king's table.

---

[c]8:13 A few Hebrew manuscripts, 1 Chronicles 18:12, Greek, Syriac; other Hebrew manuscripts "Arameans."
[d]8:18 One Hebrew manuscript, Syriac, Targum, Latin; all other Hebrew manuscripts "Jehoiada's son Benaiah, the Cherethites, the Pelethites, and David's sons were priests."

David Defeats Ammon and Aram—
I Chronicles 19:1-19

10 ¹Later the king of Ammon died, and his son Hanun became king in his place. ²David thought, "I will show kindness to Hanun as his father Nahash showed me kindness." So David sent his servants to comfort Hanun after his father's death. But when David's servants entered Ammonite territory, ³the Ammonite princes asked their master Hanun, "Do you think David is honoring your father because he sent men to comfort you? Hasn't David sent his men to explore the city, spy on it, and destroy it?" ⁴So Hanun took David's men, shaved off half of each man's beard, cut off their clothes from the waist down, and sent them away.

⁵After David was told what had happened, he sent someone to meet them because they were deeply humiliated. The king said to them, "Stay in Jericho until your beards have grown back, and then return to Jerusalem."

⁶The Ammonites realized that they had made themselves offensive to David. So they hired the Arameans from Beth Rehob and Zobah (20,000 foot soldiers), the army of the king of Maacah (1,000 men), and the men of Tob (12,000 men).

⁷After David heard about this, he sent Joab and all the elite troops. ⁸The Ammonites formed a battle line at the entrance of the city gate, while the Arameans from Zobah and Rehob and the men from Tob and Maacah remained by themselves in the open country.

⁹When Joab saw he was under attack in front and behind, he took the select troops of Israel and organized them for combat against the Arameans. ¹⁰He put his brother Abishai in charge of the rest of the troops. Abishai organized them for combat against the Ammonites.

¹¹Joab said, "If the Arameans are too strong for my troops, be ready to help me. And if the Ammonites are too strong for your troops, I'll come to help you. ¹²Be strong! Let's prove ourselves strong for our people and for the cities of our God, and the LORD will do what he considers right."

¹³Then Joab and his troops advanced to fight the Arameans, and the Arameans fled. ¹⁴When the Ammonites saw that the Arameans had fled, the Ammonites fled from Abishai and went into the city. So Joab stopped his campaign against the Ammonites and returned to Jerusalem.

¹⁵Realizing that Israel had defeated them, the Arameans reassembled their troops. ¹⁶Hadadezer sent messengers to get Arameans from beyond the Euphrates River. The Arameans came to Helam with Shobach, the commander of Hadadezer's army, leading them.

¹⁷When David was told about this, he assembled Israel's army, crossed the Jordan River, and came to Helam. The Arameans formed a battle line against David's troops and fought him. ¹⁸The Arameans fled from Israel, and David killed 700 chariot drivers and 40,000 horsemen. David struck Shobach dead.

¹⁹When all the kings who were subject to Hadadezer saw that Israel had defeated them, they made peace with Israel and became their subjects. And the Arameans were afraid to help the Ammonites anymore.

David Takes Bathsheba—
I Chronicles 20:1

11 ¹In the spring, the time when kings go out to battle, David sent Joab, his mercenaries, and Israel's army to war. They destroyed the Ammonites and attacked Rabbah, while David stayed in Jerusalem.

²Now, when evening came, David got up from his bed and walked around on the roof of the royal palace. From the roof he saw a woman bathing, and she was very pretty. ³David sent someone to ask about the woman. The man said, "She's Bathsheba, daughter of Eliam and wife of Uriah the Hittite." ⁴So David sent messengers and took her. She came to him, and he went to bed with her. (She had just cleansed herself after her monthly period.) Then she went home. ⁵The woman had become pregnant. So she sent someone to tell David that she was pregnant.

⁶Then David sent a messenger to Joab, saying, "Send me Uriah the Hittite." So Joab sent Uriah to David. ⁷When Uriah arrived, David asked him how Joab and the troops were and how the war was going.

⁸"Go home," David said to Uriah, "and wash your feet." Uriah left the royal palace, and the king sent a present to him. ⁹But Uriah slept at the entrance of the royal palace among his superior's mercenaries. He didn't go home.

¹⁰When they told David, "Uriah didn't go home," David asked Uriah, "Didn't you just come from a journey? Why didn't you go home?"

¹¹Uriah answered David, "The ark and the army of Israel and Judah are in temporary shelters, and my commander Joab and Your Majesty's mercenaries are living in the field. Should I then go to my house to eat and drink and go to bed with my wife? I solemnly swear, as sure as you're living, I won't do this!"

¹²David said to Uriah, "Then stay here today, and tomorrow I'll send you back." So Uriah stayed in Jerusalem that day and the next. ¹³David summoned him, ate and drank with him, and got him drunk. But that evening Uriah went to lie down on his bed among his superior's mercenaries. He didn't go home.

¹⁴In the morning David wrote a letter to Joab and sent it with Uriah. ¹⁵In the letter he wrote, "Put Uriah on the front line where the fighting is heaviest. Then abandon him so that he'll be struck down and die."

¹⁶Since Joab had kept the city under observation, he put Uriah at the place where he knew the experienced warriors were. ¹⁷The men of the city came out and fought Joab. Some of the people, namely, some of David's mercenaries, fell and died—including Uriah the Hittite.

¹⁸Then Joab sent a messenger to report to David all the details of the battle. ¹⁹And he commanded the messenger, "When you finish telling the king about the battle, ²⁰the king may become angry. He might ask you, 'Why did you go so close to the city to fight? Didn't you know they would shoot from the wall? ²¹Who killed Jerubbesheth's*ᵃ* son Abimelech? Didn't a woman on the wall of Thebez throw a small millstone at him and kill him? Why did you go so close to the wall?' If the king asks this, then say, 'Your man Uriah the Hittite is also dead.' "

²²The messenger left, and when he arrived, he reported to David everything Joab told him to say.*ᵇ* ²³The messenger said, "Their men overpowered us and came to attack us in the field. Then we forced them back to the entrance of the city gate. ²⁴The archers on the wall shot down at your mercenaries, and some of Your Majesty's mercenaries died. Your man Uriah the Hittite also is dead."

²⁵David said to the messenger, "This is what you are to say to Joab, 'Don't let this thing trouble you, because a sword can kill one person as easily as another. Strengthen your attack against the city, and destroy it.' Say this to encourage him."

²⁶When Uriah's wife heard that her husband Uriah was dead, she mourned for him. ²⁷When her mourning was over, David sent for her and brought her to his home, and

---

ᵃ 11:21 Or "Jerubbaal's"; see Judges 9:1.   ᵇ 11:22 Greek adds, "And David was angry with Joab. 'Why did you go so close to the city to fight? Didn't you know you would be shot at from the wall? Who killed Abimelech, Jerubbaal's son? Didn't a woman throw a millstone on him from the wall? Why did you go so close to the wall?' "

Bathsheba

"We're taking you to King David."

Bathsheba may have seemed to have a romantic life when she married David, but for her, it started as a nightmare. Bathsheba's husband, Uriah, was away fighting with the army. When King David had difficulty sleeping one night, he walked around on the roof of the royal palace. From the rooftop, David could see into Bathsheba's house as she was taking a bath.

David sent messengers to take Bathsheba from her house and bring her to the palace. David committed adultery with Bathsheba, and she became pregnant. To hide his sin, David arranged for Uriah to be in a bloody battle so he would be killed. Bathsheba had to mourn her husband knowing that she was pregnant with another man's child. It must have been difficult for Bathsheba to forgive and live with David even after he confessed his sin.

Getting to Know Bathsheba

* How do you suppose Bathsheba was able to forgive David?

* How do you usually react when someone hurts you?

* What difficult situation do you face now in which you need God's help?

Bathsheba was born around 1000 B.C.

Bathsheba means "daughter of an oath" or "seventh daughter."

Bathsheba married King David.

Bathsheba had four sons with David, including Solomon, the wisest king.

Nathan the prophet confronted David after David committed adultery with Bathsheba.

she became his wife. Then she gave birth to a son. But the LORD considered David's actions evil.

Nathan Confronts David

¹So the LORD sent Nathan to David. Nathan came to him and said, "There were two men in a certain city. One was rich, and the other was poor. ²The rich man had a very large number of sheep and cows, ³but the poor man had only one little female lamb that he had bought. He raised her, and she grew up in his home with his children. She would eat his food and drink from his cup. She rested in his arms and was like a daughter.

⁴"Now, a visitor came to the rich man. The rich man thought it would be a pity to take one of his own sheep or cattle to prepare a meal for the traveler. So he took the poor man's lamb and prepared her for the traveler."

⁵David burned with anger against the man. "I solemnly swear, as the LORD lives," he said to Nathan, "the man who did this certainly deserves to die! ⁶And he must pay back four times the price of the lamb because he did this and had no pity."

⁷"You are the man!" Nathan told David. "This is what the LORD God of Israel says: I anointed you king over Israel and rescued you from Saul. ⁸I gave you your master Saul's house and his wives. I gave you the house of Israel and Judah. And if this weren't enough, I would have given you even more. ⁹Why did you despise my word by doing what I considered evil? You had Uriah the Hittite killed in battle. You took his wife as your wife. You used the Ammonites to kill him. ¹⁰So warfare will never leave your house because you despised me and took the wife of Uriah the Hittite to be your wife.

¹¹"This is what the LORD says: I will stir up trouble against you within your own household, and before your own eyes I will take your wives and give them to someone close to you. He will go to bed with your wives in broad daylight. ¹²You did this secretly, but I will make this happen in broad daylight in front of all Israel."

¹³Then David said to Nathan, "I have sinned against the LORD."

Nathan replied, "The LORD has taken away your sin; you will not die. ¹⁴But since you have shown total contempt for the LORD by this affair, the son that is born to you must die." ¹⁵Then Nathan went home.

The LORD struck the child that Uriah's wife had given birth to for David so that the child became sick. ¹⁶David pleaded with God for the child; he fasted and lay on the ground all night. ¹⁷The older leaders in his palace stood beside him to raise him up from the ground, but he was unwilling. And he wouldn't eat with them.

¹⁸On the seventh day the child died. But David's officials were afraid to tell him that the child was dead. They thought, "While the child was alive, we talked to him, and he wouldn't listen to us. How can we tell him the child is dead? He may harm himself."

¹⁹But when David saw that his officials were whispering to one another, he realized that the child was dead. "Is the child dead?" David asked them.

"Yes, he is dead," they answered.

²⁰So David got up from the ground, bathed, anointed himself, and changed his clothes. He went into the LORD's house and worshiped. Then he went home and asked for food. They placed food in front of him, and he ate.

²¹His officials asked him, "Why are you acting this way? You fasted and cried over the child when he was alive. But as soon as the child died, you got up and ate."

²²David answered, "As long as the child was alive, I fasted and cried. I thought, 'Who knows? The LORD may be gracious to me and let the child live.' ²³But why should

I fast now that he's dead? Can I bring him back? Someday I'll go to him, but he won't come back to me."

²⁴Then David comforted his wife Bathsheba. He went to bed with her, and she later gave birth to a son. David named him Solomon. The LORD loved the child ²⁵and sent a message through the prophet Nathan to name the baby Jedidiah [The LORD's Beloved].

David Defeats the Ammonites—
I Chronicles 20:1-3

²⁶Meanwhile, Joab fought against the Ammonite city of Rabbah and captured its royal fortress. ²⁷So he sent messengers to tell David, "I fought against Rabbah and captured the fortress guarding its water supply. ²⁸Gather the rest of the troops, surround the city, and capture it. Otherwise, I will capture the city, and it will be named after me."

²⁹So David gathered all the troops and went to Rabbah. He fought against the city and captured it. ³⁰He took the gold crown from the head of Rabbah's king and put it on his own head. (The crown weighed 75 pounds and contained a precious stone.) David also took a lot of goods from the city. ³¹He brought out the troops who were there and put them to work with saws, hoes, and axes. He did the same to all the Ammonite cities. Then David and all the troops returned to Jerusalem.

The Rape of Tamar

¹After this, David's son Amnon fell in love with Tamar, the beautiful sister of David's son Absalom. ²Amnon was so obsessed with his half sister Tamar that he made himself sick. It seemed impossible for him to be alone with her because she was a virgin.

³Amnon had a friend by the name of Jonadab, a son of David's brother Shimea. Jonadab was a very clever man. ⁴He asked Amnon, "Why are you, the king's son, so worn out morning after morning? Won't you tell me?"

"I'm in love with Absalom's sister Tamar," he answered.

⁵Then Jonadab told him, "Lie down on your bed. Act sick, and when your father comes to see you, say to him, 'Please let my sister Tamar come to feed me. She can prepare a meal in front of me as I watch her, and she can feed me.'"

⁶So Amnon lay down and acted sick, and the king came to see him. Amnon asked the king, "Please let my sister Tamar come and make some bread in front of me, and she can feed me."

⁷David sent for Tamar at the palace. "Please go to your brother Amnon's home," he said, "and prepare some food for him."

⁸So Tamar went to her brother Amnon's home. He was lying down. She took dough, kneaded it, made flat bread in front of him, and cooked it. ⁹Then she took the pan and served him the bread. But he refused to eat.

"Have everyone leave me," he said. So everyone left him.

¹⁰Amnon told Tamar, "Bring the food into the bedroom so that you can feed me." Tamar took the bread she had prepared and brought it to her brother Amnon in the bedroom. ¹¹When she handed it to him to eat, he grabbed her and said, "Come to bed with me, Tamar!"

¹²"No," she told him, "don't rape me! That shouldn't be done in Israel. Don't do this godless act! ¹³Where could I go in my disgrace? And you will be considered one of the godless fools in Israel! Speak to the king. He won't refuse your request to marry me."

¹⁴But Amnon wouldn't listen to her. He grabbed his sister and raped her.
¹⁵Now, Amnon developed an intense hatred for her. His hatred for her was greater than the lust he had felt for her. "Get out of here," he told her.
¹⁶She said to him, "No, sending me away is a greater wrong than the other thing you did to me!" But he wouldn't listen to her.
¹⁷Then he called his personal servant and said, "Get rid of her. Put her out, and bolt the door behind her." ¹⁸(She was wearing a long-sleeved gown. The king's virgin daughters wore this kind of robe.) So his servant took her out and bolted the door behind her. ¹⁹Tamar put ashes on her head, tore the long-sleeved gown she had on, put her hands on her head, and went away crying.

²⁰Her brother Absalom asked her, "Has your brother Amnon been with you? Sister, be quiet for now. He's your brother. Don't dwell on this matter." So Tamar stayed there at the home of her brother Absalom and was depressed.

²¹When King David heard about this, he became very angry. But David didn't punish his son Amnon. He favored Amnon because he was his firstborn son.[a] ²²Absalom wouldn't speak at all to Amnon. He hated Amnon for raping his sister Tamar.

The Murder of Amnon

²³Two years later Absalom had sheepshearers at Baal Hazor near Ephraim. He invited all the king's sons.[b] ²⁴Absalom went to the king and said, "Since I have sheepshearers, Your Majesty and your officials are invited ˌto feastˌ with me."

²⁵"No, Son," the king answered Absalom. "If we all go, we'll be a burden to you." Even when Absalom continued to urge[c] him, David did not want to go, though he did give Absalom his blessing.

²⁶So Absalom said, "If you won't go, then please let my brother Amnon go with us."

"Why should he go with you?" the king asked him. ²⁷But when Absalom urged him, he let Amnon and all ˌthe rest ofˌ the king's sons go with him.

²⁸Then Absalom gave an order to his servants. "Watch now," he said. "When Amnon begins to feel good from drinking ˌtoo muchˌ wine, I'll tell you, 'Attack Amnon.' Then kill him. Don't be afraid. I've given you the order, haven't I? Be strong and courageous."

²⁹Absalom's servants did to Amnon as Absalom had ordered. Then all the king's sons got up, mounted their mules, and fled. ³⁰While they were on their way, David heard this rumor: "Absalom has killed all the king's sons, and not a single one is left." ³¹The king stood up, tore his clothes, and lay down on the ground. All his servants were standing beside him with their clothes torn ˌto show their griefˌ.

³²Then Jonadab, the son of David's brother Shimea, said, "Sir, don't think that all the young men, all the king's sons, have been killed. Only Amnon is dead. Absalom decided to do this the day his half brother raped his sister Tamar. ³³You shouldn't burden your heart with the idea that all the king's sons are dead, Your Majesty. Only Amnon is dead. ³⁴Absalom has fled."

When the servant who kept watch looked up, he saw many people coming down the road beside the mountain west of him. ³⁵Then Jonadab told the king, "The king's sons have come. It's just as I said." ³⁶When he finished speaking, the king's sons arrived and cried loudly. The king and all his men also cried very bitterly.

³⁷Absalom, however, fled to Geshur's King Talmai, Ammihud's son. But the king mourned for his son Amnon every day. ³⁸Absalom, having fled to Geshur, stayed there three years. ³⁹King David began to long for Absalom once people had consoled him over Amnon's death.

---

[a] 13:21 Dead Sea Scrolls, Greek, Latin add this sentence.   [b] 13:23 The time when sheep were sheared was also a time of rejoicing and feasting.   [c] 13:25 Dead Sea Scrolls; Masoretic Text "press," also in verse 27.

Women's World   Cosmetics / *2 Samuel 14:1-2*

Women in Bible times wanted to look beautiful. They applied olive oil to their skin to make it soft and smooth. Young women applied colored powders to their face with brushes; they put on eye shadow with "Kohl sticks," dark powder in a stick form. However, we might not agree with every ancient idea of beauty; women in Bible times often applied bright orange henna to the palms of their hands, as well as to their feet and nails.

The Bible does criticize women who overused cosmetics to advertise their sexuality (Jeremiah 4:30; Ezekiel 23:40). But many bottles, tweezers, spoons, and other beauty applicators found in Palestine and Syria by archaeologists show that the women of Bible times wanted to look attractive. The Bible does not say it's wrong to use cosmetics to look your best.

Absalom Returns to Jerusalem

14 ¹Joab, Zeruiah's son, knew the king was still thinking about Absalom. ²So Joab sent someone to Tekoa to get a clever woman from there. He told her, "Please act like a mourner, and dress in mourning clothes. Don't rub olive oil on yourself,*ᵃ* but act like a woman who has been mourning for the dead for a long time. ³Go to the king, and tell him this. . . ." Then Joab told her exactly what to say.

⁴The woman from Tekoa came*ᵇ* to the king and immediately bowed down with her face touching the ground. "Help me, Your Majesty," she said.

⁵The king asked her, "What can I do for you?"

She answered, "I'm a widow; my husband is dead. ⁶I had two sons who quarreled in the field, and there was no one to separate them. One killed the other. ⁷Then the entire family turned against me. They said, 'Give us the man who killed his brother so that we can kill him because he took his brother's life. We're going to destroy the one who now would be the heir.' In this way they wish to extinguish the one burning coal that is left for me. They will not let my husband's name or descendants remain on the face of the earth."

⁸"Go home," the king told the woman. "I will order someone to take care of this matter."

⁹The woman from Tekoa said to the king, "Let me be held responsible for the sin,

---

ᵃ 14:2 A cosmetic treatment of the skin.   *ᵇ* 14:4 Many Hebrew manuscripts, Greek, Syriac, Targum, Latin; some Hebrew manuscripts "said."

Your Majesty. Let my father's family be held responsible. Your Majesty and your throne are innocent."

¹⁰The king said, "If anyone says anything against you, bring him to me. He'll never harm you again."

¹¹She said, "Your Majesty, please pray to the Lᴏʀᴅ your God in order to keep an avenger from doing more harm by destroying my son."

"I solemnly swear, as the Lᴏʀᴅ lives," he said, "not a hair on your son's head will fall to the ground."

¹²The woman said, "Please let me say something else to you."

"Speak," he said.

¹³"Why have you devised something like this against God's people?" she said. "When you say this, you condemn yourself because you haven't brought back the one you banished! ¹⁴We are all going to die; we are all like water that is poured on the ground and can't be gathered up. But doesn't God forgive a person? He never plans to keep a banished person in exile.

¹⁵"I've come to say this to you because the people have frightened me. So I thought, 'I will speak to the king about this. Maybe the king will do something for me, his subject. ¹⁶Maybe the king will listen and rescue me, his subject, from the man who wants to cut off both me and my son from ₎our₎ God-given inheritance.' ¹⁷I thought that you would reassure me. You are like God's Messenger, who is able to distinguish right from wrong. May the Lᴏʀᴅ your God be with you!"

¹⁸The king said to the woman, "Please don't refuse to answer the question I'm going to ask you."

The woman responded, "Please speak, Your Majesty."

¹⁹"Did Joab put you up to this?" the king asked.

The woman answered, "I solemnly swear on your life, Your Majesty, you are absolutely right. Yes, your servant Joab ordered me ₎to do this₎. He told me to say exactly what I said. ²⁰Your servant Joab has done this to portray the matter in a different light. You are as wise as God's Messenger, who knows everything on earth."

²¹Then the king told Joab, "This is what you'll do. Bring back the young man Absalom."

²²Joab quickly bowed down with his face touching the ground, and he blessed the king. He said, "Today I know that you have been kind to me because you have done what I wanted."

²³So Joab went to Geshur and brought Absalom back to Jerusalem. ²⁴But the king said, "Absalom should return to his own house. He will not see me." So Absalom returned to his house and didn't see the king.

²⁵Now, no one in all Israel was praised for his good looks as much as Absalom was. He had no blemish from head to toe. ²⁶At the end of every year, he used to cut his hair because it became heavy for him. When he cut the hair on his head and weighed it, it weighed five pounds according to the royal standard. ²⁷Absalom had three sons and one daughter. His daughter Tamar was a beautiful woman.

²⁸Absalom stayed in Jerusalem two full years without seeing the king. ²⁹So Absalom sent for Joab in order to send him to the king, but Joab refused to come. Absalom sent for him a second time, but he still refused to come. ³⁰So Absalom said to his servants, "Look, Joab's field is next to mine. He has barley in it. Go and set it on fire." So Absalom's servants set it on fire.

Joab's servants came to him ₎in grief₎ and said, "Absalom's servants have set ₎your₎ field on fire."ᶜ

ᶜ14:30 Dead Sea Scrolls, Greek, and Latin add this sentence.

³¹Then Joab immediately went to Absalom at his home. "Why did your servants set my field on fire?" he asked.

³²Absalom answered Joab, "I sent someone to tell you to come here because I wanted to send you to the king to ask him why I had to come from Geshur. It would be better for me if I were still there. Let me see the king now! If I'm guilty of a sin, he should kill me."

³³Joab went to the king and told him this. The king then called for Absalom, who came to the king and bowed down with his face touching the ground. And the king kissed Absalom.

David Overthrown

15 ¹Soon after this, Absalom acquired a chariot, horses, and 50 men to run ahead of him. ²Absalom used to get up early and stand by the road leading to the city gate. When anyone had a case to be tried by King David, Absalom would ask, "Which city are you from?"

After the person had told him which tribe in Israel he was from, ³Absalom would say, "Your case is good and proper, but the king hasn't appointed anyone to hear it." ⁴He would add, "I wish someone would make me judge in the land. Then anyone who had a case to be tried could come to me, and I would make sure that he got justice." ⁵When anyone approached him and bowed down, Absalom would reach out, take hold of him, and kiss him. ⁶This is what he did for all Israelites who came to the king to have him try their case. So Absalom stole the hearts of the people of Israel.

⁷Four years later Absalom said to the king, "Let me go to Hebron and keep the vow I made to the Lord. ⁸I made a vow while I was living at Geshur in Aram. I said, 'If the Lord will bring me back to Jerusalem, I will serve the Lord.' "

⁹"Go in peace," the king told him.

So he went to Hebron. ¹⁰But Absalom sent his loyal supporters to all the tribes of Israel and said, "When you hear the sound of the ram's horn, say, 'Absalom has become king in Hebron.' "

¹¹Two hundred men invited from Jerusalem went with Absalom. They went innocently, knowing nothing about Absalom's plans. ¹²While Absalom was offering sacrifices, he sent for Ahithophel, David's adviser, to come from his home in Giloh. Meanwhile, the conspiracy grew stronger, and the number of people siding with Absalom kept getting larger.

¹³Someone came to tell David, "The hearts of the people of Israel are with Absalom."

Good Morning, God
2 Samuel 15:14-21

A good friend who loves the Lord is worth a lot. When David and his men were running away from Absalom, a foreigner named Ittai asked to join them. David gave Ittai permission to go back and stay with Absalom where he would have an easier life. But Ittai chose to stay with David. How can you be a loyal friend like Ittai? Who needs your encouragement today? Ask God to show you someone you can be a friend to today.

Lord, help me to be a loyal friend. Please bring good Christian friends who will be loyal to me.

David Flees Jerusalem

¹⁴David told all his men who were with him in Jerusalem, "Let's flee immediately, or none of us will escape from Absalom. Let's leave right away, or he'll catch up to us and bring disaster on us when he massacres the city."

¹⁵The king's servants told him, "No matter what happens, we are Your Majesty's servants."

¹⁶The king left on foot, and his whole household followed him except ten concubines[a] whom the king left behind to take care of the palace. ¹⁷As the king and his troops were leaving the city on foot, they stopped at the last house. ¹⁸All his mercenaries passed by him; all the Cherethites, all the Pelethites, Ittai, and all 600 men who had followed him from Gath were marching past the king.

¹⁹The king asked Ittai from Gath, "Why should you go with us? Go back, and stay with King Absalom. You are a foreigner, an exile from your homeland. ²⁰You came to us just yesterday. Should I make you wander around with me when I don't even know where I'm going? Go back, and take your countrymen with you. May the LORD always show you kindness."

²¹But Ittai answered the king, "I solemnly swear, as the LORD and the king live: Wherever you are, whether you're dead or alive, I'll be there."

²²So David told Ittai, "Go ahead and keep marching." So Ittai from Gath marched on with all his men and all the families who were with him.

²³The whole country was crying loudly as all the troops were passing by. The king was crossing the Kidron Valley, and all the people were moving down the road toward the desert. ²⁴Zadok and all the Levites with him were carrying the ark of God's promise. They set down the ark of God beside Abiathar until all the troops had withdrawn from the city.

²⁵The king told Zadok, "Take God's ark back to the city. If the LORD looks favorably on me, he will allow me to come back and see both it and its[b] dwelling place again. ²⁶But if he says, 'I'm not pleased with you,' let him do to me what he considers right."

²⁷"Aren't you a seer?"[c] the king asked Zadok the priest. "Go back to the city peacefully, and take your son Ahimaaz and Abiathar's son Jonathan with you. ²⁸I'll wait at the river crossings in the desert until I receive a message from you." ²⁹So Zadok and Abiathar took the ark of God back to Jerusalem and stayed there.

³⁰David cried as he went up the Mount of Olives. He covered his head and walked barefoot. And all of the troops with him covered their heads and cried as they went.

³¹Then David was told, "Ahithophel is among those conspiring with Absalom." So David prayed, "LORD, make Ahithophel's advice foolish."

³²When David came to the top of the Mount of Olives, where people worshiped God, Hushai from Archi's family was there to meet him. His clothes were torn, and he had dirt on his head. ³³David told him, "If you go with me, you will only be a burden to me. ³⁴But if you go back to the city and say to Absalom, 'Your Majesty, I'll be your servant. I was your father's servant in the past, but now I'll be your servant,' then you'll help me by undoing Ahithophel's advice. ³⁵The priests Zadok and Abiathar will be with you there. When you hear anything from the royal palace, tell it to the priests Zadok and Abiathar. ³⁶They have two sons with them: Zadok has Ahimaaz, and Abiathar has Jonathan. Send them to report to me anything you hear."

³⁷So Hushai, David's friend, went to the city as Absalom was entering Jerusalem.

---

[a] 15:16 A concubine is considered a wife except she has fewer rights under the law. [b] 15:25 Or "his." [c] 15:27 A seer is a prophet.

16 ¹When David had gone over the top of the Mount of Olives, Ziba, Mephibosheth's servant, met him with a pair of saddled donkeys. They were loaded with 200 loaves of bread, 100 bunches of raisins, 100 pieces of ripened fruit, and a full wineskin.

²"Why did you bring these?" David asked Ziba.

"The donkeys are for the king's family to ride on," Ziba answered. "The bread and the ripe fruit are for your servants to eat. The wine is for those who become tired and thirsty in the desert."

³"Where is your master Saul's grandson?" the king asked.

"He's staying in Jerusalem," Ziba answered the king. "He said, 'Today the house of Israel will give me back my grandfather's kingdom.' "

⁴The king told Ziba, "In that case everything that belonged to Mephibosheth now belongs to you."

"I sincerely thank you," said Ziba. "I hope to remain in your good graces, Your Majesty."

⁵When King David came to Bahurim, a man who was a distant cousin of Saul came out cursing. His name was Shimei, son of Gera. ⁶He threw stones at David and David's servants, although all the people and all the warriors were shielding David. ⁷Shimei cursed and said, "Get out! Get out, you bloodthirsty man! You worthless person! ⁸The LORD is paying you back for all the blood you spilled in the family of Saul, whom you succeeded as king. The LORD is giving the kingship to your son Absalom. Now you're in trouble because you're a bloodthirsty man."

⁹Abishai, Zeruiah's son, asked the king, "Why should this dead dog curse you, Your Majesty? Let me go over there and tear off his head."

¹⁰But the king said, "You don't think like me at all, sons of Zeruiah. Let him curse. If the LORD has told him, 'Curse David,' should anyone ask, 'Why do you do that?' " ¹¹David told Abishai and all his servants, "My own son, my own flesh and blood, is trying to kill me. Why, then, shouldn't this Benjaminite do this? Leave him alone. Let him curse, since the LORD has told him to do it. ¹²Maybe the LORD will see my misery and turn his curse into a blessing for me today."

Gossip
2 Samuel 16:5-14

It hurts when people say mean things to you. It hurts when they laugh at you. So what can you do? It's okay to tell a parent or God how you feel. It's not okay to try to get even. God doesn't want you to take revenge or to say mean things about others. You know how words can hurt.

all you can be

¹³As David and his men went along the road, Shimei was walking along the hillside parallel to him. Shimei cursed, hurled stones, and threw dirt at David. ¹⁴The king and all the people with him finally arrived at their destination and rested there.

Absalom Enters Jerusalem

15Meanwhile, Absalom and all Israel's troops came to Jerusalem, and Ahithophel was with him. 16When David's friend Hushai from Archi's family came to Absalom, he said, "Long live the king! Long live the king!"

17"Is that how loyal you are to your friend?" Absalom asked Hushai. "Why didn't you go with him?"

18Hushai answered Absalom, "No, I want to be with the one whom the Lord, these people, and all Israel have chosen. I will be his friend and stay with him. 19And besides, whom should I serve? Shouldn't it be his son? As I served your father, so I'll serve you."

20Then Absalom asked Ahithophel, "What's your advice? What should we do?"

21Ahithophel told Absalom, "Sleep with your father's concubines*a* whom he left to take care of the palace. Then all Israel will hear about how you have made your father despise you. Everyone who is with you will support you even more."

22So a tent was put up on the roof for Absalom, and he slept with his father's concubines in plain sight of Israel.

23In those days both David and Absalom thought that Ahithophel's advice was like getting an answer from God.

Absalom Pursues David

1Ahithophel said to Absalom, "Let me choose 12,000 men and leave tonight to go after David. 2I'll attack him while he's tired and weak, and I'll cause him to panic. All the people with him will flee, but I'll kill only him. 3I'll return all the people to you as a bride is returned to her husband. Since you will be seeking the life of only one man,*a* all the people will have peace." 4Absalom and all the leaders of Israel approved this plan.

5Absalom said, "Please call Hushai, who is descended from Archi's family, and let us hear what he, too, has to say."

6When Hushai arrived, Absalom said to him, "Ahithophel has told us his plan. Should we do what he says? If not, tell us."

7"This time Ahithophel's advice is no good," Hushai said to Absalom. 8"You know your father and his men. They are warriors as fierce as a wild bear whose cubs have been stolen. Your father is an experienced soldier. He will not camp with the troops tonight. 9He has already hidden in one of the ravines or some other place. If some of our soldiers are killed in the initial attack, others will definitely hear about it and say, 'The troops that support Absalom have been defeated.' 10Even the bravest man with a heart like a lion would lose his courage, because all Israel knows that your father is a warrior and the men with him are brave. 11So my advice is to gather all Israel's troops from Dan to Beersheba, since they are as numerous as the sand on the seashore. Lead them into battle yourself. 12Then we'll attack him wherever we find him. We'll fall on him as dew falls on the ground. Neither he nor any of his men will be left alive. 13If he retreats into a city, all Israel will bring ropes to that city and drag it into a valley so that not even a pebble will be found there."

14Absalom and all the people of Israel said, "The advice of Hushai from Archi's family is better than Ahithophel's advice." (The Lord had commanded Ahithophel's good advice to be defeated in order to ruin Absalom.)

15Then Hushai told the priests Zadok and Abiathar, "Ahithophel advised Absalom and the leaders of Israel to do one thing, but I advised them to do something else.

---

*a*16:21 A concubine is considered a wife except she has fewer rights under the law.   *a*17:3 "as a bride . . . only one man" Greek; Hebrew meaning uncertain.

¹⁶Now send messengers quickly to tell David, 'Don't rest tonight in the river crossings in the desert, but make sure you cross the river, or Your Majesty and all the troops with him will be wiped out.' "

¹⁷Jonathan and Ahimaaz were waiting at En Rogel. They could not risk being seen coming into the city, so a servant girl was to go and tell them, and they were to go and tell King David. ¹⁸But a young man saw Jonathan and Ahimaaz and told Absalom. So both of them left quickly and came to the home of a man in Bahurim who had a cistern in his courtyard, and they went down into it. ¹⁹The man's wife took a cover, spread it over the top of the cistern, and scattered some grain*ᵇ* over it so that no one could tell it was there.

²⁰Absalom's servants came to the woman at her home. "Where are Ahimaaz and Jonathan?" they asked.

The woman said, "They've crossed the stream."

The servants looked for them but did not find them. So Absalom's servants returned to Jerusalem.

²¹After Absalom's servants left, both men came out of the cistern and went and told King David. "Leave right away," they told David. "Cross the river quickly because this is what Ahithophel has advised against you. . . ."

²²David and all the troops with him left to cross the Jordan River. When the dawn came, everyone had crossed the Jordan River.

²³When Ahithophel saw that his advice hadn't been followed, he saddled his donkey, left, and went home to his own city. He gave instructions to his family. Then he hanged himself, died, and was buried in his father's tomb.

²⁴David had already come to Mahanaim by the time Absalom and all the men of Israel with him crossed the Jordan River. ²⁵Absalom appointed Amasa to take Joab's place as commander of the army. (Amasa was the son of a man named Ithra, a descendant of Ishmael.*ᶜ* His mother was Abigail,*ᵈ* the daughter of Nahash and sister of Joab's mother Zeruiah.) ²⁶The Israelites and Absalom camped in the region of Gilead.

²⁷When David came to Mahanaim, Shobi, son of Nahash from Rabbah in Ammon, and Machir, son of Ammiel from Lo Debar, and Barzillai from Rogelim in Gilead ²⁸brought supplies and food for David and his troops: bedding, bowls, pots, wheat, barley, flour, roasted grain, beans, lentils,*ᵉ* ²⁹honey, buttermilk, sheep, and calves. They brought these things because they thought, "The troops in the desert are hungry, exhausted, and thirsty."

David Defeats Absalom

18 ¹David called together the troops that were with him. He appointed commanders in charge of regiments and battalions. ²David put a third of the troops under Joab's command, another third under Joab's brother Abishai (Zeruiah's son), and the last third under Ittai from Gath.

"I am going into battle with you," the king said to the troops.

³"You're not going with us," the troops said. "If we flee, they won't care about us, and if half of us die, they won't care either. But you're worth 10,000 of us. It's better for you to be ready to send us help from the city."

⁴"I'll do what you think best," the king responded. So the king stood by the gate while all the troops marched out by battalions and regiments.

---

*ᵇ*17:19 Hebrew meaning uncertain.   *ᶜ*17:25 Greek, 1 Chronicles 2:17; Masoretic Text "the Israelite."   *ᵈ*17:25 Or "Ishmael's descendant Ithra, who slept with Abigail."   *ᵉ* 17:28 Greek, Latin, Syriac; Masoretic Text adds "and roasted grain."

⁵The king ordered Joab, Abishai, and Ittai, "Treat the young man Absalom gently for my sake." All the troops heard him give all the commanders this order regarding Absalom.

⁶So the troops went out to the country to fight Israel in the forest of Ephraim. ⁷There David's men defeated Israel's army, and the massacre was sizable that day— 20,000 men. ⁸The fighting spread over the whole country. That day the woods devoured more people than the battle.

⁹Absalom happened to come face to face with some of David's men. He was riding on a mule, and the mule went under the tangled branches of a large tree. Absalom's head became caught in the tree. So he was left hanging*ᵃ* in midair when the mule that was under him ran away. ¹⁰A man who saw this told Joab, "I saw Absalom hanging in a tree."

¹¹"What! You saw that!" Joab said to the man who told him. "Why didn't you strike him to the ground? Then I would have felt obligated to give you four ounces of silver and a belt."

¹²But the man told Joab, "Even if I felt the weight of 25 pounds of silver in my hand, I wouldn't raise my hand against the king's son. We heard the order the king gave you, Abishai, and Ittai: 'Protect the young man Absalom for my sake.'*ᵇ* ¹³If I had done something treacherous to him, would you have stood by me? Like everything else, it wouldn't stay hidden from the king."

¹⁴Then Joab said, "I shouldn't waste time with you like this." He took three sharp sticks and plunged them into Absalom's heart while he was still alive in the tree. ¹⁵Then ten of Joab's armorbearers surrounded Absalom, attacked him, and killed him.

¹⁶Joab blew the ram's horn to stop their fighting , and the troops returned from pursuing Israel. ¹⁷They took Absalom, threw him into a huge pit in the forest, and piled a large heap of stones over him. Meanwhile, all Israel fled and went back to their homes.

¹⁸(While he was still living, Absalom had taken a rock and set it up for himself in the king's valley. He said, "I have no son to keep the memory of my name alive." He called the rock by his name, and it is still called Absalom's Monument today.)

¹⁹Then Ahimaaz, Zadok's son, said, "Let me run and bring the king the good news that the Lᴏʀᴅ has freed him from his enemies."

²⁰But Joab told him, "You won't be the man carrying good news today. You can carry the news some other day. You must not deliver the news today because the king's son is dead." ²¹Then Joab said to a man from Sudan, "Go, tell the king what you saw." The messenger bowed down with his face touching the ground in front of Joab and then ran off.

²²Ahimaaz, Zadok's son, spoke to Joab again, "Whatever may happen, I also want to run after the Sudanese messenger."

"Now, son, why should you deliver the message?" Joab asked. "You won't be rewarded for this news."

²³"Whatever happens, I'd like to run," replied Ahimaaz.

"Run," Joab told him. So Ahimaaz ran along the valley road and got ahead of the Sudanese messenger.

²⁴David was sitting between the two gates while the watchman walked along the roof of the gate by the wall. As he looked, he saw a man running alone. ²⁵The watchman called and alerted the king.

"If he's alone," the king said, "he has good news to tell." The runner continued to come closer.

ᵃ18:9 Dead Sea Scrolls, Greek, Latin, Syriac; Masoretic Text "he was put." ᵇ18:12 Two Hebrew manuscripts, Greek, Syriac, Targum, Latin; meaning of other Hebrew manuscripts uncertain.

²⁶When the watchman saw another man running, the watchman called, "There's ⌊another⌋ man running alone."

The king said, "This one is also bringing good news."

²⁷The watchman said, "It seems to me that the first one runs like Ahimaaz, Zadok's son."

"He's a good man," the king said. "He must be coming with good news."

²⁸Then Ahimaaz came up to the king, greeted him, and bowed down in front of him. Ahimaaz said, "May the Lord your God be praised. He has handed over the men who rebelled against Your Majesty."

²⁹"Is the young man Absalom alright?" the king asked.

Ahimaaz answered, "I saw a lot of confusion when Joab sent me away, but I didn't know what it meant."

³⁰"Step aside, and stand here," the king said. He stepped aside and stood there.

³¹Then the Sudanese messenger came. "Good news for Your Majesty!" he said. "Today the Lord has freed you from all who turned against you."

³²"Is the young man Absalom alright?" the king asked.

The Sudanese messenger answered, "May your enemies and all who turned against you be like that young man!"ᶜ

³³The king was shaken⌊by the news⌋. He went to the room above the gate and cried. "My son Absalom!" he said as he went. "My son, my son Absalom! I wish I had died in your place! Absalom, my son, my son!"

David Restored to the Throne

ᵃ ¹Joab was told, "The king is crying and mourning for Absalom." ²The victory of that day was turned into mourning because all the troops heard that the king was grieving for his son. ³That day the troops sneaked into the city as if they had fled from battle and were ashamed of it. ⁴The king covered his face and cried loudly, "My son Absalom! Absalom, my son, my son!"

⁵Then Joab came into the house. "Today you have made all your men feel ashamed," he said. "They saved your life and the lives of your sons, daughters, wives, and concubinesᵇ today. ⁶You love those who hate you and hate those who love you. Today, you have made it clear that your commanders and servants mean nothing to you. I think you would be pleased if Absalom were alive and all of us were dead. ⁷Now, get up, go out, and encourage your men. I swear to you by the Lord that if you don't go out, no one will stay with you tonight, and that will be worse than all the trouble you've had in your entire life."

⁸The king sat in the gateway. When all the troops were told, "The king is sitting in the gateway," they came to the king.

Meanwhile, Israel had fled and went back to their own homes. ⁹All the people in all the tribes of Israel were arguing with one another, saying, "The king rescued us from our enemies and saved us from the Philistines, but now he has fled from Absalom and left the country. ¹⁰However, Absalom, whom we anointed to rule us, has died in battle. Why is no one talking about bringing back the king?"

¹¹What all Israel was saying reached the king at his house. So King David sent ⌊this message⌋ to the priests Zadok and Abiathar: "Ask the leaders of Judah, 'Why should you be the last ⌊tribe⌋ to bring the king back to his palace? ¹²You are my relatives, my own flesh and blood. Why should you be the last to bring back the king?'

ᶜ18:32 2 Samuel 18:33 in English Bibles is 2 Samuel 19:1 in the Hebrew Bible.   ᵃ19:1 2 Samuel 19:1-43 in English Bibles is 2 Samuel 19:2-44 in the Hebrew Bible.   ᵇ19:5 A concubine is considered a wife except she has fewer rights under the law.

¹³And tell Amasa, 'Aren't you my flesh and blood? May God strike me dead unless you are given Joab's place to serve me always as the commander of the army.' "

¹⁴All the people of Judah were in total agreement. So they sent the king this message: "Come back with all your servants."

¹⁵The king came back to the Jordan River, and the people of Judah came to Gilgal to meet the king and bring him across the Jordan River. ¹⁶Shimei, Gera's son from the tribe of Benjamin and the town of Bahurim, hurried down with the people of Judah to meet King David. ¹⁷One thousand people from Benjamin were with him. And Ziba, the servant of Saul's family, rushed to the Jordan River across from the king. Ziba brought his 15 sons and 20 servants. ¹⁸They crossed the river to bring over the king's family and to do anything else the king wanted.

Shimei, Gera's son, bowed down in front of the king as he was going to cross the Jordan River. ¹⁹He pleaded with the king, "Don't remember the crime I committed the day you left Jerusalem. Don't hold it against me or even think about it, Your Majesty. ²⁰I know I've sinned. Today I've come as the first of all the house of Joseph to meet you."

²¹But Abishai, Zeruiah's son, replied, "Shouldn't Shimei be put to death for cursing the LORD's anointed king?"

²²David responded, "Are you sure we're from the same family, sons of Zeruiah? You are my enemies today. Should anyone in Israel be killed today? Don't I know that I'm king of Israel again?"

²³The king promised Shimei, "You won't die," and the king swore to it.

²⁴Mephibosheth, Saul's grandson, went to meet the king. He had not tended to his feet, trimmed his mustache, or washed his clothes from the day the king left until he came home safely. ²⁵When he came from Jerusalem to meet the king, the king asked him, "Why didn't you go with me, Mephibosheth?"

²⁶He answered, "My servant deceived me, Your Majesty. Since I am disabled, I said, 'Saddle the donkey for me, and I'll ride on it and go with the king.' ²⁷He told you lies about me, Your Majesty. However, you are like God's Messenger. Do what you think is right. ²⁸You could have killed anyone in my entire family, Your Majesty. Instead, you've seated me with those who eat at your table. So I no longer have the right to complain to the king."

²⁹The king asked him, "Why do you keep talking about it? I've said that you and Ziba should divide the land."

³⁰"Let him take it all," Mephibosheth told the king. "It's enough for me that you've come home safely."

³¹Barzillai, the man from Gilead, came from Rogelim with the king to the Jordan River to send him on his way. ³²Barzillai was an elderly man, 80 years old. Because he was a very rich man, he had provided the king with food while he was staying at Mahanaim.

³³The king told Barzillai, "Cross the river with me. I'll provide for you in Jerusalem."

³⁴Barzillai replied, "I don't have much longer to live. I shouldn't go with Your Majesty to Jerusalem. ³⁵I'm 80 years old now. How can I tell what is pleasant and what is not? Can I taste what I eat or drink? Can I still hear the singing of men and women? Why should I now become a burden to you, Your Majesty? ³⁶I'll just cross the Jordan River with you. Why should you give me such a reward? ³⁷Please let me go back so that I can die in my city near the grave of my father and mother. But here is Chimham. Let him go across with you. And do for him what you think is right."

³⁸"Chimham will go across with me," the king said. "I will do for him whatever you want. Anything you wish I'll do for you."

³⁹All the troops crossed the Jordan River, and then the king crossed. The king kissed Barzillai and blessed him. Then Barzillai went back home.

⁴⁰The king crossed the river to Gilgal, and Chimham went with him. All the troops from Judah and half of the troops from Israel brought the king across.

⁴¹Then all the people of Israel kept coming to the king. They asked, "Why did our cousins, the people of Judah, kidnap you and bring Your Majesty and your family and men across the Jordan River?"

⁴²All the people of Judah answered the people of Israel, "Because the king is our relative. Why are you angry about this? Did we eat the king's food, or did he give us any gifts?"ᶜ

⁴³The people of Israel answered the people of Judah, "We have ten times your interest in the king and a greater claim on David than you have. Why, then, do you despise us? Weren't we the first to suggest bringing back our king?"

But the people of Judah spoke ˌevenˌ more harshly than the people of Israel.

Sheba's Rebellion

¹A good-for-nothing man by the name of Sheba, Bichri's son, from the tribe of Benjamin happened to be at Gilgal. He blew a ram's horn ˌto announceˌ,

"We have no share in David's kingdom.
We won't receive an inheritance from Jesse's son.
     Everyone to his own tent, Israel!"

²So all the people of Israel left David to follow Sheba, Bichri's son. But the people of Judah remained loyal to their king ˌon his wayˌ from the Jordan River to Jerusalem.

³When David came to his palace in Jerusalem, he took the ten concubinesᵃ he had left to look after the palace and put them in a house under guard. He provided for them but no longer slept with them. So they lived like widows in confinement until they died.

⁴The king told Amasa, "Call the people of Judah together for me, and in three days be here yourself." ⁵Amasa went to call Judah together, but he took longer to do it than David had given him.

⁶David then told Abishai, "Sheba, son of Bichri, will do us more harm than Absalom. Take my men and go after him, or he will find some fortified cities and take the best ones for himself."ᵇ

⁷So Joab's men, the Cherethites, Pelethites, and all the soldiers went with Abishai. They left Jerusalem to pursue Sheba, Bichri's son. ⁸When they were at the large rock in Gibeon, Amasa met them there. Joab wore a military uniform, and strapped over it at his hip was a sword in a scabbard. As he stepped forward, the sword dropped ˌintoˌ his handˌ. ⁹"How are you, my brother?" Joab asked Amasa. He took hold of Amasa's beard with his right hand to kiss him. ¹⁰Amasa wasn't on his guard against the sword in Joab's ˌleftˌ hand. Joab stabbed him in the stomach, and his intestines poured out on the ground. (He died without being stabbed again.) Then Joab and his brother Abishai pursued Sheba, son of Bichri. ¹¹One of Joab's young men stood beside Amasaᶜ and said, "Anyone who favors Joab and is on David's side should follow Joab." ¹²Amasa was wallowing in his blood in the middle of the road. When the man saw that all the troops stopped as they came to the body, he carried Amasa from the road to the field

---

ᶜ19:42 Greek; Hebrew meaning uncertain.   ᵃ20:3 Hebrew "concubines/wives"; a concubine is considered a wife except she has fewer rights under the law.   ᵇ20:6 Hebrew meaning of this phrase uncertain.   ᶜ20:11 Greek, Latin; Masoretic Text "him."

and threw a sheet over him. ¹³As soon as he was moved from the road, everyone followed Joab and pursued Sheba, Bichri's son.

¹⁴Sheba passed through all the tribes of Israel to Abel (Beth Maacah). All the Berites were gathered together and followed him to the city. ¹⁵Joab's army came and attacked him in Abel (Beth Maacah). They put up a dirt ramp against the city, and it stood level with the outer wall. All the troops with Joab were trying to destroy the wall and tear it down.

¹⁶Then a clever woman called from the city, "Listen, listen! Tell Joab to come here so that I can talk to him."

¹⁷He came near, and she asked, "Are you Joab?"

"I am," he answered.

"Listen to what I have to say," she told him.

"I'm listening," he answered.

¹⁸So she said, "There's an old saying: 'Be sure to ask at Abel before doing anything.. That's the way they settle matters.' ¹⁹We are peaceful and faithful Israelites. Are you trying to destroy a mother city in Israel? Why should you swallow up what belongs to the Lord?"

²⁰Joab answered, "That's unthinkable! I don't wish to swallow it, up or destroy it.. ²¹That isn't the case. A man from the mountains of Ephraim by the name of Sheba, son of Bichri, has rebelled against King David. Give him to me, and I'll withdraw from the city."

"That's fine," the woman told Joab. "His head will be thrown to you from the wall." ²²Then the woman went to all the people with her clever plan. They cut off Sheba's head and threw it to Joab. He blew the ram's horn, and everyone scattered and withdrew from the city and went home. Joab went back to the king in Jerusalem.

David's Officials

²³Now, Joab was put in charge of Israel's whole army. Benaiah, son of Jehoiada, was in charge of the Cherethites and Pelethites. ²⁴Adoram was in charge of forced labor. Jehoshaphat, son of Ahilud, was the royal historian. ²⁵Sheva was the royal scribe. Zadok and Abiathar were priests. ²⁶And Ira, a descendant of Jair, was a priest to David.

David and the People of Gibeon

¹In the time of David, there was a famine for three successive years, and David asked the Lord's advice about it. The Lord answered, "It's because of Saul and his family. They are guilty of murder because they killed the people of Gibeon."

²(The Gibeonites were not a part of Israel but were left over from the Amorites. Although the Israelites had sworn to spare them, Saul, in his eagerness, tried to destroy them for Israel and Judah.)

The king called the Gibeonites ³and asked them, "What can I do for you? What should I give you to make peace with you so that you will bless what belongs to the Lord?"

⁴"We do not want silver or gold from Saul's family," the Gibeonites answered him. "And none of us wants to kill anyone in Israel."

The king asked, "What are you saying that I should do for you?"

⁵They answered the king, "Give us seven of the male descendants of the man who wanted to finish us off. He planned to wipe us out to keep us from staying anywhere in Israel's territory. ⁶We will execute them in the Lord's presence at Saul's town Gibeah." (It was Saul whom the Lord had chosen.)

"I will give them to you," the king said.

[7]But the king spared Mephibosheth, Jonathan's son and Saul's grandson, because of the oath in the Lord's name between David and Jonathan, son of Saul. [8]The king took Armoni and Mephibosheth, the two sons whom Rizpah (Aiah's daughter) gave birth to for Saul, and five sons whom Merab[a] (Saul's daughter) gave birth to for Adriel, son of Barzillai from Meholah. [9]The king handed them over to the Gibeonites, who executed them on the mountain in the Lord's presence. All seven died together. They were killed at the beginning of the harvest, when people started harvesting barley.

[10]Rizpah (Aiah's daughter) took sackcloth and stretched it out on the rock for herself from the beginning of the harvest until the sky rained on the dead bodies. She wouldn't let any birds land on them during the day or any wild animals come near them during the night.

[11]When David was told what Saul's concubine[b] Rizpah (Aiah's daughter) had done, [12]David went and took the bones of Saul and of his son Jonathan from the citizens of Jabesh Gilead. They had stolen them from the public square of Beth Shean, where the Philistines had hung them the day they killed Saul at Gilboa. [13]When David brought up the bones of Saul and Jonathan, his men gathered the bones of those who had been executed. [14]Then they buried the bones of Saul and his son Jonathan in the land of Benjamin, in Zela, in the tomb of Saul's father Kish. They did everything the king ordered. After that, God answered the prayers for the land.

The Giants of the Philistines Defeated—
1 Chronicles 20:4-8

[15]Once again there was a battle between the Philistines and Israel. So David and his men went to fight the Philistines, but David became exhausted. [16]A descendant of Haraphah named Benob, who had a bronze spear weighing 7½ pounds which he wore on a new belt, captured David and intended to kill him. [17]But Abishai, son of Zeruiah, came to help David. He attacked the Philistine and killed him. Then David's men swore an oath, saying, "You'll never go into battle with us again. The lamp of Israel must never be extinguished."

[18]After this, there was another battle with the Philistines at Gob. Then Sibbecai from Hushah killed Saph, another descendant of Haraphah. [19]When more fighting broke out with the Philistines at Gob, Elhanan, son of Jaare Oregim from Bethlehem, killed Goliath of Gath. (The shaft of Goliath's spear was like a beam used by weavers.) [20]In another battle at Gath, there was a tall man who had a total of 24 fingers and toes: six fingers on each hand and six toes on each foot. He also was a descendant of Haraphah. [21]When he challenged Israel, Jonathan, son of David's brother Shimei, killed him. [22]These four were descendants of Haraphah from Gath, and David and his men killed them.

David's Song of Deliverance—
Psalm 18:1-50

[1]David sang this song to the Lord when the Lord rescued him from all his enemies, especially from Saul. [2]He said,

> The Lord is my rock and my fortress and my Savior,
> [3]   my God, my rock in whom I take refuge, my shield,
>   the strength of my salvation, my stronghold,
>   my refuge, and my Savior who saved me from violence.

---

[a]21:8 1 Samuel 18:19, two Hebrew manuscripts, some Greek manuscripts, Syriac, Targum; other Hebrew and Greek manuscripts "Mical."   [b]21:11 A concubine is considered a wife except she has fewer rights under the law.

4   The LORD should be praised.
         I called on him, and I was saved from my enemies.

5   The waves of death had surrounded me.
         The torrents of destruction had overwhelmed me.
6   The ropes of the grave had surrounded me.
         The clutches of death had confronted me.

7   I called on the LORD in my distress.
         I called to my God for help.
             He heard my voice from his temple,
                 and my cry for help reached his ears.

8   Then the earth shook and quaked.
         Even the foundations of the heavens trembled.
         They shook violently because he was angry.
9   Smoke went up from his nostrils,
         and a raging fire came out of his mouth.
             Glowing coals flared up from it.
10   He spread apart the heavens
         and came down with a dark cloud under his feet.
11   He rode on one of the angels[a] as he flew,
         and he soared on the wings of the wind.
12   He surrounded himself with darkness.
         He made the dark rain clouds his covering.
13   Out of the brightness in front of him, he made lightning.
14   The LORD thundered from heaven.
         The Most High made his voice heard.
15   He shot arrows and scattered them.
         He flashed streaks of lightning and threw them into confusion.
16   Then the ocean floor could be seen.
         The foundations of the earth were laid bare
             at the LORD's stern warning,
             at the blast of the breath from his nostrils.

Good Morning, God

2 Samuel 22:1-7

What would you say is unfair about your life right now? Many unfair things happened to David, yet he never doubted God's love or goodness. Whenever David was in danger, he prayed to the Lord. God rescued him and gave him strength to go on. No one has an easy, perfect life—not even David. His life reminds us that God may not take away our troubles. But God does promise to help us through them.

Thank you, Lord, that you are always here for me when I need help.

17 He reached down from high above and took hold of me.
   He pulled me out of the raging water.
18 He rescued me from my strong enemy
      and from those who hated me,
         because they were too strong for me.
19 On the day when I faced disaster, they confronted me,
      but the Lord became my defense.
20   He brought me out to a wide-open place.
         He rescued me because he was pleased with me.

21 The Lord rewarded me
      because of my righteousness,
      because my hands are clean.
   He paid me back
22   because I have kept the ways of the Lord
         and I have not wickedly turned away from my God,
23   because all his judgments are in front of me
         and I have not turned away from his laws.
24   I was innocent as far as he was concerned.
         I have kept myself from guilt.
25 The Lord paid me back
      because of my righteousness,
      because he can see that I am clean.

26 ⸢In dealing⸣ with faithful people you are faithful,
      with innocent warriors you are innocent,
27   with pure people you are pure.
   ⸢In dealing⸣ with devious people you are clever.

28 You save humble people,
      but your eyes bring down arrogant people.
29 O Lord, you are my lamp.
      The Lord turns my darkness into light.
30   With you I can attack a line of soldiers.
         With my God I can break through barricades.

31 God's way is perfect!
      The promise of the Lord has proven to be true.
      He is a shield to all those who take refuge in him.
32   Who is God but the Lord?
            Who is a rock other than our God?
33 God arms me with strength.[b]
   His perfect way sets me free.
34   He makes my feet like those of a deer
         and gives me sure footing on high places.
35   He trains my hands for battle
         so that my arms can bend an ⸢archer's⸣ bow of bronze.
36 You have given me the shield of your salvation.
   Your help makes me great.
37 You make a wide path for me to walk on
      so that my feet do not slip.

---
b 22:33 Dead Sea Scrolls, Psalm 18:33, Greek, Syriac, Latin; Masoretic Text "my refuge is strength."

38 I chased my enemies and destroyed them.
 I did not return until I had ended their lives.
39 I ended their lives by shattering them.
  They were unable to get up.
  They fell under my feet.
40 You armed me with strength for battle.
 You made my opponents bow at my feet.
41 You made my enemies turn their backs to me,
  and I destroyed those who hated me.
42 They looked, but there was no one to save them.
 They looked to the LORD, but he did not answer them.
43 I beat them into a powder as fine as the dust on the ground.
 I crushed them and stomped on them like the dirt on the streets.
44 You rescued me from my conflicts with my people.
 You kept me as the leader of nations.
  A people I did not know will serve me.
45   Foreigners will cringe in front of me.
   As soon as they hear of me, they will obey me.
46   Foreigners will lose heart,
   although they are armed[c] in their fortifications.

47 The LORD lives!
  Thanks be to my rock!
   May God, the rock of my salvation, be glorified.
48 God gives me vengeance!
  He brings people under my authority.
49 He frees me from my enemies.
   You lift me up above my opponents.
   You rescue me from violent people.
50 That is why I will give thanks to you, O LORD, among the nations
  and make music to praise your name.
51 He gives great victories to his king.
 He shows mercy to his anointed,
  to David, and to his descendant[d] forever.

David's Last Words

23 ¹These are the last words of David:

  "Here is the declaration by David, son of Jesse—
   the declaration by the man whom God raised up,[a]
  whom the God of Jacob anointed,
   the singer of Israel's psalms:

2 "The Spirit of the LORD spoke through me.
 His words were on my tongue.
3 The God of Israel spoke to them.
 The rock of Israel told me,
  'The one who rules humans with justice rules with the fear of God.
4   He is like the morning light as the sun rises,

---

c22:46 Hebrew meaning uncertain.   d22:51 Or "to his descendants."   a23:1 Dead Sea Scrolls, Greek; Masoretic Text "who was raised up high."

> like a morning without clouds,
> like the brightness after a rainstorm.
> The rain makes the grass grow from the earth.'

5 "Truly, God considers my house to be that way,
> because he has made a lasting promise[b] to me,
> with every detail arranged and assured.
> He promised everything that helps me,
> everything that pleases me.
> Truly, he makes these things happen.

6 "Worthless people are like thorns.
> All of them are thrown away, because they cannot be picked by hand.

7 > A person who touches them uses iron tools,
> or the shaft of a spear.
> Fire[c] will burn them up completely wherever they are."

David's Three Fighting Men—
1 Chronicles 11:10-19

8These are the names of David's fighting men: Josheb Basshebeth from Tahkemon's family was leader of the three. He used a spear[d] to kill 800 men on one occasion.

9Next in rank to him was Eleazar, another one of the three fighting men. He was the son of Dodo and grandson of Aho. Eleazar was with David at Pas Dammim[e] when the Philistines gathered there for battle. When the soldiers from Israel retreated, 10he attacked and killed Philistines until his hand got tired and stuck to his sword. So the Lord won an impressive victory that day. The army returned to Eleazar, but they only returned to strip the dead.

11Next in rank to him was Shammah, the son of Agee from Harar. The Philistines had gathered at Lehi, where there was a field of ripe lentils. When the troops fled from the Philistines, 12he stood in the middle of the field and defended it by killing Philistines. So the Lord won an impressive victory.

13At harvest time three of the thirty leading men came to David at the cave of Adullam when a troop from the Philistine army was camping in the valley of Rephaim. 14While David was in the fortified camp, Philistine troops were at Bethlehem. 15When David became thirsty, he said, "I wish I could have a drink of water from the well at the city gate of Bethlehem." 16So the three fighting men burst into the Philistine camp and drew water from the well. They brought it to David, but he refused to drink it. He poured it out as an offering to the Lord and said, 17"It's unthinkable that I would do this, Lord. This is the blood of men who risked their lives!" So he refused to drink it.

These are the things which the three fighting men did.

David's Thirty Fighting Men—
1 Chronicles 11:20-47

18Joab's brother Abishai, Zeruiah's son, was the leader of the thirty. He used his spear to kill 300 men. He was as famous as the three 19and was honored more than they were. So he became their captain, but he didn't become a member of the three.

20Benaiah, son of Jehoiada, was from Kabzeel and was a brave man who did many things. He killed two distinguished soldiers from Moab. He also went into a pit and

---

[b]23:5 Or "covenant." [c]23:7 Or "The fire." [d]23:8 1 Chronicles 11:11; Greek "drew his sword"; Hebrew meaning of Masoretic Text uncertain. [e]23:9 1 Chronicles 11:13; Masoretic Text "when [the Philistines] challenged."

killed a lion on the day it snowed. [21]And he killed a handsome Egyptian. The Egyptian had a spear in his hand. Benaiah went to him with a club, grabbed the spear from him, and killed him with it. [22]These are the things that Benaiah, son of Jehoiada, did. He was as famous as the three fighting men. [23]He was honored more than the thirty, but he was not a member of the three. David put him in charge of his bodyguards.

[24]One of the thirty was Joab's brother Asahel. The thirty leading men were,
Elhanan (son of Dodo) from Bethlehem,
[25]   Shammah from Harod,
Elika from Harod,
[26]   Helez the Paltite,
Ira (son of Ikkesh) from Tekoa,
[27]   Abiezer from Anathoth,
Mebunnai (son of Hushai),
[28]   Zalmon (descendant of Ahohi),
Maharai from Netophah,
[29]   Heleb (son of Baanah) from Netophah,
Ittai (son of Ribai) from Gibeah in Benjamin,
[30]   Benaiah from Pirathon,
Hiddai from the Gaash ravines,
[31]   Abi Albon from Beth Arabah,
Azmaveth from Bahurim,
[32]   Elihba from Shaalbon,
Bene Jashen,
[33]   Jonathan (son of Shammah the Hararite),
Ahiam (son of Sharar the Hararite),
[34]   Eliphelet (son of Ahasbai and grandson of a man from Maacah),
Eliam (son of Ahithophel) from Gilo,
[35]   Hezrai from Carmel,
Paarai from Arabah,
[36]   Igal (son of Nathan) from Zobah,
Bani from the tribe of Gad,
[37]   Zelek from Ammon,
Naharai from Beeroth, armorbearer for Zeruiah's son Joab,
[38]   Ira (descendant of Ithra),
Gareb (descendant of Ithra),
[39]   Uriah the Hittite—
37 in all.

David's Sin—He Takes a Census—
I Chronicles 21:1-30

24 [1]The LORD became angry with Israel again, so he provoked David to turn against Israel. He said, "Go, count Israel and Judah."

[2]King David said to Joab, the commander of the army who was with him, "Go throughout the tribes of Israel from Dan to Beersheba and count the people. That way I will know how many there are."

[3]Joab responded to the king, "May the LORD your God multiply the people a hundred times over, and may Your Majesty live to see it. But why does Your Majesty wish to do this?"

[4]However, the king overruled Joab and the commanders of the army. So they left the king in order to count the people of Israel. [5]They crossed the Jordan River and

camped at Aroer, south of the city in the middle of the valley. Then they went to Gad and to Jazer. ⁶They went to Gilead and to Tahtim Hodshi and then to Dan Jaan and around toward Sidon. ⁷They went to the fortified city of Tyre and all the cities of the Hivites and the Canaanites. Then they went to Beersheba in the Negev of Judah. ⁸When they had covered the whole country, they came to Jerusalem after 9 months and 20 days. ⁹Joab reported the census figures to the king: In Israel there were 800,000 able-bodied men who could serve in the army, and in Judah there were 500,000.

¹⁰After David counted the people, his conscience troubled him. David said to the LORD, "I have committed a terrible sin by what I have done. LORD, please forgive me because I have acted very foolishly."

¹¹When David got up in the morning, the LORD spoke his word to the prophet Gad, David's seer.ᵃ ¹²"Go and tell David, 'This is what the LORD says: I'm offering you three choices. Choose the one you want me to do to you.' "

¹³When Gad came to David, he told David this and asked, "Should seven years of famine come to you and your land, or three months during which you flee from your enemies as they pursue you, or should there be a three-day plague in your land? Think it over, and decide what answer I should give the one who sent me."

¹⁴"I'm in a desperate situation," David told Gad. "Please let us fall into the LORD's hands because he is very merciful. But don't let me fall into human hands."

¹⁵So the LORD sent a plague among the Israelites from that morning until the time he had chosen. Of the people from Dan to Beersheba, 70,000 died. ¹⁶But when the Messenger stretched out his arm to destroy Jerusalem, the LORD changed his mind about the disaster. "Enough!" he said to the Messenger who was destroying the people. "Put down your weapon." The Messenger of the LORD was at the threshing floorᵇ of Araunah the Jebusite.

¹⁷When David saw the Messenger who had been killing the people, he said to the LORD, "I've sinned. I've done wrong. What have these sheep done? Please let your punishment be against me and against my father's family."

¹⁸That day Gad came to David and said to him, "Go, set up an altar for the LORD at Araunah the Jebusite's threshing floor."

¹⁹David went as Gad had told him and as the LORD had commanded him. ²⁰When Araunah looked down and saw the king and his men coming toward him, he went out and bowed down with his face touching the ground in front of the king. ²¹"Why has Your Majesty come to me?" Araunah asked.

David answered, "To buy the threshing floor from you and to build an altar for the LORD. Then the plague on the people will stop."

²²Araunah said to David, "Take it, Your Majesty, and offer whatever you think is right. There are oxen for the burnt offering, and there are threshers and oxen yokesᶜ for firewood." ²³All this Araunah gave to the king and said, "May the LORD your God accept you."

²⁴"No!" the king said to Araunah. "I must buy it from you at a fair price. I won't offer the LORD my God burnt sacrifices that cost me nothing."

So David bought the threshing floor and the oxen for 1¼ pounds of silver. ²⁵David built an altar for the LORD there and sacrificed burnt offerings and fellowship offerings. So the LORD heard the prayers for the country, and the plague on Israel stopped.

ᵃ24:11 A seer is a prophet. ᵇ24:16 A threshing floor is an outdoor area where grain is separated from its husks. ᶜ24:22 A thresher is a device used to separate grain from its husks. A yoke is a wooden bar placed over the necks of work animals so that they can pull plows or carts.

1 Kings

This book tells about the kings that followed David. Solomon, David's son, was wise, rich, and famous. Solomon built a great temple for the Lord. After his reign, the kingdom was divided. In the north, 10 tribes kept the name Israel. In the south, two tribes became the nation of Judah. Most of the kings in both the north and the south were evil. God had to send prophets to warn the kings and encourage the people to worship God again.

This queen came from a distant country to hear Solomon's wisdom. What did she bring him? See 1 Kings 10.

Whatever Happened to
Solomon's Gold?

How much gold did Solomon have?

The gold that Solomon earned every year weighed 49,950 pounds. At $400 an ounce, a year's supply of gold was worth 320 million dollars!

What did Solomon do with all his gold?

Solomon built cities. Every cup and utensil in his palace was made of gold. But most of the gold was used to cover the floors and walls of God's temple.

Where did Solomon's gold go?

Five years after Solomon died, Shishak, king of Egypt, attacked Jerusalem. Shishak took all the gold back to Egypt. Osorkon, Shishak's son, put the gold in the temples of Egypt's gods.

What's In It For Me?

I will be wise like Solomon if I . . .

THINK BEFORE I ACT.

SEEK THE ADVICE OF THOSE I RESPECT.

LEARN TO JUDGE BETWEEN RIGHT AND WRONG.

ASK GOD TO GIVE ME UNDERSTANDING.

LIVE BY WHAT THE BIBLE SAYS.

Never Trust Anyone Over 30 Years Old?

Do you and your friends know better than your parents and other grown-ups? Solomon's son Rehoboam thought he did.

When Rehoboam became king, he "ignored the advice the older leaders gave him" (1 Kings 12:8). Rehoboam took the advice of his young friends—and 10 of Israel's 12 tribes rebelled against him!

The truth is, wisdom often comes with age. Older people aren't *always* right, of course. But it is usually a good idea to listen to them. Rehoboam realized too late that he should have listened to his older advisers.

Of course, the oldest and wisest being of all is God. He was around before the universe began! If you want really good advice, look in God's word. Then you'll be wise, too.

ROYAL
RIDDLES

What did 700
wives cost
Solomon?

His wisdom.
(See 1 Kings 11.)

What did the ravens tell the widow?

Getting Elijah's food is for the birds!
(See 1 Kings 17.)

Why did Jezebel kill the vineyard owner?

She couldn't stand Ahab's whine.
(See 1 Kings 21.)

How to Recognize the Real Thing

Jeroboam was the first ruler of the Northern Kingdom. Jeroboam was afraid that if his people went to worship the Lord at the temple in Jerusalem, they would choose Solomon's son Rehoboam as ruler. So Jeroboam started his own false religion. What's the difference between false and true religion?

False Religion	True Religion
Ignores God's ways	Exposes sin
1 Kings 12:30-33	1 Kings 16:1-2
Causes stubbornness	Leads to humility
1 Kings 19:1-2	1 Kings 21:29
Leads to injustice	Brings justice and mercy
1 Kings 21:11-15	1 Kings 18:13; 21:20-23
Brings punishment	Brings blessings
1 Kings 11:9-13; 14:6-11	1 Kings 3:10-14; 17:14

1 Kings

David's Old Age

1 ¹King David had grown old, and although he was covered with blankets, he couldn't get warm. ²His officials told him, "Your Majesty, let us search for a young woman who has never been married. She can stay with you and be your servant. She can lie in your arms and keep you warm."

³So they searched throughout Israel for a beautiful, young woman. They found Abishag from Shunem and brought her to the king. ⁴The woman was very beautiful. She became the king's servant and took care of him, but the king did not make love to her.

Adonijah Plots to Become King

⁵Adonijah, son of Haggith,ᵃ was very handsome. His mother gave birth to him after Maacah had Absalom.ᵇ Adonijah was boasting that he was king. So he got a chariot and horses and 50 men to run ahead of him. ⁶His father had never confronted him by asking why he was doing this. ⁷But Adonijah had discussed his actions with Joab (son of Zeruiah) and with the priest Abiathar, so they supported him. ⁸But the priest Zadok, Benaiah (son of Jehoiada), the prophet Nathan, Shimei, Rei, and David's ⌊thirty⌋ fighting men did not join Adonijah.

⁹Adonijah sacrificed sheep, cattle, and fattened calves at Zoheleth Rock near En Rogel. He had invited all his brothers, the king's ⌊other⌋ sons, all the men of Judah, and the king's officials. ¹⁰But he didn't invite the prophet Nathan, Benaiah, the fighting men, or his brother Solomon.

The Prophet Nathan Helps Solomon Become King

¹¹Then Nathan asked Solomon's mother Bathsheba, "Haven't you heard that Adonijah, Haggith's son, has become king, and our master David doesn't ⌊even⌋ know about it? ¹²Bathsheba, let me give you some advice about how to save your life and your son's life. ¹³Go to King David and ask him, 'Your Majesty, didn't you swear to me that my son Solomon will be king after you, and that he will sit on your throne? Why is Adonijah acting as king?' ¹⁴And while you're still there talking to the king, I'll come in and confirm what you have said."

¹⁵Bathsheba went to the king in his private room. The king was very old, and Abishag from Shunem was taking care of him. ¹⁶Bathsheba knelt and bowed down in front of the king. "What do you want?" the king asked.

¹⁷"Sir," she answered, "you took an oath to the LORD your God. You said that my son Solomon will be king after you, and that he will sit on your throne. ¹⁸But now, you see, Adonijah has become king, and you don't ⌊even⌋ know anything about it, Your Majesty. ¹⁹He has sacrificed many fattened calves, bulls, and sheep. He has invited all the king's sons, Abiathar the priest, and Joab the commander of the army ⌊to his feast⌋. But he hasn't invited your servant Solomon. ²⁰All Israel is looking to you, Your Majesty, to tell them who should succeed you on your throne. ²¹Otherwise, my son

---

ᵃ 1:5 Adonijah's mother was Haggith; his father was David. He was David's oldest living son.   ᵇ 1:5 "very handsome . . . Absalom." These words are the last part of verse 6 (in Hebrew). They have been placed at the beginning of verse 5 to express the complex Hebrew sentence structure more clearly in English.

Anointing / *1 Kings 1*

To anoint means to pour on or rub with olive oil. Solomon and other kings, as well as priests and sometimes prophets, were shown to be selected by God when they were anointed with oil. Women used perfumed oil to keep their skin smooth in the dry climate. Special guests were also honored by anointing with oil. Olive oil mixed with herbs became medical treatment for wounds and sores.

Solomon and I will be treated like criminals when you lie down in death with your ancestors."

²²While she was still talking to the king, the prophet Nathan arrived. ²³The servants told the king, "The prophet Nathan is here." When he came to the king, he bowed down in front of him. ²⁴Nathan said, "Your Majesty, you must have said that Adonijah will be king after you and that he will sit on your throne, ²⁵because today he went and sacrificed many bulls, fattened calves, and sheep. He invited all the king's sons, the army's commanders, and the priest Abiathar to his feast. They are eating and drinking with him and saying, 'Long live King Adonijah!' ²⁶But he didn't invite me or the priest Zadok or Benaiah, who is Jehoiada's son, or your servant Solomon. ²⁷Did you allow this to happen without telling me who would sit on your throne next?"

²⁸Then King David answered, "Call Bathsheba in here." So she stood in front of him, ²⁹and he swore an oath. He said, "I solemnly swear, as the LORD who has saved my life from all trouble lives, ³⁰I will do today exactly what I swore to you by the LORD God of Israel. Your son Solomon will be king after me. He will sit on my throne."

³¹Then Bathsheba bowed down with her face touching the ground in front of the king. "May Your Majesty, King David, live forever!" she said.

³²King David said, "Summon the priest Zadok, the prophet Nathan, and Benaiah, son of Jehoiada." So they came to the king, ³³and he said, "Take my officials with you. Put my son Solomon on my mule, and take him to Gihon. ³⁴Have the priest Zadok and the prophet Nathan anoint him king of Israel there. Then blow the ram's horn and say, 'Long live King Solomon!' ³⁵Follow him back here when he comes to sit on my throne. He will be king in place of me. I have appointed him to be the leader of Israel and Judah."

³⁶"So be it!" Benaiah, son of Jehoiada, answered the king. "The LORD your God says so too. ³⁷As the LORD has been with you, so may he be with Solomon. May Solomon be an even greater king than you, King David."

³⁸Then the priest Zadok, the prophet Nathan, Benaiah (son of Jehoiada), the

Cherethites, and the Pelethites put Solomon on King David's mule and brought him to Gihon. [39]The priest Zadok took the container of olive oil from the tent and anointed Solomon. They blew the ram's horn, and all the people said, "Long live King Solomon!" [40]All the people followed him, blew flutes, and celebrated so loudly that their voices shook the ground.

Adonijah's Plot Fails

[41]Adonijah and all his guests heard this as they finished eating. When Joab heard the sound of the horn, he asked, "What's the reason for the noise in the city?" [42]He was still speaking when Jonathan, son of the priest Abiathar, arrived. "Come in," Adonijah said. "You're an honorable man, so you must be bringing good news."

[43]"Not at all," Jonathan answered Adonijah. "His Majesty King David has made Solomon king. [44]The king has sent the priest Zadok, the prophet Nathan, Benaiah (son of Jehoiada), the Cherethites, and the Pelethites with him. They have put him on the king's mule. [45]The priest Zadok and the prophet Nathan have anointed him king at Gihon. They have come from there celebrating, so the city is excited. That is the sound you heard. [46]Solomon is now seated on the royal throne. [47]Furthermore, the royal officials have come to congratulate His Majesty King David, saying, 'May your God make Solomon's name more famous than yours and his reign greater than your reign.' The king himself bowed down on his bed [48]and said, 'Praise the Lord God of Israel who has let me see the heir to my throne.' "

[49]Adonijah's guests were frightened, so they got up and scattered in all directions. [50]Adonijah was afraid of Solomon. He got up, went to the tent of meeting, and took hold of the horns of the altar.[a] [51]Someone told Solomon, "Adonijah is afraid of you, King Solomon. He is holding on to the horns of the altar and saying, 'Make King Solomon swear to me today that he will not have me killed.' "

[52]Solomon said, "If he will behave like an honorable man, not one hair on his head will fall to the ground. But if he does anything wrong, he will die." [53]King Solomon sent men to take him from the altar. Adonijah bowed down in front of King Solomon. "Go home," Solomon told him.

David's Advice to Solomon—
I Chronicles 29:26-30

[1]When David was about to die, he instructed his son Solomon, [2]"I'm about to leave this world. Be strong and mature. [3]Fulfill your duty to the Lord your God. Obey his directions, laws, commands, rules, and written instructions as they are recorded in Moses' Teachings. Then you'll succeed in everything you do wherever you may go. [4]You'll succeed because the Lord will keep the promise he made to me: 'If your descendants are faithful to me with all their hearts and lives, you will never fail to have an heir on the throne of Israel.'

[5]"You know what Joab (Zeruiah's son) did to me and to the two commanders of Israel's army—Abner, son of Ner, and Amasa, son of Jether. Joab killed them. When there was peace, he shed blood as if it were wartime. With their blood he stained the belt around his waist and the shoes on his feet. [6]Use your wisdom. Don't let that gray-haired, old man go to his grave peacefully.

[7]"Be kind to the sons of Barzillai from Gilead. Let them eat at your table. They helped me when I was fleeing from your brother Absalom.

[8]"Shimei, son of Gera from Bahurim in Benjamin, is still with you. He cursed me

---

[a] 1:50 Holding on to the horns of the altar was an appeal for mercy.

repeatedly when I went to Mahanaim. But when he came to meet me at the Jordan River, I took an oath by the LORD and said, 'As long as I'm king, I won't have you killed.' ⁹Now, don't let him go unpunished. You are wise and know what to do to him: Put that gray-haired, old man into his grave by slaughtering him."

¹⁰David lay down in death with his ancestors and was buried in the City of David. ¹¹He ruled as king of Israel for 40 years. He ruled for 7 years in Hebron and for 33 years in Jerusalem.

Solomon Establishes His Authority

¹²Solomon sat on his father David's throne, and his power was firmly established.

¹³Then Adonijah, son of Haggith, went to Bathsheba, Solomon's mother. "Is this a friendly visit?" she asked.

"Yes," he answered. ¹⁴Then he added, "I have a matter to discuss with you."

"What is it?" she asked.

¹⁵He said, "You know the kingship was mine. All Israel expected me to be their king. But the kingship has been turned over to my brother because the LORD gave it to him. ¹⁶Now I want to ask you for one thing. Don't refuse me."

"What is it?" she asked.

¹⁷He said, "Please ask King Solomon to give me Abishag from Shunem as my wife. He will not refuse you."

¹⁸"Very well," Bathsheba answered. "I will talk to the king for you."

¹⁹Bathsheba went to King Solomon to talk to him on Adonijah's behalf. The king got up to meet her and bowed down in front of her. Then he sat on his throne. He had a throne brought for his mother, and she sat at his right side.

²⁰"I'm asking you for one little thing," she said. "Don't refuse me."

"Ask, Mother," the king told her. "I won't refuse you."

²¹She replied, "Let Abishag from Shunem be given to your brother Adonijah as his wife."

²²King Solomon then said, "Why do you ask that Abishag from Shunem be given to Adonijah? That would be the same as giving him the kingship. After all, he is my older brother. The priest Abiathar and Joab (Zeruiah's son) are supporting him."

²³King Solomon took an oath by the LORD and said, "May God strike me dead if Adonijah doesn't pay with his life for this request! ²⁴The LORD set me on my father David's throne and gave me a dynasty as he promised. So I solemnly swear, as the LORD who has established me lives, that Adonijah will be put to death today." ²⁵King Solomon gave this task to Benaiah, son of Jehoiada. Benaiah attacked and killed Adonijah.

²⁶The king told the priest Abiathar, "Go to your land in Anathoth. You deserve to die, but I won't kill you at this time because you carried the ark of the Almighty LORD ahead of my father David and because you shared all my father's sufferings." ²⁷So Solomon removed Abiathar as the LORD's priest and fulfilled the LORD's word spoken at Shiloh about Eli's family.

²⁸The news reached Joab. (He had supported Adonijah, although he hadn't supported Absalom.) So Joab fled to the LORD's tent and clung to the horns of the altar. ²⁹After King Solomon heard that Joab had fled to the altar in the tent of the LORD, Solomon sent Benaiah, son of Jehoiada, to kill Joab.

³⁰When Benaiah came to the tent of the LORD, he told Joab, "The king says, 'Come out.'"

"No," Joab answered, "I'll die here."

So Benaiah reported to the king what Joab had said and how he had answered.

³¹The king answered, "Do as he said. Kill him, and bury him. You can remove the innocent blood—the blood which Joab shed—from me and my father's family. ³²The LORD will repay him for the slaughter he caused. Joab killed two honorable men who were better than he was. He used his sword to kill Abner (who was the son of Ner and the commander of Israel's army) and Amasa (who was the son of Jether and the commander of Judah's army). Joab did this without my father's knowledge. ³³The responsibility for their blood will fall on Joab and his descendants forever. But may David, his descendants, family, and throne always receive peace from the LORD."

³⁴Then Benaiah, son of Jehoiada, went and attacked Joab, killed him, and buried him at his home in the desert. ³⁵The king then appointed Benaiah, son of Jehoiada, to replace Joab as commander of the army. King Solomon also replaced Abiathar with the priest Zadok.

³⁶The king summoned Shimei and said to him, "Build a house for yourself in Jerusalem, and stay there. Don't leave the city to go anywhere else. ³⁷But the day you leave and cross the brook in the Kidron Valley, you can be certain that you will die. You will be responsible for your own death."

³⁸"Very well," Shimei answered. "I'll do just what Your Majesty said."

So Shimei stayed in Jerusalem for a long time. ³⁹But after three years, two of Shimei's slaves fled to Gath's King Achish, son of Maacah. Shimei was told that his slaves were in Gath, ⁴⁰so he saddled his donkey and went to Achish in Gath to search for his slaves. Shimei went to Gath and got his slaves.

⁴¹After Solomon heard that Shimei had gone from Jerusalem to Gath and back, ⁴²he summoned Shimei. Solomon asked him, "Didn't I make you take an oath by the LORD? Didn't I warn you that if you left the city to go anywhere, you could be certain that you would die? Didn't you say to me, 'Very well. I'll do just what you said'? ⁴³Why didn't you keep your oath to the LORD and obey the command I gave you? ⁴⁴Shimei, you know in your heart all the evil that you did to my father David. The LORD is going to pay you back for the evil you have done. ⁴⁵But King Solomon is blessed, and David's dynasty will always be firmly established by the LORD."

⁴⁶Then the king gave orders to Benaiah, son of Jehoiada. He went to attack and kill Shimei.

Solomon's power as king was now firmly established.

Solomon's Marriage—
2 Chronicles 1:1

³ ¹Solomon became the son-in-law of Pharaoh (the king of Egypt). After marrying Pharaoh's daughter, Solomon brought her to the City of David until he finished building his own house, the LORD's house, and the wall around Jerusalem.

²The people were still sacrificing at other worship sites because a temple for the name of the LORD had not yet been built. ³Solomon loved the LORD and lived by his father David's rules. However, he still sacrificed and burned incense at these other worship sites.

Solomon Requests Wisdom From God—
2 Chronicles 1:2-13

⁴King Solomon went to Gibeon to sacrifice because it was the most important place of worship. Solomon sacrificed 1,000 burnt offerings on that altar.

⁵In Gibeon the LORD appeared to Solomon in a dream at night. He said, "What can I give you?"

⁶Solomon responded, "You've shown great love to my father David, who was your

servant. He lived in your presence with truth, righteousness, and commitment. And you continued to show him your great love by giving him a son to sit on his throne today.

[7]"Lord my God, although I'm young and inexperienced, you've made me king in place of my father David. [8]I'm among your people whom you have chosen. They are too numerous to count or record. [9]Give me a heart that listens so that I can judge your people and tell the difference between good and evil. After all, who can judge this great people of yours?"

[10]The Lord[a] was pleased that Solomon asked for this. [11]God replied, "You've asked for this and not for a long life, or riches for yourself, or the death of your enemies. Instead, you've asked for understanding so that you can do what is right. [12]So I'm going to do what you've asked. I'm giving you a wise and understanding heart so that there will never be anyone like you. [13]I'm also giving you what you haven't asked for—riches and honor—so that no other king will be like you as long as you live. [14]And if you follow me and obey my laws and commands as your father David did, then I will also give you a long life."

[15]Solomon woke up and realized it had been a dream. He went to Jerusalem and stood in front of the ark of the Lord's promise. He sacrificed burnt offerings and fellowship offerings and held a banquet for all his officials.

Solomon's Wisdom in Action

[16]A short time later two prostitutes came to the king and stood in front of him. [17]One woman said to him, "Sir, this woman and I live in the same house. I gave birth to a son while she was with me in the house. [18]Two days later this woman also gave birth to a son. We were alone. No one else was with us. Just the two of us were in the house. [19]That night this woman's son died because she rolled over on top of him. [20]So she got up during the night and took my son, who was beside me, while I was asleep. She held him in her arms. Then she laid her dead son in my arms. [21]When I got up in the morning to nurse my son, he was dead! I took a good look at him and realized that he wasn't my son at all!"

Good Morning, God

1 Kings 3:5-14

If you could receive anything from God, what would you ask for? When King Solomon prayed, he asked God for wisdom to tell the difference between good and evil. God was pleased that Solomon was not greedy or selfish in his prayers. Some people only pray about themselves and the things they want. Their prayers often seem more like "wish lists" than worship. What does Solomon's humble request teach you about prayer?

Dear Father, please help me pray for the things you want me to have.

---

[a]3:10 Many Hebrew manuscripts, Greek; other Hebrew manuscripts "Lord."

²²The other woman said, "No! My son is alive—your son is dead."
The first woman kept on saying, "No! Your son is dead—my son is alive." So they
argued in front of the king.

²³The king said, "This one keeps saying, 'My son is alive—your son is dead,' and
that one keeps saying, 'No! Your son is dead—my son is alive.' "

²⁴So the king told his servants to bring him a sword. When they brought it, ²⁵he
said, "Cut the living child in two. Give half to the one and half to the other."

²⁶Then the woman whose son was still alive was deeply moved by her love for the
child. She said to the king, "Please, sir, give her the living child. Please don't kill him!"
But the other woman said, "He won't be mine or yours. Cut him in two."

²⁷The king replied, "Give the living child to the first woman. Don't kill him. She is
his mother."

²⁸All Israel heard about the decision the king made. They respected the king very
highly, because they saw he possessed wisdom from God to do what was right.

Solomon's Administration—
2 Chronicles 9:26

4 ¹When King Solomon was the king of all Israel, ²these were his officials:
Azariah, son of Zadok, was the chief priest.

³**Elihoreph** and **Ahijah**, the sons of Shisha, were scribes.
Jehoshaphat, son of Ahilud, was the royal historian.

⁴**Benaiah**, son of Jehoiada, was commander of the army.
Zadok and **Abiathar** were priests.

⁵**Azariah**, son of Nathan, was in charge of the district governors.
Zabud, son of Nathan, was the king's adviser.

⁶**Ahishar** was in charge of the palace.
Adoniram, son of Abda, was in charge of forced labor.

⁷Solomon appointed 12 district governors in Israel. They were to provide food
for the king and his palace. Each one had to supply food for one month every year.
⁸Their names were

Benhur, who was in charge of the hills of Ephraim,

⁹**Bendeker**, who was in charge of Makaz, Shaalbim, Beth Shemesh, and Elon Beth
Hanan, and

¹⁰**Benhesed**, who was in charge of Arubboth, Socoh, and the entire region of
Hepher.

¹¹**Benabinadab** had the entire region of Dor.
(Solomon's daughter Taphath was his wife.)

¹²**Baana**, son of Ahilud, had Taanach, Megiddo, and all of Beth Shean.
(This was near Zarethan, below Jezreel, from Beth Shean to Abel Meholah and
over to Jokmeam.)

¹³**Bengeber** was in charge of Ramoth Gilead; he had the settlements of Jair, a
descendant of Manasseh, in Gilead.
He also had the territory of Argob in Bashan, 60 large cities with walls and bronze
bars across their gates.

¹⁴**Ahinadab**, son of Iddo, was in charge of Mahanaim.

¹⁵**Ahimaaz** was in charge of Naphtali.
(He also married Solomon's daughter Basemath.)

¹⁶**Baana**, son of Hushai, was in charge of Asher and Aloth.

¹⁷**Jehoshaphat**, son of Paruah, was in charge of Issachar.

¹⁸**Shimei**, son of Ela, was in charge of Benjamin.

¹⁹**Geber**, son of Uri, was in charge of Gilead, the territory of King Sihon the Amorite and King Og of Bashan. (There was only one governor in that territory.)ᵃ

²⁰The people of Judah and Israel were as numerous as the sand on the seashore. They ate and drank and lived happily.ᵇ

²¹Solomon ruled all the kingdoms from the Euphrates River to the country of the Philistines and as far as the Egyptian border. These kingdoms paid taxes and were subject to Solomon as long as he lived.

²²Solomon's food supply for one day was 180 bushels of flour, 360 bushels of coarse flour, ²³10 fattened cows, 20 cows from the pasture, and 100 sheep in addition to deer, gazelles, fallow deer, and fattened birds. ²⁴He controlled all the territory west of the Euphrates River from Tiphsah to Gaza and all of its kings. So he lived in peace with all the neighboring countries. ²⁵As long as Solomon lived, Judah and Israel (from Dan to Beersheba) lived securely, everyone under his own vine and fig tree.

²⁶Solomon had stalls for 40,000 chariot horses. He also had 12,000 chariot soldiers.ᶜ ²⁷Each of the governors provided food for one month every year for King Solomon and all who ate at his table. The governors saw to it that nothing was in short supply. ²⁸They brought their quota of barley and straw for the chariot horses to the proper places.

Solomon's Wisdom

²⁹God gave Solomon wisdom—keen insight and a mind as limitless as the sand on the seashore. ³⁰Solomon's wisdom was greater than that of all the eastern people and all the wisdom of the Egyptians. ³¹He was wiser than anyone, than Ethan the Ezrahite, or Heman, Calcol, or Darda, Mahol's sons. His fame spread to all the nations around him.

³²Solomon spoke 3,000 proverbs and wrote 1,005 songs. ³³He described and classified trees—from the cedar in Lebanon to the hyssop growing out of the wall. He described and classified animals, birds, reptiles, and fish. ³⁴People came from every nation to hear his wisdom; they came from all the kings of the earth who had heard about his wisdom.

Preparations for Building the Temple—
2 Chronicles 2:1-13, 15-18

5 ᵃ¹King Hiram of Tyre sent his officials to Solomon when he heard that Solomon had been anointed king to succeed his father. Hiram had always been David's friend.

²Solomon sent word to Hiram, by saying, ³"You know that my father David was surrounded by war. He couldn't build a temple for the name of the Lord our God until the Lord let him defeat his enemies. ⁴But the Lord my God has surrounded me with peace. I have no rival and no trouble. ⁵Now I'm thinking of building a temple for the name of the Lord my God as the Lord spoke to my father David: 'Your son, whom I will put on your throne to succeed you, will build a temple for my name.' ⁶So order men to cut down cedars from Lebanon for me. My workers will work with your workers. I will pay you whatever wages you ask for your workers. You know we don't have any skilled lumberjacks like those from Sidon."

⁷Hiram was very glad to hear what Solomon had said. Hiram responded, "May the Lord be praised today. He has given David a wise son to rule this great nation."

ᵃ4:19 "There was . . . territory" Masoretic Text; Greek "There was also one governor in the territory of Judah."
ᵇ4:20 1 Kings 4:21-34 in English Bibles is 1 Kings 5:1-14 in the Hebrew Bible.   ᶜ4:26 Or "12,000 cavalry horses."
ᵃ5:1 1 Kings 5:1-18 in English Bibles is 1 Kings 5:15-32 in the Hebrew Bible.

[8]Hiram sent men to Solomon to say, "I've received the message you sent me. I will do everything you want in regard to the cedar and cypress logs. [9]My workers will bring logs from Lebanon to the sea, and I will have them make them into rafts to go by sea to any place you specify. There I will have them taken apart, and you can use them. You can pay me by providing food for my palace." [10]So Hiram gave Solomon all the cedar and cypress wood he wanted. [11]Solomon gave Hiram 120,000 bushels of wheat and 120,000 gallons of pure olive oil. Solomon paid Hiram this much every year.

[12]The LORD gave Solomon wisdom as he had promised. There was peace between Hiram and Solomon, and they made a treaty with one another.

[13]King Solomon forced 30,000 men from all over Israel to work for him. [14]He sent a shift of 10,000 men to Lebanon for a month. They would spend one month in Lebanon and two months at home. Adoniram was in charge of forced labor.

[15]Solomon had 70,000 men who carried heavy loads, 70,000 who quarried stone in the mountains, [16]and 3,300 foremen who were in charge of the workers. [17]The king commanded them to quarry large, expensive blocks of stone in order to provide a foundation of cut stone for the temple. [18]Solomon's workmen, Hiram's workmen, and men from Gebal quarried the stone and prepared the logs and stone to build the temple.

The Temple Built in Seven Years—
2 Chronicles 3:1-14

[1]Solomon began to build the LORD's temple 480 years after Israel left Egypt. He began building in the month of Ziv (the second month) of the fourth year of his reign over Israel. [2]The temple that King Solomon built for the LORD was 90 feet long, 30 feet wide, and 45 feet high. [3]The entrance hall in front of the main room of the temple was the same length as the shorter side of the temple. It extended 15 feet in front of the temple. [4]He also made latticed windows for the temple.

[5]He built an annex containing side rooms all around the temple. This annex was next to the walls of the main building and the inner sanctuary. [6]The interior of the lowest story of the annex was 7½ feet wide, the second story was 9 feet wide, and the third story was 10½ feet wide. Solomon made ledges all around the temple so that this annex would not be fastened to the walls of the temple.

[7]The temple was built with stone blocks that were finished at the quarry. No hammer, chisel, or any other iron tool made a sound at the temple construction site.

[8]The entrance to the first story[a] was on the south side of the temple. A staircase went up to the middle story and then to the third story.

[9]When he had finished building the walls, he roofed the temple with rows of cedar beams and planks.[b] [10]He built each story of the annex 7½ feet high alongside the entire temple. Its cedar beams were attached to the temple.

[11]The LORD spoke to Solomon, saying, [12]"This concerns the temple you are building: If you live by my laws, follow my rules, and keep my commands, I will fulfill the promise I made about you to your father David. [13]I will live among the Israelites and never abandon my people."

[14]When Solomon had finished building the temple's frame, [15]he began to line the inside walls of the temple with cedar boards. He paneled the inside of the temple with wood from floor to ceiling. He covered the floor of the temple with cypress planks.

[16]He sectioned off a 30-foot-long room at the rear of the temple with cedar boards from the floor to the rafters. He built it to serve as an inner room, the most holy place. [17]The 60-foot-long room at the front of the temple served as the main hall. [18]Gourds

---

[a]6:8 Greek, Targum; Masoretic Text "second story." [b]6:9 Hebrew meaning uncertain.

and flowers were carved into the cedar paneling inside the temple. Everything was covered with cedar. No stone could be seen.

¹⁹He prepared the inner room of the temple in order to put the ark of the Lord's promise there. ²⁰The inner room was 30 feet long, 30 feet wide, and 30 feet high. Solomon covered it and the cedar altar with pure gold. ²¹He covered the inside of the temple with pure gold. He put golden chains across the front of the inner room which was covered with gold. ²²He covered the entire inside of the temple with gold. He also covered the entire altar in the inner room with gold.

²³In the inner room he made two 15-foot-tall angels*ᶜ* out of olive wood. ²⁴Each wing of the angels was 7½ feet long. The distance from the tip of one wing to the tip of the other was 15 feet. ²⁵Both angels had a 15-foot wingspan. Both had the same measurements and the same shape. ²⁶Each was 15 feet high. ²⁷Solomon put the angels in the inner room of the temple. The wings of the angels extended so that the wing of one of the angels touched the one wall, and the wing of the other touched the other wall. Their remaining wings touched each other in the center of the room. ²⁸He covered the angels with gold.

²⁹He carved angels, palm trees, and flowers into the walls all around the inner and outer rooms of the temple. ³⁰He covered the floor of the inner and outer rooms of the temple with gold.

³¹He made doors for the entrance to the inner room out of olive wood. The doorposts had five sides. ³²The two doors were made out of olive wood. He carved angels, palm trees, and flowers into them and covered them with gold. The gold was hammered onto the angels and the palm trees.

³³In the same way he made square doorposts out of olive wood for the temple's entrance. ³⁴He made two doors from cypress. Each of the doors had two folding panels. ³⁵On them he carved angels, palm trees, and flowers. He evenly covered them with gold.

³⁶He built the inner courtyard with three courses of finished stones and a course of finished cedar beams.

³⁷In the month of Ziv of the fourth year of Solomon's reign, the foundation of the Lord's temple was laid. ³⁸In the month of Bul (the eighth month) of the eleventh year of his reign, the temple was finished according to all its plans and specifications. He spent seven years building it.

The Palace Built in 13 Years

7 ¹Solomon took 13 years to finish building his palace. ²He built a hall named the Forest of Lebanon. It was 150 feet long, 75 feet wide, and 45 feet high. It had four rows of cedar pillars supporting cedar beams. ³The hall was covered with cedar above the side rooms, which were supported by 45 pillars (15 per row).*ᵃ* ⁴The windows were in three rows facing each other on opposite sides of the palace. ⁵All the doors and doorframes were square. There were three doors facing each other on opposite sides of the palace.

⁶Solomon made the Hall of Pillars 75 feet long and 45 feet wide. In front of the hall was an entrance hall with pillars.

⁷He made the Hall of Justice, where he sat on his throne and served as judge. The hall was covered with cedar from floor to ceiling.*ᵇ*

⁸His own private quarters were in a different location than the Hall of Justice,

---

ᶜ6:23 Or "cherubim." ᵃ7:3 Hebrew meaning of this verse uncertain. ᵇ7:7 Latin, Syriac; Masoretic Text "floor to floor."

but they were similar in design. Solomon also built private quarters like this for his wife, Pharaoh's daughter.

⁹From the foundation to the roof, all these buildings, including the large courtyard, were built with high-grade stone blocks. The stone blocks were cut to size and trimmed with saws on their inner and outer faces. ¹⁰The foundation was made with large, high-grade stones (some 12 feet long, others 15 feet long). ¹¹Above the foundation were cedar beams and high-grade stone blocks, which had been cut to size. ¹²The large courtyard had three layers of cut stone blocks and a layer of cedar beams, like the inner courtyard of the Lord's temple and the entrance hall.

The Temple Furnishings—
2 Chronicles 2:13-14; 3:15-5:1

¹³King Solomon had Hiram brought from Tyre. ¹⁴Hiram was the son of a widow from the tribe of Naphtali. His father, a native of Tyre, was a skilled bronze craftsman. Hiram was highly skilled, resourceful, and knowledgeable about all kinds of bronze craftsmanship. He came to King Solomon and did all his bronze work.

¹⁵He made two bronze pillars. Each was 27 feet high and 18 feet in circumference. ¹⁶He made two capitals of cast bronze to put on top of the pillars. Each capital was 7½ feet high. ¹⁷He also made seven rows of filigree and chains for each capital. ¹⁸After he made the pillars, he made two rows of decorations around the filigree to cover the capitals which were above the pillars.ᶜ He made the capitals identical to each other. ¹⁹The capitals on top of the pillars in the entrance hall were lily-shaped. Each was six feet high. ²⁰Two hundred pomegranates in rows were directly above the bowl-shaped parts around the filigree on the capitals on both pillars.

²¹Hiram set up the pillars in the temple's entrance hall. He set up the pillar on the right and named it Jachin [He Establishes]. Then he set up the pillar on the left and named it Boaz [In Him Is Strength]. ²²There were lily-shaped capitals at the top of the pillars. He finished the work on the pillars.

²³Hiram made a pool from cast metal. It was 15 feet in diameter. It was round, 7½ feet high, and had a circumference of 45 feet. ²⁴Under the rim were two rows of gourds all around the 45-foot circumference of the pool. They were cast in metal when the pool was cast. ²⁵The pool was set on 12 metal bulls. Three bulls faced north, three faced west, three faced south, and three faced east. The pool was set on them, and their hindquarters were toward the center of the pool. ²⁶The pool was three inches thick. Its rim was like the rim of a cup, shaped like a lily's bud. It held 12,000 gallons.

²⁷He made ten bronze stands. Each stand was 6 feet square and 4½ feet high. ²⁸The stands were made this way: They had side panels set in frames. ²⁹On the panels set in frames were lions, oxen, and angels.ᵈ These were also on the frames. Above and below the lions and the cattle were engraved designs. ³⁰Each stand had four bronze wheels on bronze axles and four supports beneath the basin. The supports were made of cast metal with designs on the sides. ³¹Each had a 1½-foot-deep opening in the center to the circular frame on top. The opening was round, formed like a pedestal, and was two feet wide. Around the opening there were engravings. But the panels were square, not round. ³²The four wheels were under the panels, and the axles were attached to the stand. Each wheel was two feet high. ³³The wheels were made like chariot wheels. The axles, rims, spokes, and hubs were all cast metal. ³⁴The four supports at the four corners of each stand were part of the stand. ³⁵The top of each stand had a round, nine-inch-high band. Above the stand were supports which were

---

ᶜ7:18 Many Hebrew manuscripts, Greek, Syriac; other Hebrew manuscripts "pomegranates."   ᵈ7:29 Or "cherubim."

part of the panels. ³⁶Hiram engraved angels, lions, palm trees, and designs in every available space on the supports and panels. ³⁷This is the way he made the ten stands. All of them were cast in the same mold, identical in size and shape.

³⁸Hiram also made ten bronze basins. Each basin held 240 gallons. Every basin was six feet wide. There was one basin on each of the ten stands. ³⁹He put five stands on the south side of the temple and five on the north side of the temple. He set the pool on the south side of the temple in the southeast corner. ⁴⁰Hiram also made pots, shovels, and bowls.

So Hiram finished all the work for King Solomon on the LORD's temple: ⁴¹2 pillars, the bowl-shaped capitals on top of the 2 pillars, and 2 sets of filigree to cover the 2 bowl-shaped capitals on top of the pillars, ⁴²400 pomegranates for the 2 sets of filigree (2 rows of pomegranates for each filigree to cover the 2 bowl-shaped capitals on the pillars), ⁴³10 stands and 10 basins on the stands, ⁴⁴1 pool, 12 bulls under the pool, ⁴⁵pots, shovels, and bowls. Hiram made all these utensils out of polished bronze for the LORD's temple at King Solomon's request. ⁴⁶The king cast them in foundries in the Jordan Valley between Succoth and Zarethan. ⁴⁷Solomon left all the products unweighed because so much bronze was used. No one tried to determine how much the bronze weighed.

⁴⁸Solomon made all the furnishings for the LORD's temple: the gold altar, the gold table on which the bread of the presence was placed, ⁴⁹lamp stands of pure gold (five on the south side and five on the north in front of the inner room), flowers, lamps, gold tongs, ⁵⁰dishes, snuffers, bowls, saucers, incense burners of pure gold, the gold sockets for the doors of the inner room (the most holy place), and the doors of the temple.

⁵¹All the work King Solomon did on the LORD's temple was finished. He brought the holy things that had belonged to his father David—the silver, gold, and utensils—and put them in the storerooms of the LORD's temple.

The LORD Comes to His Temple—
2 Chronicles 5:2-14

8 ¹Then Solomon assembled the respected leaders of Israel, all the heads of the tribes, and the leaders of the Israelite families. They came to King Solomon in Jerusalem to take the ark of the LORD's promise from the City of David (that is, Zion). ²All the people of Israel gathered around King Solomon at the Festival of Booths in the month of Ethanim, the seventh month.

³When all the leaders of Israel had arrived, the priests picked up the LORD's ark. ⁴They brought the ark, the tent of meeting, and all the holy utensils in it to the temple. The priests and the Levites carried them ⁵while King Solomon with the whole assembly from Israel were offering countless sheep and cattle sacrifices in front of the ark. ⁶The priests brought the ark of the LORD's promise to its place in the inner room of the temple (the most holy place) under the wings of the angels.ª

⁷When the angels' outstretched wings were over the place where the ark rested, the angels became a covering above the ark and its poles. ⁸The poles were so long that their ends could be seen in the holy place by anyone standing in front of the inner room, but they couldn't be seen outside. (They are still there today.) ⁹There was nothing in the ark except the two stone tablets Moses put there at Horeb, where the LORD made a promise to the Israelites after they left Egypt.

¹⁰When the priests left the holy place, a cloud filled the LORD's temple. ¹¹The priests couldn't serve because of the cloud. The LORD's glory filled his temple.

ª 8:6 Or "cherubim."

Solomon Addresses the People—
2 Chronicles 6:1-11

[12]Then Solomon said, "The LORD said he would live in a dark cloud. [13]I certainly have built you a high temple, a home for you to live in permanently."

[14]Then the king turned around and blessed the whole assembly of Israel while they were standing. [15]"Thanks be to the LORD God of Israel. With his mouth he made a promise to my father David; with his hand he carried it out. He said, [16]'Ever since I brought my people Israel out of Egypt, I didn't choose any city in any of the tribes of Israel as a place to build a temple for my name. But now I've chosen David to rule my people Israel.'

[17]"My father David had his heart set on building a temple for the name of the LORD God of Israel. [18]However, the LORD said to my father David, 'Since you had your heart set on building a temple for my name, your intentions were good. [19]But you must not build the temple. Instead, your own son will build the temple for my name.' [20]The LORD has kept the promise he made. I have taken my father David's place, and I sit on the throne of Israel as the LORD promised. I've built the temple for the name of the LORD God of Israel. [21]I've made a place there for the ark which contains the LORD's promise that he made to our ancestors when he brought them out of Egypt."

Solomon's Prayer—
2 Chronicles 6:12-42

[22]In the presence of the entire assembly of Israel, Solomon stood in front of the LORD's altar. He stretched out his hands toward heaven [23]and said,

"LORD God of Israel,
   there is no god like you in heaven above or on earth below.
You keep your promise[b] of mercy to your servants,
   who obey you wholeheartedly.
[24]   You have kept your promise to my father David, your servant.
   With your mouth you promised it.
   With your hand you carried it out as it is today.

[25]   "Now, LORD God of Israel,
   keep your promise to my father David, your servant.
      You said, 'You will never fail to have an heir
         sitting in front of me on the throne of Israel
         if your descendants are faithful to me
            as you have been faithful to me.'

[26]   "So now, God of Israel,
   may the promise you made to my father David,
      your servant, come true.

[27]   "Does God really live on earth?
   If heaven itself, the highest heaven, cannot hold you,
      then how can this temple that I have built?
[28]   Nevertheless, my LORD God, please pay attention to my prayer for mercy.
   Listen to my cry for help as I pray to you today.
[29]   Night and day may your eyes be on this temple,
      the place about which you said, 'My name will be there.'

---

[b]8:23 Or "covenant."

Listen to me as I pray toward this place.
30 Hear the plea for mercy
that your people Israel and I pray toward this place.
Hear us when we pray to heaven, the place where you live.
Hear and forgive.

31 "If anyone sins against another person
and is required to take an oath
and comes to take the oath in front of your altar in this temple,
32 then hear that person in heaven, take action, and make a decision.
Condemn the guilty person with the proper punishment,
but declare the innocent person innocent.

33 "An enemy may defeat your people Israel
because they have sinned against you.
But when your people turn to you, praise your name, pray,
and plead with you in this temple,
34 then hear them in heaven, forgive the sins of your people Israel,
and bring them back to the land that you gave to their ancestors.

35 "When the sky is shut and there's no rain
because they are sinning against you,
and they pray toward this place, praise your name,
and turn away from their sin because you made them suffer,
36 then hear them in heaven.
Forgive the sins of your servants, your people Israel.
Teach them the proper way to live.
Then send rain on the land,
which you gave to your people as an inheritance.

37 "There may be famine in the land.
Plant diseases, heat waves, funguses, locusts,
or grasshoppers may destroy crops.
Enemies may blockade Israel's city gates.
During every plague or sickness
38 hear every prayer for mercy,
made by one person or by all the people in Israel,
whose consciences bother them,
who stretch out their hands toward this temple.
39 Hear them in heaven, where you live.
Forgive them, and take action.
Give each person the proper reply.
(You know what is in their hearts,
because you alone know what is in the hearts of all people.)
40 Then, as long as they live in the land that you gave to our ancestors,
they will fear you.

41 "People will hear about your great name,
mighty hand, and powerful arm.*c*
So when people who are not Israelites

---

*c*8:41 The first sentence of verse 42 (in Hebrew) has been placed in verse 41 to express the complex Hebrew
paragraph structure more clearly in English.

come from distant countries because of your name

42   to pray facing this temple,

43   hear them in heaven, the place where you live.
      Do everything they ask you
            so that all the people of the world may know your name
            and fear you like your people Israel
            and learn also that this temple which I built bears your name.

44   "When your people go to war against their enemies
            (wherever you may send them)
                  and they pray to you, O LORD, toward the city you have chosen
                  and the temple I built for your name,

45   then hear their prayer for mercy in heaven,
            and do what is right for them.

46   "They may sin against you.
            (No one is sinless.)
      You may become angry with them and hand them over to an enemy
            who takes them to another country as captives,
                  whether it is far or near.

47   If they come to their senses,
            are sorry for what they've done,
                  and plead with you in the land where they are captives,
                        saying, 'We have sinned. We have done wrong.
                        We have been wicked,'

48   if they change their attitude toward you
            in the land of their enemies where they are captives,
      if they pray to you
            toward the land that you gave their ancestors,
                  and the city you have chosen,
                  and the temple I have built for your name,

49   then in heaven, the place where you live, hear their prayer for mercy.
      Do what is right for them.

50   Forgive your people, who have sinned against you.
            Forgive all their wrongs when they rebelled against you,

Good Morning, God
1 Kings 8:46-51

How many times will God forgive the same mistake? The Israelites kept turning away from God to do wrong. Solomon asked God to hear the prayers of those who were sorry for their sins. He asked God to have mercy on the people each time they stopped doing wrong and followed God. Each time we are truly sorry for our sins, God will forgive us—even if we make the same mistakes.

Father, thank you for forgiving me when I ask for forgiveness.

and cause those who captured them to have mercy on them
⁵¹   because they are your own people
         whom you brought out of Egypt
         from the middle of an iron smelter.

⁵²   "May your eyes always see my plea and your people Israel's plea
         so that you will listen to them whenever they call on you.
⁵³   After all, you, Lord God, set them apart from all the people of the world
         to be your own as you promised through your servant Moses
         when you brought our ancestors out of Egypt."

Solomon Blesses the People

⁵⁴When Solomon finished praying this prayer for mercy to the Lord, he stood in front of the Lord's altar, where he had been kneeling with his hands stretched out toward heaven. ⁵⁵Then he stood and in a loud voice blessed the entire assembly of Israel, ⁵⁶"Thanks be to the Lord! He has given his people Israel rest, as he had promised. None of the good promises he made through his servant Moses has failed to come true. ⁵⁷May the Lord our God be with us as he was with our ancestors. May he never leave us or abandon us. ⁵⁸May he bend our hearts toward him. Then we will follow him and keep his commands, laws, and rules, which he commanded our ancestors ˌto keepˌ. ⁵⁹May these words which I have prayed to the Lord be near the Lord our God day and night. Then he will give me and his people Israel justice every day as it is needed. ⁶⁰In this way all the people of the world will know that the Lord is God and there is no otherˌ godˌ. ⁶¹May your hearts be committed to the Lord our God. Then you will live by his laws and keep his commands as you have today."

Solomon Offers Sacrifices—
2 Chronicles 7:4-10

⁶²Then the king and all Israel offered sacrifices to the Lord. ⁶³Solomon sacrificed 22,000 cattle and 120,000 sheep as fellowship offerings to the Lord. So the king and all the people of Israel dedicated the Lord's temple.

⁶⁴On that day the king designated the courtyard in front of the Lord's temple as a holy place. He sacrificed the burnt offerings, grain offerings, and the fat from the fellowship offerings because the bronze altar in front of the Lord was too small to hold all of them.

⁶⁵At that time Solomon and all Israel celebrated the Festival ˌof Boothsˌ. A large crowd had come from ˌthe territory betweenˌ the border of Hamath and the River of Egypt to be near the Lord our God for seven days.^d ⁶⁶On the eighth day he dismissed the people. They blessed the king and went to their tents. They rejoiced with cheerful hearts for all the blessings the Lord had given his servant David and his people Israel.

The LORD Answers Solomon's Prayer—
2 Chronicles 7:11-22

¹Solomon finished building the Lord's temple, the royal palace, and everything ˌelseˌ he wanted to build. ²Then the Lord appeared to him a second time, as he had appeared to him in Gibeon. ³The Lord said to him,

         "I have heard your prayer for mercy that you made to me.
         I have declared that this temple which you have built is holy

---

^d8:65 Greek; Masoretic Text adds ". . . and seven ˌmoreˌ days, fourteen days ˌtotalˌ."

so that my name may be placed there forever.
My eyes and my heart will always be there.

4 "If you will be faithful to me as your father David was
(with a sincere and upright heart),
do everything I command,
and keep my laws and rules,
5 then I will establish your royal dynasty over Israel forever
as I promised your father David when I said,
'You will never fail to have an heir on the throne of Israel.'
6 But if you and your descendants dare to turn away from me
and do not keep my commands and laws that I gave to you,
and follow and serve other gods and worship them,
7 then I will cut Israel out of the land I gave them.
I will reject this temple that I declared holy for my name.
Israel will be an example
and an object of ridicule for all the people of the world.
8 Everyone passing by this temple, as impressive as it is, will be appalled.
They will gasp and ask,
'Why did the LORD do these things to this land and this temple?'
9 They will answer themselves,
'They abandoned the LORD their God,
who brought their ancestors out of Egypt.
They adopted other gods, worshiped, and served them.
That is why the LORD brought this disaster on them.' "

Solomon Completes His Construction—
2 Chronicles 8:1-18

10 It took Solomon 20 years to build the two houses (the LORD's house and the royal palace). 11 When King Solomon had finished, he gave King Hiram of Tyre 20 cities in Galilee. (Hiram had supplied Solomon with as much cedar and cypress lumber and gold as he wanted.) 12 Hiram left Tyre to see the cities Solomon gave him. However, they didn't please him. 13 "What kind of cities have you given me, brother?" he asked. So he named it the region of Cabul [Good for Nothing]. (They're still called that today.) 14 Hiram had sent the king 9,000 pounds of gold.

15 This is the record of the forced laborers whom King Solomon drafted to build the LORD's house, his own house, the Millo,[a] the walls of Jerusalem, and the cities of Hazor, Megiddo, and Gezer. 16 (The king of Egypt captured Gezer, burned it down, and killed the Canaanites living there. Then he gave it to his daughter, Solomon's wife, as a wedding present.) 17 So Solomon rebuilt Gezer, Lower Beth Horon, 18 Baalath, Tadmor in the desert (inside the country), and 19 all the storage cities that he owned. He also built cities for his chariots, cities for his war horses, and whatever else he wanted to build in Jerusalem, Lebanon, or the entire territory that he governed.

20 The Amorites, Hittites, Perizzites, Hivites, and Jebusites had been left in the land because the Israelites had not been able to claim them for God by destroying them.[b] They were not Israelites, 21 but they had descendants who were still in the land.

---

[a]9:15 The exact place referred to as "the Millo" is unknown. [b]9:20 "because the Israelites. . . ." This clause from verse 21 (in Hebrew) has been placed in verse 20 to express the complex Hebrew paragraph structure more clearly in English.

Solomon drafted them for slave labor. (They are still slaves today.) [22]But Solomon didn't make any of the Israelites slaves. Instead, they were soldiers, officials, officers, generals, and commanders of his chariot and cavalry units.

[23]These were the officers in charge of Solomon's projects: 550 foremen for the people who did the work.

[24]Pharaoh's daughter moved from the City of David to the palace that Solomon had built for her. Then he built the Millo.

[25]Three times a year Solomon sacrificed burnt offerings and fellowship offerings on the altar he built for the LORD. He burnt them on the altar that was in the LORD's presence. And he finished the temple.

[26]King Solomon also built a fleet near the Red Sea coast at Ezion Geber by Elath in Edom. [27]Hiram sent his own servants who were experienced seamen with the fleet. Along with Solomon's servants [28]they went to Ophir, got 31,500 pounds of gold, and brought it to King Solomon.

The Queen of Sheba Visits Solomon—
2 Chronicles 9:1-12

10 [1]The queen of Sheba heard about Solomon's reputation. (He owed his reputation to the name of the LORD.) So she came to test him with riddles. [2]She arrived in Jerusalem with a large group of servants, with camels carrying spices, a very large quantity of gold, and precious stones. When she came to Solomon, she talked to him about everything she had on her mind. [3]Solomon answered all her questions. No question was too difficult for the king to answer.

[4]When the queen of Sheba saw all of Solomon's wisdom, the palace he built, [5]the food on his table, his officers' seating arrangement, the organization of his officials and the uniforms they wore, his cupbearers,[a] and the burnt offerings that he sacrificed at the LORD's temple, she was breathless. [6]She told the king, "What I heard in my country about your words and your wisdom is true! [7]But I didn't believe the reports until I came and saw it with my own eyes. I wasn't even told half of it. Your wisdom and wealth surpass the stories I've heard. [8]How blessed your men must be! How blessed these servants of yours must be because they are always stationed in front of you, listening to your wisdom! [9]Thank the LORD your God, who is pleased with you. He has put you on the throne of Israel. Because of your God's eternal love for the people of Israel, he has made you king so that you would maintain justice and righteousness."

[10]She gave the king 9,000 pounds of gold, a very large quantity of spices, and precious stones. Never again was such a large quantity of spices brought into Israel as those that the queen of Sheba gave King Solomon.

[11]Hiram's fleet that brought gold from Ophir also brought a large quantity of sandalwood and precious stones from Ophir. [12]With the sandalwood the king made supports for the LORD's temple and the royal palace, and lyres and harps for the singers. Never again was sandalwood like this imported into Israel, nor has any been seen there to this day.

[13]King Solomon gave the queen of Sheba anything she wanted, whatever she asked for, besides what he had given her out of his royal generosity. Then she and her servants went back to her country.

---

[a] 10:5 A cupbearer was a trusted royal official who ensured that the king's drink was not poisoned.

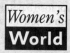

Chariots / *1 Kings 10:26-29*

In Old Testament times, chariots were used by armies just as the tanks of modern warfare are used by today's soldiers. Hundreds of chariots rushing at soldiers on foot must have been a terrifying sight. But the Israelites didn't need chariots as long as they depended on God. God told them, "When you go to war against your enemies, you may see horses, chariots, and armies larger than yours. Don't be afraid of them, because the LORD your God, who brought you out of Egypt, will be with you" (Deuteronomy 20:1).

Solomon's Wealth—
2 Chronicles 9:13-25, 27-28; 1:14-17

¹⁴The gold that came to Solomon in one year weighed 49,950 pounds, ¹⁵not counting the gold which came from the merchants, the traders' profits, all the Arab kings, and the governors of the country.

¹⁶King Solomon made 200 large shields of hammered gold, using 15 pounds of gold on each shield. ¹⁷He also made 300 small shields of hammered gold, using four pounds of gold on each shield. The king put them in the hall which he called the Forest of Lebanon.

¹⁸The king also made a large ivory throne and covered it with fine gold. ¹⁹Six steps led to the throne. Carved into the back of the throne was a calf's head. There were armrests on both sides of the seat. Two lions stood beside the armrests. ²⁰Twelve lions stood on six steps, one on each side. Nothing like this had been made for any other kingdom.

²¹All King Solomon's cups were gold, and all the utensils for the hall which he called the Forest of Lebanon were fine gold. (Nothing was silver, because it wasn't considered valuable in Solomon's time.) ²²The king had a fleet headed for Tarshish with Hiram's fleet. Once every three years the Tarshish fleet would bring gold, silver, ivory, apes, and monkeys.

²³In wealth and wisdom King Solomon was greater than all the other kings of the world. ²⁴The whole world wanted to listen to the wisdom that God gave Solomon. ²⁵So everyone who came brought him gifts: articles of silver and gold, clothing, weapons, spices, horses, and mules. This happened year after year.

²⁶Solomon built up his army with chariots and war horses. He had 1,400 chariots and 12,000 war horses. He stationed some in chariot cities and others with himself in Jerusalem. ²⁷The king made silver as common in Jerusalem as stones, and he made cedars as plentiful as fig trees in the foothills.

²⁸Solomon's horses were imported from Egypt and Kue. The king's traders bought them from Kue for a fixed price. ²⁹Each chariot was imported from Egypt for 15 pounds of silver and each horse for 6 ounces of silver. For the same price they obtained horses to export to all the Hittite and Aramean kings.

Solomon's Idolatry

¹King Solomon loved many foreign women in addition to Pharaoh's daughter. He loved Hittite women and women from Moab, Ammon, Edom, and Sidon. ²They came from the nations about which the LORD had said to the people of Israel, "Never intermarry with them. They will surely tempt you to follow their gods." But Solomon was obsessed with their love. ³He had 700 wives who were princesses and 300 wives who were concubines.ᵃ ⁴In his old age, his wives tempted him to follow other gods. He was no longer committed to the LORD his God as his father David had been. ⁵Solomon followed Astarte (the goddess of the Sidonians) and Milcom (the disgusting idol of the Ammonites). ⁶So Solomon did what the LORD considered evil. He did not wholeheartedly follow the LORD as his father David had done. ⁷Then Solomon built an illegal worship site on the hill east of Jerusalem for Chemosh (the disgusting idol of Moab) and for Molech (the disgusting idol of the Ammonites). ⁸He did these things for each of his foreign wives who burned incense and sacrificed to their gods.

God Pronounces Judgment on Solomon

⁹So the LORD became angry with Solomon because his heart had turned from the LORD God of Israel, who had appeared to him twice. ¹⁰God had given him commands about this. He told him not to follow other gods. But Solomon did not obey God's command. ¹¹The LORD told Solomon, "Because this is your attitude and you have no respect for my promisesᵇ or my laws that I commanded you to keep, I will certainly tear the kingdom away from you. I will give it to one of your servants. ¹²But I will not do it in your lifetime because of your father David. I will tear it away from the hands of your son. ¹³However, I will not tear the whole kingdom away from you. I will give your son one tribe for my servant David's sake and for the sake of Jerusalem, the city that I chose."

Rebellions Against Solomon

¹⁴The LORD raised up Hadad the Edomite as a rival to Solomon. Hadad was from the Edomite royal family. ¹⁵When David had conquered Edom, Joab, the commander of the army, went to bury those killed in battle and killed every male in Edom. ¹⁶(Joab and all Israel stayed there six months until they had destroyed every male in Edom.) ¹⁷Hadad was a young boy at the time. He and some of his father's Edomite servants fled to Egypt. ¹⁸They left Midian and went to Paran. Taking some men from Paran with them, they went to Pharaoh (the king of Egypt). Pharaoh gave Hadad a home, a food allowance, and land.

¹⁹Pharaoh approved of Hadad. So he gave Hadad his sister-in-law, the sister of Queen Tahpenes, to be Hadad's wife. ²⁰Tahpenes' sister had a son named Genubath. Tahpenes presented the boy to Pharaoh in the palace, and Genubath lived in the palace among Pharaoh's children.

²¹When Hadad heard in Egypt that David had lain down in death with his ancestors

---

ᵃ11:3 A concubine is considered a wife except she has fewer rights under the law.   ᵇ11:11 Or "covenant."

and that Joab, the commander of the army, had died, he said to Pharaoh, "Let me go to my own country."

²²Pharaoh asked him, "What don't you have here that makes you eager to go home?"

"Nothing," he said. "But let me leave anyway."

²³God also raised up Rezon, son of Eliada, as a rival to Solomon. Rezon fled from his master, King Hadadezer of Zobah, ²⁴after David killed the men of Zobah. Rezon gathered men and became the leader of a troop of warriors. They went to Damascus, settled there, and ruled a kingdom in Damascus. ²⁵In addition to the trouble that Hadad caused, Rezon was Israel's rival as long as Solomon lived. He ruled Aram and despised Israel.

²⁶There was also Jeroboam, who was the son of Nebat and an Ephrathite from Zeredah. His mother Zeruah was a widow. He was one of Solomon's officers, but he rebelled against the king.

²⁷This was the situation when he rebelled against the king: Solomon was building the Millo*c* and repairing a break in the wall of the City of David. ²⁸Solomon saw that Jeroboam was a very able and hard-working man. So he put Jeroboam in charge of all forced labor from the tribes of Joseph.

²⁹At that time Jeroboam left Jerusalem. The prophet Ahijah from Shiloh met him on the road. The two of them were alone in the open country, and Ahijah had on new clothes. ³⁰Ahijah took his new garment and tore it into 12 pieces.

³¹He told Jeroboam, "Take 10 pieces because this is what the LORD God of Israel says: I am going to tear the kingdom out of Solomon's hands and give ten tribes to you. ³²He will have one tribe left because of my servant David and Jerusalem, the city I have chosen from all the tribes of Israel. ³³I will do this because he has abandoned me and worshiped Astarte (the goddess of the Sidonians), Chemosh (the god of Moab), and Milcom (the god of Ammon). He has not followed my ways. He did not do what I consider right or keep my laws and decrees as his father David did.

³⁴"I will not take the whole kingdom from him. Instead, I will allow him to be ruler as long as he lives because of my servant David whom I chose, who obeyed my commands and laws. ³⁵But I will take the kingdom away from his son and give you ten tribes. ³⁶I will give his son one tribe so that my servant David will always have a lamp in my presence in Jerusalem, the city where I chose to place my name.

³⁷"I will choose you so that you can rule everything you desire. You will be king of Israel. ³⁸If you will do all I command you, follow my ways, and do what I consider right by obeying my laws and commands as my servant David did, then I will be with you. I will build a permanent dynasty for you as I did for David. And I will give you Israel. ³⁹I will make David's descendants suffer for this, but not always."

⁴⁰Then Solomon tried to kill Jeroboam, but Jeroboam fled to King Shishak of Egypt. He stayed in Egypt until Solomon died.

Solomon's Death—
2 Chronicles 9:29-31

⁴¹Aren't the rest of Solomon's acts—everything he did—and his wisdom written in the records of Solomon? ⁴²The length of Solomon's reign in Jerusalem over all Israel was 40 years. ⁴³Solomon lay down in death with his ancestors and was buried in the City of David. His son Rehoboam succeeded him as king.

---

*c*11:27 The exact place referred to as "the Millo" is unknown.

King Rehoboam Foolishly Rejects Israel's Request—
2 Chronicles 10:1-19

12 ¹Rehoboam went to Shechem because all Israel had gone to Shechem to make him king. ²Jeroboam (Nebat's son) was still in Egypt, where he had fled from King Solomon. When he heard ⸢about Rehoboam⸣, he returned from Egypt.ᵃ ³Israel⸣ sent for Jeroboam and invited him back. Jeroboam and the entire assembly of Israel went to speak to Rehoboam. They said, ⁴"Your father made us carry a heavy burden. Reduce the hard work and lighten the heavy burden he put on us, and we will serve you."

⁵He said to them, "Leave and come back the day after tomorrow." So the people left.

⁶King Rehoboam sought advice from the older leaders who had served his father Solomon while he was still alive. He asked, "What do you advise? How should I respond to these people?"

⁷They told him, "If you will serve these people today, humble yourself, and speak gently, then they will always be your servants."

⁸But he ignored the advice the older leaders gave him. He sought advice from the young men who had grown up with him and were serving him. ⁹He asked them, "What is your advice? How should we respond to these people who are asking me to lighten the burden my father put on them?"

¹⁰The young men who had grown up with him answered, "This is what you should tell them: 'My little finger is heavier than my father's whole body.ᵇ ¹¹If my father put a heavy burden on you, I will add to it. If my father punished you with whips, I will punish you with scorpions.' "

¹²So Jeroboam and all the people came back to Rehoboam two days later, as the king had instructed them. ¹³The king answered the people harshly. He ignored the advice the older leaders gave him. ¹⁴He spoke to them as the young men advised. He said, "If my father made your burden heavy, I will add to it. If my father punished you with whips, I will punish you with scorpions." ¹⁵The king refused to listen to the people because the LORD was directing these events to carry out the promise he had made to Jeroboam (Nebat's son) through Ahijah from Shiloh.

¹⁶When all Israel saw that the king refused to listen to them, the people answered the king,

> "What share do we have in David's kingdom?
> We won't receive an inheritance from Jesse's son.

Advice
1 Kings 12:6-20

It helps to talk about problems. If you have a problem, you can ask friends what they think. You can also talk with an older person. Pick a godly person whom you respect and who will listen and suggest ways that may help you.

ᵃ12:2 2 Chronicles 10:2, Greek, Latin; Masoretic Text "remained in Egypt."   ᵇ12:10 Hebrew meaning uncertain.

To your own tents, Israel!
Now look after your own house, David!"

So Israel went home to their own tents. ¹⁷But Rehoboam ruled the Israelites who lived in the cities of Judah.

¹⁸Then King Rehoboam sent Adoram to Israel. He was in charge of forced labor, but they stoned him to death. So King Rehoboam got on his chariot as fast as he could and fled to Jerusalem. ¹⁹Israel has rebelled against David's dynasty to this day.

King Jeroboam Establishes Idolatry in Israel—
2 Chronicles 11:1-17

²⁰When all Israel heard that Jeroboam had returned, they sent men to invite him to the assembly. They made him king of all Israel. Only the tribe of Judah remained loyal to David's dynasty.

²¹When Rehoboam came to Jerusalem, he gathered all the people of Judah and the tribe of Benjamin, 180,000 of the best soldiers, to fight against the people of Israel and return the kingdom to Rehoboam, son of Solomon.

²²But God spoke his word to Shemaiah, the man of God. He said, ²³"Speak to Judah's King Rehoboam, son of Solomon, and all the people of Judah and Benjamin, and the rest of the people. ²⁴This is what the LORD says: Don't wage war against your relatives from Israel. Everyone, go home. What has happened is my doing." So they obeyed the word of the LORD. They returned ˌhome·, as the LORD told them.

²⁵Jeroboam rebuilt Shechem in the hills of Ephraim and lived there. Then he left that place and built Penuel. ²⁶He said to himself, "The kingdom will probably return to David's dynasty now. ²⁷King Rehoboam of Judah, the former master of these people, will regain popularity if they go to sacrifice in the LORD's temple in Jerusalem. Then they will kill me and return to King Rehoboam of Judah."

²⁸After seeking advice, the king made two golden calves. He said, "You've been worshiping in Jerusalem long enough. Israel, here are your gods who brought you out of Egypt." ²⁹He put one in Bethel and the other in Dan. ³⁰Worshiping them became ˌIsrael's· sin. The people went as far as Dan to worship the one calf. ³¹Jeroboam built worship sites on hilltops. He appointed men who were not descended from Levi to be priests.

³²Jeroboam appointed a festival on the fifteenth day of the eighth month, just like the festival in Judah. He went to the altar in Bethel to sacrifice to the calves he had made. He appointed priests from the illegal worship sites ˌto serve· in Bethel. ³³He went to his altar in Bethel to burn an offering on the fifteenth day of the eighth month, ˌthe festival· he had invented for the Israelites.

A Prophet Announces God's Judgment

13 ¹A man of God from Judah had come to Bethel. When he arrived, Jeroboam was standing at the altar to offer a sacrifice. ²By a command of the LORD, this man condemned the altar. "Altar, altar! This is what the LORD says: There will be a son born in David's family line. His name will be Josiah. Here on you Josiah will sacrifice the priests from the illegal worship sites who offer sacrifices on you. Human bones will be burned on you."

³That day the man of God ˌalso· gave ˌthem· a miraculous sign, saying, "This is the sign that the LORD will give you: You will see the altar torn apart. The ashes on it will be poured ˌon the ground·."

⁴When King Jeroboam heard the man of God condemning the altar in Bethel, he pointed to the man across the altar. "Arrest him," he said. But the arm that he used to point to the man of God was paralyzed so that he couldn't pull it back. ⁵The altar was torn apart, and the ashes from the altar were poured on the ground. This was the miraculous sign the man of God performed at the LORD's command.

⁶Then the king asked the man of God, "Please make an appeal to the LORD your God, and pray for me so that I can use my arm again." So the man of God made an appeal to the LORD, and the king was able to use his arm again, as he had earlier.

⁷The king told the man of God, "Come home with me; have something to eat and drink, and I will give you a gift."

⁸The man of God told the king, "Even if you gave me half of your palace, I would never go with you to eat or drink there. ⁹When the LORD spoke to me, he commanded me not to eat or drink or go back on the same road I took." ¹⁰So the man of God left on another road and didn't go back on the road he had taken to Bethel.

A Prophet Disobeys God

¹¹An old prophet was living in Bethel. His sons told him everything the man of God did in Bethel that day and the exact words he had spoken to the king. When they told their father, ¹²he said to them, "Which road did he take?" (His sons had seen which road the man of God from Judah had taken.) ¹³The old prophet told his sons, "Saddle the donkey for me." After they had saddled the donkey for him, he got on it.

¹⁴He went after the man of God and found him sitting under an oak tree. The old prophet asked him, "Are you the man of God who came from Judah?"

"Yes," he answered.

¹⁵"Come home with me, and eat a meal," the old prophet replied.

¹⁶The man of God said, "I'm not allowed to go back with you. I'm not allowed to eat or drink with you. ¹⁷When the LORD spoke to me, he told me not to eat or drink there or go back on the road I took to get there."

¹⁸The old prophet said, "I'm also a prophet, like you. An angel spoke the word of the LORD to me. He said, 'Bring him home with you so that he may have something to eat and drink.'" (But the old prophet was lying.)

¹⁹The man of God went back with him and ate and drank in his home. ²⁰When they were sitting at the table, the LORD spoke his word to the old prophet who had brought back the man of God. ²¹The LORD also called to the man of God. He said, "This is what the LORD says: You rebelled against the words from the LORD's mouth and didn't obey the command that the LORD your God gave you. ²²You came back, ate, and drank at this place about which he told you, 'Don't eat or drink there.' That is why your dead body will not be allowed to be placed in the tomb of your ancestors."

²³After the old prophet had something to eat and drink, he saddled the donkey for the prophet whom he had brought back. ²⁴The man of God left. A lion found him as he traveled on the road and killed him. His dead body was thrown on the road. The donkey and the lion were standing by the body. ²⁵People who passed by saw the body lying on the road and the lion standing by the body. They talked about it in the city where the old prophet was living.

²⁶When the old prophet who had brought the man of God back from the road heard about it, he said, "It's the man of God who rebelled against the words from the LORD's mouth! The LORD gave him to the lion. It tore him to pieces and killed him as the word of the LORD had told him."

²⁷Then the old prophet told his sons to saddle his donkey for him. So they did. ²⁸He found the body of the man thrown on the road. He also found the donkey and

the lion standing beside it. The lion had not eaten the body, nor had it torn the donkey to pieces. ²⁹The old prophet picked up the body of the man of God, laid it on the donkey, and brought it back. He came to his own city to mourn for him and to bury him. ³⁰He laid the body of the man of God in his own tomb and mourned over the man, saying, "Oh no, my brother, my brother!" ³¹After he had buried the man of God, he said to his sons, "When I die, bury me in the tomb where the man of God was buried. Lay my bones beside his bones. ³²The things that he announced by a command of the LORD against the altar in Bethel and all the illegal worship sites in the cities of Samaria will happen."

³³Even after this, Jeroboam didn't change his evil ways, but he once again made some men priests for the illegal worship sites. He took all who were willing and appointed them to be priests at the worship sites. ³⁴Appointing illegal priests became the sin of Jeroboam's family so that it had to be destroyed and wiped off the face of the earth.

Jeroboam's Son Dies

14

¹At that time Abijah, son of Jeroboam, got sick. ²Jeroboam told his wife, "Go to Shiloh, but disguise yourself so that people will not recognize you as my wife. The prophet Ahijah, who told me I would be king of these people, is there. ³Take ten loaves of bread, some raisins,ᵃ and a jar of honey with you, and go to him. He will tell you what will happen to the boy." ⁴Jeroboam's wife did this. She left, went to Shiloh, and came to the home of Ahijah.

Ahijah couldn't see. His eyesight had failed because he was old. ⁵However, the LORD had told Ahijah, "Jeroboam's wife is coming to ask you about her son who is sick. When she comes, she will pretend to be someone else." He also told Ahijah what to say to her.

⁶Ahijah heard her footsteps when she came into the room. He said, "Come in. You're Jeroboam's wife. Why are you pretending to be someone else? I've been told to give you some terrible news. ⁷Tell Jeroboam, 'This is what the LORD God of Israel says: I picked you out of the people and made you a leader over my people Israel. ⁸I tore the kingdom away from David's heirs and gave it to you. But you have not been like my servant David. He obeyed my commands and faithfully followed me by doing only what I considered right. ⁹You have done more evil things than everyone before you. You made other gods, metal idols, for yourself. You made me furious and turned your back to me.

¹⁰" 'That is why I will bring disaster on Jeroboam's house. I will destroy every maleᵇ in his house, whether slave or freeman in Israel. I will burn down Jeroboam's house. It will burn like manure until it is gone. ¹¹If anyone from Jeroboam's house dies in the city, dogs will eat him. If anyone dies in the country, birds will eat him.' The LORD has said this!

¹²"Get up, and go home. The moment you set foot in the city the child will die. ¹³All Israel will mourn for him and bury him. He is the only one of Jeroboam's family who will be ˌproperlyˌ buried. He was the only one in Jeroboam's house in whom the LORD God of Israel found anything good. ¹⁴The LORD will appoint a king over Israel. That king will destroy Jeroboam's house. This will happen today. It will happen right now.ᶜ

¹⁵"The LORD will strike Israel like cattails which shake in the water. He will uproot Israel from this good land which he gave their ancestors. He will scatter them

---

ᵃ14:3 Or "cakes."   ᵇ14:10 Hebrew uses a coarse term for "male" here.   ᶜ14:14 Hebrew meaning of these two sentences uncertain.

beyond the Euphrates River because they dedicated poles to the goddess Asherah and made the LORD furious. [16]So the LORD will desert Israel because of Jeroboam's sins, the sins which he led Israel to commit."

[17]Jeroboam's wife got up, left, and went to Tirzah. When she walked across the threshold of her home, the boy died. [18]All Israel buried him and mourned for him as the LORD had said through his servant, the prophet Ahijah.

[19]Everything else concerning Jeroboam, his wars, and his reign is written in the official records of the kings of Israel. [20]Jeroboam ruled for 22 years. Then he lay down in death with his ancestors. His son Nadab succeeded him as king.

King Rehoboam of Judah—
2 Chronicles 12:13-14

[21]Rehoboam, son of Solomon, ruled Judah. He was 41 years old when he began to rule. He ruled for 17 years in Jerusalem, the city that the LORD chose from all the tribes of Israel, the city where the LORD put his name. Rehoboam's mother was an Ammonite woman named Naamah.

[22]The people of Judah did what the LORD considered evil. Their sins made him more angry than anything their ancestors had done. [23]They built worship sites for themselves and put up large stones and Asherah poles to worship on every high hill and under every large tree. [24]There were even male prostitutes in the temples of idols throughout the land. The people of Judah did all the disgusting practices done by the nations that the LORD had forced out of the Israelites' way.

King Shishak Takes the Temple Treasures—
2 Chronicles 12:2, 9-11, 15-16

[25]In the fifth year of Rehoboam's reign, King Shishak of Egypt attacked Jerusalem. [26]He took the treasures from the LORD's temple and the royal palace. He took them all. He took all the gold shields Solomon had made. [27]So King Rehoboam made bronze shields to replace them and put them by the entrance to the royal palace, where the captains of the guards were stationed. [28]Whenever the king went into the LORD's temple, guards carried the shields and then returned them to the guardroom.

[29]Isn't everything else concerning Rehoboam—everything he did—written in the official records of the kings of Judah? [30]There was war between Rehoboam and Jeroboam as long as they lived. [31]Rehoboam lay down in death with his ancestors and was buried with them in the City of David. (His mother was an Ammonite woman named Naamah.) His son Abijam succeeded him as king.

King Abijam of Judah—
2 Chronicles 13:1, 2, 22; 14:1

15 [1]In the eighteenth year of the reign of Jeroboam (Nebat's son), Abijam began to rule Judah. [2]He ruled for three years in Jerusalem. His mother was named Maacah, daughter of Abishalom. [3]He followed the sinful example his father had set and wasn't committed to the LORD his God as his ancestor David had been. [4]But for David's sake the LORD his God made Abijam a lamp in Jerusalem. He appointed David's descendant to rule after him and protected Jerusalem. [5]The LORD did this because David did what the LORD considered right: David never failed to do anything the LORD commanded him to do his entire life (except in the matter concerning Uriah the Hittite).

[6]There was war between Abijam[a] and Rehoboam throughout their lives.

[7]Isn't everything else about Abijam—everything he did—written in the official

---

[a] 15:6 Some Hebrew manuscripts; other Hebrew manuscripts "Jeroboam."

records of the kings of Judah? There was war between Abijam and Jeroboam. ⁸Abijam lay down in death with his ancestors and was buried in the City of David. His son Asa succeeded him as king.

King Asa of Judah—
2 Chronicles 14:2, 3; 15:16-18

⁹In Jeroboam's twentieth year as king of Israel, Asa began to rule as king of Judah. ¹⁰He ruled 41 years in Jerusalem. His grandmother was named Maacah, daughter of Abishalom.

¹¹Asa did what the LORD considered right, as his ancestor David had done. ¹²He forced the male temple prostitutes out of the land and got rid of the idols his father had made. ¹³He also removed his grandmother Maacah from the position of queen mother because she made a statue of the repulsive goddess Asherah. Asa cut the statue down and burned it in the Kidron Valley. ¹⁴Although the illegal worship sites were not torn down, Asa remained committed to the LORD his entire life. ¹⁵He brought into the LORD's temple the silver, the gold, and the utensils he and his father had set apart as holy.

King Asa's War With King Baasha—
2 Chronicles 15:19; 16:1-6, 11-14; 17:1

¹⁶There was war between Asa and King Baasha of Israel as long as they lived. ¹⁷King Baasha of Israel invaded Judah and fortified Ramah to keep anyone from going to or coming from King Asa of Judah.

¹⁸Then Asa took all the silver and gold that was left in the treasuries of the LORD's temple and the royal palace and turned them over to his officials. King Asa sent them to Damascus to Aram's King Benhadad, son of Tabrimmon and grandson of Hezion. ¹⁹He said, "There's a treaty between you and me as there was between your father and my father. I'm sending you a present of silver and gold. Now break your treaty with King Baasha of Israel so that he will leave me alone."

²⁰Benhadad did what King Asa requested. He sent his generals and their armies to attack the cities of Israel. He conquered Ijon, Dan, Abel Beth Maacah, and the entire area around Chinneroth with the entire territory of Naphtali. ²¹When Baasha heard the news, he stopped fortifying Ramah and lived in Tirzah. ²²Then King Asa drafted everyone in Judah and excused no one. He made them carry the stones and lumber from Ramah. Baasha had been using those to fortify the city. King Asa used the materials to fortify Geba in Benjamin and Mizpah.

Good Morning, God
1 Kings 15:1-3

When people are leaders, they have big jobs. They can lead people to do right or wrong. Most of the kings of Israel were evil. They led the people of Israel to do things the Lord hated. But even when leaders do wrong, we must try to do what we know is right. Then we will be leading others in the right direction. How can you become a good leader?

Lord God, give our leaders wisdom to obey you, and help me to be a good leader.

²³Isn't everything else about Asa—all his heroic acts, everything he did, and the cities he fortified—written in the official records of the kings of Judah? But when he was old, he had a foot disease. ²⁴Asa lay down in death with his ancestors. He was buried with his ancestors in the city of his ancestor, David. His son Jehoshaphat succeeded him as king.

King Baasha Overthrows Nadab, Son of Jeroboam

²⁵Nadab, son of Jeroboam, began to rule Israel in Asa's second year as king of Judah. He ruled for two years. ²⁶He did what the LORD considered evil, living as his father did, leading Israel into the same sins.

²⁷Then Baasha, son of Ahijah from the tribe of Issachar, plotted against Nadab. Baasha assassinated him in the Philistine city of Gibbethon while Nadab and the Israelite forces were attacking it. ²⁸The assassination happened in Asa's third year as king of Judah. Baasha succeeded Nadab as king of Israel. ²⁹As soon as he was king, he killed everyone else in Jeroboam's family. He did not spare a soul, as the LORD had spoken through his servant Ahijah from Shiloh. ³⁰This was because of Jeroboam's sins and the sins which he led Israel to commit. Those sins made the LORD God of Israel furious.

³¹Isn't everything else about Nadab—everything he did—written in the official records of the kings of Israel? ³²There was war between Asa and Baasha as long as they lived. ³³In Asa's third year as king of Judah, Baasha, son of Ahijah, began to rule Israel in Tirzah. He ruled for 24 years. ³⁴He did what the LORD considered evil. He lived like Jeroboam and led Israel into committing the same sins.

The LORD Condemns King Baasha

¹The LORD spoke his word to Jehu, Hanani's son, against Baasha. ²He said, "I raised you from the dust and made you leader of my people Israel. But you have lived like Jeroboam. You have led my people to sin, and their sins make me furious. ³So I will destroy Baasha and his family. I will make his family like the family of Jeroboam (Nebat's son). ⁴Dogs will eat anyone from Baasha's family who dies in the city. Birds will eat anyone from his family who dies in the country."

⁵Isn't everything else about Baasha—what he did and his heroic acts—written in the official records of the kings of Israel? ⁶Baasha lay down in death with his ancestors and was buried in Tirzah. His son Elah succeeded him as king. ⁷In addition, the LORD spoke his word to the prophet Jehu, Hanani's son, against Baasha and his family because of all the things Baasha did which the LORD considered evil. Baasha's actions, which made the LORD furious, were like the sin of Jeroboam's family. The LORD was also furious because Baasha destroyed Jeroboam's family.

Zimri Overthrows King Elah, Son of Baasha

⁸Elah, son of Baasha, began to rule Israel in Asa's twenty-sixth year as Judah's king. He ruled in Tirzah for two years. ⁹But Zimri, the general who commanded half of Elah's chariots, plotted against him. Elah was getting drunk in Tirzah at Arza's house. (Arza was in charge of the palace in Tirzah.) ¹⁰Zimri entered Arza's house, attacked Elah, and killed him in Asa's twenty-seventh year as king of Judah. Zimri succeeded Elah as king of Israel. ¹¹At the beginning of Zimri's reign, as soon as he was on his throne, he killed Baasha's entire family. He didn't spare any of Baasha's male*ᵃ* relatives or friends. ¹²So Zimri destroyed Baasha's entire family, as the LORD had spoken through the prophet Jehu. ¹³This was for all the sins committed by Baasha and

---

ᵃ16:11 Hebrew uses a coarse term for "male" here.

his son Elah. They sinned, led Israel to sin, and made the LORD God of Israel furious because of their worthless idols. [14]Isn't everything else about Elah—everything he did—written in the official records of the kings of Israel?

King Zimri Rules for Seven Days

[15]In Asa's twenty-seventh year as Judah's king, Zimri ruled for seven days in Tirzah while the army was camped near the Philistine city of Gibbethon. [16]When the army heard that Zimri had plotted against the king and killed him, the Israelite troops in the camp made Omri, the commander of the army, king of Israel.

[17]Omri and the Israelite troops with him left Gibbethon and attacked Tirzah. [18]When Zimri saw that the city had been captured, he went into the stronghold in the royal palace and burned down the palace over his own head. He died [19]because of the sins he had committed—the things the LORD considered evil. Zimri lived like Jeroboam and led Israel to sin. [20]Isn't everything else about Zimri and his plot written in the official records of the kings of Israel?

Omri Defeats Tibni

[21]Then the army of Israel was divided into two factions. Half of the army followed Tibni, son of Ginath, and wanted to make him king. The other half followed Omri. [22]But the half which followed Omri was stronger than the half which followed Tibni, Ginath's son. Tibni died, and Omri became king. [23]Omri began to rule Israel in Asa's thirty-first year as king of Judah. He ruled for 12 years, 6 of them in Tirzah.

[24]Omri bought a hill from Shemer for 150 pounds of silver. He fortified the hill and built the city of Samaria on it. He named the city after its former owner, Shemer.

King Omri of Israel

[25]Omri did what the LORD considered evil. He did more evil things than all the kings before him. [26]He lived exactly like Jeroboam (Nebat's son). He sinned and led Israel to sin with worthless idols, and the Israelites made the LORD God of Israel furious.

[27]Isn't everything else about Omri—what he did and his heroic acts—written in the official records of the kings of Israel? [28]Omri lay down in death with his ancestors and was buried in Samaria. His son Ahab succeeded him as king.

King Ahab Introduces Worship of Baal Into Israel

[29]Ahab, son of Omri, began to rule Israel in Asa's thirty-eighth year as king of Judah. He ruled for 22 years in Samaria. [30]Ahab, son of Omri, did what the LORD considered evil. He was worse than all the kings who were before him. [31]It wasn't enough that he committed the same sins as Jeroboam (Nebat's son). He also married Jezebel, daughter of King Ethbaal of Sidon. Ahab then served and worshiped Baal. [32]He built the temple of Baal in Samaria and set up an altar there. [33]Ahab made poles dedicated to the goddess Asherah. He did more to make the LORD God of Israel furious than all the kings of Israel who came before him.

[34]In Ahab's time Hiel from Bethel rebuilt Jericho.

> Laying the foundation
>   cost him his firstborn son, Abiram.
> Setting up the city doors
>   cost him his youngest son, Segub.

The LORD had spoken this through Joshua, son of Nun.

Elijah Prophesies a Drought

17 ¹Elijah, who was from Tishbe but had settled in Gilead, said to Ahab, "I solemnly swear, as the LORD God of Israel whom I serve lives, there will be no dew or rain during the next few years unless I say so."

²Then the LORD spoke his word to Elijah: ³"Leave here, turn east, and hide beside the Cherith River, which is east of the Jordan River. ⁴You can drink from the stream, and I've commanded ravens to feed you there."

⁵Elijah left and did what the word of the LORD had told him. He went to live by the Cherith River, which is east of the Jordan River. ⁶Ravens brought him bread and meat in the morning and in the evening. And he drank from the stream.

⁷But after some time the stream dried up because no rain had fallen in the land.

Elijah and the Widow at Zarephath

⁸Then the LORD spoke his word to Elijah: ⁹"Get up, go to Zarephath (which belongs to Sidon), and stay there. I've commanded a widow there to feed you."

¹⁰He got up and went to Zarephath. As he came to the town's entrance, a widow was gathering wood. He called to her, "Please bring me a drink of water." ¹¹As she was going to get it, he called to her again, "Please bring me a piece of bread too."

¹²She said, "I solemnly swear, as the LORD your God lives, I didn't bake any bread. I have one handful of flour in a jar and a little oil in a jug. I'm gathering wood. I'm going to prepare something for myself and my son so that we can eat it and then die."

¹³Then Elijah told her, "Don't be afraid. Go home, and do as you've said. But first make a small loaf and bring it to me. Then prepare something for yourself and your son. ¹⁴This is what the LORD God of Israel says: Until the LORD sends rain on the land, the jar of flour will never be empty and the jug will always contain oil."

¹⁵She did what Elijah had told her. So she, Elijah, and her family had food for a long time. ¹⁶The jar of flour never became empty, and the jug always contained olive oil, as the LORD had promised through Elijah.

¹⁷Afterwards, the son of the woman who owned the house got sick. He got so sick that finally no life was left in him. ¹⁸The woman asked Elijah, "What do you and I have in common, man of God?ᵃ Did you come here to remind me of my sin and kill my son?"

¹⁹He said to her, "Give me your son." Elijah took him from her arms, carried him to the upstairs room where he was staying, and laid him on his own bed. ²⁰Then he called to the LORD, "LORD my God, have you brought misery on the widow I'm staying with by killing her son?" ²¹Then Elijah stretched himself over the boy three times and called to the LORD, "LORD my God, please make this child's life return to him." ²²The LORD heard Elijah's request, and the child's life returned to him. He was alive again.

²³Elijah took the child, brought him down from the upstairs room of the house, and gave him to his mother. He said, "Look! Your son is alive."

²⁴The woman said to Elijah, "Now I'm convinced that you are a man of God and that the word of the LORD from your mouth is true."

Elijah Comes to King Ahab

18 ¹A while later in the third year of the drought, the LORD spoke his word to Elijah: "Present yourself to Ahab. I will allow rain to fall on the ground." ²So Elijah went to present himself to Ahab.

The famine was particularly severe in Samaria. ³Ahab sent for Obadiah, who was

---

ᵃ 17:18 Hebrew meaning of this sentence uncertain.

in charge of the palace. Obadiah was a devout worshiper of the LORD. ⁴(When Jezebel was killing the LORD's prophets, Obadiah had hidden 100 prophets in caves. He put 50 prophets in each cave and kept them alive by providing bread and water for them.) ⁵Ahab told Obadiah, "Let's go throughout the countryside to every spring and stream. If we can find grass, then we can keep the horses and mules alive and not lose any animals." ⁶So they split up in order to cover the entire countryside. Ahab went one way by himself, and Obadiah went the other way by himself.

⁷Obadiah was on the road when he met Elijah. Obadiah recognized him and immediately bowed down to the ground. "Is it you, my master Elijah?" he asked.

⁸"Yes," Elijah answered him. "Tell your master that Elijah is here."

⁹Obadiah asked, "What have I done wrong to make you hand me over to Ahab to be killed? ¹⁰I solemnly swear, as the LORD your God lives, my master has searched for you in every region and kingdom. When people would say, 'He isn't here,' my master made that kingdom or region take an oath that they hadn't found you.

¹¹"Now you say, 'Tell your master that Elijah is here.' ¹²This is what will happen: When I leave you, the LORD's Spirit will take you away to some unknown place. I'll tell Ahab, but he won't be able to find you. Then he will kill me.

"I have been faithful to the LORD since I was a child. ¹³Haven't you heard what I did when Jezebel killed the LORD's prophets? Haven't you heard how I hid 100 of the LORD's prophets in caves? I hid 50 prophets in each cave and provided bread and water for them. ¹⁴Now you say that I should tell my master that Elijah is here. He will kill me."

¹⁵Elijah said, "I solemnly swear, as the LORD of Armies whom I serve lives, I will present myself to Ahab."

¹⁶So Obadiah went to tell Ahab.

Elijah and the Prophets of Baal on Mount Carmel

Ahab went to meet Elijah. ¹⁷When he saw Elijah, Ahab said, "Is that you, you troublemaker of Israel?"

¹⁸Elijah answered, "I haven't troubled Israel. You and your father's family have done it by disobeying the LORD's commands and following the various Baal gods. ¹⁹Order all Israel to gather around me on Mount Carmel. And bring the 450 prophets of Baal and 400 prophets of Asherah who eat at Jezebel's table."

²⁰Ahab sent word to all the Israelites and brought the prophets together on Mount Carmel. ²¹Elijah stood up in front of all the people and asked them, "How long will you try to have it both ways? If the LORD is God, follow him; if Baal is God, follow him." The people didn't say a word.

²²So Elijah told the people, "I'm the only surviving prophet of the LORD, but there are 450 prophets of Baal. ²³Give us two bulls. Let the prophets of Baal choose one for themselves, cut it into pieces, lay it on the wood, but not set it on fire. I'll do the same with the other bull.

²⁴"You call on the name of your gods, but I will call on the name of the LORD. The god who answers by fire is the real God."

All the people answered, "That's fine."

²⁵Elijah told the prophets of Baal, "Choose one bull for yourselves. Prepare yours first, because there are more of you. Call on the name of your god, but don't set the wood on fire."

²⁶They took the bull he gave them, prepared it, and called on the name of Baal from morning until noon. They said, "Baal, answer us!" But there wasn't a sound or an answer. So they danced around the altar they had made. ²⁷At noon Elijah started to

make fun of them. "Shout louder, since he is a god. Maybe he's thinking, relieving himself, or traveling! Maybe he's sleeping, and you have to wake him!" ²⁸So they shouted louder. They also cut themselves with swords and spears until their blood flowed. (This is what their ritual called for.) ²⁹In the afternoon they continued to rant and rave until the time for the evening sacrifice. But there was no sound, no answer, no attention given to them.

³⁰Then Elijah said to all the people, "Come over here." So all the people came to him. He rebuilt the LORD's altar that had been torn down. ³¹Elijah took 12 stones, one for each of the tribes named after Jacob's sons. (The LORD had spoken his word to Jacob: "Your name will be Israel.") ³²Elijah built an altar in the LORD's name with those stones. He also made a trench that could hold 12 quarts of grain around the altar. ³³He arranged the wood, cut up the bull, and put it on the wood.

³⁴He said, "Fill four jars with water. Pour the water on the offering and on the wood." Then he said, "Do it again," and they did it again. Then he said, "Do it a third time," and they did it a third time. ³⁵The water flowed around the altar, and even the trench was filled with water.

³⁶When it was time to offer the sacrifice, the prophet Elijah stepped forward. He said, "LORD God of Abraham, Isaac, and Israel, make known today that you are God in Israel and that I'm your servant and have done all these things by your instructions. ³⁷Answer me, LORD! Answer me! Then these people will know that you, LORD, are God and that you are winning back their hearts."

³⁸So a fire from the LORD fell down and consumed the burnt offering, wood, stones, and dirt. The fire even dried up the water that was in the trench. ³⁹All the people saw it and immediately bowed down to the ground. "The LORD is God!" they said. "The LORD is God!"

⁴⁰Elijah told them, "Seize the prophets of Baal. Don't let any of them escape." The people seized them, and Elijah took them to the Kishon River and slaughtered them there.

The Drought Ends

⁴¹Then Elijah told Ahab, "Get up, eat, and drink. It sounds like a heavy rain is coming ‚." ⁴²Ahab got up to eat and drink.

Elijah went to the top of Carmel and bowed down on the ground to pray. ⁴³He said to his servant, "Please go back to ‚Mount Carmel‚, and look toward the sea."

He went up, looked, ‚came back,‚ and said, "There's nothing."

Seven times Elijah told him, "Go back."

⁴⁴After the seventh time the servant said, "A little cloud like a man's hand is coming from the sea."

Elijah said, "Go and tell Ahab, 'Prepare ‚ your chariot‚, and leave before the rain delays you.'"

⁴⁵Gradually, the sky grew darker with clouds and wind, and there was a heavy rain. Ahab got into his chariot to go back to Jezreel. ⁴⁶The LORD's power was on Elijah. He hiked up his robe and ran ahead of Ahab until they came to Jezreel.

Elijah Flees From Jezebel

19 ¹Ahab told Jezebel everything Elijah had done, including how he had executed all the prophets. ²Then Jezebel sent a messenger to Elijah. She said, "May the gods strike me dead if by this time to-morrow I don't take your life the way you took the lives of Baal's prophets."

³Frightened, Elijah fled to save his life. He came to Beersheba in Judah and left his

servant there. ⁴Then he traveled through the wilderness for a day. He sat down under a broom plant and wanted to die. "I've had enough now, LORD," he said. "Take my life! I'm no better than my ancestors." ⁵Then he lay down and slept under the broom plant.

An angel touched him and said, "Get up and eat." ⁶When he looked, he saw near his head some bread baked on hot stones and a jar of water. So he ate, drank, and went to sleep again.

⁷The angel of the LORD came back and woke him up again. The angel said, "Get up and eat, or your journey will be too much for you."

⁸He got up, ate, and drank. Strengthened by that food, he traveled for 40 days and nights until he came to Horeb, the mountain of God. ⁹There he went into a cave and spent the night.

Then the LORD spoke his word to Elijah. He asked, "What are you doing here, Elijah?"

¹⁰He answered, "LORD God of Armies, I have eagerly served you. The Israelites have abandoned your promises,ᵃ torn down your altars, and executed your prophets. I'm the only one left, and they're trying to take my life."

¹¹God said, "Go out and stand in front of the LORD on the mountain."

As the LORD was passing by, a fierce wind tore mountains and shattered rocks ahead of the LORD. But the LORD was not in the wind. After the wind came an earthquake. But the LORD wasn't in the earthquake. ¹²After the earthquake there was a fire. But the LORD wasn't in the fire. And after the fire there was a quiet, whispering voice. ¹³When Elijah heard it, he wrapped his face in his coat, went out, and stood at the entrance of the cave.

Depression
1 Kings 19:8-18

Sometimes you don't want to get out of bed. You feel tired. You feel sad and hopeless. It's called depression, and even a great hero like Elijah got depressed. God wasn't angry with Elijah for feeling depressed. God helped him feel better. He gave Elijah a job to do—just as you have a job at school. And he gave Elijah a friend. If you don't give up, God will help you get over your depression, too.

Then the voice said to him, "What are you doing here, Elijah?"

¹⁴He answered, "LORD God of Armies, I have eagerly served you. The Israelites have abandoned your promises, torn down your altars, and executed your prophets. I'm the only one left, and they're trying to take my life."

¹⁵The LORD told him, "Go back to the wilderness near Damascus, the same way you came. When you get there, anoint Hazael as king of Aram. ¹⁶Anoint Jehu, son of Nimshi, as king of Israel. And anoint Elisha, son of Shaphat, from Abel Meholah as prophet to take your place. ¹⁷If anyone escapes from Hazael's sword, Jehu will kill him. And if anyone escapes from Jehu's sword, Elisha will kill him. ¹⁸But I still have 7,000 people in Israel whose knees have not knelt to worship Baal and whose mouths have not kissed him."

ᵃ 19:10 Or "covenant."

The Call of Elisha

¹⁹Elijah found Elisha, son of Shaphat. Elisha was plowing behind 12 pairs of oxen. He was using the twelfth pair. Elijah took off his coat and put it on Elisha. ²⁰So Elisha left the oxen, ran after Elijah, and said, "Please let me kiss my father and mother goodbye. Then I will follow you."

"Go back," Elijah answered him. "I'm not stopping you."

²¹Elisha left him, took two oxen, and butchered them. He boiled the meat, using the oxen's yoke*ᵇ* for firewood,. He gave the meat to the people to eat. Then he left to follow and assist Elijah.

King Ahab Defeats King Benhadad

20 ¹King Benhadad of Aram gathered together his whole army. With him were 32 kings along with their horses and chariots. He went to blockade Samaria and fight against it. ²He sent messengers into the city to King Ahab of Israel. They told Ahab, "This is what Benhadad says: ³Your silver and gold are mine. Your beloved wives and children are mine."

⁴The king of Israel answered, "As you say, Your Majesty. I and everything I have are yours."

⁵But Benhadad sent messengers back ,to Ahab,. They said, "Benhadad has sent this message to you: 'Your silver, gold, wives, and children are mine. Give ,them to me,. ⁶At this time tomorrow I'm going to send my servants to search your palace and your servants' houses. They will take anything that you consider valuable.' "

⁷Then the king of Israel called for all the leaders of the country. He said, "You can see how this man is looking for trouble. When he sent for my wives, children, silver, and gold, I didn't refuse him."

⁸All the leaders and all the people told him, "Don't listen to him. Don't agree ,to his demands,."

⁹Ahab told Benhadad's messengers, "Tell His Majesty, 'I did everything your messengers told me the first time, but I can't do this.' " The messengers left to take back his answer.

¹⁰Then Benhadad sent Ahab the following message: "May the gods strike me dead if there will be enough dust left from Samaria to give a handful to each soldier who follows me."

¹¹The king of Israel answered, "The saying goes, 'Don't brag about a victory before you have even dressed for battle.' "

¹²Benhadad heard this as he and his allies were drinking in their tents. He told his officers to get ready. So they got ready ,to attack, the city.

¹³Then a prophet came to King Ahab of Israel and said, "This is what the LORD says: Have you seen this large army? I will hand it over to you today. Then you will know that I am the LORD."

¹⁴Ahab asked, "How ,will this be done,?"

The prophet answered, "This is what the LORD says: by using the young officers of the district governors."

"Who will start the battle?" Ahab asked.

"You will," the prophet answered.

¹⁵Ahab counted the young officers of the district governors. There were 232. After counting them, he counted all the Israelite soldiers. There were 7,000. ¹⁶They attacked at noon, when Benhadad was in his tent getting drunk with the 32 kings who were his allies. ¹⁷The young officers of the district governors went out first.

ᵇ19:21 A yoke is a wooden bar placed over the necks of work animals so that they can pull plows or carts.

Benhadad had sent men to watch the city. They informed him that some men had come out of Samaria.

¹⁸He said, "Take them alive, whether they have come out to make peace or to fight."

¹⁹The young officers of the district governors led an attack, and the troops followed them. ²⁰Each officer killed his opponent. The Arameans fled, and Israel pursued them. King Benhadad of Aram escaped on a horse with the cavalry. ²¹The king of Israel went out and destroyed the horses and chariots and decisively defeated the Arameans.

Ahab Spares Benhadad

²²Then the prophet came to the king of Israel and said, "Reinforce your army. Consider what you have to do. When spring comes, the king of Aram will attack again."

²³Meanwhile, the officers of King Benhadad of Aram told him, "Their god is a god of the hills. That is why they were stronger than we were. However, if we fight them on the plain, we will be stronger than they are. ²⁴This is what we must do: Remove all of the kings from their positions, and substitute governors for them. ²⁵Recruit an army as many horses and chariots as the one which was defeated. Then, if we fight them on the plain, we will be stronger than they are." He took their advice and followed it.

²⁶Spring came, and Benhadad organized the Aramean army and went to Aphek to fight Israel. ²⁷When the Israelite troops had been organized and given provisions, they went to meet the enemy. The Israelites, while camped opposite the Arameans who filled the country, seemed like two newborn goats.^a

²⁸The man of God came again. He said to the king of Israel, "This is what the LORD says: Because the Arameans said that the LORD is a god of the hills but not a god of the valleys, I will hand over their entire army to you. Then you will know that I am the LORD."

²⁹They camped facing one another for seven days, and on the seventh day the battle started. The Israelites killed 100,000 Aramean foot soldiers in one day. ³⁰The survivors fled to Aphek, the city where the wall fell on 27,000 of them. Benhadad had also fled. He came to the city and hid in an inner room.

³¹His officers told him, "We have heard that the kings of Israel are merciful. Allow us to dress in sackcloth, put ropes around our necks, and go to the king of Israel. Maybe he'll let you live." ³²So they dressed in sackcloth and put ropes around their necks. They went to the king of Israel and said, "Your servant Benhadad says, 'Please let me live.' "

Ahab asked, "He's still alive? He's my brother."

³³The men, watching for a good sign, were quick to take him at his word. "Benhadad is your brother," they said.

Ahab said, "Bring him here." When Benhadad arrived, Ahab had him come up on the chariot with him.

³⁴Benhadad told him, "I will give back the towns my father took from your father. You may set up trading centers in Damascus as my father did in Samaria."

Ahab said, "If you will put this into a treaty, I will let you go." So Ahab made a treaty with Benhadad and let him go.

³⁵A disciple of the prophets spoke to a friend as the word of the LORD had told him. The disciple said, "Punch me," but the man refused to punch him. ³⁶The disciple said, "Since you didn't obey the LORD, a lion will kill you when you leave me." When the friend left, a lion found him and killed him.

---

^a20:27 Hebrew meaning of this sentence uncertain.

³⁷Then the disciple found another man. He said, "Punch me." The man punched him hard and wounded him.

³⁸Then the prophet, disguised with a bandage over his eyes, waited for the king by the road. ³⁹When the king passed by, the disciple called to him. "I went to fight in the battle. A man turned around and brought a prisoner to me. He said, 'Guard this prisoner. If he gets away, you will pay for his life with your own life or be fined 75 pounds of silver.' ⁴⁰But while I was busy doing other things, he got away."

The king of Israel told him, "That's your own penalty. You have determined it yourself."

⁴¹Then he quickly took the bandage off his eyes. The king of Israel recognized him as one of the prophets.

⁴²The prophet told him, "This is what the LORD says: You let the man go. He was claimed by God and should have been killed. For that reason your life will be taken in place of his life and your people in place of his people."

⁴³Resentful and upset, the king of Israel went home to Samaria.

Ahab Takes Naboth's Vineyard

21 ¹This is what happened next. Naboth from Jezreel had a vineyard in Jezreel next to the palace of King Ahab of Samaria.

²Ahab told Naboth, "Give me your vineyard. It will become my vegetable garden because it is near my house. I will give you a better vineyard for it. Or if you prefer, I will pay you a fair price for it."

³Naboth told Ahab, "The LORD has forbidden me to give you what I inherited from my ancestors."

⁴Resentful and upset, Ahab went home because of what Naboth from Jezreel had told him. (Naboth had said, "I will not give you what I inherited from my ancestors.") So Ahab lay on the couch, turned his face from everyone, and refused to eat.

⁵His wife Jezebel came to him and asked, "Why are you so resentful of everything? Why don't you eat?"

⁶He told her, "I talked to Naboth from Jezreel. I said to him, 'Sell me your vineyard. Or, if you like, I'll give you another vineyard for it.' But he said, 'I won't give you my vineyard.' "

⁷His wife Jezebel said to him, "Aren't you king of Israel? Get up, eat, and cheer up. I'll give you the vineyard belonging to Naboth from Jezreel."

⁸So Jezebel wrote letters, signed them with Ahab's name, and sealed them with his seal. She sent them to the respected leaders and nobles living in Naboth's city. ⁹In these letters she wrote: "Announce a fast. Seat Naboth as leader of the people. ¹⁰Have two good-for-nothing men sit opposite him and accuse him of cursing God and the king. Then stone him to death outside the city."

¹¹The men in Naboth's city—the respected leaders and nobles who lived there—did what Jezebel asked them to do. They did just as she had written in the letters she sent. ¹²They announced a fast and had Naboth seated as the leader of the people. ¹³The two good-for-nothing men came in and sat opposite him. In front of the people, these men accused Naboth of cursing God and the king. So the people stoned him to death outside the city. ¹⁴Then the leaders sent this message to Jezebel: "Naboth has been stoned to death."

¹⁵Jezebel received the message and said to Ahab, "Get up! Confiscate the vineyard which Naboth from Jezreel refused to sell you. He's dead now."

¹⁶When he heard about Naboth's death, Ahab went to confiscate the vineyard.

¹⁷Then the LORD spoke his word to Elijah from Tishbe: ¹⁸"Go, meet King Ahab of

City Gates / *1 Kings 22:1-12*

Women with food or goods to sell usually offered them near the city gates, where anyone going in or out of the city could see them. Normally, one day a week was market day, when people from miles around brought their products to sell just outside the city gates. Women would plan to buy their food and supplies on this day.

Israel, who lives in Samaria. He went to confiscate Naboth's vineyard. ¹⁹Tell him, 'This is what the LORD asks: Have you murdered someone just to confiscate a vineyard?' Then tell him, 'This is what the LORD says: At the place where the dogs licked up Naboth's blood, the dogs will lick up your blood.' "

²⁰Ahab asked Elijah, "So you've found me, my enemy?"

Elijah answered, "I found you. Because you sold yourself to do what the LORD considers evil. ²¹So I am going to bring evil on you. I will destroy your descendants. I will destroy every male*a* in Ahab's house, whether slave or freeman in Israel. ²²I will make your family like the family of Jeroboam (Nebat's son) and like the house of Baasha, son of Ahijah, because you made me furious. You led Israel to sin."

²³Then the LORD also spoke through Elijah about Jezebel: "The dogs will eat Jezebel inside the walls of Jezreel. ²⁴If anyone from Ahab's house dies in the city, dogs will eat him. If anyone dies in the country, birds will eat him."

²⁵There was no one else like Ahab. At the urging of his wife, he sold himself to do what the LORD considered evil. ²⁶He did many disgusting things as a result of worshiping idols as the Amorites had done. (The LORD confiscated their land for Israel.)

²⁷When Ahab heard these things, he tore his clothes in distress, and dressed in sackcloth. He fasted, lay in sackcloth, and walked around depressed.

²⁸Then the LORD spoke his word to Elijah from Tishbe: ²⁹"Do you see how Ahab is humbling himself in my presence? Because he's humbling himself in my presence, I will not let any evil happen to his family while he is alive. I will bring evil on it during his son's lifetime."

Micaiah Prophesies Against King Ahab—
2 Chronicles 18:1-34

¹For three years there was no war between Aram and Israel. ²In the third year King Jehoshaphat of Judah went to visit the king of Israel.

³The king of Israel asked his staff, "Do you know that Ramoth in Gilead belongs to us, and we are doing nothing to take it back from the king of Aram?" ⁴Then he asked Jehoshaphat, "Will you go with me to fight at Ramoth in Gilead?"

---

*a*21:21 Hebrew uses a coarse term for "male" here.

Jehoshaphat told the king of Israel, "I will do what you do. My troops will do what your troops do. My horses will do what your horses do." ⁵Then Jehoshaphat said to the king of Israel, "But first, find out what the word of the LORD is ⸢in this matter⸣."

⁶So the king of Israel called 400 prophets together. He asked them, "Should I go to war against Ramoth in Gilead or not?"

"Go," they said. "The Lord*ᵃ* will hand over Ramoth to you."

⁷But Jehoshaphat asked, "Isn't there a prophet of the LORD whom we could ask?"

⁸The king of Israel told Jehoshaphat, "We can ask the LORD through Micaiah, son of Imlah, but I hate him. He doesn't prophesy anything good about me, only evil."

Jehoshaphat answered, "The king must not say that."

⁹The king of Israel called for an officer and said, "Quick! ⸢Get⸣ Micaiah, son of Imlah!"

¹⁰The king of Israel and King Jehoshaphat of Judah were dressed in royal robes and seated on thrones. They were on the threshing floorᵇ at the entrance to the gate of Samaria. All the prophets were prophesying in front of them. ¹¹Zedekiah, son of Chenaanah, made iron horns and said, "This is what the LORD says: With these horns you will push the Arameans to their destruction." ¹²All the other prophets made the same prophecy. They said, "Attack Ramoth in Gilead, and you will win. The LORD will hand it over to you."

¹³The messenger who went to call Micaiah told him, "The prophets have all told the king the same good message. Make your message agree with their message. Say something good."

¹⁴Micaiah answered, "I solemnly swear, as the LORD lives, I will tell him whatever the LORD tells me."

¹⁵When he came to the king, the king asked him, "Micaiah, should we go to war against Ramoth in Gilead or not?"

Micaiah said to him, "Attack and you will win. The LORD will hand it over to you."

¹⁶The king asked him, "How many times must I make you take an oath in the LORD's name to tell me nothing but the truth?"

¹⁷So Micaiah said, "I saw Israel's troops scattered in the hills like sheep without a shepherd. The LORD said, 'These ⸢sheep⸣ have no master. Let each one go home in peace.' "

¹⁸The king of Israel said to Jehoshaphat, "Didn't I tell you he wouldn't prophesy anything good about me, only evil?"

¹⁹Micaiah added, "Then hear the word of the LORD. I saw the LORD sitting on his throne, and the entire army of heaven was standing near him on his right and his left. ²⁰The LORD asked, 'Who will deceive Ahab so that he will attack and be killed at Ramoth in Gilead?' Some answered one way, while others said something else.

²¹"Then the Spirit stepped forward, stood in front of the LORD, and said, 'I will deceive him.'

" 'How?' the LORD asked.

²²"The Spirit answered, 'I will go out and be a spirit that tells lies through the mouths of all of Ahab's prophets.'

"The LORD said, 'You will succeed in deceiving him. Go and do it.'

²³"So, the LORD has put into the mouths of all these prophets of yours a spirit that makes them tell lies. The LORD has spoken evil about you."

²⁴Then Zedekiah, son of Chenaanah, went to Micaiah and struck him on the cheek. "How did the LORD's Spirit leave me to talk to you?" he asked.

ᵃ22:6 Some Hebrew manuscripts; many Hebrew manuscripts, Targum "The LORD." ᵇ22:10 A threshing floor is an outdoor area where grain is separated from its husks.

²⁵Micaiah answered, "You will find out on the day you go into an inner room to hide."

²⁶The king of Israel then said, "Send Micaiah back to Amon, the governor of the city, and to Joash, the prince. ²⁷Say, 'This is what the king says: Put this man in prison, and feed him nothing but bread and water until I come home safely.'"

²⁸Micaiah said, "If you really do come back safely, then the Lᴏʀᴅ wasn't speaking through me. Pay attention to this, everyone!"

²⁹So the king of Israel and King Jehoshaphat of Judah went to Ramoth in Gilead. ³⁰The king of Israel told Jehoshaphat, "I will disguise myself and go into battle, but you should wear your royal robes." So the king of Israel disguised himself and went into battle.

³¹The king of Aram had given orders to the 32 chariot commanders. He said, "Don't fight anyone except the king of Israel."

³²When the chariot commanders saw Jehoshaphat, they said, "He must be the king of Israel." So they turned to fight him. But when Jehoshaphat cried out, ³³the chariot commanders realized that he wasn't the king of Israel. They turned away from him.

³⁴One man aimed his bow at random and hit the king of Israel between his scale armor and his breastplate. Ahab told his chariot driver, "Turn around, and get me away from these troops. I'm badly wounded." ³⁵But the battle got worse that day, and the king was kept propped up in his chariot facing the Arameans. He died that evening. The blood from the wound had flowed into the chariot. ³⁶At sundown a cry went through the army, "Every man to his own city! Every man to his own property!"

³⁷When the king was dead, he was brought to Samaria to be buried. ³⁸His chariot was washed at the pool of Samaria, where the prostitutes bathed. The dogs licked up his blood, as the Lᴏʀᴅ had predicted.

³⁹Isn't everything else about Ahab—everything he did, the ivory palace he built, and all the cities he fortified—written in the official records of the kings of Israel? ⁴⁰Ahab lay down in death with his ancestors. His son Ahaziah succeeded him as king.

King Jehoshaphat of Judah—
2 Chronicles 20:31–21:1

⁴¹Jehoshaphat, son of Asa, became king of Judah in Ahab's fourth year as king of Israel. ⁴²Jehoshaphat was 35 years old when he began to rule, and he ruled for 25 years in Jerusalem. His mother's name was Azubah, daughter of Shilhi. ⁴³Jehoshaphat carefully followed the example his father Asa had set and did what the Lᴏʀᴅ considered right. ⁴⁴But the illegal worship sites were not torn down. The people continued to sacrifice and burn incense at these worship sites.ᶜ Jehoshaphat made peace with the king of Israel.

⁴⁵Isn't everything else about Jehoshaphat—the heroic acts he did and the wars he fought—written in the official records of the kings of Judah? ⁴⁶He rid the land of the male temple prostitutes who were left there from the time of his father Asa. ⁴⁷There was no king in Edom; instead, a deputy ruled.

⁴⁸Jehoshaphat made Tarshish-style ships to go to Ophir for gold. But they didn't go because the ships were wrecked at Ezion Geber. ⁴⁹Then Ahaziah, son of Ahab, said to Jehoshaphat, "Let my servants go with your servants in the ships." But Jehoshaphat refused.

⁵⁰Jehoshaphat lay down in death with his ancestors and was buried with them in the city of his ancestor David. His son Jehoram succeeded him as king.

ᶜ22:44 1 Kings 22:44b-53 in English Bibles is 1 Kings 22:45-54 in the Hebrew Bible.

King Ahaziah of Israel

⁵¹Ahaziah, son of Ahab, became king of Israel in Samaria during Jehoshaphat's seventeenth year as king of Judah. Ahaziah ruled Israel for two years. ⁵²He did what the LORD considered evil. He followed the example of his father and mother and of Jeroboam (Nebat's son) who led Israel to sin. ⁵³Ahaziah served Baal, worshiped him, and made the LORD God of Israel furious, as his father had done.

AN INTRODUCTION TO
2 Kings

This book continues to describe the reigns of the kings of Judah and Israel. Many kings led the people into sin. God had promised to take care of his people if they followed his ways. He gave his people many chances to return to him, but they continued to disobey. Eventually, the Northern Kingdom of Israel was destroyed by Assyria. The people of Judah also failed to remain faithful to the Lord. As a result of their disobedience, Jerusalem was destroyed, and the people of Judah were captured by the Babylonians.

Jerusalem

The army of Judah was defeated by the army of Babylon.

Headlines

MORE ROYAL RIDDLES

What did Elijah use to wash himself?
A hairbrush.
(See 2 Kings 1:8.)

What's the best thing to do before leaving Baal's temple?
Wash your hands.
(See 2 Kings 10:27.)

What if Isaiah didn't give a fig?
Hezekiah would have died!
(See 2 Kings 20:1-7.)

Why did Gehazi get a skin disease?
His itch for silver resulted in rash behavior.
(See 2 Kings 5:19-27.)

What did Sennacherib eat at Jerusalem?
His words.
(See 2 Kings 19:9-13, 35-37.)

What's In It For Me?

God is patient with people who sin. . . .

GOD WARNS WRONGDOERS.

GOD FORGIVES THOSE WHO HUMBLE THEMSELVES.

GOD WILL PUNISH THOSE WHO KEEP SINNING.

The Kings of Judah and Israel

Here's a list of all the kings of Judah and Israel. Which were good rulers, and which ones were bad? Put a check mark beside the good kings. Put an "X" beside the bad ones. Which kingdom was holier, Judah or Israel?

JUDAH

Rehoboam (1 Kings 14:21-24)
Abijam (1 Kings 15:1-8)
Asa (1 Kings 15:9-24)
Jehoshaphat (1 Kings 22:41-50)
Jehoram (2 Kings 8:16-24)
Ahaziah (2 Kings 8:25-29)
Queen Athaliah (2 Kings 11:1-20)
Joash (2 Kings 11:21–12:21)
Amaziah (2 Kings 14:1-22)
Azariah (2 Kings 15:1-7)
Jotham (2 Kings 15:32-38)
Ahaz (2 Kings 16:1-20)
Hezekiah (2 Kings 18:1–20:21)
Manasseh (2 Kings 21:1-18)
Amon (2 Kings 21:19-26)
Josiah (2 Kings 22:1–23:30)
Jehoahaz (2 Kings 23:30-35)
Jehoiakim (2 Kings 23:36–24:7)
Jehoiakin (2 Kings 24:8-16)

ISRAEL

Jeroboam (1 Kings 12:20-33)
Nadab (1 Kings 15:25-28)
Baasha (1 Kings 15:27–16:7)
Elah (1 Kings 16:8-14)
Zimri (1 Kings 16:15-20)
Omri (1 Kings 16:21-28)
Ahab (1 Kings 16:29-34)
Ahaziah (1 Kings 22:51-53)
Joram (2 Kings 3:1-3)
Jehu (2 Kings 9:1–10:36)
Jehoahaz (2 Kings 13:1-8)
Jehoash (2 Kings 13:10-13)
Jeroboam II (2 Kings 14:23-29)
Zechariah (2 Kings 15:8-12)
Shallum (2 Kings 15:10-15)
Menahem (2 Kings 15:16-22)
Pekahiah (2 Kings 15:23-26)
Pekah (2 Kings 15:27-31)
Hoshea (2 Kings 17:1-2)
Zedekiah (2 Kings 24:17-20)

2 Kings

Elijah and King Ahaziah of Israel

¹After Ahab died, Moab rebelled against Israel. ²During the rebellion King Ahaziah fell through a window lattice in his upstairs room in Samaria and injured himself. So he sent messengers ˌto Ekronˌ. He had told them, "Go ask Baalzebub, the god of Ekron, if I will recover from this injury."

³Then the angel of the Lord said to Elijah from Tishbe, "Meet the messengers of the king of Samaria, and ask them, 'Do you seek advice from Baalzebub, the god of Ekron, because ˌyou thinkˌ there is no God in Israel? ⁴This is what the Lord says: You will not get up from the bed you are lying on. Instead, you will die there.' " Then Elijah left.

⁵When the messengers returned, the king asked them, "Why have you come back so soon?"

⁶They told him that a man came to meet them and said to them, "Go back to the king who sent you. Tell him, 'This is what the Lord says: Do you send messengers to seek advice from Baalzebub, the god of Ekron, because ˌyou thinkˌ there is no God in Israel? You will not get up from the bed you are lying on. Instead, you will die there.' "

⁷The king asked them, "What was the man like who told you this?"

⁸They replied, "He was hairy and had a leather belt around his waist."

"That's Elijah from Tishbe," the king answered.

⁹The king sent an army officer with 50 men to Elijah. When the officer found Elijah sitting on top of a hill, he told Elijah, "Man of God, the king says, 'Come down.' "

¹⁰Elijah answered the officer, "If I'm a man of God, fire will come from heaven and burn up you and your 50 men." Then fire came from heaven and burned up the officer and his 50 men.

¹¹The king sent another officer with 50 men to Elijah. The officer said, "Man of God, this is what the king says: Come here right away!"

¹²Elijah answered the officer, "If I'm a man of God, fire will come from heaven and burn up you and your 50 men." Then God's fire came from heaven and burned up the officer and his 50 men.

¹³The king sent a third officer with 50 men. The officer of the third group went up the hill and knelt in front of Elijah. The officer begged him, "Man of God, please treat my life and the lives of these 50 servants of yours as something precious. ¹⁴Fire has come from heaven and burned up the first two officers and their 100 men. But treat my life as something precious."

¹⁵The angel of the Lord told Elijah, "Go with him. Don't be afraid of him." So Elijah got up and went with him to the king. ¹⁶Elijah told the king, "This is what the Lord says: You sent messengers to seek advice from Baalzebub, the god of Ekron. Is this because ˌyou thinkˌ there is no God in Israel whose word you can seek? You will not get up from the bed you are lying on. Instead, you will die there."

¹⁷So Ahaziah died as the Lord had predicted through Elijah. Joram succeeded him as king because Ahaziah had no son.ᵃ ¹⁸Isn't everything else about Ahaziah—the things he did—written in the official records of the kings of Israel?

ᵃ 1:17 Greek; Masoretic Text ". . . succeeded him in Jehoshaphat's son Jehoram's second year as king of Judah, because Ahaziah had no son."

Elijah Taken to Heaven

2

¹When the LORD was going to take Elijah to heaven in a windstorm, Elijah and Elisha left Gilgal. ²Elijah said to Elisha, "Please stay here because the LORD is sending me to Bethel."

Elisha answered, "I solemnly swear, as the LORD lives and as you live, I will not abandon you." So they went to Bethel.

³Some of the disciples of the prophets at Bethel came to Elisha. They asked him, "Do you know that the LORD is going to take your master from you today?"

He answered, "Yes, I know. Be quiet."

⁴Elijah said, "Elisha, please stay here because the LORD is sending me to Jericho."

Elisha answered, "I solemnly swear, as the LORD lives and as you live, I will not abandon you." So they went to Jericho.

⁵Then some of the disciples of the prophets who were in Jericho approached Elisha. They asked, "Do you know that the LORD is going to take your master from you today?"

He answered, "Yes, I know. Be quiet."

⁶Elijah said to Elisha, "Please stay here because the LORD is sending me to the Jordan River."

Elisha answered, "I solemnly swear, as the LORD lives and as you live, I will not abandon you."

⁷Fifty disciples of the prophets stood at a distance as Elijah and Elisha stood by the Jordan River. ⁸Elijah took his coat, rolled it up, and struck the water with it. The water divided to their left and their right, and the two men crossed the river on dry ground.

⁹While they were crossing, Elijah asked Elisha, "What should I do for you before I'm taken from you?"

Elisha answered, "Let me inherit a double share of your spirit."

¹⁰Elijah said, "You have asked for something difficult. If you see me taken from you, it will be yours. Otherwise, it will not."

Witnessing

2 Kings 2:1-18

People don't fly off to heaven in a windstorm these days. But people who believe Jesus is their Savior will be in heaven someday. Invite your friends to church and Sunday school to hear about Jesus. Or tell them yourself how much Jesus loves them. What friend would you like to introduce to Jesus? Start praying for him or her today.

be all you can be

¹¹As they continued walking and talking, a fiery chariot with fiery horses separated the two of them, and Elijah went to heaven in a windstorm.

¹²When Elisha saw this, he cried out, "Master! Master! Israel's chariot and horses!" When he couldn't see Elijah anymore, he grabbed his own garment and tore it in two to show his grief. ¹³Then he picked up Elijah's coat (which had fallen off Elijah), went back, and stood on the bank of the Jordan River. ¹⁴He took the coat and struck the water with it. He asked, "Where is the LORD God of Elijah?" As he struck the water, it divided to his left and his right, and Elisha crossed the river.

¹⁵The disciples of the prophets who were at Jericho saw him from a distance. They said, "Elijah's spirit rests on Elisha!" Then they went to meet him and bowed in front of him with their faces touching the ground. ¹⁶They said to him, "There are 50 strong men here with us. Please let them go and search for your master. Maybe the Lord's Spirit lifted him up and dropped him on one of the hills or in one of the valleys."

Elisha answered, "Don't send them to look." ¹⁷But the disciples kept urging him to send the men, until he was embarrassed. So he said, "Send them." They sent 50 men who searched for three days without finding him. ¹⁸They returned to Elisha in Jericho, where he was waiting. He said, "Didn't I tell you not to go?"

Elisha Purifies Jericho's Water

¹⁹The people of the city of Jericho told Elisha, "This city's location is as good as you will ever find. But the water is bad, and the land cannot grow crops."

²⁰Elisha said, "Bring me a new jar, and put salt in it." They brought it to him. ²¹He went to the spring and threw the salt into it. Then he said, "This is what the Lord says: I have purified this water. No more deaths or crop failures will come from this water." ²²To this day the water is still pure, as Elisha had said.

²³From there he went to Bethel. As he walked along the road, some boys came out of the city and mocked him. They said, "Go away, baldy! Go away!"

²⁴Looking back, he saw them and cursed them in the Lord's name. Two bears came out of the woods and tore 42 of these youths apart. ²⁵He left that place, went to Mount Carmel, and returned to Samaria.

King Joram of Israel

3 ¹Joram,ᵃ son of Ahab, became king of Israel in Samaria during Jehoshaphat's eighteenth year as king of Judah. He ruled for 12 years. ²He did what the Lord considered evil, but he didn't do what his father or mother had done. He put away the sacred stone that his father had set up and dedicated to Baal. ³But he would not give up the sins that Jeroboam (Nebat's son) led Israel to commit. Joram would not turn away from those sins.

King Mesha of Moab Defeated

⁴King Mesha of Moab raised sheep. Each year he had to pay the king of Israel 100,000 male lambs and the wool from 100,000 rams. ⁵But when Ahab died, the king of Moab rebelled against the new king of Israel. ⁶King Joram immediately left Samaria to prepare Israel's army for war. ⁷He sent this message to King Jehoshaphat of Judah: "The king of Moab has rebelled against me. Will you fight Moab with me?"

Jehoshaphat answered, "I'll go. I will do what you do. My troops will do what your troops do. My horses will do what your horses do."

⁸Joram asked, "Which road should we take?"

Jehoshaphat answered, "The road through the desert of Edom."

⁹So the king of Israel, the king of Judah, and the king of Edom took an indirect route to Moab. After seven days they ran out of water for the army and the animals. ¹⁰The king of Israel said, "Oh no! The Lord has put the three of us at the mercy of the people of Moab."

¹¹But Jehoshaphat asked, "Isn't there a prophet of the Lord whom we could ask?"

One of the officials of the king of Israel answered, "Elisha, the son of Shaphat, is here. He used to be Elijah's assistant."ᵇ

ᵃ3:1 In the Masoretic Text this king of Israel is also called Jehoram, a longer form of Joram.　ᵇ3:11 Or "He used to pour water on Elijah's hands."

¹²Jehoshaphat said, "The Lord's word is with him." So King Jehoshaphat of Judah, the king of Israel, and the king of Edom went to Elisha.

¹³Elisha asked the king of Israel, "Why did you come to me? Go to your father's prophets or your mother's prophets."

The king of Israel answered him, "No. The Lord has called the three of us in order to put us at Moab's mercy."

¹⁴Elisha answered, "I solemnly swear, as the Lord of Armies whom I serve lives, I wouldn't even bother to look at you or notice you if it weren't for my respect for King Jehoshaphat of Judah. ¹⁵But get me someone to play some music."

While the musician was playing, the Lord's power came over Elisha. ¹⁶He said, "This is what the Lord says: Make this valley full of ditches. ¹⁷You will not see wind or rain, but this valley will be filled with water. You, your cattle, and your other animals will drink. ¹⁸The Lord considers that an easy thing to do. In addition, he will put Moab at your mercy. ¹⁹You will defeat every walled city and every important city. You will cut down every good tree, seal all the wells, and use rocks to ruin every good piece of land."

²⁰That is what happened in the morning. At the time of the grain offering, water flowed from Edom and filled the countryside.

²¹All the people of Moab heard that the kings had come to fight them. So all men old enough to bear arms were called to fight. They stood at the border. ²²When the Moabites got up early in the morning as the sun was rising over the water, they saw the water from a distance. It was as red as blood. ²³They said, "It's blood! The kings have been fighting one another and have killed each other. Now, Moabites, let's take their goods!"

²⁴So when the Moabites came to Israel's camp, the Israelites attacked them, and they fled from the Israelites. Israel went after the Moabites and defeated them. ²⁵Then Israel tore down the cities, each man throwing rocks on every good field until it was covered. They sealed every well and cut down every good tree. Only the stones in the walls of Kir Hareseth were left. Soldiers surrounded Kir Hareseth and attacked it with slings and stones. ²⁶When the king of Moab saw he was losing the battle, he took 700 swordsmen to try to break through to the king of Edom. But they couldn't do it. ²⁷Then he took his firstborn son, who would have succeeded him as king, and sacrificed him on the wall as a burnt offering. There was bitter anger against the Israelites. So they went home to their own country.

Elisha and the Widow's Olive Oil

4 ¹One of the wives of a disciple of the prophets called to Elisha, "Sir, my husband is dead! You know how he feared the Lord. Now a creditor has come to take my two children as slaves."

²Elisha asked her, "What should I do for you? Tell me, what do you have in your house?"

She answered, "I have nothing in the house except a jar of olive oil."

³Elisha said, "Borrow many empty containers from all your neighbors. ⁴Then close the door behind you and your children, and pour oil into all those containers. When one is full, set it aside."

⁵So she left him and closed the door behind her and her children. The children kept bringing containers to her, and she kept pouring. ⁶When the containers were full, she told her son, "Bring me another container."

He told her, "There are no more containers." So the olive oil stopped flowing. ⁷She went and told the man of God.

He said, "Sell the oil, and pay your debt. The rest is for you and your children."

Elisha Brings a Shunem Woman's Son Back to Life

⁸One day Elisha was traveling through Shunem, where a rich woman lived. She had invited him to eat ⌊with her⌋. So whenever he was in the area, he stopped in to eat. ⁹She told her husband, "I know he's a holy man of God. And he regularly travels past our house. ¹⁰Let's make a small room on the roof and put a bed, table, chair, and lamp stand there for him. He can stay there whenever he comes to visit us."

¹¹One day he came ⌊to their house⌋, went into the upstairs room, and rested there. ¹²He told his servant Gehazi, "Call this Shunem woman."

Gehazi called her, and she stood in front of him. ¹³Elisha said to Gehazi, "Ask her what we can do for her, since she has gone to a lot of trouble for us. Maybe she would like us to speak to the king or the commander of the army for her."

She answered, "I'm already living among my own people."

¹⁴"What should we do for her?" Elisha asked.

Gehazi answered, "Well, she has no son, and her husband is old."

¹⁵Elisha said, "Call her." So Gehazi called her, and she stood in the doorway. ¹⁶Elisha said, "At this time next spring, you will hold a baby boy in your arms."

She answered, "Don't say that, sir. Don't lie to me. You're a man of God."

¹⁷But the woman became pregnant and had a son at that time next year, as Elisha had told her.

¹⁸Several years later the boy went to his father, who was with the harvest workers. ¹⁹⌊Suddenly,⌋ he said to his father, "My head! My head!"

The father told his servant, "Carry him to his mother."

²⁰The servant picked him up and brought him to his mother. The boy sat on her lap until noon, when he died. ²¹She took him upstairs and laid him on the bed of the man of God, left ⌊the room⌋, and shut the door behind her. ²²She called her husband and said, "Please send me one of the servants and one of the donkeys. I will go quickly to the man of God and come back again."

²³Her husband asked, "Why are you going to him today? It isn't a New Moon Festival or a day of worship."

But she said goodbye to him.

²⁴She saddled the donkey. Then she told her servant, "Lead on. Don't slow down unless I tell you." ²⁵So she came to the man of God at Mount Carmel.

When he saw her coming at a distance, he told his servant Gehazi, "There is the woman from Shunem. ²⁶Run to meet her and ask her how she, her husband, and the boy are doing."

"Everyone's fine," she answered.

²⁷When she came to the man of God at the mountain, she took hold of his feet. Gehazi went to push her away. But the man of God said, "Leave her alone. She is bitter. The Lord has hidden the reason from me. He hasn't told me."

²⁸The woman said, "I didn't ask you for a son. I said, 'Don't raise my hopes.' "

²⁹The man of God told Gehazi, "Put on a belt, take my shepherd's staff in your hand, and go. Whenever you meet anyone, don't stop to greet him. If he greets you, don't stop to answer him. Lay my staff on the boy's face."

³⁰The boy's mother said, "I solemnly swear, as the Lord and you live, I will not leave without you." So Elisha got up and followed her.

³¹Gehazi went ahead of them and put the staff on the boy's face, but there was no sound or sign of life. So Gehazi came back to meet the man of God. Gehazi told him, "The boy didn't wake up."

³²When Elisha came to the house, the dead boy was lying on Elisha's bed. ³³He went into the room, closed the door, and prayed to the Lord. ³⁴Then he lay on the boy,

putting his mouth on the boy's mouth, his eyes on the boy's eyes, his hands on the boy's hands. He crouched over the boy's body, and it became warm. [35]Elisha got up, walked across the room and came back, and then got back on the bed and crouched over him. The boy sneezed seven times and opened his eyes. [36]Elisha called Gehazi and said, "Call the Shunem woman." Gehazi called her. When she came to him, he said, "Take your son."

[37]Then she immediately bowed at his feet. She took her son and left.

Elisha and the Poisoned Food

[38]When Elisha went back to Gilgal, there was a famine in the country. One day, while the disciples of the prophets were meeting with him, he told his servant, "Put a large pot on the fire, and cook some stew for the disciples of the prophets."

[39]One of them went into the field to gather vegetables and found a wild vine. He filled his clothes with wild gourds. Then he cut them into the pot of stew without knowing what they were. [40]They dished out the food for the men to eat. As they were eating the stew, they cried out, "There's death in the pot, man of God!" So they couldn't eat it.

[41]Elisha said, "Bring some flour." He threw it into the pot and said, "Dish it out for the people to eat." Then there was nothing harmful in the pot.

Elisha Feeds a Hundred People

[42]A man from Baal Shalisha brought bread made from the first harvested grain, 20 barley loaves, and fresh grain to the man of God. The man of God said, "Give it to the people to eat."

[43]But his servant asked, "How can I set this in front of a hundred people?"

"Give it to the people to eat," the man of God said. "This is what the LORD says: They will eat and even have some left over."

[44]The servant set it in front of them. They ate and had some left over, as the LORD had predicted.

Elisha Heals Naaman

[1]Naaman, the commander of the Aramean king's army, was respected and highly honored by his master. The LORD had given Aram a victory through Naaman. This man was a good soldier, but he had a skin disease.

[2]Once, when the Arameans went on raids, they had brought back a little girl from Israel. She became the servant of Naaman's wife. [3]The girl told her mistress, "If only

Good Morning, God
2 Kings 4:32-36

When was a time you prayed about something but weren't sure God would answer? People sometimes think certain prayers are too big for God to answer. Not Elisha. God gave Elisha the power to bring a boy back to life. We serve the same God! No task is too great for God's awesome power. What will you pray about today?

God, thank you for doing powerful things for people who pray.

my master were with the prophet in Samaria. Then the prophet could cure him of his skin disease."

⁴Naaman went to his master and told him what the girl from Israel had said.

⁵The king of Aram said, "You may go. I will also send a letter to the king of Israel." When Naaman left, he took 750 pounds of silver, 150 pounds of gold, and 10 sets of clothing with him. ⁶He brought the letter to the king of Israel. It read, "I'm sending my officer Naaman with this letter. Cure him of his skin disease."

⁷When the king of Israel read the letter, he tore his clothes in distress. He asked, "Am I God? Can I kill someone and then bring him back to life? This man sends someone to me so that I can cure his skin disease! All of you should realize and understand that he's trying to pick a fight with me."

⁸But when Elisha, the man of God, heard that the king of Israel had torn his clothes, he sent a messenger to the king. He asked, "Why did you tear your clothes? Please let Naaman come to me and find out that there is a prophet in Israel."

⁹Naaman came with his horses and chariot and stopped at the entrance to Elisha's home. ¹⁰Elisha sent a messenger to him. He said, "Wash yourself seven times in the Jordan River, and your skin will be healthy and clean."ᵃ

¹¹But Naaman became angry and left. He said, "I thought he would at least come out of his house, stand somewhere, call on the name of the LORD his God, wave his hand over the infected place, and heal the skin disease. ¹²The Abana and Pharpar Rivers in Damascus have better water than any of the rivers in Israel. Couldn't I wash in them and be clean?" So he turned around and left in anger.

¹³But Naaman's servants went to him and said, "Master, if the prophet had asked you to do some extraordinary act, wouldn't you have done it? Why shouldn't you do as he said: 'Wash and be clean'?"

¹⁴So he went to dip himself in the Jordan River seven times, as the man of God had instructed him. His skin became healthy again like a little child's skin. ¹⁵Then he and all his men returned to the man of God. Naaman stood in front of Elisha and said, "Now I know that there's no god in the whole world, except the God of Israel. So please accept a present from me."

¹⁶Elisha said, "I solemnly swear, as the LORD whom I serve lives, I will not accept it." Naaman urged him to take it, but he refused.

¹⁷So Naaman said, "If you won't take it, please have someone give me as much dirt as a pair of mules can carry. From now on I will sacrifice to the LORD alone. I will not offer any burnt offering or sacrifice to any other gods. ¹⁸May the LORD forgive me when my master goes to the temple of Rimmon to worship, leans on my arm, and I have to bow down in the temple of Rimmon. When I do this, may the LORD forgive me for this one thing."

¹⁹Elisha told Naaman, "Go in peace."

After Elisha had left him and gone some distance, ²⁰Gehazi, the servant of Elisha (the man of God), thought, "My master let this Aramean Naaman go without accepting what he had brought. As sure as the LORD lives, I'll run after Naaman and get something from him." ²¹So Gehazi went after Naaman. When Naaman saw Gehazi running after him, he got down from his chariot to speak to him. "Is something wrong?" he asked.

²²Gehazi answered, "No. My master has sent me. He says, 'Just now two young men from the disciples of the prophets in the hills of Ephraim have arrived. Please give them 75 pounds of silver and two sets of clothing.' "

ᵃ5:10 "Clean" refers to anything that Moses' Teachings say is presentable to God.

Naaman's Slave Girl

"If only my master were with the prophet [Elisha] in Samaria.
Then the prophet could cure him of his skin disease."

Naaman's Slave Girl was just a girl when she was taken from her home in Israel. She must have missed her family. She had no one to teach her about God anymore. The girl was given to Naaman, the commander of the Aramean king's army. Naaman gave the little girl to his wife to be her servant.

Naaman was an honored military man. He was an important man in his country, but he had a terrible skin disease called leprosy. The slave girl told Naaman's wife about a prophet in Israel who could heal Naaman. When

Naaman's wife told her husband, he went to Israel and was healed by the prophet Elisha. Naaman then realized that God was the one true God. Because of the courage of the young slave girl, Naaman was healed from his disease and learned about the Lord.

Naaman's slave girl was born around 850 B.C.

We don't know the slave girl's name.

The slave girl was taken captive in a raid on Israel.

The slave girl was given to Naaman's wife to be her servant.

The slave girl cared enough about her master to speak up and tell Naaman's wife how Naaman could be cured of his skin disease.

Getting to Know the Slave Girl

* Why is this young girl remembered even though we don't know her name?
* How was the slave girl able to tell her master about God?
* Have you ever told anyone—even an adult—about God?

Naaman's slave girl was taken from Israel to live in Aram.

²³Naaman replied, "Please let me give you 150 pounds of silver." Naaman urged him to take the silver. Naaman tied up 150 pounds of silver in two bags with two sets of clothing. He gave them to a couple of his own servants to carry in front of Gehazi.

²⁴When Gehazi came to the Ophel in Samaria, he took these things and put them away in the house. Then he dismissed the men, and they left. ²⁵He went and stood in front of his master.

Elisha asked him, "Where were you, Gehazi?"

"I didn't go anywhere," he answered.

²⁶Then Elisha said to him, "I went with you in spirit when the man turned around in his chariot to speak to you. How could you accept silver, clothes, olive orchards, vineyards, sheep, cattle, or slaves? ²⁷Naaman's skin disease will cling to you and your descendants permanently!"

When he left Elisha, Gehazi had a disease that made his skin as flaky as snow.

Elisha and the Floating Ax Head

¹The disciples of the prophets said to Elisha, "The place where we're staying is too small for us. ²Let's go to the Jordan River. Each of us can get some logs and make a place for us to live there."

Elisha said, "Go ahead."

³Then one of the disciples asked, "Won't you please come with us?"

Elisha answered, "I'll go."

⁴So he went with them. They came to the Jordan River and began to cut down trees. ⁵As one of them was cutting down a tree, the ax head fell into the water. He cried out, "Oh no, master! It was borrowed!"

⁶The man of God asked, "Where did it fall?" When he showed Elisha the place, Elisha cut off a piece of wood. He threw it into the water at that place and made the ax head float. ⁷Elisha said, "Pick it up." The disciple reached for it and picked it up.

The Aramean Army Is Struck With Blindness

⁸Whenever the king of Aram was fighting against Israel, he asked for advice from his officers about where they were to camp.

⁹So the man of God would send a message to the king of Israel, "Be careful not to go by that place. The Arameans are hiding there." ¹⁰Then the king of Israel would send someone to the place that the man of God told him about. Elisha warned them so that they would be on their guard. He did this repeatedly.

Kindness
2 Kings 6:21-23

The Lord struck the enemies of Israel with blindness so that they were captured by Elisha. Then Joram, King of Israel, asked Elisha if he should kill them. Elisha's response probably surprised the king. He told King Joram to let them eat, drink, and return home. Elisha wanted King Joram to show kindness to their enemies. Who can you show kindness to? It is easy to be kind to people who are kind to us. But God expects us to be kind to everyone. In his mercy God has been kind to us, even when we don't deserve his kindness.

be all you can be

¹¹The king of Aram was very angry about this. He called his officers and asked them, "Won't you tell me who among us is a spy for the king of Israel?"

¹²One of his officers answered, "No one, Your Majesty. Elisha, the prophet in Israel, tells the king of Israel everything you say—even what you say in your bedroom."

¹³The king said, "Find out where he is. Then I will send men to capture him."

The king was told, "He is in Dothan." ¹⁴So the king sent horses and chariots and a large fighting unit there. They came at night and surrounded the city.

¹⁵When the servant of the man of God got up in the morning and went outside, he saw troops, horses, and chariots surrounding the city. Elisha's servant asked, "Master, what should we do?"

¹⁶Elisha answered, "Don't be afraid. We have more forces on our side than they have on theirs." ¹⁷Then Elisha prayed, "Lord, please open his eyes so that he may see." The Lord opened the servant's eyes and let him see. The mountain around Elisha was full of fiery horses and chariots.

¹⁸As the Arameans came down to get him, Elisha prayed to the Lord, "Please strike these people with blindness." The Lord struck them with blindness, as Elisha had asked. ¹⁹Elisha told them, "This isn't the way! This isn't the city. Follow me, and I will lead you to the man you're looking for." So he led them into Samaria. ²⁰When they came into Samaria, Elisha said, "Lord, open the eyes of these men, and let them see." The Lord opened their eyes and let them see that they were in the middle of Samaria.

²¹When the king of Israel saw them, he asked Elisha, "Master, should I kill them? Should I kill them?"

²²Elisha answered, "Don't kill them. Do you kill everyone you take captive in combat? Give them food and water. Let them eat and drink. Then let them go back to their master."

²³So the king prepared a great feast for them. They ate and drank, and then he sent them back to their master. After this, Aramean troops didn't raid Israel's territory anymore.

The Aramean Army Blockades Samaria

²⁴Later King Benhadad of Aram assembled his whole army. They went to Samaria and blockaded it. ²⁵The shortages caused by the blockade of Samaria became so severe that a donkey's head sold for two pounds of silver and a half-pint of dove[a] manure for two ounces of silver.

²⁶As the king of Israel was walking on the city wall, a woman cried to him, "Help me, Your Majesty!"

²⁷He answered, "If the Lord doesn't help you, how can I help you? I can't give you something from the threshing floor[b] or the winepress." ²⁸Then the king asked her, "What's the matter?"

She answered, "This woman told me, 'Give up your son. Let's eat him today. We'll eat my son tomorrow.' ²⁹So we boiled my son and ate him. The next day I told her, 'Give up your son. We'll eat him,' but she hid her son."

³⁰When the king heard the woman say this, he tore his clothes in distress. As he was walking on the city wall, the people saw that he was wearing sackcloth under his clothes. ³¹He said, "May God strike me dead if the head of Elisha, son of Shaphat, stays on his body today."

³²Elisha was sitting in his home with the city's leaders. The king had sent one of

---

a 6:25 Or "pigeon."   b 6:27 A threshing floor is an outdoor area where grain is separated from its husks.

his men ahead of him to Elisha's house. But before the messenger arrived, Elisha asked the leaders, "Do you see how this murderer has sent someone to tear off my head? When the messenger comes, close the door. Hold it shut because the king will be following him."

³³While he was still talking to them, the messenger arrived. He said to Elisha, "This severe famine is from the Lord. Why should I wait any longer for the Lord to help us?"

¹Elisha answered, "Listen to the word of the Lord! This is what the Lord says: About this time tomorrow 24 cups of the best flour will sell for half an ounce of silver in the gateway to Samaria. And 48 cups of barley will sell for half an ounce of silver."

²The servant on whose arm the king was leaning answered the man of God, "Could this happen even if the Lord poured rain through windows in the sky?"

Elisha replied, "You will see it with your own eyes, but you won't eat any of it."

The Aramean Army Flees

³Four men with skin diseases were at the entrance of the city gate. One of them asked, "Why are we sitting here waiting to die? ⁴If we go into the city, the famine is also there, and we'll still die. But if we stay here, we'll die. So let's go to the Aramean camp. If they give us something to keep us alive, we'll live. But if they kill us, we'll die anyway." ⁵So they started out at dusk to go into the Aramean camp. When they came to the edge of the camp, no one was there.

⁶(The Lord had made the Aramean army hear what sounded like chariots, horses, and a large army. The Aramean soldiers said to one another, "The king of Israel has hired the Hittite and Egyptian kings to attack us!" ⁷So at dusk they fled. They abandoned the camp as it was with its tents, horses, and donkeys and ran for their lives.)

⁸When the men with skin diseases came to the edge of the camp, they went into a tent, ate and drank, and carried off the silver, gold, and clothes they found in that tent. They went away and hid them. Then they came back, went into another tent, carried off its contents, went away, and hid them.

⁹Then they said to one another, "What we're doing is not right. This is a day of good news, and we're not telling anyone about it. If we wait until morning when it's light out, we'll be punished. Let's bring the news to the royal palace." ¹⁰So they called the city gatekeepers and told them, "We went into the Aramean camp, and we didn't see or hear anyone. The horses and donkeys were still tied up. Even the tents were left exactly as they were."

¹¹The gatekeepers announced the news to the royal palace. ¹²So the king got up at night and told his officers what the Arameans had planned for them. He said, "They know we're starving, so they've left the camp to hide in the countryside. They're thinking, 'When they've left the city, we'll capture them alive and get into the city.' "

¹³One of his officers replied, "Please let some men take five of the horses that are left here. Those men will be no worse off than the rest of the Israelites who are dying. Let's send them to take a look." ¹⁴So they took two chariots with horses, and the king sent them to follow the Aramean army and told them to find out what happened. ¹⁵They followed them as far as the Jordan River and saw how the whole road was littered with clothes and equipment that the Arameans had thrown away in their hurry. The messengers returned and told the king about it.

¹⁶So the people went out and looted the Aramean camp. Then 24 cups of the best flour sold for half an ounce of silver, and 48 cups of barley sold for half an ounce of silver, as the Lord had predicted.

¹⁷The king appointed the servant on whose arm he used to lean to be in charge of

the gate. But the people trampled him to death in the gateway, as the man of God had predicted when the king came to him. [18](It happened exactly as the man of God told the king, "48 cups of barley will sell for half an ounce of silver. And 24 cups of the best flour will sell for half an ounce of silver. This will happen about this time tomorrow in the gateway to Samaria." [19]Then the servant answered the man of God, "Could this happen even if the LORD poured rain through windows in the sky?" Elisha answered, "You will see it with your own eyes, but you won't eat any of it.") [20]So this is what happened to the king's servant: The people trampled him to death in the gateway.

Elisha Helps a Shunem Woman Get Her Land Back

8 [1]Elisha had told the woman whose son he had brought back to life, "Go away with your family. Stay wherever you can. The LORD has decided to send a famine on this country, and it will last seven years."

[2]The woman did what the man of God told her. She and her family went to live in Philistine territory for seven years. [3]At the end of seven years, the woman came home from Philistine territory but left again to make an appeal to the king about her house and land.

[4]The king was talking to Gehazi, the servant of the man of God. He said, "Please tell me about all the great things Elisha has done." [5]While Gehazi was telling the king how Elisha brought a dead child back to life, the mother ˌcame toˌ make an appeal to the king about her house and land.

Gehazi said, "Your Majesty, this is the woman, and this is her son whom Elisha brought back to life."

[6]When the king asked the woman ˌabout thisˌ, she told him the story. So the king assigned to her an attendant to whom he said, "Restore all that is hers, including whatever her property produced from the day she left the country until now."

Elisha Prophesies to Hazael

[7]Elisha went to Damascus. King Benhadad of Aram, who was sick, was told, "The man of God has come here."

[8]The king told Hazael, "Take a present, and meet the man of God. Ask the LORD through him, 'Will I recover from this illness?'"

[9]Hazael went to meet Elisha. He took with him a present and all kinds of goods from Damascus. He had loaded the goods on 40 camels. He stood in front of Elisha and said, "Your humble servant King Benhadad of Aram has sent me to you. He asks whether he will recover from this illness."

[10]Elisha replied, "Tell him that he will get better, although the LORD has shown me that he is actually going to die." [11]He stared at him until he became embarrassed. Then the man of God began to cry.

[12]"Sir, why are you crying?" Hazael asked.

Elisha answered, "I know the evil you will do to the Israelites: You will set their fortresses on fire, kill their best young men, smash their little children, and rip open their pregnant women."

[13]But Hazael asked, "How can a dog like me do such a significant thing?"

Elisha answered, "The LORD has shown me that you will become king of Aram." [14]Hazael left Elisha and went to his master Benhadad, who asked him what Elisha had said.

Hazael answered, "He told me that you will get better."

[15]But the next day Hazael took a blanket, soaked it in water, and smothered the king with it. Hazael ruled as king in his place.

King Jehoram of Judah—
2 Chronicles 21:2-11; 21:16–22:1

¹⁶Joram (Ahab's son) was in his fifth year as king of Israel when Jehoram,ᵃ son of King Jehoshaphat of Judah, began to rule. Jehoram ruled while Jehoshaphat was still king of Judah. ¹⁷He was 32 years old when he began to rule, and he ruled for 8 years in Jerusalem. ¹⁸He followed the ways of the kings of Israel, as Ahab's family had done, because his wife was Ahab's daughter. So he did what the LORD considered evil. ¹⁹But for David's sake the LORD didn't want to destroy Judah. The LORD had told David that he would always give him and his descendants a ˌshiningˌ lamp.

²⁰During Jehoram's time Edom rebelled against Judah and chose its own king. ²¹Jehoram took all his chariots to attack Zair. The Edomites and their chariot commanders surrounded him, but he got up at night, broke through their lines, and his troops fled home. ²²So Edom rebelled against Judah's rule and is still independent today. At that time Libnah also rebelled. ²³Isn't everything else about Jehoram—everything he did—written in the official records of the kings of Judah? ²⁴Jehoram lay down in death with his ancestors and was buried with them in the City of David. His son Ahaziah succeeded him as king.

King Ahaziah of Judah—
2 Chronicles 22:2-6

²⁵Joram (Ahab's son) was in his twelfth year as king of Israel when Jehoram's son Ahaziah became king of Judah. ²⁶Ahaziah was 22 years old when he began to rule, and he ruled for one year in Jerusalem. His mother was Athaliah, the granddaughter of King Omri of Israel. ²⁷Ahaziah followed the ways of Ahab's family. He did what the LORD considered evil, as Ahab's family had done, because he was related to Ahab's family by marriage.

²⁸Ahaziah went with Ahab's son Joram to fight against King Hazael of Aram at Ramoth Gilead. There the Arameans wounded Joram. ²⁹King Joram returned to Jezreel to let his wounds heal. (He had been wounded by the Arameans at Ramah when he fought against King Hazael of Aram.) Then Jehoram's son Ahaziah went to Jezreel to see Ahab's son Joram, who was sick.

Jehu Is Anointed King of Israel

¹The prophet Elisha called one of the disciples of the prophets. He said, "Put on your belt. Take this flask of olive oil, and go to Ramoth Gilead. ²When you arrive there, look for Jehu, son of Jehoshaphat and grandson of Nimshi. Go inside, and have him get up and leave his companions. Take him into an inner room. ³Take the flask of oil, pour it on his head, and say, 'This is what the LORD says: I have anointed you king of Israel.' Then open the door and leave immediately."

⁴The young man, the servant of the prophet, went to Ramoth Gilead. ⁵When he arrived there, the army's generals were sitting together. He said, "I have something to tell you, General."

Jehu asked, "Which one of us?"

He answered, "You, General!"

⁶Jehu got up and went into the house. The prophet poured olive oil on his head and told him, "This is what the LORD God of Israel says: I have anointed you king of the LORD's people, ˌkingˌ of Israel. ⁷You will destroy the family of your master Ahab. I will get revenge on Jezebel for shedding the blood of my servants the prophets and

---

ᵃ8:16 In the Masoretic Text this king of Judah is also called Joram, a shorter form of Jehoram.

all the LORD's other servants. [8]Ahab's entire family will die. I will destroy every male*a* from Ahab's family, whether slave or freeman in Israel. [9]I will make Ahab's family like the family of Jeroboam (Nebat's son) and like the family of Baasha, son of Ahijah. [10]Dogs will eat Jezebel inside the walls of Jezreel, and no one will bury her." Then he opened the door and left.

[11]Jehu came out to his master's officials. One of them asked him, "Is everything alright? Why did this lunatic come to you?"

He answered, "You know the man and the kind of things he says."

[12]They said, "That's not an answer. Please tell us."

Jehu replied, "We talked for a while, and he said to me, 'This is what the LORD says: I have anointed you king of Israel.' "

[13]Then each one of them immediately took off his coat and laid it on the stairs below him. They blew a ram's horn and said, "Jehu is king!"

Jehu Kills King Joram, King Ahaziah, and Queen Jezebel—
2 Chronicles 22:7-9

[14]So Jehu, son of Jehoshaphat and grandson of Nimshi, plotted against Joram. (Joram and all Israel were guarding Ramoth Gilead against King Hazael of Aram. [15]But King Joram had returned to Jezreel to recover from the wounds he received while fighting King Hazael of Aram.)

Then Jehu said, "If you want me to be king, don't let anyone escape from the city to take the news to Jezreel." [16]So Jehu got on his chariot and drove to Jezreel because Joram was lying in bed there. (King Ahaziah of Judah had come to see Joram.)

[17]The watchman standing on the tower in Jezreel saw Jehu's troops coming. He said, "I see some troops."

So Joram said, "Take a chariot driver, send him to meet them, and ask, 'Is everything alright?' "

[18]So a chariot driver rode off, met Jehu, and said, "The king asks, 'Is everything alright?' "

Jehu replied, "Why should that matter to you? Follow me."

So the watchman announced, "The messenger you sent has reached them, but he isn't coming back."

[19]Then Joram sent out a second driver. When he came to them, he said, "The king asks, 'Is everything alright?' "

Jehu replied, "Why should that matter to you? Follow me."

[20]So the watchman announced, "He has reached them, but he isn't coming back. The troop's leader is driving like a lunatic, like Jehu, grandson of Nimshi."

[21]"Hitch the horses to the chariot," Joram ordered. When that was done, King Joram of Israel and King Ahaziah of Judah went to meet Jehu, each in his own chariot. They found him in the field that belonged to Naboth from Jezreel.

[22]When Joram saw Jehu, he asked, "Is everything alright, Jehu?"

Jehu answered, "How can everything be alright as long as your mother continues her idolatry and witchcraft?"

[23]As Joram turned his chariot around and tried to flee, he said to Ahaziah, "It's a trap, Ahaziah!" [24]But Jehu took his bow and shot Joram between the shoulders. The arrow came out of his chest, and he slumped over in his chariot.

[25]Then Jehu said to his attendant Bidkar, "Take him away, and throw him into the

---

*a*9:8 Hebrew uses a coarse term for "male" here.

field that belonged to Naboth from Jezreel. Remember when you and I were driving our chariots behind his father Ahab? The LORD revealed this prophecy about him: [26]"Just as I saw the blood of Naboth and his sons yesterday, I will pay you back in this field,' declares the LORD. Now take him and throw him into the field as the LORD predicted."

[27]When King Ahaziah of Judah saw this, he fled on the road leading to Beth Haggan. Jehu pursued him and ordered, "Shoot him down in his chariot." They shot him at Gur Pass, which is near Ibleam. Ahaziah continued to flee until he got to Megiddo, where he died. [28]His servants brought him in a chariot to Jerusalem. They buried him in a tomb with his ancestors in the City of David. [29](Ahaziah had become king of Judah in the eleventh year that Joram, Ahab's son, was king of Israel.)

[30]When Jehu arrived in Jezreel, Jezebel heard about it. She put on eye shadow, fixed her hair, and looked out of a second-story window. [31]When Jehu entered the gateway, she asked, "Is everything alright, Zimri, murderer of your master?"

[32]Looking up at the window, he asked, "Is anyone on my side? Anyone?" Then two or three eunuchs looked out at him.

[33]He said, "Throw her down." They threw her down, and some of her blood splattered on the wall and the horses. The horses trampled her.

[34]He went inside, ate, and drank. Then he said, "Take care of this woman who had a curse on her. After all, she was a king's daughter." [35]But when they went out to bury her, they couldn't find any of her body except her skull, feet, and hands. [36]They came back and told him.

Jehu said, "The LORD spoke through his servant Elijah from Tishbe. He said, 'Dogs will eat Jezebel's body inside the walls of Jezreel. [37]Jezebel's corpse will be like manure on the ground in the fields surrounding Jezreel so that no one will be able to say that this is Jezebel.' "

Jehu Kills King Ahab's and King Ahaziah's Heirs

10 [1]Ahab had 70 male heirs in Samaria. So Jehu wrote letters to the officials of Jezreel, the respected leaders, and the guardians of Ahab's descendants in Samaria. The letters read, [2]"Your master's heirs are with you, and you have chariots, horses, fortified cities, and weapons. As soon as this letter reaches you, [3]choose the best and most honest of your master's heirs, and put him on Ahab's throne. Fight for your master's family."

[4]But they panicked. They said, "If two kings couldn't stand up to him, how can we stand up to him?" [5]So the official in charge of the palace, the mayor of the city, the respected leaders, and the guardians sent this message to Jehu: "We are your servants. We'll do everything you tell us. We won't make anyone king. Do what you think is best."

[6]So he wrote them a second letter. It read, "If you are on my side and ready to listen to me, bring the heads of your master's heirs to me in Jezreel about this time tomorrow."

The 70 male heirs were staying with the city's most powerful men. These men had raised them. [7]When the letter came to the men, they slaughtered all 70 heirs. They put the heads in baskets and sent them to Jehu in Jezreel. [8]A messenger told him, "They've brought the heads of the king's heirs."

Jehu said, "Put them in two piles at the entrance to the gateway until morning." [9]In the morning he stood there. He told the people, "You are innocent. I plotted against my master and killed him. But who killed all these men? [10]You can be sure that the word of the LORD spoken about Ahab's family will be fulfilled. The LORD will do what he said through his servant Elijah."

¹¹Jehu also killed every member of Ahab's household who was left in Jezreel: all the most powerful men, friends, and priests. Not one of them was left.

¹²Then Jehu left for Samaria. When he came to Beth Eked of the Shepherds, ¹³he found some relatives of King Ahaziah of Judah. "Who are you?" he asked.

They answered, "We're Ahaziah's relatives. We've come to greet the families of the king and the queen mother."

¹⁴Jehu ordered, "Capture them!"

Jehu's men captured and slaughtered 42 of them at a cistern near Beth Eked. They didn't leave any survivors.

¹⁵When he left that place, he met Jehonadab, son of Rechab, who was coming to meet him. Jehu greeted him and asked, "Are you as loyal to me as I am to you?"

"I am," Jehonadab answered.

So Jehu said, "If you are, give me your hand."

When he gave Jehu his hand, Jehu helped him up into the chariot. ¹⁶Jehu said, "Come with me. See how devoted I am to the LORD." So he had Jehonadab ride on his chariot. ¹⁷When they arrived in Samaria, Jehu killed the rest of Ahab's family, every member who was left in Samaria. He wiped them out, as the LORD had told Elijah.

Jehu Kills Baal's Prophets

¹⁸Then Jehu brought all the people together. He said, "Ahab served Baal a little, but Jehu will serve him a lot. ¹⁹Summon all the prophets, servants, and priests of Baal. Make sure no one is missing because I have a great sacrifice to offer Baal. Whoever is missing will not live." (Jehu was deceiving them. He actually wanted to destroy those who worshiped Baal.)

²⁰Jehu said, "Call a holy assembly to honor Baal." So they did. ²¹Jehu sent messengers to all the Israelites. All the worshipers of Baal came, and there wasn't one who didn't come. They went into the temple of Baal and filled it from one end to the other.

²²Then Jehu told the man in charge of the priests' robes, "Bring out the robes for all the worshipers of Baal." So he brought out robes for them. ²³Jehu and Jehonadab, son of Rechab, went into the temple of Baal and said to the worshipers of Baal, "Make sure that there are no worshipers of the LORD here with you. Only the worshipers of Baal should be here." ²⁴So they went in to offer sacrifices and burnt offerings. But Jehu had stationed 80 of his men outside. He said to them, "If any of the people I'm putting in your hands escape, you will pay for their lives with yours."

Good Morning, God
2 Kings 10:28-31

When Jehu was named the king of Israel, he could hardly contain his excitement. He did everything right. He even stopped the people from worshiping the false god Baal in Israel. Unfortunately, his enthusiasm ran out of steam. Before long, he was worshiping idols again. Like Jehu, it's easy to be excited about God for a short while. But God wants you to wholeheartedly obey him in the long run, too.

Lord, help me to follow you all my life.

²⁵When the burnt offerings had been made, Jehu said to the guards and attendants, "Kill them. Don't let anyone get away." So they used swords to kill the Baal worshipers and threw out the bodies until the guards and attendants came to the stronghold in the temple of Baal. ²⁶Then they brought out the large sacred stone of the temple of Baal and burned it. ²⁷They destroyed the sacred stone of Baal and the temple of Baal and made it into a latrine. It is still a latrine today.

²⁸So Jehu got rid of Baal worship throughout Israel. ²⁹But Jehu did not turn away from the sins that Jeroboam (Nebat's son) led Israel to commit—the worship of the golden calves that were at Bethel and Dan.

³⁰The LORD said to Jehu, "You did what I consider right, and you did it well. You did everything I wanted done to Ahab's family. That is why four generations of your descendants will sit on the throne of Israel."

³¹But Jehu didn't wholeheartedly obey the teachings of the LORD God of Israel. He didn't turn away from the sins that Jeroboam led Israel to commit. ³²So in those days the LORD began to take away some of Israel's territory. Hazael defeated Jehu's army throughout Israel's territory ³³east of the Jordan River: the entire region of Gilead (the territory belonging to Gad, Reuben, and Manasseh) from Aroer, which is near the Arnon River, to Gilead and Bashan.

³⁴Isn't everything else about Jehu—everything he did, all his heroic acts— written in the official records of the kings of Israel? ³⁵Jehu lay down in death with his ancestors and was buried in Samaria. His son Jehoahaz succeeded him as king. ³⁶Jehu ruled as king of Israel in Samaria for 28 years.

The Priest Jehoiada Opposes Queen Athaliah—
2 Chronicles 22:10–23:21

¹When Ahaziah's mother, Athaliah, saw that her son was dead, she began to destroy the entire royal family. ²But Jehosheba, daughter of King Jehoram and sister of Ahaziah, took Ahaziah's son Joash. She saved him from being killed with the king's other sons, and in a bedroom she hid him and his nurse from Athaliah. So Joash wasn't killed ³but was hidden with her in the LORD's temple for six years while Athaliah ruled the country.

⁴In the seventh year of Athaliah's reign, Jehoiada sent for the company commanders of the Carites and the guards and had them come to him in the LORD's temple. He made an agreement with them, put them under oath in the LORD's temple, and showed them the king's son. ⁵He ordered them, "This is what you must do: One third of you, those who are on duty on the day of worship, must guard the royal palace. ⁶Another third must be at Sur Gate. And another third must be at the gate behind the guards. You will guard the king's residence.ᵃ ⁷Then your two groups who normally go off duty on the day of worship must guard the king at the LORD's temple. ⁸Surround the king. Each man should have his weapons in his hand. Kill anyone who tries to break through your ranks. Stay with the king wherever he goes."

⁹The company commanders did as the priest Jehoiada had ordered them. Each commander took his men who were coming on duty on the day of worship as well as those who were about to go off duty and came to the priest Jehoiada. ¹⁰He gave the commanders the spears and the shields that had belonged to King David but were now in the LORD's temple. ¹¹The guards stood with their weapons in their hands. They were stationed around the king and around the altar and the temple (from the south side to the north side of the temple). ¹²Then Jehoiada brought out the king's son, gave

---

ᵃ 11:6 Hebrew meaning uncertain.

him the crown and the religious instructions, and made him king by anointing him. As the guards clapped their hands, they said, "Long live the king!"

[13]When Athaliah heard the noise made by the guards and the other people, she went into the LORD's temple, where the people were. [14]She looked, and the king was standing by the pillar according to custom. The commanders and the trumpeters were by his side. All the people of the land were rejoicing and blowing trumpets. As Athaliah tore her clothes in distress, she cried, "Treason, treason!"

[15]Then the priest Jehoiada ordered the company commanders who were in charge of the army, "Take her out of the temple. Use your sword to kill anyone who follows her." (The priest had said, "She must not be killed in the LORD's temple.") [16]So they arrested her as she came to the street where the horses enter the royal palace, and there she was killed.

[17]Jehoiada made a promise to the LORD on behalf of the king and his people that they would be the LORD's people. He made other promises between the king and the people. [18]Then all the people of the land went to the temple of Baal and tore it down. They smashed Baal's altars and his statues and killed Mattan, the priest of Baal, in front of the altars.

Next, the priest appointed officials to be in charge of the LORD's temple. [19]He took the company commanders of the Carites and the guards and all the people of the land, and they brought the king from the LORD's temple. They went down the street that goes through Guards' Gate to the royal palace. Then Joash sat on the royal throne. [20]All the people of the land were celebrating. But the city was quiet because they had killed Athaliah with a sword at the royal palace.[b]

King Joash of Judah—
2 Chronicles 24:1-23

[21]Joash[c] was seven years old when he began to rule.

[a][1]Joash began to rule in Jehu's seventh year as king of Israel, and he ruled for 40 years in Jerusalem. His mother was Zibiah from Beersheba. [2]Joash did what the LORD considered right, as long as the priest Jehoiada instructed him. [3]But the illegal places of worship weren't torn down. The people continued to offer sacrifices and burn incense at these worship sites.

[4]Joash told the priests, "Collect all the holy contributions that are brought into the LORD's temple—the money each person is currently required to bring and all the money brought voluntarily to the LORD's temple. [5]Each of the priests should receive it from the donors and use it to make repairs on the temple where they are needed."

[6]But by Joash's twenty-third year as king, the priests still had not repaired the temple. [7]So King Joash called for Jehoiada and the other priests and asked them, "Why aren't you repairing the damage in the temple? Don't take any more money from the donors for your own use. Instead, use it to make repairs on the temple." [8]The priests agreed neither to receive money from the people for personal use nor to be responsible for repairing the temple.

[9]Then the priest Jehoiada took a box, drilled a hole in its lid, and put it at the right side of the altar as one comes into the LORD's temple. The priests who guarded the entrance put the money that was brought to the LORD's temple in the box. [10]Whenever they saw a lot of money in the box, the king's scribe and the chief priest would collect and count the money that was donated in the LORD's temple. [11]Then they would

---

[b]11:20 2 Kings 11:21 in English Bibles is 2 Kings 12:1 in the Hebrew Bible.   [c]11:21 In the Masoretic Text this king of Judah is also called Jehoash, a longer form of Joash.   [a]12:1 2 Kings 12:1-21 in English Bibles is 2 Kings 12:2-22 in the Hebrew Bible.

Jehosheba

"I must get Joash to the temple."

Jehosheba saved baby Joash from Queen Athaliah, the mother of King Ahaziah. When the King died, Queen Athaliah wanted to rule. She quickly ordered her grandchildren, who would have taken the throne, to be killed so she could take her son's place.

Jehosheba was the half sister of the dead king. When she saw what was happening, Jehosheba acted quickly. She saved Joash from being killed with the other princes. Jehosheba hid Joash and his nanny in the Lord's temple for six years. Because of Jehosheba's courage and quick thinking, the rightful heir was finally brought to the throne.

During the seventh year of Queen Athaliah's reign, Jehoiada the priest brought Joash out of hiding and crowned him king. Jehoiada helped young King Joash do what was right in God's eyes. Together they worked to rid Israel of idol worship and bring the people back to the Lord.

Jehosheba was born around 850 B.C.

Jehosheba means "Yahweh [God] is abundance."

Jehosheba was the sister of King Ahaziah.

Jehosheba was the daughter of King Jehoram.

Jehosheba saved the life of her nephew, Prince Joash, when evil Queen Athaliah seized the throne and killed the other princes.

Getting to Know Jehosheba

* What do you think would have happened if Jehosheba hadn't rescued Joash?
* What kind of ruler was Queen Athaliah?
* What did Jehosheba's courage mean to the nation of Israel?
* Have you ever done something difficult because you knew it was what God wanted you to do?

Jehosheba hid Joash in the temple. Joash lived in the temple for six years before he became king.

give the money that had been weighed to the men who had been appointed to work on the LORD's temple. They used it to pay the carpenters, builders, [12]masons, and stonecutters. They also used it to buy wood and cut stones to make repairs on the LORD's temple and to buy anything else that they needed for the temple repairs. [13]But no silver bowls, snuffers, dishes, trumpets, or any other gold and silver utensils were made for the LORD's temple with the money that was brought. [14]Instead, the money was given to the workmen, and they used it to repair the temple. [15]They didn't require the men who were entrusted with the money for the workers to give an account, because they were honest people. [16]The money from the guilt offerings and the offerings for sin was not brought into the LORD's temple. It belonged to the priests.

[17]At this time King Hazael of Aram fought against Gath and conquered it. He was also determined to attack Jerusalem. [18]So King Joash of Judah took all the gifts his ancestors Kings Jehoshaphat, Jehoram, and Ahaziah of Judah, had dedicated to the LORD, the things he had dedicated to the LORD, and all the gold that could be found in the storerooms of the LORD's temple and the royal palace. He sent these things to King Hazael of Aram, who called off the attack on Jerusalem.

King Joash Is Assassinated—
2 Chronicles 24:24-27

[19]Isn't everything else about Joash—everything he did—written in the official records of the kings of Judah? [20]His own officials plotted against him and killed him at Beth Millo on the road that goes down to Silla. [21]Joash's officials Jozacar, son of Shimeath, and Jehozabad, son of Shomer, executed him. They buried him with his ancestors in the City of David. His son Amaziah succeeded him as king.

King Jehoahaz of Israel

[1]Ahaziah's son King Joash of Judah was in his twenty-third year as king of Judah when Jehoahaz,[a] son of Jehu, began to rule in Samaria as king of Israel. He ruled for 17 years. [2]He did what the LORD considered evil. He continued to commit the sins that Jeroboam (Nebat's son) led Israel to commit. He never gave up committing those sins. [3]So the LORD became angry with Israel and put it at the mercy of King Hazael of Aram and Hazael's son Benhadad as long as they lived.

[4]Then Jehoahaz pleaded with the LORD, and the LORD heard him because he saw how the Aramean king was oppressing Israel. [5]So the LORD gave the Israelites someone to save them, and they were freed from Aram's power. They were able to live in their homes again as they had done before. [6]But they didn't turn away from the sins that Jeroboam and his dynasty led Israel to commit. They continued to commit those sins. In addition, the pole dedicated to the goddess Asherah remained standing in Samaria.

[7]Jehoahaz had no army left except for 50 horses, 10 chariots, and 10,000 foot soldiers because the king of Aram had destroyed the rest. He had made them like dust that people trample. [8]Isn't everything else about Jehoahaz—everything he did, his heroic acts—written in the official records of the kings of Israel? [9]Jehoahaz lay down in death with his ancestors and was buried in Samaria. His son Jehoash[b] ruled as king in his place.

---

[a] 13:1 In the Masoretic Text this king of Israel is also called Joahaz, a shorter form of Jehoahaz.   [b] 13:9 In the Masoretic Text this king of Israel is also called Joash, a shorter form of Jehoash.

King Jehoash of Israel

¹⁰In Joash's thirty-seventh year as king of Judah, Jehoahaz's son Jehoash began to rule Israel in Samaria. He ruled for 16 years. ¹¹He did what the LORD considered evil and never gave up committing the sins that Jeroboam led Israel to commit. He continued to commit them. ¹²Isn't everything else about Jehoash—everything he did, his heroic acts when he fought against King Amaziah of Judah—written in the official records of the kings of Israel? ¹³Jehoash lay down in death with his ancestors and was buried with the kings of Israel in Samaria. Then Jeroboam claimed the throne.

The Death of Elisha

¹⁴Elisha became fatally ill. King Jehoash of Israel visited him, cried over him, and said, "Master! Master! Israel's chariot and horses!"

¹⁵Elisha told him, "Get a bow and some arrows." So he got a bow and some arrows. ¹⁶Then Elisha told the king of Israel, "Take the bow in your hand." So the king picked up the bow. Elisha laid his hands on the king's hands. ¹⁷Elisha said, "Open the window that faces east." So the king opened it. "Shoot," Elisha said, and the king shot. Then Elisha said, "That is the arrow of the LORD's victory, the arrow of victory against Aram. You will completely defeat the Arameans at Aphek." ¹⁸Then Elisha said, "Take the arrows." So the king took them. "Stomp on them," he told the king of Israel. The king stomped three times and stopped.

¹⁹Then the man of God became angry with him. "You should have stomped five or six times!" he said. "Then you would have completely defeated the Arameans. But now you will only defeat the Arameans three times."

²⁰Elisha died and was buried. Moabite raiding parties used to invade the country in the spring. ²¹One day some people who were burying a man saw one of these raiding parties. So they quickly put the man into Elisha's tomb. But when the body touched Elisha's bones, the man came back to life and stood up.

²²King Hazael of Aram oppressed Israel as long as Jehoahaz ruled. ²³But the LORD was kind and merciful to the Israelites because of his promise*ᶜ* to Abraham, Isaac, and Jacob. He didn't want to destroy the Israelites, and even now he hasn't turned away from them.

²⁴King Hazael of Aram died, and his son Benhadad succeeded him as king. ²⁵Then Jehoash, son of Jehoahaz, reconquered the cities that Benhadad had taken from his father Jehoahaz. Jehoash defeated Benhadad three times and recovered those cities of Israel.

King Amaziah of Judah—
2 Chronicles 25:1-13

14 ¹Jehoahaz's son King Jehoash was in his second year as king of Israel when King Amaziah, son of Joash of Judah, began to rule. ²Amaziah was 25 years old when he began to rule, and he ruled for 29 years in Jerusalem. His mother was Jehoaddin from Jerusalem.

³He did what the LORD considered right, but not exactly what his ancestor David had done. He did everything his father Joash had done. ⁴But the illegal places of worship were still not torn down. The people continued to offer sacrifices and burn incense at these worship sites.

⁵As soon as he had a firm control over the kingdom, he executed the officials who had killed his father, the former king. ⁶But he didn't execute their children. He obeyed

---

ᶜ13:23 Or "covenant."

the Lord's command written in the Book of Moses' Teachings: "Parents must never be put to death for the crimes of their children, and children must never be put to death for the crimes of their parents. Each person must be put to death for his own crime."

⁷Amaziah killed 10,000 Edomites in the Dead Sea region and took the city of Sela in battle. He gave it the name Joktheel, which is still its name today.

King Amaziah's Defeat and Death—
2 Chronicles 25:14–26:2

⁸Then Amaziah sent messengers to King Jehoash, son of Jehoahaz and grandson of Jehu of Israel, to declare war on Israel.

⁹King Jehoash of Israel sent this message to King Amaziah of Judah: "A thistle in Lebanon sent a message to a cedar in Lebanon. It said, 'Let your daughter marry my son,' but a wild animal from Lebanon came along and trampled the thistle. ¹⁰You certainly defeated Edom, and now you have become arrogant. Enjoy your fame, but stay home. Why must you invite disaster and your own defeat and take Judah with you?"

¹¹But Amaziah wouldn't listen. So King Jehoash of Israel attacked, and King Amaziah of Judah met him in battle at Beth Shemesh in Judah. ¹²Israel defeated the army of Judah, and the Judeans fled to their homes. ¹³King Jehoash of Israel captured King Amaziah, son of Joash and grandson of Ahaziah of Judah, at Beth Shemesh and went to Jerusalem. He tore down a 600-foot section of the wall around Jerusalem from Ephraim Gate to Corner Gate. ¹⁴He took all the gold, silver, and all the utensils he found in the Lord's temple and in the royal palace treasury. He also took hostages. Then he returned to Samaria.

¹⁵Isn't everything else about Jehoash—what he did, his heroic acts when he fought against King Amaziah of Judah—written in the official records of the kings of Israel? ¹⁶Jehoash lay down in death with his ancestors and was buried with the kings of Israel in Samaria. His son Jeroboam succeeded him as king.

¹⁷Joash's son King Amaziah of Judah lived 15 years after the death of Jehoahaz's son King Jehoash of Israel. ¹⁸Isn't everything else about Amaziah written in the official records of the kings of Judah? ¹⁹Conspirators in Jerusalem plotted against him, so he fled to Lachish. But they sent men to Lachish after him and killed him there. ²⁰They brought him back by horse, and he was buried in Jerusalem, in the City of David, with his ancestors.

²¹All the people of Judah took Azariah, who was 16 years old, and made him king in place of his father Amaziah. ²²Azariah rebuilt Elath and returned it to Judah after King Amaziah lay down in death with his ancestors.

King Jeroboam II of Israel

²³Joash's son Amaziah was in his fifteenth year as king of Judah when Jehoash's son King Jeroboam of Israel began to rule in Samaria. Jeroboam ruled for 41 years. ²⁴He did what the Lord considered evil. He didn't turn away from any of the sins that Jeroboam (Nebat's son) led Israel to commit.

²⁵He restored Israel's boundaries from the border of Hamath to the Dead Sea as the Lord God of Israel predicted through his servant Jonah, the prophet from Gath Hepher and the son of Amittai. ²⁶The Lord did this because he saw how bitterly everyone in Israel was suffering. No slave or free person could help Israel. ²⁷Since the Lord had said he was not going to wipe out Israel's name completely, he saved them through Jeroboam, son of Jehoash.

²⁸Isn't everything else about Jeroboam—everything he did, his heroic acts when

he fought, how he recovered Damascus and Hamath for Israel[a]—written in the official records of the kings of Israel? [29]Jeroboam lay down in death with his ancestors, the kings of Israel. His son Zechariah succeeded him as king.

King Azariah of Judah—
2 Chronicles 26:3-5

[1]In Jeroboam's twenty-seventh year as king of Israel, Amaziah's son Azariah[a] began to rule as king of Judah. [2]He was 16 years old when he began to rule, and he ruled for 52 years in Jerusalem. His mother was Jecoliah from Jerusalem.

[3]He did what the LORD considered right, as his father Amaziah had done. [4]But the illegal places of worship were still not torn down. The people continued to offer sacrifices and burn incense at these worship sites.

Azariah's Skin Disease—
2 Chronicles 26:21-23

[5]The LORD inflicted the king with a skin disease that lasted until the day the king died. So the king lived in a separate house. The king's son Jotham was in charge of the palace and governed the country.

[6]Isn't everything else about Azariah—everything he did—written in the official records of the kings of Judah? [7]Azariah lay down in death with his ancestors and was buried with them in the City of David. His son Jotham succeeded him as king.

King Zechariah of Israel Rules for Six Months

[8]In Azariah's thirty-eighth year as king of Judah, Jeroboam's son Zechariah was king of Israel in Samaria for six months. [9]He did what the LORD considered evil, as his ancestors had done. He didn't turn away from the sins that Jeroboam (Nebat's son) led Israel to commit. [10]Shallum, son of Jabesh, plotted against Zechariah, attacked him at Kabal Am, killed him, and succeeded him as king. [11]Everything else about Zechariah is written in the official records of the kings of Israel. [12]It happened exactly as the LORD had told Jehu: "Four generations of your descendants will sit on the throne of Israel."

King Shallum of Israel Rules for One Month

[13]Shallum, son of Jabesh, became king in Azariah's thirty-ninth year as king of Judah. Shallum ruled for an entire month in Samaria. [14]Then Menahem, son of Gadi, came from Tirzah to Samaria, attacked Shallum (son of Jabesh), killed him, and succeeded him as king. [15]Everything else about Shallum—all about his conspiracy—is written in the official records of the kings of Israel. [16]Then Menahem attacked Tiphsah, everyone there, and its territory. Because the city didn't open its gates for him, he attacked it and ripped open all its pregnant women.

King Menahem of Israel

[17]In Azariah's thirty-ninth year as king of Judah, Menahem, son of Gadi, began to rule as king of Israel. He ruled for 10 years in Samaria. [18]He did what the LORD considered evil. During his entire life he never turned away from the sins that Jeroboam (Nebat's son) led Israel to commit.

[19]King Pul of Assyria came to attack the country. So Menahem gave Pul 75,000 pounds of silver to gain his support and help strengthen his hold on the kingdom.

---

[a] 14:28 Syriac; Masoretic Text "for Judah in Israel."   [a] 15:1 In the Masoretic Text this king of Judah is also called Uzziah.

²⁰Menahem raised the money from all the wealthy men in Israel. Each gave 20 ounces of silver for the king of Assyria. Then the king of Assyria left the country. ²¹Isn't everything else about Menahem—everything he did—written in the official records of the kings of Israel? ²²Menahem lay down in death with his ancestors, and his son Pekahiah succeeded him as king.

King Pekahiah of Israel

²³In Azariah's fiftieth year as king of Judah, Menahem's son Pekahiah began to rule. Pekahiah was king of Israel in Samaria for two years. ²⁴He did what the LORD considered evil. He didn't turn away from the sins that Jeroboam (Nebat's son) led Israel to commit. ²⁵His officer Pekah, son of Remaliah, plotted against him. With 50 men from Gilead, Pekah attacked Pekahiah, Argob, and Arieh in the fortress of the royal palace in Samaria. Pekah killed him and succeeded him as king. ²⁶Everything else about Pekahiah—everything he did—is written in the official records of the kings of Israel.

King Pekah of Israel

²⁷In Azariah's fifty-second year as king of Judah, Pekah, son of Remaliah, began to rule Israel in Samaria. He ruled for 20 years. ²⁸He did what the LORD considered evil. He did not turn away from the sins that Jeroboam (Nebat's son) led Israel to commit. ²⁹In the days of King Pekah of Israel, King Tiglath Pileser of Assyria took Ijon, Abel Beth Maacah, Janoah, Kedesh, Hazor, Gilead, Galilee, and the entire territory of Naphtali. He also took the people away to Assyria as captives. ³⁰Hoshea, son of Elah, plotted against Pekah, son of Remaliah. Hoshea attacked him and killed him. Hoshea began to rule as king in his place in the twentieth year that Jotham, son of Azariah, was king of Judah. ³¹Everything else about Pekah—everything he did—is written in the official records of the kings of Israel.

King Jotham of Judah—
2 Chronicles 27:1-9

³²In the second year that King Pekah, son of Remaliah, ruled Israel, Jotham, son of Azariah, began to rule as king of Judah. ³³He was 25 years old when he began to rule. He ruled for 16 years in Jerusalem. His mother was Jerusha, daughter of Zadok. ³⁴He did what the LORD considered right, as his father Azariah had done. ³⁵But the illegal places of worship were not torn down. The people continued to offer sacrifices and burn incense at these worship sites. Jotham built the Upper Gate of the LORD's temple. ³⁶Isn't everything else about Jotham—everything he did—written in the official records of the kings of Judah?

³⁷In those days the LORD began to use King Rezin of Aram and Pekah, son of Remaliah, to attack Judah. ³⁸Jotham lay down in death with his ancestors and was buried with them in the city of his ancestor David. His son Ahaz succeeded him as king.

King Ahaz of Judah—
2 Chronicles 28:1-27

16 ¹Pekah, son of Remaliah, was in his seventeenth year as king of Israel when King Ahaz, son of Jotham, began to rule as king of Judah. ²Ahaz was 20 years old when he began to rule. He ruled for 26 years in Jerusalem. He didn't do what the LORD his God considered right, as his ancestor David had done. ³He followed the example of the kings of Israel and even sacrificed his son by burning him alive. Sacrificing children was one of the disgusting things done by the nations that the LORD had forced out of the Israelites' way. [4]He offered sacrifices and burned incense as an offering at the illegal worship sites, which were on hills and under every large tree.

[5]Then King Rezin of Aram and King Pekah, son of Remaliah of Israel, came to wage war against Jerusalem. They blockaded Ahaz but couldn't get him to fight. [6]At that time King Rezin of Aram drove the Judeans out of Elath and gave it back to Edom.[a] The Edomites came to Elath and still live there today.

[7]Ahaz sent messengers to King Tiglath Pileser of Assyria to say, "I'm your servant, your son. Come and save me from the kings of Aram and Israel who are attacking me." [8]Ahaz took the silver and gold he found in the LORD's temple and in the treasury in the royal palace and sent them to the king of Assyria as a present.

[9]The king of Assyria listened to him and attacked Damascus. He captured it, took the people to Kir as captives, and killed Rezin.

[10]Then King Ahaz went to Damascus to meet King Tiglath Pileser of Assyria. He saw an altar there in Damascus. So King Ahaz sent the priest Urijah a model of the altar and a set of detailed plans. [11]Urijah built an altar exactly like the model King Ahaz sent from Damascus. He finished it before Ahaz returned home from Damascus.

[12]When the king came from Damascus, he saw the altar. The king approached the altar and went up to it. [13]He sacrificed his burnt offering and grain offering, poured out his wine offering, and sprinkled the blood of his fellowship offering on the altar. [14]But he moved the bronze altar dedicated to the LORD. It had been in front of the temple between his altar and the LORD's temple. Ahaz put it on the north side of his altar. [15]King Ahaz gave this command to the priest Urijah: "On this great altar you must burn the morning burnt offerings and the evening grain offering, the king's burnt offerings and grain offerings, and the burnt offerings, grain offerings, and wine offerings of all the people of the land. Sprinkle all the blood of the burnt offerings and other sacrifices on it. I will use the bronze altar for prayer." [16]The priest Urijah did what King Ahaz had commanded.

[17]King Ahaz cut off the side panels of the bronze stands used in the temple and removed the basin from each of them. He took the bronze pool down from the bronze bulls that were under it and set it on a stone base. [18]Ahaz removed the covered walkway used on the day of worship. This walkway had been built in the temple. He also removed the outer entrance for the king from the LORD's temple. He did this to please the king of Assyria. [19]Isn't everything else about Ahaz—the things he did—written in the official records of the kings of Judah? [20]Ahaz lay down in death with his ancestors and was buried with them in the City of David. His son Hezekiah succeeded him as king.

King Hoshea of Israel

[1]In Ahaz's twelfth year as king of Judah, Hoshea, son of Elah, began to rule as king of Israel in Samaria. He ruled for nine years. [2]He did what the LORD considered evil, but he didn't do what the kings of Israel before him had done.

The Fall of Samaria

[3]King Shalmaneser of Assyria defeated Hoshea, who became his servant and was required to make annual payments to him. [4]The king of Assyria found Hoshea to be a traitor. (Hoshea had sent messengers to King Dais of Egypt and had stopped making annual payments to the king of Assyria.) So the king of Assyria arrested him and put him in prison. [5]Then the king of Assyria attacked the entire country. He attacked Samaria

---

[a] 16:6 Masoretic Text "Aram." (The Hebrew words for "Aram" and "Edom" are nearly identical.)

and blockaded it for three years. ⁶In Hoshea's ninth year as king of Israel, the king of Assyria captured Samaria and took the Israelites to Assyria as captives. He settled them in Halah, along the Habor River in Gozan, and in the cities of the Medes.

⁷The Israelites sinned against the LORD their God, who brought them out of Egypt and rescued them from the power of Pharaoh (the king of Egypt). They worshiped other gods ⁸and lived by the customs of the nations that the LORD had forced out of the Israelites' way. They also did what their kings wanted them to do. ⁹The Israelites secretly did things against the LORD their God that weren't right:

They built for themselves illegal places of worship in all of their cities, from the smallest watchtower to the largest fortified city.

¹⁰They set up sacred stones and poles dedicated to the goddess Asherah on every high hill and under every large tree.

¹¹At all the illegal places of worship, they sacrificed in the same way as the nations that the LORD had removed from the land ahead of them.

They did evil things and made the LORD furious.

¹²They served idols, although the LORD had said, "Never do this."

¹³The LORD had warned Israel and Judah through every kind of prophet and seer,ᵃ "Turn from your evil ways, and obey my commands and decrees as I commanded your ancestors in all my teachings, the commands I sent to you through my servants the prophets." ¹⁴But they refused to listen. They became as impossible to deal with as their ancestors who refused to trust the LORD their God. ¹⁵They rejected his decrees, the promiseᵇ he made to their ancestors, and the warnings he had given them. They went after worthless idols and became as worthless as the idols. They behaved like the nations around them, although the LORD had commanded them not to do that. ¹⁶They abandoned all the commands of the LORD their God:

They made two calves out of cast metal.

They made a pole dedicated to the goddess Asherah.

They prayed to the entire army of heaven.

They worshiped Baal.

¹⁷They sacrificed their sons and daughters by burning them alive.

They practiced black magic and cast evil spells.

They sold themselves by doing what the LORD considered evil, and they made him furious.

¹⁸The LORD became so angry with Israel that he removed them from his sight. Only the tribe of Judah was left. ¹⁹Even Judah didn't obey the commands of the LORD their God but lived according to Israel's customs. ²⁰So the LORD rejected all of Israel's descendants, made them suffer, handed them over to those who looted their property, and finally turned away from Israel.

²¹When he tore Israel away from the family of David, the people of Israel made Jeroboam (Nebat's son) king. Jeroboam forced Israel away from the LORD and led them to commit a serious sin. ²²The Israelites followed all the sins Jeroboam committed and never turned away from them. ²³Finally, the LORD turned away from Israel as he had said he would through all his servants, the prophets. So the people of Israel were taken from their land to Assyria as captives, and they are still there today.

Assyria Brings Foreign People to Settle in Israel

²⁴The king of Assyria brought people from Babylon, Cuthah, Avva, Hamath, and Sepharvaim and settled them in the cities of Samaria in place of the Israelites. They took over Samaria and lived in its cities.

ᵃ17:13 A seer is a prophet. ᵇ17:15 Or "covenant."

²⁵When they first came to live there, they didn't worship the LORD. So the LORD sent lions to kill some of them. ²⁶Then someone said to the king of Assyria, "The people you took as captives and settled in the cities of Samaria don't know the customs of the god of that country, so he sent lions. Now the lions are killing them because they don't know the customs of the god of this country."

²⁷The king of Assyria gave this command: "Bring one of the priests you captured from there. Let him go back to teach them the customs of the god of that country." ²⁸So one of the priests who had been taken prisoner from Samaria went to live in Bethel. He taught them how to worship the LORD.

²⁹But each group that settled in Samaria continued to make its own gods. They put them at the illegal places of worship, which the people of Samaria had made. Each group did this in the cities where they lived:

³⁰The people from Babylon made Succoth Benoth.

The people from Cuth made Nergal.

The people from Hamath made Ashima.

³¹The people from Avva made Nibhaz and Tartak.

The people from Sepharvaim burned their children for Adrammelech and Anammelech, the gods of Sepharvaim.

³²So while these people were worshiping the LORD, they also appointed all kinds of people to serve as priests for the shrines at their illegal places of worship. ³³They worshiped the LORD but also served their own gods according to the customs of the nations from which they had come.

³⁴Today they are still following their customs, as they've done from the beginning. They don't fear the LORD or live by the decrees, customs, teachings, or commands that the LORD gave to the descendants of Jacob (whom he named Israel). ³⁵When the LORD made a promise to Israel, he commanded, "Never worship other gods, bow down to them, serve them, or sacrifice to them. ³⁶Instead, worship the LORD, who used his great power and a mighty arm to bring you out of Egypt. Bow down to the LORD, and sacrifice to him. ³⁷Faithfully obey the laws, rules, teachings, and commands that he wrote for you: 'Never worship other gods. ³⁸Never forget the promise I made to you. Never worship other gods. ³⁹Instead, worship the LORD your God, and he will rescue you from your enemies.'"

⁴⁰The people of Israel had refused to listen and made up their own rules, as they had done from the beginning. ⁴¹These other nations worshiped the LORD but also served their own idols. So did their children and their grandchildren. They still do whatever their ancestors did.

King Hezekiah of Judah—
2 Chronicles 29:1-2

18 ¹King Hoshea, son of Elah, had been king in Israel for three years when King Hezekiah, son of Ahaz of Judah, began to rule as king. ²Hezekiah was 25 years old when he began to rule, and he ruled for 29 years in Jerusalem. His mother was Abi, daughter of Zechariah.

³He did what the LORD considered right, as his ancestor David had done. ⁴He got rid of the illegal places of worship, crushed the sacred stones, and cut down the poles dedicated to the goddess Asherah. He even crushed the bronze snake that Moses had made because up to that time the Israelites had been burning incense to it. They called it Nehushtan. ⁵Hezekiah trusted the LORD God of Israel. No king among all the kings of Judah was like Hezekiah. ⁶He was loyal to the LORD and never turned away from him. He obeyed the commands that the LORD had given through Moses, ⁷so the LORD was

with him. He succeeded in everything he tried: He rebelled against the king of Assyria and wouldn't serve him anymore. [8]He conquered the Philistines from the smallest watchtower to the largest fortified city all the way to Gaza and its territory.

The Fall of Samaria

[9]In Hezekiah's fourth year as king (which was the seventh year in the reign of King Hoshea, son of Elah of Israel) King Shalmaneser of Assyria attacked Samaria, blockaded it, [10]and captured it at the end of three years. Samaria was taken in Hezekiah's sixth year as king (which was Hoshea's ninth year as king of Israel). [11]The king of Assyria took the Israelites to Assyria as captives. He put them in Halah, along the Habor River in Gozan, and in the cities of the Medes. [12]This happened because they refused to obey the LORD their God and disregarded the conditions of the promise[a] he made to them. They refused to obey everything that Moses, the LORD's servant, had commanded.

The LORD Rescues Judah From the Assyrians—
2 Chronicles 32:1-23; Isaiah 36:1-37:20

[13]In Hezekiah's fourteenth year as king, King Sennacherib of Assyria attacked all the fortified cities of Judah and captured them. [14]Then King Hezekiah of Judah sent this message to the king of Assyria at Lachish: "I have done wrong. Go away, and leave me alone. I'll pay whatever penalty you give me."

So the king of Assyria demanded that King Hezekiah of Judah pay 22,500 pounds of silver and 2,250 pounds of gold. [15]Hezekiah gave him all the silver that could be found in the LORD's temple and in the royal palace treasury. [16]At that time Hezekiah stripped the gold off the doors and doorposts of the LORD's temple. (Earlier Hezekiah had them covered with gold.) He gave the gold to the king of Assyria.

[17]Then the king of Assyria sent his commander-in-chief, his quartermaster, and his field commander with a large army from Lachish to King Hezekiah at Jerusalem. They came there and stood at the channel for the Upper Pool on the road to the Laundryman's Field. [18]When they called for King Hezekiah, Eliakim, who was in charge of the palace and was the son of Hilkiah, Shebnah the scribe, and Joah, who was the royal historian and the son of Asaph, went out to the field commander.

[19]He said to them, "Tell Hezekiah, 'This is what the great king, the king of Assyria, says: What makes you so confident? [20]You give useless advice about getting ready for war. Whom, then, do you trust for support in your rebellion against me? [21]Now, look! When you trust Egypt, you're trusting a broken stick for a staff. If you lean on it, it stabs your hand and goes through it. This is what Pharaoh (the king of Egypt) is like for everyone who trusts him. [22]Suppose you tell me, "We're trusting the LORD our God." He's the god whose places of worship and altars Hezekiah got rid of. He told Judah and Jerusalem, "Worship at this altar in Jerusalem." '

[23]"Now, make a deal with my master, the king of Assyria. I'll give you 2,000 horses if you can put riders on them. [24]How can you defeat my master's lowest-ranking officers when you trust Egypt for chariots and horses?

[25]"Have I come to destroy this place without the LORD on my side? The LORD said to me, 'Attack this country, and destroy it.' "

[26]Then Eliakim (son of Hilkiah), Shebnah, and Joah said to the field commander, "Speak to us in Aramaic, since we understand it. Don't speak to us in the Judean language as long as there are people on the wall listening."

[a]18:12 Or "covenant."

Women's World

Languages / *2 Kings 18:26*

How many languages do you know? The field commander from Assyria knew Hebrew and Aramaic. The picture shows how different from English Hebrew and Aramaic are. The first column contains the English alphabet. The second column contains the Aramaic alphabet. The third column contains the Hebrew alphabet.

²⁷But the field commander asked them, "Did my master send me to tell these things only to you and your master? Didn't he send me to the men sitting on the wall who will have to eat their own excrement and drink their own urine with you?"

²⁸Then the field commander stood and shouted loudly in the Judean language, "Listen to the great king, the king of Assyria. ²⁹This is what the king says: Don't let Hezekiah deceive you. He can't rescue you from me. ³⁰Don't let Hezekiah get you to trust the LORD by saying, 'The LORD will certainly rescue us, and this city will not be put under the control of the king of Assyria.' ³¹Don't listen to Hezekiah, because this is what the king of Assyria says: Make peace with me! Come out and give yourselves up to me! Everyone will eat from his own grapevine and fig tree and drink from his own cistern. ³²Then I will come and take you away to a country like your own. It's a country with grain and new wine, a country with bread and vineyards, a country with olive trees, olive oil, and honey. Live! Don't die! Don't listen to Hezekiah when he tries to mislead you by saying to you, 'The LORD will rescue us.' ³³Did any of the gods of the nations rescue their countries from the king of Assyria? ³⁴Where are the gods of Hamath and Arpad? Where are the gods of Sepharvaim, Hena, and Ivvah? Did they rescue Samaria from my control? ³⁵Did the gods of those countries rescue them from my control? Could the LORD then rescue Jerusalem from my control?"

³⁶But the people were silent and didn't say anything to him because the king commanded them not to answer him.

³⁷Then Eliakim, who was in charge of the palace and was the son of Hilkiah, Shebna the scribe, and Joah, who was the royal historian and the son of Asaph, went to Hezekiah with their clothes torn in grief. They told him the message from the field commander. ¹When King Hezekiah heard the message, he tore his clothes in grief, covered himself with sackcloth, and went into the LORD's temple. ²Then he sent Eliakim, who was in charge of the palace, Shebna the scribe, and the leaders of the priests, clothed in sackcloth, to the prophet Isaiah, son of Amoz.

³They said to him, "This is what Hezekiah says: Today is a day filled with misery, punishment, and disgrace. We are like a woman who is about to give birth but doesn't have the strength to do it. ⁴The LORD your God may have heard all the words of the field commander. His master, the king of Assyria, sent him to defy the living God. The LORD your God may punish him because of the message that the LORD your God heard. Pray for the few people who are left."

⁵So King Hezekiah's men went to Isaiah. ⁶Isaiah answered them, "Say this to your master, 'This is what the LORD says: Don't be afraid of the message that you heard when the Assyrian king's assistants slandered me. ⁷I'm going to put a spirit in him so that he will hear a rumor and return to his own country. I'll have him assassinated in his own country.' "

⁸The field commander returned and found the king of Assyria fighting against Libnah. He had heard that the king left Lachish. ⁹Now, Sennacherib heard that King Tirhakah of Sudan was coming to fight him.

Sennacherib sent messengers to Hezekiah, saying, ¹⁰"Tell King Hezekiah of Judah, 'Don't let the god whom you trust deceive you by saying that Jerusalem will not be put under the control of the king of Assyria. ¹¹You heard what the kings of Assyria did to all countries, how they totally destroyed them. Will you be rescued? ¹²Did the gods of the nations which my ancestors destroyed rescue Gozan, Haran, Rezeph, and the people of Eden who were in Telassar? ¹³Where is the king of Hamath, the king of Arpad, and the king of the cities of Sepharvaim, Hena, and Ivvah?' "

¹⁴Hezekiah took the letters from the messengers, read them, and went to the LORD's temple. He spread them out in front of the LORD ¹⁵and prayed to the LORD, "LORD of Armies, God of Israel, you are enthroned over the angels.ᵃ You alone are God of all the kingdoms of the world. You made heaven and earth. ¹⁶Turn your ear toward me, LORD, and listen. Open your eyes, LORD, and see. Listen to the message that Sennacherib sent to defy the living God. ¹⁷It is true, LORD, that the kings of Assyria have leveled nations.ᵇ ¹⁸They have thrown the gods from these countries into fires because these gods aren't real gods. They're only wooden and stone statues made by human hands. So the Assyrians have destroyed them. ¹⁹Now, LORD our God, rescue us from Assyria's control so that all the kingdoms on earth will know that you alone are the LORD God."

Isaiah's Prophecy Against King Sennacherib of Assyria—
Isaiah 37:21-38

²⁰Then Isaiah, son of Amoz, sent a message to Hezekiah, "This is what the LORD God of Israel says: You prayed to me about King Sennacherib of Assyria. I have heard you. ²¹This is the message that the LORD speaks to him,

> 'My dear people in Zion despise you and laugh at you.
> My people in Jerusalem shake their heads behind your back.
²²   Whom are you defying and slandering?
>   Against whom are you shouting?
>   Who are you looking at so arrogantly?
>   It is the Holy One of Israel!
²³   Through your servantsᶜ you defy the Lord and say,
>   "With my many chariots I'll ride up the high mountains,
>   up the slopes of Lebanon.
>   I'll cut down its tallest cedars and its finest cypresses.
>   I'll come to its most distant borders
>   and its most fertile forests.
²⁴   I'll dig wells and drink foreign water.
>   I'll dry up all the streams of Egypt
>   with the trampling of my feet."

ᵃ19:15 Or "cherubim."   ᵇ19:17 Greek; Masoretic Text "nations and their country."   ᶜ19:23 Isaiah 37:24; Masoretic Text "kings."

²⁵ " 'Haven't you heard? I did this long ago.
   I planned it in the distant past.
      Now I make it happen so that you will turn fortified cities
         into piles of rubble.
²⁶ Those who live in these cities are weak, discouraged, and ashamed.
   They will be like plants in the field,
      like fresh, green grass on the roofs,
         scorched before it sprouted.
²⁷ I know when you get up and sit down,
      when you go out and come in,
         and how you rage against me.
²⁸ Since you rage against me and your boasting has reached my ears,
      I will put my hook in your nose
         and my bridle in your mouth.
   I will make you go back the way you came.

²⁹" 'And this will be a sign for you, Hezekiah: You will eat what grows by itself this year and next year. But in the third year you will plant and harvest, plant vineyards, and eat what is produced. ³⁰Those few people from the nation of Judah who escape will again take root and produce crops. ³¹Those few people will go out from Jerusalem, and those who escape will go out of Mount Zion. The Lord is determined to do this.'

³²"This is what the Lord says about the king of Assyria:

He will never come into this city,
   shoot an arrow here,
   hold a shield in front of it,
      or put up dirt ramps to attack it.
³³ He will go back the way he came,
      and he won't come into this city,"
         declares the Lord of Armies.
³⁴ "I will shield this city to rescue it for my sake
      and for the sake of my servant David."

³⁵It happened that night. The Lord's angel went out and killed 185,000 soldiers in the Assyrian camp. When the Judeans got up early in the morning, they saw all the corpses.
³⁶Then King Sennacherib of Assyria left. He went home to Nineveh and stayed there. ³⁷While he was worshiping in the temple of his god Nisroch, Adrammelech and Sharezer assassinated him and escaped to the land of Ararat. His son Esarhaddon succeeded him as king.

Hezekiah's Illness—
2 Chronicles 32:24; Isaiah 38:1-8, 21-22

20 ¹In those days Hezekiah became sick and was about to die. The prophet Isaiah, son of Amoz, came to him and said, "This is what the Lord says: Give final instructions to your household, because you're about to die. You won't get well."

²Hezekiah turned to the wall and prayed to the Lord, ³"Please, Lord, remember how I've lived faithfully and sincerely in your presence. I've done what you consider right." And he cried bitterly.

⁴Isaiah hadn't gone as far as the middle courtyard when the Lord spoke his word

to him: ⁵"Go back and say to Hezekiah, leader of my people, 'This is what the LORD God of your ancestor David says: I've heard your prayer. I've seen your tears. Now I'm going to heal you. The day after tomorrow you will go to the LORD's temple. ⁶I'll give you 15 more years to live. I'll rescue you and defend this city from the control of the king of Assyria for my sake and for the sake of my servant David.' "

⁷Then Isaiah said, "Get a fig cake, and put it on the boil so that the king will get well."

⁸Hezekiah asked Isaiah, "What is the sign that the LORD will heal me and that I'll go to the LORD's temple the day after tomorrow?"

⁹Isaiah said, "This is your sign from the LORD that he will do what he promises. Do you want the shadow to go forward ten steps or come back ten steps?"

¹⁰Hezekiah replied, "It's easy for the shadow to extend ten more steps forward. No, let it come back ten steps."

¹¹Then the prophet Isaiah called on the LORD, and the LORD made the shadow that had gone down on Ahaz's stairway go back up ten steps.

Hezekiah Shows the Babylonians His Treasures—
2 Chronicles 32:31-33; Isaiah 39:1-8

¹²At that time Baladan's son, King Merodach Baladan of Babylon, sent letters and a present to Hezekiah because he heard that Hezekiah had been sick. ¹³Hezekiah was so happy with them that he showed the messengers his warehouse: the silver, gold, balsam, fine olive oil, his entire armory, and everything in his treasury. Hezekiah showed them everything in his palace and every corner of his kingdom.

¹⁴Then the prophet Isaiah came to King Hezekiah and asked, "What did these men say? And where did they come from?"

Hezekiah answered, "They came to me from the distant country of Babylon."

¹⁵Isaiah asked, "What did they see in your palace?"

Hezekiah answered, "They saw everything in my palace, and I showed them everything in my treasury."

¹⁶Isaiah said to Hezekiah, "Hear the word of the LORD! ¹⁷The LORD says, 'The days are going to come when everything in your palace, everything your ancestors have stored up to this day, will be taken away to Babylon. Nothing will be left. ¹⁸Some of your own descendants will be taken away. They will become officials in the palace of the king of Babylon.' "

¹⁹Hezekiah said to Isaiah, "The LORD's word that you have spoken is good." He added, "Isn't it enough if there is peace and security as long as I live?"

Good Morning, God
2 Kings 20:1-6

When King Hezekiah was told he was about to die, he cried bitterly. The Lord heard Hezekiah's sorrow and had compassion for him. God gave Hezekiah another 15 years to live. Some people might make fun of you for expressing your feelings.

Hezekiah's story reminds us that God cares about the way we feel. He will comfort us when we need to cry.

Lord, thank you for giving me feelings and healthy ways to express them.

²⁰Isn't everything else about Hezekiah, all his heroic acts and how he made the pool and tunnel to bring water into the city, written in the official records of the kings of Judah? ²¹Hezekiah lay down in death with his ancestors. His son Manasseh succeeded him as king.

King Manasseh of Judah—
2 Chronicles 33:1-20

¹Manasseh was 12 years old when he began to rule, and he ruled for 55 years in Jerusalem. His mother's name was Hephzibah.

²He did what the LORD considered evil by copying the disgusting things done by the nations that the LORD had forced out of the Israelites' way. ³He rebuilt the illegal places of worship that his father Hezekiah had destroyed. He set up altars dedicated to Baal and made a pole dedicated to the goddess Asherah as King Ahab of Israel had done. Manasseh, like Ahab, worshiped and served the entire army of heaven. ⁴He built altars in the LORD's temple, where the LORD had said, "I will put my name in Jerusalem." ⁵In the two courtyards of the LORD's temple, he built altars for the entire army of heaven. ⁶He burned his son as a sacrifice, consulted fortunetellers, cast evil spells, and appointed royal mediums and psychics. He did many things that made the LORD furious. ⁷Manasseh had an idol of Asherah made. Then he set it up in the temple, where the LORD had said to David and his son Solomon, "I have chosen this temple and Jerusalem from all the tribes of Israel. I will put my name here forever. ⁸I will never again make Israel's feet wander from the land that I gave to their ancestors if they will obey all the commands and all the Teachings that my servant Moses gave them." ⁹(But they wouldn't obey.) Manasseh misled Israel so that they did more evil things than the nations that the LORD had destroyed when the Israelites arrived in the land.

¹⁰Then the LORD spoke through his servants the prophets: ¹¹"King Manasseh of Judah has done disgusting things, things more evil than what the Amorites who were here before him had done. Manasseh has also made Judah sin by worshiping his idols. ¹²So this is what I, the LORD God of Israel, said: I'm going to bring such a disaster on Jerusalem and Judah that the ears of everyone who hears about it will ring. ¹³I will measure Jerusalem with the measuring line used for Samaria and the plumb line used for Ahab's dynasty. I will wipe out Jerusalem in the same way that a dish is wiped out and turned upside down. ¹⁴I will abandon the rest of my people. I will put them under the control of their enemies, and they will become property that their enemies capture. ¹⁵I will do this because they have done what I consider evil and have been making me furious from the time their ancestors left Egypt until this day."

¹⁶In addition to his sin that he led Judah to commit in front of the LORD, Manasseh also killed a lot of innocent people from one end of Jerusalem to the other. ¹⁷Isn't everything else about Manasseh—everything he did, the sins he committed—written in the official records of the kings of Judah? ¹⁸Manasseh lay down in death with his ancestors. He was buried in the garden of his own palace, in the garden of Uzza. His son Amon succeeded him as king.

King Amon of Judah—
2 Chronicles 33:21-25

¹⁹Amon was 22 years old when he began to rule, and he ruled for 2 years in Jerusalem. His mother was Meshullemeth, daughter of Haruz from Jotbah. ²⁰He did what the LORD considered evil, as his father Manasseh had done. ²¹He lived like his father in every way and worshiped and prayed to the idols his father had worshiped. ²²He abandoned the LORD God of his ancestors and didn't live the LORD's way. ²³Amon's

officials plotted against him and killed him in his palace. [24]Then the people of the land killed everyone who had plotted against King Amon. They made his son Josiah king in his place. [25]Isn't everything else about Amon—the things he did—written in the official record of the kings of Judah? [26]He was buried in his tomb in the garden of Uzza. His son Josiah succeeded him as king.

King Josiah of Judah—
2 Chronicles 34:1-2

[1]Josiah was 8 years old when he began to rule, and he was king for 31 years in Jerusalem. His mother was Jedidah, daughter of Adaiah from Bozkath. [2]Josiah did what the LORD considered right. He lived in the ways of his ancestor David and never stopped.

The Book of the LORD's Teachings Found in the Temple—
2 Chronicles 34:8-28

[3]In Josiah's eighteenth year as king of Judah, he sent the scribe Shaphan, son of Azaliah and grandson of Meshullam, to the LORD's temple with these instructions: [4]"Go to the chief priest Hilkiah. Have him count the money that has been brought into the LORD's temple, the money that the doorkeepers have collected from the people. [5]Give some of it to the foremen who are in charge of the LORD's temple. They should give it to the workmen who are making repairs on the LORD's temple. [6](These workers include the carpenters, builders, and masons.) Also, use the rest of the money to buy lumber and quarried stones to repair the temple. [7]Since the workmen are honest, don't require them to account for the money you give them."

[8]The chief priest Hilkiah told the scribe Shaphan, "I have found the Book of Moses' Teachings in the LORD's temple." Hilkiah gave the book to Shaphan, who then read it.

[9]The scribe Shaphan went to the king and reported, "We have taken the money donated in the temple and have given it to the workmen who are in charge of the LORD's temple." [10]Then the scribe Shaphan told the king, "The priest Hilkiah has given me a book." And Shaphan read it to the king.

[11]When the king heard what the book of the Teachings said, he tore his clothes in distress. [12]Then the king gave an order to the priest Hilkiah, to Ahikam (son of Shaphan), Achbor (son of Micaiah), the scribe Shaphan, and the royal official Asaiah. He said, [13]"On behalf of the people, all of Judah, and me, ask the LORD about the words in this book that has been found. The LORD's fierce anger is directed towards us because our ancestors did not obey the things in this book or do everything written in it."[a]

[14]So the priest Hilkiah, Ahikam, Achbor, Shaphan, and Asaiah went to talk to the prophet Huldah. She was the wife of Shallum, son of Tikvah and grandson of Harhas. Shallum was in charge of the royal wardrobe. Huldah was living in the Second Part of Jerusalem.

[15]She told them, "This is what the LORD God of Israel says: Tell the man who sent you to me, [16]This is what the LORD says: I'm going to bring disaster on this place and on the people living here according to everything written in the book that the king of Judah has read. [17]I will do this because they have abandoned me and sacrificed to other gods in order to make me furious. Therefore, my burning anger directed at this place will never be extinguished.' "

[18]Huldah added, "But tell Judah's king who sent you to me to ask the LORD a question, 'This is what the LORD God of Israel says about the words you heard: [19]You had a change of heart and humbled yourself in front of the LORD when you heard my

---
[a]22:13 Masoretic Text adds "about us."

words against this place and those who live here. I had said that those who live here will be destroyed and cursed. You also tore your clothes ˌin distressˌ and cried in front of me. So I will listen ˌto youˌ, declares the Lord. ²⁰That is why I'm going to bring you to your ancestors. I'm going to bring you to your grave in peace, and your eyes will not see any of the disaster I'm going to bring on this place.' "

So they reported this to the king.

King Josiah's Religious Reforms—
2 Chronicles 34:29-33, 4-7; 35:1-27; 36:1

¹Then the king sent for all the respected leaders of Judah and Jerusalem to join him. ²The king, everyone in Judah, everyone living in Jerusalem, the priests, the prophets, and all the people (young and old) went to the Lord's temple. Josiah read everything written in the Book of the Promiseᵃ found in the Lord's temple so that they could hear it. ³The king stood beside the pillar and made a promise to the Lord that he would follow the Lord and obey his commands, instructions, and laws with all his heart and soul. He confirmed the terms of the promise written in this book. And all the people joined in the promise.

⁴Then the king ordered the chief priest Hilkiah, the priests who served under Hilkiah, and the doorkeepers to take out of the Lord's temple all the utensils that had been made for Baal, Asherah, and the entire army of heaven. Josiah burned the utensils outside Jerusalem in an open field near the Kidron Brook. Then he carried their ashes to Bethel.

⁵He got rid of the pagan priests whom the kings of Judah had appointed to sacrifice at the illegal places of worship in the cities of Judah and all around Jerusalem. They had been sacrificing to Baal, the sun god, the moon god, the zodiac, and the entire army of heaven. ⁶He took the pole dedicated to the goddess Asherah from the temple to the Kidron Valley outside Jerusalem. He burned it in the Kidron Valley, ground it to dust, and threw its ashes on the tombs of the common people. ⁷He tore down the houses of the male temple prostitutes who were in the Lord's temple, where women did weaving for Asherah.

⁸He brought all the priests out of the cities of Judah from Geba to Beersheba and made the places where those priests sacrificed unclean.ᵇ He tore down the worship site at the entrance of the Gate of Joshua, the gate named after the mayor of the city. (The worship site was to the left of anyone going through the city gate.)

⁹The priests of the illegal worship sites had never gone to the Lord's altar in Jerusalem. Instead, they ate their unleavened bread among the other worshipers.

¹⁰Josiah also made Topheth in the valley of Ben Hinnom unclean so that people would never again sacrifice their sons or daughters by burning them to the god Molech.

¹¹He removed the horses that Judah's kings had dedicated to the sun god at the entrance of the Lord's temple. They were in the temple courtyard near the room of the eunuch Nathan Melech. He also burned the chariots of the sun god, ¹²the altars that Judah's kings had made and placed on the roof of Ahaz's upstairs room, and the altars Manasseh had made in the two courtyards of the Lord's temple. The king tore them down from there, crushed them, and dumped their rubble in the Kidron Valley.

¹³The king made the illegal places of worship east of Jerusalem unclean. They were on the southern part of the Hill of Destruction. King Solomon of Israel had built them for Astarte (the disgusting goddess of the Sidonians), Chemosh (the disgusting god of Moab), and Milcom (the disgusting god of the Ammonites). ¹⁴Josiah crushed the

---

ᵃ 23:2 Or "Covenant." ᵇ 23:8 "Unclean" refers to anything that Moses' Teachings say is not presentable to God.

sacred stones, cut down the poles dedicated to Asherah, and filled their places with human bones. [15]He also tore down the altar at Bethel—the place of worship made by Jeroboam (Nebat's son), who had made Israel sin. He tore down both the altar and the place of worship. They burned the worship site, crushing it to powder and burning the pole dedicated to Asherah.

[16]When Josiah turned and saw the tombs on the hill there, he sent men to take the bones out of the tombs and burn them on the altar to make it unclean. This fulfilled the word of the LORD announced by the man of God. [17]Then he asked, "What is this monument that I see?"

The people of the city answered him, "It's the tomb of the man of God who came from Judah to announce that you would do these things to the altar of Bethel."

[18]So Josiah said, "Let him rest. Don't disturb his bones." So they left his bones with the bones of the prophet who had come from Samaria.

[19]Josiah also got rid of all the temples at the illegal places of worship in the cities of Samaria. The kings of Israel had built these places to make the LORD furious. He did to them everything that he had done to the worship places at Bethel. [20]He slaughtered all the priests of the illegal worship sites on their altars and then burned human bones on them. He went back to Jerusalem.

[21]The king ordered all the people to celebrate the Passover for the LORD their God as it is written in this Book of the Promise. [22]The Passover had never been celebrated like this during the time of the judges who governed Israel or during the entire time of the kings of Israel and Judah. [23]But in the eighteenth year of King Josiah's reign, this Passover was celebrated in Jerusalem for the LORD.

[24]Josiah also got rid of the mediums, psychics, family idols, other idols, and disgusting gods that could be seen in the land of Judah and in Jerusalem. He did this to confirm the words of the Teachings written in the book that the priest Hilkiah found in the LORD's temple.

[25]No king before Josiah had turned to the LORD with all his heart, soul, and strength, as directed in Moses' Teachings. No other king was like Josiah.

[26]But the LORD still didn't turn his hot, burning anger from Judah. After all, Manasseh had done all these things to make him furious. [27]The LORD had said, "I will put Judah out of my sight as I put Israel out of my sight. I will reject Jerusalem, the city that I chose, and I will reject the temple where I said my name would be."

[28]Isn't everything else about Josiah—everything he did—written in the official records of the kings of Judah?

[29]In Josiah's days Pharaoh Necoh (the king of Egypt) came to help the king of Assyria at the Euphrates River. King Josiah went to attack Necoh. When Pharaoh saw him at Megiddo, Pharaoh killed him. [30]His officers put his dead body in a chariot and brought it from Megiddo to Jerusalem. They buried Josiah in his tomb.

King Jehoahaz of Judah—
2 Chronicles 36:1-4

Then the people of the land took Josiah's son Jehoahaz, anointed him, and made him king in place of his father. [31]Jehoahaz was 23 years old when he became king, and he was king for 3 months in Jerusalem. His mother was Hamutal, daughter of Jeremiah from Libnah. [32]He did what the LORD considered evil, as his ancestors had done. [33]Pharaoh Necoh made him a prisoner at Riblah in the territory of Hamath during his reign[c] in Jerusalem and fined the country 7,500 pounds of silver and 75 pounds of gold.

---

[c]23:33 Or "to keep him from ruling."

³⁴Then Pharaoh Necoh made Josiah's son Eliakim king in place of his father Josiah and changed Eliakim's name to Jehoiakim. He took Jehoahaz away to Egypt, where he died. ³⁵Jehoiakim gave Pharaoh the silver and the gold. But he had to tax the country to pay the silver Pharaoh had demanded. He taxed each person according to his wealth so that he could get the silver and gold from the people of the land and give it to Pharaoh Necoh.

King Jehoiakim of Judah—
2 Chronicles 36:5-8

³⁶Jehoiakim was 25 years old when he began to rule, and he was king for 11 years in Jerusalem. His mother was Zebidah, daughter of Pedaiah from Rumah. ³⁷Jehoiakim did what the LORD considered evil, as his ancestors had done.

¹During Jehoiakim's reign King Nebuchadnezzar of Babylon attacked Judah, and Jehoiakim became subject to him for three years. Then Jehoiakim turned against him and rebelled.

²The LORD sent raiding parties of Babylonians, Arameans, Moabites, and Ammonites against Jehoiakim to destroy Judah as the LORD had predicted through his servants the prophets. ³Without a doubt, this happened to Judah because the LORD had commanded it to happen. He wanted to remove the people of Judah from his sight because of Manasseh's sins—everything he had done, ⁴including the innocent blood he had shed. He had a lot of innocent people in Jerusalem killed, and the LORD refused to forgive him.

⁵Isn't everything else about Jehoiakim—everything he did—written in the official records of the kings of Judah? ⁶Jehoiakim lay down in death with his ancestors, and his son Jehoiakin succeeded him as king.

⁷The king of Egypt didn't leave his own country again because the king of Babylon had taken all the territory from the River of Egypt to the Euphrates River. This territory had belonged to the king of Egypt.

King Jehoiakin of Judah—
2 Chronicles 36:9-10

⁸Jehoiakin was 18 years old when he began to rule as king. He was king for three months in Jerusalem. His mother was Nehushta, daughter of Elnathan from Jerusalem. ⁹Jehoiakin did what the LORD considered evil, as his father had done.

¹⁰At that time the officers of King Nebuchadnezzar of Babylon attacked Jerusalem. (The city was blockaded.) ¹¹King Nebuchadnezzar of Babylon arrived while his officers were blockading the city. ¹²King Jehoiakin of Judah, his mother, officials, generals, and eunuchs surrendered to the king of Babylon. In the eighth year of his reign, the king of Babylon captured Jehoiakin. ¹³He also took away all the treasures in the LORD's temple and the royal palace. As the LORD had predicted, Nebuchadnezzar stripped the gold off all the furnishings that King Solomon of Israel had made for the LORD's temple. ¹⁴He captured all Jerusalem, all the generals, all the soldiers (10,000 prisoners), and all the craftsmen and smiths. Only the poorest people of the land were left. ¹⁵He took Jehoiakin to Babylon as a captive. He also took the king's mother, wives, eunuchs, and the leading citizens of the land from Jerusalem as captives to Babylon. ¹⁶The king of Babylon brought all 7,000 of the prominent landowners, 1,000 craftsmen and smiths, and all the men who could fight in war as captives to Babylon.

King Zedekiah of Judah—
2 Chronicles 36:11-13; Jeremiah 52:1-3

[17]The king of Babylon made King Jehoiakin's Uncle Mattaniah king in his place and changed Mattaniah's name to Zedekiah. [18]Zedekiah was 21 years old when he began to rule, and he ruled for 11 years in Jerusalem. His mother was Hamutal, daughter of Jeremiah from Libnah. [19]Zedekiah did what the LORD considered evil, as Jehoiakim had done.

[20]The LORD became angry with Jerusalem and Judah and threw the people out of his sight.

Zedekiah rebelled against the king of Babylon.

The Fall of Jerusalem—
2 Chronicles 36:19-21; Jeremiah 39:1-10; 40:5-9; 41:1-3, 16-18; 52:4-30

[1]On the tenth day of the tenth month of the ninth year of Zedekiah's reign, King Nebuchadnezzar of Babylon attacked Jerusalem with his entire army. They set up camp and built dirt ramps around the city walls. [2]The blockade of the city lasted until Zedekiah's eleventh year as king. [3]On the ninth day of the fourth[a] month, the famine in the city became so severe that the common people had no food.

[4]The enemy broke through the city walls that night. All Judah's soldiers left on the road of the gate between the two walls beside the king's garden. While the Babylonians were attacking the city from all sides, the king took the road to the plain of Jericho. [5]The Babylonian army pursued King Zedekiah and caught up with him in the plain of Jericho. His entire army had deserted him. [6]The Babylonians captured the king, brought him to the king of Babylon at Riblah, and passed sentence on him. [7]They slaughtered Zedekiah's sons as he watched, and then they blinded Zedekiah. They put him in bronze shackles and took him to Babylon.

[8]On the seventh day of the fifth month of Nebuchadnezzar's nineteenth year as king of Babylon, Nebuzaradan, who was the captain of the guard and an officer of the king of Babylon, came to Jerusalem. [9]He burned down the LORD's temple, the royal palace, and all the houses in Jerusalem. Every important building was burned down. [10]The entire Babylonian army that was with the captain of the guard tore down the walls around Jerusalem.

[11]Nebuzaradan, the captain of the guard, captured the few people left in the city, those who surrendered to the king of Babylon, and the rest of the population. [12]The captain of the guard left some of the poorest people in the land to work in the vineyards and on the farms.

[13]The Babylonians broke apart the bronze pillars of the LORD's temple, the stands, and the bronze pool in the LORD's temple. They shipped the bronze to Babylon. [14]They took the pots, shovels, snuffers, dishes, and all the bronze utensils used in the temple service. [15]The captain of the guard took all of the incense burners and bowls that were made of gold or silver. [16]The bronze from the two pillars, the pool, and the stands that Solomon had made for the LORD's temple couldn't be weighed. [17]One pillar was 27 feet high and had a bronze capital on it that was 4½ feet high. The filigree and the pomegranates around the capital were all made of bronze. The second pillar and its filigree were the same.

[18]The captain of the guard took the chief priest Seraiah, the second priest Zephaniah, and the 3 doorkeepers. [19]From the city he also took an army commander, 5 men who had access to the king whom he found in the city, the scribe who was in charge

---
[a]25:3 Jeremiah 39:2; 52:6; Masoretic Text omits "fourth."

of the militia, and 60 of the common people whom he found in the city. [20]Nebuzaradan, the captain of the guard, took them and brought them to the king of Babylon at Riblah. [21]The king of Babylon executed them at Riblah in the territory of Hamath. So the people of Judah were captives when they left their land.

[22]King Nebuchadnezzar of Babylon appointed Gedaliah, son of Ahikam and grandson of Shaphan, to govern the remaining people in the land of Judah. [23]When all the army commanders and their men heard that the king of Babylon had appointed Gedaliah, they went to Gedaliah at Mizpah. They were Ishmael (son of Nethaniah), Johanan (son of Kareah), Seraiah (son of Tanhumeth from Netophah), and Jaazaniah from Beth Maacah and their men. [24]Gedaliah swore an oath to them and their men. He said, "Don't be afraid of the Babylonian officers. Live in this country, serve the king of Babylon, and you will prosper."

[25]In the seventh month Ishmael (son of Nethaniah and grandson of Elishama, a descendant of the kings) went with ten men to kill Gedaliah and the Judeans and Babylonians who were with him at Mizpah. [26]Then people of all classes and the army commanders left for Egypt because they were afraid of the Babylonians.

King Jehoiakin Released From Prison—
Jeremiah 52:31-34

[27]On the twenty-seventh day of the twelfth month of the thirty-seventh year of the imprisonment of King Jehoiakin of Judah, King Evil Merodach of Babylon, in the first year of his reign, freed King Jehoiakin of Judah from prison. [28]He treated him well and gave him a special position higher than the other kings who were with him in Babylon. [29]Jehoiakin no longer wore prison clothes, and he ate his meals in the king's presence as long as he lived. [30]The king of Babylon gave him a daily food allowance as long as he lived.

1 Chronicles

This book describes David's rule as king of
Israel. It was written to remind
Israel of God's faithfulness. It tells of
the good works of King David,
especially of his plans to worship
God at a great temple. However,
the book does not mention David's
sin with Bathsheba or his family troubles.
When God forgives, he doesn't keep a
record of our wrongs. But the Lord never
forgets the good things we do.

Why is David dancing for joy?
See 1 Chronicles 15.

A Job for
Everyone

Look at all the different jobs people had when David was king. Some were warriors. Some were priests who led worship. There were artists, builders, secretaries, judges, farmers, and shepherds. Every job was important because each person helped to make the kingdom a success.

Do you have a special job in your family? The work you do helps your family become a success. Because families are important to God, doing your job is a way you can serve God now.

What's In It For Me?

There are lots of ways I can serve God . . .

PRAY TO THE LORD.
SING A HYMN.
HELP MY PARENTS.
BRING A FRIEND TO CHURCH.
GIVE TO SOMEONE IN NEED.

Do Families Matter?

What difference does your family make in your community? Today we know that families make a big difference in people's lives. That's why politicians talk a lot about "strengthening the family."

Family is very important in the Bible. The Israelites kept careful records of their families. These records are called *genealogies*. The first nine chapters of 1 Chronicles record the genealogies of the Jews who returned to their homeland after being captives in Babylon.

Family is important to us, too. God designed the family, starting with Adam and Eve. God intended families to be a blessing. We can be thankful for the family we have. Even if we live with only one parent, other relatives, or adoptive or foster parents, we can find love in our family. If our family teaches us to grow up to love God and do what's right, we're blessed in our family.

There's something else worth remembering about families. No matter who we live with, we have God as our Heavenly Father. He loves us, and he will always be there for us.

RIDDLES

Which tribe makes a good sandwich?
Reuben

Which tribe wore blue jeans?
Levi

What has four wheels and sits in the driveway?
Issachar

1 Chronicles

The Genealogy of Isaac's Descendants—
Genesis 5:1-32; 10:1-32; 11:10-26; 25:1-4, 12-16; 36:1-43

¹Adam, Seth, Enosh, ²Kenan, Mahalalel, Jared, ³Enoch, Methuselah, Lamech, ⁴Noah: Shem, Ham, and Japheth.

⁵Japheth's descendants were Gomer, Magog, Madai, Javan, Tubal, Meshech, and Tiras. ⁶Gomer's descendants were Ashkenaz, Riphath, and Togarmah. ⁷Javan's descendants were the people from Elishah, Tarshish, Cyprus, and Rhodes.

⁸Ham's descendants were Cush, Egypt, Put, and Canaan. ⁹Cush's descendants were Seba, Havilah, Sabta, Raama, and Sabteca. Raama's descendants were Sheba and Dedan. ¹⁰Cush was the father of Nimrod, the first mighty warrior on the earth. ¹¹Egypt was the ancestor of the Ludites, Anamites, Lehabites, Naphtuhites, ¹²Pathrusites, Casluhites (from whom the Philistines came), and the Caphtorites. ¹³Canaan was the father of Sidon his firstborn, then Heth, ¹⁴also the Jebusites, the Amorites, the Girgashites, ¹⁵the Hivites, the Arkites, the Sinites, ¹⁶the Arvadites, the Zemarites, and the Hamathites.

¹⁷The descendants of Shem were Elam, Asshur, Arpachshad, Lud, Aram, Uz, Hul, Gether, and Meshech. ¹⁸Arpachshad was the father of Shelah, and Shelah was the father of Eber. ¹⁹Two sons were born to Eber. The name of the one was Peleg [Division], because in his day the earth was divided. His brother's name was Joktan. ²⁰Joktan was the father of Almodad, Sheleph, Hazarmaveth, Jerah, ²¹Hadoram, Uzal, Diklah, ²²Ebal, Abimael, Sheba, ²³Ophir, Havilah, and Jobab. All these were sons of Joktan.

²⁴Shem, Arpachshad, Shelah, ²⁵Eber, Peleg, Reu, ²⁶Serug, Nahor, Terah, ²⁷Abram (that is, Abraham). ²⁸Abraham's sons were Isaac and Ishmael.

²⁹This is their list of descendants: Ishmael's firstborn was Nebaioth, then Kedar, Adbeel, Mibsam, ³⁰Mishma, Dumah, Massa, Hadad, Tema, ³¹Jetur, Naphish, and Kedemah. These were the sons of Ishmael.

³²Keturah, Abraham's concubine,ᵃ gave birth to the following sons: Zimran, Jokshan, Medan, Midian, Ishbak, and Shuah. Jokshan's sons were Sheba and Dedan. ³³The sons of Midian were Ephah, Epher, Hanoch, Abida, and Eldaah. All these were descendants of Keturah.

³⁴Abraham was the father of Isaac. Isaac's sons were Esau and Israel. ³⁵Esau's sons were Eliphaz, Reuel, Jeush, Jalam, and Korah. ³⁶Eliphaz's sons were Teman and Omar, Zephi and Gatam, Kenaz and Amalek, son of Timna.ᵇ ³⁷Reuel's sons were Nahath, Zerah, Shammah, and Mizzah. ³⁸Seir's sons were Lotan, Shobal, Zibeon, Anah, Dishon, Ezer, and Dishan. ³⁹Lotan's sons were Hori and Homam. Timna was Lotan's sister. ⁴⁰Shobal's sons were Alian, Manahath, Ebal, Shephi, and Onam. Zibeon's sons were Aiah and Anah. ⁴¹Anah's son was Dishon. Dishon's sons were Hamran, Eshban, Ithran, and Cheran. ⁴²Ezer's sons were Bilhan, Zaavan, and Jaakan. Dishan's sons were Uz and Aran.

⁴³These were the kings who ruled Edom before any king ruled the people of Israel: Bela, son of Beor, and the name of his ͺcapitalͺ city was Dinhabah. ⁴⁴After Bela died, Jobab, son of Zerah from Bozrah, succeeded him as king. ⁴⁵After Jobab died,

---

ᵃ1:32 A concubine is considered a wife except she has fewer rights under the law.   ᵇ1:36 Genesis 36:12, Greek; Masoretic Text "Kenaz, and Timnath, and Amalek."

Husham from the land of the Temanites succeeded him as king. ⁴⁶After Husham died, Hadad, son of Bedad, who defeated the Midianites in the country of Moab, succeeded him as king, and the name of his ˎcapitalˎ city was Avith. ⁴⁷After Hadad died, Samlah from Masrekah succeeded him as king. ⁴⁸After Samlah died, Shaul from Rehoboth on the river succeeded him as king. ⁴⁹After Shaul died, Baal Hanan, son of Achbor, succeeded him as king. ⁵⁰After Baal Hanan died, Hadad succeeded him as king, and the name of his ˎcapitalˎ city was Pai. His wife's name was Mehetabel, daughter of Matred and granddaughter of Mezahab. ⁵¹Then Hadad died.

The tribal leaders of Edom were Timna, Aliah, Jetheth, ⁵²Oholibamah, Elah, Pinon, ⁵³Kenaz, Teman, Mibzar, ⁵⁴Magdiel, and Iram. These were the tribal leaders of Edom.

Israel's Twelve Sons—
Genesis 35:16-26

¹These were Israel's sons: Reuben, Simeon, Levi, Judah, Issachar, Zebulun, ²Dan, Joseph, Benjamin, Naphtali, Gad, and Asher.

Judah's Descendants—
Genesis 46:12

³Judah's sons were Er, Onan, and Shelah. These three were born to him by Bathshua, a Canaanite woman. The LORD considered Er, Judah's firstborn, evil, so the LORD killed Er. ⁴Tamar, Judah's daughter-in-law, gave birth to Judah's sons Perez and Zerah. Judah had five sons in all.

⁵Perez's sons were Hezron and Hamul. ⁶Zerah's sons were Zimri, Ethan, Heman, Calcol, and Dara*ᵃ*—five in all. ⁷Carmi's son was Achar, who caused trouble for Israel by taking goods that were claimed by God. ⁸Ethan's son was Azariah.

⁹The sons born to Hezron were Jerahmeel, Ram, and Chelubai. ¹⁰Ram was the father of Amminadab. Amminadab was the father of Nahshon, leader of Judah's people. ¹¹Nahshon was the father of Salma, and Salma was the father of Boaz. ¹²Boaz was the father of Obed, and Obed was the father of Jesse. ¹³Jesse was the father of Eliab (his firstborn), Abinadab (his second son), Shimea (his third son), ¹⁴Nethanel (his fourth son), Raddai (his fifth son), ¹⁵Ozem (his sixth son), and David (his seventh son). ¹⁶Their sisters were Zeruiah and Abigail. Zeruiah's three sons were Abishai, Joab, and Asahel. ¹⁷Abigail was the mother of Amasa, whose father was Jether, a descendant of Ishmael.

¹⁸Hezron's son was Caleb. Caleb and his wife Azubah had a son named Jerioth.

Rewards
1 Chronicles 2:9-17

It's great when others praise you. Maybe you have terrific grades. Maybe you're good at sports. Maybe you're always kind or willing to help others. All the names listed in the first chapters of this Bible book remind us that God keeps track of everyone. He knows the good things you do and remembers them, too.

---

*ᵃ*2:6 Some Hebrew manuscripts; other Hebrew manuscripts, 1 Kings 5:11, Greek, Syriac, Targum, Egyptian "Darda."

Her other sons were Jesher, Shobab, and Ardon. ¹⁹After Azubah died, Caleb married Ephrath. She gave birth to Hur. ²⁰Hur was the father of Uri, and Uri was the father of Bezalel.

²¹Afterwards, Hezron slept with the daughter of Machir, the man who first settled Gilead. Hezron had married her when he was 60 years old. She gave birth to Segub. ²²Segub was the father of Jair, who had 23 towns in Gilead. ²³Geshur and Aram captured Havvoth Jair with Kenath and its villages (60 cities in all). All of these people were descendants of Machir, the man who first settled Gilead. ²⁴After Hezron died in Caleb Ephrathah, Hezron's wife Abijah gave birth to Ashhur, who first settled Tekoa.

²⁵Jerahmeel (the firstborn son of Hezron) fathered Ram (his firstborn), then Bunah, Oren, Ozem, and Ahijah. ²⁶Jerahmeel had another wife. Her name was Atarah, and she was the mother of Onam.

²⁷The sons of Ram (the firstborn son of Jerahmeel) were Maaz, Jamin, and Eker. ²⁸Onam's sons were Shammai and Jada. Shammai's sons were Nadab and Abishur. ²⁹The name of Abishur's wife was Abihail. She gave birth to Ahban and Molid. ³⁰Nadab's sons were Seled and Appaim, but Seled died without children. ³¹Appaim's son was Ishi, and Ishi's son was Sheshan, and Sheshan's son was Ahlai. ³²The sons of Jada (Shammai's brother) were Jether and Jonathan. Jether died without children. ³³Jonathan's sons were Peleth and Zaza. These were the descendants of Jerahmeel.

³⁴Sheshan had no sons, but he had daughters. He had an Egyptian slave named Jarha. ³⁵Sheshan let Jarha marry one of his daughters. She gave birth to Attai. ³⁶Attai was the father of Nathan. Nathan was the father of Zabad. ³⁷Zabad was the father of Ephlal. Ephlal was the father of Obed. ³⁸Obed was the father of Jehu. Jehu was the father of Azariah. ³⁹Azariah was the father of Helez. Helez was the father of Eleasah. ⁴⁰Eleasah was the father of Sismai. Sismai was the father of Shallum. ⁴¹Shallum was the father of Jekamiah. Jekamiah was the father of Elishama.

⁴²The descendants of Caleb (Jerahmeel's brother) were his firstborn son Mesha, who first settled Ziph, and the sons of Mareshah, who first settled Hebron. ⁴³Hebron's sons were Korah, Tappuah, Rekem, and Shema. ⁴⁴Shema was the father of Raham, who first settled Jorkeam. Rekem was the father of Shammai. ⁴⁵Shammai's son was Maon, who first settled Beth Zur. ⁴⁶Ephah, Caleb's concubine,ᵇ was the mother of Haran, Moza, and Gazez. Haran was the father of Gazez. ⁴⁷Jahdai's sons were Regem, Jotham, Geshan, Pelet, Ephah, and Shaaph. ⁴⁸Maacah, Caleb's concubine, was the mother of Sheber and Tirhanah. ⁴⁹Also, she was the mother of Shaaph, who first settled Madmannah, and of Sheva, who first settled Machbenah and Gibea. Caleb's daughter was Achsah. ⁵⁰These people were the descendants of Caleb.

The sons of Hur, the firstborn son of Ephrath, were Shobal, who first settled Kiriath Jearim, ⁵¹Salma, who first settled Bethlehem, and Hareph, who first settled Beth Gadar. ⁵²Shobal, who first settled Kiriath Jearim, had these descendants: Haroeh, half of the Manahathites, ⁵³the families of Kiriath Jearim, the Ithrites, the Puthites, the Shumathites, and the Mishraites. From these people came the Zorahites and Eshtaolites.

⁵⁴The descendants of Salma, who first settled Bethlehem, were the Netophathites, Atroth, who first settled Beth Joab, half of the Manahathites, the Zorites, ⁵⁵and the families of scribes who lived at Jabez. These families were the people of Tira, Shimea, and Sucah. These people are the Kenites who came from Hammath. They first settled Beth Rechab.

ᵇ2:46 A concubine is considered a wife except she has fewer rights under the law.

Judah's Descendants: The Royal Family—
2 Samuel 3:2-5; 5:5, 13-16

¹These were David's sons who were born to him while he was in Hebron: His first son was Amnon, born, to Ahinoam from Jezreel. The second was Daniel, born, to Abigail from Carmel. ²The third was Absalom, born to Maacah (the daughter of King Talmai) from Geshur. The fourth was Adonijah, whose mother was Haggith. ³The fifth was Shephatiah, born, to Abital. The sixth was Ithream, born, to David's wife Eglah. ⁴Six sons were born to him in Hebron, where he ruled for seven years and six months. He ruled for 33 years in Jerusalem.

⁵These ,children, were born to David in Jerusalem: Shimea, Shobab, Nathan, and Solomon (the mother of these four was Ammiel's daughter Bathshua) and ⁶Ibhar, Elishama, Eliphelet, ⁷Nogah, Nepheg, Japhia, ⁸Elishama, Eliada, and Eliphelet (nine ,by other wives,). ⁹All of these were David's sons. Besides these, there were the sons of the concubines.ᵃ Tamar was their sister.

¹⁰Solomon's son was Rehoboam. Rehoboam's son was Abijah. Abijah's son was Asa. Asa's son was Jehoshaphat. ¹¹Jehoshaphat's son was Joram. Joram's son was Ahaziah. Ahaziah's son was Joash. ¹²Joash's son was Amaziah. Amaziah's son was Azariah. Azariah's son was Jotham. ¹³Jotham's son was Ahaz. Ahaz's son was Hezekiah. Hezekiah's son was Manasseh. ¹⁴Manasseh's son was Amon. Amon's son was Josiah. ¹⁵Josiah's firstborn son was Johanan, the second was Jehoiakim, the third was Zedekiah, and the fourth was Shallum. ¹⁶Jehoiakim's son was Jeconiah, whose son was Zedekiah.

¹⁷The descendants of the prisoner Jeconiah were his son Shealtiel, ¹⁸then Malchiram, Pedaiah, Shenazzar, Jekamiah, Hoshama, and Nedabiah. ¹⁹Pedaiah's sons were Zerubbabel and Shimei. Zerubbabel's sons were Meshullam and Hananiah, and Shelomith was their sister. ²⁰There were also five other sons: Hashubah, Ohel, Berechiah, Hasadiah, and Jushab Hesed. ²¹Hananiah's sons were Pelatiah and Jeshaiah. Jeshaiah's son was Rephaiah.ᵇ Rephaiah's son was Arnan. Arnan's son was Obadiah. Obadiah's son was Shecaniah.ᶜ ²²Shecaniah's son was Shemaiah. Shemaiah's six sons were Hattush, Igal, Bariah, Neariah, and Shaphat. ²³Neariah's three sons were Elioenai, Hizkiah, and Azrikam. ²⁴Elioenai's seven sons were Hodaviah, Eliashib, Pelaiah, Akkub, Johanan, Delaiah, and Anani.

More of Judah's Descendants

¹Judah's descendants were Perez, Hezron, Carmi, Hur, and Shobal. ²Reaiah, son of Shobal, was the father of Jahath. Jahath was the father of Ahumai and Lahad. These were the families of the Zorathites.

³These were the first settlers in Etam: Jezreel, Ishma, and Idbash. Their sister's name was Hazelelponi. ⁴Penuel was the father of Gedor, and Ezer was the father of Hushah. These were the sons of Hur, the firstborn of Ephrathah, who first settled Bethlehem.

⁵Ashhur, who first settled Tekoa, had two wives, Helah and Naarah. ⁶Naarah gave birth to Ahuzzam, Hepher, Temeni, and Haahashtari. These were Naarah's sons. ⁷Helah's sons were Zereth, Izohar, and Ethnan. ⁸Koz was the father of Anub and Zobebah, and he was the ancestor of the families of Aharhel, son of Harum.

⁹Jabez was more honorable than his brothers. His mother had named him Jabez [Painful], because she said that his birth was painful. ¹⁰Jabez prayed to the God of Israel,

---

ᵃ3:9 A concubine is considered a wife except she has fewer rights under the law. ᵇ3:21 Some Hebrew manuscripts, Greek, Latin; other Hebrew manuscripts "and Jeshiah, the sons of Rephaiah." ᶜ3:21 Greek, Latin; Masoretic Text "the sons of Arnan, the sons of Obadiah, the sons of Shecaniah."

"Please bless me and give me more territory. May your power be with me and free me from evil so that I will not be in pain." God gave him what he prayed for.

¹¹Chelub, Shuhah's brother, was the father of Mehir, who was the father of Eshton. ¹²Eshton was the first to settle Beth Rapha. He was the father of Paseah and Tehinnah, who first settled the city of Nahash. These were the men from Recah.

¹³Kenaz's sons were Othniel and Seraiah. The sons of Othniel were Hathath and Meonothai.ᵃ ¹⁴Meonothai was the father of Ophrah. Seraiah was the father of Joab, who first settled the valley of Craftsmen. (It was named this because they were craftsmen.) ¹⁵The sons of Caleb, son of Jephunneh, were Iru, Elah, and Naam. Elah's son was Kenaz.

¹⁶Jehallelel's sons were Ziph, Ziphah, Tiria, and Asarel. ¹⁷Ezrah's sons were Jether, Mered, Epher, and Jalon. His wife gave birth to Miriam, Shammai, and Ishbah, who first settled Eshtemoa. ¹⁸His Judean wife was the mother of Jered, who first settled Gedor, Heber, who first settled Soco, and Jekuthiel, who first settled Zanoah.

¹⁹The sons of Hodiah's wife, the sister of Naham, first settled Keilah of the Garmites and Eshtemoa of the Maacathites. ²⁰Shimon's sons were Amnon, Rinnah, Ben Hanan, and Tilon. Ishi's sons were Zoheth and Ben Zoheth.

²¹The descendants of Shelah, son of Judah, were Er, who first settled Lecah, Laadah, who first settled Mareshah, families of the guild of linen workers at Beth Ashbea, ²²Jokim, Joash, Saraph, and the men of Cozeba. Saraph ruled Moab and Jashubi Lehem (according to ancient records). ²³They were the potters who lived at Netaim and Gederah. They lived there with the king and did his work.

Simeon's Descendants

²⁴Simeon's sons were Nemuel, Jamin, Jarib, Zerah, and Shaul. ²⁵Shaul's son was Shallum. Shallum's son was Mibsam. Mibsam's son was Mishma. ²⁶Mishma's son was Hammuel. Hammuel's son was Zaccur. Zaccur's son was Shimei. ²⁷Shimei had 16 sons and 6 daughters. But his brothers didn't have many children, so their entire family didn't become as large as the people of Judah.

²⁸Simeon's descendants lived in Beersheba, Moladah, Hazar Shual, ²⁹Bilhah, Ezem, Tolad, ³⁰Bethuel, Hormah, Ziklag, ³¹Beth Marcaboth, Hazar Susim, Beth Biri, and Shaaraim. These were their cities until David became king. ³²Their five cities were Etam, Ain, Rimmon, Tochen, and Ashan. ³³They also had all the villages around these cities as far as the city of Baal. These places were where they lived, and they had their own genealogical records:

³⁴Meshobab, Jamlech, Joshah (son of Amaziah), ³⁵Joel, Jehu (son of Joshibiah, grandson of Seraiah, and great-grandson of Asiel), ³⁶Elioenai, Jaakobah, Jeshohaiah, Asaiah, Adiel, Jesimiel, Benaiah, and ³⁷Ziza (son of Shiphi, grandson of Allon, great-grandson of Jedaiah, a descendant of Shimri and Shemaiah). ³⁸These who are mentioned by name were leaders in their families, and the number of people in their households increased.

³⁹They moved to the outskirts of Gedor, on the east side of the valley, to find pasture for their flocks. ⁴⁰They found pasture that was rich and good. The land was vast, peaceful, and quiet because the Hamites used to live there. ⁴¹In the days of King Hezekiah of Judah, the men listed here knocked down tents and killed the Meunites. They claimed the Meunites for God and destroyed them. (Even today no Meunites live there.) They lived in that land in place of the Meunites in order to have pasture for their flocks. ⁴²Ishi's sons Pelatiah, Neariah, Rephaiah, and Uzziel led 500 of Simeon's male descendants to Mount Seir. ⁴³They killed the Amalekites who were left. Simeon's descendants still live there today.

ᵃ4:13 Greek; Masoretic Text omits "and Meonothai."

Reuben's Descendants

5 ¹These are the sons of Reuben, Israel's firstborn. (Although he was the firstborn, his rights as firstborn were given to his nephews, Joseph's sons, because he dishonored his father's bed. However, Joseph couldn't be listed in the genealogy as the firstborn son. ²Even though Judah was more prominent than his brothers and the prince was to come from him, Joseph received the rights as firstborn.)

³The sons of Reuben, Israel's firstborn, were Hanoch, Pallu, Hezron, and Carmi. ⁴Joel's son was Shemaiah. Shemaiah's son was Gog. Gog's son was Shimei. ⁵Shimei's son was Micah. Micah's son was Reaiah. Reaiah's son was Baal. ⁶Baal's son was Beerah. King Tiglath Pilneser of Assyria took him away as a captive. He was leader of the tribe of Reuben. ⁷Beerah's brothers according to their families, when they were enrolled in the genealogical records according to their ancestry, were as follows: The first was Jeiel, then Zechariah ⁸and Bela (son of Azaz, grandson of Shema, and great-grandson of Joel).

Reuben's descendants lived in Aroer as far as Nebo and Baal Meon. ⁹Some of them lived eastward as far as the edge of the desert that extends to the Euphrates River, because they had so much livestock in Gilead. ¹⁰In Saul's day they fought a war against the Hagrites, defeated them, and lived in their tents throughout the entire region east of Gilead.

Gad's Descendants

¹¹Gad's descendants lived next to Reuben's descendants in Bashan as far east as Salcah. ¹²One family descended from Gad's first son Joel. Another family descended from Gad's second son Shapham. Other families descended from Gad's sons Janai and Shaphat in Bashan. ¹³Their seven relatives by families were Michael, Meshullam, Sheba, Jorai, Jacan, Zia, and Eber. ¹⁴These were the sons of Abihail, who was the son of Huri, grandson of Jaroah, and great-grandson of Gilead. Gilead was the son of Michael, grandson of Jeshishai, great-grandson of Jahdo, and great-great-grandson of Buz. ¹⁵Ahi, son of Abdiel and grandson of Guni, was the head of their families. ¹⁶They lived in Gilead, in Bashan and its villages, and in the entire pastureland of Sharon to its extreme edges. ¹⁷All these people were recorded in genealogical records in the days of King Jotham of Judah and King Jeroboam of Israel.

Reuben, Gad, and Manasseh Fight Hagar's Descendants

¹⁸The descendants of Reuben, Gad, and half of the tribe of Manasseh had 44,760 soldiers ready to go to war. They were skilled fighters who could carry shields and swords and shoot arrows. ¹⁹They went to war against Hagar's descendants (including Jetur, Naphish, and Nodab) ²⁰and received help while fighting them. Hagar's descendants and the nations with them were handed over to Reuben's descendants. They had called out to God during the battle, and he answered their prayers because they trusted him. ²¹They confiscated the Hagrites' livestock: 50,000 of their camels, 250,000 sheep and goats, and 2,000 donkeys. They captured 100,000 people. ²²Many were killed in battle because this was God's war. Reuben, Gad, and half of the tribe of Manasseh lived in the Hagrites' land until the Assyrians captured them.

The Leaders of the Tribe of Manasseh East of the Jordan River

²³Half of the tribe of Manasseh lived in the land from Bashan to Baal Hermon, Senir, and Mount Hermon. The tribe members were numerous. ²⁴These were the heads of Manasseh's families: Epher, Ishi, Eliel, Azriel, Jeremiah, Hodaviah, and Jahdiel. They were soldiers who were famous heads of their families.

The Assyrians Capture Gad, Reuben, and Half of the Tribe of Manasseh

²⁵But Gad, Reuben, and half of the tribe of Manasseh were unfaithful to the God of their ancestors. They chased after the gods of the people of the land as if they were prostitutes. God had destroyed these people as the Israelites arrived. ²⁶Then the God of Israel led King Pul of Assyria (King Tiglath Pilneser of Assyria) to take Reuben, Gad, and half of the tribe of Manasseh into captivity. He brought them to Halah, Habor, Hara, and the Gozan River. They are still there today.

Levi's Descendants

*¹Levi's sons were Gershon, Kohath, and Merari. ²Kohath's sons were Amram, Izhar, Hebron, and Uzziel. ³Amram's children were Aaron, Moses, and Miriam. Aaron's sons were Nadab, Abihu, Eleazar, and Ithamar.

⁴Eleazar was the father of Phinehas. Phinehas was the father of Abishua. ⁵Abishua was the father of Bukki. Bukki was the father of Uzzi. ⁶Uzzi was the father of Zerahiah. Zerahiah was the father of Meraioth. ⁷Meraioth was the father of Amariah. Amariah was the father of Ahitub. ⁸Ahitub was the father of Zadok. Zadok was the father of Ahimaaz. ⁹Ahimaaz was the father of Azariah. Azariah was the father of Johanan. ¹⁰Johanan was the father of Azariah. (He was the one who served as priest in the temple Solomon built in Jerusalem.) ¹¹Azariah was the father of Amariah. Amariah was the father of Ahitub. ¹²Ahitub was the father of Zadok. Zadok was the father of Shallum. ¹³Shallum was the father of Hilkiah. Hilkiah was the father of Azariah. ¹⁴Azariah was the father of Seraiah. Seraiah was the father of Jehozadak. ¹⁵Jehozadak was taken captive when the Lord used Nebuchadnezzar to take Judah and Jerusalem away into captivity.

¹⁶Levi's sons were Gershom, Kohath, and Merari. ¹⁷These are the names of Gershom's sons: Libni and Shimei. ¹⁸Kohath's sons were Amram, Izhar, Hebron, and Uzziel. ¹⁹Merari's sons were Mahli and Mushi.

These are the descendants of Levi's sons. They are grouped by families: ²⁰Gershom's son was Libni. Libni's son was Jahath. Jahath's son was Zimmah. ²¹Zimmah's son was Joah. Joah's son was Iddo. Iddo's son was Zerah. Zerah's son was Jeatherai.

²²These were Kohath's descendants: Kohath's son was Amminadab. Amminadab's son was Korah. Korah's son was Assir. ²³Assir's son was Elkanah. Elkanah's son was Ebiasaph. Ebiasaph's son was Assir. ²⁴Assir's son was Tahath. Tahath's son was Uriel. Uriel's son was Uzziah. Uzziah's son was Shaul. ²⁵Elkanah's sons were Amasai and Ahimoth. ²⁶Ahimoth's son was Elkanah. Elkanah's son was Zophai. Zophai's son was Nahath. ²⁷Nahath's son was Eliab. Eliab's son was Jeroham. Jeroham's son was Elkanah. ²⁸Samuel's sons were Joel, who was his firstborn, and Abijah, who was his second son.

²⁹These were Merari's descendants: Merari's son was Mahli. Mahli's son was Libni. Libni's son was Shimei. Shimei's son was Uzzah. ³⁰Uzzah's son was Shimea. Shimea's son was Haggiah. Haggiah's son was Asaiah.

³¹David put men in charge of the music in the Lord's temple after the ark was placed there permanently. ³²They served as musicians in the courtyard in front of the tent of meeting until Solomon built the Lord's temple in Jerusalem. They performed their duties according to the regulations set down for them.

³³These are the men who served (their descendants also served):

*6:1 1 Chronicles 6:1-81 in English Bibles is 1 Chronicles 5:27–6:66 in the Hebrew Bible.

The musician Heman was from Kohath's family line. Heman was the son of Joel, who was the son of Samuel, [34]who was the son of Elkanah, who was the son of Jeroham, who was the son of Eliel, who was the son of Toah, [35]who was the son of Zuph, who was the son of Elkanah, who was the son of Mahath, who was the son of Amasai, [36]who was the son of Elkanah, who was the son of Joel, who was the son of Azariah, who was the son of Zephaniah, [37]who was the son of Tahath, who was the son of Assir, who was the son of Ebiasaph, who was the son of Korah, [38]who was the son of Izhar, who was the son of Kohath, who was the son of Levi, who was the son of Israel.

[39]Heman's relative Asaph stood on his right. He was the son of Berechiah, who was the son of Shimea, [40]who was the son of Michael, who was the son of Baaseiah, who was the son of Malchiah, [41]who was the son of Ethni, who was the son of Zerah, who was the son of Adaiah, [42]who was the son of Ethan, who was the son of Zimmah, who was the son of Shimei, [43]who was the son of Jahath, who was the son of Gershom, who was the son of Levi.

[44]On the left was Ethan, one of Heman's relatives descended from Merari. Ethan was the son of Kishi, who was the son of Abdi, who was the son of Malluch, [45]who was the son of Hashabiah, who was the son of Amaziah, who was the son of Hilkiah, [46]who was the son of Amzi, who was the son of Bani, who was the son of Shemer, [47]who was the son of Mahli, who was the son of Mushi, who was the son of Merari, who was the son of Levi.

[48]Their relatives, the Levites, were assigned all the other duties in the tent, the house of God.

[49]Aaron and his descendants offered sacrifices on the altar for burnt offerings and on the altar for incense. They did all the work in the most holy place and removed Israel's sins to make Israel acceptable to God. They did exactly what God's servant Moses had commanded.

[50]These were Aaron's descendants: His son was Eleazar. Eleazar's son was Phinehas. Phinehas' son was Abishua. [51]Abishua's son was Bukki. Bukki's son was Uzzi. Uzzi's son was Zerahiah. [52]Zerahiah's son was Meraioth. Meraioth's son was Amariah. Amariah's son was Ahitub. [53]Ahitub's son was Zadok. Zadok's son was Ahimaaz.

The Cities Belonging to Levi's Descendants

[54]These are the places where Levi's descendants lived, the places where they settled in the territory chosen for them when lots were drawn:

The first lot was drawn for the descendants of Aaron from the family descended from Kohath. [55]They were given Hebron in the territory of Judah as well as the pastureland around it, [56]but the fields belonging to the city and its villages were given to Caleb, son of Jephunneh. [57]Aaron's descendants were given Hebron as a city of refuge, Libnah with its pastureland, Jattir, Eshtemoa with its pastureland, [58]Hilen with its pastureland, Debir with its pastureland, [59]Ashan with its pastureland, and Beth Shemesh with its pastureland. [60]From the tribe of Benjamin, Aaron's descendants received Geba with its pastureland, Alemeth with its pastureland, and Anathoth with its pastureland. There was a total of 13 cities for their families.

[61]The rest of Kohath's descendants received 10 cities chosen by lot from the families of half of the tribe of Manasseh. [62]The families of Gershom's descendants were given 13 cities chosen by lot from the tribes of Issachar, Asher, Naphtali, and the part of the tribe of Manasseh that lived in Bashan.

⁶³The families of Merari's descendants were given 12 cities chosen by lot from the tribes of Reuben, Gad, and Zebulun. ⁶⁴So the Israelites gave the Levites the cities with their pasturelands. ⁶⁵They gave them the cities chosen by lot and mentioned here by name from the tribes of Judah, Simeon, and Benjamin. ⁶⁶Some of the families of Kohath's descendants had cities chosen by lot from the tribe of Ephraim. ⁶⁷They were given these cities of refuge: Shechem with its pastureland in the hills of Ephraim, Gezer with its pastureland, ⁶⁸Jokmeam with its pastureland, Beth Horon with its pastureland, ⁶⁹Aijalon with its pastureland, and Gath Rimmon with its pastureland. ⁷⁰From half of the tribe of Manasseh, they were given Aner with its pastureland and Bileam with its pastureland for the families of the rest of Kohath's descendants.

⁷¹Gershom's descendants received Golan in Bashan with its pastureland and Ashtaroth with its pastureland from the families of half of the tribe of Manasseh. ⁷²From the tribe of Issachar, they received Kedesh with its pastureland, Daberath with its pastureland, ⁷³Ramoth with its pastureland, and Anem with its pastureland. ⁷⁴From the tribe of Asher, they received Mashal with its pastureland, Abdon with its pastureland, ⁷⁵Hukok with its pastureland, and Rehob with its pastureland. ⁷⁶From the tribe of Naphtali, they received Kedesh in Galilee with its pastureland, Hammon with its pastureland, and Kiriathaim with its pastureland.

⁷⁷The rest of Merari's descendants received Rimmono with its pastureland and Tabor with its pastureland from the tribe of Zebulun. ⁷⁸From the tribe of Reuben,ᵇ Merari's descendants received land east of the Jordan River and across from Jericho: Bezer in the wilderness with its pastureland, Jahzah with its pastureland, ⁷⁹Kedemoth with its pastureland and Mephaath with its pastureland. ⁸⁰From the tribe of Gad, they received Ramoth in Gilead with its pastureland, Mahanaim with its pastureland, ⁸¹Heshbon with its pastureland, and Jazer with its pastureland.

Issachar's Descendants

¹Issachar's four sons were Tola, Puah, Jashub, and Shimron. ²Tola's sons were Uzzi, Rephaiah, Jeriel, Jahmai, Ibsam, and Shemuel. These men were heads of the families of Tola. They were soldiers grouped according to their ancestry. In David's day there were 22,600 of them. ³The five descendants of Uzzi were Izrahiah and Izrahiah's sons Michael, Obadiah, Joel, and Isshiah. All of them were heads of families. ⁴They had many wives and children. So in addition to these men grouped according to their ancestry and families, there were 36,000 soldiers. ⁵Their relatives (that is, all of Issachar's families) were fighting men. A total of 87,000 of them was recorded in the genealogy.

Benjamin's Descendants

⁶Benjamin had three sons: Bela, Becher, and Jediael. ⁷Bela's five sons were Ezbon, Uzzi, Uzziel, Jerimoth, and Iri. They were heads of families and fighting men. In the genealogy 22,034 of them were recorded. ⁸Becher's sons were Zemirah, Joash, Eliezer, Elioenai, Omri, Jeremoth, Abijah, Anathoth, and Alemeth. These were all of Becher's sons. ⁹In the genealogy 22,200 of them were recorded according to their ancestry (the heads of their families and fighting men). ¹⁰Jediael's son was Bilhan. Bilhan's sons

ᵇ6:78 The last part of verse 79 has been moved to verse 78 to express the complex Hebrew sentence structure more clearly in English.

were Jeush, Benjamin, Ehud, Chenaanah, Zethan, Tarshish, and Ahishahar. ¹¹All of these men were Jediael's descendants. They headed families that produced 17,200 fighting men who could go to war. ¹²The Shuppites and Huppites were Ir's descendants. The Hushites were descendants of someone else.

Naphtali's Descendants

¹³Naphtali's sons were Jahziel, Guni, Jezer, and Shallum. They were Bilhah's grandsons.

Manasseh's Descendants Who Lived West of the Jordan River

¹⁴Manasseh's sons were Asriel and Machir. Their mother was Manasseh's Aramean concubine.ᵃ Machir was the first to settle Gilead. ¹⁵He married a wife from the Huppites and Shuppites. His wife'sᵇ name was Maacah. The name of his second son was Zelophehad. Zelophehad had only daughters. ¹⁶Maacah, Machir's wife, had a son, and she named him Peresh. His brother's name was Sheresh, whose sons were Ulam and Rakem. ¹⁷Ulam's son was Bedan. These were the people of Gilead, descendants of Machir (son of Manasseh). ¹⁸Bedan's sister Hammolecheth gave birth to Ishhod, Abiezer, and Mahlah. ¹⁹Shemida's sons were Ahian, Shechem, Likhi, and Aniam.

Ephraim's Descendants

²⁰Ephraim's son was Shuthelah. Shuthelah's son was Bered. Bered's son was Tahath. Tahath's son was Eleadah. Eleadah's son was Tahath. ²¹Tahath's son was Zabad. Zabad's son was Shuthelah.

Ephraim's sons Ezer and Elead were killed by the men of Gath when they came to take their livestock. ²²Their father Ephraim mourned a long time, even though his brothers tried to comfort him. ²³Then he slept with his wife, and she became pregnant. She gave birth to a son, and Ephraim named him Beriah [Tragedy], because tragedy had come to his home. ²⁴Beriah's daughter was Sheerah, who built Upper and Lower Beth Horon and Uzzen Sheerah. ²⁵Beriah's son was Rephah. Rephah's son was Resheph. Resheph's son was Telah. Telah's son was Tahan. ²⁶Tahan's son was Ladan. Ladan's son was Ammihud. Ammihud's son was Elishama. ²⁷Elishama's son was Nun. Nun's son was Joshua.

²⁸The land and homes of Ephraim's descendants were in Bethel and its villages, Naaran to the east, Gezer with its villages to the west, Shechem and its villages, and as far as Gaza and its villages. ²⁹Next to Manasseh were Beth Shean and its villages, Taanach and its villages, Megiddo and its villages, and Dor and its villages. The descendants of Joseph, son of Israel, live in these cities.

Asher's Descendants

³⁰Asher's sons were Imnah, Ishvah, Ishvi, and Beriah. Their sister was Serah. ³¹Beriah's sons were Heber and Malchiel, who first settled Birzaith. ³²Heber was the father of Japhlet, Shomer, Hotham, and their sister Shua. ³³Japhlet's sons were Pasach, Bimhal, and Ashvath. These were Japhlet's sons. ³⁴The sons of his brother Shomer were Rohgah, Jehubbah, and Aram. ³⁵His brother Helem's sons were Zophah, Imna, Shelesh, and Amal. ³⁶Zophah's sons were Suah, Harnepher, Shual, Beri, Imrah, ³⁷Bezer, Hod, Shamma, Shilsha, Ithran, and Beera. ³⁸Jether's sons were Jephunneh, Pispa, and Ara. ³⁹Ulla's sons were Arah, Hanniel, and Rizia. ⁴⁰All of these men were Asher's

---

ᵃ7:14 A concubine is considered a wife except she has fewer rights under the law. ᵇ7:15 Or "sister's."

descendants—heads of their families, outstanding men, soldiers, and distinguished leaders. Their military roster had 26,000 recorded in it.

Benjamin's Descendants

¹Benjamin was the father of Bela (his firstborn), Ashbel (his second son), Aharah (his third son), ²Nohah (his fourth son), and Rapha (his fifth son). ³Bela's sons were Addar, Gera, Abihud, ⁴Abishua, Naaman, Ahoah, ⁵Gera, Shephuphan, and Huram.

⁶These were Ehud's sons, who were heads of the families living in Geba and who were taken away as captives to Manahath: ⁷Naaman, Ahijah, and Gera. Gera led the rest of them away as captives. He was the father of Uzza and Ahihud.

⁸Shaharaim divorced his wives Hushim and Baara. But later in Moab, ⁹he and his wife Hodesh had the following sons: Jobab, Zibia, Mesha, Malcam, ¹⁰Jeuz, Sachia, and Mirmah. All of Shaharaim's sons became heads of families. ¹¹He and Hushim were the parents of Abitub and Elpaal. ¹²Elpaal's sons were Eber, Misham, and Shemed (who built Ono, Lod, and Lod's villages).

¹³Beriah and Shema were the heads of the families who lived in Aijalon. They forced out the people living in Gath. ¹⁴Their brothers*a* were Shashak and Jeremoth. ¹⁵Beriah's sons were Zebadiah, Arad, Eder, ¹⁶Michael, Ishpah, and Joha. ¹⁷Elpaal's sons were Zebadiah, Meshullam, Hizki, Heber, ¹⁸Ishmerai, Izliah, and Jobab. ¹⁹Shimei's sons were Jakim, Zichri, Zabdi, ²⁰Elienai, Zillethai, Eliel, ²¹Adaiah, Beraiah, and Shimrath. ²²Shashak's sons were Ishpan, Eber, Eliel, ²³Abdon, Zichri, Hanan, ²⁴Hananiah, Elam, Anthothijah, ²⁵Iphdeiah, and Penuel. ²⁶Jeroham's sons were Shamsherai, Shehariah, Athaliah, ²⁷Jaareshiah, Elijah, and Zichri. ²⁸These were the heads of families listed by their ancestry. They were the heads of families. They lived in Jerusalem.

²⁹Jeiel,*b* who first settled Gibeon, lived in Gibeon, and his wife's name was Maacah. ³⁰His firstborn son was Abdon, then Zur, Kish, Baal, Nadab, ³¹Gedor, Ahio, Zecher, ³²and Mikloth, who was the father of Shimeah. They lived next to their relatives in Jerusalem. ³³Ner was the father of Kish. Kish was the father of Saul. Saul was the father of Jonathan, Malchishua, Abinadab, and Eshbaal. ³⁴Jonathan's son was Meribbaal, and Meribbaal was the father of Micah. ³⁵Micah's sons were Pithon, Melech, Tarea, and Ahaz. ³⁶Ahaz was the father of Jehoaddah. Jehoaddah was the father of Alemeth, Azmaveth, and Zimri. Zimri was the father of Moza. ³⁷Moza was the father of Binea. Binea's son was Raphah. Raphah's son was Eleasah. Eleasah's son was Azel. ³⁸Azel had six sons. Their names were Azrikam, Bocheru, Ishmael, Sheariah, Obadiah, and Hanan. All of these men were Azel's sons. ³⁹His brother Eshek's sons were Ulam (the firstborn), Jeush (the second son), and Eliphelet (the third son). ⁴⁰Ulam's sons were soldiers, skilled archers. They had many sons and grandsons, 150 in all. All of these men were Benjamin's descendants.

The People Who Lived in Jerusalem

¹All Israel was recorded in the genealogies in the Book of the Kings of Israel and Judah. The Israelites were taken away to Babylon as captives because they had sinned. ²The first to settle again on their property in their own cities were some Israelites, the priests, the Levites, and the temple servants.

³Jerusalem was settled by descendants of Judah, Benjamin, Ephraim, and Manasseh:

⁴From the descendants of Perez, son of Judah, was Uthai, who was the son of Ammihud, grandson of Omri, and great-grandson of Imri. (Imri's father

---

a 8:14 Greek; Masoretic Text "Ahio."   *b* 8:29 Dead Sea Scrolls, Greek, Targum, Latin, 1 Chronicles 9:35; Masoretic Text omits "Jeiel."

was Bani.) ⁵From the descendants of Shilah were Asaiah (the firstborn) and his sons. ⁶And from the descendants of Zerah were Jeuel and their relatives, 690 in all.

⁷From the descendants of Benjamin were Sallu (son of Meshullam, grandson of Hodaviah, and great-grandson of Hassenuah), ⁸Ibneiah (son of Jeroham), Elah (son of Uzzi and grandson of Michri), and Meshullam (son of Shephatiah, grandson of Reuel, and great-grandson of Ibniah), ⁹and their relatives according to their ancestry. All of these men were heads of their families. A total of 956 of them lived in Jerusalem.

¹⁰From the priests were Jedaiah, Jehoiarib, Jachin, ¹¹and Azariah. Azariah was the son of Hilkiah, grandson of Meshullam, and great-grandson of Zadok. Zadok's father was Meraioth, the son of Ahitub (the official in charge of God's temple). ¹²Also from the priests were Adaiah (son of Jeroham, grandson of Pashhur, and great-grandson of Malchiah) and Maasai (son of Adiel, grandson of Jahzerah, and great-grandson of Meshullam, whose father was Meshillemith, son of Immer). ¹³Their relatives who were heads of their families totaled 1,760 soldiers. They served in God's temple and settled in Jerusalem.

¹⁴From the Levites descended from Merari were Shemaiah (son of Hasshub, grandson of Azrikam, and great-grandson of Hashabiah), ¹⁵Bakbakkar, Heresh, Galal, Mattaniah (son of Mica, grandson of Zichri, and great-grandson of Asaph), ¹⁶Obadiah (son of Shemaiah, grandson of Galal, and great-grandson of Jeduthun), and Berechiah (son of Asa and grandson of Elkanah, who lived in the villages belonging to the Netophathites).

¹⁷The gatekeepers were Shallum, Akkub, Talmon, Ahiman, and their relatives. (Shallum was in charge.) ¹⁸Formerly, they were stationed at the king's gate on the east side. They were the gatekeepers for the Levite quarters.

¹⁹Shallum (son of Kore, grandson of Ebiasaph, great-grandson of Korah) and the members of his family (Korah's descendants) were responsible for serving as watchmen at the entrances to the tent, as their ancestors had been in charge of guarding the entrances to the LORD's camp. ²⁰(Phinehas, Eleazar's son, had been the official in charge of the gatekeepers, and the LORD was with him.) ²¹Zechariah, son of Meshelemiah, was the keeper at the entrance to the tent of meeting. ²²The men chosen to be gatekeepers at the entrances totaled 212. Their genealogies were recorded in their villages. David and the seer*ᵃ* Samuel appointed them to these positions because they were trustworthy. ²³So they and their descendants were assigned to be gatekeepers for the LORD's house, that is, the tent.

²⁴The gatekeepers were on the four sides (east, west, north, and south). ²⁵Their relatives had to come from their villages from time to time. They would come to serve under the gatekeepers' supervision for a period of seven days. ²⁶The four chief Levite gatekeepers were in charge of the rooms and treasures in God's temple because of their faithfulness. ²⁷They would spend the night stationed around God's temple because they had to guard it and open it every morning.

²⁸Some of them were in charge of the utensils for worship. They would count them when they brought them in and when they took them out. ²⁹Other descendants of Korah were placed in charge of the utensils, the holy utensils, the flour, wine, olive oil, incense, and spices. ³⁰Some of the priests' sons prepared the mixture of spices. ³¹Mattithiah, a Levite, the firstborn son of Shallum, Korah's descendant, was entrusted with preparing the flat bread. ³²Some of their Kohathite relatives were responsible for setting the bread out in rows every day of worship.

ᵃ9:22 A seer is a prophet.

³³These were the musicians who were the heads of the Levite families. They lived in rooms in the temple and were free from other duties because they were on duty day and night. ³⁴They were the heads of the Levite families according to their ancestry. These head Levites lived in Jerusalem.

Saul's Descendants

³⁵Jeiel, who first settled Gibeon, lived in Gibeon, and his wife's name was Maacah. ³⁶His firstborn son was Abdon, then Zur, Kish, Baal, Nadab, ³⁷Gedor, Ahio, Zechariah, and Mikloth. ³⁸Mikloth was the father of Shimeam. They lived next to their relatives in Jerusalem. ³⁹Ner was the father of Kish. Kish was the father of Saul. Saul was the father of Jonathan, Malchishua, Abinadab, and Eshbaal. ⁴⁰Jonathan's son was Meribbaal, and Meribbaal was the father of Micah. ⁴¹Micah's sons were Pithon, Melech, and Tarea. ⁴²Ahaz was the father of Jarah. Jarah was the father of Alemeth, Azmaveth, and Zimri. Zimri was the father of Moza. ⁴³Moza was the father of Binea. Binea's son was Rephaiah. Rephaiah's son was Eleasah. Eleasah's son was Azel. ⁴⁴Azel had six sons. Their names were Azrikam, Bocheru, Ishmael, Sheariah, Obadiah, and Hanan. All of these men were Azel's sons.

The Death of Saul—
1 Samuel 31:1-13

10 ¹When the Philistines fought against Israel, the men of Israel fled from the Philistines and were killed in battle on Mount Gilboa. ²The Philistines caught up to Saul and his sons. They killed Jonathan, Abinadab, and Malchishua, Saul's sons. ³The heaviest fighting was against Saul. When the archers got him in their range, he was wounded by them.

⁴Saul told his armorbearer, "Draw your sword! Stab me, or these godless men will come and make fun of me." But his armorbearer refused because he was terrified. So Saul took the sword and fell on it. ⁵When the armorbearer saw that Saul was dead, he also fell on the sword and died. ⁶So Saul, his three sons, and his dynasty died together.

⁷When all the people of Israel in the valley saw that their army had fled and that Saul and his sons were dead, they abandoned their cities. So the Philistines came to live in these cities.

⁸The next day, when the Philistines came to strip the dead, they found Saul and his sons lying on Mount Gilboa. ⁹They stripped him and took his head and his armor. Then they sent men throughout Philistine territory to tell their idols and the people this good news. ¹⁰They put his armor in the temple of their gods and fastened his head to the temple of Dagon.

¹¹When all the people of Jabesh Gilead heard about everything the Philistines had done to Saul, ¹²all the fighting men came and took away the dead bodies of Saul and his sons and brought them to Jabesh. They buried the bones under the oak tree in Jabesh. Then they fasted seven days.

¹³So Saul died because of his unfaithfulness to the LORD: He did not obey the word of the LORD. He asked a medium to request information from a dead person. ¹⁴He didn't request information from the LORD. So the LORD killed him and turned the kingship over to David, Jesse's son.

David Anointed King of Israel—
2 Samuel 5:1-3

11 ¹All Israel gathered around David at Hebron. "We are your own flesh and blood," they said. ²"Even in the past when Saul ruled, you were the one who led Israel on its campaigns to war. The LORD your God has said to you, 'You will be shepherd of my people Israel, the leader of my people Israel.' "

³All the leaders of Israel had come to Hebron. David made an agreement with them at Hebron in front of the LORD. So they anointed David king of Israel, as the LORD had spoken through Samuel.

David Captures Jerusalem—
2 Samuel 5:6-10

⁴David and all Israel went to Jerusalem (that is, Jebus). The Jebusites were living in that region. ⁵They told David, "You will never get in here." But David captured the fortress Zion (that is, the City of David).

⁶Now, David said, "Whoever is the first to kill a Jebusite will be made a general and a prince." Zeruiah's son Joab was the first to go ˌinto Jerusalemˌ, so he became the general.

⁷David lived in the fortress, so it was called the City of David. ⁸He built the city ˌof Jerusalemˌ around it, starting from the Millo*ᵃ* and making a complete circuit. Joab rebuilt the rest of the city. ⁹David continued to grow more powerful because the LORD of Armies was with him.

David's Three Fighting Men—
2 Samuel 23:8-17

¹⁰Now, these were the commanders of David's fighting men, who exercised power with him in his kingdom, and with all Israel they made him king according to the LORD's word to Israel. ¹¹The first of David's fighting men was Jashobeam, son of Hachmon, the leader of the three.*ᵇ* He used his spear to kill 300 men on one occasion. ¹²Next in rank to him was Eleazar, another one of the three fighting men. He was the son of Dodo and grandson of Aho. ¹³Eleazar was with David at Pas Dammim when the Philistines gathered there for battle. There was a field of ripe barley. When the troops fled from the Philistines, ¹⁴they stood in the middle of the field and defended it by killing Philistines. So the LORD saved ˌthemˌ with an impressive victory. ¹⁵Once three of the thirty leading men went down to David's rock at the cave of Adullam when the army of the Philistines was camping in the valley of Rephaim. ¹⁶While David was in the fortified camp, Philistine troops were in Bethlehem.

¹⁷David was thirsty and said, "I wish I could have a drink of water from the cistern at the city gate of Bethlehem." ¹⁸So the three burst into the Philistine camp and drew water from the cistern. They brought it to David, but he refused to drink it. He poured it out ˌas an offeringˌ to the LORD ¹⁹and said, "It's unthinkable that I would do this, God. Should I drink the blood of these men who risked their lives? They had to risk their lives to get this water." So he refused to drink it.

These are the things which the three fighting men did.

David's Thirty Fighting Men—
2 Samuel 23:18-39

²⁰Joab's brother Abishai was the leader of the thirty. He used his spear to kill 300 men, but he was not one of the three, ²¹although he was honored more than they were. So he became their captain but didn't become a member of the three.

²²Benaiah, son of Jehoiada, was from Kabzeel and was a brave man who did many things. He killed two distinguished soldiers from Moab. He also went into a cistern

---

ᵃ 11:8 The exact place referred to as "the Millo" is unknown. *ᵇ* 11:11 2 Samuel 23:8, Greek; Masoretic Text "thirty."

and killed a lion on the day it snowed. ²³He killed an eight-foot-tall Egyptian. The Egyptian had a spear like a weaver's beam in his hand. But Benaiah went to him with a club, grabbed the spear away from him, and killed him with it. ²⁴These are the things that Benaiah, son of Jehoiada, did. He was as famous as the three fighting men. ²⁵He was honored more than the thirty, but he was not a member of the three. David put him in charge of his bodyguards.

²⁶The distinguished fighting men were
   Joab's brother Asahel,
   Elhanan (son of Dodo) from Bethlehem,
²⁷Shammoth from Harod,
   Helez the Pelonite,
²⁸Ira (son of Ikkesh) from Tekoa,
   Abiezer from Anathoth,
²⁹Sibbecai (son of Hushai),
   Ilai (descendant of Ahohi),
³⁰Maharai from Netophah,
   Heled (son of Baanah) from Netophah,
³¹Ithai (son of Ribai) from Gibeah in Benjamin,
   Benaiah from Pirathon,
³²Hurai from the Gaash ravines,
   Abiel from Beth Arabah,
³³Azmaveth from Bahurim,
   Eliahba from Shaalbon,
³⁴Bene Hashem from Gizon,
   Jonathan (son of Shage the Hararite),
³⁵Ahiam (son of Sachar the Hararite),
   Eliphal (son of Ur),
³⁶Hepher the Mecherathite,
   Ahijah the Pelonite,
³⁷Hezro from Carmel,
   Naari (son of Ezbai),
³⁸Joel (son of Nathan),
   Mibhar (son of Hagri),
³⁹Zelek from Ammon,
   Naharai from Beroth, armorbearer for Zeruiah's son Joab,
⁴⁰Ira (descendant of Ithra),
   Gareb (descendant of Ithra),
⁴¹Uriah the Hittite,
   Zabad (son of Ahlai),
⁴²Adina (son of Shiza) from the tribe of Reuben (who was leader of the tribe of Reuben and had his own group of thirty soldiers),
⁴³Hanan (son of Maacah),
   and Joshaphat the Mithnite,
⁴⁴Uzzia from Ashteroth,
   Shama and Jeiel (sons of Hotham from Aroer),
⁴⁵Jediael (son of Shimri) and
   his brother Joha the Tizite,
⁴⁶Eliel the Mahavite,
   Jeribai and Joshaviah (sons of Elnaam),
   Ithmah from Moab,

[47]Eliel,
Obed, and
Jaasiel the Mezobaite.

The Men Who Helped David Become King

12 [1]These are the men who came to David at Ziklag when he was banished by Saul, son of Kish. They were among the soldiers who went into battle with David. [2]They were armed with bows and could sling stones or shoot arrows with either their right or their left hands. They were Saul's relatives, from the tribe of Benjamin. [3]Ahiezer was the leader, then Joash (they were the sons of Shemaah from Gibeah), Azmaveth's sons Jeziel and Pelet, Beracah and Jehu from Anathoth, [4]Ishmaiah from Gibeon (one of the thirty fighting men and one of their leaders),[a] Jeremiah, Jahaziel, Johanan, and Jozabad from Gederah, [5]Eluzai, Jerimoth, Bealiah, Shemariah, and Shephatiah from Haruph, [6]Elkanah, Isshiah, Azarel, Joezer, and Jashobeam (Korah's descendants), [7]and Joelah and Zebadiah, Jeroham's sons from Gedor.

[8]Some men left Gad to join David at the fortified camp in the desert. They were warriors, trained soldiers, able to fight with shields and spears. They looked like lions and were as fast as gazelles on the hills. [9]Ezer was the first of these soldiers. The second was Obadiah. The third was Eliab. [10]The fourth was Mishmannah. The fifth was Jeremiah. [11]The sixth was Attai. The seventh was Eliel. [12]The eighth was Johanan. The ninth was Elzabad. [13]The tenth was Jeremiah. The eleventh was Machbannai. [14]These descendants of Gad were army officers. The least able one was in command of 100 men, and the best one was in command of 1,000. [15]In the first month of the year, these men crossed the Jordan River when it was flooding its banks. They chased away all the people in the valleys to the east and west.

[16]Some of the men of Benjamin and Judah came to David at the fortified camp. [17]David went to meet them. He told them, "If you've come to help me as friends would, then you may join me. But if you've come to betray me to my enemies, even though I haven't committed a crime, may the God of our ancestors see this and judge you."

[18]Then the Spirit gave Amasai, the leader of the thirty, the strength to say,

"We are yours, David.
We are with you, son of Jesse.
    Success, success to you!
    Success to those who help you,
        because your God is helping you."

So David welcomed them and made them officers over his troops.

[19]Some men from Manasseh had deserted Saul's army to join David when he went with the Philistines to attack Saul. (However, David didn't help the Philistines because their rulers sent him away after considering the matter. They said, "It will cost us our heads when he deserts and joins his master Saul.") [20]When David went to Ziklag, these men from Manasseh deserted to join him: Adnah, Jozabad, Jediael, Michael, Jozabad, Elihu, and Zillethai. Each one was an officer over 1,000 men in Manasseh. [21]They helped David fight raiding parties because they were all warriors, commanders in the army. [22]From day to day, men came to help David until he had an army as large as God's army.

---

[a] 12:4 1 Chronicles 12:4b-40 in English Bibles is 1 Chronicles 12:5-41 in the Hebrew Bible.

²³These are the numbers of the men equipped for war. The men joined David at Hebron to turn Saul's kingship over to David, as the LORD had said.

²⁴From Judah's descendants there were 6,800 men equipped for war. They carried shields and spears. ²⁵From Simeon's descendants there were 7,100 warriors. ²⁶From Levi's descendants there were 4,600 ²⁷as well as Jehoiada (leader of Aaron's families). With him there were 3,700 men, ²⁸and Zadok, a young warrior from whose family came 22 officers. ²⁹From Benjamin's descendants, Saul's relatives, there were 3,000 men, though most of them remained loyal to Saul's family. ³⁰From Ephraim's descendants there were 20,800 warriors who were famous among their families. ³¹From half of the tribe of Manasseh there were 18,000 who had been designated by name to make David king. ³²From Issachar's descendants there were 200 leaders who understood the times and knew what Israel should do. Their relatives were under their command. ³³From Zebulun there were 50,000 experienced soldiers. They were equipped for battle with every kind of weapon. Their loyalty was unquestioned.ᵇ ³⁴From Naphtali there were 1,000 commanders. With them were 37,000 who fought with shields and spears. ³⁵From Dan there were 28,600 ready for battle. ³⁶From Asher there were 40,000 experienced soldiers ready for battle. ³⁷From the east side of the Jordan River, from Reuben, Gad, and half the tribe of Manasseh, there were 120,000 soldiers ready to fight with all kinds of weapons.

³⁸All of these soldiers, who were prepared for battle, came with a single purpose to Hebron—to make David king of all Israel. The rest of Israel also had agreed to make David king. ³⁹They ate and drank with David for three days because their relatives in Judah had provided enough for them. ⁴⁰Also, their neighbors as far as the territories of Issachar, Zebulun, and Naphtali brought food on donkeys, camels, mules, and oxen. There was plenty of flour, fig cakes, raisins, wine, olive oil, cattle, and sheep, because Israel was celebrating.

David Has the Ark Brought to Obed Edom's House—
2 Samuel 6:1-11

13 ¹David consulted with every officer who commanded a regiment or battalion. ²Then he told the whole assembly of Israel, "If you approve and if the LORD our God has consented,ᵃ we will send an invitation to the rest of our relatives in every region of Israel and to the priests and Levites in their cities and pasturelands so that they may join us. ³Then we'll bring back our God's ark, which we ignored while Saul was king."

⁴The whole assembly agreed to this because the people considered it the right thing to do. ⁵So David gathered all Israel from the Shihor River near Egypt to the border of Hamath in order to bring God's ark from Kiriath Jearim.

⁶David and all Israel went to Baalah in Kiriath Jearim, which is in Judah, to bring

---

ᵇ12:33 Hebrew meaning of this sentence uncertain. ᵃ13:2 Hebrew meaning uncertain.

God's ark to Jerusalem. (The LORD is enthroned over the angels[b] on the ark, where his name is used.) [7]David and his men put God's ark on a new cart from Abinadab's home. Uzzah and Ahio guided the cart. [8]David and all Israel were celebrating in God's presence with all their might, with songs, with lyres, harps, tambourines, cymbals, and trumpets.

[9]But when they came to Chidon's threshing floor,[c] the oxen stumbled. So Uzzah reached out to grab the ark. [10]The LORD became angry with Uzzah and killed him for reaching for the ark. He died in God's presence.

[11]David was angry because the LORD had struck Uzzah so violently. (That place is still called Perez Uzzah [The Striking of Uzzah] today.) [12]David was afraid of God that day. "How can I bring God's ark to my city?" he asked. [13]So he didn't bring God's ark to his home, the City of David. Instead, he rerouted it to the home of Obed Edom, who was from Gath. [14]God's ark stayed at the home of Obed Edom with his family for three months, and the LORD blessed Obed Edom's family and everything he owned.

David's Palace, Wives, and Children in Jerusalem—
2 Samuel 5:11-16

[1]King Hiram of Tyre sent messengers to David, along with cedarwood, masons, and carpenters to build a palace for David. [2]So David realized that the LORD had established him as king of Israel and that his kingdom was made famous for the sake of Israel, the LORD's people.

[3]David married more wives in Jerusalem and fathered more sons and daughters. [4]These are the names of the children who were born to him in Jerusalem: Shammua, Shobab, Nathan, Solomon, [5]Ibhar, Elishua, Elpelet, [6]Nogah, Nepheg, Japhia, [7]Elishama, Beeliada, and Eliphelet.

David Defeats the Philistines—
2 Samuel 5:17-25

[8]When the Philistines heard that David had been anointed king of Israel, all of them came to attack David. But David heard about it and went out to meet them. [9]The Philistines had come and raided the valley of Rephaim.

[10]David asked God, "Should I attack the Philistines? Will you hand them over to me?"

The LORD answered him, "Attack! I will hand them over to you."

[11]So David and his men attacked and defeated the Philistines at Baal Perazim. David said, "Using my power like an overwhelming flood, God has overwhelmed my enemies." That is why they call that place Baal Perazim [The Lord Overwhelms]. [12]The Philistines left their gods there, so David ordered that the gods be burned.

[13]The Philistines again raided the valley. [14]Once more David asked God.

God answered him, "Don't go after them. Circle around, and come at them in front of the balsam trees. [15]As you hear the sound of marching in the tops of the balsam trees, then go out and fight because God has gone ahead of you to defeat the Philistine army."

[16]David did as God ordered him, and his men defeated the Philistine army from Gibeon to Gezer. [17]David's fame spread through all lands, and the LORD made all the nations fear him.

---

[b]13:6 Or "cherubim." [c]13:9 A threshing floor is an outdoor area where grain is separated from its husks.

David Brings the Ark to Jerusalem—
2 Samuel 6:12-19a

15 ¹After David constructed buildings for himself in the City of David, he prepared a place for God's ark and set up a tent for it. ²Then David insisted that only the Levites carry God's ark because the LORD had chosen them to carry his ark and to serve him forever.

³David called together all Israel at Jerusalem to bring the LORD's ark to the place he had prepared for it. ⁴David also called together Aaron's descendants and the Levites. ⁵Leading Kohath's descendants was Uriel, who came with 120 of his relatives. ⁶Leading Merari's descendants was Asaiah, who came with 220 of his relatives. ⁷Leading Gershom's descendants was Joel, who came with 130 of his relatives. ⁸Leading Elizaphan's descendants was Shemaiah, who came with 200 of his relatives. ⁹Leading Hebron's descendants was Eliel, who came with 80 of his relatives. ¹⁰Leading Uzziel's descendants was Amminadab, who came with 112 of his relatives.

¹¹David called for the priests Zadok and Abiathar and for the Levites Uriel, Asaiah, Joel, Shemaiah, Eliel, and Amminadab. ¹²He said to them, "You are the heads of the Levite families. You and your relatives must perform the ceremonies to make yourselves holy. Then bring the ark of the LORD God of Israel to the place I prepared for it. ¹³Because you weren't there the first time, the LORD our God struck us. We hadn't dedicated our lives to serving him in the way ˌheˌ designated."

¹⁴So the priests and the Levites made themselves holy in order to move the ark of the LORD God of Israel. ¹⁵The Levites carried God's ark on their shoulders. They used poles as Moses had commanded according to the LORD's instructions.

¹⁶David told the Levite leaders to appoint some of their relatives to serve as musicians. They were expected to play music on harps, lyres, and cymbals to produce joyful music for singing. ¹⁷So the Levites appointed Heman, son of Joel, and from his relatives they appointed Asaph, Berechiah's son. From their own relatives, Merari's descendants, they appointed Ethan, son of Kushaiah. ¹⁸In addition, they appointed their relatives from the second division: Zechariah,*ᵃ* Jaaziel, Shemiramoth, Jehiel, Unni, Eliab, Benaiah, Maaseiah, Mattithiah, Eliphelehu, and Mikneiah. Obed Edom and Jeiel were appointed gatekeepers. ¹⁹The musicians Heman, Asaph, and Ethan were appointed to play bronze cymbals. ²⁰Zechariah, Jaziel, Shemiramoth, Jehiel, Unni, Eliab, Maaseiah, and Benaiah were appointed to play harps according to *alamoth.ᵇ* ²¹Mattithiah, Eliphelehu, Mikneiah, Obed Edom, Jeiel, and Azaziah were appointed to play lyres and to conduct the *sheminith.ᶜ* ²²Chenaniah, a Levite leader, instructed others how to sing prophetic songs because he was skilled at it. ²³Berechiah and Elkanah were gatekeepers for the ark. ²⁴The priests Shebaniah, Joshaphat, Nethanel, Amasai, Zechariah, Benaiah, and Eliezer blew trumpets in front of God's ark. Obed Edom and Jehiah were doorkeepers for the ark.

²⁵So David, the leaders of Israel, and the army's commanders joyfully went to get the ark of the LORD's promise from Obed Edom's house. ²⁶Because God helped the Levites who carried the ark of the LORD's promise, they sacrificed seven bulls and seven rams. ²⁷David was dressed in a fine linen robe, as were all the Levites who carried the ark, the ˌLevitesˌ who wereˌ singers, and Chenaniah, the leader of the musicians' prophetic songs. David also wore a linen ephod.*ᵈ*

²⁸All Israel brought the ark of the LORD's promise with shouts of joy and the sounding of rams' horns, trumpets, cymbals, harps, and lyres. ²⁹When the ark of the

---

ᵃ 15:18 Greek; Masoretic Text adds "Ben," or "son." ᵇ 15:20 Unknown musical term. ᶜ 15:21 Unknown musical term.
ᵈ 15:27 *Ephod* is a technical term for a part of the priest's clothing. Its exact usage and shape are unknown.

LORD's promise came to the City of David, Saul's daughter Michal looked out of a window and saw King David dancing and celebrating, so she despised him.

16 ¹The men carrying the ark set it inside the tent David had put up for it. They presented burnt offerings and fellowship offerings in God's presence. ²When David had finished sacrificing burnt offerings and fellowship offerings, he blessed the people in the name of the LORD. ³He also distributed to every person in Israel—both men and women—a loaf of bread, a date cake, and a raisin cake.

The Levites Lead the Worship in Jerusalem—
2 Samuel 6:19b-20a; Psalms 96:1-13; 105:1-15; 106:1, 47-48

⁴David appointed some Levites to serve in front of the LORD's ark by offering prayers, thanks, and praise to the LORD God of Israel. ⁵Asaph was the head; Zechariah was second, then Jeiel, Shemiramoth, Jehiel, Mattithiah, Eliab, Benaiah, Obed Edom, and Jeiel with harps and lyres. Asaph played the cymbals. ⁶The priests Benaiah and Jahaziel played trumpets all the time in front of the ark of God's promise. ⁷For the first time David entrusted Asaph and his relatives with the task of singing songs of thanks to the LORD:

8   "Give thanks to the LORD.
     Call on his name.
     Make known among the nations what he has done.
9   Sing to him.
     Make music to praise him.
     Meditate on all the miracles he has done.
10   Brag about his holy name.
     Let the hearts of those who seek the LORD rejoice.
11   Search for the LORD and his strength.
     Always seek his presence.
12   Remember the miracles he performed,
         the amazing things he did and the judgments he pronounced,
13   you descendants of Israel, his servant,
         you descendants of Jacob, his chosen ones.

14   "He is the LORD our God.
     His judgments are pronounced throughout the earth.
15   Remember his promise* forever,
         the word that he commanded for a thousand generations,
16   the promise that he made to Abraham,
             and his sworn promise to Isaac.
17   He confirmed it as a law for Jacob,
         as an everlasting promise to Israel,
18   by saying, 'I will give you Canaan.
         It is your share of the inheritance.'

19   "While they were few in number,
         a small group of foreigners living in that land,
20   they wandered from nation to nation
             and from one kingdom to another.
21   He didn't permit anyone to oppress them.
     He warned kings about them:

ª 16:15 Or "covenant."

22   'Do not touch my anointed ones
         or harm my prophets.'

23   "Sing to the LORD, all the earth!
         Day after day announce that the LORD saves his people.
24   Tell people about his glory.
           Tell all the nations about his miracles.

25   "The LORD is great!
         He should be highly praised.
         He should be feared more than all other gods
26   because all the gods of the nations are idols.
      The LORD made the heavens.
27   Splendor and majesty are in his presence.
      Strength and joy are where he is.

28   "Give to the LORD, you families of the nations.
      Give to the LORD glory and power.
29   Give to the LORD the glory his name deserves.
         Bring an offering, and come to him.
         Worship the LORD in his holy splendor.
30   Tremble in his presence, all the earth!

      "The earth stands firm; it cannot be moved.
31   Let the heavens rejoice and the earth be glad.
         Say to the nations, 'The LORD rules as king!'
32   Let the sea and everything in it roar like thunder.
      Let the fields and everything in them rejoice.
33   Then the trees in the forest will sing with joy
           in the presence of the LORD when he comes to judge the earth.

34   "Give thanks to the LORD because he is good,
         because his mercy endures forever.
35   Say, 'Rescue us, O God our Savior.
         Gather us and save us from the nations
            so that we may give thanks to your holy name
            and make your praise our glory.'
36   Thanks be to the LORD God of Israel
         from everlasting to everlasting."

Then all the people said amen and praised the LORD.

³⁷David left Asaph and his relatives to serve continually in front of the ark of the LORD's promise, as the daily work required. ³⁸David also left Obed Edom and 68 of his relatives to serve there. Obed Edom (Jeduthun's son) and Hosah were to be gatekeepers. ³⁹David left Zadok and his priestly relatives to serve in the LORD's tent at the place of worship in Gibeon. ⁴⁰They were ordered to sacrifice burnt offerings to the LORD. This happened on the altar of burnt offerings continually, morning and evening, as written in the LORD's Teachings that he gave Israel. ⁴¹With Zadok and his relatives were Heman, Jeduthun, and the rest of the Levites who had been selected, chosen by name, to give thanks to the LORD by singing, "His mercy endures forever." ⁴²Also, Heman and Jeduthun played trumpets, cymbals, and the other musical instruments that accompany sacred songs. Jeduthun's sons were stationed at the gate.

⁴³Then all the people went home. David went back to bless his family.

David's Wish to Build a House for God—
2 Samuel 7:1-29

17 [1]When David was living in his house, he said to the prophet Nathan, "I'm living in a house made of cedar, while the ark of the LORD's promise is inside a tent."

[2]Nathan told David, "Do everything you have in mind, because God is with you."

[3]But that same night God spoke his word to Nathan: [4]"Say to David, my servant, 'This is what the LORD says: You must not build this house for me to live in. [5]I haven't lived in a house from the day I brought Israel out of Egypt to this day, but I've gone from tent site to tent site, moving the tent of meeting from one location to another. [6]In all the places I've moved with all Israel, did I ever ask any of the judges of Israel whom I ordered to be shepherds of my people why they didn't build me a house of cedar?'

[7]"Now this is what you will say to my servant David: 'This is what the LORD of Armies says: I took you from the pasture where you followed sheep so that you could be the leader of my people Israel. [8]I was with you wherever you went, and I destroyed all your enemies in front of you. I will make your name like the names of the greatest people on earth. [9]I will make a place for my people Israel and plant them there. They will live in their own place and not be troubled anymore. The wicked will no longer frighten them as they used to do [10]ever since I appointed judges to rule my people Israel. I will crush all your enemies. I even tell you that I, the LORD, will build a house for you.

[11]"'When the time comes for you to go and be with your ancestors, I will send one of your descendants. He will be one of your sons. I will establish his kingdom. [12]He will build a house for me, and I will establish his throne forever. [13]I will be his Father, and he will be my Son. And I will never stop showing him my love as I did to your predecessor. [14]I will place him in my royal house forever, and his throne will be established forever.'"

[15]Nathan told David all these words and everything he had seen.

[16]Then King David went into the tent and sat in front of the LORD. "Who am I, LORD God," he asked, "and why is my house so important that you have brought me this far? [17]And this you consider to be a small act, God. You've spoken about the distant future of my house. LORD God, you've shown me the generation of the great man.[a]

[18]"What more can I do for you in light of the honor you have given to me and since

Good Morning, God
1 Chronicles 17:11-14

If you want proof that the Bible is true, remember that everything predicted in the Bible either has or will come true. One example is when God told David that one of David's descendants would be the Son of God. About 1,000 years later, Christ was born. His family descended from David, just like God said. Share this example with a friend who may need proof that the Bible is true.

Thank you that everything written in the Bible is true.

---
[a] 17:17 Hebrew meaning of this sentence uncertain.

you know me so well! ¹⁹Lᴏʀᴅ, you've done this great thing for my sake and your own desire. You made this great thing known to me.

²⁰"Lᴏʀᴅ, there is no one like you, and there is no other god except you, as we have heard with our own ears. ²¹Who is like your people Israel? It is the one nation on earth that God came to free in order to make its people his own, to make your name known, and to do great and wonderful things for them. You forced the nations and their gods out of the way of your people, whom you freed from Egypt. ²²You made the people of Israel to be your people forever. And you, Lᴏʀᴅ, became their God.

²³"Now, Lᴏʀᴅ, faithfully keep the promise you made to me and my house forever. Do as you promised. ²⁴Your name will endure and be respected forever when people say, 'The Lᴏʀᴅ of Armies, the God of Israel, is Israel's God.' And the house of David, your servant, will be established in your presence. ²⁵You, my God, have revealed especially to me that you will build me a house. That is why I have found the courage to pray to you.

²⁶"Almighty Lᴏʀᴅ, you are God. You promised me this good thing. ²⁷Now, you were pleased to bless my house so that it may continue in your presence forever. Indeed, you, Lᴏʀᴅ, have blessed it. It will be blessed forever."

David's Successes—
2 Samuel 8:1-18

18 ¹After this, David defeated and crushed the Philistines. He took Gath and its surrounding villages from them.

²He also defeated Moab, and the Moabites became David's subjects and paid taxes to him.

³When David went to establish his control over the territory along the Euphrates River, he defeated King Hadadezer at Hamath. ⁴David took 1,000 chariots, 7,000 horsemen, and 20,000 foot soldiers from him. David also disabled all but 100 of their horses so that they couldn't pull chariots.

⁵When the Arameans from Damascus came to help King Hadadezer of Zobah, David killed 22,000 of them. ⁶David put troops in the Aramean kingdom of Damascus, and the Arameans became his subjects and paid taxes to him. Everywhere David went, the Lᴏʀᴅ gave him victories.

⁷David took the gold shields that Hadadezer's servants carried, and he brought them to Jerusalem. ⁸David also took a large quantity of bronze from Tibhath and Cun, Hadadezer's cities. (Later, Solomon used it to make the pool, pillars, and utensils for the temple.)

⁹When King Tou of Hamath heard that David had defeated the whole army of Zobah's King Hadadezer, ¹⁰he sent his son Hadoram to greet King David and congratulate him for fighting and defeating Hadadezer. (There had often been war between Hadadezer and Tou.) ¹¹King David dedicated all the articles of gold, silver, and bronze to the Lᴏʀᴅ, along with the silver and gold he had taken from other nations—from Edom, Moab, Ammon, the Philistines, and Amalek.

¹²Zeruiah's son Abishai killed 18,000 Edomites in the Dead Sea region. ¹³He put troops in Edom, and all its people became David's subjects. Everywhere David went, the Lᴏʀᴅ gave him victories.

¹⁴So David ruled all Israel. He did what was fair and right for all his people. ¹⁵Zeruiah's son Joab was in charge of the army. Ahilud's son Jehoshaphat was the royal historian. ¹⁶Ahitub's son Zadok and Abiathar's son Abimelech*ᵃ* were priests. Shavsha

---

*ᵃ18:16 Most Hebrew manuscripts; some Hebrew manuscripts, 2 Samuel 8:17, Greek, Syriac, Latin, Arabic "Ahimelech."

was the royal scribe. ¹⁷Jehoiada's son Benaiah was commander of the Cherethites and the Pelethites. And David's sons were his main officials.

David Defeats Ammon and Aram—
2 Samuel 10:1-19

¹Later King Nahash of Ammon died, and his son became king in his place. ²David thought, "I will show kindness to Hanun because his father Nahash showed me kindness." So David sent messengers to comfort Hanun after his father's death. But when David's servants entered Ammonite territory to comfort Hanun, ³the Ammonite princes asked Hanun, "Do you think David is honoring your father because he sent men to comfort you? Haven't his servants come to explore, destroy, and spy on the country?" ⁴So Hanun took David's men, shaved them, cut off their clothes from the waist down, and sent them away.

⁵After people told David what had happened to the men, he sent someone to meet them because they were deeply humiliated. The king said to them, "Stay in Jericho until your beards have grown back, and then return to Jerusalem."

⁶The Ammonites realized that they had made themselves offensive to David. So Hanun and the Ammonites sent 75,000 pounds of silver to hire chariots and horses from the Arameans in Upper Mesopotamia, Maacah, and Zobah. ⁷They hired 32,000 chariots and the king of Maacah with his army. They camped near Medeba. The Ammonites gathered for the battle from their cities.

⁸After David heard about this, he sent Joab and all the elite troops. ⁹The Ammonites formed a battle line at the entrance of the city, while the Arameans from Zobah and Rehob and the kings who had come remained by themselves in the open country.

¹⁰When Joab saw he was under attack in front and behind, he took the select troops of Israel and organized them for combat against the Arameans. ¹¹He put his brother Abishai in charge of the rest of the troops. They organized for combat against the Ammonites.

¹²Joab said, "If the Arameans are too strong for my troops, be ready to help me. And if the Ammonites are too strong for your troops, I'll help you. ¹³Be strong! Let's prove ourselves strong for our people and for the cities of our God, and the LORD will do what he considers right."

¹⁴Then Joab and his troops advanced to fight the Arameans, and the Arameans fled. ¹⁵When the Ammonites saw that the Arameans had fled, they, too, fled from Joab's brother Abishai and went into the city. So Joab returned to Jerusalem.

¹⁶Realizing that Israel had defeated them, the kings sent messengers to get other Arameans from beyond the Euphrates River. Shophach, the commander of Hadadezer's army, led them.

¹⁷When David was told about this, he assembled Israel's army, crossed the Jordan, and confronted them. David formed a battle line against the Arameans, and they fought him. ¹⁸The Arameans fled from Israel, and David killed 7,000 chariot drivers and 40,000 foot soldiers. David also killed Shophach. ¹⁹When all the kings who were subject to Hadadezer saw that Israel had defeated them, they made peace with David and became his subjects. And the Arameans were no longer willing to help the Ammonites.

David Defeats the Philistines—
2 Samuel 11:1; 12:26-31; 21:15-22

¹In the spring, the time when kings go out to battle, Joab led the army to war. They destroyed the Ammonites and came to Rabbah to attack it, while David

stayed in Jerusalem. Joab defeated Rabbah and tore it down. ²He took the gold crown from the head of Rabbah's king and put it on David's head. (The crown was found to weigh 75 pounds, and in it was a precious stone.) David also took a lot of goods from the city. ³He brought out the troops who were there and put them to work with saws, hoes, and axes.ᵃ He did the same to all the Ammonite cities. Then David and all the troops returned to Jerusalem.

⁴After this, war broke out with the Philistines at Gezer. Then Sibbecai from Hushahᵇ killed Sippai, a descendant of Haraphah, and the Philistines were defeated. ⁵When more fighting broke out with the Philistines, Elhanan, son of Jair, killed Lahmi, the brother of Goliath from Gath. (The shaft of Lahmi's spear was like a beam used by weavers.) ⁶In another battle at Gath, there was a tall man who had 24 fingers and toes: six fingers on each hand and six toes on each foot. He also was a descendant of Haraphah. ⁷When he challenged Israel, Jonathan, son of David's brother Shimea, killed him. ⁸These men were the descendants of Haraphah from Gath, and David and his men killed them.

David Counts the People—
2 Samuel 24:1-25

21 ¹Satan attempted to attack Israel by provoking David to count the Israelites. ²David said to Joab and the leaders of the people, "Go, count Israel from Beersheba to Dan. Bring me the results so that I may know how many people there are."

³Joab responded, "May the Lord multiply his people a hundred times over. But, Your Majesty, aren't they all your servants? Why are you trying to do this? Why do you wish to make Israel guilty of this sin?"

⁴However, the king overruled Joab. So Joab left, went throughout Israel, and returned to Jerusalem. ⁵Joab reported the census figures to David: In Israel there were 1,100,000 men who could serve in the army, and in Judah there were 470,000 who could serve in the army. ⁶Joab didn't include Levi and Benjamin in the number because he was disgusted with the king's order.

⁷God considered the census to be sinful, so he struck Israel with a plague.

⁸David said to God, "I have committed a terrible sin by doing this thing. Forgive me because I have acted very foolishly."

⁹The Lord spoke to Gad, David's seer.ᵃ ¹⁰"Go and tell David, 'This is what the Lord says: I'm offering you three choices. Choose the one you want me to do to you.'"

¹¹When Gad came to David, he said, "This is what the Lord says: 'Take your pick: ¹²either three years of famine, or three months during which your enemies will chase you away when their swords catch up to you, or three days of the Lord's sword—a plague in the land with the Messenger of the Lord destroying the whole country of Israel.' Decide what answer I should give the one who sent me."

¹³"I'm in a desperate situation," David told Gad. "Please let me fall into the Lord's hands because he is extremely merciful. But don't let me fall into human hands."

¹⁴So the Lord sent a plague on Israel, and 70,000 Israelites died. ¹⁵God also sent a Messenger to Jerusalem to destroy it, but as he was destroying it, the Lord reconsidered and changed his mind about the disaster. "Enough!" he said to the destroying Messenger. "Put down your weapon." The Messenger of the Lord was standing by the threshing floorᵇ of Ornan the Jebusite.

ᵃ20:3 One Hebrew manuscript, 2 Samuel 12:31; other Hebrew manuscripts "saws." ᵇ20:4 Or "a descendant of Hushah." ᵃ21:9 A seer is a prophet. ᵇ21:15 A threshing floor is an outdoor area where grain is separated from its husks.

[16]When David looked up, he saw the Messenger of the LORD standing between heaven and earth. The Messenger had a sword in his hand and stretched it over Jerusalem. David and the leaders were dressed in sackcloth. They bowed down with their faces touching the ground. [17]David said to God, "I'm the one who ordered the people to be counted. I am the one who sinned and did wrong. What have these sheep done? LORD my God, let your punishment be against me and my father's family, but don't punish your people with a plague."

[18]The LORD's Messenger told Gad to tell David to go and set up an altar for the LORD at Ornan the Jebusite's threshing floor. [19]David went as Gad had told him in the LORD's name.

[20]Now, Ornan had turned around and seen the Messenger. Ornan's four sons who were with him hid, but Ornan kept on threshing the wheat. [21]When David arrived, Ornan looked up and saw him. So he left the threshing floor and bowed down with his face touching the ground in front of David. [22]David said to Ornan, "Let me have the land this threshing floor is on. I'll build an altar for the LORD on it. Sell it to me for the full price. Then the plague on the people will stop."

[23]Ornan said to David, "Take it, Your Majesty, and do whatever you think is right. I'll give you oxen for the burnt offering, threshers[c] for firewood, and wheat for the grain offering. I'll give you everything."

[24]"No," King David told Ornan, "I insist on buying it for the full price. I won't take what is yours for the LORD and offer burnt sacrifices that cost me nothing." [25]So David gave Ornan 15 pounds of gold for that place.

[26]David built an altar for the LORD there and sacrificed burnt offerings and fellowship offerings. He called on the LORD, and the LORD answered him by sending fire from heaven on the altar for burnt offerings. [27]So the LORD spoke to the Messenger, and he put his sword back in its scabbard.

[28]At that time, when David saw the LORD had answered him at the threshing floor of Ornan the Jebusite, he offered sacrifices there. [29]The LORD's tent that Moses made in the desert and the altar for burnt offerings were at the worship site at Gibeon. [30]However, David couldn't go there to consult God because he was frightened by the sword of the LORD's Messenger. [1]Then David said, "This is where the LORD God's temple will be. Israel's altar for burnt offerings will also be here."

David Helps Solomon Prepare to Build the Temple

[2]David ordered the foreigners living in Israel to gather. He appointed some of them to cut stones to build God's temple. [3]David prepared a large quantity of iron for nails and fittings on the doors of the gates. He also prepared so much bronze that it couldn't be weighed. [4]The men of Sidon and Tyre brought David so many cedar logs that the logs couldn't be counted.

[5]David thought, "My son Solomon is young and inexperienced, and the temple that will be built for the LORD must be magnificent, large, famous, praised, and honored in all other countries. I'll prepare the building materials for him." So David prepared many materials for Solomon before he died.

[6]He summoned his son Solomon and commanded him to build a temple for the LORD God of Israel. [7]David told his son Solomon, "I had my heart set on building a temple for the name of the LORD, my God. [8]But the LORD spoke his word to me by saying, 'You have caused a lot of bloodshed and fought in a lot of wars. You must not

---

[c]21:23 Threshers are devices used to separate grain from its husks.

build a temple for my name because you have caused so much bloodshed in my presence. ⁹You will have a son who will be a peaceful man. I will give him peace from all the enemies around him. His name will be Solomon [Peace], and in his time I will give Israel peace and quiet. ¹⁰He will build a temple for my name. He will be my son, and I will be his father. I will establish the throne of his kingdom permanently over Israel.' "

¹¹David continued, "Now, son, the Lord will be with you. You will be successful, and you will build the temple of the Lord your God as he predicted you would. ¹²The Lord will give you insight and understanding as he commands you to take charge of Israel and to follow the Teachings of the Lord your God. ¹³Then you will succeed if you will carefully obey the laws and decrees the Lord commanded Moses to give to Israel. Be strong and courageous. Don't be afraid or terrified.

¹⁴"Despite my troubles I've made preparations for the Lord's temple. There are 7,500,000 pounds of gold, 75,000,000 pounds of silver, and so much bronze and iron that it can't be weighed. I've also prepared wood and stones, and you may add to them. ¹⁵You have many kinds of workers: stonecutters, masons, carpenters, and men skilled in every kind of work. ¹⁶The gold, silver, bronze, and iron are more than can be counted. So get to work! May the Lord be with you."

¹⁷David ordered all the leaders of Israel to help his son Solomon. ¹⁸David said, "Isn't the Lord your God with you? Hasn't he given you peace with all your neighbors? He put the people who live in this country under my power, and the country has been conquered by the Lord and his people. ¹⁹So dedicate your hearts and lives to serving the Lord your God. Start building the holy place of the Lord God so that you can bring the ark of the Lord's promise and God's holy utensils into the temple that will be built for the Lord's name."

The Levites Are Organized to Serve in the Temple

¹When David had grown old and had lived out his years, he made his son Solomon king of Israel. ²He gathered all the officials of Israel and the priests and Levites. ³Every male Levite who was at least 30 years old was counted. There were 38,000. ⁴Of these, 24,000 were appointed to supervise the work on the Lord's temple, 6,000 were appointed to be officers and judges, ⁵4,000 were appointed to be gatekeepers, and 4,000 were appointed to praise the Lord with the instruments David had made for praising God. ⁶David organized the Levites into divisions based on which of Levi's sons (Gershon, Kohath, or Merari) they were descended from.

⁷Ladan and Shimei were Gershon's descendants. ⁸Ladan had three sons: Jehiel was the first, then Zetham, and Joel. ⁹Shimei had three sons: Shelomith, Haziel, and Haran. They were the heads of Ladan's families. ¹⁰Shimei's sons were Jahath, Zina,ᵃ Jeush, and Beriah. They were Shimei's four sons. ¹¹Jahath was the first, and Ziza was the second. Jeush and Beriah didn't have many sons, so they were given an assignment as one family.

¹²Kohath had four sons: Amram, Izhar, Hebron, and Uzziel. ¹³Amram's sons were Aaron and Moses. Aaron and his sons were forever designated to dedicate the most holy things to God, to offer sacrifices to the Lord, to serve him, and always give the blessing in his name. ¹⁴The sons of Moses, the man of God, were counted with the tribe of Levi. ¹⁵Moses' sons were Gershom and Eliezer. ¹⁶Gershom's only son was Shebuel. ¹⁷Eliezer's only son was Rehabiah. Eliezer had no other sons, but Rehabiah had many sons. ¹⁸Izhar's only son was Shelomith. ¹⁹Hebron's first son was Jeriah; his

---

ᵃ 23:10 Most Hebrew manuscripts; one Hebrew manuscript, Greek, Latin "Ziza" (see verse 11).

second was Amariah; his third was Jahaziel; his fourth was Jekameam. [20]Uzziel's first son was Micah; his second was Isshiah.

[21]Merari's sons were Mahli and Mushi. Mahli's sons were Eleazar and Kish. [22]Eleazar died without having any sons. He only had daughters. Their cousins, the sons of Kish, married them. [23]Mushi had three sons: Mahli, Eder, and Jeremoth.

[24]These were Levi's descendants, who were grouped according to their families. The heads of their families were registered by name as they were counted. Everyone who served in the LORD's temple was at least 20 years old. [25]David had said, "The LORD God of Israel has given his people rest. He will now live in Jerusalem forever. [26]The Levites will no longer have to carry the tent and all the utensils used in worship."

[27]David's last instructions were to count the Levites who were at least 20 years old. [28]They were appointed to stand beside Aaron's descendants to serve in the LORD's temple. They were appointed to be in charge of the courtyards and the temple rooms, to ensure that all the holy things were clean,[b] and to serve in God's temple. [29]They were also responsible for the rows of bread, the flour for the grain offerings, the unleavened bread wafers, and the bread made in frying pans. In addition, they were responsible for mixing the ingredients and keeping track of all weights and measures. [30]They were appointed to stand to give thanks and praise to the LORD every morning. They were appointed to do the same thing in the evening. [31]They were appointed to stand in front of the LORD in the required numbers whenever burnt offerings were made—on weekly worship days, at New Moon Festivals, and on appointed annual festivals. [32]They were appointed to follow the regulations for the tent of meeting and the holy place and to help their relatives, Aaron's descendants, as they served in the LORD's temple.

The Organization of the Priests

[1]The divisions of Aaron's descendants were as follows: Aaron's sons were Nadab and Abihu, Eleazar and Ithamar. [2]Nadab and Abihu died before their father died, and neither had any children. So Eleazar and Ithamar served as priests.

[3]David, Eleazar's descendant Zadok, and Ithamar's descendant Ahimelech divided Aaron's descendants into groups for service. [4]Since Eleazar's descendants had more men who were family heads than Ithamar's descendants, they were divided so that Eleazar's descendants had 16 family leaders and Ithamar's descendants had 8 family leaders. [5]Both groups were divided impartially by drawing lots so that there were officers for the holy place and officers for God among both Eleazar's and Ithamar's descendants. [6]The scribe Shemaiah was a son of Nethanel and a descendant of Levi. Shemaiah recorded their names in the presence of the king, the princes, the priest Zadok, Ahimelech (son of Abiathar), and the family leaders of the priests and Levites. One family was chosen for Eleazar, another for Ithamar.

[7]The first lot drawn was for Jehoiarib, the second for Jedaiah, [8]the third for Harim, the fourth for Seorim, [9]the fifth for Malchiah, the sixth for Mijamin, [10]the seventh for Hakkoz, the eighth for Abijah, [11]the ninth for Jeshua, the tenth for Shecaniah, [12]the eleventh for Eliashib, the twelfth for Jakim, [13]the thirteenth for Huppah, the fourteenth for Jeshebeab, [14]the fifteenth for Bilgah, the sixteenth for Immer, [15]the seventeenth for Hezir, the eighteenth for Happizzez, [16]the nineteenth for Pethahiah, the twentieth for Jehezkel, [17]the twenty-first for Jachin, the twenty-second for Gamul, [18]the twenty-third for Delaiah, the twenty-fourth for Maaziah. [19]These were their priestly groups when they went to serve at the LORD's temple. Their ancestor Aaron made these rules for them, as the LORD God of Israel had commanded him.

---

[b]23:28 "Clean" refers to anything that Moses' Teachings say is presentable to God.

The Organization of the Levites

²⁰The following men were leaders, for Levi's descendants from Kohath,:
    Jehdeiah (for Amram's descendants through Shubael),
²¹ Isshiah (for Amram's descendants, through Rehabiah),
²² Jahath (for Izhar's descendants through Shelomoth),
²³ Jeriah (for Hebron's descendants*),
    Amariah (the second of Hebron's descendants,),
    Jahaziel (the third of Hebron's descendants,),
    Jekameam (the fourth of Hebron's descendants,),
²⁴ Shamir (for Uzziel's descendants through Micah),
²⁵ and Zechariah (for Uzziel's, descendants through Micah's brother
    Isshiah).

²⁶The following men were leaders from Levi's descendants from Merari:
    Mahli, Mushi, and Merari's son Jaaziah,
²⁷ Shoham, Zaccur, and Ibri (for Merari's descendants through his son Jaaziah),
²⁸ Eleazar (who had no sons, for Mahli's descendants),
²⁹ Jerahmeel (for Mahli's, descendants through Kish),
³⁰ Mahli, Eder, and Jerimoth (for Mushi's descendants).

These were Levi's descendants according to their families. ³¹They drew lots as their relatives, Aaron's descendants, had done. They drew them in front of King David, Zadok, Ahimelech, and the leaders of the families of the priests and Levites. The families of the oldest brother were treated the same way as those of the youngest.

David Appoints Musicians for the Temple

25 ¹David and the army commanders appointed the sons of Asaph, Heman, and Jeduthun to serve as prophets with lyres, harps, and cymbals. This is the list of the men who performed this service:

²From the sons of Asaph were Zaccur, Joseph, Nethaniah, and Asharelah. (They were directed by Asaph, who served as a prophet under the king's direction.)

³From the sons of Jeduthun were Gedaliah, Zeri, Jeshaiah, Shimei, Hashabiah, Mattithiah. (The six brothers were directed by their father, the prophet Jeduthun. They thanked and praised the LORD as they played lyres.)

⁴From the sons of Heman were Bukkiah, Mattaniah, Uzziel, Shebuel, Jerimoth, Hananiah, Hanani, Eliathah, Giddalti, Romamti Ezer, Joshbekashah, Mallothi, Hothir, and Mahazioth. ⁵(All of them were the sons of the king's seer* Heman. They were given to him to make him prominent, as God had promised. So God gave Heman 14 sons and 3 daughters.)

⁶All these Levites, sang at the LORD's temple under the direction of their fathers Asaph, Jeduthun, and Heman. They played cymbals, lyres, and harps for worship in God's temple under the direction of the king. ⁷They, along with their relatives, were trained, skilled musicians for the LORD. There were 288 of them.

⁸They drew lots for their assignment of duties, the youngest as well as the oldest, the skilled musicians, along with the students.

⁹The first lot drawn chose Joseph, the son of Asaph.
    The second chose Gedaliah, his sons, and his relatives—12 men.
¹⁰The third chose Zaccur, his sons, and his relatives—12 men.
¹¹The fourth chose Izri, his sons, and his relatives—12 men.

ª24:23 Greek, 1 Chronicles 23:19; Masoretic Text lacks "for Hebron's descendants." ª25:5 A seer is a prophet.

¹²The fifth chose Nethaniah, his sons, and his relatives—12 men.

¹³The sixth chose Bukkiah, his sons, and his relatives—12 men.

¹⁴The seventh chose Jesarelah, his sons, and his relatives—12 men.

¹⁵The eighth chose Jeshaiah, his sons, and his relatives—12 men.

¹⁶The ninth chose Mattaniah, his sons, and his relatives—12 men.

¹⁷The tenth chose Shimei, his sons, and his relatives—12 men.

¹⁸The eleventh chose Azarel, his sons, and his relatives—12 men.

¹⁹The twelfth chose Hashabiah, his sons, and his relatives—12 men.

²⁰The thirteenth chose Shubael, his sons, and his relatives—12 men.

²¹The fourteenth chose Mattithiah, his sons, and his relatives—12 men.

²²The fifteenth chose Jeremoth, his sons, and his relatives—12 men.

²³The sixteenth chose Hananiah, his sons, and his relatives—12 men.

²⁴The seventeenth chose Joshbekashah, his sons, and his relatives—12 men.

²⁵The eighteenth chose Hanani, his sons, and his relatives—12 men.

²⁶The nineteenth chose Mallothi, his sons, and his relatives—12 men.

²⁷The twentieth chose Eliathah, his sons, and his relatives—12 men.

²⁸The twenty-first chose Hothir, his sons, and his relatives—12 men.

²⁹The twenty-second chose Giddalti, his sons, and his relatives—12 men.

³⁰The twenty-third chose Mahazioth, his sons, and his relatives—12 men.

³¹The twenty-fourth chose Romamti Ezer, his sons, and his relatives—12 men.

David Appoints Gatekeepers for the Temple

26 ¹The following were the divisions of the gatekeepers: For Korah's descendants there was Meshelemiah, the son of Kore, from the descendants of Asaph. ²Meshelemiah's sons were Zechariah (the firstborn), Jediael (the second), Zebadiah (the third), Jathniel (the fourth), ³Elam (the fifth), Jehohanan (the sixth), and Eliehoenai (the seventh).

⁴Also for Korah's descendants, there were Obed Edom's sons Shemaiah (the firstborn), Jehozabad (the second), Joah (the third), Sachar (the fourth), Nethanel (the fifth), ⁵Ammiel (the sixth), Issachar (the seventh), and Peullethai (the eighth). God had blessed Obed Edom. ⁶His son Shemaiah had sons who ruled their families because they were soldiers. ⁷Shemaiah's sons were Othni, and Othni's skilled brothers Rephael, Obed, Elzabad, as well as Elihu and Semachiah. ⁸All of these people were Obed Edom's descendants. They, their sons, and their relatives were skilled and had the ability to perform the service. Obed Edom's family included 62 men.

⁹Meshelemiah's sons and relatives were 18 skilled men.

Good Morning, God
1 Chronicles 25:6-7

Does singing music that praises God make you happy? God is glad when we sing praises to him. King David appointed musicians who played cymbals, harps, and lyres. They also sang songs of praise. Singing praises to God pleases him. And it makes us happy, too. Put it to the test. The next time you feel sad, try singing praise songs and see how it can change your attitude.

Thank you, God, for making me glad when I praise you!

¹⁰From the descendants of Merari there were Hosah's sons. Shimri was the head, although he was not the firstborn. His father appointed him head. ¹¹Hosah's other sons were Hilkiah (the second), Tebaliah (the third), and Zechariah (the fourth). There were 13 sons and relatives of Hosah.

¹²These divisions of gatekeepers through their head men were assigned duties with their relatives to serve in the LORD's temple. ¹³They drew lots by families, youngest and oldest alike, for every gate. ¹⁴Shelemiah was chosen for the east side. His son Zechariah, a counselor who displayed insight, was chosen for the north side. ¹⁵Obed Edom was chosen for the south side, and his sons were chosen for the storerooms. ¹⁶Shuppim and Hosah were chosen for the west side with Shallecheth Gate at the gateway that goes to the palace.

One squad of guards served its watch after another. ¹⁷On the east side there were six Levites. On the north there were four every day. On the south there were four every day. At the storerooms there were four, two at each entrance. ¹⁸At the courtyard[a] on the west there were four Levites at the gateway to the palace and two at the courtyard itself. ¹⁹These were the divisions of the gatekeepers among Korah's and Merari's descendants.

David Appoints Treasurers for the Temple

²⁰Ahijah, a Levite, was in charge of the treasuries in God's temple and the treasuries of the gifts dedicated to God. ²¹There were also, the descendants of Ladan, who was descended from Gershon. Those who served, for Ladan, the descendant of Gershon, were the heads of Ladan's families: Jehiel ²²and, Jehiel's sons Zetham and Joel. They were in charge of the treasuries in the LORD's temple. ²³For the descendants of Amram, Izhar, Hebron, and Uzziel, ²⁴there was Shebuel, a descendant of Moses' son Gershom. He was the highest-ranking official in charge of the treasuries. ²⁵From his relatives on Eliezer's side of the family was Shelomith. (Eliezer's son was Rehabiah; his grandson was Jeshaiah; his great-grandson was Joram. Joram's son was Zichri; his grandson was Shelomith.) ²⁶He and his relatives were in charge of all the treasuries of the gifts dedicated to God that King David, the heads of families, the commanders of regiments and battalions, and the commanders of the army had donated. ²⁷(They had donated some of the loot taken in battle to support the LORD's temple.) ²⁸Everything that Samuel the seer,[b] Saul (son of Kish), Abner (son of Ner), and Joab (son of Zeruiah) had donated—everything that had been donated—was under the supervision of Shelomith and his relatives.

David Appoints Levites to Oversee Israel's Worship

²⁹From Izhar's descendants Chenaniah and his sons were assigned duties. They served as officials and judges outside the temple, in Israel. ³⁰From Hebron's descendants Hashabiah and his 1,700 skilled, male relatives were appointed to serve Israel west of the Jordan River. They did everything the LORD wanted them to do, and they served the king. ³¹Jeriah was the head of Hebron's descendants. In the fortieth year of David's reign, the ancestry of Hebron's descendants was researched family by family. Warriors from these families were found at Jazer in Gilead. ³²Jeriah's relatives were 2,700 skilled men, who were heads of families. King David appointed them to be overseers in every matter involving God or the king for the tribes of Reuben, Gad, and half of the tribe of Manasseh.

---

a 26:18 Hebrew meaning uncertain.   b 26:28 A seer is a prophet.

David's Government Officials

27 ¹This is a list of Israelite family heads, regiment and battalion commanders, and officers who were serving the king in all the army's units. Throughout each year they came for a month at a time and then left. Each unit consisted of 24,000 men.

²Jashobeam, son of Zabdiel, was in charge of the first unit, the one during the first month. In his unit there were 24,000. ³He was a descendant of Perez, and he was head of all of the army's officers for the first month.

⁴Dodai, Ahoh's descendant, was in charge of the unit during the second month. It was his unit. (Mikloth was one of its leaders.) In Dodai's unit there were 24,000.

⁵The third commander of the army during the third month was Benaiah, son of the priest Jehoiada. He was the head, and in his unit there were 24,000. ⁶This Benaiah was one of the thirty fighting men and commander of the thirty as well as his own unit. His son was Ammizabad.

⁷Asahel, Joab's brother, was in charge of the fourth unit during the fourth month, and after him was his son Zebadiah. In his unit there were 24,000.

⁸Shamhuth, Izrah's descendant, was commander of the fifth unit during the fifth month. In his unit there were 24,000.

⁹Ira, the son of Ikkesh from Tekoa, was in charge of the sixth unit during the sixth month. In his unit there were 24,000.

¹⁰Helez, a Pelonite from the descendants of Ephraim, was in charge of the seventh unit during the seventh month. In his unit there were 24,000.

¹¹Sibbecai, a descendant of Zerah from Hushah, was in charge of the eighth unit during the eighth month. In his unit there were 24,000.

¹²Abiezer, a member of the tribe of Benjamin from Anathoth, was in charge of the ninth unit during the ninth month. In his unit there were 24,000.

¹³Mahrai, a descendant of Zerah from Netophah, was in charge of the tenth unit during the tenth month. In his unit there were 24,000.

¹⁴Benaiah, a member of the tribe of Ephraim from Pirathon, was in charge of the eleventh unit during the eleventh month. In his unit there were 24,000.

¹⁵During the twelfth month, the twelfth unit was commanded by Heldai from Netophah. He was Othniel's descendant. In his unit there were 24,000.

¹⁶The following officers were in charge of the tribes of Israel:

for the tribe of Reuben	Eliezer, son of Zichri
for the tribe of Simeon	Shephatiah, son of Maacah
¹⁷for the tribe of Levi	Hashabiah, son of Kemuel
for the family of Aaron	Zadok
¹⁸for the tribe of Judah	Elihu, one of David's brothers
for the tribe of Issachar	Omri, son of Michael
¹⁹for the tribe of Zebulun	Ishmaiah, son of Obadiah
for the tribe of Naphtali	Jerimoth, son of Azriel
²⁰for the tribe of Ephraim	Hoshea, son of Azaziah
for half of the tribe of Manasseh	Joel, son of Pedaiah
²¹for the half of Manasseh in Gilead	Iddo, son of Zechariah
for the tribe of Benjamin	Jaasiel, son of Abner
²²for the tribe of Dan	Azarel, son of Jeroham

These were the commanders of Israel's tribes.

²³David didn't count those under 20 years old, because the Lord had promised that the people of Israel would be as numerous as the stars in the sky. ²⁴Joab, son of Zeruiah, started to count them but didn't finish. God was angry with Israel because of this, and the report from it was never included in the official records of King David.

²⁵These were all the commanders in charge of King David's property:[a]

for the royal treasuries	Azmaveth, son of Adiel
for the goods in the fields, cities, villages, and watchtowers	Jonathan, son of Uzziah
²⁶for the farm workers in the fields	Ezri, son of Chelub
²⁷for the vineyards	Shimei from Ramah
for storing wine that came from the vineyards	Zabdi from Shepham
²⁸for the olive and fig trees in the foothills	Baal Hanan from Gedor
for storing olive oil	Joash
²⁹for the herds grazing in Sharon	Shitrai from Sharon
for the herds in the valleys	Shaphat, son of Adlai
³⁰for the camels	Obil, a descendant of Ishmael
for the donkeys	Jehdeiah from Meronoth
³¹for the flocks	Jaziz from Hagar

³²David's uncle Jonathan, an educated man who possessed insight, was David's adviser. Jonathan and Jehiel, son of Hachmoni, were in charge of the king's sons. ³³Ahithophel was the king's adviser. Hushai, a descendant of Archi, was the king's friend. ³⁴Jehoiada (son of Benaiah) and Abiathar succeeded Ahithophel. Joab was the commander of the royal army.

David's Public Assembly at Jerusalem

28 ¹David held a meeting in Jerusalem for all the leaders of Israel—the leaders of the tribes, the leaders of the army units that served the king, the commanders of regiments and battalions, the officials in charge of all the property and livestock belonging to the king and his sons, the palace officials, the soldiers, and the fighting men.

²David stood in front of them and said, "Listen to me, my relatives and subjects. I had my heart set on building the temple where the ark of the Lord's promise could be placed. This temple would be a stool for our God's feet, and I have made preparations to build it. ³But God told me, 'You must not build the temple for my name. You have fought wars and caused bloodshed.' ⁴Yet, from my entire family the Lord God of Israel chose me to be king of Israel permanently. He had chosen the tribe of Judah to lead Israel. From the families of Judah he chose my father's family. From among my father's sons he was pleased to make me king of all Israel. ⁵And of all my sons (the Lord has given me many sons) he chose my son Solomon to sit on the throne of the Lord's kingdom to rule Israel.

⁶"He told me, 'Your son Solomon will build my temple and my courtyards because I have chosen him to be my son. I will be his father. ⁷I will establish his kingdom forever if he will remain determined to obey my commands and laws, as he is doing today.' ⁸Now, leaders, I order you in the sight of Israel (the Lord's congregation) and as our God listens to dedicate your lives to doing everything the Lord your God has commanded. Then you will be able to possess this good land and leave it as an inheritance to your descendants.

[9]"And you, my son Solomon, learn to know your father's God. Serve the LORD wholeheartedly and willingly because he searches every heart and understands every thought we have. If you dedicate your life to serving him, he will accept you. But if you abandon him, he will reject you from then on. [10]So be careful, because the LORD has chosen you to build the temple as his holy place. Be strong, and do it."

[11]Then David gave his son Solomon the plans for the entrance hall and the temple, its storerooms, upper rooms, inner rooms, and the room for the throne of mercy. [12]He gave him plans for the courtyards of the LORD's temple and for all the rooms around it. (These rooms served as treasuries for God's temple and the gifts dedicated to God.) [13]He determined the divisions of priests and Levites. He planned all the work done for worship in the LORD's temple. He designed all the utensils for worship in the LORD's temple. [14]David specified the weight of gold to be used for each of the utensils for worship, [15]the weight of the gold lamp stands and their gold lamps (that is, the weight of gold for each lamp stand and its lamps), the weight of silver for each silver lamp stand and its lamps (according to the use of each lamp stand for worship), [16]the weight of gold for each table with the rows of bread, and the silver for the silver tables, [17]the pure gold for the forks, bowls, and pitchers, the weight of each gold bowl, the weight of each silver bowl, [18]and the refined gold for the altar of incense. He also gave Solomon the plans for the chariot, that is, the gold angels[a] with their wings spread to cover the ark of the LORD's promise. [19]David said, "All this was written for me by the LORD's hand. He made all the details of the plan clear to me."

[20]David also told his son Solomon, "Be strong and courageous, and do the work. Don't be afraid or terrified. The LORD God, my God, will be with you. He will not abandon you before all the work on the LORD's temple is finished. [21]Here are also the divisions of the priests and Levites for every type of worship in God's temple. You have with you every skilled worker to do all the work. In addition, all the leaders and people are at your command."

29 [1]Then King David said to the whole assembly, "My son Solomon, the one whom God has chosen, is young and inexperienced. Yet, the work is important because this palace is not for a person but for the LORD God. [2]With all my might I gathered the materials for the temple of my God: gold for gold objects, silver for silver objects, bronze for bronze objects, iron for iron objects, wood for wooden objects, onyx stones and settings, black stones, stones of different colors, gems, and marble. [3]Moreover, I delight in the temple of my God. I have a personal treasury of gold and silver that I'm giving to my God's temple in addition to everything else I gathered for the holy temple. [4]There are 225,000 pounds of gold from Ophir and 525,000 pounds of refined silver. They are to be used to cover the walls of the buildings, [5]to make gold objects, silver objects, and everything else the craftsmen will make. Who else is willing to make an offering and dedicate himself to the LORD today?"

[6]Then the leaders of the families, the leaders of the tribes of Israel, the commanders of regiments and battalions, and the officials in charge of the king's work gave generously. [7]They gave 375,186 pounds of gold, 750,000 pounds of silver, 135,000 pounds of bronze, and 7,500,000 pounds of iron for the work on God's temple. [8]Whoever happened to have precious stones gave them to Jehiel, Gershon's descendant, for the treasury of the LORD's temple. [9]The people were overjoyed that the leaders gave so generously and wholeheartedly to the LORD.

King David was also overjoyed, and [10]he praised the LORD while the whole assembly watched. David said,

---

[a]28:18 Or "cherubim."

"May you be praised, Lord God of Israel,
      our father forever and ever.*a*

11   Greatness, power, splendor, glory, and majesty are yours, Lord,
         because everything in heaven and on earth is yours.
         The kingdom is yours, Lord,
            and you are honored as head of all things.

12   Riches and honor are in front of you.
         You rule everything.
         You hold power and strength in your hands,
            and you can make anyone great and strong.

13   "Our God, we thank you
         and praise your wonderful name.

14   But who am I and who are my people
            that you enable us to give so generously?
         Everything comes from you.
         We give you only what has come from your hands.

15   To you we are all like our ancestors—
         foreigners without permanent homes.
            Our days are as fleeting as shadows on the ground.
            There's no hope for them.

16"Lord, our God, all this wealth that we gathered to build a temple for your holy name is from you. All of it is yours. 17I know, my God, that you examine hearts and delight in honesty. With an honest heart I have willingly offered all these things. I've been overjoyed to see your people here offering so willingly to you. 18Lord God of our ancestors Abraham, Isaac, and Israel, always watch over your people's deepest thoughts. Keep their hearts directed toward you. 19Make my son Solomon completely committed to you, so that he will obey your commands, requests, and laws and do everything to build the palace I have planned."

Good Morning, God
1 Chronicles 29:14-18

David didn't have to share his money. He could have spent his money on himself or anything else he pleased. After all, he was the king. But David realized God looks closely into the hearts of all people. God sees hearts that are stingy and others that are filled with selfishness. But God found honesty in David's heart because David admitted that God owned every penny he had. If God looked in your heart today, what would he see?

Father, help me to have an honest heart that is willing to share.

---

*a*29:10 Or "May you be praised forever and ever, Lord God of our ancestor Israel."

Solomon Is Made King

²⁰Then David said to the whole assembly, "Praise the Lord your God!" So the whole assembly praised the Lord God of their ancestors and knelt in front of the Lord and the king.

²¹The next day they sacrificed to the Lord. They sacrificed burnt offerings to the Lord: 1,000 bulls, 1,000 rams, 1,000 lambs, wine offerings, and many sacrifices for all Israel. ²²That day they ate and drank as they joyfully celebrated in front of the Lord. For the second time they made David's son Solomon king. On the Lord's behalf they anointed Solomon to be leader and Zadok to be the priest.

²³Then Solomon sat on the Lord's throne as king in place of his father David. Solomon was successful and all Israel obeyed him. ²⁴All the leaders and soldiers and all of King David's sons pledged their loyalty to King Solomon. ²⁵The Lord made Solomon extremely powerful, as all Israel could see. The people of Israel gave him royal honor like no king of Israel before him ever had.

David's Reign—
1 Kings 2:10-12

²⁶David, son of Jesse, had ruled all Israel. ²⁷He ruled as king of Israel for 40 years. He ruled for 7 years in Hebron and for 33 in Jerusalem. ²⁸He died at a very old age. His long life was full of wealth and honor. Then his son Solomon succeeded him as king.

²⁹Everything about King David from first to last is written in the records of the seer *ᵇ* Samuel, the prophet Nathan, and the seer Gad. ³⁰It includes everything about his reign, his power, and the things that happened to him, Israel, and all the other kingdoms.

---

*ᵇ*29:29 A seer is a prophet.

2 Chronicles

Second Chronicles describes how God was faithful
to David's descendants when they were faithful to
him and tells about the rule of Judah's kings who tried
to follow God. God helps leaders who rely on him. But
trouble comes to a nation when its leaders turn away
from God. Eventually, wicked kings led the
people away from God, and the people
were taken away as captives to Babylon.
But 2 Chronicles ends with some
good news. After many years in
captivity, the Jews in Babylon
returned home.

Headlines

Temple Too Small for God
2 Chronicles 2, page 551

Sugar 'n' Spice 'n' Everything Nice
2 Chronicles 9, page 560

Shishak Steals From God
2 Chronicles 12, page 564

Don't Listen to Mom!
2 Chronicles 22, page 574

God Shuts Up Sennacherib
2 Chronicles 32, page 586

King Wears Nose Ring
2 Chronicles 33, page 587

Prophet Comforts King
2 Chronicles 34, page 589

Why hide a baby from its own
grandmother? See 2 Chronicles 22.

If Kids Were
Queens

Imagine if you were queen of your own country! You could do just about anything you wanted. What are some of the things you would do? Declare longer summer vacations? Have pizza and ice cream for supper every day?

Joash became king of Judah when he was just seven years old! And he became one of Judah's best kings! Check out a couple of the things Joash did when he was both a kid and a king:

He cleaned up:
See 2 Chronicles 24:4-5.

He collected:
See 2 Chronicles 24:6-11.

What's In It For Me?

If I am faithful to God, he gives me . . .

PEACE.
SUCCESS.
BLESSINGS.
CONFIDENCE.
ETERNAL
LIFE.

Are Doctors Bad Medicine?

Is it wrong for a Christian to go to a doctor? Some people think so. They believe a person who is sick should just pray for healing.

King Asa probably would have been healed if he had asked God for help (2 Chronicles 16:12). When he relied only on his doctors, Asa's disease got worse. Asa didn't ask the Lord for help.

We should always ask God for help and healing. But that doesn't mean God won't use medicine to answer our prayers! Hezekiah prayed when he was sick. God told Isaiah to use a fig cake as a treatment for the king's boil (2 Kings 20:7). That was medicine.

Is God against doctors? No, God even chose a physician to write two books of the Bible—Luke and Acts. God could heal us without medicine. But today God has given us wonderful medicines and wise doctors who prescribe them. It's OK to go to the doctor when you're sick. But be sure to ask God for healing, too.

Proud or
Humble?

We can choose to be proud or humble. Proud people ignore God's word. Humble people admit when they're wrong and try to please God. Which is better?

Uzziah followed God for many years. Then he became proud and broke God's law (2 Chronicles 26:16). God punished Uzziah with a skin disease. He had to live in a house away from other people for the rest of his life.

King Manasseh was the most evil king Judah ever had. He was cruel, worshiped idols, and practiced witchcraft. So God allowed the king of Assyria to capture Manasseh and put him in prison. Then Manasseh humbled himself (2 Chronicles 33:12-13). He admitted to God that he was wrong, and God forgave him. God even gave Manasseh his kingdom back!

The Road to Revival

Every good king in Judah led the people back to the Lord. Who were the good kings, and what did they do?

1. This king was the first to lead a revival.

_____ **(2 Chronicles 15:8-15)**

2. This king sent teachers throughout the land to teach people the law of God.

_____ **(2 Chronicles 17:7-9)**

3. This king made a collection box to repair God's temple.

_____ **(2 Chronicles 24:4-11)**

4. This king reopened the temple.

_____ **(2 Chronicles 29:5-36)**

5. This king ground idols to powder.

_____ **(2 Chronicles 34:3-4)**

2 Chronicles

God Appears to Solomon—
I Kings 3:1-15; 10:26-29

¹Solomon, son of David, strengthened his position over the kingdom. The LORD his God was with him and made him very powerful.

²Solomon spoke to all Israel—to the commanders of regiments and battalions, judges, every prince, and the heads of Israel's families. ³Then Solomon and the entire assembly went to the place of worship in Gibeon because God's tent of meeting was there. Moses, the LORD's servant, had made the tent in the desert. ⁴(However, David had already brought God's ark from Kiriath Jearim to a place he had prepared for it. He had put up a tent for it in Jerusalem.) ⁵The bronze altar that Bezalel, son of Uri and grandson of Hur, had made was in front of the LORD's tent. There Solomon and the assembly worshiped the LORD. ⁶In the LORD's presence Solomon went to the bronze altar in front of the tent of meeting and sacrificed 1,000 burnt offerings on it.

⁷That night God appeared to Solomon. He said, "What can I give you?"

⁸Solomon responded to God, "You've shown great love to my father David, and you've made me king in his place. ⁹Now, LORD God, you've kept the promise you made to my father David. You've made me king of people who are as numerous as specks of dust on the ground. ¹⁰Give me wisdom and knowledge so that I may lead these people. After all, who can judge this great people of yours?"

¹¹God replied to Solomon, "I know this request is from your heart. You didn't ask for riches, fortunes, honor, or the death of those who hate you. You didn't even ask for a long life. Instead, you've asked for wisdom and knowledge to judge my people, over whom I made you king. ¹²So wisdom and knowledge will be given to you. I will also give you riches, fortunes, and honor like no other king before or after you."

¹³Solomon went from the tent of meeting at the place of worship in Gibeon to Jerusalem. And he ruled Israel.

¹⁴Solomon built up his army with chariots and war horses. He had 1,400 chariots and 12,000 war horses. He stationed some in chariot cities and others with himself in Jerusalem.

¹⁵The king made silver and gold as common in Jerusalem as stones, and he made cedars as plentiful as fig trees in the foothills.

¹⁶Solomon's horses were imported from Egypt and Kue. The king's traders bought them from Kue for a fixed price. ¹⁷They imported each chariot from Egypt for 15 pounds of silver and each horse for 6 ounces of silver. For the same price they obtained horses to export to all the Hittite and Aramean kings.

Solomon Assembles the Labor and Materials for the Temple—
I Kings 5:1-18; 7:13-14

ᵃ¹Solomon gave orders to begin building the temple for the LORD's name and a royal palace for himself.

²Solomon drafted 70,000 men to carry heavy loads, 80,000 to quarry stones in

---

ᵃ2:1 2 Chronicles 2:1-18 in English Bibles is 2 Chronicles 1:18–2:17 in the Hebrew Bible.

the mountains, and 3,600 foremen. ³Solomon sent word to King Huram of Tyre by saying, "Do what you did for my father David. You sent him cedar so that he could build a palace to live in. ⁴I want to build the temple for the name of the LORD my God. I want to dedicate it to him, burn sweet-smelling incense in his presence, and have rows of bread there continually. I want to sacrifice burnt offerings every morning and evening, on weekly worship days, New Moon Festivals, and during the annual festivals appointed by the LORD our God. (These festivals are always to be celebrated by Israel.) ⁵The temple I am building will be great because our God is greater than all other gods. ⁶But who is able to build him a temple when heaven itself, the highest heaven, cannot hold him? Who am I to build him a temple except as a place to sacrifice in his presence?

⁷"Send me a man who has the skill to work with gold, silver, bronze, and iron as well as purple, dark red, and violet cloth. He should know how to make engravings with the skilled men whom my father David provided for me in Judah and Jerusalem. ⁸Send me cedar, cypress, and sandalwood from Lebanon. I know that your servants are skilled Lebanese lumberjacks. My workers will work with your workers. ⁹They'll prepare plenty of lumber for me, because the temple I want to build will be large and astonishing. ¹⁰I will give your lumberjacks 120,000 bushels of ground wheat, 120,000 bushels of barley, 200,000 gallons of wine, and 200,000 gallons of olive oil."

¹¹Then King Huram of Tyre responded to Solomon by sending a letter that said, "Because the LORD loves his people, he made you their king." ¹²Huram added, "May the LORD God of Israel be praised. He made the heavens and the earth and has given King David a wise son who has insight and intelligence and can build the LORD's temple and a royal palace. ¹³And now, I'm sending a man with skill and intelligence—Huram Abi. ¹⁴He was the son of a woman from the tribe of Dan, and his father is a native of Tyre. Huram knows how to work with gold, silver, bronze, iron, stone, wood, purple, violet, and dark red cloth, and linen. He also knows how to make all kinds of engravings and follow any set of plans that will be given to him. He can work with your skilled workmen and the skilled workmen of His Majesty David, your father. ¹⁵Your Majesty may now send the wheat, barley, olive oil, and wine he promised the workers. ¹⁶We will cut all the lumber you need in Lebanon. Then we will make rafts out of it and send them to you in Joppa by sea. You can take it from there to Jerusalem."

¹⁷Solomon counted all the men who were foreigners in the land of Israel, as his father David had counted them. Solomon counted 153,600 foreigners. ¹⁸He made 70,000 of them carry heavy loads, 80,000 of them quarry stone in the mountains, and 3,600 of them supervise the work as foremen.

The Temple Built and Furnished—
I Kings 6:1-38; 7:13-51

3 ¹Solomon began to build the LORD's temple in Jerusalem on Mount Moriah, where the LORD appeared to his father David. There David had prepared the site on the threshing floor*ᵃ* of Ornan the Jebusite. ²He began to build on the second day in the second month of the fourth year of his reign.

³This is how Solomon laid the foundation to build God's temple. It was 90 feet long and 30 feet wide. (They used the old standard measurement.) ⁴The entrance hall in front of the main room was 30 feet wide (the same as the width of the temple) and 30 feet high. He covered its inside walls with pure gold. ⁵He paneled the larger building with cypress, overlaid it with fine gold, and decorated it with designs in the form

---

ᵃ 3:1 A threshing floor is an outdoor area where grain is separated from its husks.

of palm trees and chains. [6]He covered the building with gems to beautify it and used gold from Parvaim. [7]He also overlaid the building, the rafters, the threshold, the walls, and the doors with gold, and he carved angels[b] into the walls.

[8]He made the most holy place. It was as long as the temple was wide, 30 feet long. It was also 30 feet wide. He overlaid it with 45,000 pounds of fine gold. [9]The gold nails weighed 20 ounces. He also overlaid the upper rooms with gold.

[10]In the most holy place he made two sculptured angels and covered them with gold. [11]The combined length of the angels' wings was 30 feet. A wing of one of the angels was 7½ feet long and touched the wall of the building. Its other wing was 7½ feet long and touched one wing of the other. [12]The wing of the other one of the angels was 7½ feet long and touched the other wall of the building. Its other wing was 7½ feet long and touched the wing of the first. So the angels' combined wingspan was 30 feet. [13]They stood on their feet and faced the main hall. [14]Solomon made the canopy of violet, purple, and dark red cloth and of linen and decorated it with angels.

[15]He made two pillars for the front of the temple. They were 53 feet long, and the capital on each pillar was 7½ feet high. [16]He made chains for the inner room and also put them on the capitals. He made 100 pomegranates and put them on the chains. [17]He set up the pillars in front of the temple, one on the right and the other on the left. He named the one on the right Jachin [He Establishes] and the one on the left Boaz [In Him Is Strength].

[1]He made a bronze altar 30 feet long, 30 feet wide, and 15 feet high. [2]Huram made a pool from cast metal. It was 15 feet in diameter. It was round, 7½ feet high, and had a circumference of 45 feet. [3]Under the rim were two rows of figurines shaped like bulls all around the 45-foot circumference of the pool. They were cast in metal when the pool was cast. [4]The pool was set on 12 metal bulls. Three bulls faced north, three faced west, three faced south, and three faced east. The pool was set on them, and their hindquarters were toward the center of the pool. [5]The pool was three inches thick. Its rim was like the rim of a cup, shaped like a lily's bud. It held 18,000 gallons.

[6]Huram also made ten basins for washing and put five on the south side and five on the north side. The priests rinsed the meat prepared for the burnt offerings in them. They used the pool to wash themselves.

[7]Huram made ten gold lamp stands according to their specifications and put them in the temple, five on the south side and five on the north side. [8]He made ten tables and put them in the temple, five on the south side and five on the north side. And he made 100 gold bowls.

[9]He also made the priests' courtyard and the large courtyard and its doors. He covered the doors with bronze. [10]He set the pool on the south side in the southeast corner. [11]Huram also made the pots, shovels, and bowls.

So Huram finished the work for King Solomon in God's temple: [12]2 pillars, bowl-shaped capitals on top of the 2 pillars, and 2 sets of filigree to cover the 2 bowl-shaped capitals on top of the pillars, [13]400 pomegranates for the 2 sets of filigree (2 rows of pomegranates for each filigree to cover the 2 bowl-shaped capitals on the pillars), [14]10 stands and 10[a] basins on the stands, [15]1 pool and the 12 bulls under it, [16]pots, shovels, and three-pronged forks. Huram made all of them out of polished bronze for the Lord's temple at King Solomon's request. [17]The king cast them in foundries in the Jordan Valley between Succoth and Zeredah. [18]Solomon made so many of these products that no one tried to determine how much the bronze weighed.

---

[b]3:7 Or "cherubim."   [a]4:14 1 Kings 7:43, Greek; Masoretic Text "he made stands, and he made basins. . . ."

¹⁹Solomon made all the furnishings for God's temple: the gold altar, the gold tables on which the bread of the presence was placed, ²⁰lamp stands and lamps of pure gold (to burn as directed in front of the inner room), ²¹flowers, lamps, pure gold tongs, ²²snuffers, basins, dishes, incense burners of pure gold, the gold entrance to the temple, the gold doors of the inner ⌐room⌐ (the most holy place), and the gold doors of the temple.

¹All the work Solomon did on the LORD's temple was finished. He brought the holy things that had belonged to his father David—the silver, gold, and all the utensils—and put them in the storerooms of God's temple.

The LORD Comes to His Temple—
I Kings 8:1-11

²Then Solomon assembled the respected leaders of Israel, all the heads of the tribes, and the leaders of the Israelite families. They came to Jerusalem to take the ark of the LORD's promise from the City of David (that is, Zion). ³All the men of Israel gathered around the king at the Festival ⌐of Booths⌐ in the seventh month.

⁴When all the leaders of Israel had arrived, the Levites picked up the ark. ⁵They brought the ark, the tent of meeting, and all the holy utensils in it ⌐to the temple⌐. The priests and the Levites carried them ⁶while King Solomon and the whole assembly from Israel were offering countless sheep and cattle sacrifices in front of the ark. ⁷The priests brought the ark of the LORD's promise to its place in the inner room of the temple (the most holy place) under the wings of the angels.^a

⁸The angels' outstretched wings were over the place where the ark ⌐rested⌐ so that the angels became a covering above the ark and its poles. ⁹The poles were so long that their ends could be seen in the holy place by anyone standing in front of the inner room,^b but they couldn't be seen outside. (They are still there today.) ¹⁰There was nothing in the ark except the two tablets Moses placed there at Horeb, where the LORD made a promise to the Israelites after they left Egypt.

¹¹All the priests who were present had performed the ceremonies to make themselves holy to God without regard to staying in their divisions. ¹²All the Levites who were musicians—Asaph, Heman, Jeduthun, their sons, and their relatives—were dressed in fine linen and stood east of the altar with cymbals, harps, and lyres. With the musicians were 120 priests blowing trumpets. When the priests left the holy place,^c ¹³the trumpeters and singers praised and thanked the LORD in unison. Accompanied by trumpets, cymbals, and other musical instruments, they sang in praise to the LORD: "He is good; his mercy endures forever." Then the LORD's temple was filled with a cloud. ¹⁴The priests couldn't serve because of the cloud. The LORD's glory filled God's temple.

Solomon Addresses the People—
I Kings 8:12-21

¹Then Solomon said, "The LORD said he would live in a dark cloud. ²But I have built you a high temple, a home for you to live in permanently."

³Then the king turned around and blessed the whole assembly from Israel while they were standing. ⁴"Thanks be to the LORD God of Israel. With his mouth he made a promise to my father David; with his hand he carried it out. He said, ⁵"Ever since I

---

^a5:7 Or "cherubim." ^b5:9 A few Hebrew manuscripts, 1 Kings 8:8, Greek; other Hebrew manuscripts "The poles extended so long from the ark that their ends could be seen by anyone standing in front of the inner room."
^c5:12 The first part of verse 11 (in Hebrew) has been placed just before verse 13 to express the complex Hebrew sentence structure more clearly in English.

brought my people Israel out of Egypt, I didn't choose any city from the tribes of Israel as a place to build a temple for my name. And I didn't choose any man to be prince over my people Israel. [6]But now I've chosen Jerusalem to be a place for my name; I've chosen David to rule my people Israel.'

[7]"My father David had his heart set on building a temple for the name of the LORD God of Israel. [8]However, the LORD said to my father David, 'Since you had your heart set on building a temple for my name, your intentions were good. [9]But you must not build the temple. Instead, your own son will build the temple for my name.' [10]The LORD has kept the promise he made. I've taken my father David's place, and I sit on the throne of Israel as the LORD promised. I've built the temple for the name of the LORD God of Israel. [11]I've put the ark which contains the LORD's promise to Israel there."

Solomon's Prayer—
I Kings 8:22-53; Psalm 132:1, 8-10

[12]In the presence of the entire assembly of Israel, Solomon stood in front of the LORD's altar. He stretched out his hands to pray. [13](Solomon had made a bronze platform 7½ feet long, 7½ feet wide, and 4½ feet high. He put it in the middle of the courtyard. He stood on the platform, knelt in front of the entire assembly, and stretched out his hands toward heaven.) [14]He said,

"LORD God of Israel,
  there is no god like you in heaven or on earth.
You keep your promise[a] of mercy to your servants,
  who obey you wholeheartedly.
[15] You have kept your promise to my father David, your servant.
  With your mouth you promised it.
  With your hand you carried it out as it is today.

[16] "Now, LORD God of Israel,
  keep your promise to my father David, your servant.
  You said, 'You will never fail to have an heir
    sitting in front of me on the throne of Israel
    if your descendants are faithful to me
      as you have been faithful to me.'

Good Morning, God
2 Chronicles 6:18-21

The temple was a place where God chose to live during Solomon's time. People turned toward the temple when they prayed to show their faith in God. We don't have a temple today because God lives in our hearts! We can turn to him in prayer wherever we go. We can sing, cry, or talk to him anytime. He's always listening because he lives inside us.

Lord, thank you for making your home in my heart.

---

[a]6:14 Or "covenant."

17 "So now, Lord God of Israel,
    may the promise you made to David, your servant, come true.

18 "Does God really live on earth with people?
    If heaven itself, the highest heaven, cannot hold you,
    then how can this temple that I have built?

19 Nevertheless, my Lord God, please pay attention to my prayer for mercy.
    Listen to my cry for help as I pray to you.

20   Day and night may your eyes be on this temple,
        the place about which you said your name will be there.
    Listen to me as I pray toward this place.

21 Hear the plea for mercy
    that your people Israel and I pray toward this place.
    Hear us in heaven, the place where you live.
    Hear and forgive.

22 "If anyone sins against another person
        and is required to take an oath
            and comes to take the oath in front of your altar in this temple,

23 then hear ˌthat personˌ in heaven, take action, and make a decision.
    Repay the guilty person with the proper punishment,
        but declare the innocent person innocent.

24 "An enemy may defeat your people Israel
    because they have sinned against you.
        But when your people turn, praise your name, pray,
            and plead with you in this temple,

25 then hear ˌthemˌ in heaven, forgive the sins of your people Israel,
    and bring them back to the land
        that you gave to them and their ancestors.

26 "When the sky is shut and there's no rain
    because they are sinning against you
        and they pray toward this place, praise your name,
            and turn away from their sin because you made them suffer,

27 then hear ˌthemˌ in heaven.
    Forgive the sins of your servants, your people Israel.
    Teach them the proper way to live.
        Then send rain on the land,
            which you gave to your people as an inheritance.

28 "There may be famine in the land.
    Plant diseases, heat waves, funguses, locusts,
        or grasshoppers may destroy crops.
    Enemies may blockade Israel's city gates.
    During every plague or sickness

29   ˌhearˌ every prayer for mercy
        made by one person or by all the people in Israel,
            all who know suffering or pain,
                who stretch out their hands toward this temple.

30 Hear ˌthemˌ in heaven, where you live.
    Forgive ˌthemˌ, and give each person the proper reply.

(You know what is in their hearts,
because you alone know what is in people's hearts.)
31 Then, as long as they live in the land that you gave to our ancestors,
they will fear you and follow you.

32 "People who are not Israelites
will come from distant countries because of your great name,
mighty hand, and powerful arm.
When they come to pray facing this temple,
33 then hear them in heaven, the place where you live.
Do everything they ask you
so that all the people of the world may know your name
and fear you like your people Israel
and learn that this temple which I built bears your name.

34 "When your people go to war against their enemies
(wherever you may send them)
and they pray to you toward this city you have chosen
and the temple I built for your name,
35 then hear their prayer for mercy in heaven,
and do what is right for them.

36 "They may sin against you.
(No one is sinless.)
You may become angry with them and hand them over to an enemy
who takes them to another country as captives,
whether it is far or near.
37 If they come to their senses,
are sorry for what they've done,
and plead with you in the land where they are captives,
saying, 'We have sinned. We have done wrong.
We have been wicked,'
38 if they change their attitude toward you
in the land where they are captives,
if they pray to you
toward the land that you gave their ancestors,
and the city you have chosen,
and the temple I have built for your name,
39 then in heaven, the place where you live, hear their prayer for mercy.
Do what is right for them.
Forgive your people, who have sinned against you.

40 "Finally, my God, may your eyes be open and your ears attentive
to the prayers offered in this place.

41 "Now arise, and come to your resting place, LORD God—
you and the ark of your power.
Clothe your priests, LORD God, with salvation.
Let your godly ones rejoice in what is good.
42 LORD God, do not reject your anointed one.
Remember your mercy to your servant David!"

Women's World — **Solomon's Temple**
2 Chronicles 7:4-10

The temple in Jerusalem was the one and only place Israelites were to offer sacrifices. Three times each year the Jews came to the temple for worship festivals. Solomon built the temple in 960 B.C., but in 586 B.C. it was destroyed by the Babylonians. About a thousand years after Solomon started his temple, Jesus taught in a much larger temple built on the same spot.

God's people were joyful when they came to the temple to worship. The one place to worship reminded them that there is only one God. And the sacrifices offered there helped all the Israelites remember that God forgives sins.

Solomon Offers Sacrifices—
I Kings 8:62-66

7 ¹When Solomon finished praying, fire came down from heaven and consumed the burnt offerings and the other sacrifices, and the LORD's glory filled the temple. ²The priests couldn't go into the LORD's temple because the LORD's glory had filled the LORD's temple. ³When all the Israelites saw the fire come down and the LORD's glory on the temple, they knelt down with their faces on the pavement. They worshiped and praised the LORD, ˌby saying, "He is good; his mercy endures forever."

⁴Then the king and all the people offered sacrifices to the LORD. ⁵King Solomon offered 22,000 cattle and 120,000 sheep as sacrifices to the LORD. So the king and all the people dedicated God's temple.

⁶The priests were standing at their posts. So were the Levites who had the LORD's musical instruments which King David made for praising the LORD with "his mercy endures forever" and which he used to offer praise. The priests were opposite the Levites blowing trumpets while all Israel was standing ˌthereˌ.

⁷Solomon designated the courtyard in front of the LORD's temple as a holy place. He sacrificed the burnt offerings, grain offerings, and the fat because the bronze altar that he had made and that was in front of the LORD was not able to hold all of them.

⁸At that time Solomon and all Israel celebrated the Festival ˌof Boothsˌ. A very large crowd had come from ˌthe territory between ˌthe border of Hamath and the River of Egypt. ⁹On the eighth day there was an assembly. They had observed the dedication of the altar for seven days and celebrated the festival for ˌanotherˌ seven days. ¹⁰On the twenty-third day of the seventh month, Solomon dismissed the people to their tents. They rejoiced with cheerful hearts for all the blessings the LORD had given David, Solomon, and his people Israel.

The LORD Answers Solomon's Prayer—
I Kings 9:1-9

¹¹Solomon finished the LORD's temple and the royal palace and completed everything he had in mind for the LORD's temple and his own palace. ¹²Then the LORD appeared to him at night. He said to Solomon,

"I have heard your prayer
    and have chosen this place for myself as a temple for sacrifices.
¹³ I may shut the sky so that there is no rain,
    or command grasshoppers to devour the countryside,
    or send an epidemic among my people.
¹⁴ However, if my people, who are called by my name,
    will humble themselves,
    pray, search for me, and turn from their evil ways,
    then I will hear their prayer from heaven, forgive their sins,
    and heal their country.
¹⁵ My eyes will be open,
    and my ears will pay attention to those prayers at this place.
¹⁶ I have chosen and declared this temple holy
    so that my name may be placed there forever.
My eyes and my heart will always be there.

¹⁷ "If you will be faithful to me as your father David was,
    do everything I command,
    and obey my laws and rules,
¹⁸ then I will establish your royal dynasty
    as I said in a promise to your father David,
    'You will never fail to have an heir ruling Israel.'
¹⁹ But if you and your descendants turn away from me
    and abandon my commands and laws that I gave you,
    and follow and serve other gods and worship them,
²⁰ then I will uproot Israel from the land I gave them.
I will reject this temple that I declared holy for my name.
I will make it an example
    and an object of ridicule for all the people of the world.
²¹ Everyone passing by this impressive temple will be appalled.
They will ask,
    'Why did the LORD do these things to this land and this temple?'
²² They will answer themselves,
    'They abandoned the LORD God of their ancestors,
    who brought them out of Egypt.
They adopted other gods, worshiped, and served them.
That is why he brought this disaster on them.' "

Solomon Completes His Construction—
I Kings 9:10-28

8 ¹It took Solomon 20 years to build the LORD's house and his own house. ²He rebuilt the cities Huram gave him, and he had Israelites live in them.
³Then Solomon went to Hamath Zobah and conquered it. ⁴He rebuilt Tadmor in the desert and built all the storage cities in Hamath. ⁵He rebuilt Upper Beth Horon and Lower Beth Horon into cities fortified with walls, double-door gates, and bars.

⁶He also rebuilt Baalath and all the storage cities that he owned. He built all the cities for his chariots, all the cities for his war horses, and whatever else he wanted to build in Jerusalem, Lebanon, or the entire territory that he governed.

⁷The Hittites, Perizzites, Hivites, and Jebusites had been left in the land because the Israelites had not been able to destroy them.ᵃ They were not Israelites, ⁸but they had descendants who were still in the land. Solomon drafted them for slave labor. (They are still slaves today.) ⁹But Solomon didn't make any of the Israelites slaves for his projects. Instead, they were the soldiers, officers, generals, and commanders of his chariot and cavalry units.

¹⁰These were the officers in charge of King Solomon's projects: 250 foremen for the people who did the work.

¹¹Solomon brought Pharaoh's daughter from the City of David to a palace he had built for her. He said, "My wife will not live in the palace of King David of Israel because these places where the LORD's ark has come are holy."

¹²Then Solomon sacrificed burnt offerings to the LORD on the LORD's altar that he built in front of the entrance hall. ¹³He sacrificed every day, on weekly worship days, on the New Moon Festivals, and on the three annual festivals (the Festival of Unleavened Bread, the Festival of Weeks, and the Festival of Booths) as Moses had commanded. ¹⁴As Solomon's father David had directed, he set up the divisions of priests for their service and the divisions of Levites for their appointed places. The Levites were to lead in praising the LORD and to serve beside the priests by doing whatever needed to be done each day. Solomon also set up divisions of doorkeepers at every gate because this is what David, the man of God, had commanded. ¹⁵No one neglected the king's orders to the priests or the Levites in any matter, including the temple's finances. ¹⁶All of Solomon's work was carried out from the day the foundation of the LORD's temple was laid until it was completed. The LORD's temple was now finished.

¹⁷Then Solomon went to the coast near Ezion Geber and Elath in Edom. ¹⁸Huram sent his own servants and his experienced sailors with ships to Solomon. They went with Solomon's servants to Ophir, got 33,750 pounds of gold, and brought it to King Solomon.

The Queen of Sheba Visits Solomon—
I Kings 10:1-13

9 ¹The queen of Sheba heard about Solomon's reputation. So she came to Jerusalem to test him with riddles. She arrived with a large group of servants, with camels carrying spices, a large quantity of gold, and precious stones. When she came to Solomon, she talked to him about everything she had on her mind. ²Solomon answered all her questions. No question was too difficult for Solomon to answer.

³When the queen of Sheba saw Solomon's wisdom, the palace he built, ⁴the food on his table, his officers' seating arrangement, the organization of his officials and the uniforms they wore, his cupbearersᵃ and their uniforms, and the burnt offerings that he sacrificed at the LORD's temple, she was breathless. ⁵She told the king, "What I heard in my country about your words and your wisdom is true! ⁶But I didn't believe the reports until I came and saw it with my own eyes. I wasn't even told about half of the extent of your wisdom. You've surpassed the stories I've heard. ⁷How blessed your men must be! How blessed these servants of yours must be because

---

ᵃ8:7 "because the Israelites. . . ." This clause has been moved from verse 8 (in Hebrew) to express the complex Hebrew sentence structure more clearly in English.   ᵃ9:4 A cupbearer was a trusted royal official who ensured that the king's drink was not poisoned.

Household Furnishings

2 Chronicles 9:1-24

The typical Old Testament home had a stone or mud ledge along the wall where people could sit. At night people wrapped their coats around themselves and slept on the floor. This wealthy person's home had cushioned benches on both sides of the room. It also had stools, a low table, and a brazier, or metal container, for heating. It even had a lamp stand with a bronze (not clay) lamp! Although this wealthy person had more than most people, Solomon had riches far above these.

they are always stationed in front of you and listen to your wisdom! [8]Thank the Lord your God, who is pleased with you. He has put you on his throne to be king on behalf of the Lord your God. Because of your God's love for the people of Israel, he has established them permanently and made you king over them so that you would maintain justice and righteousness."

[9]She gave the king 9,000 pounds of gold, a very large quantity of spices, and precious stones. Never was there such a large quantity of spices ͵in Israel͵ as those that the queen of Sheba gave King Solomon.

[10]Huram's servants and Solomon's servants who brought gold from Ophir also brought sandalwood and precious stones. [11]With the sandalwood the king made gateways to the Lord's temple and the royal palace, and lyres and harps for the singers. No one had ever seen anything like them in Judah.

[12]King Solomon gave the queen of Sheba anything she wanted, whatever she asked for, more than what she had brought him. Then she and her servants went back to her country.

Solomon's Wealth—
I Kings 5:1; 10:14-29

[13]The gold that came to Solomon in one year weighed 49,950 pounds, [14]not counting ͵the gold͵ which the merchants and traders brought. All the Arab kings and governors of the land also brought gold and silver to Solomon.

[15]King Solomon made 200 large shields of hammered gold, using 15 pounds of gold on each shield. [16]He also made 300 small shields of hammered gold, using 7½ pounds of gold on each shield. The king put them in the hall ͵named͵ the Forest of Lebanon.

[17]The king also made a large ivory throne and covered it with pure gold. [18]Six steps led to the throne, which had a gold footstool attached to it. There were armrests on both sides of the seat. Two lions stood beside the armrests. [19]Twelve lions stood on six steps, one on each side. Nothing like this had been made for any other kingdom.

²⁰All King Solomon's cups were gold, and all the utensils for the hall named the Forest of Lebanon were fine gold. (Silver wasn't considered valuable in Solomon's time.) ²¹The king had ships going to Tarshish with Huram's sailors. Once every three years the Tarshish ships would bring gold, silver, ivory, apes, and monkeys.

²²In wealth and wisdom King Solomon was greater than all the other kings of the world. ²³All the kings of the world wanted to listen to the wisdom that God gave Solomon. ²⁴So everyone who came brought him gifts: articles of silver and gold, clothing, weapons, spices, horses, and mules. This happened year after year.

²⁵Solomon had 4,000 stalls for horses and chariots, and 12,000 war horses. He stationed some in chariot cities and others with himself in Jerusalem. ²⁶He ruled all the kings from the Euphrates River to the country of the Philistines and as far as the Egyptian border. ²⁷The king made silver as common in Jerusalem as stones, and he made cedars as plentiful as fig trees in the foothills. ²⁸Horses were imported for Solomon from Egypt and from all other countries.

Solomon's Death—
1 Kings 11:41-43

²⁹Aren't the rest of Solomon's acts from first to last written in the records of Nathan the prophet, in the prophecy of Ahijah from Shiloh, and in Iddo the seer's[b] visions about Jeroboam (son of Nebat)?

³⁰Solomon ruled in Jerusalem over all Israel for 40 years. ³¹Solomon lay down in death with his ancestors and was buried in the City of David. His son Rehoboam succeeded him as king.

King Rehoboam Foolishly Rejects Israel's Request—
1 Kings 12:1-19

10 ¹Rehoboam went to Shechem because all Israel had gone to Shechem to make him king. ²Jeroboam (Nebat's son) was still in Egypt, where he had fled from King Solomon. When he heard about Rehoboam, he returned from Egypt. ³Israel sent for Jeroboam and invited him back. Jeroboam and all Israel went to speak to

Good Morning, God
....
2 Chronicles 10:6-11

Imagine that you needed help with a certain problem. Who do you think would give you better advice: a friend or an older Christian adult? Young King Rehoboam followed the foolish advice of his friends instead of the wise direction from some older adult leaders. It may be tempting to listen to our friends instead of adults because our peers often tell us what we like to hear. But remember Rehoboam's mistake, and be careful when seeking advice. Ask God to give you godly, wise adults to turn to when you need help.

Lord, guide me in asking for advice. Help me find people who will give me good and wise counsel.

---

[b] 9:29 A seer is a prophet.

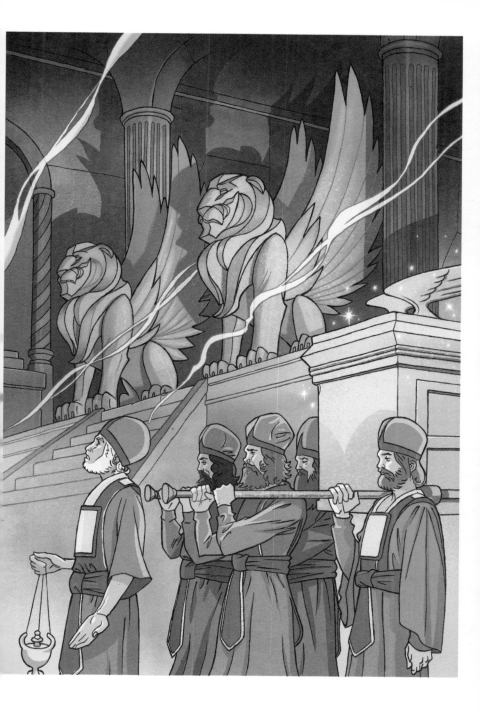

The Lord Comes to His Temple

The Lord Comes to His Temple

2 Chronicles 5:2–7

2 Then Solomon assembled the respected leaders of Israel, all the heads of the tribes, and the leaders of the Israelite families. They came to Jerusalem to take the ark of the Lord's promise from the City of David (that is, Zion). **3** All the men of Israel gathered around the king at the Festival ˻of Booths˼ in the seventh month.

4 When all the leaders of Israel had arrived, the Levites picked up the ark. **5** They brought the ark, the tent of meeting, and all the holy utensils in it ˻to the temple˼. The priests and the Levites carried them **6** while King Solomon and the whole assembly from Israel were offering countless sheep and cattle sacrifices in front of the ark. **7** The priests brought the ark of the Lord's promise to its place in the inner room of the temple (the most holy place) under the wings of the angels.

Rehoboam. They said, [4]"Your father made us carry a heavy burden. Reduce the hard work and lighten the heavy burden he put on us, and we will serve you."

[5]He said to them, "Come back the day after tomorrow." So the people left.

[6]King Rehoboam sought advice from the older leaders who had served his father Solomon while he was still alive. He asked, "What do you advise? How should I respond to these people?"

[7]They told him, "If you are good to these people and try to please them by speaking gently to them, then they will always be your servants."

[8]But he ignored the advice the older leaders gave him. He sought advice from the young men who had grown up with him and were serving him. [9]He asked them, "What is your advice? How should we respond to these people who are asking me to lighten the burden my father put on them?"

[10]The young men who had grown up with him answered, "This is what you should tell them: 'My little finger is heavier than my father's whole body.[a] [11]If my father put a heavy burden on you, I will add to it. If my father punished you with whips, I will punish you with scorpions.' "

[12]So Jeroboam and all the people came back to Rehoboam two days later, as the king had instructed them. [13]The king answered them harshly. He ignored the older leaders' advice. [14]He spoke to them as the young men advised. He said, "If my father made your burden heavy, I will add to it. If my father punished you with whips, I will use scorpions." [15]The king refused to listen to the people because the LORD was directing these events to carry out the promise he had made to Jeroboam (Nebat's son) through Ahijah from Shiloh.

[16]When all Israel saw that the king refused to listen to them, the people answered the king,

"What share do we have in David's kingdom?
We won't receive an inheritance from Jesse's son.
Everyone to his own tent, Israel!
Now look after your own house, David!"

So all Israel went home to their own tents. [17]But Rehoboam ruled the Israelites who lived in the cities of Judah.

[18]Then King Rehoboam sent Hadoram to the Israelites. He was in charge of forced labor, but they stoned him to death. So King Rehoboam got on his chariot as fast as he could and fled to Jerusalem. [19]Israel has rebelled against David's dynasty to this day.

Israel's Priests Come to Judah—
1 Kings 12:21-33

[1]When Rehoboam came to Jerusalem, he gathered the people of Judah and Benjamin, 180,000 of the best soldiers, to fight against Israel and return the kingdom to Rehoboam.

[2]But God spoke his word to Shemaiah, the man of God. He said, [3]"Speak to Judah's King Rehoboam, son of Solomon, and all Israel in Judah and Benjamin. [4]This is what the LORD says: Don't wage war against your relatives. Everyone, go home. What has happened is my doing." So they obeyed the word of the LORD. They turned back from their attack on Jeroboam.

[5]Rehoboam lived in Jerusalem and built fortified cities in Judah. [6]He rebuilt

---

[a] 10:10 Hebrew meaning uncertain.

Bethlehem, Etam, Tekoa, [7]Beth Zur, Soco, Adullam, [8]Gath, Mareshah, Ziph, [9]Adoraim, Lachish, Azekah, [10]Zorah, Aijalon, and Hebron. These were fortified cities in Judah and Benjamin. [11]He strengthened them and put army officers with reserves of food, olive oil, and wine in them. [12]In each city he stored shields and spears. He made the cities very secure. So Rehoboam held on to Judah and Benjamin.

[13]The priests and Levites in every region of Israel sided with Rehoboam. [14]The priests abandoned their land and property and went to Judah and Jerusalem because Jeroboam and his descendants rejected them as the LORD's priests. [15]Instead, Jeroboam appointed his own priests for the illegal worship sites and the goat and calf statues he had made as idols. [16]People from every tribe of Israel who were determined to seek the LORD God of Israel followed the Levitical priests to Jerusalem to sacrifice to the LORD God of their ancestors.

[17]So they strengthened the kingdom of Judah by supporting Rehoboam, son of Solomon, for three years. During those three years they lived the way David and Solomon had lived.

Rehoboam's Family

[18]Rehoboam married Mahalath, daughter of Jerimoth. (Jerimoth was the son of David and Abihail. Abihail was the daughter of Eliab, son of Jesse.) [19]Mahalath gave birth to the following sons: Jeush, Shemariah, and Zaham.

[20]After marrying Mahalath, he married Maacah, Absalom's granddaughter. She gave birth to Abijah, Attai, Ziza, and Shelomith. [21]Rehoboam loved Maacah, Absalom's granddaughter, more than all his other wives and concubines.[a] (He had 18 wives and 60 concubines. He fathered 28 sons and 60 daughters.)

[22]Rehoboam appointed Abijah, son of Maacah, as family head and prince among his brothers. By doing this, Rehoboam could make him king. [23]He wisely placed his sons in every region of Judah and Benjamin, in every fortified city. He gave them allowances and obtained many wives for them.

King Shishak Takes the Temple Treasures—
I Kings 14:21-31

[1]When Rehoboam had established his kingdom and made himself strong, he and all Israel abandoned the LORD's teachings. [2]In the fifth year of Rehoboam's reign, King Shishak of Egypt attacked Jerusalem. This happened because all Israel was not loyal to the LORD. [3]Shishak had 1,200 chariots, 60,000 horses, and an army of countless Libyans, Sukkites, and Sudanese from Egypt.

[4]He captured the fortified cities in Judah and then came to Jerusalem.

[5]The prophet Shemaiah came to Rehoboam and the leaders of Judah who had gathered in Jerusalem because of Shishak. Shemaiah said to them, "This is what the LORD says: You have abandoned me, so I will abandon you. I will hand you over to Shishak." [6]Then the commanders of Israel and the king humbled themselves. "The LORD is right!" they said.

[7]When the LORD saw that they had humbled themselves, he spoke his word to Shemaiah: "They have humbled themselves. I will not destroy them. In a little while I will give them an escape. I will not use Shishak to pour my anger on Jerusalem. [8]But they will become his servants so that they can learn the difference between serving me and serving foreign kings."

[9]King Shishak of Egypt attacked Jerusalem and took the treasures from the LORD's

---

[a] 11:21 A concubine is considered a wife except she has fewer rights under the law.

temple and the royal palace. He took them all. He took the gold shields Solomon had made. ¹⁰So King Rehoboam made bronze shields to replace them and put them by the entrance to the royal palace, where the captains of the guards were stationed. ¹¹Whenever the king went into the LORD's temple, guards carried the shields and then returned them to the guardroom.

¹²After Rehoboam humbled himself, the LORD was no longer angry with him and didn't completely destroy him. So things went well in Judah.

¹³King Rehoboam strengthened his position in Jerusalem and ruled. He was 41 years old when he began to rule. He ruled for 17 years in Jerusalem, the city that the LORD chose from all the tribes of Israel, the city where the LORD put his name. (Rehoboam's mother was an Ammonite woman named Naamah.) ¹⁴He did evil things because he was not serious about dedicating himself to serving the LORD.

¹⁵Aren't the events concerning Rehoboam from first to last written in the records of the prophet Shemaiah and the records of the seer*ᵃ Iddo in the genealogies? There was war between Rehoboam and Jeroboam as long as they lived. ¹⁶Rehoboam lay down in death with his ancestors and was buried in the City of David. His son Abijah succeeded him as king.

King Abijah's War With King Jeroboam—
I Kings 15:1-8

¹In the eighteenth year of the reign of Jeroboam, Abijah began to rule Judah. ²He ruled for three years in Jerusalem. His mother was named Micaiah, daughter of Uriel from Gibeah.

There was war between Abijah and Jeroboam.

³Abijah prepared for battle with an army of 400,000 of the best soldiers, while Jeroboam arranged to oppose him with 800,000 of the best professional soldiers.

⁴Then Abijah stood on Mount Zemaraim in the mountains of Ephraim. He called out, "Jeroboam and all Israel, listen to me! ⁵Don't you know that the LORD God of Israel gave the kingdom of Israel to David and his descendants forever in a permanent promise?*ᵃ ⁶But Jeroboam (Nebat's son) rebelled against his master. He had been the servant of David's son Solomon. ⁷Worthless, good-for-nothing men gathered around him. They opposed Rehoboam, son of Solomon, when Rehoboam was too young and inexperienced to challenge them. ⁸Do you now intend to challenge the LORD's kingdom, which has been placed in the hands of David's descendants? You are a large crowd, and you have the gold calves that Jeroboam made to be your gods. ⁹You forced out the LORD's priests who were Aaron's descendants, and you forced out the Levites so that you could appoint your own priests, as the people in foreign countries do. Anyone who has a young bull and seven rams can be ordained as a priest of nonexistent gods.

¹⁰"However, the LORD is our God. We haven't abandoned him. The priests who serve the LORD are Aaron's descendants, and the Levites assist them. ¹¹They sacrifice burnt offerings to the LORD every morning and every evening. They offer sweet-smelling incense and rows of bread on the clean*ᵇ table. The lamps on the gold lamp stand burn every evening. We're following the instructions the LORD our God gave us, but you have abandoned him. ¹²God is with us as our leader. His priests will sound their trumpets to call ¸the army¸ to fight you. Men of Israel, don't wage war against the LORD God of your ancestors. You won't succeed."

¹³But Jeroboam had set an ambush to attack them from behind. So Jeroboam's army was in front of Judah, and the ambush was behind them. ¹⁴When Judah's soldiers looked

---

ᵃ12:15 A seer is a prophet. ᵃ13:5 Or "covenant." ᵇ13:11 "Clean" refers to anything that Moses' Teachings say is presentable to God.

around, the battle was in front of them and behind them. They cried out to the LORD, the priests blew the trumpets, ¹⁵and the men of Judah shouted. When they shouted, God attacked Jeroboam and all Israel in front of Abijah and Judah. ¹⁶The Israelites fled from Judah's ⌈army⌉, and God handed them over to Judah. ¹⁷So Abijah and his men defeated them decisively, and 500 of the best men of Israel were killed. ¹⁸So the Israelites were humbled at that time, and the men of Judah won because they trusted the LORD God of their ancestors. ¹⁹Abijah pursued Jeroboam and captured some of his cities: Bethel and its villages, Jeshanah and its villages, and Ephron and its villages.

²⁰Jeroboam never regained power during Abijah's time. The LORD caused Jeroboam to become sick, and Jeroboam died.

²¹But Abijah became strong. He married 14 wives and fathered 22 sons and 16 daughters.

²²Everything else about Abijah—how he lived and what he said—is written in the history by the prophet Iddo.

ᵃ¹Abijah lay down in death with his ancestors and was buried in the City of David. His son Asa succeeded him as king. In Asa's time the land had peace for ten years.

King Asa of Judah—
I Kings 15:9-15

²Asa did what the LORD his God considered good and right.

³He got rid of the altars of foreign gods, broke down the sacred stones, and cut down the poles dedicated to the goddess Asherah. ⁴He told the people of Judah to dedicate their lives to serving the LORD God of their ancestors and follow his teachings and commands. ⁵He got rid of the illegal places of worship and the altars for incense in all the cities of Judah. The kingdom was at peace during his reign.

⁶He built fortified cities in Judah because the land had peace. There was no war during those years because the LORD gave him a time of peace. ⁷So Asa told Judah, "Let's build these cities and make walls around them with towers and doors that can be barred. The country is still ours because we have dedicated our lives to serving the LORD our God. We have dedicated our lives to him, and he has surrounded us with peace." So they built the cities, and everything went well.

⁸Asa had an army of 300,000 Judeans who were armed with large shields and spears and 280,000 Benjaminites who were armed with small shields and bows. All of these men were good fighting men.

⁹Then Zerah from Sudan came with 1,000,000 men and 300 chariots to attack Asa. Zerah got as far as Mareshah. ¹⁰Asa went to confront him, and the two armies set up their battle lines in the Zephathah Valley at Mareshah.

¹¹Asa called on the LORD his God. He said, "LORD, there is no one except you who can help those who are not strong so that they can fight against a large ⌈army⌉. Help us, LORD our God, because we are depending on you. In your name we go against this large crowd. You are the LORD our God. Don't let anyone successfully oppose you."

¹²The LORD attacked the Sudanese army in front of Asa and Judah. The Sudanese army fled. ¹³Asa and his troops pursued them as far as Gerar. Many of the Sudanese died in battle. As a result, the Sudanese army couldn't fight again. It was crushed in front of the LORD and his army. The LORD's army captured a lot of goods. ¹⁴It attacked all the cities around Gerar because the cities were afraid of the LORD. The army looted all the cities because there were many things to take. ¹⁵It also attacked those who

---
ᵃ14:1 2 Chronicles 14:1-15 in English Bibles is 2 Chronicles 13:23–14:14 in the Hebrew Bible.

were letting their cattle graze and captured many sheep and camels. Then it returned to Jerusalem.

¹God's Spirit came to Azariah, son of Oded. ²Azariah went to Asa and said to him, "Listen to me, Asa and all you men from Judah and Benjamin. The Lord is with you when you are with him. If you will dedicate your lives to serving him, he will accept you. But if you abandon him, he will abandon you. ³For a long time Israel was without the true God, without a priest who taught correctly, and without Moses' Teachings. ⁴But when they were in trouble, they turned to the Lord God of Israel. When they searched for him, he let them find him. ⁵At those times no one could come and go in peace, because everyone living in the land had a lot of turmoil. ⁶One nation crushed another nation; one city crushed another. God had tormented them with every kind of trouble. ⁷But you must remain strong and not become discouraged. Your actions will be rewarded."

⁸When Asa heard the prophet Oded's words of prophecy, he was encouraged and put away the detestable idols from all of Judah, Benjamin, and the cities he had captured in the mountains of Ephraim. He also repaired the Lord's altar in front of the Lord's entrance hall.

⁹Then Asa gathered all the people from Judah and Benjamin and the foreigners who had come from Ephraim, Manasseh, and Simeon. (Many of them had come to him from Israel when they saw that Asa's God, the Lord, was with him.) ¹⁰In the third month of the fifteenth year of Asa's reign, they gathered in Jerusalem. ¹¹On that day they sacrificed to the Lord a part of the loot they had brought with them: 700 cattle and 7,000 sheep. ¹²They made an agreement with one another to dedicate their lives to serving the Lord God of their ancestors with all their heart and soul. ¹³All people (young or old, male or female) who refused to dedicate their lives to the Lord God of Israel were to be killed. ¹⁴Asa and the people swore their oath to the Lord with shouts, singing, and the blowing of trumpets and rams' horns. ¹⁵All the people of Judah were overjoyed because of the oath, since they took the oath wholeheartedly. They took great pleasure in looking for the Lord, and he let them find him. So the Lord surrounded them with peace.

¹⁶King Asa also removed his grandmother Maacah from the position of queen mother because she made a statue of the repulsive goddess Asherah. Asa cut the statue down, crushed it, and burned it in the Kidron Valley. ¹⁷Although the illegal worship sites in Israel were not taken down, Asa remained committed to the Lord his entire life. ¹⁸He brought into God's temple the silver, the gold, and the utensils he and his father had set apart as holy.

King Asa's War With King Baasha—
I Kings 15:16-24
¹⁹There was no war until the thirty-fifth year of Asa's reign.

¹In the thirty-sixth year of Asa's reign, King Baasha of Israel invaded Judah and fortified Ramah to keep anyone from going to or coming from King Asa of Judah.

²Then Asa brought out all the silver and gold that was left in the treasuries of the Lord's temple and the royal palace. He sent them to Damascus to Aram's King Benhadad. ³He said, "There's a treaty between you and me as there was between your father and my father. I'm sending you silver and gold. Now break your treaty with King Baasha of Israel so that he will leave me alone."

⁴Benhadad did what King Asa requested. He sent his generals and their armies to attack the cities of Israel. He conquered Ijon, Dan, Abel Maim, and all the storage

cities in the territory of Naphtali. ⁵When Baasha heard the news, he stopped fortifying Ramah and abandoned his work on it.

⁶Then King Asa took everyone in Judah to Ramah. He made them carry the stones and lumber from Ramah. Baasha had been using those to fortify the city. Asa used the materials to fortify Geba in Benjamin and Mizpah.

⁷At that time the seer*ᵃ* Hanani came to King Asa of Judah and said to him, "Because you depended on the king of Syria and did not depend on the Lord your God, the army of the king of Aram has escaped your grasp. ⁸Weren't the Sudanese and Libyans a large army with many chariots and drivers? But when you depended on the Lord, he handed them over to you. ⁹The Lord's eyes scan the whole world to find those whose hearts are committed to him and to strengthen them. You acted foolishly in this matter. So from now on, you will have to fight wars."

¹⁰Asa was furious at the seer. He was so angry with Hanani that he put Hanani in prison. Asa also oppressed some of the people at that time in his reign.

¹¹Everything about Asa from first to last is written in the Book of the Kings of Judah and Israel.

¹²In the thirty-ninth year of his reign, Asa got a foot disease that became progressively worse. Instead of asking the Lord for help, he went to doctors.

¹³Asa lay down in death with his ancestors. He died in the forty-first year of his reign. ¹⁴They buried him in the tomb that he had prepared for himself in the City of David. They laid him on a bed full of spices and blended perfumes. And they burned a bonfire in his honor.

King Jehoshaphat of Judah

¹Asa's son Jehoshaphat succeeded him as king. Jehoshaphat strengthened himself to wage war against Israel. ²He put troops in all the fortified cities of Judah and placed military posts in Judah and in the cities of Ephraim that his father Asa had captured.

³The Lord was with Jehoshaphat, who lived in the old way like his ancestor David. Jehoshaphat didn't dedicate his life to serving other gods—the Baals. ⁴Instead, he dedicated his life to his ancestor's God and lived by God's commands. Jehoshaphat did not do what Israel was doing. ⁵So the Lord established Jehoshaphat's power over the kingdom. All the people of Judah gave gifts to Jehoshaphat, and he had a lot of riches and honor. ⁶He had the confidence to live the way the Lord wanted him to live. He also got rid of the illegal places of worship and poles dedicated to the goddess Asherah in Judah.

⁷In the third year of his reign, he sent his officers Ben Hail, Obadiah, Zechariah, Nethanel, and Micaiah to teach in the cities of Judah. ⁸With them were the Levites Shemaiah, Nethaniah, Zebadiah, Asahel, Shemiramoth, Jehonathan, Adonijah, Tobijah, Tob Adonijah, and the priests Elishama and Jehoram. ⁹They taught in Judah. They had the Book of the Lord's Teachings with them when they taught the people in all the cities of Judah.

¹⁰Fear of the Lord came to all the kingdoms around Judah. As a result, they didn't wage war against Jehoshaphat. ¹¹Some of the Philistines brought gifts and silver as taxes. The Arabs also brought him flocks: 7,700 rams and 7,700 male goats. ¹²So Jehoshaphat became more and more powerful. He built fortresses and cities where supplies were stored in Judah. ¹³He had large supplies of food in the cities of Judah and an army of professional soldiers with him in Jerusalem. ¹⁴The following is a

---

ᵃ 16:7 A seer is a prophet.

breakdown of these soldiers. They are listed by families. Judah's regimental commanders were Commander Adnah (with 300,000 fighting men), [15]next to him Commander Jehohanan (with 280,000), [16]and next to him Amasiah, Zichri's son, who volunteered to serve the LORD (with 200,000 fighting men). [17]From Benjamin there was the fighting man Eliada (with 200,000 armed men with bows and shields), [18]and next to him was Jehozabad (with him was an army of 180,000 armed men). [19]These were the men who served the king in addition to those whom the king put in the fortified cities throughout Judah.

Micaiah Prophesies Against King Ahab—
1 Kings 22:1-40

[1]Jehoshaphat was wealthy and honorable and became Ahab's in-law. [2]A few years later he went to visit Ahab in Samaria. Ahab slaughtered many sheep and cattle for a banquet in honor of Jehoshaphat and the people who were with him. And Ahab persuaded Jehoshaphat to attack Ramoth in Gilead with him.

[3]King Ahab of Israel asked King Jehoshaphat of Judah, "Will you go with me to Ramoth in Gilead?"

Jehoshaphat told the king of Israel, "I will do what you do. My troops will do what your troops do. ⸤We will join⸥ your troops in battle." [4]Then Jehoshaphat said to the king of Israel, "But first, find out what the word of the LORD is ⸤in this matter⸥."

[5]So the king of Israel called 400 prophets together. He asked them, "Should we go to war against Ramoth in Gilead or not?"

"Go," they said. "God will hand over Ramoth to you."

[6]But Jehoshaphat asked, "Isn't there a prophet of the LORD whom we could ask?"

[7]The king of Israel told Jehoshaphat, "We can ask the LORD through Micaiah, son of Imla, but I hate him. Nothing he prophesies about me is good; it's always evil."

Jehoshaphat answered, "The king must not say that."

[8]The king of Israel called for an officer and said, "Quick! ⸤Get⸥ Micaiah, son of Imla!"

[9]The king of Israel and King Jehoshaphat of Judah were dressed in royal robes and seated on thrones. They were sitting on the threshing floor[a] at the entrance to the gate of Samaria. All the prophets were prophesying in front of them. [10]Zedekiah, son of Chenaanah, made iron horns and said, "This is what the LORD says: With these horns you will push the Arameans to their destruction." [11]All the other prophets made the same prophecy. They said, "Attack Ramoth in Gilead, and you will win. The LORD will hand it over to you."

[12]The messenger who went to call Micaiah told him, "The prophets have all told the king the same good message. Make your message agree with their message. Say something good."

[13]Micaiah answered, "I solemnly swear, as the LORD lives, I will tell him whatever my God says to me."

[14]When he came to the king, the king asked him, "Micaiah,[b] should we go to war against Ramoth in Gilead or not?"

Micaiah said, "Attack and you will win. They will be handed over to you."

[15]The king asked him, "How many times must I make you take an oath in the LORD's name to tell me nothing but the truth?"

[16]So Micaiah said, "I saw Israel's troops scattered in the hills like sheep without a shepherd. The LORD said, 'These sheep have no master. Let each one go home in peace.' "

---

[a]18:9 A threshing floor is an outdoor area where grain is separated from its husks.   [b]18:14 1 Kings 22:15; Masoretic Text "Micah."

¹⁷The king of Israel said to Jehoshaphat, "Didn't I tell you he wouldn't prophesy anything good about me?"

¹⁸Micaiah added, "Then hear the word of the LORD. I saw the LORD sitting on his throne, and the entire army of heaven was standing on his right and his left. ¹⁹The LORD asked, 'Who will deceive King Ahab of Israel so that he will attack and be killed at Ramoth in Gilead?' Some answered one way, while others were saying something else.

²⁰"Then the Spirit stepped forward, stood in front of the LORD, and said, 'I will deceive him.'

" 'How?' the LORD asked.

²¹"The Spirit answered, 'I will go out and be a spirit that tells lies through the mouths of all of Ahab's prophets.'

"The LORD said, 'You will succeed in deceiving him. Go and do it.'

²²"So the LORD has put into the mouths of these prophets of yours a spirit that makes them tell lies. The LORD has spoken evil about you."

²³Zedekiah, son of Chenaanah, went to Micaiah and struck him on the cheek. "Which way did the Spirit go when he left me to talk to you?" he asked.

²⁴Micaiah answered, "You will find out on the day you go into an inner room to hide."

²⁵The king of Israel then said, "Send Micaiah back to Amon, the governor of the city, and to Joash, the prince. ²⁶Say, 'This is what the king says: Put this man in prison, and feed him nothing but bread and water until I return home safely.' "

²⁷Micaiah said, "If you really do come back safely, then the LORD wasn't speaking through me. Pay attention to this, everyone!"

Lying

2 Chronicles 18:11-27

be all you can be

Does God allow lying? Not at all. The "lying spirit" in this story fooled the false prophets. But God's prophet Micaiah told the whole truth when he was asked.

That's an example for all Christians to follow. Be a girl whose word others can trust.

²⁸So the king of Israel and King Jehoshaphat of Judah went to Ramoth in Gilead. ²⁹The king of Israel told Jehoshaphat, "I will disguise myself and go into battle, but you should wear your royal robes." So the king of Israel disguised himself and went into battle.

³⁰The king of Aram had given orders to the chariot commanders. He said, "Don't fight anyone except the king of Israel."

³¹When the chariot commanders saw Jehoshaphat, they said, "He must be the king of Israel." So they surrounded him in order to fight him. But when Jehoshaphat cried out, the LORD helped him. God drew them away from him, ³²and the chariot commanders realized that Jehoshaphat wasn't the king of Israel. Then they turned away from him.

³³One man aimed his bow at random and hit the king of Israel between his scale armor and his breastplate. Ahab told the chariot driver, "Turn around, and get me away from

these troops. I'm badly wounded." ³⁴But the battle got worse that day, and the king propped himself up in his chariot facing the Arameans until evening. At sundown he died.

King Jehoshaphat's Religious Reforms

¹King Jehoshaphat of Judah returned safely to his home in Jerusalem. ²Jehu, son of the seer *ª* Hanani, asked King Jehoshaphat, "Why do you help wicked people and love those who hate the LORD? The LORD's anger is directed toward you because you have done this. ³However, you've done some good things: You've burned the Asherah poles in this country, and you've wholeheartedly dedicated your life to serving God."

⁴While Jehoshaphat was living in Jerusalem, he regularly went to the people between Beersheba and the mountains of Ephraim. He brought the people back to the LORD God of their ancestors. ⁵He appointed judges in the country, in each fortified city of Judah. ⁶He told the judges, "Pay attention to what you're doing. When you judge, you aren't doing it for a human but for the LORD. He will be with you when you hear a case. ⁷May you have the fear of the LORD in you. Be careful about what you do. The LORD our God is never unjust. He is impartial and never takes bribes."

⁸In Jerusalem Jehoshaphat also appointed some Levites, priests, and family heads from Israel to administer the LORD's laws and decide cases. They lived in Jerusalem. ⁹He ordered them, "Do this wholeheartedly—with the fear of the LORD and with faithfulness. ¹⁰Warn your relatives living in other cities about every case they bring to you, even if the case involves bloodshed or commands, rules, or regulations derived from Moses' Teachings. Then your relatives will not become guilty in front of the LORD. Otherwise, he will become angry with you and your relatives. Do this, and you won't be guilty of anything . ¹¹Now, the chief priest Amariah will be in charge of you in every matter involving the LORD. Zebadiah, who is the son of Ishmael and the leader of the tribe of Judah, will be in charge of every matter involving the king. The Levites will serve as officers of the court. Be strong, and do your job. May the LORD be with those who do right."

King Jehoshaphat Defeats Judah's Enemies

¹Later the Moabites, Ammonites, and some of the Meunites *ª* came to wage war against Jehoshaphat. ²Some men reported to Jehoshaphat, "A large crowd is coming against you from the other side of the Dead Sea, from Edom. *ᵇ* The crowd is already in Hazazon Tamar" (also called En Gedi).

³Frightened, Jehoshaphat decided to ask for the LORD's help. He announced a fast throughout Judah. ⁴The people of Judah gathered to seek the LORD's help. They came from every city in Judah.

⁵In the new courtyard at the LORD's temple, Jehoshaphat stood in front of the people. ⁶He said, "LORD God of our ancestors, aren't you the God in heaven? You rule all the kingdoms of the nations. You possess power and might, and no one can oppose you. ⁷Didn't you, our God, force those who were living in this country out of Israel's way? Didn't you give this country to the descendants of your friend Abraham to have permanently? ⁸His descendants have lived in it and built a holy temple for your name in it. They said, ⁹'If evil comes in the form of war, flood, *ᶜ* plague, or famine, we will stand in front of this temple and in front of you because your name is in this temple. We will cry out to you in our troubles, and you will hear us and save us.'

ª 19:2 A seer is a prophet.   *ª* 20:1 Greek; Masoretic Text "and some of the Ammonites."   *ᵇ* 20:2 One Hebrew manuscript, Latin; other Hebrew manuscripts "Aram."   *ᶜ* 20:9 Greek; Masoretic Text "judgment."

¹⁰"The Ammonites, Moabites, and the people of Mount Seir have come here. However, you didn't let Israel invade them when they came out of Egypt. The Israelites turned away from them and didn't destroy them. ¹¹They are now paying us back by coming to force us out of your land that you gave to us. ¹²You're our God. Won't you judge them? We don't have the strength to face this large crowd that is attacking us. We don't know what to do, so we're looking to you."

¹³All the people from Judah, their infants, wives, and children were standing in front of the LORD. ¹⁴Then the LORD's Spirit came to Jahaziel. (He was the son of Zechariah, grandson of Benaiah, great-grandson of Jeiel, whose father was Mattaniah, a Levite descended from Asaph.) ¹⁵Jahaziel said, "Pay attention to me, everyone from Judah, everyone living in Jerusalem, and King Jehoshaphat. This is what the LORD says to you: Don't be frightened or terrified by this large crowd. The battle isn't yours. It's God's. ¹⁶Tomorrow go into battle against them. They will be coming up the Ziz Pass. You will find them at the end of the valley in front of the Jeruel Desert. ¹⁷You won't fight this battle. Instead, take your position, stand still, and see the victory of the LORD for you, Judah and Jerusalem. Don't be frightened or terrified. Tomorrow go out to face them. The LORD is with you."

¹⁸Jehoshaphat bowed down with his face touching the ground. Everyone from Judah and the people who lived in Jerusalem immediately bowed down in front of the LORD. ¹⁹The Levites, descendants of Kohath and Korah, stood up to praise the LORD God of Israel with very loud songs.

²⁰They got up early in the morning and went to the desert of Tekoa. As they were leaving, Jehoshaphat stopped and said, "Listen to me, people of Judah and those living in Jerusalem. Trust the LORD your God, and believe. Believe his prophets, and you will succeed."

²¹After he had advised the people, he appointed people to sing to the LORD and praise him for the beauty of his holiness. As they went in front of the troops, they sang, "Thank the LORD because his mercy endures forever!" ²²As they started to sing praises, the LORD set ambushes against the Ammonites, Moabites, and the people of Mount Seir who had come into Judah. They were defeated. ²³Then the Ammonites and Moabites attacked the people from Mount Seir and annihilated them. After they had finished off the people of Seir, they helped destroy one another.

²⁴The people of Judah went to the watchtower in the desert and looked for the crowd. Corpses were lying on the ground. No one had escaped. ²⁵When Jehoshaphat and his troops came to take the loot, they found among them a lot of goods, clothes,ᵈ and valuables. They found more than they could carry. They spent three days collecting the loot. ²⁶On the fourth day they gathered in the valley of Beracah. Because they thanked the LORD there, that place is still called the valley of Beracah [Thanks] today.

²⁷All the men of Judah and Jerusalem returned to Jerusalem. They rejoiced while Jehoshaphat led them. The LORD gave them a reason to rejoice about what had happened to their enemies. ²⁸So they brought harps, lyres, and trumpets to the LORD's temple in Jerusalem.

²⁹The fear of the LORD came over the kingdoms in that area when they heard how the LORD waged war against Israel's enemies. ³⁰Jehoshaphat's kingdom was peaceful, since his God surrounded him with peace.

ᵈ20:25 Latin; Masoretic Text "corpses."

Summary of Jehoshaphat's Reign—
I Kings 22:41-50

³¹Jehoshaphat ruled as king of Judah. He was 35 years old when he began to rule, and he ruled for 25 years in Jerusalem. His mother's name was Azubah, daughter of Shilhi. ³²Jehoshaphat carefully followed the example his father Asa had set and did what the LORD considered right. ³³But the illegal worship sites on the hills were not torn down. The people still didn't have their hearts set on the God of their ancestors.

³⁴Everything else about Jehoshaphat from first to last is written in the records of Jehu, son of Hanani, which is included in the Book of the Kings of Israel.

³⁵After this, King Jehoshaphat of Judah allied himself with King Ahaziah of Israel, who led him to do evil. ³⁶Jehoshaphat joined him in making ships to go to Tarshish. They made the ships in Ezion Geber. ³⁷Then Eliezer, son of Dodavahu from Mareshah, prophesied against Jehoshaphat. He said, "The LORD will destroy your work because you have allied yourself with Ahaziah." So the ships were wrecked and couldn't go to Tarshish.

King Jehoram of Judah—
I Kings 22:51; 2 Kings 8:17-19

21 ¹Jehoshaphat lay down in death with his ancestors and was buried with them in the City of David. His son Jehoram succeeded him as king. ²He had the following brothers, sons of Jehoshaphat: Azariah, Jehiel, Zechariah, Azariahu, Michael, and Shephatiah. All were the sons of King Jehoshaphat of Israel. ³Their father gave them many gifts: silver, gold, and other expensive things, along with fortified cities in Judah. But Jehoshaphat gave the kingdom to Jehoram, who was the firstborn.

⁴After Jehoram had taken over his father's kingdom, he strengthened his position and then executed all his brothers and some of the officials of Israel. ⁵Jehoram was 32 years old when he became king, and he ruled for 8 years in Jerusalem. ⁶He followed the ways of the kings of Israel, as Ahab's family had done, because his wife was Ahab's daughter. So he did what the LORD considered evil. ⁷But the LORD, recalling the promiseᵃ he had made to David, didn't want to destroy David's family. The LORD had told David that he would always give him and his descendants a shining lamp.

Edom Wins Independence From Judah—
2 Kings 8:20-24a

⁸During Jehoram's time Edom rebelled against Judah and chose its own king. ⁹Jehoram took all his chariot commanders to attack. The Edomites and their chariot commanders surrounded him, but he got up at night and broke through their lines. ¹⁰So Edom rebelled against Judah's rule and is still independent today. At the same time Edom rebelled, Libnah rebelled because Jehoram had abandoned the LORD God of his ancestors. ¹¹Jehoram made illegal places of worship in the hills of Judah. This caused the inhabitants of Jerusalem to chase after foreign gods as if they were prostitutes. So he led Judah astray.

¹²Then a letter came to him from the prophet Elijah. It read, "This is what the LORD God of your ancestor David says: You haven't followed the ways of your father Jehoshaphat or the ways of King Asa of Judah. ¹³Instead, you have followed the ways of the kings of Israel. You, like Ahab's family, have caused Judah and the inhabitants of Jerusalem to chase after foreign gods as if they were prostitutes. You have killed your brothers, your father's family. Your brothers were better than you. ¹⁴The LORD will

---

ᵃ21:7 Or "covenant."

strike a great blow to your people, your sons, your wives, and all your property because you did this. [15]You will suffer from a chronic intestinal disease until your intestines come out."

[16]The LORD prompted the Philistines and the Arabs who lived near the people of Sudan to attack Jehoram. [17]They fought against Judah, broke into the country, and took away everything that could be found in the royal palace. They even took Jehoram's sons and wives. The only son left was Ahaziah,[b] Jehoram's youngest son. [18]After this, the LORD struck Jehoram with an incurable intestinal disease. [19]Two years later, as his life was coming to an end, his intestines fell out because of his sickness. He died a painful death.

His people did not make a bonfire in his honor as they had done for his ancestors. [20]He was 32 years old when he became king, and he ruled for 8 years in Jerusalem. No one was sorry to see him die. He was buried in the City of David but not in the tombs of the kings.

King Ahaziah of Judah—
2 Kings 8:24b-29; 9:14-29

[1]The people of Jerusalem made Jehoram's youngest son Ahaziah king in his place, because the raiders who came to the camp with the Arabs had killed all the older sons. So Jehoram's son Ahaziah became king of Judah. [2]Ahaziah[a] was 42 years old when he began to rule, and he ruled for one year in Jerusalem. His mother was Athaliah, the granddaughter of Omri. [3]Ahaziah also followed the ways of Ahab's family, because his mother gave him advice that led him to sin. [4]He did what the LORD considered evil, as Ahab's family had done. After his father died, they advised him to do what Ahab's family had done. They did this to destroy him.

[5]Ahaziah followed their advice and went with Ahab's son King Joram[b] of Israel to fight against King Hazael of Aram at Ramoth Gilead. There the Arameans wounded Joram. [6]Joram returned to Jezreel to let his wounds heal. (He had been wounded by the Arameans at Ramah when he fought against King Hazael of Aram.) Then Jehoram's son Ahaziah[c] went to Jezreel to see Ahab's son Joram, who was sick.

[7]God brought about Ahaziah's downfall when he went to Joram. He went with Joram to meet Jehu, grandson of Nimshi. (The LORD had anointed Jehu to destroy Ahab's family.) [8]When Jehu was executing judgment on Ahab's family, he found Judah's leaders (Ahaziah's nephews) who were serving Ahaziah, and he killed them. [9]He searched for Ahaziah, and Jehu's men captured him while he was hiding in Samaria. They brought him to Jehu and killed him. Then they buried him. They explained, "Ahaziah is Jehoshaphat's grandson. Jehoshaphat dedicated his life to serving the LORD with all his heart." But no one in Ahaziah's family was able to rule as king.

The Priest Jehoiada Opposes Queen Athaliah—
2 Kings 11:1-20

[10]When Ahaziah's mother, Athaliah, saw that her son was dead, she began to destroy the entire royal family of the house of Judah. [11]But Jehoshebath, daughter of the king and sister of Ahaziah, took Ahaziah's son Joash. She saved him from being killed with the king's other sons, and she put him and his nurse in a bedroom. Jehoshebath was the daughter of King Jehoram and wife of Jehoiada the priest. Because she was also Ahaziah's sister, she hid Joash from Athaliah. So he wasn't killed.

[b]21:17 In the Masoretic Text this king of Judah is also called Jehoahaz, an alternate form of Ahaziah.   [a]22:2 In the Masoretic Text this king of Judah is also called Jehoahaz, an alternate form of Ahaziah.   [b]22:5 In the Masoretic Text this king of Israel is also called Jehoram, a longer form of Joram.   [c]22:6 Some Hebrew manuscripts, 2 Kings 8:29, Greek, Syriac, Latin; other Hebrew manuscripts "Azariah."

¹²Joash was with the priests. He was hidden in God's temple for six years while Athaliah ruled the country.

¹In the seventh year of Athaliah's reign, Jehoiada strengthened his position by making an agreement with the company commanders: Azariah, son of Jeroham, Ishmael, son of Jehohanan, Azariah, son of Obed, Maaseiah, son of Adaiah, and Elishaphat, son of Zichri. ²They went around Judah, gathered the Levites from all the cities of Judah and the leaders of the families of Israel, and came to Jerusalem. ³The whole assembly made an agreement with the king in God's temple.

Then Jehoiada said to them, "Here is the king's son. He should be king, as the Lord said about David's descendants. ⁴This is what you must do: One third of you, the priests and Levites who are on duty on the day of worship, must guard the gates. ⁵Another third must be at the royal palace. And another third must be at Foundation Gate. All the people must be in the courtyards of the Lord's temple. ⁶No one should come into the Lord's temple except the priests and the Levites who are on duty with them. They may enter because they are holy, but all other people should follow the Lord's regulations. ⁷The Levites should surround the king. Each man should have his weapon in his hand. Kill anyone who tries to come into the temple. Stay with the king wherever he goes."

⁸So the Levites and all the Judeans did what the priest Jehoiada had ordered them. Each took his men who were coming on duty on the day of worship as well as those who were about to go off duty. Jehoiada had not dismissed the priestly divisions.

⁹Jehoiada gave the commanders the spears and the small and large shields that had belonged to King David but were now in God's temple. ¹⁰All the troops stood with their weapons drawn. They were stationed around the king and around the altar and the temple (from the south side to the north side of the temple). ¹¹Then they brought out the king's son, gave him the crown and the religious instructions, and Jehoiada and his sons made him king by anointing him. They said, "Long live the king!"

¹²When Athaliah heard the people running and praising the king, she went into the Lord's temple, where the people were. ¹³She looked, and the king was standing by the pillar at the entrance. The commanders and the trumpeters were by his side. All the people of the land were rejoicing and blowing trumpets. The singers were leading the celebration with songs accompanied by musical instruments. As Athaliah tore her clothes in distress, she said, "Treason, treason!"

¹⁴Then the priest Jehoiada brought the company commanders who were in charge of the army out of the temple. He said to them, "Take her out of the temple. Use your sword to kill anyone who follows her." (The priest had said, "Don't kill her in the Lord's temple.") ¹⁵So they arrested her as she entered Horse Gate of the royal palace, and they killed her there.

¹⁶Jehoiada made a promise to the Lord on behalf of the king and his people that they would be the Lord's people. ¹⁷Then all the people went to the temple of Baal and tore it down. They smashed Baal's altars and his statues and killed Mattan, the priest of Baal, in front of the altars.

¹⁸Next, Jehoiada appointed officials to be in charge of the Lord's temple under the direction of the priests and Levites.*ª* (David had arranged them in divisions for the Lord's temple. They were appointed to sacrifice burnt offerings to the Lord as it is written in Moses' Teachings. They made these offerings with joy and singing as David had directed.) ¹⁹Jehoiada appointed gatekeepers for the gates of the Lord's temple so that no one who was unclean*ᵇ* for any reason could enter.

---

*ª*23:18 A few Hebrew manuscripts, Greek, Syriac, Latin; most Hebrew manuscripts "Levitical priests."
*ᵇ*23:19 "Unclean" refers to anything that Moses' Teachings say is not presentable to God.

[20]He took the company commanders, the nobles, the people's governors, and all the people of the land, and they brought the king from the LORD's temple. They went through Upper Gate to the royal palace and seated the king on the royal throne. The nobles, the governors of the people, and [21]all the people of the land were celebrating. But the city was quiet because they had killed Athaliah with a sword.

King Joash of Judah—
2 Kings 11:21–12:14

24 [1]Joash[a] was 7 years old when he began to rule, and he ruled for 40 years in Jerusalem. His mother was Zibiah from Beersheba. [2]Joash did what the LORD considered right, as long as the priest Jehoiada lived.

[3]Jehoiada got Joash two wives, and Joash had sons and daughters.

[4]After this, Joash wanted to renovate the LORD's temple. [5]He gathered the priests and the Levites and said to them, "Go to the cities of Judah, and collect money throughout Israel to repair the temple of your God every year. Do it immediately!" But the Levites didn't do it immediately.

[6]So the king called for the chief priest Jehoiada and asked him, "Why didn't you require the Levites to bring the contributions from Judah and Jerusalem? The LORD's servant Moses and the assembly had required Israel to give contributions for the use of the tent containing the words of God's promise." [7](The sons of that wicked woman Athaliah had broken into God's temple and used all the holy things of the LORD's temple to worship other gods—the Baals.)

[8]The king issued an order, and they made a box and placed it outside the gate of the LORD's temple. [9]Then they issued a proclamation in Judah and Jerusalem that the contributions should be brought to the LORD. (In the desert the LORD's servant Moses had required Israel to make contributions.) [10]All the officials and all the people were overjoyed. They brought the money and dropped it into the box until it was full. [11]Whenever the Levites brought the box to the king's officers and they saw a lot of money, the king's scribe and the chief priest's officer would empty the box and put it back in its place. They would do this every day, so they collected a lot of money. [12]The king and Jehoiada would give the money to the foremen who were working on the LORD's temple, and they hired masons and carpenters to renovate the LORD's temple. They also hired men who worked with iron and bronze to repair the LORD's temple. [13]As the men worked, the project progressed under the foremen's guidance. They restored God's temple to its proper condition and reinforced it.

[14]When they finished, they brought the rest of the money to the king and Jehoiada, who used it to make utensils for the LORD's temple. They made dishes and gold and silver utensils for the service and for the offerings. As long as Jehoiada lived, they sacrificed burnt offerings in the LORD's temple.

Joash's Sin Leads to His Assassination—
2 Kings 12:17-21

[15]When Jehoiada was old and had lived out his years, he died. He was 130 years old when he died. [16]He was buried in the City of David with the kings because of the good he had done in Israel for God and the temple.

[17]After he died, the officials of Judah bowed in front of the king with their faces touching the ground. Then the king listened to their advice. [18]They abandoned the temple of the LORD God of their ancestors and worshiped idols and the poles dedicated

---

[a]24:1 In the Masoretic text this king of Judah is also called Jehoash, a longer form of Joash.

to the goddess Asherah. This offense of theirs brought God's anger upon Judah and Jerusalem.

¹⁹The Lord sent them prophets to bring them back to himself. The prophets warned them, but they wouldn't listen. ²⁰God's Spirit gave Zechariah, son of the priest Jehoiada, strength. Zechariah stood in front of the people and said to them, "This is what God says: Why are you breaking the Lord's commands? You won't prosper that way! The Lord has abandoned you because you have abandoned him." ²¹But they plotted against Zechariah, and by the king's order they stoned him to death in the courtyard of the Lord's temple. ²²King Joash did not remember how kind Zechariah's father, Jehoiada, had been to him. Instead, he killed Jehoiada's son. As Zechariah died, he said, "May the Lord see ˌthisˌ and get revenge!"

²³At the end of the year, the Aramean army attacked Joash. They came to Judah and Jerusalem and destroyed all the people's leaders. The Arameans sent all the loot they took from Judah and Jerusalem to the king of Damascus. ²⁴The Aramean army had come with a small number of men, but the Lord handed Joash's large army over to them because Joash's soldiers had abandoned the Lord God of their ancestors. So the Arameans carried out ˌthe Lord'sˌ judgment on Joash. ²⁵When the Arameans withdrew, they left him suffering from many wounds. His own officials plotted against him for murdering the son of the priest Jehoiada. They killed Joash in his bed. When he died, they buried him in the City of David, but they didn't bury him in the tombs of the kings. ²⁶These were the men who conspired against him: Zabad, son of an Ammonite woman named Shimeath, and Jehozabad, son of a Moabite woman named Shimrith. ²⁷The record about his sons, the many divine revelations against him, and the rebuilding of God's temple is in the notes made in the Book of the Kings. His son Amaziah succeeded him as king.

King Amaziah of Judah—
2 Kings 14:1-7

25 ¹Amaziah was 25 years old when he began to rule, and he ruled for 29 years in Jerusalem. His mother was Jehoaddan from Jerusalem. ²He did what the Lord considered right, but he did not do it wholeheartedly. ³As soon as he had firm control over the kingdom, he executed the officials who killed his father, the former king. ⁴But he didn't execute their children. He obeyed the Lord's command written in the Book of Moses' Teachings: "Parents must never be put to death for the crimes of their children, and children must never be put to death for the crimes of their parents. Each person must be put to death for his own crime."

⁵Amaziah called the people of Judah together and assigned them by families to regiment and battalion commanders for all of Judah and Benjamin. He organized those who were at least 20 years old and found that he had 300,000 of the best men for the army, those who could handle a spear and a shield. ⁶He also hired 100,000 soldiers from Israel for 7,500 pounds of silver.

⁷But a man of God came to him and said, "Your Majesty, Israel's army must not go with you, because the Lord isn't with Israel. He's not with these men from Ephraim. ⁸If you go into battle with them, no matter how courageous you are, God will use the enemy to defeat you, because God has the power to help you or to defeat you."

⁹Amaziah asked the man of God, "What should I do about the 7,500 pounds of silver I gave the troops from Israel?"

The man of God answered, "The Lord can give you much more than that."

¹⁰Then Amaziah dismissed the troops that had come to him from Ephraim. But they became furious with Judah and returned home.

[11]Amaziah courageously led his troops. When he came to the Dead Sea region, he killed 10,000 men from Seir.[a] [12]The Judeans captured another 10,000 alive, took them to the top of a cliff, and threw them off the top of the cliff so that they were dismembered.

[13]The troops that Amaziah sent back so that they couldn't go with him into battle raided the towns in Judah from Samaria to Beth Horon. They killed 3,000 people and took a lot of goods.

King Amaziah's Sin Leads to His Defeat—
2 Kings 14:8-20

[14]After Amaziah came back from defeating the Edomites, he brought the gods of the people of Seir, set them up as his gods, bowed down to them, and burned sacrifices to them. [15]The Lord became angry with Amaziah. He sent him a prophet who asked him, "Why do you dedicate your life to serving the gods of those people? Those gods couldn't save their own people from you."

[16]As he was talking, the king asked him, "Did we make you an adviser to the king? Stop! Do you want me to have you killed?"

The prophet stopped. He said, "I know that God has decided to destroy you because you did this, but you refuse to listen to my advice."

[17]After getting advice from his advisers, King Amaziah of Judah sent messengers to King Jehoash,[b] son of Jehoahaz and grandson of Jehu of Israel, to declare war on Israel.

[18]King Jehoash of Israel sent this message to King Amaziah of Judah: "A thistle in Lebanon sent a message to a cedar in Lebanon. It said, 'Let your daughter marry my son,' but a wild animal from Lebanon came along and trampled the thistle. [19]You say you defeated Edom, and now you've become arrogant enough to look for more fame. Stay home! Why must you invite disaster and your own defeat and take Judah with you?"

[20]But Amaziah wouldn't listen. (God made this happen because he wanted to hand over the Judeans to Jehoash because they had sought help from Edom's gods.) [21]So King Jehoash of Israel attacked, and King Amaziah of Judah met him in battle at Beth Shemesh in Judah. [22]Israel defeated the army of Judah, and the Judeans fled to their homes. [23]King Jehoash of Israel captured King Amaziah, son of Joash and grandson of Ahaziah of Judah, at Beth Shemesh and brought him to Jerusalem. He tore down a 600-foot section of the wall around Jerusalem from Ephraim Gate to Corner Gate. [24]He took all the gold, silver, and all the utensils he found in God's temple with Obed Edom and in the royal palace treasury. He also took hostages. Then he returned to Samaria.

[25]Joash's son King Amaziah of Judah lived 15 years after the death of Jehoahaz's son King Jehoash of Israel. [26]Isn't everything else about Amaziah, from beginning to end, written in the Book of the Kings of Judah and Israel? [27]After Amaziah turned away from the Lord, conspirators in Jerusalem plotted against him. Amaziah fled to Lachish, but they sent men to Lachish after him and killed him there. [28]They brought him back by horse and buried him in the city of Judah with his ancestors.

---

[a]25:11 Seir is another name for Edom.   [b]25:17 In the Masoretic Text this king of Israel is also called Joash, a shorter form of Jehoash.

King Uzziah of Judah—
2 Kings 14:21–15:3

26 [1]All the people of Judah took Uzziah, who was 16 years old, and made him king in place of his father Amaziah. [2]Uzziah rebuilt Elath and returned it to Judah after King Amaziah lay down in death with his ancestors. [3]Uzziah was 16 years old when he began to rule, and he ruled for 52 years in Jerusalem. His mother was Jecoliah from Jerusalem. [4]He did what the LORD considered right, as his father Amaziah had done. [5]He dedicated his life to serving God in the days of Zechariah, who taught him to fear God. As long as he dedicated his life to serving the LORD, the LORD gave him success.

[6]Uzziah went to wage war against the Philistines. He tore down the walls of Gath, Jabneh, and Ashdod. He built cities near Ashdod and elsewhere among the Philistines. [7]God helped him when he attacked the Philistines, the Arabs who lived in Gur Baal, and the Meunites. [8]The Ammonites paid taxes to Uzziah, and his fame spread to the border of Egypt because he became very powerful. [9]Uzziah built towers in Jerusalem at Corner Wall, Valley Gate, and the Angle, and he reinforced them. [10]He built towers in the desert. He dug many cisterns because he had a lot of herds in the foothills and the plains. He had farmers and vineyard workers in the mountains and the fertile fields because he loved the soil.

[11]Uzziah had an army of professional soldiers. They were ready to go to war in their companies based on the number organized by the scribe Jeiel and the officer Maaseiah. They were commanded by Hananiah, one of the king's officials. [12]The total number of family heads among these warriors was 2,600. [13]Under them was an army of 307,500 soldiers. They were a powerful force that could support the king against the enemy. [14]For the entire army Uzziah prepared shields, spears, helmets, armor, bows, and stones for slings. [15]In Jerusalem he made machines designed by inventive people. The machines were placed on the towers and corners to shoot arrows and hurl large stones.

King Uzziah Is Cursed With a Skin Disease—
2 Kings 15:5-7

Uzziah's fame spread far and wide because he had strong support until he became powerful. [16]But when he became powerful, his pride destroyed him. He was unfaithful to the LORD his God. He went into the LORD's temple to burn incense on

Good Morning, God
2 Chronicles 26:15b-19

God gave King Uzziah great success because he obeyed God. Uzziah became known throughout the land due to his powerful armies. But soon all this fame made Uzziah proud. Uzziah forgot that his obedience to God was the key to his success. So God punished him with a terrible skin disease. Do you want to be successful in life? Remember Uzziah's story, and follow God's formula for success: obedience.

Lord, help me remember that everything I have is from you. Help me to obey you always.

the incense altar. [17]The priest Azariah went in after him with 80 of the Lord's courageous priests. [18]They opposed King Uzziah. They said to him, "Uzziah, you have no right to burn incense as an offering to the Lord. That right belongs to the priests, Aaron's descendants, who have been given the holy task of burning incense. Get out of the holy place because you have been unfaithful. The Lord God will not honor you for this."

[19]Uzziah, who held an incense burner in his hand, became angry. While he was angry with the priests, a skin disease broke out on his forehead. This happened in front of the priests in the Lord's temple as Uzziah was at the incense altar. [20]When the chief priest Azariah and all the priests turned toward him, a skin disease was on his forehead. They rushed him away. Uzziah was in a hurry to get out because the Lord had inflicted him with the disease.

[21]King Uzziah had a skin disease until the day he died. Since he had a skin disease, he lived in a separate house and was barred from the Lord's temple. His son Jotham was in charge of the royal palace and governed the country.

[22]Everything else about Uzziah, from beginning to end, is recorded by the prophet Isaiah, son of Amoz. [23]Uzziah lay down in death with his ancestors and was buried with them in a field containing tombs that belonged to the kings. People said, "He had a skin disease." His son Jotham succeeded him as king.

King Jotham of Judah—
2 Kings 15:32-38

27 [1]Jotham was 25 years old when he began to rule. He ruled for 16 years in Jerusalem. His mother was Jerushah, daughter of Zadok. [2]He did what the Lord considered right, as his father Uzziah had done. But unlike his father, he didn't illegally enter the Lord's temple. Nevertheless, the people continued their corrupt ways.

[3]Jotham built the Upper Gate of the Lord's temple and did extensive building of the wall at the Ophel. [4]He built cities in the hills of Judah, and he built forts and towers in the wooded areas. [5]He fought with the king of the Ammonites and conquered them. That year the Ammonites gave him 7,500 pounds of silver, 60,000 bushels of wheat, and 60,000 bushels of barley. The Ammonites gave him the same amount for two more years. [6]Jotham grew powerful because he was determined to live as the Lord his God wanted.

[7]Everything else about Jotham—all his wars and his life—is written in the Book of the Kings of Israel and Judah. [8]He was 25 years old when he began to rule as king. He ruled for 16 years in Jerusalem. [9]Jotham lay down in death with his ancestors, and they buried him in the City of David. His son Ahaz succeeded him as king.

King Ahaz of Judah—
2 Kings 16:1-20

28 [1]Ahaz was 20 years old when he began to rule. He ruled for 26 years in Jerusalem. He didn't do what the Lord considered right, as his ancestor David had done. [2]He followed the example of the kings of Israel and even made metal idols for worshiping other gods—the Baals. [3]He burned sacrifices in the valley of Ben Hinnom and sacrificed his son by burning him alive, one of the disgusting things done by the nations that the Lord had forced out of the Israelites' way. [4]He offered sacrifices and burned incense as an offering at the illegal worship sites, which were on hills and under every large tree.

[5]So the Lord his God handed him over to the king of Aram, who defeated him, captured many prisoners, and brought them to Damascus. He also handed him over to the king of Israel, who decisively defeated him. [6]In one day Pekah, son of Remaliah, killed

120,000 soldiers in Judah because they had abandoned the LORD God of their ancestors. [7]Zichri, a fighting man from Ephraim, killed Maaseiah, who was the king's son, Azrikam, who was in charge of the palace, and Elkanah, who was the king's second-in-command. [8]The Israelites captured 200,000 women, boys, and girls from their relatives the Judeans. They also took a lot of goods from Judah and brought them to Samaria.

[9]A prophet of the LORD named Oded was there. He went to meet the army coming home to Samaria. He said to them, "The LORD God of your ancestors handed Judah over to you in his anger. You killed them in a rage that reaches up to heaven. [10]Now you intend to enslave the men and women of Judah and Jerusalem. But aren't you also guilty of sinning against the LORD your God? [11]Listen to me. Return these prisoners you have captured from your relatives, because the LORD is very angry with you."

[12]Then Azariah, son of Jehohan, Berechiah, son of Meshillemoth, Jehizkiah, son of Shallum, and Amasa, son of Hadlai (some leaders of Ephraim) opposed those coming home from the army. [13]They said to the army, "Don't bring the prisoners here. You'll make us responsible for this sin against the LORD. Do you intend to add to all our sins? The LORD is very angry with Israel because we have already sinned."

[14]So the army left the prisoners and the loot in front of the leaders and the whole assembly. [15]Then the men who were mentioned by name took charge of the prisoners and gave clothes from the loot to all the prisoners who were naked. They provided clothes for them, gave them sandals, gave them something to eat and drink, and let them bathe. They put everyone who was exhausted on donkeys and brought them to Jericho (the City of Palms) near their own people. Then they returned to Samaria.

[16]At that time King Ahaz sent for help from the kings of Assyria. [17]The Edomites had again invaded and defeated Judah and captured prisoners. [18]The Philistines had raided the foothills and the Negev in Judah. They captured and began living in Beth Shemesh, Aijalon, Gederoth, Soco and its villages, Timnah and its villages, and Gimzo and its villages. [19]The LORD humbled Judah because of King Ahaz of Israel. Ahaz had spread sin throughout Judah and was unfaithful to the LORD.

[20]King Tillegath Pilneser of Assyria attacked Ahaz. Instead of strengthening Ahaz, Tillegath Pilneser made trouble for him. [21]Ahaz took some of the things from the LORD's temple, the royal palace, and the princes, and he gave them to the king of Assyria. But that didn't help him. [22]When he had this trouble, King Ahaz became more unfaithful to the LORD. [23]He sacrificed to the gods of Damascus, the gods who had defeated him. He thought, "The gods of the kings of Aram are helping them. I'll sacrifice to them so that they will help me." But they ruined him and all Israel.

[24]Ahaz collected the utensils in God's temple, cut them up, and closed the doors to the LORD's temple. He made altars for himself on every corner in Jerusalem. [25]And in each city of Judah, he made places of worship to sacrifice to other gods. So he made the LORD God of his ancestors angry.

[26]Everything else about him—everything from beginning to end—is written in the Book of the Kings of Judah and Israel. [27]Ahaz lay down in death with his ancestors and was buried in the city of Jerusalem because they didn't put him into the tombs of the kings of Israel. His son Hezekiah succeeded him as king.

King Hezekiah Rededicates the Temple—
2 Kings 18:1-3

29 [1]Hezekiah began to rule as king when he was 25 years old. He ruled for 29 years in Jerusalem. His mother was Abijah, daughter of Zechariah. [2]He did what the LORD considered right, as his ancestor David had done.

³In the first month of his first year as king, he opened the doors of the LORD's temple and repaired them. ⁴He brought the priests and Levites together in the square on the east side ˻of the temple˼.

⁵He said to them, "Listen to me, Levites. Perform the ceremonies to make the temple of the LORD God of your ancestors holy. Remove anything that has been corrupted from the holy place. ⁶Our ancestors were unfaithful and did what the LORD our God considered evil. They deserted him. They turned away from the LORD's tent*ᵃ* and turned their backs on him. ⁷They also shut the doors of the ˻temple's˼ entrance hall, extinguished the lamps, and didn't burn incense or sacrifice burnt offerings in the holy place to the God of Israel. ⁸So the LORD was angry with Judah and Jerusalem. He made them something that shocks and terrifies people and that people ridicule, as you can see with your own eyes. ⁹Our fathers were killed in battle, and our sons, daughters, and wives are prisoners because of this. ¹⁰Now I intend to make a pledge to the LORD God of Israel so that he may turn his burning anger away from us. ¹¹Don't be negligent, my sons. The LORD has chosen you to stand in front of him, serve him, be his servants, and burn sacrifices."

¹²So the Levites started to work.

From Kohath's descendants were Mahath, son of Amasai, and Joel, son of Azariah.

From Merari's descendants were Kish, son of Abdi, and Azariah, son of Jehallelel.

From Gershon's descendants were Joah, son of Zimmah, and Eden, son of Joah. ¹³From Elizaphan's descendants were Shimri and Jeiel.

From Asaph's descendants were Zechariah and Mattaniah. ¹⁴From Heman's descendants were Jehiel and Shimei.

From Jeduthun's descendants were Shemaiah and Uzziel.

¹⁵These men gathered their relatives and performed the ceremonies to make themselves holy. Then they obeyed the king's order from the LORD's word and entered the temple to make it clean.*ᵇ* ¹⁶The priests entered the LORD's temple to make it clean. They carried into the courtyard every unclean thing that they found in the LORD's temple. Then the Levites took the unclean items outside the city to the Kidron Brook. ¹⁷They started on the first day of the first month. On the eighth day they went into the LORD's entrance hall, and for eight days they performed the ceremonies to make the LORD's temple holy. They finished on the sixteenth day of the first month.

¹⁸Then they went to King Hezekiah. They said ˻to him˼, "We have made all of the LORD's temple clean. This includes the altar for burnt offerings, all its utensils, the table for the rows of bread and all its utensils, ¹⁹and all the utensils King Ahaz refused to use during his reign when he was unfaithful. We have restored them and made them holy. They are in front of the LORD's altar."

²⁰Early in the morning Hezekiah gathered the leaders of the city and went to the LORD's temple. ²¹They brought seven bulls, seven rams, seven lambs, and seven male goats as an offering for sin for the kingdom, the holy place, and Judah. Hezekiah told the priests, Aaron's descendants, to sacrifice the animals on the LORD's altar.

²²So they slaughtered the bulls, and the priests sprinkled the blood on the altar. Then they slaughtered the rams and sprinkled the blood on the altar. After that, they slaughtered the lambs and sprinkled the blood on the altar. ²³Then they brought the male goats for the offering for sin in front of the king and the assembly, who laid their hands on them. ²⁴The priests slaughtered the goats and made their blood an offering for sin at the altar to make peace with the LORD for Israel. The king had said that the burnt offerings and offerings for sin should be for all Israel.

---

*ᵃ*29:6 Or "the place where the LORD lives." *ᵇ*29:15 "Clean" refers to anything that Moses' Teachings say is presentable to God.

²⁵He had the Levites stand in the LORD's temple with cymbals, harps, and lyres as David, the king's seer° Gad, and the prophet Nathan had ordered. This command came from the LORD through his prophets. ²⁶The Levites stood with David's instruments, and the priests had the trumpets. ²⁷Then Hezekiah ordered the sacrificing of burnt offerings on the altar. When the burnt offerings started, the songs to the LORD started. These songs were accompanied by trumpets and the instruments of King David of Israel. ²⁸The whole assembly bowed down with their faces touching the ground, singers began to sing, and the trumpets blew until the burnt offering was finished. ²⁹When the burnt offerings were finished, the king and everyone who was with him kneeled and bowed down. ³⁰Then King Hezekiah and the leaders told the Levites to praise the LORD with the words of David and the seer Asaph. They joyfully sang praises, bowed down, and worshiped.

³¹Hezekiah said, "You have dedicated your lives to the LORD. Come, bring sacrifices and thank offerings to the LORD's temple."

The assembly brought sacrifices and thank offerings, and everyone who was willing brought burnt offerings. ³²The burnt offerings brought by the assembly totaled 70 bulls, 100 rams, and 200 lambs. All of these were burnt offerings to the LORD. ³³The animals dedicated as holy sacrifices were 600 bulls and 3,000 sheep. ³⁴But the priests needed more help to skin all the burnt offerings. So their relatives, the Levites, helped them until the work was completed and the priests could make themselves holy. The Levites were more diligent in making themselves holy than the priests were. ³⁵There were many burnt offerings in addition to the fat of the fellowship offerings and wine offerings that accompanied the burnt offerings. So the worship in the LORD's temple was reestablished. ³⁶Hezekiah and all the people were overjoyed because of what God had done for the people. Everything had happened so quickly.

Hezekiah Celebrates the Passover

30 ¹Hezekiah sent a message to all Israel and Judah and wrote letters to the tribes of Ephraim and Manasseh. He invited them to come to the LORD's temple in Jerusalem to celebrate the Passover of the LORD God of Israel.

²The king, his officials, and the whole assembly in Jerusalem decided to celebrate the Passover in the second month. ³They couldn't celebrate it at the regular time because not enough priests had performed the ceremonies to make themselves holy and the people hadn't gathered in Jerusalem. ⁴The king and the whole assembly considered their plan to be the right thing to do. ⁵So they decided to send an announcement throughout Israel from Beersheba to Dan. They summoned everyone to come to Jerusalem to celebrate the Passover of the LORD God of Israel. These people had not celebrated it in large numbers as the written instructions said they should.

⁶Messengers took letters from the king and his officials throughout Israel and Judah. The king's order said, "Israelites, return to the LORD God of Abraham, Isaac, and Israel. Then he will return to the few of you who escaped from the power of the kings of Assyria. ⁷Don't be like your ancestors and your relatives who were unfaithful to the LORD God of their ancestors. He made them something that shocks people, as you have seen. ⁸Don't be impossible to deal with like your ancestors. Reach out for the LORD. Come to his holy place that he made holy forever. Serve the LORD your God, and he will turn his burning anger away from you. ⁹When you return to the LORD, your relatives and children will find compassion from those who captured them. They will return to this land. The LORD your God is merciful and compassionate. He will not turn his face away from you if you return to him."

°29:25 A seer is a prophet.

¹⁰So the messengers went from city to city in the territories of Ephraim and Manasseh, as far as Zebulun. But the people ridiculed them. ¹¹However, some people from Asher, Manasseh, and Zebulun humbled themselves and came to Jerusalem. ¹²Also, God guided the people of Judah so that they united to carry out the command which the king and the leaders gave from the LORD's word.

¹³Many people gathered in Jerusalem to celebrate the Festival of Unleavened Bread in the second month. They formed a large assembly.

¹⁴Then the people got rid of the idols' altars in Jerusalem. They got rid of all the altars for incense by dumping them in the Kidron Valley.

¹⁵They slaughtered the Passover lamb on the fourteenth day of the second month. The priests and Levites were ashamed, so they performed the ceremonies to make themselves holy. Then they brought burnt offerings to the LORD's temple. ¹⁶They stood in their regular places as instructed by Moses' Teachings. (Moses was a man of God.) The priests sprinkled the blood they received from the Levites. ¹⁷Many people in the assembly had not made themselves holy. So the Levites had to kill the Passover lambs for all who weren't clean*ᵃ* and couldn't make their lambs holy for the LORD.

¹⁸Many people from Ephraim, Manasseh, Issachar, and Zebulun had not made themselves clean. So they ate the Passover, but not in the way the written instructions said they should. Hezekiah prayed for them: "May the good LORD forgive ¹⁹those who have their hearts set on dedicating their lives to serving God. May the LORD God of their ancestors do this for those who are not clean as required for the holy place." ²⁰The LORD listened to Hezekiah and healed the people.

²¹So the Israelites in Jerusalem celebrated the Festival of Unleavened Bread for seven days with great joy. Each day the Levites and priests praised the LORD in song. They played the LORD's instruments loudly. ²²Hezekiah spoke encouraging words to all the Levites who had the skills to serve the LORD. They ate the festival meals for seven days, sacrificed fellowship offerings, and confessed their sins to the LORD God of their ancestors.

²³Then the whole assembly decided to celebrate the festival for seven more days. So they joyfully celebrated for seven more days. ²⁴King Hezekiah of Judah provided 1,000 bulls and 7,000 sheep as sacrifices for the assembly. The leaders provided 1,000 bulls and 10,000 sheep for the assembly. So a large number of priests were able to perform the ceremonies to make themselves holy.

Good Morning, God
2 Chronicles 30:21-27

King Hezekiah knew how to celebrate! He invited people from all around to come together and celebrate God's goodness. Everyone feasted, sang praise songs, played instruments, and prayed. They had such a good time, that they continued the party through the next week! How would you throw a party to celebrate God? Who would you invite?

Thank you, Lord, for people like Hezekiah who know how to celebrate you.

ᵃ 30:17 "Clean" refers to anything that Moses' Teachings say is presentable to God.

²⁵The whole assembly from Judah, the priests, the Levites, the whole assembly from Israel, the foreigners who came from Israel, and those who lived in Judah rejoiced. ²⁶The city of Jerusalem was filled with joy. Nothing like this had happened in Jerusalem since the days of King Solomon of Israel.

²⁷Then the Levitical priests blessed the people. Their voices were heard, and their prayers went to God's holy place in heaven.

Hezekiah Reforms Judah's Worship

31 ¹When this was over, all the Israelites who were there went to the cities in Judah. They crushed the sacred stones, cut down the poles dedicated to the goddess Asherah, and tore down the illegal places of worship and the altars throughout Judah, Benjamin, Ephraim, and Manasseh. The Israelites destroyed all of these things. Then all the Israelites returned to their own cities. Each person went to his own property.

²Hezekiah assigned the priests and the Levites to divisions. Each priest or Levite was put in a division based on the service he performed: sacrificing burnt offerings, sacrificing fellowship offerings, serving, giving thanks, or praising within the gates of the LORD's camp.

³He set aside part of the king's property for burnt offerings, the morning and evening offerings, burnt offerings on the weekly worship days, the New Moon Festivals, and the annual festivals, as it is written in the LORD's Teachings. ⁴He told the people living in Jerusalem to give the priests and Levites the portions they were due so that they could devote themselves to the LORD's Teachings. ⁵As soon as the word spread, the Israelites brought plenty of offerings from the first of their produce: grain, new wine, fresh olive oil, honey, and every crop from the fields. They brought large quantities, a tenth of everything. ⁶The people of Israel and Judah who were living in the cities of Judah brought a tenth of their cattle and sheep and a tenth of the holy things they had dedicated to the LORD their God. They piled these holy things in heaps. ⁷In the third month they started piling them up, and in the seventh month they finished. ⁸When Hezekiah and the leaders saw the heaps, they praised the LORD and his people Israel.

⁹Hezekiah asked the priests and the Levites about the heaps. ¹⁰The chief priest Azariah from Zadok's family said, "Since the people started to bring the offerings to the LORD's temple, we have had all we wanted to eat and plenty to spare. The LORD has blessed his people, and there's a lot left over."

¹¹Then Hezekiah told them to prepare storerooms in the LORD's temple. After they had prepared them, ¹²they faithfully brought in the contributions, the offerings of one-tenth of the crops, and the gifts dedicated to God. The Levite Conaniah was in charge of these things, and his brother Shimei was his assistant. ¹³King Hezekiah and Azariah, who was in charge of God's temple, appointed Jehiel, Azaziah, Nahath, Asahel, Jerimoth, Jozabad, Eliel, Ismachiah, Mahath, and Benaiah to serve under Conaniah and his brother Shimei. ¹⁴Kore, son of Imnah the Levite, was the gatekeeper at East Gate and had to take care of the freewill offerings made to God. His responsibility was to distribute the offerings made to the LORD and the holy gifts dedicated to God. ¹⁵Eden, Miniamin, Jeshua, Shemaiah, Amariah, and Shecaniah served under him in the cities belonging to the priests. They were to distribute the offerings faithfully to all their relatives, young and old, by their divisions. ¹⁶They were appointed to distribute them to males who were at least three years old. The way they were enrolled in the genealogical records did not matter. The six men who served under Kore were to distribute the offerings to everyone who went to the LORD's temple to perform the

daily service that each division was responsible for. [17]They were to distribute offerings to the priests who were enrolled by families and to the Levites who were at least 20 years old. Distribution was based on the way they served in their divisions. [18]The priests and Levites were enrolled with their wives, sons, daughters, and other people who depended on them—the whole community. The priests and Levites had to be faithful in keeping themselves holy for the holy work. [19]Men were appointed to give a portion of the offerings to all the males in the priestly families and to everyone listed in the genealogies of the Levites. These men were Aaron's descendants, priests who lived in the pasturelands of every Levite city.

[20]This is what Hezekiah did throughout Judah. He did what was good and right and true to the LORD his God. [21]Hezekiah incorporated Moses' Teachings and commands into worship and dedicated his life to serving God. Whatever he did for the worship in God's temple, he did wholeheartedly, and he succeeded.

God Saves Judah From the Assyrians—
2 Kings 18:13–19:37; Isaiah 36:1–37:38

[1]After everything Hezekiah had done so faithfully, King Sennacherib of Assyria came to invade Judah. He set up camp to attack the fortified cities. He intended to conquer them himself.

[2]When Hezekiah saw that Sennacherib had come to wage war against Jerusalem, [3]he, his officers, and his military staff made plans to stop the water from flowing out of the springs outside the city. They helped him do it. [4]A large crowd gathered as they stopped all the springs and the brook that flowed through the land. They said, "Why should the kings of Assyria find plenty of water?"

[5]Hezekiah worked hard. He rebuilt all the broken sections of the wall, made the towers taller, built another wall outside the city wall, strengthened the Millo[a] in the City of David, and made plenty of weapons and shields. [6]He appointed military commanders over the troops and gathered the commanders in the square by the city gate. He spoke these words of encouragement: [7]"Be strong and courageous. Don't be frightened or terrified by the king of Assyria or the crowd with him. Someone greater is on our side. [8]The king of Assyria has human power on his side, but the LORD our God is on our side to help us and fight our battles." So the people were encouraged by what King Hezekiah of Judah said.

[9]After this, while King Sennacherib of Assyria and all his royal forces were attacking Lachish, he sent his officers to King Hezekiah of Judah and to all of the people in Judah who were in Jerusalem to say: [10]"This is what King Sennacherib of Assyria says: Why are you so confident as you live in Jerusalem while it is blockaded? [11]Isn't Hezekiah misleading you and abandoning you to die from hunger and thirst when he says, 'The LORD our God will rescue us from the king of Assyria?' [12]Isn't this the same Hezekiah who got rid of the LORD's places of worship and altars and told Judah and Jerusalem, 'Worship and sacrifice at one altar?' [13]Don't you know what I and my predecessors have done to the people of all other countries? Were any of the gods of these other nations ever able to rescue their countries from me? [14]Were the gods of these nations able to rescue their people from my control? My predecessors claimed and destroyed those nations. Is your God able to rescue you from my control? [15]Don't let Hezekiah deceive you or persuade you like this. Don't believe him. No god of any nation or kingdom could save his people from me or my ancestors. Certainly, your God will not rescue you from me!"

ª32:5 The exact place referred to as "the Millo" is unknown.

¹⁶Sennacherib's officers said more against the LORD God and his servant Hezekiah. ¹⁷Sennacherib wrote letters cursing the LORD God of Israel. These letters said, "As the gods of the nations in other countries couldn't rescue their people from me, Hezekiah's God cannot rescue his people from me." ¹⁸Sennacherib's officers shouted loudly in the Judean language to the troops who were on the wall of Jerusalem. They tried to frighten and terrify the troops so that they could capture the city. ¹⁹They spoke about the God of Jerusalem as if he were one of the gods made by human hands and worshiped by the people in other countries.

²⁰Then King Hezekiah and the prophet Isaiah, son of Amoz, prayed about this and called to heaven. ²¹The LORD sent an angel who exterminated all the soldiers, officials, and commanders in the Assyrian king's camp. Humiliated, Sennacherib returned to his own country. When he went into the temple of his god, some of his own sons killed him with a sword. ²²So the LORD saved Hezekiah and the people living in Jerusalem from King Sennacherib of Assyria and from everyone else. The LORD gave them peace with all their neighbors.

²³Many people still went to Jerusalem to bring gifts to the LORD and expensive presents to King Hezekiah of Judah. From then on, he was considered important by all the nations.

Other Events in Hezekiah's Life—
2 Kings 20:1-21; Isaiah 38:1-8, 21-22; 39:1-8

²⁴In those days Hezekiah became sick and was about to die. He prayed to the LORD, who answered him and gave him a miraculous sign. ²⁵But Hezekiah was conceited, so he didn't repay the LORD for his kindness. The LORD became angry with him, with Judah, and with Jerusalem. ²⁶Hezekiah and the people living in Jerusalem humbled themselves when they realized they had become conceited. So the LORD didn't vent his anger on them during Hezekiah's time.

²⁷Hezekiah became richer and was highly honored. He prepared storerooms for himself to hold silver, gold, precious stones, spices, shields, and all kinds of valuables. ²⁸He made sheds to store his harvests of grain, new wine, and fresh olive oil, and he made barns for all his cattle and stalls for his flocks. ²⁹He made cities for himself because he had many sheep and cattle. God had given him a lot of property. ³⁰Hezekiah was the one who stopped the water from flowing from the upper outlet of Gihon. He channeled the water directly underground to the west side of the City of David. Hezekiah succeeded in everything he did.

³¹When the leaders of Babylon sent ambassadors to ask him about the miraculous sign that had happened in the land, God left him. God did this to test him, to find out everything that was in Hezekiah's heart.

³²Everything else about Hezekiah, including his devotion to God, is written in the vision of the prophet Isaiah, son of Amoz, and in the records of the kings of Judah and Israel. ³³Hezekiah lay down in death with his ancestors. He was buried in the upper tombs of David's descendants. When Hezekiah died, all of Judah and the people in Jerusalem honored him. His son Manasseh succeeded him as king.

King Manasseh of Judah—
2 Kings 21:1-20

¹Manasseh was 12 years old when he began to rule, and he ruled for 55 years in Jerusalem.

²He did what the LORD considered evil by copying the disgusting things done by the nations that the LORD had forced out of the Israelites' way. ³He rebuilt the illegal

places of worship that his father Hezekiah had torn down. He set up altars dedicated to other gods—the Baals—and made a pole dedicated to the goddess Asherah as King Ahab of Israel had done. Manasseh, like Ahab, worshiped and served the entire army of heaven. [4]He built altars in the Lord's temple, where the Lord had said, "My name will be in Jerusalem forever." [5]In the two courtyards of the Lord's temple, he built altars for the entire army of heaven. [6]He burned his son as a sacrifice in the valley of Ben Hinnom, consulted fortunetellers, cast evil spells, practiced witchcraft, and appointed royal mediums and psychics. He did many things that made the Lord furious. [7]Manasseh had a carved idol made. Then he set it up in God's temple, where God had said to David and his son Solomon, "I have chosen this temple and Jerusalem from all the tribes of Israel. I will put my name here forever. [8]I will never again remove Israel from the land that I set aside for their ancestors if they will obey all the commands, all the teachings, the ordinances, and the regulations I gave through Moses." [9]Manasseh misled Judah and the inhabitants of Jerusalem so that they did more evil things than the nations that the Lord had destroyed when the Israelites arrived in the land.

[10]When the Lord spoke to Manasseh and his people, they wouldn't even pay attention. [11]So the Lord made the army commanders of the king of Assyria invade Judah. They took Manasseh captive, put a hook in his nose, put him in bronze shackles, and brought him to Babylon.

[12]When he experienced this distress, he begged the Lord his God to be kind and humbled himself in front of the God of his ancestors. [13]He prayed to the Lord, and the Lord accepted his prayer and listened to his request. The Lord brought him back to his kingdom in Jerusalem. Then Manasseh knew that the Lord is God.

[14]After this, Manasseh rebuilt the outer wall of the City of David from west of Gihon Spring in the valley to the entrance of Fish Gate. He made the wall go around the Ophel, and he built it very high. He put army commanders in every fortified city in Judah.

[15]Manasseh got rid of the foreign gods and the idol in the Lord's temple. He got rid of the altars he had built in the temple on the Lord's mountain and in Jerusalem. [16]He built the Lord's altar and sacrificed fellowship offerings and thank offerings on it. And he told Judah to serve the Lord God of Israel. [17]The people continued to sacrifice at the illegal places of worship, but they sacrificed only to the Lord their God.

[18]Everything else about Manasseh—including his prayer to his God and the words that the seers[a] spoke to him in the name of the Lord God of Israel—are in the records of the kings of Israel. [19]His prayer and how God accepted it are written in the records of Hozai. The things he did before he humbled himself are also written there. This includes all his sins and unfaithfulness and the places where he built illegal worship sites and set up idols and poles dedicated to the goddess Asherah.

[20]Manasseh lay down in death with his ancestors. They buried him in his own palace. His son Amon succeeded him as king.

King Amon of Judah—
2 Kings 21:19-26

[21]Amon was 22 years old when he began to rule, and he ruled for 2 years in Jerusalem. [22]He did what the Lord considered evil, as his father Manasseh had done. Amon sacrificed to all the idols his father Manasseh had made, and he worshiped them. [23]He didn't humble himself in front of the Lord as his father Manasseh had humbled himself. Instead, Amon continued to sin.

---

[a]33:18 Seers are prophets.

²⁴His officials plotted against him and killed him in his palace. ²⁵Then the people of the land killed everyone who had plotted against King Amon. They made his son Josiah king in his place.

King Josiah Reforms Judah's Worship—
2 Kings 22:1-2; 23:4-20

34 ¹Josiah was 8 years old when he began to rule, and he was king for 31 years in Jerusalem. ²He did what the LORD considered right. He lived in the ways of his ancestor David and never stopped living this way.

³In the eighth year of his reign, while he was still a boy, he began to dedicate his life to serving the God of his ancestor David. In his twelfth year as king, he began to make Judah and Jerusalem clean*ᵃ* by destroying the illegal places of worship, poles dedicated to the goddess Asherah, carved idols, and metal idols. ⁴He had the altars of the various Baal gods torn down. He cut down the incense altars that were above them. He destroyed the Asherah poles, carved idols, and metal idols. He ground them into powder and scattered the powder over the tombs of those who had sacrificed to them. ⁵He burned the bones of the priests on their altars. So he made Judah and Jerusalem clean. ⁶In the cities of Manasseh, Ephraim, Simeon, and as far as Naphtali, he removed all their temples,*ᵇ* ⁷tore down the altars, beat the Asherah poles and idols into powder, and cut down all the incense altars everywhere in Israel. Then he went back to Jerusalem.

King Josiah Rededicates Judah to God's Promise—
2 Kings 22:3–23:4

⁸In the eighteenth year of his reign as he was making the land and the temple clean, Josiah sent Shaphan, son of Azaliah, Maaseiah, the mayor of the city, and Joah, the royal historian and son of Joahaz, to repair the temple of the LORD his God. ⁹They came to the chief priest Hilkiah and gave him the money that had been brought to God's temple, the money that the Levite doorkeepers had collected from the tribes of Manasseh and Ephraim, from all who were left in Israel, from everyone in the tribes of Judah and Benjamin, and from the inhabitants of Jerusalem. ¹⁰They gave the money to the foremen who were in charge of the LORD's temple. These foremen gave it to the workmen who were restoring and repairing the temple. ¹¹(These workers included carpenters and builders.) They were to buy quarried stones and wood for the fittings and beams of the buildings that the kings of Judah had allowed to become run-down. ¹²The men did their work faithfully under the supervision of Jahath and Obadiah (Levites descended from Merari), and Zechariah and Meshullam (descendants of Kohath). The Levites, who were skilled musicians, ¹³also supervised the workers and directed all the workmen on the various jobs. Some of the Levites served as scribes, officials, or gatekeepers.

¹⁴When they brought out the money that had been deposited in the LORD's temple, the priest Hilkiah found the book of the LORD's Teachings written by Moses. ¹⁵Hilkiah told the scribe Shaphan, "I have found the book of the Teachings in the LORD's temple." Hilkiah gave the book to Shaphan.

¹⁶Shaphan took the book to the king and reported, "We are doing everything you told us to do. ¹⁷We took the money that was donated in the LORD's temple and gave it to the supervisors and the workmen." ¹⁸Then the scribe Shaphan told the king, "The priest Hilkiah has given me a book." And Shaphan read it to the king.

ᵃ 34:3 "Clean" refers to anything that Moses' Teachings say is presentable to God.   ᵇ 34:6 Hebrew meaning of "he removed all their temples" uncertain.

Huldah

"Huldah, please tell us what the LORD has to say to us."

Huldah was a prophet when Josiah became king. In his twelfth year as king, Josiah began to rid Judah and Jerusalem of idol worship. Then he began to repair the LORD's temple. That is where the book of the LORD's Teaching was found. When King Josiah read the book, he tore his clothes because he was so upset at how God's laws had been broken.

Josiah told his officials to "ask the LORD about the words in this book." Now at this time, there lived a famous prophet called Habakkuk. He wrote one of the books of the Bible. But that's not who the officials went to about this important matter. Instead, they immediately thought of the prophet Huldah. They asked Huldah about the book that they had found.

Huldah told the officials God's message for Israel. The message was then taken to King Josiah who continued massive reforms in Israel.

Huldah was born around 625 B.C.

Huldah means "weasel."

Huldah was a prophet.

Getting to Know Huldah

✴ Why did the king's officials go to Huldah to ask about the Book of the LORD's Teachings?

✴ Who do you go to for advice?

✴ Who comes to you for advice?

King Josiah's officials consulted Huldah about the book of the LORD's Teachings after finding the book while repairing the temple.

¹⁹When the king heard what the Teachings said, he tore his clothes ₍in distress₎. ²⁰Then the king gave an order to Hilkiah, Ahikam (son of Shaphan), Abdon (son of Micah), the scribe Shaphan, and the royal official Asaiah. He said, ²¹"On behalf of those who are left in Israel and Judah and me, ask the LORD about the words in this book that was found. The LORD's fierce anger has been poured on us because our ancestors did not obey the word of the LORD by doing everything written in this book."

²²So Hilkiah and the king's officials went to talk to the prophet Huldah about this matter. She was the wife of Shallum, son of Tokhath and grandson of Hasrah. Shallum was in charge of the ₍royal₎ wardrobe. Huldah was living in the Second Part of Jerusalem. ²³She told them, "This is what the LORD God of Israel says: Tell the man who sent you to me, ²⁴'This is what the LORD says: I'm going to bring disaster on this place and on the people living here according to the curses written in the book that was read to the king of Judah. ²⁵I will do this because they have abandoned me and sacrificed to other gods in order to make me furious. Therefore, my anger will be poured on this place and will never come to an end.'"

²⁶₍Huldah added,₎ "Tell Judah's king who sent you to me to ask the LORD a question, 'This is what the LORD God of Israel says about the words you heard: ²⁷You had a change of heart and humbled yourself in front of God when you heard my words against this place and those who live here. You humbled yourself, tore your clothes ₍in distress₎, and cried in front of me. So I will listen ₍to you₎, declares the LORD. ²⁸That is why I'm going to bring you to your ancestors. I'm going to bring you to your grave in peace, and your eyes will not see any of the disaster I'm going to bring on this place and those who live here.'"

So they reported this to the king.

²⁹Then the king sent for all the respected leaders of Judah and Jerusalem to join him. ³⁰The king, everyone in Judah, everyone living in Jerusalem, the priests, the Levites, and all the people (young and old) went up to the LORD's temple. He read everything written in the Book of the Promise*ᵉ* found in the LORD's temple so that they could hear it. ³¹The king stood in his place and made a promise to the LORD that he would follow the LORD and obey his commands, instructions, and laws with all his heart and soul. He said he would live by the terms of the promise written in this book. ³²He also made all those found in Jerusalem and Benjamin join with him ₍in the promise₎. Then the people of Jerusalem lived according to the promise of God, the God of their ancestors.

³³Josiah got rid of all the disgusting idols throughout Israelite territory. He made all people found in Israel serve the LORD their God. As long as he lived, they didn't stop following the LORD God of their ancestors.

King Josiah Celebrates the Passover—
2 Kings 23:21-23

35 ¹Josiah celebrated the Passover for the LORD in Jerusalem. The Passover lamb was slaughtered on the fourteenth day of the first month. ²Josiah appointed the priests to their duties and encouraged them to serve in the LORD's temple. ³He told the Levites, who instructed all Israel and performed ceremonies to make themselves holy to the LORD, "Put the holy ark in the temple that Solomon, son of David and king of Israel, built. It shouldn't be carried on your shoulders any longer. Serve the LORD your God and his people Israel. ⁴Get yourselves ready with the family groups of your divisions, which are listed in the records of King David of Israel and the records

---

ᵉ34:30 Or "Covenant."

of his son Solomon. [5]Stand in the holy place representing the family divisions of your relatives, the people of Israel. Let the Levites be considered a part of each family. [a] [6]Slaughter the Passover lamb, perform the ceremonies to make yourselves holy, and prepare the lambs for the other Israelites as the LORD instructed us through Moses."

[7]Josiah provided the people with 33,000 sheep and goats to be sacrificed as Passover offerings for all who were present. In addition, he provided 3,000 bulls. (These animals were the king's property.) [8]His officials also voluntarily gave animals to the people, priests, and Levites. Hilkiah, Zechariah, and Jehiel, the men in charge of God's temple, gave the priests 2,600 sheep and goats and 300 bulls for Passover sacrifices. [9]Conaniah and his brothers Shemaiah and Nethanel, and Hashabiah, Jeiel, and Jozabad, the leaders of the Levites, gave the Levites 5,000 sheep and goats and 500 bulls as Passover sacrifices.

[10]So the service was prepared. The priests took their positions with the Levites according to their divisions, as the king had ordered. [11]They slaughtered the Passover lambs. The priests sprinkled the blood with their hands while the Levites skinned the lambs. [12]They set aside the burnt offerings to give them to the laypeople according to their family divisions. The laypeople could then present them to the LORD as written in the Book of Moses. The Levites did the same with the bulls. [13]They roasted the Passover lambs according to the directions. They boiled the holy offerings in pots, kettles, and pans and immediately served them to all the people. [14]Later, they prepared the animals for themselves and for the priests because the priests (Aaron's descendants) were sacrificing the burnt offerings and the fat until that evening.

So the Levites prepared the animals for themselves and the priests. [15]The singers (Asaph's descendants) were in their places as David, Asaph, Heman, and the king's seer [b] Jeduthun had commanded. The gatekeepers were stationed at each gate. They didn't need to leave their work, because their relatives, the Levites, prepared animals for them.

[16]So everything was arranged that day for the worship of the LORD. The Passover was celebrated, and the burnt offerings were sacrificed on the LORD's altar as King Josiah had commanded. [17]The Israelites who were present celebrated the Passover at that time. They also celebrated the Festival of Unleavened Bread for seven days.

[18]Never had a Passover like this been celebrated in Israel during the time of the prophet Samuel or the kings of Israel. They did not celebrate the Passover as Josiah celebrated it with priests, Levites, all of Judah, the people of Israel who could be found, and the inhabitants of Jerusalem. [19]In the eighteenth year of Josiah's reign, this Passover was celebrated.

Josiah's Sin Leads to His Death—
2 Kings 23:28-30a

[20]After all this, when Josiah had repaired the temple, King Neco of Egypt came to fight a battle at Carchemish at the Euphrates River. Josiah went to attack him. [21]But Neco sent messengers to Josiah to say, "What's your quarrel with me, king of Judah? I'm not attacking you. I've come to fight those who are at war with me. God told me to hurry. God is with me, so stop now or else he will destroy you."

[22]But Josiah would not stop his attack. He disguised himself as he went into battle. He refused to listen to Neco's words, which came from God, and he went to fight in the valley of Megiddo.

[23]Some archers shot King Josiah. The king told his officers, "Take me away because I'm badly wounded."

---

[a] 35:5 Hebrew meaning of this sentence uncertain.   [b] 35:15 A seer is a prophet.

²⁴His officers took him out of the chariot and brought him to Jerusalem in his other chariot. He died and was buried in the tombs of his ancestors. All Judah and Jerusalem mourned for Josiah. ²⁵Jeremiah sang a funeral song about Josiah. All the male and female singers still sing funeral songs about Josiah today. This became a tradition in Israel. They are written in the Book of the Funeral Songs.

²⁶Everything else about Josiah—including his devotion to God by following what is written in the Lord's Teachings ²⁷and his acts from first to last—are written in the records of the kings of Israel and Judah.

King Jehoahaz of Judah—
2 Kings 23:30b-35

36 ¹Then people of the land took Josiah's son Jehoahaz and made him king in Jerusalem in place of his father. ²Jehoahaz was 23 years old when he became king, and he was king in Jerusalem for 3 months. ³The king of Egypt removed him from office in Jerusalem and fined the country 7,500 pounds of silver and 75 pounds of gold. ⁴The king of Egypt made Jehoahaz's brother Eliakim king of Judah and Jerusalem and changed Eliakim's name to Jehoiakim. Neco took Jehoahaz away to Egypt.

King Jehoiakim of Judah—
2 Kings 23:36–24:7

⁵Jehoiakim was 25 years old when he began to rule, and he ruled for 11 years in Jerusalem. He did what the Lord his God considered evil. ⁶King Nebuchadnezzar of Babylon attacked Jehoiakim and put him in bronze shackles to take him to Babylon. ⁷Nebuchadnezzar also brought some of the utensils of the Lord's temple to Babylon. He put them in his palace in Babylon.

⁸Everything else about Jehoiakim—the disgusting things he did and all the charges against him—is written in the Book of the Kings of Israel and Judah. His son Jehoiakin succeeded him as king.

King Jehoiakin of Judah—
2 Kings 24:8-17

⁹Jehoiakin was eight years old when he began to rule as king. He was king for three months and ten days in Jerusalem. He did what the Lord considered evil.

¹⁰In the spring King Nebuchadnezzar sent for Jehoiakin and brought him to Babylon with the valuable utensils from the Lord's temple. Nebuchadnezzar made Jehoiakin's uncle Zedekiah king of Judah and Jerusalem.

King Zedekiah of Judah—
2 Kings 24:18–25:21; Jeremiah 39:1-10; 52:1-27

¹¹Zedekiah was 21 years old when he began to rule, and he ruled for 11 years in Jerusalem. ¹²He did what the Lord his God considered evil and didn't humble himself in front of the prophet Jeremiah, who spoke for the Lord. ¹³Zedekiah also rebelled against King Nebuchadnezzar. Nebuchadnezzar had made Zedekiah swear an oath of allegiance to him in God's name. But Zedekiah became so stubborn and so impossible to deal with that he refused to turn back to the Lord God of Israel.

¹⁴All the officials, the priests, and the people became increasingly unfaithful and followed all the disgusting practices of the nations. Although the Lord had made the temple in Jerusalem holy, they made the temple unclean.ᵃ ¹⁵The Lord God of their

---

ᵃ36:14 "Unclean" refers to anything that Moses' Teachings say is not presentable to God.

ancestors repeatedly sent messages through his messengers because he wanted to spare his people and his dwelling place. [16]But they mocked God's messengers, despised his words, and made fun of his prophets until the LORD became angry with his people. He could no longer heal them.

[17]So he had the Babylonian king attack them and execute their best young men in their holy temple. He didn't spare the best men or the unmarried women, the old people or the sick people. God handed all of them over to him. [18]He brought to Babylon each of the utensils from God's temple, the treasures from the LORD's temple, and the treasures of the king and his officials. [19]They burned God's temple, tore down Jerusalem's walls, burned down all its palaces, and destroyed everything of value. [20]The king of Babylon took those who weren't executed to Babylon to be slaves for him and his sons. They remained captives until the Persian Empire began to rule. [21]This happened so that the LORD's words spoken through Jeremiah would be fulfilled. The land had its years of rest and was made acceptable again. While it lay in ruins, the land had its 70 years of rest.

King Cyrus Allows the Jews to Return From Babylon—
Ezra 1:1-3

[22]The promise the LORD had spoken through Jeremiah was about to come true in Cyrus' first year as king of Persia. The LORD inspired the king to make this announcement throughout his whole kingdom and then to put it in writing.

[23]This is what King Cyrus of Persia says: The LORD God of heaven has given me all the kingdoms of the world. And he has ordered me to build a temple for him in Jerusalem (which is in Judah). May the LORD God be with all of you who are his people. You may go.

AN INTRODUCTION TO

Ezra

After being captives in Babylon for 70 years, some of the Jews returned home. But Jerusalem lay in ruins. The book of Ezra tells how the people rebuilt God's temple in spite of hostile neighbors.

King Cyrus ruled the Persian empire. Why would God help a pagan king? See Ezra 1:1.

What's In It For Me?

Strong faith helps me when I . . .

HAVE TO LIVE WITH SOMEONE ELSE'S CHOICES FOR ME.

STAND UP FOR MY RIGHTS.

GET DISCOURAGED BY OTHERS.

HAVE MY TRUST IN GOD CHALLENGED.

MAKE DECISIONS ABOUT RIGHT AND WRONG.

Headlines

King Dishes Out Gold!
Ezra 1, page 598

King Sends Orders— Building Stopped
Ezra 4, page 602

New King Sticks Up for Jews
Ezra 6, page 605

Bad Marriages Cause Hair Loss
Ezra 9:3, page 609

Hometown Girls Best
Ezra 10, page 611

Moving to a
New Home

Leaving your home and going to someplace new can be scary. But some Jews who lived in Babylon for 70 years decided to go to Jerusalem, the city of God. They knew God had special plans for their future in the land he had given to their ancestors.

When you move to a new place, you can be excited, not scared. God has special plans for you, too: a new home, a new church, new friends, and new things to do! When you move, you can write to your old friends and tell them about what's happening in your new world.

Solve This Mystery

Jenny was working on a school project. Clarissa and Tracy thought it looked good, so they asked Jenny if they could help. "No thanks," said Jenny. She knew they just wanted to take credit for her work.

After that, Clarissa and Tracy started playing dirty tricks on Jenny. They told the teacher that Jenny was cheating. Then they stole some of her supplies to keep her from finishing her project. They even threatened to smash her project!

What happened to Jenny was a lot like what happened to the Jews who were rebuilding the temple. Read their story in Ezra 4.

Here is the mystery. Read Ezra 6 and suppose Jenny's story ends the same way. What will happen to Jenny's project? What will happen to Clarissa and Tracy?

Name Game

The exiles missed things from home. Fill in the missing letters in these names taken from the book of Ezra. Put the letters together, and you will find out what the exiles were missing!

1. _ nat_ _ _ h (2:23), _alluch & Sh_ _ _ (10:29).
   They were missing:

   _____

2. _rah (2:5), Tab _ _o _ _ (2:43). They were missing:

   _____

3. B_ni (2:10), _e_aah (2:35) & Hash_m (2:19) & _ibbar
   (2:20), _ _bai (8:11), Azga_ (8:12). They were missing:

   _____

Ezra

Cyrus Allows the Jews to Return From Babylon—
2 Chronicles 36:22-23

¹The promise the LORD had spoken through Jeremiah was about to come true in Cyrus' first year as king of Persia. The LORD inspired the king to make this announcement throughout his whole kingdom and then to put it in writing.

²This is what King Cyrus of Persia says: The LORD God of heaven has given me all the kingdoms of the world. And he has ordered me to build a temple for him in Jerusalem (which is in Judah). ³May God be with all of you who are his people. You may go to Jerusalem (which is in Judah) and build a temple for the LORD God of Israel. He is the God who is in Jerusalem. ⁴All who choose to remain behind, wherever they may be living, should provide the people who are leaving with silver, gold, supplies, livestock, and freewill offerings to be used in God's temple in Jerusalem.

Sheshbazzar Returns With the Temple Furnishings

⁵Then the heads of the families of Judah and Benjamin, the priests, and the Levites—everyone God had inspired—came forward to rebuild the LORD's temple in Jerusalem. ⁶All their neighbors who were remaining behind provided them with articles made from silver and gold, supplies, livestock, and valuable gifts besides everything that was freely offered. ⁷King Cyrus brought out the utensils belonging to the LORD's temple. Nebuchadnezzar had taken these utensils from Jerusalem and put them in the temple of his own god. ⁸King Cyrus of Persia put the treasurer Mithredath in charge of bringing them out. So Mithredath made a list of them for Prince Sheshbazzar of Judah.ᵃ ⁹This is the inventory:

	gold dishesᵇ	30
	silver dishes	1,000
	knivesᶜ	29
10	gold bowls	30
	other silver bowls	410
	other utensils	1,000

¹¹The gold and silver utensils totaled 5,400.

Sheshbazzar took all these utensils with him when the exiles left Babylon to go to Jerusalem.

Those Who Returned With Zerubbabel—
Nehemiah 7:6-7

¹These were the people in the province. They were the ones who left the place where the exiles had been taken captive. (King Nebuchadnezzar of Babylon had taken them to Babylon.) These exiles returned to Jerusalem and Judah. All of them went to their own cities. ²They went with Zerubbabel, Jeshua, Nehemiah, Seraiah, Reelaiah, Mordecai, Bilshan, Mispar, Bigvai, Rehum, and Baanah.

ᵃ 1:8 Or "for Sheshbazzar, the leader of Judah." ᵇ 1:9 Hebrew meaning of this word uncertain. ᶜ 1:9 Hebrew meaning of this word uncertain.

Families Listed by Ancestor—
Nehemiah 7:8-25

This is the number of Israelite men from the people in exile:

3	the descendants of Parosh	2,172
4	of Shephatiah	372
5	of Arah	775
6	of Pahath Moab, that is, of Jeshua and Joab	2,812
7	of Elam	1,254
8	of Zattu	945
9	of Zaccai	760
10	of Bani	642
11	of Bebai	623
12	of Azgad	1,222
13	of Adonikam	666
14	of Bigvai	2,056
15	of Adin	454
16	of Ater, that is, Hezekiah	98
17	of Bezai	323
18	of Jorah	112
19	of Hashum	223
20	of Gibbar	95

Families Listed by Cities—
Nehemiah 7:26-38

21	The people of Bethlehem	123
22	of Netophah	56
23	of Anathoth	128
24	of Azmaveth	42
25	of Kiriath Jearim, Chephirah, and Beeroth	743
26	of Ramah and Geba	621
27	of Michmas	122
28	of Bethel and Ai	223
29	of Nebo	52
30	of Magbish	156
31	of the other Elam	1,254
32	of Harim	320
33	of Lod, Hadid, and Ono	725
34	of Jericho	345
35	of Senaah	3,630

Priests—
Nehemiah 7:39-42

36 These priests returned from exile:

	the descendants of Jedaiah (through the family of Jeshua)	973
37	of Immer	1,052
38	of Pashhur	1,247
39	of Harim	1,017

Levites—
Nehemiah 7:43-45

[40]These Levites returned from exile:
the descendants of Jeshua and Kadmiel, that is,
of Hodaviah   74
[41]These singers returned from exile:
the descendants of Asaph   128
[42]These gatekeepers returned from exile:
the descendants of Shallum, Ater, Talmon,
Akkub, Hatita, and Shobai   139

Temple Servants—
Nehemiah 7:46-56

[43]These temple servants returned from exile: the descendants of Ziha, Hasupha, Tabbaoth, [44]Keros, Siaha, Padon, [45]Lebanah, Hagabah, Akkub, [46]Hagab, Shalmai, Hanan, [47]Giddel, Gahar, Reaiah, [48]Rezin, Nekoda, Gazzam, [49]Uzza, Paseah, Besai, [50]Asnah, Meunim, Nephusim, [51]Bakbuk, Hakupha, Harhur, [52]Bazluth, Mehida, Harsha, [53]Barkos, Sisera, Temah, [54]Neziah, and Hatipha.

Descendants of Solomon's Servants—
Nehemiah 7:57-60

[55]These descendants of Solomon's servants returned from exile: the descendants of Sotai, Hassophereth, Peruda, [56]Jaalah, Darkon, Giddel, [57]Shephatiah, Hattil, Pochereth Hazzebaim, and Ami.

[58]The temple servants and the descendants of Solomon's servants totaled 392.

Those of Unknown Origin—
Nehemiah 7:61-65

[59]The following people came from Tel Melah, Tel Harsha, Cherub, Addan, and Immer, but they couldn't prove they were Israelites on the basis of their father's family or their genealogy: [60]the descendants of Delaiah, Tobiah, and Nekoda. These people totaled 652.

[61]These descendants of the priests couldn't prove their families were Israelites: the descendants of Hobaiah, Hakkoz, and Barzillai (who had married one of the daughters of Barzillai from Gilead and took that family name). [62]These people searched for their family names in the genealogical records, but their names couldn't be found there. For this reason they were considered contaminated and couldn't be priests. [63]The governor told them not to eat any of the most holy food until a priest could use the Urim and Thummim[a] to settle the problem.

The Total of the People and Animals Returning From Exile—
Nehemiah 7:66-69

[64]The whole assembly totaled 42,360. [65]In addition to the male and female servants who numbered 7,337, they also had 200 male and female singers. [66]They had 736 horses, 245 mules, [67]435 camels, and 6,720 donkeys.

---

[a]2:63 The Urim and Thummim were used by the chief priest to determine God's answer to questions.

Gifts Given for the Temple—
Nehemiah 7:70-73

⁶⁸When some of the heads of the families came to the LORD's temple in Jerusalem, they contributed freewill offerings to help rebuild God's temple on its ⌊former⌋ site. ⁶⁹They contributed as much as they could to the treasury for this work: 1,030 pounds of gold, 5,740 pounds of silver, and 100 robes for the priests.

⁷⁰The priests, the Levites, some of the people, the singers, the gatekeepers, and the temple servants settled in their own cities. All the other Israelites settled in their own cities.

Worship at the Temple Site Begins Again

3 ¹When the seventh month came, the people gathered together in Jerusalem. (The Israelites had already settled in their cities.) ²Then Jozadak's son Jeshua and his relatives ⌊who were⌋ priests and Shealtiel's son Zerubbabel and his relatives built an altar for the God of Israel. They built it in order to sacrifice burnt offerings. They ⌊followed the directions⌋ written in Moses' Teachings. (Moses was a man of God.) ³So they rebuilt the altar on its original site, though they were afraid of the people in the neighboring regions. They sacrificed burnt offerings on it to the LORD every morning and evening.

⁴Following the written directions, they celebrated the Festival of Booths. Each day they sacrificed the required number of burnt offerings. ⁵After that, they sacrificed the daily burnt offerings, the offerings for the New Moon Festival and all the other holy festivals of the LORD, and all the freewill offerings brought to the LORD. ⁶They started to bring these burnt offerings to the LORD on the first day of the seventh month, even though the foundation of the LORD's temple had not yet been laid.

Work on the Temple Begins

⁷So they gave money to the stonecutters and carpenters. Then they gave food, drink, and olive oil to the men from Sidon and Tyre in exchange for cedar, which the men would bring by sea from Lebanon to Joppa as King Cyrus of Persia had authorized them to do.

⁸Zerubbabel (who was Shealtiel's son), Jeshua (who was Jozadak's son), and the rest of the Jews, (the priests, Levites, and all the others who had come back from exile to Jerusalem) began to rebuild the temple. This happened in the second month of the second year following their return to ⌊the site⌋ of God's house in Jerusalem.

Good Morning, God
Ezra 3:12-13

When the Jews gathered to begin rebuilding the Lord's temple, some cried, while others cheered. The older people were sad because they remembered how beautiful the old temple used to be. Others were excited about the future! Sometimes change is hard. You might feel sad when you think about the past. But when your life changes, remember that God might have greater plans for your future.

Thank you, Lord, for giving me joy today and hope for the future.

They began by appointing the Levites who were at least 20 years old to direct the work on the LORD's house. ⁹Then Jeshua with his sons and relatives and Kadmiel with his sons who were Judah's descendants joined Henadad's family and their sons and relatives, the Levites, in directing those working on God's house.

A Celebration After the Laying of the Temple's Foundation

¹⁰The builders laid the foundation of the LORD's temple. Then the priests who were dressed in their robes took their places with trumpets, and the Levites who were Asaph's descendants took their places with cymbals to praise the LORD according to the instructions of King David of Israel. ¹¹As they praised and gave thanks to the LORD, they sang antiphonally:

"He is good; his mercy toward Israel endures forever."

Then all the people shouted, "Praise the LORD," because the foundation for the house of the LORD had been laid.

¹²But many of the priests, Levites, and the heads of the families who were old enough to have seen the first temple with their own eyes began to sob when they saw the foundation of this temple. Many others shouted for joy. ¹³No one could distinguish between the joyful shouts and the loud sobbing because the people were shouting so loudly. The noise was heard from far away.

The Samaritans Stop the Work

¹When the enemies of Judah and Benjamin heard that the people who returned from exile were building a temple for the LORD God of Israel, ²they approached Zerubbabel and the heads of the families. They told them, "We want to help you build because we worship the same God you worship. We have been sacrificing to him*a* since the time of King Esarhaddon of Assyria, who brought us here."

³But Zerubbabel, Jeshua, and the rest of the heads of Israel's families told them, "It isn't right for your people and our people to build a temple for our God together. We must build it alone for the LORD God of Israel, as King Cyrus of Persia ordered us to do."

⁴Then the people of that region discouraged the people of Judah and made them afraid to continue building. ⁵They bribed officials to keep the people of Judah from carrying out their plans throughout the reign of King Cyrus of Persia until the reign of King Darius of Persia.

⁶When Xerxes began to rule, the enemies of Judah and Jerusalem wrote a letter in which they made an accusation against the inhabitants of Judah and Jerusalem.

⁷Bishlam, Mithredath, Tabeel, and the rest of their group wrote to him when Artaxerxes was king of Persia. The letter was written with the Aramaic script and translated into the Aramaic language.

⁸Rehum the commander and Shimshai the scribe wrote another letter against the people of Jerusalem to King Artaxerxes. ⁹At that time, Rehum the commander and Shimshai the scribe were with the others of their group—the people from Denya, Partakka, Tarpel, Persia, Erech, Babylon, Susa, (that is, those of Elam), ¹⁰and the rest of the people whom the great and noble Assurbanipal deported. (Assurbanipal settled them in the cities of Samaria and the rest of the lands west of the Euphrates River.) ¹¹This is the copy of the letter they sent to him:

To King Artaxerxes,

---

a 4:2 Dead Sea Scrolls, Greek, Syriac, Egyptian; Masoretic Text "We have not sacrificed."

From your servants, the people west of the Euphrates:

¹²Your Majesty, you should know that the Jews who came to us from you are now in Jerusalem. They are rebuilding that rebellious and wicked city. They are close to finishing the walls. The foundations are already in place. ¹³You should also know that if this city is rebuilt and its walls are finished, the Jews will no longer pay taxes, fees, and tolls.

Ultimately, this will hurt the king's income. ¹⁴Now, because we are paid by your palace, it isn't right for us to watch something happen that will dishonor the king. So we are sending this letter to inform you ¹⁵that you should search the official records of your predecessors. You will find in those official records that this city has been rebellious and has been a threat to kings and provinces. This city has a history of rebelliousness. That's why this city was destroyed. ¹⁶We want the king to know that if this city is rebuilt and its walls are finished, you will have nothing left of your province, west of the Euphrates River.

¹⁷Then the king sent this reply:

To Rehum the commander, Shimshai the scribe, and the rest of their group living in Samaria, and to others west of the Euphrates River:
I wish you peace and prosperity!

¹⁸The letter you sent me has been read word for word in my presence. ¹⁹I gave the order, and a search was made. I discovered that this city has a long history of uprisings against kings. Its inhabitants are guilty of treason and rebellion. ²⁰Jerusalem has had powerful kings who have ruled the whole province, west of the Euphrates. Taxes, fees, and tolls were paid to them. ²¹So order these men to stop rebuilding. Keep this city from being rebuilt until I give the order. ²²Be careful not to neglect your duty in this matter. Why should I, the king, suffer any more harm?

²³Rehum the commander, Shimshai the scribe, and their group hurried to Jerusalem after hearing a copy of King Artaxerxes' letter. They forced the Jews to stop rebuilding.
²⁴Then the work on God's temple in Jerusalem was stopped. Nothing more was done until Darius' second year as king of Persia.

Work Resumed on the Temple

¹The prophet Haggai and Zechariah, grandson of Iddo, prophesied to the Jews in Judah and Jerusalem in the name of Israel's God, who was over them. ²Then Zerubbabel, who was Shealtiel's son, and Jeshua, who was Jozadak's son, began to rebuild God's temple in Jerusalem. God's prophets were with them and supported them.

³At the same time, Governor Tattenai from the province west of the Euphrates River, Shethar Bozenai, and their group went to the Jews and asked them, "Who gave you permission to rebuild this temple and finish its walls?" ⁴They also asked the Jews for the names of the men who were working on this building.

⁵But the leaders of the Jews were under God's watchful eye. They couldn't be stopped until Darius received a report and sent a reply to it.

Permission Requested From Darius

⁶Here is a copy of the letter Governor Tattenai from the province west of the Euphrates River, Shethar Bozenai and his group (the Persians west of that river) sent to King Darius. ⁷They sent him the following report:

To King Darius,
We wish you peace and prosperity in everything you do.

⁸Your Majesty should know that we went to the province of Judah, to the temple of the great God. The temple is being built with large stones and with wooden beams laid in its walls. The builders are doing an excellent job and making rapid progress. ⁹We asked their leaders the following question: "Who gave you permission to rebuild this temple and finish its walls?" ¹⁰For your information, we also asked them for their names so that we would have a record of the men who were their leaders. ¹¹This was their reply to us:

"We are the servants of the God of heaven and earth. We are rebuilding the temple that was originally built many years ago by a great king of Israel. ¹²But because our ancestors made the God of heaven angry, he handed them over to King Nebuchadnezzar of Babylon (a Chaldean). So Nebuchadnezzar destroyed this temple and deported its people to Babylon. ¹³However, in the first year of the reign of King Cyrus of Babylon, Cyrus gave permission for God's temple to be rebuilt. ¹⁴In addition, Cyrus took out of a temple in Babylon the gold and silver utensils that belonged to God's temple. (Nebuchadnezzar had taken them out of God's temple in Jerusalem and brought them into a temple in Babylon.) Cyrus gave them to a man named Sheshbazzar, whom he had made governor. ¹⁵Cyrus told him, 'Take these utensils. Place them in the temple in Jerusalem. Rebuild God's temple on its original site.' ¹⁶Then Sheshbazzar laid the foundation of God's temple in Jerusalem. The temple has been under construction from that time until now, but it still isn't finished."

Success
Ezra 5:3-17

be all you can be

"You'll never pass this test." "You're not good enough to get a part in the school play." "The choir director will never let you sing a solo." It's easy to give up if others discourage you. But God is your helper. Ask for his help as you work hard to achieve your goals. Keep doing your best; God will be with you.

¹⁷If it pleases Your Majesty, allow someone to search the king's archives in Babylon to determine whether King Cyrus gave permission for the temple of God to be rebuilt in Jerusalem. Then please send us Your Majesty's decision on this matter.

King Darius Finds King Cyrus' Memorandum

¹Then King Darius gave the order to search the library where the archives were stored in Babylon. ²A scroll was found in the palace of Ecbatana, which is in the province of Media. This was written on it:

MEMORANDUM

³Date: Cyrus' first year as king
From: King Cyrus
Subject: God's temple in Jerusalem.

The temple should be rebuilt as a place to offer sacrifices. Its foundation should be laid. It should be 90 feet high and 90 feet wide ⁴with three rows of large stones and a row of wood. The king's palace will pay for it. ⁵In addition, Cyrus took out of a temple in Babylon the gold and silver utensils that belonged to God's temple. (Nebuchadnezzar had taken them out of God's temple in Jerusalem and brought them into a temple in Babylon.) They should be returned to their proper place in the temple in Jerusalem. You should put each one in God's temple.

⁶Governor Tattenai from the province west of the Euphrates, Shethar Bozenai, and those of your group (the Persians west of the river):

You must stay away from there. ⁷Don't interfere with the work on God's temple. Let the governor of the Jews and the leaders of Judah rebuild God's temple on its original foundation. ⁸I am issuing this decree about how you must help the Jewish leaders rebuild God's temple:

The cost for this should be paid out of the king's own money from the taxes on the province west of the Euphrates. Full payment should be made to these men so that the work is not interrupted. ⁹Also, whatever the priests in Jerusalem need for burnt offerings to the God of heaven—young bulls, rams, lambs, wheat, salt, wine, and olive oil—should be provided for them each day. Make sure that nothing is omitted. ¹⁰Then they can offer sacrifices that please the God of heaven and pray for the life of the king and his sons.

¹¹I am also issuing a decree that if anyone tampers with my orders, that person should be impaled on a beam torn from his own house and his house should be turned into a pile of rubble.[a] ¹²May the God whose name is worshiped there cause the downfall of each king and nation who tries to tamper with my orders or tries to destroy the temple of the God in Jerusalem.

I, Darius, have issued a decree. It's to be carried out exactly as ordered.

¹³Then Governor Tattenai from the province west of the Euphrates River, Shethar Bozenai, and their group did exactly what King Darius had ordered. ¹⁴So the Jewish leaders continued to make progress because of the message from the prophet Haggai

---

^a6:11 Hebrew meaning of this word uncertain.

and Zechariah, the grandson of Iddo. They finished building as the God of Israel had ordered and as Cyrus, Darius, and Artaxerxes (the kings of Persia) had ordered. [15]This temple was finished on the third day of the month of Adar in the sixth year of King Darius' reign.

The Temple Is Completed and Dedicated

[16]Then the people of Israel, the priests, the Levites, and the others who had returned from exile celebrated at the dedication of God's temple. [17]At the dedication of God's temple, they sacrificed 100 bulls, 200 rams, and 400 lambs. They sacrificed 12 male goats as an offering for sin, one goat for each of the tribes of Israel.

[18]The priests were assigned to their divisions and the Levites to their groups to lead the worship of God in Jerusalem by following the directions written in the Book of Moses.

The Passover Is Celebrated

[19]On the fourteenth day of the first month, those who had returned from exile celebrated the Passover. [20]Since the priests and Levites had cleansed themselves, all of them were now clean.[b] They killed the Passover lambs for all the people who had returned from exile, for the rest of the priests, and for themselves. [21]The lambs were eaten by the Israelites who had returned from exile and by all who had separated themselves from the unclean practices of the non-Jews in the land to worship the LORD God of Israel. [22]So for seven days they celebrated the Festival of Unleavened Bread because the LORD had made them joyful. The LORD had made the king of Assyria change his mind so that he supported the people in their work on the temple of God, the God of Israel.

Ezra's Family Background

[1]After these things, during the reign of King Artaxerxes of Persia, Ezra left Babylon.

Ezra was the son of Seraiah, who was the son of Azariah, who was the son of Hilkiah, [2]who was the son of Shallum, who was the son of Zadok, who was the son of Ahitub, [3]who was the son of Amariah, who was the son of Azariah, who was the son of Meraioth, [4]who was the son of Zerahiah, who was the son of Uzzi, who was the son of Bukki, [5]who was the son of Abishua, who was the son of Phinehas, who was the son of Eleazer, who was the son of Aaron (the first priest).

[6]As a scribe, Ezra was an expert in Moses' Teachings, which the LORD God of Israel had given. The king gave Ezra everything he requested because the LORD his God was guiding him.

[7]Some Israelites (including priests, Levites, singers, gatekeepers, and temple servants) went to Jerusalem in Artaxerxes' seventh year as king. [8]In that same year in the fifth month, Ezra arrived in Jerusalem. [9]He had left Babylon on the first day of the first month, and on the first day of the fifth month, he arrived in Jerusalem, since his God was good to him. [10]Ezra was determined to study the LORD's Teachings, live by them, and teach their rules and regulations in Israel.

King Artaxerxes' Letter to Ezra

[11]This is a copy of the letter that King Artaxerxes gave Ezra the priest and scribe, a man with a thorough knowledge of the LORD's commands and laws for Israel:

---

[b]6:20 "Clean" refers to anything that Moses' Teachings say is presentable to God.

¹²From: Artaxerxes, king of kings
To: Ezra the priest, a scribe for the Teachings of the God of Heaven:
          I wish you peace and prosperity!

¹³I have issued a decree that any Israelites who are in my kingdom and want to go with you to Jerusalem may go. This also includes the priests and Levites. ¹⁴I, the king, and my seven advisers are sending you to evaluate the situation in Judah and Jerusalem on the basis of your God's Teachings, which you hold in your hands. ¹⁵Also, you must take the silver and gold that the king and his advisers willingly contributed to the God of Israel, the God whose temple is in Jerusalem. ¹⁶Take any silver and gold that you find in the whole province of Babylon when you take the gifts contributed by the people and the priests. They willingly contributed these gifts for the temple of their God in Jerusalem. ¹⁷You must use this money to buy bulls, rams, lambs, grain, and wine to offer on the altar of the temple of your God in Jerusalem. ¹⁸You and your relatives may do whatever you think is right with the rest of the silver and gold. However, what you do must conform to the will of your God. ¹⁹The utensils that have been given to you so that they can be used in your God's temple must all be presented to the God of Jerusalem. ²⁰You may use the king's treasury to pay for anything else that you must provide for your God's temple.

²¹I, King Artaxerxes, order all the treasurers in the province west of the Euphrates River to do exactly what Ezra the priest, a scribe for the Teachings of the God of Heaven, asks you to do. ²²You may give him up to 7,500 pounds of silver, 100 measures of wheat, 600 gallons of wine, 600 gallons of olive oil, and as much salt as he needs. ²³Whatever the God of heaven has commanded must be carried out in detail for the temple of the God of heaven. Why should God become angry with the king's empire and his sons? ²⁴Furthermore, we are notifying you that you are forbidden to make any priest, Levite, singer, gatekeeper, servant, or worker in the temple of this God pay any taxes, fees, or tolls.

²⁵You, Ezra, using your God's wisdom—the Teachings you hold in your hands—will appoint judges and administrators for all the people who know your God's Teachings and live in the province west of the Euphrates River. In addition, you will teach anyone who doesn't know the Teachings.

²⁶Whoever will not strictly follow your God's Teachings and the king's

Good Morning, God

Ezra 7:21-26

God gave Ezra the important task of teaching the people to obey God's laws. Even though King Artaxerxes did not follow God, God used him to help Ezra with this task. God enabled Ezra to have the king's respect and support so that Ezra could fulfill his mission. Ezra's life reminds us that

God is in control of every situation. He will give you everything you need to do whatever he asks you to do.

Father, thank you for providing all I need to carry out your plans.

orders should be promptly exiled, have his goods confiscated, be imprisoned or be sentenced to die.

27 I, Ezra, said: Thanks be to the LORD God of our ancestors. He put this into the king's mind to make the LORD's temple in Jerusalem beautiful. 28 He made the king, his advisers, and all the king's powerful officials treat me kindly.

I was encouraged because the LORD my God was guiding me. So I gathered leaders in Israel to go with me.

The List of Those Returning From Babylon

8 1 These are the leaders of the families and the genealogy of those who left Babylon with me during the reign of King Artaxerxes:

2	from the family of Phinehas:	Gershom
	from the family of Ithamar:	Daniel
3	from the family of David:	Hattush, son of Shecaniah
	from the family of Parosh:	Zechariah, with 150 males whose genealogies were known
4	from the family of Pahath Moab:	Eliehoenai, son of Zerahiah, with 200 males
5	from the family of Zattu:ª	Shecaniah, son of Jahaziel, with 300 males
6	from the family of Adin:	Ebed, son of Jonathan, with 50 males
7	from the family of Elam:	Jeshaiah, son of Athaliah, with 70 males
8	from the family of Shephatiah:	Zebadiah, son of Michael, with 80 males
9	from the family of Joab:	Obadiah, son of Jehiel, with 210 males
10	from the family of Bani:ᵇ	Shelomith, son of Josiphiah, with 160 males
11	from the family of Bebai:	Zechariah, son of Bebai, with 38 males
12	from the family of Azgad:	Johanan, son of Hakkatan, with 110 males
13	from the family of Adonikam:	Eliphelet, Jeuel, and Shemaiah, who arrived later with 60 males
14	from the family of Bigvai:	Uthai and Zabbud, with 70 males.

The People Prepare for Their Journey

15 I had this group gather by the river that flows to Ahava, and we camped there for three days. I noticed laypeople and priests there, but I didn't find any Levites. 16 Then I sent for Eliezer, Ariel, Shemaiah, Elnathan, Jarib, Elnathan, Nathan, Zechariah, and Meshullam (who were leading men) and for Joiarib and Elnathan (who were wise). 17 I sent them to Iddo, the leader in Casiphia. I told them to tell Iddo and his relatives, the temple servants in Casiphia, that they should bring us men who can serve in our God's temple. 18 God was guiding us, so Iddo and his relatives brought us someone competent, Sherebiah, who was a descendant of Mahli, Levi, and Israel. They brought

ª 8:5 Greek; Masoretic Text omits "of Zattu."   ᵇ 8:10 Greek; Masoretic Text omits "of Bani."

us 18 of Sherebiah's sons and relatives. ¹⁹They also brought Hashabiah, Jeshaiah (who was a descendant of Merari), 20 of Jeshaiah's relatives and their sons, ²⁰and 220 temple servants. They were descended from the temple servants whom David and his officials had appointed to work for the Levites. These were all listed by name.

²¹Then I announced a fast there at the Ahava River so that we might humble ourselves in the presence of our God to ask him for a safe journey for ourselves, for our little ones, and for all our goods. ²²I was ashamed to ask the king for an armed escort with cavalry to help us against an enemy attack on the way. We had already told the king, "Our God works things out for the good of everyone who dedicates his life to serving him, but his power and his anger oppose everyone who abandons him." ²³So we fasted and asked our God for a safe journey, and he answered our prayer.

²⁴Then I selected 12 leaders from the priests—Sherebiah, Hashabiah, and 10 of their relatives. ²⁵I weighed for them the silver, the gold, and the utensils. These were the contributions that the king, his advisers, his officials, and all the Israelites had contributed for our God's temple. ²⁶I weighed the contributions for them to guard: about 24 tons of silver, 100 silver utensils weighing 150 pounds apiece, 7,500 pounds of gold, ²⁷20 gold bowls weighing 18 pounds apiece, and two utensils of fine polished bronze that were as precious as gold. ²⁸I told them, "You and the utensils are holy to the LORD. The silver and gold are freewill offerings to the LORD God of your ancestors. ²⁹Guard them carefully. In Jerusalem, inside the storerooms of the LORD's temple, weigh these items. Do this in front of the chief priests, Levites, and the leaders of Israel's families." ³⁰So the priests and the Levites took charge of the silver, the gold, and the utensils. They were responsible for bringing these items to the temple of our God in Jerusalem.

The People Arrive in Jerusalem

³¹Then we left the Ahava River on the twelfth day of the first month to go to Jerusalem. God was guiding us, and he rescued us from our enemies and from ambushes along the way. ³²When we reached Jerusalem, we rested for three days. ³³On the fourth day we weighed the silver, the gold, and the utensils in our God's temple. We put them under the supervision of Meremoth, son of the priest Uriah, as well as Eleazar, the son of Phinehas. The Levites, Jeshua's son Jozabad, and Binnui's son Noadiah, assisted them. ³⁴Everything was counted and weighed, and the entire weight was recorded at that time.

³⁵The exiles who had come back from captivity sacrificed burnt offerings to the God of Israel: 12 bulls for all Israel, 96 rams, 77 lambs, and 12 male goats for an offering for sin. All of these animals were burnt offerings for the LORD.

³⁶The exiles delivered the king's orders to the king's satraps and governors in the province west of the Euphrates River. These officials then gave their support to the people and the temple of God.

Ezra Leads the People in Prayer

9 ¹After these things had been done, the leaders came to me and said, "The people of Israel, including the priests and Levites, have failed to keep themselves separate from the neighboring groups of people and from the disgusting practices of the Canaanites, Hittites, Perizzites, Jebusites, Ammonites, Moabites, Egyptians, and Amorites. ²The Israelites and their sons have married some of these foreign women. They have mixed our holy race with the neighboring groups of people. Furthermore, the leaders and officials have led the way in being unfaithful."

³When I heard this, I tore my clothes in distress, pulled hair from my scalp and

my beard, and sat down in shock. [4]Since the former exiles had been unfaithful, everyone who gathered around me there trembled at the words of the God of Israel. I sat in shock until the evening sacrifice. [5]At the evening sacrifice I got up from my misery, and with my clothes torn, I knelt down, stretched out my hands to the LORD my God in prayer, [6]and said,

"I am ashamed, my God. I am embarrassed to look at you. Our sins have piled up over our heads, and our guilt is so overwhelming that it reaches heaven. [7]From our ancestors' days until now, we have been deep in guilt. Our kings and our priests have been handed over to foreign kings to be executed. We have been taken captive, robbed, and humiliated, as we still are today because of our sins. [8]And now, for a brief moment, the LORD our God has been kind enough to leave us a few survivors from Babylon and to give us a secure hold on his holy place. Our God has made our eyes light up and has given us new opportunities while we were slaves. [9]We are slaves, but our God hasn't abandoned us in our slavery. Instead, he has made the kings of Persia treat us kindly. He did this to give us an opportunity to rebuild our God's temple and restore its ruins and to give us a protective wall in Judah and Jerusalem.

[10]"And now, our God, what can we say after all this? We have abandoned your commandments! [11]The commandments you gave us through your servants the prophets, said, 'The land you are going to take possession of has been polluted by its perverted people and by their disgusting practices that have filled it with wickedness from one end to another. [12]So never let your daughters marry their sons or your sons marry their daughters, and never seek peace or trade with them. Then you will be strong, be able to eat the good things the land produces, and be able to give this land as a long-lasting inheritance to your children.'

[13]"After all that has happened to us because of the evil things we have done and because of our overwhelming guilt, you, our God, have punished us far less than we deserve and have permitted a few of us to survive. [14]If we break your commandments again and intermarry with people doing these disgusting things, you will become even more angry with us until you finally destroy us and no survivors are left. [15]LORD God of Israel, because you are fair, a few of us continue to remain as survivors. Look at us. All of us are guilty. None of us can stand in your presence because of this."

Good Morning, God

Ezra 9:3-5

When Ezra arrived in Jerusalem, he saw that many Israelites no longer obeyed God's laws. Ezra was disappointed and hurt. But instead of yelling at the people or giving up on his relationship with them, he cried out to God. What do you do when you are hurt or upset? Do you talk to God about how you feel? Learn from Ezra, and let God help you when you feel hurt.

Lord, help me to be more like Ezra and trust you with my problems.

Nehemiah Overcomes Opposition from Sanballat

Nehemiah Overcomes Opposition from Sanballat

Nehemiah 4:4–9

⁴ ˌNehemiah prayed,ˌ "Our God, hear us. We are despised. Turn their insults back on them, and let them be robbed in the land where they are prisoners. ⁵ Don't ignore their guilt, and don't let their sins disappear from your records. They have insulted you in front of these builders."

⁶ So we rebuilt the wall, which was rebuilt to about half its ˌoriginalˌ height. The people worked with determination.

⁷ When Sanballat, Tobiah, the Arabs, the Ammonites, and the people from Ashdod heard that the repair work on the walls of Jerusalem was making progress and that the gaps were being filled in, they became furious. ⁸ All of them plotted to attack Jerusalem to create confusion. ⁹ But we prayed to our God and set guards to protect us day and night.

The People Take Action

10 ¹While Ezra was praying, confessing these sins, crying, and throwing himself down in front of God's temple, a large crowd of Israelite men, women, and children gathered around him. They also began to cry bitterly. ²Then Shecaniah, son of Jehiel, one of the descendants of Elam, interrupted by saying to Ezra, "We have been unfaithful to our God by marrying foreign women who came from the people around us. However, there is still hope for Israel. ³So we must now make a promise to our God to get rid of all foreign women and the children born from them, as my lord Ezra and the others who tremble at the commandments of our God have advised us to do. We must do what Moses' Teachings tell us. ⁴Get up! It's your duty to take action. We are with you, so be strong and take action."

⁵Then Ezra got up and made the leaders, priests, Levites, and all the rest of Israel swear to do what they had said. So they took an oath. ⁶Then Ezra left the front of God's temple and went to the room of Jehohanan, son of Eliashib. Ezra didn't eat any food or drink any water while he was there. He was mourning because these former exiles had been so unfaithful.

⁷Then he sent a proclamation throughout Judah and Jerusalem that all the former exiles must gather in Jerusalem. ⁸If any of them didn't come within three days as the leaders and the older men had advised, then they would lose all their property and be excluded from the community of former exiles. ⁹Then all the men of Judah and Benjamin gathered within three days in Jerusalem. On the twentieth day of the ninth month, all the people sat in the courtyard of God's temple. They were trembling because of this matter and shivering because of the heavy rain.

¹⁰Ezra the priest stood up and said to them, "You have been unfaithful by marrying foreign women, and now you have added to Israel's guilt. ¹¹Confess to the LORD God of your ancestors what you have done, and do what he wants. Separate yourselves from the people of this land and from your foreign wives."

¹²Then the whole assembly shouted in reply, "Yes! We will do as you say. ¹³But the crowd is too large, and it's the rainy season. We can't take care of this outside. Besides, there are so many of us who are involved in this sin that it can't be taken care of in a day or two. ¹⁴Let our leaders represent the whole community. At a set time, everyone who has married a foreign woman must meet with the leaders and judges of each city until our God's burning anger has turned away from us in this matter."

¹⁵(Only Jonathan, Asahel's son, and Jahzeiah, Tikvah's son, opposed this. Meshullam and Shabbethai, the Levite, supported Jonathan and Jahzeiah.)

¹⁶The former exiles did this. Ezra the priest chose men who were heads of families. He chose one from each family division. (They were all listed by name.) They sat down on the first day of the tenth month to investigate the matter. ¹⁷By the first day of the first month, they had finished dealing with all the men who had married foreign women.

¹⁸Among the descendants of the priests, the following were married to foreign women: Maaseiah, Eliezer, Jarib, and Gedaliah, a descendant of Jeshua (who was Jozadak's son) and his brothers. ¹⁹They shook hands as a pledge that they would get rid of their wives. They sacrificed a ram from their flock as an offering for guilt because they were guilty.

Those Who Were Guilty of Marrying Foreign Women

²⁰ From the descendants of Immer: Hanani and Zebadiah
²¹ From the descendants of Harim: Maaseiah, Elijah, Shemaiah, Jehiel, and Uzziah

[22] From the descendants of Pashhur:	Elioenai, Maaseiah, Ishmael, Nethanel, Jozabad, and Elasah
[23] From the Levites:	Jozabad, Shimei, Kelaiah (that is, Kelita), Pethahiah, Judah, and Eliezer
[24] From the singers:	Eliashib
From the gatekeepers:	Shallum, Telem, and Uri
[25] From the other Israelites:	
From the descendants of Parosh:	Ramiah, Izziah, Malchiah, Mijamin, Eleazar, Malchiah, and Benaiah
[26] From the descendants of Elam:	Mattaniah, Zechariah, Jehiel, Abdi, Jeremoth, and Elijah
[27] From the descendants of Zattu:	Elioenai, Eliashib, Mattaniah, Jeremoth, Zabad, and Aziza
[28] From the descendants of Bebai:	Jehohanan, Hananiah, Zabbai, and Athlai
[29] From the descendants of Bani:	Meshullam, Malluch, Adaiah, Jashub, Sheal, and Jeremoth
[30] From the descendants of Pahath Moab:	Adna, Chelal, Benaiah, Maaseiah, Mattaniah, Bezalel, Binnui, and Manasseh
[31] From the descendants of Harim:	Eliezer, Isshiah, Malchiah, Shemaiah, Shimeon, [32]Benjamin, Malluch, and Shemariah
[33] From the descendants of Hashum:	Mattenai, Mattattah, Zabad, Eliphelet, Jeremai, Manasseh, and Shimei
[34] From the descendants of Bani:	Maadai, Amram, Uel, [35]Benaiah, Bedeiah, Cheluhi, [36]Vaniah, Meremoth, Eliashib, [37]Mattaniah, Mattenai, Jaasau
[38] From the descendants of Binnui:	Shimei, [39]Shelemiah, Nathan, Adaiah, [40]Machnadebai, Shashai, Sharai, [41]Azarel, Shelemiah, Shemariah, [42]Shallum, Amariah, and Joseph
[43] From the descendants of Nebo:	Jeiel, Mattithiah, Zabad, Zebina, Jaddai, Joel, and Benaiah

[44]All of these men had married foreign women. Some of these women had given birth to children.[a]

---

[a] 10:44 Hebrew meaning of this sentence uncertain.

Nehemiah

In Bible times, all important cities needed walls for protection. Nehemiah was an official in Babylon. He wanted to return to Judah to rebuild the walls of God's city, Jerusalem—not a simple task. Nehemiah is a good example to follow when you have a tough job to do.

Headlines

Two-Second Prayer Answered
Nehemiah 2:4-5, page 616

Planned Ambush Foiled!
Nehemiah 4:11-23, page 619

Nehemiah to Run Away?
Nehemiah 6:10-14, page 621

People Have Wall Party
Nehemiah 12, page 632

What's so interesting that the whole family listens? See Nehemiah 8.

Leaders Set an
Example

Should we expect more from leaders than from other people? Nehemiah thought so. When Nehemiah received a death threat, he refused to hide or run away. Nehemiah would not let his enemies give him "a bad reputation" (Nehemiah 6:11-13).

Nehemiah's life is a lesson for anyone who wants to lead. A good leader doesn't just tell others what to do; a good leader sets an example for others.

What's In It For Me?

I can accomplish what I set out to do . . .

BY SETTING A GOAL.

BY DOING WHAT IS RIGHT.

BY HOLDING ON TO MY PRINCIPLES.

BY BEING STRONG WHEN TROUBLE COMES.

BY ENCOURAGING FRIENDS TO JOIN ME.

BY ASKING GOD TO HELP ME.

Should You Avoid a Fight?

We all know it's wrong to start a fight. But what if someone else tries to pick a fight with you? Nehemiah 4 tells how Nehemiah's enemies tried to pick a fight with him. They threatened him and plotted to attack the Jews who were working on Jerusalem's walls. Instead of quitting, Nehemiah continued to do what God wanted him to do. And his enemies backed down!

It's best to avoid a fight. But if someone tries to make you do something wrong, it's OK to stand up for yourself and what you believe. Don't let others intimidate you into doing wrong.

How Do We Serve God?

The building blocks show Nehemiah's plan for following God:

1. Remember God's ways (Nehemiah 8).

2. Confess sins to God (Nehemiah 9).

3. Promise obedience to God (Nehemiah 10).

4. Celebrate God's goodness (Nehemiah 12:27-47).

Nehemiah

Distressing News

¹These are the words of Nehemiah, son of Hacaliah:

During the month of Chislev, in Artaxerxes' twentieth year as king, while I was in the fortress at Susa, ²one of my brothers, Hanani, arrived with some men from Judah. I asked them about the Jews who had survived captivity and about Jerusalem. ³They told me, "Those who survived captivity are in the province. They are enduring serious troubles and being insulted. The wall of Jerusalem has been broken down, and its gates have been destroyed by fire."

Nehemiah's Prayer

⁴When I heard this, I sat down and cried. I mourned for days. I continued to fast and pray to the God of heaven. ⁵I said,

"LORD God of heaven, great and awe-inspiring God, you faithfully keep your promise*a* and show mercy to those who love you and obey your commandments. ⁶Open your eyes, and pay close attention with your ears to what I, your servant, am praying. I am praying to you day and night about your servants the Israelites. I confess the sins that we Israelites have committed against you as well as the sins that my father's family and I have committed. ⁷We have done you a great wrong. We haven't obeyed the commandments, laws, or regulations that you gave us through your servant Moses. ⁸Please remember what you told us through your servant Moses: 'If you are unfaithful, I will scatter you among the nations. ⁹But if you return to me and continue to obey my commandments, though your people may be driven to the most distant point on the horizon, I will come and get you from there and bring you to the place where I chose to put my name.' ¹⁰These are your servants and your people whom you have saved by your great power and your strong hand. ¹¹Lord, please pay attention to my prayer and to the prayers of all your other servants who want to worship your name. Please give me success today and make this man, King Artaxerxes, show me compassion."

I was cupbearer*b* to the king at this time.

The King Shows Compassion to Nehemiah

¹In the month of Nisan, in Artaxerxes' twentieth year as king, after some wine was brought for the king, I picked up the cup of wine and gave it to the king. I had never been sad in his presence before.

²The king asked me, "Why do you look so sad? You aren't sick, are you? You must be troubled about something." (I was really afraid.)

³"May the king live forever!" I said to the king. "Why shouldn't I look sad when the city, the place where my ancestors are buried, is in ruins and its gates are burned down?"

---

a 1:5 Or "covenant."   *b* 1:11 A cupbearer was a trusted official who ensured that the king's drink was not poisoned.

⁴"What do you want?" the king asked me.

So I prayed to the God of heaven, ⁵and I asked the king, "If it pleases Your Majesty, and you are willing to grant my request, let me go to Judah, to the city where my ancestors are buried, so that I can rebuild it."

⁶Then, while the queen was sitting beside him, the king asked me, "How long will you be gone, and when will you come back?" When I gave him a specific date, he was willing to let me go.

⁷I also asked the king, "If it pleases Your Majesty, let me have letters addressed to the governors of the province west of the Euphrates River. In the letters tell them to grant me safe conduct until I arrive in Judah. ⁸Also, let me have a letter addressed to Asaph, the supervisor of Your Majesty's forest. In the letter order him to give me wood for the gates of the fortress near the temple, for the city wall, and for the house I'll move into." (The king let me have the letters, because God was guiding me.)

Nehemiah Goes to Jerusalem

⁹I went to the governors of the province west of the Euphrates River and gave them the king's letters. (The king had sent army officers and cavalry to be with me.) ¹⁰But when Sanballat the Horonite and Tobiah the Ammonite servant heard this, they were very upset that someone had come to give the people of Israel so much assistance.

Nehemiah Surveys the Damage to Jerusalem's Walls

¹¹I went to Jerusalem and was there for three days. ¹²During the night I went out with a few men without telling anyone what my God had inspired me to do for Jerusalem. The only animal I had was the one I was riding. ¹³I went through Valley Gate that night toward Snake Fountain and Dung Gate and examined the places where the walls of Jerusalem were broken down and where its gates had been burned. ¹⁴Passing through Fountain Gate, I arrived at King's Pool, but the animal I was riding couldn't get through. ¹⁵So I went through the valley that night and examined the wall. Then I turned back, entered Valley Gate, and returned.

¹⁶The officials didn't know where I had gone or what I had done. I hadn't yet told the Jews, the priests, the leaders, the other officials, or any of the rest who would be doing the work. ¹⁷Then I told them, "You see the trouble we're in. Jerusalem is in ruins, and its gates are burned down. Let's rebuild the wall of Jerusalem, and we will no longer be insulted." ¹⁸Then I told them that my God had been guiding me and what the king had told me.

They replied, "Let's begin to rebuild." So they encouraged one another to begin this God-pleasing work.

¹⁹When Sanballat the Horonite, Tobiah the Ammonite servant, and Geshem the Arab heard about this, they made fun of us and ridiculed us. They asked, "What are you doing? Are you going to rebel against the king?"

²⁰"The God of heaven will give us success," I answered them. "We, his servants, are going to rebuild. You have no property or claim or historic right in Jerusalem."

A List of the People Rebuilding Jerusalem's Walls

3 ¹The chief priest Eliashib and his relatives, the priests, started by rebuilding Sheep Gate. They dedicated it and set its doors in place. They rebuilt as far as the Tower of the Hundred, which they dedicated, and then as far as the Tower of Hananel. ²The men from Jericho were rebuilding next to Eliashib. Zaccur, son of Imri, was next to them. ³The sons of Hassenaah rebuilt Fish Gate. They laid its beams and set its doors, locks, and bars in place. ⁴Next to them Meremoth, son of Uriah and grandson of Hakkoz, made repairs. Next to them Meshullam, son of Berechiah and grandson of Meshezabel, made repairs. Next to them Zadok, son of Baana, made repairs. ⁵Next to them the men from Tekoa made repairs. However, the nobles wouldn't lower themselves to work under supervisors.

⁶Joiada, Paseah's son, and Meshullam, Besodeiah's son, made repairs on Old Gate. They laid its beams and set its doors, locks, and bars in place. ⁷Next to them Melatiah from Gibeon and Jadon from Meronoth, with men from Gibeon and Mizpah, made repairs on the wall. They did this under the authority of the governor from the province west of the Euphrates River. ⁸Next to them Uzziel, Harhaiah's son, a goldsmith, made repairs. Next to him Hananiah, a perfume maker, made repairs. They left out part of Jerusalem as far as Broad Wall. ⁹Next to them Rephaiah, Hur's son, an official in charge of half a district of Jerusalem, made repairs. ¹⁰Next to them Jedaiah, Harumaph's son, made repairs across from his own home. Next to them Hattush, Hashabneiah's son, made repairs. ¹¹Malchiah, Harim's son, and Hasshub, Pahath Moab's son, made repairs on a section that included the Tower of the Ovens. ¹²Next to them Shallum, Hallohesh's son, an official in charge of half a district of Jerusalem, made repairs with the help of his daughters.

¹³Hanun and the people of Zanoah repaired Valley Gate. They rebuilt it and set its doors, locks, and bars in place, and they repaired 1,500 feet of the wall, as far as Dung Gate. ¹⁴Dung Gate itself was repaired by Malchiah, Rechab's son, the official in charge of the district of Beth Hakkerem. He rebuilt it and set its doors, locks, and bars in place.

Chores

Nehemiah 3:1-5

Do you ever get tired of doing your chores? Do you ever wish that you could trade chores with your brother or sister? Try doing chores together. You help with the dishes, and your brother or sister can help you with the raking. It's more fun to do things together. And when you work side by side, things get done faster, too.

be you all can be

¹⁵Shallun, Col Hozeh's son, the official in charge of the district of Mizpah, repaired Fountain Gate. He rebuilt it, put a roof over it, and set its doors, locks, and bars in place. He also made repairs on the wall of the Pool of Shelah by the King's Garden as far as the stairs going down from the City of David. ¹⁶After him Nehemiah, Azbuk's son, the official in charge of half the district of Beth Zur, made repairs all the way to a point across from the tombs of David as far as the pool and the soldiers' barracks. ¹⁷After him the Levites, including Rehum (Bani's son), made repairs. Next to him Hashabiah, the official in charge of half the district of Keilah, made repairs for his district. ¹⁸After him their relatives made repairs. This included Binnui, Henadad's son, the official in charge of half the district of Keilah. ¹⁹Next to him Ezer, Jeshua's son, the official in charge of Mizpah, repaired a section across from the ascent to the Armory

at the Angle. ²⁰After him Baruch, Zabbai's son,ᵃ made repairs on a section from the Angle to the door of the house of the chief priest Eliashib. ²¹After him Meremoth, son of Uriah and grandson of Hakkoz, made repairs on a section from the door of Eliashib's house to the end of Eliashib's house. ²²After him the priests who lived in that area made repairs. ²³After them Benjamin and Hasshub made repairs across from their own homes. After them Azariah, son of Maaseiah and grandson of Ananiah, made repairs next to his home. ²⁴After him Binnui, Henadad's son, made repairs on a section from Azariah's home to the Angle and to the corner of the wall. ²⁵Palal, Uzai's son, made repairs across from the Angle and the upper tower that projects from the king's palace to the guards' courtyard. After him Pedaiah, Parosh's son, ²⁶and the temple servants who were living on the Ophel made repairs on the wall as far as a point across from Water Gate toward the east and the projecting tower. ²⁷After him the men from Tekoa repaired a section across from the large projecting tower as far as the Wall of the Ophel.

²⁸Above Horse Gate the priests made repairs. Each priest made repairs across from his own home. ²⁹After them Zadok, Immer's son, made repairs across from his own home. After him Shemaiah, Shecaniah's son, the guard at East Gate, made repairs. ³⁰After him Hananiah, Shelemiah's son, and Hanun, Zalaph's sixth son, repaired another section. After him Meshullam, Berechiah's son, made repairs across from his living quarters. ³¹After him Malchiah, one of the goldsmiths, made repairs as far as the building that housed the temple servants and merchants across from Inspection Gate and as far as the upper room at the corner. ³²The goldsmiths and merchants made repairs between the upper room at the corner and Sheep Gate.

Sanballat Ridicules the Jews

4 ᵃ¹When Sanballat heard we were rebuilding the wall, he became enraged and made fun of the Jews. ²In front of his allies and the army from Samaria, he said, "What do these miserable Jews think they're doing? Can they rebuild it by themselves? Are they going to offer sacrifices? Can they finish it in a day? Will they get the stones out of the rubbish heaps, burned as these stones are, and give them new strength?"

³Tobiah the Ammonite, who was beside Sanballat, said, "Even a fox would make their stone wall collapse if it walked on top of what they're building!"

Nehemiah Overcomes Opposition From Sanballat

⁴Nehemiah prayed, "Our God, hear us. We are despised. Turn their insults back on them, and let them be robbed in the land where they are prisoners. ⁵Don't ignore their guilt, and don't let their sins disappear from your records. They have insulted you in front of these builders."

⁶So we rebuilt the wall, which was rebuilt to about half its original height. The people worked with determination.

⁷When Sanballat, Tobiah, the Arabs, the Ammonites, and the people from Ashdod heard that the repair work on the walls of Jerusalem was making progress and that the gaps were being filled in, they became furious. ⁸All of them plotted to attack Jerusalem to create confusion. ⁹But we prayed to our God and set guards to protect us day and night.

¹⁰Then the people of Judah said, "The work crews are worn out, and there is too much rubble. We can't continue to rebuild the wall."

ᵃ3:20 Masoretic Text; Dead Sea Scrolls, Syriac, Latin, Egyptian "Zaccai's son." ᵃ4:1 Nehemiah 4:1-23 in English Bibles is Nehemiah 3:33–4:17 in the Hebrew Bible.

[11]Our enemies said, "Before they know what is happening or see a thing, we will be right in the middle of them. We'll kill them and bring the work to an end."

[12]Jews who were living near our enemies warned us ten times that our enemies would attack us from every direction.[b]

[13]That is why I positioned people by their families behind the wall where it was lowest and most exposed. The people were armed with swords, spears, and bows. [14]I looked them over and proceeded to tell the nobles, the leaders, and the rest of the people, "Don't be afraid of our enemies. Remember how great and awe-inspiring the LORD is. Fight for your brothers, your sons, your daughters, your wives, and your homes."

[15]When our enemies heard that we knew about their plots and that God had prevented their plans from being successful, we all went back to the work on the wall. Each person performed his own job. [16]From that day on, half of my men worked on the wall, and the other half were wearing body armor and holding spears, shields, and bows. The leaders stood behind all the Judeans [17]who were rebuilding the wall. The workers who were carrying loads did the work with one hand and held their weapons with the other, [18]and each builder had his sword fastened to his side. The man who was supposed to sound the trumpet alarm was with me. [19]I told the nobles, the leaders, and the rest of the people, "So much work has to be done in different places that we are widely separated from one another on the wall. [20]When you hear the trumpet, assemble around me. Our God will fight for us!"

[21]So we continued to work. Half of us held spears from early dawn until the stars came out. [22]At that time I told the people, "Every man and his servant should stay overnight in Jerusalem so that we can set a guard at night and work during the day." [23]My brothers, my servants, and the guards assigned to me never changed their clothes. Neither did I. We each kept our weapons at hand.

The Poor Complain About Their Rich Relatives

[1]Then some of the people, the men and their wives, complained publicly about their Jewish relatives. [2]Some of them said, "We have large families! We need some grain if we are going to eat and stay alive." [3]Others said, "We've had to mortgage our fields, our vineyards, and our homes in order to get some grain because of this famine." [4]Others said, "We've had to borrow money to pay the king's taxes on our fields and vineyards. [5]We have the same flesh and blood as our relatives. Our children are just like theirs. Yet, we have to force our sons and daughters to become slaves. Some of our daughters have already become slaves. But we can't do anything else when our fields and vineyards belong to others."

Nehemiah Stops the Rich From Taking Advantage of the Poor

[6]I became furious when I heard their complaint and what they had to say. [7]After thinking it over, I confronted the nobles and the leaders. I told them, "You are charging interest on loans made to your own relatives." I arranged for a large meeting to deal with them. [8]Then I told them, "We have done our best to buy back our Jewish relatives who had been sold to other nations. Now you are selling your Jewish relatives so that we have to buy them back again!" They were unable to say anything. [9]I added, "What you're doing is wrong. Shouldn't you live in the fear of our God to keep our enemies from ridiculing us? [10]My brothers, my servants, and I are lending money

---

[b]4:12 Hebrew meaning of this verse uncertain.

and grain to the poor. But we must stop charging them interest. ¹¹You must return their fields, their vineyards, their olive orchards, and their homes today. Also, you must return the interest on the money, grain, new wine, and olive oil you've been charging them."

¹²They responded, "We'll return it and not try to get it from them again . We'll do what you say." Then I called the priests and made them swear to do what they promised. ¹³I brushed off my clothes and said, "In the same way, may God brush off from home and work everyone who refuses to keep this promise. In the same way, may everyone be brushed off and left with nothing." Then the whole congregation said amen and praised the LORD. The people did what they had promised.

Nehemiah Never Takes What Is Rightfully His as Governor

¹⁴During the 12 years that I was governor of Judah, from the twentieth year of King Artaxerxes' reign to the thirty-second year of his reign, my brothers and I never ate any food that was paid for by the governor's food allowance. ¹⁵Those who were governors before me had made life difficult for the people by taking from them food and wine plus one pound of silver. Even the governors' servants took advantage of their power over the people. But I didn't do that, because I feared God. ¹⁶Instead, I put my best effort into the work on this wall, and we bought no land. All my men gathered here for work. ¹⁷I fed 150 Jewish leaders and their people who came to us from the surrounding nations. ¹⁸Preparing one ox and six choice sheep was necessary every day. Poultry was prepared for me. Once every ten days a supply of wine was ordered. Yet, in spite of all this, I never demanded anything from the governor's food allowance, because these people were already carrying a heavy load.

Nehemiah's Prayer

¹⁹Remember me, my God. Consider everything that I have done for these people.

Sanballat Tries to Harm Nehemiah

6 ¹Sanballat, Tobiah, Geshem the Arab, and the rest of our enemies heard that I had rebuilt the wall and that no gaps had been left in it (although at that time I had not yet hung the doors in the city gates). ²Then Sanballat and Geshem sent this

Good Morning, God
Nehemiah 5:14-18

Imagine working really hard and refusing to get paid for your work! Nehemiah didn't accept any money for being governor. Nehemiah did not want to be compared to the governors before him. They took advantage of their powerful position, and the people suffered. Sometimes leaders like power. They boss people around and hurt others. A godly leader should always think about the needs of the people she is leading. How can you be a godly leader like Nehemiah?

Father, help me remember the feelings of others when I am a leader.

message to me: "Let's meet in Hakkephirim on the plain of Ono." They were planning to harm me.

³I sent messengers to tell them, "I'm working on an important project and can't get away. Why should the work stop while I leave to meet with you?" ⁴They sent the same message to me four times, and I answered them the same way. ⁵When Sanballat sent me the same message a fifth time, his servant held in his hand an unsealed letter. ⁶In it was written:

> It has been reported throughout the nations, and Geshem has confirmed it, that you and the Jews are planning to rebel. That's why you're rebuilding the wall. According to this report, you want to become their king. ⁷You've appointed prophets to announce about you in Jerusalem, 'There's a king in Judah!' This report will get back to the king. So let's talk about this.

⁸Then I sent someone to tell him, "None of your accusations are true. You are making them up out of your own imagination."

⁹They were all trying to intimidate us. They thought we would give up and not finish the work.

But God made me strong.

¹⁰One day, I went to the home of Shemaiah, son of Delaiah and grandson of Mehetabel. Shemaiah who was confined to his house, said, "Let's meet in the house of God, inside the temple, and close the temple doors. Some men are coming at night to kill you."

¹¹But I asked, "Should a man like me run away? Would a man like me go into the temple to save his life? I won't go."

¹²Then I realized that God hadn't sent him. Instead, Tobiah and Sanballat had hired him to prophesy against me. ¹³He was hired to intimidate me into doing this so that I would sin. Then they could give me a bad reputation in order to discredit me.

¹⁴Nehemiah prayed, "My God, remember what Tobiah and Sanballat have done. Also, remember the female prophet Noadiah and the rest of the prophets who have been trying to intimidate me."

The Wall Rebuilt in Spite of Opposition

¹⁵The wall was finished on the twenty-fifth day of the month of Elul. The wall took 52 days to finish. ¹⁶When all our enemies heard about this, all the surrounding nations were afraid and lost their self-confidence. They realized we had done this work with the help of our God.

Traitors on the Inside

¹⁷In those days the nobles of Judah sent many letters to Tobiah, and Tobiah sent many letters back to them. ¹⁸Many in Judah had promised to support Tobiah because he was the son-in-law of Shecaniah, Arah's son. In addition, Tobiah's son Jehohanan had married the daughter of Meshullam, Berechiah's son. ¹⁹The nobles were singing Tobiah's praises to me and reporting to him what I said. Tobiah kept sending letters to intimidate me.

Nehemiah Places Hanani and Hananiah in Charge of Guarding the City Gates

⁷ ¹The gatekeepers, the singers, and the Levites were assigned their duties after the wall had been rebuilt and I had hung the doors. ²I put my brother Hanani and Hananiah, the commander of the fortress, in charge of Jerusalem. Hananiah was a

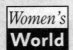

Cities / *Nehemiah 7:1-4*

The ancient city of Nineveh was surrounded by an 8-mile-long wall. The city had a population of about 175,000 people. The walled cities or towns in Israel were much smaller. In King David's time, the city of Jerusalem held only about 3,500 people. Even in Jesus' time, Jerusalem's population numbered only about 40,000.

Throughout ancient Israel's history, most cities in Israel covered only 5 or 10 acres. They were built on the tops or sides of hills. The city wall might be 20 feet thick. But inside the wall there was room for only 100 to 150 small, one-story houses.

These cities had narrow streets and alleys. The streets wound around to courtyards, where outdoor ovens served five or six households. The people who lived in cities and towns worked in fields outside the walls during the day. Larger and more important Old Testament cities were called "mothers." Near these cities were unwalled villages, called "daughters," with just ten or twelve houses.

The cities mentioned in the New Testament were different from the Old Testament cities. They were larger centers of trade and government. Some New Testament cities had many public buildings—theaters, temples, baths, and gymnasiums. They also had a large marketplace where farmers and others could sell their goods. When the apostle Paul visited one of these cities, Philippi, about 50,000 people lived there. Rome, then the largest city in the world, contained one million people; the entire Roman Empire numbered about 58 million people.

trustworthy man, and he feared God more than most people do. ³I told them, "The gates of Jerusalem should not be opened at the hottest time of the day. While the gatekeepers are still standing there, they should shut the doors and bar them. Order some of the men in Jerusalem to stand guard, some at their posts and others in front of their homes." ⁴The city was large and wide-open. Few people were in it, and no houses were being built.

The First Jewish Exiles Who Returned to Jerusalem

[5]Then my God put the idea into my head that I should gather the nobles, leaders, and people so that they could check their genealogy. I found the book with the genealogy of those who came back the first time. I found the following written in it:

[6]These were the people in the province. They were the ones who left the place where the exiles had been taken captive. King Nebuchadnezzar of Babylon had taken them captive. They returned to Jerusalem and Judah. All of them went to their own cities. [7]They went with Zerubbabel, Jeshua, Nehemiah, Azariah, Raamiah, Nahamani, Mordecai, Bilshan, Mispereth, Bigvai, Nehum, and Baanah.

Families Listed by Ancestor—
Ezra 2:3-20

This is the number of Israelite men from the people in exile:

[8]	the descendants of Parosh	2,172
[9]	of Shephatiah	372
[10]	of Arah	652
[11]	of Pahath Moab, that is, of Jeshua and Joab	2,818
[12]	of Elam	1,254
[13]	of Zattu	845
[14]	of Zaccai	760
[15]	of Binnui	648
[16]	of Bebai	628
[17]	of Azgad	2,322
[18]	of Adonikam	667
[19]	of Bigvai	2,067
[20]	of Adin	655
[21]	of Ater, that is, Hezekiah	98
[22]	of Hashum	328
[23]	of Bezai	324
[24]	of Hariph	112
[25]	of Gibeon	95

Families Listed by Towns—
Ezra 2:21-35

[26]	the people of Bethlehem and Netophah	188
[27]	of Anathoth	128
[28]	of Beth Azmaveth	42
[29]	of Kiriath Jearim, Chephirah, and Beeroth	743
[30]	of Ramah and Geba	621
[31]	of Michmas	122
[32]	of Bethel and Ai	123
[33]	of the other Nebo	52
[34]	of the other Elam	1,254
[35]	of Harim	320
[36]	of Jericho	345
[37]	of Lod, Hadid, and Ono	721
[38]	of Senaah	3,930

Priests—
Ezra 2:36-39

[39]These priests returned from exile:

the descendants of Jedaiah (through the family of Jeshua)	973
[40] of Immer	1,052
[41] of Pashhur	1,247
[42] of Harim	1,017

Levites—
Ezra 2:40-42

[43]These Levites returned from exile:

the descendants of Jeshua, that is, of Kadmiel and, of Hodeiah	74

[44]These singers returned from exile:

the descendants of Asaph	148

[45]These gatekeepers returned from exile:

the descendants of Shallum, Ater, Talmon, Akkub, Hatita, and Shobai	138

Temple Servants—
Ezra 2:43-54

[46]These temple servants returned from exile: the descendants of Ziha, Hasupha, Tabbaoth, [47]Keros, Sia, Padon, [48]Lebanah, Hagabah, Shalmai, [49]Hanan, Giddel, Gahar, [50]Reaiah, Rezin, Nekoda, [51]Gazzam, Uzza, Paseah, [52]Besai, Meunim, Nephusheshim, [53]Bakbuk, Hakupha, Harhur, [54]Bazlith, Mehida, Harsha, [55]Barkos, Sisera, Temah, [56]Neziah, and Hatipha.

Descendants of Solomon's Servants—
Ezra 2:55-58

[57]These descendants of Solomon's servants returned from exile: the descendants of Sotai, Sophereth, Perida, [58]Jaala, Darkon, Giddel, [59]Shephatiah, Hattil, Pochereth Hazzebaim, and Amon.

[60]The temple servants and the descendants of Solomon's servants totaled 392.

Those of Unknown Origin—
Ezra 2:59-63

[61]The following people came from Tel Melah, Tel Harsha, Cherub, Addan, and Immer, but they couldn't prove they were Israelites on the basis of their father's family or their genealogy: [62]the descendants of Delaiah, Tobiah, and Nekoda. These people totaled 642.

[63]These priests couldn't prove they were Israelites: the descendants of Hobaiah, Hakkoz, and Barzillai (who had married one of the daughters of Barzillai from Gilead and took that family name). [64]These people searched for their family names in the genealogical records, but their names couldn't be found there. For this reason they were considered contaminated and couldn't be priests. [65]The governor told them not to eat any of the most holy food until a priest could use the Urim and Thummim[a] to settle the problem.

---

[a]7:65 The Urim and Thummim were used by the chief priest to determine God's answer to questions.

The Total of the People and Animals Returning From Exile—
Ezra 2:64-67

⁶⁶The whole assembly totaled 42,360. ⁶⁷In addition to the male and female servants who numbered 7,337, they also had 245 male and female singers. ⁶⁸They had 736 horses, 245 mules,ᵇ ⁶⁹435 camels, and 6,720 donkeys.

Gifts Given for the Temple—
Ezra 2:68-70

⁷⁰Some of the heads of the families contributed to this work. The governor contributed the following to the treasury: nearly 18 pounds of gold, 50 bowls, and 530 robes for the priests. ⁷¹Some of the heads of the families contributed to the treasury for this work: 337 pounds of gold and 3,215 pounds of silver. ⁷²The rest of the people contributed 337 pounds of gold, 2,923 pounds of silver, and 67 robes for the priests.

⁷³The priests, Levites, the gatekeepers, the singers, some of the people, the temple servants, and the rest of Israel settled in their own cities. When the seventh month came, the people of Israel were in their own cities.

The Public Reading of Moses' Teachings

¹When the seventh month came, all the people gathered together in the court yard in front of Water Gate. They told Ezra the scribe to bring the Book of Moses' Teachings, which the Lord had commanded Israel to follow. ²Then Ezra the priest brought the Teachings in front of the assembly. This included men, women, and any children who could understand what they heard. This took place on the first day of the seventh month. ³From daybreak until noon, he read from it in the courtyard in front of Water Gate to the men, women, and children who could understand it. All the people listened to the Book of Moses' Teachings.

⁴Ezra the scribe stood on a raised wooden platform made for this occasion. Mattithiah, Shema, Anaiah, Uriah, Hilkiah, and Maaseiah stood beside him on his right. Pedaiah, Mishael, Malchiah, Hashum, Hashbaddanah, Zechariah, and Meshullam stood beside him on his left. ⁵Ezra, standing higher than all the other people, opened the book in front of all the people. As he opened it, all the people stood up. ⁶Ezra thanked the Lord, the great God. All the people responded, "Amen! Amen!" as they raised their hands and then bowed with their faces to the ground and worshiped the Lord. ⁷The Levites—Jeshua, Bani, Sherebiah, Jamin, Akkub, Shabbethai, Hodiah, Maaseiah, Kelita, Azariah, Jozabad, Hanan, and Pelaiah—explained the Teachings to the people while they were standing there. ⁸They read the Book of God's Teachings clearly and explained the meaning so that the people could understand what was read.

⁹Then Nehemiah the governor, Ezra the priest and scribe, and the Levites who taught the people told them, "This is a holy day for the Lord your God. Don't mourn or cry." All the people were crying as they listened to the reading of God's Teachings. ¹⁰Then he told them, "Go, eat rich foods, drink sweet drinks, and send portions to those who cannot provide for themselves. Today is a holy day for the Lord. Don't be sad because the joy you have in the Lord is your strength." ¹¹So the Levites calmed all the people by saying, "Listen. Today is a holy day. Don't be sad."

¹²Then all the people went to eat and drink and to send portions. They had a big, joyful celebration because they understood the words that had been explained to them.

ᵇ7:68 Some Hebrew manuscripts omit "They had . . . mules." In those manuscripts verses 69-73 are numbered as 68-72.

The Festival of Booths Is Observed

¹³On the second day the leaders of the families of all the people, including the priests and the Levites, met with Ezra the scribe to study the words of God's Teachings. ¹⁴They found written in the Teachings that the Lord had given an order through Moses that the people of Israel should live in booths during a festival in the seventh month. ¹⁵They should announce this command and send this message throughout all their cities and Jerusalem: "Go to the mountains, and get branches—olive and wild olive, myrtle, palm, and other thick-leaved branches—to make booths as it is written."

¹⁶So the people went to get branches to make booths for themselves. Some made booths on their roofs, others in their courtyards, in the courtyards of God's temple, in the open area by Water Gate, or in the open area at Ephraim Gate.

¹⁷The whole assembly that had come back from exile made booths and lived in them. From the time of Jeshua (son of Nun) to that day, the people of Israel had not done this. There was a big, joyful celebration. ¹⁸Day by day, from the first day of the festival to the last day, Ezra continued to read from the Book of God's Teachings. The people celebrated the festival for seven days, and on the eighth day, they had a closing festival assembly in accordance with the regulations.

A Day of Fasting and Confession

¹When the Israelites assembled on the twenty-fourth day of this month, they fasted, wore sackcloth, and threw dirt on their heads. ²Those who were descendants of Israel separated themselves from all foreigners. They stood and confessed their sins as well as the wicked things their ancestors had done. ³They stood in their places, and for one-fourth of the day, they listened as the Book of the Teachings of the Lord their God was read, and for another fourth of the day, they confessed their sins and worshiped the Lord their God.

A Day of Prayer

⁴Then Jeshua, Bani, Kadmiel, Shebaniah, Bunni, Sherebiah, Bani, and Chanani stood on the stairs built for the Levites and cried loudly to the Lord their God. ⁵Then the Levites—Jeshua, Kadmiel, Bani, Hashabneiah, Sherebiah, Hodiah, Shebaniah, and Pethahiah—said, "Stand up, and thank the Lord your God:

Creation

From everlasting to everlasting your glorious name is praised
  and lifted high above all blessing and praise.
6   You alone are the Lord.
  You made heaven, the highest heaven, with all its armies.
  You made the earth and everything on it, the seas and everything in them.
  You give life to them all, and the armies of heaven worship you.

Abraham

7   You are the Lord, the God who chose Abram
  and took him from Ur of the Chaldeans
  and gave him the name Abraham.
8   You found that his heart was faithful to you.
  You made a promise*ᵈ* to him to give the land of the Canaanites, Hittites,

---

ᵈ9:8 Or "covenant."

Amorites, Perizzites, Jebusites, and Girgashites to his descendants.
You kept your promise because you are fair.

The Exodus

9   You saw how our ancestors suffered in Egypt,
   and you heard them crying at the Red Sea.
10   You performed miraculous signs and did amazing things to Pharaoh
   and all his servants and all the people in his land
      because you knew how arrogantly they were treating our ancestors.
   You made a name for yourself, a name which remains to this day.
11   You divided the sea in front of them
      so that they could walk through the sea on dry ground.
   You threw into deep water those who pursued your people
      as someone throws a stone into raging water.

Wandering in the Wilderness

12   You led them during the day by a column of smoke
      and during the night by a column of fire to give them light
         to see the way they should go.
13   You came from heaven to Mount Sinai and spoke with them from heaven.
   You gave them fair rules, trustworthy teachings,
      and good laws and commandments.
14   You taught them about your holy day of worship.
   You gave them commandments, laws, and teachings
      through your servant Moses.
15   You gave them bread from heaven to satisfy their hunger
      and made water flow from a rock to quench their thirst.
   You told them to take possession of the land
      that you swore you would give them.
16   But they—our own ancestors—acted arrogantly.
   They became stubborn and wouldn't obey your commands.
17   They refused to listen.
   They forgot the miracles you performed for them.
   They became stubborn and appointed a leader
      to take them back to slavery in Egypt.
   But you are a forgiving God,
      one who is compassionate, merciful, patient,
         and always ready to forgive.
   You never abandoned them,
18   even when they made a metal statue of a calf for themselves
         and said, 'This is your god who took you out of Egypt.'
   They committed outrageous sins.
19   But because of your endless compassion,
      you didn't abandon them in the desert.
         The column of smoke didn't leave them during the day,
            but it led them on their way.
         The column of fire didn't leave them during the night,
            but it gave them light to see the way they should go.
20   You gave them your good Spirit to teach them.
   You didn't keep your manna to yourself.

You gave them water to quench their thirst.
21 You provided for them in the desert for 40 years,
      and they had everything they needed.
    Their clothes didn't wear out, and their feet didn't swell.

Conquest of Canaan
22 You gave kingdoms and nations to the Israelites
      and assigned them their boundaries.
        So they took possession of the land of Sihon,
          the land of the king of Heshbon,
            and the land of King Og of Bashan.
23 You made their children as numerous as the stars in the sky.
    You brought them into the land you told their parents to enter and possess.
24 Their children took possession of the land.
    You defeated for them the Canaanites, who lived in the land.
    You handed the Canaanite kings and their people over to them
      to do whatever they wanted with the Canaanites.
25 The Israelites captured fortified cities and a rich land.
    They took possession of houses filled with all sorts of good things,
      cisterns, vineyards, olive trees,
        and plenty of fruit trees.
          So they ate and were satisfied and grew fat.
            They enjoyed the vast supply of good things you gave them.

Israel's Rebellion
26 But they were defiant and rebelled against you.
    They threw your teachings over their shoulders
      and killed your prophets who warned them to turn back to you.
        They committed outrageous sins.
27 You handed them over to their enemies, who made them suffer.
      When they began to suffer, they cried to you.
    You heard them from heaven.
    You gave them saviors to rescue them from their enemies
      because of your endless compassion.
28 As soon as they felt some relief,
      they were again doing what you considered evil.
    You abandoned them to their enemies, who conquered them.
    They cried to you again, and you heard them from heaven.
    You rescued them many times because of your compassion.
29 You warned them in order to bring them back to your teachings,
      but they became arrogant and would not obey your commandments.
    They sinned by not following your regulations.
      If anyone follows them, he will find life in them.
    But they gave you the cold shoulder,
      became impossible to deal with, and wouldn't listen.
30 You were patient with them for many years.
    You warned them by your Spirit through your prophets.
      However, they wouldn't listen.
        So you handed them over to the people in the surrounding nations.
31 But your compassion is endless.

You didn't destroy them or abandon them.
You are a merciful and compassionate God.

The Present

32 And now, our God, you are the great, mighty, and awe-inspiring God.
You faithfully keep your promises.
Do not consider all the hardships
that we have been going through as unimportant.
The hardships have come to our kings, leaders, priests, prophets,
ancestors, and all your people
from the time of the kings of Assyria until now.
33 But you were fair about everything that has happened to us.
You have been faithful, but we have been wicked.
34 Our kings, leaders, priests, and ancestors didn't obey your teachings.
They didn't pay attention to your commandments or the warnings
that you gave them.
35 When they lived in their own kingdom and enjoyed the many good things
that you gave them in a vast, fertile land
which was set in front of them, they didn't serve you
or turn away from their wicked lives.
36 Look ‚at us‚ now. We're slaves!
In the land you gave our ancestors,
they could eat its produce and ‚enjoy‚ its good things.
But now we're slaves!
37 The many products ‚from our land‚ go to the kings you put over us.
This is because of our sins.
These kings have control over our bodies,
and they do as they please with our livestock.
We are in agony.[b]

An Agreement in Writing

38"We are making a binding agreement ‚and putting it‚ in writing because of all this.
Our leaders, Levites, and priests are putting their seals on the document."

[a]1The following people sealed the agreement: Governor Nehemiah (son of Hacaliah), Zedekiah, 2Seraiah, Azariah, Jeremiah, 3Pashhur, Amariah, Malchiah, 4Hattush, Shebaniah, Malluch, 5Harim, Meremoth, Obadiah, 6Daniel, Ginnethon, Baruch, 7Meshullam, Abijah, Mijamin, 8Maaziah, Bilgai, and Shemaiah. These were the priests.

9These were the Levites: Jeshua (son of Azaniah), Binnui (of the sons of Henadad), Kadmiel, 10and their relatives Shebaniah, Hodiah, Kelita, Pelaiah, Hanan, 11Mica, Rehob, Hashabiah, 12Zaccur, Sherebiah, Shebaniah, 13Hodiah, Bani, and Beninu.

14These were the leaders of the people: Parosh, Pahath Moab, Elam, Zattu, Bani, 15Bunni, Azgad, Bebai, 16Adonijah, Bigvai, Adin, 17Ater, Hezekiah, Azzur, 18Hodiah, Hashum, Bezai, 19Hariph, Anathoth, Nebai, 20Magpiash, Meshullam, Hezir, 21Meshezabel, Zadok, Jaddua, 22Pelatiah, Hanan, Anaiah, 23Hoshea, Hananiah, Hasshub, 24Hallohesh, Pilha, Shobek, 25Rehum, Hashabnah, Maaseiah, 26Ahiah, Hanan, Anan, 27Malluch, Harim, and Baanah.

---

[b]9:37 Nehemiah 9:38 in English Bibles is Nehemiah 10:1 in the Hebrew Bible. [a]10:1 Nehemiah 10:1-39 in the English Bible is Nehemiah 10:2-40 in the Hebrew Bible.

²⁸The rest of the people took an oath. These people included the priests, Levites, gatekeepers, singers, temple servants, and all who had separated themselves from the inhabitants of the land for the sake of God's Teachings. Their wives, sons, daughters, and everyone who is capable of understanding also took an oath. ²⁹They joined their relatives, the nobles, in binding themselves with a curse and an oath to follow God's teachings given by Moses, God's servant. They also bound themselves to follow all the commandments, rules, and regulations of the LORD our Lord.

³⁰We will not allow our daughters to marry the inhabitants of the land or allow their daughters to marry our sons. ³¹If the inhabitants of the land bring merchandise or grain to sell on the day of worship, we won't buy anything from them on the day of worship or any other holy day. During the seventh year, we won't plant the fields or collect any debts.

³²Also, we take upon ourselves the obligation to give an eighth of an ounce of silver every year for worship in our God's temple: ³³for rows of the bread of the presence, and for the daily grain offerings and daily burnt offerings, on the weekly days of worship, and on the New Moon Festivals, and at the appointed annual festivals, for the holy gifts and offerings for sin that make peace with God for Israel, and for all the other work in the temple of our God.

³⁴We priests, Levites, and laypeople have drawn lots to decide the order in which the heads of our families should bring wood to our God's temple to burn on the altar of the LORD our God at appointed times every year according to the directions in the Teachings. ³⁵We have drawn lots to decide who should bring the first produce harvested and the first fruit from every tree each year to the LORD's temple. ³⁶Following the directions in the Teachings, we have drawn lots to decide who should bring the firstborn of our sons, our cattle, and our flocks to the priests serving in our God's temple. ³⁷Also, we have drawn lots to decide who should bring the best of our coarse flour, contributions, fruit from every tree, new wine, and olive oil to the priests, to the storerooms. We will bring for the Levites one-tenth of the produce from our fields, because the Levites are the ones who collect one-tenth of the produce from all our farm communities. ³⁸A priest—one of Aaron's descendants—should be with the Levites when they collect the tenth. Then the Levites should bring one-tenth of these tenths to our God's temple, into the rooms of the storehouses there. ³⁹The Israelites and the Levites should bring into the storerooms their contributions of grain, new wine, and olive oil. They should bring these products to the place where the utensils of the holy place are and where the priests who serve and the gatekeepers and the singers are. We won't neglect our God's temple.

New Residents for Jerusalem

11 ¹The leaders of the people settled in Jerusalem. The rest of the people drew lots to bring one out of every ten to live in Jerusalem, the holy city. The remaining nine-tenths were supposed to live in the other cities. ²The people blessed everyone who willingly offered to live in Jerusalem.

³These were the officials of the province who settled in Jerusalem. Some Israelites, priests, Levites, temple servants, and descendants of Solomon's servants settled in the cities of Judah. They lived on their own property in their own cities.

⁴Some of the descendants of Judah and of Benjamin settled in Jerusalem. The

descendants of Judah were Athaiah, who was the son of Uzziah, who was the son of Zechariah, who was the son of Amariah, who was the son of Shephatiah, who was the son of Mahalalel, who was the son of Perez; ⁵Maaseiah was the son of Baruch, who was the son of Col Hozeh, who was the son of Hazaiah, who was the son of Adaiah, who was the son of Joiarib, who was the son of Zechariah, who was the son of Shiloni. ⁶All the descendants of Perez who settled in Jerusalem were 468 outstanding men. ⁷These are the descendants of Benjamin: Sallu, who was the son of Meshullam, who was the son of Joed, who was the son of Pedaiah, who was the son of Kolaiah, who was the son of Maaseiah, who was the son of Ithiel, who was the son of Jeshaiah, ⁸and after him, Gabbai and Sallai. The number of Benjamin's descendants totaled 928. ⁹Joel, son of Zichri, was in charge, and Judah, son of Senuah, was second-in-command over the city.

¹⁰These were the priests: Jedaiah (son of Joiarib), Jachin, ¹¹Seraiah, who was the son of Hilkiah, who was the son of Meshullam, who was the son of Zadok, who was the son of Meraioth, who was the son of Ahitub, who was the supervisor of God's temple. ¹²From Seraiah's relatives 822 did the work in the temple. Also, Adaiah worked in the temple. He was the son of Jeroham, who was the son of Pelaliah, who was the son of Amzi, who was the son of Zechariah, who was the son of Pashhur, who was the son of Malchiah. ¹³Adaiah's relatives, the heads of the families, totaled 242. Amashsai was the son of Azarel, who was the son of Ahzai, who was the son of Meshillemoth, who was the son of Immer. ¹⁴Their relatives, who were warriors, totaled 128. The man in charge of them was Zabdiel, son of Haggedolim.

¹⁵These were the Levites: Shemaiah who was the son of Hasshub, who was the son of Azrikam, who was the son of Hashabiah, who was the son of Bunni. ¹⁶Shabbethai and Jozabad, Levite leaders, who were in charge of the work outside God's temple. ¹⁷Mattaniah was the son of Mica, who was the son of Zabdi, who was the son of Asaph, the leader who led the prayer of thanksgiving. The Levite leader Bakbukiah was the second-in-command among his relatives; and so was Abda who was the son of Shammua, who was the son of Galal, who was the son of Jeduthum. ¹⁸All the Levites in the holy city totaled 284.

¹⁹These were the gatekeepers: Akkub, Talmon, and their relatives who guarded the gates totaled 172.

²⁰The rest of the Israelites, priests, and Levites lived in all the cities of Judah. Everyone lived on his own inherited property. ²¹But the temple servants lived on Mount Ophel with Ziha and Gishpa in charge of them. ²²The man in charge of the Levites in Jerusalem was Uzzi, who was the son of Bani, who was the son of Hashabiah, who was the son of Mattaniah, who was the son of Mica from Asaph's descendants who were the singers in charge of worship in God's temple. ²³They were under orders from the king, orders that determined which duties they should perform day by day. ²⁴Pethahiah, son of Meshezabel, one of the descendants of Zerah, Judah's son, was the king's adviser on all matters concerning the people.

²⁵Many people lived in villages that had fields. Some people of Judah lived in Kiriath Arba and its villages, in Dibon and its villages, in Jekabzeel and its villages, ²⁶in Jeshua, Moladah, and Beth Pelet, ²⁷in Hazar Shual, in Beersheba and its villages, ²⁸in Ziklag, and in Meconah and its villages, ²⁹in En Rimmon, Zorah, Jarmuth, ³⁰Zanoah, and Adullam and their villages, in Lachish and its fields, and in Azekah and its villages. So they settled in the land from Beersheba to the Valley of Hinnom.

³¹Benjamin's descendants live in the area of Geba, in Michmash, Aija, Bethel and its villages, ³²in Anathoth, Nob, Ananiah, ³³Hazor, Ramah, Gittaim, ³⁴Hadid, Zeboim,

Neballat, [35]Lod, Ono, and in the valley of the Craftsmen. [36]Some divisions of Levites in Judah were assigned to Benjamin.

The Priest and Levites Who Returned to Jerusalem With Zerubbabel

12 [1]These are the priests and Levites who came back with Zerubbabel (Shealtiel's son) and Jeshua: Seraiah, Jeremiah, Ezra, [2]Amariah, Malluch, Hattush, [3]Shecaniah, Rehum, Meremoth, [4]Iddo, Ginnethoi, Abijah, [5]Mijamin, Maadiah, Bilgah, [6]Shemaiah, Joiarib, Jedaiah, [7]Sallu, Amok, Hilkiah, and Jedaiah. These were the leaders of the priests and of their relatives at the time of Jeshua.

[8]The Levites were Jeshua, Binnui, Kadmiel, Sherebiah, Judah, and Mattaniah, who with his relatives was in charge of the thanksgiving hymns. [9]Their relatives Bakbukiah and Unno stood across from them in worship.

[10]Jeshua was the father of Joiakim. Joiakim was the father of Eliashib. Eliashib was the father of Joiada. [11]Joiada was the father of Jonathan. Jonathan was the father of Jaddua.

[12]At the time of Joiakim, these were the priests who were the leaders of their families: From Seraiah, Meraiah; from Jeremiah, Hananiah; [13]from Ezra, Meshullam; from Amariah, Jehohanan; [14]from Malluchi, Jonathan; from Shebaniah, Joseph; [15]from Harim, Adna; from Meraioth, Helkai; [16]from Iddo, Zechariah; from Ginnethon, Meshullam; [17]from Abijah, Zichri; from Miniamin, from Moadiah, Piltai; [18]from Bilgah, Shammua; from Shemaiah, Jehonathan; [19]from Joiarib, Mattenai; from Jedaiah, Uzzi; [20]from Sallai, Kallai; from Amok, Eber; [21]from Hilkiah, Hashabiah; from Jedaiah, Nethanel.

[22]The names of the family heads of the Levites and the priests at the time of Eliashib, Joiada, Johanan, and Jaddua were recorded until the reign of Darius the Persian. [23]The names of the family heads of the Levites were recorded in the Book of Chronicles until the time of Johanan, grandson of Eliashib. [24]The heads of the Levites were Hashabiah, Sherebiah, and Jeshua (son of Kadmiel). They and their relatives stood in groups across from one another to sing hymns of praise and thanksgiving antiphonally as David, the man of God, had ordered. [25]Mattaniah, Bakbukiah, Obadiah, Meshullam, Talmon, and Akkub were gatekeepers standing guard at the storehouses by the gates. [26]They lived in the days of Joiakim, son of Jeshua, grandson of Jozadak, and in the days of Nehemiah the governor and of Ezra the priest and scribe.

Jerusalem's Wall Is Dedicated to God

[27]When the wall of Jerusalem was going to be dedicated, they went to wherever the Levites lived and had them come to Jerusalem to celebrate the dedication joyfully with hymns of thanksgiving, with songs and cymbals, and with harps and lyres. [28]So the groups of singers came together from the countryside around Jerusalem, from the villages of Netophah, [29]from Beth Gilgal, and from the region of Geba and Azmaveth. The singers had built villages for themselves around Jerusalem. [30]The priests and the Levites cleansed themselves. Then they cleansed the people, the gates, and the wall.

[31]Then I had the leaders of Judah come up on the wall, and I arranged two large choirs to give thanks and march in procession. One choir went to the right on the wall to Dung Gate. [32]Hoshaiah and half of the leaders of Judah followed them. [33]Azariah, Ezra, Meshullam, [34]Judah, Benjamin, Shemaiah, and Jeremiah also followed. [35]So did some priests with trumpets: Zechariah, who was the son of Jonathan, who was the son of Shemaiah, who was the son of Mattaniah, who was the son of Micaiah, who was the son of Zaccur, who was the son of Asaph. [36]Also, these relatives of Zechariah

followed: Shemaiah, Azarel, Milalai, Gilalai, Maai, Nethanel, Judah, and Hanani with the musical instruments of David, the man of God. Ezra the scribe led them. [37]At Fountain Gate they went straight up the stairs of the City of David. There the wall rises past David's palace and reaches Water Gate on the east.

[38]The other choir went to the left. I followed them with the other half of the people. We walked on the wall, past the Tower of the Ovens, as far as Broad Wall, [39]then past Ephraim Gate, over Old Gate and Fish Gate, and by the Tower of Hananel and the Tower of the Hundred, as far as Sheep Gate. The choir stopped at Guard's Gate. [40]So both choirs stood in God's temple, as did I and the half of the leaders who were with me. [41]Likewise, these priests stood in God's temple: Eliakim, Maaseiah, Miniamin, Micaiah, Elioenai, Zechariah, and Hananiah with trumpets, [42]and Maaseiah, Shemaiah, Eleazar, Uzzi, Jehohanan, Malchiah, Elam, and Ezer. The singers sang under the direction of Jezrahiah.

[43]That day they offered many sacrifices and rejoiced because God had given them reason to rejoice. The women and children rejoiced as well. The sound of rejoicing in Jerusalem could be heard from far away.

[44]On that day men were put in charge of the storerooms for the contributions, the first produce harvested, and a tenth of the people's money. They stored in those rooms the gifts designated by Moses' Teachings for the priests and Levites from the fields around the cities. The people of Judah were pleased with the ministry of the priests and Levites. [45]They were doing what their God required, what needed to be done for cleansing. The singers and the gatekeepers did what David and his son Solomon had ordered them to do. [46]Long ago in the time of David and Asaph, there had been directors for the singers to lead ⌊in singing⌋ the songs of praise and hymns of thanksgiving to God. [47]At the time of Zerubbabel and Nehemiah, all the Israelites were giving gifts for the daily support of the singers and the gatekeepers. They set aside holy gifts for ⌊the daily support of⌋ the Levites, and the Levites set aside holy gifts for support of Aaron's descendants.

13 [1]On that day the Book of Moses was read while the people were listening. They heard the passage that no Ammonite or Moabite should ever be admitted into God's assembly. [2](After all, they didn't welcome the Israelites with food and water. Instead, they hired Balaam to curse the Israelites. But our God turned the curse into a blessing.) [3]After the people heard this Teaching, they separated the non-Israelites from the Israelites.

[4]Even before this, the priest Eliashib, who was related to Tobiah and had been put in charge of the storerooms of our God's temple, [5]had provided a large room for Tobiah. Previously, this room had been used to store grain offerings, incense, utensils, a tenth of all the grain harvested, new wine, and olive oil. These things belonged by law to the Levites, singers, and gatekeepers. The contributions for the priests had also been stored there.

Nehemiah Evicts Tobiah From the Temple

[6]While all of this was taking place, I wasn't in Jerusalem. In the thirty-second year of King Artaxerxes' reign in Babylon, I returned to the king. Later, I asked the king for permission to return. [7]I went to Jerusalem and discovered the evil thing Eliashib had done by providing Tobiah with a room in God's temple. [8]I was furious. So I threw all of Tobiah's household goods out of the room. [9]Then I told them to cleanse the rooms, and I put back in there the utensils from God's temple, the offerings, and the incense.

Nehemiah Ensures That the Levites Receive Their Portion of the Offerings

¹⁰I learned that the Levites had not been given their portions. So each of the Levites and singers, who conducted the worship in the temple, had left for their own fields. ¹¹I reprimanded the leaders. "Why is God's temple being neglected?" I asked. So I brought the Levites back together and put them back in their places of service. ¹²Then all Judah brought a tenth of all the grain harvested, new wine, and olive oil to the storerooms. ¹³I appointed the following men to be in charge of the storerooms: Shelemiah the priest, Zadok the scribe, and Pedaiah the Levite, and I appointed Hanan, son of Zaccur and grandson of Mattaniah to help them. Since they could be trusted, I made them responsible for distributing the portions to their relatives.

¹⁴Nehemiah prayed, "Remember me for what I have done, my God, and don't wipe out the good things that I have done for your temple and for the worship that is held there."

Nehemiah Ensures That No Work Is Done on the Day of Worship

¹⁵In those days I saw people in Judah stomping grapes in the winepresses on the day of worship. I saw them bringing in loads of wine, grapes, figs, and every other kind of load. They piled the loads on donkeys and brought them into Jerusalem on the day of worship. I warned them about selling food on that day. ¹⁶People from Tyre who lived in Jerusalem were bringing in fish and all kinds of goods. They were selling them on the day of worship to the people of Judah, even in Jerusalem. ¹⁷I reprimanded the nobles of Judah and asked them, "What is this evil thing you're doing? How dare you treat the day of worship as unholy! ¹⁸Isn't this what your ancestors did, with the results that our God brought all these evils on us and on this city? Now you're making him even more angry with Israel by treating the day of worship as unholy."

¹⁹Before the day of worship, when the gates of Jerusalem were cleared of traffic, I ordered the doors to be shut and not to be reopened until after the day of worship. I stationed some of my men by the gates to make sure that no loads could be brought in on the day of worship. ²⁰Once or twice merchants and those who sell all kinds of goods spent the night outside Jerusalem. ²¹I warned them. "Why are you spending the night in front of the wall?" I asked them. "If you do it again, I'll arrest you." After that, they no longer came on the day of worship. ²²Then I told the Levites to cleanse themselves and guard the gates to keep the day of worship holy.

Good Morning, God

Nehemiah 13:23-27

Ezra and Nehemiah had to constantly remind the people about God's law and their promise to obey it. Many times the people gladly obeyed God. But after a while, they got tired of doing right and began to disobey. Sometimes God puts people in our lives to remind us to do what is right. Listen to those who take the time to remind you of God's laws.

Dear Lord, help me listen to good advice from others.

Nehemiah prayed, "Remember me also for this, my God, and spare me, since you are very kind."

Nehemiah Dissolves Marriages to Foreigners

²³In those days I saw some Jews who had married women from Ashdod, Ammon, and Moab. ²⁴Half their children spoke the language of Ashdod or one of the other languages, but they couldn't understand the language of Judah well enough to speak it. ²⁵So I reprimanded those Jews, cursed them, beat some of them, and pulled out their hair. I made them swear by God: "We won't allow our daughters to marry their sons, and we won't allow their daughters to marry us or our sons." ²⁶I said, "Wasn't it because of marriages like these that King Solomon of Israel sinned? There wasn't a king like him among all nations. God loved him, and God made him king of all Israel. But his non-Israelite wives led him to sin. ²⁷Should we follow your example, commit such a serious crime against our God, and be unfaithful to him by marrying non-Israelite women?"

²⁸Even one of Joiada's sons was a son-in-law of Sanballat from Beth Horon. (Joiada was the son of the chief priest Eliashib.) I chased Joiada's son away from me.

²⁹Nehemiah prayed, "Remember them, my God, because they have contaminated the priestly office and the promise* you made to the priests and Levites."

³⁰So I cleansed them from everything that was foreign. I assigned duties to the priests and Levites. Each one had his own assignment. ³¹I also arranged for delivering wood at regular times and for bringing the first produce to be harvested.

Nehemiah prayed, "Remember me, my God, for my benefit."

---

*13:29 Or "covenant."

AN INTRODUCTION TO
Esther

Esther was a beautiful
young Jewish woman
who became queen of
Persia. When an evil
enemy plotted to kill all
the Jews, Esther per-
suaded the king to save
her people, and the
enemy was put to death.
Esther's story shows
that God can use people
to bring about his plans.

Headlines

Queen Disobeys King
Esther 1, page 639

**Esther's Plan to
Save Millions**
Esther 5, page 645

**Wife Warns
Hateful Haman**
Esther 6, page 645

Turnabout's Fair Play
Esther 8, page 647

Esther Starts a Holiday!
Esther 9, page 648

Esther took a big chance in
going to King Xerxes. Why?
See Esther 4.

Where Is God in Our News?

We read about the many miracles God did in the Bible. Why don't we read in our newspapers about what God is doing today? Is God on vacation?

Of course not! But God does not need to perform miracles to influence events. God can also work through everyday circumstances and use ordinary people.

The story of Esther is a perfect example of God working through events and people. God isn't mentioned once in the whole book of Esther. Instead, God uses events, like Queen Vashti's rebellion against King Xerxes, to cause Esther to be made the new queen. And later, when King Xerxes couldn't sleep the night before Esther's banquet, he read about how Mordecai uncovered a plot to kill him. Was this all by accident? No, the Lord was able to arrange all these things to save his people.

God may not be mentioned in today's news, but he is at work in our world. And he works in each of our lives, too!

Who's the Boss?

Trouble between men and women has been going on for a long time. Just take a look at Esther:

1. Queen Vashti didn't like being ordered to show off at Xerxes' banquet. *So she refused to come!*

2. King Xerxes got angry when Queen Vashti refused. He was the king! What would people think if he could not order his wife around? *So he divorced her!*

King Xerxes and Queen Vashti are examples of what happens to relationships when pride and power get in the way. Things turn out a lot better when men and women both have less pride and more respect for one another.

What's In It For Me?

No matter what happens . . .

GOD IS IN CHARGE.

GOD USES NORMAL PEOPLE TO MAKE A DIFFERENCE.

GOD, NOT CHANCE, CONTROLS EVENTS.

GOD HAS A PURPOSE FOR EVERYTHING.

638

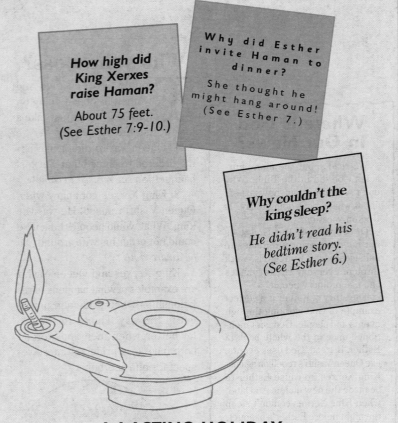

How high did King Xerxes raise Haman?

About 75 feet. (See Esther 7:9-10.)

Why did Esther invite Haman to dinner?

She thought he might hang around! (See Esther 7.)

Why couldn't the king sleep?

He didn't read his bedtime story. (See Esther 6.)

A LASTING HOLIDAY

Today, the Jews still celebrate God's rescue of their people through Esther. They celebrate it with a holiday called "Purim."

Where did the holiday get its name?

From the word *Pur*. Pur were dice used by Haman to choose the date for killing the Jews.

When is Purim celebrated?

Purim is celebrated on the 14th and 15th of the month of Adar in the Jewish religious calendar (that's during the month of March).

How is Purim celebrated?

The Jews eat lots of food and sing songs. Friends exchange presents and give to the poor. Men, women, and children come to the synagogue for a reading of Esther's exciting story. Every time Haman's name is spoken, the audience boos and hisses.

For some fun, get your family together to read the book of Esther. *Boo* when Haman is mentioned, and *cheer* when Haman's plan is foiled!

Esther

Queen Vashti Disobeys King Xerxes

1 ¹In the days of Xerxes the following events took place. This was the same Xerxes who ruled over 127 provinces from India to Sudan. ²At the time when King Xerxes sat on the royal throne in the fortress of Susa, ³he held a banquet in the third year of his reign. The banquet was for all his officials and advisers, that is, the military officers of the Persians and Medes, the nobles and officials of the provinces who had access to him. ⁴He showed them the enormous wealth of his kingdom and the costly splendor of his greatness for many days, 180 to be exact. ⁵When those days were over, the king held a banquet lasting seven days. This banquet was held in the enclosed garden of the king's palace for all people in the fortress of Susa, whatever their rank.

⁶The garden had white and violet linen curtains. These curtains were attached to silver rods and marble pillars by cords made of white and purple fine linen. Gold and silver couches were on a mosaic pavement of purple rock, white marble, pearl-like stone, and black marble. ⁷People drank from golden cups. No two cups were alike. The king also provided plenty of royal wine out of his royal generosity. ⁸The drinking followed this rule: Drink as you please. (The king had ordered all the waiters in his palace to let everyone do as he pleased.)

⁹Queen Vashti also held a banquet for the women at the royal palace of King Xerxes.

¹⁰On the seventh day when the king was drunk on wine, he ordered Mehuman, Biztha, Harbona, Bigtha, Abagtha, Zethar, and Carcas, the seven eunuchs who served under King Xerxes, ¹¹to bring Queen Vashti in front of the king, wearing her royal crown. He wanted to show the people, especially the officials, her beauty, because she was very attractive. ¹²But Queen Vashti refused the king's command that the eunuchs delivered to her. As a result, the king became very angry, and his rage burned inside him.

¹³Now, the king usually asked for advice from all the experts in royal decrees and decisions, ¹⁴from those closest to him—Carshena, Shethar, Admatha, Tarshish, Meres, Marsena, and Memucan. These seven officials of the Persians and Medes had access to the king and held the highest rank in the kingdom. The king asked these wise men who knew the times,[a] ¹⁵"According to the royal decrees, what must we do with Queen Vashti since she did not obey King Xerxes' command, which the eunuchs delivered?"

¹⁶Then Memucan spoke up in the presence of the king and the officials, "Queen Vashti has done wrong, not only against the king but also against all the officials and all the people in every province of King Xerxes. ¹⁷The news of what the queen has done will spread to all women, and they will despise their husbands. They will say, 'King Xerxes ordered Queen Vashti to be brought to him, but she would not come.' ¹⁸Today the wives of the officials in Persia and Media who have heard what the queen did will talk back to all the king's officials. There will be contempt and short tempers. ¹⁹If it pleases you, Your Majesty, issue a royal decree. It should be recorded in the decrees of the Persians and Medes, never to be repealed, that Vashti may never again appear in front of King Xerxes. Furthermore, Your Majesty, you should give her royal position to another woman who is more worthy than she. ²⁰When you issue your decree, your whole kingdom, great as it is, will hear it. Then all the wives will honor their husbands, regardless of their status."

---

[a] 1:14 The first part of verse 13 (in Hebrew) has been placed just before verse 15 to express the complex Hebrew sentence structure more clearly in English.

²¹The king and his officials approved of this, and so the king did as Memucan suggested. ²²He sent official documents to all the king's provinces, to each province in its own script and to the people in each province in their own language: "Let every husband be the ruler in his own house and speak with authority."ᵇ

Esther Becomes Queen

¹Later, when King Xerxes got over his raging anger, he remembered Vashti, what she had done, and what had been decided against her.

²So the king's personal staff said to him, "Search for attractive young virgins for the king. ³And appoint scouts in all the provinces of your kingdom to gather all the attractive young virgins and bring them to the fortress of Susa, to the women's quarters. There, in the care of the king's eunuch Hegai, the guardian of the women, they will have their beauty treatment. ⁴Then the young woman who pleases you, Your Majesty, will become queen instead of Vashti."

The king liked the suggestion, and so he did just that.

⁵In the fortress of Susa there was a Jew from the tribe of Benjamin named Mordecai. He was the son of Jair, the grandson of Shimei, and the great-grandson of Kish. ⁶(Kish had been taken captive from Jerusalem together with the others who had gone into exile along with Judah's King Jehoiakin,ᵃ whom King Nebuchadnezzar of Babylon had carried away.) ⁷Mordecai had raised Hadassah, also known as Esther, his uncle's daughter, because she was an orphan. The young woman had a beautiful figure and was very attractive. When her father and mother died, Mordecai adopted her as his own daughter.

⁸When the king's announcement and decree were heard, many young women were gathered together and brought to the fortress of Susa. They were placed in the care of Hegai. Esther also was taken to the king's palace and placed in the care of Hegai, the guardian of the women. ⁹The young woman pleased him and won his affection. So he immediately provided her with the beauty treatment, a daily supply of food, and seven suitable female servants from the king's palace. Then he moved her and her servants to the best place in the women's quarters.

¹⁰Esther did not reveal her nationality or her family background, because Mordecai had ordered her not to. ¹¹Every day Mordecai would walk back and forth in front of the courtyard of the women's quarters to find out how Esther was and what was happening to her.

¹²Each young woman had her turn to go to King Xerxes after she had completed the required 12-month treatment for women. The time of beauty treatment was spent as follows: six months using oil of myrrh and six months using perfumes and other treatments for women.

¹³After that, the young woman would go to the king. Anything she wanted to take with her from the women's quarters to the king's palace was given to her. ¹⁴She would go in the evening and come back in the morning to the other quarters for women. There she would be in the care of the king's eunuch Shaashgaz, the guardian of the concubines.ᵇ She never went to the king again unless the king desired her and requested her by name.

¹⁵(Esther was the daughter of Abihail, Mordecai's uncle. Mordecai had adopted her as his own daughter.)

When Esther's turn came to go to the king, she asked only for what the king's eunuch Hegai, the guardian of the women, advised. Everyone who saw Esther liked

ᵇ1:22 Hebrew meaning uncertain. ᵃ2:6 Masoretic Text "Jeconiah," an alternate form of Jehoiakin.
ᵇ2:14 A concubine is considered a wife except she has fewer rights under the law.

her. ¹⁶So Esther was taken to King Xerxes in his royal palace in the month of Tebeth, the tenth month, in the seventh year of his reign.

¹⁷Now, the king loved Esther more than all the other women and favored her over all the other virgins. So he put the royal crown on her head and made her queen instead of Vashti. ¹⁸Then the king held a great banquet for Esther. He invited all his officials and his advisers. He also declared that day a holiday in the provinces, and he handed out gifts from his royal generosity.

Mordecai Saves the King's Life

¹⁹When the virgins were gathered a second time, Mordecai was sitting at the king's gate. ²⁰Esther still had not revealed her family background or nationality, as Mordecai had ordered her. Esther always did whatever Mordecai told her, as she did when she was a child.

²¹In those days, while Mordecai was sitting at the king's gate, Bigthan and Teresh, two of the king's eunuchs who guarded the entrance, became angry and planned to kill King Xerxes. ²²But Mordecai found out about it and informed Queen Esther. Then Esther told the king, on behalf of Mordecai. ²³When the report was investigated and found to be true, the dead bodies of Bigthan and Teresh were hung on a pole. The matter was written up in the king's presence in his official record of daily events.

Haman's Plot

3 ¹Later, King Xerxes promoted Haman. (Haman was the son of Hammedatha and was from Agag.) He gave Haman a position higher in authority than all the other officials who were with him. ²All the king's advisers were at the king's gate, kneeling and bowing to Haman with their faces touching the ground, because the king had commanded it. But Mordecai would not kneel and bow to him.

³Then the king's advisers at the king's gate asked Mordecai, "Why do you ignore the king's command?" ⁴Although they asked him day after day, he paid no attention to them. So they informed Haman to see if Mordecai's actions would be tolerated, since Mordecai had told them that he was a Jew.

⁵When Haman saw that Mordecai did not kneel and bow to him, Haman was infuriated. ⁶Because the king's advisers had informed him about Mordecai's nationality, he thought it beneath himself to kill only Mordecai. So Haman planned to wipe out Mordecai's people—all the Jews in the entire kingdom of Xerxes.

⁷In Xerxes' twelfth year as king, *Pur* (which means *the lot*) was thrown in front of

Good Morning, God

Esther 3:1-6

Haman had a problem with pride. He didn't like a Jew named Mordecai because Mordecai would not kneel and bow to him. So Haman decided not only to punish Mordecai, but to punish all the Jews. However, God used a humble but brave woman named Esther to stop Haman's plan. Pride can cause people to do foolish things. Strive to be humble like Esther so God can use you for good.

Father, help me not to let pride get me into trouble.

Haman for every day of every month, from Nisan, the first month, until Adar, the twelfth month.

⁸Now, Haman told King Xerxes, "Your Majesty, there is a certain nationality scattered among—but separate from—the nationalities in all the provinces of your kingdom. Their laws differ from those of all other nationalities. They do not obey your decrees. So it is not in your interest to tolerate them, Your Majesty. ⁹If you approve, have the orders for their destruction be written. For this I will pay 750,000 pounds of silver to your treasurers to be put in your treasury."

¹⁰At that, the king removed his signet ring and gave it to Haman, the enemy of the Jews. (Haman was the son of Hammedatha and was from Agag.) ¹¹The king told Haman, "You can keep your silver and do with the people whatever you like."

Haman Prepares to Kill the Jews

¹²On the thirteenth day of the first month the king's scribes were summoned. All Haman's orders were written to the king's satraps, the governors of every province, and the officials of every people. They wrote to each province in its own script and to the people in each province in their own language. The orders were signed in the name of King Xerxes and sealed with the king's ring. ¹³Messengers were sent with official documents to all the king's provinces. The people were ordered to wipe out, kill, and destroy all the Jews—young and old, women and children—on a single day, the thirteenth day of the twelfth month, the month of Adar. Their possessions were also to be seized. ¹⁴A copy of the document was made public in a decree to every province. All the people were to be ready for this day.

¹⁵The messengers hurried out as the king told them. The decree was also issued at the fortress of Susa. So the king and Haman sat down to drink a toast, but the city of Susa was in turmoil.

¹When Mordecai found out about everything that had been done, he tore his clothes and put on sackcloth and ashes. He went into the middle of the city and cried loudly and bitterly. ²He even went right up to the king's gate. (No one could enter it wearing sackcloth.)

³In every province touched by the king's command and decree, the Jews went into mourning, fasting, weeping, and wailing. Many put on sackcloth and ashes.

Esther's Problem

⁴Esther's servants and eunuchs came and informed her about Mordecai. The queen was stunned. She sent clothing for Mordecai to put on in place of his sackcloth, but he refused to accept it. ⁵Then Esther called for Hathach, one of the king's eunuchs appointed to serve her. She commanded him to go to Mordecai and find out what was going on and why.

⁶So Hathach went out to Mordecai in the city square in front of the king's gate. ⁷Mordecai informed him about everything that had happened to him. He told him the exact amount of silver that Haman had promised to pay into the king's treasury to destroy the Jews. ⁸He also gave him a copy of the decree that was issued in Susa. The decree gave permission to exterminate the Jews. Hathach was supposed to show it to Esther to inform and command her to go to the king, beg him for mercy, and appeal to him for her people. ⁹So Hathach returned and told Esther what Mordecai had said.

¹⁰Esther spoke to Hathach and commanded him to say to Mordecai, ¹¹"All the king's advisers and the people in the king's provinces know that no one approaches the king in the throne room without being summoned. By law that person must be put to death. Only if the king holds out the golden scepter to him will he live. I, myself, have not

Esther

"Your Majesty, spare my life. That is my request. And spare the life of my people."

Esther was a Jewish orphan girl. Her older cousin, Mordecai, adopted Esther and raised her as if she were his own daughter.

When the king wanted a new queen, all the beautiful young girls were required to go to the palace. Esther went, too. Everyone who met Esther liked her very much. Before long, the king chose Esther to become his new queen. Esther never told anyone she was Jewish because Mordecai had told her not to.

The king's number one adviser, Haman, hated the Jews. He asked for the king's permission to destroy all of the Jews. Esther and Mordecai came up with a plan to stop Haman; however, Esther would have to risk death by approaching the king to ask for help. With God's help, Esther saved her people.

644

Esther was born around 475 B.C.

Esther means "star."

Esther was named queen by King Xerxes.

Esther saved the Jewish people from destruction.

Getting to Know Esther

* How did God use Esther to save his people?
* How was Esther brave?
* What would have happened if Esther hadn't obeyed God and Mordecai?
* How is God using you now?

Queen Esther and Mordecai developed a plan to save the Jewish people. The plan became a law when they sealed it with the king's signet ring.

been summoned to enter the king's presence for 30 days now." ¹²So Esther's servants told Mordecai what Esther said.

¹³Mordecai sent this answer back to Esther, "Do not imagine that just because you are in the king's palace you will be any safer than all the rest of the Jews. ¹⁴The fact is, even if you remain silent now, someone else will help and rescue the Jews, but you and your relatives will die. And who knows, you may have gained your royal position for a time like this."

¹⁵Esther sent this reply back to Mordecai, ¹⁶"Assemble all the Jews in Susa. Fast for me: Do not eat or drink at all for three entire days. My servants and I will also fast. After that, I will go to the king, even if it is against a royal decree. If I die, I die."

¹⁷Mordecai did just as Esther had commanded him.

Esther Brings Her Request to the King

¹On the third day Esther put on her royal robes. She stood in the courtyard of the king's palace, facing the king's throne room. The king was sitting on the royal throne inside the palace, facing the entrance.

²When the king saw Queen Esther standing in the entrance, she won his favor. So the king held out the golden scepter that was in his hand to Esther. Esther went up to him and touched the top of the scepter.

³Then the king asked her, "What is troubling you, Queen Esther? What would you like? Even if it is up to half of the kingdom, it will be granted to you."

⁴So Esther answered, "If it pleases you, Your Majesty, come today with Haman to a dinner I have prepared for you."

⁵The king replied, "Bring Haman right away, and do whatever Esther asks." So the king and Haman came to the dinner that Esther had prepared.

⁶While they were drinking wine, the king asked Esther, "What is your request? It will be granted to you. What would you like? Even if it is up to half of the kingdom, it will be granted."

⁷Esther answered, "My request? What would I like? ⁸Your Majesty, come with Haman to a dinner I will prepare for you. And tomorrow I will answer you, Your Majesty. If I have found favor with you, Your Majesty, and if it pleases you, Your Majesty, may you then grant my request and do what I would like."

Meanwhile, Haman Is Disgraced Because of Mordecai

⁹When Haman left that day, he was happy and feeling good. But when Haman saw Mordecai at the king's gate, neither getting up nor trembling in his presence, Haman was furious with Mordecai. ¹⁰However, Haman controlled himself. He went home and sent for his friends and his wife Zeresh.

¹¹Then Haman began to relate in detail to them how very rich he was, the many sons he had, and all about how the king promoted him to a position over the officials and the king's advisers. ¹²Haman went on to say, "What's more, Queen Esther allowed no one except me to come with the king to the dinner she had prepared. And again tomorrow I am her invited guest together with the king. ¹³Yet, all this is worth nothing to me every time I see Mordecai the Jew sitting at the king's gate."

¹⁴Then his wife Zeresh and all his friends said to him, "Have a pole set up, 75 feet high, and in the morning ask the king to have Mordecai's dead body hung on it. Then go with the king to the dinner in good spirits."

Haman liked the idea, so he had the pole set up.

¹That night the king could not sleep. So he told a servant to bring the official daily records, and they were read to the king. ²The records showed how Mordecai had

informed him that Bigthan and Teresh, two of the king's eunuchs who guarded the entrance, had plotted a rebellion against King Xerxes.

[3]The king asked, "How did I reward and promote Mordecai for this?"

The king's personal staff replied, "Nothing was done for him."

[4]The king asked, "Who is in the courtyard?" At that moment, Haman came through the courtyard to the king's palace to ask the king about hanging Mordecai on the pole he had prepared for him.

[5]The king's staff answered him, "Haman happens to be standing in the courtyard." "Let him come in," the king said.

[6]So Haman came in. The king then asked him, "What should be done for the man whom the king wishes to reward?"

Haman thought to himself, "Whom would the king wish to reward more than me?" [7]So Haman told the king, "This is what should be done: [8]The servants should bring a royal robe that the king has worn and a horse that the king has ridden, one that has a royal crest on its head. [9]Give the robe and the horse to one of the king's officials, who is a noble. Put the robe on the man whom the king wishes to reward and have him ride on the horse in the city square. The king's servants are also to shout ahead of him, 'This is what is done for the man whom the king wishes to reward.'"

[10]The king told Haman, "Hurry, take the robe and the horse as you said. Do this for Mordecai the Jew who sits at the king's gate. Do not omit anything you have said."

[11]So Haman took the robe and the horse. He put the robe on Mordecai and had him ride in the city square, shouting ahead of him, "This is what is done for the man whom the king wishes to reward."

[12]After that, Mordecai returned to the king's gate, but Haman hurried home. He was in despair and covered his head. [13]There, Haman began to relate in detail to his wife Zeresh and to all his friends everything that had happened to him. Then his counselors and his wife Zeresh told him, "You are starting to lose power to Mordecai. If Mordecai is of Jewish descent, you will never win out over him. He will certainly lead to your downfall."

[14]While they were still speaking with him, the king's eunuchs arrived and quickly took Haman to the dinner Esther had prepared.

Esther Brings About Haman's Downfall

7 [1]So the king and Haman came to have dinner with Queen Esther. [2]On the second day, while they were drinking wine, the king asked Esther, "What is your request, Queen Esther? It will be granted to you. And what would you like? Even if it is up to half of the kingdom, it will be granted."

[3]Then Queen Esther answered, "If I have found favor with you, Your Majesty, and if it pleases you, Your Majesty, spare my life. That is my request. And spare the life of my people. That is what I ask for. [4]You see, we—my people and I—have been sold so that we can be wiped out, killed, and destroyed. If our men and women had only been sold as slaves, I would have kept silent because the enemy is not worth troubling you about, Your Majesty."

[5]Then King Xerxes interrupted Queen Esther and said, "Who is this person? Where is the person who has dared to do this?"

[6]Esther answered, "Our vicious enemy is this wicked man Haman!" Then Haman became panic-stricken in the presence of the king and queen.

[7]The king was furious as he got up from dinner and went into the palace garden. But Haman stayed to beg Queen Esther for his life, because he saw that the king had a terrible end in mind for him. [8]When the king returned from the palace garden to the

palace dining room, Haman was falling on the couch where Esther was lying. The king thought, "Is he even going to rape the queen while I'm in the palace?" Then the king passed sentence on him, and servants covered Haman's face.

⁹Harbona, one of the eunuchs present with the king, said, "What a coincidence! The 75-foot pole Haman made for Mordecai, who spoke up for the well-being of the king, is still standing at Haman's house."

The king responded, "Hang him on it!" ¹⁰So servants hung Haman's ¸dead body¸ on the very pole he had prepared for Mordecai. Then the king got over his raging anger.

8 ¹On that same day King Xerxes gave the property of Haman, the enemy of the Jews, to Queen Esther. Also, Mordecai came to the king because Esther had told him how Mordecai was related to her. ²Then the king took off his signet ring, which he had taken from Haman, and gave it to Mordecai. And Esther put Mordecai in charge of Haman's property.

Esther Brings Her Request to the King

³Esther spoke again to the king. She fell down at his feet crying and begged him to have mercy and to undo the evil plot of Haman, who was from Agag, and his conspiracy against the Jews. ⁴The king held out his golden scepter to Esther, and Esther got up and stood in front of the king. ⁵She said, "Your Majesty, if it pleases you, and if I have found favor with you, if you consider my cause to be reasonable and if I am pleasing to you, cancel the official orders ¸concerning¸ the plot of Haman (who was the son of Hammedatha and was from Agag). He signed ¸the order¸ to destroy the Jews in all your provinces, Your Majesty. ⁶I cannot bear to see my people suffer such evil. And I simply cannot bear to see the destruction of my relatives."

⁷King Xerxes said to Queen Esther and Mordecai the Jew, "I have given Haman's property to Esther, and Haman's ¸dead body¸ was hung on the pole because he tried to kill the Jews. ⁸You write what you think is best for the Jews in the king's name. Seal it also with the king's signet ring, because whatever is written in the king's name and sealed with the king's signet ring cannot be canceled."

Mordecai Uses His Position to Save the Jews

⁹At that time on the twenty-third day of Sivan, the third month, the king's scribes were summoned. What Mordecai had ordered was written to the Jews and to the satraps, governors, and officers of the 127 provinces from India to Sudan. It was written to each province in its own script, to each people in their own language, and to the Jews in their own script and their own language.

¹⁰Mordecai wrote in King Xerxes' name and sealed the official documents with the king's signet ring. Then he sent them by messengers who rode special horses bred for speed. ¸He wrote¸ ¹¹that the king had given permission for the Jews in every city to assemble, to defend themselves, to wipe out, to kill, and to destroy every armed force of the people and province that is hostile to them, even women and children, and to seize their goods. ¹²This was permitted¸ on one day in all the provinces of King Xerxes, on the thirteenth day of Adar, the twelfth month. ¹³The copy of the document was made public in a decree to every province for all people. On that day the Jews were to be ready to take revenge on their enemies.

¹⁴The messengers rode the king's fastest horses. They left quickly, in keeping with the king's command. The decree was issued also in the fortress of Susa.

¹⁵Mordecai went out from the presence of the king wearing the royal violet and white robe, a large gold crown, and a purple outer robe of fine linen. And the city of Susa cheered and rejoiced.

¹⁶So the Jews were cheerful, happy, joyful, and successful. ¹⁷In every province and every city where the king's message and decree arrived, the Jews were happy and joyful, feasting and enjoying a holiday. Then many common people pretended to be Jews because they were terrified of the Jews.

The Jews Defend Themselves

9 ¹On the thirteenth day of Adar, the twelfth month, the king's command and decree were to be carried out. On that very day, when the enemies of the Jews expected to overpower them, the exact opposite happened: The Jews overpowered those who hated them.

²The Jews assembled in their cities throughout all the provinces of King Xerxes to kill those who were planning to harm them. No one could stand up against them, because all the people were terrified of them. ³All the officials of the provinces, the satraps, the governors, and the king's treasurers assisted the Jews because they were terrified of Mordecai. ⁴Mordecai was an important man in the king's palace. Moreover, his reputation was spreading to all the provinces, since Mordecai was becoming more and more powerful.

⁵Then with their swords, the Jews attacked all their enemies, killing them, destroying them, and doing whatever they pleased to those who hated them. ⁶In the fortress of Susa the Jews killed and wiped out 500 men. ⁷They also killed Parshandatha, Dalphon, Aspatha, ⁸Poratha, Adalia, Aridatha, ⁹Parmashta, Arisai, Aridai, and Vaizatha. ¹⁰These were the ten sons of Haman, who was the son of Hammedatha and the enemy of the Jews. But the Jews did not seize any of their possessions.

¹¹On that day the number of those killed in the fortress of Susa was reported to the king. ¹²So the king said to Queen Esther, "In the fortress of Susa the Jews have killed and wiped out 500 men and Haman's 10 sons. What must they have done in the rest of the king's provinces! Now, what is your request? It will be granted to you. And what else would you like? It, too, will be granted."

¹³Esther said, "If it pleases you, Your Majesty, allow the Jews in Susa to do tomorrow what was decreed for today. Let them hang Haman's ten sons on poles."

¹⁴The king commanded this, issuing a decree in Susa. And so they hung Haman's ten sons on poles.

¹⁵The Jews in Susa also assembled on the fourteenth day of the month of Adar and killed 300 men in Susa, but they did not seize any of their possessions. ¹⁶The other Jews who were in the king's provinces had also assembled to defend and free themselves

Good Morning, God

Esther 9:1

The Jews were upset because they feared they would soon die. Just when the Jews were about to be killed, God provided a way for them to be saved. Their crisis was turned into a celebration! God proved once again that no job is impossible for him. When God's people had no power to fight sin, he sent Jesus to give us hope. God has given you a wonderful gift of salvation through Jesus. Like the Jews in this story, you have reason to celebrate!

Lord, thank you for rescuing me from sin!

from their enemies. They killed 75,000 of those who hated them, but they did not seize any of their possessions. ¹⁷This was on the thirteenth day of the month of Adar. On the fourteenth they rested and made it a day of feasting and celebration. ¹⁸But the Jews in Susa had assembled on the thirteenth and fourteenth. They rested on the fifteenth and made it a day of feasting and celebration. ¹⁹That is why the Jews who live in the villages and in the unwalled towns make the fourteenth day of the month of Adar a holiday for feasting and celebration. They also send gifts of food to one another.

The Festival of Purim Instituted by Esther and Mordecai

²⁰Now, Mordecai wrote these things down and sent official letters to all the Jews in all the provinces of King Xerxes, near and far. ²¹He established the fourteenth and fifteenth days of the month of Adar as days they must observe every year. ²²They were to observe them just like the days when the Jews freed themselves from their enemies. In that month their grief turned to joy and their mourning into a holiday. He declared that these days are to be days for feasting and celebrating and for sending gifts of food to one another, especially gifts to the poor.

²³So the Jews accepted as tradition what they had begun, as Mordecai had written to them. ²⁴It was because Haman, the enemy of all the Jews, had plotted against the Jews to destroy them. (Haman was the son of Hammedatha and was from Agag.) Haman had the *Pur* (which means *the lot*) thrown in order to determine when to crush and destroy them. ²⁵But when this came to the king's attention, he ordered, in the well-known letter, that the evil plan Haman had plotted against the Jews should turn back on his own head. As a result, they hung Haman and his sons on poles.

²⁶So the Jews called these days Purim, based on the word *Pur*. Therefore, because of everything that was said in this letter—both what they had seen and what had happened to them— ²⁷the Jews established a tradition for themselves and their descendants and for anyone who would join them. The tradition was that a person should never fail to observe these two days every year, as they were described and at their appointed time. ²⁸So these days must be remembered and observed in every age, family, province, and city. These days of Purim must not be ignored among the Jews, and the importance of these days must never be forgotten by the generations to come.

²⁹Abihail's daughter Queen Esther and Mordecai the Jew wrote with full authority in order to establish with this second letter the well-known celebration of Purim. ³⁰Mordecai sent official documents granting peace and security to all the Jews in the 127 provinces of the kingdom of Xerxes. ³¹He did this in order to establish these days of Purim at the appointed time. Mordecai the Jew and Queen Esther established them for themselves, as they had established for themselves and their descendants the practices of fasting with sadness. ³²Esther's command had established these practices of Purim, and they are written in a book.

Mordecai's Greatness

10 ¹King Xerxes levied a tax on the country and the islands of the sea. ²All his acts of power and might along with the whole account of the greatness of Mordecai, whom the king had promoted, are recorded in the history of the kings of the Medes and Persians. ³Mordecai the Jew was ranked second only to King Xerxes. He was greatly respected by, and popular with, all of the other Jews, since he provided for the good of his people and spoke for the welfare of his fellow Jews.

Job

J ob was a good man who loved God and helped the poor. But terrible things happened to him. Job and three of his friends wondered if God was punishing him. They wondered if he had sinned. Job and his friends learned that bad things can happen even to good people. And Job learned to trust God when bad times came along.

What advice did Job's wife give? See Job 2.

Comforting a Friend

What would you do to make a sad friend feel better? Give her a present? Tell her a joke? Do a special favor that your friend would really appreciate?

Sometimes all you need to do is love and listen. That's all Job wanted from his friends. It may not sound like much, but listening shows your friend that you care. And that can be the best comfort of all.

We Can Trust God

Who do you trust to keep you from harm? Your parents? That's good because parents do watch out for their kids. But even they can't watch over you all the time.

But you have another parent, too—your Heavenly Father! He watches out for you every moment of the day. Just as he did for Job, the Lord puts a "protective fence" around you (Job 1:10). And even when things go wrong, you can trust God to make them right again— just as he did for Job. God has promised us that "all things work together for the good of those who love God" (Romans 8:28).

When Bad Things Happen

When something bad happens to us, it's easy to feel that we're being punished. That's how Job felt. He wanted to know why God was being so unfair and causing bad things to happen to him. Job hadn't done anything wrong!

But bad things can happen to good people. And we may never know why. Even after talking with God, Job didn't learn why he had suffered. But Job did learn to trust God in good times and in bad times, even when things didn't make sense.

We may never understand exactly why bad things happen in our lives, either. But we do know that God always cares about us. We can turn to him for help because the Lord will "rescue the weak person" (Psalm 35:10). God will always be there with us when we need him most.

What's In It For Me?

When bad things happen, I know that . . .

GOD STILL LOVES ME.

EVERYONE SUFFERS AT TIMES.

EVIL IN THE WORLD CAUSES SUFFERING.

PAIN TEACHES US TO RELY ON GOD.

I CAN PRAY TO GOD FOR HELP.

GOD WILL RESCUE ME IN THE END.

Job

Job's Life

1 ¹A man named Job lived in Uz. He was a man of integrity: He was decent, he feared God, and he stayed away from evil. ²He had seven sons and three daughters. ³He owned 7,000 sheep and goats, 3,000 camels, 1,000 oxen, 500 donkeys, and a large number of servants. He was the most influential person in the Middle East.

⁴His sons used to go to each other's homes, where they would have parties. (Each brother took his turn having a party.) They would send someone to invite their three sisters to eat and drink with them.

⁵When they finished having their parties, Job would send for them in order to cleanse them from sin. He would get up early in the morning and sacrifice burnt offerings for each of them. Job thought, "My children may have sinned and cursed God in their hearts." Job offered sacrifices for them all the time.

Satan Challenges the LORD

⁶One day when the sons of God came to stand in front of the LORD, Satan the Accuser came along with them.

⁷The LORD asked Satan, "Where have you come from?"

Satan answered the LORD, "From wandering all over the earth."

⁸The LORD asked Satan, "Have you thought about my servant Job? No one in the world is like him! He is a man of integrity: He is decent, he fears God, and he stays away from evil."

⁹Satan answered the LORD, "Haven't you given Job a reason to fear God? ¹⁰Haven't you put a protective fence around him, his home, and everything he has? You have blessed everything he does. His cattle have spread out over the land. ¹¹But now stretch out your hand, and strike everything he has. I bet he'll curse you to your face."

¹²The LORD told Satan, "Everything he has is in your power, but you must not lay a hand on him!"

Then Satan left the LORD's presence.

Job's First Crisis

¹³One day when Job's sons and daughters were eating and drinking wine in their oldest brother's home, ¹⁴a messenger came to Job. He said, "While the oxen were plowing and the donkeys were grazing nearby, ¹⁵men from Sheba attacked. They took the livestock and massacred the servants. I'm the only one who has escaped to tell you."

¹⁶While he was still speaking, another ⸤messenger⸣ came and said, "A fire from God fell from heaven and completely burned your flocks and servants. I'm the only one who has escaped to tell you."

¹⁷While he was still speaking, another ⸤messenger⸣ came and said, "The Chaldeans formed three companies and made a raid on the camels. They took the camels and massacred the servants. I'm the only one who has escaped to tell you."

¹⁸While he was still speaking, another ⸤messenger⸣ came and said, "Your sons and your daughters were eating and drinking wine at their oldest brother's home ¹⁹when suddenly a great storm swept across the desert and struck the four corners of the

house. It fell on the young people, and they died. I'm the only one who has escaped to tell you."

²⁰Job stood up, tore his robe in grief, and shaved his head. Then he fell to the ground and worshiped. ²¹He said,

> "Naked I came from my mother,
> and naked I will return.
> The LORD has given,
> and the LORD has taken away!
> May the name of the LORD be praised."

²²Through all this Job did not sin or blame God for doing anything wrong.

Satan Challenges the LORD Again

¹One day when the sons of God came to stand in front of the LORD, Satan the Accuser came along with them. ²The LORD asked Satan, "Where have you come from?"

Satan answered the LORD, "From wandering all over the earth."

³The LORD asked Satan, "Have you thought about my servant Job? No one in the world is like him! He is a man of integrity: He is decent, he fears God, and he stays away from evil. And he still holds on to his principles. You're trying to provoke me into ruining him for no reason."

⁴Satan answered the LORD, "Skin for skin! Certainly, a man will give everything he has for his life. ⁵But stretch out your hand, and strike his flesh and bones. I bet he'll curse you to your face."

⁶The LORD told Satan, "He is in your power, but you must spare his life!"

Job's Second Crisis

⁷Satan left the LORD's presence and struck Job with painful boils from the soles of his feet to the top of his head. ⁸Job took a piece of broken pottery to scratch himself as he sat in the ashes.

⁹His wife asked him, "Are you still holding on to your principles? Curse God and die!"

¹⁰He said to her, "You're talking like a godless fool. We accept the good that God gives us. Shouldn't we also accept the bad?"

Through all this Job's lips did not utter one sinful word.

¹¹When Job's three friends heard about all the terrible things that had happened to him, each of them came from his home—Eliphaz of Teman, Bildad of Shuah, Zophar of Naama. They had agreed they would go together to sympathize with Job and comfort him.

¹²When they saw him from a distance, they didn't even recognize him. They cried out loud and wept, and each of them tore his own clothes in grief. They threw dust on their heads. ¹³Then they sat down on the ground with him for seven days and seven nights. No one said a word to him because they saw that he was in such great pain.

Job Speaks
Job Curses the Day He Was Born

¹After all this, Job finally opened his mouth and cursed the day he was born. ²Job said,

³   "Scratch out the day I was born
>   and the night that said, 'A boy has been conceived!'

4   "That day—
        let it be pitch-black.
        Let God above not ˌevenˌ care about it.
        Let no light shine on it.
5   Let the darkness and long shadows claim it as their own.
        Let a dark cloud hang over it.
        Let the gloom terrify it.

6   "That night—
        let the blackness take it away.
        Let it not be included in the days of the year
            or be numbered among the months.
7   Let that night be empty.
        Let no joyful singing be heard in it.
8   Let those who curse the day[a]
            (those who know how to wake up Leviathan[b])
                curse that night.
9   Let its stars turn dark before dawn.
        Let it hope for light and receive none.
        Let it not see the first light of dawn
10   because it did not shut the doors of the womb ˌfrom which I cameˌ
            or hide my eyes from trouble.

Why Did I Survive at Birth?

11 "Why didn't I die as soon as I was born
        and breathe my last breath when I came out of the womb?
12 Why did knees welcome me?
    Why did breasts let me nurse?
13 Instead of being alive,
        I would now be quietly lying down.
        I would now be sleeping peacefully.
14   I would be with the kings and the counselors of the world

Good Morning, God
Job 3:1-5

Have you ever felt so down that you wished you had never been born? That's how Job felt when he wrote these verses. But don't stop reading here. When you read the end of Job's story, you'll find that Job discovers hope in God. Even when things get bad, God can use the hard times for your good. Life isn't easy—not even for Christians. But we have hope because we have God.

Father, I know that sometimes life is hard. But thank you that you never leave me.

---

[a]3:8 Or "those who curse the sea." [b]3:8 Hebrew meaning uncertain.

who built for themselves what are now ruins.
15 I would be with princes
who had gold,
who filled their homes with silver.
16 I would be buried like a stillborn baby.
I would not exist.
I would be like infants who never saw the light.
17 There the wicked stop their raging.
There the weary are able to rest.
18 There the captives have no troubles at all.
There they do not hear the shouting of the slave driver.
19 There you find both the unimportant and important people.
There the slave is free from his master.

Why Do I Go on Living?

20 "Why give light to one in misery
and life to those who find it so bitter,
21 to those who long for death but it never comes—
though they dig for it more than for buried treasure?
22 They are ecstatic,
delighted to find the grave.
23 Why give light to those whose paths have been hidden,
to those whom God has fenced in?

24 "When my food is in front of me, I sigh.
I pour out my groaning like water.
25 What I fear most overtakes me.
What I dread happens to me.
26 I have no peace!
I have no quiet!
I have no rest!
And trouble keeps coming!"

Eliphaz Speaks
Be Patient and Listen, Job

4 ¹Then Eliphaz from Teman replied to Job.

2 "If someone tries to talk to you, will you become impatient?
But who can keep from talking?
3 Certainly, you have instructed many people:
When hands were weak, you made them strong.
4 When someone stumbled, you lifted him up with your words.
When knees were weak, you gave them strength.
5 But trouble comes to you, and you're impatient.
It touches you, and you panic.
6 Doesn't your fear of God give you confidence
and your lifetime of integrity give you hope?

Only Evil People Suffer

7 "Now think about this:
Which innocent person ever died an untimely death?

Find me a decent person who has been destroyed.
8 Whenever I saw those who plowed wickedness and planted misery,
    they gathered its harvest.
9   God destroys them with his breath
        and kills them with a blast of his anger.
10 Though the roar of the lion
    and the growl of the ferocious lion is loud,
        the young lions have had their teeth knocked out.
11   The old lions die without any prey to eat,
        and the cubs of the lioness are scattered.

12 "I was told something secretly
    and heard something whispered in my ear.
13 With disturbing thoughts from visions in the night,
  when deep sleep falls on people,
14   fear and trembling came over me,
        and all my bones shook.
15 A spirit passed in front of me.
    It made my hair stand on end.
16   Something stood there.
      I couldn't tell what it was.
    A vague image was in front of my eyes.
    I heard a soft voice:
17   'Can any mortal be righteous to God?
    Can any human being be pure to his maker?'

18 "You see, God doesn't trust his own servants,
    and he accuses his angels of making mistakes.
19   How much more will he accuse those who live in clay houses
        that have their foundation in the dust.
           Those houses can be crushed quicker than a moth!
20   From morning to evening, they are shattered.
        They will disappear forever without anyone paying attention.
21   Haven't the ropes of their tent been loosened?
        Won't they die without wisdom?

Eliphaz Continues: Seek God's Help, Job

5 1 "Cry out!
    Is there anyone to answer you?
        To which of the holy ones will you turn?
2 Certainly, anger kills a stubborn fool,
    and jealousy murders a gullible person.
3 I have seen a stubborn fool take root,
    but I quickly cursed his house.
4 His children are far from help.
    They are crushed at the city gate,
        and no one is there to rescue them.
5 What a stubborn fool gathers, hungry people eat.
    They take it even from among the thorns,
        and thirsty people pant after his wealth.[a]

---

[a] 5:5 Hebrew meaning of the last two lines uncertain.

6 Certainly, sorrow doesn't come from the soil,
and trouble doesn't sprout from the ground.
7 But a person is born for trouble as surely as sparks fly up ˻from a fire˼.

8 "But I would seek God's help
and present my case to him.
9 He does great things that ˻we˼ cannot understand
and miracles that ˻we˼ cannot count.
10 He gives rain to the earth
and sends water to the fields.
11 He places lowly people up high.
He lifts those who mourn to safety.
12 He keeps shrewd people from carrying out their plans
so that they cannot do anything successfully.
13 He catches the wise with their own tricks.
The plans of schemers prove to be hasty.
14 In the daytime they meet darkness
and grope in the sunlight as if it were night.

15 "But he saves ˻other people˼ from their slander
and the needy from the power of the mighty.
16 Then the poor have hope
while wrongdoing shuts its mouth.

Blessing Comes When God Corrects You

17 "Blessed is the person whom God corrects.
That person should not despise discipline from the Almighty.
18 God injures, but he bandages.
He beats you up, but his hands make you well.
19 He will keep you safe from six troubles,
and when the seventh one comes, no harm will touch you:

20 "In famine he will save you from death,
and in war he will save you from the sword.

21 "When the tongue lashes out, you will be safe,
and you will not be afraid of destruction when it comes.

22 "You will be able to laugh at destruction and starvation,
so do not be afraid of wild animals on the earth.

23 "You will have a binding agreement with the stones in the field,
and wild animals will be at peace with you.

24 "You will know peace in your tent.
You will inspect your house and find nothing missing.

25 "You will find that your children are many
and your descendants are like the grass of the earth.

26 "You will come to your grave at a ripe old age
like a stack of hay in the right season.

27 "We have studied all of this thoroughly! This is the way it is.
Listen to it, and learn it for yourself."

Job Speaks
God Has Attacked Me Without Cause

6 ¹Then Job replied to his friends,

2   "If only my grief could be weighed,
     if only my misery could be laid on the scales with it,
3   then they would be heavier than the sand of the seas.
      I spoke carelessly
4   because the arrows of the Almighty have found their target in me,
       and my spirit is drinking their poison.
      God's terrors line up in battle against me.

5   "Does a wild donkey bray when it's eating grass,
     or does an ox make a sound over its hay?
6   Is tasteless food eaten without salt,
     or is there any flavor in the white of an egg?[a]
7   I refuse to touch such things.
     They are disgusting to me.[b]

8   "How I wish that my prayer would be answered—
     that God would give me what I'm hoping for,
9   that God would finally be willing to crush me,
     that he would reach out to cut me off.
10   Then I would still have comfort.
      I would be happy despite my endless pain,
       because I have not rejected the words of the Holy One.
11   What strength do I have left that I can go on hoping?
     What goal do I have that I would want to prolong my life?
12   Do I have the strength of rocks?
     Does my body have the strength of bronze?
13   Am I not completely helpless?
     Haven't my skills been taken away from me?

Good Morning, God
Job 6:14

Talk about having a bad day! Job's herds were stolen and killed. All of his children died. On top of that, Job became infected with terrible sores all over his body. He certainly didn't need his so-called friends to show up with bad news. Instead of trying to help Job or comfort him, they told him his terrible situation was his own fault! Encourage your friends when you see them hurting. Don't add to their pain. Who can you encourage today?

Lord, help me be a loving friend.

---

[a]6:6 Hebrew meaning of "white of an egg" uncertain.   [b]6:7 Hebrew meaning of this line uncertain.

Esther Brings Her Request to the King

Esther Brings Her Request to the King

Esther 4:15–5:3

15 Esther sent this reply back to Mordecai, **16** "Assemble all the Jews in Susa. Fast for me: Do not eat or drink at all for three entire days. My servants and I will also fast. After that, I will go to the king, even if it is against a royal decree. If I die, I die."

17 Mordecai did just as Esther had commanded him.

Esther Brings Her Request to the King

5 **1** On the third day Esther put on her royal robes. She stood in the courtyard of the king's palace, facing the king's throne room. The king was sitting on the royal throne inside the palace, facing the entrance.

2 When the king saw Queen Esther standing in the entrance, she won his favor. So the king held out the golden scepter that was in his hand to Esther. Esther went up to him and touched the top of the scepter.

3 Then the king asked her, "What is troubling you, Queen Esther? What would you like? Even if it is up to half of the kingdom, it will be granted to you."

You Have Not Treated Me Like True Friends

14 "A friend should treat a troubled person kindly,
 even if he abandons the fear of the Almighty.
15 My brothers have been as deceptive as seasonal rivers,
 like the seasonal riverbeds that flood.
16   They are dark with ice.
       They are hidden by snow.*c*
17   They vanish during a scorching summer.
       In the heat their riverbeds dry up.
18   They change their course.
       They go into a wasteland and disappear.
19 Caravans from Tema look for them.
 Travelers from Sheba search for them.
20 They are ashamed because they relied on the streams.
 Arriving there, they are disappointed.

21 "So you are as unreliable to me as they are.*d*
 You see something terrifying, and you are afraid.
22 Did I ever say, 'Give me a gift,'
 or 'Offer me a bribe from your wealth,'
23 or 'Rescue me from an enemy,'
 or 'Ransom me from a tyrant'?
24 Teach me, and I'll be silent.
 Show me where I've been wrong.
25 How painful an honest discussion can be!
 In correcting me, you correct yourselves!
26   Do you think my words need correction?
       Do you think they're what a desperate person says to the wind?
27   Would you also throw dice for an orphan?
       Would you buy and sell your friend?

28 "But now, if you're willing, look at me.
 I won't lie to your face.
29 Please change your mind.
       Don't permit any injustice.
       Change your mind because I am still right about this!
30 Is there injustice on my tongue,
 or is my mouth unable to tell the difference between right and wrong?

Job Speaks About the Futility of Human Existence

7 1 "Isn't a mortal's stay on earth difficult
 like a hired hand's daily work?
2 Like a slave, he longs for shade.
 Like a hired hand, he eagerly looks for his pay.
3   Likewise, I have been given months that are of no use,
       and I have inherited nights filled with misery.
4   When I lie down, I ask,
       'When will I get up?'
       But the evening is long,

---

*c*6:16 Hebrew meaning of this verse uncertain. *d*6:21 Hebrew meaning of this line uncertain.

and I'm exhausted from tossing about until dawn.
5 My body is covered with maggots and scabs.
My skin is crusted over with sores; then they ooze.
6 My days go swifter than a weaver's shuttle.
They are spent without hope.
7 Remember, my life is only a breath,
and never again will my eyes see anything good.
8 The eye that watches over me will no longer see me.
Your eye will look for me, but I'll be gone.
9 As a cloud fades away and disappears,
so a person goes into the grave and doesn't come back again.
10 He doesn't come back home again,
and his household doesn't recognize him anymore.
11 So I won't keep my mouth shut,
but I will speak from the distress that is in my spirit
and complain about the bitterness in my soul."

Job Says to God: Leave Me Alone

12 "Am I the sea or a sea monster
that you have set a guard over me?
13 When I say,
'My couch may give me comfort.
My bed may help me bear my pain,'
14 then you frighten me with dreams
and terrify me with visions.
15 My throat would rather be choked.
My body*a* would prefer death to these dreams.
16 I hate my life; I do not want to live forever.
Leave me alone because my days are so brief.

17 "What is a mortal that you should make so much of him,
that you should be concerned about him?
18 What is he that you should inspect him every morning
and examine him every moment?
19 Why don't you stop looking at me
long enough to let me swallow my spit?*b*
20 If I sin, what can I possibly do to you
since you insist on spying on people?
Why do you make me your target?
I've become a burden even to myself.
21 Why don't you forgive my disobedience
and take away my sin?
Soon I'll lie down in the dust.
Then you will search for me, but I'll be gone!"

Bildad Speaks
You Are Unjustly Accusing God of Doing Evil, Job

8 ¹Then Bildad from Shuah replied to Job,

---

a 7:15 Or "bones." *b* 7:19 English equivalent of this verse difficult.

2 "How long will you say these things?
   How long will your words be so windy?
3 Does God distort justice,
   or does the Almighty distort righteousness?
4 If your children sinned against him,
   he allowed them to suffer the consequences of their sinfulness.
5 If you search for God
   and plead for mercy from the Almighty,
6 if you are moral and ethical,
   then he will rise up on your behalf
   and prove your righteousness by rebuilding your home.[a]
7 Then what you had in the past will seem small
   compared with the great prosperity you'll have in the future.

Learn From Past Generations

8 "Ask the people of past generations.
   Find out what their ancestors had learned.
9 We have only been around since yesterday, and we know nothing.
   Our days on earth are only a fleeting shadow.
10 Won't their words teach you?
   Won't they share their thoughts with you?

God Does Not Punish the Innocent Person

11 "Can papyrus grow up where there is no swamp?
   Can rushes grow tall without water?
12 Even if they were fresh and not cut,
   they would wither quicker than grass.
13 The same thing happens to all who forget God.
   The hope of the godless dies.
14 His confidence is easily shattered.
   His trust is a spider's web.
15 If one leans on his house, it collapses.
   If one holds on to it, it will not support his weight.
16 He is like a well-watered plant in the sunshine.
   The shoots spread over his garden.
17 Its roots weave through a pile of stones.
   They cling to a stone house.
18 But when it is uprooted from its place,
   the ground denies it and says, 'I never saw you!'
19 That is its joy in this life,
   and others sprout from the same ground to take its place.

20 "Certainly, God does not reject a person of integrity
   or give a helping hand to wicked people.
21 He will fill your mouth with laughter
   and your lips with happy shouting.
22 Those who hate you will be clothed with shame,
   and the tent of the wicked will cease to exist."

---

[a]8:6 English equivalent of this line difficult.

Job 9

Job Speaks
The Futility of Arguing With God

⁹ ¹Then Job replied to his friends,,

2 "Yes, I know that this is true.
  But how can a mortal be declared righteous to God?
3 If he wished to debate with God,
  he wouldn't be able to answer one question in a thousand.

4 "God is wise in heart and mighty in power.
  Who could oppose him and win?
5 He moves mountains without their knowing it,
  and he topples them in his anger.
6 He shakes the earth from its place,
  and its pillars tremble.
7 He commands the sun not to rise.
  He doesn't let the stars come out.
8 He stretches out the heavens by himself
  and walks on the waves of the sea.
9 He made the constellations, Ursa Major, Orion, and the Pleiades,
  and the clusters of stars in the south.
10 He does great things that are unsearchable
  and miracles that cannot be numbered.
11 He passes alongside of me, and I don't even see him.
  He goes past me, and I don't even notice him.
12 He takes something away, but, who can stop him?
  Who is going to ask him, 'What are you doing?'
13 God does not hold back his anger.
  Even Rahab's*ᵃ* helpers bow humbly in front of him.

14 "How can I possibly answer God?
  How can I find the right words to speak, with him?
15 Even if I were right, I could not answer him,.
  I would have to plead for mercy from my judge.
16 If I cried out and he answered me,
  I do not believe that he would listen to me.
17 He would knock me down with a storm
  and bruise me without a reason.
18 He would not let me catch my breath.
  He fills me with bitterness.
19 If it is a matter of strength,
    then he is the mighty one.
  If it is about justice,
    who will charge me with a crime?
20 If I am righteous, my own mouth would condemn me.
  It would declare that I am corrupt even if I am a man of integrity.
21 If I am a man of integrity, I have no way of knowing it.
  I hate my life!
22 It is all the same.

ᵃ9:13 Rahab is the name of a demonic creature who opposes God.

That is why I say,
　'He destroys both the man of integrity and the wicked.'
23 When a sudden disaster brings death,
　he makes fun of the despair of innocent people.
24 The earth is handed over to the wicked.
　He covers the faces of its judges.
　　If he isn't the one doing this, who is?

25 "My days go by more quickly than a runner.
　They sprint away.
　They don't see anything good.
26 　They pass by quickly like boats made from reeds,
　　like an eagle swooping down on its prey.
27 Even if I say, 'I will forget my complaining;
　I will change my expression and smile,'
28 I still dread everything I must suffer.
　I know that you won't declare me innocent.
29 I've already been found guilty.
　Why should I work so hard for nothing?
30 If I wash myself with lye soap[b]
　and cleanse my hands with bleach,
31 then you would plunge me into a muddy pit,
　and my own clothes would find me disgusting.
32 A human like me cannot answer God,
　'Let's take our case to court.'
33 There is no mediator between us
　to put his hand on both of us.
34 God should take his rod away from me,
　and he should not terrify me.[c]
35 Then I would speak and not be afraid of him.
　But I know that I am not like that."[d]

Job Says to God: I Hate My Life

10 1 "I hate my life.
I will freely express my complaint.
I will speak as bitterly as I feel.
2 I will say to God,
　'Don't condemn me.
　　Let me know why you are quarreling with me.
3 　　What do you gain by mistreating me,
　　　by rejecting the work of your hands
　　　　while you favor the plans of the wicked?
4 Do you actually have human eyes?
Do you see as a mortal sees?
5 　Are your days like a mortal's days?
　Are your years like a human's years?
6 　　Is that why you look for guilt in me
　　　and search for sin in me?

---

[b]9:30 Or "with water made from snow."　[c]9:33-34 Or "If there were a mediator between us to put his hand on both of us, he would remove his rod from me, and no longer terrify me."　[d]9:35 Hebrew meaning of this line uncertain.

7   You know I'm not guilty,
        but there is no one to rescue me from your hands.

8   " 'Your hands formed me and made every part of me,
        then you turned to destroy me.*

9   Please remember that you made me out of clay
        and that you will return me to the dust again.

10 Didn't you pour me out like milk
        and curdle me like cheese?

11 Didn't you dress me in skin and flesh
        and weave me together with bones and tendons?

12 You gave me life and mercy.
     Your watchfulness has preserved my spirit.

13 But in your heart you hid these things.
     I know this is what you did.

14 " 'If I sin, you watch me
        and will not free me from my guilt.

15 How terrible it will be for me if I'm guilty!
        Even if I'm righteous, I dare not lift up my head.
     I am filled with disgrace
        while I look on my misery.

16 Like a proud, ferocious lion you hunt me down.
        You keep working your miracles against me.*

17 You keep finding new witnesses against me.
     You keep increasing your anger toward me.
     You keep bringing new armies against me.

18 " 'Why did you take me out of the womb?
        I wish I had breathed my last breath
           before anyone had laid eyes on me.

19 Then it would be as if I had never existed,
        as if I had been carried from the womb to the tomb.

20 " 'Isn't my life short enough?
        So stop ˎthisˎ, and leave me alone.
           Let me smile a little

21   before I go away
              to a land of darkness and gloom,

22   to a dismal land of long shadows and confusion
                   where light is as bright as darkness.
                      I'll never return.' "

Zophar Speaks
Your Words Call for an Answer, Job

11 ¹Then Zophar from Naama replied ˎto Jobˎ,

2   "Shouldn't someone answer this flood of words?
        Should a good public speaker be acquitted?

3   Should your empty talk silence others
        so that you can make fun of us without any shame?

---

*10:8 Hebrew meaning of this line uncertain.   *10:16 Hebrew meaning of this verse uncertain.

4   You say, 'My teaching is morally correct,'
    and, 'As you can see, I'm innocent.'
5   I only wish God would speak
    and open his mouth ⸢to talk⸣ to you.
6   He would tell you the secrets of wisdom,
        because ⸢true⸣ wisdom is twice ⸢as great as your wisdom⸣,[a]
        and you would know that God forgets your sin.

God Can Do as He Pleases

7   "Can you discover God's hidden secrets,
    or are you able to find the Almighty's limits?
8   ⸢God's wisdom is⸣ higher than heaven.
    What can you do?
    It is deeper than ⸢the depths⸣ of hell.
    What can you know?
9   It is longer than the earth
    and wider than the sea.
10   If God comes along and imprisons ⸢someone⸣,
    and then calls a court into session, who can stop him?
11   He knows who the scoundrels are.
        And when he sees sin, doesn't he pay attention to it?
12   But an empty-headed person will gain understanding
        when a wild donkey is born tame.

Confess Your Sin and Be Forgiven

13   "If you want to set your heart right,
    then pray to him.
14   If you're holding on to sin, put it far away,
    and don't let injustice live in your tent.
15   Then you will be able to show your face without being ashamed,
    and you will be secure ⸢and⸣ unafraid.
16   ⸢Then⸣ you will forget your misery
    and remember it like water that has flowed downstream.
17   Then your life will be brighter than the noonday sun.
    The darkness in your life will become like morning.
18   You will feel confident because there's hope,
    and you will look around and rest in safety.
19   You will lie down with no one to frighten you,
    and many people will try to gain your favor.
20   But the wicked will lose their eyesight.
    Their escape route will be closed.
        Their only hope is to take their last breath."[b]

Job Speaks
My Friends Have No Wisdom

12 ¹Then Job replied ⸢to his friends⸣,

2   "You certainly are ⸢wise⸣ people,
    and when you die, wisdom will die.

ᵃ11:6 Hebrew meaning of this line uncertain.   ᵇ11:20 Hebrew meaning of
ᵃ12:6 Hebrew meaning "who have lived a long time."

3 Like you, I have a mind.
    I am not inferior to you.
        But who doesn't know these things?
4 I am a laughingstock to my neighbors.
    I am one who calls on God and expects an answer.
    A man of integrity, a man who is righteous, has become a laughingstock.

5 "A person who has an easy life has no appreciation for misfortune.
    He thinks it is the fate of those who slip up.
6 ₁But₁ robbers' tents are prosperous,
        and there is security for those who provoke God,
            for those whose god is their power.*

7 "Instead, ask the animals, and they will teach you.
    Ask the birds, and they will tell you.
8 Or speak with the earth, and it will teach you.
    Even the fish will relate ₁the story₁ to you.
9 What creature doesn't know that the LORD's hands made it?
10 The life of every living creature
        and the spirit in every human body are in his hands.
11 Doesn't the ear distinguish sounds
        and the tongue taste food?

Wisdom Comes From God

12 "Wisdom is with the ancient one.
    The one who has had many days has insight.*
13 God has wisdom and strength.
    Advice and insight are his.
14   When he tears ₁something₁ down, it cannot be rebuilt.
        When he puts someone in prison, that person cannot be freed.
15   When he holds back the waters, there is a drought.
        When he releases them, they flood the earth.

Good Morning, God

Job 12:5

Many girls and boys have serious problems in their families. Because their lives are so different, sometimes it's hard for those who come from loving homes to understand those who have family problems. Job said, "A person who has an easy life has no appreciation for misfortune." If you know someone who is having a hard time, take time to listen to his or her problems. You don't have to understand or relate completely; just listen. You can help others by being their friend.

Dear Lord, help me to be a good listener so I can help others.

ᵃf this line uncertain.   ᵇ12:12 Or "Wisdom is with the elderly, and understanding with those

16 "God has power and priceless wisdom.
He owns ⸤both⸥ the deceiver and the person who is deceived.

17 He leads counselors away barefoot
and makes fools out of judges.

18 He loosens kings' belts
and strips them of their pants.

19 He leads priests away barefoot
and misleads those who serve in a temple.

20 He makes trusted advisers unable to speak
and takes away the good judgment of respected leaders.

21 He pours contempt on influential people
and unbuckles the belt of the mighty.

22 He uncovers mysteries ⸤hidden⸥ in the darkness
and brings gloom into the light.

23 He makes nations important and then destroys them.
He makes nations large and leads them away.

24 He takes away the common sense of a country's leaders
and makes them stumble about in a pathless wilderness.

25 They grope in the dark with no light,
and he makes them stumble like drunks.

Job Continues: You Are Not Listening to Me

1 "My eye has certainly seen all of this!
My ear has heard and understood it.

2 After all, I know it as well as you do.
I am not inferior to you.

3 However, I want to speak to the Almighty,
and I wish to argue my case in front of God.

4 But you are smearing me with lies.
All of you are worthless physicians.

5 I wish you would keep silent.
For you, that would be wisdom.

6 Please listen to my argument,
and pay attention to my plea.

Your Wisdom Misrepresents God

7 "Will you talk wickedly for God
and talk deceitfully on his behalf?

8 Will you favor him
⸤as⸥ if you were arguing in court on God's behalf?

9 Will it go well when he cross-examines you?
Will you try to trick him as one mortal tricks another?

10 Will he really defend you
if you secretly favor ⸤him⸥?

11 Doesn't his majesty terrify you?
Doesn't the fear of him fall upon you?

12 "Your recollections are worthless proverbs.ᵃ
Your answers are absolutely useless.ᵇ

ᵃ 13:12 Or "proverbs of ashes." ᵇ 13:12 Or "are just answers of clay."

13 Be quiet, because I want to speak.
    Let whatever may happen to me ˌhappenˌ!
14 I am biting off more than I can chew
    and taking my life in my own hands.
15 If God would kill me, I would have no hope ˌleftˌ.[c]
    Nevertheless, I will defend my behavior to his face.
16 This also will be my salvation
    because no godless person could face him.

Job Speaks to God

17 "Listen carefully to my words.
    Hear my declaration.
18 I have prepared my case.
    I know that I will be declared righteous.
19 Who can make a case against me?
    If someone could, I'd be silent and die.

20 "Please don't do two things to me
    so that I won't have to hide from you:
21   Stop oppressing me.
       Don't let your terror frighten me.
22   Then call, and I'll answer.
       Otherwise, I'll speak, and you'll answer me.
23 How many crimes and sins have I committed?
       Make me aware of my disobedience and my sin.
24 Why do you hide your face ˌfrom meˌ and consider me your enemy?
25 Are you trying to make a fluttering leaf tremble
    or trying to chase dry husks?
26   You write down bitter accusations against me.
       You make me suffer for the sins of my youth.
27   You put my feet in shackles.
       You follow my trail by engraving marks on the soles of my feet.
28 I am like worn-out wineskins,
    like moth-eaten clothes.

Job Continues: Consider My Frail Human Nature, God

14 ¹ "A person who is born of a woman is short-lived
    and is full of trouble.
² He comes up like a flower; then he withers.
    He is like a fleeting shadow; he doesn't stay long.
³ You observe this
    and call me to account to you.

⁴ "If only an unclean person could become clean![a]
    It's not possible.
⁵ If the number of his days
    and the number of his months are determined by you,
       and you set his limit,
    then he cannot go past it.

ᶜ13:15 Or "If God would kill me, I would still have hope."   ª14:4 "Unclean" refers to anything that Moses' Teachings
say is not presentable to God. "Clean" refers to anything that Moses' Teachings say is presentable to God.

6 Look away from him, and he will cease to be.[b]
  Meanwhile, he loves life as a laborer loves work.

7 There is hope for a tree when it is cut down.
  It will sprout again.
  Its shoots will not stop sprouting.

8 If its roots grow old in the ground
  and its stump dies in the soil,

9 merely a scent of water will make it sprout
  and grow branches like a plant.

10 But a human dies and is powerless.
   A person breathes his last breath, and where is he?

11 ‚As‚ water drains out of a lake,
   or ‚as‚ a river dries up completely,

12 so each person lies down
   and does not rise until the heavens cease to exist.
   He does not wake up.
   He is not awakened from his sleep.

13 I wish you would hide me in Sheol
   and keep me hidden there until your anger cools.
   Set a specific time for me when you will remember me.

14 "If a person dies, will he go on living?
   I will wait for my relief to come
   as long as my hard labor continues.

15 You will call, and I will answer.
   You will long for the person your hands have made.

16 Though now you count my steps,
   you will not keep ‚a record of‚ my sins.

17 My disobedience will be closed up in a bag,
   and you will cover over my sins.

18 As surely as a mountain falls
   and rocks are dislodged,

19 ‚so‚ water wears away stone,
   floods wash away soil from the and,
   and you destroy a mortal's hope.

20 You overpower him forever, and he passes away.
   You change his appearance and send him away.

21 His sons are honored, and he doesn't know it.
   Or they become unimportant, and he doesn't realize it.

22 He feels only his body's pain.
   He is only worried about himself."

Eliphaz Speaks
You Are Speaking Sinfully, Job

15 [1]Then Eliphaz from Teman replied ‚to Job‚,

2 "Should a wise person answer with endless details
  and fill his stomach with the east wind?

3 Should he argue with words that don't help,
  with speeches that don't help ‚anyone‚?

---

[b]14:6 Hebrew meaning uncertain.

4 Yes, you destroy the fear of God,
   and diminish devotion to God.
5 Your sin teaches you what to say.
   You choose to talk with a sly tongue.
6 Your own mouth condemns you, not I.
   Your lips testify against you.

You Are Not the Only Wise Person, Job

7 "Were you the first human to be born?
   Were you delivered before the hills existed?
8 Did you listen in on God's council meeting
   and receive a monopoly on wisdom?
9 What do you know that we don't know?
   What do you understand that we don't?
10 Both the old and the gray-haired are among us.
   They are older than your father.
11 Isn't God's comfort enough for you,
   even when gently spoken to you?
12 Why have your emotions carried you away?
   Why do your eyes flash
13 when you turn against God
   and spit these words out of your mouth?
14 Why should a mortal be considered faultless
   or someone born of a woman be considered righteous?
15 If God doesn't trust his holy ones,
   and the heavens are not pure in his sight,
16 how much less will he trust the one who is disgusting and corrupt,
   the one who drinks wickedness like water.

I Want to Tell You What I Know

17 "I'll tell you; listen to me!
   I'll relate what I have seen.
18 I'll tell you what wise people have declared
   and what was not kept secret from their ancestors.
19   (The land was given to them alone,
      and no stranger passed through their land.)

The Tortured Life of the Wicked Person

20 "The wicked person is tortured all his days.
   Only a few years are reserved for the ruthless person.
21   Terrifying sounds are in his ears.
      While he enjoys peace, the destroyer comes to him.
22   He doesn't believe he'll return from the dark.
      He is destined to be killed with a sword.
23   He wanders around for food and asks, 'Where is it?'ᵃ
      He knows that his ruin is close at hand.

24 "The day of darknessᵇ troubles him.
   Distress and anguish terrify him

ᵃ 15:23 Or "He wanders around as if he were food for vultures."   ᵇ 15:24 The Hebrew text divides verses 23 and 24 at this point.

25 He stretches out his hand against God
    and attacks the Almighty like a warrior.
26 He stubbornly charges at him with a thick shield.

27 "His face is bloated with fat,
    and he is fat around the waist.
28 He lives in ruined cities
    where no one dwells,
        in houses that are doomed to be piles of rubble.
29 He won't get rich,
    and his wealth won't last.
        His possessions won't spread out over the land.

30 "He won't escape the darkness.
    A flame will shrivel his branches.
    He will be blown away by his own breath.
31 He shouldn't trust in worthless things and deceive himself
    because he will get worthless things in return.
32 It will happen before his time has come,
    and his branch will not become green.
33 He will drop his unripened grapes like a vine
    and throw off his blossoms like an olive tree
34   because a mob of godless people produces nothing,
        and fire burns up the tents of those who offer bribes.ᶜ
35   They conceive trouble and give birth to evil.
        Their wombs produce deception."

Job Speaks
My Friends Do Not Help Ease My Pain

¹Then Job replied ˌto his friendsˌ,

2 "I have heard many things like this before.
    You are all pathetic at comforting me.
3 Will ˌyourˌ long-winded speeches never end?
    What disturbs you that you keep on answering ˌmeˌ?
4 I, too, could speak like you
    if we could trade places.
    I could string words together against you
        and shake my head at you.
5 I could encourage you with my mouth,
    and my quivering lips could ease ˌyour painˌ.
6 If I speak, my pain is not eased.
    If I stop talking, how much of it will go away?

7 "But now, God has worn me out.
    You, ˌGod,ˌ have destroyed everyone who supports me.
8 You have shriveled me up, which itself is a witness ˌagainst meˌ.
    My frail body rises up and testifies against me.

ᶜ15:34 Or "those who take bribes."

Job Describes What God Has Done to Him

9 "God's anger tore me ˻apart˼ and attacked me.
He gritted his teeth at me.
My opponent looked sharply at me.

10 People gaped at me with wide-open mouths.
In scorn they slapped my cheeks.
They united against me.

11 God handed me over to unjust people
and threw me into the hands of wicked people.

12 I was at ease, and he shattered me.
He grabbed me by the back of the neck and smashed ˻my skull˼.
He set me up as his target,

13 and his archers surrounded me.
He slashes open my kidneys without mercy
and spills my blood*a* on the ground.

14 He inflicts wound after wound on me.
He lunges at me like a warrior.

15 "I have sewn sackcloth over my skin,
and I have thrown my strength in the dust.

16 My face is red from crying,
and dark shadows encircle my eyes,

17 although my hands have done nothing violent,
and my prayer is sincere.

Job Appeals His Case to Heaven

18 "Earth, don't cover my blood.
Don't ever let my cry ˻for justice˼ be stopped.

19 Even now, look! My witness is in heaven,
and the one who testifies for me is above,

20 the spokesman for my thoughts.*b*
My eyes drip ˻with tears˼ to God

22 because in a few short years I will take the path of no return.*c*

21 But my witness will plead for a human in front of God.
The Son of Man will plead for his friend!

Job Pleads With God to Declare Him Honest

17 1 "My spirit is broken.
My days have been snuffed out.
The cemetery ˻is waiting˼ for me.

2 Certainly, mockers are around me.
My eyes are focused on their opposition.

3 Please guarantee my bail yourself.
Who else will guarantee it with a handshake?

4 You have closed their minds so that they cannot understand.*a*
That is why you will not honor them.

5 (Whoever turns in friends to get their property
should have his children's eyesight fail.)

---

*a*16:13 Or "bile." *b*16:20 Or "my friends mock me." *c*16:22 Verse 22 has been placed before verse 21 to express the complex Hebrew sentence structure more clearly in English. *a*17:4 English equivalent difficult.

Job Says to His Friends: I'm Still Wiser Than You

6 "Now he has made me a laughingstock for many people.
    Now they spit in my face.
7 Now my eyes are blurred from grief.
    Now all my limbs are like a shadow.
8 Decent people are shocked by this,
        and it stirs up the innocent against godless people.
9 Yet, the righteous person clings to his way,
        and the one with clean hands grows stronger.

10 "But now, all of you, come and try again!
        I won't find one wise man among you.
11 My days are passing by.
        My plans are broken.
            My dreams are shattered.
12 You say that night is day.
        Light has nearly become darkness.
13 If I look for the grave as my home
        and make my bed in the darkness,
14 if I say to the pit, 'You are my father,'
        and to the worm, 'You are my mother and sister,'
15 then where is my hope?
        Can you see any hope left in me?
16 Will hope go down with me to the gates of the grave?
        Will my hope rest with me in the dust?"

Bildad Speaks
Why Do You Think You Are So Great, Job?

¹Then Bildad from Shuah replied to Job,

2 "How long before your words will end?
        Think it through, and then we'll talk.
3 Why do you think of us as cattle?
    Why are we considered stupid in your eyes?
4 Why do you rip yourself apart in anger?
        Should the earth be abandoned for your sake
            or a boulder be dislodged?

What a Wicked Person Can Expect From Life

5 "Indeed, the light of the wicked is snuffed out.
        The flame of his fire stops glowing.
6 The light in his tent becomes dark,
        and the lamp above him is snuffed out.

7 "His healthy stride is shortened,
        and his own planning trips him up.
8 His own feet get him tangled in a net
        as he walks around on its webbing.
9 A trap catches his heel.
        A snare holds him.
10 A rope is hidden on the ground for him.
        A trap is on his path to catch him.

11 "Terrors suddenly pounce on him from every side
      and chase him every step he takes.
12 Hunger undermines his strength.
      Disaster is waiting beside him.
13 His skin is eaten away by disease.
      Death's firstborn son eats away at the limbs of his body.
14   He is dragged from the safety of his tent
          and marched off to the king of terrors.
15 Fire lives in his tent.
      Sulfur is scattered over his home.
16   His roots dry up under him.
      His branches wither over him.
17   All memory about him will vanish from the earth,
          and his reputation will not be known on the street corner.
18   He will be driven from the light into the dark
          and chased out of the world.
19   He will not have any children or descendants among his people
          or any survivor where he used to live.
20 People in the west are shocked by what happens to him.
      People in the east are seized with horror.
21 This is what happens to the homes of wicked people
      and to those who do not know God.

Job Speaks
Admit That God Is Mistreating Me

19 ¹Then Job replied to his friends,

2 "How long will you torment me
      and depress me with words?
3 You have insulted me ten times now.
      You're not even ashamed of mistreating me.
4 Even if it were true that I've made a mistake without realizing it,
      my mistake would affect only me.
5 If you are trying to make yourselves look better than me
      by using my disgrace as an argument against me,
6 then I want you to know that God has wronged me
      and surrounded me with his net.
7 Indeed, I cry, 'Help! I'm being attacked!' but I get no response.
   I call for help, but there is no justice.

What God Has Done to Me

8 "God has blocked my path so that I can't go on.
      He has made my paths dark.
9 He has stripped me of my honor.
      He has taken the crown off my head.
10 He beats me down on every side until I'm gone.
      He uproots my hope like a tree.
11 He is very angry at me.
      He considers me to be his enemy.
12 His troops assemble against me.

> They build a ramp to attack me
>> and camp around my tent.

13 "My brothers stay far away from me.
My friends are complete strangers to me.

14 My relatives and my closest friends have stopped coming.
My house guests have forgotten me.

15 My female slaves consider me to be a stranger.
I am like a foreigner to them.

16 I call my slave, but he doesn't answer, though I beg him.

17 My breath offends my wife.
I stink to my own children.

18 Even young children despise me.
> If I stand up, they make fun of me.

19 All my closest friends are disgusted with me.
> Those I love have turned against me.

20 I am skin and bones,
>> and I have escaped only by the skin of my teeth.

21 "Have pity on me, my friends!
Have pity on me because God's hand has struck me down.

22 Why do you pursue me as God does?
Why are you never satisfied with my flesh?

Job's Confidence in His Defender

23 "I wish now my words were written.
I wish they were inscribed on a scroll.

24 I wish they were forever engraved on a rock
with an iron stylus and lead.[a]

25 But I know that my defender lives,
and afterwards, he will rise on the earth.

26 Even after my skin has been stripped off my body,
I will see God in my own flesh.

27 I will see him with my own eyes,
not with someone else's.
My heart fails inside me!

Job Warns His Friends

28 "You say,
'We will persecute him!
The root of the problem is found in him.'

29 Fear death,
because ˻your anger˼ is punishable by death.
> Then you will know there is a judge."

Zophar Speaks
Here Is My Answer

20 ¹Then Zophar from Naama replied ˻to Job˼,

2 "My disturbing thoughts make me answer,
and because of them I am upset.

---

[a] 19:24 The order of the lines has been reversed because the English equivalent is difficult.

3   I have heard criticism that makes me ashamed,
        but a spirit beyond my understanding gives me answers.

A Wicked Person's Joy Is Short, His Pain Long

4   "Don't you know
        that from ancient times,
            from the time humans were placed on earth,
5   the triumph of the wicked is short-lived,
                and the joy of the godless person lasts only a moment?
6   If his height reaches to the sky
    and his head touches the clouds,
7   he will certainly rot[a] like his own feces.
  Those who have seen him will say, 'Where is he?'
8   He will fly away like a dream and not be found.
    He will be chased away like a vision in the night.
9   Eyes that saw him will see him no more.
    His home will not look at him again.
10   His children will have to ask the poor for help.
    His own hands will have to give back his wealth.
11   His bones, once full of youthful vigor,
        will lie down with him in the dust.

12   "Though evil is sweet in his mouth
    and he hides it under his tongue. . . .
13   Though he savors it and won't let go of it
    and he holds it on the roof of his mouth,
14   the food in his belly turns sour.
    It becomes snake venom in his stomach.
15   He vomits up the riches that he swallowed.
        God forces them out of his stomach.
16   The godless person sucks the poison of snakes.
        A viper's fang kills him.
17   He won't be able to drink from the streams
    or from the rivers of honey and buttermilk.
18   He will give back what he earned without enjoying it.
    He will get no joy from the profits of his business
19   because he crushed and abandoned the poor.
    He has taken by force a house that he didn't build.
20   He will never know peace in his heart.
    He will never allow anything he desires to escape his grasp.

21   "Nothing is left for him to eat.
        His prosperity won't last.
22   Even with all his wealth
        the full force of misery comes down on him.
23   Let that misery fill his belly.
        God throws his burning anger at the godless person
            and makes his wrath come down on him like rain.
24   If that person flees from an iron weapon,

---

[a] 20:7 Or "he will be dead forever."

25   a bronze bow will pierce him.
He pulls it out, and it comes out of his back.
The glittering point comes out of his gallbladder.

26   "Terrors come quickly to the godless person:
Total darkness waits in hiding for his treasure.
A fire that no one fans will burn him.
Whatever is left in his tent will be devoured.

27   Heaven exposes his sin.
Earth rises up against him.

28   A flood will sweep away his house,
a flash flood on the day of his anger.

29   This is the reward God gives to the wicked person,
the inheritance God has appointed for him."

Job Speaks
Comfort Me by Listening to Me

21 ¹Then Job replied to his friends,,

2   "Listen carefully to my words,
and let that be the comfort you offer me.

3   Bear with me while I speak.
Then after I've spoken, you may go on mocking.

4   Am I complaining about a person?
Why shouldn't I be impatient?

5   Look at me, and be shocked,
and put ,your, hand over ,your, mouth.

6   When I remember it, I'm terrified,
and shuddering seizes my body.

Wicked People Do Not Suffer for Their Sins

7   "Why do the wicked go on living, grow old,
and even become more powerful?

8   They see their children firmly established with them,
and they get to see their descendants.

9   Their homes are free from fear,
and God doesn't use his rod on them.

10   Their bulls are fertile when they breed.
Their cows give birth to calves and never miscarry.

11   They send their little children out ,to play,
like a flock of lambs,
and their children dance around.

12   They sing with the tambourine and lyre,
and they are happy with the music of the flute.

13   They spend their days in happiness,
and they go peacefully to the grave.

14   But they say to God,
'Leave us alone.
We don't want to know your ways.

15   Who is the Almighty that we should serve him?
What do we gain if we pray to him?'

16 Anyhow, isn't their happiness in their own power?
   (The plan of the wicked is foreign to my way of thinking.)

17 "How often is the lamp of the wicked snuffed out?
   How often does disaster happen to them?
   How often does an angry God give them pain?

18 How often are they like straw in the wind
   or like husks that the storm sweeps away?

19 "You say, 'God saves a person's punishment for his children.'
   God should pay back that person
   so that he would know that it is a punishment.

20 His eyes should see his own ruin.
   He should drink from the wrath of the Almighty.

21 How can he be interested in his family after he's gone,
   when the number of his months is cut short?

No One Understands How God Deals With Humans

22 "Can anyone teach God knowledge?
   Can anyone judge the Most High?

23 One person dies in his prime
   and feels altogether happy and contented.

24 His stomach is full of milk,
   and his bones are strong and healthy.

25 Another person, never having tasted happiness,
   dies with a bitter soul.

26 Together they lie down in the dust,
   and worms cover them.

My Friends Have Betrayed Me

27 "You see, I know your thoughts
   and the schemes you plot against me

28 because you ask,
   'Where is the house of the influential person?
   Where is the tent where wicked people live?'

29 Haven't you asked travelers?
   But you didn't pay attention to their directions.

30 On the day of disaster the wicked person is spared.
   On the day of God's anger he is rescued.

31 Who will tell him to his face how he lived?
   Who will pay him back for what he did?

32 He is carried to the cemetery,
   and his grave is guarded.

33 The soil in the creekbed is sweet to him.
   Everyone follows him.
   Countless others went before him.

34 How can you comfort me with this nonsense
   when your answers continue to betray me?"

Eliphaz Speaks
Admit You Are Wicked, Job

22 ¹Then Eliphaz from Teman replied ⌊to Job⌋,

² "Can a human be of any use to God
   when even a wise person is only useful to himself?
³ Is the Almighty pleased when you are righteous?
   Does he gain anything when you follow the path of integrity?
⁴ Does God correct you
   and bring you into a court of law because you fear him?

⁵ "Aren't you really very wicked?
   Is there no end to your wrongdoing?
⁶ For no reason you take your brothers' goods as security for a loan
   and strip them of their clothes.ᵃ
⁷ You don't even give a tired person a drink of water,
   and you take food away from hungry people.
⁸   A strong person owns the land.
     A privileged person lives in it.
⁹ You send widows away empty-handed,
   and the arms of orphans are broken.
¹⁰ That is why traps are all around you
   and great fear suddenly grips you.
¹¹ ⌊That is why⌋ darkness surrounds you and you cannot see
   and a flood of water covers you.

¹² "Isn't God high above in the heavens?
   Look how high the highest stars are!
¹³ You ask, 'What does God know?
   Can he judge ⌊anything⌋ from behind a dark cloud?
¹⁴ Thick clouds surround him so that he cannot see.
   He walks above the clouds.'ᵇ

¹⁵ "Are you following the old path that wicked people have taken?
¹⁶ They are snatched up before their time.
   A river washes their foundation away.
¹⁷ They told God, 'Leave us alone!
   What can the Almighty do for us?'
¹⁸ Yet, he filled their homes with good things.
   (The plan of the wicked is foreign to my way of thinking.)
¹⁹ The righteous saw it and were glad,
   and the innocent made fun of them by saying,
²⁰   'Indeed, their wealth has been wiped out,
       and a fire has burned up what ⌊little⌋ they had left.'

Make Peace With God

²¹ "Be in harmony and at peace with God.
   In this way you will have prosperity.
²² Accept instruction from his mouth,
   and keep his words in your heart.
²³ If you return to the Almighty, you will prosper.

ᵃ22:6 Clothes were often used as security deposits for loans in biblical times.   ᵇ22:14 English equivalent difficult.

If you put wrongdoing out of your tent,
24 and lay your gold down in the dust,
and put your gold from Ophir among the pebbles in the rivers,
25 then the Almighty will become your gold
and your large supply of silver.
26 Then you will be happy with the Almighty
and look up toward God.
27 You will pray to him, and he will listen to you,
and you will keep your vow to him.
28 When you promise to do something, you will succeed,
and light will shine on your path.
29 When others are discouraged, you will say, 'Cheer up!'
Then he will save the humble person.*c*
30 He will rescue one who is not innocent.
That person will be rescued by your purity."

Job Speaks
Where Can I Find God?

23 ¹Then Job replied to his friends,

2 "My complaint is bitter again today.
I try hard to control my sighing.

3 "If only I knew where I could find God!
I would go where he lives.
4 I would present my case to him.
I would have a mouthful of arguments.
5 I want to know the words he would use to answer me.
I want to understand the things he would say to me.
6 Would he sue me and hide behind great legal maneuvers?
No, he certainly would press charges against me.
7 Then decent people could argue with him,
and I would escape my judgment forever.
8 However, if I go east, he isn't there.

Good Morning, God
Job 23:10-12

Job realized his tough situation was a test to see if he would remain faithful to God. In these verses, Job compared his life to gold. Gold is precious and valuable. God considers each of us precious and valuable—even more so than gold. When times get tough, remember Job's determination to be faithful to God. And think gold!

Father, help me to remember I am precious and valuable, even when I'm having problems.

---

*c*22:29 Or "you will say, 'It's conceit.' But he will save the humble person."

If I go west, I can't find him.
9   If I go northward, where he is at work, I can't observe him.
If I turn southward, I can't see him.
10 ⌞I can't find him⌟ because he knows the road I take.
When he tests me,
I'll come out as pure as gold.
11 I have followed his footsteps closely.
I have stayed on his path and did not turn from it.
12 I have not left his commands behind.
I have treasured his words in my heart.

God Is Against Me

13 "But God is one of a kind.
Who can make him change his mind?
He does whatever he wants!
14 He will carry out ⌞his⌟ orders concerning me
as he does with so many other things.[a]
15 That is why I'm terrified of him.
When I think of it, I'm afraid of him.
16 God has discouraged me.
The Almighty has filled me with terror.
17 But I am not silenced by the dark
or by the thick darkness that covers my face.

Job Continues: Why Doesn't God Punish Those Who Do Evil?

24 1 "Why doesn't the Almighty set aside times ⌞for punishment⌟?
Why don't those who are close to him see his days ⌞of judgment⌟?

2 "⌞People⌟ move boundary markers.
They steal flocks and tend them as shepherds.
3 They drive away the orphan's donkey.
They take the widow's ox as security for a loan.
4 They force needy people off the road.
All the poor people of the country go into hiding.
5 Like wild donkeys in the desert,
poor people go out to do their work, looking for food.
The plains provide food for their children.
6 They harvest animal food in the field ⌞to feed themselves⌟.
They pick the leftover grapes in the wicked person's vineyard.
7 All night they lie naked
without a covering from the cold.
8 They are drenched by the rainstorms in the mountains.
They hug the rocks because they can't find shelter.

9 "⌞People⌟ snatch the ⌞nursing⌟ orphan from a breast
and take a poor woman's baby as security for a loan.
10 ⌞That is why⌟ the poor go around naked.
They are hungry, yet they carry bundles of grain.

---

[a] 23:14 Hebrew meaning uncertain.

11   They press out olive oil between rows ⸤of olive trees⸥.
      They stomp on grapes in wine vats, yet they are thirsty.
12   Those dying in the city groan.
              Wounded people cry for help,
                  but God pays no attention to their prayers.

13   "Such people are among those who rebel against the light.
          They are not acquainted with its ways.
              They do not stay on its paths.
14   At dawn murderers rise; they kill the poor and needy.
      At night they become thieves.
15   Adulterers watch for twilight.
          They say, 'No one is watching us,' as they cover their faces.
16   In the dark, they break into houses,
          ⸤but⸥ by day they lock themselves in.
      They do not ⸤even⸥ know the light,
17   because morning and deep darkness are the same to them,
              because they are familiar with the terrors of deep darkness.
18   Such people are like scum on the surface of the water.
          Their property is cursed in the land.
      People do not travel the road that goes to their vineyards.
19   ⸤Just as⸥ drought and heat steal water from snow,
          so the grave steals people who sin.
20   The womb forgets them.
              Worms feast on them.
                  No one remembers them anymore,
                      and wickedness is snapped like a twig.
21   These men take advantage of childless women.
      These men show no kindness to widows.
22   ⸤God⸥ will drag away ⸤these⸥ mighty men by his power.
          These people may prosper,
              but they will never feel secure about life.
23   ⸤God⸥ may let them feel confident and self-reliant,
          but his eyes are on their ways.
24   ⸤Such people⸥ may be prosperous for a little while,
          but then they're gone.
      They are brought down low and disappear like everything else.[a]
      They wither like heads of grain.

25   "If it isn't so, who can prove I'm a liar
          and show that my words are worthless?"

Bildad Speaks
No One Is Righteous to God

25   [1]Then Bildad from Shuah replied ⸤to Job⸥,

2   "Authority and terror belong to God.
          He establishes peace in his high places.
3   Is there any ⸤limit to the⸥ number of his troops?

---

[a]24:24 Hebrew meaning of this line uncertain.

Is there anyone on whom his light does not rise?

4   How can a person be righteous to God?
How can anyone born of a woman be pure?

5   Even the moon isn't bright,
and the stars aren't pure in his sight.

6   How much less pure is a mortal—who is only a maggot—
a descendant of Adam—who is only a worm!"

Job Speaks
My Friends Have Offered Useless Advice

¹Then Job replied ˻to his friends˼,

2   "You have helped the person who has no power
and saved the arm that isn't strong.

3   You have advised the person who has no wisdom
and offered so much assistance.

4   To whom have you spoken ˻these˼ words,
and whose spirit has spoken through you?

God's Power Over Creation

5   "The souls of the dead tremble beneath the water,
and so do the creatures living there.

6   Sheol is naked in God's presence,
and Abaddon has no clothing.

7   "He stretches out his heavens*ᵃ* over empty space.
He hangs the earth on nothing whatsoever.

8   He holds the water in his thick clouds,
and the clouds don't ˻even˼ split under its ˻weight˼.

9   He covers his throne*ᵇ*
by spreading his cloud over it.

10   He marks the horizon on the surface of the water
at the boundary where light meets dark.

11   The pillars of heaven tremble
and are astonished when he yells at them.

12   With his power he calmed the sea.
With his insight he killed Rahab ˻the sea monster˼.

13   With his wind the sky was cleared.
With his hand he stabbed the fleeing snake.

14   "These are only glimpses of what he does.
We ˻only˼ hear a whisper of him!
Who can understand the thunder of his power?"

Job Continues: I Insist I Am Innocent

¹Job continued his poems and said,

2   "I swear an oath
by God, the one who has taken away my rights,
by the Almighty, who has made my life bitter:

ᵃ 26:7 Or "the north." ᵇ 26:9 Or "the face of the moon."

3   'As long as there is one breath ˻left˼ in me
            and God's breath fills my nostrils,
4   my lips will not say anything wrong,
                and my tongue will not mumble anything deceitful.'
5   It's unthinkable for me to admit that you are right.
            Until I breathe my last breath, I will never give up my claim of integrity.
6   I cling to my righteousness and won't let go.
      My conscience won't accuse me as long as I live.

7   "Let my enemy be ˻treated˼ like wicked people.
      Let anyone who attacks me be ˻treated˼ like unrighteous people.
8   After all, what hope does the godless person have when he is cut off,
            when God takes away his life?
9   Will God hear his cry when trouble comes upon him?
10   Can he be happy with the Almighty?
      Can he call on God at all times?

What God Has in Store for Wicked People

11   "I will teach you about God's power.
      I will not hide what the Almighty has done.
12   Certainly, you have all seen it.
            Why then do you chatter on about such nonsense?
13   This is what God has waiting for the wicked person,
            the inheritance that tyrants receive from the Almighty:
14   If he has many children, swords will kill them,
                and his descendants won't have enough food.
15   Those who survive him will be buried by a plague,
                and their widows won't cry ˻for them˼.
16   Though he collects silver like dust
                and piles up clothing like dirt,
17   righteous people will wear what he piles up,
                      and the innocent will divide the silver
                          ˻among themselves˼.
18   He builds his house like a moth,
                like a shack that a watchman makes.
19   He may go to bed rich, but he'll never be rich again.
                When he opens his eyes, nothing will be left.
20   Terrors overtake him like a flood.
                A windstorm snatches him away at night.
21   The east wind carries him away, and he's gone.
                      It sweeps him from his place.
22   It hurls itself at him without mercy.
                      He flees from its power.
23   It claps its hands over him.
                      It whistles at him from his own place.

Job Continues: Wisdom Is Inaccessible to Humans

28   1   "There is a place where silver is mined
                and a place where gold is refined.

2   Iron is taken from the ground,
        and rocks are melted for their copper.
3   Humans bring an end to darkness there,
        and search to the limit of the gloomy, pitch-black rock.
4   They open up a mineshaft far from civilization,
        where no one has set foot.
    In this shaft, men dangle and swing back and forth.

5   "Above the ground food grows,
        but beneath it the food decays as if it were burned by fire.
6   That place's stones are sapphire.*
        Its dust contains gold.
7   No bird of prey knows the way to it.
        No hawk's eye has ever seen it.
8   No proud beast has ever walked on it.
        No ferocious lion has ever passed over it.

9   "Humans exert their power on the flinty rocks
        and overturn mountains at their base.
10   They cut out mineshafts in the rocks.
        Their eyes see every precious thing.
11   They explore*b* the sources of rivers
        so that they bring hidden treasures to light.

Wisdom Is Inaccessible to Decay and Death

12   "Where can wisdom be found?
    Where does understanding live?
13   No mortal knows where it is.*c*
        It cannot be found in this world of the living.
14   The deep ocean says, 'It isn't in me.'
        The sea says, 'It isn't with me.'
15   You cannot obtain it with solid gold
        or buy it for any amount of silver.
16   It can't be bought with the gold from Ophir
        or with precious onyx or sapphire.
17   Neither gold nor glass can equal its value.
        Nor can gold ornaments, jewels, or crystal*d*
18   be exchanged for it.
    Wisdom is more valuable than gems.
19   Topaz from Ethiopia cannot equal its value.
        It cannot be bought for any amount of pure gold.

20   "Where does wisdom come from?
    Where does understanding live?
21   It is hidden from the eyes of every living being,
        hidden even from the birds in the air.
22   Decay and Death say,
        'We've heard a rumor about it.'

---

*28:6 Hebrew meaning uncertain. *b*28:11 Or "dam up." *c*28:13 Or "how valuable it is." *d*28:17 Hebrew meaning uncertain.

Wisdom Is Accessible Only to the Creator

23 "God understands the way to it.
   He knows where it lives
24   because he can see to the ends of the earth
      and observe everything under heaven.
25   When he gave the wind its force
         and measured the water ⸢in the sea⸣,
26   when he made rules for the rain
         and set paths for the thunderstorms,
27   then he saw it and announced it.
         He confirmed it and examined it.
28   So he told humans,
            'The fear of the Lord is wisdom!
            To stay away from evil is understanding.' "

Job Continues: My Glorious Past

1 Job continued his poems and said,

2 "If only my life could be like it used to be,
   in the days when God watched over me,
3   when he made his lamp shine on my head,
     when I walked through the dark in his light.
4 If only I were in the prime of my life ⸢again⸣,
   when God was an adviser in my tent.
5 When the Almighty was still with me
   and my children were around me,
6   my steps were bathed in buttermilk,
        and the rocks poured streams of olive oil on me.
7 When I went through the city gate
   and took my seat in the town square,
8   young men saw me and kept out of sight.
        Old men stood up straight out of respect ⸢for me⸣.
9   Princes held back ⸢their⸣ words
        and put their hands over their mouths.
10   The voices of nobles were hushed,
        and their tongues stuck to the roofs of their mouths.

11 "⸢Any⸣ ears that heard me blessed me.
   ⸢Any⸣ eyes that saw me spoke well of me,
12   because I rescued the poor who called ⸢for help⸣,
      and the orphans who had no one to help them.
13 I received a blessing from the dying.
   I made the widow's heart sing for joy.
14 I put on righteousness, and it was my clothing.
   I practiced justice, and it was my robe and my turban.
15 I was eyes for the blind person.
   I was feet for the lame person.
16 I was father to the needy.
   I carefully investigated cases brought by strangers.
17 I broke the teeth of the wicked person
   and made him drop the prey out of his mouth.

18 "I thought, 'I may die in my own house,
    but I will make my days as numerous as the sand.
19 My roots will grow toward the water,
    and dew will lie on my branches all night.
20 My power will be fresh every day,
    and the bow in my hand will remain new.'

21 "People listened to me eagerly,
    quietly waiting for my advice.
22 After I had spoken, they wouldn't speak again.
    After all, my words fell gently on them.
23 They were as eager to hear me as they were for rain.
    They opened their mouths wide as if waiting for a spring shower.
24 When I smiled at them, they could hardly believe it,
    but the expression on my face did not change.*
25 I decided how they should live.
    I sat as their leader.
    I lived like a king among his troops,
    like one who comforts mourners.

Job Talks About His Present Misery

1 "But now those who are younger than I am laugh at me.
    I didn't think their fathers were fit to sit with the dogs of my flock.
2 Of what use to me was the strength of their hands?
    Their strength is gone.
3 Shriveled up from need and hunger,
    they gnaw at the dry and barren ground during the night.*
4 They pick saltwort from the underbrush,
    and the roots of the broom plant are their food.*
5 They are driven from the community.
    People shout at them in the same way they shout at thieves.
6 They have to live in dry riverbeds,
    in holes in the ground, and among rocks.
7 They howl in bushes
    and huddle together under thornbushes.
8 Godless fools and worthless people
    are forced out of the land with whips.

9 "And now they make fun of me with songs.
    I have become a joke to them.
10 Since they consider me disgusting, they keep their distance from me
    and don't hesitate to spit in my face.
11 Because God has untied my cord and has made me suffer,
    they are no longer restrained in my presence.
12 They have attacked me on my right side like a mob.
    They trip my feet
    and then prepare ways to destroy me.*
13 Yes, they remove all traces of my path in order to destroy me.

---

*29:24 Hebrew meaning uncertain.   *30:3 Hebrew meaning of this line uncertain.   *30:4 Or "they use the roots of the
broom plant for warmth."   *30:12 Hebrew meaning of this verse uncertain.

No one is there to help me against them.
¹⁴ They come through a wide hole in the wall.
    They crawl through the ruins.
¹⁵ Terrors are directed toward me.
    They blow away my dignity like the wind.
    My prosperity vanishes like a cloud.

¹⁶ "Now my life is pouring out of me.
    Days of suffering seize me.
¹⁷ At night God pierces my bones.
    My body^d doesn't rest.
¹⁸ With great strength he grabs my clothes.
    He seizes me by the collar of my robe.
¹⁹   He throws me into the dirt
        so that I become like dust and ashes.

Job Calls on God for Help

²⁰ "I call to you for help,
        but you don't answer me.
        I stand up, but you just look at me.
²¹ You have begun to treat me cruelly.
    With your mighty hand you assault me.
²² You pick me up and let the wind carry me away.
    You toss me around with a storm.
²³ I know you will lead me to death,
        to the dwelling place appointed for all living beings.

Job Says: I Am Being Punished by God

²⁴ "But God doesn't stretch out his hand against one who is ruined
        when that person calls for help in his disaster.
²⁵ Didn't I cry for the person whose days were difficult?
    Didn't my soul grieve for the poor?
²⁶ When I waited for good, evil came.
    When I looked for light, darkness came.
²⁷ My insides are churning and won't calm down.
    Days of misery are ahead of me.
²⁸ I walk in the dark without the sun.
    I stand up in public and call for help.
²⁹ I'm a brother to jackals
        and a companion of ostriches.
³⁰ My skin turns dark and peels.
    My body burns with fever.
³¹ So my lyre is used for mourning
        and my flute for loud weeping.

Job Wonders What Sin He May Have Committed

31 ¹ "I have made an agreement with my eyes.
        Then how can I look with lust at a virgin?
² What would God above do to me?

---
^d30:17 Hebrew meaning uncertain.

What would be my inheritance from the Almighty on high?
3 Aren't there catastrophes for wicked people
      and disasters for those who do wrong?
4 Doesn't he see my ways
      and count all my steps?

5 "If I have walked with lies
      or my feet have run after deception,
6 ₋then₋ let God weigh me on honest scales,
      and he will know I have integrity.

7 "If my steps have left the ₋proper₋ path,
      or my heart has followed ₋the desire of₋ my eyes,
      or my hands are stained ₋with sin₋,
8 ₋then₋ let someone else eat what I have planted,
      and let my crops be uprooted.

9 "If I have been seduced by a woman
      or I have secretly waited near my neighbor's door,
10 ₋then₋ let my wife grind for another ₋man₋,
      and let other ₋men₋ kneel over her.
11 That would be a scandal,
      and that would be a criminal offense.
12 It would be a fire that burns even in Abaddon.
      It would uproot my entire harvest.

13 "If I have abused the rights of my servants, male or female,
      when they have disagreed with me,
14 then what could I do if God rises up?
      If he examines me, how could I answer him?
15 Didn't he who made me in my mother's belly make them?
      Didn't the same God form us in the womb?

16 "If I have refused the requests of the poor
      or made a widow's eyes stop ₋looking for help₋,
17 or have eaten my food alone
      without letting the orphan eat any of it. . . .
18 (From my youth the orphan grew up with me
      as though I were his father,
         and from my birth I treated the widow kindly.)
19 If I have seen anyone die because he had no clothes
      or a poor person going naked. . . .
20 (If his body didn't bless me,
      or the wool from my sheep didn't keep him warm. . . .)
21 If I have shaken my fist at an orphan
      because I knew that others would back me up in court,
22 ₋then₋ let my shoulder fall out of its socket,
      and let my arm be broken at the elbow.

23 "A disaster from God terrifies me.
      In the presence of his majesty I can do nothing.

24 "If I put my confidence in gold
      or said to fine gold, 'I trust you'. . . .

Job

**Job showed his despair by tearing his clothes
and sitting in ashes.**

Job was "decent" and "stayed away from evil" (Job 1). How did Job show he was a decent man? Chapter 31 tells us Job was truthful and didn't try to deceive people. Job was faithful to his wife. He never abused anyone working for him. Job helped people in need. He was rich, but he was generous and used his money to help others. He welcomed travelers and fed them. Job didn't worry about what others thought of him, but always tried to do right.

No wonder Job and his friends couldn't understand when terrible things happened to him!

In the end, God gave Job more than he had lost. Job learned that he could trust God whatever happened. And Job's friends learned not to think someone had sinned just because bad things happened to that person.

Getting to Know Job

* How did Job's life show his character?
* Do you think Job was popular with others? Why or why not?
* What makes someone popular these days?
* If you had to choose between being popular and being obedient to God, which would you choose? Why?

Job lived around 2000 B.C.

Job was a good man, but bad things happened to him.

Job's friends thought he must have sinned and was being punished by God.

Job was considered wealthy because he had many animals. After Job's illness, God restored Job's wealth.

²⁵ If I enjoyed being very rich
    because my hand had found great ˏwealthˌ. . . .
²⁶ If I saw the light shine
    or the moon move along in its splendor
²⁷   so that my heart was secretly tempted,
        and I threw them a kiss with my hand,
²⁸ then that, too, would be a criminal offense,
    and I would have denied God above.

²⁹ "If I enjoyed the ruin of my enemy
    or celebrated when harm came to him
³⁰   (even though I didn't speak sinfully
        by calling down a curse on his life). . . .

³¹ "If the people who were in my tent had said,
    'We wish we had never filled ˏour stomachsˌ with his food'. . . .
³²   (The visitor never spent the night outside,
        because I opened my door to the traveler.)

³³ "If I have covered my disobedience like Adam
    and kept my sin to myself,
³⁴   because I dreaded the large, noisy crowd
        and because the contempt of the ˏlocalˌ mobs terrified me
        so that I kept quiet and didn't go outside. . . .

³⁵ "If only I had someone who would listen to me!
    Look, here is my signature!
    Let the Almighty answer me.
    Let the prosecutor write ˏhis complaintˌ on a scroll.
³⁶   I would certainly carry it on my shoulder
        and place it on my head like a crown.
³⁷   I would tell him the number of my steps
        and approach him like a prince.

³⁸ "If my land has cried out against me,
    and its furrows have wept. . . .
³⁹ If I have eaten its produce without paying for it
    and made its owners breathe their last,
⁴⁰ ˏthenˌ let it grow thistles instead of wheat,
    and foul-smelling weeds instead of barley."

This is the end of Job's words.

Elihu Decides to Speak to Job

¹These three men stopped answering Job because Job thought he was righteous. ²Then Elihu, son of Barachel, a descendant of Buz from the family of Ram, became very angry with Job because Job thought he was more righteous than God. ³Elihu was also very angry with Job's three friends because they had found no answer. They made it look as if God*ᵃ* were wrong. ⁴Elihu waited as they spoke to Job because they were older than he was. ⁵When Elihu saw that the three men had no further responses, he became very angry.

---

^a32:3 Masoretic Text "Job." At times some scribes would alter the text when they thought it was disrespectful to God.

Elihu Speaks
The Reason for Elihu's Discourse

⁶So Elihu, son of Barachel, the descendant of Buz, replied ˌto Jobˌ,

"I am young, and you are old.
That's why I refrained from speaking
   and was afraid to tell you what I know.
⁷ I thought, 'Age should speak,
   and experience should teach wisdom.'
⁸ However, there is in humans a Spirit,
   the breath of the Almighty, that gives them understanding.
⁹ People do not become wise merely because they live long.
   They don't understand what justice is merely because they're old.

¹⁰ "That is why I say, 'Listen to me!
   Let me tell you what I know.'
¹¹ I waited for you to speak.
   I listened for you to share your understanding
      until you could find the right words.
¹² I've paid close attention to you,
   but none of you refuted Job.
      None of you has an answer to what he says.
¹³ So don't say, 'We've found wisdom.
   Let God, not humans, defeat him.'
¹⁴ Job did not choose his words to refute me,
   so I won't answer him with your speeches.

¹⁵ "Job's friends have been overwhelmed and don't have any more answers.
   They don't have another word to say.
¹⁶ Should I wait because they don't speak,
   because they stand there and don't have any more answers?

¹⁷ "I'll give my answer.
   I'll tell you what I know.
¹⁸ I'm full of words.
   The Spirit within me forces me ˌto speakˌ.
¹⁹ My belly is like ˌaˌ bottle ofˌ wine that has not been opened,
   like new wineskins that are ready to burst.
²⁰ I must speak to get relief.
   I must open my mouth and answer.
²¹ I won't be partial toward anyone
   or flatter anyone.
²² I don't know how to flatter.
   If I did, my maker would soon carry me away.

Elihu Continues: Listen, Job

33
¹ "Please, Job, listen to my words
   and consider everything I say.
² I've opened my mouth.
   The words are on the tip of my tongue.
³ My words are straight from the heart,
   and I sincerely speak the knowledge that is on my lips.

4 "God's Spirit has made me.
  The breath of the Almighty gives me life.
5   Answer me if you can.
      Present your case to me, and take your stand.
6   Indeed, I stand in front of God as you do.
      I, too, was formed from a piece of clay.
7   You certainly don't need to be terrified of me.
      I won't put too much pressure on you.

God Doesn't Have to Answer You, Job

8 "But you spoke directly to me,
    and I listened to your words.
9   You said, 'I'm pure—without any rebellious acts against God.
    I'm clean; I have no sin.
10   God is only looking for an excuse to attack me.
      He considers me his enemy.
11   He puts my feet in the stocks and watches all my paths.'
12 You aren't right about this!
      I've got an answer for you:
        God is greater than any mortal.
13 Why do you quarrel with him
      since he doesn't answer any questions?

Two Ways God Warns People

14 "God speaks in one way,
      even in two ways without people noticing it:
15   In a dream, a prophetic vision at night,
          when people fall into a deep sleep,
          when they sleep on their beds,
16   he opens people's ears
            and terrifies them with warnings.
17   He warns them to turn away from doing wrong
            and to stop being arrogant.[a]
18   He keeps their souls from the pit
            and their lives from crossing the River of Death.
19   In pain on their sickbeds, they are disciplined
          with endless aching in their bones
20   so that their whole being hates food
            and they lose their appetite for a delicious meal.
21   Their flesh becomes so thin that it can't be seen.
            Their bones, not seen before, will be exposed.
22   Their souls approach the pit.
            Their lives come close to those already dead.

A Third Way God Warns People

23 "If they have a messenger for them,
    a spokesman, one in a thousand,
      to tell people what is right for them,

---

[a] 33:17 Or "and cover a person's pride."

²⁴ then he will have pity on them and say,
   'Free them from going into the pit.
      I have found a ransom.'
²⁵ Then their flesh will become softer than a child's.
   They will go back to the days of their youth.
²⁶ They will pray to God, who will be pleased with them.
   They will see God's face and shout for joy
      as he restores their righteousness.ᵇ
²⁷ Each one sings in front of other people and says,
   'I sinned and did wrong instead of what was right,
      and it did me no good.
²⁸ The messenger has freed my soul from going into the pit,
      and my life will see the light.'
²⁹ Truly, God does all this two or three times with people
³⁰ to turn their souls away from the pit
      and to enlighten them with the light of life.

Pay Attention, Job

³¹ "Pay attention, Job! Listen to me!
   Keep quiet, and let me speak.
³² If you have a response, answer me.
      Speak, because I'd be happy if you were right.
³³ If not, you listen to me.
   Keep quiet, and I'll teach you wisdom."

Elihu Continues: Listen, Everyone

¹ Elihu continued to speak to Job and his friends,,
² "Listen to my words, you wise men.
   Open your ears to me, you intelligent men.
³ The ear tests words
      like the tongue tastes food.
⁴ Let's decide for ourselves what is right
   and agree among ourselves as to what is good,
⁵ because Job has said,
   'I'm righteous, but God has taken away my rights.
⁶ I'm considered a liar in spite of my rights.
   I've been wounded by a deadly arrow,
      though I haven't been disobedient.'
⁷ What person is like Job,
   who drinks scorn like water,
⁸ who travels with troublemakers
      and associates with evil people?
⁹ He says, 'It doesn't do any good to try to please God.'
¹⁰ "You people who have understanding, listen to me.
   It is unthinkable that God would ever do evil
      or that the Almighty would ever do wicked things.
¹¹ God will repay humanity for what it has done
      and will give each person what he deserves.

ᵇ33:26 Or "restores them to his righteousness."

12   Certainly, God will never do anything evil,
            and the Almighty will never pervert justice.
13   Who put him in charge of the earth?
        Who appointed him to be over the whole world?
14   If he thought only of himself
            and withdrew his Spirit and his breath,
15   all living beings would die together,
                and humanity would return to dust.

God Is Fair

16   "If you understand, listen to this.
            Open your ears to my words!
17   Should anyone who hates justice be allowed to govern?
                Will you condemn the one who is righteous and mighty?
18   Should anyone even, say to a king,
                'You good-for-nothing scoundrel!'
                or to nobles, 'You wicked people!'
19   The one who is righteous and mighty
                does not grant special favors to princes
                    or prefer important people over poor people
                        because his hands made them all.
20   They die suddenly in the middle of the night.
            People have seizures and pass away.
            Mighty people are taken away but not by human hands.
21   God's eyes are on a person's ways.
        He sees all his steps.
22   There's no darkness or deep shadow
                where troublemakers can hide.
23   He doesn't have to set a time for a person
            in order to bring him to divine judgment.
24   He breaks mighty people into pieces without examining them
            and puts others in their places.
25   He knows what they do,
            so he overthrows them at night, and they're crushed.
26   In return for their evil, he strikes them in public,
27   because they turned away from following him
                and didn't consider any of his ways.
28   They forced the poor to cry out to him,
                    and he hears the cry of those who suffer.
29   If he keeps quiet, who can condemn him?
        If he hides his face, who can see him
            whether it is a nation or a single person?
30   He does this, so that godless people cannot rule
            and so that they cannot trap people.

31   "But suppose such a person says to God, 'I am guilty,
            I will stop my immoral behavior.
32   Teach me what I cannot see.
            If I've done wrong, I won't do it again.'
33   Should God reward you on your own terms since you have rejected his?

You must choose, not I.
Tell me what you know. Speak!

Elihu Makes an Appeal to God

34 "People of understanding, the wise people
who listen to me, will say,
35   'Job speaks without knowledge.
His words show no insight.'
36 "My Father, let Job be thoroughly tested
for giving answers like wicked people do.
37   He adds disobedience to his sin.
He claps his hands to insult us.
He multiplies his words against God."

Elihu Continues: I Will Answer You and Your Friends, Job

1 Elihu continued to speak to Job and his friends,
2 "Do you think this is right
when you say, 'My case is more just than God's,'
3 when you ask, 'What benefit is it to you?'
and, 'What would I gain by sinning?'
4 I will answer you and your friends.

Human Behavior Cannot Change God

5 "Look at the heavens and see.
Observe the clouds high above you.
6   If you've sinned, what effect can you have on God?
If you've done many wrongs, what can you do to him?
7   If you're righteous, what can you give him,
or what can he get from you?
8 Your wickedness affects only someone like yourself.
Your righteousness affects only the descendants of Adam.
9   The weight of oppression makes them cry out.
The power of mighty people makes them call for help.
10   But no one asks,
'Where is God, my Creator,
who inspires songs in the night,
11   who teaches us more than he teaches the animals of the earth,
who makes us wiser than the birds in the sky?'
12   Then they cry out, but he doesn't answer them
because of the arrogance of those evil people.
13 "Surely, God doesn't listen to idle complaints.
The Almighty doesn't even pay attention to them.
14   Although you say that you pay attention to him,
your case is in front of him, but you'll have to wait for him.
15   And now you say that his anger doesn't punish anyone,
and he isn't too concerned about evil.ª

ª 35:15 Hebrew meaning of this verse uncertain.

16 Job opens his mouth for no good reason
    and talks a lot without having any knowledge."

Elihu Continues: Hear Me Out

36 1 Elihu continued to speak ˌto Jobˌ,

2 "Be patient with me a little longer, and I will show you
    that there is more to be said in God's defense.

3 I will get my knowledge from far away
    and prove that my Creator is fair.

4 Certainly, my words are not lies.
    The one who knows everything is ˌspeakingˌ with you.

God's Justice Is Beyond Human Understanding

5 "Certainly, God is mighty.
    He doesn't despise anyone.
    He is mighty and brave.

6 He doesn't allow the wicked person to live.
    He grants justice to those who are oppressed.

7 He doesn't take his eyes off righteous people.
    He seats them on thrones with kings to honor them forever.

8 However, if righteous people are bound in chains
    and tangled in ropes of misery,

9 he tells them what they've done wrong
    and that they've behaved arrogantly.

10 He makes them listen to his warning
    and orders them to turn away from wrong.

11 "If righteous people listen and serve ˌhimˌ,
    they will live out their days in prosperity
    and their years in comfort.

12 But if they don't listen,
    they will cross the River ˌof Deathˌ
    and die like those who have no knowledge.

13 But those who have godless hearts remain angry.
    They don't even call for help when he chains them up.

14 They die while they're young,
    or they live on as male prostitutes in the temples of idols.

15 He rescues suffering people through their suffering,
    and he opens their ears through distress.

16 "Yes, he lured you away from the jaws of trouble
    into an open area where you were not restrained,
    and your table was covered with rich foods.

17 But you are given the judgment evil people deserve.
    A fair judgment will be upheld.

18 Be careful that you are not led astray with riches.
    Don't let a large bribe turn you ˌto evil waysˌ.

19 Will your riches save you from having to suffer?
    Will all your mighty strength help you?

20 Don't look forward to the night,

when people disappear from their places.

21 Be careful! Don't turn to evil,
because you have chosen evil instead of suffering.*

22 "God does great things by his power.
Is there any teacher like him?
23 Who can tell him which way he should go?
Who can say to him, 'You did wrong'?
24 Remember that you should praise his work.
People have sung about it.
25 Every person has seen it.
Mortals have looked at it from a distance.

26 "Certainly, God is so great
that he is beyond our understanding.
The number of his years cannot be counted.
27 He collects drops of water.
He distills rain from his mist,
28 which then drips from the clouds.
It pours down on many people.
29 Can anyone really understand how clouds spread out
or how he thunders from his dwelling place?
30 Look, he scatters his flashes of lightning around him
and covers the depths of the sea.
31 This is how he uses the rains to provide for people
and to give them more than enough food.
32 He fills his hands with lightning
and orders it to hit the target.
33 The thunder announces his coming.
The storm announces his angry wrath.

Elihu Continues: God's Ways Are Beyond Human Understanding

37 1 "My heart pounds because of this
and jumps out of its place.
2 Listen! Listen to the roar of God's voice,
to the rumbling that comes from his mouth.
3 He flashes his lightning everywhere under heaven.
His light flashes to the ends of the earth.
4 It is followed by the roar of his voice.
He thunders with his majestic voice.
He doesn't hold the lightning back when his thunder is heard.
5 God's voice thunders in miraculous ways.
It does great things that we cannot understand.

6 "He says to the snow, 'Fall to the ground,'
and to the pouring rain, 'Rain harder!'
7 He makes it impossible to do anything*
so that people will recognize his work.

---

* 36:21 Hebrew meaning of verses 17-21 uncertain. The first two words of verse 18 (in Hebrew) were added to the end of verse 17 to express the complex Hebrew sentence structure more clearly in English.   * 37:7 Or "He seals up every person's hand."

8 Animals go into their dens
  and stay in their lairs.
9 A storm comes out of its chamber.
  It is cold because of the strong winds.[b]
10 God's breath produces ice,
   and the seas freeze over.
11 Yes, he loads the thick clouds with moisture
   and scatters his lightning from the clouds.
12 He guides the clouds as they churn round and round
   over the face of the inhabited earth
   to do everything he orders them.
13 Whether for discipline,
   or for ˌthe good ofˌ his earth,
   or out of mercy,
   he makes the storm appear.

14 "Open your ears to this, Job.
   Stop and consider God's miracles.
15 Do you know how God controls them
   and makes the lightning flash from his clouds?
16 Do you know how the clouds drift
   (these are the miracles of the one who knows everything),
17 you whose clothes are hot and sweaty,
   when the earth is calm under a south wind?
18 Can you stretch out the skies with him
   and make them as firm as a mirror made of metal?
19 Teach us what we should say to him.
   We are unable to prepare ˌa caseˌ because of darkness.
20 Should he be told that I want to speak?
   Can a person speak when he is confused?
21 People can't look at the sun
   when it's bright among the clouds
   or after the wind has blown and cleared those clouds away.
22 A golden light comes from the north.
   A terrifying majesty is around God.
23 The Almighty, whom we can't reach,
   is great in power and judgment,
   has more than enough righteousness,
   and does not oppress.
24 That is why people should fear him.
   He does not respect those who think they're wise."

The LORD Speaks
Who Is Able to Challenge Me?

38 ¹Then the LORD answered Job out of the storm.

2 "Who is this that belittles my advice
   with words that do not show any knowledge ˌabout itˌ?
3 Brace yourself like a man!
   I will ask you, and you will teach me.

---

[b]37:9 Hebrew meaning uncertain.

The LORD Speaks About Creation

4 "Where were you when I laid the foundation of the earth?
   Tell me if you have ˌsuchˌ insight.

5 Who determined its dimensions?
   Certainly, you know!
Who stretched a measuring line over it?

6 On what were its footings sunk?
Who laid its cornerstone

7   when the morning stars sang together
     and all the sons of God shouted for joy?

8 "Who shut the sea behind gates
   when it burst through and came out of the womb,

9   when I clothed it with clouds
    and wrapped it up in dark clouds,

10 when I set a limit for it
    and put up bars and gates,

11 when I said, 'You may come this far but no farther.
    Here your proud waves will stop'?

12 "Have you ever given orders to the morning
   or assigned a place for the dawn

13   so that it could grab the earth by its edges
      and shake wicked people out of it?

14 The earth changes like clay stamped by a seal,
   and ˌparts of itˌ stand out like ˌfolds inˌ clothing.

15 Wicked people are deprived of their light,
   and an arm raised ˌin victoryˌ is broken.

16 Have you gone to the springs in the sea
   or walked through the valleys of the ocean depths?

17 Have the gateways to death been revealed to you,
   or have you seen the gateways to total darkness?

18 Have you ˌevenˌ considered how wide the earth is?
   Tell me, if you know all of this!

19 "What is the way to the place where light lives?
   Where is the home of darkness

20   so that you may lead it to its territory,
      so that you may know the path to its home?

21 You must know because you were born then
   and have lived such a long time!

22 Have you been to the warehouses where snow is stored
   or seen the warehouses for hail

23   that I have stored up for the time of trouble,
      for the day of battle and war?

24 Which is the way to the place where light is scattered
   and the east wind is spread across the earth?

25 "Who made a channel for the flooding rains
   and a path for the thunderstorms

26   to bring rain on a land where no one lives,
      on a desert where there are no humans,

27   to saturate the desolate wasteland
         in order to make it sprout with grass?
28   Does the rain have a father?
       Who gave birth to the dewdrops?
29   From whose womb came the ice,
       and who has given birth to the frost in the air?
30   The water hardens like a stone,
         and the surface of the ocean freezes over.

31   "Can you connect the chains of the constellation Pleiades
       or untie the ropes of Orion?
32   Can you bring out the constellations at the right time
       or guide Ursa Major with its cubs?
33   Do you know the laws of the sky
       or make them rule the earth?
34   Can you call to the clouds
       and have a flood of water cover you?
35   Can you send lightning flashes so that they may go and say to you,
       'Here we are'?
36   Who put wisdom in the heart
       or gave understanding to the mind?[a]
37   Who is wise enough to count the clouds
       or pour out the water jars of heaven
38   when the dirt hardens into clumps
         and the soil clings together?

The Lioness

39   "Can you hunt prey for the lioness
       and satisfy the hunger of her cubs
40   as they crouch in their dens
         and lie ready to ambush from their lairs?

The Crow

41   "Who provides food for the crow
       when its young ones cry to God
       and wander around in need of food?

The LORD Continues: The Mountain Goats

39 ¹   "Do you know the time when the mountain goats give birth?
Do you watch the does when they are in labor?
2   Can you count the months they are pregnant
       or know the time when they'll give birth?
3   They kneel down to give birth and deliver their young.
         Then the pain of giving birth is over.
4   Their young are healthy and grow up in the wild.
         They leave and don't come back.

---

[a] 38:36 Hebrew meaning uncertain.

The Wild Donkey

5 "Who lets the wild donkey go free?
Who unties the ropes of the wild donkey?

6   I gave it the desert to live in
and the salt flats as its dwelling place.

7   It laughs at the noise of the city
and doesn't even listen to the shouting of its master.

8   It explores the mountains for its pasture
and looks for anything green.

The Wild Ox

9 "Will the wild ox agree to serve you,
or will it stay at night beside your feeding trough?

10   Can you guide a wild ox in a furrow,
or will it plow the valleys behind you?

11   Can you trust it just because it's so strong
or leave your labor to it?

12   Can you rely on it to bring your grain back
and take it to your threshing floor?[a]

The Ostrich

13 "Does the ostrich flap its wings in joy,
or do its wings lack feathers?[b]

14   It lays its eggs on the ground
and warms them in the dust.

15   It forgets that a foot may crush them
or a wild animal may trample them.

16   It acts harshly toward its young as if they weren't its own.
It is not afraid that its work is for nothing

17   because God has deprived it of wisdom
and did not give it any understanding.

18   It laughs at the horse and its rider when it gets up to flee.

The Horse

19 "Can you give strength to a horse
or dress its neck with a flowing mane?

20   Can you make it leap like a locust,
when its snorting causes terror?

21   It paws in strength and finds joy in its power.
It charges into battle.

22   It laughs at fear,
is afraid of nothing,
and doesn't back away from swords.

23   A quiver of arrows rattles on it
along with the flashing spear and javelin.

24   Anxious and excited, the horse eats up the ground
and doesn't trust the sound of the ram's horn.

25   As often as the horn sounds, the horse says, 'Aha!'

---

[a] 39:12 A threshing floor is an outdoor area where grain is separated from its husks.   [b] 39:13 Or "Do its wings compare well with the wings and feathers of the stork?"

and it smells the battle far away—
the thundering ,orders, of the captains and the battle cries.

The Birds of Prey

26 "Does your understanding make a bird of prey fly
and spread its wings toward the south?
27 Is it by your order that the eagle flies high
and makes its nest on the heights?
28 It perches for the night on a cliff.
Its fortress is on a jagged peak.
29 From there it seeks food,
and its eyes see it from far away.
30 Its young ones feed on blood.
It is found wherever there are dead bodies."

The LORD Speaks

40 ¹The LORD responded to Job,

2 "Will the person who finds fault with the Almighty correct him?
Will the person who argues with God answer him?"

Job Speaks

³Job answered the LORD,

4 "I'm so insignificant. How can I answer you?
I will put my hand over my mouth.
5 I spoke once, but I can't answer—
twice, but not again."

The LORD Speaks
Can You Be Like Me, Job?

⁶Then the LORD responded to Job out of a storm,

7 "Brace yourself like a man!
I will ask you, and you will teach me.

8 "Would you undo my justice?
Would you condemn me so that you can be righteous?
9 Do you have power like God's?
Can you thunder with a voice like his?
10 Then dress yourself in majesty and dignity.
Clothe yourself in splendor and glory.
11 Unleash your outbursts of anger.
Look at all who are arrogant, and put them down.
12 Look at all who are arrogant, and humble them.
Crush wicked people wherever they are.
13 Hide them completely in the dust,
and cover their faces in the hidden place.
14 Then even I will praise you
because your right hand can save you.

Can You Conquer Behemoth, Job?

15 "Look at Behemoth,ᵃ which I made along with you.
  It eats grass as cattle do.

16 Look at the strength in its back muscles,
  the power in its stomach muscles.

17 It makes its tail stiff like a cedar.
  The ligaments of its thighs are intertwined.

18 Its bones are bronze tubes.
  They are like iron bars.

19 Behemoth is the first of God's conquests.
  Its maker approaches it with his sword.

20 The hills bring it food,
  and all the wild animals play there.

21 It lies down under the lotus plants
  in a hiding place among reeds and swamps.

22 Lotus plants provide it with cover.
  Poplars by the stream surround it.

23 Though the river flows powerfully against it, it's not alarmed.
  It's confident even, when the Jordan rushes against its mouth.

24 Can anyone blind its eyesᵇ
  or pierce its nose with snares?

The LORD Continues: Can You Conquer Leviathan, Job?

41

ᵃ1 "Can you pull Leviathanᵇ out of the water with a fishhook
  or tie its tongue down with a rope?

2 Can you put a ring through its nose
  or pierce its jaw with a hook?

3 Will it plead with you for mercy
  or speak tenderly to you?

4 Will it make an agreement with you
  so that you can take it as your permanent slave?

5 Can you play with it like a bird
  or keep it on a leash for your girls?

6 Will traders bargain over it
  and divide it among the merchants?

7 Can you fill its hide with harpoons
  or its head with fishing spears?

8 Lay your hand on it.
  Think of the struggle!
  Don't do it again!

9 Certainly, any hope of defeating it is a false hope.
  Doesn't the sight of it overwhelm you?

10 No one is brave enough to provoke Leviathan.
  Then who can stand in front of me?ᶜ

11 Who can confront me that I should repay him?
  Everything under heaven belongs to me!

ᵃ40:15 The Hebrew word [Behemoth] means "beast, animal." ᵇ40:24 Or "catch it with a trap." ᵃ41:1 Job 41:1-34 in English Bibles is Job 40:25–41:26 in the Hebrew Bible. ᵇ41:1 Hebrew meaning uncertain. ᶜ41:10 Some Hebrew manuscripts; many Hebrew manuscripts "it."

12 "I will not be silent about Leviathan's limbs,
    its strength, or its graceful form.
13 Who can skin its hide?
    Who can approach it with a harness?
14 Who can open its closed mouth?
    Its teeth are surrounded by terror.
15 Its back has rows of scales that are tightly sealed.
16   One is so close to the other
        that there is no space between them.
17   Each is joined to the other.
        They are locked together and inseparable.
18 When Leviathan sneezes, it gives out a flash of light.
    Its eyes are like the first rays of the dawn.
19   Flames shoot from its mouth.
        Sparks of fire fly from it.
20   Smoke comes from its nostrils
        like a boiling pot heated over brushwood.
21 Its breath sets coals on fire,
    and a flame pours from its mouth.
22 Strength resides in its neck,
    and power dances in front of it.
23 The folds of its flesh stick to each other.
    They are solid and cannot be moved.
24 Its chest is solid like a rock,
    solid like a millstone.

25 "The mighty are afraid when Leviathan rises.
    Broken down, they draw back.
26 A sword may strike it but not pierce it.
    Neither will a spear, lance, or dart.
27   It considers iron to be like straw
        and bronze to be like rotten wood.
28 An arrow won't make it run away.
    Stones from a sling turn to dust against it.
29   It considers clubs to be like stubble,
        and it laughs at a rattling javelin.
30 Its underside is like sharp pieces of broken pottery.
    It stretches out like a threshing*d* sledge on the mud.
31   It makes the deep sea boil like a pot.
        It stirs up the ocean like a boiling kettle.
32   It leaves a shining path behind it
        so that the sea appears to have silvery hair.
33 Nothing on land can compare to it.
    It was made fearless.
34 It looks down on all high things.
    It is king of everyone who is arrogant."

---

*d*41:30 Threshing is the process of beating stalks to separate them from the grain.

Job Speaks
I Admit That I Was Wrong

42 ¹Then Job answered the LORD,

² "I know that you can do everything
   and that your plans are unstoppable.

³ "You said, 'Who is this that belittles my advice
   without having any knowledge about it?'
      Yes, I have stated things I didn't understand,
         things too mysterious for me to know.

⁴ "You said, 'Listen now, and I will speak.
   I will ask you, and you will teach me.'

⁵   I had heard about you with my own ears,
            but now I have seen you with my own eyes.

⁶   That is why I take back what I said,
            and I sit in dust and ashes to show that I am sorry."

Job's Life Is Restored

⁷After the LORD had said those things to Job, the LORD said to Eliphaz from Teman, "I'm very angry with you and your two friends because you didn't speak what is right about me as my servant Job has done. ⁸So take seven young bulls and seven rams. Go to my servant Job, and make a burnt offering for yourselves. My servant Job will pray for you. Then I will accept his prayer not to treat you as godless fools. After all, you didn't speak what is right about me as my servant Job has done."

⁹Then Eliphaz of Teman, Bildad of Shuah, and Zophar of Naama went and did what the LORD had told them to do. And the LORD accepted Job's prayer.

¹⁰After Job prayed for his friends, the LORD restored Job's prosperity and gave him twice as much as he had before. ¹¹Then all his brothers and sisters and everyone who had previously known him came to him. They ate with him at his house, sympathized with him, and comforted him for all the evil the LORD had brought to him. Each one gave him some money[a] and a gold ring.

¹²The LORD blessed the latter years of Job's life more than the earlier years. He had 14,000 sheep and goats, 6,000 camels, 2,000 oxen, and 1,000 donkeys. ¹³He also had seven sons and three daughters. ¹⁴He named the first daughter Jemimah, the second Cassia, and the third Keren Happuch. ¹⁵Nowhere in the whole country could be found women who were as beautiful as Job's daughters. Their father gave them and their brothers an inheritance.

¹⁶Job lived 140 years after this. He saw his children, grandchildren, and great-grandchildren.[b] ¹⁷Then at a very old age, Job died.

---

[a] 42:11 Hebrew meaning uncertain.   [b] 42:16 Or "grandchildren, four generations."

AN INTRODUCTION TO
Psalms

Psalms is a book of poems written to and about God. David wrote 73 of the 150 psalms. Some of the psalms are songs for praising God and remembering his goodness. In other psalms, the writers tell about sad, happy, and even angry feelings. By reading Psalms, we can learn how to pray and express our thoughts and feelings to our loving Lord.

Headlines

God Made Us Special!
Psalm 8, page 715

David Sings Love Song
Psalm 18, page 722

God Cleans Up Born Sinner
Psalm 51, page 755

God Is Your Guardian
Psalm 121, page 833

Brothers and Sisters in Harmony!
Psalm 133, page 838

God Knows All About You
Psalm 139, page 842

What's it like "when brothers and sisters live together in harmony"? See Psalm 133.

Write Your
Own Psalm

Many of the psalms praise God. In fact, the Jewish name for Psalms is "The Book of Praises."

You can praise God by writing your own psalm. First read Psalms 103 and 148. These are good examples of praise psalms. Then go outside and take a look around you. What do you see that shows God's wisdom? What do you see that shows God's care for creation? What do you see that is beautiful? What has God created that makes you feel happy? Put these things in a poem to God.

Congratulations! You've just made your own psalm!

What Do People Think of God?

Polls have shown that most people in the United States believe in God. But when they say "God," what do they mean? Do they think of God as some distant power? Do they see God as a kind old grandfather up in heaven? The book of Psalms tells us a lot about God. It describes who God is and describes our relationship with him.

God is our rock (Psalm 28). He is firm, strong, and trustworthy. God is our shepherd (Psalm 23). He leads us and takes care of us. God is our stronghold (Psalm 144). He protects us from harm. And God is our savior (Psalm 88). He rescues us and saves our lives.

We can learn a lot from Psalms about our relationship with God. Isn't it great to have a God who is our rock, our shepherd, our stronghold, and our savior, too?

What's In It For Me?

Psalms teaches me . . .

I CAN TALK TO HIM ABOUT EVERYTHING.

GOD KNOWS ALL THAT IS IN MY MIND.

GOD PROTECTS ME AND CARES FOR ME.

GOD IS MY FATHER, AND I AM HIS CHILD.

GOD LOVES ME, AND I LOVE HIM.

RIDDLE:
What's the subject of the longest song in the world?

God's great love. The song lasts forever. (See Psalm 89:1.)

In Bible times people loved riddles.
Here are some riddles to try out on
your friends or your parents.

RIDDLES:

*What does the
fool say to
himself?*

There is no God.
(See Psalm 14:1.)

*Why are believers
brighter than
unbelievers?*

Because the Lord
is their light.
(See Psalm 27:1.)

*What can God
clean that you
can't even touch?*

Your heart.
(See Psalm 51:10.)

God Has Feelings, Too

Some people think of God as a strange being who isn't like us at all. But the Bible says that God created us in his image (Genesis 1:27). He made us with feelings because he has feelings, too.

The Lord feels anger when someone is greedy (Psalm 78:29-31). He feels merciful toward people who are discouraged (Psalm 42:8). Most of all, the Lord feels love and compassion for people who obey him (Psalm 103:13). Because God has feelings like we do, we can know that when we tell him all our feelings, he will understand.

Psalm 119

Psalm 119 praises the word of God.
Why is God's word "a lamp for my feet
and a light for my path" (verse 105)?
The Bible . . .

is a true and trustworthy guide (verses 149-151).

guides us away from wickedness (verse 110).

gives blessings to those who obey God (verses 1-3).

brings the believer happiness (verse 77).

leads us to an everlasting reward (verse 112).

Psalms

BOOK ONE
Psalms 1–41

Psalm 1

1   Blessed is the person who does not
       follow the advice of wicked people,
          take the path of sinners,
             or join the company of mockers.
2   Rather, he delights in the teachings of the Lord
       and reflects on his teachings day and night.
3   He is like a tree planted beside streams—
       a tree that produces fruit in season
          and whose leaves do not wither.
    He succeeds in everything he does.[a]

4   Wicked people are not like that.
    Instead, they are like husks that the wind blows away.
5   That is why wicked people will not be able to stand in the judgment
          and sinners will not be able to stand where righteous people gather.

6   The Lord knows the way of righteous people,
       but the way of wicked people will end.

Psalm 2

1   Why do the nations gather together?
    Why do their people devise useless plots?
2   Kings take their stands.
       Rulers make plans together
          against the Lord and against his Messiah[a] by saying,
3   "Let's break apart their chains
             and shake off their ropes."

4   The one enthroned in heaven laughs.
    The Lord makes fun of them.
5   Then he speaks to them in his anger.
       In his burning anger he terrifies them by saying,
6   "I have installed my own king on Zion, my holy mountain."

7   I will announce the Lord's decree.
    He said to me:
       "You are my Son.

---

[a] 1:3 Or "and its leaves do not wither, and whatever it produces thrives."   [a] 2:2 Or "anointed one."

Today I have become your Father.
8   Ask me, and I will give you the nations as your inheritance
and the ends of the earth as your own possession.
9   You will break them with an iron scepter.
You will smash them to pieces like pottery."

10   Now, you kings, act wisely.
Be warned, you rulers of the earth!
11   Serve the Lord with fear, and rejoice with trembling.
12   Kiss the Son, or he will become angry
and you will die on your way
because his anger will burst into flames.
Blessed is everyone who takes refuge in him.

Psalm 3

A psalm by David when he fled from his son Absalom.

1   O Lord, look how my enemies have increased!
Many are attacking me.
2   Many are saying about me,
"Even with God on his side,
he won't be victorious."   *Selah*

3   But you, O Lord, are a shield that surrounds me.
You are my glory.
You hold my head high.

4   I call aloud to the Lord,
and he answers me from his holy mountain.   *Selah*
5   I lie down and sleep.
I wake up again because the Lord continues to support me.
6   I am not afraid of the tens of thousands
who have taken positions against me on all sides.

7   Arise, O Lord!
Save me, O my God!
You have slapped all my enemies in the face.
You have smashed the teeth of wicked people.
8   Victory belongs to the Lord!
May your blessing rest on your people.   *Selah*

Psalm 4

For the choir director; with stringed instruments; a psalm by David.

1   Answer me when I call, O God of my righteousness.
You have freed me from my troubles.
Have pity on me, and hear my prayer!

2   You important people,
how long are you going to insult my honor?
How long are you going to love what is empty
and seek what is a lie?   *Selah*

3 Know that the LORD singles out godly people for himself.
  The LORD hears me when I call to him.
4 Tremble and do not sin.
  Think about this on your bed and remain quiet.   *Selah*
5 Offer the sacrifices of righteousness
  by trusting the LORD.

6 Many are saying, "Who can show us anything good?"
  Let the light of your presence shine on us, O LORD.
7 You put more joy in my heart
  than when their grain and new wine increase.
8 I fall asleep in peace the moment I lie down
  because you alone, O LORD, enable me to live securely.

Psalm 5

For the choir director; for flutes; a psalm by David.

1 Open your ears to my words, O LORD.
  Consider my innermost thoughts.
2 Pay attention to my cry for help, my king and my God,
  because I pray only to you.
3 In the morning, O LORD, hear my voice.
  In the morning I lay my needs in front of you,
  and I wait.

4 You are not a God who takes pleasure in wickedness.
  Evil will never be your guest.
5 Those who brag cannot stand in your sight.
  You hate all troublemakers.
6 You destroy those who tell lies.
  The LORD is disgusted with bloodthirsty and deceitful people.

7 But I will enter your house because of your great mercy.
  Out of reverence for you, I will bow toward your holy temple.
8 O LORD, lead me in your righteousness because of those who spy on me.
  Make your way in front of me smooth.

9 Nothing in their mouths is truthful.
  Destruction comes from their hearts.
  Their throats are open graves.
  They flatter with their tongues.

10 Condemn them, O God.
   Let their own schemes be their downfall.
   Throw them out for their many crimes
   because they have rebelled against you.
11 But let all who take refuge in you rejoice.
   Let them sing with joy forever.
   Protect them, and let those who love your name triumph in you.
12 You bless righteous people, O LORD.
   Like a large shield, you surround them with your favor.

Psalm 6

For the choir director; with stringed instruments, on the *sheminith;*[a] a psalm by David.

1 O Lord, do not punish me in your anger
or discipline me in your rage.
2 Have pity on me, O Lord, because I am weak.
Heal me, O Lord, because my bones shake with terror.
3 My soul has been deeply shaken with terror.
But you, O Lord, how long. . . ?
4 Come back, O Lord.
Rescue me.
Save me because of your mercy!
5 In death, no one remembers you.
In the grave, who praises you?
6 I am worn out from my groaning.
My eyes flood my bed every night.
I soak my couch with tears.
7 My eyes blur from grief.
They fail because of my enemies.
8 Get away from me, all you troublemakers,
because the Lord has heard the sound of my crying.
9 The Lord has heard my plea for mercy.
The Lord accepts my prayer.
10 All my enemies will be put to shame and deeply shaken with terror.
In a moment they will retreat and be put to shame.

Psalm 7

A *shiggaion*[a] by David; he sang it to the Lord about the slanderous words of Cush, a descendant of Benjamin.

1 O Lord my God, I have taken refuge in you.
Save me, and rescue me from all who are pursuing me.
2 Like a lion they will tear me to pieces
and drag me off with no one to rescue me.
3 O Lord my God,
if I have done this—
if my hands are stained with injustice,
4 if I have paid back my friend with evil
or rescued someone who has no reason to attack me—[b]
5 then let the enemy chase me and catch me.
Let him trample my life into the ground.
Let him lay my honor in the dust. *Selah*
6 Arise in anger, O Lord.
Stand up against the fury of my attackers.
Wake up, my God.[c]

---

[a]6:1 Unknown musical term.   [a]7:1 Unknown musical term.   [b]7:4 Hebrew meaning of this line uncertain.
[c]7:6 Greek; Masoretic Text "Wake up to me."

You have already pronounced judgment.
    Let an assembly of people gather around you.
        Take your seat high above them.
8   The LORD judges the people of the world.
Judge me, O LORD,
        according to my righteousness,
        according to my integrity.

9   Let the evil within wicked people come to an end,
        but make the righteous person secure,
            O righteous God who examines thoughts and emotions.
10   My shield is God above,
        who saves those whose motives are decent.

11   God is a fair judge,
        a God who is angered by injustice every day.
12   If a person does not change, God sharpens his sword.
            By bending his bow, he makes it ready to shoot.
13   He prepares his deadly weapons
            and turns them into flaming arrows.
14   See how that person conceives evil,
        is pregnant with harm,
            and gives birth to lies.
15   He digs a pit and shovels it out.
        Then he falls into the hole that he made for others.
16   His mischief lands back on his own head.
His violence comes down on top of him.

17   I will give thanks to the LORD for his righteousness.
I will make music to praise the name of the LORD Most High.

Psalm 8

For the choir director; on the *gittith*;[a] a psalm by David.

1   O LORD, our Lord, how majestic is your name throughout the earth!

Your glory is sung above the heavens.[b]
2   From the mouths of little children and infants,
        you have built a fortress against your opponents
        to silence the enemy and the avenger.

3   When I look at your heavens,
        the creation of your fingers,
            the moon and the stars that you have set in place—
4   what is a mortal that you remember him
            or the Son of Man that you take care of him?
5   You have made him a little lower than yourself.
            You have crowned him with glory and honor.
6   You have made him rule what your hands created.
            You have put everything under his control:
7   all the sheep and cattle, the wild animals,

---

a8:1 Unknown musical term.   b8:1 Hebrew meaning of this line uncertain.

8   the birds, the fish,
         whatever swims in the currents of the seas.

9   O L ORD , our Lord, how majestic is your name throughout the earth!

Psalm 9

For the choir director; according to *muth labben;*[a] a psalm by David.[b]

1   I will give you, thanks, O L ORD ,
         with all my heart.
    I will tell about all the miracles
         you have done.
2   I will find joy and be glad
         about you.
    I will make music to praise
         your name, O Most High.

3   When my enemies retreat,
         they will stumble
         and die in your presence.
4   You have defended
         my just cause:
    You sat down on your throne
         as a fair judge.
5   You condemned nations.
    You destroyed
         wicked people.
    You wiped out their names
         forever and ever.
6   The enemy is finished—
         in ruins forever.
    You have uprooted their cities.
    Even the memory of them
         has faded.

7   Yet, the L ORD is enthroned
         forever.
    He has set up his throne
         for judgment.
8   He alone judges the world with righteousness.
    He judges its, people fairly.
9   The L ORD is a stronghold for the oppressed,
         a stronghold in times of trouble.
10   Those who know your name trust you, O L ORD ,
         because you have never deserted those who seek your help.
11   Make music to praise the L ORD , who is enthroned in Zion.
         Announce to the nations what he has done.

God's World

Psalm 8:3-8

God made people special. Because we are so special, God lets us take care of the world he made. There are things you can do to help take care of your world. You can take good care of your pets.

You can do your part to protect the plants and animals that make our world such a wonderful place. You can also start recycling. Can you think of other ways you can help take care of God's world?

be all you can be

---

a 9:1 Or *"almuth labben"*; unknown musical term.   b 9:1 Some Hebrew manuscripts, Greek, and Latin treat Psalms 9 and 10 as one psalm.

12 The one who avenges murder has remembered oppressed people.
He has never forgotten their cries.
13 Have pity on me, O LORD.
Look at what I suffer because of those who hate me.
You take me away from the gates of death
14 so that I may recite your praises one by one
in the gates of Zion
and find joy in your salvation.

15 The nations have sunk into the pit they have made.
Their feet are caught in the net they have hidden ˻to trap others˼.
16 The LORD is known by the judgment he has carried out.
The wicked person is trapped
by the work of his own hands. *Higgaion Selah*
17 Wicked people, all the nations who forget God,
will return to the grave.
18 Needy people will not always be forgotten.
Nor will the hope of oppressed people be lost forever.
19 Arise, O LORD.
Do not let mortals gain any power.
Let the nations be judged in your presence.
20 Strike them with terror, O LORD.
Let the nations know that they are ˻only˼ mortal. *Selah*

Psalm 10

1 Why are you so distant, LORD?
Why do you hide yourself in times of trouble?

2 The wicked person arrogantly pursues oppressed people.
He will be caught in the schemes that he planned.
3 The wicked person boasts about his selfish desires.
He blesses robbers, but he curses the LORD.
4 He turns up his nose ˻and says˼, "God doesn't care."
His every thought ˻concludes˼, "There is no God."
5 He always seems to succeed.
Your judgments are beyond his understanding.
He spits at all his opponents.
6 He says to himself, "Nothing can shake me.
I'll never face any trouble."
7 His mouth is full of cursing, deception, and oppression.
Trouble and wrongdoing are on the tip of his tongue.
8 He waits in ambush in the villages.
From his hiding places he kills innocent people.
His eyes are on the lookout for victims.
9 He lies in his hiding place like a lion in his den.
He hides there to catch oppressed people.
He catches oppressed people when he draws them into his net.
10 ˻His˼ victims are crushed.
They collapse,
and they fall under ˻the weight of˼ his power.

11 He says to himself,
   "God has forgotten.
   He has hidden his face.
   He will never see it!"

12 Arise, O Lord!
   Lift your hand, O God.
   Do not forget oppressed people!
13   Why does the wicked person despise God?
   Why does he say to himself, "God doesn't care"?
14 You have seen it.; yes, you have taken note of trouble and grief
   and placed them under your control.
   The victim entrusts himself to you.
You alone have been the helper of orphans.
15   Break the arm of the wicked and evil person.
   Punish his wickedness until you find no more.

16 The Lord is king forever and ever.
   The nations have vanished from his land.
17 You have heard the desire of oppressed people, O Lord.
   You encourage them.
You pay close attention to them
18   in order to provide justice for orphans and oppressed people
   so that no mere mortal will terrify them again.

Psalm 11

For the choir director; by David.

1 I have taken refuge in the Lord.
   How can you say to me:
   "Flee to your mountain like a bird?
2   Wicked people bend their bows.
     They set their arrows against the strings
      to shoot in the dark at people whose motives are decent.
3   When the foundations ,of life, are undermined,
     what can a righteous person do?"

4 The Lord is in his holy temple.
The Lord's throne is in heaven.
   His eyes see.
   They examine Adam's descendants.
5 The Lord tests righteous people,
   but he hates wicked people and the ones who love violence.
6   He rains down fire and burning sulfur upon wicked people.
   He makes them drink from a cup filled with scorching wind.
7 The Lord is righteous.
   He loves a righteous way of life.
   Decent people will see his face.

Psalm 12

For the choir director; on the *sheminith*; a psalm by David.

1 Help, O LORD.
   No godly person is left.
   Faithful people have vanished from among Adam's descendants!
2 All people speak foolishly.
   They speak with flattering lips. They say one thing but mean another.
3 May the LORD cut off every flattering lip
   and every bragging tongue
4   that has said,
        "We will overcome with our tongues.
        With lips such as ours, who can be our master?"

5 "Because oppressed people are robbed and needy people groan,
   I will now arise," says the LORD.
   "I will provide safety for those who long for it."
6 The promises of the LORD are pure,
   like silver refined in a furnace[a] and purified seven times.
7 O LORD, you will protect them.
   You will keep each one safe from those people forever.
8   Wicked people parade around
        when immorality increases among Adam's descendants.

Psalm 13

For the choir director; a psalm by David.

1 How long, O LORD? Will you forget me forever?
   How long will you hide your face from me?
2 How long must I make decisions alone
   with sorrow in my heart day after day?
   How long will my enemy triumph over me?

3 Look at me! Answer me, O LORD my God!
   Light up my eyes,
   or else I will die
4   and my enemy will say, "I have overpowered him."
        My opponents will rejoice because I have been shaken.

5 But I trust your mercy.
   My heart finds joy in your salvation.
6 I will sing to the LORD because he has been good to me.

Psalm 14[a]

For the choir director; by David.

1 Godless fools say in their hearts,
      "There is no God."
   They are corrupt.
   They do disgusting things.

---

[a] 12:6 Hebrew meaning uncertain.   [a] 14:1 Psalm 14 is virtually identical in wording to Psalm 53.

There is no one who does good things.

2 The LORD looks down from heaven on Adam's descendants
    to see if there is anyone who acts wisely,
        if there is anyone who seeks help from God.

3 Everyone has turned away.
    Together they have become rotten to the core.
        No one, not even one person, does good things.

4 Are all those troublemakers,
    those who devour my people as if they were devouring food,
        so ignorant that they do not call on the LORD?

5 There they are—panic-stricken
    because God is with the person who is righteous.

6 They put the advice of oppressed people to shame
    because the LORD is their refuge.

7 If only salvation for Israel would come from Zion!
When the LORD restores the fortunes of his people,
    Jacob will rejoice.
    Israel will be glad.

Psalm 15

A psalm by David.

1 O LORD, who may stay in your tent?
Who may live on your holy mountain?

2 The one who walks with integrity,
    does what is righteous,
    and speaks the truth within his heart.

3 The one who does not slander with his tongue,
    do evil to a friend,
    or bring disgrace on his neighbor.

4 The one who despises those rejected by God
    but honors those who fear the LORD.

The one who makes a promise and does not break it,
    even though he is hurt by it.

5 The one who does not collect interest on a loan
    or take a bribe against an innocent person.

Whoever does these things will never be shaken.

Psalm 16

A *miktam*[a] by David.

1 Protect me, O God, because I take refuge in you.
2 I said to the LORD,
    "You are my Lord. Without you, I have nothing good."
3 Those who lead holy lives on earth

---

[a] 16:1 Unknown musical term.

are the noble ones who fill me with joy.[b]
4 Those who quickly chase after other gods multiply their sorrows.
I will not pour out their sacrificial offerings of blood
or use my lips to speak their names.

5 The LORD is my inheritance and my cup.
You are the one who determines my destiny.
6 Your boundary lines mark out pleasant places for me.
Indeed, my inheritance is something beautiful.

7 I will praise the LORD, who advises me.
My conscience warns me at night.
8 I always keep the LORD in front of me.
When he is by my side, I cannot be moved.
9 That is why my heart is glad and my soul rejoices.
My body rests securely
10 because you do not abandon my soul to the grave
or allow your holy one to decay.
11 You make the path of life known to me.
Complete joy is in your presence.
Pleasures are by your side forever.

Psalm 17

A prayer by David.

1 Hear my plea for justice, O LORD.
Pay attention to my cry.
Open your ears to my prayer,
which comes from lips free from deceit.
2 Let the verdict of my innocence come directly from you.
Let your eyes observe what is fair.

3 You have probed my heart.
You have confronted me at night.
You have tested me like silver,
but you found nothing wrong.
I have determined that my mouth will not sin.
4 I have avoided cruelty because of your word.
In spite of what others have done,
5 my steps have remained firmly in your paths.
My feet have not slipped.
6 I have called on you because you answer me, O God.
Turn your ear toward me.
Hear what I have to say.
7 Reveal your miraculous deeds of mercy,
O Savior of those who find refuge by your side
from those who attack them.
8 Guard me as if I were the pupil in your eye.
Hide me in the shadow of your wings.

---

[b]16:3 English equivalent of this verse difficult.

9   Hide me from wicked people who violently attack me,
        from my deadly enemies who surround me.
10   They have shut out all feeling.ᵃ
        Their mouths have spoken arrogantly.
11   They have tracked me down.
        They have surrounded me.
        They have focused their attention on throwing me to the ground.
12   Each one of them is like a lion eager to tear its prey apart
            and like a young lion crouching in hiding places.

13   Arise, O Lord; confront them!
        Bring them to their knees!
        With your sword rescue my life from wicked people.
14   With your power rescue me from mortals, O Lord,
            from mortals who enjoy their inheritance only in this life.
            You fill their bellies with your treasure.
            Their children are satisfied with it,
                and they leave what remains to their children.

15   I will see your face when I am declared innocent.
        When I wake up, I will be satisfied with seeing you.

Psalm 18ᵃ

For the choir director; by David, the servant of the Lord. He sang this song to the Lord when the Lord rescued him from all his enemies, especially from Saul. He said,

1   I love you, O Lord, my strength.
2   The Lord is my rock and my fortress and my Savior,
        my God, my rock in whom I take refuge,
            my shield, and the strength of my salvation,
                my stronghold.
3   The Lord should be praised.
        I called on him, and I was saved from my enemies.

4   The ropes of death had become tangled around me.
        The torrents of destruction had overwhelmed me.
5   The ropes of the grave had surrounded me.
            The clutches of death had confronted me.

6   I called on the Lord in my distress.
        I cried to my God for help.
            He heard my voice from his temple,
                and my cry for help reached his ears.

7   Then the earth shook and quaked.
        Even the foundations of the mountains trembled.
            They shook violently because he was angry.
8   Smoke went up from his nostrils,
        and a raging fire came out of his mouth.
            Glowing coals flared up from it.

ᵃ17:10 Hebrew meaning uncertain.   ᵃ18:1 Psalm 18 is virtually identical in wording to 2 Samuel 22.

⁹ He spread apart the heavens
    and came down with a dark cloud under his feet.
¹⁰ He rode on one of the angels*ᵇ* as he flew,
    and he soared on the wings of the wind.
¹¹ He made the darkness his hiding place,
    the dark rain clouds his covering.
¹² Out of the brightness in front of him,
    those rain clouds passed by with hailstones and lightning.
¹³ The Lord thundered in the heavens.
    The Most High made his voice heard with hailstones and lightning.
¹⁴ He shot his arrows and scattered them.
    He flashed streaks of lightning and threw them into confusion.
¹⁵   Then the ocean floor could be seen.
    The foundations of the earth were laid bare
        at your stern warning, O Lord,
        at the blast of the breath from your nostrils.

¹⁶ He reached down from high above and took hold of me.
    He pulled me out of the raging water.
¹⁷ He rescued me from my strong enemy
    and from those who hated me,
        because they were too strong for me.
¹⁸ On the day when I faced disaster, they confronted me,
    but the Lord came to my defense.
¹⁹   He brought me out to a wide-open place.
    He rescued me because he was pleased with me.

²⁰ The Lord rewarded me
    because of my righteousness,
    because my hands are clean.
He paid me back
²¹   because I have kept the ways of the Lord
    and I have not wickedly turned away from my God,
²² because all his judgments are in front of me
    and I have not turned away from his laws.
²³   I was innocent as far as he was concerned.
    I have kept myself from guilt.
²⁴ The Lord paid me back
    because of my righteousness,
    because he can see that my hands are clean.

²⁵ ⌞In dealing⌟ with faithful people you are faithful,
    with innocent people you are innocent,
²⁶   with pure people you are pure.
⌞In dealing⌟ with devious people you are clever.

²⁷ You save humble people,
    but you bring down a conceited look.
²⁸ O Lord, you light my lamp.
    My God turns my darkness into light.

ᵇ 18:10 Or "cherubim."

29   With you I can attack a line of soldiers.
With my God I can break through barricades.

30   God's way is perfect!
The promise of the Lord has proven to be true.
He is a shield to all those who take refuge in him.

31   Who is God but the Lord?
Who is a rock except our God?

32   God arms me with strength
and makes my way perfect.

33   He makes my feet like those of a deer
and gives me sure footing on high places.

34   He trains my hands for battle
so that my arms can bend an archer's bow of bronze.

35   You have given me the shield of your salvation.
Your right hand supports me.
Your gentleness makes me great.

36   You make a wide path for me to walk on
so that my feet do not slip.

37   I chased my enemies and caught up with them.
I did not return until I had ended their lives.

38   I wounded them so badly that they were unable to get up.
They fell under my feet.

39   You armed me with strength for battle.
You made my opponents bow at my feet.

40   You made my enemies turn their backs to me,
and I destroyed those who hated me.

41   They cried out for help, but there was no one to save them.
They cried out to the Lord, but he did not answer them.

42   I beat them into a powder as fine as the dust blown by the wind.
I threw them out as though they were dirt on the streets.

43   You rescued me from my conflicts with the people.
You made me the leader of nations.
A people I did not know will serve me:

44   As soon as they hear of me, they will obey me.
Foreigners will cringe in front of me.

45   Foreigners will lose heart,
and they will tremble when they come out of their fortifications.

46   The Lord lives!
Thanks be to my rock!
May God my Savior be honored.

47   God gives me vengeance!
He brings people under my authority.

48   He saves me from my enemies.
You lift me up above my opponents.
You rescue me from violent people.

49   That is why I will give thanks to you, O Lord, among the nations
and make music to praise your name.

⁵⁰ He gives great victories to his king.
He shows mercy to his anointed,
   to David, and to his descendant*c* forever.

Psalm 19

For the choir director; a psalm by David.

¹ The heavens declare the glory of God,
   and the sky displays what his hands have made.
² One day tells a story to the next.
One night shares knowledge with the next
³   without talking,
   without words,
   without their voices being heard.
⁴ ⌞Yet,⌟ their sound has gone out into the entire world,
   their message to the ends of the earth.
He has set up a tent in the heavens for the sun,
⁵   which comes out of its chamber like a bridegroom.
      Like a champion, it is eager to run its course.
⁶   It rises from one end of the heavens.
      It circles around to the other.
         Nothing is hidden from its heat.

⁷ The teachings of the LORD are perfect.
   They renew the soul.
The testimony of the LORD is dependable.
   It makes gullible people wise.
⁸ The instructions of the LORD are correct.
   They make the heart rejoice.
The command of the LORD is radiant.
   It makes the eyes shine.
⁹ The fear of the LORD is pure.
   It endures forever.
The decisions of the LORD are true.
   They are completely fair.
¹⁰ They are more desirable than gold, even the finest gold.
They are sweeter than honey, even the drippings from a honeycomb.
¹¹   As your servant I am warned by them.
      There is a great reward in following them.

¹² Who can notice every mistake?
   Forgive my hidden faults.
¹³   Keep me from sinning.
Do not let anyone gain control over me.
   Then I will be blameless,
      and I will be free from any great offense.

¹⁴ May the words from my mouth and the thoughts from my heart
   be acceptable to you, O LORD, my rock and my defender.

---

c 18:50 Or "to his descendants."

Psalm 20

For the choir director; a psalm by David.

1 The LORD will answer you in times of trouble.
   The name of the God of Jacob will protect you.
2 He will send you help from his holy place
    and support you from Zion.
3 He will remember all your grain offerings
    and look with favor on your burnt offerings.   *Selah*
4 He will give you your heart's desire
    and carry out all your plans.

5 We will joyfully sing about your victory.
   We will wave our flags in the name of our God.
   The LORD will fulfill all your requests.

6 Now I know that the LORD will give victory to his anointed king.
    He will answer him from his holy heaven
      with mighty deeds of his powerful hand.
7 Some rely on chariots and others on horses,
    but we will boast in the name of the LORD our God.
8   They will sink to their knees and fall,
      but we will rise and stand firm.

9 Give victory to the king, O LORD.
   Answer us when we call.

Psalm 21

For the choir director; a psalm by David.

1 The king finds joy in your strength, O LORD.
    What great joy he has in your victory!
2 You gave him his heart's desire.
    You did not refuse the prayer from his lips.   *Selah*
3 You welcomed him with the blessings of good things
    and set a crown of fine gold on his head.
4 He asked you for life.
    You gave him a long life, forever and ever.
5 Because of your victory his glory is great.
   You place splendor and majesty on him.
6   Yes, you made him a blessing forever.
    You made him glad with the joy of your presence.
7   Indeed, the king trusts the LORD,
      and through the mercy of the Most High, he will not be moved.

8 Your hand will discover all your enemies.
   Your powerful hand will find all who hate you.
9   When you appear, you will make them burn like a blazing furnace.
     The LORD will swallow them up in his anger.
       Fire will devour them.
10   You will destroy their children from the earth
    and their offspring from among Adam's descendants.

11 Although they scheme and plan evil against you,
    they will not succeed.
12 They turn their backs and flee,
    because you aim your bow at their faces.[a]

13 Arise, O Lord, in your strength.
We will sing and make music to praise your power.

Psalm 22

For the choir director; according to *ayyeleth hashachar;*[a] a psalm by David.

1 My God, my God,
    why have you abandoned me?
    Why are you so far away from helping me,
        so far away from the words of my groaning?
2 My God,
    I cry out by day, but you do not answer—
        also at night, but I find no rest.

3 Yet, you are holy, enthroned on the praises of Israel.
4 Our ancestors trusted you.
    They trusted, and you rescued them.
5   They cried to you and were saved.
    They trusted you and were never disappointed.

6 Yet, I am a worm and not a man.
I am scorned by humanity and despised by people.
7 All who see me make fun of me.
    Insults pour from their mouths.
    They shake their heads and say,
8   "Put yourself in the Lord's hands.
        Let the Lord save him!
        Let God rescue him since he is pleased with him!"
9 Indeed, you are the one who brought me out of the womb,
    the one who made me feel safe at my mother's breasts.
10 I was placed in your care from birth.
    From my mother's womb you have been my God.

11 Do not be so far away from me.
    Trouble is near, and there is no one to help.
12   Many bulls have surrounded me.
        Strong bulls from Bashan have encircled me.
13   They have opened their mouths to attack me
        like ferocious, roaring lions.
14 I am poured out like water,
    and all my bones are out of joint.
        My heart is like wax.
        It has melted within me.
15 My strength is dried up like pieces of broken pottery.
My tongue sticks to the roof of my mouth.

---

[a]21:12 Hebrew meaning of this verse uncertain.   [a]22:1 Unknown musical term.

You lay me down in the dust of death.
16 Dogs have surrounded me.
A mob has encircled me.
They have pierced my hands and feet.
17   I can count all my bones.
People stare.
They gloat over me.
18 They divide my clothes among themselves.
They throw dice for my clothing.

19 Do not be so far away, O LORD.
Come quickly to help me, O my strength.
20 Rescue my soul from the sword,
my life from vicious dogs.
21 Save me from the mouth of the lion
and from the horns of wild oxen.

You have answered me.

22 I will tell my people about your name.
I will praise you within the congregation.
23 All fear the LORD, praise him!
All you descendants of Jacob, glorify him!
Stand in awe of him, all you descendants of Israel.
24 The LORD has not despised or been disgusted
with the plight of the oppressed one.
He has not hidden his face from that person.
The LORD heard when that oppressed person
cried out to him for help.
25 My praise comes from you while I am among those assembled for worship.
I will fulfill my vows in the presence of those who fear the LORD.
26 Oppressed people will eat until they are full.
Those who look to the LORD will praise him.
May you live forever.
27 All the ends of the earth will remember and return to the LORD.
All the families from all the nations will worship you
28 because the kingdom belongs to the LORD
and he rules the nations.
29 All prosperous people on earth will eat and worship.
All those who go down to the dust will kneel in front of him,
even those who are barely alive.
30 There will be descendants who serve him,
a generation that will be told about the Lord.
31 They will tell people yet to be born about his righteousness—
that he has finished it.

Psalm 23

A psalm by David.

1   The LORD is my shepherd.
I am never in need.

2 He makes me lie down in green pastures.
He leads me beside peaceful waters.
3 He renews my soul.
He guides me along the paths of righteousness
for the sake of his name.
4 Even though I walk through the dark valley of death,
because you are with me, I fear no harm.
Your rod and your staff give me courage.

5 You prepare a banquet for me while my enemies watch.
You anoint my head with oil.
My cup overflows.

6 Certainly, goodness and mercy will stay close to me all the days of my life,
and I will remain in the LORD's house for days without end.

Psalm 24

A psalm by David.

1 The earth and everything it contains are the LORD's.
The world and all who live in it are his.
2 He laid its foundation on the seas
and set it firmly on the rivers.

3 Who may go up the LORD's mountain?
Who may stand in his holy place?
4 The one who has clean hands and a pure heart
and does not long for what is false*
or lie when he is under oath.
5 This person will receive a blessing from the LORD
and righteousness from God, his savior.
6 This is the person who seeks him,
who searches for the face of the God of Jacob.*   *Selah*

7 Lift your heads, you gates.
Be lifted, you ancient doors,
so that the king of glory may come in.

8 Who is this king of glory?
The LORD, strong and mighty!
The LORD, heroic in battle!

9 Lift your heads, you gates.
Be lifted, you ancient doors,
so that the king of glory may come in.

10 Who, then, is this king of glory?
The LORD of Armies is the king of glory!   *Selah*

---

*24:4 Hebrew meaning uncertain.   *24:6 A few Hebrew manuscripts, Greek, Syriac; Masoretic Text "your face, Jacob."

Psalm 25[a]

By David.

1 To you, O LORD, I lift my soul.
2 I trust you, O my God.
     Do not let me be put to shame.
     Do not let my enemies triumph over me.
3 No one who waits for you will ever be put to shame,
     but all who are unfaithful will be put to shame.
4 Make your ways known to me, O LORD,
     and teach me your paths.
5 Lead me in your truth and teach me
     because you are God, my savior.
       I wait all day long for you.
6 Remember, O LORD, your compassionate and merciful deeds.
     They have existed from eternity.
7 Do not remember the sins of my youth or my rebellious ways.
     Remember me, O LORD, in keeping with your mercy and your goodness.

8 The LORD is good and decent.
     That is why he teaches sinners the way they should live.
9 He leads humble people to do what is right,
     and he teaches them his way.
10 Every path of the LORD is ˌone ofˌ mercy and truth
     for those who cling to his promise[b] and written instructions.

11 For the sake of your name, O LORD,
     remove my guilt, because it is great.
12 Who, then, is this person that fears the LORD?
     He is the one whom the LORD will teach which path to choose.
13 He will enjoy good things in life,
     and his descendants will inherit the land.
14 The LORD advises those who fear him.
     He reveals to them the intent of his promise.

15 My eyes are always on the LORD.
     He removes my feet from traps.
16 Turn to me, and have pity on me.
     I am lonely and oppressed.
17 Relieve my troubled heart,
     and bring me out of my distress.
18 Look at my misery and suffering,
     and forgive all my sins.
19 See how my enemies have increased in number,
     how they have hated me with vicious hatred!
20 Protect my life, and rescue me!
     Do not let me be put to shame.
       I have taken refuge in you.
21 Integrity and honesty will protect me because I wait for you.
22 Rescue Israel, O God, from all its troubles!

---

[a] 25:1 Psalm 25 is a poem in Hebrew alphabetical order.   [b] 25:10 Or "covenant."

Psalm 26

By David.

1   Judge me favorably, O LORD,
      because I have walked with integrity
      and I have trusted you without wavering.
2   Examine me, O LORD, and test me.
   Look closely into my heart and mind.
3   I see your mercy in front of me.
      I walk in the light of your truth.
4   I did not sit with liars,
         and I will not be found among hypocrites.
5   I have hated the mob of evildoers
         and will not sit with wicked people.
6   I will wash my hands in innocence.
   I will walk around your altar, O LORD,
7   so that I may loudly sing a hymn of thanksgiving
         and tell about all your miracles.

8   O LORD, I love the house where you live,
      the place where your glory dwells.

9   Do not sweep away my soul along with hardened sinners
      or my life along with bloodthirsty people.
10   Evil schemes are in their hands.
      Their right hands are full of bribes.
11 But I walk with integrity.
   Rescue me, and have pity on me.
12 My feet stand on level ground.
   I will praise the LORD with the choirs in worship.

Psalm 27

By David.

1   The LORD is my light and my salvation.
      Who is there to fear?
   The LORD is my life's fortress.
      Who is there to be afraid of?

2   Evildoers closed in on me to tear me to pieces.
      My opponents and enemies stumbled and fell.
3   Even though an army sets up camp against me,
         my heart will not be afraid.
      Even though a war breaks out against me,
         I will still have confidence in the LORD.

4   I have asked one thing from the LORD.
   This I will seek:
      to remain in the LORD's house all the days of my life
         in order to gaze at the LORD's beauty
         and to search for an answer in his temple.
5   He hides me in his shelter when there is trouble.

He keeps me hidden in his tent.
He sets me high on a rock.

6　Now my head will be raised above my enemies who surround me.
I will offer sacrifices with shouts of joy in his tent.
I will sing and make music to praise the LORD.

7　Hear, O LORD, when I cry aloud.
Have pity on me, and answer me.

8　When you said,
"Seek my face,"
my heart said to you,
"O LORD, I will seek your face."[a]

9　Do not hide your face from me.
Do not angrily turn me away.
You have been my help.
Do not leave me!
Do not abandon me, O God, my savior!

10　Even if my father and mother abandon me,
the LORD will take care of me.

11　Teach me your way, O LORD.
Lead me on a level path
because I have enemies who spy on me.

12　Do not surrender me to the will of my opponents.
False witnesses have risen against me.
They breathe out violence.

13　I believe that I will see the goodness of the LORD
in this world of the living.

14　Wait with hope for the LORD.
Be strong, and let your heart be courageous.
Yes, wait with hope for the LORD.

Psalm 28

By David.

1　O LORD, I call to you.
O my rock, do not turn a deaf ear to me.
If you remain silent,
I will be like those who go into the pit.

2　Hear my prayer for mercy when I call to you for help,
when I lift my hands toward your most holy place.

3　Do not drag me away with wicked people,
with troublemakers who speak of peace with their neighbors
but have evil in their hearts.

4　Pay them back for what they have done,
for their evil deeds.
Pay them back for what their hands have done,
and give them what they deserve.

---

[a] 27:8 Hebrew meaning uncertain; Greek "My heart said to you, 'I have sought your face. O LORD, I will seek your face.'"

5 The Lord will tear them down and never build them up again,
  because they never consider what he has done
    or what his hands have made.

6 Thank the Lord!
  He has heard my prayer for mercy!
7 The Lord is my strength and my shield.
  My heart trusted him, so I received help.
  My heart is triumphant; I give thanks to him with my song.

8 The Lord is the strength of his people
  and a fortress for the victory of his Messiah.[a]
9 Save your people, and bless those who belong to you.
  Be their shepherd, and carry them forever.

Psalm 29

A psalm by David.

1 Give to the Lord, you heavenly beings.
  Give to the Lord glory and power.
2 Give to the Lord the glory his name deserves.
  Worship the Lord in ⌊his⌋ holy splendor.

3 The voice of the Lord rolls over the water.
    The God of glory thunders.
    The Lord shouts over raging water.
4 The voice of the Lord is powerful.
  The voice of the Lord is majestic.
5 The voice of the Lord breaks the cedars.
    The Lord splinters the cedars of Lebanon.
6   He makes Lebanon skip along like a calf
      and Mount Sirion like a wild ox.
7 The voice of the Lord strikes with flashes of lightning.
8 The voice of the Lord makes the wilderness tremble.
    The Lord makes the wilderness of Kadesh tremble.
9 The voice of the Lord splits the oaks[a]
    and strips ⌊the trees of⌋ the forests bare.
    Everyone in his temple is saying, "Glory!"

10 The Lord sat enthroned over the flood.
   The Lord sits enthroned as king forever.
11 The Lord will give power to his people.
   The Lord will bless his people with peace.

Psalm 30

A psalm by David sung at the dedication of the temple.

1 I will honor you highly, O Lord,
    because you have pulled me out ⌊of the pit⌋,
    and have not let my enemies rejoice over me.

---

[a]28:8 Or "anointed one."   [a]29:9 Hebrew meaning of "splits the oaks" uncertain.

Dancing / *Psalm 30*

In Bible times, Hebrew men and women danced in separate groups. The people danced to celebrate military victories. They danced at weddings. And the Israelites danced when they came to Jerusalem to worship the Lord.

Hebrew words for dancing describe the dancer leaping, skipping, whirling, twisting, and turning. God's people danced enthusiastically to express great joy in many areas of life.

2 O Lord my God,
     I cried out to you for help,
       and you healed me.
3 O Lord, you brought me up from the grave.
     You called me back to life
       from among those who had gone into the pit.
4 Make music to praise the Lord, you faithful people who belong to him.
     Remember his holiness by giving thanks.
5 His anger lasts only a moment.
     His favor lasts a lifetime.
       Weeping may last for the night,
         but there is a song of joy in the morning.

6 When all was well with me, I said,
     "I will never be shaken."
7 O Lord, by your favor you have made my mountain stand firm.
     When you hid your face, I was terrified.
8 I will cry out to you, O Lord.
     I will plead to the Lord for mercy:
9   "How will you profit if my blood is shed,
         if I go into the pit?
       Will the dust of my body give thanks to you?
       Will it tell about your truth?"
10 Hear, O Lord, and have pity on me!
     O Lord, be my helper!
11 You have changed my sobbing into dancing.
     You have removed my sackcloth and clothed me with joy

¹² so that my soul*^a may praise you with music and not be silent.
O Lord my God, I will give thanks to you forever.

Psalm 31

For the choir director; a psalm by David.

¹ I have taken refuge in you, O Lord.
    Never let me be put to shame.
        Save me because of your righteousness.
²   Turn your ear toward me.
    Rescue me quickly.
    Be a rock of refuge for me,
        a strong fortress to save me.
³ Indeed, you are my rock and my fortress.
    For the sake of your name, lead me and guide me.
⁴   You are my refuge,
        so pull me out of the net that they have secretly laid for me.
⁵   Into your hands I entrust my spirit.
        You have rescued me, O Lord, God of truth.

⁶ I hate those who cling to false gods, but I trust the Lord.
⁷ I will rejoice and be glad because of your mercy.
    You have seen my misery.
    You have known the troubles in my soul.
⁸   You have not handed me over to the enemy.
    You have set my feet in a place where I can move freely.

⁹ Have pity on me, O Lord, because I am in distress.
    My eyes, my soul, and my body waste away from grief.
¹⁰ My life is exhausted from sorrow,
    my years from groaning.
    My strength staggers under the weight of my guilt,
    and my bones waste away.
¹¹ I have become a disgrace because of all my opponents.
    I have become someone dreaded by my friends, even by my neighbors.
    Those who see me on the street run away from me.
¹² I have faded from memory as if I were dead
    and have become like a piece of broken pottery.
¹³ I have heard the whispering of many people—
    terror on every side—
        while they made plans together against me.
        They were plotting to take my life.

¹⁴ I trust you, O Lord.
    I said, "You are my God."

¹⁵ My future is in your hands.
    Rescue me from my enemies, from those who persecute me.
¹⁶   Smile on me.
    Save me with your mercy.

---

*30:12 Or "glory."

17 O Lord, I have called on you, so do not let me be put to shame.
Let wicked people be put to shame.
Let them be silent in the grave.

18 Let their lying lips be speechless,
  since they speak against righteous people with arrogance and contempt.

19 Your kindness is so great!
  You reserve it for those who fear you.
    Adam's descendants watch
    as you show it to those who take refuge in you.

20 You hide them in the secret place of your presence
  from those who scheme against them.
  You keep them in a shelter,
    safe from quarrelsome tongues.

21 Thank the Lord!
  He has shown me the miracle of his mercy
  in a city under attack.

22 When I was panic-stricken, I said,
  "I have been cut off from your sight."
  But you heard my pleas for mercy when I cried out to you for help.

23 Love the Lord, all you godly ones!
  The Lord protects faithful people,
    but he pays back in full those who act arrogantly.

24 Be strong, all who wait with hope for the Lord,
  and let your heart be courageous.

Psalm 32

A psalm by David; a *maskil*.[a]

1 Blessed is the person whose disobedience is forgiven
  and whose sin is pardoned.

2 Blessed is the person whom the Lord no longer accuses of sin
  and who has no deceitful thoughts.

3 When I kept silent about my sins,
  my bones began to weaken because of my groaning all day long.

4 Day and night your hand lay heavily on me.
  My strength shriveled in the summer heat.   *Selah*

5 I made my sins known to you, and I did not cover up my guilt.
  I decided to confess them to you, O Lord.
    Then you forgave all my sins.   *Selah*

6 For this reason let all godly people pray to you
  when you may be found.
    Then raging floodwater will not reach them.

7 You are my hiding place.
  You protect me from trouble.
  You surround me with joyous songs of salvation.   *Selah*

---

a 32:1 Unknown musical term.

8 ⌞The LORD says,⌟
    "I will instruct you.
    I will teach you the way that you should go.
    I will advise you as my eyes watch over you.
9 Don't be stubborn like a horse or mule.
    ⌞They need⌟ a bit and bridle
        in their mouth
            to restrain them,
        or they will not come
            near you."

10 Many heartaches
        await wicked people,
    but mercy surrounds those
        who trust the LORD.

11 Be glad and find joy in the LORD,
        you righteous people.
    Sing with joy, all whose motives
        are decent.

Psalm 33

1 Joyfully sing to the LORD,
        you righteous people.
    Praising ⌞the LORD⌟ is proper
        for decent people.
2 Give thanks with a lyre
        to the LORD.
    Make music for him
        on a ten-stringed harp.
3 Sing a new song to him.
    Play beautifully and joyfully
        on stringed instruments.

4 The word of the LORD is correct,
        and everything he does
            is trustworthy.
5 The LORD loves righteousness and justice.
        His mercy fills the earth.
6 The heavens were made by the word of the LORD
        and all the stars by the breath of his mouth.
7 He gathers the water in the sea like a dam
        and puts the oceans in his storehouses.
8 Let all the earth fear the LORD.
    Let all who live in the world stand in awe of him.
9 He spoke, and it came into being.
    He gave the order, and there it stood.

10 The LORD blocks the plans of the nations.
    He frustrates the schemes of the people of the world.
11 The LORD's plan stands firm forever.

Prayer
Psalm 32

God will forgive you if you make the wrong choice. But it's better to make right choices. How can you know what is the right thing to do? God promises, "I will teach you the way that you should go" (verse 8). Ask God what he wants you to do. Read the Bible. And then choose to do right.

be all you can be

His thoughts stand firm in every generation.
12 Blessed is the nation whose God is the Lord.
Blessed are the people he has chosen as his own.
13 The Lord looks down from heaven.
He sees all of Adam's descendants.
14 From the place where he sits enthroned,
    he looks down upon all who live on earth.
15 The one who formed their hearts
    understands everything they do.

16 No king achieves a victory with a large army.
No warrior rescues himself by his own great strength.
17 Horses are not a guarantee for victory.
    Their great strength cannot help someone escape.
18 The Lord's eyes are on those who fear him,
    on those who wait with hope for his mercy
19   to rescue their souls from death
        and keep them alive during a famine.

20 We wait for the Lord.
He is our help and our shield.
21 In him our hearts find joy.
In his holy name we trust.
22 Let your mercy rest on us, O Lord,
    since we wait with hope for you.

Psalm 34 [a]

By David when he pretended to be insane in the presence of Abimelech; Abimelech threw him out, so David left.

1 I will thank the Lord at all times.
My mouth will always praise him.
2 My soul will boast about the Lord.
    Those who are oppressed will hear it and rejoice.
3 Praise the Lord's greatness with me.
Let us highly honor his name together.
4 I went to the Lord for help.
    He answered me and rescued me from all my fears.
5 All who look to him will be radiant. [b]
    Their faces will never be covered with shame.
6 Here is a poor man who called out.
    The Lord heard him and saved him from all his troubles.
7 The Messenger of the Lord camps around those who fear him,
    and he rescues them.
8 Taste and see that the Lord is good.
    Blessed is the person who takes refuge in him.
9 Fear the Lord, you holy people who belong to him.
    Those who fear him are never in need.

---

[a] 34:1 Psalm 34 is a poem in Hebrew alphabetical order.   [b] 34:5 Hebrew meaning uncertain.

10 Young lions go hungry and may starve,
　　but those who seek the Lord's help have all the good things they need.
11 Come, children, listen to me.
　　I will teach you the fear of the Lord.
12 Which of you wants a full life?
　　Who would like to live long enough to enjoy good things?
13 　　Keep your tongue from saying evil things
　　　　and your lips from speaking deceitful things.
14 　　Turn away from evil, and do good.
　　　　Seek peace, and pursue it!
15 The Lord's eyes are on righteous people.
　　His ears hear their cry for help.
16 The Lord confronts those who do evil
　　in order to wipe out all memory of them from the earth.
17 Righteous people cry out.
　　The Lord hears and rescues them from all their troubles.
18 The Lord is near to those whose hearts are humble.
　　He saves those whose spirits are crushed.
19 The righteous person has many troubles,
　　but the Lord rescues him from all of them.
20 　　The Lord guards all of his bones.
　　　　Not one of them is broken.
21 Evil will kill wicked people,
　　and those who hate righteous people will be condemned.
22 The Lord protects the souls of his servants.
　　All who take refuge in him will never be condemned.

Psalm 35

By David.

1 O Lord, attack those who attack me.
　　Fight against those who fight against me.
2 　　Use your shields, both small and large.
　　　　Arise to help me.
3 　　Hold your spear to block the way of those who pursue me.
　　　　Say to my soul, "I am your savior."

4 Let those who seek my life be put to shame and disgraced.
　　Let those who plan my downfall be turned back in confusion.
5 Let them be like husks blown by the wind
　　as the Messenger of the Lord chases them.
6 Let their path be dark and slippery
　　as the Messenger of the Lord pursues them.
7 For no reason they hid their net in a pit.
　　For no reason they dug the pit to trap me.
8 Let destruction surprise them.
　　Let the net that they hid catch them.
　　Let them fall into their own pit and be destroyed.
9 My soul will find joy in the Lord
　　and be joyful about his salvation.

10 All my bones will say, "O Lord, who can compare with you?
    You rescue the weak person from the one who is too strong for him
        and weak and needy people from the one who robs them."

11 Malicious people bring charges against me.
    They ask me things I know nothing about.
12 I am devastated
    because they pay me back with evil instead of good.
13 But when they were sick, I wore sackcloth.
    I humbled myself with fasting.
        When my prayer returned unanswered,
14   I walked around as if I were mourning for my friend or my brother.
        I was bent over as if I were mourning for my mother.

15 Yet, when I stumbled,
        they rejoiced and gathered together.
    They gathered together against me.
        Unknown attackers tore me apart without stopping.
16   With crude and abusive mockers,
            they grit their teeth at me.
17 O Lord, how long will you look on?
    Rescue me from their attacks.
    Rescue my precious life from the lions.
18   I will give you thanks in a large gathering.
    I will praise you in a crowd of worshipers.

19 Do not let my treacherous enemies gloat over me.
    Do not let those who hate me for no reason wink at me.
20   They do not talk about peace.
        Instead, they scheme against the peaceful people in the land.
21   They open their big mouths and say about me,
            "Aha! Aha! Our own eyes have seen it."
22 You have seen it, O Lord.
    Do not remain silent.
    O Lord, do not be so far away from me.
23   Wake up, and rise to my defense.
        Plead my case, O my God and my Lord.
24   Judge me by your righteousness, O Lord my God.
    Do not let them gloat over me
25   or think, "Aha, just what we wanted!"
    Do not let them say, "We have swallowed him up."
26 Let those who gloat over my downfall
        be thoroughly put to shame and confused.
    Let those who promote themselves at my expense
        be clothed with shame and disgrace.
27 Let those who are happy when I am declared innocent
        joyfully sing and rejoice.
    Let them continually say, "The Lord is great.
        He is happy when his servant has peace."
28 Then my tongue will tell about your righteousness,
        about your praise all day long.

Psalm 36

For the choir director; by David, the LORD's servant.

1 There is an inspired truth about the wicked person
who has rebellion in the depths of his heart:
He is not terrified of God.
2 He flatters himself and does not hate or ˌevenˌ recognize his guilt.
3 The words from his mouth are ˌnothing butˌ trouble and deception.
He has stopped doing what is wise and good.
4 He invents trouble while lying on his bed
and chooses to go the wrong direction.
He does not reject evil.

5 O LORD, your mercy reaches to the heavens,
your faithfulness to the skies.
6 Your righteousness is like the mountains of God,
your judgments like the deep ocean.
You save people and animals, O LORD.
7 Your mercy is so precious, O God,
that Adam's descendants take refuge
in the shadow of your wings.
8 They are refreshed with the rich foods in your house,
and you make them drink from the river of your pleasure.
9 Indeed, the fountain of life is with you.
In your light we see light.
10 Continue to show your mercy to those who know you
and your righteousness to those whose motives are decent.
11 Do not let the feet of arrogant people step on me
or the hands of wicked people push me away.
12 Look at the troublemakers who have fallen.
They have been pushed down and are unable to stand up again.

Psalm 37[a]

By David.

1 Do not be preoccupied with evildoers.
Do not envy those who do wicked things.
2 They will quickly dry up like grass
and wither away like green plants.
3 Trust the LORD, and do good things.
Live in the land, and practice being faithful.
4 Be happy with the LORD,
and he will give you the desires of your heart.
5 Entrust your ways to the LORD.
Trust him, and he will act ˌon your behalfˌ.
6 He will make your righteousness shine like a light,
your just cause like the noonday sun.
7 Surrender yourself to the LORD, and wait patiently for him.

_____

[a]37:1 Psalm 37 is a poem in Hebrew alphabetical order.

Do not be preoccupied with an evildoer, who succeeds in his way
    when he carries out his schemes.
8 Let go of anger, and leave rage behind.
    Do not be preoccupied.
      It only leads to evil.
9 Evildoers will be cut off
    from their inheritance,
    but those who wait with hope
      for the LORD
      will inherit the land.

10 In a little while a wicked person
    will vanish.
    Then you can carefully
      examine where he was,
    but there will be no trace
      of him.
11 Oppressed people
    will inherit the land
    and will enjoy unlimited peace.
12 The wicked person plots against
    a righteous one
    and grits his teeth at him.
13 The Lord laughs at him
    because he has seen
      that his time is coming.
14 Wicked people pull out their
      swords and bend their bows
    to kill oppressed
      and needy people,
    to slaughter those
      who are decent.
15 But their own swords
    will pierce their hearts,
    and their bows will be broken.

16 The little that the righteous person has is better
    than the wealth of many wicked people.
17 The arms of wicked people will be broken,
    but the LORD continues to support righteous people.
18 The LORD knows the daily struggles of innocent people.
    Their inheritance will last forever.
19 They will not be put to shame in trying times.
    Even in times of famine they will be satisfied.
20 But wicked people will disappear.
    The LORD's enemies will vanish like the best part of a meadow.
    They will vanish like smoke.
21 A wicked person borrows, but he does not repay.
    A righteous person is generous and giving.
22 Those who are blessed by him will inherit the land.
    Those who are cursed by him will be cut off.

Hatred

Psalm 37:1-9

Did you ever think (or even say out loud), "I hate him!" Or have you ever lain in bed thinking about what you would like to do to get back at someone? Psalm 37 tells us not to waste time thinking about evildoers. Our job is to trust the Lord and to do good things. Let go of your anger. Trust in God and be happy in him.

be all you can be

²³ A person's steps are directed by the LORD,
and the LORD delights in his way.
²⁴ When he falls, he will not be thrown down headfirst
because the LORD holds on to his hand.
²⁵ I have been young, and now I am old,
but I have never seen a righteous person abandoned
or his descendants begging for food.
²⁶ He is always generous and lends freely.
His descendants are a blessing.
²⁷ Avoid evil, do good, and live forever.
²⁸ The LORD loves justice,
and he will not abandon his godly ones.
They will be kept safe forever,
but the descendants of wicked people will be cut off.
²⁹ Righteous people will inherit the land
and live there permanently.
³⁰ The mouth of the righteous person reflects on wisdom.
His tongue speaks what is fair.
³¹ The teachings of his God are in his heart.
His feet do not slip.
³² The wicked person watches the righteous person
and seeks to kill him.
³³ But the LORD will not abandon him to the wicked person's power
or condemn him when he is brought to trial.
³⁴ Wait with hope for the LORD, and follow his path,
and he will honor you by giving you the land.
When wicked people are cut off, you will see it.

³⁵ I have seen a wicked person acting like a tyrant,
spreading himself out like a large cedar tree.
³⁶ But he moved on, and now there is no trace of him.
I searched for him, but he could not be found.
³⁷ Notice the innocent person,
and look at the decent person,
because the peacemaker has a future.
³⁸ But rebels will be completely destroyed.
The future of wicked people will be cut off.
³⁹ The victory for righteous people comes from the LORD.
He is their fortress in times of trouble.
⁴⁰ The LORD helps them and rescues them.
He rescues them from wicked people.
He saves them because they have taken refuge in him.

Psalm 38

A psalm by David; to be kept in mind.^a

¹ O LORD, do not angrily punish me
or discipline me in your wrath.

---

^a38:1 Hebrew meaning of "to be kept in mind" uncertain.

2 Your arrows have struck me.
 Your hand has struck me hard.
3 No healthy spot is left on my body
  because of your rage.
 There is no peace in my bones
  because of my sin.
4 My guilt has overwhelmed me.
 Like a heavy load, it is more than I can bear.
5 My wounds smell rotten.
 They fester because of my stupidity.
6 I am bent over and bowed down very low.
 All day I walk around in mourning.
7 My insides are filled with burning pain,
  and no healthy spot is left on my body.
8 I am numb and completely devastated.
 I roar because my heart's in turmoil.
9 You know all my desires, O Lord,
  and my groaning has not been hidden from you.
10 My heart is pounding.
  I have lost my strength.
   Even the light of my eyes has left me.
11 My loved ones and my friends keep their distance
  and my relatives stand far away because of my sickness.
12 Those who seek my life lay traps for me.
 Those who are out to harm me talk about ruining me.
  All day long they think of ways to deceive me.
13 But I am like a person who cannot hear
  and like a person who cannot speak.
14 I am like one who cannot hear
  and who can offer no arguments.
15 But I wait with hope for you, O Lord.
 You will answer, O Lord, my God.
16 I said, "Do not let them gloat over me.
  When my foot slips,
   do not let them promote themselves at my expense."
17 I am ready to fall.
 I am continually aware of my pain.
18 I confess my guilt.
 My sin troubles me.
19 My mortal enemies are growing stronger.
  Many hate me for no reason.
20 They pay me back with evil instead of good,
  and they accuse me because I try to do what is good.
21 Do not abandon me, O Lord.
 O my God, do not be so distant from me.
22 Come quickly to help me, O Lord, my savior.

Psalm 39

For the choir director; for Jeduthun; a psalm by David.

¹ I said,
  "I will watch my ways so that I do not sin with my tongue.
  I will bridle my mouth while wicked people are in my presence."
² I remained totally speechless.
  I kept silent, although it did me no good.
    While I was deep in thought, my pain grew worse.
³   My heart burned like a fire flaring up within me.
  Then I spoke with my tongue:
⁴   "Teach me, O Lᴏʀᴅ, about the end of my life.
  Teach me about the number of days I have left
    so that I may know how temporary my life is.
⁵ Indeed, you have made the length of my days only a few inches.
  My life span is nothing compared to yours.
  Certainly, everyone alive is like a whisper in the wind. *Selah*
⁶   Each person who walks around is like a shadow.
    They are busy for no reason.
      They accumulate riches without knowing who will get them."

⁷ And now, Lord, what am I waiting for?
  My hope is in you!
⁸ Rescue me from all my rebellious acts.
  Do not disgrace me in front of godless fools.
⁹ I remained speechless.
  I did not open my mouth
    because you are the one who has done this.
¹⁰ Remove the sickness you laid upon me.
  My life is over because you struck me with your hand.
¹¹ With stern warnings you discipline people for their crimes.
  Like a moth you eat away at what is dear to them.
  Certainly, everyone is like a whisper in the wind. *Selah*

¹² Listen to my prayer, O Lᴏʀᴅ.
  Open your ear to my cry for help.
  Do not be deaf to my tears,
    for I am a foreign resident with you,
      a stranger like all my ancestors.
¹³ Look away from me so that I may smile again
    before I go away and am no more.

Psalm 40

For the choir director; a psalm by David.

¹ I waited patiently for the Lᴏʀᴅ.
  He turned to me and heard my cry for help.
² He pulled me out of a horrible pit,
    out of the mud and clay.
  He set my feet on a rock
    and made my steps secure.

³   He placed a new song in my mouth,
      a song of praise to our God.
         Many will see this and worship.
         They will trust the Lord.

⁴ Blessed is the person
      who places his confidence in the Lord
         and does not rely on arrogant people
         or those who follow lies.

⁵ You have done many miraculous things, O Lord my God.
  You have made many wonderful plans for us.
      No one compares to you!
  I will tell others about your miracles,
      which are more than I can count.

⁶ You were not pleased with sacrifices and offerings.
  You have dug out two ears for me.ᵃ
  You did not ask for burnt offerings or sacrifices for sin.

⁷   Then I said, "I have come!
      (It is written about me in the scroll of the book.)

⁸   I am happy to do your will, O my God."
  Your teachings are deep within me.

⁹ I will announce the good news of righteousness
      among those assembled for worship.
         I will not close my lips.
            You know that, O Lord.

¹⁰ I have not buried your righteousness deep in my heart.
   I have been outspoken about your faithfulness and your salvation.
   I have not hidden your mercy and your truth
      from those assembled for worship.

¹¹ Do not withhold your compassion from me, O Lord.
   May your mercy and your truth always protect me.

¹²   Countless evils have surrounded me.
      My sins have caught up with me so that I can no longer see.
         They outnumber the hairs on my head.
            I have lost heart.

¹³ O Lord, please rescue me!
   Come quickly to help me, O Lord!ᵇ

¹⁴ Let all those who seek to end my life
      be confused and put to shame.
   Let those who want my downfall
      be turned back and disgraced.

¹⁵ Let those who say to me, "Aha! Aha!"
      be stunned by their own shame.

¹⁶ Let all who seek you rejoice and be glad because of you.
   Let those who love your salvation continually say,
      "The Lord is great!"

¹⁷ But I am oppressed and needy.
   May the Lord think of me.

ᵃ40:6 Hebrew meaning of this line uncertain. ᵇ40:13 Verses 13–17 are virtually identical in wording to Psalm 70.

You are my help and my savior.
O my God, do not delay!

Psalm 41

For the choir director; a psalm by David.

1 Blessed is the one who has concern for helpless people.
  The Lᴏʀᴅ will rescue him in times of trouble.
2 The Lᴏʀᴅ will protect him and keep him alive.
  He will be blessed in the land.
  Do not place him at the mercy of his enemies.
3 The Lᴏʀᴅ will support him on his sickbed.
  You will restore this person to health when he is ill.

4 I said, "O Lᴏʀᴅ, have pity on me!
  Heal my soul because I have sinned against you."
5 My enemies say terrible things about me:
  "When will he die, and when will his family name disappear?"
6 When one of them comes to visit me, he speaks foolishly.
  His heart collects gossip.
  ⌊Then⌋ he leaves to tell others.
7 Everyone who hates me whispers about me.
  They think evil things about me and say,
8 "A devilish disease has attached itself to him.
  He will never leave his sickbed."
9 Even my closest friend whom I trusted,
  the one who ate my bread,
  has lifted his heel against me.
10 Have pity on me, O Lᴏʀᴅ!
  Raise me up so that I can pay them back
11 and my enemy cannot shout in triumph over me.
  When you do this, I know that you are pleased with me.
12 You defend my integrity,
  and you set me in your presence forever.

13 Thank the Lᴏʀᴅ God of Israel through all eternity!
  Amen and amen!

BOOK TWO
Psalms 42–72

Psalm 42

For the choir director; a *maskil*ᵃ by Korah's descendants.

1 As a deer longs for flowing streams,
  so my soul longs for you, O God.

ᵃ42:1 Unknown musical term.

2   My soul thirsts for God, for the living God.
     When may I come to see God's face?
3   My tears are my food day and night.
     People ask me all day long, "Where is your God?"
4   I will remember these things as I pour out my soul:
     how I used to walk with the crowd
        and lead it in a procession to God's house.
         I sang songs of joy and thanksgiving
            while crowds of people celebrated a festival.

5   Why are you discouraged, my soul?
     Why are you so restless?
       Put your hope in God,
         because I will still praise him.
           He is my savior and my God.

6   My soul is discouraged.
     That is why I will remember you
       in the land of Jordan, on the peaks of Hermon, on Mount Mizar.
7   One deep sea calls to another at the roar of your waterspouts.
     All the whitecaps on your waves have swept over me.[b]
8   The Lord commands his mercy during the day,
     and at night his song is with me—
       a prayer to the God of my life.
9   I will ask God, my rock,
        "Why have you forgotten me?
        Why must I walk around in mourning
          while the enemy oppresses me?"
10   With a shattering blow to my bones,
        my enemies taunt me.
          They ask me all day long, "Where is your God?"

11   Why are you discouraged, my soul?
     Why are you so restless?
       Put your hope in God,
         because I will still praise him.
           He is my savior and my God.

Psalm 43

1   Judge me, O God,
     and plead my case against an ungodly nation.
   Rescue me from deceitful and unjust people.
2   You are my fortress, O God!
      Why have you rejected me?
      Why must I walk around in mourning
        while the enemy oppresses me?
3   Send your light and your truth.
     Let them guide me.
     Let them bring me to your holy mountain
       and to your dwelling place.

---

b 42:7 Hebrew meaning of this verse uncertain.

4 Then let me go to the altar of God, to God my highest joy,
   and I will give thanks to you on the lyre, O God, my God.

5 Why are you discouraged, my soul?
   Why are you so restless?
      Put your hope in God,
         because I will still praise him.
            He is my savior and my God.

Psalm 44

For the choir director; a *maskil* by Korah's descendants.

1 O God,
      we have heard it with our own ears.
      Our ancestors have told us
         about the miracle you performed in their day,
            in days long ago.
2 By your power you forced nations out of the land,
      but you planted our ancestors there.
   You shattered many groups of people,
      but you set our ancestors free.*
3 It was not with their swords that they took possession of the land.
   They did not gain victory with their own strength.
   It was your right hand, your arm,
      and the light of your presence that did it,
         because you were pleased with them.

4 You alone are my king, O God.
   You won those victories for Jacob.
5   With you we can walk over our enemies.
     With your name we can trample those who attack us.
6   I do not rely on my bow,
           and my sword will never save me.
7 But you saved us from our enemies.
   You put to shame those who hate us.
8 All day long we praise our God.
   We give thanks to you forever.   *Selah*

9 But now you have rejected and disgraced us.
      You do not even go along with our armies.
10   You make us retreat from the enemy.
         Those who hate us rob us at will.
11   You hand us over to be butchered like sheep
         and scatter us among the nations.
12   You sell your people for almost nothing,
         and at that price you have gained nothing.
13   You made us a disgrace to our neighbors
         and an object of ridicule and contempt to those around us.
14   You made our defeat a proverb among the nations
         so that people shake their heads at us.

---

*44:2 Or "and you sent them away."

¹⁵ All day long my disgrace is in front of me.
  Shame covers my face
¹⁶   because of the words of those who insult and slander us,
      because of the presence of the enemy and the avenger.

¹⁷ Although all of this happened to us,
  we never forgot you.
  We never ignored your promise.*ᵇ*
¹⁸ Our hearts never turned away.
  Our feet never left your path.
¹⁹ Yet, you crushed us in a place for jackals
  and covered us with the shadow of death.

²⁰ If we forgot the name of our God
  or stretched out our hands to pray to another god,
²¹   wouldn't God find out,
      since he knows the secrets in our hearts?
²² Indeed, we are being killed all day long because of you.
  We are thought of as sheep to be slaughtered.

²³ Wake up! Why are you sleeping, O Lord?
  Awake! Do not reject us forever!
²⁴   Why do you hide your face?
      Why do you forget our suffering and misery?
²⁵   Our souls are bowing in the dust.
      Our bodies cling to the ground.
²⁶   Arise! Help us!
         Rescue us because of your mercy!

Psalm 45

For the choir director; according to *shoshannim;*ᵃ a *maskil* by Korah's descendants; a love song.

¹ My heart is overflowing with good news.
  I will direct my song to the king.
  My tongue is a pen for a skillful writer.

² You are the most handsome of Adam's descendants.
    Grace is poured on your lips.
      That is why God has blessed you forever.
³ O warrior, strap your sword to your side
    with your splendor and majesty.
⁴ Ride on victoriously in your majesty
    for the cause of truth, humility, and righteousness.
  Let your right hand teach you awe-inspiring things.
⁵ Your arrows are sharp in the heart of the king's enemies.
    Nations fall beneath you.
⁶ Your throne, O God, is forever and ever.
  The scepter in your kingdom is a scepter for justice.
⁷ You have loved what is right and hated what is wrong.

ᵇ44:17 Or "covenant."   ᵃ45:1 Unknown musical term.

That is why God, your God, has anointed you,
    rather than your companions, with the oil of joy.
8 All your robes are fragrant, with myrrh, aloes, and cassia.
    From ivory palaces the music of stringed instruments delights you.
9 The daughters of kings are among your noble ladies.
    The queen takes her place at your right hand
      and wears gold from Ophir.

10 Listen, daughter! Look closely!
    Turn your ear toward me.
    Forget your people, and forget your father's house.
11   The king longs for your beauty.
      He is your Lord.
        Worship him.

12 The people of Tyre, the richest people,
    want to win your favor with a gift.
13 The daughter of the king is glorious inside the palace.
    Her dress is embroidered with gold.
14 Wearing a colorful gown, she is brought to the king.
    Her bridesmaids follow her.
      They will be brought to you.
15   With joy and delight they are brought in.
      They enter the palace of the king.

16 Your sons will take the place of your father.
    You will make them princes over the whole earth.

17 I will cause your name to be remembered throughout every generation.
    That is why the nations will give thanks to you forever and ever.

Psalm 46

For the choir director; a song by the descendants of Korah; according to *alamoth.*[a]

1 God is our refuge and strength,
    an ever-present help in times of trouble.
2 That is why we are not afraid
    even when the earth quakes
      or the mountains topple into the depths of the sea.
3   Water roars and foams,
      and mountains shake at the surging waves.   *Selah*

4 There is a river
    whose streams bring joy to the city of God,
      the holy place where the Most High lives.
5 God is in that city.
    It cannot fall.
      God will help it at the break of dawn.
6 Nations are in turmoil, and kingdoms topple.
      The earth melts at the sound of God's voice.

---

[a] 46:1 Unknown musical term.

7 The Lord of Armies is with us.
The God of Jacob is our stronghold. *Selah*

8 Come, see the works of the Lord,
the devastation he has brought to the earth.
9 He puts an end to wars all over the earth.
He breaks an archer's bow.
He cuts spears in two.
He burns chariots.
10 Let go of your concerns!
Then you will know that I am God.
I rule the nations.
I rule the earth.

11 The Lord of Armies is with us.
The God of Jacob is our stronghold. *Selah*

Psalm 47

For the choir director; a psalm by Korah's descendants.

1 Clap your hands, all you people.
Shout to God with a loud, joyful song.
2 We must fear the Lord, the Most High.
He is the great king of the whole earth.
3 He brings people under our authority
and puts nations under our feet.
4 He chooses our inheritance for us,
the pride of Jacob, whom he loved. *Selah*

5 God has gone up with a joyful shout.
The Lord has gone up with the sound of a ram's horn.
6 Make music to praise God.
Play music for him!
Make music to praise our king.
Play music for him!
7 God is the king of the whole earth.
Make your best music for him!
8 God rules the nations.
He sits upon his holy throne.

9 The influential people from the nations gather together
as the people of the God of Abraham.
The rulers of the earth belong to God.
He rules everything.

Psalm 48

A song; a psalm by Korah's descendants.

1 The Lord is great.
He should be highly praised.
His holy mountain is in the city of our God.

2　　　Its beautiful peak is the joy of the whole earth.
　　　　Mount Zion is on the northern ridge.
　　　　　It is the city of the great king.
3　　God is in its palaces.
　　He has proved that he is a stronghold.

4　　The kings have gathered.
　　　They marched together.
5　　　　When they saw Mount Zion,
　　　　　they were astonished.
　　　　　They were terrified and ran away in fear.
6　　　　　Trembling seized them
　　　　　　like the trembling that a woman experiences during labor.
7　　With the east wind you smash the ships of Tarshish.

8　　The things we had only heard about, we have now seen
　　　in the city of the Lord of Armies,
　　　　in the city of our God.
　　　　　God makes Zion stand firm forever.　　　　　　　*Selah*
9　　Inside your temple we carefully reflect on your mercy, O God.
10　　Like your name, O God,
　　　your praise reaches to the ends of the earth.
　　Your right hand is filled with righteousness.
11　　Let Mount Zion be glad
　　　and the cities of Judah rejoice
　　　　because of your judgments.

12　　Walk around Zion.
　　　Go around it.
　　　　Count its towers.
13　　　　Examine its embankments.
　　　　　Walk through its palaces.
　　Then you can tell the next generation,
14　　"This God is our God forever and ever.
　　　He will lead us beyond death."

Psalm 49

For the choir director; a psalm by Korah's descendants.

1　　Listen to this, all you people.
　　Open your ears, all who live in the world—
2　　　common people and important ones,
　　　　rich people and poor ones.
3　　My mouth will speak wise sayings,
　　　the insights I have carefully considered.
4　　I will turn my attention to a proverb.
　　I will explain my riddle with the music of a lyre.
5　　　Why should I be afraid in times of trouble,
　　　　when slanderers surround me with evil?
6　　　　They trust their riches
　　　　　and brag about their abundant wealth.

7 No one can ever buy back another person
    or pay God a ransom for his life.
8   The price to be paid for his soul is too costly.
        He must always give up
9   in order to live forever and never see the pit.

10 Indeed, one can see that wise people die,
    that foolish and stupid people meet the same end.
    They leave their riches to others.
11 Although they named their lands after themselves,
    their graves*ᵃ* have become their homes for ages to come,
    their dwelling places throughout every generation.

12 But mortals will not continue here with what they treasure.
    They are like animals that die.

13 This is the final outcome for fools and their followers
    who are delighted by what they say: *Selah*
14   Like sheep, they are driven to hell
        with death as their shepherd.
        (Decent people will rule them in the morning.)
    Their forms will decay in the grave,
        far away from their comfortable homes.
15 But God will buy me back from the power of hell
    because he will take me.   *Selah*
16 Do not be afraid when someone becomes rich,
    when the greatness of his house increases.
17   He will not take anything with him when he dies.
        His greatness cannot follow him.
18 Even though he blesses himself while he is alive
    (and they praise you when you do well for yourself),
19   he must join the generation of his ancestors,
        who will never see light again.

20 Mortals, with what they treasure, still don't have understanding.
    They are like animals that die.

Psalm 50

A psalm by Asaph.

1 The Lᴏʀᴅ, the only true God, has spoken.
    He has summoned the earth
        from where the sun rises to where it sets.
2 God shines from Zion,
    the perfection of beauty.
3 Our God will come and will not remain silent.
    A devouring fire is in front of him
        and a raging storm around him.
4 He summons heaven and earth to judge his people:
5   "Gather around me, my godly people
        who have made a pledge to me through sacrifices."

ᵃ 49:11 Greek, Syriac, Targum; Masoretic Text "their insides."

6 The heavens announce his righteousness
   because God is the judge.

Selah

7 "Listen, my people, and I will speak.
   Listen, Israel, and I will testify against you:
   I am God, your God!
8 I am not criticizing you for your sacrifices or burnt offerings,
   which are always in front of me.
9 ⌊But⌋ I will not accept ⌊another⌋ young bull from your household
   or a single male goat from your pens.
10 Every creature in the forest,
   ⌊even⌋ the cattle on a thousand hills, is mine.
11 I know every bird in the mountains.
   Everything that moves in the fields is mine.
12 If I were hungry, I would not tell you,
   because the world and all that it contains are mine.
13 Do I eat the meat of bulls or drink the blood of goats?
14 Bring ⌊your⌋ thanks to God as a sacrifice,
   and keep your vows to the Most High.
15 Call on me in times of trouble.
   I will rescue you, and you will honor me."

16 But God says to wicked people,
   "How dare you quote my decrees
   and mouth my promises!*
17 You hate discipline.
   You toss my words behind you.
18 When you see a thief, you want to make friends with him.
   You keep company with people who commit adultery.
19 You let your mouth say anything evil.
   Your tongue plans deceit.
20 You sit and talk against your own brother.
   You slander your own mother's son.
21 When you did these things, I remained silent.
   ⌊That⌋ made you think I was like you.
   I will argue my point with you
   and lay it all out for you to see.
22 Consider this, you people who forget God.
   Otherwise, I will tear you to pieces,
   and there will be no one left to rescue you.
23 Whoever offers thanks as a sacrifice honors me.
   I will let everyone who continues in my way
   see the salvation that comes from God."

Psalm 51

For the choir director; a psalm by David when the prophet Nathan came to him
after David's adultery with Bathsheba.

1 Have pity on me, O God, in keeping with your mercy.
   In keeping with your unlimited compassion, wipe out my rebellious acts.

---

*50:16 Or "covenant."

2 Wash me thoroughly from my guilt,
   and cleanse me from my sin.
3 I admit that I am rebellious.
   My sin is always in front of me.
4 I have sinned against you, especially you.
   I have done what you consider evil.
   So you hand down justice when you speak,
      and you are blameless when you judge.

5 Indeed, I was born guilty.
   I was a sinner when my mother
      conceived me.
6 Yet, you desire truth
      and sincerity.*
   Deep down inside me
      you teach me wisdom.
7 Purify me from sin with hyssop,*
      and I will be clean.*
   Wash me, and I will be
      whiter than snow.
8 Let me hear ⌊sounds of⌋ joy
      and gladness.
   Let the bones that you
      have broken dance.
9 Hide your face from my sins,
      and wipe out all
      that I have done wrong.

10 Create a clean heart in me,
      O God,
   and renew a faithful spirit
      within me.
11 Do not force me away
      from your presence,
   and do not take
      your Holy Spirit from me.
12 Restore the joy of your salvation to me,
   and provide me with a spirit of willing obedience.

13 ⌊Then⌋ I will teach your ways to those who are rebellious,
   and sinners will return to you.
14 Rescue me from the guilt of murder,
   O God, my savior.
   Let my tongue sing joyfully about your righteousness!
15 O Lord, open my lips,
   and my mouth will tell about your praise.
16 You are not happy with any sacrifice.
   Otherwise, I would offer one ⌊to you⌋.
   You are not pleased with burnt offerings.

Forgiveness
Psalm 51:1-12

It's important to apologize when we're sorry. But the first person to talk to when we do wrong is God. When we admit doing wrong, God forgives us and gives us a joyful heart. So when you do something wrong, don't wait. Say "I'm sorry" to God right away.

Sorry

be all you can be

---

*51:6 Hebrew meaning uncertain.   *51:7 Branches from the hyssop plant were used in purification rites.
*51:7 "Clean" refers to anything that Moses' Teachings say is presentable to God.

17　　The sacrifice pleasing to God is a broken spirit.
　　　　O God, you do not despise a broken and sorrowful heart.
18　　Favor Zion with your goodness.
　　　　Rebuild the walls of Jerusalem.
19　　Then you will be pleased with sacrifices offered in the right spirit—
　　　　with burnt offerings and whole burnt offerings.
　　　　Young bulls will be offered on your altar.

Psalm 52

For the choir director; a *maskil*; a psalm by David when Doeg (who was from Edom) told Saul that David had come to Ahimelech's home.

1　　Why do you brag about the evil you've done, you hero?
　　　　The mercy of God lasts all day long!
2　　Your tongue makes up threats.
　　　　It's like a sharp razor, you master of deceit.
3　　You prefer evil to good.
　　　　You prefer lying to speaking the truth.　　　　　　　　　*Selah*
4　　You love every destructive accusation, you deceitful tongue!

5　　But God will ruin you forever.
　　　　He will grab you and drag you out of your tent.
　　　　He will pull your roots out of this world of the living.　　*Selah*
6　　Righteous people will see this, and be struck with fear.
　　　　They will laugh at you and say,
7　　　"Look at this person who refused to make God his fortress!
　　　　Instead, he trusted his great wealth
　　　　　and became strong through his greed."

8　　But I am like a large olive tree in God's house.
　　　　I trust the mercy of God forever and ever.
9　　I will give thanks to you forever
　　　　for what you have done.
　　　In the presence of your godly people,
　　　　I will wait with hope in your good name.

Psalm 53 [a]

For the choir director; according to *mahalath*,[b] a *maskil* by David.

1　　Godless fools say in their hearts,
　　　　"There is no God."
　　　They are corrupt.
　　　They do disgusting things.
　　　　There is no one who does good things.
2　　God looks down from heaven on Adam's descendants
　　　　to see if there is anyone who acts wisely,
　　　　　if there is anyone who seeks help from God.
3　　Everyone has fallen away.
　　　　Together they have become rotten to the core.

---

[a]53:1 Psalm 53 is virtually identical in wording to Psalm 14.　　[b]53:1 Unknown musical term.

No one, not even one person, does good things.

4 Are all those troublemakers,
   those who devour my people as if they were devouring food,
      so ignorant that they do not call on God?
5 There they are—panic-stricken—
   but there was no reason to panic,
      because God has scattered the bones
         of those who set up camp against you.[c]
   You put them to shame.
   After all, God has rejected them.

6 If only salvation for Israel would come from Zion!
   When God restores the fortunes of his people,
      Jacob will rejoice.
      Israel will be glad.

Psalm 54

For the choir director; on stringed instruments; a *maskil* by David when people from the city of Ziph told Saul that David was hiding among them.

1 O God, save me by your name,
   and defend me with your might.
2 O God, hear my prayer,
   and open your ears to the words from my mouth.

3 Strangers have attacked me.
   Ruthless people seek my life.
      They do not think about God.[a]   *Selah*

4 God is my helper!
   The Lord is the provider for my life.
5   My enemies spy on me.
      Pay them back with evil.
      Destroy them with your truth!

6 I will make a sacrifice to you along with a freewill offering.
   I will give thanks to your good name, O Lord.
7   Your name rescues me from every trouble.
      My eyes will gloat over my enemies.

Psalm 55

For the choir director; on stringed instruments; a *maskil* by David.

1 Open your ears to my prayer, O God.
   Do not hide from my plea for mercy.
2 Pay attention to me, and answer me.
   My thoughts are restless, and I am confused
3   because my enemy shouts at me
         and a wicked person persecutes me.
         They bring misery crashing down on me,
            and they attack me out of anger.

---

c53:5 Hebrew meaning uncertain.   a54:3 Hebrew meaning of this line uncertain.

⁴ My heart is in turmoil.
   The terrors of death have seized me.
⁵ Fear and trembling have overcome me.
   Horror has overwhelmed me.
⁶ I said, "If only I had wings like a dove—
   I would fly away and find rest.
⁷ Indeed, I would run far away.
   I would stay in the desert.   *Selah*
⁸ I would hurry to find shelter
   from the raging wind and storm."

⁹ Completely confuse their language, O Lord,
   because I see violence and conflict in the city.
¹⁰ Day and night they go around on ˻top of˼ the city walls.
   Trouble and misery are everywhere.
¹¹ Destruction is everywhere.
   Oppression and fraud never leave the streets.ᵃ

¹² If an enemy had insulted me,
   then I could bear it.
   If someone who hated me had attacked me,
   then I could hide from him.
¹³ But it is you, my equal,
   my best friend,
   one I knew so well!
¹⁴ We used to talk to each other in complete confidence
   and walk into God's house with the festival crowds.

¹⁵ Let death suddenly take ˻wicked people˼!
   Let them go into the grave while they are still alive,
   because evil lives in their homes as well as in their hearts.
¹⁶ But I call on God,
   and the Lᴏʀᴅ saves me.
¹⁷ Morning, noon, and night I complain and groan,
   and he listens to my voice.
¹⁸ With ˻his˼ peace, he will rescue my soul
   from the war waged against me,
   because there are many ˻soldiers fighting˼ against me.
¹⁹ God will listen.
   The one who has sat enthroned from the beginning
   will deal with them.   *Selah*
   They never change. They never fear God.
²⁰ ˻My best friend˼ has betrayed his friends.
   He has broken his solemn promise.
²¹ His speech is smoother than butter,
   but there is war in his heart.
   His words are more soothing than oil,
   but they are like swords ready to attack.
²² Turn your burdens over to the Lᴏʀᴅ,
   and he will take care of you.

ᵃ55:11 Or "its marketplace."

He will never let the righteous person stumble.
23 But you, O God, will throw ˏwicked peopleˏ into the deepest pit.
Bloodthirsty and deceitful people will not live out half their days.
But I will trust you.

Psalm 56

For the choir director; according to *yonath elem rechokim*;[a] a *miktam* by David
when the Philistines captured him in Gath.

1 Have pity on me, O God, because people are harassing me.
All day long warriors oppress me.
2 All day long my enemies spy on me.
They harass me.
There are so many
fighting against me.
3 Even when I am afraid,
I still trust you.
4 I praise the word of God.
I trust God.
I am not afraid.
What can mere flesh
ˏand bloodˏ do to me?
5 All day long my enemies twist
my words.
Their every thought
is an evil plan against me.
6 They attack, and then they hide.
They watch my every step
as they wait to take my life.
7 With the wrong they do,
can they escape?
O God, angrily make
the nations fall.
8 (You have kept a record
of my wanderings.
Put my tears in your bottle.
They are already
in your book.)
9 Then my enemies will retreat
when I call ˏto youˏ.
This I know: God is on my side.
10 I praise the word of God.
I praise the word of the LORD.
11 I trust God.
I am not afraid.
What can mortals do to me?

Fear

Psalm 56

**What do you do when
people twist your words
or lie about you? What if
other kids tease you on the
bus or at school? When David's
enemies picked on him, he told
God his troubles. Then David
told himself, "I trust God. I am
not afraid." With God on your
side, you don't have to give up
and hide. Trust God to show
you how to respond to those
who harass you.**

be
all you
can be

---

[a] 56:1 Unknown musical term.

¹² I am bound by my vows to you, O God.
I will keep my vows by offering songs of thanksgiving to you.
¹³ You have rescued me from death.
You have kept my feet from stumbling
so that I could walk in your presence, in the light of life.

Psalm 57

For the choir director; *al tashcheth*;^a a *miktam* by David when he fled from Saul into the cave.

¹ Have pity on me, O God. Have pity on me,
because my soul takes refuge in you.
I will take refuge in the shadow of your wings
until destructive storms pass by.
² I call to God Most High,
to the God who does everything for me.
³ He sends his help from heaven and saves me.
He disgraces the one who is harassing me.   *Selah*
God sends his mercy and his truth!
⁴ My soul is surrounded by lions.
I must lie down with man-eating lions.
Their teeth are spears and arrows.
Their tongues are sharp swords.
⁵   May you be honored above the heavens, O God.
Let your glory extend over the whole earth.

⁶ My enemies spread out a net to catch me.
(My soul is bowed down.)^b
They dug a pit to trap me,
but then they fell into it.   *Selah*

⁷ My heart is confident, O God.
My heart is confident.
I want to sing and make music.^c
⁸   Wake up, my soul!^d
Wake up, harp and lyre!
I want to wake up at dawn.
⁹ I want to give thanks to you among the people, O Lord.
I want to make music to praise you among the nations
¹⁰   because your mercy is as high as the heavens.
Your truth reaches the skies.

¹¹   May you be honored above the heavens, O God.
Let your glory extend over the whole earth.

Psalm 58

For the choir director; *al tashcheth*; a *miktam* by David.

¹ Do you rulers really give fair verdicts?
Do you judge Adam's descendants fairly?

---

^a57:1 Unknown musical term.   ^b57:6 Hebrew meaning of this line uncertain.   ^c57:7 Verses 7-11 are virtually identical in wording to Psalm 108:1-5.   ^d57:8 Or "my glory."

2   No, you invent new crimes on earth,
        and your hands spread violence.

3   Even, inside the womb wicked people are strangers to God.
    From their birth liars go astray.
4   They have poisonous venom like snakes.
        They are like a deaf cobra that shuts its ears
5   so that it cannot hear the voice of a snake charmer
            or of anyone trained to cast spells.

6   O God, knock the teeth out of their mouths.
        Break the young lions' teeth, O Lord.
7   Let them disappear like water that drains away.
        When they aim their bows, let their arrows miss the target.*
8   Let them become like a snail that leaves behind a slimy trail
            or like a stillborn child who never sees the sun.
9   Let God, sweep them away
            faster than a cooking pot is heated by burning twigs.*

10 Righteous people will rejoice when they see God take revenge.
        They will wash their feet in the blood of wicked people.
11 Then people will say,
        "Righteous people certainly have a reward.
        There is a God who judges on earth."

Psalm 59

For the choir director; *al tashcheth*; a *miktam* by David when Saul sent men to
watch David's home and kill him.

1   Rescue me from my enemies, O my God.
        Protect me from those who attack me.
2   Rescue me from troublemakers.
        Save me from bloodthirsty people.
3   They lie in ambush for me right here!
            Fierce men attack me, O Lord,
                but not because of any disobedience,
4   or any sin, or any guilt on my part.
            They hurry to take positions against me.
    Wake up, and help me; see for yourself.
5   O Lord God of Armies, God of Israel,
        arise to punish all the nations.
        Have no pity on any traitors.   *Selah*

6   They return in the evening.
            They howl like dogs.
            They prowl the city.

7   See what pours out of their mouths—
        swords from their lips!
            They think, "Who will hear us?"

---

*58:7 Hebrew meaning of this sentence uncertain.   *58:9 Hebrew meaning uncertain.

8   O LORD, you laugh at them.
     You make fun of all the nations.

9   O my strength, I watch for you!
         God is my stronghold, my merciful God!

10 God will come to meet me.
     He will let me gloat over those who spy on me.
11 Do not kill them.
         Otherwise, my people may forget.
     Make them wander aimlessly by your power.
     Bring them down, O Lord, our shield,
12   because of the sins from their mouths
             and the words on their lips.
     Let them be trapped by their own arrogance
         because they speak curses and lies.
13 Destroy them in your rage.
     Destroy them until not one of them is left.
         Then they will know that God rules Jacob
             to the ends of the earth.   *Selah*

14   They return in the evening.
         They howl like dogs.
         They prowl the city.

15 They wander around to find something to eat.
         If they are not full enough,
             they will stay all night.
16 But I will sing about your strength.
         In the morning I will joyfully sing about your mercy.
             You have been my stronghold
                 and a place of safety in times of trouble.
17   O my strength, I will make music to praise you!
         God is my stronghold, my merciful God!

Psalm 60

For the choir director; according to *shushan eduth;*[a] a *miktam* by David; for
teaching. When David fought Aram Naharaim and Aram Zobah, and when Joab
came back and killed 12,000 men from Edom in the Dead Sea region.

1   O God, you have rejected us.
         You have broken down our defenses.
         You have been angry.
             Restore us!
2   You made the land quake.
     You split it wide open.
         Heal the cracks in it
             because it is falling apart.
3   You have made your people experience hardships.
     You have given us wine that makes us stagger.

---

[a] 60:1 Unknown musical term.

4 Yet, you have raised a flag for those who fear you
  so that they can rally to it
    when attacked by bows ⸢and arrows⸣.   *Selah*
5 Save ⸢us⸣ with your powerful hand, and answer us
  so that those who are dear to you may be rescued.[b]

6 God has promised the following through his holiness:
  "I will triumph!
  I will divide Shechem.
  I will measure the valley of Succoth.
7   Gilead is mine.
    Manasseh is mine.
    Ephraim is the helmet on my head.
    Judah is my scepter.
8   Moab is my washtub.
    I will throw my shoe over Edom.
    I will shout in triumph over Philistia."

9 Who will bring me into the fortified city?
  Who will lead me to Edom?
10 Isn't it you, O God, who rejected us?
    Isn't it you, O God, who refused to accompany our armies?

11 Give us help against the enemy
   because human assistance is worthless.
12   With God we will display great strength.
     He will trample our enemies.

Psalm 61

For the choir director; on a stringed instrument; by David.

1 Listen to my cry for help, O God.
  Pay attention to my prayer.
2   From the ends of the earth, I call to you
    when I begin to lose heart.
  Lead me to the rock that is high above me.
3   You have been my refuge,
    a tower of strength against the enemy.
4 I would like to be a guest in your tent forever
  and to take refuge under the protection of your wings.   *Selah*
5   O God, you have heard my vows.
    You have given me the inheritance
    that belongs to those who fear your name.
6 Add days upon days to the life of the king.
  May his years endure throughout every generation.
7 May he sit enthroned in the presence of God forever.
  May mercy and truth protect him.
8   Then I will make music to praise your name forever,
    as I keep my vows day after day.

---

[b] 60:5 Verses 5-12 are virtually identical in wording to Psalm 108:6-13.

Psalm 62

For the choir director; according to Jeduthun; a psalm by David.

1 My soul waits calmly for God alone.
  My salvation comes from him.
2 He alone is my rock and my savior—my stronghold.
  I cannot be severely shaken.

3 How long will all of you attack a person?
  How long will you try to murder him,
    as though he were a leaning wall or a sagging fence?
4   They plan to force him out of his high position.
  They are happy to lie.
  They bless with their mouths,
    but in their hearts they curse.   *Selah*

5 Wait calmly for God alone, my soul,
    because my hope comes from him.
6 He alone is my rock and my savior—my stronghold.
  I cannot be shaken.

7 My salvation and my glory depend on God.
    God is the rock of my strength, my refuge.
8 Trust him at all times, you people.
  Pour out your hearts in his presence.
    God is our refuge.   *Selah*

9 Common people are only a whisper in the wind.
  Important people are only a delusion.
    When all of them are weighed on a scale, they amount to nothing.
    They are less than a whisper in the wind.
10 Do not count on extortion to make you rich.
  Do not hope to gain anything through robbery.
    When riches increase, do not depend on them.

11 God has spoken once.
  I have heard it said twice:
    "Power belongs to God.
12   Mercy belongs to you, O Lord.
    You reward a person based on what he has done."

Psalm 63

A psalm by David when he was in the wilderness of Judah.

1 O God, you are my God.
    At dawn I search for you.
  My soul thirsts for you.
  My body longs for you
    in a dry, parched land where there is no water.
2 So I look for you in the holy place
    to see your power and your glory.
3 My lips will praise you

Knives and Swords
Psalm 64

The same Hebrew words are used for *knives* and *swords*. Knives were used as both tools and weapons. But they were not used for eating. Hebrew swords were straight, with the blade sharpened on both sides of the point. Other nations had curved swords, used for slashing. These were sharpened on only one side, with the other side thickened to add weight. Psalm 64:3 reminds us that the tongue can be like a sword and can do real harm to others.

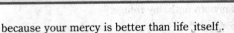

because your mercy is better than life ⌐itself⌐.
4   So I will thank you as long as I live.
I will lift up my hands ⌐to pray⌐ in your name.
5   You satisfy my soul with the richest foods.
My mouth will sing ⌐your⌐ praise with joyful lips.
6   As I lie on my bed, I remember you.
Through the long hours of the night, I think about you.
7   You have been my help.
In the shadow of your wings, I sing joyfully.
8   My soul clings to you.
Your right hand supports me.

9   But those who try to destroy my life
will go into the depths of the earth.
10   They will be cut down by swords.
Their dead bodies will be left as food for jackals.
11   But the king will find joy in God.
Everyone who takes an oath by God will brag,
but the mouths of liars will be shut.

Psalm 64

For the choir director; a psalm by David.

1   Hear my voice, O God, when I complain.
Protect my life from a terrifying enemy.
2   Hide me from the secret plots of criminals,
from the mob of troublemakers.
3   They sharpen their tongues like swords.
They aim bitter words like arrows

4   to shoot at innocent people from their hiding places.
     They shoot at them suddenly, without any fear.
5   They encourage one another in their evil plans.
     They talk about setting traps and say,
         "Who can see them?"
6   They search for the perfect crime and say,
         "We have perfected a foolproof scheme!"
             Human nature and the human heart are a mystery!

7   But God will shoot them with an arrow.
         Suddenly, they will be struck dead.
8   They will trip over their own tongues.
         Everyone who sees them will shake his head.
9   Everyone will be afraid and conclude,
         "This is an act of God!"
             They will learn from what he has done.

10   Righteous people will find joy in the LORD and take refuge in him.
     Everyone whose motives are decent will be able to brag.

Psalm 65

For the choir director; a psalm by
David; a song.

1   You are praised with silence
         in Zion, O God,
         and vows made to you
             must be kept.
2   You are the one
         who hears prayers.
     Everyone will come to you.
3   Various sins overwhelm me.
     You are the one who forgives
         our rebellious acts.
4   Blessed is the person you choose
     and invite to live with you
         in your courtyards.
     We will be filled with good
         food from your house,
         from your holy temple.

5   You answer us with awe-inspiring
         acts done in righteousness,
     O God, our savior,
         the hope of all the ends
             of the earth
             and of the most distant sea,
6   the one who set
         the mountains in place
         with his strength,

Nature

Psalm 65:8-13

**Take a walk outdoors
after a rain shower. Stop
to look at the sky and
smell the freshness of the
earth. Bend over and look at
a flower. Climb a tree and lie
on its rough limb. Everything
we smell and taste and feel
is a gift from God. Tell God
how much you appreciate his
good gifts.**

the one who is clothed with power,
7   the one who calms the roar of the seas,
          their crashing waves,
             and the uproar of the nations.
8 Those who live at the ends of the earth are in awe of your miraculous signs.
   The lands of the morning sunrise and evening sunset sing joyfully.

9 You take care of the earth, and you water it.
   You make it much richer than it was.
          (The river of God is filled with water.)
   You provide grain for them.
          Indeed, you even prepare the ground.
10 You drench plowed fields ˌwith rainˌ
          and level their clumps of soil.
   You soften them with showers
          and bless what grows in them.
11 You crown the year with your goodness,
          and richness overflows wherever you are.
12   The pastures in the desert overflow ˌwith richnessˌ.
          The hills are surrounded with joy.
13   The pastures are covered with flocks.
          The valleys are carpeted with grain.
             All of them shout triumphantly. Indeed, they sing.

Psalm 66

For the choir director; a song; a psalm.

1 Shout happily to God, all the earth!
2 Make music to praise the glory of his name.
   Make his praise glorious.
3 Say to God,
          "How awe-inspiring are your deeds!
          Your power is so great that your enemies will cringe in front of you.
4   The whole earth will worship you.
          It will make music to praise you.
          It will make music to praise your name."   *Selah*
5 Come and see what God has done—
          his awe-inspiring deeds for Adam's descendants.
6   He turned the sea into dry land.
          They crossed the river on foot.
             We rejoiced because of what he did there.
7   He rules forever with his might.
          His eyes watch the nations.
             Rebels will not be able to oppose him.   *Selah*

8 Thank our God, you nations.
   Make the sound of his praise heard.
9   He has kept us alive
          and has not allowed us to fall.
10 You have tested us, O God.
   You have refined us in the same way silver is refined.

¹¹ You have trapped us in a net.
  You have laid burdens on our backs.
¹² You let people ride over our heads.
  We went through fire and water,
    but then you brought us out and refreshed us.

¹³ I will come into your temple with burnt offerings.
  I will keep my vows to you,
¹⁴   the vows made by my lips and spoken by my own mouth
    when I was in trouble.
¹⁵ I will offer you a sacrifice of fattened livestock for burnt offerings
    with the smoke from rams.
  I will offer cattle and goats.   *Selah*

¹⁶ Come and listen, all who fear God,
    and I will tell you what he has done for me.
¹⁷   With my mouth I cried out to him.
    High praise was on my tongue.
¹⁸ If I had thought about doing anything sinful,
    the Lord would not have listened to me.
¹⁹ But God has heard me.
    He has paid attention to my prayer.

²⁰ Thanks be to God,
    who has not rejected my prayer
    or taken away his mercy from me.

Psalm 67

For the choir director; on stringed instruments; a psalm; a song.

¹ May God have pity on us and bless us!
  May he smile on us.   *Selah*
²   Then your ways will be known on earth,
    your salvation throughout all nations.

³ Let everyone give thanks to you, O God.
  Let everyone give thanks to you.
⁴ Let the nations be glad and sing joyfully
    because you judge everyone with justice
    and guide the nations on the earth.   *Selah*
⁵ Let the people give thanks to you, O God.
  Let all the people give thanks to you.
⁶   The earth has yielded its harvest.
  May God, our God, bless us.
⁷ May God bless us,
    and may all the ends of the earth worship him.

Psalm 68

For the choir director; a psalm by David; a song.

¹ God will arise.
  His enemies will be scattered.

Those who hate him will flee from him.

2   Blow them away like smoke.
Let wicked people melt in God's presence like wax next to a fire.

3   But let righteous people rejoice.
Let them celebrate in God's presence.
Let them overflow with joy.

4   Sing to God; make music to praise his name.
Make a highway for him to ride through the deserts.*
The LORD is his name.
Celebrate in his presence.

5   The God who is in his holy dwelling place
is the father of the fatherless and the defender of widows.

6   God places lonely people in families.
He leads prisoners out of prison into productive lives,
but rebellious people must live in an unproductive land.

7   O God, when you went in front of your people,
when you marched through the desert,   *Selah*
8   the earth quaked and the sky poured
in the presence of the God of Sinai,
in the presence of the God of Israel.

9   You watered the land with plenty of rain, O God.
You refreshed it when your land was exhausted.
10   Your flock settled there.
Out of your goodness, O God,
you provided for oppressed people.

11   The Lord gives instructions.
The women who announce the good news are a large army.
12   They say, "The kings of the armies flee; they run away.
The women who remained at home will divide the goods.
13   Though you stayed among the sheep pens,
you will be like the wings of a dove covered with silver,
its feathers with yellow gold.
14   Meanwhile, the Almighty was still scattering kings there
like snow falling on Mount Zalmon."

15   The mountain of Bashan is the mountain of God.
The mountain of Bashan is the mountain with many peaks.
16   Why do you look with envy, you mountains with many peaks,
at the mountain where God has chosen to live?
Certainly, the LORD will live there forever.

17   The chariots of God are twenty thousand in number,
thousands upon thousands.
The Lord is among them.
The God of Sinai is in his holy place.
18   You went to the highest place.
You took prisoners captive.

---

*68:4 Or "Lift a song to him who rides upon the clouds."

You received gifts from people,
    even from rebellious people, so that the Lord God may live there.

19 Thanks be to the Lord,
    who daily carries our burdens for us.
        God is our salvation.   *Selah*

20 Our God is the God of victories.
    The Almighty Lord is our escape from death.

21 Certainly, God will crush the heads of his enemies
    and destroy even the hair on the heads
        of those who continue to be guilty.

22 The Lord said, "I will bring them back from Bashan.
    I will bring them back from the depths of the sea

23   so that you, my people, may bathe[b] your feet in blood
        and the tongues of your dogs
           may lick the blood of your enemies."

24 Your festival processions, O God, can be seen by everyone.
    They are the processions for my God, my king, into the holy place.

25   The singers are in front.
    The musicians are behind them.
    The young women beating tambourines are between them.

26   Thank God, the Lord, the source of Israel, with the choirs.

27   Benjamin, the youngest, is leading them,
        next, the leaders of Judah with their noisy crowds,
        then, the leaders of Zebulun,
        then, the leaders of Naphtali.

28 Your God has decided you will be strong.
    Display your strength, O God,
        as you have for us before.

29 Kings will bring you gifts
    because of your temple high above Jerusalem.

30 Threaten the beast who is among the cattails,
    the herd of bulls with the calves of the nations,
        until it humbles itself with pieces of silver.
    Scatter the people who find joy in war.[c]

31 Ambassadors will come from Egypt.
    Sudan will stretch out its hands to God in prayer.

32 You kingdoms of the world, sing to God.
    Make music to praise the Lord.   *Selah*

33   God rides through the ancient heaven, the highest heaven.
    Listen! He makes his voice heard, his powerful voice.

34   Acknowledge the power of God.
    His majesty is over Israel, and his power is in the skies.

35 God, the God of Israel, is awe-inspiring in his holy place.
    He gives strength and power to his people.
        Thanks be to God!

---

[b] 68:23 Greek, Targum, Syriac; Masoretic Text "shatter." [c] 68:30 Hebrew meaning of this verse uncertain.

Psalm 69

For the choir director; according to *shoshannim*; by David.

1   Save me, O God!
        The water is already up to my neck!
2   I am sinking in deep mud.
        There is nothing to stand on.
    I am in deep water.
        A flood is sweeping me away.
3   I am exhausted from crying for help.
        My throat is hoarse.
    My eyes are strained ⸢from⸣ looking for my God.
4   Those who hate me for no reason
            outnumber the hairs on my head.
        Those who want to destroy me are mighty.
            They have no reason to be my enemies.
    I am forced to pay back what I did not steal.

5   O God, you know my stupidity,
        and the things of which I am guilty are not hidden from you.
6   Do not let those who wait with hope for you
        be put to shame because of me, O Almighty Lord of Armies.
    Do not let those who come to you for help
        be humiliated because of me, O God of Israel.

7   Indeed, for your sake I have endured insults.
        Humiliation has covered my face.
8   I have become a stranger to my ⸢own⸣ brothers,
        a foreigner to my mother's sons.
9   Indeed, devotion for your house has consumed me,
        and the insults of those who insult you have fallen on me.
10   I cried and fasted, but I was insulted for it.
11   I dressed myself in sackcloth, but I became the object of ridicule.
12   Those who sit at the gate gossip about me,
            and drunkards make up songs about me.

13   May my prayer come to you at an acceptable time, O Lord.
        O God, out of the greatness of your mercy,
            answer me with the truth of your salvation.
14   Rescue me from the mud.
        Do not let me sink ⸢into it⸣.
    I want to be rescued from those who hate me
        and from the deep water.
15   Do not let floodwaters sweep me away.
        Do not let the ocean swallow me up,
            or the pit close its mouth over me.
16   Answer me, O Lord, because your mercy is good.
    Out of your unlimited compassion, turn to me.
17   I am in trouble, so do not hide your face from me.
        Answer me quickly!
18   Come close, and defend my soul.
        Set me free because of my enemies.

19 You know that I have been insulted, put to shame, and humiliated.
   All my opponents are in front of you.

20 Insults have broken my heart, and I am sick.
   I looked for sympathy, but there was none.
   I looked for people to comfort me, but I found no one.

21   They poisoned my food,
         and when I was thirsty, they gave me vinegar to drink.

22 Let the table set for them become a trap
   and a snare for their friends.

23 Let their vision become clouded so that they cannot see.
   Let their thighs continually shake.

24 Pour your rage on them.
   Let your burning anger catch up with them.

25 Let their camp be deserted
   and their tents empty.

26 They persecute the one you have struck,
   and they talk about the pain of those you have wounded.

27 Charge them with one crime after another.
   Do not let them be found innocent.

28 Let their names be erased from the Book of Life.
   Do not let them be listed with righteous people.

29 I am suffering and in pain.
   Let your saving power protect me, O God.

30 I want to praise the name of God with a song.
   I want to praise its greatness with a song of thanksgiving.

31 This will please the LORD more than ˻sacrificing˼ an ox
   or a bull with horns and hoofs.

32 Oppressed people will see ˻this˼ and rejoice.
   May the hearts of those who look to God for help be refreshed.

33 The LORD listens to needy people.
   He does not despise his own who are in prison.

34 Let heaven and earth, the seas, and everything that moves in them,
   praise him.

35 When God saves Zion, he will rebuild the cities of Judah.
   His servants will live there and take possession of it.

36   The descendants of his servants will inherit it.
         Those who love him will live there.

Psalm 70 [a]

For the choir director; by David; to be kept in mind.

1 Come quickly to rescue me, O God!
  Come quickly to help me, O LORD!

2 Let those who seek my life
    be confused and put to shame.
  Let those who want my downfall
    be turned back and disgraced.

---

[a] 70:1 Psalm 70 is virtually identical in wording to Psalm 40:13-17.

3 Let those who say, "Aha! Aha!"
  be turned back because of their own shame.
4 Let all who seek you rejoice and be glad because of you.
  Let those who love your salvation continually say,
    "God is great!"

5 But I am oppressed and needy.
  O God, come to me quickly.
    You are my help and my savior.
      O LORD, do not delay!

Psalm 71

1 I have taken refuge in you, O LORD.
    Never let me be put to shame.
2 Rescue me and free me because of your righteousness.
  Turn your ear toward me, and save me.
3   Be a rock on which I may live,
      a place where I may always go.
        You gave the order to save me!
    Indeed, you are my rock and my fortress.
4 My God, free me from the hands of a wicked person,
    from the grasp of one who is cruel and unjust.
5 You are my hope, O Almighty LORD.
  You have been my confidence ever since I was young.
6 I depended on you before I was born.
    You took me from my mother's womb.
      My songs of praise constantly speak about you.
7 I have become an example to many people,
    but you are my strong refuge.
8 My mouth is filled with your praise,
    with your glory all day long.

9 Do not reject me when I am old
    or abandon me when I lose my strength.
10 My enemies talk about me.
    They watch me as they plot to take my life.
11 They say, "God has abandoned him.
    Pursue him and grab him because there is no one to rescue him."
12 O God, do not be so distant from me.
  O my God, come quickly to help me.
13 Let those who accuse me come to a shameful end.
  Let those who want my downfall be covered
      with disgrace and humiliation.
14 But I will always have hope.
    I will praise you more and more.
15 My mouth will tell about your righteousness,
    about your salvation all day long.
      Even then, it is more than I can understand.
16 I will come with the mighty deeds of the Almighty LORD.
  I will praise your righteousness, yours alone.

¹⁷ O God, you have taught me ever since I was young,
   and I still talk about the miracles you have done.
¹⁸ Even when I am old and gray, do not abandon me, O God.
   Let me live to tell the people of this age
      what your strength has accomplished,
         to tell about your power to all who will come.

¹⁹ Your righteousness reaches to the heavens, O God.
   You have done great things.
      O God, who is like you?
²⁰ You have made me endure many terrible troubles.
   You restore me to life again.
   You bring me back from the depths of the earth.
²¹ You comfort me and make me greater than ever.

²² Because of your faithfulness, O my God,
   even I will give thanks to you as I play on a lyre.
   I will make music with a harp to praise you, O Holy One of Israel.
²³ My lips will sing with joy when I make music to praise you.
   My soul, which you have rescued, also will sing joyfully.
²⁴ My tongue will tell about your righteousness all day long,
   because those who wanted my downfall
      have been disgraced and put to shame.

Psalm 72

By Solomon.

¹ O God, give the king your justice
   and the king's son[a] your righteousness
²   so that he may judge your people with righteousness
      and your oppressed ˌpeopleˌ with justice.

³ May the mountains bring peace to the people
   and the hills bring righteousness.
⁴ May he grant justice to the people who are oppressed.
   May he save the children of needy people
   and crush their oppressor.
⁵ May they fear you as long as the sun and moon ˌshine,ˌ—
   throughout every generation.
⁶ May he be like rain that falls on ˌfreshlyˌ cut grass,
   like showers that water the land.
⁷ May righteous people blossom in his day.
   May there be unlimited peace until the moon no longer ˌshinesˌ.

⁸ May he rule from sea to sea,
   from the Euphrates River to the ends of the earth.
⁹ May the people of the desert kneel in front of him.
   May his enemies lick the dust.
¹⁰ May the kings from Tarshish and the islands bring presents.
   May the kings from Sheba and Seba bring gifts.

---

[a] 72:1 According to ancient Jewish and Christian tradition, "king" and "king's son" refer to the Messiah.

11 May all kings worship him.
    May all nations serve him.

12   He will rescue the needy person who cries for help
            and the oppressed person who has no one's help.

13   He will have pity on the poor and needy
            and will save the lives of the needy.

14   He will rescue them from oppression and violence.
            Their blood will be precious in his sight.

15 May he live long.
    May the gold from Sheba be given to him.
    May the people pray for him continually.
    May they praise him all day long.

16 May there be plenty of grain in the land.
    May it wave in the breeze on the mountaintops,
        its fruit like the treetops of Lebanon.
    May those from the city flourish like the grass on the ground.

17 May his name endure forever.
    May his name continue as long as the sun shines.
    May all nations be blessed through him and call him blessed.

18 Thank the Lord God, the God of Israel,
        who alone does miracles.

19 Thanks be to his glorious name forever.
    May the whole earth be filled with his glory.

                    Amen and amen!

20 The prayers by David, son of Jesse, end here.

BOOK THREE
Psalms 73–89

Psalm 73

A psalm by Asaph.

1   God is truly good to Israel,
        to those whose lives are pure.

2   But my feet had almost stumbled.
        They had almost slipped

3   because I was envious of arrogant people
                when I saw the prosperity that wicked people enjoy.

4   They suffer no pain.
    Their bodies are healthy.

5   They have no drudgery in their lives like ordinary people.
    They are not plagued with problems like others.

6   That is why they wear arrogance like a necklace
        and acts of violence like clothing.

7 Their eyes peer out from their fat faces,^a
    and their imaginations run wild.
8 They ridicule.
  They speak maliciously.
  They speak arrogantly about oppression.
9 They verbally attack heaven,
    and they order people around on earth.
10 That is why God's people turn to wickedness^b
    and swallow their words.
11 Then wicked people ask, "What does God know?"
    "Does the Most High know anything?"
12 Look how wicked they are!
    They never have a worry.
      They grow more and more wealthy.

13 I've received no reward for keeping my life pure
    and washing my hands of any blame.
14 I'm plagued with problems all day long,
    and every morning my punishment begins again.
15 If I had said, "I will continue to talk like that,"
    I would have betrayed God's people.

16 But when I tried to understand this,
    it was too difficult for me.
17 Only when I came into God's holy place
    did I finally understand what would happen to them.

18 You put them in slippery places
    and make them fall into ruin.
19 They are suddenly destroyed.
  They are completely swept away by terror!
20 As someone gets rid of a dream when he wakes up,
    so you, O Lord, get rid of the thought of them
      when you wake up.

Good Morning, God

Psalm 73:2-5

Asaph didn't think it was fair that he should have problems when wicked people had it so easy. He wondered, *What's the point of trying to do good?* Then he realized that when everything is going great, people often think they don't need God. Imagine what it would be like to live without God! On the other hand, we can actually grow closer to God through our trials because they remind us how much we need his help.

Thank you, Lord, for my trials because they keep me close to you.

---

^a73:7 Hebrew meaning uncertain.   ^b73:10 Hebrew meaning uncertain.

21 When my heart was filled with bitterness
      and my mind was seized with envy,
22   I was stupid, and I did not understand.
      I was like a dumb animal in your presence.
23 Yet, I am always with you.
      You hold on to my right hand.
24   With your advice you guide me,
          and in the end you will take me to glory.
25 As long as I have you,
      I don't need anyone else in heaven or on earth.
26 My body and mind may waste away,
      but God remains the foundation of my life
        and my inheritance forever.
27 Without a doubt, those who are far from you will die.
    You destroy all who are unfaithful to you.

28 Being united with God is my highest good.
      I have made the Almighty LORD my refuge
        so that I may report everything that he has done.

Psalm 74

A *maskil*[a] by Asaph.

1   Why, O God, have you rejected us forever?
    Why does your anger
      smolder against the sheep in your care?

2   Remember your congregation.
      Long ago you made it your own.
      You bought this tribe to be your possession.
        This tribe is Mount Zion, where you have made your home.
3   Turn your steps toward[b] these pathetic ruins.
      The enemy has destroyed everything in the holy temple.

4   Your opponents have roared inside your meeting place.
      They have set up their own emblems as symbols.
5   Starting from its entrance, they hacked away
          like a woodcutter in a forest.[c]
6   They smashed all its carved paneling with axes and hatchets.
7   They burned your holy place to the ground.
      They dishonored the place where you live among us.
8   They said to themselves, "We will crush them."
      They burned every meeting place of God in the land.

9   We no longer see miraculous signs.
      There are no prophets anymore.
        No one knows how long this will last.
10 How long, O God, will the enemy insult us?
    Will the enemy despise you forever?
11 Why do you hold back your hand, especially your right hand?

---

[a]74:1 Unknown musical term.   [b]74:3 Hebrew meaning uncertain.   [c]74:5 Hebrew meaning of this verse uncertain.

Take your hands out of your pockets.
Destroy your enemies!*ᵈ*

12 And yet, from long ago God has been my king,
the one who has been victorious throughout the earth.
13 You stirred up the sea with your own strength.
You smashed the heads of sea monsters in the water.
14 You crushed the heads of Leviathan*ᵉ*
and gave them to the creatures of the desert for food.
15 You opened the springs and brooks.
You dried up the ever-flowing rivers.
16 The day and the night are yours.
You set the moon and the sun in their places.
17 You determined all the boundaries of the earth.
You created summer and winter.

18 Remember how the enemy insulted you, O Lord.
Remember how an entire nation of godless fools despised your name.
19 Do not hand over the soul of your dove to wild animals.
Do not forget the life of your oppressed people forever.
20 Consider your promise*ᶠ*
because every dark corner of the land is filled with violence.
21 Do not let oppressed people come back in disgrace.
Let weak and needy people praise your name.
22 Arise, O God!
Fight for your own cause!
Remember how godless fools insult you all day long.
23 Do not forget the shouting of your opponents.
Do not forget the uproar made by those who attack you.

Psalm 75

For the choir director; *al tashcheth*; a psalm by Asaph; a song.

1 We give thanks to you, O God; we give thanks.
You are present, and your miracles confirm that.

2 When I choose the right time,
I will judge fairly.
3 When the earth and everyone who lives on it begin to melt,
I will make its foundations as solid as rock.   *Selah*

4 I said to those who brag, "Don't brag,"
and to wicked people,
"Don't raise your weapons.
5 Don't raise your weapons so proudly
or speak so defiantly."

6 The ⌊authority⌋ to reward someone does not ⌊come⌋
from the east,
from the west,
or ⌊even⌋ from the wilderness.

---

*ᵈ*74:11 Hebrew meaning of this verse uncertain. *ᵉ*74:14 Hebrew meaning uncertain. *ᶠ*74:20 Or "covenant."

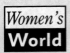

Music / *Psalm 76*

The Israelites played music at weddings and other happy occasions. Women sang as they worked, and musicians entertained at the king's court. Armies marched off to war to music; women sang and danced when their men returned. Music in the Bible is also often associated with worship.

   Many psalms were set to music and sung. Temple musicians played many different musical instruments. King David, famous as a great warrior and leader, was also a skilled harpist. David wrote many of the worship songs in the book of Psalms.

7   God alone is the judge.
         He punishes one person and rewards another.
8   A cup is in the LORD's hand.
         (Its foaming wine is thoroughly mixed with spices.)
      He will empty it,
         ₁and₁ all the wicked people on earth
            will have to drink every last drop.

9   But I will speak ₁about your miracles₁ forever.
         I will make music to praise the God of Jacob.
10   I will destroy all the weapons of wicked people,
         but the weapons of righteous people will be raised proudly.

Psalm 76

For the choir director; on stringed instruments; a psalm by Asaph; a song.

1   God is known in Judah.
         His name is great in Israel.
2   His tent is in Salem.
         His home is in Zion.
3   There he destroyed flaming arrows,
            shields, swords, and weapons of war.   *Selah*

4   You are the radiant one.
         You are more majestic than the ancient mountains.[a]
5   Brave people were robbed.

---

[a] 76:4 Greek, Syriac; Masoretic Text "mountains of prey."

They died.
  None of the warriors were able to lift a hand.
6 At your stern warning, O God of Jacob,
    chariot riders and horses were put to sleep.

7 You alone must be feared!
  Who can stand in your presence when you become angry?
8 From heaven you announced a verdict.
  The earth was fearful and silent
9   when you rose to judge, O God,
    when you rose to save every oppressed person on earth. *Selah*

10 Even angry mortals will praise you.
  You will wear the remainder of ˌtheirˌ anger.[b]
11 Make vows to the Lord your God, and keep them.
  Let everyone around him bring gifts to the one who must be feared.
12 He cuts short the lives of influential people.
  He terrifies the kings of the earth.

Psalm 77

For the choir director; according to Jeduthun; a psalm by Asaph.

1 Loudly, I cried to God.
  Loudly, I cried to God
    so that he would open his ears to ˌhearˌ me.
2 On the day I was in trouble, I went to the Lord for help.
  At night I stretched out my hands in prayer without growing tired.
    Yet, my soul refused to be comforted.

3 I sigh as I remember God.
  I begin to lose hope as I think about him. *Selah*
4   (You keep my eyelids open.)
  I am so upset that I cannot speak.
5 I have considered the days of old,
    the years long ago.
6 I remember my song in the night
    and reflect ˌon itˌ.
  My spirit searches ˌfor an answerˌ:
7   Will the Lord reject ˌmeˌ for all time?
  Will he ever accept me?
8   Has his mercy come to an end forever?
  Has his promise been canceled throughout every generation?
9   Has God forgotten to be merciful?
  Has he locked up his compassion because of his anger? *Selah*
10   Then I said, "It makes me feel sick
    that the power of the Most High is no longer the same."[a]

11 I will remember the deeds of the Lord.
  I will remember your ancient miracles.
12 I will reflect on all your actions
    and think about what you have done.

---

[b]76:10 Hebrew meaning of this line uncertain. [a]77:10 Hebrew meaning of this line uncertain.

13 O God, your ways are holy!
        What god is as great as our God?
14 You are the God who performs miracles.
        You have made your strength known among the nations.
15 With your might you have defended your people,
        the descendants of Jacob and Joseph.   *Selah*

16 The water saw you, O God.
        The water saw you and shook.
            Even the depths of the sea trembled.
17 The clouds poured out water.
        The sky thundered.
            Even your arrows flashed in every direction.
18 The sound of your thunder rumbled in the sky.*ᵇ*
        Streaks of lightning lit up the world.
            The earth trembled and shook.

19 Your road went through the sea.
        Your path went through raging water,
            but your footprints could not be seen.
20 Like a shepherd, you led your people.
        You had Moses and Aaron take them by the hand.

Psalm 78

A *maskil* by Asaph.

1   Open your ears to my teachings, my people.
        Turn your ears to the words from my mouth.
2   I will open my mouth to illustrate points.
        I will explain what has been hidden long ago,
3   things that we have heard and known about,
                things that our parents have told us.
4   We will not hide them from our children.
                We will tell the next generation
                    about the LORD's power and great deeds
                        and the miraculous things he has done.

5   He established written instructions for Jacob's people.
        He gave his teachings to Israel.
        He commanded our ancestors to make them known to their children
6   so that the next generation would know them.
                Children yet to be born ⸢would learn them⸣.
                They will grow up and tell their children
7   to trust God, to remember what he has done,
                    and to obey his commands.
8   Then they will not be like their ancestors,
                a stubborn and rebellious generation.
                    Their hearts were not loyal.
                    Their spirits were not faithful to God.

---

*ᵇ*77:18 Hebrew meaning of this line uncertain.

9   The men of Ephraim, well-equipped with bows ⸢and arrows⸣,
      turned ⸢and ran⸣ on the day of battle.
10   They had not been faithful to God's promise.[a]
         They refused to follow his teachings.
11   They forgot what he had done—
           the miracles that he had shown them.

12   In front of their ancestors he performed miracles
       in the land of Egypt, in the fields of Zoan.
13   He divided the sea and led them through it.
         He made the waters stand up like a wall.
14   He guided them by a cloud during the day
           and by a fiery light throughout the night.
15   He split rocks in the desert.
         He gave them plenty to drink, an ocean of water.
16   He made streams come out of a rock.
         He made the water flow like rivers.

17   They continued to sin against him,
       to rebel in the desert against the Most High.
18   They deliberately tested God by demanding the food they craved.
19   They spoke against God by saying,
       "Can God prepare a banquet in the desert?
20   True, he did strike a rock,
         and water did gush out,
           and the streams did overflow.
       But can he also give us bread or provide us, his people, with meat?"

21   When the Lord heard this, he became furious.
       His fire burned against Jacob
         and his anger flared up at Israel
22   because they did not believe God
             or trust him to save them.

23   In spite of that, he commanded the clouds above
       and opened the doors of heaven.
24   He rained manna down on them to eat
           and gave them grain from heaven.
25   Humans ate the bread of the mighty ones,
           and God sent them plenty of food.

26   He made the east wind blow in the heavens
       and guided the south wind with his might.
27   He rained meat down on them like dust,
           birds like the sand on the seashore.
28   He made the birds fall in the middle of his camp,
               all around his dwelling place.

29   They ate more than enough.
       He gave them what they wanted,
30   but they still wanted more.

---

a 78:10 Or "covenant."

While the food was still in their mouths,
    the anger of God flared up against them.
    He killed their strongest men
        and slaughtered the best young men in Israel.

32 In spite of all this, they continued to sin,
    and they no longer believed in his miracles.

33 He brought their days to an end like a whisper in the wind.
    He brought their years to an end in terror.

34 When he killed some of them, the rest searched for him.
    They turned from their sins and eagerly looked for God.

35 They remembered that God was their rock,
    that the Most High was their defender.

36 They flattered him with their mouths
    and lied to him with their tongues.

37 Their hearts were not loyal to him.
    They were not faithful to his promise.

38 But he is compassionate.
    He forgave their sin.
    He did not destroy them.
    He restrained his anger many times.
    He did not display all of his fury.

39 He remembered that they were only flesh and blood,
    a breeze that blows and does not return.

40 How often they rebelled against him in the wilderness!
How often they caused him grief in the desert!

41 Again and again they tested God,
    and they pushed the Holy One of Israel to the limit.

42 They did not remember his power—
    the day he freed them from their oppressor,

43   when he performed his miraculous signs in Egypt,
        his wonders in the fields of Zoan.

44 He turned their rivers into blood
    so that they could not drink from their streams.

45 He sent a swarm of flies that bit them
    and frogs that ruined them.

46 He gave their crops to grasshoppers
    and their produce to locusts.

47 He killed their vines with hail
    and their fig trees with frost.

48 He let the hail strike their cattle
    and bolts of lightning strike their livestock.

49 He sent his burning anger, rage, fury, and hostility against them.
He sent an army of destroying angels.

50 He cleared a path for his anger.
He did not spare them.
He let the plague take their lives.

51 He slaughtered every firstborn in Egypt,
   the ones born in the tents of Ham when their fathers were young.
52 But he led his own people out like sheep
   and guided them like a flock through the wilderness.
53 He led them safely.
   They had no fear while the sea covered their enemies.
54 He brought them into his holy land,
   to this mountain that his power had won.
55 He forced nations out of their way
   and gave them the land of the nations as their inheritance.
   He settled the tribes of Israel in their own tents.

56 They tested God Most High and rebelled against him.
   They did not obey his written instructions.
57 They were disloyal and treacherous like their ancestors.
   They were like arrows shot from a defective bow.
58 They made him angry because of their illegal worship sites.
   They made him furious because they worshiped idols.
59 When God heard, he became furious.
   He completely rejected Israel.
60 He abandoned his dwelling place in Shiloh,
   the tent where he had lived among humans.
61 He allowed his power to be taken captive
   and handed his glory over to an oppressor.
62 He let swords kill his people.
   He was furious with those who belonged to him.
63 Fire consumed his best young men,
   so his virgins heard no wedding songs.
64 His priests were cut down with swords.
   The widows ⌞of his priests⌟ could not even weep ⌞for them⌟.
65 Then the Lord woke up like one who had been sleeping,
   like a warrior sobering up from ⌞too much⌟ wine.
66 He struck his enemies from behind
   and disgraced them forever.

67 He rejected the tent of Joseph.
   He did not choose the tribe of Ephraim,
68 but he chose the tribe of Judah,
   Mount Zion which he loved.
69 He built his holy place to be like the high heavens,
   like the earth which he made to last for a long time.

70 He chose his servant David.
   He took him from the sheep pens.
71 He brought him from tending the ewes that had lambs
   so that David could be the shepherd of the people of Jacob,
   of Israel, the people who belonged to the LORD.
72 With unselfish devotion David became their shepherd.
   With skill he guided them.

Psalm 79

A psalm by Asaph.

1 O God, the nations have invaded the land that belongs to you.
   They have dishonored your holy temple.
   They have left Jerusalem in ruins.
2 They have given the dead bodies of your servants
     to the birds for food.
   They have given the flesh of your godly ones
     to the animals.
3 They have shed the blood of your people around Jerusalem
     as though it were water.
       There is no one to bury your people.

4 We have become a disgrace to our neighbors,
     an object of ridicule and contempt to those around us.
5 How long, O Lord?
   Will you remain angry forever?
   Will your fury continue to burn like fire?
6 Pour your fury on the nations that do not know you,
     on the kingdoms that have not called you.
7 They have devoured Jacob.
   They have destroyed his home.
8 Do not hold the crimes of our ancestors against us.
   Reach out to us soon with your compassion,
     because we are helpless.
9 Help us, O God, our savior, for the glory of your name.
   Rescue us, and forgive our sins for the honor of your name.
10 Why should the nations be allowed to say,
   "Where is their God?"
   Let us watch as the nations learn
     that there is punishment for shedding the blood of your servants.
11 Let the groans of prisoners come into your presence.
   With your powerful arm rescue those who are condemned to death.
12 Pay each one of our neighbors back
     with seven times the number of insults they used to insult you, O Lord.
13 Then we, your people, the flock in your pasture,
     will give thanks to you forever.
     We will praise you throughout every generation.

Psalm 80

For the choir director; according to *shoshannim eduth*; by Asaph; a psalm.

1 Open your ears, O Shepherd of Israel,
     the one who leads the descendants of Joseph like sheep,
     the one who is enthroned over the angels.[a]

---

[a] 80:1 Or "cherubim."

2 Appear in front of Ephraim, Benjamin, and Manasseh.
  Wake up your power, and come to save us.

3 O God, restore us and smile on us
  so that we may be saved.

4 O Lord God, commander of armies, how long will you smolder in anger
  against the prayer of your people?
5 You made them eat tears as food.
  You often made them drink their own tears.
6 You made us a source of conflict to our neighbors,
  and our enemies made fun of us.

7 O God, commander of armies, restore us and smile on us
  so that we may be saved.

8 You brought a vine from Egypt.
  You forced out the nations and planted it.
9 You cleared the ground for it
  so that it took root and filled the land.
10 Its shade covered the mountains.
   Its branches covered the mighty cedars.
11 It reached out with its branches to the Mediterranean Sea.
   Its shoots reached the Euphrates River.

12 Why did you break down the stone fences around this vine?
   All who pass by are picking its fruit.
13 Wild boars from the forest graze on it.
   Wild animals devour it.
14 O God, commander of armies, come back!
   Look from heaven and see!
Come to help this vine.
15 Take care of what your right hand planted,
   the son you strengthened for yourself.
16 The vine has been cut down and burned.
   Let them be destroyed by the threatening look on your face.

17 Let your power rest on the man you have chosen,
   the son of man you strengthened for yourself.
18 Then we will never turn away from you.
   Give us life again, and we will call on you.

19 O Lord God, commander of armies, restore us, and smile on us
   so that we may be saved.

Psalm 81

For the choir director; on the *gittith;*[a] by Asaph.

1 Sing joyfully to God, our strength.
  Shout happily to the God of Jacob.
2 Begin a psalm, and strike a tambourine.
  Play lyres and harps with their pleasant music.

---

[a]81:1 Unknown musical term.

³ Blow the ram's horn on the day of the new moon,
   on the day of the full moon,
   on our festival days.
⁴ This is a law for Israel,
   a legal decision from the God of Jacob.
⁵   These are the instructions God set in place for Joseph
      when Joseph rose to power over Egypt.

I heard a message I did not understand:
⁶   "I removed the burden from his shoulder.
      His hands were freed from the basket.
⁷   When you were in trouble, you called out ˌto meˌ, and I rescued you.
      I was hidden in thunder, but I answered you.
      I tested your ˌloyaltyˌ at the oasis of Meribah.   *Selah*
⁸   Listen, my people, and I will warn you.
      Israel, if you would only listen to me!
⁹   Never keep any strange god among you.
      Never worship a foreign god.
¹⁰   I am the Lᴏʀᴅ your God, the one who brought you out of Egypt.
      Open your mouth wide, and I will fill it.

¹¹   "But my people did not listen to me.
      Israel wanted nothing to do with me.
¹²   So I let them go their own stubborn ways
       and follow their own advice.
¹³ If only my people would listen to me!
   If only Israel would follow me!
¹⁴   I would quickly defeat their enemies.
       I would turn my power against their foes.
¹⁵   Those who hate the Lᴏʀᴅ would cringe in front of him,
        and their time ˌfor punishmentˌ would last forever.
¹⁶ But I would feed Israel with the finest wheat
   and satisfy them with honey from a rock."

Psalm 82

A psalm by Asaph.

¹ God takes his place in his own assembly.
   He pronounces judgment among the gods:
²   "How long are you going to judge unfairly?
      How long are you going to side with wicked people?"   *Selah*

³ Defend weak people and orphans.
   Protect the rights of the oppressed and the poor.
⁴ Rescue weak and needy people.
   Help them escape the power of wicked people.

⁵ Wicked people do not know or understand anything.
   As they walk around in the dark,
   all the foundations of the earth shake.
⁶ I said, "You are gods.
   You are all sons of the Most High.

7   You will certainly die like humans
        and fall like any prince."

8   Arise, O God!
        Judge the earth, because all the nations belong to you.

Psalm 83

A song; a psalm by Asaph.

1   O God, do not remain silent.
        Do not turn a deaf ear to me.
        Do not keep quiet, O God.

2   Look, your enemies are in an uproar.
        Those who hate you hold their heads high.

3   They make plans in secret against your people
            and plot together against those you treasure.

4   They say, "Let's wipe out their nation
            so that the name of Israel will no longer be remembered."

5   They agree completely on their plan.
        They form an alliance against you:

6   the tents from Edom and Ishmael,
            Moab and Hagar,

7   Gebal, Ammon, and Amalek,
            Philistia, along with those who live in Tyre.

8   Even Assyria has joined them.
            They helped the descendants of Lot.   *Selah*

9   Do to them what you did to Midian,
        to Sisera and Jabin at the Kishon River.

10   They were destroyed at Endor.
        They became manure to fertilize the ground.

11   Treat their influential people as you treated Oreb and Zeeb.
        Treat all their leaders like Zebah and Zalmunna.

12   They said, "Let's take God's pasturelands for ourselves."

13   O my God, blow them away like tumbleweeds,*a*
        like husks in the wind.

14   Pursue them with your storms,
        and terrify them with your windstorms

15   the way fire burns a forest
            and flames set mountains on fire.*b*

16   Let their faces blush with shame, O Lord,
        so that they must look to you for help.

17   Let them be put to shame and terrified forever.
        Let them die in disgrace

18   so that they must acknowledge you.
            Your name is the Lord.
            You alone are the Most High God of the whole earth.

---

*a*83:13 Or "whirling dust." *b*83:15 Verse 15 (in Hebrew) has been placed in front of verse 14 to express the complex Hebrew sentence structure more clearly in English.

Psalm 84

For the choir director; on the *gittith*; a psalm by Korah's descendants.

1 Your dwelling place is lovely, O Lord of Armies!
2 My soul longs and yearns
for the Lord's courtyards.
My whole body shouts for joy to the living God.
3 Even sparrows find a home,
and swallows find a nest for themselves.
There they hatch their young
near your altars, O Lord of Armies,
my king and my God.
4 Blessed are those who live in your house.
They are always praising you.   Selah

5 Blessed are those who find strength in you.
Their hearts are on the road that leads to you.*
6 As they pass through a valley where balsam trees grow,*
they make it a place of springs.
The early rains cover it with blessings.*
7 Their strength grows as they go along
until each one of them appears
in front of God in Zion.

8 O Lord God, commander of armies, hear my prayer.
Open your ears, O God of Jacob.   Selah
9 Look at our shield, O God.
Look with favor on the face of your anointed one.
10 One day in your courtyards is better than a thousand anywhere else.
I would rather stand in the entrance to my God's house
than live inside wicked people's homes.
11 The Lord God is a sun and shield.
The Lord grants favor and honor.
He does not hold back any blessing
from those who live innocently.

12 O Lord of Armies, blessed is the person who trusts you.

Psalm 85

For the choir director; a psalm by Korah's descendants.

1 You favored your land, O Lord.
You restored the fortunes of Jacob.
2 You removed your people's guilt.
You pardoned all their sins.   Selah
3 You laid aside all your fury.
You turned away from your burning anger.

---

*84:5 Hebrew meaning of this line uncertain.   *84:6 Or "As they pass through the valley of Weeping."
*84:6 Or "pools."

4 Restore us, O God, our savior.
Put an end to your anger against us.
5 Will you be angry with us forever?
Will you ever let go of your anger in the generations to come?
6 Won't you restore our lives again
so that your people may find joy in you?
7 Show us your mercy, O Lord,
by giving us your salvation.

8 I want to hear what God the Lord says,
because he promises peace to his people, to his godly ones.
But they must not go back to their stupidity.
9 Indeed, his salvation is near those who fear him,
and his glory will remain in our land.

10 Mercy and truth have met.
Righteousness and peace have kissed.
11 Truth sprouts from the ground,
and righteousness looks down from heaven.
12 The Lord will certainly give us what is good,
and our land will produce crops.
13 Righteousness will go ahead of him
and make a path for his steps.

Psalm 86

A prayer by David.

1 Turn your ear toward me, O Lord.
Answer me, because I am oppressed and needy.
2 Protect me, because I am faithful to you.
Save your servant who trusts you. You are my God.
3 Have pity on me, O Lord,
because I call out to you all day long.
4 Give me joy, O Lord,
because I lift my soul to you.
5 You, O Lord, are good and forgiving,
full of mercy toward everyone who calls out to you.
6 Open your ears to my prayer, O Lord.
Pay attention when I plead for mercy.
7 When I am in trouble, I call out to you
because you answer me.

8 No god is like you, O Lord.
No one can do what you do.
9 All the nations that you have made
will bow in your presence, O Lord.
They will honor you.
10 Indeed, you are great, a worker of miracles.
You alone are God.
11 Teach me your way, O Lord,
so that I may live in your truth.

Focus my heart on fearing you.
12 I will give thanks to you with all my heart, O Lord my God.
I will honor you forever
13   because your mercy toward me is great.
You have rescued me from the depths of hell.

14 O God, arrogant people attack me,
and a mob of ruthless people seeks my life.
They think nothing of you.
15 But you, O Lord, are a compassionate and merciful God.
You are patient, always faithful and ready to forgive.
16 Turn toward me, and have pity on me.
Give me your strength because I am your servant.
Save me because I am the son of your female servant.
17 Grant me some proof of your goodness
so that those who hate me may see it and be put to shame.
You, O LORD, have helped me and comforted me.

Psalm 87

By Korah's descendants; a psalm; a song.

1 ⌞The city⌟ the LORD has founded ⌞stands⌟ on holy mountains.
2 The LORD loves the city of Zion
more than any other place in Jacob.
3 Glorious things are said about you, O city of God!   *Selah*

4 ⌞The LORD says,⌟ "I will add Egypt and Babylon
as well as Philistia, Tyre, and Sudan
to the list of those who acknowledge me.
Each nation ⌞will claim that it⌟ was born there."

5   But it will be said of Zion,
"Every race is born in it.
The Most High will make it secure."
6   The LORD will record this in the Book of Nations:
"Every race ⌞claims that it⌟ was born there."   *Selah*

Good Morning, God

Psalm 86:11-12

What do you like best about growing up? What do you like the least? Growing up means becoming more mature. You can show that you are growing up by putting God in the center of your life. The closer you are to God, the more mature you will be.

David is a good example to follow. Ask God to help you to pray a prayer like the one David prayed in Psalm 86.

Father, help me to grow up to be a person who stays close to you.

7   Singers and dancers will sing,
    "Zion is the source of all our blessings."

Psalm 88

A song; a psalm by Korah's descendants; for the choir director; according to
mahalath leannoth;[a] a *maskil* by Heman the Ezrahite.

1   O Lord God, my savior,
    I cry out to you during the day and at night.
2   Let my prayer come into your presence.
        Turn your ear to hear my cries.
3   My soul is filled with troubles,
    and my life comes closer to the grave.
4   I am numbered with those who go into the pit.
    I am like a man without any strength—
5   abandoned with the dead,
        like those who have been killed and lie in graves,
        like those whom you no longer remember,
            who are cut off from your power.
6   You have put me in the bottom of the pit— in deep, dark places.
7   Your rage lies heavily on me.
    You make all your waves pound on me.   *Selah*
8   You have taken my friends far away from me.
    You made me disgusting to them.
        I'm shut in, and I can't get out.
9   My eyes grow weak because of my suffering.
        All day long I call out to you, O Lord.
        I stretch out my hands to you in prayer.

10 Will you perform miracles for those who are dead?
    Will the spirits of the dead rise and give thanks to you?   *Selah*
11 Will anyone tell about your mercy in Sheol
    or about your faithfulness in Abaddon?
12 Will anyone know about your miracles in that dark place
    or about your righteousness in the place where forgotten people live?

13 I cry out to you for help, O Lord,
    and in the morning my prayer will come into your presence.

14 Why do you reject my soul, O Lord?
    Why do you hide your face from me?
15   Ever since I was young, I have been suffering and near death.
        I have endured your terrors, and now I am in despair.[b]
16   Your burning anger has swept over me.
            Your terrors have destroyed me.
17   They swirl around me all day long like water.
                They surround me on all sides.
18   You have taken my loved ones and friends far away from me.
                    Darkness is my only friend![c]

---

[a]88:1 Unknown musical term.   [b]88:15 Hebrew meaning uncertain.   [c]88:18 Hebrew meaning uncertain.

Psalm 89

A *maskil* by Ethan the Ezrahite.

1   I will sing forever about the evidence of your mercy, O Lord.
    I will tell about your faithfulness to every generation.
2   I said, "Your mercy will last forever.
    Your faithfulness stands firm in the heavens."

3   You said, "I have made a promise[a] to my chosen one.
    I swore this oath to my servant David:
4   'I will make your dynasty continue forever.
    I built your throne to last throughout every generation.'"   *Selah*

5   O Lord, the heavens praise your miracles
    and your faithfulness in the assembly of the holy ones.
6   Who in the skies can compare with the Lord?
    Who among the heavenly beings is like the Lord?
7   God is terrifying in the council of the holy ones.
    He is greater and more awe-inspiring than those who surround him.
8   O Lord God of Armies, who is like you?
    Mighty Lord, even your faithfulness surrounds you.
9   You rule the raging sea.
        When its waves rise, you quiet them.
10 You crushed Rahab;[b] it was like a corpse.
    With your strong arm you scattered your enemies.
11 The heavens are yours.
    The earth is also yours.
    You made the world and everything in it.
12 You created north and south.
        Mount Tabor and Mount Hermon sing your name joyfully.
13 Your arm is mighty.
    Your hand is strong.
    Your right hand is lifted high.
14 Righteousness and justice are the foundations of your throne.
    Mercy and truth stand in front of you.
15 Blessed are the people who know how to praise you.
        They walk in the light of your presence, O Lord.
16 They find joy in your name all day long.
    They are joyful in your righteousness
17   because you are the glory of their strength.
    By your favor you give us victory.[c]
18 Our shield belongs to the Lord.
    Our king belongs to the Holy One of Israel.

19 Once in a vision you said to your faithful ones:
    "I set a boy above warriors.[d]
    I have raised up one chosen from the people.
20 I found my servant David.
    I anointed him with my holy oil.

---

[a] 89:3 Or "covenant."   [b] 89:10 Rahab is the name of a demonic creature who opposes God.   [c] 89:17 Hebrew meaning of "give us victory" uncertain.   [d] 89:19 Hebrew meaning of this line uncertain.

21 My hand is ready to help him.
   My arm will also give him strength.
22   No enemy will take him by surprise.
      No wicked person will mistreat him.
23 I will crush his enemies in front of him
   and defeat those who hate him.
24 My faithfulness and mercy will be with him,
   and in my name he will be victorious.*
25 I will put his left hand on the sea
   and his right hand on the rivers.
26 He will call out to me,
   'You are my Father, my God, and the rock of my salvation.'
27 Yes, I will make him the firstborn.
   He will be the Most High to the kings of the earth.
28 My mercy will stay with him forever.
   My promise to him is unbreakable.
29 I will make his dynasty endure forever
   and his throne like the days of heaven.

30 "If his descendants abandon my teachings
   and do not live by my rules,
31 if they violate my laws
   and do not obey my commandments,
32 then with a rod I will punish their rebellion
   and their crimes with beatings.
33 But I will not take my mercy away from him
   or allow my truth to become a lie.
34 I will not dishonor my promise
   or alter my own agreement.
35 On my holiness I have taken an oath once and for all:
   I will not lie to David.
36 His dynasty will last forever.
   His throne will be in my presence like the sun.
37   Like the moon his throne will stand firm forever.
      It will be like a faithful witness in heaven."

38 But you have despised, rejected,
   and become angry with your anointed one.
39 You have refused to recognize the promise to your servant
   and have thrown his crown into the dirt.
40 You have broken through all his walls
   and have laid his fortified cities in ruins.
41   (Everyone who passed by robbed him.
      He has become the object of his neighbors' scorn.)
42 You held the right hand of his enemies high
   and made all of his adversaries rejoice.
43 You even took his sword out of his hand
   and failed to support him in battle.
44 You put an end to his splendor

---

*89:24 Hebrew meaning of "he will be victorious" uncertain.

and hurled his throne to the ground.
45   You cut short the days of his youth
and covered him with shame.   *Selah*

46   How long, O Lord? Will you hide yourself forever?
How long will your anger continue to burn like fire?
47   Remember how short my life is!
Have you created Adam's descendants for no reason?
48   Can a mortal go on living and never see death?
Who can set himself free from the power of the grave?   *Selah*
49   Where is the evidence of your mercy, Lord?
You swore an oath to David
on ‚the basis of‚ your faithfulness.

50   Remember, O Lord,ᶠhow your servantᵍ has been insulted.
Remember how I have carried in my heart
‚the insults‚ from so many people.
51   Your enemies insulted ‚me‚.
They insulted your Messiahʰ every step he took.

52   Thank the Lord forever.
Amen and amen!

BOOK FOUR
Psalms 90–106

Psalm 90

A prayer by Moses, the man of God.

1   O Lord, you have been our refuge throughout every generation.
2   Before the mountains were born,
before you gave birth to the earth and the world, you were God.
You are God from everlasting to everlasting.

3   You turn mortals back into dust
and say, "Return, descendants of Adam."
4   Indeed, in your sight a thousand years are like a single day,
like yesterday—already past—
like an hour in the night.
5   You sweep mortals away.
They are a dream.
They sprout again in the morning like cut grass.
6   In the morning they blossom and sprout.
In the evening they wither and dry up.

7   Indeed, your anger consumes us.
Your rage terrifies us.

ᶠ89:50 Many Hebrew manuscripts; other Hebrew manuscripts "Lord."   ᵍ89:50 Many Hebrew manuscripts, Greek, Syriac; other Hebrew manuscripts "your servants."   ʰ89:51 Or "anointed one."

8   You have set our sins in front of you.
      You have put our secret sins in the light of your presence.
9   Indeed, all our days slip away because of your fury.
      We live out our years like one ˻long˼ sigh.
10   Each of us lives for 70 years—
      or even 80 if we are in good health.
        But the best of them[a] ˻bring˼ trouble and misery.
          Indeed, they are soon gone, and we fly away.
11   Who fully understands the power of your anger?
      A person fears you more when he better understands your fury.[b]
12   Teach us to number each of our days
      so that we may grow in wisdom.

13   Return, Lord! How long. . .?
      Change your plans about ˻us,˼ your servants.
14   Satisfy us every morning with your mercy
      so that we may sing joyfully and rejoice all our days.
15   Make us rejoice for as many days as you have made us suffer,
      for as many years as we have experienced evil.
16   Let ˻us,˼ your servants, see what you can do.
      Let our children see your glorious power.
17   Let the kindness of the Lord our God be with us.
      Make us successful in everything we do.
        Yes, make us successful in everything we do.

Psalm 91

1   Whoever lives under the shelter of the Most High
      will remain in the shadow of the Almighty.
2   I will say to the Lord,
      "˻You are˼ my refuge and my fortress, my God in whom I trust."

3   He is the one who will rescue you from hunters' traps
      and from deadly plagues.
4   He will cover you with his feathers,
      and under his wings you will find refuge.
        His truth is your shield and armor.

5   You do not need to fear
      terrors of the night,
      arrows that fly during the day,
6   plagues that roam the dark,
      epidemics that strike at noon.
7   They will not come near you,
          even though a thousand may fall dead beside you
          or ten thousand at your right side.

8   You only have to look with your eyes
      to see the punishment of wicked people.

9   You, O Lord, are my refuge!

---

[a] 90:10 Hebrew meaning of "the best of them" uncertain.   [b] 90:11 Hebrew meaning of this line uncertain.

You have made the Most High your home.
10   No harm will come to you.
No sickness will come near your house.
11 He will put his angels in charge of you
    to protect you in all your ways.
12   They will carry you in their hands
      so that you never hit your foot against a rock.
13   You will step on lions and cobras.
    You will trample young lions and snakes.

14 Because you love me, I will rescue you.
    I will protect you because you know my name.
15 When you call to me, I will answer you.
    I will be with you when you are in trouble.
    I will save you and honor you.
16 I will satisfy you with a long life.
    I will show you how I will save you.

Psalm 92

A psalm; a song; for the day of worship.

1 It is good to give thanks to the LORD,
    to make music to praise your name, O Most High.
2 It is good to announce your mercy in the morning
    and your faithfulness in the evening
3   on a ten-stringed instrument and a harp
      and with a melody on a lyre.

4 You made me find joy in what you have done, O LORD.
    I will sing joyfully about the works of your hands.
5   How spectacular are your works, O LORD!
    How very deep are your thoughts!

6 A stupid person cannot know
    and a fool cannot understand
7   that wicked people sprout like grass
      and all troublemakers blossom like flowers,
      only to be destroyed forever.

8 But you, O LORD, are highly honored forever.
9   Now look at your enemies, O LORD.
    Now look at your enemies.
    They disappear, and all troublemakers are scattered.

10 But you make me as strong as a wild bull,
    and soothing lotion is poured on me.
11 My eyes gloat over those who spy on me.
    My ears hear the cries of evildoers attacking me.

12 Righteous people flourish like palm trees
    and grow tall like the cedars in Lebanon.
13   They are planted in the LORD's house.

They blossom in our God's courtyards.
14 Even when they are old, they still bear fruit.
They are always healthy and fresh.
15 They make it known that the LORD is decent.
He is my rock.
He is never unfair.

Psalm 93

1 The LORD rules as king! He is clothed with majesty.
The LORD has clothed himself; he has armed himself with power.
The world was set in place; it cannot be moved.
2 Your throne was set in place a long time ago.
You are eternal.

3 The ocean rises, O LORD.
The ocean rises with a roar.
The ocean rises with its pounding waves.
4 The LORD above is mighty—
mightier than the sound of raging water,
mightier than the foaming waves of the sea.

5 Your written testimonies are completely reliable.
O LORD, holiness is what makes your house beautiful for days without end.

Psalm 94

1 O LORD, God of vengeance,
O God of vengeance, appear!
2 Arise, O Judge of the earth.
Give arrogant people what they deserve.
3 How long, O LORD, will wicked people triumph?
How long?

4 They ramble.
They speak arrogantly.
All troublemakers brag about themselves.
5 They crush your people, O LORD.
They make those who belong to you suffer.
6 They kill widows and foreigners, and they murder orphans.
7 They say, "The LORD doesn't see it.
The God of Jacob doesn't even pay attention to it."
8 Pay attention, you stupid people!
When will you become wise, you fools?
9 God created ears.
Do you think he can't hear?
He formed eyes.
Do you think he can't see?
10 He disciplines nations.
Do you think he can't punish?
He teaches people.

Do you think he doesn't know anything?
11   The LORD knows that people's thoughts are pointless.

12   O LORD, blessed is the person
        whom you discipline and instruct from your teachings.
13   You give him peace and quiet from times of trouble
          while a pit is dug to trap wicked people.

14   The LORD will never desert his people
        or abandon those who belong to him.
15   The decisions of judges will again become fair,
          and everyone whose motives are decent will pursue justice.[a]

16   Who will stand up for me against evildoers?
     Who will stand by my side against troublemakers?
17   If the LORD had not come to help me,
          my soul would have quickly fallen silent in death.

18   When I said, "My feet are slipping,"
        your mercy, O LORD, continued to hold me up.
19   When I worried about many things,
        your assuring words soothed my soul.

20   Are wicked rulers who use the law to do unlawful things
        able to be your partners?
21   They join forces to take the lives of righteous people.
        They condemn innocent people to death.
22   The LORD has become my stronghold.
     My God has become my rock of refuge.
23   He has turned their own wickedness against them.
        He will destroy them because of their sins.
        The LORD our God will destroy them.

Psalm 95

1   Come, let's sing joyfully to the LORD.
        Let's shout happily to the rock of our salvation.
2   Let's come into his presence with a song of thanksgiving.
        Let's shout happily to him with psalms.
3   The LORD is a great God and a great king above all gods.
4   In his hand are the deep places of the earth,
          and the mountain peaks are his.
5   The sea is his.
        He made it, and his hands formed the dry land.

6   Come, let's worship and bow down.
        Let's kneel in front of the LORD, our maker,
7   because he is our God
            and we are the people in his care,
              the flock that he leads.

If only you would listen to him today!

---

[a]94:15 English equivalent of this verse difficult.

8   "Do not be stubborn like my people were at Meribah,
    like the time at Massah in the desert.
9   Your ancestors challenged me and tested me there,
        although they had seen what I had done.
10 For 40 years I was disgusted with those people.
    So I said, 'They are a people whose hearts continue to stray.
    They have not learned my ways.'
11 That is why I angrily took this solemn oath:
    'They will never enter my place of rest!' "

Psalm 96

1   Sing to the LORD a new song!
    Sing to the LORD, all the earth!
2   Sing to the LORD! Praise his name!
    Day after day announce that the LORD saves his people.
3   Tell people about his glory.
        Tell all the nations about his miracles.

4   The LORD is great!
    He should be highly praised.
    He should be feared more than all other gods
5   because all the gods of the nations are idols.
    The LORD made the heavens.
6   Splendor and majesty are in his presence.
    Strength and beauty are in his holy place.

7   Give to the LORD, you families of the nations.
    Give to the LORD glory and power.
8   Give to the LORD the glory he deserves.
    Bring an offering, and come into his courtyards.
9   Worship the LORD in his holy splendor.
    Tremble in his presence, all the earth!

10 Say to the nations, "The LORD rules as king!"
    The earth stands firm; it cannot be moved.
    He will judge people fairly.
11   Let the heavens rejoice and the earth be glad.
    Let the sea and everything in it roar like thunder.
12   Let the fields and everything in them rejoice.
    Then all the trees in the forest will sing joyfully
13   in the LORD's presence because he is coming.
    He is coming to judge the earth.
    He will judge the world with righteousness
    and its people with his truth.

Psalm 97

1   The LORD rules as king.
    Let the earth rejoice.
    Let all the islands be joyful.
2   Clouds and darkness surround him.

Righteousness and justice are the foundations of his throne.
3   Fire spreads ahead of him.
    It burns his enemies who surround him.
4   His flashes of lightning light up the world.
        The earth sees them and trembles.
5   The mountains melt like wax in the presence of the LORD,
        in the presence of the Lord of the whole earth.
6   The heavens tell about his righteousness,
        and all the people of the world see his glory.

7   Everyone who worships idols
        and brags about false gods will be put to shame.
    All the gods will bow to him.

8   Zion hears about this and rejoices.
        The people of Judah are delighted with your judgments, O LORD.
9   You, O LORD, the Most High, are above the whole earth.
    You are highest. You are above all the gods.
10 Let those who love the LORD hate evil.
        The one who guards the lives of his godly ones
            will rescue them from the power of wicked people.
11 Light dawns for righteous people*
        and joy for those whose motives are decent.
12 Find joy in the LORD, you righteous people.
        Give thanks to him as you remember how holy he is.

Psalm 98

A psalm.

1   Sing a new song to the LORD
        because he has done miraculous things.
            His right hand and his holy arm have gained victory for him.
2   The LORD has made his salvation known.
        He has uncovered his righteousness for the nations to see.
3   He has not forgotten to be merciful and faithful
            to Israel's descendants.
                All the ends of the earth have seen how our God saves them.

4   Shout happily to the LORD, all the earth.
        Break out into joyful singing, and make music.
5   Make music to the LORD with a lyre,
        with a lyre and the melody of a psalm,
6   with trumpets and the playing of a ram's horn.
    Shout happily in the presence of the king, the LORD.

7   Let the sea, everything in it,
        the world, and those who live in it roar like thunder.
8   Let the rivers clap their hands
        and the mountains sing joyfully
9   in the LORD's presence

---

*97:11 One Hebrew manuscript, Greek, Syriac, Latin; other Hebrew manuscripts "Light is planted for righteous people."

because he is coming to judge the earth.
He will judge the world with justice
and its people with fairness.

Psalm 99

1 The LORD rules as king.
Let the people tremble.
He is enthroned over the angels.[a]
Let the earth quake.
2 The LORD is mighty in Zion.
He is high above all people.
3 Let them give thanks to your great and fearful name.

He is holy!

4 The king's strength is that he loves justice.
You have established fairness.
You have done what is fair and right for Jacob.

5 Highly honor the LORD our God.
Bow down at his footstool.

He is holy!

6 Moses and Aaron were among his priests.
Samuel was among those who prayed to him.
They called to the LORD, and he answered them.
7 He spoke to them from a column of smoke.
They obeyed his written instructions and the laws that he gave them.
8 O LORD, our God, you answered them.
You showed them that you are a forgiving God
and that you are a God who punishes their sinful deeds.

9 Highly honor the LORD our God.
Bow at his holy mountain.

The LORD our God is holy!

Psalm 100

A psalm of thanksgiving.

1 Shout happily to the LORD, all the earth.
2 Serve the LORD cheerfully.
Come into his presence with a joyful song.
3 Realize that the LORD alone is God.
He made us, and we are his.[a]
We are his people and the sheep in his care.
4 Enter his gates with a song of thanksgiving.
Come into his courtyards with a song of praise.
Give thanks to him; praise his name.

---

[a]99:1 Or "cherubim."   [a]100:3 Many Hebrew manuscripts, Greek, Targum, Latin; other Hebrew manuscripts "and not we ourselves."

David, the Psalmist

David wrote poems to praise God.

David thought about God a lot. David took good care of his sheep, and he realized that God took care of him the same way. David wrote Psalm 23 to praise God for being his shepherd.

David knew that God cared about everything that happened to him. So when David felt afraid, he talked to God about his fears (Psalm 59). When David felt angry, he talked to God (Psalm 28). When David felt alone and helpless, he told God all about it (Psalm 68). David also talked to God when he felt joyful. He wrote down his words of praise (Psalm 47). Often, David just told God how wonderful he thought God was (Psalm 116).

How many of the 150 psalms did David write? Seventy-three!

David lived around 1000 B.C.

David was a famous warrior and king.

David wrote many prayers and poems praising God.

Getting to Know David

✳ Why do you suppose David liked to talk to God so much?

✳ David saw God as his shepherd. How did that help David talk honestly with God?

✳ Who do you talk to when you feel upset, angry, or afraid?

✳ If you wrote a psalm or poem to God, what would you say?

David believed worship was important.
He brought God's ark to Jerusalem and told all the people to worship in the city. The people often gathered together and sang David's psalms to worship God.

5   The LORD is good.
     His mercy endures forever.
     His faithfulness endures throughout every generation.

Psalm 101

A psalm by David.

1   I will sing about mercy and justice.
     O LORD, I will make music to praise you.
2   I want to understand the path to integrity.
       When will you come to me?

    I will live in my own home with integrity.
3   I will not put anything wicked in front of my eyes.
    I hate what unfaithful people do.
       I want no part of it.
4   I will keep far away from devious minds.
       I will have nothing to do with evil.
5   I will destroy anyone who secretly slanders his neighbor.
       I will not tolerate anyone with a conceited look or arrogant heart.
6   My eyes will be watching the faithful people in the land
       so that they may live with me.
          The person who lives with integrity will serve me.

7   The one who does deceitful things will not stay in my home.
     The one who tells lies will not remain in my presence.

8   Every morning I will destroy all the wicked people in the land
       to rid the LORD's city of all troublemakers.

Psalm 102

A prayer by someone who is suffering, when he is weary and pours out his troubles in the LORD's presence.

1   O LORD, hear my prayer,
       and let my cry for help come to you.
2   Do not hide your face from me when I am in trouble.
       Turn your ear toward me.
       Answer me quickly when I call.
3   My days disappear like smoke.
     My bones burn like hot coals.
4   My heart is beaten down and withered like grass
       because I have forgotten about eating.
5   I am nothing but skin and bones
       because of my loud groans.
6   I am like a desert owl,
       like an owl living in the ruins.
7   I lie awake.
     I am like a lonely bird on a rooftop.
8   All day long my enemies insult me.
       Those who ridicule me use my name as a curse.

⁹ I eat ashes like bread
    and my tears are mixed with my drink
¹⁰   because of your hostility and anger,
    because you have picked me up and thrown me away.
¹¹ My days are like a shadow that is getting longer,
    and I wither away like grass.

¹² But you, O LORD, remain forever.
    You are remembered throughout every generation.
¹³ You will rise and have compassion on Zion,
    because it is time to grant a favor to it.
    Indeed, the appointed time has come.
¹⁴   Your servants value Zion's stones,
    and they pity its rubble.
¹⁵ The nations will fear the LORD's name.
    All the kings of the earth will fear your glory.
¹⁶ When the LORD builds Zion,
    he will appear in his glory.
¹⁷ He will turn his attention to the prayers
    of those who have been abandoned.
    He will not despise their prayers.
¹⁸ This will be written down for a future generation
    so that a people yet to be created may praise the LORD:
¹⁹   "The LORD looked down from his holy place high above.
    From heaven he looked at the earth.
²⁰ He heard the groans of the prisoners
    and set free those who were condemned to death.
²¹   The LORD's name is announced in Zion
    and his praise in Jerusalem
²²   when nations and kingdoms gather
    to worship the LORD."

²³ He has weakened my strength along the way.
    He has reduced the number of my days.
²⁴ I said, "My God, don't take me now in the middle of my life.
    Your years continue on, throughout every generation.
²⁵ Long ago you laid the foundation of the earth.
    Even the heavens are the works of your hands.
²⁶ They will come to an end, but you will still go on.
    They will all wear out like clothing.
    You will change them like clothes,
    and they will be thrown away.
²⁷   But you remain the same, and your life will never end.
²⁸ The children of your servants will go on living here.
    Their descendants will be secure in your presence."

Psalm 103

By David.

¹ Praise the LORD, my soul!
    Praise his holy name, all that is within me.

² Praise the LORD, my soul,
    and never forget all the good he has done:
³   He is the one who forgives all your sins,
        the one who heals all your diseases,
⁴   the one who rescues your life from the pit,
        the one who crowns you with mercy and compassion,
⁵   the one who fills your life with blessings
        so that you become young again like an eagle.

⁶ The LORD does what is right and fair
    for all who are oppressed.
⁷   He let Moses know his ways.
    He let the Israelites know the things he had done.
⁸ The LORD is compassionate, merciful, patient,
    and always ready to forgive.

⁹ He will not always accuse us of wrong
    or be angry with us forever.
¹⁰ He has not treated us as we deserve for our sins
    or paid us back for our wrongs.

¹¹ As high as the heavens are above the earth—
    that is how vast his mercy is toward those who fear him.
¹² As far as the east is from the west—
    that is how far he has removed our rebellious acts from himself.
¹³ As a father has compassion for his children,
    so the LORD has compassion for those who fear him.

¹⁴ He certainly knows what we are made of.
    He bears in mind that we are dust.
¹⁵ Human life is as short-lived as grass.
    It blossoms like a flower in the field.
¹⁶   When the wind blows over the flower, it disappears,
        and there is no longer any sign of it.

¹⁷ But from everlasting to everlasting,
    the LORD's mercy is on those who fear him.
       His righteousness belongs
        to their children and grandchildren,
¹⁸   to those who are faithful to his promise,[a]
        to those who remember to follow his guiding principles.
¹⁹ The LORD has set his throne in heaven.
    His kingdom rules everything.

²⁰ Praise the LORD, all his angels,
    you mighty beings who carry out his orders
    and are ready to obey his spoken orders.
²¹ Praise the LORD, all his armies,
    his servants who carry out his will.
²² Praise the LORD, all his creatures
    in all the places of his empire.
    Praise the LORD, my soul!

---

^a103:18 Or "covenant."

Psalm 104

1 Praise the LORD, my soul!
   O LORD my God, you are very great.
      You are clothed with splendor and majesty.
2   You cover yourself with light as though it were a robe.
      You stretch out the heavens as though they were curtains.
3   You lay the beams of your home in the water.
      You use the clouds for your chariot.
      You move on the wings of the wind.
4   You make your angels winds
        and your servants flames of fire.

5 You set the earth on its foundations
      so that it can never be shaken.
6 You covered the earth with an ocean as though it were a robe.
      Water stood above the mountains
7   and fled because of your threat.
      Water ran away at the sound of your thunder.
8   The mountains rose and the valleys sank
        to the place you appointed for them.
9   Water cannot cross the boundary you set
        and cannot come back to cover the earth.

10 You make water gush from springs into valleys.
      It flows between the mountains.
11   Every wild animal drinks ˌfrom themˌ.
      Wild donkeys quench their thirst.
12   The birds live by the streams.
      They sing among the branches.
13 You water the mountains from your home above.
   You fill the earth with the fruits of your labors.

14 You make grass grow for cattle
      and make vegetables for humans to use
        in order to get food from the ground.
15 You make wine to cheer human hearts,
      olive oil to make faces shine,
        and bread to strengthen human hearts.
16 The LORD's trees, the cedars in Lebanon which he planted,
      drink their fill.
17   Birds build their nests in them.
      Storks make their homes in fir trees.
18 The high mountains are for wild goats.
   The rocks are a refuge for badgers.

19 He created the moon, which marks the seasons,
      and the sun, which knows when to set.
20   He brings darkness, and it is nighttime,
        when all the wild animals in the forest come out.
21   The young lions roar for their prey
        and seek their food from God.

22   When the sun rises,
          they gather and lie down in their dens.
23   Then people go to do their work,
              to do their tasks until evening.
24 What a large number of things you have made, O Lord!
        You made them all by wisdom.
          The earth is filled with your creatures.
25   The sea is so big and wide with countless creatures,
              living things both large and small.
26   Ships sail on it,
              and Leviathan,[a] which you made, plays in it.
27 All of them look to you to give them their food at the right time.
28   You give it to them, and they gather it up.
        You open your hand, and they are filled with blessings.
29   You hide your face, and they are terrified.
        You take away their breath, and they die and return to dust.
30   You send out your Spirit, and they are created.
        You renew the face of the earth.
31 May the glory of the Lord endure forever.
    May the Lord find joy in what he has made.
32   He looks at the earth, and it trembles.
        He touches the mountains, and they smoke.
33   I will sing to the Lord throughout my life.
        I will make music to praise my God as long as I live.
34 May my thoughts be pleasing to him.
        I will find joy in the Lord.
35 May sinners vanish from the world.
    May there no longer be any wicked people.
    Praise the Lord, my soul!

    Hallelujah!

Psalm 105

1   Give thanks to the Lord.
    Call on him.
    Make known among the nations what he has done.
2   Sing to him.
    Make music to praise him.
    Meditate on all the miracles he has performed.
3   Brag about his holy name.
    Let the hearts of those who seek the Lord rejoice.
4   Search for the Lord and his strength.
    Always seek his presence.
5   Remember the miracles he performed,
          the amazing things he did, and the judgments he pronounced,
6   you descendants of his servant Abraham,
              you descendants of Jacob, his chosen ones.

---

a 104:26 Hebrew meaning uncertain.

7 He is the LORD our God.
His judgments are pronounced throughout the earth.
8 He always remembers his promise,[a]
the word that he commanded for a thousand generations,
9 the promise that he made to Abraham,
and his sworn oath to Isaac.
10 He confirmed it as a law for Jacob,
as an everlasting promise to Israel,
11 by saying, "I will give you the land of Canaan.
It is your share of the inheritance."

12 While the people of Israel were few in number,
a small group of foreigners living in that land,
13 they wandered from nation to nation,
from one kingdom to another.
14 He didn't permit anyone to oppress them.
He warned kings about them:
15 "Do not touch my anointed ones
or harm my prophets."

16 He brought famine to the land.
He took away their food supply.
17 He sent a man ahead of them.
He sent Joseph, who was sold as a slave.
18 They hurt his feet with shackles,
and cut into his neck with an iron collar.
19 The LORD's promise tested him through fiery trials
until his prediction came true.
20 The king sent someone to release him.
The ruler of nations set him free.
21 He made Joseph the master of his palace
and the ruler of all his possessions.
22 Joseph trained the king's officers the way he wanted
and taught his respected leaders wisdom.

23 Then Israel came to Egypt.
Jacob lived as a foreigner in the land of Ham.
24 The LORD made his people grow rapidly in number
and stronger than their enemies.
25 He changed their minds so that they hated his people,
and they dealt treacherously with his servants.
26 He sent his servant Moses, and he sent Aaron, whom he had chosen.
27 They displayed his miraculous signs among them
and did amazing things in the land of Ham.
28 He sent darkness and made their land dark.
They did not rebel against his orders.
29 He turned their water into blood
and caused their fish to die.
30 He made their land swarm with frogs,
even in the kings' bedrooms.

___

a 105:8 Or "covenant."

31 He spoke, and swarms of flies and gnats
      infested their whole territory.
32 He gave them hail and lightning
      instead of rain throughout their land.
33 He struck their grapevines and fig trees
      and smashed the trees in their territory.
34 He spoke, and countless locusts and grasshoppers came.
35   They devoured all the plants in the land.
        They devoured the crops in the fields.
36 He killed all the firstborn sons,
      the first ones born in the land when their fathers were young.
37 He brought Israel out with silver and gold,
      and no one among his tribes stumbled.
38 The Egyptians were terrified of Israel,
      so they were glad when Israel left.
39 He spread out a cloud as a protective covering
      and a fire to light up the night.
40 The Israelites asked, and he brought them quail
      and filled them with bread from heaven.
41 He opened a rock, and water gushed
      and flowed like a river through the dry places.

42 He remembered his holy promise to his servant Abraham.
43 He brought his people out with joy,
      his chosen ones with a song of joy.
44 He gave them the lands of other nations,
      and they inherited what others had worked for
45   so that they would obey his laws
              and follow his teachings.

    Hallelujah!

Psalm 106

1   Hallelujah!

    Give thanks to the Lord because he is good,
      because his mercy endures forever.
2   Who can speak about all the mighty things the Lord has done?
    Who can announce all the things for which he is worthy of praise?
3   Blessed are those who defend justice
      and do what is right at all times.

4   Remember me, O Lord, when you show favor to your people.
    Come to help me with your salvation
5   so that I may see the prosperity of your chosen ones,
          find joy in our people's happiness,
            and brag with the people who belong to you.

6   We have sinned, and so did our ancestors.
    We have done wrong.
    We are guilty.
7   When our ancestors were in Egypt,

they gave no thought to your miracles.
They did not remember your numerous acts of mercy,
so they rebelled at the sea, the Red Sea.

8   He saved them because of his reputation
so that he could make his mighty power known.
9   He angrily commanded the Red Sea, and it dried up.
He led them through deep water as though it were a desert.
10 He rescued them from the power of the one who hated them.
He rescued them from the enemy.
11 Water covered their adversaries.
Not one Egyptian survived.
12   Then our ancestors believed what he said.
They sang his praise.

13 They quickly forgot what he did.
They did not wait for his advice.
14 They had an unreasonable desire for food in the wilderness.
In the desert they tested God.
15   He gave them what they asked for.
He also gave them a degenerative disease.

16 In the camp certain men became envious of Moses.
They also became envious of Aaron, the LORD's holy one.
17   The ground split open and swallowed Dathan.
It buried Abiram's followers.
18   A fire broke out among their followers.
Flames burned up wicked people.

19 At Mount Horeb they made a statue of a calf.
They worshiped an idol made of metal.
20   They traded their glorious God[a]
for the statue of a bull that eats grass.
21 They forgot God, their savior,
the one who did spectacular things in Egypt,
22   miracles in the land of Ham,
and terrifying things at the Red Sea.
23 God said he was going to destroy them,
but Moses, his chosen one, stood in his way
to prevent him from exterminating them.

24 They refused to enter the pleasant land.
They did not believe what he said.
25 They complained in their tents.
They did not obey the LORD.
26   Raising his hand, he swore
that he would kill them in the wilderness,
27   kill their descendants among the nations,
and scatter them throughout various lands.

---

[a] 106:20 Or "their glory."

28 They joined in worshiping the god Baal while they were at Peor,
   and they ate what was sacrificed to the dead.
29 They infuriated God by what they did,
   and a plague broke out among them.
30 Then Phinehas stood between God and the people,
   and the plague was stopped.
31   Because of this, Phinehas was considered righteous forever,
        throughout every generation.
32 They made God angry by the water at Meribah.
        Things turned out badly for Moses because of what they did,
33   since they made him bitter so that he spoke recklessly.

34 They did not destroy the people as the LORD had told them.
35   Instead, they intermarried with other nations.
        They learned to do what other nations did,
36   and they worshiped their idols,
              which became a trap for them.
37 They sacrificed their sons and daughters to demons.
38   They shed innocent blood,
           the blood of their own sons and daughters
              whom they sacrificed to the idols of Canaan.
                 The land became polluted with blood.
39 They became filthy because of what they did.
   They behaved like prostitutes.
40   The LORD burned with anger against his own people.
        He was disgusted with those who belonged to him.
41   He handed them over to other nations,
           and those who hated them ruled them.
42   Their enemies oppressed them
              and made them subject to their power.
43   He rescued them many times,
           but they continued to plot rebellion against him
           and to sink deeper because of their sin.
44   He saw that they were suffering
           when he heard their cry for help.
45   He remembered his promise[b] to them.
           In keeping with his rich mercy, he changed his plans.
46   He let them find compassion
           from all those who held them captive.

47 Rescue us, O LORD our God, and gather us from the nations
   so that we may give thanks to your holy name
   and make your praise our glory.

48   Thanks be to the LORD God of Israel
           from everlasting to everlasting.
              Let all the people say amen.
               Hallelujah!

---

b 106:45 Or "covenant."

BOOK FIVE
Psalms 107–150

Psalm 107

¹ Give thanks to the LORD because he is good,
   because his mercy endures forever.

² Let the people the LORD defended repeat these words.
   They are the people he defended from the power of their enemies
³   and gathered from other countries,
      from the east and from the west,
      from the north and from the south.
⁴ They wandered around the desert on a deserted road
   without finding an inhabited city.
⁵ They were hungry and thirsty.
   They began to lose hope.
⁶ In their distress they cried out to the LORD.
   He rescued them from their troubles.
⁷ He led them on a road that went straight to an inhabited city.

⁸ Let them give thanks to the LORD because of his mercy.
   He performed his miracles for Adam's descendants.
⁹ He gave plenty to drink to those who were thirsty.
   He filled those who were hungry with good food.
¹⁰ Those who lived in the dark, in death's shadow
      were prisoners in misery.
         They were held in iron chains
¹¹   because they had rebelled against God's words
            and had despised the advice given by the Most High.
¹² So he humbled them with hard work.
      They fell down, but no one was there to help them.
¹³ In their distress they cried out to the LORD.
   He saved them from their troubles.
¹⁴ He brought them out of the dark, out of death's shadow.
   He broke apart their chains.

¹⁵ Let them give thanks to the LORD because of his mercy.
   He performed his miracles for Adam's descendants.
¹⁶ He shattered bronze gates
      and cut iron bars in two.
¹⁷ Fools suffered because of their disobedience
      and because of their crimes.
¹⁸ All food was disgusting to them,
      and they came near death's gates.
¹⁹ In their distress they cried out to the LORD.
   He saved them from their troubles.
²⁰ He sent his message and healed them.
   He rescued them from the grave.

21 Let them give thanks to the LORD because of his mercy.
   He performed his miracles for Adam's descendants.
22 Let them bring songs of thanksgiving as their sacrifice.
   Let them tell in joyful songs what he has done.
23 Those who sail on the sea in ships,
   who do business on the high seas,
24   have seen what the LORD can do,
      the miracles he performed in the depths of the sea.
25 He spoke, and a storm began to blow,
   and it made the waves rise high.
26 The sailors aboard ship rose toward the sky.
   They plunged into the depths.
      Their courage melted in the face of disaster.
27   They reeled and staggered like drunks,
      and all their skills as sailors became useless.
28 In their distress they cried out to the LORD.
   He led them from their troubles.
29 He made the storm calm down,
   and the waves became still.
30   The sailors were glad that the storm was quiet.
   He guided them to the harbor they had longed for.
31 Let them give thanks to the LORD because of his mercy.
   He performed his miracles for Adam's descendants.
32 Let them glorify him when the people are gathered for worship.
   Let them praise him in the company of respected leaders.
33   He changes rivers into a desert,
      springs into thirsty ground,
34   and fertile ground into a layer of salt
         because of the wickedness of the people living there.
35   He changes deserts into lakes
      and dry ground into springs.
36   There he settles those who are hungry,
         and they build cities to live in.
37   They plant in fields and vineyards
            that produce crops.
38   He blesses them, and their numbers multiply,
      and he does not allow a shortage of cattle.

39   They became few in number and were humiliated
      because of oppression, disaster, and sorrow.
40   He poured contempt on their influential people
         and made them stumble around in a pathless desert.
41   But now he lifts needy people high above suffering
         and makes their families like flocks.
42   Decent people will see this and rejoice,
               but all the wicked people will shut their mouths.

43 Let those who think they are wise
   pay attention to these things
      so that they may understand the LORD's blessings.

Psalm 108[a]

A song; a psalm by David.

1   My heart is confident, O God.
    I want to sing and make music even with my soul.[b]
2   Wake up, harp and lyre!
    I want to wake up at dawn.
3   I want to give thanks to you among the people, O Lᴏʀᴅ.
    I want to make music to praise you among the nations
4   because your mercy is higher than the heavens.
            Your truth reaches the skies.

5   May you be honored above the heavens, O God.
    Let your glory extend over the whole earth.

6   Save ͺusͺ with your powerful hand, and answer us
    so that those who are dear to you may be rescued.

7   God has promised the following through his holiness:
    "I will triumph!
        I will divide Shechem.
        I will measure the valley of Succoth.
8   Gilead is mine.
        Manasseh is mine.
        Ephraim is the helmet on my head.
        Judah is my scepter.
9   Moab is my washtub.
        I will throw my shoe over Edom.
        I will shout in triumph over Philistia."

10 Who will bring me into the fortified city?
    Who will lead me to Edom?
11   Isn't it you, O God, who rejected us?
    Isn't it you, O God, who refused to accompany our armies?

12 Give us help against the enemy
        because human assistance is worthless.
13   With God we will display great strength.
            He will trample our enemies.

Psalm 109

For the choir director; a psalm by David.

1   O God, whom I praise, do not turn a deaf ear to me.
2   Wicked and deceitful people have opened their mouths against me.
        They speak against me with lying tongues.
3   They surround me with hateful words.
        They fight against me for no reason.
4   In return for my love, they accuse me,
        but I pray for them.[a]

---

[a]108:1 Verses 1-5 are virtually identical in wording to Psalm 57:7-11; verses 6-13 are virtually identical in wording to Psalm 60:5-12.   [b]108:1 Or "my glory."   [a]109:4 Or "but I am a man of prayer."

5 They reward me with evil instead of good
and with hatred instead of love.

6 I said, "Appoint the evil one to oppose him.
Let Satan stand beside him.

7 When he stands trial,
let him be found guilty.
Let his prayer be considered sinful.

8 Let his days be few in number.
Let someone else take his position.

9 "Let his children become fatherless and his wife a widow.

10 Let his children wander around and beg.
Let them seek help far from their ruined homes.

11 Let a creditor take everything he owns.
Let strangers steal what he has worked for.

12 Let no one be kind to him anymore.
Let no one show any pity to his fatherless children.

13 Let his descendants be cut off
and their family name be wiped out by the next generation.

14 Let the LORD remember the guilt of his ancestors
and not wipe out his mother's sin.

15 Let their guilt and sin always remain on record
in front of the LORD.
Let the LORD remove every memory of him[b] from the earth,

16 because he did not remember to be kind.

"He drove oppressed, needy,
and brokenhearted people to their graves.

17 He loved to put curses on others,
so he, too, was cursed.
He did not like to bless others,
so he never received a blessing.

18 He wore cursing as though it were clothing,
so cursing entered his body like water
and his bones like oil.

19 Let cursing be his clothing,
a belt he always wears."

20 This is how the LORD rewards those who accuse me,
those who say evil things against me.

21 O LORD Almighty, deal with me out of the goodness of your name.
Rescue me because of your mercy.

22 I am oppressed and needy.
I can feel the pain in my heart.

23 I fade away like a lengthening shadow.
I have been shaken off like a grasshopper.

24 My knees give way because I have been fasting.
My body has become lean, without any fat.

25 I have become the victim of my enemies' insults.

---

b 109:15 Or "them."

They look at me and shake their heads.
26 Help me, O Lord my God.
    Save me because of your mercy.
27   Then they will know that this is your doing,
        that you, O Lord, are the one who saved me.
28 They may curse, but you will bless.
    Let those who attack me be ashamed,
        but let me rejoice.
29 Let those who accuse me wear disgrace as though it were clothing.
    Let them be wrapped in their shame as though it were a robe.

30 With my mouth I will give many thanks to the Lord.
    I will praise him among many people,
31   because he stands beside needy people
        to save them from those who would condemn them to death.

Psalm 110

A psalm by David.

1 The Lord said to my Lord,
    "Sit in the highest position in heaven
        until I make your enemies your footstool."

2 The Lord will extend your powerful scepter from Zion.
    Rule your enemies who surround you.

3   Your people will volunteer when you call up your army.
    Your young people will come to you in holy splendor
        like dew in the early morning.*

4 The Lord has taken an oath and will not change his mind:
    "You are a priest forever, in the way Melchizedek was a priest."

5 The Lord is at your right side.
    He will crush kings on the day of his anger.
6 He will pass judgment on the nations
    and fill them with dead bodies.
        Throughout the earth he will crush ˻their˼ heads.
7 He will drink from the brook along the road.
    He will hold his head high.

Psalm 111*

1 Hallelujah!

I will give thanks to the Lord with all my heart
    in the company of decent people and in the congregation.
2 The Lord's deeds are spectacular.
    They should be studied by all who enjoy them.
3 His work is glorious and majestic.
    His righteousness continues forever.
4 He has made his miracles unforgettable.

---

*110:3 Or "You have the dew of your youth." *111:1 Psalm 111 is a poem in Hebrew alphabetical order.

The Lord is merciful and compassionate.
5 He provides food for those who fear him.
He always remembers his promise.[b]
6 He has revealed the power of his works to his people
by giving them the lands of other nations as an inheritance.
7 His works are done with truth and justice.
All his guiding principles are trustworthy.
8 They last forever and ever.
They are carried out with truth and decency.
9 He has sent salvation to his people.
He has ordered that his promise should continue forever.
His name is holy and terrifying.
10 The fear of the Lord is the beginning of wisdom.
Good sense is shown by everyone who follows ˎGod's guiding principlesˌ.
His praise continues forever.

Psalm 112[a]

1 Hallelujah!

Blessed is the person who fears the Lord
and is happy to obey his commands.
2 His descendants will grow strong on the earth.
The family of a decent person will be blessed.
3 Wealth and riches will be in his home.
His righteousness continues forever.
4 Light will shine in the dark for a decent person.
He is merciful, compassionate, and fair.

5 All goes well for the person who is generous and lends willingly.
He earns an honest living.
6 He will never fail.
A righteous person will always be remembered.
7 He is not afraid of bad news.
His heart remains secure, full of confidence in the Lord.
8 His heart is steady, and he is not afraid.
In the end he will look triumphantly at his enemies.
9 He gives freely to poor people.
His righteousness continues forever.
His head is raised in honor.
10 The wicked person sees this and becomes angry.
He angrily grits his teeth and disappears.
The hope that wicked people have will vanish.

Psalm 113

1 Hallelujah!

You servants of the Lord, praise him.
Praise the name of the Lord.

---

[b]111:5 Or "covenant." [a]112:1 Psalm 112 is a poem in Hebrew alphabetical order.

2 Thank the name of the LORD now and forever.
3 From where the sun rises to where the sun sets,
   the name of the LORD should be praised.
4 The LORD is high above all the nations.
   His glory is above the heavens.
5 Who is like the LORD our God?
   He is seated on his high throne.
6 He bends down to look at heaven and earth.
7 He lifts the poor from the dust.
   He lifts the needy from a garbage heap.
8 He seats them with influential people,
   with the influential leaders of his people.
9 He makes a woman who is in a childless home
   a joyful mother.

Hallelujah!

Psalm 114

1 When Israel left Egypt,
   when Jacob's family left people who spoke a foreign language,
2 Judah became his holy place and Israel became his kingdom.
3 The Red Sea looked at this and ran away.
   The Jordan River turned back.
4 The mountains jumped like rams.
   The hills jumped like lambs.
5 Red Sea, why did you run away?
   Jordan River, what made you turn back?
6 Mountains, what made you jump like rams?
   Hills, what made you jump like lambs?
7 Earth, tremble in the presence of the Lord,
   in the presence of the God of Jacob.
8 He turns a rock into a pool filled with water
   and turns flint into a spring flowing with water.

Psalm 115

1 Don't give glory to us, O LORD.
   Don't give glory to us.
      Instead, give glory to your name
      because of your mercy and faithfulness.
2 Why should other nations say, "Where is their God?"
3 Our God is in heaven.
   He does whatever he wants.
4 Their idols are made of silver and gold.
   They were made by human hands.*
5 They have mouths, but they cannot speak.
   They have eyes, but they cannot see.
6 They have ears, but they cannot hear.
   They have noses, but they cannot smell.

---

*115:4 Verses 4-8 are virtually identical in wording to Psalm 135:15-18.

7   They have hands, but they cannot feel.
      They have feet, but they cannot walk.
      They cannot even make a sound with their throats.
8   Those who make idols end up like them.
       So does everyone who trusts them.

9   Israel, trust the LORD.
      He is your helper and your shield.
10 Descendants of Aaron, trust the LORD.
      He is your helper and your shield.
11 If you fear the LORD, trust the LORD.
      He is your helper and your shield.
12 The LORD, who is always thinking about us, will bless us.
      He will bless the descendants of Israel.
      He will bless the descendants of Aaron.
13 He will bless those who fear the LORD,
      from the least important to the most important.
14 May the LORD continue to bless you and your children.
15 You will be blessed by the LORD, the maker of heaven and earth.
16 The highest heaven belongs to the LORD,
      but he has given the earth to the descendants of Adam.
17 Those who are dead do not praise the LORD,
      nor do those who go into the silence of the grave.
18 But we will thank the LORD now and forever.

      Hallelujah!

Psalm 116

1 I love the LORD because he hears my voice, my pleas for mercy.
2 I will call on him as long as I live
      because he turns his ear toward me.
3 The ropes of death became tangled around me.
      The horrors of the grave took hold of me.
       I experienced pain and agony.

Good Morning, God
Psalm 115:12-13

Sometimes adults don't listen very well when children try to speak. You may feel like you are ignored by some adults or that you are unimportant. But that's not how God looks at kids! The Bible says that the Lord is always thinking about everyone—even people the world might not consider important. God is interested in what children have to say. Go ahead. Say something to him right now. He is listening to you.

Lord, it's good to know I'm always on your mind and that I'm important to you.

4 But I kept calling on the name of the LORD:
  "Please, LORD, rescue me!"

5 The LORD is merciful and righteous.
  Our God is compassionate.

6 The LORD protects defenseless people.
  When I was weak, he saved me.

7 Be at peace again, my soul,
  because the LORD has been good to you.

8 You saved me from death.
  You saved my eyes from tears and, my feet from stumbling.

9 I will walk in the LORD's presence in this world of the living.

10 I kept my faith even when I said,
   "I am suffering terribly."

11 I also said when I was panic-stricken,
   "Everyone is undependable."

12 How can I repay the LORD
   for all the good that he has done for me?

13 I will take the cup of salvation
   and call on the name of the LORD.

14 I will keep my vows to the LORD
   in the presence of all his people.

15 Precious in the sight of the LORD
   is the death of his faithful ones.

16 O LORD, I am indeed your servant.
   I am your servant,
      the son of your female servant.
   You have freed me from my chains.

17 I will bring a song of thanksgiving to you as a sacrifice.
   I will call on the name of the LORD.

18 I will keep my vows to the LORD
   in the presence of all his people,

19   in the courtyards of the LORD's house,
         in the middle of Jerusalem.

Hallelujah!

Psalm 117

1 Praise the LORD, all you nations!
  Praise him, all you people of the world!

2   His mercy toward us is powerful.
     The LORD's faithfulness endures forever.

Hallelujah!

Psalm 118

1 Give thanks to the LORD because he is good,
   because his mercy endures forever.

2   Israel should say,

"His mercy endures forever."
3   The descendants of Aaron should say,
        "His mercy endures forever."
4   Those who fear the Lord should say,
        "His mercy endures forever."

5   During times of trouble I called on the Lord.
     The Lord answered me and set me free from all of them.
6   The Lord is on my side.
     I am not afraid.
       What can mortals do to me?
7   The Lord is on my side as my helper.
     I will see the defeat of those who hate me.
8   It is better to depend on the Lord
     than to trust mortals.
9   It is better to depend on the Lord
     than to trust influential people.

10   All the nations surrounded me,
     but armed with the name of the Lord, I defeated them.
11   They surrounded me. Yes, they surrounded me,
     but armed with the name of the Lord, I defeated them.
12   They swarmed around me like bees,
     but they were extinguished like burning thornbushes.
     So armed with the name of the Lord, I defeated them.
13   They pushed hard to make me fall,
     but the Lord helped me.
14   The Lord is my strength and my song.
     He is my savior.

15   The sound of joyful singing and victory is heard
     in the tents of righteous people.
     The right hand of the Lord displays strength.
16   The right hand of the Lord is held high.
     The right hand of the Lord displays strength.
17   I will not die,
     but I will live and tell what the Lord has done.
18   The Lord disciplined me severely,
     but he did not allow me to be killed.

19   Open the gates of righteousness for me.
     I will go through them and give thanks to the Lord.
20   This is the gate of the Lord
     through which righteous people will enter.

21   I give thanks to you,
     because you have answered me.
       You are my savior.
22   The stone that the builders rejected
     has become the cornerstone.
23   The Lord is responsible for this,
     and it is amazing for us to see.

24 This is the day the LORD has made.
   Let's rejoice and be glad today!
25 We beg you, O LORD, save us!
  We beg you, O LORD, give us success!
26   Blessed is the one who comes in the name of the LORD.
    We bless you from the LORD's house.
27 The LORD is God, and he has given us light.
   March in a festival procession
    with branches to the horns of the altar.
28 You are my God, and I give thanks to you.
  My God, I honor you highly.

29 Give thanks to the LORD because he is good,
   because his mercy endures forever.

Psalm 119 [a]

1 Blessed are those whose lives have integrity,
   those who follow the teachings of the LORD.
2 Blessed are those who obey his written instructions.
   They wholeheartedly search for him.
3   They do nothing wrong.
   They follow his directions.
4 You have commanded
   that your guiding principles be carefully followed.
5 I pray that my ways may become firmly established
   so that I can obey your laws.
6   Then I will never feel ashamed
    when I study all your commandments.
7 I will give thanks to you
   as I learn your regulations, which are based on your righteousness.
8 I will obey your laws.
  Never abandon me.

9 How can a young person keep his life pure?
   He can do it ⌞by holding on⌟ to your word.
10 I wholeheartedly searched for you.
   Do not let me wander away from your commandments.
11 I have treasured your promise in my heart
   so that I may not sin against you.
12 Thanks be to you, O LORD.
  Teach me your laws.
13 With my lips I have repeated
   every regulation that ⌞comes⌟ from your mouth.
14 I find joy in the way ⌞shown by⌟ your written instructions
   more than I find joy in all kinds of riches.
15 I want to reflect on your guiding principles
   and study your ways.
16 Your laws make me happy.
  I never forget your word.

---

[a] 119:1 Psalm 119 is a poem in Hebrew alphabetical order.

17 Be kind to me so that I may live
and hold on to your word.
18 Uncover my eyes
so that I may see the miraculous things in your teachings.
19 I am a foreigner in this world.
Do not hide your commandments from me.
20 My soul is overwhelmed with endless longing for your regulations.
21 You threaten arrogant people, who are condemned
and wander away from your commandments.
22 Remove the insults and contempt that have fallen on me
because I have obeyed your written instructions.
23 Even though influential people plot against me,
I reflect on your laws.
24 Indeed, your written instructions make me happy.
They are my best friends.

25 I am close to death.
Give me a new life as you promised.
26 I told you what I have done, and you answered me.
Teach me your laws.
27 Help me understand your guiding principles
so that I may reflect on your miracles.
28 I am drowning in tears.
Strengthen me as you promised.
29 Turn me away from a life of lies.
Graciously provide me with your teachings.
30 I have chosen a life of faithfulness.
I have set your regulations in front of me.
31 I have clung tightly to your written instructions.
O Lord, do not let me be put to shame.
32 I will eagerly pursue your commandments
because you continue to increase my understanding.

33 Teach me, O Lord, how to live by your laws,
and I will obey them to the end.
34 Help me understand so that I can follow your teachings.
I will guard them with all my heart.
35 Lead me on the path of your commandments,
because I am happy with them.
36 Direct my heart toward your written instructions
rather than getting rich in underhanded ways.
37 Turn my eyes away from worthless things.
Give me a new life in your ways.
38 Keep your promise to me
so that I can fear you.
39 Take away insults, which I dread,
because your regulations are good.
40 I long for your guiding principles.
Give me a new life in your righteousness.

41 Let your blessings reach me, O Lord.
Save me as you promised.

42   Then I will have an answer for the one who insults me
         since I trust your word.
43   Do not take so much as a single word of truth from my mouth.
         My hope is based on your regulations.
44   I will follow your teachings forever and ever.
45   I will walk around freely
         because I sought out your guiding principles.
46   I will speak about your written instructions in the presence of kings
         and not feel ashamed.
47   Your commandments, which I love, make me happy.
48   I lift my hands ⌞in prayer⌟ because of your commandments,
         which I love.
     I will reflect on your laws.

49   Remember the word ⌞you gave⌟ me.
         Through it you gave me hope.
50   This is my comfort in my misery:
         Your promise gave me a new life.
51   Arrogant people have mocked me with cruelty,
         yet I have not turned away from your teachings.
52   I remembered your regulations from long ago, O Lord,
         and I found comfort ⌞in them⌟.
53   I am burning with anger because of wicked people,
         who abandon your teachings.
54   Your laws have become like psalms to me
         in this place where I am only a foreigner.
55   At night I remember your name, O Lord,
         and I follow your teachings.
56   This has happened to me
         because I have obeyed your guiding principles.

57   You are my inheritance, O Lord.
         I promised to hold on to your words.
58   With all my heart I want to win your favor.
         Be kind to me as you promised.
59   I have thought about my life,
         and I have directed my feet back to your written instructions.
60   Without any hesitation I hurry to obey your commandments.
61   ⌞Though⌟ the ropes of wicked people are tied around me,
         I never forget your teachings.
62   At midnight I wake up to give thanks to you
         for the regulations, which are based on your righteousness.
63   I am a friend to everyone who fears you
         and to everyone who follows your guiding principles.
64   Your mercy, O Lord, fills the earth.
         Teach me your laws.

65   You have treated me well, O Lord,
         as you promised.
66   Teach me ⌞to use⌟ good judgment and knowledge,
         because I believe in your commandments.

67 Before you made me suffer, I used to wander off,
     but now I hold on to your word.
68 You are good, and you do good things.
     Teach me your laws.
69 Arrogant people have smeared me with lies,
     yet, I obey your guiding principles with all my heart.
70 Their hearts are cold and insensitive,
     yet, I am happy with your teachings.
71 It was good that I had to suffer
     in order to learn your laws.
72 The teachings that come, from your mouth are worth more to me
     than thousands in gold or silver.

73 Your hands created me and made me what I am.
     Help me understand so that I may learn your commandments.
74 Those who fear you will see me and rejoice,
     because my hope is based on your word.
75 I know that your regulations are fair, O LORD,
     and that you were right to make me suffer.
76 Let your mercy comfort me
     as you promised.
77 Let your compassion reach me so that I may live,
     because your teachings make me happy.
78 Let arrogant people be put to shame
     because they lied about me,
     yet, I reflect on your guiding principles.
79 Let those who fear you turn to me
     so that they can come to know your written instructions.
80 Let my heart be filled with integrity in regard to your laws
     so that I will not be put to shame.

81 My soul is weak from waiting for you to save me.
     My hope is based on your word.
82 My eyes have become strained from looking for your promise.
     I ask, "When will you comfort me?"
83 Although I have become like a shriveled and dried out wineskin,
     I have not forgotten your laws.
84 What is left of my life?
     When will you bring those who persecute me to justice?
85 Arrogant people have dug pits to trap me
     in defiance of your teachings.
86 (All your commandments are reliable.)
     Those people persecute me with lies. Help me!
87 They almost wiped me off the face of, the earth.
     But I did not abandon your guiding principles.
88 Give me a new life through your mercy
     so that I may obey the written instructions,
     which came, from your mouth.

89 O LORD, your word is established in heaven forever.
90 Your faithfulness endures throughout every generation.

Lamps / *Psalm 119:105*

The lamps in most homes were clay dishes
filled with olive oil. A bit of flax was dropped
in the oil and lit. Lamps burned all night
long in every home. These lamps
gave enough light for a person to see
his or her next step.

God's word is a "lamp for [our] feet."
The Bible shows us what steps to take in order to please God.

You set the earth in place, and it continues to stand.

91 All things continue to stand today because of your regulations,
since they are all your servants.

92 If your teachings had not made me happy,
then I would have died in my misery.

93 I will never forget your guiding principles,
because you gave me a new life through them.

94 I am yours.
Save me, because I have searched for your guiding principles.

95 The wicked people have waited for me in order to destroy me,
⌞yet⌟ I want to understand your written instructions.

96 I have seen a limit to everything else,
⌞but⌟ your commandments have no limit.

97 Oh, how I love your teachings!
They are in my thoughts all day long.

98 Your commandments make me wiser than my enemies,
because your commandments are always with me.

99 I have more insight than all my teachers,
because your written instructions are in my thoughts.

100 I have more wisdom than those with many years of experience,
because I have obeyed your guiding principles.

101 I have kept my feet ⌞from walking⌟ on any evil path
in order to obey your word.

102 I have not neglected your regulations,
because you have taught me.

103 How sweet the taste of your promise is!
It tastes sweeter than honey.

104 From your guiding principles I gain understanding.
That is why I hate every path that leads to lying.

105 Your word is a lamp for my feet
and a light for my path.

106 I took an oath, and I will keep it.
     I took an oath to follow your regulations,
       which are based on your righteousness.
107 I have suffered so much.
     Give me a new life, O Lord, as you promised.
108 Please accept the praise I gladly give you, O Lord,
       and teach me your regulations.
109 I always take my life into my own hands,
       but I never forget your teachings.
110 Wicked people have set a trap for me,
       but I have never wandered away from your guiding principles.
111 Your written instructions are mine forever.
     They are the joy of my heart.
112 I have decided to obey your laws.
     They offer a reward that never ends.

113 I hate two-faced people,
       but I love your teachings.
114 You are my hiding place and my shield.
     My hope is based on your word.
115 Get away from me, you evildoers,
       so that I can obey the commandments of my God.
116 Help me God, as you promised, so that I may live.
     Do not turn my hope into disappointment.
117 Hold me, and I will be safe,
       and I will always respect your laws.
118 You reject all who wander away from your laws,
       because their lies mislead them.*b*
119 You get rid of all wicked people on earth as if they were rubbish.
     That is why I love your written instructions.
120 My body shudders in fear of you,
       and I am afraid of your regulations.

121 I have done what is fair and right.
     Do not leave me at the mercy of those who oppress me.
122 Guarantee my well-being.
     Do not let arrogant people oppress me.
123 My eyes are strained from looking for you to save me
       and from looking for the fulfillment of your righteous promise.
124 Treat me with kindness,
       and teach me your laws.
125 I am your servant.
     Help me understand
       so that I may come to know your written instructions.
126 It is time for you to act, O Lord.*c*
     Even though people have abolished your teachings,
127   I love your commandments more than gold, more than pure gold.
128   I follow the straight paths of your guiding principles.
     I hate every pathway that leads to lying.

---

b 119:118 Hebrew meaning of this line uncertain.   *c* 119:126 One Hebrew manuscript, Latin; other Hebrew manuscripts "It is time to act for the Lord."

129 Your written instructions are miraculous.
      That is why I obey them.
130 Your word is a doorway that lets in light,
      and it helps gullible people understand.
131 I open my mouth and pant
      because I long for your commandments.
132 Turn toward me, and have pity on me
      as you have pledged to do for those who love your name.
133 Make my steps secure through your promise,
      and do not let any sin control me.
134 Save me from human oppression
      so that I may obey your guiding principles.
135 Smile on me,
      and teach me your laws.
136 Streams of tears flow from my eyes
      because others do not follow your teachings.

137 You are righteous, O Lord,
      and your regulations are fair.
138 You have issued your written instructions.
      They are fair and completely dependable.
139 My devotion for your words consumes me,
      because my enemies have forgotten your words.
140 Your promise has been thoroughly tested,
      and I love it.
141 I am unimportant and despised,
      ⌐yet⌐ I never forget your guiding principles.
142 Your righteousness is an everlasting righteousness,
      and your teachings are reliable.
143 Trouble and hardship have found me,
      but your commandments ⌐still⌐ make me happy.
144 Your written instructions are always right.
      Help me understand ⌐them⌐ so that I will live.

145 I have called out with all my heart. Answer me, O Lord.
      I want to obey your laws.
146 I have called out.
      Save me, so that I can obey your written instructions.
147 I got up before dawn, and I cried out for help.
      My hope is based on your word.
148 My eyes are wide-open throughout the nighttime hours
      to reflect on your word.
149 In keeping with your mercy, hear my voice.
      O Lord, give me a new life guided by your regulations.
150 Those who carry out plots against me are near,
      ⌐yet⌐ they are far away from your teachings.
151 You are near, O Lord,
      and all your commandments are reliable.
152 Long ago I learned from your written instructions
      that you made them to last forever.

153 Look at my misery, and rescue me,
      because I have never forgotten your teachings.
154 Plead my case for me, and save me.
      Give me a new life as you promised.
155 Wicked people are far from being saved,
      because they have not searched for your laws.
156 Your acts of compassion are many in number, O Lord.
      Give me a new life guided by your regulations.
157 I have many persecutors and opponents,
      yet I have not turned away from your written instructions.
158 I have seen traitors,
      and I am filled with disgust.
         They have not accepted your promise.
159 See how I have loved your guiding principles!
      O Lord, in keeping with your mercy, give me a new life.
160 There is nothing but truth in your word,
      and all of your righteous regulations endure forever.

161 Influential people have persecuted me for no reason,
      but it is only your words that fill my heart with terror.
162 I find joy in your promise
      like someone who finds a priceless treasure.
163 I hate lying; I am disgusted with it.
      I love your teachings.
164 Seven times a day I praise you
      for your righteous regulations.
165 There is lasting peace for those who love your teachings.
      Nothing can make those people stumble.
166 I have waited with hope for you to save me, O Lord.
      I have carried out your commandments.
167 I have obeyed your written instructions.
      I have loved them very much.
168 I have followed your guiding principles and your written instructions,
      because my whole life is in front of you.

169 Let my cry for help come into your presence, O Lord.
      Help me understand as you promised.
170 Let my plea for mercy come into your presence.
      Rescue me as you promised.
171 Let my lips pour out praise
      because you teach me your laws.
172 Let my tongue sing about your promise
      because all your commandments are fair.
173 Let your hand help me
      because I have chosen to follow your guiding principles.
174 I have longed for you to save me, O Lord,
      and your teachings make me happy.
175 Let my soul have new life so that it can praise you.
      Let your regulations help me.
176 I have wandered away like a lost lamb.

> Search for me,
>> because I have never forgotten your commandments.

Psalm 120

A song for going up to worship.

1 When I was in trouble, I cried out to the LORD,
> and he answered me.
2 O LORD, rescue me from lying lips
> and from a deceitful tongue.

3 You deceitful tongue, what can the LORD give you?
> What more can he do for you?
4   He will give you a warrior's sharpened arrows and red-hot coals.

5 How horrible it is to live as a foreigner in Meshech
> or to stay in the tents of Kedar.
6   I have lived too long with those who hate peace.
7   I am for peace, but when I talk about it,
>> they only talk about war.

Psalm 121

A song for going up to worship.

1 I look up toward the mountains.
> Where can I find help?
2 My help comes from the LORD,
> the maker of heaven and earth.
3 He will not let you fall.
> Your guardian will not fall asleep.
4 Indeed, the Guardian of Israel never rests or sleeps.
5 The LORD is your guardian.
> The LORD is the shade over your right hand.
6   The sun will not beat down on you during the day,
>> nor will the moon at night.
7 The LORD guards you from every evil.
> He guards your life.
8 The LORD guards you as you come and go,
> now and forever.

Psalm 122

A song by David for going up to worship.

1 I was glad when they said to me,
> "Let's go to the house of the LORD."
2 Our feet are standing inside your gates, Jerusalem.
3 Jerusalem is built to be a city
> where the people are united.[a]

---

[a] 122:3 Hebrew meaning of this verse uncertain.

4 All of the Lord's tribes go to that city
  because it is a law in Israel
    to give thanks to the name of the Lord.
5 The court of justice sits there.
  It consists of ˌprinces who areˌ David's descendants.

6 Pray for the peace of Jerusalem:
  "May those who love you prosper.
7 May there be peace inside your walls
    and prosperity in your palaces."
8 For the sake of my relatives and friends, let me say,
  "May it go well for you!"
9 For the sake of the house of the Lord our God,
  I will seek what is good for you.

Psalm 123

A song for going up to worship.

1 I look up to you,
    to the one who sits enthroned in heaven.
2 As servants depend on their masters,
  as a maid depends on her mistress,
    so we depend on the Lord our God
      until he has pity on us.
3 Have pity on us, O Lord.
  Have pity on us
    because we have suffered more than our share of contempt.
4 We have suffered more than our share of ridicule
    from those who are carefree.
  We have suffered more than our share of contempt
    from those who are arrogant.

Psalm 124

A song by David for going up to worship.

1 "If the Lord had not been on our side . . ."
    (Israel should repeat this.)
2 "If the Lord had not been on our side when people attacked us,
3   then they would have swallowed us alive
      when their anger exploded against us.
4   Then the floodwaters would have swept us away.
      An ˌoverflowingˌ stream would have washed us away.
5   Then raging water would have washed us away."

6 Thank the Lord, who did not let them sink their teeth into us.
7 We escaped like a bird caught in a hunter's trap.
    The trap was broken, and we escaped.
8 Our help is in the name of the Lord, the maker of heaven and earth.

Psalm 125

A song for going up to worship.

1 Those who trust the Lord are like Mount Zion,
  which can never be shaken.
    It remains firm forever.
2 As the mountains surround Jerusalem,
  so the Lord surrounds his people now and forever.

3 A wicked ruler will not be allowed to govern
  the land set aside for righteous people.
    That is why righteous people do not use their power to do wrong.

4 Do good, O Lord, to those who are good,
  to those whose motives are decent.
5 But when people become crooked,
  the Lord will lead them away with troublemakers.

Let there be peace in Israel!

Psalm 126

A song for going up to worship.

1 When the Lord restored the fortunes of Zion,
  it was as if we were dreaming.
2 Then our mouths were filled with laughter
  and our tongues with joyful songs.
Then the nations said,
  "The Lord has done spectacular things for them."

3 The Lord has done spectacular things for us.
  We are overjoyed.
4 Restore our fortunes, O Lord,
  as you restore streams to dry riverbeds in the Negev.
5 Those who cry while they plant
  will joyfully sing while they harvest.
6 The person who goes out weeping, carrying his bag of seed,
  will come home singing, carrying his bundles of grain.

Psalm 127

A song by Solomon for going up to worship.

1 If the Lord does not build the house,
  it is useless for the builders to work on it.
If the Lord does not protect a city,
  it is useless for the guard to stay alert.
2 It is useless to work hard for the food you eat
  by getting up early and going to bed late.
    The Lord gives food to those he loves while they sleep.

3 Children are an inheritance from the Lord.
They are a reward from him.

4   The children born to a man when he is young
       are like arrows in the hand of a warrior.
5   Blessed is the man who has filled his quiver with them.
          He will not be put to shame
             when he speaks with his enemies in the city gate.

Psalm 128

A song for going up to worship.

1   Blessed are all who fear the LORD
       and live his way.

2   You will certainly eat what your own hands have provided.
          Blessings to you!
          May things go well for you!
3   Your wife will be like a fruitful vine inside your home.
     Your children will be like young olive trees around your table.
4   This is how the LORD will bless the person who fears him.
5   May the LORD bless you from Zion
             so that you may see Jerusalem prospering
             all the days of your life.
6   May you live to see your children's children.

Let there be peace in Israel!

Psalm 129

A song for going up to worship.

1   "From the time I was young, people have attacked me . . ."
          (Israel should repeat this.)
2   "From the time I was young, people have attacked me,
          but they have never overpowered me.
3   They have plowed my back ⸤like farmers plow fields⸥.
          They made long slashes ⸤like furrows⸥."
4   The LORD is righteous.
          He has cut me loose
             from the ropes that wicked people tied around me.
5   Put to shame all those who hate Zion.
          Force them to retreat.
6   Make them be like grass on a roof,
             like grass that dries up before it produces a stalk.
7   It will never fill the barns of those who harvest
             or the arms of those who gather bundles.
8   Those who pass by will never say ⸤to them⸥,
                  "May you be blessed by the LORD"
                  or "We bless you in the name of the LORD."

Psalm 130

A song for going up to worship.

1   O LORD, out of the depths I call to you.
2   O Lord, hear my voice.

Let your ears be open to my pleas for mercy.
3 O Lord, who would be able to stand
if you kept a record of sins?
4 But with you there is forgiveness
so that you can be feared.
5 I wait for the Lord, my soul waits,
and with hope I wait for his word.
6 My soul waits for the Lord
more than those who watch for the morning,
more than those who watch for the morning.
7 O Israel, put your hope in the Lord,
because with the Lord there is mercy
and with him there is unlimited forgiveness.
8 He will rescue Israel from all its sins.

Psalm 131

A song by David for going up to worship.

1 O Lord, my heart is not conceited.
My eyes do not look down on others.
I am not involved in things too big or too difficult for me.
2 Instead, I have kept my soul calm and quiet.
My soul is content as a weaned child is content in its mother's arms.
3 Israel, put your hope in the Lord now and forever.

Psalm 132

A song for going up to worship.

1 O Lord, remember David and all the hardships he endured.
2 Remember how he swore an oath to the Lord
and made this vow to the Mighty One of Jacob:
3 "I will not step inside my house,
4 get into my bed, shut my eyes, or close my eyelids
5 until I find a place for the Lord,
a dwelling place for the Mighty One of Jacob."

6 Now, we have heard about the ark of the promise being in Ephrathah.
We have found it in Jaar.
7 Let's go to his dwelling place.
Let's worship at his footstool.
8 O Lord, arise, and come to your resting place
with the ark of your power.
9 Clothe your priests with righteousness.
Let your godly ones sing with joy.
10 For the sake of your servant David,
do not reject your anointed one.
11 The Lord swore an oath to David.
This is a truth he will not take back:
"I will set one of your own descendants on your throne.

12   If your sons are faithful to my promise[a]
      and my written instructions that I will teach them,
    then their descendants will also sit on your throne forever."

13 The Lord has chosen Zion.
   He wants it for his home.
14   "This will be my resting place forever.
    Here I will sit enthroned because I want Zion.
15   I will certainly bless all that Zion needs.
    I will satisfy its needy people with food.
16   I will clothe its priests with salvation.
    Then its godly ones will sing joyfully.
17   There I will make a horn sprout up for David.
    I will prepare a lamp for my anointed one.
18   I will clothe his enemies with shame,
      but the crown on my anointed one will shine."

Psalm 133

A song by David for going up to worship.

1 See how good and pleasant it is
   when brothers and sisters live together in harmony!
2   It is like fine, scented oil on the head,
      running down the beard—down Aaron's beard—
    running over the collar of his robes.
3   It is like dew on ⌊Mount⌋ Hermon,
    dew which comes down on Zion's mountains.
      That is where the Lord promised
      the blessing of eternal life.

Psalm 134

A song for going up to worship.

1 Praise the Lord, all you servants of the Lord,
   all who stand in the house of the Lord night after night.
2 Lift your hands toward the holy place, and praise the Lord.
3 May the Lord, the maker of heaven and earth, bless you from Zion.

Psalm 135

1 Hallelujah!

Praise the name of the Lord.
Praise him, you servants of the Lord
2   who are standing in the house of the Lord,
    in the courtyards of the house of our God.
3 Praise the Lord because he is good.
   Make music to praise his name because his name is beautiful.
4   The Lord chose Jacob to be his own
    and chose Israel to be his own special treasure.

---

a 132:12 Or "covenant."

5 I know that the LORD is great,
that our Lord is greater than all the false gods.
6 The LORD does whatever he wants in heaven or on earth,
on the seas or in all the depths of the oceans.
7 He is the one who makes the clouds rise from the ends of the earth,
who makes lightning for the thunderstorms,
and who brings wind out of his storerooms.

8 He is the one who killed every firstborn male in Egypt.
He killed humans and animals alike.
9 He sent miraculous signs and amazing things into the heart of Egypt
against Pharaoh and all his officials.
10 He is the one who defeated many nations and killed mighty kings:
11 King Sihon of the Amorites,
King Og of Bashan,
and all the kingdoms in Canaan.
12 He gave their land as an inheritance,
an inheritance to his people Israel.

13 O LORD, your name endures forever.
O LORD, you will be remembered throughout every generation.
14 The LORD will provide justice for his people
and have compassion on his servants.

15 The idols of the nations are made of silver and gold.
They were made by human hands.ᵃ
16 They have mouths, but they cannot speak.
They have eyes, but they cannot see.
17 They have ears, but they cannot hear.
They cannot breathe.
18 Those who make idols end up like them.
So does everyone who trusts them.

19 Descendants of Israel, praise the LORD.
Descendants of Aaron, praise the LORD.
20 Descendants of Levi, praise the LORD.
You people who fear the LORD, praise the LORD.
21 Thank the LORD in Zion.
Thank the one who lives in Jerusalem.

Hallelujah!

Psalm 136

1 Give thanks to the LORD because he is good,

because his mercy endures forever.

2 Give thanks to the God of gods

because his mercy endures forever.

3 Give thanks to the Lord of lords

because his mercy endures forever.

ᵃ135:15 Verses 15-18 are virtually identical in wording to Psalm 115:4-8.

4 Give thanks to the only one who does miraculous things—
          because his mercy endures forever.
5   to the one who made the heavens by his understanding—
          because his mercy endures forever.
6   to the one who spread out the earth on the water—
          because his mercy endures forever.
7   to the one who made the great lights—
          because his mercy endures forever.
8   the sun to rule the day—
          because his mercy endures forever.
9   the moon and stars to rule the night—
          because his mercy endures forever.

10 Give thanks to the one who killed the firstborn males in Egypt—
          because his mercy endures forever.
11   He brought Israel out from among them—
          because his mercy endures forever.
12   with a mighty hand and a powerful arm—
          because his mercy endures forever.

13 Give thanks to one who divided the Red Sea—
          because his mercy endures forever.
14   He led Israel through the middle of it—
          because his mercy endures forever.
15   He swept Pharaoh and his army into the Red Sea—
          because his mercy endures forever.

16 Give thanks to the one who led his people through the desert—
          because his mercy endures forever.

17 Give thanks to the one who defeated powerful kings—
          because his mercy endures forever.
18   He killed mighty kings—
          because his mercy endures forever.
19   King Sihon of the Amorites—
          because his mercy endures forever.
20   and King Og of Bashan—
          because his mercy endures forever.
21   He gave their land as an inheritance—
          because his mercy endures forever.
22   as an inheritance for his servant Israel—
          because his mercy endures forever.

23 He remembered us when we were humiliated—
          because his mercy endures forever.
24 He snatched us from the grasp of our enemies—
          because his mercy endures forever.
25 He gives food to every living creature—
          because his mercy endures forever.

26   Give thanks to the God of heaven
          because his mercy endures forever.

Psalm 137

1 By the rivers of Babylon, we sat down and cried
   as we remembered Zion.
2 We hung our lyres on willow trees.
3 It was there that those who had captured us demanded that we sing.
   Those who guarded us wanted us to entertain them.
   ⌊They said,⌋ "Sing a song from Zion for us!"

4 How could we sing the LORD's song in a foreign land?
5 If I forget you, Jerusalem,
   let my right hand forget ⌊how to play the lyre⌋.
6 Let my tongue stick to the roof of my mouth
   if I don't remember you,
   if I don't consider Jerusalem my highest joy.

7 O LORD, remember the people of Edom.
   Remember what they did the day Jerusalem ⌊was captured⌋.
   They said, "Tear it down! Tear it down to its foundation."
8 You destructive people of Babylon,
   blessed is the one who pays you back
   with the same treatment you gave us.
9 Blessed is the one who grabs your little children
   and smashes them against a rock.

Psalm 138

By David.

1 I will give thanks to you with all my heart.
   I will make music to praise you in front of the false gods.
2 I will bow toward your holy temple.
   I will give thanks to your name because of your mercy and truth.
   You have made your name and your promise greater than everything.

3 When I called, you answered me.
   You made me bold by strengthening my soul.[a]
4 All the kings of the earth will give thanks to you, O LORD,
   because they have heard the promises you spoke.
5 They will sing this about the ways of the LORD:
   "The LORD's honor is great!"
6 Even though the LORD is high above, he sees humble people ⌊close up⌋,
   and he recognizes arrogant people from a distance.

7 Even though I walk into the middle of trouble,
   you guard my life against the anger of my enemies.
   You stretch out your hand,
   and your right hand saves me.
8 The LORD will do everything for me.
   O LORD, your mercy endures forever.
   Do not let go of what your hands have made.

---

a 138:3 Hebrew meaning of this line uncertain.

Psalm 139

For the choir director; a psalm by David.

1   O Lord, you have examined me, and you know me.
2   You alone know when I sit down and when I get up.
        You read my thoughts from far away.
3   You watch me when I travel and when I rest.
        You are familiar with all my ways.
4   Even before there is a ˌsingleˌ word on my tongue,
                you know all about it, Lord.
5   You are all around me—in front of me and in back of me.
        You lay your hand on me.
6   Such knowledge is beyond my grasp.
            It is so high I cannot reach it.

7   Where can I go ˌto get awayˌ from your Spirit?
    Where can I run ˌto get awayˌ from you?
8   If I go up to heaven, you are there.
        If I make my bed in hell, you are there.
9   If I climb upward on the rays of the morning sun
            ˌorˌ land on the most distant shore of the sea where the sun sets,
10   even there your hand would guide me
                and your right hand would hold on to me.
11   If I say, "Let the darkness hide me
        and let the light around me turn into night,"
12   even the darkness is not too dark for you.
                Night is as bright as day.
                Darkness and light are the same ˌto youˌ.

13 You alone created my inner being.
    You knitted me together inside my mother.
14 I will give thanks to you
        because I have been so amazingly and miraculously made.
            Your works are miraculous, and my soul is fully aware of this.
15 My bones were not hidden from you
        when I was being made in secret,

Good Morning, God

Psalm 139:13-18

How well does God know you? He reads your thoughts, watches you, and knows what you will say before you even begin to speak. And that's not all. He knew all about you *before* you were born. He thinks of you so often that you can't even count his thoughts. Some people may know you well—like your family and friends. But God knows you the best.

Dear Father, thank you that you know me and love me.

when I was being skillfully woven in an underground workshop.

16 Your eyes saw me when I was only a fetus.
    Every day of my life was recorded in your book
        before one of them had taken place.

17 How precious are your thoughts concerning me, O God!
    How vast in number they are!

18 If I try to count them,
        there would be more of them than there are grains of sand.
        When I wake up, I am still with you.

19 I wish that you would kill wicked people, O God,
        and that bloodthirsty people would leave me alone.

20 They say wicked things about you.
        Your enemies misuse your name.

21 Shouldn't I hate those who hate you, O LORD?
    Shouldn't I be disgusted with those who attack you?

22 I hate them with all my heart.
        They have become my enemies.

23 Examine me, O God, and know my mind.
    Test me, and know my thoughts.

24 See whether I am on an evil path.
        Then lead me on the everlasting path.

Psalm 140

For the choir leader; a psalm by David.

1 Rescue me from evil people, O LORD.
    Keep me safe from violent people.

2 They plan evil things in their hearts.
    They start fights every day.

3 They make their tongues as sharp as a snake's fang.
    Their lips hide the venom of poisonous snakes.   *Selah*

4 Protect me from the hands of wicked people, O LORD.
    Keep me safe from violent people.
        They try to trip me.

5 Arrogant people have laid a trap for me.
    They have spread out a net with ropes.
    They have set traps for me along the road.   *Selah*

6 I said to the LORD, "You are my God."
        O LORD, open your ears to hear my plea for pity.

7 O LORD Almighty, the strong one who saves me,
        you have covered my head in the day of battle.

8 O LORD, do not give wicked people what they want.
        Do not let their evil plans succeed,
            or they will become arrogant.   *Selah*

9 Let the heads of those who surround me
        be covered with their own threats.

10 Let burning coals fall on them.
    Let them be thrown into a pit, never to rise again.

11   Do not let slanderers prosper on earth.
Let evil hunt down violent people with one blow after another.

12   I know that the LORD will defend the rights of those who are oppressed
and the cause of those who are needy.
13   Indeed, righteous people will give thanks to your name.
Decent people will live in your presence.

Psalm 141

A psalm by David.

1   O LORD, I cry out to you, "Come quickly."
Open your ears to me when I cry out to you.
2   Let my prayer be accepted
as sweet-smelling incense in your presence.
Let the lifting up of my hands in prayer be accepted
as an evening sacrifice.

3   O LORD, set a guard at my mouth.
Keep watch over the door of my lips.
4   Do not let me be persuaded to do anything evil
or to become involved with wickedness,
with people who are troublemakers.
Do not let me taste their delicacies.

5   A righteous person may strike me or correct me out of kindness.
It is like lotion for my head.
My head will not refuse it,
because my prayer is directed against evil deeds.
6   When their judges are thrown off a cliff,
they will listen to what I have to say.
It will sound pleasant to them.
7   As someone plows and breaks up the ground,
so our bones will be planted at the mouth of the grave.[a]

Good Morning, God

Psalm 141:3-4

It's easy to say things we shouldn't when we hear our peers gossiping, lying or saying negative things. We might even be tempted to join others who want to do something wrong. David was tempted to do the same things. So he prayed for God to guard his mouth and protect him from following troublemakers. You can pray a prayer like David's whenever you are tempted to do wrong.

Lord, I want to be like David. Protect me from saying and doing what is wrong.

[a] 141:7 Hebrew meaning of verses 5-7 uncertain.

8 My eyes look to you, Lord Almighty.
   I have taken refuge in you.
      Do not leave me defenseless.
9 Keep me away from the trap they set for me
      and from the traps set by troublemakers.
10 Let wicked people fall into their own nets,
      while I escape unharmed.

Psalm 142

A *maskil*[a] by David when he was in the cave; a prayer.

1 Loudly, I cry to the Lord.
   Loudly, I plead with the Lord for mercy.
2 I pour out my complaints in his presence
      and tell him my troubles.
3   When I begin to lose hope,
         you ˌalreadyˌ know what I am experiencing.

   ˌMy enemiesˌ have hidden a trap for me on the path where I walk.
4 Look to my right and see that no one notices me.
      Escape is impossible for me.
      No one cares about me.

5 I call out to you, O Lord.
   I say, "You are my refuge,
      my own inheritance in this world of the living."
6 Pay attention to my cry for help
      because I am very weak.
   Rescue me from those who pursue me
      because they are too strong for me.
7 Release my soul from prison
      so that I may give thanks to your name.
      Righteous people will surround me
         because you are good to me.

Psalm 143

A psalm by David.

1 O Lord, listen to my prayer.
      Open your ears to hear my urgent requests.
      Answer me because you are faithful and righteous.
2 Do not take me to court for judgment,
      because there is no one alive
         who is righteous in your presence.

3 The enemy has pursued me.
      He has ground my life into the dirt.
      He has made me live in dark places
         like those who have died long ago.

---

a 142:1 Unknown musical term.

4   That is why I begin to lose hope
        and my heart is in a state of shock.

5   I remember the days long ago.
    I reflect on all that you have done.
    I carefully consider what your hands have made.
6   I stretch out my hands to you in prayer.
        Like parched land, my soul thirsts for you.   *Selah*

7   Answer me quickly, O Lord.
        My spirit is worn out.
    Do not hide your face from me,
        or I will be like those who go into the pit.
8   Let me hear about your mercy in the morning,
        because I trust you.
    Let me know the way that I should go,
        because I long for you.
9   Rescue me from my enemies, O Lord.
        I come to you for protection.
10   Teach me to do your will, because you are my God.
    May your good Spirit lead me on level ground.
11   O Lord, keep me alive for the sake of your name.
    Because you are righteous, lead me out of trouble.
12   In keeping with your mercy, wipe out my enemies
        and destroy all who torment me,
           because I am your servant.

Psalm 144

By David.

1   Thank the Lord, my rock,
        who trained my hands to fight
        and my fingers to do battle,
2   my merciful one, my fortress,
        my stronghold, and my savior,
        my shield, the one in whom I take refuge,
        and the one who brings people under my authority.

3   O Lord, what are humans that you should care about them?
        What are mere mortals that you should think about them?
4   Humans are like a breath of air.
        Their life span is like a fleeting shadow.

5   O Lord, bend your heaven low, and come down.
        Touch the mountains, and they will smoke.
6   Hurl bolts of lightning, and scatter them.
        Shoot your arrows, and throw them into confusion.
7   Stretch out your hands from above.
        Snatch me, and rescue me from raging waters
           and from foreigners' hands.

8   Their mouths speak lies.
        Their right hands take false pledges.

9   O God, I will sing a new song to you.
        I will sing a psalm to you on a ten-stringed harp.

10   You are the one who gives victory to kings.
      You are the one who snatches your servant David
        away from a deadly sword.

11   Snatch me, and rescue me from foreigners' hands.
      Their mouths speak lies.
      Their right hands take false pledges.

12   May our sons be like full-grown, young plants.
      May our daughters be like stately columns
        that adorn the corners of a palace.

13   May our barns be filled with all kinds of crops.
      May our sheep give birth to thousands of lambs,
        tens of thousands in our fields.

14   May our cattle have many calves. [a]

      May no one break in, and may no one be dragged out.
      May there be no cries of distress in our streets.

15   Blessed are the people who have these blessings!
      Blessed are the people whose God is the LORD!

Psalm 145 [a]

A song of praise by David.

1   I will highly praise you, my God, the king.
      I will bless your name forever and ever.

2   I will bless you every day.
      I will praise your name forever and ever.

3   The LORD is great, and he should be highly praised.
      His greatness is unsearchable.

4   One generation will praise your deeds to the next.
      Each generation will talk about your mighty acts.

5   I will think about the glorious honor of your majesty
      and the miraculous things you have done.

6   People will talk about the power of your terrifying deeds,
      and I will tell about your greatness.

7   They will announce what they remember of your great goodness,
      and they will joyfully sing about your righteousness.

8   The LORD is merciful, compassionate, patient,
      and always ready to forgive.

9   The LORD is good to everyone
      and has compassion for everything that he has made.

10   Everything that you have made will give thanks to you, O LORD,
      and your faithful ones will praise you.

---

[a] 144:14 Hebrew meaning of this verse uncertain.   [a] 145:1 Psalm 145 is a poem in Hebrew alphabetical order.

11 Everyone will talk about the glory of your kingdom
   and will tell the descendants of Adam about your might
12   in order to make known your mighty deeds
      and the glorious honor of your kingdom.
13 Your kingdom is an everlasting kingdom.
   Your empire endures throughout every generation.

14 The LORD supports everyone who falls.
   He straightens the backs of those who are bent over.
15   The eyes of all creatures look to you,
      and you give them their food at the proper time.
16   You open your hand,
      and you satisfy the desire of every living thing.
17 The LORD is fair in all his ways
   and faithful in everything he does.
18 The LORD is near to everyone who prays to him,
   to every faithful person who prays to him.
19 He fills the needs of those who fear him.
   He hears their cries for help and saves them.
20 The LORD protects everyone who loves him,
   but he will destroy all wicked people.

21 My mouth will speak the praise of the LORD,
   and all living creatures will praise his holy name
      forever and ever.

Psalm 146

1 Hallelujah!

   Praise the LORD, my soul!
2 I want to praise the LORD throughout my life.
   I want to make music to praise my God as long as I live.

3 Do not trust influential people,
   mortals who cannot help you.
4   When they breathe their last breath, they return to the ground.
      On that day their plans come to an end.
5 Blessed are those who receive help from the God of Jacob.
   Their hope rests on the LORD their God,
6   who made heaven, earth,
      the sea, and everything in them.
   The LORD remains faithful forever.
7   He brings about justice for those who are oppressed.
   He gives food to those who are hungry.
   The LORD sets prisoners free.
8 The LORD gives sight to blind people.
   The LORD straightens the backs of those who are bent over.
   The LORD loves righteous people.
9 The LORD protects foreigners.
   The LORD gives relief to orphans and widows.
      But he keeps wicked people from reaching their goal.

¹⁰ The LORD rules as king forever.
Zion, your God rules throughout every generation.

Hallelujah!

Psalm 147

¹ Hallelujah!

It is good to sing psalms to our God.
It is pleasant to sing his praise beautifully.

² The LORD is the builder of Jerusalem.
He is the one who gathers the outcasts of Israel together.
³ He is the healer of the brokenhearted.
He is the one who bandages their wounds.
⁴ He determines the number of stars.
He gives each one a name.
⁵ Our Lord is great, and his power is great.
There is no limit to his understanding.
⁶ The LORD gives relief to those who are oppressed.
He brings wicked people down to the ground.

⁷ Sing to the LORD a song of thanksgiving.
Make music to our God with a lyre.
⁸ He covers the sky with clouds.
He provides rain for the ground.
He makes grass grow on the mountains.
⁹ He is the one who gives food to animals
and to young ravens when they call out.
¹⁰ He finds no joy in strong horses,
nor is he pleased by brave soldiers.
¹¹ The LORD is pleased with those who fear him,
with those who wait with hope for his mercy.

¹² Praise the LORD, Jerusalem!
Praise your God, Zion!
¹³ He makes the bars across your gates strong.
He blesses the children within you.
¹⁴ He is the one who brings peace to your borders
and satisfies your hunger with the finest wheat.
¹⁵ He is the one who sends his promise throughout the earth.
His word travels with great speed.
¹⁶ He is the one who sends snow like wool
and scatters frost like ashes.
¹⁷ He is the one who throws his hailstones like breadcrumbs.
Who can withstand his chilling blast?
¹⁸ He sends out his word and melts his hailstones.
He makes wind blow and water flow.
¹⁹ He speaks his word to Jacob,
his laws and judicial decisions to Israel.

20 He has done nothing like this for any other nation.
The other nations do not know the decisions he has handed down.

Hallelujah!

Psalm 148

1 Hallelujah!

Praise the LORD from the heavens.
Praise him in the heights above.
2 Praise him, all his angels.
Praise him, his entire heavenly army.
3 Praise him, sun and moon.
Praise him, all shining stars.
4 Praise him, you highest heaven
and the water above the sky.
5 Let them praise the name of the LORD
because they were created by his command.
6 He set them in their places forever and ever.
He made it a law that no one can break.

7 Praise the LORD from the earth.
Praise him, large sea creatures and all the ocean depths,
8   lightning and hail,
     snow and fog,
     strong winds that obey his commands,
9   mountains and all hills,
     fruit trees and all cedar trees,
10   wild animals and all domestic animals,
     crawling animals and birds,
11   kings of the earth and all its people,
     officials and all judges on the earth,
12   young men and women,
     old and young together.
13 Let them praise the name of the LORD
because his name is high above all others.
His glory is above heaven and earth.
14 He has given his people a strong leader,[a]
someone praiseworthy for his faithful ones,
for the people of Israel, the people who are close to him.

Hallelujah!

Psalm 149

1 Hallelujah!

Sing a new song to the LORD.
Sing his praise in the assembly of godly people.
2 Let Israel find joy in their creator.
Let the people of Zion rejoice over their king.

---

[a] 148:14 Or "given his people strength."

3 Let them praise his name with dancing.
Let them make music to him with tambourines and lyres,
4   because the LORD takes pleasure in his people.
He crowns those who are oppressed with victory.
5 Let godly people triumph in glory.
Let them sing for joy on their beds.
6 Let the high praises of God be in their throats
   and two-edged swords in their hands
7   to take vengeance on the nations,
       to punish the people of the world,
8   to put their kings in chains
       and their leaders in iron shackles,
9   to carry out the judgment that is written against them.
       This is an honor that belongs to all his godly ones.

Hallelujah!

Psalm 150

1 Hallelujah!

Praise God in his holy place.
Praise him in his mighty heavens.
2 Praise him for his mighty acts.
Praise him for his immense greatness.
3 Praise him with sounds from horns.
Praise him with harps and lyres.
4 Praise him with tambourines and dancing.
Praise him with stringed instruments and flutes.
5 Praise him with loud cymbals.
Praise him with crashing cymbals.

6 Let everything that breathes praise the LORD!

Hallelujah!

AN INTRODUCTION TO
Proverbs

Proverbs is a book of wise sayings. Many of them
were written by Solomon. They were collected to
help young people make good
choices. The book of Proverbs
gives advice on work,
wealth, family matters,
and moral behavior. It
tells us that wise choices
lead to blessings,
but foolish choices
lead to ruin.

Headlines

Those Bugs Are Smart!
Proverbs 6:6-8, page 863

Strong Wife Crowns Husband!
Proverbs 12:4, page 872

Big Mouth Ruins Everything!
Proverbs 13:3, page 873

Spankings Won't Kill You
Proverbs 23:13, page 888

A Real Woman!
Proverbs 31, page 900

Who's the woman,
and what happens if
you come to her party?
See Proverbs 9.

Is It Bad to Be Rich?

Most people would like to have a lot of money. But some people say that rich people are bad and their money should be taken away from them. Some rich people may be bad. But what does Proverbs say?

"It is the LORD's blessing that makes a person rich" (Proverbs 10:22). But being rich brings responsibility. The wise person with wealth gives generously (Proverbs 3:9-10 and 11:25) and cares for the less fortunate (Proverbs 14:31 and 19:17). So we should be happy when good people prosper (Proverbs 11:10-11).

However, riches in the wrong hands do lead to evil. People who are dishonest bring trouble on themselves and others (Proverbs 15:6, 27). It's harmful when foolish people are rich because they won't use their wealth wisely (Proverbs 15:16 and 19:10).

It's bad to be rich if you use your wealth selfishly instead of to do good.

Why Should We Fear God?

Proverbs 1:7 says, "fear of the LORD is the beginning of knowledge." That sounds strange! Are we supposed to be scared of God?

Not at all! When the Bible says to fear God, it means we are to *respect and obey* God. Respecting God and choosing to obey him are the first steps to living a truly wise life.

What's In It For Me?

What leads to a good and happy life? . . .

FAITH IN GOD, WHO CREATED ME.

DISCIPLINE, WHICH LEADS TO MATURITY.

HARD WORK, WHICH BRINGS REWARDS.

GIVING, WHICH BRINGS BLESSINGS IN RETURN.

WISDOM, WHICH LEADS TO RIGHTEOUS ACTION.

854

MIXED-UP PROVERBS

Can you straighten out these scrambled proverbs?

"A gracious woman wins respect, like a gold ring in a pig's snout."
(See Proverbs 11:16, 22.)

"The wisest of women will be destroyed, but a stupid one will continue to expand."
(See Proverbs 14:1, 11.)

"An evil person loves to learn, but a righteous person is a dumb animal."
(See Proverbs 12:1, 13.)

"Stupidity is fun to the LORD, and your plans will succeed!"
(See Proverbs 15:21; 16:3.)

ANIMAL ANSWERS

Wise sayings in Proverbs use examples to get their points across. Sometimes animals are mentioned to make a point. What lessons do these animals help to teach us?

Who could learn a thing or two from the ant? (See Proverbs 6:6-8.)

What's more dangerous than a bear robbed of its cubs? (See Proverbs 17:12.)

What can escape your grasp "like an eagle flying into the sky"? (See Proverbs 23:5.)

What "bites like a snake"? (See Proverbs 23:32.)

What is "like grabbing a dog by the ears"? (See Proverbs 26:17.)

Proverbs

The Reasons for Proverbs

1 ¹ The proverbs of Solomon, David's son who was king of Israel, ⌐given⌐
² to grasp wisdom and discipline,
to understand deep thoughts,
³ to acquire the discipline of wise behavior—
righteousness and justice and fairness—
⁴ to give insight to gullible people,
to give knowledge and foresight to the young—
⁵ a wise person will listen and continue to learn,
and an understanding person will gain direction—
⁶ to understand a proverb and a clever saying,
the words of wise people and their riddles.

⁷ The fear of the LORD is the beginning of knowledge.
Stubborn fools despise wisdom and discipline.

Listen to Wisdom

⁸ My son,
listen to your father's discipline,
and do not neglect your mother's teachings,
⁹ because discipline and teachings
are a graceful garland on your head
and a ⌐golden⌐ chain around your neck.

¹⁰ My son,
if sinners lure you, do not go along.
¹¹ If they say,
"Come with us.
Let's set an ambush to kill someone.
Let's hide to ambush innocent people for fun.
¹² We'll swallow them alive like the grave,
like those in good health who go into the pit.
¹³ We'll find all kinds of valuable possessions.
We'll fill our homes with stolen goods.
¹⁴ Join us.
We'll split the loot equally."

¹⁵ My son,
do not follow them in their way.
Do not even set foot on their path,
¹⁶ because they rush to do evil
and hurry to shed blood.
¹⁷ It does no good to spread a net
within the sight of any bird.
¹⁸ But these people set an ambush for their own murder.
They go into hiding only to lose their lives.
¹⁹ This is what happens to everyone

who is greedy for unjust gain.
  Greed takes away his life.

20 Wisdom sings her song in the streets.
   In the public squares she raises her voice.
21 At the corners of noisy streets she calls out.
   At the entrances to the city she speaks her words,
22   "How long will you gullible people love being so gullible?
       How long will you mockers find joy in your mocking?
       How long will you fools hate knowledge?

23   "Turn to me when I warn you.
         I will generously pour out my spirit for you.
         I will make my words known to you.

24   "I called, and you refused to listen.
       I stretched out my hands to you, and no one paid attention.
25   You ignored all my advice.
         You did not want me to warn you.
26   I will laugh at your calamity.
       I will make fun of you
         when panic strikes you,
27   when panic strikes you like a violent storm,
         when calamity strikes you like a wind storm,
         when trouble and anguish come to you.

28   "They will call to me at that time, but I will not answer.
       They will look for me, but they will not find me,
29   because they hated knowledge
           and did not choose the fear of the LORD.
30   They refused my advice.
       They despised my every warning.
31   They will eat the fruit of their lifestyle.
       They will be stuffed with their own schemes.

32   "Gullible people kill themselves because of their turning away.
       Fools destroy themselves because of their indifference.
33   But whoever listens to me will live without worry
           and will be free from the dread of disaster."

The Benefit of Wisdom

1 My son,
    if you take my words to heart,
      and treasure my commands within you,
2   if you pay close attention to wisdom,
      and let your mind reach for understanding,
3   if indeed you call out for insight,
    if you ask aloud for understanding,
4   if you search for wisdom as if it were money
      and hunt for it as if it were hidden treasure,
5   then you will understand the fear of the LORD
      and you will find the knowledge of God.

6   The L ord gives wisdom.
     From his mouth come knowledge and understanding.
7   He has reserved priceless wisdom for decent people.
     He is a shield for those who walk in integrity
8   in order to guard those on paths of justice
         and to watch over the way of his godly ones.
9   Then you will understand what is right and just and fair—
         every good course ⸤in life⸥.

10   Wisdom will come into your heart.
     Knowledge will be pleasant to your soul.
11   Foresight will protect you.
     Understanding will guard you.

12   ⸤Wisdom will⸥ save you
         from the way of evil,
         from the person who speaks devious things,
13   from those who abandon the paths of righteousness
             to walk the ways of darkness,
14   from those who enjoy doing evil,
         from those who find joy in the deviousness of evil.
15   Their paths are crooked.
             Their ways are devious.

16   ⸤Wisdom will⸥ also save you
         from an adulterous woman,
         from a loose woman with her smooth talk,
17   who leaves ⸤her husband,⸥ the closest friend of her youth,
             and forgets her marriage vows to her God.
18   Her house sinks down to death.
             Her ways lead to the souls of the dead.
19   None who have sex with her come back.
                 Nor do they ever reach the paths of life.

20   So walk in the way of good people
         and stay on the paths of righteous people.
21   Decent people will live in the land.
             People of integrity will remain in it.
22   But wicked people will be cut off from the land
                 and treacherous people will be torn[a] from it.

Using Wisdom

3 1   My son,
         do not forget my teachings,
             and keep my commands in mind,
2   because they will bring you
                 long life, good years, and peace.

3   Do not let mercy and truth leave you.
     Fasten them around your neck.
     Write them on the tablet of your heart.

---

[a] 2:22 Or "will be swept away."

4   Then you will find favor and much success
         in the sight of God and humanity.
5   Trust the LORD with all your heart,
         and do not rely on your own understanding.
6   In all your ways acknowledge him,
         and he will make your paths smooth.[a]
7   Do not consider yourself wise.
      Fear the LORD, and turn away from evil.
8   ₍Then₎ your body will be healed,
         and your bones will have nourishment.

9   Honor the LORD with your wealth
         and with the first and best part of all your income.[b]
10   Then your barns will be full,
            and your vats will overflow with fresh wine.

11   Do not reject the discipline of the LORD, my son,
         and do not resent his warning,
12   because the LORD warns the one he loves,
            even as a father warns a son with whom he is pleased.

13   Blessed is the one who finds wisdom
         and the one who obtains understanding.
14   The profit ₍gained₎ from ₍wisdom₎ is greater than
            the profit ₍gained₎ from silver.
            Its yield is better than fine gold.
15   ₍Wisdom₎ is more precious than jewels,
         and all your desires cannot equal it.
16   Long life is in ₍wisdom's₎ right hand.
            In ₍wisdom's₎ left hand are riches and honor.
17   ₍Wisdom's₎ ways are pleasant ways,
         and all its paths lead to peace.
18   ₍Wisdom₎ is a tree of life

Good Morning, God
Proverbs 3:11-12

When was a time that you hurt someone else by what you said or did? What happened as a result of your mistake? Because God loves us, he wants us to learn from our mistakes. God disciplines us so that we will know better next time. God loves you enough to remind you what he wants you to do. Take some time to thank him for his love and discipline.

Lord, thank you for loving me enough to remind me to do what you want me to.

for those who take firm hold of it.
Those who cling to it are blessed.

19 By Wisdom the Lord laid the foundation of the earth.
By understanding he established the heavens.
20 By his knowledge the deep waters were divided,
and the skies dropped dew.

21 My son,
do not lose sight of these things.
Use priceless wisdom and foresight.
22 Then they will mean life for you,
and they will grace your neck.
23 Then you will go safely on your way,
and you will not hurt your foot.
24 When you lie down, you will not be afraid.
As you lie there, your sleep will be sweet.

25 Do not be afraid of sudden terror
or of the destruction of wicked people when it comes.
26 The Lord will be your confidence.
He will keep your foot from getting caught.

27 Do not hold back anything good
from those who are entitled to it
when you have the power to do so.
28 When you have the good thing with you,
do not tell your neighbor,
"Go away!
Come back tomorrow.
I'll give you something then."

29 Do not plan to do something wrong to your neighbor
while he is sitting there with you and suspecting nothing.
30 Do not quarrel with a person for no reason
if he has not harmed you.
31 Do not envy a violent person.
Do not choose any of his ways.
32 The devious person is disgusting to the Lord.
The Lord's intimate advice is with decent people.

33 The Lord curses the house of wicked people,
but he blesses the home of righteous people.
34 When he mocks the mockers,
he is gracious to humble people.
35 Wise people will inherit honor,
but fools will bear disgrace.

Cherish Wisdom

4 1 Sons,
listen to ˻your˼ father's discipline,
and pay attention in order to gain understanding.
2 After all, I have taught you well.

Do not abandon my teachings.

3 When I was a boy learning from my father,
when I was a tender and only child of my mother,

4 they used to teach me and say to me,
"Cling to my words wholeheartedly.
Obey my commands so that you may live.

5 Acquire wisdom.
Acquire understanding.
Do not forget.
Do not turn away from the words that I have spoken.

6 Do not abandon wisdom, and it will watch over you.
Love wisdom, and it will protect you.

7 The beginning of wisdom is to acquire wisdom.
Acquire understanding with all that you have.

8 Cherish wisdom.
It will raise you up.
It will bring you honor when you embrace it.

9 It will give you a graceful garland for your head.
It will hand you a beautiful crown."

Stay on the Path of Wisdom

10 My son,
listen and accept my words,
and they will multiply the years of your life.

11 I have taught you the way of wisdom.
I have guided you along decent paths.

12 When you walk, your stride will not be hampered.
Even if you run, you will not stumble.

13 Cling to discipline.
Do not relax your grip on it.
Keep it because it is your life.

14 Do not stray onto the path of wicked people.
Do not walk in the way of evil people.

15 Avoid it.
Do not walk near it.
Turn away from it,
and keep on walking.

16 Wicked people cannot sleep
unless they do wrong,
and they are robbed of their sleep
unless they make someone stumble.

17 They eat food obtained through wrongdoing
and drink wine obtained through violence.

18 But the path of righteous people is like the light of dawn
that becomes brighter and brighter until it reaches midday.

19 The way of wicked people is like deep darkness.
They do not know what makes them stumble.

Stay Focused on Wisdom

20 My son,
  pay attention to my words.
  Open your ears to what I say.
21 Do not lose sight of these things.
  Keep them deep within your heart
22   because they are life to those who find them
    and they heal the whole body.
23 Guard your heart more than anything else,
  because the source of your life flows from it.
24 Remove dishonesty from your mouth.
  Put deceptive speech far away from your lips.
25 Let your eyes look straight ahead
  and your sight be focused in front of you.
26 Carefully walk a straight path,
  and all your ways will be secure.
27 Do not lean to the right or to the left.
  Walk away from evil.

Avoid Adultery

5 1 My son,
  pay attention to my wisdom.
  Open your ears to my understanding
2   so that you may act with foresight
    and speak with insight.

3 The lips of an adulterous woman drip with honey.
  Her kiss is smoother than oil,
4   but in the end she is as bitter as wormwood,
    as sharp as a two-edged sword.
5 Her feet descend to death.
  Her steps lead straight to hell.
6   She doesn't even think about the path of life.
    Her steps wander, and she doesn't realize it.

7 But now, sons,
  listen to me,
    and do not turn away from what I say to you.
8 Stay far away from her.
  Do not even go near her door.
9   Either you will surrender your reputation to others
    and the rest of your years to some cruel person,
10 or strangers will benefit from your strength
  and you will have to work hard in a pagan's house.
11 Then you will groan when your end comes,
  when your body and flesh are consumed.
  You will say,
12   "Oh, how I hated discipline!
    How my heart despised correction!
13   I didn't listen to what my teachers said to me,

nor did I keep my ear open to my instructors.
14   I almost reached total ruin
        in the assembly and in the congregation."

15   Drink water out of your own cistern
        and running water from your own well.
16   Why should water flow out of your spring?
            Why should your streams flow into the streets?
17   They should be yours alone,
                so do not share them with strangers.
18   Let your own fountain be blessed,
        and enjoy the girl you married when you were young,
19   a loving doe and a graceful deer.[a]
        Always let her breasts satisfy you.
        Always be intoxicated with her love.
20   Why should you, my son,
            be intoxicated with an adulterous woman
            and fondle a loose woman's breast?

21   Each person's ways are clearly seen by the LORD,
        and he surveys all his actions.
22   A wicked person will be trapped by his own wrongs,
        and he will be caught in the ropes of his own sin.
23   He will die for his lack of discipline
        and stumble around because of his great stupidity.

Avoid Disaster

6 1   My son,
        if you guarantee a loan for your neighbor
            or pledge yourself for a stranger with a handshake,
2   you are trapped by the words of your own mouth,
                caught by your own promise.

Good Morning, God
Proverbs 6:6-8

Did you know that God's word tells us to be like an ant? God doesn't expect us to live underneath the ground! But he does want us to work hard, like an ant, instead of being lazy. So God says to follow the example of ants. They work hard and store up food for the winter. No one has to stand over them telling them to work. They know what needs to be done, and they do it. How can you be more helpful around your home?

Dear God, help me not to be lazy around the house, so I can be a help to my parents.

---

[a] 5:19 Or "graceful goat."

3　Do the following things, my son, so that you may free yourself,
　　because you have fallen into your neighbor's hands:
　　　Humble yourself,
　　　　and pester your neighbor.
4　　　Don't let your eyes rest
　　　　or your eyelids close.
5　　　Free yourself like a gazelle from the hand of a hunter
　　　　and like a bird from the hand of a hunter.

6　Consider the ant, you lazy bum.
　　Watch its ways, and become wise.
7　　Although it has no overseer, officer, or ruler,
8　　　in summertime it stores its food supply.
　　　At harvest time it gathers its food.

9　How long will you lie there, you lazy bum?
　　When will you get up from your sleep?
10　　"Just a little sleep,
　　　just a little slumber,
　　　just a little nap."
11　　　Then your poverty will come to you like a drifter,
　　　　and your need will come to you like a bandit.

12　A good-for-nothing scoundrel is a person who has a dishonest mouth.
13　　He winks his eye,
　　　makes a signal with his foot,
　　　and points with his fingers.
14　　He devises evil all the time with a twisted mind.
　　　He spreads conflict.
15　　That is why disaster will come on him suddenly.
　　　In a moment he will be crushed beyond recovery.

16　There are six things that the LORD hates,
　　even seven that are disgusting to him:
17　　　arrogant eyes,
　　　a lying tongue,
　　　hands that kill innocent people,
18　　　a mind devising wicked plans,
　　　feet that are quick to do wrong,
19　　　a dishonest witness spitting out lies,
　　　　and a person who spreads conflict among relatives.

More Advice About Avoiding Adultery

20　My son,
　　obey the command of your father,
　　　and do not disregard the teachings of your mother.
21　Fasten them on your heart forever.
　　Hang them around your neck.
22　　When you walk around, they will lead you.
　　　When you lie down, they will watch over you.
　　　When you wake up, they will talk to you
23　　　　because the command is a lamp,

the teachings are a light,
and the warnings from discipline are the path of life
24   to keep you from an evil woman
and from the smooth talk of a loose woman.

25 Do not desire her beauty in your heart.
Do not let her catch you with her eyes.
26   A prostitute's price is only a loaf of bread,
but a married woman hunts for your life itself.
27 Can a man carry fire in his lap
without burning his clothes?
28 Can anyone walk on red-hot coals
without burning his feet?
29 So it is with a man who has sex with his neighbor's wife.
None who touch her will escape punishment.
30 People do not despise a thief who is hungry
when he steals to satisfy his appetite,
31   but when he is caught,
he has to repay it seven times.
He must give up all the possessions in his house.

32 Whoever commits adultery with a woman has no sense.
Whoever does this destroys himself.
33   An adulterous man will find disease[a] and dishonor,
and his disgrace will not be blotted out,
34   because jealousy arouses a husband's fury.
The husband will show no mercy when he takes revenge.
35   No amount of money will change his mind.
The largest bribe will not satisfy him.

7
1   My son,
pay attention to my words.
Treasure my commands that are within you.
2   Obey my commands so that you may live.
Follow my teachings just as you protect the pupil of your eye.
3   Tie them on your fingers.
Write them on the tablet of your heart.
4   Say to wisdom, "You are my sister."
Give the name "my relative" to understanding
5   in order to guard yourself from an adulterous woman,
from a loose woman with her smooth talk.

6   From a window in my house I looked through my screen.
7   I was looking at gullible people
when I saw a young man without much sense among youths.
8   He was crossing a street near her corner
and walking toward her house
9   in the twilight,
in the evening,
in the dark hours of the night.

---

a 6:33 Or "wounds."

10 A woman with an ulterior motive meets him.
    She is dressed as a prostitute.
11 She is loud and rebellious.
    Her feet will not stay at home.
12   One moment she is out on the street,
        the next she is at the curb,
            on the prowl at every corner.
13 She grabs him and kisses him and brazenly says to him,
14 "I have some sacrificial meat.
    Today I kept my vows.
15 That's why I came to meet you.
    Eagerly, I looked for you,
        and I've found you.
16 I've made my bed,
    with colored sheets of Egyptian linen.
17 I've sprinkled my bed with myrrh, aloes, and cinnamon.
18 Come, let's drink our fill of love until morning.
    Let's enjoy making love,
19   because my husband's not home.
        He has gone on a long trip.
20   He took lots of money with him.
        He won't be home for a couple of weeks."

21 With all her seductive charms, she persuades him.
    With her smooth lips, she makes him give in.
22   He immediately follows her
        like a steer on its way to be slaughtered,
        like a ram hobbling into captivity[a]
23   until an arrow pierces his heart,
        like a bird darting into a trap.
    He does not realize that it will cost him his life.

24 Now, sons,
    listen to me.
    Pay attention to the words from my mouth.
25   Do not let your heart be turned to her ways.
    Do not wander onto her paths,
26   because she has brought down many victims,
        and she has killed all too many.
27   Her home is the way to hell
        and leads to the darkest vaults of death.

Wisdom's Announcement

8 1 Does not wisdom call out?
    Does not understanding raise its voice?
2 ⌞Wisdom⌟ takes its stand on high ground,
    by the wayside where the roads meet,
3   near the gates to the city.
    At the entrance ⌞wisdom⌟ sings its song,

---

[a] 7:22 Hebrew meaning of this line uncertain.

4 "I am calling to all of you,
  and my appeal is to all people.
5   You gullible people, learn how to be sensible.
    You fools, get a heart that has understanding.[a]
6 Listen! I am speaking about noble things,
  and my lips will say what is right.
7 My mouth expresses the truth,
  and wickedness is disgusting to my lips.
8 Everything I say is fair,
  and there is nothing twisted or crooked in it.
9   All of it is clear to a person who has understanding
    and right to those who have acquired knowledge.
10 Take my discipline, not silver,
   and my knowledge rather than fine gold,
11   because wisdom is better than jewels.
     Nothing you desire can equal it.

Wisdom's Authority

12 "I, Wisdom, live with insight,
   and I acquire knowledge and foresight.
13   To fear the Lord is to hate evil.
   I hate pride, arrogance, evil behavior, and twisted speech.
14   Advice and priceless wisdom are mine.
   I, Understanding, have strength.
15   Through me kings reign,
     and rulers decree fair laws.
16   Through me princes rule,
     so do nobles and all fair judges.
17 I love those who love me.
   Those eagerly looking for me will find me.
18 I have riches and honor,
   lasting wealth and righteousness.
19 What I produce is better than gold, pure gold.
   What I yield is better than fine silver.
20 I walk in the way of righteousness, on the paths of justice,
21   to give an inheritance to those who love me
     and to fill their treasuries.

Wisdom as Creator

22 "The Lord already possessed me long ago,
   when his way began,
     before any of his works.
23 I was appointed from everlasting
   from the first,
     before the earth began.
24 I was born
   before there were oceans,
   before there were springs filled with water.

---

[a] 8:5 English equivalent difficult.

25 I was born
   before the mountains were settled in their places
      and before the hills,
26 when he had not yet made land or fields
      or the first dust of the world.

27 "When he set up the heavens, I was there.
   When he traced the horizon on the surface of the ocean,
28 when he established the skies above,
   when he determined the currents in the ocean,
29 when he set a limit for the sea
      so the waters would not overstep his command,
   when he traced the foundations of the earth,
30   I was beside him as a master craftsman.[b]
   I made him happy day after day,
      I rejoiced in front of him all the time,
31   found joy in his inhabited world,
            and delighted in the human race.

Wisdom as Lifegiver

32 "Now, sons, listen to me.
      Blessed are those who follow my ways.
33   Listen to discipline, and become wise.
      Do not leave my ways.
34   Blessed is the person who listens to me,
         watches at my door day after day,
            and waits by my doorposts.
35   Whoever finds me finds life
         and obtains favor from the LORD.
36   Whoever sins against me harms himself.
      All those who hate me love death."

Wisdom Hosts a Banquet

9 1 Wisdom has built her house.
   She has carved out her seven pillars.
2 She has prepared her meat.
   She has mixed her wine.
   She has set her table.
3 She has sent out her servant girls.
   She calls from the highest places in the city,
4   "Whoever is gullible turn in here!"

   She says to a person without sense,
5   "Come, eat my bread,
         and drink the wine I have mixed.
6   Stop being gullible and live.
      Start traveling the road to understanding."

---

[b]8:30 Hebrew meaning of "master craftsman" uncertain.

Wisdom Prolongs Life

7   Whoever corrects a mocker receives abuse.
    Whoever warns a wicked person gets hurt.
8   Do not warn a mocker, or he will hate you.
       Warn a wise person, and he will love you.
9   Give advice to a wise person,
              and he will become even wiser.
          Teach a righteous person,
              and he will learn more.

10 The fear of the Lord is the beginning of wisdom.
    The knowledge of the Holy One is understanding.

11 You will live longer because of me,
        and years will be added to your life.
12 If you are wise, your wisdom will help you.
    If you mock, you alone will be held responsible.

Stupidity Imitates Wisdom's Banquet

13 The woman Stupidity is loud, gullible, and ignorant.[a]
14 She sits at the doorway of her house.
    She is enthroned on the high ground of the city
15   and calls to those who pass by,
            those minding their own business,
16   "Whoever is gullible turn in here!"

    She says to a person without sense,
17   "Stolen waters are sweet,
            and food eaten in secret is tasty."
18 But he does not know
        that the souls of the dead are there,
        that her guests are in the depths of hell.

10 1   The proverbs of Solomon:

A Wise Son Is Righteous

    A wise son makes his father happy,
        but a foolish son brings grief to his mother.

2   Treasures gained dishonestly profit no one,
        but righteousness rescues from death.
3   The Lord will not allow a righteous person to starve,
        but he intentionally ignores the desires of a wicked person.

4   Lazy hands bring poverty,
        but hard-working hands bring riches.
5   Whoever gathers in the summer is a wise son.
    Whoever sleeps at harvest time brings shame.

6   Blessings cover the head of a righteous person,
        but violence covers the mouths of wicked people.

---

[a] 9:13 Hebrew meaning of this verse uncertain.

7 The name of a righteous person remains blessed,
  but the names of wicked people will rot away.

Proverbs Concerning the Mouth

8 The one who is truly wise accepts commands,
  but the one who talks foolishly will be thrown down headfirst.

9 Whoever lives honestly will live securely,
  but whoever lives dishonestly will be found out.

10 Whoever winks with his eye causes heartache.
  The one who talks foolishly will be thrown down headfirst.

11 The mouth of a righteous
      person is a fountain of life,
    but the mouths of wicked
      people conceal violence.

12 Hate starts quarrels,
    but love covers every wrong.

13 Wisdom is found on the lips
      of a person
      who has understanding,
    but a rod is for the back of one
      without sense.

14 Those who are wise
      store up knowledge,
    but the mouth of a stubborn fool
      invites ruin.

15 The rich person's wealth
      is his strong city.
    Poverty ruins the poor.

16 A righteous person's reward
      is life.
    A wicked person's harvest
      is sin.

17 Whoever practices discipline
      is on the way to life,
    but whoever ignores a warning
      strays.

18 Whoever conceals hatred
      has lying lips.
    Whoever spreads slander
      is a fool.

19 Sin is unavoidable
      when there is much talk,
    but whoever seals his lips is wise.

20 The tongue of a righteous person is pure silver.
    The hearts of wicked people are worthless.

21 The lips of a righteous person feed many,
    but stubborn fools die because they have no sense.

School

Proverbs 10:14

Some kids think that the things they have to learn at school don't make a lot of sense. Will you ever use the things you learn? This proverb says the wise "store up knowledge." The more you know, the better prepared you'll be for what the future holds. Time spent doing homework now can make a big difference in the rest of your life.

22 It is the LORD's blessing that makes a person rich,
  and hard work adds nothing to it.
23 Like the laughter of a fool when he carries out an evil plan,
  so is wisdom to a person who has understanding.

Righteous People Contrasted to Wicked People

24 That which wicked people dread happens to them,
  but the LORD grants the desire of righteous people.
25 When the storm has passed, the wicked person has vanished,
  but the righteous person has an everlasting foundation.
26 Like vinegar to the teeth,
  like smoke to the eyes,
  so is the lazy person to those who send him on a mission.
27 The fear of the LORD lengthens the number of days,
  but the years of wicked people are shortened.
28 The hope of righteous people leads to joy,
  but the eager waiting of wicked people comes to nothing.
29 The way of the LORD is a fortress for an innocent person
  but a ruin to those who are troublemakers.
30 A righteous person will never be moved,
  but wicked people will not continue to live in the land.
31 The mouth of a righteous person increases wisdom,
  but a devious tongue will be cut off.
32 The lips of a righteous person announce good will,
  but the mouths of wicked people are devious.

The Value of Righteousness

1 Dishonest scales are disgusting to the LORD,
  but accurate weights are pleasing to him.
2 Arrogance comes,
  then comes shame,
  but wisdom remains with humble people.
3 Integrity guides decent people,
  but hypocrisy leads treacherous people to ruin.
4 Riches are of no help on the day of fury,
  but righteousness saves from death.
5 The righteousness of innocent people makes their road smooth,
  but wicked people fall by their own wickedness.
6 Decent people are saved by their righteousness,
  but treacherous people are trapped by their own greed.
7 At the death of a wicked person, hope vanishes.
  Moreover, his confidence in strength vanishes.
8 A righteous person is rescued from trouble,
  and a wicked person takes his place.
9 With his talk a godless person can ruin his neighbor,
  but righteous people are rescued by knowledge.
10 When righteous people prosper, a city is glad.
  When wicked people die, there are songs of joy.

¹⁷ A truthful witness speaks honestly,
  but a lying witness speaks deceitfully.
¹⁸ Careless words stab like a sword,
  but the words of wise people bring healing.
¹⁹ The word of truth lasts forever,
  but lies last only a moment.
²⁰ Deceit is in the heart of those who plan evil,
  but joy belongs to those who advise peace.

²¹ No ˻lasting˼ harm comes to a righteous person,
  but wicked people have lots of trouble.
²² Lips that lie are disgusting to the Lᴏʀᴅ,
  but honest people are his delight.
²³ A sensible person ˻discreetly˼ hides knowledge,
  but foolish minds preach stupidity.
²⁴ Hard-working hands gain control,
  but lazy hands do slave labor.
²⁵ A person's anxiety will weigh him down,
  but an encouraging word makes him joyful.
²⁶ A righteous person looks out for his neighbor,
  but the path of wicked people leads others astray.
²⁷ A lazy hunter does not catchᶜ his prey,
  but a hard-working person becomes wealthy.ᵈ
²⁸ Everlasting life is on the way of righteousness.
  Eternal death is not along its path.

A Wise Son Lives Righteously

13 ¹ A wise son listens to his father's discipline,
  but a mocker does not listen to reprimands.
² A person eats well as a result of his speaking ability,
  but the appetite of treacherous people ˻craves˼ violence.
³ Whoever controls his mouth protects his own life.
  Whoever has a big mouth comes to ruin.
⁴ A lazy person craves food and there is none,
  but the appetite of hard-working people is satisfied.
⁵ A righteous person hates lying,
  but a wicked person behaves with shame and disgrace.
⁶ Righteousness protects the honest way of life,
  but wickedness ruins a sacrifice for sin.

⁷ One person pretends to be rich but has nothing.
  Another pretends to be poor but has great wealth.
⁸ A person's riches are the ransom for his life,
  but the poor person does not pay attention to threats.
⁹ The light of righteous people beams brightly,
  but the lamp of wicked people will be snuffed out.
¹⁰ Arrogance produces only quarreling,
  but those who take advice gain wisdom.
¹¹ Wealth ˻gained˼ through injustice dwindles away,
  but whoever gathers little by little has plenty.

ᶜ12:27 Hebrew meaning uncertain. ᵈ12:27 Hebrew meaning of this line uncertain.

12 Delayed hope makes one sick at heart,
   but a fulfilled longing is a tree of life.
13 Whoever despises ⸤God's⸥ words will pay the penalty,
   but the one who fears ⸤God's⸥ commands will be rewarded.

14 The teachings of a wise person are a fountain of life
   to turn ⸤one⸥ away from the grasp of death.
15 Good sense brings favor,
   but the way of treacherous people is always the same.[a]
16 Any sensible person acts with knowledge,
   but a fool displays stupidity.
17 An undependable messenger gets into trouble,
   but a dependable envoy brings healing.
18 Poverty and shame come to a person who ignores discipline,
   but whoever pays attention to constructive criticism will be honored.

19 A fulfilled desire is sweet to the soul,
   but turning from evil is disgusting to fools.
20 Whoever walks with wise people will be wise,
   but whoever associates with fools will suffer.
21 Disaster hunts down sinners,
   but righteous people are rewarded with good.
22 Good people leave an inheritance to their grandchildren,
   but the wealth of sinners is stored away for a righteous person.

23 When poor people are able to plow, there is much food,
   but a person is swept away where there is no justice.
24 Whoever refuses to spank his son hates him,
   but whoever loves his son disciplines him from early on.
25 A righteous person eats to satisfy his appetite,
   but the bellies of wicked people are always empty.

Wise People Live Righteously

14 1 The wisest of women builds up her home,
   but a stupid one tears it down with her own hands.
2 Whoever lives right fears the LORD,
   but a person who is devious in his ways despises him.
3 Because of a stubborn fool's words a whip is lifted against him,
   but wise people are protected by their speech.

4 Where there are no cattle, the feeding trough is empty,
   but the strength of an ox produces plentiful harvests.
5 A trustworthy witness does not lie,
   but a dishonest witness breathes lies.
6 A mocker searches for wisdom without finding it,
   but knowledge comes easily to a person who has understanding.

7 Stay away from a fool,
   because you will not receive knowledge from his lips.
8 The wisdom of a sensible person guides his way of life,
   but the stupidity of fools misleads them.

---

[a] 13:15 Masoretic Text; Greek "is their disaster."

9   Stubborn fools make fun of guilt,
         but there is forgiveness among decent people.
10   The heart knows its own bitterness,
         and no stranger can share its joy.
11   The houses of wicked people will be destroyed,
         but the tents of decent people will continue to expand.
12   There is a way that seems right to a person,
         but eventually it ends in death.
13   Even while laughing a heart can ache,
         and joy can end in grief.

14   A heart that turns ˎfrom Godˏ becomes bored with its own ways,
         but a good person is satisfied with God's ways.
15   A gullible person believes anything,
         but a sensible person watches his step.
16   A wise person is cautious and turns away from evil,
         but a fool is careless[a] and overconfident.
17   A short-tempered person acts stupidly,
         and a person who plots evil is hated.
18   Gullible people are gifted with stupidity,
         but sensible people are crowned with knowledge.
19   Evil people will bow to good people.
     Wicked people will bow at the gates of a righteous person.

20   A poor person is hated even by his neighbor,
         but a rich person is loved by many.
21   Whoever despises his neighbor sins,
         but blessed is the one who is kind to humble people.

22   Don't those who stray plan what is evil,
         while those who are merciful and faithful plan what is good?
23   In hard work there is always something gained,
             but idle talk leads only to poverty.
24   The crown of wise people is their wealth.
     The stupidity of fools is just that—stupidity!
25   An honest witness saves lives,
             but one who tells lies is dangerous.
26   In the fear of the Lᴏʀᴅ there is strong confidence,
         and his children will have a place of refuge.
27   The fear of the Lᴏʀᴅ is a fountain of life
         to turn ˎoneˏ away from the grasp of death.
28   A large population is an honor for a king,
         but without people a ruler is ruined.

29   A person of great understanding is patient,
         but a short temper is the height of stupidity.
30   A tranquil heart makes for a healthy body,
         but jealousy is ˎlikeˏ bone cancer.
31   Whoever oppresses the poor insults his maker,
         but whoever is kind to the needy honors him.

---

[a] 14:16 Hebrew meaning uncertain.

³² A wicked person is thrown down by his own wrongdoing,
     but even in his death a righteous person has a refuge.

³³ Wisdom finds rest in the heart of an understanding person.
     Even fools recognize this.^b

Wise Ways to Live

³⁴ Righteousness lifts up a nation,
     but sin is a disgrace in any society.

³⁵ A king is delighted with a servant who acts wisely,
     but he is furious with one who acts shamefully.

15

¹ A gentle answer turns away rage,
     but a harsh word stirs up anger.

² The tongues of wise people give good expression to knowledge,
     but the mouths of fools pour out a flood of stupidity.

³ The eyes of the LORD are everywhere.
     They watch evil people and good people.

⁴ A soothing tongue is a tree of life,
     but a deceitful tongue breaks the spirit.

⁵ A stubborn fool despises his father's discipline,
     but whoever appreciates a warning shows good sense.

⁶ Great treasure is in the house of a righteous person,
     but trouble comes along with the income of a wicked person.

⁷ The lips of wise people spread knowledge,
     but a foolish attitude does not.

⁸ A sacrifice brought by wicked people is disgusting to the LORD,
     but the prayers of decent people please him.

⁹ The way of wicked people is disgusting to the LORD,
     but he loves those who pursue righteousness.

¹⁰ Discipline is a terrible ‚burden‚ to anyone who leaves the ‚right‚ path.
     Anyone who hates a warning will die.

¹¹ If Sheol and Abaddon lie open in front of the LORD
     how much more the human heart!

¹² A mocker does not appreciate a warning.
     He will not go to wise people.

¹³ A joyful heart makes a cheerful face,
     but with a heartache comes depression.

¹⁴ The mind of a person who has understanding searches for knowledge,
     but the mouths of fools feed on stupidity.

¹⁵ Every day is a terrible day for a miserable person,
     but a cheerful heart has a continual feast.

¹⁶ Better to have a little with the fear of the LORD
     than great treasure and turmoil.

¹⁷ Better to have a dish of vegetables where there is love
     than juicy steaks where there is hate.

¹⁸ A hothead stirs up a fight,
     but one who holds his temper calms disputes.

---

^b14:33 Hebrew meaning of this line uncertain.

19 The path of lazy people is like a thorny hedge,
    but the road of decent people is an ˌopenˌ highway.

A Wise Son Brings Blessings to Others

20 A wise son makes his father happy,
    but a foolish child despises its mother.

21 Stupidity is fun to the one without much sense,
    but a person who has understanding forges straight ahead.

22 Without advice plans go wrong,
    but with many advisers they succeed.

23 A person is delighted to hear an answer from his own mouth,
    and a timely word—oh, how good!

24 The path of life for a wise person leads upward
    in order to turn him away from hell below.

25 The Lord tears down the house of an arrogant person,
    but he protects the property of widows.

26 The thoughts of evil people are disgusting to the Lord,
    but pleasant words are pure to him.

27 Whoever is greedy for unjust gain brings trouble to his family,
    but whoever hates bribes will live.

28 The heart of a righteous person carefully considers how to answer,
    but the mouths of wicked people pour out a flood of evil things.

29 The Lord is far from wicked people,
    but he hears the prayers of righteous people.

30 A twinkle in the eye delights the heart.
    Good news refreshes the body.

31 The ear that listens to a life-giving warning
    will be at home among wise people.

32 Whoever ignores discipline despises himself,
    but the person who listens to warning gains understanding.

33 The fear of the Lord is discipline ˌleading toˌ wisdom,
    and humility comes before honor.

Wisdom's Blessings Come From the Lord

16
1 The plans of the heart belong to humans,
    but an answer on the tongue comes from the Lord.

2 A person thinks all his ways are pure,
    but the Lord weighs motives.

3 Entrust your efforts to the Lord,
    and your plans will succeed.

4 The Lord has made everything for his own purpose,
    even wicked people for the day of trouble.

5 Everyone with a conceited heart is disgusting to the Lord.
    Certainly, ˌsuch a personˌ will not go unpunished.

6 By mercy and faithfulness, peace is made with the Lord.
    By the fear of the Lord, evil is avoided.

⁷ When a person's ways are pleasing to the LORD,
    he makes even his enemies to be at peace with him.

⁸ Better a few possessions gained honestly
    than many gained through injustice.

⁹ A person may plan his own journey,
    but the LORD directs his steps.

¹⁰ When a divine revelation is on a king's lips,
    he cannot voice a wrong judgment.

¹¹ Honest balances and scales belong to the LORD.
    He made the entire set of weights.

¹² Wrongdoing is disgusting to kings
    because a throne is established through righteousness.

¹³ Kings are happy with honest words,
    and whoever speaks what is right is loved.

¹⁴ A king's anger announces death,
    but a wise man makes peace with him.

¹⁵ When the king is cheerful, there is life,
    and his favor is like a cloud bringing spring rain.

¹⁶ How much better it is to gain wisdom than gold,
    and the gaining of understanding should be chosen over silver.

¹⁷ The highway of decent people turns away from evil.
    Whoever watches his way preserves his own life.

¹⁸ Pride precedes a disaster,
    and an arrogant attitude precedes a fall.

¹⁹ Better to be humble with lowly people
    than to share stolen goods with arrogant people.

²⁰ Whoever gives attention to the LORD's word prospers,
    and blessed is the person who trusts the LORD.

²¹ The person who is truly wise is called understanding,
    and speaking sweetly helps others learn.

²² Understanding is a fountain of life to the one who has it,
    but stubborn fools punish themselves with their stupidity.

²³ A wise person's heart controls his speech,
    and what he says helps others learn.

²⁴ Pleasant words are like honey from a honeycomb—
    sweet to the spirit and healthy for the body.

Words of Advice to a Wise Son

²⁵ There is a way that seems right to a person,
    but eventually it ends in death.

²⁶ A laborer's appetite works to his advantage,
    because his hunger drives him on.

²⁷ A worthless person plots trouble,
    and his speech is like a burning fire.

²⁸ A devious person spreads quarrels.
    A gossip separates the closest of friends.

²⁹ A violent person misleads his neighbor
    and leads him on a path that is not good.

30 Whoever winks his eye is plotting something devious.
 Whoever bites his lips has finished his evil work.

31 Silver hair is a beautiful crown found in a righteous life.
32 Better to get angry slowly than to be a hero.
 Better to be even-tempered than to capture a city.
33 The dice are thrown,
 but the Lord determines every outcome.

1 Better a bite of dry bread ,eaten, in peace
 than a family feast filled with strife.
2 A wise slave will become master over a son who acts shamefully,
 and he will share the inheritance with the brothers.
3 The crucible is for refining silver and the smelter for gold,
 but the one who purifies hearts ,by fire, is the Lord.
4 An evildoer pays attention to wicked lips.
 A liar opens his ears to a slanderous tongue.
5 Whoever makes fun of a poor person insults his maker.
 Whoever is happy ,to see someone's, distress
 will not escape punishment.
6 Grandchildren are the crown of grandparents,
 and parents are the glory of their children.

The Consequences of Being a Fool

7 Refined speech is not fitting for a godless fool.
 How much less does lying fit a noble person!
8 A bribe seems ,like, a jewel to the one who gives it.[a]
 Wherever he turns, he prospers.
9 Whoever forgives an offense seeks love,
 but whoever keeps bringing up the issue
 separates the closest of friends.

10 A reprimand impresses a person who has understanding
 more than a hundred lashes impress a fool.
11 A rebel looks for nothing but evil.
 Therefore, a cruel messenger will be sent ,to punish, him.
12 Better to meet a bear robbed of its cubs
 than a fool ,carried away, with his stupidity.
13 Whoever pays back evil for good—
 evil will never leave his home.
14 Starting a quarrel is ,like, opening a floodgate,
 so stop before the argument gets out of control.
15 Whoever approves of wicked people
 and whoever condemns righteous people
 is disgusting to the Lord.

16 Why should a fool have money in his hand to buy wisdom
 when he doesn't have a mind to grasp anything?
17 A friend always loves,
 and a brother is born to share trouble.
18 A person without good sense closes a deal with a handshake.

---

a 17:8 Or "who receives it."

He guarantees a loan in the presence of his friend.

19 Whoever loves sin loves a quarrel.
Whoever builds his city gate high invites destruction.

20 A twisted mind never finds happiness,
and one with a devious tongue repeatedly gets into trouble.

21 The parent of a fool has grief,
and the father of a godless fool
has no joy.

22 A joyful heart is good medicine,
but depression
drains one's strength.

23 A wicked person
secretly accepts a bribe
to corrupt the ways of justice.

24 Wisdom is directly in front
of an understanding person,
but the eyes of a fool
are looking around,
all over the world.

How Fools Live

25 A foolish son is a heartache
to his father
and bitter grief to his mother.

26 To punish an innocent person
is not good.
To strike down noble people
is not right.

27 Whoever has knowledge
controls his words,
and a person who has
understanding
is even-tempered.

28 Even a stubborn fool is thought
to be wise if he keeps silent.
He is considered intelligent
if he keeps his lips sealed.

18 ¹ A loner is out to get
what he wants for himself.
He opposes all sound reasoning.

2 A fool does not find joy in understanding
but only in expressing his own opinion.

3 When wickedness comes, contempt also comes,
and insult comes along with disgrace.

4 The words of a person's mouth are like deep waters.
The fountain of wisdom is an overflowing stream.

5 It is not good to be partial toward a wicked person,
thereby depriving an innocent person of justice.

Friends
Proverbs 17:17

Everyone wants friends, but it can be hard to find friends. Even if you've just moved to a new school or have lost friends who have moved away, there's one sure way to get friends. You can be sure to gain friends by being a friend to others. Proverbs says that "a friend always loves." If you show an interest in others and look for ways to help them, others will want you as a friend.

be all you can be

6 By talking, a fool gets into an argument,
   and his mouth invites a beating.
7 A fool's mouth is his ruin.
   His lips are a trap to his soul.
8 The words of a gossip are swallowed greedily,
   and they go down into a person's innermost being.

How to Avoid Fools and Foolishness

9 Whoever is lazy in his work is related to a vandal.
10 The name of the LORD is a strong tower.
    A righteous person runs to it and is safe.
11 A rich person's wealth is his strong city
    and is like a high wall in his imagination.
12 Before destruction a person's heart is arrogant,
    but humility comes before honor.
13 Whoever gives an answer before he listens is stupid and shameful.
14 A person's spirit can endure sickness,
    but who can bear a broken spirit?
15 The mind of a person who has understanding acquires knowledge.
    The ears of wise people seek knowledge.
16 A gift opens doors for the one who gives it
    and brings him into the presence of great people.
17 The first to state his case seems right
    until his neighbor comes to cross-examine him.
18 Flipping a coin ends quarrels
    and settles issues between powerful people.
19 An offended brother is more resistant than a strong city,
    and disputes are like the locked gate of a castle tower.
20 A person's speaking ability provides for his stomach.
    His talking provides him a living.
21 The tongue has the power of life and death,
    and those who love to talk will have to eat their own words.
22 Whoever finds a wife finds something good
    and has obtained favor from the LORD.
23 A poor person is timid when begging,
    but a rich person is blunt when replying.
24 Friends can destroy one another,[a]
    but a loving friend can stick closer than family.

19
1 Better to be a poor person who lives innocently
   than to be one who talks dishonestly and is a fool.
2 A person without knowledge is no good.
   A person in a hurry makes mistakes.
3 The stupidity of a person turns his life upside down,
   and his heart rages against the LORD.
4 Wealth adds many friends,
   but a poor person is separated from his friend.

---

a 18:24 Or "A person has friends as companions."

5 A lying witness will not go unpunished.
   One who tells lies will not escape.
6 Many try to win the kindness of a generous person,
        and everyone is a friend to a person who gives gifts.
7 The entire family of a poor person hates him.
        How much more do his friends keep their distance from him!
        When he chases them with words, they are gone.
8 A person who gains sense loves himself.
        One who guards understanding finds something good.
9 A lying witness will not go unpunished.
   One who tells lies will die.
10 Luxury does not fit a fool,
        much less a slave ruling princes.
11 A person with good sense is patient,
        and it is to his credit that he overlooks an offense.
12 The rage of a king is like the roar of a lion,
        but his favor is like dew on the grass.

A Foolish Son Brings Ruin to Others

13 A foolish son ruins his father,
        and a quarreling woman is like constantly dripping water.
14 Home and wealth are inherited from fathers,
        but a sensible wife comes from the LORD.
15 Laziness throws one into a deep sleep,
        and an idle person will go hungry.
16 Whoever obeys the law preserves his life,
        but, whoever despises the LORD's ways will be put to death.
17 Whoever has pity on the poor lends to the LORD,
        and he will repay him for his good deed.
18 Discipline your son while there is still hope.
        Do not be the one responsible for his death.
19 A person who has a hot temper will pay for it.
        If you rescue him, you will have to do it over and over.
20 Listen to advice and accept discipline
        so that you may be wise the rest of your life.
21 Many plans are in the human heart,
        but the advice of the LORD will endure.
22 Loyalty is desirable in a person,
        and it is better to be poor than a liar.
23 The fear of the LORD leads to life,
        and such a person will rest easy without suffering harm.[a]
24 A lazy person puts his fork in his food.
        He doesn't even bring it back to his mouth.
25 Strike a mocker, and a gullible person may learn a lesson.
        Warn an understanding person, and he will gain more knowledge.

---

[a] 19:23 Hebrew meaning of this line uncertain.

Foolproof Instructions

26 A son who assaults his father and who drives away his mother
    brings shame and disgrace.
27 If you stop listening to instruction, my son,
    you will stray from the words of knowledge.
28 A worthless witness mocks justice,
    and the mouths of wicked people swallow up trouble.
29 Punishments are set for mockers
    and beatings for the backs of fools.

20 1 Wine makes people mock,
    liquor makes them noisy,
        and everyone under their influence is unwise.
2 The rage of a king is like the roar of a lion.
    Whoever makes him angry forfeits his life.
3 Avoiding a quarrel is honorable.
    After all, any stubborn fool can start a fight.
4 A lazy person does not plow in the fall.*
    He looks for something in the harvest but finds nothing.
5 A motive in the human heart is like deep water,
    and a person who has understanding draws it out.
6 Many people declare themselves loyal,
    but who can find someone who is really trustworthy?
7 A righteous person lives on the basis of his integrity.
    Blessed are his children after he is gone.
8 A king who sits on his throne to judge sifts out every evil with his eyes.

9 Who can say,
    "I've made my heart pure.
    I'm cleansed from my sin"?
10 A double standard of weights and measures—
    both are disgusting to the LORD.
11 Even a child makes himself known by his actions,
    whether his deeds are pure or right.
12 The ear that hears,
    the eye that sees—
        the LORD made them both.
13 Do not love sleep or you will end up poor.
    Keep your eyes open, and you will have plenty to eat.
14 "Bad! Bad!" says the buyer.
    Then, as he goes away, he brags about his bargain.
15 There are gold and plenty of jewels,
    but the lips of knowledge are precious gems.
16 Hold on to the garment of one who guarantees a stranger's loan,
    and hold responsible the person who makes a loan on behalf of a foreigner.
17 Food gained dishonestly tastes sweet to a person,
    but afterwards his mouth will be filled with gravel.

---

*20:4 Fall was the start of the planting season in Palestine.

18   Plans are confirmed by getting advice,
        and with guidance one wages war.
19   Whoever goes around as a gossip tells secrets.
        Do not associate with a person whose mouth is always open.

20   The lamp of the person who curses his father and mother
        will be snuffed out in total darkness.[b]
21   An inheritance quickly obtained in the beginning
        will never be blessed in the end.
22   Do not say, "I'll get even with you!"
        Wait for the LORD, and he will save you.
23   A double standard of weights is disgusting to the LORD,
        and dishonest scales are no good.
24   The LORD is the one who directs a person's steps.
        How then can anyone understand his own way?
25   It is a trap for a person to say impulsively, "This is a holy offering!"
        and later to have second thoughts about those vows.

26   A wise king scatters the wicked
        and then runs them over.
27   A person's soul is the LORD's lamp.
        It searches his entire innermost being.
28   Mercy and truth protect a king,
        and with mercy he maintains his throne.
29   While the glory of young men is their strength,
        the splendor of older people is their silver hair.
30   Brutal beatings cleanse away wickedness.
        Such beatings cleanse the innermost being.

The LORD Controls Wise and Foolish People

21
1   The king's heart is like streams of water.
        Both are under the LORD's control.
        He turns them in any direction he chooses.
2   A person thinks everything he does is right,
        but the LORD weighs hearts.
3   Doing what is right and fair
        is more acceptable to the LORD than offering a sacrifice.
4   A conceited look and an arrogant attitude,
        which are the lamps of wicked people, are sins.

5   The plans of a hard-working person lead to prosperity,
        but everyone who is ,always, in a hurry ends up in poverty.
6   Those who gather wealth by lying are wasting time.
        They are looking for death.
7   The violence of wicked people will drag them away
        since they refuse to do what is just.
8   The way of a guilty person is crooked,
        but the behavior of those who are pure is moral.[a]

9   Better to live on a corner of a roof
        than to share a home with a quarreling woman.

---

[b]20:20 Or "snuffed out as darkness approaches."   [a]21:8 Hebrew meaning of this verse uncertain.

10 The mind of a wicked person desires evil
    and has no consideration for his neighbor.
11 When a mocker is punished, a gullible person becomes wise,
    and when a wise person is instructed, he gains knowledge.
12 A righteous person wisely considers the house of a wicked person.
    He throws wicked people into disasters.

13 Whoever shuts his ear to the cry of the poor will call and not be answered.
14 A gift ⸢given⸣ in secret calms anger,
    and a secret bribe calms great fury.
15 When justice is done, a righteous person is delighted,
    but troublemakers are terrified.
16 A person who wanders from the way of wise behavior
    will rest in the assembly of the dead.

17 Whoever loves pleasure will become poor.
    Whoever loves wine and expensive food will not become rich.
18 Wicked people become a ransom for righteous people,
    and treacherous people will take the place of decent people.
19 Better to live in a desert
    than with a quarreling and angry woman.
20 Costly treasure and wealth are in the home of a wise person,
    but a fool devours them.
21 Whoever pursues righteousness and mercy
    will find life, righteousness, and honor.

22 A wise man attacks a city of warriors
    and pulls down the strong defenses in which they trust.
23 Whoever guards his mouth and his tongue
    keeps himself out of trouble.
24 An arrogant, conceited person is called a mocker.
    His arrogance knows no limits.
25 The desire of a lazy person will kill him
    because his hands refuse to work.
26   All day long he feels greedy,
         but a righteous person gives and does not hold back.

27 The sacrifice of wicked people is disgusting,
    especially if they bring it with evil intent.
28 A lying witness will die,
    but a person who listens to advice will continue to speak.
29 A wicked person puts up a bold front,
    but a decent person's way of life is his own security.

30 No wisdom, no understanding, and no advice
    ⸢can stand up⸣ against the LORD.
31 The horse is made ready for the day of battle,
    but the victory belongs to the LORD.

22 1 A good name is more desirable than great wealth.
            Respect is better than silver or gold.
        2 The rich and the poor have this in common:

the Lord is the maker of them all.
3 Sensible people foresee trouble and hide from it,
   but gullible people go ahead and suffer the consequence.
4 On the heels of humility (the fear of the Lord)
   are riches and honor and life.
5 A devious person has thorns and traps ahead of him.
   Whoever guards himself will stay far away from them.
6 Train a child in the way he should go,
   and even when he is old he will not turn away from it.
7 A rich person rules poor people,
   and a borrower is a slave to a lender.
8 Whoever plants injustice will harvest trouble,
   and this weapon of his own fury will be destroyed.
9 Whoever is generous will be blessed
   because he has shared his food with the poor.
10 Drive out a mocker, and conflict will leave.
    Quarreling and abuse will stop.
11 Whoever loves a pure heart and whoever speaks graciously
    has a king as his friend.
12 The Lord's eyes watch over knowledge,
    but he overturns the words of a treacherous person.
13 A lazy person says,
    "There's a lion outside!
      I'll be murdered in the streets!"
14 The mouth of an adulterous woman is a deep pit.
    The one who is cursed by the Lord will fall into it.
15 Foolishness is firmly attached to a child's heart.
    Spanking will remove it far from him.
16 Oppressing the poor for profit
    or giving to the rich
      certainly leads to poverty.

Listen to My Advice

17 Open your ears, and hear the words of wise people,
    and set your mind on the knowledge I give you.
18   It is pleasant if you keep them in mind
        so that they will be on the tip of your tongue,
19   so that your trust may be in the Lord.
    Today I have made them known to you, especially to you.
20 Didn't I write to you previously with advice and knowledge
21   in order to teach you the words of truth
        so that you can give an accurate report to those who send you?

Living With Your Neighbor

22 Do not rob the poor because they are poor
    or trample on the rights of an oppressed person at the city gate,
23   because the Lord will plead their case
        and will take the lives of those who rob them.

Boundary Stones
Proverbs 22:28

Stones were used to mark the boundaries of people's farms. God had given each family a farm when the land was conquered in Joshua's day. Some people moved stones to get some of their neighbor's land because they were not satisfied with what God had given them. This proverb reminds us not to take what belongs to others, but to thank God for what we have.

24 Do not be a friend of one who has a bad temper,
 and never keep company with a hothead,
25 or you will learn his ways
  and set a trap for yourself.

26 Do not be found among those who make deals with a handshake,
 among those who guarantee other people's loans.
27 If you have no money to pay back a loan,
  why should your bed be repossessed?
28 Do not move an ancient boundary marker
 that your ancestors set in place.
29 Do you see a person who is efficient in his work?
 He will serve kings.
 He will not serve unknown people.

23 1 When you sit down to eat with a ruler,
  pay close attention to what is in front of you,
2   and put a knife to your throat if you have a big appetite.
3 Do not crave his delicacies,
  because this is food that deceives you.

4 Do not wear yourself out getting rich.
 Be smart enough to stop.
5 Will you catch only a fleeting glimpse of wealth before it is gone?
  It makes wings for itself like an eagle flying into the sky.

6 Do not eat the food of one who is stingy,
 and do not crave his delicacies.
7 As he calculates the cost to himself, this is what he does:
  He tells you, "Eat and drink,"
   but he doesn't really mean it.
8 You will vomit the little bit you have eaten
 and spoil your pleasant conversation.

9 Do not talk directly to a fool,
      because he will despise the wisdom of your words.
10 Do not move an ancient boundary marker
      or enter fields that belong to orphans,
11   because the one who is responsible for them is strong.
      He will plead their case against you.

Learning From Your Father

12 Live a more disciplined life,
      and listen carefully to words of knowledge.
13 Do not hesitate to discipline a child.
      If you spank him, he will not die.
14   Spank him yourself,
      and you will save his soul from hell.

15 My son,
      if you have a wise heart,
      my heart will rejoice as well.
16   My heart rejoices when you speak what is right.

17 Do not envy sinners in your heart.
      Instead, continue to fear the LORD.
18   There is indeed a future,
      and your hope will never be cut off.

19 My son,
      listen, be wise,
      and keep your mind going in the right direction.
20 Do not associate with those who drink too much wine,
      with those who eat too much meat,
21   because both a drunk and a glutton will become poor.
      Drowsiness will dress a person in rags.

22   Listen to your father since you are his son,
      and do not despise your mother because she is old.
23 Buy truth (and do not sell it),
      that is, buy wisdom, discipline, and understanding.
24 A righteous person's father will certainly rejoice.
      Someone who has a wise son will enjoy him.
25   May your father and your mother be glad.
      May she who gave birth to you rejoice.

26 My son,
      give me your heart.
      Let your eyes find happiness in my ways.
27   A prostitute is a deep pit.
      A loose woman is a narrow well.
28   She is like a robber, lying in ambush.
      She spreads unfaithfulness throughout society.

29 Who has trouble?
      Who has misery?
      Who has quarrels?

Who has a complaint?
Who has wounds for no reason?
Who has bloodshot eyes?
30   Those who drink glass after glass of wine
        and mix it with everything.
31 Do not look at wine
        because it is red,
        because it sparkles in the cup,
        because it goes down smoothly.
32   Later it bites like a snake
            and strikes like a poisonous snake.
33 Your eyes will see strange sights,
        and your mouth will say embarrassing things.
34 You will be like someone lying down in the middle of the sea
        or like someone lying down on top of a ship's mast, saying,
35   "They strike me, but I feel no pain.
        They beat me, but I'm not aware of it.
            Whenever I wake up, I'm going to look for another drink."

24 ¹ Do not envy evil people
        or wish you were with them,
    2   because their minds plot violence,
            and their lips talk trouble.

3 With wisdom a house is built.
    With understanding it is established.
4 With knowledge its rooms are filled
        with every kind of riches, both precious and pleasant.

5 A strong man knows how to use his strength,
        but a person with knowledge is even more powerful.
6   After all, with the right strategy you can wage war,
            and with many advisers there is victory.

7 Matters of wisdom are beyond the grasp of a stubborn fool.
        At the city gate he does not open his mouth.
8 Whoever plans to do evil will be known as a schemer.
9 Foolish scheming is sinful,
        and a mocker is disgusting to everyone.

10 If you faint in a crisis, you are weak.
11 Rescue captives condemned to death,
        and spare those staggering toward their slaughter.
12 When you say, "We didn't know this,"
        won't the one who weighs hearts take note of it?
        Won't the one who guards your soul know it?
        Won't he pay back people for what they do?

13 Eat honey, my son, because it is good.
        Honey that flows from the honeycomb tastes sweet.
14   The knowledge of wisdom is like that for your soul.
        If you find it, then there is a future,
            and your hope will never be cut off.

15 You wicked one,
     do not lie in ambush at the home of a righteous person.
     Do not rob his house.
16 A righteous person may fall seven times, but he gets up again.
     However, in a disaster wicked people fall.

17 Do not be happy when your enemy falls,
     and do not feel glad when he stumbles.
18 The LORD will see it, he won't like it,
     and he will turn his anger away from that person.

19 Do not get overly upset with evildoers.
     Do not envy wicked people,
20 because an evil person has no future,
     and the lamps of wicked people will be snuffed out.

21 Fear the LORD, my son.
     Fear the king as well.
     Do not associate with those who always insist upon change,
22 because disaster will come to them suddenly.
     Who knows what misery both may bring?

Learning From Wise People

23 These also are the sayings of wise people:

     Showing partiality as a judge is not good.
24 Whoever says to a guilty person, "You are innocent,"
     will be cursed by people and condemned by nations.
25 But people will be pleased with those who convict a guilty person,
     and a great blessing will come to them.
26 Giving a straight answer is ⌞like⌟ a kiss on the lips.

27 Prepare your work outside,
     and get things ready for yourself in the field.
     Afterwards, build your house.

28 Do not testify against your neighbor without a reason,
     and do not deceive with your lips.
29 Do not say,
     "I'll treat him as he treated me.
     I'll pay him back for what he has done to me."

30 I passed by a lazy person's field,
     the vineyard belonging to a person without sense.
31 I saw that it was all overgrown with thistles.
     The ground was covered with weeds,
     and its stone fence was torn down.
32 When I observed ⌞this⌟, I took it to heart.
     I saw it and learned my lesson.
33 "Just a little sleep,
     just a little slumber,
     just a little nap."

34 Then your poverty will come like a drifter,
    and your need will come like a bandit.

25 1 These also are Solomon's proverbs that were copied
    by the men of King Hezekiah of Judah.

Advice for Kings

2 It is the glory of God to hide things
    but the glory of kings to investigate them.
3 ⌊Like⌋ the high heavens and the deep earth,
    so the mind of kings is unsearchable.
4 Take the impurities out of silver,
    and a vessel is ready for the silversmith to mold.
5 Take a wicked person away from the presence of a king,
    and justice will make his throne secure.

6 Do not brag about yourself in front of a king
    or stand in the spot that belongs to notable people,
7 because it is better to be told, "Come up here,"
    than to be put down in front of a prince
        whom your eyes have seen.

8 Do not be in a hurry to go to court.
    What will you do in the end if your neighbor disgraces you?
9 Present your argument to your neighbor,
    but do not reveal another person's secret.
10 Otherwise, when he hears about it, he will humiliate you,
    and his evil report about you will never disappear.

11 ⌊Like⌋ golden apples in silver settings,
    ⌊so⌋ is a word spoken at the right time.
12 ⌊Like⌋ a gold ring and a fine gold ornament,
    ⌊so⌋ is constructive criticism to the ear of one who listens.
13 Like the coolness of snow on a harvest day,
    ⌊so⌋ is a trustworthy messenger to those who send him:
    He refreshes his masters.
14 ⌊Like⌋ a dense fog or a dust storm,
    ⌊so⌋ is a person who brags about a gift that he does not give.

15 With patience you can persuade a ruler,
    and a soft tongue can break bones.
16 When you find honey, eat only as much as you need.
    Otherwise, you will have too much and vomit.
17 Do not set foot in your neighbor's house too often.
    Otherwise, he will see too much of you and hate you.

18 ⌊Like⌋ a club and a sword and a sharp arrow,
    ⌊so⌋ is a person who gives false testimony against his neighbor.
19 ⌊Like⌋ a broken tooth and a lame foot,
    ⌊so⌋ is confidence in an unfaithful person in a ⌊time of⌋ crisis.
20 ⌊Like⌋ taking off a coat on a cold day
    or pouring vinegar on baking soda,
        so is singing songs to one who has an evil heart.

21 If your enemy is hungry, give him some food to eat,
　and if he is thirsty, give him some water to drink.
22 　In this way, you will make him feel guilty and ashamed,
　　and the Lord will reward you.

23 ˌAsˌ the north wind brings rain,
　so a whispering tongue brings angry looks.
24 Better to live on a corner of a roof
　than to share a home with a quarreling woman.
25 ˌLikeˌ cold water to a thirsty soul,
　so is good news from far away.
26 ˌLikeˌ a muddied spring and a polluted well,
　ˌsoˌ is a righteous person who gives in to a wicked person.

27 Eating too much honey is not good,
　and searching for honor is not honorable.[a]

28 ˌLikeˌ a city broken into ˌandˌ left without a wall,
　ˌsoˌ is a person who lacks self-control.

All About Fools

26 1 Like snow in summertime and rain at harvest time,
　so honor is not right for a fool.
2 Like a fluttering sparrow,
　like a darting swallow,
　　so a hastily spoken curse does not come to rest.
3 A whip is for the horse,
　a bridle is for the donkey,
　　and a rod is for the backs of fools.

4 Do not answer a fool with his own stupidity,
　or you will be like him.
5 Answer a fool with his own stupidity,
　or he will think he is wise.
6 Whoever uses a fool to send a message
　cuts off his own feet and brings violence upon himself.

7 ˌLikeˌ a lame person's limp legs,
　so is a proverb in the mouths of fools.
8 Like tying a stone to a sling,
　so is giving honor to a fool.
9 ˌLikeˌ a thorn stuck in a drunk's hand,
　so is a proverb in the mouths of fools.
10 ˌLikeˌ many people who destroy everything,
　so is one who hires fools or drifters.
11 As a dog goes back to its vomit,
　ˌsoˌ a fool repeats his stupidity.
12 Have you met a person who thinks he is wise?
　There is more hope for a fool than for him.

13 A lazy person says,
　"There's a ferocious lion out on the road!

---

[a]25:27 Hebrew meaning of this line uncertain.

14 As a door turns on its hinges,
  so the lazy person turns on his bed.
15 A lazy person puts his fork in his food.
  He wears himself out as he brings it back to his mouth.
16 A lazy person thinks he is wiser than seven people
  who give a sensible answer.

17 Like grabbing a dog by the ears,
  so is a bystander who gets involved in someone else's quarrel.
18 Like a madman who shoots flaming arrows, arrows, and death,
19 so is the person who tricks his neighbor and says, "I was only joking!"

20 Without wood a fire goes out,
  and without gossip a quarrel dies down.
21 As charcoal fuels burning coals and wood fuels fire,
  so a quarrelsome person fuels a dispute.
22 The words of a gossip are swallowed greedily,
  and they go down into a person's innermost being.

23 Like a clay pot covered with cheap silver,
  so is smooth talk that covers up an evil heart.
24 Whoever is filled with hate disguises it with his speech,
  but inside he holds on to deceit.
25 When he talks charmingly, do not trust him
  because of the seven disgusting things in his heart.
26 His hatred is deceitfully hidden,
  but his wickedness will be revealed to the community.

27 Whoever digs a pit will fall into it.
Whoever rolls a stone will have it roll back on him.
28 A lying tongue hates its victims,
  and a flattering mouth causes ruin.

All About Life

1 Do not brag about tomorrow,
  because you do not know what another day may bring.
2 Praise should come from another person
  and not from your own mouth,
  from a stranger and not from your own lips.
3 A stone is heavy, and sand weighs a lot,
  but annoyance caused by a stubborn fool is heavier than both.
4 Anger is cruel, and fury is overwhelming,
  but who can survive jealousy?

5 Open criticism is better than unexpressed love.
6 Wounds made by a friend are intended to help,
  but an enemy's kisses are too much to bear.[a]
7 One who is full despises honey,
  but to one who is hungry,
    even bitter food tastes sweet.

---

[a] 27:6 Hebrew meaning of "are too much to bear" uncertain.

8   Like a bird wandering from its nest,
        so is a husband wandering from his home.

9   Perfume and incense make the heart glad,
        but the sweetness of a friend is a fragrant forest.*b*

10   Do not abandon your friend or your father's friend.
        Do not go to a relative's home when you are in trouble.
        A neighbor living nearby is better than a relative far away.

11   Be wise, my son, and make my heart glad
        so that I can answer anyone who criticizes me.

12   Sensible people foresee trouble and hide.
        Gullible people go ahead and suffer.

13   Hold on to the garment of one who guarantees a stranger's loan,
        and hold responsible the person
            who makes a loan in behalf of a foreigner.

14   Whoever blesses his friend early in the morning with a loud voice—
        his blessing is considered a curse.

15   Constantly dripping water on a rainy day is like a quarreling woman.

16   Whoever can control her can control the wind.
        He can even pick up olive oil with his right hand.*c*

17   As iron sharpens iron,
        so one person sharpens the wits of another.

18   Whoever takes care of a fig tree can eat its fruit,
        and whoever protects his master is honored.

19   As a face is reflected in water,
        so a person is reflected by his heart.

20   Hell and decay are never satisfied,
        and a person's eyes are never satisfied.

21   The crucible is for refining silver and the smelter for gold,
        but a person is tested by the praise given to him.

22   If you crush a stubborn fool in a mortar with a pestle along with grain,*d*
        even then his stupidity will not leave him.

23   Be fully aware of the condition of your flock,
        and pay close attention to your herds.

24   Wealth is not forever.
        Nor does a crown last from one generation to the next.

25   When grass is cut short, the tender growth appears,
        and vegetables are gathered on the hills.

26   Lambs will provide you with clothing,
        and the money from the male goats will buy a field.

27   There will be enough goat milk to feed you,
                to feed your family,
                    and to keep your servant girls alive.

28   1   A wicked person flees when no one is chasing him,
            but righteous people are as bold as lions.

---

*b*27:9 Or "is sincere advice."   *c*27:16 Hebrew meaning of this line uncertain.   *d*27:22 Hebrew meaning uncertain.

2 When a country is in revolt, it has many rulers,
     but only with a person who has understanding and knowledge
        will it last a long time.
3 A poor person who oppresses poorer people
     is like a driving rain that leaves no food.
4 Those who abandon ˌGod'sˌ teachings praise wicked people,
     but those who follow ˌGod'sˌ teachings oppose wicked people.
5 Evil people do not understand justice,
     but those who seek the LORD understand everything.
6 Better to be a poor person who has integrity
     than to be rich and double-dealing.

7 Whoever follows ˌGod'sˌ teachings is a wise son.
   Whoever associates with gluttons disgraces his father.
8 Whoever becomes wealthy through ˌunfairˌ loans and interest
     collects them for the one who is kind to the poor.
9 Surely the prayer of someone who refuses
     to listen to ˌGod'sˌ teachings is disgusting.
10 Whoever leads decent people into evil will fall into his own pit,
     but innocent people will inherit good things.

11 A rich person is wise in his own eyes,
     but a poor person with understanding sees right through him.
12 When righteous people triumph, there is great glory,
     but when wicked people rise, people hide themselves.
13 Whoever covers over his sins does not prosper.
   Whoever confesses and abandons them receives compassion.
14 Blessed is the one who is always fearful ˌof sinˌ,
     but whoever is hard-hearted falls into disaster.

15 ˌLikeˌ a roaring lion and a charging bear,
     ˌsoˌ a wicked ruler is a threat to poor people.
16 A leader without understanding taxes ˌhis peopleˌ heavily,
     but those who hate unjust gain will live longer.
17 A person burdened with the guilt of murder
     will be a fugitive down to his grave.
        No one will help him.

18 Whoever lives honestly will be safe.
   Whoever lives dishonestly will fall all at once.
19 Whoever works his land will have plenty to eat.
   Whoever chases unrealistic dreams will have plenty of nothing.

20 A trustworthy person has many blessings,
     but anyone in a hurry to get rich will not escape punishment.
21 Showing partiality is not good,
     because some people will turn on you even for a piece of bread.
22 A stingy person is in a hurry to get rich,
     not realizing that poverty is about to overtake him.

23 Whoever criticizes people will be more highly regarded in the future
     than the one who flatters with his tongue.
24 The one who robs his father or his mother

and says, "It isn't wrong!" is a companion to a vandal.
25 A greedy person stirs up a fight,
　　but whoever trusts the LORD prospers.

26 Whoever trusts his own heart is a fool.
　　Whoever walks in wisdom will survive.
27 Whoever gives to the poor lacks nothing.
　　Whoever ignores the poor receives many curses.

28 When wicked people rise, people hide.
　　When they die, righteous people increase.

29

1 A person who will not bend after many warnings
　　will suddenly be broken beyond repair.
2 When righteous people increase, the people of God rejoice,
　　but when a wicked person rules, everybody groans.
3 A person who loves wisdom makes his father happy,
　　but one who pays prostitutes wastes his wealth.
4 By means of justice, a king builds up a country,
　　but a person who confiscates religious contributions tears it down.
5 A person who flatters his neighbor
　　is spreading a net for him to step into.
6 To an evil person sin is bait in a trap,
　　but a righteous person runs away from it[a] and is glad.
7 A righteous person knows the just cause of the poor.
　　A wicked person does not understand this.
8 Mockers create an uproar in a city,
　　but wise people turn away anger.
9 When a wise person goes to court with a stubborn fool,
　　he may rant and rave,
　　　　but there is no peace and quiet.
10 Bloodthirsty people hate an innocent person,
　　but decent people seek to protect his life.
11 A fool expresses all his emotions,
　　but a wise person controls them.
12 If a ruler pays attention to lies,
　　all his servants become wicked.
13 A poor person and an oppressor have this in common:
　　The LORD gives both of them sight.
14 When a king judges the poor with honesty,
　　his throne will always be secure.
15 A spanking and a warning produce wisdom,
　　but an undisciplined child disgraces his mother.
16 When wicked people increase, crime increases,
　　but righteous people will witness their downfall.
17 Correct your son, and he will give you peace of mind.
　　He will bring delight to your soul.

---

a 29:6 Hebrew meaning of "runs away from it" uncertain.

18 Without prophetic vision people run wild,
   but blessed are those who follow ⌊God's⌋ teachings.
19 A slave cannot be disciplined with words.
   He will not respond, though he may understand.
20 Have you met a person who is quick to answer?
   There is more hope for a fool than for him.
21 Pamper a slave from childhood,
   and later he will be ungrateful.[b]

22 An angry person stirs up a fight,
   and a hothead does much wrong.
23 A person's pride will humiliate him,
   but a humble spirit gains honor.
24 Whoever is a thief's partner hates his own life.
   He will not testify under oath.
25 A person's fear sets a trap ⌊for him⌋,
   but one who trusts the LORD is safe.
26 Many seek an audience with a ruler,
   but justice for humanity comes from the LORD.
27 An unjust person is disgusting to righteous people.
   A decent person is disgusting to wicked people.

30 1 The words of Agur, son of Jakeh. Agur's prophetic revelation.

Agur Speaks About God
[To God]
This man's declaration:
   "I'm weary, O God.
   I'm weary and worn out, O God.
2 I'm more ⌊like⌋ a dumb animal than a human being.
   I don't ⌊even⌋ have human understanding.
3 I haven't learned wisdom.
   I don't have knowledge of the Holy One.[a]

[To the audience]
4 "Who has gone up to heaven and come down?
   Who has gathered the wind in the palm of his hand?
   Who has wrapped water in a garment?
   Who has set up the earth from one end to the other?
   What is his name or the name of his son?
   Certainly, you must know!

5 "Every word of God has proven to be true.
   He is a shield to those who come to him for protection.
6 Do not add to his words,
   or he will reprimand you, and you will be found to be a liar.

---
[b] 29:21 Hebrew meaning uncertain.   [a] 30:3 Or "holy ones."

A Prayer

[To God]

7 "I've asked you for two things.
   Don't keep them from me before I die:
8   Keep vanity and lies far away from me.
       Don't give me either poverty or riches.
       Feed me ‚only‚ the food I need,
9   or I may feel satisfied and deny you
           and say, 'Who is the LORD?'
       or I may become poor and steal
           and give the name of my God a bad reputation.

Against Slander

[To the audience]

10 "Do not slander a slave to his master.
    The slave will curse you,
        and you will be found guilty."

Four Kinds of People

11 A certain kind of person curses his father
        and does not bless his mother.
12 A certain kind of person thinks he is pure
        but is not washed from his own feces.*b*
13 A certain kind of person looks around arrogantly
        and is conceited.
14 A certain kind of person,
        whose teeth are like swords
            and whose jaws are ‚like‚ knives,
                devours oppressed people from the earth
                and people from among humanity.

Human Bloodsuckers

15 The bloodsucking leech has two daughters—"Give!" and "Give!"

Four Things That Are Never Satisfied

Three things are never satisfied.
Four never say, "Enough!":
16   the grave,
        a barren womb,
        a land that never gets enough water,
        a fire that does not say, "Enough!"

Disrespectful Children—Their Punishment

17 The eye that makes fun of a father and hates to obey a mother
        will be plucked out by ravens in the valley
        and eaten by young vultures.

---

*b*30:12 Blunt Hebrew term but not considered vulgar.

Four Things of Intrigue

¹⁸ Three things are too amazing to me,
   even four that I cannot understand:
¹⁹   an eagle making its way through the sky,
     a snake making its way over a rock,
     a ship making its way through high seas,
     a man making his way with a virgin.

About the Woman Who Commits Adultery

²⁰ This is the way of a woman who commits adultery:
   She eats, wipes her mouth,
     and says, "I haven't done anything wrong!"

Four Things That Are Intolerable

²¹ Three things cause the earth to tremble,
   even four it cannot bear up under:
²²   a slave when he becomes king,
     a godless fool when he is filled with food,
²³   a woman who is unloved when she gets married,
     a maid when she replaces her mistress.

Four Things That Are Small—
Yet Smart and Strong

²⁴ Four things on earth are small,
   yet they are very wise:
²⁵   Ants are not a strong species,
       yet they store their food in summer.
²⁶   Rock badgers are not a mighty species,
       yet they make their home in the rocks.
²⁷   Locusts have no king,
       yet all of them divide into swarms by instinct.
²⁸   A lizard you can hold in your hands,
       yet it can even be found in royal palaces.

Four Things That Move With Dignity

²⁹ There are three things that walk with dignity,
   even four that march with dignity:
³⁰   a lion, mightiest among animals, which turns away from nothing,
³¹   a strutting rooster,ᶜ
     a male goat,
     a king at the head of his army.ᵈ

Keep Calm and Quiet

³² If you are such a godless fool as to honor yourself,
   or if you scheme,
     you had better put your hand over your mouth.
³³   As churning milk produces butter

ᶜ30:31 Hebrew meaning of this line uncertain.   ᵈ30:31 Hebrew meaning of "at the head of his army" uncertain.

and punching a nose produces blood,
    so stirring up anger *e* produces a fight.

31 ¹ The sayings of King Lemuel, a prophetic revelation,
    used by his mother to discipline him.

Advice to a Prince

² "What, my son?
    What, son to whom I gave birth?
    What, son of my prayers?
³   Don't give your strength to women
        or your power to those who ruin kings.

⁴ "It is not for kings, Lemuel.
    It is not for kings to drink wine or for rulers to crave liquor.
⁵   Otherwise, they drink and forget what they have decreed
        and change the standard of justice for all oppressed people.
⁶ Give liquor to a person who is dying
    and wine to one who feels resentful.
⁷   Such a person drinks
        and forgets his poverty
        and does not remember his trouble anymore.

⁸ "Speak out for the one who cannot speak,
    for the rights of those who are doomed.
⁹ Speak out,
    judge fairly,
        and defend the rights of oppressed and needy people."

A Poem in Hebrew Alphabetical Order

¹⁰ "Who can find a wife with a strong character?
    She is worth far more than jewels.
¹¹ Her husband trusts her with ˌallˌ his heart,
    and he does not lack anything good.
¹² She helps him and never harms him all the days of her life.

¹³ "She seeks out wool and linen ˌwith careˌ
    and works with willing hands.
¹⁴ She is like merchant ships.
    She brings her food from far away.
¹⁵ She wakes up while it is still dark
    and gives food to her family
        and portions of food to her female slaves.

¹⁶ "She picks out a field and buys it.
    She plants a vineyard from the profits she has earned.
¹⁷ She puts on strength like a belt
    and goes to work with energy.
¹⁸ She sees that she is making a good profit.
    Her lamp burns late at night.

---

e 30:33 In Hebrew there is a play on words in verse 33 where the same verb is used to express all three actions.

19   "She puts her hands on the distaff,
         and her fingers hold a spindle.
20   She opens her hands to oppressed people
         and stretches them out to needy people.
21   She does not fear for her family when it snows
            because her whole family
               has a double layer of clothing.
22   She makes quilts for herself.
      Her clothes are made of linen and purple cloth.

23   "Her husband is known at the city gates
         when he sits with the leaders of the land.

24   "She makes linen garments and sells them
         and delivers belts to the merchants.
25   She dresses with strength and nobility,
         and she smiles at the future.

26   "She speaks with wisdom,
         and on her tongue there is tender instruction.
27   She keeps a close eye on the conduct of her family,
         and she does not eat the bread of idleness.
28   Her children and her husband
         stand up and bless her.
      In addition, he sings her praises, by saying,
29   'Many women have done noble work,
            but you have surpassed them all!'

30   "Charm is deceptive, and beauty evaporates,
         but a woman who has the fear of the LORD should be praised.
31   Reward her for what she has done,
         and let her achievements praise her at the city gates."

Ecclesiastes

Solomon wrote this book when he was an old man. He wanted to know if life had any meaning. He tried pleasure. He tried wealth. He tried learning. He tried building great buildings. Finally, he decided that without God, everything is pointless.

This woman "has everything." So why isn't she happy? See Ecclesiastes 5:10.

Headlines

Money Isn't Everything?

For some people, nothing is more important than money. They make it the center of their lives. That's really too bad because only God gives life real meaning.

Solomon learned this lesson the hard way. He had more wealth than anybody, but it didn't make him happy. In fact, he ended up depressed! Solomon found out that "whoever loves money will never be satisfied with money. Whoever loves wealth will never be satisfied with more income" (Ecclesiastes 5:10). If money is the most important thing in your life, you will also end up miserable. Loving money can't make life worth living. But loving God can!

Who's Kidding Who?

Some people say you have to try things to find out if you like them. Your mom might say that about asparagus. But what if someone says that about smoking or drugs?

Solomon, who wrote Ecclesiastes, decided he would learn what was good for people by trying everything. He even "explored ways to do some foolish things" (Ecclesiastes 2:3)! What Solomon learned was "to hate life" (Ecclesiastes 2:17). In the end, he realized that the best thing to do in life is to "fear God, and keep his commands" (Ecclesiastes 12:13).

You can be wiser than wise King Solomon. You don't need to experience the bad things in life to know what is good for you. God has given you the Bible and has told you what is good!

Oops! We Goofed!

Our reporter got Solomon's sayings wrong. Can you figure out what Solomon really said?

"With a lot of whiskers comes a lot of hard work!"
See Ecclesiastes 1:18.

"A time to be bored and a time to diet."
See Ecclesiastes 3:2.

"A celebrated dope is not easily woken."
See Ecclesiastes 4:12.

"Move over! The hat's affordable and full of weevils!"
See Ecclesiastes 9:3.

"Throw your bird in the face of the otter, because you will find it aching after being dazed."
See Ecclesiastes 11:1.

What's In It For Me?

Only God . . .

CAN GIVE MY LIFE MEANING.

CAN BLESS ME WITH CONTENTMENT.

CAN MAKE MY ACHIEVEMENTS WORTHWHILE.

CAN MAKE SURE THERE IS JUSTICE.

CAN MAKE LIFE WORTH LIVING.

Ecclesiastes

Introducing the Spokesman

¹The words of the spokesman, the son of David and the king in Jerusalem.

The Theme

²"Absolutely pointless!" says the spokesman. "Absolutely pointless! Everything is pointless."

Life Is an Endless Circle

³What do people gain from all their hard work under the sun?

⁴   Generations come, and generations go,
      but the earth lasts forever.
⁵   The sun rises, and the sun sets,
      and then it rushes back to the place where it will rise ˌagainˌ.
⁶   The wind blows toward the south and shifts toward the north.
      Round and round it blows. It blows in a full circle.
⁷   All streams flow into the sea, but the sea is never full.
      The water goes back to the place where the streams began
        in order to ˌstartˌ flowing again.

⁸All of these sayings are worn-out phrases. They are more than anyone can express, comprehend, or understand. ⁹Whatever has happened before will happen ˌagainˌ. Whatever has been done before will be done ˌagainˌ. There is nothing new under the sun. ¹⁰Can you say that anything is new? It has already been here long before us. ¹¹Nothing from the past is remembered. Even in the future, nothing will be remembered by those who come after us.

The Spokesman Begins to Study Everything Under Heaven

¹²I, the spokesman, have been king of Israel in Jerusalem. ¹³With all my heart I used wisdom to study and explore everything done under heaven.

The Spokesman's General Conclusion

Mortals are weighed down with a terrible burden that God has placed on them. ¹⁴I have seen everything that is done under the sun. Look at it! It's all pointless. ˌIt'sˌ like ˌtryingˌ to catch the wind.

¹⁵   No one can straighten what is bent.
      No one can count what is not there.

The Spokesman Begins to Study Life

¹⁶I thought to myself, "I have grown wiser than anyone who ˌhas ruledˌ Jerusalem before me. I've had a lot of experience with wisdom and knowledge." ¹⁷I've used my mind to understand wisdom and knowledge as well as madness and stupidity. ˌNowˌ I know that this is ˌlikeˌ trying to catch the wind.

¹⁸   With a lot of wisdom ˌcomesˌ a lot of heartache.
      The greater ˌyourˌ knowledge, the greater ˌyourˌ pain.

The Spokesman Studies Laughter

¹I thought to myself, "Now I want to experiment with pleasure and enjoy myself." But even this was pointless. ²I thought, "Laughter doesn't make any sense. What does pleasure accomplish?"

The Spokesman Studies Wine

³I explored ways to make myself feel better by drinking wine. I also explored ways to do some foolish things. During all that time, wisdom continued to control my mind. I was able to determine whether this was good for mortals to do during their brief lives under heaven.

The Spokesman Studies Personal Achievements

⁴I accomplished some great things:

I built houses for myself.
I planted vineyards for myself.
⁵ I made gardens and parks for myself.
I planted every kind of fruit tree in them.
⁶ I made pools to water the forest of growing trees.
⁷ I bought male and female slaves.
In addition, slaves were born in my household.
I owned more herds and flocks
than anyone in Jerusalem before me.
⁸ I also gathered silver and gold for myself.
I gathered the treasures of kings and provinces.
I provided myself with male and female singers
and the pleasures men have with one concubineᵃ after another.

⁹So I grew richer than anyone in Jerusalem before me. Yet, my wisdom remained with me. ¹⁰If something appealed to me, I did it. I allowed myself to have any pleasure I wanted, since I found pleasure in my work. This was my reward for all my hard work.

¹¹But when I turned to look at all that I had accomplished and all the hard work I had put into it, I saw that it was all pointless. It was like trying to catch the wind. I gained nothing from any of my accomplishments under the sun.

Death Is the Common Destiny of All Life

¹²Then I turned my attention to experience wisdom, madness, and foolishness. For instance, what can the man who replaces the king do? Only what has already been done. ¹³But I saw that wisdom has an advantage over foolishness as light has an advantage over darkness. ¹⁴A wise person uses the eyes in his head, but a fool walks in the dark. But I have also come to realize that the same destiny waits for both of them.

¹⁵I thought to myself, "If the destiny that waits for the fool waits for me as well, then what is the advantage in being wise?" So I thought that even this is pointless.

Without God Everything Is Pointless

¹⁶Neither the wise person nor the fool will be remembered for long, since both will be forgotten in the days to come. Both the wise person and the fool will die. ¹⁷So I came to hate life because everything done under the sun seemed wrong to me. Everything was pointless. It was like trying to catch the wind.

ᵃ2:8 A concubine is considered a wife except she has fewer rights under the law.

¹⁸I came to hate everything for which I had worked so hard under the sun, because I will have to leave it to the person who replaces me. ¹⁹Who knows whether that person will be wise or foolish? He will still have control over everything under the sun for which I worked so hard and used my wisdom. Even this is pointless.

²⁰Then I fell into despair over everything for which I had worked so hard under the sun. ²¹Here is someone who had worked hard with wisdom, knowledge, and skill. Yet, he must turn over his estate to someone else, who didn't work for it. Even this is pointless and a terrible tragedy.

²²What do people get from all of their hard work and struggles under the sun? ²³Their entire life is filled with pain, and their work is unbearable. Even at night their minds don't rest. Even this is pointless.

With God Even the Simplest Things Have a Point

²⁴There is nothing better for people to do than to eat, drink, and find satisfaction in their work. I saw that even this comes from the hand of God. ²⁵Who can eat or enjoy themselves without God? ²⁶God gives wisdom, knowledge, and joy to anyone who pleases him. But to the person who continues to sin, he gives the job of gathering and collecting wealth. The sinner must turn his wealth over to the person who pleases God. Even this is pointless. It's like trying to catch the wind.

Everything in God's Own Time

3 ¹Everything has its own time, and there is a specific time for every activity under heaven:

2   a time to be born and
       a time to die,
       a time to plant and
       a time to pull out what was planted,
3   a time to kill and
       a time to heal,
       a time to tear down and
       a time to build up,
4   a time to cry and
       a time to laugh,
       a time to mourn and
       a time to dance,
5   a time to scatter stones and
       a time to gather them,ᵃ
       a time to hug and
       a time to stop hugging,
6   a time to start looking and
       a time to stop looking,
       a time to keep and
       a time to throw away,
7   a time to tear apart and
       a time to sew together,
       a time to keep quiet and
       a time to speak out,

ᵃ3:5 Hebrew meaning of these two lines uncertain.

8 a time to love and
a time to hate,
a time for war and
a time for peace.

God Gives Mortals a Sense of Eternity

[9]What do working people gain from their hard labor? [10]I have seen mortals weighed down with a burden that God has placed on them. [11]It is beautiful how God has done everything at the right time. He has put a sense of eternity in people's minds. Yet, mortals still can't grasp what God is doing from the beginning to the end of time.

[12]I realize that there's nothing better for them to do than to be cheerful and enjoy what is good in their lives. [13]It is a gift from God to be able to eat and drink and experience the good that comes from every kind of hard work.

[14]I realize that whatever God does will last forever. Nothing can be added to it, and nothing can be taken away from it. God does this so that people will fear him.

[15]Whatever has happened in the past is present now. Whatever is going to happen in the future has already happened in the past. God will call the past to account.[b]

Humans and Animals Meet the Same End

[16]I saw something else under the sun:

There is wickedness where justice should be found.
There is wickedness where righteousness should be found.

[17]I thought to myself, "God will judge righteous people as well as wicked people, because there is a specific time for every activity and every work that is done." [18]I thought to myself, "God is going to test humans in order to show them that they are like animals." [19]Humans and animals have the same destiny. One dies just like the other. All of them have the same breath of life. Humans have no advantage over animals. All of life is pointless. [20]All life goes to the same place. All life comes from the ground, and all of it goes back to the ground. [21]Who knows whether a human spirit goes upward or whether an animal spirit goes downward to the earth?

[22]I saw that there's nothing better for people to do than to enjoy their work because that is their lot in life. Who will allow them to see what will happen after them?

Better Not to Have Been Born

[1]Next, I turned to look at all the acts of oppression that make people suffer under the sun. Look at the tears of those who suffer! No one can comfort them. Their oppressors have all the power. No one can comfort those who suffer. [2]I congratulate the dead, who have already died, rather than the living, who still have to carry on. [3]But the person who hasn't been born yet is better off than both of them. He hasn't seen the evil that is done under the sun.

Hard Work Versus Laziness

[4]Then I saw that all hard work and skillful effort come from rivalry. Even this is pointless. It's like trying to catch the wind. [5]A fool folds his hands and wastes away. [6]One handful of peace and quiet is better than two handfuls of hard work and of trying to catch the wind.

---

b 3:15 Hebrew meaning of this sentence uncertain.

Those Who Are All Alone

⁷Next, I turned to look at something pointless under the sun: ⁸There are people who are all alone. They have no children or other family members. So there is no end to all the hard work they have to do. Their eyes are never satisfied with riches. But they never ask themselves, why they are working so hard and depriving themselves of good things. Even this is pointless and a terrible tragedy.

Two Are Better Than One

⁹Two people are better than one because together they have a good reward for their hard work. ¹⁰If one falls, the other can help his friend get up. But how tragic it is for the one who is all alone when he falls. There is no one to help him get up. ¹¹Again, if two people lie down together, they can keep warm, but how can one person keep warm? ¹²Though one person may be overpowered by another, two people can resist one opponent. A triple-braided rope is not easily broken.

Rulers and Fickle Citizens

¹³A young man who is poor and wise is better than an old, foolish king who won't take advice any longer.

¹⁴A young man came out of prison to rule as king, even though he had been born in poverty in that same kingdom. ¹⁵I saw all living people moving about under the sun. They sided with the second young man, the king's successor. ¹⁶There was no end to all those people, everyone whom he led.ᵃ But those who will come later will not be happy with the successor. Even this is pointless. It's like trying to catch the wind.

Don't Daydream or Speak Carelessly When You Worship

¹Watch your step when you go to the house of God.ᵃ It is better to go there and listen than to bring the sacrifices fools bring. Fools are unaware that they are doing something evil.

²Don't be in a hurry to talk. Don't be eager to speak in the presence of God. Since God is in heaven and you are on earth, limit the number of your words.

³Daydreaming comes when there are too many worries.

Careless speaking comes when there are too many words.

⁴When you make a promise to God, don't be slow to keep it because God doesn't like fools. Keep your promise. ⁵It is better not to make a promise than to make one and not keep it. ⁶Don't let your mouth talk you into committing a sin. Don't say in the presence of a temple messenger, "My promise was a mistake!" Why should God become angry at your excuse and destroy what you've accomplished?

⁷In spite of many daydreams, pointless actions, and empty words, you should still fear God.

Corrupt Officials Have Corrupt Officials Over Them

⁸Don't be surprised if you see poor people being oppressed, denied justice, or denied their rights in any district. One authority is watching over another, and they both have authorities watching over them. ⁹Yet, a king is an advantage for a country with cultivated fields.ᵇ

ᵃ4:16 Or "everyone who lived before these kings." ᵃ5:1 Ecclesiastes 5:1-20 in English Bibles is Ecclesiastes 4:17–5:19 in the Hebrew Bible. ᵇ5:9 Hebrew meaning of this verse uncertain.

The Value of Money

[10]Whoever loves money will never be satisfied with money. Whoever loves wealth will never be satisfied with more income. Even this is pointless. [11]As the number of goods increase, so do the number of people who consume them. What do owners gain from all their goods, except the opportunity to look at them?

[12]The sleep of working people is sweet, whether they eat a little or a lot. But the full stomachs that rich people have will not allow them to sleep.

Economic Ruin

[13]There is a painful tragedy that I have seen under the sun: Riches lead to the downfall of those who hoard them. [14]These hoarded riches were then lost in bad business deals. The owners had children, but now they have nothing to give them. [15]They came from their mother's womb naked. They will leave as naked as they came. They won't even be able to take a handful of their earnings with them from all their hard work.

[16]This also is a painful tragedy: They leave exactly as they came. What advantage do they gain from working so hard for the wind? [17]They spend their entire lives in darkness, in constant frustration, sickness, and resentment.

Conclusion: God Alone Gives Contentment

[18]At last I have seen what is good and beautiful: It is to eat and drink and to enjoy the good in all our hard work under the sun during the brief lives God gives us. That is our lot in life. [19]It is a gift from God when God gives some people wealth and possessions, the power to enjoy them, the ability to accept their lot in life, and the ability to rejoice in their own hard work. [20]These people won't give much thought to their brief lives because God keeps them occupied with the joy in their hearts.

The Rich Person and the Stillborn Baby

[1]There is a tragedy that I have seen under the sun. It is a terrible one for mortals. [2]God gives one person riches, wealth, and honor so that he doesn't lack anything he wants. Yet, God doesn't give him the power to enjoy any of them. Instead, a stranger enjoys them. This is pointless and is a painful tragedy.

[3]Suppose a rich person wasn't satisfied with good things while he was alive, and didn't even get an honorable burial after he died. Suppose he had a hundred children and lived for many years. No matter how long he would have lived, it still would have been better for him to have been born dead. [4]A stillborn baby arrives in a pointless birth and goes out into the darkness. The darkness then hides its name. [5]Though it has never seen the sun or known anything, the baby finds more rest than the rich person. [6]Even if the rich person lives two thousand years without experiencing anything good—don't we all go to the same place?

More Pointless Challenges

[7]Everything that people work so hard for goes into their mouths, but their appetite is never satisfied.

[8]What advantage does a wise person have over a fool? What advantage does a poor person have in knowing how to face life?

[9]It is better to look at what is in front of you than to go looking for what you want. Even this is pointless. It's like trying to catch the wind.

[10]Whatever has happened in the past already has a name. Mortals are already known for what they are. Mortals cannot argue with the one who is stronger than they.

[11]The more words there are, the more pointless they become. What advantage do mortals gain from this? [12]Who knows what may be good for mortals while they are alive, during the brief, pointless days they live? Mortals pass by like a shadow. Who will tell them about their future under the sun?

Proverbs About Life

[1]A good name is better than expensive perfume, and the day you die is better than the day you're born. [2]It is better to go to a funeral than to a banquet because that is where everyone will end up. Everyone who is alive should take this to heart! [3]Sorrow is better than laughter because, in spite of a sad face, the heart can be joyful. [4]The minds of wise people think about funerals, but the minds of fools think about banquets.

[5]It is better to listen to wise people who reprimand you than to fools who sing your praises. [6]The laughter of a fool is like the crackling of thorns burning under a pot. Even this is pointless.

[7]Oppression can turn a wise person into a fool, and a bribe can corrupt the mind.

[8]The end of something is better than its beginning. It is better to be patient than arrogant.

[9]Don't be quick to get angry, because anger is typical of fools. [10]Don't ask, "Why were things better in the old days than they are now?" It isn't wisdom that leads you to ask this!

Wisdom Gives Life

[11]Wisdom is as good as an inheritance. It is an advantage to everyone who sees the sun. [12]Wisdom protects us just as money protects us, but the advantage of wisdom is that it gives life to those who have it.

[13]Consider what God has done! Who can straighten what God has bent?

A Truth for Every Situation

[14]When times are good, be happy. But when times are bad, consider this: God has made the one time as well as the other so that mortals cannot predict their future.

Mortals Don't Get What They Deserve

[15]I have seen it all in my pointless life:

> Righteous people die in spite of being righteous.
> Wicked people go on living in spite of being wicked.

[16]Don't be too virtuous, and don't be too wise. Why make yourself miserable? [17]Don't be too wicked, and don't be a fool. Why should you die before your time is up? [18]It's good to hold on to the one and not let go of the other, because the one who fears God will be able to avoid both extremes.

The Advantages of Wisdom

[19]Wisdom will help a wise person more than ten rulers can help a city. [20]Certainly, there is no one so righteous on earth that he always does what is good and never sins.

[21]Don't take everything that people say to heart, or you may hear your own servant cursing you. [22]Your conscience knows that you have cursed others many times.

[23]I used wisdom to test all of this. I said, "I want to be wise, but it is out of my reach." [24]Whatever wisdom may be, it is out of reach. It is deep, very deep. Who can find out what it is? [25]I turned my attention to study, to explore, and to seek out wisdom

and the reason for things. I learned that wickedness is stupid and foolishness is madness.

²⁶I find that a woman whose thoughts are ˌlikeˌ traps and snares is more bitter than death itself. Even her hands are ˌlikeˌ chains. Whoever pleases God will escape her, but she will catch whoever continues to sin.

²⁷The spokesman said, "This is what I've found: I added one thing to another in order to find a reason for things. ²⁸I am still seeking a reason for things, but have not found any. I found one man out of a thousand who had it, but out of all these I didn't find one woman. ²⁹I have found only this: God made people decent, but they looked for many ways ˌto avoid being decentˌ."ᵃ

¹Who is really wise? Who knows how to explain things? Wisdom makes one's face shine, and it changes one's grim look.

The Power of Kings Versus the Power of Death

²I ˌadviseˌ you to obey the ˌking'sˌ commands because of the oath you took in God's presence. ³Don't be in a hurry to leave the king's service. Don't take part in something evil, because he can do whatever he pleases. ⁴Since a king's word has such power, no one can ask him what he is doing. ⁵Whoever obeys his commands will avoid trouble. The mind of a wise person will know the right time and the right way ˌto actˌ. ⁶There is a right time and a right way ˌto actˌ in every situation. Yet, a terrible human tragedy hangs over people.

⁷They don't know what the future will bring. So who can tell them how things will turn out? ⁸No one has the power to prevent the spiritᵃ of life from leaving. No one has control over the day of his own death. There is no way to avoid the war ˌagainst deathˌ. Wickedness will not save wicked people ˌfrom dyingˌ.

Life Is Unfair

⁹I have seen all of this, and I have carefully considered all that is done under the sun whenever one person has authority to hurt others. ¹⁰Then I saw wicked people given an ˌhonorableˌ burial. They used to go in and out of the holy place. They were praised in the city for doing such things. Even this is pointless.

The Need for Swift Justice

¹¹When a sentence against a crime isn't carried out quickly, people are encouraged to commit crimes. ¹²A sinner may commit a hundred crimes and yet live a long life. Still, I know with certainty that it will go well for those who fear God, because they fear him. ¹³But it will not go well for the wicked. They will not live any longer. Their lives are like shadows, because they don't fear God.

Enjoy Life

¹⁴There is something being done on earth that is pointless. Righteous people suffer for what the wicked do, and wicked people get what the righteous deserve. I say that even this is pointless.

¹⁵So I recommend the enjoyment ˌof lifeˌ. People have nothing better to do under the sun than to eat, drink, and enjoy themselves. This joy will stay with them while they work hard during their brief lives which God has given them under the sun.

¹⁶When I carefully considered how to study wisdom and how to look at the work

---

ᵃ7:29 English equivalent difficult. ᵃ8:8 Or "breath."

that is done on earth (even going without sleep day and night), [17]then I saw everything that God has done. No one is able to grasp the work that is done under the sun. However hard a person may search for it, he will not find its meaning. Even though a wise person claims to know, he is not able to grasp it.

Everything Is in the Hands of God

[1]Now, I have carefully thought about all this, and I explain it in this way: Righteous people and wise people, along with their accomplishments, are in God's hands. No one knows whether there will be love or hatred.

[2]Everything turns out the same way for everyone. All people will share the same destiny, whether they are righteous, wicked, or good, clean or unclean,[a] whether they offer sacrifices or don't offer sacrifices. Good people are treated like sinners. People who take oaths are treated like those who are afraid to take oaths.

Where There's Life, There's Hope

[3]This is the tragedy of everything that happens under the sun: Everyone shares the same destiny. Moreover, the hearts of mortals are full of evil. Madness is in their hearts while they are still alive. After that, they join the dead. [4]But all who are among the living have hope, because a living dog is better than a dead lion. [5]The living know that they will die, but the dead don't know anything. There is no more reward for the dead when the memory of them has faded. [6]Their love, their hate, and their passions have already vanished. They will never again take part in anything that happens under the sun.

Enjoy Life With Your Wife

[7]Go, enjoy eating your food, and drink your wine cheerfully, because God has already accepted what you've done. [8]Always wear clean clothes, and never go without lotion on your head. [9]Enjoy life with your wife, whom you love, during all your brief, pointless life. God has given you your pointless life under the sun. This is your lot in life, and what you get for the hard work that you do under the sun.

Work With All Your Might

[10]Whatever presents itself for you to do, do it with all your might, because there is no work, planning, knowledge, or skill in the grave where you're going.

Time and Unpredictable Events

[11]I saw something else under the sun. The race isn't won by fast runners, or the battle by heroes. Wise people don't necessarily have food. Intelligent people don't necessarily have riches, and skilled people don't necessarily receive special treatment. But time and unpredictable events overtake all of them. [12]No one knows when his time will come. Like fish that are caught in a cruel net or birds caught in a snare, humans are trapped by a disaster when it suddenly strikes them.

Wisdom Is Despised

[13]I also have seen this example of wisdom under the sun, and it made a deep impression on me. [14]There was a small town with a few soldiers in it, and a powerful king came to attack it. He surrounded it and blockaded it. [15]A poor, wise person was found in that town. He saved the town using his wisdom. But no one remembered

---

[a] 9:2 "Clean" refers to anything that Moses' Teachings say is presentable to God. "Unclean" refers to anything that Moses' Teachings say is not presentable to God.

that poor person. ¹⁶So I said, "Wisdom is better than strength," even though that poor person's wisdom was despised, and no one listened to what he said.

¹⁷One should pay more attention to calm words from wise people than shouting from a ruler of fools. ¹⁸Wisdom is better than weapons of war, but one sinner can destroy much that is good.

10 ¹Dead flies will make a bottle of perfume stink, and then it is spoiled. A little foolishness outweighs wisdom and honor.

Proverbs About Life in General

²A wise person's heart leads the right way. The heart of a fool leads the wrong way. ³Even when a fool goes walking, he has no sense and shows everyone else that he's a fool.

⁴If a ruler becomes angry with you, don't resign your position. If you remain calm, you can make up for serious offenses.

⁵There is a tragedy that I've seen under the sun, an error often made by rulers. ⁶Foolish people are often given high positions, and rich people are left to fill lower positions. ⁷I have seen slaves sitting on horses and influential people going on foot like slaves.

⁸Whoever digs a pit may fall into it. Whoever breaks through a stone wall may be bitten by a snake. ⁹Whoever works in a stone quarry may get hurt. Whoever splits wood may be injured.

¹⁰If an ax is blunt and the edge isn't sharpened, then one has to use more strength. But wisdom prepares the way for success. ¹¹If a snake bites before it has been charmed, then there is no advantage in being a snake charmer.

¹²A wise person's words win favors, but a fool's lips are self-destructive. ¹³A fool starts out by talking foolishness and ends up saying crazy things that are dangerous. ¹⁴He never stops talking. No one knows what the future will bring, or what will happen after death. Who can say! ¹⁵Fools wear themselves out with hard work, because they don't even know the way to town.

Talking
Ecclesiastes 10:12-14

Do you know anyone who just talks and talks? Ecclesiastes calls the person who never stops talking a fool. That person doesn't listen to others. She doesn't think about what she's saying. That kind of talk could hurt others' feelings or stir up trouble. Listen to others and try to speak only good and helpful words.

be all you can be

¹⁶How horrible it will be for any country where the king used to be a servant and where the high officials throw parties in the morning. ¹⁷A country is blessed when the king is from a noble family and when the high officials eat at the right time in order to get strength and not to get drunk.

¹⁸A roof sags because of laziness. A house leaks because of idle hands.

¹⁹A meal is made for laughter, and wine makes life pleasant, but money is the answer for everything.

²⁰Don't curse the king even in your thoughts, and don't curse rich people even in your bedroom. A bird may carry your words, or some winged creature may repeat what you say.

Live Boldly

¹Throw your bread on the surface of the water, because you will find it again after many days.

²Divide what you have into seven parts, or even into eight, because you don't know what disaster may happen on earth.

³If the clouds are full of rain, they will let it pour down on the earth. If a tree falls north or south, the tree will remain where it fell.

⁴Whoever watches the wind will never plant. Whoever looks at the clouds will never harvest.

⁵Just as you don't know how the breath of life enters the limbs of a child within its mother's womb, you also don't understand how God, who made everything, works.

⁶Plant your seed in the morning, and don't let your hands rest until evening. You don't know whether this field or that field will be profitable or whether both of them will turn out equally well.

⁷Light is sweet, and it is good for one's eyes to see the sun. ⁸Even though people may live for many years, they should enjoy every one of them. But they should also remember there will be many dark days. Everything that is coming is pointless.

Remember Your Creator While You're Young

⁹You young people should enjoy yourselves while you're young. You should let your hearts make you happy when you're young. Follow wherever your heart leads you and whatever your eyes see. But realize that God will make you give an account for all these things when he judges everyone. ¹⁰Get rid of what troubles you or wears down your body, because childhood and youth are pointless.

1　Remember your Creator when you are young,
　　before the days of trouble come
　　and the years catch up with you.
　　　They will make you say,
　　　　"I have found no pleasure in them."
2　Remember your Creator before the sun, the light, the moon,
　　and the stars turn dark, and the clouds come back with rain.
3　Remember your Creator when those who guard the house tremble,
　　strong men are stooped over,
　　　the women at the mill stop grinding
　　　because there are so few of them,
　　　　and those who look out of the windows
　　　　see a dim light.
4　Remember your Creator when the doors to the street are closed,
　　the sound of the mill is muffled,
　　　you are startled at the sound of a bird,
　　　　and those who sing songs become quiet.
5　Remember your Creator when someone is afraid of heights
　　and of dangers along the road,

the almond tree blossoms,
    the grasshopper drags itself along,
        ⌞and⌟ the caper bush has ⌞no⌟ fruit.
Mortals go to their eternal rest, and mourners go out in the streets.

6   Remember your Creator before the silver cord is snapped,
        the golden bowl is broken,
            the pitcher is smashed near the spring,
                and the water wheel is broken at the cistern.
7   Then the dust ⌞of mortals⌟ goes back to the ground as it was before,
        and the breath of life goes back to God who gave it.

8   "Absolutely pointless!" says the spokesman. "Everything is pointless!"

Lifelong Duty—Fear God and Keep His Commands

⁹Besides being wise, the spokesman also taught the people what he knew. He very carefully thought about it, studied it, and arranged it in many proverbs. ¹⁰The spokesman tried to find just the right words. He wrote the words of truth very carefully.

¹¹Words from wise people are like spurs. Their collected sayings are like nails that have been driven in firmly. They come from one shepherd. ¹²Be warned, my children, against anything more than these. People never stop writing books. Too much studying will wear out your body. ¹³After having heard it all, this is the conclusion: Fear God, and keep his commands, because this applies to everyone. ¹⁴God will certainly judge everything that is done. This includes every secret thing, whether it is good or bad.

AN INTRODUCTION TO
Song of Songs

This book is a love poem about a man and woman who are about to be married. It was probably written by Solomon. The bride and groom talk about their feelings for each other and describe what it is like to be in love. This book reminds us that love and marriage are gifts from God.

What fire comes from God and can't be put out? See Song of Songs 8:6-7.

Headlines

Wait for the Right Time
Song of Songs 2:7, page 918

What a Beautiful Bride!
Song of Songs 4:1, page 920

Groom—One in Ten Thousand
Song of Songs 5:10, page 922

You Can't Put Out Love's Fire
Song of Songs 8:6-7, page 925

CURIOUS COMPLIMENTS

How big was the bride's nose?
(See Song of Songs 7:4.)

Did she have any other strange features?
(See Song of Songs 4:3.)

How long was the bride's neck?
(See Song of Songs 7:4.)

Could her eyes fly?
(See Song of Songs 4:1.)

Song of Songs

1 ¹ The most beautiful song of Solomon.

The Young Woman Arrives in Solomon's Palace

[Bride]

² Let him kiss me with the kisses of his mouth.
   Your expressions of love are better than wine,
³   better than the fragrance of cologne.
      (Cologne should be named after you.)
   No wonder the young women love you!
⁴   Take me with you. Let's run away.
   The king has brought me into his private rooms.

[The chorus of young women]

We will celebrate and rejoice with you.
We will praise your expressions of love more than wine.
How right it is that the young women love you!

[Bride]

⁵ Young women of Jerusalem, I am dark and lovely
   like Kedar's tents,
   like Solomon's curtains.
⁶ Stop staring at me because I am so dark.
   The sun has tanned me.
My brothers were angry with me.
They made me the caretaker of the vineyards.
   I have not even taken care of my own vineyard.
⁷ Please tell me, you whom I love, where do you graze your flock?
Where does your flock lie down at noon?
⌜Tell me,⌟ or I will be considered a prostitute
   ⌜wandering⌟ among the flocks of your companions.

[The chorus of young women]

⁸ If you do not know, most beautiful of women,
   follow the tracks of the flocks,
      and graze your young goats near the shepherds' tents.

Solomon Searches for the Young Woman's Love

[Groom]

⁹ My true love, I compare you to a mare among Pharaoh's stallions.
¹⁰   Your cheeks are lovely with ornaments,
      your neck with strings of pearls.

[The chorus of young women]

¹¹ We will make gold ornaments with silver beads for you.

[Bride]

¹² While the king is at his table,
   my perfume fills the air with its fragrance.

13 My beloved is a pouch of myrrh[a]
    that lies at night between my breasts.
14 My beloved is a bouquet of henna flowers
    in the vineyards of En Gedi.

[Groom]

15 Look at you! You are beautiful, my true love!
    Look at you! You are so beautiful!
        Your eyes are like doves!

[Bride]

16 Look at you! You are handsome, my beloved, so pleasing to me!
    The leaf-scattered ground will be our couch.
17 The cedars will be the walls of our house.
    The cypress trees will be our rafters.

2
1 I am a rose of Sharon,
    a lily ˏgrowingˏ in the valleys.

[Groom]

2 Like a lily among thorns,
    so is my true love among the young women.

[Bride]

3 Like an apple tree among the trees in the forest,
    so is my beloved among the young men.
        I want to sit in his shadow.
            His fruit tastes sweet to me.
4 He leads me into a banquet room
    and looks at me with love.
5   Strengthen me with raisins
            and refresh me with apples
                because I am weak from love.
6 His left hand is under my head.
    His right hand caresses me.

7 Young women of Jerusalem, swear to me
    by the gazelles
        or by the does in the field
            that you will not awaken love
                or arouse love before its proper time.

The Young Woman Remembers One Spring Day With Her Beloved

[Bride]

8 I hear my beloved's voice.
    Look! Here he comes,
        sprinting over the mountains,
            racing over the hills.
9 My beloved is like a gazelle or a young stag.
    Look! There he stands behind our wall,

---

[a] 1:13 Myrrh is a fragrant resin used for perfumes, embalming, and deodorizers.

peeking through the window,
looking through the lattice.
10 My beloved said to me,
"Get up, my true love, my beautiful one, and come with me.
11 Look! The winter is past.
The rain is over and gone.
12 Blossoms appear in the land.
The time of the songbird has arrived.
The cooing of the mourning dove is heard in our land.
13 The green figs ripen.
The grapevines bloom and give off a fragrance.
Get up, my true love, my beautiful one, and come with me.
14 My dove, in the hiding places of the rocky crevices,
in the secret places of the cliffs,
let me see your figure and hear your voice.
Your voice is sweet, and your figure is lovely."

15 Catch the foxes for us,
the little foxes that ruin vineyards.
Our vineyards are blooming.

16 My beloved is mine, and I am his.
He is the one who grazes his flock among the lilies.
17 When the day brings a cooling breeze and the shadows flee,
turn around, my beloved.
Run like a gazelle or a young stag
on the mountains that separate us!

The Young Woman Dreams About Searching
for Her Beloved

[Bride]

1 Night after night on my bed
I looked for the one I love.
I looked for him but did not find him.
2 I will get up now and roam around the city,
in the streets, and in the squares.
I will look for the one I love.
I looked for him but did not find him.
3 The watchmen making their rounds in the city found me.
I asked, "Have you seen the one I love?"
4 I had just left them when I found the one I love.
I held on to him and would not let him go
until I had brought him into my mother's house,
into the bedroom of the one who conceived me.

5 Young women of Jerusalem, swear to me
by the gazelles
or by the does in the field,
that you will not awaken love
or arouse love before its proper time.

A Description of the Royal Procession
[The chorus of young women]

6 Who is this young woman coming up from the wilderness
   like clouds of smoke?
      She is perfumed with myrrh and incense
         made from the merchants' scented powders.

7 Look! Solomon's sedan chair![a]
   Sixty soldiers from the army of Israel surround it.

8 All of them are skilled in using swords,
      experienced in combat.
   Each one has his sword at his side
      and guards against the terrors of the night.

9 King Solomon had a carriage made for himself[b]
   from the wood of Lebanon.

10 He had its posts made out of silver,
      its top out of gold,
      its seat out of purple fabric.
      Its inside—with inlaid scenes of love—
         was made by the young women of Jerusalem.

11 Young women of Zion, come out and look at King Solomon!
   Look at his crown,
      the crown his mother placed on him on his wedding day,
         his day of joyful delight.

Solomon Is Charmed by the Young Woman
[Groom]

1 Look at you! You are beautiful, my true love.
   Look at you! You are so beautiful.
      Your eyes behind your veil are like doves.
      Your hair is like a flock of goats moving down Mount Gilead.

2 Your teeth are like a flock of sheep about to be sheared,
      sheep that come up from the washing.
         All of them bear twins, and not one has lost its young.

3 Your lips are like scarlet thread.
   Your mouth is lovely.
      Your temples behind your veil are like slices of pomegranate.

4 Your neck is like David's beautifully-designed[a] tower.
      A thousand round shields belonging to soldiers
         are hung on it.

5 Your breasts are like two fawns,
      like twin gazelles grazing among the lilies.

6 When the day brings a cool breeze and the shadows flee,
      I will go to the mountain of myrrh and the hill of incense.

7 You are beautiful in every way, my true love.
      There is no blemish on you.

8 You will come with me from Lebanon,
      from Lebanon as my bride.

---

[a] 3:7 A sedan chair is a portable chair for carrying a person of high position.   [b] 3:9 English equivalent of this phrase difficult.   [a] 4:4 Hebrew meaning of "beautifully-designed" uncertain.

You will travel with me
  from the peak of Mount Amana,
  from the mountain peaks in Senir and Hermon,
  from the lairs of lions,
  from the mountains of leopards.
9 My bride, my sister, you have charmed me.[b]
You have charmed me
  with a single glance from your eyes,
  with a single strand of your necklace.
10 How beautiful are your expressions of love, my bride, my sister!
How much better are your expressions of love than wine
  and the fragrance of your perfume than any spice.
11 Your lips drip honey, my bride.
  Honey and milk are under your tongue.
    The fragrance of your clothing is like the fragrance of Lebanon.
12 My bride, my sister is a garden that is locked,
  a garden that is locked,
  a spring that is sealed.
13 You are paradise that produces
  pomegranates and the best fruits,
  henna flowers and nard,
14 nard and saffron,
  calamus,[c] cinnamon, and all kinds of incense,[d]
  myrrh, aloes, and all the best spices.
15 You are a spring for gardens,
  a well of living water flowing from Lebanon.

[Bride]

16 Awake, north wind!
Come, south wind!
Blow on my garden!
  Let its spices flow from it.
  Let my beloved come to his garden,
    and let him eat his own precious fruit.

[Groom]

5 1 My bride, my sister, I will come to my garden.
I will gather my myrrh with my spice.
I will eat my honeycomb with my honey.
I will drink my wine with my milk.
  Eat, my friends!
  Drink and become intoxicated with expressions of love!

The Young Woman Dreams of Marriage
With Her Husband

[Bride]

2 I sleep, but my mind is awake.
Listen! My beloved is knocking.

---

[b] 4:9 "Brother" and "sister" are terms of endearment between lovers in ancient Near Eastern literature.
[c] 4:14 Calamus is a sweet-smelling spice.   [d] 4:14 Or "incense-producing trees."

[Groom]

Open to me, my true love, my sister,
   my dove, my perfect one.
My head is wet with dew,
   my hair with the dewdrops of night.

[Bride]

3 I have taken off my clothes! Why should I put them on ͵again ͵?
I have washed my feet! Why should I get them dirty ͵again ͵?
4 My beloved put his hand through the keyhole.
   My heart throbbed for him.
5   I got up to open for my beloved.
     My hands dripped with myrrh,
      and my fingers were drenched with liquid myrrh,
       on the handles of the lock.
6 I opened for my beloved,
   but my beloved had turned away. He was gone!
I almost died when he left.
I looked for him, but I did not find him.
I called for him, but he did not answer me.
7 The watchmen making their rounds in the city found me.
   They struck me!
     They wounded me!
      Those watchmen on the walls took my robe from me!

8 Young women of Jerusalem, swear to me
   that if you find my beloved
     you will tell him I am hopelessly lovesick.

[The chorus of young women]

9 Most beautiful of women,
   what makes your beloved better than any other beloved?
What makes your beloved better than any other beloved
   that you make us swear this way?

[Bride]

10 My beloved is dazzling yet ruddy.
   He stands out among 10,000 men.
11   His head is the finest gold.
   His hair is wavy, black as a raven.
12   His eyes are set like doves bathing in milk.
13   His cheeks are like a garden of spices,
     a garden that produces scented herbs.
   His lips are lilies that drip with myrrh.
14   His hands are disks of gold set with emerald.
   His chest is a block of ivory covered with sapphires.
15   His legs are columns of marble set on bases of pure gold.
   His form is like Lebanon, choice as the cedars.
16   His mouth is sweet in every way.
     Everything about him is desirable!
This is my beloved, and this is my friend, young women of Jerusalem.

Hair / *Song of Songs 6:5*

Both men and women carefully dressed and plaited their hair. For women, hair-dressers braided the hair and wove it into special patterns. Sweet-smelling ointments were used to perfume the hair. While women still like to look their best, the New Testament warns women not to rely on beauty. What really counts is good character (see 1 Peter 3:3-4).

6

[The chorus of young women]

1 Where did your beloved go, most beautiful of women?
Where did your beloved turn?
  We will look for him with you.

[Bride]

2 My beloved went to his garden,
    to the beds of spices,
      to graze his flock in the gardens and gather lilies.
3 I am my beloved's, and my beloved is mine.
  He is the one who grazes his flock among the lilies.

Solomon Desires the Young Woman More Than the Rest of His Wives

[Groom]

4 You are beautiful, my true love, like Tirzah,
    lovely like Jerusalem,
      awe-inspiring like those great cities.[a]
5 Turn your eyes away from me. They enchant me!

  Your hair is like a flock of goats moving down from Gilead.
6   Your teeth are like a flock of sheep,
      sheep that come up from the washing.
        All of them bear twins, and not one has lost its young.
7   Your temples behind your veil are like slices of pomegranate.

8 There are 60 queens, 80 concubines,[b] and countless virgins,
9   but she is unique, my dove, my perfect one.
    Her mother thinks she is unique.
    She is pure to the one who gave birth to her.

---

[a]6:4 Or "awe-inspiring as an army with flags."   [b]6:8 A concubine is considered a wife except she has fewer rights under the law.

Her sisters saw her and blessed her.
Queens and concubines saw her and praised her.

The Young Woman's Home in Shulam

[The chorus of young women]

10 Who is this young woman?
    She looks like the dawn.
    She is beautiful like the moon,
        pure like the sun,
            awe-inspiring like those heavenly bodies.

[Bride]

11 I went to the walnut grove
        to look at the blossoms in the valley,
        to see if the grapevine had budded
            and if the pomegranates were in bloom.
12 I did not know that I had become
        like the chariots of my noble people.[c]

[The chorus of young women]

13 Come back! Come back, young woman from Shulam!
    Come back! Come back so that we may look at you!

[Bride]

Why do you look at me, the young woman from Shulam,
    as you look at the dance of Mahanaim?

[The chorus of young women]

7[a]1 How beautiful are your feet in their sandals, noble daughter!
    The curves of your thighs are like ornaments,
        like the work of an artist's hands.
2   Your navel is a round bowl.
        May it always be filled with spiced wine.
    Your waist is a bundle of wheat enclosed in lilies.
3   Your breasts are like two fawns,
        twins of a gazelle.
4   Your neck is like an ivory tower.
    Your eyes are like pools in Heshbon, pools by the gate of Bath Rabbim.
    Your nose is like a Lebanese tower facing Damascus.
5   You hold your head as high as Mount Carmel.
    Your dangling curls are royal beauty.
    Your flowing locks could hold a king captive.

Solomon Longs for the Young Woman's Affection

[Groom]

6   How beautiful and charming you are, my love, with your elegance.
7   Young woman,
        your figure is like a palm tree,
            and your breasts are like its clusters.
8   I thought, "I will climb the palm tree

---

[c]6:12 Song of Songs 6:13 in English Bibles is Song of Songs 7:1 in the Hebrew Bible.   [a]7:1 Song of Songs 7:1-13 in English Bibles is Song of Songs 7:2-14 in the Hebrew Bible.

and take hold of its fruit."
May your breasts be like clusters on the vine.
  May the fragrance of your breath be like apples.
9   May your mouth taste like the best wine . . .

[Bride]
. . . that goes down smoothly to my beloved
  and glides over the lips of those about to sleep.[b]
10   I am my beloved's, and he longs for me.
11   Come, my beloved.
  Let's go into the field.
  Let's spend the night among the henna flowers.[c]
12   Let's go to the vineyards early.
  Let's see if the vines have budded,
    if the grape blossoms have opened,
    if the pomegranates are in bloom.
  There I will give you my love.
13   The mandrakes[d] give off a fragrance,
    and at our door are all kinds of precious fruits.
  I have saved new and old things
    for you alone, my beloved.

8 1 If only you were my brother,
    one who nursed at my mother's breasts.
  If I saw you on the street,
    I would kiss you, and no one would look down on me.
2   I would lead you.
  I would bring you into my mother's house.
    (She is the one who was my teacher.)
  I would give you some spiced wine to drink,
    some juice squeezed from my pomegranates.
3   His left hand is under my head.
  His right hand caresses me.

4   Young women of Jerusalem, swear to me
    that you will not awaken love
    or arouse love before its proper time!

The Young Woman's Love for Her Beloved
[The chorus of young women]
5   Who is this young woman coming from the wilderness
    with her arm around her beloved?

[Bride]
Under the apple tree I woke you up.
  There your mother went into labor with you.
    There she went into labor
    and gave birth to you!
6   Wear me as a signet ring on your heart,
    as a ring on your hand.

---

[b]7:9 Or "flowing gently over lips and teeth." [c]7:11 Or "in the villages." [d]7:13 Mandrakes were thought to stimulate sexual desire.

Love is as overpowering as death.
Devotion is as unyielding as the grave.
    Love's flames are flames of fire,
        flames that come from the Lord.
7   Raging water cannot extinguish love,
                and rivers will never wash it away.
If a man exchanged all his family's wealth for love,
    people would utterly despise him.

The Young Woman With Her Family and Her Beloved

[The brothers]

8   We have a little sister, and she has no breasts.
    What will we do for our sister on the day she becomes engaged?
9   If she is a wall, we will build a silver barrier around her.
    If she is a door, we will barricade her with cedar boards.

[Bride]

10 I am a wall, and my breasts are like towers.
        So he considers me to be one who has found peace.[a]
11 Solomon had a vineyard at Baal Hamon.
    He entrusted that vineyard to caretakers.
        Each one was to bring 25 pounds of silver
            in exchange for its fruit.
12 My own vineyard is in front of me.
        That 25 pounds is yours, Solomon,
            and 5 pounds go to those who take care of its fruit.

[Groom]

13 Young woman living in the gardens,
        while your friends are listening to your voice,
            let me hear. . . .

[Bride]

14 Come away quickly, my beloved.
        Run like a gazelle or a young stag
            on the mountains of spices.

---

[a] 8:10 In Hebrew there is a play on the words "peace" (*shalom*), "Solomon" (*Shlomo*), and "the young woman from Shulam" (*Shulamith*).

Isaiah

Isaiah met God face-to-face in the temple. Although he was terrified, Isaiah volunteered to go on a mission for God. This book contains Isaiah's warnings that God would punish the people of Judah if they kept on doing wrong. But Isaiah also tells about a future when Jesus will save God's people.

Isaiah wrote about Jesus' death 700 years before Jesus was born. See Isaiah 53.

What's In It For Me?

God has promised to . . .

- PUNISH THE WICKED FOR THEIR SINS.
- REWARD THE RIGHTEOUS WITH BLESSINGS.
- GIVE PERFECT PEACE TO THOSE WHO TRUST HIM.
- NEVER ABANDON THOSE WHO BELONG TO HIM.
- ESTABLISH HIS KINGDOM ON EARTH.
- BRING THE DEAD BACK TO LIFE AT HISTORY'S END.

Headlines

Proud Women Punished
Isaiah 3, page 933

Child Jesus Foretold
Isaiah 9, page 941

Mom Forgets, but Not God!
Isaiah 49, page 1002

Childless Women Sing for Joy
Isaiah 54, page 1011

A Whole New World!
Isaiah 65, page 1025

A World at Peace

There has never been a time without war somewhere in the world. Can you imagine a world at perfect peace? What would it be like? Isaiah 11:6-9 gives us a picture of what the world will be like when Jesus returns. In Christ's new kingdom, people will live together in peace, and even the animals will live in harmony with each other!

Family Fun
Pretend Prophecies

Wouldn't it be fun to predict the future? Play a game with your family. Everybody gets a piece of paper and writes down predictions to these questions:

1. *What color car will be the next to pass your home?*
2. *Who will be the next person to phone your home?*
3. *What time will that phone call come?*
4. *What will be the first thing that person says?*
5. *Who will be the next person to come to your door?*
6. *What color and kind of clothes will he or she be wearing?*
7. *What color will his or her hair be?*

Whoever gets the most right is declared the family's "Best Guesser." And you'll all see how difficult it is to guess future events. You'll realize how amazing the true prophecies found in the Bible really are!

Can People See the Future?

Every January, newspapers carry predictions about what will happen during the coming year. And throughout the year, psychics make claims that they can tell you what your own future holds. Can people really predict the future?

Bible prophets really could tell the future. But God told them what to say. Only God can tell things that haven't happened yet (Isaiah 46:10). That is how Isaiah was able to describe Jesus' birth (Isaiah 7:14) and tell about his death (Isaiah 53:4-12) 700 years before he was born!

There's a way to tell whose predictions come from God. Deuteronomy 18:22 says prophets who speak from the Lord will have *all* their predictions come true! Nobody around today can make that claim!

Being a Good Servant

Isaiah 42:1-4 describes Jesus, God's perfect servant. The best servants of God aren't those who draw the most attention. A good servant of God is gentle. Jesus would not break off "a damaged cattail" or put out "a smoking wick." The damaged cattail and smoking wick stand for people who seem useless or unimportant. But no one is unimportant to God. Jesus was sent to be kind to people who need help. When we are kind to others when no one else seems to care about them, we are being God's good servants, too.

Isaiah

1 ¹This is the vision which Isaiah, son of Amoz, saw about Judah and Jerusalem at the time of Kings Uzziah, Jotham, Ahaz, and Hezekiah.

The LORD Accuses Israel of Sin

² Listen, heaven, and pay attention, earth!
       The LORD has spoken,
           "I raised ⸢my⸣ children and helped them grow,
               but they have rebelled against me.
³ Oxen know their owners,
       and donkeys know where their masters feed them.
   But Israel doesn't know ⸢its owner⸣.
       My people don't understand ⸢who feeds them⸣.

⁴ "How horrible it will be for a nation that sins.
       ⸢Its⸣ people are loaded down with guilt.
           They are descendants of evildoers
               and destructive children.
       They have abandoned the LORD.
       They have despised the Holy One of Israel.
       They have turned their backs on him.

⁵ "Why do you still want to be beaten?
   Why do you continue to rebel?
       Your whole head is infected.
       Your whole heart is failing.
⁶ From the bottom of your feet to the top of your head
       there is no healthy spot left on your ⸢body⸣—
           only bruises, sores, and fresh wounds.
       They haven't been cleansed, bandaged,
           or soothed with oil.

⁷ "Your country is devastated.
   Your cities are burned down.
   Your fields are destroyed right before your eyes by foreigners.
       Your fields are devastated and taken over by foreigners.
⁸ My people Zion are left like a hut in a vineyard,
       like a shack in a cucumber field,
       like a city under attack."

⁹ If the LORD of Armies hadn't left us a few survivors,
       we would have been like Sodom and Gomorrah.

Israel's Corrupt Religion

¹⁰ Listen to the word of the LORD, you rulers of Sodom!
       Pay attention to the teachings from our God, you people of Gomorrah!
¹¹ The LORD asks, "What do your many animal sacrifices mean to me?
       I've had enough of your burnt offerings of rams

and enough fat from your fattened calves.
    I'm not pleased with the blood of bulls, lambs, or male goats.
12 When you appear in my presence,
    who asked you to trample on my courtyards?
13 Don't bring any more worthless grain offerings.
    Your incense is disgusting to me,
        so are your New Moon Festivals, your days of worship,
            and the assemblies you call.
    I can't stand your evil assemblies.
14 I hate your New Moon Festivals and your appointed festivals.
        They've become a burden to me,
            and I'm tired of putting up with them.
15 So when you stretch out your hands in prayer,
    I will turn my eyes away from you.
Even though you offer many prayers,
    I will not listen because your hands are covered with blood.

The LORD Invites Israel to Turn Away From Sin

16 "Wash yourselves! Become clean!
Get your evil deeds out of my sight.
Stop doing evil.
17 Learn to do good.
Seek justice.
Arrest oppressors.
Defend orphans.
Plead the case of widows."

18 "Come on now, let's discuss this!" says the LORD.
    "Though your sins are bright red,
        they will become as white as snow.
    Though they are dark red,
        they will become as white as wool.
19 If you are willing and obedient,
    you will eat the best from the land.
20 But if you refuse and rebel,
    you will be destroyed by swords."
The LORD has spoken.

Jerusalem's Future

21 How the faithful town has become a prostitute!
        She was full of justice,
            and righteousness lived in her.
                But now murderers live there!
22 Your silver is not pure.
Your wine is watered down.
23 Your rulers are rebels, friends with thieves.
        They all love bribes and run after gifts.
        They never defend orphans.
        They don't notice the widows' pleas.

²⁴That's why the Lord, the LORD of Armies, the Mighty One of Israel, says,

"How horrible it will be when I take revenge on my opponents!
I will avenge myself against my enemies.
²⁵   I will turn my power against you.
I will remove your impurities with bleach.
I will get rid of all your impurities.
²⁶   I will give you judges like you had long ago,
    advisers like you had in the beginning.
After that you will be called the Righteous City,
    the Faithful Town."

²⁷ Zion will be pardoned by the LORD's justice,
    and those who return will be pardoned
        by the LORD's righteousness.
²⁸ Rebels and sinners will be crushed at the same time,
    and those who abandon the LORD will come to an end.
²⁹ You will be ashamed of the oaks that you wanted to worship
    and embarrassed by the garden that you have chosen for your gods.
³⁰ You will be like an oak whose leaves wither
    and like a garden without water.
³¹ Strong people will become tinder for a fire,
    and their work will be the spark.
Both of them will burn together,
    and there will be no one to put out the fire.

The LORD Will Teach the Nations—
Micah 4:1-3

²¹This is the message which Isaiah, son of Amoz, saw about Judah and Jerusalem.

² In the last days the mountain of the LORD's house
    will be established as the highest of the mountains
    and raised above the hills.
        All the nations will stream to it.
³ Then many people will come and say,
    "Let's go to the mountain of the LORD,
    to the house of the God of Jacob.
        He will teach us his ways so that we may live by them."
The teachings will go out from Zion.
The word of the LORD will go out from Jerusalem.
⁴   Then he will judge disputes between nations
    and settle arguments between many people.
They will hammer their swords into plowblades
    and their spears into pruning shears.
Nations will never fight against each other,
    and they will never train for war again.
⁵ Come, descendants of Jacob,
    let's live in the light of the LORD.

Jewelry / *Isaiah 3:18-23*

Women in Bible times liked jewelry of
all kinds. Ezekiel 16:11-13 mentions
bracelets, necklaces, rings for the
nose, earrings, and even crowns.
Exodus 35:22 lists the same items,
along with finger rings, pins, and
pendants. It's all right to enjoy
beautiful things. But remember that
"wisdom is more precious than jewels,
and all your desires cannot equal it"
(Proverbs 3:15).

Israel's Sins

6   LORD, you have abandoned your people, the descendants of Jacob,
        because they are filled with Eastern influences.
            They are fortunetellers like the Philistines,
                and they make deals with foreigners.
7   Their land is filled with silver and gold,
        and there is no end to their treasures.
    Their land is filled with horses,
        and there is no end to their chariots.
8   Their land is filled with idols,
        and they worship what their hands have shaped
            and what their fingers have molded.
9   People will be brought down. Everyone will be humbled.
        Do not forgive them.
10 Go in among the rocks and hide underground
        because of the LORD's terrifying presence
            and the honor of his majesty.
11 The eyes of arrogant people will be humbled.
    High and mighty people will be brought down.
        On that day the LORD alone will be honored.

The Day of the LORD's Judgment

12 The LORD of Armies will have his day
        against all who are arrogant and conceited
            and all who are proud of themselves (they will be humbled),
13   against all the towering and mighty cedars of Lebanon
            and all the oaks of Bashan,

14 against all the high mountains
  and all the lofty hills,
15 against every high tower
  and every fortified wall,
16 against all the large ships of Tarshish
  and all the beautiful boats.
17 Then arrogant people will be brought down,
  and high and mighty people will be humbled.
    On that day the LORD alone will be honored.
18   Then idols will disappear completely.
19 People will go into caves in the rocks
  and into holes in the ground
    because of the LORD's terrifying presence
      and the honor of his majesty
        when he rises to terrify the earth.
20 On that day people will throw to the moles and the bats
  the silver and gold idols that they made
    for themselves to worship.
21 They will go into caves in the rocks
  and into cracks in the cliffs
    because of the LORD's terrifying presence
      and the honor of his majesty
        when he rises to terrify the earth.
22 Stop trusting people.
  Their life is in their nostrils.
    How can they be worth anything?

The LORD's Judgment on Sinners in Zion

3 1 See now, the Lord, the LORD of Armies,
  is going to take from Jerusalem and Judah
    every kind of support
      and their entire supply of food and water.
2 He will take their heroes and soldiers,
  judges and prophets,
    fortunetellers and statesmen,
3   military leaders and civilian leaders,
      counselors, skilled workers, and experts in magic.

4 "I will make boys their leaders.
  Children will govern them."

5 People will oppress each other,
  and everyone will oppress his neighbor.
The young will make fun of the old,
  and common people will make fun of their superiors.
6 A person will grab one of his relatives
  from his father's family and say,
    "You have a coat.
    You'll be our leader.
      This pile of ruins will be under your control."

7   When that day comes the relative will cry out,
      "I'm not a doctor!
      I don't have any food or a coat in my home.
      Don't make me a leader of our family."

8   Jerusalem has stumbled, and Judah has fallen,
      because what they say and what they do is against the LORD.
      They are defiant in his honored presence.

9   The look on their faces will be held against them.
   They boast about their sins,
      which are like those of the people of Sodom.
   They don't even bother to hide them.
   How horrible it will be for these people,
      because they have brought disaster on themselves.

10   Tell the righteous that blessings will come to them.
      They will taste the fruit of their labor.

11   How horrible it will be for the wicked! Disaster will strike them.
      What they have done will be done to them.

12   "Children will oppress my people.
      Women will rule them.
        My people, your guides mislead you,
          and you don't know which way to go."

13   The LORD takes his place in the courtroom.
      He stands to judge his people.

14   The LORD presents his case to the respected leaders
      and the officials of his people:
        "You have burned down the vineyard!
          Your houses are filled with goods stolen from the poor."

15   The Almighty LORD of Armies asks,
      "How can you crush my people
      and grind the faces of the poor into the ground?"

16   The LORD adds,
      "The women of Zion are arrogant.
      They walk with their noses in the air,
        making seductive glances,
        taking short little steps,
        jingling the ankle bracelets on their feet."

17   The Lord will cause sores to appear
      on the heads of the women of Zion,
      and the LORD will make their foreheads bare.

18On that day the Lord will take away their fine things: jingling anklets, headbands, crescent-shaped necklaces, 19pendants, bracelets, scarfs, 20hats, ankle bracelets, blouses, perfume boxes, charms, 21signet rings, nose rings, 22fine robes, coats, shawls, purses, 23mirrors, underwear, headdresses, and veils.

24   Instead of the smell of perfume, there will be the smell of decay.
      They will wear ropes instead of belts.
      They will have bald heads instead of beautiful hair.
      They will wear sackcloth instead of expensive clothes.

Their beauty will be scarred.[a]

25 ⌊Women,⌋ your warriors will die in combat.
Your mighty men will die in battle.

26 The gates of Zion will cry and grieve,
and Zion will sit on the ground, exhausted.

4 1 When that day comes, seven women will grab one man and say,
"We'll eat our own food and provide our own clothes.
Just let us marry you for your name.
Take away our disgrace."

The LORD's New Glory for Zion

2 When that day comes, the branch of the LORD
will be beautiful and wonderful.
The fruit of the land
will be the pride and joy of Israel's survivors.

3 Then whoever is left in Zion and whoever remains in Jerusalem will be called holy, everyone who is recorded among the living in Jerusalem. 4 The Lord will wash away the filth of Zion's people.[a] He will clean bloodstains from Jerusalem with a spirit of judgment and a spirit of burning. 5 The LORD will create a cloud of smoke during the day and a glowing flame of fire during the night over the whole area of Mount Zion and over the assembly. His glory will cover everything. 6 It will be a shelter from the heat during the day as well as a refuge and hiding place from storms and rain.

The Song About the Vineyard

5 1 Let me sing a lovesong to my beloved about his vineyard:

My beloved had a vineyard on a fertile hill.

2 He dug it up, removed its stones,
planted it with the choicest vines,
built a watchtower in it,
and made a winepress in it.

Good Morning, God
Isaiah 5:7

Who in your family likes to garden? Who in your family likes what is *grown* in a garden? Sweet juicy tomatoes, fresh orange carrots, and even lovely, fragrant roses grow in a well-tended garden. The Bible tells us we are like a garden to God. Like a garden, we grow and mature. God guides us and helps us to grow in a healthy way. Today, thank God that he is helping you grow.

Father, help me to grow into the kind of person you want me to be. Thank you that you are here to help me.

---

[a] 3:24 Dead Sea Scrolls; Masoretic Text "expensive clothes, instead of beauty."   [a] 4:4 Or "Zion's women."

Then he waited for it to produce good grapes,
    but it produced only sour, wild grapes.

3 Now then, you inhabitants of Jerusalem and Judah,
    judge between me and my vineyard!
4 What more could have been done for my vineyard
    than what I have already done for it?
When I waited for it to produce good grapes,
    why did it produce only sour, wild grapes?

5 Now then, let me tell you what I will do to my vineyard.
    I will tear away its hedge so that it can be devoured
        and tear down its wall so that it can be trampled.
6   I will make it a wasteland.
    It will never be pruned or hoed.
        Thorns and weeds will grow in it,
        and I will command the clouds not to rain on it.

7 The vineyard of the Lord of Armies is the nation of Israel,
    and the people of Judah are the garden of his delight.
He hoped for justice but saw only slaughter,
    for righteousness but heard only cries of distress.

Six Sins Condemned

8 How horrible it will be for you
    who acquire house after house and buy field after field
        until there's nothing left
        and you have to live by yourself in the land.

9 With my own ears I heard the Lord of Armies say,
    "Many houses will become empty.
    Large, beautiful houses will be without people to live in them.
10 A ten-acre vineyard will produce only six gallons of wine,
    and two quarts of seed will produce only four quarts of grain."

11 How horrible it will be for those
    who get up early to look for a drink,
    who sit up late until they are drunk from wine.
12   At their feasts there are lyres and harps,
        tambourines and flutes, and wine.
        Yet, they don't pay attention to what the Lord is doing
        or see what his hands have done.

13 "My people will go into exile
    because they don't understand what I'm doing.
    Honored men will starve,
        and common people will be parched with thirst."
14 That is why the grave's appetite increases.
    It opens its mouth very wide
        so that honored people and common people will go down into it.
    Those who are noisy and joyous will go down into it.
15 People will be brought down. Everyone will be humbled.
    And the eyes of arrogant people will be humbled.

¹⁶ The LORD of Armies will be honored when he judges.
The holy God will show himself to be holy when he does what is right.

¹⁷ Then lambs will graze as if they were in their own pasture,
and foreigners will eat among the ruins of the rich.

¹⁸ How horrible it will be for those
who string people along with lies and empty promises,
whose lives are sinful.

¹⁹ They say,
"Let God hurry and quickly do his work
so that we may see what he has in mind.
Let the plan of the Holy One of Israel happen quickly
so that we may understand what he is doing."

²⁰ How horrible it will be for those
who call evil good and good evil,
who turn darkness into light and light into darkness,
who turn what is bitter into something sweet
and what is sweet into something bitter.

²¹ How horrible it will be for those
who think they are wise
and consider themselves to be clever.

²² How horrible it will be for those
who are heroes at drinking wine,
who are champions at mixing drinks,

²³ who declare the guilty innocent for a bribe,
who take away the rights of righteous people.

The LORD Will Use Another Nation to Punish His People

²⁴ As flames burn up straw
and dry grass shrivels in flames,
so their roots will rot,
and their blossoms will blow away like dust.
They have rejected the teachings of the LORD of Armies
and have despised the word of the Holy One of Israel.

²⁵ That's why the anger of the LORD burns hot against his people,
and he is ready to use his power to strike them down.
The hills tremble,
and dead bodies lie like garbage in the streets.

Even after all this, his anger has not disappeared,
and he is still ready to use his power.

²⁶ The LORD raises up a flag for the nations far away.
With a whistle he signals those at the ends of the earth.
Look, they are coming very quickly!

²⁷ None of them grow tired or stumble.
None of them slumber or sleep.
The belts on their waists aren't loose
or their sandal straps broken.

28   Their arrows are sharpened; all their bows are ready to shoot.
     Their horses' hoofs are as hard as flint.
     Their chariot wheels are as quick as the wind.
29   They roar like a lioness.
     They growl like a young lion.
     They growl as they snatch their prey
        and carry it off to where no one can rescue it.
30   On that day they will roar over their prey
        as the sea roars.
     If they look at the land,
        they will see only darkness and distress.
     Even the light will be darkened by thick clouds.

Isaiah Is Sent With a Message for the LORD's People

¹In the year King Uzziah died, I saw the Lord sitting on a high and lofty throne. The bottom of his robe filled the temple. ²Angels*ᵃ* were standing above him. Each had six wings: With two they covered their faces, with two they covered their feet, and with two they flew. ³They called to each other and said,

     "Holy, holy, holy is the LORD of Armies!
     The whole earth is filled with his glory."

⁴Their voices shook the foundations of the doorposts, and the temple filled with smoke.

⁵So I said, "Oh, no!

     I'm doomed.
       Every word that passes through my lips is sinful.
        I live among people with sinful lips.
         I have seen the king, the LORD of Armies!"

⁶Then one of the angels flew to me. In his hand was a burning coal that he had taken from the altar with tongs. ⁷He touched my mouth with it and said, "This has touched your lips. Your guilt has been taken away, and your sin has been forgiven."

⁸Then I heard the voice of the Lord, saying, "Whom will I send? Who will go for us?"

     I said, "Here I am. Send me!"

⁹And he said, "Go and tell these people,

     'No matter how closely you listen, you'll never understand.
     No matter how closely you look, you'll never see.'
10   Make these people close-minded.
       Plug their ears.
        Shut their eyes.
        Otherwise, they may see with their eyes,
       hear with their ears,
      understand with their minds,
       and return and be healed."

¹¹I asked, "How long, O Lord?"
     And he replied,

---

*ᵃ*6:2 Or "Seraphim."

"Until the cities lie in ruins with no one living in them,
  the houses have no people,
  and the land is completely desolate."
  12 The LORD will send his people far away,
  and a large area in the middle of the land will be abandoned.
  13 Even if one out of ten people is left in it,
  the land will be burned again.
  When a sacred oak or an oak is cut down, a stump is left.
  The holy seed will be the land's stump."

The Virgin Will Have a Child

¹When Ahaz, son of Jotham and grandson of Uzziah, was king of Judah, Aram's King Rezin and Israel's King Pekah, son of Remaliah, went to Jerusalem to attack it, but they couldn't defeat it. ²When word reached David's family that the Arameans had made an alliance with Ephraim, the hearts of the king and his people were shaken as the trees of the forest are shaken by the wind.

³Then the LORD said to Isaiah, "Go out with your son Shear Jashub to meet Ahaz at the end of the ditch of the Upper Pool on the road to the Laundryman's Field. ⁴Say to him, 'Be careful, stay calm, and don't be afraid. Don't lose heart because of the fierce anger of Rezin from Aram and Remaliah's son. These two are smoldering logs.' ⁵Aram, Ephraim, and Remaliah's son have planned evil against you, saying, ⁶'Let's march against Judah, tear it apart, divide it among ourselves, and set up Tabeel's son as its king.' ⁷This is what the Almighty LORD says:

It won't take place; it won't happen.
  8 The capital of Aram is Damascus,
    and the leader of Damascus is Rezin.
      Ephraim will be shattered within 65 years
        so that it will no longer be a nation.
  9 The capital of Ephraim is Samaria,
    and the leader of Samaria is Remaliah's son.
      If you don't remain faithful,
        you won't remain standing.

¹⁰Again the LORD spoke to Ahaz, ¹¹"Ask the LORD your God for a sign. It can be anything you want."

¹²But Ahaz answered, "I won't ask; I wouldn't think of testing the LORD."

¹³"Listen now, descendants of David," Isaiah said. "Isn't it enough that you try the patience of mortals? Must you also try the patience of my God? ¹⁴So the Lord himself will give you this sign: A virgin will become pregnant and give birth to a son, and she will name him Immanuel [God Is With Us]. ¹⁵He will eat cheese and honey until he knows how to reject evil and choose good. ¹⁶Indeed, before the boy knows how to reject evil and choose good, the land of the two kings who terrify you will be deserted.

¹⁷"The LORD will bring on you, your people, and your ancestor's family a time unlike any since Ephraim broke away from Judah. He will bring the king of Assyria. ¹⁸On that day the LORD will whistle for the flies that are at the distant branches of the Nile River in Egypt and for the bees that are in Assyria. ¹⁹All of them will come and settle in the deep valleys, in the cracks in the cliffs, on all the thornbushes, and at all the water holes.

²⁰"On that day the Lord will hire the king of Assyria from beyond the Euphrates River to be a razor to shave the hair on your head, the hair on your legs, and even

your beard. ²¹On that day a person will keep alive a young cow and two sheep. ²²That person will eat cheese, because they will produce so much milk. Everyone who is left in the land will eat cheese and honey. ²³On that day, in every place where there were 1,000 vines (worth 1,000 pieces of silver), there will be briars and thorns. ²⁴People will come there with bows and arrows to hunt, because the whole land will be filled with briars and thorns. ²⁵And you will no longer be able to go to all the hills which used to be cultivated because they will be filled with briars and thorns. It will be a place for turning oxen loose and letting sheep run."

Isaiah's Child Is a Sign of the LORD's Protection of Judah

¹The LORD said to me, "Take a large writing tablet, and write on it with a pen: 'Maher Shalal Hash Baz' [The Looting Will Come Quickly; the Prey Will Be Easy]. ²I will have these dependable witnesses testify: the priest Uriah and Zechariah (son of Jeberechiah)."

³I slept with the prophet. She became pregnant and gave birth to a son. The LORD told me, "Name him Maher Shalal Hash Baz. ⁴Before the boy knows how to say 'Daddy' or 'Mommy,' the wealth of Damascus and the loot from Samaria will be carried away to the king of Assyria."

Assyria Will Invade, But It Will Not Conquer Judah

⁵The LORD spoke to me again. He said,

6 "These people have rejected the gently flowing water of Shiloah
  and find joy in Rezin and Remaliah's son."
7 That is why the Lord is going to bring against them
  the raging and powerful floodwaters of the Euphrates River—
   the king of Assyria with all his power.
 It will overflow all its channels and go over all its banks.
8 It will sweep through Judah.
 It will overflow and pass through; it will be neck-high.
 Its outspread wings will extend over your whole country, O Immanuel.

9 Be broken, you people. Be terrified.
 Listen, all you distant parts of the earth.
  Prepare for battle, but be terrified.
  Prepare for battle, but be terrified.

10 Make plans for battle, but they will never succeed.
 Give orders, but they won't be carried out,
  because God is with us!

Some in Jerusalem Will Stumble
Because They Do Not Trust the LORD

¹¹This is what the LORD said with his powerful hand on me.

 He warned me not to follow the ways of these people:
12 "Don't say that everything these people call a conspiracy
  is a conspiracy.
 Don't fear what they fear.
 Don't let it terrify you."
13 Remember that the LORD of Armies is holy.
 He is the one you should fear

and the one you should be terrified of.

14 He will be a place of safety for you.
But he will be a rock that makes people trip
and a stumbling block for both kingdoms of Israel.
He will be a trap and a snare for those who live in Jerusalem.

15 Many will stumble.
They will fall and be broken.
They will be trapped and caught.

16 Tie up the written instructions.
Seal the teachings among my disciples.

17 I will wait for the LORD,
who hides his face from the descendants of Jacob.
I will hope in him.

18 I am here with the children that the LORD has given me.
We are signs and symbols in Israel
from the LORD of Armies, who lives on Mount Zion.

19 People will say to you, "Ask for help from the mediums
and the fortunetellers, who whisper and mutter."
Shouldn't people ask their God for help instead?
Why should they ask the dead to help the living?

20 They should go to the teachings and to the written instructions.
If people don't speak these words,
it is because it doesn't dawn on them.

21 They will pass through the land when they are hard-pressed and hungry.
When they are hungry, they will be furious.
Then they will look up, cursing their king and God.

22 They will look at the earth and see only distress and gloom.
They will go in anguish and be forced into darkness.

9 ª1 But there will be no more gloom
for the land that is in distress.
God humbled the lands of Zebulun and Naphtali in earlier times.
But in the future he will bring glory to the road by the sea,
to the land across the Jordan River,
to Galilee, where foreigners live.

A Child Will Be Born as the Prince of Peace

2 The people who walk in darkness will see a bright light.
The light will shine on those who live in the land of death's shadow.

3 You will expand the nation and increase its happiness.
It will be happy in your presence
like those who celebrate the harvest
or rejoice when dividing loot.

4 You will break the yoke*ᵇ* that burdens them,
the bar that is across their shoulders,
and the stick used by their oppressor,

ª9:1 Isaiah 9:1-21 in English Bibles is Isaiah 8:23–9:20 in the Hebrew Bible.   ᵇ9:4 A yoke is a wooden bar placed over the necks of work animals so that they can pull plows or carts.

as you did in the battle against Midian.

5 Every warrior's boot marching to the sound of battle
    and every garment rolled in blood
        will be burned as fuel in the fire.

6 A child will be born for us.
A son will be given to us.
    The government will rest on his shoulders.
    He will be named:
        Wonderful Counselor,
        Mighty God,
        Everlasting Father,
        Prince of Peace.

7 His government and peace will have unlimited growth.
    He will establish David's throne and kingdom.
    He will uphold it with justice and righteousness now and forever.
The Lord of Armies is determined to do this!

The LORD's Message Against His People

8 The Lord sent a message against Jacob.
    The message is against Israel.

9 All the people of Ephraim
    and the people who live in Samaria will know it.
    With arrogant and conceited hearts they will say,

10   "Bricks have fallen,
        but we will rebuild with hand-cut stones.
    Fig trees have been cut down,
        but we will replace them with cedars."

11 The Lord will set Rezin's oppressors against Israel
    and will stir up its enemies—

12   the Arameans from the east and the Philistines from the west.
    They will devour Israel with open mouths.

Even after all this, his anger will not disappear,
    and he is still ready to use his power.

13 But the people have not returned to the one who struck them,
    nor have they sought the Lord of Armies.

Good Morning, God
Isaiah 9:6

A nickname often tells us something about a person. It may reveal the person's personality or a special characteristic. More than 700 years before Jesus was born, the prophet Isaiah wrote several names that would describe Jesus. Read them aloud in verse 6. What things do these names tell you about our Savior?

I praise you, God, for sending your son, Jesus Christ, to earth!

14 So in one day the LORD will cut off from Israel
    both head and tail,
    both palm branches and cattails.
15   Respected and honored leaders are the head.
      Prophets who teach lies are the tail.
16   Those who guide these people lead them astray.
          Those who are guided by them will be destroyed.
17 That is why the Lord isn't happy with their young men,
    nor will he show compassion for their orphans and widows.
        Every one of them is a godless evildoer,
          and every mouth speaks foolishness.

    Even after all this, his anger will not disappear,
      and he is still ready to use his power.

18 Surely wickedness burns like fire.
    It burns up briars and thorns.
    It sets the underbrush in the forest on fire,
      and it whirls upward in clouds of smoke.
19 The land is scorched by the fury of the LORD of Armies,
    and the people are like fuel for the fire.
   No one shows concern for others:
20   On the right, one gobbles up food and is still hungry.
      On the left, another eats and is never full.
        Each person eats the flesh from his own arm.
21 Manasseh is against Ephraim.
   Ephraim is against Manasseh.
      Together they attack Judah.

   Even after all this, his anger will not disappear,
     and he is still ready to use his power.

10
1   How horrible it will be for those who make unjust laws
       and who make oppressive regulations.
2   They deprive the poor of justice.
       They take away the rights of the needy among my people.
       They prey on widows and rob orphans.
3 What will you do on the day
     you are called to account for these things,
       when the disaster comes from far away?
   Where will you run for help?
   Where will you leave your wealth?
4   Nothing's left but to crouch among prisoners
       and to fall with those who are killed.

   Even after all this, his anger will not disappear,
     and he is still ready to use his power.

The LORD's Message Against Assyria

5 "How horrible it will be for Assyria!
     It is the rod of my anger.
       My fury is the staff in the Assyrians' hands.

6 I send them against a godless nation.
In my fury I order them against the people
to take their belongings, loot them,
and trample on them like mud in the streets.
7 But that's not what they intend to do.
Their minds don't work that way.
Their purpose is to destroy and put an end to many nations.
8 They ask, 'Aren't all our commanders kings?
9 Isn't Calno like Carchemish?
Isn't Hamath like Arpad?
Isn't Samaria like Damascus?'
10 My power has reached kingdoms which have idols.
They had more carved statues than Jerusalem or Samaria.
11 I will do to Jerusalem and its idols
what I've done to Samaria and its idols."

12When the Lord has finished all his work on Mount Zion and in Jerusalem, he will
punish the king of Assyria for all his boasting and all his arrogance. 13The king will say,

"I did this with my own two powerful hands.
I did this with my wisdom, because I am so clever.
I've eliminated the boundaries of nations.
I've looted treasuries.
I've brought down people like a mighty man.
14 I've found the riches of nations as one finds a nest.
I've gathered the whole world as one gathers abandoned eggs.
Not one of them flapped a wing, opened its mouth, or peeped."

15 Can an ax attack the person who cuts with it?
Can a saw make itself greater than the person who saws with it?
A rod cannot move the person who lifts it.
A wooden stick cannot pick up a person.
16 That is why the Almighty Lord of Armies
will send a degenerative disease against brave men.
A flame will be turned into a raging fire under his power.
17 Israel's light will become a flame.
Its Holy One will become a fire.
He will burn up and devour the weeds and thornbushes in one day.
18 The majestic forest and the orchard
will destroy both body and soul.
They will be like a sick person wasting away.
19 The trees that remain in the forest will be so few that
a child could count them.

20 At that time the remaining few Israelites,
the survivors of Jacob's descendants
will no longer depend on the one who struck them.
They will only depend on the Lord, the Holy One of Israel.
21 A few, the remaining few of Jacob, will return to the mighty God.
22 Although your people Israel may be
as numerous as the grains of sand on the seashore,
only a few will return.

Destruction will be complete and fair.

23 The Almighty LORD of Armies will carry out this destruction
    throughout the world as he has determined.

24 The Almighty LORD of Armies says:
    My people who live in Zion,
        don't be afraid of the Assyrians when they strike with a rod
            or when they raise their staff against you
                as the Egyptians did.

25 Very soon I will unleash my fury,
    and my anger will destroy them.

26 Then the LORD of Armies will raise his whip against them.
    As he struck down Midian at the Rock of Oreb
        and raised his staff over the water,
            so he will lift it as he did in Egypt.

27 At that time their burden will be removed from your shoulders.
    Their yoke[a] will be removed from your neck.
    The yoke will be torn away because you have grown fat.

28 They come to Aiath.
    They pass through Migron.
    They store their equipment at Michmash.

29 They go through the mountain pass and lodge at Geba for the night.
    The people in Ramah tremble; the people in Saul's Gibeah flee.

30 Cry aloud, you people in Gallim!
Pay attention, you people in Laishah and miserable Anathoth!

31 The people in Madmenah flee; those who live in Gebim take shelter.

32 This day they stopped at Nob.
    They shake their fist at the mountain of my people Zion,
        at the mountain of Jerusalem.

33 Now look! The Almighty LORD of Armies
    will trim the branches with terrifying power.
    The highest trees will be cut down.
    The tallest ones will be brought down.

34 He will cut down the underbrush of the forest with an ax.
    Lebanon will fall in front of the Mighty One.

The LORD's Kingdom Will Be Ruled by a Shoot From Jesse's Stump

11

1 Then a shoot will come out from the stump of Jesse,
    and a branch from its roots will bear fruit.

2 The Spirit of the LORD will rest on him—
    the Spirit of wisdom and understanding,
    the Spirit of advice and power,
    the Spirit of knowledge and fear of the LORD.

3 He will gladly bear the fear of the LORD.
He will not judge by what his eyes see
    or decide by what his ears hear.

---

[a] 10:27 A yoke is a wooden bar placed over the necks of work animals so that they can pull plows or carts.

4 He will judge the poor justly.
   He will make fair decisions for the humble people on earth.
   He will strike the earth with a rod from his mouth.
   He will kill the wicked with the breath from his lips.

5 Justice will be the belt around his waist.
   Faithfulness will be the belt around his hips.

6 Wolves will live with lambs.
   Leopards will lie down with goats.
   Calves, young lions, and year-old lambs will be together,
      and little children will lead them.

7 Cows and bears will eat together.
      Their young will lie down together.
   Lions will eat straw like oxen.

8 Infants will play near cobras' holes.
   Toddlers will put their hands into vipers' nests.

9 They will not hurt or destroy anyone anywhere on my holy mountain.
      The world will be filled with the knowledge of the LORD
      like water covering the sea.

10 At that time the root of Jesse will stand as a banner
      for the people to gather around.
      The nations will come to him.
         His resting place will be glorious.

11 At that time the Lord will use his power again
      to recover what remains of his people
         in Assyria, Upper and Lower Egypt,
            Sudan, Elam, Babylonia, Hamath,
            and the islands of the sea.

12 He will raise a banner for the nations to gather around.
   He will gather the outcasts of Israel
      and bring together the scattered people of Judah
         from the four corners of the earth.

13 Ephraim's jealousy will vanish,
      and Judah's opponents will come to an end.
   Ephraim won't be jealous of Judah,
      and Judah won't oppose Ephraim.

14 They will swoop down on the slopes of Philistia in the west.
      Together they will loot the people of the east.
   They will conquer Edom and Moab.
      The people of Ammon will be subject to them.

15 The LORD will dry up the gulf of the Egyptian Sea.
   He will wave his hand over the Euphrates River with his scorching wind
      and divide it into seven streams
         so that people can walk over it in their sandals.

16 There will be a highway
      for the remaining few of his people left in Assyria
         like there was for Israel when it came out of Egypt.

A Hymn of Praise From the LORD's People in His Kingdom

12 ¹At that time you will say,

"I will praise you, O LORD.
Although you had been angry with me,
    you turned your anger away from me, and you comforted me.
² Look! God is my Savior.
I am confident and unafraid,
    because the LORD is my strength and my song.
He is my Savior."

³With joy you will draw water from the springs of salvation.
⁴At that time you will say,

"Praise the LORD.
Call on his name.
Make his deeds known among the nations.
Make them remember that his name is highly honored.
⁵ Make music to praise the LORD.
    He has done wonderful things.
        Let this be known throughout the earth.
⁶ Shout loudly, and sing with joy, people of Zion!
The Holy One of Israel is great. He is among you."

Babylon Will Be Punished

13 ¹This is the divine revelation which Isaiah, son of Amoz, saw about Babylon.

² Raise a banner on the bare mountaintop.
    Call loudly to them.
        Signal them with your hand to enter the nobles' gates.
³ I've commanded my holy ones.
I've called my mighty men to carry out my anger.
    They find joy in my triumphs.
⁴ Listen to the noise on the mountains.
    It is like the sound of a large army.
    It is the sound of kingdoms and nations gathering together.
The LORD of Armies is assembling his army for battle.
⁵ His army is coming from a distant land,
    from the ends of heaven.
The LORD is coming with the weapons of his fury
    to destroy the whole world.

⁶ Cry loudly, for the day of the LORD is near.
    It will come like destruction from the Almighty.
⁷ That is why every hand will hang limp,
    and everyone's courage will fail.
⁸   They'll be terrified.
        Pain and anguish will seize them.
        They'll writhe like a woman giving birth to a child.
        They'll look at one another in astonishment.
        Their faces will be burning red.

9   The day of the LORD is going to come.
         It will be a cruel day with fury and fierce anger.
             He will make the earth desolate.
             He will destroy its sinners.
10   The stars in the sky and their constellations
         won't show their light anymore.
     The sun will be dark when it rises.
     The moon won't shine.
11   I will punish the world for its evil
         and the wicked for their wrongdoing.
     I will put an end to arrogant people
         and humble the pride of tyrants.
12   I will make people harder to find than pure gold
         and human beings more rare than gold from Ophir.
13   I will make heaven tremble,
         and the earth will be shaken from its place
             when the LORD of Armies is angry.
             At that time he will be very angry.

14   They'll be like hunted gazelle
         and like sheep with no one to gather them.
     Everyone will return to his own people
         and flee to his own land.
15   Whoever is found will be stabbed to death.
     Whoever is captured will be executed.
16   Their little children will be smashed to death right before their eyes.
         Their houses will be looted and their wives raped.

17   I'm going to stir up the Medes against them.
         They don't care for silver and aren't happy with gold.
18   But their bows will smash the youth.
         They'll have no compassion for babies,
             nor will they look with pity on children.

19   Babylon, the jewel of the kingdoms,
         the proud beauty of the Chaldeans,
             will be like Sodom and Gomorrah when God destroyed them.
20   It will never be inhabited again,
         and no one will live in it for generations.
             Arabs won't pitch their tents there.
             Shepherds won't let their flocks rest there.
21   Desert animals will lie down there.
         Their homes will be full of owls.
             Ostriches will live there,
                 and wild goats will skip about.
22   Hyenas will howl in Babylon's strongholds,
         and jackals will howl in its luxurious palaces.

     Its time has almost come.
     Its days will not be extended.

Israel Will Be Rescued From Babylon

14 ¹ The LORD will have compassion for Jacob and again choose Israel.
He will resettle them in their own country.
Foreigners will join them
and unite with the descendants of Jacob.
² People will take them
and bring them to their own place.
The nation of Israel will possess nations
as male and female slaves in the LORD's land.
They will take their captors captive
and rule their oppressors.

³ When that day comes, the LORD will give you relief
from your pain and suffering,
from the hard slavery you were forced to do.
⁴ Then you will mock the king of Babylon with this saying,
"How the tyrant has come to an end!
How his attacks have come to an end!"
⁵ The LORD has broken the staff of the wicked,
the scepter of rulers.
⁶ They struck the people with fury,
with blows that didn't stop.
They ruled nations in anger,
persecuting them without restraint.
⁷ The whole earth rests and is peaceful.
It breaks out into shouts of joy.
⁸ Even the cypresses rejoice over you.
The cedars of Lebanon say,
"Since you have fallen,
no lumberjack has come to attack us."

⁹ Sheol below wakes up to meet you when you come.
It wakes up the ghosts of the dead,
all who were leaders on earth.
It raises all who were kings of the nations from their thrones.
¹⁰ All of them will greet you,
"You also have become weak like us!
You have become like one of us!"
¹¹ Your pride has been brought down to Sheol
along with the music of your harps.
Maggots are spread out like a bed under you,
and worms cover you.

¹² How you have fallen from heaven, you morning star, son of the dawn!
How you have been cut down to the ground, you conqueror of nations!
¹³ You thought,
"I'll go up to heaven and set up my throne above God's stars.
I'll sit on the mountain far away in the north
where the gods assemble.
¹⁴ I'll go above the top of the clouds.
I'll be like the Most High."

15 But you've been brought down to Sheol,
   to the deepest part of the pit.
16 Those who see you stare at you; they look at you closely and say,
   "Is this the man who made the earth tremble,
      who shook the kingdoms,
17   who made the world like a desert and tore down its cities,
      who didn't let his prisoners go home?"

18 All the kings of the nations, all of them,
   have been buried with honor, each in his own tomb.
19 But you are thrown out of your tomb like a rejected branch.
   You are covered with those who were killed in battle.
   You go down to the stones of the pit like a trampled corpse.
20 You won't be joined by the kings in the tomb,
   because you have destroyed your land and killed your people.

   The descendants of the wicked will never be mentioned again.
21 Prepare a place to slaughter their sons
   because of their ancestors' guilt.
      They won't be able to rise, possess the earth,
      and rebuild cities all over it.

22 "I'll rise up against them," declares the LORD of Armies.
   "I'll cut off the name of the survivors from Babylon,
   its offspring and descendants," declares the LORD.
23   "It will become the possession of herons.
      It will become pools of water.
   I'll sweep it with the broom of destruction,"
   declares the LORD of Armies.

Assyria Will Be Punished

24 The LORD of Armies has taken an oath:
   "It will happen exactly as I've intended.
   It will turn out exactly as I've planned.
25   I'll crush Assyria on my land.
      I'll trample it underfoot on my mountains.
   Then its yoke[a] will be removed from my people,
      and its burden will be removed from their shoulders."

26 This is the plan determined for the whole earth.
   This is how he will use his power against all the nations.
27   The LORD of Armies has planned it. Who can stop it?
      He is ready to use his power. Who can turn it back?

The Philistines Will Be Punished

28 This was the divine revelation in the year King Ahaz died.

29 All you Philistines, don't rejoice
   that the rod of the one who struck you is broken,
      because a viper will come from that snake's root,
         and his descendant will be a flying, fiery serpent.

---

[a] 14:25 A yoke is a wooden bar placed over the necks of work animals so that they can pull plows or carts.

30 The poorest of the poor will eat,
  and the needy will lie down in safety.
    But I will put your root to death with famine
      and kill off your survivors.
31 Cry loudly in the gate!
    Cry out in the city!
      Be frightened, all you Philistines!
  Smoke comes from the north,
    and there are no stragglers in its ranks.
32 How should we answer the messengers from the nations?
    ⌊Tell them that⌋ the LORD has laid Zion's foundation,
      and his humble people will find refuge in it.

Moab Will Be Punished

15 ¹This is the divine revelation about Moab.

  In a single night Ar in Moab is laid waste and destroyed!
  In a single night Kir in Moab is laid waste and destroyed!
² The people of Dibon go to the temple,
    to the worship sites, to cry.
  Moab wails over Nebo and Medeba.
    Every head is shaved bald, and every beard is cut off.ᵃ
³ In their streets they wear sackcloth.
    On their roofs and in their city squares everyone wails and cries.
⁴ Heshbon and Elealeh also cry out.
    Their voices are heard as far away as Jahaz.
  Moab's armed men cry out.
    Their courage is gone.
⁵ My heart cries out for Moab.
    Its people flee as far as Zoar at Eglath Shelishiyah.
      They go up the mountain road to Luhith.
      They cry loudly over the destruction on the way to Horonaim.
⁶ The Nimrim Brook has run dry!
    The grass dries up,
      the vegetation withers,
        and nothing green is left.
⁷ That is why they carry the wealth that they have earned and stored up
    over Willow Ravine.
⁸ Cries for help echo throughout the land of Moab.
    Their wailing echoes as far as Eglaim.
    Their wailing echoes as far as Beer Elim.
⁹ The water in Dimon is red with blood,
    yet I will bring even more on Dimon.
      A lion will attack the fugitives from Moab
        and the survivors from Adamah.ᵇ

16 ¹ Send lambs to the ruler of the land.ᵃ
    Send lambs from Sela through the desert to my people at Mount Zion.

ᵃ15:2 The shaving of the head and the beard are signs of a people going into exile. ᵇ15:9 Or "the survivors in the countryside." ᵃ16:1 Masoretic Text; Targum "They have sent lambs to the ruler of the land."

2   Moab's daughters are like fluttering birds,
         like scattered nestlings,
             at the shallow crossings of the Arnon River.

3   Give us advice.
         Make a decision.
             At high noon make your shadow as dark as night.
                 Hide the fugitives.
                     Don't betray the refugees.
4   Let the fugitives from Moab stay with you a while.
                         Be their refuge from the destroyer.
     Ruthless people will come to an end.
         The destruction will end.
             The one who tramples others will be gone.

5   Then the LORD will set up a trusted king.
         He will rule faithfully.
             He is from the tent of David.
             He judges and searches for justice.
             He is quick to do what is right.

6   We've heard of the arrogance of Moab's people.
         They are very arrogant.
     We've heard of their boasting, arrogance, and conceit,
         but their boasts aren't true.

7   That is why Moab will wail.
         Everyone will wail for Moab.
     Mourn and grieve over the raisin cakes of Kir Hareseth.[b]

8   The fields of Heshbon and the vineyards of Sibmah wither.
     Rulers of the nations have cut off their grapes.
         The grapevines once reached as far as Jazer
             and strayed out into the desert.
         Their shoots had spread out over the sea.

9   I will cry for the grapevines of Sibmah
         as Jazer cries for them.
             I will drench you with my tears, Heshbon and Elealeh.
     The shouts of joy for your ripened fruits
         and your harvest will be silenced.

10   Joy and delight have vanished from the orchards.
         No songs are sung.
         No shouts are raised.
         No one stomps on grapes in the winepresses,
             because I have put an end to the shouts of joy.

11   That is why my heart mourns for Moab like a harp.
         My soul mourns for Kir Hareseth.

12   When the people of Moab appear at the worship site,
         they will only wear themselves out.
     They will come into the holy place to pray,
         but they won't be able to.

---

b 16:7 Hebrew meaning of this line uncertain.

¹³This is the message that the Lord spoke about Moab in the past. ¹⁴But now the Lord says, "Moab's honor will be despised within three years. I will count them like workers count the years left of their contracts.ᶜ In spite of their great number, the survivors will be very few and powerless."

Damascus and Israel Will Be Punished

¹This is the divine revelation about Damascus.

> "Damascus will no longer be a city.
>> It will become a pile of rubble.
² The cities of Aroer will be deserted.
>> These cities will be used for sheep, which will lie down in them.
>> There will be no one to disturb those sheep.
³ Fortified cities will disappear from Ephraim,
>> and the kingdom will disappear from Damascus.
> The remaining few from Aram will share Israel's honor,"
>> declares the Lord of Armies.

⁴ "When that day comes, the honor of Jacob's people will fade away,
>> and they will become skin and bones.
⁵ That time will be like harvesting bundles of grain by the armful.
> It will be like gathering grain in the Rephaim Valley.
⁶ Only a few people will survive.
>> They will be like an olive tree that has been beaten.
>> Only two or three olives are left
>>> at the top of the highest branch,
>>>> four or five olives on the rest of the branches,"
>>> declares the Lord God of Israel.

⁷ When that day comes, they will look to their maker,
>> and their eyes will look to the Holy One of Israel.
⁸ They won't look to the altars made by their hands
>> or to the Asherah poles or incense altars
>>> which their fingers molded.

⁹ When that day comes, the fortified cities
>> which other people abandoned because of the Israelites
>> will be like abandoned woods and undergrowth.
> So it will become a wasteland.

¹⁰ You have forgotten the God of your salvation.
> You haven't remembered the rock, your stronghold.
> Instead, you have planted the best plants
>> and have set out the imported grapevines.
¹¹ On the day you plant, you will make it grow.ᵃ
> On the morning you set out the seedling, you will make it sprout.
>> But the harvest will become a rotting pileᵇ
>> on a day of grief and incurable pain.

¹² How horrible it will be for many people!
> They will roar like the roaring sea.

ᶜ16:14 Hebrew meaning of this sentence uncertain. ᵃ17:11 Hebrew meaning of this line uncertain. ᵇ17:11 Or "But the harvest will flee."

> The noise that the people make
> > will be like the noise from rushing water.
>
> 13   The people will make noise like raging water.
> > But the Lord will yell at them, and they will run far away.
> > > They will be chased away
> > > > like husks on the mountains being blown by the wind,
> > > > like whirling dust being blown by a storm.
>
> 14   In the evening there will be sudden terror.
> > Before morning they will be gone.
> > This will be the fate of those who looted us,
> > > the destiny of those who robbed us.

Sudan Will Be Punished

18 ¹ How horrible it will be for the land of whirring wings
> which lies beyond the rivers of Sudan.
>
> 2   It sends messengers by sea
> > in boats made of reeds
> > > skimming over the surface of the water.
> > Go, swift messengers, to a tall and smooth-skinned people,
> > > a people who are feared far and near,
> > > a strong and aggressive nation,
> > > > whose land is divided by rivers.
>
> 3   Look when someone raises a flag on the mountains.
> > Listen when someone blows a ram's horn,
> > > all you inhabitants of the world who live on the earth.

⁴This is what the Lord says to me:

> I will keep quiet and watch from my dwelling place.
> > My presence will be like scorching heat in the sunshine,
> > > like heavy dew in the heat of the harvest.
>
> 5   Before the harvest, when blossoms are gone
> > and grapes are ripening from blossoms,
> > he will cut off the shoots with pruning shears
> > > and chop off the spreading branches.
>
> 6   They will be left for the birds of prey on the mountains
> > and the wild animals.
> > > The birds of prey will feed on them in the summer,
> > > > and all the wild animals on earth
> > > > > will feed on them in the winter.
>
> 7   At that time gifts will be brought to the Lord of Armies
> > from a tall and smooth-skinned people,
> > a people who are feared far and near,
> > a strong and aggressive nation,
> > > whose land is divided by rivers.
> > They will be brought to Mount Zion,
> > > the place where the name of the Lord of Armies is.

Weaving / *Isaiah 19:9-10*

To make cloth, women stripped fibers from dried flax or wool to make into thread. The threads were crisscrossed and pulled snug on looms to make cloth. One type of loom was a ground loom. Rows of pegs were driven in the ground, and threads were tied between the pegs. Then other threads were woven between them.

The women made clothing from the cloth they had woven. Women in Israel worked as hard as their husbands (see Proverbs 31:19-22). Their handmade clothing helped the family to be as comfortable as possible.

Egypt Will Be Punished

19 ¹This is the divine revelation about Egypt.

The Lord is riding on a fast-moving cloud and is coming to Egypt.
  Egypt's idols will tremble in his presence.
  Egypt's courage will fail.

² "I will turn one Egyptian against another.
They will fight—
  brother against brother,
  neighbor against neighbor,
  city against city,
  kingdom against kingdom.

³ The Egyptians will lose courage.
  I will unravel their plans.
They will turn to idols, ghosts,
  mediums, and fortunetellers.

⁴ I will hand over the Egyptians to a harsh master.
  A strong king will rule them,"
    declares the Almighty Lord of Armies.

⁵ The water in the Nile River will be dried up,ᵃ
  and the river will be dry and empty.

⁶ The canals will stink.
  Egypt's streams will be emptied and dried up.
  The reeds and cattails will wither.

⁷ The rushes by the Nile, by the edge of the Nile,

ᵃ 19:5 Or "Then the water of the sea will be dried up."

and all the fields planted beside the Nile
will dry up, be blown away, and disappear.
8 Fishermen will cry.
All who cast their lines into the Nile will mourn.
Those who spread their nets on the water will sigh.
9 Linenworkers and weavers will be ashamed.
10 Egypt's weavers will be crushed.
Those who work for money will be distressed.
11 The leaders of Zoan are nothing but fools.
The wisest of Pharaoh's counselors gives stupid advice.
How can you tell Pharaoh,
"I'm a descendant of wise men,
a descendant of ancient kings"?
12 Where are your wise men now?
Let them tell you.
Let them explain what the Lord of Armies
is planning against Egypt.
13 The leaders of Zoan are acting foolishly.
The leaders of Memphis are led astray.
The leaders who are the cornerstones of its tribes mislead the Egyptians.
14 The Lord mixes up their minds.
So they lead the Egyptians astray
like a drunk who staggers in his vomit.
15 No one—leaders or followers, important or unimportant—
can do anything for Egypt.

16At that time Egyptians will act like women. They will tremble and be terrified because the Lord of Armies will shake his fist at them. 17The land of Judah will terrify the Egyptians. Whenever they are reminded of Judah, they will be terrified of it because of what the Lord of Armies is planning against it.

18When that day comes, five cities in Egypt will have people that speak the language of Canaan and swear allegiance to the Lord of Armies. One of the cities will be called Heliopolis.*b*

19When that day comes, an altar for the Lord will be in the middle of Egypt, and a stone marker for the Lord will be near its border. 20These objects will be a sign and a witness that the Lord of Armies is in Egypt. When the people cry to the Lord because of those who oppress them, he will send a savior and defender to rescue them. 21So the Lord will make himself known to the Egyptians. The Egyptians will know the Lord when that day comes. They will worship with sacrifices and food offerings. They will make vows to the Lord and carry them out. 22The Lord will strike Egypt with a plague. When he strikes them, he will also heal them. Then they will come back to the Lord. And he will respond to their prayers and heal them.

23When that day comes, a highway will run from Egypt to Assyria. The Assyrians will come to Egypt and the Egyptians to Assyria, and the Egyptians will worship with the Assyrians. 24When that day comes, Israel will be one-third of God's people, along with Egypt and Assyria. They will be a blessing on the earth. 25The Lord of Armies will bless them, saying, "My people Egypt, the work of my hands Assyria, and my possession Israel are blessed."

---

b 19:18 Dead Sea Scrolls, some Hebrew manuscripts, Greek, Targum, Latin, Egyptian; Masoretic Text "City of Destruction."

Those Who Were Allied With Egypt Will Be Ashamed

20 [1]In the year when King Sargon of Assyria sent his commander-in-chief to fight against Ashdod, he captured it. [2]At that time the LORD told Isaiah, son of Amoz, "Take off the sackcloth that you are wearing, and take off your sandals!" Isaiah did this and walked around barefoot and naked.

[3]Then the LORD said, "My servant Isaiah has gone barefoot and naked for three years as a sign and as an omen to Egypt and Sudan. [4]The king of Assyria will lead away both the young and the old—captives from Egypt and exiles from Sudan. They will be barefoot and naked. Their buttocks will be exposed in order to disgrace Egypt. [5]Then the people will be shattered and ashamed because Sudan was their hope and Egypt was their beauty. [6]When that day comes, those who live on this coastland will say, 'Look at what has happened to our hope. We ran to Egypt for help to be rescued from the king of Assyria. How can we escape?' "

Babylon Has Fallen

21 [1]This is the divine revelation about the desert by the sea.

Like a storm sweeping through the Negev,
  an invader will come from the desert,
    from a terrifying land.
[2] I was shown a harsh vision.
  The traitor betrays.
  The destroyer destroys.
    Go to war, Elam!
    Surround them, Media!
I will put an end to all the groaning.
[3] That is why my body is full of trembling.
Pain grips me like the pain of childbirth.
  I'm disturbed by what I hear.
  I'm terrified by what I see.
[4] I'm confused.
  I'm shaking with terror.
The twilight hours I longed for make me tremble.
[5] Set the table.
  Spread the rugs by the table.
    Eat. Drink.
Get up, you leaders!
Prepare your shields for battle!

[6]This is what the Lord says to me:

Post a watchman.
  Have him report whatever he sees.
[7] He will see chariots, pairs of horsemen,
  riders on donkeys, and riders on camels.
    Let him watch carefully, very carefully.
[8] The watchman[a] called,
  "Sir, I stand on the watchtower every day.
    Every night, I stand guard at my post.
[9]   Look! Here come chariots and horsemen in pairs."

---

[a] 21:8 Syriac, Dead Sea Scrolls; Masoretic Text, Targum "lion"; Greek "Uriah."

Then he said,
"Babylon has fallen! It has fallen!
All the idols they worship lie shattered on the ground."

10 You, my people, have been threshed and winnowed.[b]
I make known to you what I heard from the LORD of Armies,
the God of Israel.

Someone Calling From Seir

11This is the divine revelation about Dumah.[c]

Someone is calling to me from Seir,
"Watchman, how much of the night is left?
Watchman, how much of the night is left?"

12 The watchman answers,
"Morning is coming, and night will come again.
If you need to ask, come back and ask."

Arabia Will Be Punished

13This is the divine revelation about Arabia.

You caravan of travelers from the people of Dedan
will spend the night in the forest of Arabia.

14 Bring water for the thirsty,
you inhabitants of the land of Tema.
Bring food to the fugitives.

15 They flee from swords,
from swords ready to kill,
from bows ready to shoot,
and from the thick of battle.

16This is what the Lord says to me: All of Kedar's honor will be gone in another year. I will count it like workers count the years left on their contracts.[d] 17The remaining number of archers, Kedar's mighty archers, will be few. The LORD God of Israel has spoken.

Judah Will Be Punished

22 1This is the divine revelation about the valley of Vision.

What's the matter with you?
Why do all of you go up on the roofs?

2 You are a city filled with shouting,
a town filled with noise and excitement.
Your people weren't killed with swords.
Your dead didn't die in battle.

3 All your leaders fled together
and were captured without their bows and arrows.
All those who were found were taken prisoner
before any of them could get far away.

4 That is why I say,

---

[b]21:10 Threshing is the process of beating stalks to separate them from the grain. Winnowing is the process of separating husks from grain.   [c]21:11 The exact location of Dumah is unknown.   [d]21:16 Hebrew meaning of this sentence uncertain.

"Turn away from me
so that I can cry bitterly.
Don't try to comfort me
because of the destruction brought on my people."

5 The Almighty Lord of Armies has chosen a special day.
It will be a day of confusion and trampling
in the valley of Vision,
a day of tearing down walls and crying for help
in the mountains.
6 Elam takes its quiver of arrows,
manned chariots, and horsemen.
Kir uncovers its shields.
7 Then your fertile valleys will be filled with chariots,
and horsemen will stand ready in front of the gate.
8 On that day the Lord will remove the defenses of Judah.

You will look for weapons in the House of the Forest.[a]
9 You will see how many places in David's wall are broken.
You will store water in the Lower Pool.
10 You will count the houses in Jerusalem.
You will tear down those houses in order to fortify the walls.
11 You will build a reservoir between the two walls
to hold the water of the Old Pool.
You didn't look to Jerusalem's maker.
You didn't see the one who formed it long ago.
12 On that day the Almighty Lord of Armies
will call for crying and for mourning,
for shaving your heads and for wearing sackcloth.
13 Instead, you will rejoice, celebrate,
slaughter cattle, and butcher sheep.
You will eat meat, drink wine, and say,
"Let's eat and drink because tomorrow we're going to die."

14The Lord of Armies revealed this to me: "Certainly, this wrong will not be forgiven even when you die," says the Almighty Lord of Armies.

Shebna's Position Will Be Given to Eliakim

15This is what the Almighty Lord of Armies says:

Go to Shebna, the man in charge of the palace, and say to him,
16 "What are you doing here?
What right do you have to dig a tomb for yourself?
What right do you have to cut it out in a prominent place?
What right do you have to carve out
a resting place for yourself in the rock?
17 Look, mighty man!
The Lord will throw you out.
He will grab you.
18 He will wrap you up tightly like a turban.

---

a 22:8 "The House of the Forest" is a storehouse for weapons and other items. It was built by Solomon as part of the temple complex.

He will throw you far away into another land.
    There you will die.
    There your splendid chariots will remain.
    There you will become a disgrace to your master's household.

19   "I will remove you from your office
        and do away with your position.
20   When that day comes, I will call my servant Eliakim, son of Hilkiah.
21   I will dress him in your linen robe
        and fasten it with your belt.
    I will give him your authority,
        and he will be like a father to those who live in Jerusalem
            and to the nation of Judah.
22   I will place the key of the house of David around his neck.
    What he opens no one will shut.
    What he shuts no one will open.
23   I will fasten him firmly in place like a peg,
        and he will be a source of honor for his father's household.
24   They will hang on him the whole weight of his father's household,
        descendants and offspring and all the little utensils,
            from bowls to jars of every kind."

25The Lord of Armies declares,

"On that day the peg which I firmly fastened in place will be removed.
    It will be cut off and will fall,
        and everything hanging on it will be destroyed."

The Lord has spoken.

Tyre Will Be Punished

23 ¹This is the divine revelation about Tyre.

    Cry loudly, you ships of Tarshish!
        Your port at Tyre is destroyed.
            Word has come to the ships from Cyprus.
2   Be silent, you inhabitants of the coastland, you merchants from Sidon.
        Your messengers have crossed the sea.
3   The grain of Shihor is on the Mediterranean.
        The harvest of the Nile River is brought to Tyre.
            Tyre became the marketplace for the nations.

4   Be ashamed, Sidon, because the stronghold by the sea has spoken,
        "I've never been in labor or given birth.
        I've raised no sons.
        I've brought up no daughters."
5   When the news reaches Egypt,
        the Egyptians will shudder over the news about Tyre.

6   Travel to Tarshish!
    Cry loudly, you inhabitants of the seacoast!
7   Is this your bustling city founded in the distant past?
    Is this the city that sent its people to settle in distant lands?
8   Who planned such a thing against Tyre, the city that produced kings?

Its merchants are princes.
Its traders are among the honored people of the world.
9 The Lord of Armies planned this
in order to dishonor all arrogant people
and to humiliate all the honored people of the world.
10 Travel through your country like the Nile, people of Tarshish.
You no longer have a harbor.
11 The Lord has stretched his hand over the sea to shake kingdoms.
He has commanded that Canaan's fortifications be destroyed.
12 He says, "You will no longer be joyful,
my dear abused people Sidon."
Get up, and travel to Cyprus.
Even there you will find no rest.
13 Look at the land of the Babylonians.
These people will be gone.
Assyria gave this land to the desert animals.
Assyria set up battle towers,
stripped palaces bare,
and turned these places into ruins.

14Cry loudly, you ships of Tarshish, because your fortress will be destroyed. 15When that day comes, Tyre will be forgotten for 70 years, the lifetime of one king. At the end of the 70 years, Tyre will be like the prostitute in this song:

16 "Take your lyre.
Go around in the city, you forgotten prostitute.
Make sweet music.
Sing many songs so that you'll be remembered."

17At the end of 70 years the Lord will come to help Tyre. Then she will go back to earning money as a prostitute. She will become a prostitute for all the world's kingdoms. 18Her profits and her earnings will be turned over to the Lord for his holy purpose. It won't be stored or hoarded. Her merchandise will belong to those who live in the presence of the Lord so that they will have plenty of food and expensive clothing.

The Lord's Great Triumph

24 1 The Lord is going to turn the earth into a desolate wasteland.
He will mar the face of the earth and scatter the people living on it.
2 The same will happen to people and priests,
male slaves and masters,
female slaves and masters,
buyers and sellers,
lenders and borrowers,
debtors and creditors.
3 The earth will be completely laid waste and stripped
because the Lord has spoken.

4 The earth dries up and withers.
The world wastes away and withers.
The great leaders of the earth waste away.
5 The earth is polluted by those who live on it

because they've disobeyed the Lord's teachings,
 violated his laws,
  and rejected the everlasting promise.[a]

6 That is why a curse devours the earth,
 and its people are punished for their guilt.
That is why those who live on the earth are burned up,
 and only a few people are left.

7 New wine dries up, and grapevines waste away.
 All happy people groan.

8 Joyful tambourine music stops.
 Noisy celebrations cease.
  Joyful harp music stops.

9 People no longer drink wine when they sing.
 Liquor tastes bad to its drinkers.

10 The ruined city lies desolate.
 The entrance to every house is barred shut.

11 People in the streets call for wine.
All joy passes away,
 and the earth's happiness is banished.

12 The city is left in ruins.
 Its gate is battered to pieces.

13 That is the way it will be on earth among the nations.
 They will be like an olive tree which has been shaken
  or like what's left after the grape harvest.

14 They raise their voices.
  They shout for joy.
   From the sea they sing joyfully about the Lord's majesty.

15 Honor the Lord in the east.
Honor the name of the Lord God of Israel along the coastlands.

16 From the ends of the earth we hear songs of praise
 that honor the Righteous One.

But I kept saying,
 "I'm wasting away! I'm wasting away!
  How horrible it is for me!
   Traitors continue to betray,
    and their treachery grows worse and worse."

17 Disasters, pits, and traps
 are in store for those who live on earth.

18 Whoever flees from news of a disaster will fall into a pit.
Whoever climbs out of that pit will be caught in a trap.
The floodgates in the sky will be opened,
 and the foundations of the earth will shake.

19 The earth will be completely broken.
The earth will shake back and forth violently.
The earth will stagger.

20 The earth will stumble like a drunk
 and sway like a shack in the wind.

---

[a] 24:5 Or "covenant."

Its disobedience weighs heavy on it.
It will fall and not get up again.

21 On that day the LORD will punish heaven's armies in heaven
and earth's kings on earth.

22 They'll be gathered like prisoners in a jail
and locked in prison.
After a long time they'll be punished.

23 The moon will be embarrassed.
The sun will be ashamed,
because the LORD of Armies will rule
on Mount Zion and in Jerusalem.
He will be glorious
in the presence of his respected leaders.

The LORD Protects the Weak

1 O LORD, you are my God.
I will highly honor you; I will praise your name.
You have done miraculous things.
You have been completely reliable
in carrying out your plans from long ago.

2 You have turned cities into ruins,
fortified cities into piles of rubble,
and foreigners' palaces into cities that will never be rebuilt.

3 That is why strong people will honor you,
and cities ruled by the world's tyrants will fear you.

4 You have been a refuge for the poor,
a refuge for the needy in their distress,
a shelter from the rain, and shade from the heat.
(A tyrant's breath is like a rainstorm against a wall,

5 like heat in a dry land.)
You calm the uproar of foreigners.
The song of tyrants is silenced
like heat that is ⌞reduced⌟ by the shadow of a cloud.

Death Will Be Swallowed Up

6 On this mountain the LORD of Armies will prepare for all people
a feast with the best foods,
a banquet with aged wines,
with the best foods and the finest wines.

7 On this mountain he will remove
the veil of grief covering all people
and the mask covering all nations.

8 He will swallow up death forever.
The Almighty LORD will wipe away tears from every face,
and he will remove the disgrace of his people from the whole earth.
The LORD has spoken.

9 On that day ⌞his people⌟ will say,
"This is our God; we have waited for him, and now he will save us.

This is the LORD; we have waited for him.
    Let us rejoice and be glad because he will save us."

10 The LORD's power will be on this mountain.
    Moab will be trampled beneath him
        like straw that is trampled in a pile of manure.
11 The Moabites will stretch out their hands in the manure
    like swimmers who stretch out their hands to swim.
    The LORD will humble those arrogant people
        despite the movements of their hands.*a*
12 He will bring down Moab's high fortified walls,
    level them, and throw them into the dust on the ground.

The LORD's People Praise Him for Salvation

26 ¹On that day this song will be sung in the land of Judah:

We have a strong city.
    Its walls and fortifications
        provide safety.
2 Open the gates, and let
        the righteous nation come in,
    the nation
        that remains faithful.
3 With perfect peace you will
        protect those whose minds
        cannot be changed,
    because they trust you.
4 Trust the LORD always,
        because the LORD,
           the LORD alone,
        is an everlasting rock.
5 He has brought down
        those who live high
        in the towering city.
    He levels it.
    He levels it to the ground
        and throws it into the dust.
6 Feet trample it,
        the feet of the oppressed,
        the footsteps of the poor.
7 The path of the righteous
        is level.
    O Upright One, you make
        the road of the righteous
        smooth.
8 Certainly, we wait with hope
        for you, O LORD,
    as we follow the path
        of your guiding principles.

Trust
Isaiah 26:3-4

Can your friends talk you into things? When you say "no," but they reply, "Aw, come on," do you change your mind? Sometimes it's OK to do what others do. But be careful not to change your mind and do things that are wrong. Trust God enough to say "no" to actions that he says are wrong. Don't change your mind about doing right.

be you can be all

---

a 25:11 Hebrew meaning of "despite the movements of their hands" uncertain.

We want to remember you and your name.

9 With my soul I long for you at night.
  Yes, with my spirit I eagerly look for you.
When your guiding principles are on earth,
  those who live in the world learn to do what is right.

10 Although the wicked are shown pity,
  they do not learn to do what is right.
  They do what is wrong in the upright land
    and do not see the majesty of the Lord.

11 O Lord, your power is visible, but they do not see it.
  They will see how devoted your people are,
    and they will be put to shame.
Your burning anger will destroy your enemies.

12 O Lord, you will establish peace for us,
  since you have done everything for us.

13 O Lord, our God, you are not the only master to rule us,
  but we acknowledge only you.

14 The wicked are dead.
  They are no longer alive.
    The spirits of the dead won't rise.
You have punished them, destroyed them,
  and wiped out all memory of them.

15 You have expanded the nation, O Lord.
You have expanded the nation.
You are honored.
You have extended all the land's boundaries.

16 O Lord, the people have come to you in trouble.
  They were humbled by oppression, by your discipline upon them.[a]

17 O Lord, when we are with you,
  we are like pregnant women ready to give birth.
    They writhe and cry out in their labor pains.

18 We were pregnant; we writhed with labor pains
  only to give birth to the wind.
We weren't able to bring salvation to the land,
  and no new people were born on earth.

19 Your dead will live.
Their corpses will rise.
Those who lie dead in the dust will wake up and shout for joy,
  because your dew is a refreshing dew,
    and the earth will revive the spirits of the dead.

20 My people, go to your rooms,
  and shut the doors behind you.
Hide for a little while until his fury has ended.

21 The Lord is going to come out from his dwelling place
  to punish those who live on earth for their sins.
    The earth will uncover the blood shed on it
      and will no longer cover up its dead bodies.

---

a 26:16 Hebrew meaning of this line uncertain.

The LORD's People Will Worship on His Holy Mountain

27 [1] On that day the LORD will use his fierce and powerful sword
to punish Leviathan,[a] that slippery snake,
Leviathan, that twisting snake.
He will kill that monster which lives in the sea.

[2] On that day sing about a delightful vineyard.
[3]   I, the LORD, watch over it.
I water it continually.
I watch over it day and night
so that no one will harm it.
[4]   I am no longer angry.
If only thorns and briars would confront me!
I would fight them in battle and set all of them on fire.
[5]   Or else let them come to me for protection.
Let them make peace with me.
Yes, let them make peace with me.

[6] In times to come Jacob will take root.
Israel will blossom, bud,
and fill the whole world with fruit.

[7] Will the LORD hurt Israel as he hurt others who hurt them?
Will he kill them as he killed others?
[8] He punished Israel by sending it away.
He removed it with a fierce blast from the east winds.[b]
[9] In this way the wrongdoings of the descendants of Jacob are covered up.
This is the way they will turn from their sins—
when they turn all the altar stones into powdered chalk
and no poles dedicated to the goddess Asherah
or incense altars are left standing.
[10] The fortified city is isolated.
The homestead is left deserted, abandoned like the desert.
Calves will graze there.
They will lie down.
They will feed on the branches.
[11] When the branches are dried up,
they will be broken off.
Women will come and build a fire with them.
These people don't understand these things.
That is why their maker won't have compassion on them,
and their Creator won't have pity on them.

[12] On that day the LORD will begin his threshing[c]
from the flowing stream of the Euphrates River
to the brook of Egypt.
People of Israel, you will be gathered one by one.

[13] On that day a ram's horn will be blown loudly.
Those who are dying in Assyria

---

[a]27:1 Hebrew meaning uncertain.   [b]27:8 Hebrew meaning of this verse uncertain.   [c]27:12 Threshing is the process
of beating stalks to separate them from the grain.

and those who are banished to Egypt
 will come and worship the LORD
  on the holy mountain in Jerusalem.

Ephraim Will Fall

28 ¹ How horrible it will be for the arrogant drunks of Ephraim.
  Their glorious beauty is like a withered flower.
   They are at the entrance to a fertile valley
    where they lie drunk from wine.
² The Lord has one who is strong and powerful.
  He is like a hailstorm, a destructive wind.
  He is like a thunderstorm, an overwhelming flood.
  He will throw them to the ground forcefully.
³ The arrogant drunks of Ephraim will be trampled underfoot.
⁴ Their glorious beauty is like a withered flower.
  They are at the entrance to a fertile valley.
  They will be like figs that ripened early.
   As soon as someone sees them,
    they will be taken and eaten.

⁵ When that day comes, the LORD of Armies will be
  like a glorious crown for his few remaining people.
⁶ He will give a spirit of justice to those who judge.
  He will give strength to those who defend the city gates in battle.

⁷ Priests and prophets stagger from wine and wobble from too much liquor.
  They stagger from too much liquor
   and become confused from too much wine.
  They wobble because of their liquor.
  They stagger when they see visions.
  They swerve as they judge.
⁸ All the tables are covered with vomit and excrement.
  There isn't a clean place left.
⁹ To whom will they make the message understood?
  To whom will they explain this message?
   To children just weaned from milk?
   To those just taken from their mother's breasts?
¹⁰ They speak utter nonsense.[a]

¹¹ The LORD will speak to these people.
  He will mock them by speaking in a foreign language.
¹² He will say to them,
   "This is a place for comfort.
    This is a place of rest for those who are tired.
     This is a place for them to rest."
  But they weren't willing to listen.
¹³ The LORD speaks utter nonsense to them.
   That is why they will fall backwards.
   That is why they will be hurt, trapped, and captured.

---

[a] 28:10 Or "Command for command, command for command, line for line, line for line, a little here, a little there." Also in verse 13.

A Message to Jerusalem

14 So hear the word of the LORD, you foolish talkers
　　who rule the people in Jerusalem.
15 You say, "We made a treaty with death
　　and an agreement with the grave.
　When the overwhelming disaster passes by,
　　it won't matter to us,
　　　　because we have taken refuge in our lies,
　　　　　and falsehood is our hiding place."

16This is what the Almighty LORD says:

　I am going to lay a rock in Zion,
　　a rock that has been tested,
　　a precious cornerstone,
　　a solid foundation.
　　　Whoever believes in him will not worry.
17 I will make justice a measuring line
　　and righteousness a plumb line.
　Hail will sweep away your refuge of lies,
　　and floodwaters will wash away your hiding place.
18 Your treaty with death will be wiped away.
　Your agreement with the grave will not stand.
　When the overwhelming disaster passes by,
　　you will be trampled by it.
19 　　Each time it passes by it will take you.
　　　It will pass by morning after morning,
　　　　during the day and during the night.
　　　　　Understanding this message brings only terror.
20 The bed is too short to stretch out on.
　The blanket is too narrow to serve as a cover.
21 The LORD will rise as he did on Mount Perazim.
　He will wake up as he did in Gibeon Valley.
　　He will do his work, his unexpected work,
　　　and perform his deeds, his mysterious deeds.
22 Now stop laughing, or your chains will be tightened,
　　because I have heard that the Almighty LORD of Armies
　　　has finally determined to destroy the whole land.

23 Open your ears, and listen to me!
　Pay attention, and hear me!
24 Does a farmer go on plowing every day so he can plant?
　Does he continue to break up the soil and make furrows in the ground?
25 　When he has smoothed its surface,
　　　doesn't he scatter black cumin seed and plant cumin?
　　　Doesn't he plant wild wheat in rows?
　　　Doesn't he put barley in its own area
　　　　and winter wheat at its borders?
26 God will guide him in judgment,
　　and his God will teach him.

27 Black cumin isn't threshed[b] with a sledge,
and wagon wheels aren't rolled over cumin.
Black cumin is beaten with a rod
and cumin with a stick.
28 Grain is ground into flour, but the grinding eventually stops.
It will be threshed.
The wheels of his cart will roll over it,
but his horses won't crush it.
29 All of this has come from the Lord of Armies.
His counsel is wonderful, and his wisdom is great.

The Lord's Word Will Be Hidden From Some but Revealed to Others

29

1 How horrible it will be for you Ariel, Ariel,[a]
the city where David camped.
Let year after year go by.
Let your annual festivals go on.
2 I will torment Ariel,
and the city will be filled with people grieving and mourning.
The city will become like Ariel.
3 I will set up war camps all around you.
I will blockade you with towers.
I will put up mounds of dirt around you.
4 When you have fallen, you will speak as you lie on the ground.
Your words will be muffled by the dust.
Your voice will come out of the ground like that of a ghost.
Your words will be whispered from the dust.
5 Your many enemies will be like fine dust.
Your many foes will be like husks blown by the wind.
All of this will happen suddenly, unexpectedly.
6 The Lord of Armies will punish you
with thunder, earthquakes, and loud noises,
with windstorms, rainstorms, and fire storms.
7 The armies from all the nations will go to war against Ariel.
They will go to war against it, blockade it, and torment it.
All of this will be like a dream, like a vision in the night.
8 They will be like hungry people who dream that they're eating
and wake up to find they're hungry.
They will be like thirsty people who dream that they're drinking
and wake up to find they're lightheaded and parched with thirst.
This is what will happen to the armies from all the nations
that fight against Mount Zion.

9 If you confuse yourselves, you will be confused.
If you blind yourselves, you will be blinded.
You are drunk, but not from wine.
You stagger, but not from liquor.
10 The Lord has poured out on you a spirit of deep sleep.

---

[b]28:27 Threshing is the process of beating stalks to separate them from the grain. [a]29:1 *Ariel* is an unknown Hebrew word which may mean "lion of God," "mountain of God," or "fireplace."

Pottery / *Isaiah 29:16*

Every Hebrew home used pottery, and most villages in Israel had a potter, a person who made pottery. The potter found good clay, mixed it with water and grit, and worked it with his feet to remove air pockets. He placed lumps of clay on a potter's wheel, which he turned by hand or foot as he shaped the clay pottery.

Women visited pottery shops to buy pottery containers of all sizes and shapes. Giant jars held grain and olive oil; large jugs were used to carry water. Clay pots became cooking utensils. Potters also produced shallow bowls, dishes, and even lamps.

Archaeologists who find a pottery container today can usually tell within 50 years when it was made by studying its texture, design, shape, and decorations.

He will shut your eyes. (Your eyes are the prophets.)
He will cover your heads. (Your heads are the seers.[b])

¹¹To you all these visions will be like words in a book that is closed and sealed. You give this book to someone who can read, saying, "Please read this."
He answers, "I can't read it. It's sealed."
¹²Then you give the book to someone who can't read, saying, "Please read this."
He answers, "I can't read."
¹³The Lord says,

"These people worship me with their mouths
and honor me with their lips.
But their hearts are far from me,
and their worship of me is based on rules made by humans.
¹⁴ That is why I am going to do something completely amazing
for these people once again.
The wisdom of their wise people will disappear.
The intelligence of their intelligent people will be hidden."

¹⁵ How horrible it will be for those
who try to hide their plans from the LORD.
Their deeds are done in the dark,
and they say, "No one can see us"
and "No one can recognize us."

---

[b]29:10 A seer is a prophet.

16 You turn things upside down!
> Is the potter no better than his clay?
> Can something that has been made
>> say about its maker, "He didn't make me"?
> Can a piece of pottery
>> say about the potter, "He doesn't understand"?

17 In a very short time Lebanon will be turned into a fertile field
> and the fertile field will be considered a forest.

18 When that day comes, the deaf will hear the words written in the book.
> The blind will see out of their gloom and darkness.

19 Humble people again will find joy in the LORD.
> The poorest of people will find joy in the Holy One of Israel.

20 Tyrants will be gone.
> Mockers will be finished.
> All who look for ways to do wrong will come to an end:

21 > those who make people sin with words,
> those who lay traps for judges,
> those who, without any reason, deny justice
>> to people who are in the right.

22 This is what the LORD, who saved Abraham, says about the descendants of Jacob:

> Jacob will no longer be ashamed.
> Jacob's face will no longer turn pale.

23 > When they see all their children,
>> the children I made with my hands,
>> they will acknowledge my name as holy.
>> They will treat the Holy One of Jacob as holy.
>> They will stand in terror of the God of Israel.

24 Then those who are wayward in spirit will gain understanding,
> and those who complain will accept instruction.

Judah Should Trust the LORD, Not Egypt

30 1 The LORD declares,

> "How horrible it will be for those rebellious children.
>> They carry out plans, but not mine.
>> They make alliances against my will.
>> They pile sin on top of sin.

2 > They go to Egypt without asking me.
> They look for shelter under Pharaoh's protection
>> and look for refuge in Egypt's shadow.

3 But Pharaoh's protection will be their shame,
> and the refuge in Egypt's shadow will be their disgrace.

4 Although Pharaoh's officials are in Zoan
> and his messengers have reached Hanes,

5 > the people of Judah will be put to shame
>> because that nation can't help them.
>> That nation can't give aid or help to them.
>> It can only offer shame and disgrace."

⁶This is the divine revelation about the animals in the Negev.

"My people travel through lands
  where they experience distress and hardship.
    Lions and lionesses live there.
    Vipers and poisonous snakes live there.
They carry their riches on the backs of young donkeys
  and their treasures on the humps of camels
    to a nation that can't help them.
7 Egypt's help is completely useless.
    That is why I call it, 'Rahab*ᵃ* who sits still.'
8 Now, write this on a tablet for them, and inscribe it in a book
    so that it will be there in the future as a permanent witness.
9 These people are rebellious and deceitful children,
    children who refuse to listen to the Lord's teachings.
10 They say to the seers,*ᵇ* 'Don't see the future.'
  They say to those who have visions,
    'Don't have visions that tell us what is right.
    Tell us what we want to hear. See illusions.
11   Get out of our way! Stop blocking our path!
      Get the Holy One of Israel out of our sight.' "

¹²This is what the Holy One of Israel says:

You have rejected this warning,
  trusted oppression and deceit,
    and leaned on them.
13 That is why your sin will be
    like a high wall with a bulging crack, ready to fall.
    All of a sudden it will fall.
14 It will break like pottery.
  It will be smashed, and nothing will be left of it.
    No piece will be big enough to carry live coals from a fireplace
    or to dip water from a reservoir.

¹⁵This is what the Almighty Lord, the Holy One of Israel, says:

You can be saved by returning to me.
You can have rest.
You can be strong by being quiet and by trusting me.
  But you don't want that.
16   You've said, "No, we'll flee on horses."
      So you flee.
    You've added, "We'll ride on fast horses."
      So those who chase you will also be fast.
17 One thousand people will flee when one person threatens them,
  and you will flee when five threaten you.
      Then you will be left alone
        like a flagpole on top of a mountain,
        like a signpost on a hill.
18 The Lord is waiting to be kind to you.

---

*ᵃ*30:7 Rahab is the name of a demonic creature who opposes God. *ᵇ*30:10 A seer is a prophet.

He rises to have compassion on you.
>> The LORD is a God of justice.
>> Blessed are all those who wait for him.

The LORD Will Heal His People's Wounds

[19]You will live in Zion, in Jerusalem. You won't cry anymore. The LORD will certainly have pity on you when you cry for help. As soon as he hears you, he will answer you. [20]The Lord may give you troubles and hardships. But your teacher will no longer be hidden from you. You will see your teacher with your own eyes. [21]You will hear a voice behind you saying, "This is the way. Follow it, whether it turns to the right or to the left." [22]Then you will dishonor your silver-plated idols and your gold-covered statues. You will throw them away like clothing ruined by stains. You will say to them, "Get out!"

[23]The Lord will give you rain for the seed that you plant in the ground, and the food that the ground provides will be rich and nourishing. When that day comes, your cattle will graze in large pastures. [24]The oxen and the donkeys which work the soil will eat a mixture of food that has been winnowed[c] with forks and shovels. [25]There will be brooks and streams on every lofty mountain and every high hill. When the day of the great slaughter comes, towers will fall. [26]Then the light of the moon will be like the light of the sun. The light of the sun will be seven times as strong, like the light of seven days. When that day comes, the LORD will bandage his people's injuries and heal the wounds he inflicted.

27 The name of the LORD is going to come from far away.
>> His anger is burning.
>> His burden is heavy.
>> His lips are filled with fury.
>> His tongue is like a devouring flame.
28 His breath is like an overflowing stream.
>>> It rises neck high,
>>>> sifting the nations with a sieve of destruction,
>>>>> placing a bit in the mouths of the people
>>>>>> to lead them astray.
29 You will sing a song
>> like the song you sing on a festival night.
>> Your hearts will be happy like someone going out with a flute
>>> on the way to the LORD's mountain, to the rock of Israel.
30 The LORD will make his majestic voice heard.
>> He will come down with all his might,
>>> with furious anger,
>>> with fire storms, windstorms, rainstorms, and hailstones.
31 At the sound of the LORD, the people of Assyria will be shattered.
>> He will strike them with his rod.
32 To the sound of tambourines and lyres, the LORD will pound on them.
>> He will fight them in battle, swinging his fists.
33 Topheth was prepared long ago.
>> It was made ready for the king.
>> It was made deep and wide

---

[c]30:24 Winnowing is the process of separating husks from grain.

and piled high with plenty of burning logs.
The LORD's breath will be like a flood of burning sulfur,
   setting it on fire.

The LORD, Not the Egyptians, Will Protect
His People From Assyria

31

¹ How horrible it will be for those
   who go to Egypt for help,
   who rely on horses,
   who depend on many chariots,
   who depend on very strong war horses.
     They don't look to the Holy One of Israel.
     They don't seek the LORD.
²   He is wise and can bring about disaster.
     He doesn't take back his words.
     He rises against wicked people
       and against those who help troublemakers.
³ The Egyptians are humans, not gods.
   Their horses are flesh and blood, not spirit.
When the LORD uses his powerful hand,
   the one who gives help will stumble,
     and the one who receives help will fall.
     Both will die together.

⁴This is what the LORD said to me:

A lion, even a young lion, growls over its prey
   when a crowd of shepherds is called to fight it.
     It isn't frightened by their voices
     or disturbed by the noise they make.
So the LORD of Armies will come to fight for
   Mount Zion and its hill.
⁵ The LORD of Armies will defend Jerusalem like a hovering bird.
   He will defend it and rescue it.
   He will pass over it and protect it.
⁶ You people of Israel, return to the one
   whom you have so violently rebelled against.
⁷ When that day comes, all of you will reject
   the silver and gold idols
     that your sinful hands have made.
⁸ Then Assyrians will be killed with swords not made by human hands.
   Swords not made by human hands will destroy them.
   They will flee from battle,
     and their young men will be made to do forced labor.
⁹ In terror they will run to their stronghold,*a*
     and their officers will be frightened at the sight of the battle flag.

The LORD declares this. His fire is in Zion and his furnace is in Jerusalem.

---

a 31:9 Hebrew meaning of this line uncertain.

The LORD Will Pour Out His Spirit and Bring Peace

32 ¹ A king will rule with fairness,
   and officials will rule with justice.
² Then each ruler will be like a shelter from the wind
   and a hiding place from the rain.
They will be like streams on parched ground
   and the shade of a large rock in a weary land.
³ Then the vision of those who can see won't be blurred,
   and the ears of those who can hear will pay attention.
⁴ Then those who are reckless will begin to understand,
   and those who stutter will speak quickly and clearly.
⁵ Godless fools will no longer be called nobles,
   nor will scoundrels be considered gentlemen.
⁶ Godless fools speak foolishness,
   and their minds plan evil
      in order to do ungodly things.
They speak falsely about the LORD.
They let people go hungry
   and withhold water from thirsty people.
⁷ The tricks of scoundrels are evil.
   They devise wicked plans in order to ruin poor people with lies,
      even when needy people plead for justice.
⁸ But honorable people act honorably
   and stand firm for what is honorable.

⁹ Get up, and listen to me, you pampered women.
Hear what I say, you overconfident daughters.
¹⁰ In a little less than a year
      you overconfident women will tremble,
         because the grape harvest will fail
            and no fruit will be brought in ⌊from the fields⌋.
¹¹ Shudder, you pampered women.
Tremble, you overconfident women.
Take off your clothes, walk around naked,
   and wear sackcloth around your waists.
¹² Beat your breasts as you mourn for the fields,
   for the vines bearing grapes.

Good Morning, God
Isaiah 32:8

When it comes to doing what's right, God wants us to be like steel that can't bend. Honorable people stand firm for the truth. Sometimes we start out to do what's right, but we are soon tempted to change our minds. We must be careful not to bend when we have the chance to stand for what is right.

God, give me courage to stand firm for what is right.

13 Mourn for my people's land where thorns and briars will grow.
Mourn for all the happy homes in a joyful city.

14 Palaces will be deserted.
Noisy cities will be abandoned.
Fortresses and watchtowers will become permanent caves.
They will be a delight for wild donkeys and pastures for flocks

15 until the Spirit is poured on us from on high.
Then the wilderness will be turned into a fertile field,
and the fertile field will be considered a forest.

16 Then justice will live in the wilderness,
and righteousness will be at home in the fertile field.

17 Then an act of righteousness will bring about peace,
calm, and safety forever.

18 My people will live in a peaceful place,
in safe homes and quiet places of rest.

19 The forest will be flattened because of hail,
and the city will be completely leveled.

20 Blessed are those who plant beside every stream
and those who let oxen and donkeys roam freely.

The LORD Will Rescue Jerusalem From Assyria

33

1 How horrible it will be for you, you destroyer,
although you haven't been destroyed.
How horrible it will be for you, you traitor,
although you haven't been betrayed.
When you've finished destroying, you will be destroyed.
When you've finished being a traitor, you will be betrayed.

2 O LORD, have pity on us.
We wait with hope for you.
Be our strength in the morning.
Yes, be our savior in times of trouble.

3 People flee from the noise of ˌyourˌ army.
Nations scatter when you attack.

4 You nations, your loot is gathered as grasshoppers harvest a crop.
Like swarming locusts, people rush for your loot.

5 The LORD is honored because he lives on high.
He will fill Zion with justice and righteousness.

6 He will be the foundation of your future.
The riches of salvation are wisdom and knowledge.
The fear of the LORD is ˌyourˌ treasure.

7 Heroes cry in the streets.
Messengers of peace cry bitterly.

8 Highways are deserted.
Travelers stop traveling.
Agreements are broken.
Witnesses[a] are rejected.
People are no longer respected.

---

a 33:8 Dead Sea Scrolls; Masoretic Text "Cities."

9 The country grieves and wastes away.
  Lebanon is ashamed and is decaying.
  Sharon has become like a wilderness.
  Bashan and Carmel are shaken.

10 The LORD says, "Now I will arise.
   Now I will get up.
   Now I will be lifted up."
11 You will be pregnant with hay.
   You will give birth to straw.
   Your breath will be a fire which will burn you up.
12 People will be cremated.
   They will be set on fire like dry thornbushes.

13 Hear what I have done, you people who are far away!
   Acknowledge my might, you people who are near!
14 The sinners in Zion are terrified.
   Trembling seizes the ungodly.
   Can any of us live through a fire that destroys?
   Can any of us live through a fire that burns forever?
15 The person who does what is right and speaks the truth will live.
   He rejects getting rich by extortion and refuses to take bribes.
   He refuses to listen to those who are plotting murders.
   He doesn't look for evil things to do.
16 This person will live on high.
   His stronghold will be a fortress made of rock.
   He will have plenty of food
   and a dependable supply of water.

17 Your eyes will see how handsome the king is.
   You will see a land that stretches into the distance.
18 Your mind will be thinking of the terrors in the past.
   Where are the scribes?
   Where are the tax collectors?
   Where are those who counted the towers?
19 You will no longer see those savage people,
   those people with an unrecognizable language,
   with a foreign language that you can't understand.
20 Look at Zion, the city of our festivals.
   Your eyes will see Jerusalem as a peaceful place.
   It is a tent that can't be moved.
   Its tent pegs will never be pulled out,
   and none of its ropes will be broken.
21 The LORD will be our mighty defender
   in a place surrounded by wide rivers and streams.
   Ships with oars won't travel on them.
   Stately ships won't sail on them.
22 The LORD is our judge.
   The LORD is our lawgiver.
   The LORD is our king.
   The LORD is our savior.

23   Your ropes hang loose,
         your mast isn't secure,
            and your sail isn't spread out.
      A large amount of loot will be distributed.
      Lame people will carry off your loot.
24   No one who lives in Zion will say, "I'm sick."
      The sins of its inhabitants will be forgiven.

The Fall of Edom Is a Glimpse of the LORD's Judgment

34 ¹ Come close, you nations, and listen.
         Pay attention, you people.
            The earth, everyone in it,
               the world, and everything on it will listen.
2   The LORD is angry with all the nations.
      He is furious with all their armies.
         He has claimed them for destruction.
         He has handed them over to be slaughtered.
3   Their dead bodies will be thrown out.
            A stench will rise from their corpses.
               Mountains will be red with their blood.
4   All the stars in the sky will rot.
      The heavens will be rolled up like a scroll.
      The stars will fall
         like leaves from a grapevine,
         like green figs from a fig tree.
5   When my sword is covered with blood in the heavens,
         it will fall on Edom
            and on the people I've claimed for destruction.
6   The LORD's sword is covered with blood.
      It is covered with fat,
         with the blood of lambs and goats,
         with the fat of rams' kidneys.
      The LORD will receive a sacrifice in Bozrah,
         a huge slaughter in the land of Edom.
7   Wild oxen will be killed with them,
         young bulls along with rams.
      Their land will be drenched with blood.
      Their dust will be covered with fat.

8   The LORD will have a day of vengeance,
         a year of revenge in defense of Zion.
9   Edom's streams will be turned to tar.
         Its soil will be turned to burning sulfur.
         Its land will become blazing tar.
10   They will not be extinguished day or night,
            and smoke will always go up from them.
      Edom will lie in ruins for generations.
         No one will ever travel through it.
11   Pelicans and herons will take possession of the land.
            Owls and crows will live there.

He will stretch the measuring line of chaos
and the plumb line of destruction over it.
12 There are no nobles to rule a kingdom.
All of its princes have disappeared.
13 Its palaces are covered with thorns.
Its fortresses have nettles and thistles.
It will become a home for jackals
and a place for ostriches.
14 Hyenas will meet with jackals.
Male goats will call to their mates.
Screech owls will rest there
and find a resting place for themselves.
15 Owls will make their nests there, lay eggs, and hatch them.
They will gather their young
in the shadow of their wings.
Vultures also will gather there,
each one with its mate.

16 Search the LORD's book, and read it.
Not one of these animals will be missing.
Not one will lack a mate,
because the LORD has commanded it,
and his Spirit will gather them together.
17 He is the one who throws dice for them,
and his hand divides up the land for them with a measuring line.
They will possess it permanently
and live there for generations.

The LORD's People Will Have Joy

1 The desert and the dry land will be glad,
and the wilderness will rejoice and blossom.
2 Like a lily the land will blossom.
It will rejoice and sing with joy.
It will have the glory of Lebanon, the majesty of Carmel and Sharon.
Everyone will see the glory of the LORD, the majesty of our God.

3 Strengthen limp hands.
Steady weak knees.
4 Tell those who are terrified,
"Be brave; don't be afraid.
Your God will come with vengeance, with divine revenge.
He will come and rescue you."

5 Then the eyes of the blind will be opened,
and the ears of the deaf will be unplugged.
6 Then those who are lame will leap like deer,
and those who cannot speak will shout for joy.
Water will gush out into the desert,
and streams will gush out into the wilderness.
7 Then the hot sand will become a pool,
and dry ground will have springs.

Grass will become cattails and rushes
    in the home of jackals.
8   A highway will be there, a roadway.
    It will be called the Holy Road.
        Sinners won't travel on it.
    It will be for those who walk on it.
        Godless fools won't wander onto it.
9   Lions won't be there.
    Wild animals won't go on it.
        They won't be found there.
    But the people reclaimed by the LORD will walk on it.
10   The people ransomed by the LORD will return.
        They will come to Zion singing with joy.
            Everlasting happiness will be on their heads as a crown.
            They will be glad and joyful.
            They will have no sorrow or grief.

The LORD Rescues Judah From the Assyrians—
2 Kings 18:13–19:19

36 ¹In Hezekiah's fourteenth year as king, King Sennacherib of Assyria attacked all the fortified cities of Judah and captured them. ²Then the king of Assyria sent his field commander with a large army from Lachish to King Hezekiah at Jerusalem. He stood at the channel for the Upper Pool on the road to Laundryman's Field.

³Eliakim, who was in charge of the palace and was the son of Hilkiah, Shebna the scribe, and Joah, who was the royal historian and the son of Asaph, went out to the field commander. ⁴He said to them, "Tell Hezekiah, 'This is what the great king, the king of Assyria, says: What makes you so confident? ⁵You give useless advice about getting ready for war. Whom, then, do you trust for support in your rebellion against me? ⁶Look! When you trust Egypt, you're trusting a broken stick for a staff. If you lean on it, it stabs your hand and goes through it. This is what Pharaoh (the king of Egypt) is like for everyone who trusts him. ⁷Suppose you tell me, "We're trusting the LORD our God." He's the god whose places of worship and altars Hezekiah got rid of. Hezekiah told Judah and Jerusalem, "Worship at this altar." '

⁸"Now, make a deal with my master, the king of Assyria. I'll give you 2,000 horses if you can put riders on them. ⁹How can you defeat my master's lowest-ranking officers when you trust Egypt for chariots and horses?

¹⁰"Have I come to destroy this country without the LORD on my side? The LORD said to me, 'Attack this country, and destroy it.' "

¹¹Then Eliakim, Shebna, and Joah said to the field commander, "Speak to us in Aramaic, since we understand it. Don't speak to us in the Judean language as long as there are people on the wall listening."

¹²But the field commander asked, "Did my master send me to tell these things only to you and your master? Didn't he send me to the men sitting on the wall who will have to eat their own excrement and drink their own urine with you?"

¹³Then the field commander stood and shouted loudly in the Judean language, "Listen to the great king, the king of Assyria. ¹⁴This is what the king says: Don't let Hezekiah deceive you. He can't rescue you. ¹⁵Don't let Hezekiah get you to trust the LORD by saying, 'The LORD will certainly rescue us, and this city will not be put under the control of the king of Assyria.' ¹⁶Don't listen to Hezekiah, because this is what the king of Assyria says: Make peace with me! Come out, and give yourselves up to

me! Everyone will eat from his own grapevine and fig tree and drink from his own cistern. ¹⁷Then I will come and take you away to a country like your own. It's a country with grain and new wine, a country with bread and vineyards. ¹⁸Don't let Hezekiah mislead you by saying to you, 'The Lord will rescue us.' Did any of the gods of the nations rescue their countries from the king of Assyria? ¹⁹Where are the gods of Hamath and Arpad? Where are the gods of Sepharvaim? Did they rescue Samaria from my control? ²⁰Did the gods of these countries rescue them from my control? Could the Lord then rescue Jerusalem from my control?' "

²¹They were silent and didn't say anything to him because the king commanded them not to answer him.

²²Then Eliakim, who was in charge of the palace and was son of Hilkiah, Shebna the scribe, and Joah, who was the royal historian and the son of Asaph, went to Hezekiah with their clothes torn in grief. They told him the message from the field commander.

37 ¹When King Hezekiah heard the message, he tore his clothes in grief, covered himself with sackcloth, and went into the Lord's temple. ²Then he sent Eliakim, who was in charge of the palace, Shebna the scribe, and the leaders of the priests, clothed in sackcloth, to the prophet Isaiah, son of Amoz.

³They said to him, "This is what Hezekiah says: Today is a day filled with misery, punishment, and disgrace. We are like a woman who is about to give birth but doesn't have the strength to do it. ⁴The Lord your God may have heard the words of the field commander. His master, the king of Assyria, sent him to defy the living God. The Lord your God may punish him because of the message that the Lord your God heard. Pray for the few people who are left."

⁵So King Hezekiah's men went to Isaiah. ⁶Isaiah answered them, "Say this to your master, 'This is what the Lord says: Don't be afraid of the message that you heard when the Assyrian king's assistants slandered me. ⁷I'm going to put a spirit in him so that he will hear a rumor and return to his own country. I'll have him assassinated in his own country.' "

⁸The field commander returned and found the king of Assyria fighting against Libnah. He had heard that the king left Lachish. ⁹Now, Sennacherib heard that King Tirhakah of Sudan was coming to fight him.

When he heard this, he again sent messengers to Hezekiah, saying, ¹⁰"Tell King Hezekiah of Judah, 'Don't let the god whom you trust deceive you by saying that Jerusalem will not be put under the control of the king of Assyria. ¹¹You heard what the kings of Assyria did to all countries, how they totally destroyed them. Will you be rescued? ¹²Did the gods of the nations which my ancestors destroyed rescue Gozan, Haran, Rezeph, and the people of Eden who were in Telassar? ¹³Where is the king of Hamath, the king of Arpad, and the king of the cities of Sepharvaim, Hena, and Ivvah?' "

¹⁴Hezekiah took the letter from the messengers, read it, and went to the Lord's temple. He spread it out in front of the Lord ¹⁵and prayed to the Lord, ¹⁶"Lord of Armies, God of Israel, you are enthroned over the angels.ᵃ You alone are God of the kingdoms of the world. You made heaven and earth. ¹⁷Turn your ear toward me, Lord, and listen. Open your eyes, Lord, and see. Listen to the entire message that Sennacherib sent to defy the living God. ¹⁸It is true, Lord, that the kings of Assyria have leveled every country.ᵇ ¹⁹They have thrown the gods from these countries into fires because these gods aren't real gods. They're only wooden and stone statues made by human hands. So the Assyrians have destroyed them. ²⁰Now, Lord our God, rescue

---

ᵃ37:16 Or "cherubim."   ᵇ37:18 Dead Sea Scrolls, Greek; Masoretic Text "every country and their country."

us from Assyria's control so that all the kingdoms on earth will know that you alone are the LORD."

Isaiah's Prophecy Against King Sennacherib of Assyria—
2 Kings 19:20-37

²¹Then Isaiah, son of Amoz, sent a message to Hezekiah, "This is what the LORD God of Israel says: You prayed to me about King Sennacherib of Assyria. ²²This is the message that the LORD speaks to him,

'My dear people in Zion despise you and laugh at you.
My people in Jerusalem shake their heads behind your back.
23   Whom are you defying and slandering?
          Against whom are you shouting?
            Who are you looking at so arrogantly?
            It is the Holy One of Israel!
24   Through your servants you defy the Lord and say,
        "With my many chariots I'll ride up the high mountains,
          up the slopes of Lebanon.
            I'll cut down its tallest cedars and its finest cypresses.
            I'll come to its most distant heights
              and its most fertile forests.
25   I'll dig wells and drink water.
            I'll dry up all the streams of Egypt
              with the trampling of my feet."

26   " 'Haven't you heard? I did this long ago.
        I planned it in the distant past.
          Now I make it happen so that you will turn fortified cities
            into piles of rubble.
27   Those who live in these cities are weak, discouraged, and ashamed.
      They will be like plants in the field,
          like fresh, green grass on the roofs,
          dried up by the east wind.
28   I know when you get up and sit down,
        when you go out and come in,
          and how you rage against me.
29   Since you rage against me and your boasting has reached my ears,

Good Morning, God
Isaiah 37:16-19

Some people believe that everyone worships the same god—people just know him by different names. But the Bible says that there is only one true God. He alone made the heavens and earth. Other gods are made by people. But our God created everything. He alone is worthy to be called "God."

God, you are awesome!

I will put my hook in your nose
    and my bridle in your mouth.
I will make you go back the way you came.

³⁰" 'And this will be a sign for you, Hezekiah: You will eat what grows by itself this year, and the next year you will eat what comes up by itself. But in the third year you will plant and harvest, plant vineyards, and eat what is produced. ³¹Those few people from the nation of Judah who escape will again take root and produce crops. ³²Those few people will go out from Jerusalem, and those who escape will go out from Mount Zion. The LORD of Armies is determined to do this.'

³³"This is what the LORD says about the king of Assyria:

He will never come into this city,
    shoot an arrow here,
    hold a shield in front of it,
        or put up dirt ramps to attack it.
³⁴ He will go back the way he came,
    and he won't come into this city,"
        declares the LORD of Armies.
³⁵ "I will shield this city to rescue it for my sake
    and for the sake of my servant David."

³⁶The LORD's angel went out and killed 185,000 ₍soldiers₎ in the Assyrian camp. When the Judeans got up early in the morning, they saw all the corpses.
³⁷Then King Sennacherib of Assyria left. He went home to Nineveh and stayed there. ³⁸While he was worshiping in the temple of his god Nisroch, Adrammelech and Sharezer, his sons, assassinated him and escaped to the land of Ararat. His son Esarhaddon succeeded him as king.

Hezekiah's Illness—
2 Kings 20:1-11; 2 Chronicles 32:24

38 ¹In those days Hezekiah became sick and was about to die. The prophet Isaiah, son of Amoz, came to him and said, "This is what the LORD says: Give final instructions to your household, because you're about to die. You won't get well."

²Hezekiah turned to the wall and prayed to the LORD. ³"Please, LORD, remember how I've lived faithfully and sincerely in your presence. I've done what you consider right." And he cried bitterly.

⁴Then the LORD spoke his word to Isaiah, ⁵"Go and say to Hezekiah, 'This is what the LORD God of your ancestor David says: I've heard your prayer. I've seen your tears. I'm going to give you 15 more years to live. ⁶I'll rescue you and defend this city from the control of the king of Assyria.' "

²¹Then Isaiah said, "Take a fig cake, and place it over the boil so that the king will get well."

²²Hezekiah asked, "What is the sign that I'll go to the LORD's temple?"ᵃ

⁷Isaiah said, "This is your sign from the LORD that he will do what he promises. ⁸The sun made a shadow that went down the stairway of Ahaz's upper palace. I'm going to make the shadow go back ten steps." So the sun on the stairway went back up the ten steps it had gone down.

⁹King Hezekiah of Judah wrote this after he was sick and became well again:

ᵃ38:22 Verses 21 and 22 have been placed after verse 6 to express the complex Hebrew paragraph structure more clearly in English. See 2 Kings 20:6-9.

10 I thought that in the prime of my life
        I would go down to the gates of Sheol
            and be robbed of the rest of my life.
11 I thought that I wouldn't see the LORD in this world.
    Even with all the people in the world,
        I thought I would never see another person.
12 My life was over.
        You rolled it up like a shepherd's tent.
        You rolled up my life like a weaver.
        You cut me off from the loom.
            You ended my life in one day.
13 I cried out until morning
        as if a lion had crushed all my bones.
        You ended my life in one day.
14 I chirped like swallows and cranes.
    I cooed like doves.
    My eyes were tired from looking up to heaven.
        I've suffered miserably, O Lord!
            Please help me!

15 What can I say now that he has spoken to me?
    He has done this.
    I will be careful the rest of my life because of my bitter experience.*b*
16 Lord, people live in spite of such things,
        and I have the will to live in spite of them.
    You give me health and keep me alive.
17 Now my bitter experience turns into peace.
    You have saved me and kept me from the rotting pit.
        You have thrown all my sins behind you.
18 Sheol doesn't thank you!
    Death doesn't praise you!
        Those who go down to the pit cannot expect you to be faithful.
19 Those who are living praise you as I do today.
    Fathers make your faithfulness known to their children.
20 The LORD is going to rescue me,
        so let us play stringed instruments.
        We live our lives in the LORD's temple.

Hezekiah Shows the Babylonians His Treasures—
2 Kings 20:12-19; 2 Chronicles 32:31-33

39 ¹At that time Baladan's son, King Merodach Baladan of Babylon, sent letters and a present to Hezekiah. He had heard that Hezekiah had been sick and had recovered. ²Hezekiah was so happy with them that he showed the messengers his warehouse: the silver, gold, balsam, fine olive oil, his entire armory, and everything in his treasury. Hezekiah showed them everything in his palace and every corner of his kingdom.

³Then the prophet Isaiah came to King Hezekiah and asked, "What did these men say? And where did they come from?"

Hezekiah answered, "They came to me from the distant country of Babylon."

---

*b*38:15 Hebrew meaning of this line uncertain.

⁴Isaiah asked, "What did they see in your palace?"

Hezekiah answered, "They saw everything in my palace, and I showed them everything in my treasury."

⁵Isaiah said to Hezekiah, "Hear the word of the Lord of Armies! ⁶The Lord says, 'The days are going to come when everything in your palace, everything your ancestors have stored up to this day, will be taken away to Babylon. Nothing will be left. ⁷Some of your own descendants will be taken away. They will become officials in the palace of the king of Babylon.' "

⁸Hezekiah said to Isaiah, "The Lord's word that you have spoken is good." He added, "Just let there be peace and security as long as I live."

Comfort My People

40 ¹ "Comfort my people! Comfort them!" says your God.
² "Speak tenderly to Jerusalem and announce to it
    that its time of hard labor is over
    and its wrongs have been paid for.
    It has received from the Lord double for all its sins."

³A voice cries out in the desert:

"Clear a way for the Lord.
Make a straight highway in the wilderness for our God.
⁴   Every valley will be raised.
    Every mountain and hill will be lowered.
    Steep places will be made level.
    Rough places will be made smooth.
⁵   Then the Lord's glory will be revealed
        and all people will see it together.
        The Lord has spoken."

⁶A voice called, "Call out!"
I asked, "What should I call out?"

"Call out: All people are like grass,
    and all their beauty is like a flower in the field.
⁷   Grass dries up,
        and flowers wither when the Lord's breath blows on them.
        Yes, people are like grass.
⁸   Grass dries up,
        and flowers wither,
        but the word of our God will last forever."

⁹   Go up a high mountain, Zion.
        Tell the good news!
    Call out with a loud voice, Jerusalem.
        Tell the good news!
    Raise your voice without fear.
        Tell the cities of Judah:
        "Here is your God!"

¹⁰   The Almighty Lord is coming with power
        to rule with authority.
        His reward is with him,

and the people he has won arrive ahead of him.
11 Like a shepherd he takes care of his flock.
    He gathers the lambs in his arms.
    He carries them in his arms.
    He gently helps the sheep and their lambs.

God Gives Strength to Those Who Depend on Him

12 Who has measured the water of the sea[a] with the palm of his hand
    or measured the sky with the length of his hand?
Who has held the dust of the earth in a bushel basket
    or weighed the mountains on a scale and the hills on a balance?
13 Who has directed the Spirit of the LORD
    or instructed him as his adviser?
14   Whom did he consult?
    Who gave him understanding?
    Who taught him the right way?
    Who taught him knowledge?
    Who informed him about the way to understanding?

15 The nations are like a drop in a bucket
    and are considered to be like dust on a scale.
The weight of the islands is like fine dust.
16 All the trees in Lebanon are not enough to burn an offering.
    Its wild animals are not enough for a single burnt offering.
17 All the nations amount to nothing in his presence.
    He considers them less than nothing and worthless.
18 To whom, then, can you compare God?
To what statue can you compare him?

19 Craftsmen make idols.
    Goldsmiths cover them with gold.
        Silversmiths make silver chains for them.
20 The poorest people choose wood that will not rot
    and search out skillful craftsmen
        to set up idols that will not fall over.
21 Don't you know?
    Haven't you heard?
        Haven't you been told from the beginning?
        Don't you understand the foundations of the earth?
22 God is enthroned above the earth,
    and those who live on it are like grasshoppers.
He stretches out the sky like a canopy
    and spreads it out like a tent to live in.
23 He makes rulers unimportant
    and makes earthly judges worth nothing.
24 They have hardly been planted.
They have hardly been sown.
They have hardly taken root in the ground.
    Then he blows on them and they wither,
        and a windstorm sweeps them away like straw.

---

[a] 40:12 Dead Sea Scrolls; Masoretic Text "Who has measured the water."

²⁵ "To whom, then, can you compare me?
Who is my equal?" asks the Holy One.

²⁶ Look at the sky and see.
Who created these things?
Who brings out the stars one by one?
He calls them all by name.
Because of the greatness of his might and the strength of his power,
not one of them is missing.

²⁷ Jacob, why do you complain?
Israel, why do you say,
"My way is hidden from the LORD,
and my rights are ignored by my God"?

²⁸ Don't you know?
Haven't you heard?
The eternal God, the LORD, the Creator of the ends of the earth,
doesn't grow tired or become weary.
His understanding is beyond reach.

²⁹ He gives strength to those who grow tired
and increases the strength of those who are weak.

³⁰ Even young people grow tired and become weary,
and young men will stumble and fall.

³¹ Yet, the strength of those who wait with hope in the LORD
will be renewed.
They will soar on wings like eagles.
They will run and won't become weary.
They will walk and won't grow tired.

The Nations Chose Idols, but the LORD Chose Israel

41 ¹ "Be silent and listen to me, you coastlands.
Let the people gain new strength.
Let them come near and speak.
Let us come together for judgment.

² "Who has raised up from the east
someone to whom the LORD gives victory with every step he takes?

Good Morning, God
Isaiah 40:28-31

Have you ever been so tired that you felt like you couldn't go on? When was the last time you wondered if God was really listening to your prayers? Isaiah 40 tells us that God understands when we feel discouraged and defeated. He will give us the strength to keep going. We must simply trust him to do so. When you're feeling down, remember God can make you soar high like an eagle.

Thank you, Lord, for strength to keep going when the going gets rough.

Nations are handed over to him.
He defeats kings.
With his sword he turns them into dust.
With his bow he turns them into straw blown by the wind.

3   He chases them, marching by safely
on a path his feet have never traveled before.

4 Who has accomplished this?
Who has determined the course of history from the beginning?
I, the LORD, was there first, and I will be there to the end.
I am the one!"

5 The coastlands have seen him and are afraid.
The ends of the earth tremble.
They have come near and gathered together.

6 People help their neighbors
and say to their relatives, "Be brave!"

7 Craftsmen encourage goldsmiths.
Metalsmiths encourage blacksmiths who work at their anvils.
They say that their soldering is good.
And they fasten things with nails so they won't move.

8 "But you are my servant Israel,
Jacob, whom I have chosen,
the descendant of Abraham, my dear friend.

9 I have taken you from the ends of the earth
and called you from its most distant places.
I said to you, 'You are my servant.
I've chosen you; I haven't rejected you.'

10 Don't be afraid, because I am with you.
Don't be intimidated; I am your God.
I will strengthen you.
I will help you.
I will support you with my victorious right hand.

11 "Everyone who is angry with you
will be ashamed and disgraced.
Those who oppose you
will be reduced to nothing and disappear.

12 You will search for your enemies,
but you will not find them.
Those who are at war with you
will be reduced to nothing and no longer exist.

13 I, the LORD your God, hold your right hand
and say to you, 'Don't be afraid; I will help you.'

14 Don't be afraid, Jacob, you worm.
You people of Israel, I will help you,"
declares the LORD, your Defender, the Holy One of Israel.

15 "I am going to make you into a new threshing*a* sledge
with sharp, double-edged teeth.
You will thresh the mountains and crush them to dust.

---

a 41:15 Threshing is the process of beating stalks to separate them from the grain.

You will turn the hills into straw.
¹⁶ You will winnow^b them.
   The wind will carry them away.
   The windstorm will scatter them.
But you will find joy in the L<small>ORD</small>
   and praise the Holy One of Israel.

¹⁷ "The poor and needy are looking for water, but there is none.
   Their tongues are parched with thirst.
I, the L<small>ORD</small>, will answer them.
I, the God of Israel, will not abandon them.
¹⁸ I will make rivers flow on bare hilltops.
   I will make springs flow through valleys.
      I will turn deserts into lakes.
      I will turn dry land into springs.
¹⁹ I will plant cedar, acacia, myrtle, and wild olive trees in the desert.
   I will place cedar, fir, and cypress trees together in the wilderness.
²⁰ People will see and know.
Together they will consider and understand
   that the L<small>ORD</small>'s power has done this,
   that the Holy One of Israel has created it.

²¹ "Present your case," says the L<small>ORD</small>.
   "Bring forward your best arguments," says Jacob's king.
²² "Bring ˻ your idols ˼ so they can tell us what's going to happen.
   Explain past events that your idols told you about
      so that we may consider them
         and know what their outcome will be.
            Tell us about future events.
²³ Tell us what's going to happen
      so that we may know that you are gods.
   Yes, do something, good or evil,
      to intimidate us and make us afraid.
²⁴ You are nothing!
You can't do anything!
   Whoever chooses you is disgusting.

²⁵ "I have raised up someone from the north, and he has come.
   He will call on my name from the east.
   He will attack rulers as if they were mud,
      as if he were treading on clay like a potter.
²⁶ Who revealed this from the beginning so that we could know it?
Who revealed this from the past so that we could say that he was right?
   No one revealed it.
   No one announced it.
   No one heard your words.
²⁷ I was the first to tell Zion, 'Look, here they are.'
I gave Jerusalem a messenger with the good news.
²⁸ When I look, there is no one.
   There is no one to advise them.

---

^b41:16 Winnowing is the process of separating husks from grain.

When I ask them a question,
   will they give an answer?
29 All of them are nothing.*c*
   They can't do anything.
   Their statues are nothing but air."

The LORD's Servant Will Bring Righteousness to the World

42
1 Here is my servant, whom I support.
   Here is my chosen one, with whom I am pleased.
   I have put my Spirit on him.
     He will bring justice to the nations.
2 He will not cry out or raise his voice.
   He will not make his voice heard in the streets.
3 He will not break off a damaged cattail.
   He will not even put out a smoking wick.
   He will faithfully bring about justice.
4 He will not be discouraged or crushed
   until he has set up justice on the earth.
   The coastlands will wait for his teachings.

5 The LORD God created the heavens and stretched them out.
   He shaped the earth and all that comes from it.
   He gave life to the people who are on it
   and breath to those who walk on it.

This is what the LORD God says:

6 I, the LORD, have called you to do what is right.
   I will take hold of your hand.
   I will protect you.
   I will appoint you as my promise*ᵃ* to the people,
   as my light to the nations.
7   You will give sight to the blind,
     bring prisoners out of prisons,
      and bring those who live in darkness
      out of dungeons.
8 I am the LORD; that is my name.
   I will not give my glory to anyone else
   or the praise I deserve to idols.
9 What I said in the past has come true.
   I will reveal new things before they happen.

A Song About the LORD, the Warrior

10 Sing a new song to the LORD.
   Sing his praise from the ends of the earth,
     you people who sail on the seas
     and all the creatures that live in them,
     you coastlands and all who live on them.
11 Let those who live in the desert and its cities raise their voices.
   Let those who live in the settlements of Kedar praise him.

---

*c*41:29 Dead Sea Scrolls, Syriac, Targum; Masoretic Text "They are false." *ᵃ*42:6 Or "covenant."

Let those who live in Sela sing for joy.
Let them shout from the tops of the mountains.
12   Let them give glory to the LORD
and announce his praise on the coastlands.
13 The LORD marches out like a warrior.
He prepares himself for battle like a soldier.
He shouts, gives the battle cry, and overpowers his enemies.

14 I have been silent for a long time.
I kept quiet and held myself back.
But like a woman in childbirth I will cry out.
    I will gasp and pant.
15 I will lay waste to mountains and hills.
I will dry up all their vegetation.
I will turn rivers into islands.
I will dry up ponds.
16 I will lead the blind on unfamiliar roads.
I will lead them on unfamiliar paths.
I will turn darkness into light in front of them.
I will make rough places smooth.
    These are the things I will do for them,
    and I will never abandon them.
17   Then those who trust idols
      and those who say to statues,
        "You are our gods"
        will be turned away and put to shame.

The LORD Will Bring Israel Home

18 Listen, you deaf people.
Look, you blind people, so that you can see.
19 Who is blind except my servant
    or deaf like the messenger I send?
Who is blind like the one who has my trust
    or blind like the servant of the LORD?
20 You have seen much, but you do not observe anything.
Your ears are open, but you hear nothing.
21 The LORD is pleased because he does what is right.
He praises the greatness of his teachings and makes them glorious.
22   But these people are robbed and looted.
    They are all trapped in pits and hidden in prisons.
    They have become prey with no one to rescue them.
    They have become loot with no one to say, "Give it back."
23 Who among you will listen to this?
Is there anyone who will pay attention and listen in the future?
24 Who gave Jacob away as loot
    and handed Israel over to robbers?
Wasn't it the LORD, against whom we have sinned?
    They didn't want to live his way.
    They didn't obey his teachings.
25 So he poured out his burning anger and the horrors of war on them.

It engulfed them in flames, but they did not understand.
It burned them, but they did not take it to heart.

43 ¹The LORD created Jacob and formed Israel. Now, this is what the LORD says:

Do not be afraid, because I have reclaimed you.
I have called you by name; you are mine.

2   When you go through the sea, I am with you.
When you go through rivers, they will not sweep you away.
When you walk through fire, you will not be burned,
and the flames will not harm you.

3   I am the LORD your God, the Holy One of Israel, your Savior.
Egypt is the ransom I exchanged for you.
Sudan and Seba are the price I paid for you.

4   Since you are precious to me, you are honored and I love you.
I will exchange others for you.
Nations will be the price I pay for your life.

5   Do not be afraid, because I am with you.
I will bring your descendants from the east
and gather you from the west.

6   I will say to the north, "Give them up,"
and to the south, "Do not keep them."
Bring my sons from far away
and my daughters from the ends of the earth.

7   Bring everyone who is called by my name,
whom I created for my glory,
whom I formed and made.

8   Bring the people who are blind but still have eyes,
the people who are deaf but still have ears.

9   All nations have gathered together, and people have assembled.
Who among them could have revealed this?
Who among them could have foretold this to us?
They should bring their witnesses to prove that they were right.
Let the people hear them. Then they will say that it is true.

10 "You are my witnesses," declares the LORD.
"I have chosen you as my servant
so that you can know and believe in me
and understand that I am the one ˌwho did thisˌ.
No god was formed before me,
and there will be none after me.

11 I alone am the LORD,
and there is no savior except me.

12 I have revealed it to you, I have saved you,
and I have announced it to you.
There was no foreign ˌgodˌ among you.
You are my witnesses that I am God," declares the LORD.

13 "From the ˌfirstˌ day I was the one ˌwho did thisˌ.
No one can rescue people from my power.
When I do something, who can undo it?"

¹⁴This is what the L<small>ORD</small>, your Defender, the Holy One of Israel, says:

> For your sake I will send ˏan armyˎ to Babylon.
> I will bring back all the Babylonian refugees
>   in the ships that they take pride in.
> ¹⁵ I am the L<small>ORD</small>, your Holy One,
> the Creator of Israel, your King.

Despite the People of Israel's Past Sin, the L<small>ORD</small> Will Forgive Them

> ¹⁶ The L<small>ORD</small> makes a path through the sea
> and a road through the strong currents.
> ¹⁷ He leads chariots and horses, an army and reinforcements.
> (They lie down together and do not get up ˏagainˎ.
> They are extinguished and snuffed out like a wick.)

This is what the L<small>ORD</small> says:

> ¹⁸ Forget what happened in the past,
> and do not dwell on events from long ago.
> ¹⁹ I am going to do something new.
> It is already happening. Don't you recognize it?
>   I will clear a way in the desert.
>   I will make rivers on dry land.
> ²⁰ Wild animals, jackals, and ostriches will honor me.
> I will provide water in the desert.
> I will make rivers on the dry land for my chosen people to drink.
> ²¹ I have formed these people for myself.
> They will praise me.

> ²² Jacob, you have not prayed to me.
> Israel, you have grown tired of me.
> ²³ You did not bring me sheep for your burnt offerings
> or honor me with your sacrifices.
> I did not burden you by requiring grain offerings
>   or trouble you by requiring incense offerings.
> ²⁴ You did not buy me any sugar cane with ˏyourˎ money
> or satisfy me with the best part of your sacrifices.
> Rather, you burdened me with your sins
>   and troubled me with your wrongdoings.

> ²⁵ I alone am the one who is going to wipe away your rebellious actions
> for my own sake.
>   I will not remember your sins ˏanymoreˎ.
> ²⁶ Remind me ˏof what happenedˎ.
> Let us argue our case together.
>   State your case so that you can prove you are right.
> ²⁷ Your first ancestor sinned,
> and your priests rebelled against me.
> ²⁸ That is why I will corrupt the leaders of the holy place.
> I will claim Jacob for destruction.
> I will set up Israel for ridicule.

Idolatry / *Isaiah 44*

Pagan women worshiped goddesses like Asherah, who is symbolized by a wooden pole. But how could a wooden pole help anyone? Our God is real and powerful. He is the only one worthy of being worshiped. Idols made by human hands have no power to help or to save people.

44 ¹ But now listen, my servant Jacob,
     Israel, whom I have chosen.
² The LORD made you, formed you in the womb, and will help you.

This is what the LORD says:

     Don't be afraid, my servant Jacob,
        Jeshurun,ᵃ whom I have chosen.
³ I will pour water on thirsty ground and rain on dry land.
     I will pour my Spirit on your offspring
        and my blessing on your descendants.
⁴ They will spring up with the grass
        as poplars spring up by streams.
⁵ One person will say, "I belong to the LORD."
     Another will call on the name of Jacob.
        Another will write on his hand, "The LORD's,"
           and he will adopt the name of Israel.

The Nations Form Idols, but the LORD Formed Israel

⁶ The LORD is Israel's king and defender.
     He is the LORD of Armies.

This is what the LORD says:

     I am the first and the last,
        and there is no God except me.
⁷ If there is anyone like me, let him say so.
     Let him tell me what happened
        when I established my people long ago.
     Then let him predict what will happen to them.
⁸ Don't be terrified or afraid.

ᵃ44:2 "Jeshurun" is another name for Israel.

Didn't I make this known to you long ago?
     You are my witnesses.
          Is there any God except me?
               There is no ,other, rock; I know of none.

⁹All who make idols are nothing. Their precious treasures are worthless. Their own witnesses do not see or know anything, so they will be put to shame. ¹⁰Nothing comes from making gods or casting metal idols. ¹¹Everyone associated with the gods will be put to shame. The craftsmen themselves are only human. Let them all get together and take their stand. They will be frightened and ashamed together.

¹²Blacksmiths shape iron into tools. They work them over the coals and shape them with hammers, working them with their strong arms. They get hungry, and their strength fails. If they don't drink water, they will faint.

¹³Carpenters measure blocks of wood with ,chalk, lines. They mark them with pens. They carve them with chisels and mark them with compasses. They carve them into forms of people, beautiful people, so the idols can live in shrines.

¹⁴They cut down cedars for themselves. Then they choose fir trees or oaks. They let them grow strong among the trees in the forest. Then they plant cedars, and the rain makes them grow. ¹⁵These trees become ,fuel, for people to burn. So they take some of them and warm themselves with them. They start fires and bake bread. They also make gods from these trees and worship them. They make them into carved statues and bow in front of them. ¹⁶Half of the wood they burn in the fire. Over this half they roast meat that they can eat until they are full. They also warm themselves and say, "Ah! We are warm. We can see the fire!" ¹⁷But the rest of the wood they make into gods, carved statues. They bow to them and worship them. They pray to them, saying, "Rescue us, because you are our gods."

¹⁸They don't know or understand anything. Their eyes are plastered shut, so they can't see. And their minds are closed, so they can't understand. ¹⁹No one stops to think. No one has enough knowledge or understanding to say, "I burned half of the wood in the fire. I also baked bread over its coals. I roasted meat and ate it. Now I am making the rest of the wood into a disgusting thing and bowing to a block of wood." ²⁰They eat ashes because they are deceived. Their own misguided minds lead them astray. They can't rescue themselves or ask themselves, "Isn't what I hold in my right hand a false god?"

21   Remember these things, Jacob:
          You are my servant, Israel.
               I formed you; you are my servant.
                    Israel, I will not forget you.
22   I made your rebellious acts disappear like a thick cloud
          and your sins like the morning mist.
     Come back to me, because I have reclaimed you.

23   Sing with joy, you heavens, because the Lord has done this.
     Rejoice, you deep places of the earth.
     Break into shouts of joy, you mountains,
          you forests and every tree in them.
               The Lord has reclaimed Jacob.
                    He will display his glory in Israel.

Through Cyrus the LORD Will Set Israel Free

24 The LORD reclaimed you.
    He formed you in the womb.

This is what the LORD says:

    I, the LORD, made everything.
    I stretched out the heavens by myself.
    I spread out the earth all alone.
25   I cause the signs of false prophets to fail
      and make fools of fortunetellers.
    I make wise men retreat
      and turn their knowledge into foolishness.

26 He confirms the word of his servant
      and fulfills the plan of his messengers.
    He says about Jerusalem, "It will be inhabited."
    He says about the cities of Judah, "They will be rebuilt."
    He says about their ruins, "I will restore them."
27 He says to the deep water, "Dry up."
    So I will dry up your rivers.
28 He says about Cyrus, "He is my shepherd.
    He will do everything I want him to do."
    He says about Jerusalem, "It will be rebuilt."
    He says about the temple, "Your foundation will be laid."

45 1 This is what the LORD says about Cyrus, his[a] anointed one:

    I have held him by his right hand
      so he could conquer the nations ahead of him,
        strip kings of their power,
          and open doors ahead of him
            so that the gates would not be shut.
2 I will go ahead of you, Cyrus, and smooth out the rough places.
    I will break down the bronze doors and cut through the iron bars.
3 I will give you treasures from dark places and hidden stockpiles.
    Then you will know that I, the LORD God of Israel,
      have called you by name.

4 For the sake of my servant Jacob,
    Israel, my chosen one,
      I have called you by name.
      I have given you a title of honor, although you don't know me.
5 I am the LORD, and there is no other.
    There is no other God besides me.
      I will strengthen you, although you don't know me,
6   so that from the east to the west people will know
          that there is no God except me.
    I am the LORD, and there is no other.
7 I make light and create darkness.

I make blessings and create disasters.
I, the Lord, do all these things.

8 Rain down from above, you heavens,
 and pour down righteousness, you skies.
  Let the earth open.
   Let salvation and righteousness sprout.
   Let them spring up.
 I, the Lord, have created them.

9 How horrible it will be for the one who quarrels with his maker.
 He is pottery among other earthenware pots.
  Does the clay ask the one who shapes it, "What are you making?"
  Does your work say to you, "There are no handles"?
10 How horrible it will be for the one
  who says to his father, "Why did you conceive me?"
  or to his mother, "Why did you go through labor pains for me?"

11 The Lord is the Holy One and the maker of Israel.

This is what the Lord says:

 Ask me about what is going to happen to my children!
 Are you going to give me orders concerning my handiwork?
12 I made the earth and created humans on it.
 I stretched out the heavens with my own hands.
 I commanded all the stars to shine.
13 I prepared Cyrus for my righteous purpose.
 I will make all his roads straight.
  He will build my city and let my exiles go free
   without any payment or any reward, says the Lord of Armies.

14This is what the Lord says:

 The products from Egypt, the merchandise from Sudan,
  and the important Sabaeans will come to you.
   They will belong to you.
   They will follow you.
   They will come to you in chains.
   They will bow to you and pray to you,
    "Certainly God is with you alone, and there is no other God."

15 Certainly, you are a God who has hidden himself.
 You are the God of Israel, the Savior!
16 Those who make idols will be ashamed and disgraced.
 They will go away completely disgraced.
17 Israel has been saved by the Lord forever.
 You will never again be ashamed or disgraced.
18 The Lord created the heavens.
 God formed the earth and made it.
 He set it up.
 He did not create it to be empty
  but formed it to be inhabited.

This is what the LORD says:

I am the LORD, and there is no other.
19 I haven't spoken privately or in some dark corner of the world.
I didn't say to Jacob's descendants,
"Search for me in vain!"
I, the LORD, speak what is fair and say what is right.

20 Come here, you refugees from the nations.
Ignorant people carry wooden idols
and pray to gods that cannot save anyone.
21 Speak and present your case. Yes, let them consult one another.
Who revealed this in the distant past and predicted it long ago?
Wasn't it I, the LORD?
There is no other God except me.
There is no other righteous God and Savior besides me.

22 Turn to me and be saved, all who live at the ends of the earth,
because I am God, and there is no other.
23 I have bound myself with an oath.
A word has gone out from my righteous mouth that will not be recalled,
"Every knee will bow to me
and every tongue will swear allegiance."
24 It will be said of me,
"Certainly, righteousness and strength are found in the LORD alone."

All who are angry with him will come to him and be ashamed.
25 All the descendants of Israel will be declared righteous,
and they will praise the LORD.

Babylon's Idols Will Go Into Captivity

46 1 The god Bel bows down; the god Nebo stoops low.
Their statues are seated on animals and cattle.
The gods that you carry are burdens, a load for weary people.
2 These gods stoop low and bow down together.
They aren't able to escape with heavy loads.
They go away into captivity.

3 Listen to me, descendants of Jacob,
the few people left of the nation of Israel.
I've carried you since your birth.
I've taken care of you from the time you were born.
4 Even when you're old, I'll take care of you.
Even when your hair turns gray, I'll support you.
I made you and will continue to care for you.
I'll support you and save you.

5 To whom will you compare me and make me equal?
To whom will you compare me so that we can be alike?

6 People pour gold out of their bags and weigh silver on scales.
They hire a goldsmith. He makes it into a god.
They bow down and worship it.

7   They lift it on their shoulders and carry it.
          They set the idol in its place, and it stands there.
               It doesn't move from its place.
               If they cry to it for help, it can't answer.
               It can't rescue them from their distress.

8   Remember this, and take courage.
          Recall your rebellious acts.
9   Remember the first events,
          because I am God, and there is no other.
               I am God, and there's no one like me.
10   From the beginning I revealed the end.
          From long ago I told you things that had not yet happened, saying,
               "My plan will stand, and I'll do everything I intended to do."
11   I will call a bird of prey from the east.
          I will call someone for my plan from a faraway land.
          I have spoken, and I will bring it about.
          I have planned it, and I will do it.
12   Listen to me, you stubborn people who are far from being righteous.
13   I'll bring my righteousness near; it isn't far away.
          My salvation will not be delayed.
               I'll provide salvation for Zion
               and bring my glory to Israel.

Babylon's Fall

47 ¹   Go, sit in the dirt,
               virgin princess of Babylon!
          Sit on the ground, not on a throne,
               princess of the Babylonians!
                    You will no longer be called soft and delicate.
2   Take millstones and grind flour.
          Remove your veil.
               Take off your skirt.
                    Uncover your legs, and cross the river.
3   People will see you naked.
          People will see your shame.
          I will take revenge.
          I won't spare anyone.

4   Our defender is the Holy One of Israel.
          His name is the LORD of Armies.

5   Go into the dark, and sit in silence,
          princess of the Babylonians!
               You will no longer be called the queen of kingdoms.
6   I was angry with my people.
          I dishonored those who belong to me.
          I put them under your control.
               You showed them no mercy.
               You placed a heavy burden on old people.
7   You said, "I will always be a queen."

> You didn't carefully consider these things
>   or keep in mind how they would end.

8   Now then, listen to this, you lover of pleasure.
>   You live securely and say to yourself,
>   "I'm the only one, and there's no one else.
>   I won't live as a widow.
>   I won't suffer the loss of children."

9   In one day both of these will happen to you instantly:
>   the loss of your children and your husband.
> All this will happen to you in spite of
>   your evil magic and your many spells.

10   You feel safe in your wickedness
>   and say, "No one can see me."
> Your wisdom and knowledge have led you astray,
>   so you say to yourself,
>   "I'm the only one, and there's no one else."

11   But evil will happen to you.
>   You won't know how to keep it away.
> Disaster will strike you.
>   You won't be able to stop it.
> Destruction will overtake you suddenly.
>   You won't expect it.

12   Keep practicing your spells and your evil magic.
>   You have practiced them ever since you were young.
>   You may succeed.
>   You may cause terror.

13   You are worn out by your many plans.
> Let your astrologers and your stargazers,
>   who foretell the future month by month,
>   come to you, rise up, and save you.

14   They are like straw.
>   Fire burns them.
> They can't rescue themselves from the flames.
> There are no glowing coals to keep them warm
>   and no fire for them to sit by.

15   This is how it will be for those who have worked with you,
>   for those who have been with you ever since you were young.
>   They will go their own ways,
>   and there will be no one to save you.

The LORD Will Refine His People Before He Rescues Them From Babylon

48 ¹ Listen to this, descendants of Jacob!
>   You are given the name of Israel.
>   You are descended from Judah.ᵃ
>   You take oaths by the name of the LORD.
>   You acknowledge the God of Israel,

ᵃ 48:1 Dead Sea Scrolls; Masoretic Text "the fountain of Judah."

but you are not honest or sincere.
2 You call yourselves ⌊citizens⌋ of the holy city.
    You depend on the God of Israel.
    His name is the LORD of Armies.

3 From the beginning I revealed to you what would happen.
    These words came out of my mouth,
        and I made them known.
    Suddenly, I acted, and they happened.
4 I know that you are stubborn.
    Like iron, you are hardheaded.
    Like bronze, nothing gets through your thick skull.
5 That is why I revealed to you what would happen long ago.
    I told you about them before they happened.
    ⌊I did this⌋ so you couldn't say,
        "My gods have done these things.
    My carved idols and my metal idols
        have commanded them to happen."
6 You've heard these words.
    Now look at all this.
        Won't you admit it?

From now on I will reveal to you new things,
    hidden things that you do not know.
7 They are created now, not in the past.
    You haven't heard about them before today,
        so you can't say that you already knew about them.
8 You have never heard about them.
    You have never known about them.
        Your ears have never been open to hear them before.
I know that you've acted very treacherously
    and that you have been called a rebel since you were born.
9 For my name's sake I'll be patient.
For my glory's sake I'll hold my anger back from you,
    rather than destroy you.
10 I have refined you,
        but not like silver.
I have tested you in the furnace of suffering.
11 I am doing this for myself, only for myself.
        Why should my name be dishonored?
I will not give my glory to anyone else.

12 Listen to me, Jacob,
    Israel, whom I have called.
        I am the one.
        I am the first and the last.
13 My hand laid the foundation of the earth.
    My right hand stretched out the heavens.
        When I call for them, they both stand.
14 Gather together, all of you, and listen.
        What idol has revealed such things?

The LORD loves Cyrus.
>> He will carry out the LORD's plan against Babylon.
>> He will use his strength against the Babylonians.

15 I alone have spoken.
>> I have called him.
>>> I will bring him here, and he will succeed.

16 Come here. Listen to this:
>> From the beginning I have spoken nothing in private.
>> From the time it took place, I was there.

Now the Almighty LORD has sent me and his Spirit.

17This is what the LORD, your Defender, the Holy One of Israel, says:

I am the LORD your God.
>> I teach you what is best for you.
>> I lead you where you should go.
18 If only you had listened to my commands!
>> Your peace would be like a river that never runs dry.
>> Your righteousness would be like waves on the sea.
19 Your descendants would be like sand.
>> Your children would be like its grains.
>>> Their names would not be cut off or wiped out in my presence.

20 Leave Babylon; flee from the Babylonians!
>> Shout for joy as you tell it and announce it.
>>> Shout it out to the ends of the earth.
>>>> Say that the LORD has reclaimed his servant Jacob.
21 They weren't thirsty when he led them through the deserts.
>> He made water flow from a rock for them.
>> He split a rock, and water gushed out.

22 "There is no peace for the wicked," says the LORD.

The LORD's Servant Will Bring Salvation to the Nations

49 1 Listen to me, you islands.
>> Pay attention, you people far away.
>>> Before I was born, the LORD chose me.
>>> While I was in my mother's womb, he recorded my name.
2 He made my tongue like a sharp sword
>> and hid me in the palm of his hand.
He made me like a sharpened arrow
>> and hid me in his quiver.

3 He said to me,
>> "You are my servant Israel.
>>> I will display my glory through you."
4 But I said,
>> "I have worked hard for nothing.
>>> I have used my strength, but I didn't accomplish anything.
>>>> Yet, certainly my case is in the LORD's hands,
>>>> and my reward is with my God."

⁵ The LORD formed me in the womb to be his servant
in order to bring Jacob back to him
and gather Israel to him.
(The LORD honors me,
and my God has become my strength.)

⁶Now, the Lord says,

"You are not just my servant
who restores the tribes of Jacob
and brings back those in Israel whom I have preserved.
I have also made you a light for the nations
so that you would save people all over the world."

⁷ The LORD is the defender of Israel, its Holy One.

This is what the LORD says to the despised one, to the one scorned by the nation, to the slave of rulers:

Kings will see ˌyouˌ and stand.
Princes will see ˌyouˌ and bow.
The LORD is faithful.
The Holy One of Israel has chosen you.

⁸This is what the LORD says:

In the time of favor I will answer you.
In the day of salvation I will help you.
I will protect you.
I will appoint you as my promiseᵃ to the people.
You will restore the land.
You will make them inherit the desolate inheritance.
⁹ You will say to the prisoners, "Come out,"
and to those who are in darkness, "Show yourselves."

They will graze along every path,
and they will find pastures on every bare hill.
¹⁰ They will never be hungry or thirsty,
nor will the sun or the burning, hot wind strike them.
The one who has compassion on them will lead them
and guide them to springs.
¹¹ I will turn all my mountains into roads,
and my highways will be restored.
¹² They will come from far away.
They will come from the north and from the west,
and they will come from the land of Sinim.

¹³ Sing with joy, you heavens!
Rejoice, you earth!
Break into shouts of joy, you mountains!
The LORD has comforted his people
and will have compassion on his humble people.

ᵃ 49:8 Or "covenant."

The LORD Has Not Forgotten Israel

14   But Zion said, "The LORD has abandoned me.
         My Lord has forgotten me."

15   Can a woman forget her nursing child?
         Will she have no compassion on the child from her womb?
         Although mothers may forget,
              I will not forget you.

16   I have engraved you on the palms of my hands.
         Your walls are always in my presence.

17   Your children will hurry back.
         Those who destroyed you and laid waste to you will leave you.

18   Look up, look around, and watch!
         All of your children are gathering together and returning to you.
         "I solemnly swear as I live," declares the LORD,
              "you will wear all of them like jewels
              and display them on yourself as a bride would."

19   Though you are destroyed and demolished and your land is in ruins,
         you will be too crowded for ⌊your⌋ people now.
              Those who devoured you will be long gone.

20   The children taken from you will say to you,
         "This place is too crowded for me.
         Make room for me to live here."

21   Then you will ask yourself,
         "Who has fathered these ⌊children⌋ for me?
              I was childless and unable to have children.
              I was exiled and rejected.
         Who raised these ⌊children⌋ for me?
              I was left alone.
         Where have they come from?"

22This is what the Almighty LORD says:

    I will lift my hand ⌊to signal⌋ the nations.
    I will raise my flag for the people.
         They will bring your sons in their arms
              and carry your daughters on their shoulders.

23   Then kings will be your foster fathers,
         and their queens will nurse you.
    They will bow in front of you
         with their faces touching the ground.
    They will lick the dust at your feet.
         Then you will know that I am the LORD.
              Those who wait with hope for me will not be put to shame.

24   Can loot be taken away from mighty men
         or prisoners be freed from conquerors?

25This is what the LORD says:

    Prisoners will be freed from mighty men.
    Loot will be taken away from tyrants.

I will fight your enemies,
and I will save your children.
²⁶ I will make your oppressors eat their own flesh,
and they will become drunk on their own blood
as though it were new wine.
Then all humanity will know that I am the LORD, who saves you,
the Mighty One of Jacob, who reclaims you.

The LORD's People Were Sold Because of Their Sin

¹This is what the LORD says:

Where are your mother's divorce papers?
Did I give her any to get rid of her?
To which of my creditors did I sell you?
You were sold because of your sins.
I got rid of your mother because of your rebellion.
² Why was no one here when I came?
Why was no one here to answer when I called?
Am I too weak to reclaim you?
Don't I have the power to rescue you?
I dry up the sea with my command,
and I turn rivers into deserts.
Their fish stink because there is no water,
and people die of thirst.
³ I clothe the heavens in darkness
and cover them with sackcloth.

The LORD's Servant Trusts in the LORD's Help

⁴ The Almighty LORD will teach me what to say,
so I will know how to encourage weary people.
Morning after morning he will wake me
to listen like a student.
⁵ The Almighty LORD will open my ears.
I will not rebel, nor will I turn away from him.
⁶ I will offer my back to those who whip me
and my cheeks to those who pluck hairs out of my beard.
I will not turn my face away from those who humiliate me
and spit on me.

⁷ The Almighty LORD helps me.
That is why I will not be ashamed.
I have set my face like a flint.
I know that I will not be put to shame.
⁸ The one who pronounces me innocent is near.
Who will bring a case against me?
Let us confront each other!
Who accuses me?
Let him confront me!
⁹ The Almighty LORD helps me.
Who will find me guilty?

> They will all wear out like a garment.
> > Moths will eat them.

10 Who among you fears the LORD
> and obeys his servant?
> Let those who walk in darkness and have no light
> > trust the name of the LORD
> > > and depend upon their God.

11 But all of you light fires
> and arm yourselves with flaming torches.
> So walk in your own light
> > and among the torches you have lit.

> This is what you will receive from me:
> > You will be tormented.

The LORD Will Save His People

51 ¹ Listen to me, you people who pursue what is right and seek the LORD.
> Look to the rock from which you were cut
> > and to the quarry from which you were dug.
² Look to Abraham, your ancestor,
> and to Sarah, from whom you are descended.
> When I called Abraham, he was childless.
> > I blessed him and gave him many descendants.
³ So the LORD will comfort Zion.
> He will comfort all those who live among its ruins.
> He will make its desert like Eden.
> He will make its wilderness like the garden of the LORD.
> > Joy and gladness will be found in it,
> > > thanksgiving and the sound of singing.

⁴ Pay attention to me, my people.
> Open your ears to hear me, my nation.
> > My teachings will go out from me.
> > My justice will become a light for the people.
⁵ My righteousness is near.
> My salvation is on the way.
> I will bring justice to people.
> > The coastlands put their hope in me,
> > > and they wait eagerly for me.
⁶ Look at the sky.
> Look at the earth below.
> > The sky will vanish like smoke.
> > The earth will wear out like clothing,
> > > and those who live there will die like flies.
> But my salvation will last forever,
> > and my righteousness will never fail.

⁷ Listen to me, you people who know righteousness,
> > you people who have my teachings in your hearts.
> Don't be afraid of being insulted by people.

Don't be discouraged by their ridicule.
8   Moths will eat them like clothing.
       Worms will devour them like wool.
   But my righteousness will last forever,
       and my salvation will last throughout every generation.

9   Wake up! Wake up! Clothe yourself with strength, O Lord!
   Wake up as you did in days long past, as in generations long ago.
   Didn't you cut Rahab[a] into pieces and stab the serpent?
10 Didn't you dry up the sea, the water of the great ocean?
       You made a road in the depths of the sea
           so that the people reclaimed by the Lord
           might pass through it.
11 The people ransomed by the Lord will return.
       They will come to Zion singing with joy.
           Everlasting happiness will be on their heads as a crown.
           They will be glad and joyful.
           They will have no sorrow or grief.

12 I alone am the one who comforts you.
   Why, then, are you afraid of mortals, who must die,
       of humans, who are like grass?
13 Why have you forgotten the Lord, your Creator?
       He stretched out the heavens
           and laid the foundations of the earth.
   Why should you live in constant fear of the fury
       of those who oppress you,
       of those who are ready to destroy you?
   Where is the fury of those who oppress you?
14 Chained prisoners will be set free.
       They will not die in prison.
       They will not go without food.
15 I am the Lord your God who stirs up the sea
       and makes its waves roar.
           My name is the Lord of Armies.
16 I put my words in your mouth
       and sheltered you in the palm of my hand.
   I stretched out the heavens,
       laid the foundations of the earth,
           and said to Zion, "You are my people."

Wake Up, Jerusalem

17 Wake up! Wake up!
   Stand up, Jerusalem!
       You drank from the cup in the Lord's hand.
       That cup was filled with his anger.
       You drank from the bowl, the cup that makes people stagger,
           and you drained it!
18 From all the children she gave birth to,

---

[a]51:9 Rahab is the name of a demonic creature who opposes God.

there was no one to guide her.
From all the children she raised,
    there was no one to take her by the hand.
19 Twice as many disasters have happened to you.
    Who will feel sorry for you?
Violence, destruction, famine, and war have happened to you.
    Who will comfort you?
20 Your children have fainted.
    They lie sleeping at every street corner.
    They are like an antelope caught in a net.
    They experience the anger of the Lord,
        the fury of your God.

21 Listen to this, you humble people
    who are drunk but not from wine.
22 The Lord your God defends his people.

This is what your master says:

I'm taking from your hand the cup that makes people stagger,
    the bowl, the cup of my fury.
        You will never drink from it again.
23 I will put it in the hands of those who made you suffer.
    They said to you, "Lie down so that we can walk over you."
        So you made your back like the ground
        and like a street for them to cross.

Wake Up, Zion

52 ¹ Wake up! Wake up! Clothe yourself with strength, Zion!
    Put on your beautiful clothes, holy city of Jerusalem.
        Godless and evil people will no longer come to you.
2 Shake the dust from yourselves.
    Get up, captive Jerusalem.
    Free yourself from the chains around your neck, captive people of Zion.

³This is what the Lord says: You were sold, but no price was paid. You will be bought back, but without money.

⁴This is what the Almighty Lord says: In the beginning my people went to Egypt to live there as foreigners. Later the Assyrians oppressed them for no reason. ⁵So what do I find here? asks the Lord. My people are taken away for no reason. Their rulers are screaming, declares the Lord. And my name is cursed all day long. ⁶Now my people will know my name. When that day comes, ⌊they will know⌋ that I am the one who says, "Here I am!"

7 How beautiful on the mountains are the feet of the messenger
    who announces the good news, "All is well."
        He brings the good news,
        announces salvation,
            and tells Zion that its God rules as king.
8 Listen! Your watchmen raise their voices
    and shout together joyfully.
        When the Lord brings Zion back,

they will see it with their own eyes.

9 Break out into shouts of joy, ruins of Jerusalem.
   The Lord will comfort his people.
      He will reclaim Jerusalem.
10 The Lord will show his holy power to all the nations.
   All the ends of the earth will see the salvation of our God.

11 Run away! Run away!
   Get away from there!
   Do not touch anything unclean.*
   Get away from it!
   Make yourselves pure,
      you Levites who carry the utensils for the Lord's temple.

12 You will not go away in a hurry,
      nor will you go away quickly.
   The Lord will go ahead of you.
   The God of Israel will guard you from behind.

The Suffering Servant

13 My servant will be successful.
   He will be respected, praised, and highly honored.
14 Many will be shocked by him.*
      His appearance will be so disfigured
         that he won't look like any other man.
      His looks will be so disfigured
         that he will hardly look like a human.
15 He will cleanse many nations with his blood.
   Kings will shut their mouths because of him.
      They will see things that they had never been told.
      They will understand things that they had never heard.

53 1 Who has believed our message?
   To whom has the Lord's power been revealed?

Good Morning, God

Isaiah 53:5

Would you take the punishment for someone else's wrongdoing? Seven hundred years before the birth of Christ, Isaiah said that an innocent person would one day pay the price for everyone's sin. Isaiah was talking about Jesus. The price of sin is death.

Jesus paid the penalty for our sin by dying on a cross. But he came back to life, and now he lives forever!

God, thank you for loving me so much that you let your Son die for me!

---

*52:11 "Unclean" refers to anything that Moses' Teachings say is not presentable to God.   *52:14 Two Hebrew manuscripts, Syriac, Targum; Masoretic Text "you."

2   He grew up in his presence like a young tree,
        like a root out of dry ground.
    He had no form or majesty that would make us look at him.
    He had nothing in his appearance that would make us desire him.
3   He was despised and rejected by people.
    He was a man of sorrows, familiar with suffering.
    He was despised like one from whom people turn their faces,
        and we didn't consider him to be worth anything.
4   He certainly has taken upon himself our suffering
        and carried our sorrows,
            but we thought that God had wounded him,
                beat him, and punished him.
5   He was wounded for our rebellious acts.
    He was crushed for our sins.
        He was punished so that we could have peace,
            and we received healing from his wounds.

6   We have all strayed like sheep.
    Each one of us has turned to go his own way,
        and the Lord has laid all our sins on him.
7   He was abused and punished,
        but he didn't open his mouth.
    He was led like a lamb to the slaughter.
    He was like a sheep that is silent
        when its wool is cut off.
        He didn't open his mouth.

8   He was arrested, taken away, and judged.
        Who would have thought that he would be removed
            from the world?
    He was killed because of my people's rebellion.
9   He was placed in a tomb with the wicked.
    He was put there with the rich when he died,
        although he had done nothing violent
            and had never spoken a lie.

10 Yet, it was the Lord's will to crush him with suffering.
    When the Lord has made his life a sacrifice for our wrongdoings,
        he will see his descendants for many days.
            The will of the Lord will succeed through him.
11   He will see and be satisfied
            because of his suffering.
    My righteous servant will acquit many people
        because of what he has learned through suffering .
    He will carry their sins as a burden.

12 So I will give him a share among the mighty,
        and he will divide the prize with the strong,
            because he poured out his life in death
                and he was counted with sinners.
            He carried the sins of many.
                He intercedes for those who are rebellious.

The LORD's Compassion for the Women Without Children

54 ¹ Sing with joy, you childless women who never gave birth to children.
Break into shouts of joy, you women who never had birth pains.
  "There will be more children of women who have been deserted
    than there are children of married women," says the LORD.

² Expand the space of your tent.
  Stretch out the curtains of your tent, and don't hold back.
  Lengthen your tent ropes, and drive in the tent pegs.

³ You will spread out to the right and left.
  Your descendants will take over other nations,
    and they will resettle deserted cities.

⁴ Don't be afraid, because you won't be put to shame.
Don't be discouraged, because you won't be disgraced.
  You'll forget the shame you've had since you were young.
  You won't remember the disgrace of your husband's death anymore.

⁵   Your husband is your maker.
      His name is the LORD of Armies.
    Your defender is the Holy One of Israel.
      He is called the God of the whole earth.

⁶ "The LORD has called you as if you were
    a wife who was abandoned and in grief,
    a wife who married young and was rejected," says your God.

⁷ "I abandoned you for one brief moment,
    but I will bring you back with unlimited compassion.

⁸ I hid my face from you for a moment in a burst of anger,
    but I will have compassion on you with everlasting kindness,"
      says the LORD your defender.

⁹ "To me this is like Noah's floodwaters, when I swore an oath
    that Noah's floodwaters would never cover the earth again.
So now I swear an oath not to be angry with you or punish you.

¹⁰ The mountains may move, and the hills may shake,
    but my kindness will never depart from you.
    My promise*ᵃ* of peace will never change,"
      says the LORD, who has compassion on you.

¹¹ "You suffering, comfortless, storm-ravaged city!
    I will rebuild your city with precious stones.
    I will reset your foundations with sapphires.

¹²   I will rebuild your towers with rubies,
      your gates with sparkling stones,
        and all your walls with precious stones."

¹³ All your children will be taught by the LORD,
    and your children will have unlimited peace.

¹⁴ You will be established in righteousness.
You will be far from oppression,
    so you will not be afraid.
You will be far from destruction,
    so it won't come near you.

---

*ᵃ*54:10 Or "covenant."

15 "If anyone attacks you, it will not be my doing.
   Whoever attacks you will be defeated by you.
16 I've created blacksmiths to fan the coals into flames
      and to produce useful weapons.
   I've also created destroyers to bring destruction.
17 No weapon that has been made to be used against you will succeed.
      You will have an answer for anyone who accuses you.
         This is the inheritance of the LORD's servants.
            Their victory comes from me," declares the LORD.

The LORD's Word Will Accomplish Its Task

55 ¹ "Listen! Whoever is thirsty, come to the water!
      Whoever has no money can come, buy, and eat!
         Come, buy wine and milk. You don't have to pay; its free!
2 Why do you spend money on what cannot nourish you
      and your wages on what does not satisfy you?
   Listen carefully to me:
      Eat what is good, and enjoy the best foods.
3 Open your ears, and come to me!
   Listen so that you may live!
   I will make an everlasting promiseᵃ to you—
      the blessings I promised to David.
4 I made him a witness to people,
      a leader and a commander for people.
5 You will summon a nation that you don't know,
      and a nation that doesn't know you will run to you
         because of the LORD your God,
         because of the Holy One of Israel.
            He has honored you."

6 Seek the LORD while he may be found.
   Call on him while he is near.
7 Let wicked people abandon their ways.
   Let evil people abandon their thoughts.
   Let them return to the LORD,
      and he will show compassion to them.
   Let them return to our God,
      because he will freely forgive them.

8 "My thoughts are not your thoughts,
      and my ways are not your ways," declares the LORD.
9 "Just as the heavens are higher than the earth,
      so my ways are higher than your ways,
         and my thoughts are higher than your thoughts."

10 "Rain and snow come down from the sky.
      They do not go back again until they water the earth.
         They make it sprout and grow
            so that it produces seed for farmers
               and food for people to eat.

ᵃ 55:3 Or "covenant."

11 My word, which comes from my mouth, is like the rain and snow.
    It will not come back to me without results.
    It will accomplish whatever I want
        and achieve whatever I send it to do."

12 You will go out with joy and be led out in peace.
    The mountains and the hills
        will break into songs of joy in your presence,
            and all the trees will clap their hands.
13 Cypress trees will grow where thornbushes grew.
    Myrtle trees will grow where briars grew.
        This will be a reminder of the Lord's name
            and an everlasting sign that will never be destroyed.

Salvation for All People

56 ¹This is what the Lord says:

Preserve justice, and do what is right.
    My salvation is about to come.
    My righteousness is about to be revealed.

2 Blessed is the one who does these things
    and the person who holds on to them.
Blessed is the one who keeps the day of worship from becoming unholy
    and his hands from doing anything wrong.

³Foreigners who have joined the Lord should not say, "The Lord will separate us from his people." Castrated men should not say, "We're only dead trees!" ⁴This is what the Lord says: ⌊I will remember⌋ the castrated men who keep my days of worship, choose what pleases me, and faithfully observe the conditions of my promise.ᵃ ⁵Inside my house and within my walls, I will give them something better than sons and daughters. I will give them a monument and a name. I will give them a permanent name that will not be forgotten. ⁶And ⌊I will remember⌋ the foreigners who have joined the Lord to worship him, to love the Lord's name, and to be his servants. All of them will keep the day of worship from becoming unholy and will faithfully observe the conditions of my promise. ⁷Then I will bring them to my holy mountain and make them happy in my house of prayer. Their burnt offerings and their sacrifices will be acceptable on my altar, because my house will be called a house of prayer for all nations.

⁸The Almighty Lord, who gathers the scattered people of Israel, declares, "I will gather still others besides those I have already gathered."

The Sins of Israel Bring the LORD's Anger

9 All you animals in the field,
    all you animals in the forest,
        come and eat.
10 ⌊Israel's⌋ watchmen are blind.
    None of them know anything.
    All of them are like dogs that are unable to bark.
    They lie around dreaming; they love to sleep.
11 These dogs have huge appetites.

ᵃ56:4 Or "covenant."

They are never full.
They are the shepherds,
  but they don't understand.
All of them have turned to go their own ways.
  Each one seeks his own gain.
12 Each one cries,
  "Let me get some wine,
    and we'll fill ourselves with liquor.
      And tomorrow will be like today, only better."

1 Righteous people die,
  and no one cares.
Loyal people are taken away,
  and no one understands.
Righteous people are spared when evil comes.
2 When peace comes,
  everyone who has lived honestly will rest on his own bed.

Israel's Idolatry

3 But you—come here,
  you children of witches,
    you descendants of adulterers and prostitutes!
4 Whom are you making fun of?
Whom are you making a face at?
Whom are you sticking out your tongue at?
  Aren't you rebellious children,
    descendants of liars?
5 You burn with lust under oak trees
  and under every large tree.
You slaughter children in the valleys
  and under the cracks in the rocks.
6 Your idols are among the smooth stones in the ravine.
  They are your destiny.
You have given them wine offerings
  and sacrificed grain offerings to them.
Do you think I am pleased with all this?

7 You've made your bed on a high and lofty mountain.
You've gone to offer sacrifices there.
8 You've set up your idols beside doors and doorposts.
You've uncovered yourself to the idols.
  You've distanced yourself from me.
You've made your bed with them.
You've made a deal with those you have pleasure with in bed.
You've seen them naked.
9 You've journeyed to the king with perfumed oils
  and put on plenty of perfume.
You've sent your ambassadors far away
  and sent them down to Sheol.
10 You've tired yourself out with many journeys.
  You didn't think that it was hopeless.

You've found renewed strength,
  so you didn't faint.

11 Whom did you dread and fear so much that you lied to me?
  You haven't remembered me or cared about me.
I've been silent for a long time.
  Is that why you don't fear me?

12 I'll tell you about your righteous ways and what you have done,
  but they won't help you.

13 When you cry for help,
    let your collection of idols save you.
      A wind will carry them all away.
      A breath will take them away.
        But whoever trusts me will possess the land
          and inherit my holy mountain.

14 It will be said:
    "Build a road! Build a road!
      Prepare the way!
        Remove every obstacle in the way of my people!"

15 The High and Lofty One lives forever, and his name is holy.

This is what he says:

I live in a high and holy place.
  But I am with those who are crushed and humble.
    I will renew the spirit of those who are humble
      and the courage of those who are crushed.

16 I will not accuse you forever.
I will not be angry with you forever.
  Otherwise, the spirits, the lives of those I've made,
    would grow faint in my presence.

17 I was angry because of their sinful greed,
  so I punished them, hid from them, and remained angry.
    But they continued to be sinful.

18 I've seen their sinful ways, but I'll heal them.
I'll guide them and give them rest.
I'll comfort them and their mourners.

19 I'll create praise on their lips:
    "Perfect peace to those both far and near."
"I'll heal them," says the LORD.

20 But the wicked are like the churning sea.
    It isn't quiet,
      and its water throws up mud and slime.

21 "There is no peace for the wicked," says my God.

Worship the LORD as He Wants to Be Worshiped

58 1 Cry aloud! Don't hold back!
    Raise your voice like a ram's horn.
      Tell my people about their rebellion
        and the descendants of Jacob about their sins.

2 They look for me every day and want to know my ways.
    They act as if they were a nation that has done what is right
        and as if they haven't disregarded God's judgment ⌊on them⌋.
    They ask me for just decrees.
    They want God to be near them.

3 Why have we fasted if you are not aware of it?
    Why have we inflicted pain on ourselves if you don't pay attention?

    Don't you see that on the days you fast,
        you do what you want to do?
            You mistreat all your workers.
4 Don't you see that when you fast,
        you quarrel and fight and beat your workers?
            The way you fast today keeps you from being heard in heaven.
5 Is this the kind of fasting I have chosen?
        Should people humble themselves for ⌊only⌋ a day?
    Is fasting just bowing your head like a cattail
        and making your bed from sackcloth and ashes?
    Is this what you call fasting?
    Is this an acceptable day to the LORD?

6 This is the kind of fasting I have chosen:
    Loosen the chains of wickedness,
        untie the straps of the yoke,ᵃ
            let the oppressed go free,
                and break every yoke.
7 Share your food with the hungry,
        take the poor and homeless into your house,
            and cover them with clothes when you see ⌊them⌋ naked.
                Don't refuse to help your relatives.

8 Then your light will break through like the dawn,
        and you will heal quickly.
    Your righteousness will go ahead of you,
        and the glory of the LORD will guard you from behind.
9 Then you will call, and the LORD will answer.
    You will cry for help, and he will say, "Here I am!"

    Get rid of that yoke.
        Don't point your finger and say wicked things.

10 If you give some of your own food to ⌊feed⌋ those who are hungry
        and to satisfy ⌊the needs of⌋ those who are humble,
    then your light will rise in the dark,
        and your darkness will become as bright as the noonday sun.
11 The LORD will continually guide you
        and satisfy you even in sun-baked places.
    He will strengthen your bones.
        You will become like a watered garden
            and like a spring whose water does not stop flowing.

ᵃ 58:6 A yoke is a wooden bar placed over the necks of work animals so that they can pull plows or carts.

12 Your people will rebuild the ancient ruins
   and restore the foundations of past generations.
   You will be called the Rebuilder of Broken Walls
   and the Restorer of Streets Where People Live.

13 If you stop trampling on the day of worship
   and doing as you please on my holy day,
   if you call the day of worship a delight
   and the LORD's holy day honorable,
   if you honor it by not going your own way,
   by not going out when you want, and by not talking idly,
14 then you will find joy in the LORD.
   I will make you ride on the heights of the earth.
   I will feed you with the inheritance of your ancestor Jacob.
   The LORD has spoken.

The LORD Will Turn His People From Wrongdoing

59 ¹ The LORD is not too weak to save
   or his ear too deaf to hear.
2 But your wrongs have separated you from your God,
   and your sins have made him hide his face
   so that he doesn't hear you.
3 Your hands are stained with blood,
   and your fingers are stained with sin.
   You speak lies,
   and you mutter wicked things.
4 No one calls for justice,
   and no one pleads his case truthfully.
   People trust pointless arguments and speak lies.
   They conceive trouble and give birth to evil.
5 They hatch viper eggs
   and weave spiderwebs.
        Those who eat their eggs will die.
           When an egg is crushed, a poisonous snake is hatched.
6 Their webs can't be used for clothes,
   nor can they cover themselves with their works.
   Their works are evil.
   Their hands have committed acts of violence.
7 Their feet run to do evil.
   They hurry to shed innocent blood.
   Their plans are evil.
   Ruin and destruction are on their highways.
8 They don't know the way of peace.
   There's no justice on their highways.
   They've made their paths crooked.
   Whoever walks on them will never know peace.

9 That is why justice is far from us,
   and righteousness doesn't reach us.
   We hope for light, but we walk in darkness.
   We hope for brightness, but we walk in gloom.

10 We grope like blind men along a wall.
We grope like people without eyes.
We stumble at noon as if it were twilight.
We are like dead people among healthy people.
11 We all growl like bears.
We coo like doves.
We hope for justice, but there is none.
We hope for salvation, but it's far from us.

12   You are aware of our many rebellious acts.
         Our sins testify against us.
         Our rebellious acts are with us.
We know our wrongdoings.
13 We have rebelled and denied the LORD.
We have turned away from our God.
We have spoken about oppression and revolt.
We have conceived and uttered lies in our hearts.
14   Justice is turned back,
         and righteousness stands far away.
     Truth has fallen in the street,
         and honesty can't come in.
15   Truth is missing.
         Those who turn away from evil make themselves victims.

The LORD sees it, and he's angry
     because there's no justice.
16 He sees that there's no one to help.
He's astounded that there's no one to intercede.
     So with his own power he wins a victory.
     His righteousness supports him.
17 He puts on righteousness like a coat of armor
     and a helmet of salvation on his head.
He wears clothes of vengeance.
He wraps himself with fury as a coat.
18 He will pay them back according to their deeds.
He will pay back his opponents with wrath and punish his enemies.
He will pay back the people who live on the coastlands.
19 The people of the west will fear the name of the LORD.
     Those in the east will fear his glory.
He will come like a rushing stream.
     The wind of the LORD pushes him.

20   "Then a Savior will come to Zion,
         to those in Jacob who turn from rebellion," declares the LORD.

21"This is my promise[a] to them," says the LORD. "My Spirit, who is on you, and my words that I put in your mouth will not leave you. They will be with your children and your grandchildren permanently," says the LORD.

---

[a] 59:21 Or "covenant."

The LORD Will Be Jerusalem's Glory

60 ¹ Arise! Shine! Your light has come,
　　and the glory of the LORD has dawned.
² Darkness now covers the earth,
　　and thick darkness covers the nations.
　But the LORD dawns,
　　and his glory appears over you.
³ Nations will come to your light,
　　and kings will come to the brightness of your dawn.

⁴ "Look up, look around, and watch.
　　All of your people assemble and come to you.
　　　Your sons come from far away.
　　　Your daughters are carried in their arms.
⁵ Then you will see this and rejoice,
　　and your heart will be thrilled with joy,
　　　because the riches of the sea will be brought to you.
　　　The wealth of the nations will come to you.

⁶ "Many camels will cover your ⌞land⌟,
　　young camels from Midian and Ephah.
　Everyone from Sheba will come.
　　They will bring gold and incense.
　　They will sing the praises of the LORD.
⁷ All of the flocks from Kedar will gather and come to you.
　The rams of Nebaioth will serve you.
　　They will be sacrificed as acceptable ⌞offerings⌟ on my altar.
　　So I will honor my beautiful temple.

⁸ "Who are these people that fly by like clouds,
　　like doves to their nests?
⁹ Certainly, the coastlands wait with hope for me.
　　The ships from Tarshish are the first to bring your children
　　　from far away.
　　Their silver and their gold comes with them
　　　to honor the name of the LORD your God, the Holy One of Israel,
　　　because he has honored you.

¹⁰ "Foreigners will rebuild your walls,
　　and their kings will serve you.
　　In my anger I struck you,
　　　but in my favor I have compassion on you.
¹¹ Your gates will always be open.
　　They will never be closed day or night
　　　so that people may bring you the wealth of nations,
　　　with their kings led as prisoners.
¹² Nations and kingdoms that do not serve you will be destroyed.
　The nations will certainly be ruined.

¹³ "Lebanon's glory will come to you:
　　Cedar, fir, and cypress trees will come to beautify my holy place,
　　　and I will honor the place where my feet rest.

14 The descendants of those who oppress you will bow in front of you.
All who despise you will bow at your feet.
> They will call you the city of the LORD,
>> Zion, the city of the Holy One of Israel.

15 "You have been abandoned and hated; no one has passed through you.
> But now I will make you a source of everlasting pride,
>> a joy for all generations.

16 You will drink milk from other nations
> and nurse at royal breasts.
>> Then you will know that I am the LORD, your Savior,
>>> the Mighty One of Jacob, your Defender.

17 I will bring gold instead of bronze.
I will bring silver instead of iron,
> bronze instead of wood, and iron instead of stone.
I will appoint peace as your governor and righteousness as your ruler.

18 No longer will you hear about violence in your land
> or desolation and destruction within your borders.
>> You will call your walls Salvation and your gates Praise.

19 The sun will no longer be your light during the day,
> nor will the brightness of the moon give you light,
>> But the LORD will be your everlasting light.
>>> Your God will be your glory.

20 Your sun will no longer go down,
> nor will your moon disappear.
>> The LORD will be your everlasting light,
>>> and your days of sadness will be over.

21 Then all your people will be righteous,
> and they will possess the land permanently.
>> They will be the seedling I have planted,
>>> the honored work of my hands.

22 The smallest of them will become a family.
The weakest of them will become a mighty nation.
> At the right time I, the LORD, will make it happen quickly."

The LORD Will Anoint His Servant With His Spirit

61 1 The Spirit of the Almighty LORD is with me
> because the LORD has anointed me
>> to deliver good news to humble people.
He has sent me
> to heal those who are brokenhearted,
>> to announce that captives will be set free
>>> and prisoners will be released.

2 ⸢He has sent me⸣
> to announce the year of the LORD's good will
>> and the day of our God's vengeance,
> to comfort all those who grieve.

3 ⸢He has sent me⸣
> to provide for all those who grieve in Zion,
>> to give them crowns instead of ashes,

the oil of joy instead of tears of grief,
and clothes of praise instead of a spirit of weakness.

They will be called Oaks of Righteousness,
the Plantings of the Lord,
so that he might display his glory.

4 They will rebuild the ancient ruins.
They will restore the places destroyed long ago.
They will renew the ruined cities,
the places destroyed generations ago.
5 Foreigners will come forward and become shepherds for your flocks,
and children of foreigners will work your fields and vineyards.
6 You will be called the priests of the Lord.
You will be called the servants of our God.
You will consume the wealth of the nations.
You will boast in their splendor.
7 You will receive a double measure of wealth instead of your shame.
You will sing about your wealth instead of being disgraced.
That is why you will have a double measure of wealth in your land.
You will have everlasting joy.
8 I, the Lord, love justice.
I hate robbery and wrongdoing.
I will faithfully reward my people's work.
I will make an everlasting promise[a] to them.
9 Then their offspring will be known among the nations
and their descendants among the people.
Everyone who sees them will recognize
that they are the descendants whom the Lord has blessed.
10 I will find joy in the Lord.
I will delight in my God.
He has dressed me in the clothes of salvation.
He has wrapped me in the robe of righteousness
like a bridegroom with a priest's turban,
like a bride with her jewels.
11 Like the ground that brings forth its crops
and like a garden that makes the seed in it grow,
so the Almighty Lord will make righteousness and praise
spring up in front of all nations.

Jerusalem's Salvation Is Coming

62 1 For Zion's sake I will not remain silent.
For Jerusalem's sake I will not rest,
until its righteousness shines like the dawn
and its salvation burns brightly like a torch.
2 The nations will see your righteousness.
All kings will see your glory.
You will be given a new name
that the Lord will announce.

---

a 61:8 Or "covenant."

³ Then you will be a beautiful crown in the hand of the LORD,
   a royal crown in the hand of your God.
⁴ You will no longer be called Deserted,
   and your land will no longer be called Destroyed.
But you will be named My Delight,
   and your land will be named Married.
The LORD is delighted with you,
   and your land will be married.
⁵ As a young man marries a woman,
   so your sons will marry you.
As a bridegroom rejoices over his bride,
   so your God will rejoice over you.

⁶ I have posted watchmen on your walls, Jerusalem.
   They will never be silent day or night.
Whoever calls on the LORD, do not give yourselves any rest,
⁷   and do not give him any rest until he establishes Jerusalem
     and makes it an object of praise throughout the earth.
⁸ The LORD has sworn with his right hand and with his mighty arm,
   "I will never again let your enemies eat your grain,
     nor will foreigners drink the new wine which you made."
⁹   Those who harvest grain
       will eat it and praise the LORD.
     Those who gather grapes
       will drink wine in my holy courtyards.

¹⁰ Go through! Go through the gates!
   Prepare a way for the people!
   Build up! Build up the highway!
   Clear away the stones!
   Raise a flag for the people!

¹¹ The LORD has announced to the ends of the earth:
   "Tell my people Zion,
     'Your Savior is coming.
     His reward is with him,
       and the people he has won arrive ahead of him.'"

¹² They will be called Holy People, Those Reclaimed by the LORD,
   and you will be called Sought After, a City Not Deserted.

The LORD Alone Wins His Victory

63 ¹ Who is this coming from Bozrah in Edom
   with his clothes stained bright red?
Who is this dressed in splendor,
   going forward with great strength?

"It is I, the LORD. I am coming to announce my victory.
   I am powerful enough to save ⌊you⌋."

² Why are your clothes red
   and your garments like those who trample grapes in a winepress?

3 "I have trampled alone in the winepress.
  No one was with me.
In my anger I trampled on people.
In my wrath I stomped on them.
Their blood splattered my clothes
  so all my clothing has been stained.
4 I planned the day of vengeance.
The year for my reclaiming ⌊you⌋ has come.
5 I looked, but there was no help.
I was astounded that there was no ⌊outside⌋ support.
  So with my own power I won a victory.
  My anger supported me.
6   In my anger I trampled on people.
  In my wrath I made them drunk
    and poured their blood on the ground."

The Lord's People Pray for His Help

7 I will acknowledge the Lord's acts of mercy,
  and ⌊sing⌋ the praises of the Lord,
    because of everything that the Lord has done for us.
    He has done many good things for the nation of Israel
      because of his compassion and his unlimited mercy.
8 He said, "They are my people,
  children who will not lie to me."
  So he became their Savior.
9 In all their troubles he was troubled,
  and he was the Messenger who saved them.
In his love and compassion he reclaimed them.
He always held them and carried them in the past.
10 But they rebelled and offended his Holy Spirit.
  So he turned against them as their enemy; he fought against them.

11 Then his people remembered Moses and the distant past.
  Where is the one who brought them out of the sea
    with the shepherds of his flock?
  Where is the one who put his Holy Spirit in them?
12 Where is the one who sent his powerful arm
    to support the right hand of Moses?
  Where is the one who divided the water in front of them
    to make an everlasting name for himself?
13 Where is the one who led them through the deep water?
Like horses in the wilderness,
  they didn't stumble.
14 Like animals going down into a valley,
  they were given rest by the Lord's Spirit.
    In this way you guided your people
      to make an honored name for yourself.

15 Look down and see from heaven, from your holy and beautiful dwelling.
  Where is your determination and might?
  Where is the longing of your heart and your compassion?

Don't hold back.

16 You are our Father.
　　Even though Abraham doesn't know us
　　and Israel doesn't pay attention to us,
　　　O Lord, you are our Father.
　　　　Your name is our Defender From Everlasting.

17 O Lord, why do you let us wander from your ways
　　and become so stubborn that we are unable to fear you?
　　　Return for the sake of your servants.
　　　They are the tribes that belong to you.

18 Your holy people possessed the land for a little while.
　　Our enemies have trampled on your holy place.

19 We have become like those whom you never ruled,
　　like those who are not called by your name.

64 ^{a}1 If only you would split open the heavens and come down!
　　　　The mountains would quake at your presence.
2 　　Be like the fire that kindles brushwood and makes water boil.
　　Come down to make your name known to your enemies.
　　　The nations will tremble in your presence.

3 When you did awe-inspiring things that we didn't expect,
　　you came down and the mountains quaked in your presence.

4 No one has ever heard,
　　no one has paid attention,
　　　and no one has seen any god except you.
　　　　You help those who wait for you.

5 You greeted the one who gladly does right and remembers your ways.
　　You showed your anger, because we've sinned.
　　　We've continued to sin for a long time.
　　　　Can we still be saved?

6 We've all become unclean,^{b}
　　and all our righteous acts are like permanently stained rags.
　　All of us shrivel like leaves,
　　　and our sins carry us away like the wind.

7 No one calls on your name
　　or tries to hold on to you.
　　　You have hidden your face from us.
　　　You have let us be ruined by our sins.

8 But now, Lord, you are our Father.
　　We are the clay, and you are our potter.
　　We are the work of your hands.

9 Don't be too angry, Lord.
　　Don't remember our sin forever.
　　　Now look, we are all your people.

10 Your holy cities have become a desert.
　　Zion has become a desert.
　　Jerusalem is a wasteland.

---

^{a}64:1 Isaiah 64:1-12 in English Bibles is Isaiah 63:19b–64:11 in the Hebrew Bible.　^{b}64:6 "Unclean" refers to anything that Moses' Teachings say is not presentable to God.

¹¹ Our holy and beautiful temple, where our ancestors praised you,
  has been burned to the ground.
  All that we valued has been ruined.
¹² Despite these things, Lord, will you hold back?
  Will you be silent and make us suffer more than we can bear?

The LORD Answers His People's Prayer

65 ¹ I was ready to answer those who didn't ask.
  I was found by those who weren't looking for me.
  I said, "Here I am! Here I am!"
  to a nation that didn't worship me.
² I stretched out my hands all day long to stubborn people.
  They chose to go the wrong direction.
  They followed their own plans.
³ These people constantly and openly provoked me.
  They offered sacrifices in gardens
  and burnt incense on brick altars.
⁴ They sat among the graves and spent their nights in caves.
  They ate pork and in their pots made broth from unclean foods.
⁵ They said, "Stay away! Don't touch me!
  I'm holier than you are."
  They have become like smoke in my nose,
  like a smoldering fire all day long.

⁶ "Look! It is written in front of me.
  I will not be silent, but I will repay.
  I will repay you in full.
⁷ I will repay you for your sins
  and for the sins of your ancestors," says the Lord.
  They burnt incense on the mountains and slandered me on the hills,
  so I will be the first to pay them back in full.

⁸This is what the Lord says:

When someone finds juice for new wine in a cluster of grapes,
  another person will say,
  "Don't destroy it, because there's a blessing in it."
In the same way, I will do this for my servants:
  I will not destroy everything.
⁹ I will bring with me Jacob's descendant,
  one who will inherit my mountains from Judah.
  My chosen ones will inherit them.
  My servants will live there.
¹⁰ The Sharon Plain will be a pasture for flocks.
  The Achor Valley will be a resting place for cattle
  and for my people who search for me.
¹¹ You have abandoned the Lord
  and forgotten my holy mountain.
You have prepared a table for the god of good fortune
  and offered cups full of spiced wine to the goddess of destiny.
¹² Now I will destine you for death.

All of you will bow to be slaughtered.
    I called, but you didn't answer.
    I spoke, but you didn't listen.
        You did what I consider evil.
        You chose what I don't like.

¹³This is what the LORD God says:

My servants will eat, but you will be hungry.
My servants will drink, but you will be thirsty.
My servants will be glad, but you will be ashamed.
¹⁴ My servants will sing because of the gladness in their hearts.
    But you will cry because of your sadness
        and wail because of your depression.
¹⁵ Your name will be used as a curse by my chosen ones.
    The Almighty LORD will kill you
        and call his servants by another name.
¹⁶ Whoever asks for a blessing in the land
    will be blessed by the God of Truth.
Whoever swears an oath in the land
    will swear by the God of Truth.
        Past troubles are forgotten.
        They are hidden from my eyes.

¹⁷ I will create a new heaven and a new earth.
    Past things will not be remembered.
    They will not come to mind.
¹⁸ Be glad, and rejoice forever in what I'm going to create,
    because I'm going to create Jerusalem to be a delight
        and its people to be a joy.
¹⁹ I will rejoice about Jerusalem and be glad about my people.
Screaming and crying will no longer be heard in the city.
²⁰ There will no longer be an infant who lives for only a few days
    or an old man who doesn't live a long life.
Whoever lives to be a hundred years old will be thought of as young.
Whoever dies before he is a hundred years old will be cursed as a sinner.
²¹   They will build houses and live there.

Good Morning, God

Isaiah 65:19-25

What do you think life will be like in heaven? What do you want it to be like? Our life forever with God will be wonderful. We will not remember painful memories of the past. No one will hurt and no one will cry. No one will die, either. Because the world we live in now is full of sin, unfair things often happen. But remember, a new life in heaven is waiting for you!

Thank you, Lord, for giving me the hope of heaven.

They will plant vineyards and eat fruit from them.
22 They will not build homes and have others live there.
They will not plant and have others eat from it.
My people will live as long as trees,
and my chosen ones will enjoy what they've done.
23 They will never again work for nothing.
They will never again give birth to children who die young,
because they will be offspring blessed by the LORD.
The LORD will bless their descendants as well.
24 Before they call, I will answer.
While they're still speaking, I will hear.
25 Wolves and lambs will feed together,
lions will eat straw like oxen,
and dust will be food for snakes.
"They will not hurt or destroy anyone anywhere on my holy mountain,"
says the LORD.

The People of the LORD's New Creation

66 ¹This is what the LORD says:

Heaven is my throne.
The earth is my footstool.
Where can you build a house or resting place for me?
2 I have made all these things.
"That is why all these things have come into being,"
declares the LORD.
I will pay attention to those
who are humble and sorry for their sins,
and who tremble at my word.

3 Whoever kills a bull is like someone who kills a person.
Whoever sacrifices a lamb is like someone who breaks a dog's neck.
Whoever offers a grain sacrifice
is like someone who offers pig's blood.
Whoever burns incense is like someone who worships an idol.
People have certainly chosen their own ways,
and their souls delight in detestable things.

4 So I will choose harsh treatment for them
and bring on them what they fear.
I called, but no one answered.
I spoke, but they didn't listen.
They did what I consider evil.
They chose what I don't like.

⁵Listen to the word of the LORD, all who tremble at his word.

Your relatives, who hate you and exclude you for my name's sake, say,
"Let the LORD show his glory; then we will see your joy."
But they will be put to shame.
6 Listen to the uproar from the city.
Listen to the sound from the temple.

It is the sound of the L ORD
    paying back his enemies as they deserve.

7 Before a woman goes into labor, she gives birth.
Before she has labor pains, she delivers a child.
8   Who has heard of such a thing?
   Who has seen such things?
      Can a country be born in one day?
      Can a nation be born in a moment?
When Zion went into labor,
    she also gave birth to her children.
9 "Do I bring a mother to the moment of birth
    and not let her deliver?" asks the L ORD.
"Do I cause a mother to deliver
    and then make her unable to have children?" asks your God.
10 All who love Jerusalem, be happy and rejoice with her.
All who mourn for her, be glad with her.
11   You will nurse and be satisfied from her comforting breasts.
   You will nurse to your heart's delight at her full breasts.

12 This is what the L ORD says:

I will offer you peace like a river
    and the wealth of the nations like an overflowing stream.
      You will nurse and be carried in Jerusalem's arms
        and cuddled on her knees.
13 As a mother comforts her child,
    so will I comfort you.
      You will be comforted in Jerusalem.
14 When you see it, your heart will rejoice
    and you will flourish like new grass.
The power of the L ORD will be made known to his servants,
    but he will condemn his enemies.
15 The L ORD will come with fire
    and with his chariots like a thunderstorm.
      He will pay them back with his burning anger
        and punish them with flames of fire.
16 The L ORD will judge with fire,
    and he will judge all people with his sword.
      Many people will be struck dead by the L ORD.

17 People make themselves holy
    and prepare themselves for their garden rituals.
      They go into the garden
        and devour pork, disgusting things, and mice.
      "They will come to an end at the same time,"
        declares the L ORD.
18 Because of their actions and their thoughts,[a]
    I am coming to gather the nations of every language.
    They will come and see my glory.

---

[a] 66:18 Hebrew meaning of this line uncertain.

¹⁹ I will set up a sign among them
   and send some of their survivors to the nations:
      to Tarshish, Put and Lud, Meshech, Rosh, Tubal, Javan,
         and to the distant coastlands
            who have not heard of my fame or seen my glory.
   They will tell about my glory among the nations.

²⁰ They will bring all your relatives
   from every nation like a grain offering to the Lord.
   "They will come on horses, in chariots, in wagons,
      on mules and camels to my holy mountain, Jerusalem,"
         declares the Lord.
   They will come like the people of Israel who bring
      their grain offerings in clean dishes to the Lord's temple.

²¹ "I will make some of them priests and Levites," declares the Lord.

²² "The new heaven and earth that I am about to make
      will continue in my presence," declares the Lord.
   "So your descendants and your name
      will also continue in my presence.

²³ From one month to the next and from one week to the next
      all people will come to worship me," declares the Lord.

²⁴ Then they will go out
   and look at the corpses of those who have rebelled against me.
      The worms that eat them will not die.
      The fire that burns them will not go out.
      All humanity will be disgusted by them.

AN INTRODUCTION TO

Jeremiah

Jeremiah's mission was to warn the people of Judah that God would punish them. For over 40 years, Jeremiah warned his people. But instead of listening, the people got angry and threatened Jeremiah. Later, Jeremiah's prophecies came true. Babylon conquered Judah and made all the Jews captives.

Headlines

God Must Punish Jerusalem
Jeremiah 6:6, page 1043

Hometown Turns on Jeremiah
Jeremiah 11:21, page 1053

No Wife for Prophet
Jeremiah 16, page 1059

Prophet Goes Into Real Estate
Jeremiah 32, page 1084

Jeremiah Jailed
Jeremiah 38, page 1092

In Jeremiah's time, women were hired to weep at funerals. Why is this woman teaching a young girl to cry? See Jeremiah 9:17-21.

God Has a Plan for
Your Life

Jeremiah was shocked when God told him he had a mission for the prophet. "I'm too young!" twenty-year-old Jeremiah thought. "God couldn't have plans for me at this age!"

But God had made plans for Jeremiah before he was born (Jeremiah 1:5). Don't think just because you're young that God doesn't have plans for you. He knew you even before you were born, too.

God probably won't tell you those plans ahead of time. But if you follow Jesus faithfully, someday you'll be able to look back on your life and say, "Wow! God had it planned all along!"

For a special promise, see Jeremiah 29:11.

What's In It For Me?

It is worth obeying God . . .

EVEN WHEN OTHERS ARE MEAN TO ME.

EVEN WHEN I AM LEFT OUT OF SOMEONE ELSE'S FUN.

EVEN WHEN I DON'T GET WHAT I WANT.

BECAUSE GOD HAS PROMISED TO CARE FOR ME ALWAYS.

Why Was the Temple Destroyed?

Jeremiah warned the people of Jerusalem that their sins would lead to the destruction of God's temple. What did they do wrong?

1. They were unfair and oppressed the poor (Jeremiah 7:5-6).

2. They continued to sin and break God's law (Jeremiah 7:9).

3. They refused to stop worshiping other gods (Jeremiah 7:9).

4. They made the temple "a gathering place for thieves" (Jeremiah 7:11).

5. They would not listen to God's message through the prophets and would not change their ways (Jeremiah 7:13).

Jeremiah

The Prophet Jeremiah

¹These are the words of Jeremiah, son of Hilkiah. He was one of the priests at Anathoth in the territory of Benjamin. ²The LORD spoke his word to Jeremiah when King Josiah, son of Amon, was in his thirteenth year as king of Judah. ³The LORD also spoke when Jehoiakim, son of Josiah, was king of Judah and during the 11 years that Zedekiah, another son of Josiah, was king of Judah. The LORD continued to speak to Jeremiah until the people of Jerusalem were taken away into captivity in the fifth month of the year.

The LORD Gives Jeremiah a Message for His People

⁴The LORD spoke his word to me,

5   "Before I formed you in the womb,
          I knew you.
       Before you were born,
          I set you apart for my holy purpose.
          I appointed you to be a prophet to the nations."

⁶I, Jeremiah, said, "Almighty LORD, I do not know how to speak. I am only a boy!" ⁷But the LORD said to me, "Don't say that you are only a boy. You will go wherever I send you. You will say whatever I command you to say. ⁸Don't be afraid of people. I am with you, and I will rescue you," declares the LORD.

⁹Then the LORD stretched out his hand and touched my mouth. The LORD said to me,

       "Now I have put my words in your mouth.
10   Today I have put you in charge of nations and kingdoms.
          You will uproot and tear down.
          You will destroy and overthrow.
          You will build and plant."

¹¹Again the LORD spoke his word to me and asked, "Jeremiah, what do you see?" I answered, "I see a branch of an almond tree." ¹²Then the LORD said to me, "Right. I am watching to make sure that my words come true."ᵃ ¹³Again the LORD spoke his word to me and asked, "What do you see?" I answered, "I see a boiling pot, and its top is tilted away from the north." ¹⁴Then the LORD said to me,

       "Disaster will be poured out from the north
          on all those who live in the land.
15   I am going to call every family and kingdom from the north,"
          declares the LORD.
          "They will come, and they will set up their thrones
             at the entrance of Jerusalem's gates.
          They will attack all the walls around the city

ᵃ 1:11-12 There is a play on words here between Hebrew *shaked* (almond tree) and *shoked* (watching).

and all the cities of Judah.

¹⁶ I will pass sentence on my people because of all their wickedness.
> They abandoned me,
>> burned incense to other gods,
>>> and worshiped what their hands have made.

¹⁷ Brace yourself, Jeremiah!
> Stand up, and say to them whatever I tell you to say.
> Don't be terrified in their presence,
>> or I will make you even more terrified in their presence.

¹⁸ Today I have made you like a fortified city,
> an iron pillar, and a bronze wall.
>> You will be able to stand up to the whole land.
>> You will be able to stand up to Judah's kings,
>>> its officials, its priests, and all the common people.

¹⁹
> They will fight you, but they will not defeat you.
> I am with you, and I will rescue you," declares the LORD.

The People Continue to Reject the LORD's Love for Them

¹The LORD spoke his word to me,

² "Go and announce to Jerusalem,
> 'This is what the LORD says:
>> I remember the unfailing loyalty of your youth,
>>> the love you had for me as a bride.
>> I remember how you followed me into the desert,
>>> into a land that couldn't be farmed.

³ Israel was set apart for the LORD.
> It was the best part of the harvest.
>> All who devoured it became guilty,
>>> and disaster struck them,' " declares the LORD.

⁴ Listen to the word of the LORD, descendants of Jacob,
> all the families in the nation of Israel.

⁵ This is what the LORD says:
> What did your ancestors find wrong with me
>> that they went so far away from me?
> They followed worthless idols and became worthless themselves.

⁶ They didn't ask, "Where is the LORD,
> who brought us from Egypt?
>> He led us through the desert,
>>> through a wasteland and its pits,
>>>> a land of drought and the shadow of death.
>>>>> No one lives there or travels there."

⁷
> I brought them into a fertile land
>> to eat its fruit and its produce.
>>> They came and made my land unclean.^a
>>> They made my property disgusting.

⁸ The priests didn't ask, "Where is the LORD?"
> Those who deal with my teachings didn't know me.
> The rulers rebelled against me.

---

^a2:7 "Unclean" refers to anything that Moses' Teachings say is not presentable to God.

Women's World

Cisterns / *Jeremiah 2*

Cisterns were bell-shaped hollows made
in the rock and plastered to hold water.
Many hillside homes in Israel had a
series of cisterns to collect water during
the rainy season and store it for dry
times. Some household cisterns held
enough liquid to provide water for 6 to
12 people for a year. One giant cistern in
the city of Jerusalem held almost 3
million gallons of water!

> The prophets prophesied in the name of Baal
> and followed statues that couldn't help them.

9 "That is why I am bringing charges against you," declares the LORD,
      "and I am bringing charges against your grandchildren.
10 Go over to the coasts of Cyprus, and see.
      Send ₍someone₎ to Kedar, and observe closely.
        See if there has ever been anything like this.
11 Has any nation ever exchanged gods?
      (Their gods aren't really gods.)
      Yet, my people have exchanged their Glory
        for something that doesn't help them.
12 Be horrified over this, heaven.
      Be terribly afraid," declares the LORD.
13 "My people have done two things wrong.
      They have abandoned me,
        the fountain of life-giving water.
      They have also dug their own cisterns,
        broken cisterns that can't hold water.

14 "Are the people of Israel slaves?
      Were they born into slavery?
        Why, then, have they become someone's property?
15 Young lions have roared very loudly at them.
      Young lions have turned the land into a wasteland.
        The cities have been burned down, and everyone has left.
16 People from Noph and Tahpanhes have cracked your skulls, Israel.
17 You have brought this on yourself
      by abandoning the LORD your God
        when he led you on his way.
18 You won't gain anything by going to Egypt

to drink water from the Nile River.
You won't gain anything by going to Assyria
to drink water from the Euphrates River.

19 Your own wickedness will correct you,
and your unfaithful ways will punish you.
You should know and see how evil and bitter it is for you
if you abandon the LORD your God and do not fear me,"
declares the Almighty LORD of Armies.

20 "Long ago you broke off your yoke,[b] tore off your chains,
and said that you wouldn't be a slave.
You lay down and acted like a prostitute
on every high hill and under every large tree.

21 I planted you like a choice grapevine from the very best seed.
Now you have turned against me and have become a wild vine.

22 Even if you wash with detergent and use a lot of soap,
I would still see the stains from your wickedness,"
declares the Almighty LORD.

23 "How can you say that you haven't dishonored yourselves
and haven't followed other gods—the Baals?
Look how you've behaved in the valley.
Acknowledge what you've done.
You are like a young camel that swiftly runs here and there.

24 You are like a wild donkey that is used to the desert,
sniffing the wind while in heat.
All who look for you won't get tired.
They will find you during your monthly period.

25 Don't run until your feet are bare and your throats are dry.
But you say that it's useless.
You love foreign gods and follow them.

26 "As a thief feels ashamed when he's caught,
so the nation of Israel will feel ashamed.
Their kings, princes, priests,
and prophets will also feel ashamed.

27 You call wood your father.
You call stone your mother.
You've turned your backs, not your faces, to me.
But when you're in trouble, you ask me to come and rescue you.

28 Where are the gods that you made for yourselves?
Let them come and rescue you when you're in trouble.
You have as many gods as you have cities, Judah!

29 "Why do you complain about me?
All of you have rebelled against me," declares the LORD.

30 "I have punished your children without results.
They didn't respond to correction.
You killed my prophets like a raging lion.

31 "Consider the word of the LORD, people of this generation.
Haven't I been a desert, a land of thick darkness, for Israel?

---

[b] 2:20 A yoke is a wooden bar placed over the necks of work animals so that they can pull plows or carts.

Why do my people say that they are free to wander around
    and no longer come to me?
 32 A young woman can't forget her jewelry or a bride her veils.
    Yet, my people have forgotten me for countless days.
33 You carefully planned ways to look for love.
    You taught your ways to wicked women.
34 You have the blood from poor and innocent people
    on your clothes.
    You didn't kill them for breaking in to your home.
35 In spite of all this you say, 'I'm innocent.
    God will turn his anger from me,
      because I haven't sinned.'
36 You change your mind so easily.
You will be put to shame by Egypt
    as you were put to shame by Assyria.
37 You will also leave this place with your hands over your head,
    because the Lord has rejected those you trust.
    You will not be helped by them."

3 ¹A saying:

If a man divorces his wife
    and she leaves him and marries another man,
      her first husband shouldn't go back to her again.
      The land would become thoroughly polluted.
"You have acted like a prostitute who has many lovers.
    And now you want to come back to me!" declares the Lord.

2 "Look at the bare hills, and see.
    You have had sex with men in every place.
    You sat by the roadside waiting for them like a nomad in the desert.
    You have polluted the land with your prostitution and wickedness.
3 So the rain has been withheld, and there have been no spring showers.
Yet, you have the shameless look of a prostitute,
    and you refuse to blush.
4 But now you are calling to me.
    You say, 'Father! You have been my companion
      ever since I was young.
5   He won't hold a grudge forever.
    He won't always be angry.'
You have said and done all the evil things that you could."

The Lord Offers to Forgive the Ten Tribes of Israel Despite Their Idolatry

⁶When Josiah was king, the Lord asked me, "Did you see what unfaithful Israel did? She went up every high mountain and under every large tree, and she acted like a prostitute there. ⁷I thought that after she had done all this that she would come back to me. But she didn't come back, and her treacherous sister Judah saw her. ⁸Judah saw that I sent unfaithful Israel away because of her adultery and that I gave Israel her divorce papers. But treacherous Judah, her sister, wasn't afraid. She also acted like a prostitute. ⁹Because she wasn't concerned about acting like a prostitute, she

polluted the land and committed adultery with standing stones and wood pillars. ¹⁰Even after all this, Israel's treacherous sister Judah didn't wholeheartedly come back to me. She was deceitful," declares the LORD.

¹¹Then the LORD said to me, "Unfaithful Israel was less guilty than treacherous Judah. ¹²Go and proclaim these things to the north:

> " 'Come back, unfaithful Israel.
>> It is the LORD speaking.
>>> I will no longer frown on you
>>>> because I'm merciful,' declares the LORD.
>>> 'I will no longer be angry with you.

¹³ Admit that you've done wrong!
>> You have rebelled against the LORD your God.
>> You have given yourself to strangers under every large tree.
>> You have not obeyed me,' declares the LORD.

¹⁴"Come back, you rebellious people," declares the LORD. "I'm your husband. I will take you, one from every city and two from every family, and bring you to Zion. ¹⁵I will give you shepherds after my own heart. They will be shepherds who feed you with knowledge and insight. ¹⁶In those days you will be fertile, and your population will increase in the land," declares the LORD. "People will no longer talk about the ark of the LORD's promise. It will no longer come to mind. They won't remember it, miss it, or make another one. ¹⁷At that time they will call Jerusalem the throne of the LORD. All nations will gather in Jerusalem because the name of the LORD will be found there. They will no longer follow their own stubborn, evil ways. ¹⁸In those days the nation of Judah will live with the nation of Israel. They will come together from the land of the north to the land that I gave their ancestors as their own property.

¹⁹ "I wanted to treat you like children
>> and give you a pleasant land,
>>> the most beautiful property among the nations.
>> I thought that you would call me Father and wouldn't turn away from me.
²⁰ But like a wife who betrays her husband,
>> so you, nation of Israel, betrayed me," declares the LORD.

²¹ The sound of crying is heard on the hills.
>> It is the crying and the pleading of the people of Israel.
>>> They have become crooked
>>>> and have forgotten the LORD their God.
²² "Come back, you rebellious people,
>> and I will forgive you for being unfaithful."

Here we are!
>> We have come to you because you are the LORD our God.
²³ Truly, the noise from the hills, from the mountains,
>> is the noise of false worship.
Truly, the LORD our God will rescue us.
²⁴ Ever since we were young,
>> the shameful worship ͺof Baalͺ
>>> has taken everything our ancestors worked for,
>>>> their flocks and herds, their sons and daughters.
²⁵ We must lie down in our shame

and be covered by our disgrace.
Ever since we were young, we and our ancestors have sinned
against the Lord our God.
We haven't obeyed the Lord our God.

4 ¹The Lord declares,

"If you come back, Israel,
if you come back to me,
if you take your disgusting idols out of my sight
and you don't wander away from me,
² if you take the oath, "As the Lord lives . . ."
in an honest, fair, and right way,
then the nations will be blessed,
and they will be honored by me."

The Lord Will Bring Destruction on Judah From the North

³This is what the Lord says to the people of Judah and to Jerusalem:

Plow your unplowed fields,
and don't plant among thorns.
⁴ Be circumcised by the Lord,
and get rid of the foreskins of your hearts,
people of Judah and inhabitants of Jerusalem.
If you don't, my fury will flare up like a fire.
It will burn, and no one will be able to put it out,
because of the evil you do.

⁵ Report this message in Judah.
Make it heard in Jerusalem.
Say, "Blow the ram's horn throughout the land."
Shout loudly and say, "Gather together!
Let's go into the fortified cities."
⁶ Raise the flag to signal people to go to Zion.
Take cover!
Don't just stand there!
I'm bringing disaster and widespread destruction from the north.
⁷ A lion has come out of its lair.
A destroyer of nations has set out.
He has left his place to destroy your land.
Your cities will be ruined, and no one will live in them.
⁸ So put on sackcloth, mourn, and cry
because the Lord's burning anger hasn't turned away from us.

⁹ "When that day comes," declares the Lord,
"the king and the leaders will lose their courage.
The priests will be stunned.
The prophets will be amazed and astonished."
¹⁰ I said, "Almighty Lord,
you certainly have deceived these people and Jerusalem.
You said that everything would go well for them,
but a sword is held at their throats."

11 At that time it will be said to these people and to Jerusalem:
"A hot wind from the heights will blow in the desert
on the tracks of my people.
It will not be a wind that winnows[a] or cleanses.
12 It will be a stronger wind than that.
It will come from me.
Now, I will pass sentence on them."

13 The enemy comes up like clouds.
His chariots are like a raging wind.
His horses are faster than eagles.
How horrible it will be for us! We will be destroyed!
14 Jerusalem, wash the evil from your heart
so that you may be rescued.
Don't continue making evil plans.
15 A message is heard from Dan,
and a report of disaster comes from the mountains of Ephraim.
16 Warn the nations about these things.
Bring them to the attention of Jerusalem.
"Hostile troops are coming from a distant country.
They are shouting battle cries against the cities of Judah.
17 They surround them like men guarding a field,
because Judah has rebelled against me,"
declares the LORD.
18 "You brought this on yourself.
This is your punishment.
It is bitter.
It breaks your heart."

19 My anguish, my anguish!
I writhe in pain.
My heart is beating wildly!
My heart is pounding!
I can't keep quiet
because I hear a ram's horn sounding the alarm for war.
20 One disaster follows another.
The whole land is ruined.
My tents are suddenly destroyed.
Their curtains are torn in an instant.
21 How long must I see the battle flag and hear the sound of rams' horns?

22 "My people are fools. They don't know me.
They are stupid people. They don't understand.
They are experts in doing wrong,
and they don't know how to do good."

23 I see the earth. It's formless and empty.
I see the sky. Its lights are gone.
24 I see the mountains. They are shaking,
and the hills are swaying.

---

a 4:11 Winnowing is the process of separating husks from grain.

25 I see that there are no people,
  and every bird has flown away.
26 I see that the fertile land has become a desert,
  and all its cities are torn down
    because of the LORD and his burning anger.

27This is what the LORD says:

The whole earth will be ruined,
  although I will not destroy it completely.
28 The earth will mourn, and the sky will grow black.
  I have spoken, and I have planned it.
  I won't change my plans, and I won't turn back.

29 All the people in the city will flee
  at the sound of riders and archers.
    They will go off into the thickets
      and climb among the rocks.
The entire city will be abandoned, and no one will live in it.

30 You are going to be destroyed!
  What are you going to do?
    Why do you dress in red and put on gold jewelry?
    Why do you wear eye shadow?
      You are making yourself beautiful for nothing.
      Your lovers reject you; they want to kill you.

31 I hear a woman in labor.
I hear the woman cry with anguish as she gives birth to her first child.
  My people Zion are gasping for breath.
  They are stretching out their hands, saying,
    "How horrible it is for us!
    We're defenseless in the presence of murderers!"

Judah's Complete Rejection of the LORD

5 1 Walk around the streets of Jerusalem.
Look around, and think about these things.
Search the city squares.
See if you can find anyone
  who does what is right and seeks the truth.
    Then I will forgive Jerusalem.
2 People say, "As the LORD lives. . . ."
  Yet, they lie when they take this oath.
3 LORD, your eyes look for the truth.
  You strike these people, but they don't feel it.
  You crush them, but they refuse to be corrected.
    They are more stubborn than rocks.
    They refuse to turn back.
4 I thought, "These are poor, foolish people.
  They don't know the way of the LORD
    and the justice that God demands.
5 Let me go to important people and speak to them.

They know the way of the LORD
  and the justice that God demands."
    But they, too, had broken off their yokes[a]
      and torn off their chains.
6 That is why a lion from the forest will attack them.
  A wolf from the wilderness will destroy them.
  A leopard will lie in ambush outside their cities.
    All who leave the cities will be torn to pieces,
      because they rebel so often
        and they become more and more unfaithful.

7 "Why should I forgive you?
  Your children abandoned me.
    They took godless oaths.
    They committed adultery, even though I satisfied their needs.
    They traveled in crowds to the houses of prostitutes.
8 They are like well-fed stallions that are wild with desire.
  They neigh for their neighbors' wives.
9 I will punish them for these things," declares the LORD.
  "I will punish this nation.

10 "Go among Jerusalem's rows of grapevines and destroy them,
  but don't destroy all of them.
  Cut off the branches because they don't belong to the LORD.
11 The nations of Israel and Judah are unfaithful to me,"
  declares the LORD.
12 They lie about the LORD and say,
  "He doesn't exist!
    Nothing bad will happen to us.
    We won't experience war or famine.
13 The prophets are nothing but windbags.
  The LORD hasn't spoken through them,
    so let what they say happen to them."

14This is what the LORD God of Armies says:

Because you've talked like this,
  I'm going to put my words in your mouth like a fire.
    These people will be like wood.
    My words will burn them up.
15 Nation of Israel, I'm going to bring a nation from far away
  to attack you, declares the LORD.
    It is a nation that has lasted a long time.
    It is an ancient nation.
      You don't know the language of this nation.
      You can't understand what its people say.
16 Their arrow quivers are like open graves.
  They are all mighty warriors.
17   They will devour your harvest and your food.
    They will devour your sons and your daughters.
    They will devour your flocks and your cattle.

---

[a]5:5 A yoke is a wooden bar placed over the necks of work animals so that they can pull plows or carts.

> They will devour your grapevines and your fig trees.
> With their swords they will destroy
>   the fortified cities you trust.

18 Yet, even in those days, declares the LORD,
    I won't destroy all of you.

¹⁹They will ask, "Why has the LORD our God done all this to us?" Answer them, "You have abandoned me and served foreign gods in your land. So you will serve foreigners in a land that isn't yours."

20 "Tell this to the descendants of Jacob, and make this heard in Judah:
21 Hear this, you stupid and senseless people!
> You have eyes, but you cannot see.
> You have ears, but you cannot hear.
22 Don't you fear me?" asks the LORD.
> "Don't you tremble in my presence?
> I made the sand a boundary for the sea,
>   a permanent barrier that it cannot cross.
>   Although the waves toss continuously,
>   they can't break through.
>   Although they roar, they can't cross it.
23 But these people are stubborn and rebellious.
> They have turned aside and wandered away from me.
24 They don't say to themselves,
> 'We should fear the LORD our God.
> He sends rain at the right time,
>   the autumn rain and the spring rain.
> He makes sure that we have harvest seasons.'
25 Your wickedness has turned these things away.
> Your sins have kept good things away from you.

26 "Wicked people are found among my people.
> They lie in ambush like bird catchers.
> They set traps and catch people.
27 Like cages filled with birds, their houses are filled with deceit.
> That is why they become powerful and rich.
28 They grow big and fat.
> Their evil deeds have no limits.
> They have no respect for the rights of others.
> They have no respect for the rights of orphans.
>   But they still prosper.
> They don't defend the rights of the poor.
29 I will punish them for these things," declares the LORD.
> "I will punish this nation.

30 "Something horrible and disgusting is happening in the land:
31 Prophets prophesy lies.
> Priests rule under the prophets' directions,
>   and my people love this.
> But what will you do in the end?"

The LORD's Rejection of Judah

6 ¹ "Take cover, people of Benjamin!
Run away from Jerusalem!
Blow the ram's horn in Tekoa.
Raise the flag over Beth Hakkerem,
　　because disaster and widespread destruction
　　are coming from the north.

² "My people Zion are like lovely pastures.
³ With their flocks, shepherds will come to them,
　　pitch their tents all around them,
　　and each of them will tend his own flock.
⁴ ⸢The shepherds say,⸣ 'Prepare yourselves for war against Zion.
　　Let's attack at noon!
　　　How horrible it will be for us. The day is passing,
　　　and the shadows of evening are growing longer.
⁵ 　Let's attack at night and destroy its palaces.' "

⁶This is what the LORD of Armies says:

Cut down its trees.
Build up dirt mounds to attack Jerusalem.
　This city must be punished.
　　There is nothing but oppression in it.
⁷ As a well keeps its water fresh,
　so Jerusalem keeps its evil fresh.
　　Violence and destruction can be heard in it.
　　　I see that it is sick and wounded.
⁸ Pay attention to my warning, Jerusalem,
　or I will turn away from you.
I will make your land desolate,
　a land where no one will live.

⁹This is what the LORD of Armies says:

Thoroughly pick through the faithful few of Israel
　like someone picks through a grapevine.
　　Like someone picking grapes, pass your hand over its branches again.

¹⁰ Whom can I speak to?
Whom can I give a warning to?
Who will listen?
　Their ears are plugged,
　　and they aren't able to pay attention.
　When the LORD speaks his word to them,
　　they show contempt for it and object to it.
¹¹ I am filled with the anger of the LORD.
I am tired of holding it in.

"Pour it out on the children in the street
　and on the gangs of young men.
A man and his wife will be taken away
　as well as very old people.
¹² Their households, their fields, and their wives

will be turned over to others.
I will use my power against those who live in the land,"
declares the LORD.

13 "All of them, from the least important to the most important,
are eager to make money dishonestly.
All of them, from prophets to priests, act deceitfully.

14 They treat my people's wounds as though they were not serious, saying,
'Everything is alright! Everything is alright!'
But it's not alright.

15 Are they ashamed when they do disgusting things?
No, they're not ashamed.
They don't even know how to blush.
So they will die with those who die.
They will be brought down when I punish them," says the LORD.

16 This is what the LORD says:

Stand at the crossroads and look.
Ask which paths are the old, reliable paths.
Ask which way leads to blessings.
Live that way, and find a resting place for yourselves.
But you said that you wouldn't live that way.

17 I posted watchmen over you.
Pay attention to the sound of the ram's horn.
But you said that you wouldn't pay attention.

18 Listen, you nations,
and learn, you witnesses, what will happen to them.

19 Listen, earth!
I'm going to bring disaster on these people.
It is the result of their own plots,
because they won't pay attention to my words.
They reject my teachings.

20 Incense that comes from Sheba is no good to me.
Sugar cane that comes from a distant land is no good to me.
I won't accept your burnt offerings.
I'm not pleased with your sacrifices.

21 This is what the LORD says:

I'm going to lay stumbling blocks in front of these people.
Parents and children will stumble over them.
Neighbors and their friends will die.

22 This is what the LORD says:

An army is going to come from the north.
A great nation is preparing itself in the distant parts of the earth.

23 Its people take hold of bows and spears.
They are cruel and have no compassion.
They sound like the roaring sea.
They ride on horses.
They march like soldiers ready for battle
against my people Zion.

24 We have heard the news about them.
    Our hands hang limp.
We are gripped by anguish and pain
    like a woman giving birth to a child.
25 Don't go into the field or walk on the road.
    The enemy has a sword.
      Terror is all around.
26 Wear sackcloth, and roll around in ashes, my people.
    Mourn as if you have lost your only child, and cry bitterly.
The destroyer will suddenly attack us.

27 "Jeremiah, I have put you in charge of testing and refining my people.
    You will know how to test their ways.
28   They are all vicious rebels.
    They go around slandering.
    They are all like bronze and iron.
    They corrupt themselves.
29 The bellows of the blast furnace blow fiercely
    to make the fire melt away the lead.
    It is useless to go on refining
      because the impurities can't be removed.
30 People will call them useless silver
    because the LORD has rejected them."

Judah Trusts the Wrong Things

1 The LORD spoke his word to Jeremiah. He said, 2 "Stand at the gate of the LORD's house, and announce from there this message: 'Listen to the word of the LORD, all you people of Judah who go through these gates to worship the LORD. 3 This is what the LORD of Armies, the God of Israel, says: Change the way you live and act, and I will let you live in this place. 4 Do not trust the words of this saying, "This is the LORD's temple, the LORD's temple, the LORD's temple!" It's a lie.

5 " 'Suppose you really change the way you live and act and you really treat each other fairly. 6 Suppose you do not oppress foreigners, orphans, and widows, or kill anyone in this place. And suppose you do not follow other gods that lead you to your own destruction. 7 Then I will let you live in this place, in the land that I gave permanently to your ancestors long ago.

8 " 'You are trusting the words of a saying. It's a lie that cannot help you. 9 You steal, murder, commit adultery, lie when you take oaths, burn incense as an offering to Baal, and run after other gods that you do not know. 10 Then you stand in my presence in the house that is called by my name. You think that you're safe to do all these disgusting things. 11 The house that is called by my name has become a gathering place for thieves. I have seen what you are doing,' " declares the LORD.

12 " 'But go to my place that was at Shiloh, where I first made a dwelling place for my name. See what I did to Shiloh because of the evil done by my people Israel. 13 You have done the same things the people did at Shiloh,' " declares the LORD. " 'Although I spoke to you again and again, you did not listen. When I called you, you did not answer. 14 So what I did to Shiloh I will now do to the house that is called by my name. This is the place I gave to you and to your ancestors, the place where you feel so safe. 15 I will force you out of my sight as I forced out all your relatives, all of Ephraim's descendants.'

¹⁶"Jeremiah, don't pray for these people. Don't cry or pray for them. Don't plead with me, because I will not listen to you. ¹⁷Don't you see what they are doing in the cities of Judah and in the streets of Jerusalem? ¹⁸Children gather wood, fathers light fires, and women knead dough to make cakes for the queen of heaven. They pour out wine offerings to other gods in order to make me furious. ¹⁹They aren't really provoking me," declares the Lord. "But they are ˌharmingˌ themselves to their own shame.

²⁰"This is what the Almighty Lord says: My anger and fury will be poured out on this place, on humans and animals, and on trees and crops. My anger and fury will burn and not be put out.

²¹"This is what the Lord of Armies, the God of Israel, says: Add your burnt offerings to your sacrifices, and eat the meat. ²²When I brought your ancestors out of Egypt, I did not tell them anything about burnt offerings and sacrifices. ²³But I did tell them this, 'Obey me, and I will be your God, and you will be my people. Live the way I told you to live so that things will go well for you.' ²⁴But they didn't obey me or pay attention to me. They followed their own plans and their stubborn, evil ways. They went backward and not forward. ²⁵From the time that your ancestors left Egypt until now, I have sent all my servants the prophets to you again and again. ²⁶But you didn't obey me or pay attention to me. You became impossible to deal with, and you were worse than your ancestors.

²⁷"Jeremiah, you will say all these things to them, but they will not obey you. You will call to them, but they will not respond to you. ²⁸You will say to them, 'This is the nation that did not obey the Lord their God. They did not accept discipline. Truth has disappeared and vanished from their lips.'

²⁹"Cut off your hair and throw it away. Sing a song of mourning on the bare hills, because in his anger the Lord has rejected and abandoned the people of this generation. ³⁰The people of Judah have done what I consider evil," declares the Lord. "They set up their detestable idols in the house that is called by my name. They have made it unclean.ᵃ ³¹They have built worship sites at Topheth in the valley of Ben Hinnom in order to burn their sons and daughters as sacrifices. I did not ask for this. It never entered my mind.

³²"That is why the days are coming," declares the Lord, "when that place will no longer be known as Topheth or the valley of Ben Hinnom. Instead, it will be known as Slaughter Valley. They will bury ˌpeopleˌ at Topheth because no other place will be left. ³³The dead bodies of these people will become food for birds and animals, and no one will be there to frighten them away. ³⁴In the cities of Judah and in the streets of Jerusalem, I will banish the sounds of joy and happiness and the sounds of brides and grooms, because the land will be a wasteland."

8 ¹The Lord declares, "At that time the bones of the kings and the leaders of Judah, the bones of the priests and the prophets, and the bones of the others who lived in Jerusalem will be taken out of their graves. ²They will be spread out and exposed to the sun, the moon, and all the stars in the sky. These are the things that they had loved, served, gone after, sought, and worshiped. Their bones will not be gathered or buried, but they will become manure on the ground.

³"Then the few who remain from these wicked people will want to die rather than live where I will scatter them," declares the Lord of Armies.

ᵃ7:30 "Unclean" refers to anything that Moses' Teachings say is not presentable to God.

The LORD's Judgment on Judah's False Religion

4"Say to them, 'This is what the LORD says:

> When someone falls, he gets back up.
> When someone turns away from me, he returns.

5 The people of Jerusalem turned away from me without ever returning.
> They still cling to deceit.
> They refuse to return.

6 I have paid attention and listened,
> but they weren't honest.
>> They don't turn away from their wickedness and ask,
>> "What have we done?"
> They go their own ways like horses charging into battle.

7 Even storks know when it's time to return.
> Mourning doves, swallows, and cranes know
>> when it's time to migrate.
>> But my people don't know
>> that I, the LORD, am urging them to return.

8 " 'How can you say that you are wise
> and that you have the LORD's teachings?
The scribes have used their pens to turn these teachings into lies.

9 Wise people are put to shame, confused, and trapped.
> They have rejected the word of the LORD.
> They don't really have any wisdom.

10 That is why I will give their wives to other men
> and their fields to new owners.
All of them, from the least important to the most important,
> are eager to make money dishonestly.
All of them, from prophets to priests, act deceitfully.

11 They treat my dear people's wounds
> as though they were not serious, saying,
>> "Everything is alright! Everything is alright!"
>> But it's not alright.

12 Are they ashamed that they do disgusting things?
> No, they're not ashamed.
> They don't even know how to blush.
So they will die with those who die.
They will be brought down when I punish them,' " says the LORD.

13 " 'I would have gathered their harvest,' " declares the LORD,
> " 'but there are no grapes on the vine.
> There are no figs on the tree,
>> and the leaves have dried up.
>> What I have given them will be taken away.' "

14 Why are we just sitting here? Let's get up!
Let's go into the fortified cities and die there.
> The LORD our God has condemned us to die.
> He has given us poison to drink
>> because we have sinned against the LORD.

15 We hoped for peace, but nothing good has happened.

We hoped for a time of healing, but there's only terror.

16　　The snorting of horses can be heard from Dan.
　　　The neighing of stallions makes the whole land tremble.
　　　　They are coming to devour the land and everything in it,
　　　　　the city and its people.

17　　"I am going to send snakes among you,
　　　　vipers that can't be charmed.
　　　　They will bite you," declares the LORD.

Jeremiah's Grief Over His People's Punishment

18　　Sorrow has overwhelmed me.
　　　I am sick at heart!

19　　The cry from my dear people comes from a distant land:
　　　　"Isn't the LORD in Zion?
　　　　Isn't Zion's king still there?"
　　　They make me furious with their idols, with their foreign gods.

20　　The harvest is past,
　　　　the summer has ended,
　　　　　and we haven't been saved.

21　　I am crushed because my dear people have been crushed.
　　　I mourn; terror grips me.

22　　Isn't there medicine in Gilead?
　　　　Aren't there doctors there?
　　　　　Then why hasn't the health of my dear people been restored?

9 [a]1　"I wish that my head were filled with water
　　　and my eyes were a fountain of tears
　　　　so that I could cry day and night
　　　　　for my dear people who have been killed.

2　　I wish I had a place to stay in the desert.
　　　I would abandon my people and go away from them.
　　　　They are all adulterers,
　　　　　a mob of traitors.

3　　They use their tongues like bows that shoot arrows.
　　　　Lies and dishonesty rule the land.[b]
　　　They go from one evil thing to another,
　　　　and they don't know me," declares the LORD.

4　　"Beware of your neighbors.
　　　Don't trust your relatives.
　　　　Every relative cheats.
　　　　Every neighbor goes around slandering.

5　　Everyone cheats his neighbor.
　　　　No one speaks the truth.
　　　My people train their tongues to speak lies.
　　　They wear themselves out doing wrong.

6　　Oppression follows oppression.[c]

---

[a]9:1 Jeremiah 9:1-26 in English Bibles is Jeremiah 8:23-9:25 in the Hebrew Bible.　[b]9:3 Greek; Masoretic Text
"They bend their tongue. Their bow is falsehood. And not for truth are they strong in the land."　[c]9:6 Greek;
Masoretic Text "Your sitting is in the midst of deceit."

Deceit follows deceit.
They refuse to acknowledge me," declares the LORD.

7This is what the LORD of Armies says:

I will now refine them with fire and test them.
What else can I do for my dear people?
8   Their tongues are like deadly arrows.
They speak deceitfully.
People speak politely to their neighbors,
but they think of ways to set traps for them.
9   I will punish them for these things, declares the LORD.
I will punish this nation.
I still won't be satisfied.

10   I will cry and weep for the mountains.
I will sing a funeral song for the pastures in the wilderness.
They are destroyed so that no one can travel through them.
No one can hear the sound of cattle.
Birds and cattle have fled.
They are gone.
11   I will turn Jerusalem into a pile of rubble, a home for jackals.
I will destroy the cities of Judah so that no one can live there.
12   No one is wise enough to understand this.
To whom has the LORD revealed this
so that they can explain it?
The land dies; it has been ruined like the desert
so that no one can travel through it.

13The LORD answered,

"They've abandoned my teachings that I placed in front of them.
They didn't obey me, and they didn't follow them.
14   They followed their own stubborn ways and other gods—the Baals,
as their ancestors taught them."

15This is what the LORD of Armies, the God of Israel, says:

Good Morning, God
Jeremiah 9:7-9

When was the last time someone hurt your feelings with careless words? Jeremiah describes a person's tongue as being like an arrow. We have the ability to hurt people deeply, simply by the things we say to them or about them. Are you using your words as ammunition to cause someone else pain? God reminds us in the Bible that he will punish us for misusing our tongue.

Lord, help my words to be pleasant, not painful.

I am going to feed these people bitterness
  and give them poison to drink.
16 I will scatter them among nations
  that they and their ancestors haven't heard of.
I will send armies after them until I've wiped them out.

17This is what the Lord of Armies says:

Consider this:
  Call for the women who cry at funerals.
  Send for those who are the most skilled.
18 They should come quickly and cry for us.
  Our eyes will run with tears.
  Our eyelids will flow with water.
19 The sound of crying is heard from Zion.
  "We're ruined! We're very ashamed.
  We must leave our land because our homes have been torn down."

20 Listen to the word of the Lord, you women,
  and open your ears to hear his words.
    Teach your daughters how to cry.
    Teach your neighbors funeral songs.
21 Death has come through our windows and entered our palaces.
  Death has cut down the children in the streets
    and the young men in the market places.

22This is what the Lord says:

Dead bodies will fall like manure on the field.
  They will be like grain that has been cut but not gathered.

The Lord Is the Only True God

23This is what the Lord says:

Don't let wise people brag about their wisdom.
Don't let strong people brag about their strength.
Don't let rich people brag about their riches.
24 If they want to brag, they should brag that they understand and know me.
  They should brag that I, the Lord, act out of love, righteousness,
    and justice on the earth.
      This kind of bragging pleases me, declares the Lord.

25 "The days are coming," declares the Lord,
  "when I will punish all who are circumcised.
26 I will punish Egypt, Judah, Edom, Ammon, and Moab.
I will punish all who shave the hair on their foreheads
  or live in the desert.
    Even though these nations are circumcised,
      all Israel has uncircumcised hearts."

1Listen to the message that the Lord has spoken to you, nation of Israel. 2This
is what the Lord says:

Don't learn the practices of the nations.
Don't be frightened by the signs in the sky

because the nations are frightened by them.

3 The religion of the people is worthless.
Woodcutters cut down trees from the forest.
The hands of craftsmen prepare them with axes.

4 Craftsmen decorate them with silver and gold
and fasten them together with hammers and nails
so that they won't fall over.

5 These trees are like scarecrows in cucumber gardens.
They aren't able to speak.
They have to be carried, because they can't walk.
Don't be afraid of them.
They can't harm you.
They can't do you any good either.

6 No one is like you, O Lord.
You are great.
Your name is powerful.

7 Everyone fears you, O King of the Nations.
This is what you deserve.
No one is like you among all the wise people in the nations
or in all their kingdoms.

8 They are complete idiots.
They learn nonsense from wooden idols.

9 Hammered silver is brought from Tarshish and gold from Uphaz.
Craftsmen and goldsmiths shape these metals.
The clothing for the idols is blue and purple,
all made by skilled workers.

10 But the Lord is the only God.
He is the living God and eternal king.
The earth trembles when he is angry.
The nations can't endure his fury.

11 Tell them this: These gods will disappear from the earth
and from under heaven because they didn't make heaven and earth.

12 The Lord made the earth by his power.
He set up the world by his skill.
He stretched out the world by his understanding.

13 He speaks, and the water in the sky produces a storm.
He makes clouds rise from the ends of the earth.
He makes lightning flash with the rain.
He brings wind out of his storehouses.

14 Everyone is stupid and ignorant.
Metalsmiths are put to shame by their idols.
Their statues are false gods.
They can't breathe.

15 They are worthless jokes.
When they are punished, they disappear.

16 Jacob's God isn't like them.
He made everything,

and Israel is the tribe that belongs to him.
His name is the Lord of Armies.

17   Pick up your bags. You are being blockaded.

18This is what the Lord says:

I am going to throw out those who live in the land at this time
and cause trouble for them so that they will feel it.

19   Oh, I'm wounded!
My wound is serious.
Then I thought that this is my punishment, and I will bear it.

20   My tent is destroyed, and all my ropes are broken.
My children have left me and have disappeared.
There's no one to set up my tent again
or put up my tent curtains.

21   The shepherds are foolish.
They don't look to the Lord for help.
That is why they won't succeed,
and all their flocks will be scattered.

22   The report has arrived.
A tremendous uproar is coming from the land of the north.
Its army will destroy Judah's cities
and make them homes for jackals.

23   O Lord, I know that the way humans act is not under their control.
Humans do not direct their steps as they walk.

24   Correct me, O Lord, but please be fair.
Don't correct me when you're angry.
Otherwise, you'll reduce me to nothing.

25   Pour out your fury on the nations who don't know you
and on people who don't worship you.
They have devoured the descendants of Jacob.
They have devoured them completely.
They have destroyed their homes.

Judah Has Disobeyed the Terms of the LORD's Promise

11 ¹This is the message that the Lord spoke to Jeremiah. He said, ²"Listen to the terms of this promise,ᵃ and tell them to the people of Judah and to those who live in Jerusalem. ³Say to them, 'This is what the Lord, the God of Israel, says: Cursed is anyone who doesn't listen to the terms of this promise. ⁴I made this promise to your ancestors when I brought them out of Egypt, which was an iron smelter. I said, "Obey me, and do everything that I have told you to do. Then you will be my people, and I will be your God. ⁵I will keep the oath I made to your ancestors and give them a land flowing with milk and honey, the land you still have today." ' "

I answered, "Yes, Lord."

⁶The Lord said to me, "Announce all these things in the cities of Judah and in the streets of Jerusalem: Listen to the terms of this promise, and keep them. ⁷I solemnly warned your ancestors when I brought them out of Egypt, and the warning still applies to you today. I solemnly warned them to obey me. ⁸But they didn't obey me or

---

pay attention to me. They followed their own stubborn, evil ways. So I punished them, because they did not keep all the terms of the promise, the terms that I commanded them to keep."

⁹The LORD said to me, "Conspiracy exists among the people of Judah and among those who live in Jerusalem. ¹⁰They've gone back to the evil ways of their ancestors and refused to obey my words. They are following other gods and worshiping them. The nations of Israel and Judah have rejected the promise that I made to their ancestors. ¹¹This is what the LORD says: I'm going to bring a disaster on them that they can't escape. Although they will cry out to me, I won't listen to them. ¹²Then the cities of Judah and those who live in Jerusalem will cry to the gods to whom they've been sacrificing. But these gods will never rescue them when they're in trouble. ¹³Judah, you have as many gods as you have cities. You have set up many altars in Jerusalem to sacrifice to Baal. You have as many altars as there are streets in Jerusalem. ¹⁴Jeremiah, don't pray for these people. Don't cry or pray for them. I won't listen when they call to me for help in times of trouble.

15 "What right do these people I love have to be in my house
        when they do so many devious things?
    Can the meat from their sacrifices turn disaster away from them?
        They rejoice when they do evil."

16 The LORD called you a large olive tree
        that has beautiful fruit to look at.
    He will set fire to you with a mighty storm,
        and your branches will be broken.
17 The LORD of Armies planted you.
        He has pronounced disaster on you.
    This is because of the evil things
        that Israel and Judah have done.
    They have made him furious by burning incense
        as an offering to Baal.

Jeremiah's Life Is Threatened

¹⁸The LORD revealed their plot to me so that I would understand. He showed me what they were doing. ¹⁹I was like a trusting lamb brought to the slaughter. I didn't know that they were plotting against me. They were saying, "Let's destroy the tree with its fruit. Let's cut Jeremiah off from this world of the living so that we won't be reminded of him anymore."

20 O LORD of Armies, you judge fairly
        and test motives and thoughts.
    I want to see you take revenge on them,
        because I've brought my case to you.

²¹This is what the LORD says: The people of Anathoth want to kill you. They say, "Don't prophesy in the name of the LORD, or we'll kill you."

²²This is what the LORD of Armies says: I'm going to punish them. The young men will die because of war. Their sons and daughters will die because of famine. ²³I will bring a disaster on the people of Anathoth. It will be a year of punishment. There will be no survivors.

Jeremiah's Question

12 ¹ O Lord, even if I would argue my case with you,
  you would always be right.
    Yet, I want to talk to you about your justice.
      Why do wicked people succeed?
      Why do treacherous people have peace and quiet?
²   You plant them, and they take root.
        They grow, and they produce fruit.
        They speak well of you with their lips,
          but their hearts are far from you.
³ You know me, O Lord.
  You see me and test my devotion to you.
    Drag them away like sheep to be slaughtered.
    Prepare them for the day of slaughter.
⁴ How long will the land mourn?
  How long will the plants in every field remain dried up?
    The animals and the birds are dying,
      because people are wicked.
    They think that God*ᵃ* doesn't know what they are doing.

The LORD's Reply

⁵ "If you have raced against others on foot, and they have tired you out,
  how can you compete with horses?
If you stumble in open country,
  how can you live in the jungle along the Jordan River?
⁶ Even your relatives and members of your father's household betray you.
    They have also formed a mob to find you.
    Don't trust them when they say good things about you.

⁷ "I have abandoned my nation.
I have left my own people.
I have handed the people I love over to their enemies.
⁸ My people have turned on me like a lion in the forest.
    They roar at me, so I hate them.
⁹ My people are like a colorful bird of prey.
Other birds of prey surround it.
    Go, gather all the animals in the field,
      and bring them to devour it.
¹⁰ Many shepherds have destroyed my vineyard.
    They've trampled my property.
    They've turned my pleasant property into a wasteland.
¹¹   They've left it a wasteland.
      Devastated, it mourns in my presence.
      The whole land is destroyed,
        but no one takes this to heart.
¹² Looters swarm all over the bare hills in the desert.
    The Lord's sword destroys them
      from one end of the land to the other.
      No one will be safe.

ᵃ12:4 Greek; Masoretic Text "he."

¹³ My people planted wheat, but they harvested thorns.
They worked until they became sick, but they gained nothing by it.
They were disappointed by their harvests
because of the burning anger of the LORD.

¹⁴"This is what I, the LORD, say about all my evil neighbors who take the inheritance that I gave my people Israel: I am going to uproot those neighbors from their lands. I will also uproot the people of Judah from among them. ¹⁵After I've uprooted them, I will have compassion on them again. I will return them to their inheritance and to their lands. ¹⁶Suppose they learn carefully the ways of my people. Suppose they take an oath in my name, 'As the LORD lives . . .' as they taught my people to take an oath in the name of Baal. Then they will build homes among my people. ¹⁷But suppose they don't listen. Then I will uproot that nation and destroy it," declares the LORD.

Jeremiah's Linen Belt

¹This is what the LORD said to me: "Buy a linen belt. Put it around your waist. Don't let it get wet." ²So I bought the belt, as the LORD had told me, and put it around my waist.

³The LORD spoke his word to me again. He said, ⁴"Take the belt that you bought, the one you're wearing. Go to the Euphrates River, and bury it there in a crack in the rocks." ⁵So I went and buried it by the Euphrates, as the LORD had told me.

⁶After many days the LORD said to me, "Go to the Euphrates, and get the belt from where I told you to bury it." ⁷So I went back to the Euphrates and dug it up. I got the belt from where I had buried it. Now the belt was ruined. It was good for nothing.

⁸Then the LORD spoke his word to me. He said, ⁹"This is what the LORD says: This is how I will destroy Judah's arrogance and Jerusalem's extreme arrogance. ¹⁰These wicked people refuse to listen to me. They go their own stubborn ways and follow other gods in order to serve them and worship them. They are like this good-for-nothing belt. ¹¹As a belt clings to a person's waist, so I have made the entire nation of Israel and the entire nation of Judah cling to me," declares the LORD. "I did this so that they would be my people and bring fame, praise, and honor to me. However, they wouldn't listen.

¹²"Give this message to them, 'This is what the LORD God of Israel says: Every bottle will be filled with wine.' Then they will say to you, 'We know that every bottle will be filled with wine.' ¹³Say to them, 'This is what the LORD says: I'm going to make everyone who lives in this land drunk. The kings who sit on David's throne, the priests, the prophets, and all those who live in Jerusalem will become drunk. ¹⁴Then I will smash them like bottles against each other. I will smash parents and children together, declares the LORD. I will have no pity, mercy, or compassion when I destroy them.' "

¹⁵ Listen, and pay attention!
Don't be arrogant. The LORD has spoken.
¹⁶ Honor the LORD your God before it gets dark,
before your feet stumble on the mountains in the twilight.
You will look for light,
but the LORD will turn it into the shadow of death
and change it into deep darkness.
¹⁷ If you won't listen,
I will cry secretly over your arrogance.

I will cry bitterly, and my eyes will flow with tears
because the LORD's flock will be taken captive.

18 Say to the king and his mother,
"Come down from your thrones,
because your crowns have fallen off your heads."

19 The cities in the Negev will be locked up,
and there will be no one to reopen them.
All the people of Judah will be taken away into captivity.

20 Look up, and see those who are coming from the north.
Where is the flock that was given to you—your beautiful sheep?

21 What will you say
when God makes the people you thought were your friends
your new masters?
Won't pain grip you like a woman in labor?

22 If you ask yourself,
"Why do these things happen to me?"
it's because you have so many sins.
Your clothes have been torn off
and your limbs are bare.

23 Can Ethiopians change the color of their skin
or leopards change their spots?
Can you do good
when you're taught to do wrong?

24 "I will scatter you like straw that is blown away by a desert wind.

25 This is your fate, the destiny I have planned for you,"
declares the LORD.
"You have forgotten me and trusted false gods.

26 I will also tear off your clothes,
and your shame will be seen.

27 I have seen you commit adultery and squeal with delight.
I have seen you act like a shameless prostitute
on the hills and in the fields.
How horrible it will be for you, Jerusalem!
Will you ever be clean?"[a]

The LORD Sends a Drought

14 [1]The LORD spoke his word to Jeremiah about the drought.

2 Judah mourns; its gates fall apart.
The people of Judah sit in mourning on the ground.
Their cry goes up from Jerusalem.

3 Important people send their assistants out for water.
They go to the cisterns, but they don't find any water.
They come back with their containers empty.
They cover their heads, because they are ashamed and disgraced.

4 The ground is cracked because there has been no rain in the land.
The farmers are disappointed. They cover their heads.

5 Even deer in the fields give birth and abandon their young

---

[a] 13:27 "Clean" refers to anything that Moses' Teachings say is presentable to God.

because there's no grass.
6   Wild donkeys stand on the bare hills.
    They sniff the air like jackals.
    Their eyesight fails because they have no green plants.

7   Do something, Lord, for the sake of your name,
    even though our sins testify against us.
    We have been unfaithful and have sinned against you.
8   You are Israel's hope,
    the one who saves it in times of trouble.
    Why should you be like a stranger in the land,
    like a traveler who stays only one night?
9   Why should you be like someone taken by surprise,
    like a strong man who cannot help?
    You, O Lord, are among us.
    We are called by your name.
    Don't leave us!

¹⁰This is what the Lord says about these people: They love to wander. They don't keep their feet where they belong. So the Lord isn't happy with them. He will remember their crimes and punish their sins.

¹¹The Lord said to me, "Don't pray for the good of these people. ¹²Even if they go without food, I won't listen to their cries for help. Even if they sacrifice burnt offerings and grain offerings, I won't be pleased with them. But I will destroy these people with wars, famines, and plagues."

¹³Then I said, "Almighty Lord, prophets are saying to them, 'You won't see wars or famines, because I, the Lord, will give you lasting peace in this place.'"

¹⁴Then the Lord told me, "These are the lies that the prophets are telling in my name: They claim that I sent them, commanded them, and spoke to them. They dreamed up the visions they tell you. Their predictions are worthless. They are the products of their own imagination.

¹⁵"I didn't send these prophets. Yet, they prophesy in my name that there will be no wars or famines in this land. So this is what I, the Lord, say about them: Wars and famines will bring an end to these prophets. ¹⁶The people they prophesy to will be thrown out into the streets of Jerusalem. They will be victims of famines and wars. No one will bury them, their wives, their sons, or their daughters. I will pour on them the destruction that they deserve.

¹⁷"Say this to them:

    'My eyes flow with tears day and night without stopping
    because my dear people will suffer massive destruction.
    It will be a very serious blow.'"

18   If I go to the field, I see those killed because of war.
    If I go to the city, I see those sick because of famine.
    Prophets and priests wander through a land they haven't heard of.
19   Have you completely rejected Judah?
    Do you despise Zion?
    Why have you struck us so hard that we cannot heal?
    We hope for peace, but no good comes from it.
    We hope for a time of healing, but there's only terror.
20   O Lord, we realize our wickedness

and the wrongs done by our ancestors.
We have sinned against you.

21 For the sake of your name, don't despise us.
Don't dishonor your glorious throne.
Remember your promise[a] to us; don't break it.

22 The worthless gods of the nations can't make it rain.
By themselves, the skies can't give showers.
But you can, O LORD our God.
We have hope in you because you do all these things.

15 ¹Then the LORD said to me, "Even if Moses and Samuel were standing in front of me, I would not feel sorry for these people. Send them away from me, and let them go. ²When they ask you where they should go, say to them, 'This is what the LORD says:

Those who are destined to die will die.
Those who are destined to die in wars will die in wars.
Those who are destined to die in famines will die in famines.
Those who are destined to die in captivity will die in captivity.'

³"I will devise four ways to punish them," declares the LORD. "I will send swords to kill, dogs to drag away, and birds and animals to devour and destroy. ⁴I will make these people a horrifying sight to all the kingdoms on the earth. This will happen because of what Judah's King Manasseh, son of Hezekiah, did in Jerusalem.

5 No one will take pity on you, Jerusalem.
No one will mourn for you.
No one will bother to ask how you are doing.

6   You have left me," declares the LORD.
"You have turned your back on me.
So I will use my power against you and destroy you.
I'm tired of showing compassion to you.

7 "I will separate them with a winnowing[a] shovel at the city gates.
I will make them childless.
I will destroy my people because they will not change their ways.

8 Their widows will be more numerous
than the grains of sand on the seashore.
At noontime I will send a destroyer against the mothers of young men.
I will suddenly bring anguish and terror to them.

9   A mother who gives birth to seven sons will grow faint
and breathe her last.
She will die, ashamed and humiliated,
while it is still daylight.
I will put survivors from these people to death
in the presence of their enemies," declares the LORD.

Jeremiah Complains Bitterly

10 I'm so miserable! Why did my mother give birth to me?
I am a man who argues and quarrels with the whole earth.

---

[a] 14:21 Or "covenant."   [a] 15:7 Winnowing is the process of separating husks from grain.

I have never lent or borrowed anything.
>Yet, everyone curses me.

¹¹The Lord said,

"I will certainly rescue you for a good reason.
I will certainly make your enemies plead with you
>in times of disaster and in times of distress.
¹²   (No one can break iron, iron from the north, or bronze.)
¹³ I will give away your wealth and treasures as loot
>as the price for all the sins that you have committed
>>throughout your territory.
¹⁴ I will make you serve your enemies in a land that you haven't heard of,
>because my anger has started a fire.
>>It will burn you."

¹⁵ O Lord, you understand.
Remember me, take care of me,
>and take revenge on those who persecute me.
Be patient, and don't take me away.
You should know that I've been insulted because of you.

¹⁶ Your words were found, and I devoured them.
Your words are my joy and my heart's delight,
>because I am called by your name, O Lord God of Armies.
¹⁷ I didn't keep company with those who laugh and have fun.
I sat alone because your hand was on me.
>You filled me with outrage.
¹⁸ Why is my pain unending
>and my wound incurable, refusing to heal?
Will you disappoint me like a stream
>that dries up in summertime?

¹⁹This is what the Lord says:

If you will return, I will take you back.
If you will speak what is worthwhile and not what is worthless,
>you will stand in my presence.
The people will return to you, but you will not return to them.
²⁰ I will make you like a solid bronze wall in front of these people.
They will fight you, but they will not defeat you.
>I am with you, and I will save you and rescue you,
>>declares the Lord.
²¹ I will rescue you from the power of wicked people
>and free you from the power of tyrants.

The Lord Tells Jeremiah Not to Marry

¹The Lord spoke his word to me. He said, ²"Don't marry! Don't have any sons or daughters in this place! ³This is what the Lord says about the sons and daughters born in this place and about the mothers and fathers who have children in this land: ⁴They will die horrible deaths. No one will mourn for them or bury them. They will be like manure on the ground. Wars and famines will bring them to an end. Their bodies will be food for birds and animals.

⁵"This is what the LORD says: Don't go into a house where people are grieving. Don't go to mourn or to grieve for them. I'm taking my peace, love, and compassion away from these people," declares the LORD. ⁶"Old and young alike will die in this land. No one will mourn for them or bury them. No one will cut his own body or shave his own head for them. ⁷No one will offer food to comfort those who mourn the dead. No one will give a consoling drink to those who have lost their fathers or mothers.

⁸"Don't even go into a home where there is a banquet. Don't sit with them to eat and drink. ⁹This is what the LORD of Armies, the God of Israel, says: I'm going to put a stop to the sounds of joy and happiness and the sounds of brides and grooms in this place. This will happen in your lifetime, while you watch.

¹⁰"When you tell the people all these things, they will ask you, 'Why does the LORD threaten us with all these disasters? What have we done wrong? How have we sinned against the LORD our God?' ¹¹Then say to them, 'It's because your ancestors abandoned me, declares the LORD. They followed other gods, served them, worshiped them, and abandoned me. They didn't obey my teachings. ¹²You have done worse than your ancestors. All of you are following your own stubborn, evil ways that keep you from obeying me. ¹³So I will throw you out of this land into a land that you and your ancestors haven't heard of. There you will serve other gods day and night because I will no longer have pity on you.'

¹⁴"That is why the days are coming," declares the LORD, "when people will no longer begin an oath with, 'The LORD brought the people of Israel out of Egypt. As the LORD lives. . . .' ¹⁵But they will say, 'The LORD brought the people of Israel out of the land of the north and all the lands where he had scattered them. As the LORD lives. . . .' They will say this because I will bring them back to the land that I gave their ancestors.

¹⁶"I'm going to send for many fishermen," declares the LORD, "and they will catch the people of Israel. After that, I will send for many hunters, and they will hunt for them on every mountain and hill and even in the cracks in the rocks. ¹⁷I see everything that they do. They can't hide anything from me. Their wickedness can't be hidden; I can see it. ¹⁸First, I will have them pay twice as much for their wickedness and their sin, because they have polluted my land. They have filled my property with the lifeless statues of their detestable and disgusting idols."

¹⁹   The LORD is my strength and my fortress,
       my refuge in times of trouble.
     Nations come to you from the most distant parts of the world
       and say, "Our ancestors have inherited lies,
         worthless and unprofitable gods."

²⁰   "People can't make gods for themselves.
       They aren't really gods.
²¹   That is what I will teach them.
       This time I will make my power and my strength known to them.
       Then they will know that my name is the LORD."

17 ¹   The LORD says, "Judah's sin is written with an iron pen.
       It is engraved with a diamond point
         on the tablet of their hearts and on the horns of their altars.
²   Even their children remember their altars
       and their poles dedicated to the goddess Asherah
         beside large trees on high hills

3 and on mountains in the open country.[a]
I will turn your wealth and all your treasures into loot.
I will do this because of your worship sites and your sin
   throughout all your territory.
4   You will lose the inheritance that I gave you.
I will make you serve your enemies in a land that you haven't heard of.
I will do this because you have stirred up the fire of my anger.
   It will burn forever.

5 "This is what the LORD says:

Cursed is the person who trusts humans,
   who makes flesh and blood his strength
      and whose heart turns away from the LORD.
6 He will be like a bush in the wilderness.
He will not see when something good comes.
He will live in the dry places in the desert,
   in a salty land where no one can live.
7 Blessed is the person who trusts the LORD.
   The LORD will be his confidence.
8 He will be like a tree that is planted by water.
   It will send its roots down to a stream.
   It will not be afraid in the heat of summer.
   Its leaves will turn green.
   It will not be anxious during droughts.
   It will not stop producing fruit.

9 "The human mind is the most deceitful of all things. It is incurable.
   No one can understand how deceitful it is.
10 I, the LORD, search minds and test hearts.
   I will reward each person for what he has done.
   I will reward him for the results of his actions.
11 A person who gets rich dishonestly is like a partridge
   that hatches eggs it did not lay.
      During his lifetime, he will lose his wealth.
      In the end, he will be a godless fool."

12 Our holy place is a glorious throne,
   highly honored from the beginning.
13 O LORD, the Hope of Israel, all who abandon you will be put to shame.
   Those who turn away from you will be written in dust,
      because they abandon the LORD,
         the fountain of life-giving water.

14 Heal me, O LORD, and I will be healed.
   Rescue me, and I will be rescued.
      You are the one I praise.
15 People keep asking me,
   "Where is the word of the LORD?
      Let it come."
16 I have not run away from being your shepherd,

---

[a] 17:3 Greek; Masoretic Text "on my mountain."

and I have not longed for the day of destruction.
  You know what came out of my mouth.
17   Do not terrorize me.
  You are my refuge on the day of disaster.
18   Put my persecutors to shame,
    but do not let me be put to shame.
  Terrify them,
    but do not let me be terrified.
  Bring the day of disaster on them,
    and destroy them completely.

The Blessing That Comes From Observing the Day of Worship as a Holy Day

19This is what the Lord said to me: Stand at People's Gate, where the kings of Judah go in and out. Then stand at every gate in Jerusalem. 20Tell everyone: "Listen to the word of the Lord, you kings of Judah, all the people of Judah, and all those who live in Jerusalem, and go through these gates. 21This is what the Lord says: Watch out! If you value your lives, do not carry anything on the day of worship or bring it through the gates of Jerusalem. 22Do not bring anything out of your homes on the day of worship. Do not do any work, but observe the day of worship as a holy day, as I told your ancestors. 23Your ancestors did not obey me or pay attention to me. They were impossible to deal with and would not listen or accept discipline.

24"Now," declares the Lord, "you must listen to me and not bring anything through the gates of this city on the day of worship. You must observe the day of worship as a holy day by not doing any work on it. 25If you do this, then the kings and princes who sit on David's throne will come through the gates of this city. They and their princes will ride in chariots and on horses along with the people of Judah and those who live in Jerusalem. This city will always have people living in it.

26"People will come from the cities of Judah, from all around Jerusalem, from the territory of Benjamin, from the foothills, from the mountains, and from the Negev. They will bring burnt offerings, sacrifices, grain offerings, and incense. They will also bring thank offerings to the Lord's temple. 27But you must listen to me and observe the day of worship as a holy day by not carrying anything through the gates of Jerusalem on the day of worship. If you don't do this, I will set its gates on fire. The fire will burn down the palaces in Jerusalem, and you won't be able to put it out."

The People of Israel Are Like Clay for a Potter

18 1The Lord spoke his word to Jeremiah. He said, 2"Go to the potter's house. There I will give you my message."

3I went to the potter's house, and he was working there at his wheel. 4Whenever a clay pot he was working on was ruined, he would rework it into a new clay pot the way he wanted to make it.

5The Lord spoke his word to me. The Lord asked, 6"Nation of Israel, can't I do with you as this potter does with clay? Nation of Israel, you are like the clay in the potter's hands.

7"At one time I may threaten to tear up, break down, and destroy a nation or a kingdom. 8But suppose the nation that I threatened turns away from doing wrong. Then I will change my plans about the disaster I planned to do to it.

9"At another time I may promise to build and plant a nation or a kingdom. 10But suppose that nation does what I consider evil and doesn't obey me. Then I will change my plans about the good that I promised to do to it.

¹¹"Now say to the people of Judah and to those who live in Jerusalem, 'This is what the Lord says: I'm going to prepare a disaster and make plans against you. Turn from your evil ways, change your lives, and do good.'

¹²"But they will answer, 'It's useless! We'll live the way we want to. We'll go our own stubborn, evil ways.'

¹³"This is what the Lord says:

Ask among the nations if anyone has ever heard anything like this.
  The people of Israel have done a very horrible thing.
¹⁴ The rocky slopes of Lebanon are never without snow.
  The cool mountain streams never dry up.
¹⁵ But my people have forgotten me.
    They burn incense as an offering to worthless idols,
      and they stumble along the way, on the ancient path.
    They go on side roads and not on major highways.
¹⁶ Their land will become desolate
    and something to be hissed at forever.
  Everyone who will pass by it will be stunned and shake his head.
¹⁷ Like the east wind I will scatter them in front of the enemy.
  On the day of their disaster,
    I will show them my back, not my face."

¹⁸Then they said, "Let's plot against Jeremiah, because the teachings of the priests, the advice of wise people, and the word of the prophets won't disappear. Accuse him! Pay no attention to anything he says."

¹⁹ Pay attention to me, O Lord,
    and listen to what my accusers say.
²⁰ Good should not be paid back with evil.
    They dig a pit to take my life.
      Remember how I stood in your presence and pleaded for them
        in order to turn your anger away from them.
²¹ Now, hand their children over to famine.
    Pour out their blood by using your sword.
      Then their wives will become childless widows.
        Their husbands will be put to death.
        Their young men will be struck down in battle.
²² Make them cry out from their homes
    when you suddenly send troops against them,
      because they dug a pit to catch me and hid snares for my feet.
²³ But you, O Lord, know that they plan to kill me.
    Don't forgive their crimes.
    Don't wipe their sins out of your sight.
    Make them stumble in your presence.
    Deal with them when you get angry.

Israel Will Be Smashed Like a Clay Jar

19 ¹This is what the Lord says: Go and buy a clay jar from a potter. Take along some of the leaders of the people and some of the leaders of the priests. ²Go to the valley of Ben Hinnom at the entrance to Potsherd Gate. Announce there the things I plan to do. ³Say, "Listen to the word of the LORD, you kings of Judah and those who live in Jerusalem. This is what the LORD of Armies, the God of Israel, says: I'm going to bring such a disaster on this place that the ears of everyone who hears about it will ring.

⁴"The people, their ancestors, and the kings of Judah have abandoned me. They have made this place unrecognizable by burning incense as an offering to other gods that they hadn't heard of. They have filled this place with the blood of innocent people. ⁵They have built worship sites to burn their children as sacrifices to Baal. I didn't ask them or command them to do this. It never entered my mind.

⁶"That is why the days are coming, declares the LORD, when this place will no longer be called Topheth or the valley of Ben Hinnom. Instead, it will be called Slaughter Valley. ⁷I will smash the plans of Judah and Jerusalem in this place. I will cut them down with swords in front of their enemies and with the hands of those who want to kill them. I will give their bodies as food to birds and to animals. ⁸I will devastate this city. It will become something to hiss at. Everyone who goes by it will be stunned and hiss with contempt at all the disasters that happen to it. ⁹I will make the people eat the flesh of their sons and daughters. They will eat each other's flesh during blockades and hardships that their enemies impose on them when they want to kill them."

¹⁰The LORD says, "Then smash the jar in front of the men who went with you. ¹¹Say to them, 'This is what the LORD of Armies says: I will smash these people and this city as this potter's jar was smashed beyond repair. They will bury the dead in Topheth until there's no other place to bury them. ¹²That's what I will do to this place and to those who live in it, declares the LORD. I will make this city like Topheth. ¹³The houses in Jerusalem, the houses of the kings of Judah, and all the rooftops of the houses will be unclean*ª* like this city Topheth. This is because people burned incense to the entire army of heaven and poured out wine offerings to other gods.' "

¹⁴Then Jeremiah left Topheth, where the LORD had sent him to prophesy. He stood in the courtyard of the LORD's temple and said to all the people, ¹⁵"This is what the LORD of Armies, the God of Israel, says: I'm going to bring on this city and on all its towns the disasters that I threatened. They've become impossible to deal with, and they refuse to obey me."

Pashhur Imprisons Jeremiah

20 ¹Now the priest, Immer's son Pashhur, the chief officer of the LORD's temple, heard Jeremiah prophesying these things. ²Pashhur struck the prophet Jeremiah and put him in prison at Upper Benjamin Gate that was in the LORD's temple.

³The next day when Pashhur took Jeremiah out of prison, Jeremiah said to him, "The LORD doesn't call you Pashhur, but he calls you Terror Everywhere. ⁴This is what the LORD says: I'm going to make you terrify yourself and all your friends. Their enemies' swords will kill them, and you will see it with your own eyes. I will hand all of Judah over to the king of Babylon. He will take the people away as captives to Babylon or kill them with swords. ⁵I will hand all the riches of this city over to their enemies. This will include all its produce, all its valuables, and all the treasures of the kings of Judah. Their enemies will loot them, take them away, and bring them to Babylon. ⁶And you, Pashhur, and all those who live in your house will go into captivity. You will go to Babylon, and you will die there. You will be buried there together with all your friends to whom you prophesied these lies."

ª 19:13 "Unclean" refers to anything that Moses' Teachings say is not presentable to God.

Jeremiah

Jeremiah showed what captivity would be like
for God's disobedient people.

Jeremiah was not popular. When he told the people of Judah to
surrender to Babylon, his listeners got angry. They reported Jeremiah
to the government. They threatened to hurt Jeremiah. They called him a
traitor. Even Jeremiah's close friends wanted to see him punished. But
Jeremiah was only telling the people what God told him to say.

Being rejected and disliked hurt Jeremiah. Sometimes he was angry with
God. Sometimes Jeremiah even wished he had never been born.

But Jeremiah didn't quit. He told God how he felt. And then Jeremiah
kept right on doing the job God had given him.

Jeremiah lived to be very old, and he saw the things he had preached
about come true.

Jeremiah lived around 600 B.C.

Jeremiah was a prophet in the southern kingdom of Judah.

For 40 years Jeremiah warned Judah that they would be defeated by the Babylonians.

Because the people never listened to Jeremiah, he wept for them.

Getting to Know Jeremiah

✳ What does it feel like when others reject you or don't seem to like you?

✳ Why did Jeremiah keep preaching?

✳ Why is Jeremiah one of the true heroes of the Bible?

✳ Did you ever wonder if boys can feel very sad? What do Jeremiah's feelings tell you about emotions?

When the Babylonians attacked Jerusalem, they threw Jeremiah in a deep, muddy cistern where water was stored.

King Nebuchadnezzar of Babylon took the people of Jerusalem captive. But he let Jeremiah go.

Jeremiah Prays to the LORD

7 O LORD, you have deceived me, and I was deceived.
      You overpowered me and won.
        I've been made fun of all day long.
          Everyone mocks me.
8 Each time I speak, I have to cry out and shout,
        "Violence and destruction!"
      The word of the LORD has made me the object of insults
        and contempt all day long.
9 I think to myself, "I can forget the LORD
        and no longer speak his name."
      But his word is inside me like a burning fire shut up in my bones.
        I wear myself out holding it in, but I can't do it any longer.
10 I have heard many people whispering,
        "Terror is everywhere!
          Report him! Let's report him!"
      All my closest friends are waiting to see me stumble.
        They say, "Maybe he will be tricked.
          Then we can overpower him and take revenge on him."
11 But the LORD is on my side like a terrifying warrior.
        That is why those who persecute me will stumble. They can't win.
          They will be very ashamed that they can't succeed.
            Their eternal shame will not be forgotten.
12 But the LORD of Armies examines the righteous.
        He sees their motives and thoughts.
      I want to see you take revenge on them,
        because I've brought my case to you.
13 Sing to the LORD! Praise the LORD!
        He has rescued the lives of needy people
          from the power of wicked people.

14 Cursed is the day that I was born,
        the day that my mother gave birth to me.
          May it not be blessed.
15 Cursed is the man who made my father very happy with the news
        that he had just become the father of a baby boy.
16 May that man be like the cities
        that the LORD destroyed without pity.
      May he hear a cry of alarm in the morning
        and a battle cry at noon.
17 If only he had killed me while I was in the womb.
        Then my mother would have been my grave,
          and she would have always been pregnant.
18 Why did I come out of the womb?
        All I've seen is trouble and grief.
          I will finish my days in shame.

Jerusalem Will Be Captured by the Babylonians

21 ¹The LORD spoke his word to Jeremiah when King Zedekiah sent Pashhur, son of Malchiah, and the priest Zephaniah, son of Maaseiah, to Jeremiah. They said,

²"Consult the Lord for us, because King Nebuchadnezzar of Babylon is attacking us. Maybe the Lord will perform miracles for us so that Nebuchadnezzar will retreat."

³Jeremiah responded to them, "This is what you should say to Zedekiah, ⁴This is what the Lord God of Israel says: I'm going to take your weapons away from you. You are using these weapons to fight the king of Babylon as well as the Babylonians who are now blockading you outside the wall. I will bring the Babylonians inside this city. ⁵I will fight you in anger, fury, and rage with my powerful hand and my mighty arm. ⁶I will defeat those who live in this city, both people and animals. They will die from a terrible plague. ⁷Afterwards, declares the Lord, I will hand over Judah's King Zedekiah, his officials, the people, and everyone else in this city who survives the plague, war, and famine. They will be handed over to King Nebuchadnezzar of Babylon and to their enemies who want to kill them. Nebuchadnezzar will kill them with swords. He won't spare them, show them compassion, or care for them.'

⁸"Say to these people, 'This is what the Lord says: I am going to give you the choice of life or death. ⁹Those who live in this city will die in the war, famine, or plague. Those of you who go out and surrender to the Babylonians will live. You will escape with your lives. ¹⁰I've decided to harm this city, not to do good to it, declares the Lord. It will be handed over to the king of Babylon, and he will burn it down.'

¹¹"Say to the nation of the king of Judah, 'Listen to the word of the Lord, ¹²descendants of David. This is what the Lord says:

> Judge fairly every morning.
> Rescue those who have been robbed from those who oppress them.
> Otherwise, my fury will break out and burn like fire.
> No one will be able to put it out
> because of the evil things you have done.

¹³   " 'I'm against you, Jerusalem.
> You are the city that is in the valley
> and on the rock in the plain,' "
> declares the Lord.
> " 'But you ask, "Who can attack us?
> Who can enter our places of refuge?"

¹⁴   " 'I will punish you because of the evil things you have done,' "
> declares the Lord.
> " 'I will start a fire in your forests,
> and it will burn up everything around you.' "

Warnings to the Wicked Kings

22 ¹This is what the Lord says: Go to the palace of the king of Judah, and speak this message there: ²"Listen to the word of the Lord, you officials, you people who come into these gates, and you, king of Judah, the one sitting on David's throne. ³This is what the Lord says: Judge fairly, and do what is right. Rescue those who have been robbed from those who oppress them. Don't mistreat foreigners, orphans, or widows, and don't oppress them. Don't kill innocent people in this place. ⁴If you do what I say, then the kings who sit on David's throne will ride through the gates of this palace in chariots and on horses along with their officials and their people. ⁵But if you don't do what I say, I will take an oath on myself," declares the Lord, "that this palace will become a pile of rubble.

⁶"This is what the Lord says about the palace of the king of Judah:

This palace is like Gilead to me,
　　like the top of Lebanon.
I will certainly turn it into a desert,
　　into cities that no one lives in.
7　I will send people to destroy you.
　　They will have their own weapons.
　　They will cut down your finest cedar trees
　　　　and throw them on a fire.

8"People from many nations will pass by this city and ask each other, 'Why has
the LORD done this to this important city?' 9The answer will be: 'They rejected the
promise*ᵃ* of the LORD their God. They worshiped other gods and served them.' "

10　Don't cry for the dead.
　　Don't shake your heads at them.
　　Cry bitterly for those who are taken away,
　　　　because they won't come back to see their homeland.

11This is what the LORD says about King Josiah's son Shallum, who succeeded his
father as king of Judah and left this place: He will never come back here again. 12He
will die in the place where he was taken captive, and he will never see this land again.

13　"How horrible it will be for the person who builds his house dishonestly
　　　　and his upper rooms through injustice.
　　He makes his neighbors work for nothing
　　　　and doesn't pay them for their work.
14　He says, 'I will build a large house for myself with big upper rooms.'
　　He cuts out windows in it,
　　　　panels the rooms with cedar,
　　　　and paints them red.
15　Do you think you're a better king than others
　　　　because you use more cedar?
　　Your father ate and drank and did what is fair and right.
　　　　Everything went well for him.
16　He defended the cause of the poor and needy.
　　　　Everything went well for him.
　　Isn't this what it means to know me?" asks the LORD.
17　"But your eyes and your mind are set on nothing but dishonest profits.
　　　　You kill innocent people and violently oppress your people."

18This is what the LORD says about Jehoiakim, son of Judah's King Josiah:

People won't mourn for him and say,
　　"How horrible it is for my brother and sister!"
They won't mourn for him and say,
　　"How horrible it is for my master and his splendor!"
19　He will receive a donkey's burial.
　　He will be dragged off and thrown outside the gates of Jerusalem.

20　"Go to Lebanon and cry! Raise your voice in Bashan!
　　Cry out from Abarim, because all your lovers are defeated."

ᵃ22:9 Or "covenant."

21 I spoke to you when you were prosperous,
   but you said that you wouldn't listen.
   This is how you've been ever since you were young.
   You don't listen to me.
22 The wind will blow away all your shepherds,
   and your lovers will go into captivity.
   Then you will be ashamed and disgraced by all your wickedness.
23 You live in Lebanon and have your nest in the cedars.
   But you will groan when pain strikes you,
   pain like a woman giving birth to a child.

24"As I live," declares the LORD, "even though you, Jehoiakim,[b] son of Judah's King Jehoiakim, are the signet ring on my right hand, I will pull you off my hand. 25I will hand you over to those who want to kill you, those you fear—King Nebuchadnezzar of Babylon and the Babylonians. 26I will throw you and your mother into another land. You weren't born there, but you will die there. 27You will want to return to this land, but you won't be allowed to come home."

28 This Jehoiakin is like a rejected and broken pot that no one wants.
   Is that why he and his descendants will be thrown out
   and cast into another land they've never heard of?
29 O land, land, land!
   Listen to the word of the LORD.

30This is what the LORD says:

Write this about Jehoiakin: He will be childless.
   He won't prosper in his lifetime.
   None of his descendants will succeed him as king.
   They won't sit on David's throne and rule Judah again.

The Righteous Branch

1"How horrible it will be for the shepherds who are destroying and scattering the sheep in my care," declares the LORD. 2"This is what I, the LORD God of Israel, said to the shepherds who take care of my people: You have scattered my sheep and chased them away. You have not taken care of them, so now I will take care of you by punishing you for the evil you have done," declares the LORD.

3"Then I will gather the remaining part of my flock from all the countries where I chased them. I will bring them back to their pasture, and they will be fertile and increase in number. 4I will put shepherds over them. Those shepherds will take care of them. My sheep will no longer be afraid or terrified, and not one of them will be missing," declares the LORD.

5   "The days are coming," declares the LORD,
    "when I will grow a righteous branch for David.
    He will be a king who will rule wisely.
    He will do what is fair and right in the land.
6   In his lifetime, Judah will be saved,
        and Israel will live in safety.
        This is the name that he will be given:
        The LORD Our Righteousness.

---

b22:24 Masoretic Text "Coniah," an alternate form of Jehoiakim.

⁷"That is why the days are coming," declares the LORD, "when people's oaths will no longer be, 'The LORD brought the people of Israel out of Egypt. As the LORD lives. . . .' ⁸Instead, their oaths will be, 'The LORD brought the descendants of the nation of Israel out of the land of the north and all the lands where he*ᵃ* had scattered them. As the LORD lives. . . .' At that time they will live in their own land.

Warnings to the False Prophets

⁹"Say this about the prophets:

I am deeply disturbed.
     All my bones tremble.
I am like a drunk,
     like a person who has had too much wine,
          because of the LORD and his holy words.
¹⁰   The land is filled with adulterers.
The land mourns because of the curse.
     Pastures in the wilderness have dried up.
          The people are evil,
               and they use their strength to do the wrong things.
¹¹   The prophets and priests are godless.
     Even in my temple I've found them doing evil," declares the LORD.
¹²   "That is why their own way will become
     like slippery paths in the dark.
They will be chased away, and they will fall down in the dark.
     I will bring disaster on them.
          It is time for them to be punished," declares the LORD.

¹³"Say this about the prophets of Samaria:

I saw something disgusting.
     The prophets of Samaria prophesied by Baal
          and led my people Israel astray.

¹⁴"Say this about the prophets of Jerusalem:

I see something horrible.
     The prophets of Jerusalem commit adultery and live a lie.
          They support those who do evil
               so that no one turns back from his wickedness.
          They are all like Sodom to me,
               and those who live in Jerusalem are like Gomorrah."

¹⁵This is what the LORD of Armies says about the prophets:

I will give them wormwood to eat and poison to drink.
     The prophets of Jerusalem have spread godlessness
          throughout the land.

¹⁶This is what the LORD of Armies says:

Don't listen to what the prophets are saying to you.
     They fill you with false hope.
     They speak about visions that they dreamed up.

ᵃ23:8 Greek; Masoretic Text "I."

These visions are not from the Lord.

17   They keep saying to those who despise me,
        "The Lord says, 'Everything will go well for you.' "
     They tell all who live by their own stubborn ways,
        "Nothing bad will happen to you."

18   Who is in the Lord's inner circle
        and sees and hears his word?
     Who pays attention and listens to his word?

19   The storm of the Lord will come with his anger.
        Like a windstorm, it will swirl down on the heads of the wicked.

20   The anger of the Lord will not turn back
        until he has done everything he intends to do.
     In the last days you will understand this clearly.

21   I didn't send these prophets,
        yet they ran with their message.
     I didn't speak to them,
        yet they prophesied.

22   If they had been in my inner circle,
        they would have announced my words to my people.
     They would have turned back from their evil ways
        and the evil they have done.

23   "I am a God who is near.
        I am also a God who is far away," declares the Lord.

24   "No one can hide so that I can't see him," declares the Lord.
        "I fill heaven and earth!" declares the Lord.

²⁵"I've heard the prophets who speak lies in my name. They say, 'I had a dream! I had a dream!' ²⁶How long will these prophets continue to lie and deceive? ²⁷They tell each other the dreams they had, because they want to make my people forget my name, as their ancestors forgot my name because of Baal. ²⁸The prophet who has a dream should tell his dream. However, the person who has my word should honestly speak my word. What does grain have to do with straw?" asks the Lord. ²⁹"Isn't my word like fire or like a hammer that shatters a rock?" asks the Lord. ³⁰"I'm against the prophets who steal my words from each other," declares the Lord. ³¹"I'm against the prophets who speak their own thoughts and say that they speak for me. ³²I'm against those who prophesy dreams they made up," declares the Lord. "They tell the dreams they made up and lead my people astray with their lies and their wild talk. I didn't send them or command them to go. They don't help these people at all," declares the Lord.

³³"When these people, the prophets, or the priests ask you, 'What revelation has the Lord burdened you with now?' say to them, 'You are the burden! I will abandon you, declares the Lord.' ³⁴Suppose the prophets, the priests, or these people say, 'This is the Lord's revelation!' I will punish them and their families. ³⁵They should ask their neighbors and their relatives, 'What is the Lord's answer?' and 'What did the Lord say?' ³⁶They should never again say, 'This is the Lord's revelation,' because each person's word becomes the revelation. They will twist the words of the living God, the Lord of Armies, our God.

³⁷"Jeremiah, say this to the prophets, 'What was the Lord's answer to you?' and 'What did the Lord say?' ³⁸Suppose they say, 'This is the Lord's revelation!' Then say, 'This is what the Lord says: Because you have said, "This is the Lord's revelation!"

Baskets / *Jeremiah 24*

Baskets woven from fibers were
commonplace in homes in Bible
times. Basket weaving became an
important skill for both men and
women.

One basket, called a *spyris* by the
Greeks, was large enough for the
apostle Paul to ride in when he was let
down over the city wall of Damascus
(Acts 9:25).

even though I commanded you not to repeat this saying, ³⁹I will certainly forget you.
I will throw you out of my presence and out of the city that I gave you and your ancestors. ⁴⁰I will bring eternal disgrace and shame on you. It will never be forgotten.' "

The Two Fig Baskets

24 ¹King Nebuchadnezzar of Babylon took Jehoiakin^a (son of King Jehoiakim of
Judah), the princes of Judah, the skilled workers, and the builders from Jerusalem into captivity and brought them to Babylon. After this, the LORD showed me two
baskets of figs set in front of the LORD's temple. ²One basket had very good figs, like
figs that ripen first. The other basket had very bad figs. These figs were so bad that
they couldn't be eaten.

³Then the LORD asked me, "What do you see, Jeremiah?"

I answered, "Figs. Figs that are very good. I also see figs that are very bad, so
bad that they can't be eaten."

⁴The LORD spoke his word to me, ⁵"This is what the LORD God of Israel says: The
captives of Judah, whom I sent away from here to Babylon, are like these good figs. I
will look kindly on them. ⁶I will watch over them for their own good, and I will bring
them back to this land. I will build them up and not tear them down. I will plant them
and not uproot them. ⁷I will give them the desire to know that I am the LORD. They
will be my people, and I will be their God, because they will wholeheartedly come
back to me.

⁸"But this is what the LORD says about the bad figs that are so bad that they can't
be eaten. The LORD says, 'Like these bad figs, I will abandon King Zedekiah of Judah,
his princes, the remaining few in Jerusalem who stayed behind in this land, and those
who are living in Egypt. ⁹I will make them a horrifying sight to all the kingdoms of
the earth. They will be a disgrace and an example. They will become something ridiculed and cursed wherever I scatter them. ¹⁰I will send wars, famines, and plagues
until they disappear from the land that I gave to them and their ancestors.' "

---

^a24:1 Masoretic Text "Jeconiah," an alternate form of Jehoiakin.

Judgment on Judah and the Nations

25 ¹The Lord spoke his word to Jeremiah about all the people of Judah when Jehoiakim, son of Josiah, was in his fourth year as king. (This was the first year that Nebuchadnezzar was king of Babylon.) ²The prophet Jeremiah spoke to all the people of Judah and to everyone who lived in Jerusalem. He said, ³"For 23 years, from the time that Josiah, son of Amon, was in his thirteenth year as king of Judah until today, the Lord continued to speak his word to me. So I have spoken to you again and again, but you have not listened.

⁴"Even though the Lord has sent all his servants the prophets to you, you haven't listened or paid attention to them. ⁵The prophets said, 'Turn from your evil ways and the evil you have done, and live in the land that the Lord permanently gave to you and your ancestors. ⁶Don't follow other gods to serve and worship them. Don't make me furious about the idols your hands have shaped. Then I won't harm you. ⁷But you haven't listened to me, declares the Lord. You have made me furious about the idols your hands have shaped and have brought harm upon yourselves.'

⁸"This is what the Lord of Armies says: You did not listen to my words, ⁹so I'm going to send for all the families from the north. I will also send for my servant King Nebuchadnezzar of Babylon, declares the Lord. I will bring the families from the north to attack this land, its people, and all these surrounding nations. I'm going to destroy them and turn them into something terrible, something ridiculed, and something permanently ruined. ¹⁰I will take from them the sounds of joy and happiness, the sounds of brides and grooms, the sound of mills, and the light of lamps. ¹¹This whole land will be ruined and become a wasteland. These nations will serve the king of Babylon for 70 years.

¹²"When the 70 years are over, I will punish the king of Babylon and that nation for their crimes, declares the Lord. I will turn Babylon into a permanent wasteland. ¹³I will bring on that land all the disasters I threatened to do to it, everything that Jeremiah prophesied against all the nations, everything written in this book. ¹⁴Many nations and great kings will make slaves of the people of Babylon, and I will pay them back for what they have done."

¹⁵This is what the Lord God of Israel said to me: Take from my hand this cup filled with the wine of my fury, and make all the nations to whom I'm sending you drink from it. ¹⁶When they drink from it, they will stagger and go insane because of the wars that I'm going to send them.

¹⁷So I took the cup from the Lord's hand. I made all the nations to whom the Lord sent me drink from it: ¹⁸Jerusalem and the cities of Judah as well as its kings and officials. When they drank from it, they became wastelands and ruins, something ridiculed and cursed, until today.

¹⁹I also made these people drink from it: Pharaoh king of Egypt, his servants, officials, all his people, ²⁰and all the foreign people living among them; all the kings of the land of Uz; all the kings of Philistia, those from the cities of Ashkelon, Gaza, and Ekron, and the people left in Ashdod; ²¹Edom, Moab, and the people of Ammon; ²²all the kings of Tyre and Sidon, and the kings on the seacoast; ²³Dedan, Tema, Buz, and all who shave the hair on their foreheads; ²⁴all the kings of Arabia, and all the kings of the foreign people living in the desert; ²⁵all the kings of Zimri, all the kings of Elam, and all the kings of Media; ²⁶all the kings of the north, near and far, one after another— all the kingdoms of the earth. Last of all, the king of Sheshach will drink from the cup.

²⁷The Lord said, "Say to them, 'This is what the Lord of Armies, the God of Israel, says: Drink, get drunk, vomit, fall down, and don't get up because of the wars that I'm going to send you.' ²⁸But if they refuse to take the cup from your hand and

drink from it, say to them, 'This is what the LORD of Armies says: You must drink from it! ²⁹I am going to bring disaster on the city that is named after me. Do you think you'll go unpunished? You will not go unpunished! I'm declaring war on all those who live on earth, declares the LORD of Armies.'

³⁰"That is why you will prophesy all these things to them and say,

'The LORD roars from above.
　He thunders from his holy dwelling place.
　He roars against his land.
　He shouts like those who stomp grapes.
　He shouts against all those who live on earth.
31　　The sound is echoing to the ends of the earth
　　　because the LORD has brought charges against the nations.
　He will judge all humans.
　He will kill the wicked, declares the LORD.'

³²"This is what the LORD of Armies says:

Disaster is spreading from nation to nation.
A great storm is brewing from the distant corners of the earth."

³³On that day those killed by the LORD will stretch from one end of the earth to the other. They will not be mourned, taken away, or buried. They will become like manure on the ground.

34　Mourn, you shepherds, and cry.
　Roll in the dust, you leaders of the flock.
　　The time has come for you to be slaughtered.
　　The time has come for you to be scattered,
　　　and you will break like fine pottery.
35　There will be no place for the shepherds to flee,
　　no escape for the leaders of the flock.
36　The shepherds are crying
　　and the leaders of the flock are mourning
　　　because the LORD is stripping their pasture.
37　The peaceful pastures are destroyed by the LORD's burning anger.
38　He has left his lair like a lion.
　　Their land has been ruined
　　　because of the heat of the oppressor,
　　　because of the fury of his anger.

Jeremiah Is Arrested

¹The LORD spoke his word when Judah's King Jehoiakim, son of Josiah, began to rule. He said, ²"This is what the LORD says: Stand in the courtyard of the LORD's temple, and speak to all the people who come from the cities of Judah to worship in the LORD's temple. Tell them everything that I command you to tell them. Don't leave out a single word. ³Maybe they'll listen, and they'll turn from their evil ways. Then I'll change my plan about the disaster I intend to bring on them because of the evil they have done."

⁴The LORD added, "Also say to them, 'This is what the LORD says: Suppose you don't listen to me and don't follow my teachings that I set in front of you. ⁵Suppose you don't listen to the words of my servants the prophets, whom I sent to you again

and again, even though you didn't listen. ⁶Then I will do to this temple what I did to Shiloh. I will turn this city into something that will be cursed by all the nations on earth.' "

⁷The priests, the prophets, and all the people heard Jeremiah speaking these things in the LORD's temple. ⁸But as soon as Jeremiah finished saying everything that the LORD had commanded him to say, the priests, the prophets, and all the people grabbed him and said, "You must die! ⁹Why do you prophesy in the LORD's name that this temple will be like Shiloh and this city will become a pile of rubble with no one living here?" Then all the people crowded around Jeremiah in the LORD's temple.

¹⁰When the officials of Judah heard about these things, they went from the king's palace to the LORD's temple. They sat at the entrance of New Gate to the LORD's temple. ¹¹Then the priests and the prophets said to the officials and all the people, "This man is condemned to die because he prophesied against this city as you yourselves have heard."

¹²Then Jeremiah said to all the officials and all the people, "The LORD sent me to prophesy everything that you have heard me say against this temple and against this city. ¹³Now, change your ways and what you are doing, and listen to the LORD your God. Then the LORD will change his plan about the disaster that he intends to bring on you.

¹⁴"My life is in your hands. Do with me whatever you think is good and right. ¹⁵But know for certain that if you put me to death, you, this city, and the people living in it will be guilty of killing an innocent person. The LORD has certainly sent me to speak all these things to you."

¹⁶Then the officials and all the people said to the priests and prophets, "This man should not be condemned to die. He has spoken to us in the name of the LORD our God."

¹⁷Then some of the leaders in the land got up and said to the entire crowd, ¹⁸"Micah from Moresheth prophesied at the time of Judah's King Hezekiah and said to all the people of Judah, 'This is what the LORD of Armies says:

> Zion will be plowed like a field,
>> Jerusalem will become a pile of rubble,
>>> and the temple mountain will become a worship site
>>>> covered with trees.'

¹⁹Did Judah's King Hezekiah and all the people of Judah put Micah to death? No! Hezekiah feared the LORD and sought the LORD's favor. So the LORD changed his plan about the disaster he intended to bring on them. But we are about to bring a bigger disaster on ourselves."

²⁰There was another man prophesying in the name of the LORD. His name was Uriah, son of Shemaiah, from Kiriath Jearim. He prophesied against this city and this land as Jeremiah did. ²¹When King Jehoiakim and all his personal troops and officials heard what Uriah said, the king wanted to put him to death. But Uriah heard about it and fled in fear to Egypt. ²²King Jehoiakim sent soldiers to Egypt: Elnathan (son of Achbor) and other soldiers along with him. ²³They brought Uriah from Egypt and took him to King Jehoiakim. The king executed Uriah and threw his body into the burial ground for the common people. ²⁴Ahikam, son of Shaphan, supported Jeremiah. So Jeremiah was not handed over to the people to be put to death.

The Yoke of Babylon Will Be on Judah

27 ¹When Zedekiah, son of King Josiah of Judah, began to rule, the LORD spoke his word to Jeremiah.

²This is what the LORD said to me: Make leather straps and a wooden yoke,ᵃ and strap the yoke on your neck. ³Then send messages to the kings of Edom, Moab, Ammon, Tyre, and Sidon, with messengers who have come to King Zedekiah of Judah in Jerusalem. ⁴Give them an order for their masters: "This is what the LORD of Armies, the God of Israel, says: Say this to your masters, ⁵'I used my great strength and my powerful arm to make the earth along with the people and the animals on it. I give it to anyone I please. ⁶Now I have handed all these countries over to my servant King Nebuchadnezzar of Babylon. I have even made wild animals serve him. ⁷All nations will serve him, his son, and his grandson until Babylon is defeated. Then many nations and great kings will make him their slave.

⁸'" 'Suppose nations or kingdoms won't serve or surrender to King Nebuchadnezzar of Babylon. I will punish those nations by wars, famines, and plagues, until I have put an end to them by Nebuchadnezzar's power, declares the LORD. ⁹Don't listen to prophets, mediums, interpreters of dreams, fortunetellers, or sorcerers who tell you that you'll never serve the king of Babylon. ¹⁰They are prophesying lies to you. They will cause you to be taken far from your lands. I'll scatter you, and you will die. ¹¹But suppose a nation surrenders to the king of Babylon and serves him. I will let it stay in its own land. People will farm the land and live on it,' " declares the LORD.

¹²I spoke the same message to King Zedekiah of Judah, "Surrender to the king of Babylon, serve him and his people, and you will stay alive. ¹³Why should you and your people die in wars, famines, and plagues? The LORD has threatened the nations that don't serve the king of Babylon. ¹⁴Don't listen to the prophets who tell you that you'll never serve the king of Babylon. They are prophesying lies to you. ¹⁵I didn't send them, declares the LORD. They prophesy lies in my name. So I will scatter you, and you and the prophets will die."

¹⁶I also spoke this message to the priests and all the people. "This is what the LORD said to me: Don't listen to the prophets who tell you that the utensils of the LORD's temple will be brought back from Babylon soon. They are prophesying lies to you. ¹⁷Don't listen to them. Instead, serve the king of Babylon, and live. Why should this city be turned into rubble? ¹⁸If they are prophets and the LORD is speaking to them, they should beg the LORD of Armies not to allow the utensils that are left in the LORD's temple, in the royal palace of Judah, and in Jerusalem to be taken away to Babylon.

¹⁹⁻²⁰"Babylon's King Nebuchadnezzar took Jehoiakin,ᵇ son of King Jehoiakim of Judah, into captivity from Jerusalem to Babylon along with all the nobles of Judah and Jerusalem. But he didn't take the pillars, the bronze pool, the stands, and the rest of the utensils that are left in this city. ²¹This is what the LORD of Armies, the God of Israel, says about the utensils that are left in the LORD's temple, in the royal palace of Judah, and in Jerusalem: ²²They will be taken to Babylon and stay there until I come for them, declares the LORD. I will take them from there and bring them back to this place."

Hananiah's False Prophecy

28 ¹In that same year, early in the rule of King Zedekiah of Judah, in the fifth month of his fourth year as king, the prophet Hananiah, son of Azzur, from Gibeon, spoke to me in the LORD's temple. He said to me in front of the priests and all the

---

ᵃ 27:2 A yoke is a wooden bar placed over the necks of work animals so that they can pull plows or carts.
ᵇ 27:19-20 Masoretic Text "Jeconiah," an alternate form of Jehoiakin.

people, ²"This is what the LORD of Armies, the God of Israel, says: I will break the yoke*ᵃ* of the king of Babylon. ³Within two years I will bring back all the utensils of the LORD's temple that King Nebuchadnezzar of Babylon took from this place and carried off to Babylon. ⁴I will also bring back to this place Jehoiakin, son of King Jehoiakim of Judah, and all the captives of Judah who went to Babylon, declares the LORD. So I will break the yoke of the king of Babylon."

⁵The prophet Jeremiah replied to the prophet Hananiah in front of the priests and all the people standing in the LORD's temple. ⁶He said, "Amen! May the LORD do this! May the LORD make your prophecy come true and bring back the utensils of the LORD's temple and all the captives from Babylon to this place. ⁷But now listen to this message that I am speaking to you and to all the people: ⁸Long ago, the prophets who preceded you and me prophesied wars, disasters, and plagues against many countries and great kingdoms. ⁹But the prophet who prophesied peace was recognized as a prophet that the LORD sent only if the message of the prophet came true."

¹⁰Then the prophet Hananiah took the yoke off the neck of the prophet Jeremiah and broke it. ¹¹Hananiah said in front of all the people, "This is what the LORD says: In the same way, I will break the yoke of King Nebuchadnezzar of Babylon off the neck of all the nations within two years." Then the prophet Jeremiah went on his way.

¹²After the prophet Hananiah broke the yoke off the neck of the prophet Jeremiah, the LORD spoke his word to Jeremiah. He said, ¹³"Tell Hananiah, 'This is what the LORD says: You have broken the wooden yoke, but I*ᵇ* will replace it with an iron yoke. ¹⁴This is what the LORD of Armies, the God of Israel, says: I will put an iron yoke on the necks of all these nations so that they will serve King Nebuchadnezzar of Babylon. They will serve him! I will even make wild animals serve him.'"

¹⁵Then Jeremiah told the prophet Hananiah, "Now listen, Hananiah, the LORD hasn't sent you. You have made these people believe a lie. ¹⁶This is what the LORD says: I'm going to remove you from the face of the earth. You will die this year because you have encouraged rebellion against the LORD."

¹⁷So the prophet Hananiah died in the seventh month of that year.

Jeremiah Writes to the Captives in Babylon

29 ¹The prophet Jeremiah sent a letter from Jerusalem to the rest of the leaders among the captives. He also sent it to the priests, the prophets, and all the people that Nebuchadnezzar took away as captives from Jerusalem to Babylon. ²(This was after King Jehoiakin*ᵃ* and his mother, the court officials, the leaders of Judah and Jerusalem, the craftsmen, and metal workers left Jerusalem.) ³He sent the letter with Shaphan's son Elasah and Hilkiah's son Gemariah, whom King Zedekiah of Judah had sent to King Nebuchadnezzar in Babylon. The letter said:

⁴This is what the LORD of Armies, the God of Israel, says to all those who were taken captive from Jerusalem to Babylon: ⁵Build houses, and live in them. Plant gardens, and eat what they produce. ⁶Get married, and have sons and daughters. Find wives for your sons, and let your daughters get married so that they can have sons and daughters. Grow in number there; don't decrease. ⁷Work for the good of the city where I've taken you as captives, and pray to the LORD for that city. When it prospers, you will also prosper.

⁸This is what the LORD of Armies, the God of Israel, says: Don't let the prophets or the mediums who are among you trick you. Don't even listen

---

ᵃ 28:2 A yoke is a wooden bar placed over the necks of work animals so that they can pull plows or carts. ᵇ 28:13 Greek; Masoretic Text "you." ᵃ 29:2 Masoretic Text "Jeconiah," an alternate form of Jehoiakin.

to your own dreams. ⁹These people are prophesying lies to you in my name. I didn't send them, declares the LORD.

¹⁰This is what the LORD says: When Babylon's 70 years are over, I will come to you. I will keep my promise to you and bring you back to this place. ¹¹I know the plans that I have for you, declares the LORD. They are plans for peace and not disaster, plans to give you a future filled with hope. ¹²Then you will call to me. You will come and pray to me, and I will hear you. ¹³When you look for me, you will find me. When you wholeheartedly seek me, ¹⁴I will let you find me, declares the LORD. I will bring you back from captivity. I will gather you from all the nations and places where I've scattered you, declares the LORD. I will bring you back from the place where you are being held captive.

¹⁵You've said that the LORD has given you prophets in Babylon. ¹⁶But this is what the LORD says about the king who sits on David's throne and about all the people who live in this city, the people who are your relatives and who weren't taken away as captives: ¹⁷The LORD of Armies says: I'm going to send them wars, famines, and plagues. These people are like rotten figs to me, figs that are so bad that they can't be eaten. ¹⁸I will chase them with wars, famines, and plagues. I will make them a horrifying sight to all the kingdoms on the earth. They will become something cursed, ridiculed, and hissed at, and they will be a disgrace among all the nations where I scatter them. ¹⁹They didn't listen to me, declares the LORD. I sent them my servants the prophets again and again, but they refused to listen, declares the LORD.

²⁰So listen to the word of the LORD, all you captives who were sent away from Jerusalem to Babylon.

²¹This is what the LORD of Armies, the God of Israel, says about Kolaiah's son Ahab and about Maaseiah's son Zedekiah, who prophesy lies to you in my name: I'm going to hand them over to King Nebuchadnezzar of Babylon. I will kill them as you watch. ²²Because of them, all the captives from Judah who are in Babylon will use this curse: May the LORD curse you as he cursed Zedekiah and Ahab, whom the king of Babylon burned to death. ²³They have done shameful things in Israel. They committed adultery with their neighbors' wives and spoke lies in my name. I didn't command them to do this. I know what they have done. I'm a witness, declares the LORD.

²⁴The LORD says, "Say to Shemaiah from Nehelam, ²⁵This is what the LORD of Armies, the God of Israel, says: You sent letters in your own name to all the people who are in Jerusalem, to the priest Zephaniah, son of Maaseiah, and to all the priests. These letters said: ²⁶The LORD made you priest instead of Jehoiada so that there would be officials for the LORD's temple. You should put any lunatic who acts like a prophet in prison and in shackles. ²⁷Now, why haven't you arrested Jeremiah from Anathoth? After all, he acts like a prophet among you. ²⁸That's why Jeremiah sent this message to us in Babylon: You will be captives a long time. Build houses, and live in them. Plant gardens, and eat what they produce.' "

²⁹The priest Zephaniah read this letter to the prophet Jeremiah.

³⁰Then the LORD spoke his word to Jeremiah. He said, ³¹"Send this message to all the captives: 'This is what the LORD says about Shemaiah from Nehelam: Shemaiah prophesied to you, but I didn't send him. He has made you believe a lie. ³²The LORD says: I will punish Shemaiah from Nehelam. I will also punish his descendants. No one from his family will be left alive. He will not see the blessings that I'm going to send my people, declares the LORD, because he has encouraged rebellion against the LORD.' "

Israel's Glorious Future

30 ¹The LORD spoke his word to Jeremiah. He said, ²"This is what the LORD God of Israel says: Write in a book everything that I tell you. ³The days are coming," declares the LORD, "when I will bring my people Israel and Judah back from captivity. I will bring them back to the land that I gave their ancestors, and they will take possession of it."

⁴This is the message that the LORD spoke about Israel and Judah: ⁵"This is what the LORD says:

"We hear cries of fear, cries of panic, not cries of peace.
6   Ask now, and see: Can a man give birth to a child?
     Why, then, do I see every strong man holding his stomach in pain
       like a woman giving birth to a child?
     Why has every face turned pale?
7   How terrible that day will be!
     There will be no other day like it.
     It will be a time of calamity for the descendants of Jacob,
       but they will be rescued from it.

⁸"On that day," declares the LORD of Armies, "I will break the yokes *a* off your necks and tear off your ropes. Foreigners will no longer make you serve them. ⁹You will serve the LORD your God and David your king. I will establish him for you.

10   "Don't be afraid, my servant Jacob," declares the LORD.
     Don't be terrified, Israel.
     I'm going to rescue you from a faraway place.
     I'm going to rescue your descendants from where they are captives.
     The descendants of Jacob will again have peace and security,
       and no one will frighten them.
11   I am with you, and I will rescue you," declares the LORD.
     "I will completely destroy all the nations where I scattered you,
       but I will not completely destroy you.
     I will correct you with justice.
     I won't let you go entirely unpunished.

¹²"This is what the LORD says:

     Your wound is incurable.
     Your injury is beyond healing.
13   No one argues that you should be healed.
     No medicine will heal you.
14   All your lovers have forgotten you,
       and they don't want you anymore.
     I've punished you as an enemy would.
     I've corrected you as a cruel person would.
     You are very wicked, and you have many sins.
15   Why do you cry about your wound, your injury that can't be cured?
     I've done this to you.
     You are very wicked, and you have many sins.
16   That is why everyone who devours you will be devoured,
       and all your enemies will be taken away as captives.

---

a 30:8 A yoke is a wooden bar placed over the necks of work animals so that they can pull plows or carts.

Those who looted you will be looted.
Those who stole from you in war will have things stolen from them.
17 I'll restore your health and heal your wounds," declares the Lord.
"People call you an outcast:
Zion, no one cares for you.

18"This is what the Lord says:

I'm going to bring the captives back to Jacob's tents
and show compassion on their homes.
Cities will be built on the ruins,
and fortified palaces will be built in their rightful place.
19 The people who live there will sing songs of praise,
and the sound of laughter will be heard from there.
I'll make them numerous, and their number won't decrease.
I'll bring them honor, and they won't be considered unimportant.
20 Their children will be like they were long ago.
Their community will be established in my presence,
and I will punish everyone who oppresses them.
21 Their leader will be someone from their own people.
Their ruler will come from among them.
I'll bring him near, and he will come close to me.
Who would dare to come near me?" asks the Lord.
22 You will be my people, and I will be your God.
23 The storm of the Lord will come with his anger.
Like a driving wind, it will swirl down on the heads of the wicked.
24 The Lord's burning anger will not turn back
until he has done everything he intends to do.
In the last days you will understand this clearly.

Both Israel and Judah Will Be Rescued

31 1"At that time," declares the Lord, "I will be the God of all the families of Israel,
and they will be my people."
2This is what the Lord says:

The people who survived the wars have found favor in the desert.
Israel went to find its rest.

3The Lord appeared to me in a faraway place and said,

"I love you with an everlasting love.
So I will continue to show you my kindness.
4 Once again I will build you up,
and you will be rebuilt, my dear people Israel.
Once again you will take your tambourines,
and you will go dancing with happy people.
5 Once again you will plant vineyards on the mountains of Samaria.
Those who plant them will enjoy the fruit.
6 There will be a day when watchmen on the mountains of Ephraim
will call out this message:
'Arise! Let's go to Zion, to the Lord our God.' "

7This is what the Lord says:

Sing a happy song about Jacob.
Sing joyfully for the leader of the nations.
Shout, sing praise, and say,
"O Lord, rescue your people, the remaining few from Israel."

8 "I will bring them from the land of the north.
I will gather them from the farthest parts of the earth.
Blind people and lame people will return
together with pregnant women and those in labor.
A large crowd will return here.
9 They will cry as they return.
They will pray as I bring them back.
I will lead them beside streams
on a level path where they will not stumble.
I will be a Father to Israel,
and Ephraim will be my firstborn.

10 "You nations, listen to the word of the Lord.
Tell it to the distant islands.
Say, 'The one who scattered the people of Israel will gather them
and watch over them as a shepherd watches over his flock.'
11 The Lord will free the descendants of Jacob
and reclaim them from those who are stronger than they are.
12 They will come and shout for joy on top of Mount Zion.
They will stream to it to enjoy the Lord's blessings:
fresh grain, new wine, and olive oil, lambs and calves.
Their lives will be like well-watered gardens,
and they will never suffer again.
13 Then young women will rejoice and dance
along with young men and old men.
I will turn their mourning into joy.
I will comfort them.
I will give them joy in place of their sorrow.
14 I will satisfy the priests with rich food.
My people will be filled with my blessings," declares the Lord.

15This is what the Lord says:

Good Morning, God

Jeremiah 31:13

Who can make you laugh even when you feel like crying? A good friend? A special adult? Crying and sadness are a part of everyone's life. God gives us tears so we can deal with our sadness. In time, God promises to turn our sadness into joy. Remember his promise the next time you are sad, and look forward to the joy he will soon bring.

Lord, thank you for bringing joy out of sadness.

A sound is heard in Ramah,
>the sound of crying in bitter grief.
>>Rachel is crying for her children.
>>She refuses to be comforted,
>>>because they are dead.

¹⁶This is what the Lord says:

>Stop your crying, and wipe away your tears.
>>You will be rewarded for your work, declares the Lord.
>>You will return from the land of the enemy.
¹⁷ Your future is filled with hope, declares the Lord.
>>Your children will return to their own territory.

¹⁸ "I have certainly heard Ephraim mourn and say,
>'You disciplined me, and I was disciplined.
>>I was like a young, untrained calf.
>Turn me, and I will be turned,
>>because you are the Lord my God.
¹⁹ After I was turned around, I changed the way I thought and acted.
>After I was taught a lesson, I hung my head in shame.
>>I was so ashamed and humiliated,
>>>because of all the stupid things I have done
>>>>ever since I was young.'
²⁰ Is Ephraim my dear son? Is he a pleasant child?
>Even though I have often spoken against him, I still think fondly of him.
>That is why my heart longs for him,
>>and I will certainly have compassion on him," declares the Lord.

²¹ Set up landmarks!
>Put up road signs!
>>Remember the highway, the road on which you traveled.
>>Come back, my dear people Israel, come back to your cities.
²² How long will you wander around, you unfaithful people?
>The Lord will create something new on earth:
>>A woman will protect a man.

²³This is what the Lord of Armies, the God of Israel, says: When I have brought them back from captivity, they will once again use this saying in Judah and in its cities:

>"The Lord will bless you, home of righteousness, holy mountain.
²⁴ Judah and all its cities will live there together.
>>Farmers and shepherds will also live there.
²⁵ >I will give those who are weary all they need.
>>I will refresh everyone who is filled with sorrow."

²⁶At this, I woke up and looked around. My sleep had been pleasant.

²⁷"The days are coming," declares the Lord, "when I will plant the nations of Israel and Judah with people and animals. ²⁸Once I watched over them to uproot them, to tear them down, and to wreck, ruin, and hurt them. Now I will watch over them to build them up and to plant them," declares the Lord. ²⁹"When those days come, people will no longer say, 'Fathers have eaten sour grapes, and their children's teeth are set on edge.' ³⁰But each person will die for his own sin. Whoever eats sour grapes will have his own teeth set on edge.

The New Promise

³¹"The days are coming," declares the Lord, "when I will make a new promise*ᵃ* to Israel and Judah. ³²It will not be like the promise that I made to their ancestors when I took them by the hand and brought them out of Egypt. They rejected that promise, although I was a husband to them," declares the Lord. ³³"But this is the promise that I will make to Israel after those days," declares the Lord: "I will put my teachings inside them, and I will write those teachings on their hearts. I will be their God, and they will be my people. ³⁴No longer will each person teach his neighbors or his relatives by saying, 'Know the Lord.' All of them, from the least important to the most important, will know me," declares the Lord, "because I will forgive their wickedness and I will no longer hold their sins against them."

35   The Lord provides the sun to be a light during the day.
      He orders the moon and stars to be lights during the night.
      He stirs up the sea so that its waves roar.
      His name is the Lord of Armies.

This is what the Lord says:

36   Only if these laws stop working, declares the Lord,
      will Israel's descendants stop being a nation in my presence.

³⁷This is what the Lord says:

      Only if the heavens could be measured
      or the foundations of the earth could be searched,
         would I ever reject all of Israel's descendants
            because of everything that they have done, declares the Lord.

³⁸"The days are coming," declares the Lord, "when the city will be rebuilt for me from the Tower of Hananel to Corner Gate. ³⁹A measuring line will stretch from there straight to the Hill of Gareb, and then it will turn to Goah. ⁴⁰The whole valley, filled with its dead bodies and ashes, and the whole area to the Kidron Valley, as far as the corner of Horse Gate in the east, will be holy to the Lord. It will never be uprooted or torn down again."

Jeremiah Buys a Field

32 ¹The Lord spoke his word to Jeremiah during Zedekiah's tenth year as king of Judah. (This was Nebuchadnezzar's eighteenth year as king.) ²At that time the army of the king of Babylon was blockading Jerusalem.

The prophet Jeremiah was locked up in the courtyard of the prison. This prison was in the palace of the king of Judah. ³When King Zedekiah of Judah locked up Jeremiah, Zedekiah asked him, "Why are you prophesying? You are saying, 'This is what the Lord says: I'm going to hand this city over to the king of Babylon, and he will capture it. ⁴King Zedekiah of Judah will not escape from the Babylonians. He will certainly be handed over to the king of Babylon. He will talk to Nebuchadnezzar in person and look him in the eye. ⁵Nebuchadnezzar will take Zedekiah to Babylon, and Zedekiah will stay there until I deal with him, declares the Lord. When you fight the Babylonians, you won't win.' "

⁶Jeremiah said, "The Lord spoke his word to me. He said, ⁷Jeremiah, your cousin Hanamel, son of Shallum, is going to come to you and say, "Buy my field that is in Anathoth, because as the closest relative it is your responsibility to buy it.' "

ᵃ 31:31 Or "covenant."

⁸"Then, as the LORD had said, my cousin Hanamel came to me in the courtyard of the prison. He said to me, 'Please buy my field that is in Anathoth in the territory of Benjamin. It is your responsibility to purchase it, because the rights of the closest relative belong to you. Buy it for yourself.' Then I knew that the LORD had spoken to me.

⁹"So I bought the field in Anathoth from my cousin Hanamel and gave him the money. The field cost seven ounces of silver. ¹⁰I signed the deed, sealed it, had people witness the signing of the deed, and paid out the silver. ¹¹Then I took the sealed copy of the deed, containing the terms and conditions, as well as an unsealed copy. ¹²I gave the copies of the deeds to Baruch, son of Neriah and grandson of Mahseiah. I did this in the presence of my cousin Hanamel and the witnesses who had signed the deed and in the presence of all the Jews who were sitting in the courtyard of the prison. ¹³Then I gave Baruch these orders: ¹⁴"This is what the LORD of Armies, the God of Israel, says: Take both of these documents, both the sealed and the unsealed copies of the deed. Put them in a clay jar so that they will last a long time. ¹⁵This is what the LORD of Armies, the God of Israel, says: My people will again buy houses, fields, and vineyards in this land.'

¹⁶"After I had given the copies to Baruch, son of Neriah, I prayed to the LORD. I prayed, ¹⁷Almighty LORD, you made heaven and earth by your great strength and powerful arm. Nothing is too hard for you. ¹⁸You show mercy to thousands of generations. However, you punish children for the wickedness of their parents. You, God, are great and mighty. Your name is the LORD of Armies. ¹⁹You make wise plans and do mighty things. You see everything the descendants of Adam do. You reward them for the way they live and for what they do. ²⁰You performed miraculous signs and amazing things in Egypt. To this day you are still doing them in Israel. You made a name for yourself that continues to this day. ²¹You brought your people from Egypt with miraculous signs and amazing things, with a mighty hand and a powerful arm, and with great terror. ²²You gave them the land that you swore with an oath to give their ancestors, the land flowing with milk and honey. ²³They entered and took possession of it. However, they refused to obey you or to follow your teachings. They didn't do anything you commanded them to do, so you brought all this disaster on them.

²⁴" 'See how the dirt ramps have been built up around the city to capture it! Because of wars, famines, and plagues, the city will be handed over to the Babylonians who are attacking it. What you have threatened to do has happened, as you can see. ²⁵Yet you, Almighty LORD, told me to buy a field with money and get witnesses to confirm it, although the city was handed over to the Babylonians.' "

²⁶The LORD spoke his word to Jeremiah. He said, ²⁷"I am the LORD God of all humanity. Nothing is too hard for me. ²⁸This is what the LORD says: I'm going to hand this city over to the Babylonians and King Nebuchadnezzar of Babylon. They will capture it.

²⁹"The Babylonians who are attacking this city will break in, set this city on fire, and burn it down. They will burn down the houses of people who made me furious by going up to the roofs to burn incense to Baal and to pour out wine offerings to other gods. ³⁰Ever since they were young, the people of Israel and Judah have done what I consider evil. The people of Israel have made me furious by what they've done," declares the LORD. ³¹"The people in this city have made me so angry and furious from the day they built it to this day. So now I must remove this city from my presence.

³²"The people of Israel and Judah have made me furious because they are evil. The people, their kings and officials, their priests and prophets, and the Judeans and those who live in Jerusalem ³³have turned their backs, not their faces to me. I taught them

again and again, but they refused to listen and learn. ³⁴They set up their detestable idols in the temple that is called by my name, and they dishonored it. ³⁵In the valley of Ben Hinnom they built worship sites for Baal to sacrifice their sons and daughters to Molech. I didn't ask them to do this. It never entered my mind. I didn't make Judah sin.

³⁶"You have said this about the city, 'Because of wars, famines, and plagues it will be handed over to the king of Babylon.' Now this is what the Lord God of Israel says: ³⁷I am going to gather the people from all the lands where I scattered them in my anger, fury, and terrifying wrath. I will bring them back to this place and make them live here securely. ³⁸They will be my people, and I will be their God. ³⁹I will give them the same attitude and the same purpose so that they will fear me as long as they live. This will be for their own good and for the good of their children. ⁴⁰I will make an eternal promise*ᵃ* to them that I will never stop blessing them. I will make them fear me so that they will never turn away from me. ⁴¹I will enjoy blessing them. With all my heart and soul I will faithfully plant them in this land.

⁴²"This is what the Lord says: As I brought all these disasters on these people, so I will bring on them all these blessings that I have promised them. ⁴³You have said that this land is a wasteland, without people or animals living in it. You have also said that it has been handed over to the Babylonians. But people will once again buy fields in this land. ⁴⁴They will buy fields for money, sign deeds, seal them, and have people witness the signing of the deeds. This will happen in the territory of Benjamin, in the region of Jerusalem, in the cities of Judah, in the cities on the mountains, in the hill country, and in the Negev because I will bring them back from their captivity," declares the Lord.

The Lord Will Restore and Heal Judah

33 ¹While Jeremiah was still being held in the courtyard of the prison, the Lord spoke his word to him a second time. The Lord said, ²"I made the earth, formed it, and set it in place. My name is the Lord. This is what the Lord says: ³Call to me, and I will answer you. I will tell you great and mysterious things that you do not know. ⁴The houses in this city and the palaces of the kings of Judah have been torn down to be used against the dirt ramps and weapons of the Babylonians. This is what the Lord God of Israel says about this: ⁵The people of Israel fought the Babylonians. Now their houses are filled with the bodies of their own people I killed in my anger and my fury. I will hide my face from this city because of its wickedness.

⁶"But I will heal this city and restore it to health. I will heal its people, and I will give them peace and security. ⁷I will restore Judah and Israel and rebuild them as they were before. ⁸I will cleanse them from all the sins that they have committed against me. I will forgive them for all the sins that they have committed against me and for rebelling against me. ⁹Then Jerusalem will be my source of joy, praise, and honor. All the nations on earth will hear about all the blessings that I will give to Jerusalem. They will be afraid and tremble because of all the prosperity that I will provide for it.

¹⁰"This is what the Lord says: You have said that this place is ruined and that no people or animals live in it. It's true! The cities of Judah and the streets of Jerusalem are deserted. No people or animals live there. But once again you will hear ¹¹the sounds of joy and happiness and the sounds of brides and grooms. You will hear those who bring thank offerings to the Lord's temple say,

---

*ᵃ*32:40 Or "covenant."

'Give thanks to the Lord of Armies because the Lord is good,
   because his mercy endures forever.'

I will restore the fortunes of the land to what they were before," says the Lord.

¹²"This is what the Lord of Armies says: In this deserted place, where no people or animals live, and in all its cities, there will once again be pastures where shepherds can rest their flocks. ¹³In the cities on the mountains, in the foothills, in the Negev, in the territory of Benjamin, in the area around Jerusalem, and in the cities of Judah, shepherds will once again count their sheep," says the Lord.

¹⁴"The days are coming," declares the Lord, "when I will keep the promise that I made to Israel and Judah. ¹⁵In those days and at that time, I will cause a righteous branch to spring up for David. He will do what is fair and right in the land. ¹⁶In those days Judah will be saved and Jerusalem will live securely. Jerusalem will be called The Lord Our Righteousness.

¹⁷"This what the Lord says: David will never fail to have a descendant sitting on the throne of Israel. ¹⁸The Levitical priests will never fail to have a descendant in my presence to sacrifice burnt offerings, to burn grain offerings, and to prepare daily sacrifices."

¹⁹The Lord spoke his word to Jeremiah. He said, ²⁰"This is what the Lord says: Suppose you could break my arrangement*ᵃ* with day and night so that they wouldn't come at their proper time. ²¹Then my arrangement with my servant David could be broken, and he would not have a descendant to rule on his throne. The arrangement with my servants the Levitical priests could also be broken. ²²I will multiply the descendants of my servant David and the Levites who serve me like the stars of heaven that cannot be counted and the sand on the seashore that cannot be measured."

²³Then the Lord spoke his word to Jeremiah. He said, ²⁴"Haven't you noticed what these people have said? They have said that the Lord has rejected the two families he has chosen. They despise my people, and they no longer consider them a nation.

²⁵"This is what the Lord says: Suppose I hadn't made an arrangement with day and night or made laws for heaven and earth. ²⁶Then I would reject the descendants of Jacob and of my servant David. I would not let any of David's descendants rule the descendants of Abraham, Isaac, and Jacob. However, I will restore their fortunes and love them."

King Zedekiah and the People Break Their Promise

34 ¹The Lord spoke his word to Jeremiah when King Nebuchadnezzar of Babylon, his entire army, and all the kingdoms and people that he ruled were attacking Jerusalem and all its cities. He said, ²"This is what the Lord God of Israel says: Go to King Zedekiah of Judah, and tell him, 'The Lord says: I'm going to hand this city over to the king of Babylon, and he will burn it down. ³You will not escape from him. You will certainly be captured and handed over to him. You will see the king of Babylon with your own eyes, and he will talk to you face to face. Then you will go to Babylon.'

⁴" 'Listen to the word of the Lord, King Zedekiah of Judah. This is what the Lord says about you: You will not die in war. ⁵You will die peacefully. People will burn funeral fires for you as they did for your ancestors, the kings who lived before you. They will say, "Oh, master," as they mourn for you. I have spoken my word, declares the Lord.' "

⁶The prophet Jeremiah told all these things to King Zedekiah of Judah in Jerusalem. ⁷He did this when the army of the king of Babylon was attacking Jerusalem and

---

ᵃ33:20 Or "covenant."

the cities of Lachish and Azekah. These were the only fortified cities of Judah that were left.

⁸The LORD spoke his word to Jeremiah after King Zedekiah and all the people in Jerusalem promised to free their slaves. ⁹Everyone was supposed to free his Hebrew slaves, both male and female. No one was supposed to keep another Jew as a slave. ¹⁰All the officials and all the people agreed and promised to free their male and female slaves and not to keep them as slaves anymore. So they set them free. ¹¹But afterwards, they changed their minds and took back the men and women they had freed and made them their slaves again.

¹²The LORD spoke his word to Jeremiah. He said, ¹³"This is what the LORD God of Israel says: I put a condition on the promise* I made to your ancestors when I brought them from Egypt, where they were slaves. I said, ¹⁴'Every seven years each of you must free any Hebrews who sold themselves to you. When they have served you for six years, you must set them free.' But your ancestors refused to obey me or listen to me. ¹⁵Recently, you changed and did what I consider right. You agreed to free your neighbors, and you made a promise in my presence, in the temple that is called by my name. ¹⁶Now you have changed again and dishonored me. You brought back the male and female slaves that you had set free to live their own lives. You have forced them to be your male and female slaves again.

¹⁷"This is what the LORD says: You didn't obey me. You haven't freed your relatives and neighbors. Now I am going to free you," declares the LORD. "I will free you to die in wars, plagues, and famines. I will make all the kingdoms of the world horrified at the thought of you. ¹⁸I will hand over the people who have rejected my promise. They have not kept the terms of the promise which they made in my presence when they cut a calf in two and passed between its pieces. ¹⁹I will hand over the officials of Judah and Jerusalem, the palace officials, the priests, and all the common people who passed between the pieces of the calf. ²⁰I will hand them over to their enemies who want to kill them, and their corpses will be food for birds and wild animals. ²¹I will hand King Zedekiah of Judah and his officials over to their enemies who want to kill them and to the army of the king of Babylon, the army that has withdrawn from you. ²²I am going to give a command," declares the LORD. "I will bring that army back to this city to attack it, capture it, and burn it down. I will destroy the cities of Judah so that no one will live there."

The Obedient Example of the Family of Rechab

35 ¹The LORD spoke his word to Jeremiah during the reign of Jehoiakim, son of King Josiah of Judah. He said, ²"Go to the family of Rechab and talk to them. Take them into one of the side rooms in the LORD's temple, and offer them a drink of wine."

³I took Jaazaniah, who was the son of Jeremiah and the grandson of Habazziniah, and I took Jaazaniah's brothers and all his sons—the whole family of Rechab. ⁴I brought them into the LORD's temple, into the side room of the sons of Hanan. (He was Igdaliah's son, the man of God.) It was next to the room of the officials and above the side room of Maaseiah, Shallum's son, the doorkeeper. ⁵Then I set cups and pitchers filled with wine in front of the family of Rechab. I said to them, "Drink some wine."

⁶They answered, "We don't drink wine, because our ancestor Jonadab, Rechab's son, gave us this order: 'You and your descendants must never drink wine. ⁷Never build any houses or plant any fields or vineyards. You must never have any of these

---

*34:13 Or "covenant."

had dictated, the Lᴏʀᴅ spoke his word to Jeremiah. He said, ²⁸"Take another scroll, and write on it everything that was written on the scroll that King Jehoiakim of Judah burned. ²⁹Say about King Jehoiakim of Judah, 'This is what the Lᴏʀᴅ says: You burned this scroll, and you asked Jeremiah, "Why did you write that the king of Babylon will certainly come to destroy this land and take away people and animals?" ³⁰This is what the Lᴏʀᴅ says about King Jehoiakim of Judah: He will have no one to sit on David's throne, and his own corpse will be thrown out and exposed to the heat of day and the cold of night. ³¹I will punish him, his descendants, and his attendants for their wickedness. They refused to listen. So I will bring on them, on those who live in Jerusalem, and on the people of Judah all the disasters that I have threatened.' "

³²Then Jeremiah took another scroll and gave it to the scribe Baruch, son of Neriah. As Jeremiah dictated, Baruch wrote on it everything that was on the scroll that King Jehoiakim of Judah had burned. They added many similar messages.

Jeremiah Advises Zedekiah

³⁷ ¹King Nebuchadnezzar of Babylon appointed Zedekiah, son of Josiah, to be king of Judah. Zedekiah succeeded Jehoiakin, son of Jehoiakim. ²But Zedekiah, his administrators, and the common people didn't listen to what the Lᴏʀᴅ had spoken through the prophet Jeremiah.

³King Zedekiah sent Jehucal (son of Shelemiah) and the priest Zephaniah (son of Maaseiah) to the prophet Jeremiah. They asked him, "Please pray to the Lᴏʀᴅ our God for us."

⁴Jeremiah was still free to come and go among the people. The people of Jerusalem hadn't put him in prison yet. ⁵Pharaoh's army had come from Egypt, and when the Babylonians who were blockading Jerusalem heard this news, they retreated from Jerusalem.

⁶The Lᴏʀᴅ spoke his word to the prophet Jeremiah. He said, ⁷"This is what the Lᴏʀᴅ God of Israel says: Say this to the king of Judah, who sent you to get advice from me: 'Pharaoh's army has come out to help you. But it will go back to Egypt, its own land. ⁸Then the Babylonians will return. They will attack the city, capture it, and burn it down.

⁹" 'This is what the Lᴏʀᴅ says: Don't deceive yourselves by thinking that the Babylonians will leave you. They will not leave you. ¹⁰Even if you would defeat the entire Babylonian army so that they had only a few badly wounded men left in their tents, they would get up and burn down this city.' "

¹¹The Babylonian army had retreated from Jerusalem because Pharaoh's army was coming. ¹²So Jeremiah wanted to leave Jerusalem and go to the territory of Benjamin to take possession of his property there among the people. ¹³But when he came to Benjamin Gate, the captain of the guard there, whose name was Irijah, son of Shelemiah and grandson of Hananiah, arrested the prophet Jeremiah. He said, "You're deserting to the Babylonians!"

¹⁴Jeremiah answered, "That's a lie! I'm not deserting to the Babylonians." But Irijah wouldn't listen to him. Irijah arrested Jeremiah and took him to the officials. ¹⁵The officials were so angry with Jeremiah that they beat him and put him in prison in the scribe Jonathan's house, which had been turned into a prison. ¹⁶Jeremiah went into a prison cell, and he stayed there a long time.

¹⁷Then King Zedekiah sent for Jeremiah, and the king asked him privately in the palace, "Is there any message from the Lᴏʀᴅ?"

Jeremiah answered, "Yes! There is a message from the Lᴏʀᴅ. You will be handed over to the king of Babylon." ¹⁸Then Jeremiah asked King Zedekiah, "What crime have I committed against you, your administrators, or these people? Why have you put me in prison? ¹⁹Where are the prophets who told you that the king of Babylon wouldn't attack you and this land? ²⁰But now, Your Majesty, please listen, and accept my plea for mercy. Don't return me to the scribe Jonathan's house, or I will die there."

²¹King Zedekiah gave the command to have Jeremiah put in the courtyard of the prison. He gave him a loaf of bread every day from the bakers' street until all the bread in the city was gone. So Jeremiah stayed in the courtyard of the prison.

Jeremiah Is Thrown Into a Muddy Cistern

38 ¹Shephatiah (son of Mattan), Gedaliah (son of Pashhur), Jucal (son of Shelemiah), and Pashhur (son of Malchiah) heard that Jeremiah was speaking to all the people. ²They heard Jeremiah say, "This is what the LORD says: Those who stay in this city will die in wars, famines, or plagues. But those who surrender to the Babylonians will live. They will escape with their lives.

³"This is what the LORD says: This city will certainly be handed over to the army of the king of Babylon, and it will capture the city."

⁴Then the officials said to the king, "Have this man put to death. He discourages the soldiers who are left in this city and all the people by telling them such things. This man is not trying to help these people; he's trying to hurt them."

⁵King Zedekiah answered, "He's in your hands. I won't do anything to stop you."

⁶So they took Jeremiah and threw him into the cistern of Malchiah, the king's son. It was in the courtyard of the prison. They used ropes to lower Jeremiah into the cistern. There was no water in the cistern, only mud, and Jeremiah sank in the mud.

⁷But an official in the royal palace, Ebed Melech from Sudan, heard that they had put Jeremiah in the cistern. The king happened to be sitting at Benjamin Gate. ⁸Ebed Melech left the royal palace and spoke to the king at Benjamin Gate. ⁹"Your Majesty, everything that these men have done to the prophet Jeremiah is wrong. They have thrown him into the cistern, where he'll starve to death, because there's no more bread in the city."

¹⁰Then the king gave Ebed Melech from Sudan this command: "Take 30 men from here, and lift the prophet Jeremiah out of the cistern before he dies."

¹¹So Ebed Melech took the men with him and went to the royal palace, to a room under the treasury. He took rags and torn clothes from there and lowered them with ropes to Jeremiah in the cistern. ¹²Ebed Melech from Sudan said to Jeremiah, "Put these rags and torn clothes under your arms to protect you from the ropes." Jeremiah did. ¹³They used the ropes to pull Jeremiah up and lift him out of the cistern. Then Jeremiah stayed in the courtyard of the prison.

¹⁴King Zedekiah sent for the prophet Jeremiah and brought him to the third entrance in the LORD's temple. "I'm going to ask you a question," the king said to Jeremiah. "Don't hide anything from me."

¹⁵Jeremiah answered Zedekiah, "If I answer you, you'll kill me. If I give you advice, you won't listen to me."

¹⁶So King Zedekiah secretly swore an oath to Jeremiah, "The LORD gave us life. As the LORD lives, I will not kill you or hand you over to these men who want to kill you."

¹⁷Jeremiah said to Zedekiah, "This is what the LORD God of Armies, the God of Israel, says: If you surrender to the officers of the king of Babylon, you will live, and this city will not be burned. You and your household will live. ¹⁸But if you don't surrender to the officers of the king of Babylon, this city will be handed over to the Babylonians. They will burn it down, and you will not escape from them."

¹⁹King Zedekiah answered Jeremiah, "I'm afraid of the Jews who have deserted

to the Babylonians. The Babylonians may hand me over to them, and they will torture me."

²⁰Jeremiah said, "You will not be handed over to them. Obey the Lord by doing what I'm telling you. Then everything will go well for you, and you will live. ²¹But if you refuse to surrender, this is what the Lord has shown me. ²²All the women who are left in the palace of Judah's king will be brought out to the officers of the king of Babylon. These women will say:

'Your trusted friends have misled you and used you.
Your feet are stuck in the mud, and your friends have deserted you.'

²³"All your wives and children will be brought to the Babylonians. You will not escape from them. You will be captured by the king of Babylon, and this city will be burned down."

Jeremiah and Zedekiah Make an Agreement

²⁴Zedekiah said to Jeremiah, "Don't let anyone know about this conversation, or you will die. ²⁵The officials may find out that I've been talking with you. They may come to you and say, 'Tell us what you said to the king and what the king said to you. Don't hide anything from us, or we'll kill you.' ²⁶If they come to you, say to them, 'I asked the king not to send me back to Jonathan's house to die there.' "

²⁷All the officials came to Jeremiah and questioned him. He told them exactly what the king had told him to say. So they stopped questioning him, because they hadn't heard his conversation with the king. ²⁸Jeremiah stayed in the courtyard of the prison until the day Jerusalem was captured.

Jerusalem Is Captured—
2 Kings 25:1-12; 2 Chronicles 36:19-21; Jeremiah 52:4-16

¹In the tenth month of Zedekiah's ninth year as king of Judah, King Nebuchadnezzar of Babylon attacked Jerusalem with his entire army and blockaded it. ²On the ninth day of the fourth month of Zedekiah's eleventh year as king, they broke into the city.

³Then all the officers of the king of Babylon came in and sat in Middle Gate: Nergal (the quartermaster), Samgar Nebo (the chief officer), Nergal (the quartermaster and the chief fortuneteller), and all the rest of the officers of the king of Babylon.

⁴When King Zedekiah of Judah and all the soldiers saw them, they fled. They left the city at night by way of the king's garden through the gate between the two walls, and they took the road to the plain of Jericho. ⁵The Babylonian army pursued them and caught up with Zedekiah in the plain of Jericho. They arrested him and brought him to Babylon's King Nebuchadnezzar at Riblah in the territory of Hamath. The king of Babylon passed sentence on him. ⁶The king of Babylon slaughtered Zedekiah's sons as Zedekiah watched at Riblah. He also slaughtered all the leaders of Judah. ⁷Then he blinded Zedekiah, put him in bronze shackles, and took him to Babylon.

⁸The Babylonians burned down the royal palace and the people's homes, and they tore down the walls of Jerusalem. ⁹Nebuzaradan, Babylon's captain of the guard, captured the few people left in the city, those who surrendered to him, and the rest of the people. ¹⁰But Nebuzaradan, the captain of the guard, left some poor people who had nothing in the land of Judah. At that time he gave them vineyards and farms.

¹¹King Nebuchadnezzar of Babylon gave Nebuzaradan an order concerning Jeremiah. He said, ¹²"Take him, and look after him. Don't harm him in any way, but do for him whatever he asks." ¹³Nebuzaradan (the captain of the guard), Nebushazban

(the chief official), Nergal (the quartermaster and the chief fortuneteller), and all the other leaders of the king of Babylon sent for Jeremiah. [14]They took Jeremiah out of the courtyard of the prison and handed him over to Gedaliah, son of Ahikam and grandson of Shaphan, to take him home. So he lived among the people.

[15]While Jeremiah was still confined in the courtyard of the prison, the Lord spoke his word to him. The Lord said, [16]"Say to Ebed Melech from Sudan, 'This is what the Lord of Armies, the God of Israel, says: I'm going to carry out my threat against this city by bringing disaster on it instead of prosperity. At that time these things will happen as you watch. [17]But at that time I will rescue you, declares the Lord. You will not be handed over to those you fear. [18]I will certainly rescue you. You will not die in war. You will escape with your life because you trusted me, declares the Lord.'"

Jeremiah Is Freed—
2 Kings 25:22–26

[1]The Lord spoke his word to Jeremiah after Nebuzaradan, the captain of the guard, let him go at Ramah. Nebuzaradan found Jeremiah in chains along with the captives of Jerusalem and Judah who were being taken to Babylon. [2]The captain of the guard took Jeremiah aside and said to him, "The Lord your God threatened to bring this disaster on this place. [3]He has carried out his threat. The Lord did as he promised because you Israelites have sinned against him and refused to obey him. That is why this has happened to you. [4]Today I'm removing the chains from your hands. If you would like to come with me to Babylon, come, and I'll look after you. But if you don't want to come with me to Babylon, don't come. The whole land is yours. Go wherever you want.

[5]"If you wish to remain,[a] then go back to Gedaliah, son of Ahikam and grandson of Shaphan, whom the king of Babylon appointed to govern the cities of Judah. Live among the people with him, or go anywhere you want." The captain of the guard gave Jeremiah some food and a present and let him go. [6]Jeremiah went to Gedaliah, son of Ahikam, at Mizpah and lived with him among the people who were left in the land.

[7]All the army commanders and their men who were in the field heard that the king of Babylon had appointed Gedaliah, son of Ahikam, to govern the country and some of the country's poorest men, women, and children who had not been taken away to Babylon. [8]These are the commanders who went with their men to Gedaliah at Mizpah: Ishmael (son of Nethaniah), Johanan and Jonathan (sons of Kareah), Seraiah (son of Tanhumeth), the sons of Ephai from Netophah, and Jezaniah, who was the son of a man from Maacah. [9]Gedaliah, son of Ahikam and grandson of Shaphan, swore an oath to them and their men. He said, "Don't be afraid to serve the Babylonians. Live in this country, serve the king of Babylon, and you will prosper. [10]I'm going to live in Mizpah and represent you when the Babylonians come to us. Gather grapes, summer fruit, and olive oil, and put them in storage jars. Live in the cities you have taken over."

[11]Now, all the Jews who were in Moab, Ammon, Edom, and in all the other countries heard that the king of Babylon had left a few survivors in Judah and had appointed Gedaliah, son of Ahikam and grandson of Shaphan, to govern them. [12]So all the Jews returned from all the places where they had been scattered. They came to Judah and to Gedaliah at Mizpah. They gathered a large harvest of grapes and summer fruit.

[13]Kareah's son Johanan and all the army commanders who were still in the country came to Gedaliah at Mizpah. [14]They asked him, "Do you know that King Baalis of the Ammonites has sent Ishmael, Nethaniah's son, to kill you?" However, Gedaliah, son of Ahikam, didn't believe them.

---

[a]40:5 Hebrew meaning of "If you wish to remain" uncertain.

¹⁵Then Johanan, Kareah's son, secretly asked Gedaliah at Mizpah, "Let me kill Ishmael, Nethaniah's son. No one will know about it. Why should he kill you? All the Jews who have gathered around you would scatter. What is left of Judah would disappear."

¹⁶Gedaliah, son of Ahikam, told Johanan, Kareah's son, "Don't do that! What you are saying about Ishmael is a lie."

Gedaliah Is Assassinated by Ishmael—
2 Kings 25:25-26

¹In the seventh month Ishmael (son of Nethaniah and grandson of Elishama, a descendant of the royal family and of the king's officers) went with ten men to Gedaliah, son of Ahikam, at Mizpah. As they ate together at Mizpah, ²Ishmael, son of Nethaniah, and the ten men who were with him got up, drew their swords, and killed Gedaliah, son of Ahikam and grandson of Shaphan. So they assassinated the man whom the king of Babylon had appointed to govern the land. ³Ishmael also killed all the Jews who were with Gedaliah at Mizpah as well as the Babylonian soldiers that he found there.

⁴The day after the murder of Gedaliah, before anyone knew about it, ⁵80 men arrived from Shechem, Shiloh, and Samaria. Their beards were shaved off, their clothes were torn, and cuts were on their bodies. They brought grain offerings and incense to the Lord's temple. ⁶Ishmael, son of Nethaniah, left Mizpah to meet them, crying as he went. When he met them, he said to them, "Come to Gedaliah, son of Ahikam."

⁷When they came into the city, Ishmael, son of Nethaniah, and his men slaughtered them and threw them into a cistern. ⁸However, ten men from the group had said to Ishmael, "Don't kill us! We have wheat, barley, olive oil, and honey hidden in the country." So he left them alone and didn't kill them along with the others.

⁹Now, the cistern where Ishmael threw all the bodies of the men he had killed was the same one that King Asa made as a part of his defense against King Baasha of Israel. Ishmael, son of Nethaniah, filled it with the bodies.

¹⁰Then Ishmael took captive the rest of the people who were at Mizpah. He captured the king's daughters and all the other people who had been left at Mizpah. They were the people whom Nebuzaradan, the captain of the guard, had put under the control of Gedaliah, son of Ahikam. Ishmael, son of Nethaniah, took them captive and left for Ammon.

¹¹When Kareah's son Johanan and all the army commanders who were with him heard about all the crimes Ishmael, son of Nethaniah, had done, ¹²they took all their men and went to fight Ishmael. They caught up with him at the large pool in Gibeon. ¹³When all the people who were with Ishmael saw Kareah's son Johanan and all the army commanders who were with him, they were glad. ¹⁴Then all the people Ishmael had taken captive at Mizpah turned and ran to Kareah's son Johanan. ¹⁵Ishmael and eight of his men escaped from Johanan and fled to Ammon.

¹⁶Then Kareah's son Johanan and all the army commanders who were with him brought back the rest of the people of Mizpah whom he had rescued from Ishmael, son of Nethaniah, after Ishmael had killed Gedaliah, son of Ahikam. Johanan brought back men, women, children, soldiers, and commanders from Gibeon. ¹⁷When they left Gibeon, they stayed near Bethlehem at Geruth Kimham on their way to Egypt. ¹⁸They were afraid of the Babylonians because Ishmael had killed Gedaliah whom the king of Babylon had appointed to govern the land.

Jeremiah Warns the People of Judah Not to Go to Egypt

42 ¹Then all the army commanders along with Kareah's son Johanan and Hoshaiah's son Jezaniah and all the people, from the least important to the most important, came to the prophet Jeremiah. ²They said to him, "Please listen to our request, and pray to the LORD your God for all of us who are left here. As you can see, there are only a few of us left. ³Let the LORD your God tell us where we should go and what we should do."

⁴The prophet Jeremiah answered them, "I have listened to your request. I will pray to the LORD your God as you have requested, and I will tell you everything the LORD says. I won't keep anything from you."

⁵They said to Jeremiah, "May the LORD be a true and faithful witness against us if we don't do exactly what the LORD your God tells us to do. ⁶We will obey the LORD our God to whom we are sending you, whether it's good or bad. Yes, we will obey the LORD our God so that everything will go well for us."

⁷After ten days the LORD spoke his word to Jeremiah. ⁸So Jeremiah called Kareah's son Johanan, all the army commanders who were with him, and all the people from the least important to the most important. ⁹Jeremiah said to them, "You sent me to plead your case humbly to the LORD. This is what the LORD God of Israel says: ¹⁰Suppose you stay in this land. Then I will build you up and not tear you down. I will plant you and not uproot you. I will change my plans about the disaster I've brought on you. ¹¹Don't be afraid of the king of Babylon, whom you now fear. Don't be afraid of him, declares the LORD. I'm with you. I will save you and rescue you from his power. ¹²I will have compassion on you. I will make him have compassion on you and return you to your land.

¹³"But suppose you say, 'We won't stay in this land,' and you disobey the LORD your God. ¹⁴Then you say, 'We'll go to Egypt, where we won't have to see war, hear the sound of a ram's horn, or be hungry. We'll stay there.'

¹⁵"Now, listen to the word of the LORD, you people who are left in Judah. This is what the LORD of Armies, the God of Israel, says: Suppose you're determined to go to Egypt, and you go and live there. ¹⁶Then the wars you fear will catch up with you in Egypt. The famines you dread will follow you to Egypt, and you will die there. ¹⁷So all the people who decide to go and live in Egypt will die in wars, famines, and plagues. No one will survive or escape the disasters I will bring on them.

¹⁸"This is what the LORD of Armies, the God of Israel, says: As my anger and my fury were poured out on those who live in Jerusalem, so my fury will be poured out on you if you go to Egypt. You will become a curse word. You will become something ridiculed, cursed, and disgraced. You won't see this place again.

¹⁹"The LORD has told you people who are left in Judah not to go to Egypt. You need to know that I am warning you today. ²⁰You only deceived yourselves when you sent me to the LORD your God and said, 'Pray to the LORD our God for us, and tell us everything that the LORD our God says, and we'll do it.' ²¹I have told you today, but you won't obey anything the LORD your God sent me to tell you. ²²But now, you need to know that you will die in wars, famines, or plagues in the place where you want to go and live."

Jeremiah Is Forced to Go to Egypt

43 ¹So Jeremiah finished telling all the people the message from the LORD their God. He told them everything the LORD their God sent him to tell them. ²Azariah (son of Hoshaiah), Johanan (son of Kareah), and all the arrogant people said to Jeremiah, "You're lying! The LORD our God didn't send you to tell us that we must not go to live in Egypt. ³But Baruch, son of Neriah, has turned you against us in order to hand us over to the Babylonians. Then they will kill us or take us as captives to Babylon."

⁴So Johanan (son of Kareah), all the army commanders, and all the people didn't obey the LORD. They didn't stay in Judah. ⁵Johanan (son of Kareah) and all the army commanders took all the people who were left in Judah to Egypt. These were all the people who had come back to Judah from the places where they had been scattered. ⁶They took men, women, children, and the king's daughters. They took every person whom Nebuzaradan, the captain of the guard, had left with Gedaliah, son of Ahikam and grandson of Shaphan, including the prophet Jeremiah and Baruch, son of Neriah. ⁷They didn't listen to the LORD, so they went to Egypt. They went as far as Tahpanhes.

Jeremiah Prophesies That Egypt Will Be Invaded by Nebuchadnezzar

⁸Then the LORD spoke his word to Jeremiah in Tahpanhes. He said, ⁹"Take some large stones, and bury them under the brick pavement at the entrance to the Pharaoh's palace in Tahpanhes. Do this while the people of Judah watch you. ¹⁰Say to them, 'This is what the LORD of Armies, the God of Israel, says: I'm going to send for my servant King Nebuchadnezzar of Babylon. I will set his throne over these stones that I buried, and I will spread his royal canopy above them. ¹¹He will defeat Egypt. He will bring death to those who are supposed to die. He will capture those who are supposed to be captured. He will kill in battle those who are supposed to be killed in battle. ¹²He*ᵃ* will set fire to the temples of Egypt's gods. He will burn down the temples and take their gods captive. Nebuchadnezzar will put on Egypt as his coat as a shepherd puts on his coat. He will leave Egypt peacefully. ¹³At Beth Shemesh he will break the monuments in Egypt and burn down the temples of Egypt's gods.' "

The Jews in Egypt Will Be Punished for Their Idolatry

44 ¹The LORD spoke his word to Jeremiah about all the Jews living in Egypt at Migdol, Tahpanhes, Noph, and Pathros. ²This is what the LORD of Armies, the God of Israel, says: You have seen all the disasters I brought on Jerusalem and on all the cities of Judah. Today they are deserted ruins. ³It is because their people did evil, and they made me angry. They went to burn incense and serve other gods that neither you nor your ancestors heard of. ⁴I have sent my servants the prophets to you again and again to tell you not to do these detestable things that I hate. ⁵But you wouldn't listen or pay attention. You wouldn't turn from your wicked ways and wouldn't stop burning incense as an offering to other gods. ⁶That is why my fury and anger were poured out and continued to burn in the cities of Judah and on the streets of Jerusalem. So they became the desolate ruin that they are today.

⁷Now, this is what the LORD God of Armies, the God of Israel, says: Why do you bring this terrible disaster on yourselves? Why do you keep destroying men, women, children, and babies from Judah until none are left? ⁸Why do you make me angry by burning incense to other gods in Egypt, where you have come to live. You will destroy yourselves and be cursed and ridiculed by all the nations on earth. ⁹Have you forgotten the wicked things done by your ancestors, by the kings of Judah and their wives, and by you and your wives in Judah and on the streets of Jerusalem? ¹⁰You have not humbled yourselves even to this day. You haven't feared me or lived your lives by my teachings or by my decrees that I gave your ancestors.

ᵃ43:12 Greek; Masoretic Text "I."

¹¹This is what the Lord of Armies, the God of Israel, says: I'm going to bring disaster on you and destroy all of Judah. ¹²I will take away from Judah those who are left, those who were determined to go to live in Egypt. They will die in Egypt. All of them, from the least important to the most important, will die in wars or be brought to an end by famines. They will become something cursed, ridiculed, and disgraced. ¹³I will punish those living in Egypt as I punished Jerusalem with wars, famines, and plagues. ¹⁴None of the people of Judah who went to live in Egypt will survive or return to Judah, where they long to return and live. Only a few refugees will return there.

¹⁵Then all the men who knew that their wives were burning incense to other gods, all the women who were standing there, and all the people who lived at Pathros in Egypt answered Jeremiah. They said, ¹⁶"We won't listen to the message that you have spoken to us in the Lord's name. ¹⁷We will do everything we said we would do. We will burn incense to the queen of heaven and pour out wine offerings to her as our ancestors, our kings, and our officials did in the cities of Judah and on the streets of Jerusalem. We had plenty to eat then, and we lived comfortably and saw no disaster. ¹⁸But since we stopped burning incense to the queen of heaven and pouring out wine offerings to her, we have had nothing but wars and famines."

¹⁹The women added, "When we burned incense to the queen of heaven, poured out wine offerings to her, and made cakes for her with her image on them, do you think our husbands didn't approve?"

²⁰Then Jeremiah said to all the people, both men and women, to everyone who answered him, ²¹"Doesn't the Lord remember that you burned incense in the cities of Judah and on the streets of Jerusalem along with your ancestors, your kings and your officials, and the people in the land? ²²The Lord could no longer bear the wicked and detestable things you did. That is why your land has become something ruined, destroyed, and cursed. No one lives in that land today. ²³You burned incense as offerings to other gods, sinned against the Lord, and wouldn't obey him. You didn't live by his teachings, decrees, or written instructions. That is why you have met with this disaster as it is today."

²⁴Then Jeremiah said to all the people, including the women, "Listen to the word of the Lord, all you people of Judah who are in Egypt. ²⁵This is what the Lord of Armies, the God of Israel, says: You and your wives made promises, and you have kept them. You said, 'We will certainly do what we vow. We will burn incense to the queen of heaven and pour out wine offerings to her.'

"So go ahead. Keep your vows, and do what you vow. ²⁶But listen to the word of the Lord, all you people of Judah who live in Egypt. 'I swear by my great name,' says the Lord, 'that no one from Judah who lives anywhere in Egypt will ever again call on my name and take the oath, "As the Almighty Lord lives." ²⁷I am going to watch over them. I am going to watch over them to bring disasters, not blessings. In Egypt the people from Judah will die in wars and famines until everyone is gone. ²⁸Those who escape the wars will return to Judah from Egypt. Then all the people of Judah who went to live in Egypt will know whose words have come true, mine or theirs. ²⁹I will give you this sign,' declares the Lord. 'I will punish you in this place so that you will know that my threats of disaster will happen to you. ³⁰This is what the Lord says: I'm going to hand Pharaoh Hophra, king of Egypt, over to his enemies and to those who want to kill him, just as I handed over King Zedekiah of Judah to King Nebuchadnezzar of Babylon and to those who wanted to kill him.' "

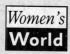

Seals / *Jeremiah 45:1*

When a letter was written on a scroll, a seal was pressed into a bit of clay used to fasten the letter. The seal was like a signature. A seal pressed into an object showed ownership. More than a thousand Hebrew seals have been found by archaeologists.

The New Testament says that when we accept Jesus, we are sealed by the Holy Spirit (Ephesians 1:13). We belong to God, and no one can ever take us away from him.

The LORD's Promise to the Scribe Baruch

45 ¹This is the message that the prophet Jeremiah spoke to Baruch, son of Neriah. Baruch wrote these things on a scroll as Jeremiah dictated them during the fourth year that Jehoiakim, son of Josiah, was king of Judah. Jeremiah said, ²"This is what the LORD God of Israel says to you, Baruch: ³You said, 'I'm so miserable! The LORD has added grief to my pain. I'm worn out from groaning. I can't find any rest.'

⁴"Say this to Baruch, 'This is what the LORD says: I will tear down what I have built. I will uproot what I have planted throughout the earth. ⁵Are you looking for great things for yourself? Don't look for them, because I'm going to bring disaster on all people, declares the LORD. But wherever you go I will let you escape with your life.' "

A Prophecy Against Egypt

46 ¹The LORD spoke this message to the prophet Jeremiah about the nations.

²This is the message about Egypt, about the army of Pharaoh Neco, king of Egypt. King Nebuchadnezzar of Babylon defeated his army at Carchemish along the Euphrates River during the fourth year that Jehoiakim, son of Josiah, was king of Judah.

3   "Get your large and small shields ready; advance into battle.
4   Harness your horses. Mount up, you horsemen.
     Take your positions, and put on your helmets.
     Polish your spears.
     Put on your armor.
5   "What do I see in them?
     They are terrified.
       They are retreating.
     Their warriors are defeated.
       They flee without looking back.
         Terror is all around them," declares the LORD.
6   "The infantry can't flee.

The warriors can't escape.
    They stumble and fall in the north by the Euphrates River.

7 Who is this, rising like the Nile River,
    like streams that flow swiftly?
8 Egypt is like the rising Nile River,
    like a river quickly overflowing its banks.
Egypt says, 'I will rise; I will cover the earth.
    I will destroy cities and the people in them.'
9 Go into battle, you horsemen.
    Drive wildly, you chariot drivers.
March into battle, you warriors,
    you warriors from Sudan and Put who carry shields,
    you warriors from Lydia who use bows and arrows.
10 That day belongs to the Almighty Lord of Armies.
    It is a day of vengeance when he will take revenge on his enemies.
      His sword will devour until it has had enough,
        and it will drink their blood until it's full.
    The Almighty Lord of Armies will offer them as sacrifices
      in the north by the Euphrates River.
11 Go to Gilead, and get medicine, dear people of Egypt.
    You have used many medicines without results; you can't be cured.
12 The nations have heard of your shame; your cry fills the earth.
One warrior will stumble over another,
    and both will fall together."

13 The Lord spoke this message to the prophet Jeremiah about the coming of King Nebuchadnezzar of Babylon, who will defeat Egypt.

14 "Tell this in Egypt; announce this in Migdol.
Make it known in Memphis and in Tahpanhes.
Say, 'Take your positions, and get ready.
    Swords will kill those around you.'
15 Why should your soldiers be cut down?
    They can't stand because the Lord will push them down.
16 They have repeatedly stumbled, and now they have fallen.
They say to each other,
    'Get up! Let's go back to our people,
      to the land where we were born,
        and escape our enemy's sword.'
17 There they will cry, 'Pharaoh, king of Egypt, is a big windbag.
He has missed his chance.'

18 "As I live," declares the king, whose name is the Lord of Armies,
    "someone who is like Mount Tabor among the mountains will come.
    Someone who is like Mount Carmel by the sea will come.
19 Pack your bags, inhabitants of Egypt,
    because you will be taken away as captives.
      Memphis will become a dreary wasteland,
        a pile of rubble where no one lives.

20 "Egypt is like a beautiful cow,
    but a horsefly from the north will attack it.

21   Egypt's hired soldiers are like fattened calves.
      They will turn and run away together.
      They won't stand their ground.
         The day of destruction is coming.
            At that time they will be punished.
22   Egypt will hiss like a snake as it slithers away.
      Its enemies will come with full force.
      They will attack it with axes like those who chop wood.
23   They will cut down the forest," declares the LORD,
      "since Egypt can't be found.
      They are more numerous than locusts; they can't be counted.
24   The people of Egypt will be put to shame.
      They will be handed over to the people from the north."

25The LORD of Armies, the God of Israel, says,

"I'm going to punish Amon, who is the god of Thebes.
      I will also punish Pharaoh, Egypt, its gods, its kings,
         and whoever trusts Pharaoh.
26   I'll hand them over to those who want to kill them,
      to King Nebuchadnezzar of Babylon and his officers.
      Afterward, they will live in peace as they did long ago,"
         declares the LORD.

27   "Don't be afraid, my servant Jacob.
Don't be terrified, Israel.
      I'm going to rescue you and your descendants from a faraway land,
         from the land where you are captives.
      Then Jacob's descendants will again have undisturbed peace,
         and no one will make them afraid.
28   Don't be afraid, my servant Jacob," declares the LORD.
      "I am with you.
      I will completely destroy all the nations where I scattered you,
         but I will not completely destroy you.
         I will correct you with justice.
         I won't let you go entirely unpunished."

A Prophecy Against Philistia

47 ¹The LORD spoke this message to the prophet Jeremiah about the Philistines before Pharaoh defeated Gaza. ²This is what the LORD says:

Water is rising in the north.
      It will become an overflowing river.
      It will overflow the land and everything in it,
         the cities and those who live in them.
People will cry out and everyone who lives in the land will cry loudly.
3   They will hear the sound of galloping war horses,
      the rattling of enemy chariots,
         and the rumbling of their wheels.
Fathers who lack courage abandon their children.
4   The time has come to destroy all the Philistines,
      to cut off from Tyre and Sidon any Philistine

who might have escaped to get help.
The LORD will destroy the Philistines
　　and anyone who is left from the island of Crete.
5 Gaza will shave its head in mourning.
Ashkelon will be destroyed.
How long will you cut yourselves, you people left on the plains?
6 You cry out, "Sword of the LORD,
　　how long will you keep on fighting?
　　　Go back into your scabbard.
　　　　Stay there and rest!"
7 How can the sword of the LORD rest?
The LORD has ordered it to attack Ashkelon and the coast.
He has put it there.

A Prophecy Against Moab

48 ¹This is what the LORD of Armies, the God of Israel, says about Moab:

How horrible it will be for Nebo; it will be destroyed.
Kiriathaim will be put to shame; it will be captured.
　　Its stronghold will be put to shame and torn down.
2 People will no longer praise Moab.
The people in Heshbon will plan Moab's destruction.
　　"Let's destroy that nation!"
You will be silenced, city of Madmen.
　　Death will come after you.
3 People will cry out from Horonaim, "Looting and great destruction!"
4 Moab will be broken.
　　Its little ones will cry out.
5 People go up the pass of Luhith, crying bitterly as they go.
　　On the road down to Horonaim they have heard
　　　the distressful cry of destruction.
6 　　"Run away! Run for your lives!
　　　Run like a wild donkey in the desert."
7 Since you trust the things you do and your treasures,
　　you will be captured.
Chemosh will go into captivity with all its priests and officials.
8 The destroyer will come to every city, and no city will escape.
The valley will be destroyed, and the plain will be laid waste
　　as the LORD has threatened.
9 Put salt on Moab.
　　It will be destroyed.
　　Its cities will become deserted ruins.
10 Cursed are those who neglect doing the LORD's work.
Cursed are those who keep their swords from killing.

11 "Moab has lived securely ever since it was young.
　　Its people are like wine left to settle in a jar.
　　　They aren't poured from one jar to another.
　　　They haven't gone into captivity.
　　　　That is why its flavor has remained the same,
　　　　and its aroma hasn't changed.

¹² That is why the days are coming," declares the LORD,
  "when I will send people to pour Moab out of its jars
    and to smash its pitchers.
¹³ Then Moab will be ashamed of Chemosh
    as the nation of Israel was ashamed when it trusted Bethel.

¹⁴ "How can you say, 'We are soldiers and warriors'?
¹⁵ The enemy will attack Moab and destroy its cities.
    Its finest young men will be slaughtered,"
      declares the king, whose name is the LORD of Armies.
¹⁶ "Moab's destruction is coming near; disaster is coming quickly.
¹⁷ Mourn over it, all of its neighbors and everyone who knows its fame.
  Say, 'Look at the strong staff, the beautiful rod, that is broken!'

¹⁸ "People of Dibon, come down from your place of honor
    and sit on the dry ground.
  The destroyers of Moab will attack you.
  They will destroy your fortresses.
¹⁹ Stand by the road in Aroer, and watch.
    Ask those who are fleeing
      and those who are escaping what is happening.
²⁰ They will answer, 'Moab is disgraced; it is defeated.
    Shout loudly, and cry.
      Tell the news in Arnon that Moab is destroyed.'

²¹"Judgment has come to all the cities on the plain: to Holon, Jahzah, Mephaath,
²²Dibon, Nebo, Beth Diblathaim, ²³Kiriathaim, Beth Gamul, Beth Meon, ²⁴Kerioth,
Bozrah, and on all the cities of Moab, far and near.

²⁵ "Moab's horn is cut off, and its arm is broken,"
    declares the LORD.
²⁶ "Get the people of Moab drunk; they have spoken against the LORD.
  They will wallow in their own vomit, and people will laugh at them.
²⁷ People of Moab, didn't you laugh at the people of Israel?
    Were they caught among thieves?
      Whenever you talk about them you shake your heads in contempt.
²⁸ People of Moab, abandon your cities.
    Live among the cliffs.
      Be like doves that make their nests at the entrance of a cave.

²⁹ "We have heard about the arrogance of Moab's people.
  They are very arrogant.
    They are very arrogant, conceited, and boastful.
³⁰ I know how arrogant they are," declares the LORD,
    "but it isn't right.
  They brag and don't do what they say.
³¹ That is why I will weep for Moab and cry for all of Moab.
  I will moan for the people of Kir Hareseth.
³² I will cry for you as Jazer cries.
  I will cry for you, grapevines of Sibmah.
    Your branches once spread as far as the sea,
      and they reached as far as the sea of Jazer.

The destroyer will destroy your ripened fruits and your grapes.
33 Joy and gladness have disappeared from the orchards and fields of Moab.
  I will stop the wine flowing from the winepresses.
    No one will stomp on grapes with shouts of joy.
      There will be shouts, but not shouts of joy.

34"The cry will be heard from Heshbon to Elealeh and Jahaz. It will be heard from Zoar to Horonaim and Eglath Shelishiyah. Even the streams of Nimrim will dry up. 35I will stop those in Moab who come to worship sites, those who bring offerings to their gods," declares the LORD. 36"That is why I moan for Moab like a flute. I sound like a flute for the people of Kir Hareseth. The wealth they gained has disappeared.

37"Every head is shaved, and every beard is cut off. There are gashes on every hand and sackcloth on every waist. 38People in Moab will mourn on every rooftop and in every street. There will be mourning everywhere, because I will break Moab like a jar that no one wants," declares the LORD. 39"They will cry, 'Look how Moab is defeated! Moab turns away in shame!' Moab has become something ridiculed and something held in contempt by everyone around it.

40"This is what the LORD says:

  The enemy will swoop down like eagles and spread their wings over Moab.
41   The cities will be taken, and the fortified places will be captured.
  On that day Moab's soldiers will be like women in childbirth.
42   Moab will be destroyed as a nation,
    because it spoke against the LORD.
43   Disasters, pits, and traps are in store for those who live in Moab,"
    declares the LORD.
44   "Whoever flees from a disaster will fall into a pit.
  Whoever climbs out of the pit will be caught in a trap.
    I will bring a year of punishment to Moab," declares the LORD.
45   "Those who flee will stand exhausted in the shadow of Heshbon.
  A fire will come out of Heshbon and a flame from Sihon.
    It will burn the foreheads of the people of Moab
      and the skulls of those noisy people.
46   How horrible it will be for you, Moab.
  You people of Chemosh will die.
    Your sons will be taken away into exile,
      and your daughters will be taken away into captivity.
47   But I will restore Moab in the last days," declares the LORD.

The judgment against Moab ends here.

A Prophecy Against Ammon

49 1This is what the LORD says about the people of Ammon:

  Doesn't Israel have any children? Doesn't it have any heirs?
    Why, then, has the god Milcom* taken over the inheritance
      of Gad's descendants?
    Why do Milcom's people live in Gad's cities?
2   That is why the days are coming, declares the LORD,
  when I will sound the battle cry against Rabbah,

---

a 49:1 Or "Molech."

where the people of Ammon live.
        It will become a pile of rubble.
        Its villages will be burned down.
    Then Israel will take possession of its inheritance, says the Lord.
³   Cry loudly, Heshbon, because Ai is destroyed.
    Cry, people of Rabbah, put on your sackcloth, and mourn.
        Run back and forth between the walls.
        Milcom will be taken away into captivity
            with its priests and officials.
⁴   Why do you brag about your valleys,
        your fertile valleys, you unfaithful people?
        You trust your treasures.
            You think, "Who would attack me?"
⁵   I am going to bring terror on you from all around,
        declares the Almighty Lord of Armies.
            Everyone will be scattered.
            No one will gather the refugees.
⁶   But afterward, I will return the captives of Ammon, declares the Lord.

A Prophecy Against Edom—
Obadiah 1-5

⁷This is what the Lord of Armies says about Edom:

    Is there no longer any wisdom in Teman?
        Has wisdom disappeared from your people?
        Has their wisdom vanished?
⁸   Turn and run.
        Hide in deep caves, inhabitants of Dedan.
            When I punish them,
                I will bring disaster on the descendants of Esau.
⁹   If people come to pick your grapes,
        won't they leave a few grapes behind?
    If thieves come during the night,
        won't they steal only until they've had enough?
¹⁰ Yet, I will strip the descendants of Esau.
        I will find their hiding places.
            They won't be able to hide.
            Their children and relatives will be destroyed.
        None of their neighbors will say,
¹¹   "Abandon your orphans, and I will keep them alive.
        Your widows can trust me."

¹²This is what the Lord says: If those who don't deserve to drink from the cup still drink from it, why should you go unpunished? You won't go unpunished. You must drink from it. ¹³I take an oath on myself, declares the Lord, that Bozrah will become a pile of rubble. It will become something horrifying, ridiculed, ruined, and cursed. All its cities will lie in ruins permanently.

¹⁴ I heard a message from the Lord.
        A messenger was sent among the nations to say,

"Assemble, and attack Edom.
  Get ready for battle."

15 "Edom, I will make you the smallest of nations
      and despised among humanity.
16   You have frightened other people.
      Your arrogance has deceived you.
        You live on rocky cliffs
          and occupy the highest places in the hills.
    Even though you build your nest as high as an eagle,
      I will bring you down from there," declares the LORD.
17 "Then Edom will become something horrible.
      Everyone who passes by it will be horrified
        and hiss at all its wounds.
18 Edom will be like Sodom, Gomorrah, and their neighboring cities
      when they were destroyed.
      No one will live there.
      No human will stay there," says the LORD.
19 "I will suddenly chase them from their places
      like a lion coming out of the jungle
        along the Jordan River into pastureland.
    I will appoint over Edom whomever I choose.
      Who is like me? Who can challenge me?
        Is there any leader who can stand up to me?"

20 Listen to the plans that the LORD is making against Edom
      and the things he intends to do to those who live in Teman.
      He will surely drag away the little ones of the flock.
      He will surely destroy the pasture
        because of the people who live in Teman.
21 The earth will quake at the sound of their downfall.
    The sound of their crying will be heard at the Red Sea.
22 The enemy will swoop down like eagles
      and spread their wings over Bozrah.
        On that day Edom's soldiers will be like women in childbirth.

A Prophecy Against Damascus

23 This is a message about Damascus.

"Hamath and Arpad are worried because they heard the bad news.
      They melt in fear.
    They are troubled like a sea that can't be calmed.
24 The people of Damascus are weak.
      They turn to flee, but panic grips them.
      Anguish and pain grip them like a woman in labor.
25 Why isn't that famous, happy city abandoned?
26 That is why its young men will die in the streets,
      and its soldiers will be silenced that day,"
        declares the LORD of Armies.
27 "I will set fire to the walls of Damascus
      and burn down Benhadad's palaces."

A Prophecy Against Kedar and Hazor

²⁸This is about the tribe of Kedar and the kingdoms of Hazor that King Nebuchadnezzar of Babylon defeated. This is what the LORD says:

> Get ready, attack Kedar,
>   and loot the people from the east.
> ²⁹ Their tents and their flocks will be taken.
> Their tent curtains, utensils, and camels will be carried away.
> People will shout to them, "Terror is all around!"
> ³⁰ Run far away! Find a place to hide,
>   inhabitants of Hazor, declares the LORD.
> King Nebuchadnezzar of Babylon has made plans against you
>   and intends to attack you.
> ³¹ Get ready! Attack the nation living peacefully and securely,
>   declares the LORD.
>   It is a nation with no gates or bars.
>   Its people live alone.
> ³² Their camels will be taken as prizes.
> Their large herds will be taken as loot.
>   I will scatter to the winds
>   those who shave the hair on their foreheads.
>   I will bring disaster on them from every side,
>   declares the LORD.
> ³³ Hazor will be a place where only jackals live.
>   It will become a permanent wasteland.
>   No one will live there.
>   No human will stay there.

A Prophecy Against Elam

³⁴Early in the rule of King Zedekiah of Judah, the LORD spoke his word to the prophet Jeremiah about Elam.

³⁵This is what the LORD of Armies says:

> I'm going to break the bows of Elam's archers,
>   the most important weapon of their strength.
> ³⁶ I'll bring the four winds
>   from the four corners of heaven against Elam
>   and scatter its people in every direction.
> There won't be a nation
>   where Elam's refugees won't go.
> ³⁷ I'll defeat the people of Elam in the presence of their enemies,
>   in the presence of those who want to kill them.
> I'll bring disaster with my burning anger, declares the LORD.
> I'll send armies after them until I put an end to them.
> ³⁸ I'll set my throne in Elam and destroy its king and officials,
>   declares the LORD.
> ³⁹ But afterward, I'll return the captives of Elam, declares the LORD.

A Prophecy Against Babylon

50 ¹This is the message that the Lord spoke about Babylon and the land of the Babylonians through the prophet Jeremiah.

² "Announce this among the nations, and spread the news.
Raise a flag, and announce it.
Don't hide anything.
Say, 'Babylon will be captured.
Bel will be put to shame.
Marduk will be filled with terror.
Babylon's statues will be put to shame.
Its idols will be filled with terror.'

³ A nation from the north will attack Babylon
and destroy its land so that no one will live in it.
People and animals will run away.

⁴ "In those days and at that time," declares the Lord,
"the people of Israel and Judah will cry as they go together
to seek the Lord their God.

⁵ They will ask which road goes to Zion and turn in that direction.
They will go there to make a permanent agreement with the Lord.
It will not be forgotten.

⁶ My people have been lost sheep.
Their shepherds have led them astray.
They wander around on the mountains.
They go from mountains to hills.
They have forgotten their resting place.

⁷ Everyone who finds them eats them.
Their enemies say, 'We're not guilty.
They have sinned against the Lord, their true pasture.
They have sinned against the Lord, the hope of their ancestors.'

⁸ "Run away from Babylon.
Leave the land of the Babylonians.
Be like the male goats that lead the flock.

⁹ I am going to stir up an alliance of strong nations from the north
and bring it against Babylon.
Those nations will take up positions against Babylon.
Babylon will be captured from the north.
Its enemy's arrows will be like skilled soldiers
who don't come back empty-handed.

¹⁰ The Babylonians will become the prize.
All who loot them will get everything they want,"
declares the Lord.

¹¹ "You are happy and excited.
You have looted the people who belong to me.
You dance around like calves on the grass
and neigh like stallions.

¹² But your mother will be greatly ashamed.
The woman who gave birth to you will be disgraced.
Babylon, you will be the least important nation.

You will become a parched desert.

13 No one will live in Babylon because of the LORD's anger.
   It will be completely abandoned.
Everyone who passes by Babylon will be horrified
   and hiss at all its wounds.

14 "Take up your positions around Babylon, all you archers with bows.
Shoot at it; don't save any arrows,
   because the people of Babylon have sinned against the LORD.

15 Shout a war cry against them on every side.
   They'll surrender.
   Their towers will fall and their walls will be torn down.
Since this is the LORD's vengeance, take revenge against them.
   Do to them what they did to others.

16 Don't allow anyone in Babylon to plant or harvest.
Everyone will turn to his own people and flee to his own homeland
   because of the enemies' swords.

17 "The people of Israel are like scattered sheep that lions have chased.
   The first to devour them was the king of Assyria.
   The last to gnaw at their bones was King Nebuchadnezzar of Babylon.

18 "This is what the LORD of Armies, the God of Israel, says:

   I am going to punish the king of Babylon and his land
      as I punished the king of Assyria.

19 I will bring the people of Israel back to their pastures.
   They will eat on Mount Carmel and Mount Bashan.
   They will eat until they are full
      on the mountains of Ephraim and Gilead.

20 In those days and at that time," declares the LORD,
   "people will look for Israel's crimes, but they will find none.
   They will look for Judah's sins, but none will be found.
      I will forgive the faithful few whom I have spared.

21 "Attack the land of Merathaim
      and the people who live in Pekod.
Claim them for me by killing them with a sword,"
      declares the LORD.
      "Do everything I commanded you.

22 The noise of battle and great destruction fills the land.

23 The hammer of the whole earth is broken and shattered.
See how desolate Babylon is of all the nations!

24 I will set traps for you, Babylon.
   You will be caught, but you won't know it.
      You will be found and captured
         because you have opposed the LORD.

25 The LORD will open his armory
   and bring out the weapons of his fury,
      because the Almighty LORD of Armies
         has a job to do in the land of the Babylonians.

26 Attack them from a distance,

open their storehouses,
    pile up their corpses like piles of grain,
        claim them for me by destroying them,
            and don't leave anyone behind.

27 Kill all their young bulls.
Let them go to be slaughtered.
How horrible it will be for them when their time has come,
    the time for them to be punished.

28 Listen! Fugitives and refugees from Babylon
    are coming to Zion to tell about
        the vengeance of the Lord our God, the vengeance for his temple.

29 "Call together the archers, the soldiers with bows, against Babylon.
Set up blockades around it. Don't let anyone escape.
    Pay the people of Babylon back for what they have done.
        Do to them what they did to others.
They have disobeyed the Lord, the Holy One of Israel.

30 That is why their young men will die in the streets,
    and all their soldiers will be silenced that day,"
        declares the Lord.

31 "I'm against you, you arrogant city,"
    declares the Almighty Lord of Armies.
"Your day has come, the time when I will punish you.

32 Those arrogant people will stumble and fall,
    and there will be no one to help them get up.
I will light a fire in their cities
    that will burn up everything around them."

33 This is what the Lord of Armies says:

All the people of Israel and Judah are oppressed.
    All their enemies have captured them.
        They refuse to let them go.

34 Their defender is strong.
    His name is the Lord of Armies.
        He will certainly take up their cause
            in order to bring rest to the land of Israel
                and unrest to the people who live in Babylon.

35 "A sword will kill the Babylonians and everyone who lives in Babylon,"
    declares the Lord.
"A sword will kill their officials and their wise men.

36 A sword will kill the false prophets.
    They will become fools.
A sword will kill their soldiers and defeat them.

37 A sword will kill their horses, their chariots,
    and all the foreigners within their ranks.
        They will become women.
A sword will destroy their treasures, and they will be looted.

38 A drought will diminish their water supply, and it will dry up.
    Babylon is a land of idols, statues that will go crazy with fear.

39   That is why desert animals will live with hyenas.

> Desert owls will also live there.
>> It will no longer be inhabited or lived in for generations.
40 Babylon will be like Sodom, Gomorrah, and their neighboring cities
>> when I, God, destroyed them.
>>> No one will live there.
>>> No human will stay there," declares the LORD.

41 "People are going to come from the north.
> A great nation and many kings will rise from the ends of the earth.
42 They will take hold of bows and spears.
>> They will be cruel and have no compassion.
>> They will sound like the sea when it roars.
>> They will ride horses.
>> They are ready for war, ready to attack you, people of Babylon.
43 The king of Babylon has heard reports about them, and he loses courage.
>> Anguish will grip him as pain grips a woman in labor.
44 I will suddenly chase them from their places
>> like a lion coming out of the jungle
>>> along the Jordan River into pastureland.
>>> I will appoint over Babylon whomever I choose.
>>>> Who is like me? Who can challenge me?
>>>> Is there any leader who can stand up to me?
45 Listen to the plans that the LORD is making against Babylon
> and the things he intends to do to the land of the Babylonians.
>> He will surely drag away the little ones of the flock.
>> He will surely destroy the pasture because of the Babylonians.
46 The earth will quake at the news that Babylon has been captured.
> Its cry will be heard among the nations."

51 1This is what the LORD says:

> I will stir up a destructive wind against Babylon
>> and against the people who live in Leb Kamai.
2 I will send people to winnow[a] Babylon,
> to winnow it and strip its land bare.
> They will attack it from every direction on the day of trouble.
3 Have the archers bend their bows.
> Have them put on their armor.
>> Don't spare Babylon's young men.
>> Completely destroy its whole army.
4 Babylon's soldiers will fall down badly wounded in their streets.
> They will lie dead in their own land.

5Israel and Judah haven't been abandoned by their God, the LORD of Armies, although their land is guilty of abandoning the Holy One of Israel.

6 Run away from Babylon!
> Run for your lives!
>> You shouldn't die because of Babylon's crimes.
> This is the time for the vengeance of the LORD.
>> He will pay the people of Babylon back for what they have done.

---

[a] 51:2 Winnowing is the process of separating husks from grain.

7   Babylon was a golden cup in the Lord's hand.
       It made the whole world drunk.
       The nations drank its wine.
          That is why the nations have gone insane.
8   Babylon will suddenly fall and be shattered.
       Cry for it.
          Bring medicine for its pain.
             Maybe it can be healed.
9   We wanted to heal Babylon, but it couldn't be healed.
       Let's abandon it and go to our own land.
          God has judged Babylon.
             Its judgment is complete.

10   The Lord has brought about our victory.
       Let's announce in Zion what the Lord our God has done.

11   Sharpen the arrows; fill the quivers.
       The Lord will stir up the spirit of the kings of the Medes
          because his plan is to destroy Babylon.
       The Lord will avenge his temple.
12   Raise your battle flag in front of the walls of Babylon.
       Strengthen the guards.
          Station watchmen.
             Prepare ambushes.
       The Lord will carry out his plans
          against the people who live in Babylon.
13   Babylon, you live beside many rivers and are rich with treasures,
       but your end has come.
          The thread of your life has been cut off.
14   The Lord of Armies has taken an oath on himself:
       "I will certainly fill you with many enemy armies.
          They will swarm like locusts.
             People will shout their victory over you."

15   The Lord made the earth by his power.
     He set up the world by his wisdom.
     He stretched out heaven by his understanding.
16   When he thunders, the water in the sky roars.
     He makes clouds rise from the ends of the earth.
     He sends lightning with the rain.
     He brings wind out of his storehouses.

17   Everyone is stupid and ignorant.
     Metalsmiths are put to shame by their idols.
          Their statues are false gods.
18   They can't breathe.
             They are worthless jokes.
                When they are punished, they will disappear.
19   Jacob's God isn't like them.
       He made everything,
          and Israel is the tribe that belongs to him.
             His name is the Lord of Armies.

20 "You are my war club and my weapon for battle.
  I will use you to crush nations.
  I will use you to destroy kingdoms.
21 I will use you to crush horses and their riders.
  I will use you to crush chariots and their drivers.
22 I will use you to crush men and women.
  I will use you to crush the old and the young.
  I will use you to crush young men and women.
23 I will use you to crush shepherds and their flocks.
  I will use you to crush farmers and their oxen.
  I will use you to crush governors and officials.

24 "In your presence I will pay back Babylon
    and all the people who live in Babylon
      for all the evil things that they did in Zion,"
        declares the LORD.

25 "I am against you, Babylon, you destructive mountain.
    You have destroyed the whole earth," declares the LORD.
  "I will use my power against you,
    roll you off the cliffs,
      and make you a scorched mountain.
26 People won't find any stones in you to use as a cornerstone.
  They won't find any stones in you to use for a foundation.
    You will become permanent ruins," declares the LORD.

27 Raise your battle flag throughout the world.
  Blow the ram's horn among the nations.
    Prepare nations to attack Babylon.
      Tell the kingdoms of Ararat, Minni, and Ashkenaz to attack it.
        Appoint a commander to lead the attack.
          Bring up horses like a swarm of locusts.
28 Prepare nations to attack Babylon.
  Prepare the king of the Medes, their governors, all their deputies,
    and all the countries that they rule.
29 The earth trembles and writhes in pain.
  The LORD carries out his plans against Babylon
    to make Babylon a wasteland so that no one will live there.
30 The warriors of Babylon have stopped fighting.
    They stay in their fortified cities.
    Their strength has failed. They have become women.
    Their buildings are set on fire.
      The bars across their gates are broken.
31 Runners run to meet runners.
  Messengers follow messengers.
      They inform the king of Babylon that his entire city is captured.
32   The river crossings have been taken.
        The enemy has burned its marshes,
          and its soldiers are terrified.

33This is what the LORD of Armies, the God of Israel, says:

The people of Babylon are like a threshing floor [b]
at the time it is trampled.
Their harvest time will come soon.

34 King Nebuchadnezzar of Babylon has devoured us.
He has thrown us into confusion.
He has turned us into empty jars.
He has swallowed us like a monster.
He has filled his belly with our delicacies.
Then he spit us out.

35 The people who live in Zion say,
"May the violence done to us be done to Babylon."
Jerusalem says,
"May the people of Babylon be held responsible for our deaths."

36This is what the LORD says:

I am going to take up your cause and get revenge for you.
I will dry up Babylon's sea and make its springs dry.

37 Babylon will become piles of rubble.
It will become a dwelling place for jackals,
something horrible, and an object of contempt,
where no one lives.

38 Its people are like roaring lions and growling lion cubs.

39 When they are excited,
I will prepare a feast for them
and make them drunk so that they will shout and laugh.
They will fall into a deep sleep and never wake up again,
declares the LORD.

40 I will take them to be slaughtered like lambs, rams, and male goats.

41 "Sheshach has been captured.
Babylon, the city that the whole world praised, has been taken captive.

42 What a horrifying sight Babylon will be to the nations!
The sea will rise over Babylon,
and its roaring waves will cover it.

43 Its cities will be ruined.
It will become a desert, a land where no one lives
and where no human travels.

44 I will punish Bel in Babylon.
I will make Bel spit out everything that it has swallowed.
Nations will no longer stream to Babylon,
and its walls will fall.

45 "Leave it, my people!
Run for your lives!
Run from the burning anger of the LORD.

46 Don't lose courage or be afraid when rumors are heard in the land.
One rumor comes one year; another rumor comes the next year.
Rumors of violence are in the land.
Rumors that one ruler will fight against another are in the land.

---

[b]51:33 A threshing floor is an outdoor area where grain is separated from its husks.

47 That is why the days are coming when I will punish Babylon's idols.
The whole country will be put to shame,
and all its soldiers will lie dead.

48 Then heaven and earth and everything in them will rejoice over Babylon,
because destroyers from the north will attack it,"
declares the LORD.

49 Because the people of Babylon have killed many Israelites
and because they have killed many people throughout the earth,
Babylon must fall.

50 You people who escaped from the sword, leave!
Don't just stand there.
Remember the LORD in a distant land, and think about Jerusalem.

51 We have been put to shame, and we have been disgraced.
Shame covers our faces, because foreigners have gone
into the holy places of the LORD's temple.

52 "That is why the days are coming," declares the LORD,
"when I will punish their idols,
and those who are wounded will moan everywhere in the land.

53 The people of Babylon might go up to heaven.
They might fortify their strongholds.
But destroyers will still come from me against them,"
declares the LORD.

54 Cries of agony are heard from Babylon.
Sounds of terrible destruction are heard
from the land of the Babylonians.

55 The LORD will destroy Babylon.
He will silence the loud noise coming from it.
Waves of enemies will come roaring in like raging water.
The noise will be heard everywhere.

56 A destroyer will attack Babylon,
its soldiers will be captured,
and their bows and arrows will be broken.

"I, the LORD, am a God who punishes evil.
I will certainly punish them.

57 I will make their officials and wise men drunk,
along with their governors, officers, and soldiers.
They will fall into a deep sleep and never wake up,"
declares the king, whose name is the LORD of Armies.

58 This is what the LORD of Armies says:

The thick walls of Babylon will be leveled,
and its high gates will be set on fire.
People exhaust themselves for nothing.
The nations wear themselves out only to have a fire.

59 This is the message that the prophet Jeremiah gave to Seraiah, son of Neriah and grandson of Mahseiah, when Seraiah went to Babylon with King Zedekiah of Judah in the fourth year of Zedekiah's rule. (Seraiah was the quartermaster.)

⁶⁰Jeremiah wrote on a scroll all the disasters that would happen to Babylon. He wrote all these things that have been written about Babylon. ⁶¹Jeremiah said to Seraiah, "When you come to Babylon, see that you read all this. ⁶²Then say, 'LORD, you have threatened to destroy this place so that no person or animal will live here, and it will become a permanent ruin.' ⁶³When you finish reading this scroll, tie a stone to it and throw it into the middle of the Euphrates River. ⁶⁴Say, 'Babylon will sink like this scroll. It will never rise again because of the disasters that I will bring on it.' "

The words of Jeremiah end here.

The Fall of Jerusalem—
2 Kings 24:18–25:26; 2 Chronicles 36:11-12; Jeremiah 39:1-10

¹Zedekiah was 21 years old when he began to rule, and he ruled for 11 years in Jerusalem. His mother's name was Hamutal, daughter of Jeremiah from Libnah. ²Zedekiah did what the LORD considered evil, as Jehoiakim had done. ³The LORD became angry with Jerusalem and Judah and threw the people out of his sight.

Zedekiah rebelled against the king of Babylon. ⁴On the tenth day of the tenth month of the ninth year of Zedekiah's reign, King Nebuchadnezzar of Babylon attacked Jerusalem with his entire army. They set up camp and built dirt ramps around the city walls. ⁵The blockade of the city lasted until Zedekiah's eleventh year as king. ⁶On the ninth day of the fourth month, the famine in the city became so severe that the common people had no food.

⁷The enemy broke through the city walls, and all Judah's soldiers fled. They left the city at night through the gate between the two walls beside the king's garden. While the Babylonians were attacking the city from all sides, they took the road to the plain of Jericho. ⁸The Babylonian army pursued King Zedekiah and caught up with him in the plain of Jericho. His entire army had deserted him. ⁹The Babylonians captured the king and brought him to the king of Babylon at Riblah in Hamath, where the king of Babylon passed sentence on him. ¹⁰The king of Babylon slaughtered Zedekiah's sons as Zedekiah watched. He also slaughtered all the officials of Judah at Riblah. ¹¹Then he blinded Zedekiah and put him in bronze shackles. The king of Babylon took him to Babylon and put him in a prison, where he stayed until he died.

¹²On the tenth day of the fifth month of Nebuchadnezzar's nineteenth year as king of Babylon, Nebuzaradan, who was the captain of the guard and an officer of the king of Babylon, came to Jerusalem. ¹³He burned down the LORD's temple, the royal palace, and all the houses in Jerusalem. Every important building was burned down. ¹⁴The entire Babylonian army that was with the captain of the guard tore down the walls around Jerusalem.

¹⁵Nebuzaradan, the captain of the guard, captured the few people left in the city, those who surrendered to the king of Babylon, and the rest of the population. ¹⁶But Nebuzaradan, the captain of the guard, left some of the poorest people in the land to work in the vineyards and on the farms.

¹⁷The Babylonians broke apart the bronze pillars of the LORD's temple, the stands, and the bronze pool in the LORD's temple. They shipped all the bronze to Babylon. ¹⁸They took the pots, shovels, snuffers, bowls, dishes, and all the bronze utensils used in the temple service. ¹⁹The captain of the guard also took pans, incense burners, bowls, pots, lamp stands, dishes, and the bowls used for wine offerings. The captain of the guard took all of the trays and bowls that were made of gold or silver. ²⁰The bronze from the 2 pillars, the pool, and the 12 bronze bulls under the stands that King Solomon had made for the LORD's temple couldn't be weighed. ²¹One pillar was 27 feet high and 18 feet in circumference. It was three inches thick and hollow. ²²The

capital that was on it was 7½ feet high with a filigree and pomegranates around it. They were all made of bronze. The second pillar was the same. It also had pomegranates. ²³There were 96 pomegranates on the sides. The total number of pomegranates on the surrounding filigree was 100.

²⁴The captain of the guard took the chief priest Seraiah, the second priest Zephaniah, and the 3 doorkeepers. ²⁵From the city he also took an army commander, 7 men who had access to the king whom he found in the city, the scribe who was in charge of the militia, and 60 common people whom he found in the city. ²⁶Nebuzaradan, the captain of the guard, took them and brought them to the king of Babylon at Riblah. ²⁷The king of Babylon executed them at Riblah in the territory of Hamath. So the people of Judah were captives as they left their land.

²⁸These are the people Nebuchadnezzar took captive: In his seventh year as king, he took 3,023 Jews. ²⁹In his eighteenth year, Nebuchadnezzar took 832 people from Jerusalem. ³⁰In Nebuchadnezzar's twenty-third year as king, Nebuzaradan, the captain of the guard, took away 745 Jews. In all, 4,600 people were taken away.

King Jehoiakin Released From Prison—
2 Kings 25:27-30

³¹On the twenty-fifth day of the twelfth month of the thirty-seventh year of the imprisonment of King Jehoiakin of Judah, King Evil Merodach of Babylon, in the first year of his reign, freed King Jehoiakin of Judah and released him from prison. ³²He treated him well and gave him a special position higher than the other kings who were with him in Babylon. ³³Jehoiakin no longer wore prison clothes, and he ate his meals in the king's presence as long as he lived. ³⁴The king of Babylon gave him a daily food allowance as long as he lived.

Lamentations

Lamentations is a book of sad funeral poems, called dirges. The poems in this book express the grief of the Jews who were taken into captivity in Babylon. Leaving their homeland made them feel like someone they loved had died.

Who is this woman, and why is she so sad? See Lamentations 1:1-22.

Better Safe Than Sorry

Doing wrong has consequences. Some people don't learn that until it's too late. The Jews who were taken to Babylon had been warned many times to stop sinning and to obey God. They didn't listen. When punishment came, they were terribly sorry!

What lesson can you learn from Lamentations? Before doing something wrong, consider the consequences. Then choose to do right instead. That way, you won't have to be sorry later on.

Headlines

Zion Has Fallen and Can't Get Up
Lamentations 1, page 1119

Prophet Calls Out From Pit
Lamentations 3:53-55, page 1125

"Has God Forgotten?"
Lamentations 5, page 1127

Lamentations

The Prophet Speaks Out: No One Offers Comfort

1 [a]**1** "Look how deserted Jerusalem is!
  Once the city was crowded with people.
  Once it was important among the nations.
    Now it is a widow.
  Once it was a princess among the provinces.
    Now it does forced labor.
2 Jerusalem cries bitterly at night with tears running down its cheeks.
  Out of all those who love the city, no one offers it comfort.
  All of Jerusalem's friends have betrayed it and become its enemies.

3 "Judah has been exiled after ˌmuchˌ suffering and harsh treatment.
  Its ˌpeopleˌ live among the nations; they find no rest.
    Those who chased them caught up with them
      in places where there was no way out.

4 "The roads to Zion are deserted.[b]
  No one comes to the annual festivals.
  No one passes through any of its gates.[c]
    Its priests are groaning.
    Its young women are made to suffer.
      Zion is bitter.
5 Its opponents are now in control.
  Its enemies have no worries.
  The LORD made Zion suffer for its many rebellious acts.
  Its children go ahead of their opponents into captivity.
6 All splendor has abandoned the people of Zion.
  Its influential people were like deer that couldn't find any pasture.
  They ran without any strength ahead of the hunters.

7 "Now, during its suffering and oppression,
  Jerusalem remembers all the treasures it had from ancient times,
    when its people fell into the power of their enemies
      with no one to help them.
  Their opponents looked on, and they laughed at Jerusalem's downfall.
8 Jerusalem has sinned so much that it has become a filthy thing.
  Everyone who used to honor it now despises it.
    They've seen it naked.
      Jerusalem groans and turns away.
9 Jerusalem's own filth ˌcoversˌ its clothes.
  It gave no thought to its future.
  Its downfall was shocking.
    No one offers it comfort.

---

[a]1:1 Chapter 1 is a poem in Hebrew alphabetical order. [b]1:4 Or "are in mourning." [c]1:4 Or "All its gates are in despair."

'O LORD, look at my suffering,
　　because my enemies have triumphed.'
10　The enemies laid their hands on all of the city's treasures.
　　Jerusalem has seen the nations enter the holy place.
　　　'O Lord, they are the same people
　　　　you have forbidden to enter your congregation.'
11　All the people are groaning as they beg for bread.
　　They trade their treasures for food to keep themselves alive.
　　　'O LORD, look and see how despised I am!' "

Zion Speaks Out: No One Offers Comfort

12　"Doesn't this affect all of you who pass by?
　　Look and see if there's any pain
　　　like the pain that the LORD has caused me,
　　　like the pain that he has made me suffer on the day of his fierce anger.
13　　He sent fire from above.
　　　He made it go deep into my bones.
　　　He spread a net for my feet.
　　　He made me turn back.
　　　He has left me devastated.
　　　He has made me sick all day long.
14　My rebellious acts are a heavy burden for me.
　　They were tied together by God's own hands.
　　They were tied around my neck.
　　　He has weakened me ˌwith themˌ.
　　　The Lord has handed me over to people I cannot oppose.*ᵈ*
15　The Lord has treated all the warriors inside my ˌwallsˌ with contempt.
　　He called an army to defeat my young men.
　　　The LORD trampled the people of Judah in a winepress.
16　I'm crying because of ˌallˌ these things.
　　My eyes—my eyes flow with tears.
　　　No one can give me the comfort I need to keep me alive.
　　　Everyone is too far away from me.
　　　　My children are devastated because my enemies have won."

17　Zion holds out its hands.
　　No one offers it comfort.
　　The LORD has given this order about Jacob:
　　　His own neighbors will become his opponents.
　　　Jerusalem has become a filthy thing among them.

18　"The LORD is right in what he did,
　　because I rebelled against his word.
　　Please listen, all you people, and look at my pain.
　　　My young women and young men have gone into captivity.
19　I called for those who love me, but they betrayed me.
　　　My priests and leaders breathed their last breath in the city,
　　　　looking for food to keep themselves alive.

---

*ᵈ*1:14 Hebrew meaning of this verse uncertain.

20 "O Lord, see the distress I'm in!
   My stomach is churning.
   My heart is pounding because I've been very bitter.
In the streets swords kill my children.
   Inside the houses it's like death.

21 "All my enemies have heard that I am groaning.
   No one offers me comfort.
All my enemies have heard about my disaster.
   They are happy that you did it.
      You have allowed the day to come,
         the one that you had announced.
      Let my enemies be like me now.ᵉ

22 Recall all of their wickedness.
   Then deal with them as you have dealt with me
      because of all my rebellious acts.
      I groan so much and feel so sick at heart."

The Prophet Speaks Out: The LORD Destroyed Zion

2 ᵃ1 "Look how the Lord has covered the people of Zion
   with the cloud of his anger!
He has thrown down Israel's beauty from heaven to earth.
He didn't even remember his footstool on the day of his anger.

2 The Lord swallowed up all of Jacob's pastures without any pity.
   He tore down the fortified cities of Judah in his fury.
He brought the kingdom of Judah and its leaders
   down to the ground in dishonor.

3 In his burning anger he cut off all of Israel's strength.
   He withdrew his right hand when they faced their enemy.
He burned like a raging fire in the land of Jacob,
   destroying everything around him.

4 Like an enemy he bent his bow.
Like an opponent his right hand held the arrow steady.
He killed all the beautiful people.
He poured out his fury like fire on the tent of Zion's people.

5 The Lord became an enemy.
   He swallowed up Israel.
   He swallowed up all of its palaces.
   He destroyed its strongholds.
   He made the people of Judah mourn and moan.

6 He stripped his own booth as if it were a garden
   and destroyed his own festivals.
The LORD wiped out the memory of festivals and days of worship in Zion.
   He expelled kings and priests because of his fierce anger.

7 The Lord rejected his altar and disowned his holy place.
   He handed the walls of Zion's palaces over to its enemies.
      The enemies made noise in the LORD's temple
         as though it were a festival day.

8 The LORD planned to destroy the wall of Zion's people.

ᵉ1:21 Hebrew meaning of this verse uncertain.   ᵃ2:1 Chapter 2 is a poem in Hebrew alphabetical order.

He marked it off with a line.
He didn't take his hand away until he had swallowed it up.
He made the towers and walls mourn.
They are completely dejected.

The Prophet Describes Jerusalem's Destruction

9 "Zion's gates have sunk into the ground.
The LORD destroyed and shattered the bars across its gates.
Its king and influential people are scattered among the nations.
There is no longer any instruction from Moses' Teachings.
Its prophets can find no visions from the LORD.
10 The respected leaders of Zion's people sit silently on the ground.
They throw dirt on their heads and put on sackcloth.
The young women of Jerusalem bow their heads to the ground.
11 My eyes are worn out with tears.
My stomach is churning.
My heart is poured out on the ground
because of the destruction of my people.
Little children and infants faint in the city streets.
12 They're asking their mothers for some bread and wine
as they faint like wounded people in the city streets.
Their lives dwindle away in their mothers' arms.

The Prophet Speaks Out: The LORD Destroyed You

13 "What example can I give you?
What parallel can I show you, people of Jerusalem?
What comparison can I make that will comfort you,
beloved people of Zion?
Your wounds are as deep as the sea.
Who can heal you?
14 Your prophets saw misleading visions about you.
They painted a good picture of you.
They didn't expose your guilt in order to make things better again.
They gave you false prophecies that misled you.
15 Everyone who walks along the road shakes a fist at you.
They hiss and shake their heads at Jerusalem's people:
'Is this the city they used to call absolutely beautiful,
the joy of the whole world?'
16 All your enemies gawk at you.
They hiss and grit their teeth.
They say, 'We've swallowed it up.
Yes, this is the day we've been waiting for.
At last we have seen it!'
17 The LORD has accomplished what he had planned to do.
He carried out the threat he announced long ago.
He tore you down without any pity, Jerusalem.
He made your enemies gloat over you.
He raised the weapons of your opponents.
18 The hearts of Jerusalem's people
cried out to the LORD, the wall of Zion's people.

Let your tears run down like a river day and night.
>> Don't let them stop.
>>> Don't let your eyes rest.

19 Get up! Cry out at night, every hour on the hour.
Pour your heart out like water in the presence of the LORD.
Lift up your hands to him in prayer,
>> for the life of your little children
>>> who faint from hunger at every street corner."

Zion Speaks Out: The LORD Destroyed Me

20 "O LORD, look and consider:
>> Have you ever treated anyone like this?
>>> Should women eat their own children,
>>>> the children they have nursed?
>>> Should priests and prophets be killed in the Lord's holy place?
21 Young and old lie on the ground in the streets.
My young women and men are cut down by swords.
>> You killed them on the day of your anger.
>> You slaughtered them without any pity.
22 You have invited those who terrorize me on every side,
>> as though they were invited to a festival.
No one escaped or survived on the day of the LORD's anger.
My enemy has murdered the children I nursed and raised."

The Prophet—A Man of Despair

3 ª1 "I am the man who has experienced suffering under the rod of God's fury.
2 God has driven me away
>> and made me walk in darkness instead of light.
3 He beat me again and again all day long.
4 He has made my flesh and my skin waste away.
He has broken my bones.
5 He has attacked me and surrounded me with bitterness and hardship.
6 He has made me live in darkness,
>> like those who died a long time ago.
7 He has blocked me so that I can't get out.
He has put heavy chains on me.
8 Even when I cry and call for help, he shuts out my prayer.
9 He has blocked my way with cut stones and made my paths crooked.
10 He is like a bear waiting to ambush me, like a lion in hiding.
11 He has forced me off the road I was taking, torn me to pieces,
>> and left me with nothing.
12 He has drawn his bow and made me the target for his arrows.
13 He has shot the arrows from his quiver into my heart.
14 I have become a laughingstock to all my people.
All day long they make fun of me with their songs.
15 He has filled me with bitterness.
He has made me drink wormwood.
16 He has ground my teeth with gravel.
He has trampled me into the dust.

ª3:1 Chapter 3 is a poem in Hebrew alphabetical order.

17   "My soul has been kept from enjoying peace.
     I have forgotten what happiness is.
18   I said, 'I've lost my strength to live, and my hope in the LORD.'
19   Remember my suffering and my aimless wandering,
         the wormwood and poison.
20   My soul continues to remember these things, and is so discouraged.

The Prophet—A Man of Hope

21   "The reason I can still find hope is that I keep this one thing in mind:
22   the LORD's mercy.
             We were not completely wiped out.
             His compassion is never limited.
23   It is new every morning.
             His faithfulness is great.
24   My soul can say, 'The LORD is my lot in life.
             That is why I find hope in him.'
25   The LORD is good to those who wait for him,
             to anyone who seeks help from him.

26   "It is good to continue to hope and wait silently
             for the LORD to save us.
27   It is good for people to endure burdens when they're young.
28   They should sit alone and remain silent
                 because the LORD has laid these burdens on them.
29   They should put their mouths in the dust.
                 Maybe a reason to hope exists.
30   They should turn their cheeks to the one who strikes them
                 and take their fill of insults.

31   "The Lord will not reject such people forever.
32   Even if he makes us suffer,
             he will have compassion
                 in keeping with the richness of his mercy.
33   He does not willingly bring suffering or grief to anyone,
34   crush any prisoner on earth underfoot,
35   deny people their rights in the presence of the Most High God,
36   or deprive people of justice in court.
                 The Lord isn't happy to see these things.
37   Who was it who spoke and it came into being?
             It was the Lord who gave the order.
38   Both good and bad come from the mouth of the Most High God.

39   "Why should any living mortal (any person)
             complain about being punished for sin?
40   Let us look closely at our ways and examine them
             and then return to the LORD.
41   Let us raise our hearts and hands to God in heaven.

42   "We have been disobedient and rebellious.
             You haven't forgiven us.
43   You covered yourself with anger and pursued us.
             You killed without pity.

44 You covered yourself with a cloud
     so that no prayer could get through it.
45 You made us the scum and trash of the nations.
46 All our enemies gawk at us.
47 Panic and pitfalls have found us, so have devastation and destruction.

48 "Streams of tears run down from my eyes
     over the ruin of my dear people.
49 My eyes will keep flowing without stopping for a moment
50   until the LORD looks down from heaven and sees.
51 What I see with my eyes disturbs me deeply
     because of all the young women in my city.*b*

52 "Those who were my enemies for no reason hunted me like a bird.
53   They threw me alive into a pit and threw rocks at me.
54   Water flowed over my head. I thought I was finished.

55 "I call your name from the deepest pit, O LORD.
56   Listen to my cry for help.
     Don't close your ears when I cry out for relief.
57 Be close at hand when I call to you. You told me not to be afraid.
58 Plead my case for me, O LORD. Reclaim my life.
59 Look at the wrong that has been done to me, O LORD.
     Give me a fair verdict.
60 Look at all their malice, all their plots against me.
61 Listen to their insults, all their plots against me.
62 The words and thoughts of those who attack me
     are directed against me all day long.
63 Look at them! Whether they are sitting or standing,
     they make fun of me in their songs.
64 Pay them back, O LORD, for what they deserve,
     for what their own hands have done.
65 Make them stubborn. Let your curse be on them.
66 Pursue them in anger, and wipe them out from under the LORD's heaven."

The Prophet Speaks Out: Zion's Suffering Was Worse Than Sodom's

4

*a*1 "Look how the gold has become tarnished!
The fine gold has changed!
The sacred stones are scattered at every street corner.

2 "Zion's precious children, who are worth their weight in fine gold,
     are now treated like clay pots,
         like those made by a potter's hands.
3 Even jackals offer their breasts to nurse their young,
     but the women of my people are as cruel as wild ostriches.
4 The tongues of nursing infants stick to the roofs of their mouths
     because of their thirst.
Little children beg for bread,
     but no one will break off a piece for them.
5 Those who used to eat delicacies are now destitute in the streets.

---

*b*3:51 Hebrew meaning of this verse uncertain.   *a*4:1 Chapter 4 is a poem in Hebrew alphabetical order.

Those who used to wear expensive clothes now pick
    through piles of garbage.
6 The punishment for my people's wickedness has been more severe
    than the punishment for the sins of Sodom.
    Sodom was destroyed instantly,
        without one human hand touching it.
7 Zion's princes were purer than snow, whiter than milk.
    Their bodies were more pink than coral.
    Their hair was like sapphires.
8 Their faces are ⌊now⌋ blacker than soot.
    No one recognizes them on the streets.
    Their skin has shriveled on their bones.
    It has become as dry as bark.
9 Those who were killed with swords are better off
    than those who are dying from starvation.
    Those who were stabbed bled to death.
    The others are dying because there is nothing in the fields to eat.
10 The hands of loving mothers cooked their own children.
    The children were used for food by my people
        when they were being destroyed ⌊by a blockade⌋.
11 The Lord's fury has accomplished his purpose.
    He unleashed his burning anger.
    He started a fire in Zion that even burned its foundations.
12 Neither the kings of the earth nor anyone living on earth could believe
    that enemies or invaders would ever get through the gates of Jerusalem.
13   ⌊They got through⌋ because of the sins of Jerusalem's prophets
        and the crimes of its priests,
           who spilled the blood of righteous people within it.
14 My people staggered blindly through the streets.
    They were so contaminated with bloodstains
        that no one would touch their clothes.
15 'Get away! You're unclean,'[b] people yelled at them.
    'Get away! Get away! Don't touch anyone.'
    When they fled and wandered around,
        the people of the nations said, 'They can't stay here any longer.'
16 The Lord himself has scattered them.
    He will no longer look favorably on them.
    They no longer respected the priests,
        nor did they honor their older leaders."

The People of Zion Speak Out

17 "We are still straining our eyes, trying in vain to find help.
    We waited and waited for a nation that didn't save us.
18   ⌊The enemy⌋ kept tracking us down,
        so we couldn't even go out into the streets.
    Our end was near.
    Our time was up.
    Our end had come.

---

b 4:15 "Unclean" refers to anything that Moses' Teachings say is not presentable to God.

19 Those who were hunting us were faster than eagles in the sky.
They chased us in the mountains and ambushed us in the wilderness.
20 The person the LORD anointed ⸢as king⸣, who is the breath of our life,
was caught in their pits.
We had thought that we would live
in our king's shadow among the nations."

The Prophet Speaks Out: Be Warned About Edom's Impending Doom

21 "Rejoice and be glad, people of Edom, inhabitants of the country of Uz.
The cup ⸢of the LORD's fury⸣ will be passed to you next.
You'll get drunk and take off all your clothes.
22 People of Zion, the punishment for your wickedness will end.
The LORD will not let you remain in exile.
People of Edom, he will punish you for your wickedness.
He will expose your sins."

A Prayer of the Prophet

5

1 "Remember, O LORD, what has happened to us.
Take a look at our disgrace!

2 "The land we inherited has been turned over to strangers.
Our homes have been turned over to foreigners.
3 We are orphans without a father.
Our mothers are like widows.
4 We have to pay to drink our own water.
We have to pay to chop our own wood.
5 ⸢Our enemies⸣ are breathing down our necks.
We are worn out ⸢and⸣ not permitted to rest.
6 We had to beg Egypt and Assyria for food.ᵃ
7 Our ancestors sinned.
Now they are gone,
⸢but⸣ we have to take the punishment for their wickedness.
8 Slaves rule us.
There is no one to rescue us from them.
9 To get our food, we have to risk our lives
in the heatᵇ of the desert.
10 Our skin is as hot as an oven from the burning heat of starvation.
11 Women in Zion are raped, so are the girls in the cities of Judah.
12 ⸢Our⸣ leaders are hung by their hands.
⸢Our⸣ older leaders are shown no respect.
13 ⸢Our⸣ young men work at the mill,
and ⸢our⸣ boys stagger under loads of wood.
14 ⸢Our⸣ older leaders have stopped meeting at the city gate,
and ⸢our⸣ young men no longer play their music.
15 There is no joy left in our hearts.
Our dancing has turned into mourning.
16 The crown has fallen from our head.

ᵃ 5:6 Or "We made a pledge to Egypt and Assyria in order to get enough food."   ᵇ 5:9 Hebrew meaning of "in the heat" uncertain.

Because we have sinned, it has been disastrous for us.

17 This is why we feel sick.
    This is why our eyes see less and less.

18   Foxes roam around on Mount Zion, which lies in ruins.

19 "But you, O LORD, sit enthroned forever,
        and your reign continues throughout every generation.

20 Why have you completely forgotten us?
    Why have you abandoned us for such a long time?

21 O LORD, bring us back to you, and we'll come back.
    Give us back the life we had long ago,

22   unless you have completely rejected us
        and are very angry with us."

Ezekiel

Ezekiel, a prophet in Babylon, had many strange and wonderful visions. He saw God in a blazing fire surrounded by angels. He also saw God's glory leave the Jerusalem temple before the city was destroyed.

God gave Ezekiel these visions so that Ezekiel could explain God's holiness to the Jews in Babylon. His final vision was of a new temple that would be built in the future.

What amazing thing is Ezekiel about to see? See Ezekiel 37.

How to Listen to a Sermon

The prophet Ezekiel gave stirring sermons. He told people what God intended to do and even acted out what would happen in the future. The people were eager to hear what Ezekiel would say next. But to them it was only entertainment. *They didn't really listen!*

Is it hard for you to listen to sermons in church? Here's how you can become a good listener. When your pastor preaches, write down three things that you hear.

(1) Write down one thing about God.

(2) Write down one thing about making wise choices.

(3) Write down one thing about how to get along better with others.

Do this, and Sunday sermons will help you live in a way that pleases God!

What's In It For Me?

Because the LORD is holy . . .

HIS PEOPLE SHOULD BE HOLY.

GOD CANNOT ALLOW SIN TO GO UNJUDGED.

GOD JUDGES EACH PERSON FAIRLY.

GOD GIVES ALL OF US AN OPPORTUNITY TO CHANGE THE WAY WE THINK AND ACT.

AFTER A PERSON CHANGES, GOD WILL FORGIVE.

Can We Eat the Bible?

The Lord unrolled a scroll of prophecies. Then he told Ezekiel to eat the scroll (see Ezekiel 2–3)! Here's what the vision of the scroll meant:

1. "Eat the scroll."   We are to make God's message a part of our lives.

2. "Speak my words."   Our mission is to tell others what we learn about God.

3. "Sweet as honey."   God's word is always good and true, even when the message is about judgment.

Ezekiel

Ezekiel Sees the LORD's Throne

1 ¹On the fifth day of the fourth month in the thirtieth year, while I was living among the exiles by the Chebar River, the sky opened, and I saw visions from God. ²On the fifth day of the month, during the fifth year of the exile of King Jehoiakin, ³the LORD spoke his word to the priest Ezekiel, son of Buzi, in Babylon by the Chebar River. The power of the LORD came over Ezekiel.

⁴As I looked, I saw a storm coming from the north. There was an immense cloud with flashing lightning surrounded by a bright light. The middle of the lightning looked like glowing metal. ⁵In the center of the cloud I saw what looked like four living creatures. They were shaped like humans, ⁶but each of them had four faces and four wings. ⁷Their legs were straight, their feet were like those of calves, and they glittered like polished bronze. ⁸They had human hands under their wings on each of their four sides. All four of them had faces and wings. ⁹Their wings touched each other. The creatures went straight ahead, and they did not turn as they moved.

¹⁰Their faces looked like this: From the front, each creature had the face of a human. From the right, each one had the face of a lion. From the left, each one had the face of a bull. And from the back, each one had the face of an eagle. ¹¹That is what their faces looked like. Their wings were spread out, pointing upward. Each creature had two wings with which they touched each other. The other two wings covered their bodies. ¹²Each of the creatures went straight ahead. They went wherever their spirit wanted to go, and they didn't turn as they moved. ¹³The living creatures looked like burning coals and torches. Fire moved back and forth between the living creatures. The fire was bright, and lightning came out of the fire. ¹⁴The living creatures ran back and forth like lightning.

¹⁵As I looked at the living creatures, I saw a wheel on the ground beside each of them. ¹⁶This is how the wheels looked and how they were made: They looked like beryl. All four wheels looked the same. They looked like a wheel within a wheel. ¹⁷Whenever they moved, they moved in any of the four directions without turning as they moved. ¹⁸The rims of the wheels were large and frightening. They were covered with eyes.

¹⁹When the living creatures moved, the wheels moved with them. When the living creatures rose from the earth, the wheels rose. ²⁰Wherever their spirit wanted to go, the creatures went. The wheels rose with them, because the spirit of the living creatures was in the wheels. ²¹So whenever the creatures moved, the wheels moved. Whenever the creatures stood still, the wheels stood still. And whenever the creatures rose from the earth, the wheels rose with them, because the spirit of the living creatures was in the wheels.

²²Something like a dome was spread over the heads of the living creatures. It looked like dazzling crystal. ²³Under the dome, each creature had two wings that were stretched out straight, touching one another. Each creature had two wings that covered its body. ²⁴When the creatures moved, I heard the sound of their wings. The sound was like the noise of rushing water, like the thunder of the Almighty, like the commotion in an army camp. When the creatures stood still, they lowered their wings.

²⁵A voice came from above the dome over their heads as they stood still with their wings lowered. ²⁶Above the dome over their heads was something that looked like a throne made of sapphire. On the throne was a figure that looked like a human. ²⁷Then I saw what he looked like from the waist up. He looked like glowing bronze with fire all around it. From the waist down, he looked like fire. A bright light surrounded him. ²⁸The brightness all around him looked like a rainbow in the clouds. It was like the Lord's glory. When I saw it, I immediately bowed down, and I heard someone speaking.

Ezekiel's Vision of a Scroll

2 ¹He said to me, "Son of man, stand up, and I will speak to you." ²As he spoke to me, the Spirit entered me, stood me on my feet, and I heard him speaking to me. ³He said to me, "Son of man, I am sending you to the people of Israel. They are people from a nation that has rebelled against me. They and their ancestors have rebelled against me to this day. ⁴I am sending you to these defiant and stubborn children. Tell them, 'This is what the Almighty Lord says.' ⁵Whether these rebellious people listen or not, they will realize that a prophet has been among them. ⁶Son of man, don't be afraid of them or the things they say. Don't be afraid, even though thorns and thistles are around you and you live among scorpions. Don't let the things they say frighten you. Don't be terrified in their presence, even though they are rebellious people. ⁷Speak my words to them whether they listen or not, because they are rebellious. ⁸But you, son of man, listen to what I say. Don't be rebellious like those rebellious people. Open your mouth, and eat what I am giving to you."

⁹As I looked, I saw a hand stretched out toward me. In it was a scroll. ¹⁰He spread the scroll in front of me. There was writing on the front and back. There were funeral songs, songs of mourning, and horrible things written on it.

3 ¹The Lord said to me, "Son of man, eat what you find. Eat this scroll. Then speak to the people of Israel." ²So I opened my mouth, and he gave me the scroll to eat. ³He said to me, "Son of man, eat this scroll I'm giving you, and fill your stomach with it." So I ate it, and it tasted as sweet as honey in my mouth.

⁴He said to me, "Son of man, go to the people of Israel, and speak my words to them. ⁵I am not sending you to people whose language is hard to understand or difficult to speak. I am sending you to Israel. ⁶I am not sending you to nations whose language is hard to understand, difficult to speak, or whose words you cannot understand. If I send you to those nations, they will certainly listen to you. ⁷But the people of Israel will refuse to listen to you because they refuse to listen to me. All the people of Israel are very stubborn and hardheaded. ⁸Yet, I will make you as stubborn and as hardheaded as they are. ⁹I will make you as hard as a diamond, harder than stone. Don't be afraid of them. Don't be terrified in their presence, even though they are rebellious people."

¹⁰He also said to me, "Son of man, take to heart everything I have spoken to you, and listen closely. ¹¹Go to the exiles, to your people. Whether they listen or not, tell them, 'This is what the Almighty Lord says.' "

¹²Then the Spirit lifted me, and behind me I heard a loud thundering voice say, "Blessed is the Lord's glory, which left this place." ¹³I also heard the noise of the wings of the living creatures touching one another and the noise of the wheels beside them as well as a loud rumbling. ¹⁴Then the Spirit lifted me and took me away. I went away feeling bitter and angry. The strong power of the Lord came over me. ¹⁵I went to Tel Abib, to the exiles who lived by the Chebar River. I sat there among them for seven days. I was stunned.

Paper / *Ezekiel 3:1-3*

Women's
World

In ancient times, some people wrote by pressing letters into wet, soft clay tablets. Others used ink to write on pieces of broken clay pots. Some important documents were written on cured animal skin that had been scraped thin. Schoolchildren practiced their writing on soft, dry clay tablets that could be rubbed smooth and used again and again. Paper was invented in Egypt, but it was very expensive.

To make paper, workers cut papyrus reeds into 12-inch sections. The inner pith was taken out and sliced into very thin strips. Strips were laid side by side; then another layer was laid in the opposite direction. The two layers were then glued together. Workers pounded the layers flat and sanded them smooth. This paper of Bible times was a little thicker than our brown wrapping paper. Often, workers glued 20 sheets of paper together and then rolled them up into a scroll. For long books, these rolls could be glued together to make a scroll 30 feet long.

Ezekiel Is Appointed to Be a Watchman

¹⁶After seven days the LORD spoke his word to me. He said, ¹⁷"Son of man, I have made you a watchman over the people of Israel. Listen to what I say, and warn them for me. ¹⁸Suppose I tell you that wicked people will surely die, but you don't warn them or speak out so that they can change their wicked ways in order to save their lives. Then these wicked people will die because of their sin, but I will hold you responsible for their deaths. ¹⁹But suppose you warn the wicked people, and they don't turn from their wicked ways. Then they will die because of their sin, but you will save yourself. ²⁰If righteous people turn from living the right way and do wrong, I will make them stumble, and they will die. If you don't warn them, they will die because of their sin, and the right things they did will not be remembered. I will hold you responsible for their deaths. ²¹But if you warn righteous people not to sin, and they don't sin, they will certainly live because they listened to the warning. You will save yourself."

The LORD Gives Ezekiel Directions to Follow

²²The power of the LORD came over me. He said, "Get up, and go to the plain. I will speak to you there." ²³I got up and went to the plain. The LORD's glory was standing there like the glory I saw by the Chebar River, and I immediately bowed down.

[24]Then the Spirit entered me and stood me on my feet. He talked to me. He said, "Go into your home, and shut yourself inside. [25]People will tie you up with ropes, son of man, so that you can't go outside. [26]I will make your tongue stick to the roof of your mouth so that you can't talk or criticize them, even though they are rebellious people. [27]But when I speak to you, I will open your mouth. You will tell them, 'This is what the Almighty Lord says.' Some will listen, and some will refuse to listen. They are rebellious people."

Ezekiel Plays Out the Blockade of Jerusalem

[1]The Lord said, "Son of man, take clay, put it in front of you, and draw a map of Jerusalem on it. [2]Set up a blockade against it, build attack walls around it, put up dirt ramps around it, have troops ready to attack it, and place battering rams all around it. [3]Then take an iron pan, and set it up as a wall between you and the city. Turn your face toward the city as if you were going to attack it, and then attack it. This is a sign for the people of Israel.

[4]"Then lie on your left side and take the punishment of the nation of Israel yourself. You will bear its punishment as many days as you lie on that side. [5]I have assigned to you one day for each year its punishment will last. So for 390 days, you will bear the punishment for the sins of the nation of Israel. [6]When you finish this, you will lie down again, this time on your right side. You will bear the punishment for the sins of the nation of Judah for 40 days, one day for each year I have assigned to you. [7]Turn your face toward the blockaded Jerusalem. Shake your fist and prophesy against it. [8]I will tie you up with ropes so that you will not be able to turn from one side to the other until you have finished attacking ˳Jerusalem˳.

[9]"Then take wheat, barley, beans, lentils, millet, and winter wheat. Put them in a container, and use them to make bread for yourself. Eat it during the 390 days that you are lying on your side. [10]The food that you eat should be weighed. Eat eight ounces of food every day at set times. [11]Measure out two-thirds of a quart of water, and drink it at set times. [12]Eat the bread as you would eat barley loaves. Bake the bread in front of people, using human excrement for fuel."

[13]Then the Lord said, "In the same way, the people of Israel will eat unclean[a]bread among the nations where I scatter them."

[14]I answered, "Almighty Lord, I have never dishonored myself. From the time I was young until now, I have never eaten an animal that died by itself or was killed by other wild animals. No unclean meat has ever entered my mouth."

[15]He said to me, "I will let you use cow manure in place of human excrement. Bake your bread over it."

[16]He also said to me, "Son of man, I am going to cut off the bread supply in Jerusalem. People will anxiously eat rationed bread and fearfully drink rationed water. [17]They will be shocked at the sight of each other because of the lack of food and water. They will waste away because of their sin."

The LORD Tells Ezekiel About the Fall of Jerusalem

[1]The Lord said, "Son of man, take a sharp blade, and use it as a barber's razor to shave your head and beard. Take scales to weigh your hair and divide it ˳into three even parts˳. [2]When the blockade is over, burn one-third of your hair in a fire in the middle of the city. Take another third, and cut it up with a blade around the city. Then scatter the remaining third to the wind, and I will draw a sword and go after it. [3]Take

---

[a]4:13 "Unclean" refers to anything that Moses' Teachings say is not presentable to God.

a few strands of hair, and wrap them in the hem of your clothes. ⁴Later, take some of them, and throw them in a fire and burn them up. From there a fire will spread throughout the whole nation of Israel.

⁵"This is what the Almighty LORD says: This is Jerusalem! I have placed it in the center of the nations with countries all around it. ⁶The people of Jerusalem have rebelled against my rules and my laws more than the surrounding nations. They have rejected my rules, and they don't live by my laws.

⁷"So this is what the Almighty LORD says: People of Jerusalem, you have caused more trouble than the nations around you. You haven't lived by my laws or obeyed my rules. You haven't even lived up to the standards of the nations around you.

⁸"So this is what the Almighty LORD says: I, too, am against you, and I will punish you in front of the nations. ⁹Because of all the detestable things that you do, I will do things to you that I have never done before and will never do again. ¹⁰That is why parents will eat their children, and children will eat their parents. I will punish you and scatter whoever is left to the wind.

¹¹"As I live, declares the Almighty LORD, because you have dishonored my holy worship place with all your disgusting and detestable things, I will have you killed. I will not have compassion for you or feel sorry for you. ¹²One-third of you will die in plagues and be devoured in famines. Another third will die in battles against those around you. I will scatter the remaining third to the wind, and I will pursue them with a sword.

¹³"I will unleash my anger. I will use my fury against you, and I will get revenge. When my fury is unleashed against you, you will know that I, the LORD, spoke to you while I was angry. ¹⁴I will turn you into a wasteland and an object of ridicule among the nations around you and in the presence of everyone who passes by you. ¹⁵The nations that are around you will ridicule you and laugh at you. When I punish you because of my anger, fury, and fierce revenge, you will become something ridiculed and something horrible. I, the LORD, have spoken. ¹⁶When I shoot my destructive arrows of famine at you, I will shoot to kill you. I will bring more and more famines into your land, and I will cut off your food supply. ¹⁷I will send famines and wild animals against you, and they will rob you of your children. I will send plagues, violence, and wars to kill you. I, the LORD, have spoken."

A Prophecy Against the Mountains of Israel

6 ¹The LORD spoke his word to me. He said, ²"Son of man, look toward the mountains of Israel, and prophesy against them. ³Say this, 'You mountains of Israel, listen to the word of the Almighty LORD! This is what the Almighty LORD says to the mountains and hills and to the ravines and valleys: I am going to attack you with a sword and destroy your worship sites. ⁴Your altars will be destroyed, and your incense burners will be smashed. I will kill people in front of your idols. ⁵I will lay the dead bodies of the people of Israel in front of your idols, and I will scatter their bones around your altars. ⁶Wherever people live, the cities will be ruined, and the worship sites will be wrecked. Your altars will be ruined and demolished. Your idols will be smashed and completely destroyed. Your incense burners will be cut down, and everything you have done will be wiped out. ⁷People will be killed, and they will fall among you. Then you will know that I am the LORD.

⁸"'But I will let some people live. Some people will escape the battle among the nations and be scattered throughout the countries. ⁹Then those who escape will remember me among the nations where they are taken captive. I was hurt by their adulterous hearts, which turned away from me, and by their eyes, which lusted after

idols. They will hate themselves for the evil and disgusting things that they have done. ¹⁰Then you will know that I am the LORD and that the disaster I promised was not an empty threat.

¹¹" 'This is what the Almighty LORD says: Clap your hands, stomp your feet, and say, "Oh no!" because the people of Israel have done evil and disgusting things. So they will die in wars, famines, and plagues. ¹²Plagues will kill those who are far away. Those who are near will die in wars, and anyone who is left and has escaped will die in famines. This is how I will unleash my anger. ¹³Then you will know that I am the LORD.

" 'Those who are killed will lie beside the idols around their altars. They will lie on every high hill, on all the mountaintops, and under every large tree and every leafy oak. These are the places where they made offerings to their disgusting idols. ¹⁴I will use my power against them and destroy the land, from the desert to Diblah. Then they will know that I am the LORD.' "

The LORD's Judgment on Israel

7 ¹The LORD spoke his word to me. He said, ²"Son of man, this is what the Almighty LORD says to the people in the land of Israel: The end is coming! The end is coming to the four corners of the earth. ³Now the end is coming for you. I will send my anger against you. I will judge you for the way you have lived, and I will punish you for all the detestable things that you have done. ⁴I will not have compassion for you or feel sorry for you. I will pay you back for the way you have lived and for the detestable things you have done. Then you will know that I am the LORD.

⁵"This is what the Almighty LORD says: One disaster after another is coming. ⁶The end is coming. The end is coming. It is stirring itself up against you. It is coming! ⁷Destruction is coming to you, inhabitants of the land. The time is coming. The day is near. There will be confusion. There will be no joy in the mountains. ⁸Soon I will pour out my fury on you and unleash my anger on you. I will judge you for the way you have lived, and I will punish you for all the detestable things that you have done. ⁹I will not have compassion or feel sorry. I will pay you back for the way you have lived and for the detestable things that you are still doing. Then you will know that I am the LORD and that I am the one attacking you.

¹⁰"The day is near! It is coming! Destruction is coming! Wrongdoing has blossomed. Arrogance has flourished. ¹¹Violence has grown into a weapon for punishing wickedness. None of the people will be left. None of that crowd, none of their wealth, and nothing of value will be left. ¹²The time is coming. The day is near. Buyers will not rejoice, and sellers will not mourn, because my fury will be against the whole crowd. ¹³Sellers will not live long enough to buy back what they have sold. The visions against that crowd will not change. Because of their sins, none of the people will live. ¹⁴They have blown a ram's horn, and everything is ready. But no one will go into battle, because my fury is against their whole crowd.

¹⁵"Outside are swords, and inside are plagues and famines. Whoever is in a field will die in battle. Whoever is in the city will be devoured by famines and plagues. ¹⁶Those who survive will escape to the mountains. They will moan like doves in the valleys. They will moan because of their sins. ¹⁷Every hand will hang limp, and every knee will be as weak as water. ¹⁸They will put on sackcloth, and horror will cover them. All their faces will be covered with shame, and every head will be shaved. ¹⁹They will throw their silver and gold into the streets like garbage. Their silver and gold won't be able to rescue them on the day of the LORD's anger. It will no longer satisfy their hunger or fill their stomachs. Their silver and gold caused them to fall into sin.

²⁰They were proud of their beautiful jewels and used them to make disgusting and detestable statues of false gods. That is why I will make their jewels disgusting. ²¹I will hand their jewels over to foreigners as loot and to the most evil people on earth as prizes. These foreigners will dishonor the people of Israel. ²²I will turn my face away from the people of Israel, and foreigners will dishonor my treasured place. Robbers will go in and dishonor it.

²³"Get the chains ready! The land is filled with murder, and the city is filled with violence. ²⁴So I will send the most evil nation, and it will take possession of people's houses. I will stop those who are strong from feeling proud, and their holy places will be dishonored. ²⁵Anguish is coming. People will look for peace, but there will be none. ²⁶One disaster will happen after another. One rumor will follow another. People will ask for a vision from a prophet. The teachings of priests and the advice of leaders will disappear. ²⁷Kings will mourn, and princes will give up hope. The common people will lose their courage. I will give them what they deserve and judge them as they have judged others. Then they will know that I am the Lord."

Idolatry in Jerusalem

8 ¹On the fifth day of the sixth month in the sixth year, I was sitting in my home. Judah's leaders were sitting in front of me. The power of the Almighty Lord came over me. ²As I looked, I saw something that looked like a human. From the waist down its body looked like fire, and from the waist up its body looked like glowing metal. ³It stretched out what looked like a hand and grabbed me by the hair on my head. In these visions from God, the Spirit carried me between heaven and earth. He took me to Jerusalem, to the entrance to the north gate of the inner courtyard of the temple. That was where an idol that stirs up God's anger was located. ⁴There I saw the glory of Israel's God as I did in the vision that I saw in the valley.

⁵God said to me, "Son of man, look toward the north." So I looked toward the north, and there in the entrance to the north gate beside the altar, I saw the idol that stirs up God's anger.

⁶He asked me, "Son of man, do you see what the people of Israel are doing? The people of Israel are doing very disgusting things here, things that will force me to go far away from my holy place. But you will see even more disgusting things."

⁷Then he took me to the entrance of the courtyard. As I looked, I saw a hole in the wall. ⁸He said to me, "Son of man, dig through the wall." So I dug through the wall, and I saw a door.

⁹He said to me, "Go in, and see the wicked, disgusting things that the people of Israel are doing here." ¹⁰So I went in and looked. I saw that the walls were covered with drawings of every kind of crawling creature, every kind of disgusting animal, and all the idols in the nation of Israel. ¹¹In front of these drawings stood 70 of Israel's leaders. Jaazaniah, son of Shaphan, was standing with the leaders. Each of them was holding an incense burner in his hand, and a cloud of incense went up.

¹²God asked me, "Son of man, do you see what the leaders of the nation of Israel are doing in secret? Each of them is in the room where his god is, and each one of them is thinking, 'The Lord doesn't see me. The Lord has abandoned this land.' "

¹³Then he said to me, "You will see even more disgusting things that they are doing."

¹⁴He brought me to the entrance of the north gate of the Lord's temple. Women were sitting there and crying for the god Tammuz. ¹⁵He asked me, "Son of man, do you see this? You will see even more disgusting things than these."

¹⁶Then he brought me into the inner courtyard of the Lord's temple. There at the

entrance to the LORD's temple, between the entrance and the altar, were about 25 men who had their backs turned to the LORD's temple. They were facing east and worshiping the rising sun. [17]He asked me, "Son of man, do you see this? Isn't it bad enough that the people of Judah have done these disgusting things that you have seen here? Yet, they also fill the land with violence and continue to provoke me even more. Look how they insult me in the worst possible way.[a] [18]So I will take action because I'm angry, and I won't have compassion for them or feel sorry for them. Even if they shout in my ears, I won't listen to them."

The LORD Orders the Destruction of the Temple in Jerusalem

9 [1]Then I heard the LORD call out with a loud voice. He said, "Come here, those who are going to punish this city. Each of you should bring your weapon with you." [2]So six men came from the upper north gate. Each one brought a deadly weapon with him. Among them was a person dressed in linen who was carrying paper and pen. The men came in and stood by the bronze altar. [3]Then the glory of the God of Israel went up from the angels,[a] where it had been, to the temple's entrance. The LORD called to the person dressed in linen who was carrying paper and pen.

[4]The LORD said to that person, "Go throughout the city of Jerusalem, and put a mark on the foreheads of those who sigh and groan about all the disgusting things that are being done in the city."

[5]Then he said to the others as I was listening, "Follow him throughout the city and kill. Don't have any compassion, and don't feel sorry. [6]Kill old men, young men, old women, young women, and children. But don't come near anyone who has a mark on him. Start with my holy place." So they started with the old men in front of the temple.

[7]He said to them, "Dishonor the temple! Fill its courtyards with dead people, and then leave." So they went out and killed the people in the city.

[8]As they were killing people, I was left alone. So I immediately bowed down. I cried, "Almighty LORD, will you destroy everyone who is left in Israel while you pour out your anger on Jerusalem?"

[9]He answered me, "The wickedness of the nations of Israel and Judah is terrible. The land is filled with murder, and the city is filled with wrongdoing. They think that the LORD has abandoned the land and that he doesn't see. [10]But I will not have compassion or feel sorry. I will do to them what they have done to others."

[11]Then the person dressed in linen who was carrying paper and pen reported, "I did everything you commanded."

The Glory of the LORD Leaves His Temple

10 [1]As I looked at the dome over the heads of the angels,[a] I saw something that looked like a throne made of sapphire. [2]The LORD said to the person dressed in linen, "Go between the wheels under the angels, and fill your hands with burning coals. Then scatter them over the city." So he went between the wheels as I watched.

[3]The angels were standing on the south side of the temple as the person went. A cloud filled the inner courtyard. [4]The LORD's glory rose from the angels to the entrance of the temple, the cloud filled the temple, and the brightness of the LORD's glory filled the courtyard. [5]The sound of the angels' wings was heard as far as the outer courtyard. It was like the sound of the Almighty God when he speaks.

---

[a]8:17 Hebrew meaning uncertain. [a]9:3 Or "cherubim." [a]10:1 Or "cherubim."

⁶After the LORD had commanded the person dressed in linen to take burning coals from between the wheels beside the angels, the person went in and stood beside one of the wheels. ⁷One of the angels reached into the fire that was between the angels and took out some coals. This angel put them in the hands of the person dressed in linen. The person took them and left.

⁸The angels appeared to have what looked like human hands under their wings. ⁹As I looked, I saw four wheels beside the angels, one wheel beside each of the angels. The wheels looked like beryl. ¹⁰All four wheels looked the same. Each was like a wheel within a wheel. ¹¹Whenever the angels moved, they moved in any of the four directions without turning as they moved. They always moved in the direction they faced without turning as they moved. ¹²Their entire bodies, their backs, hands, wings, and wheels were covered with eyes. Each of the angels had a wheel. ¹³I heard that the wheels were called the whirling wheels. ¹⁴Each of the angels had four faces. The first was the face of an angel, the second was the face of a human, the third was the face of a lion, and the fourth was the face of an eagle.

¹⁵The angels rose. These were the living creatures that I saw at the Chebar River. ¹⁶When the angels moved, the wheels moved beside them. When the angels lifted their wings to rise from the ground, the wheels didn't leave their side. ¹⁷When the angels stood still, the wheels stood still. When the angels rose, the wheels rose with them. The spirit of the living creatures was in the wheels. ¹⁸Then the glory of the LORD left the temple's entrance and stood over the angels. ¹⁹The angels lifted their wings and rose from the ground. I was watching them as they left with the wheels beside them. The angels stood at the door to the east gate of the LORD's temple, and the glory of the God of Israel was above them.

²⁰These are the living creatures that I saw under the God of Israel at the Chebar River. I realized that they were angels. ²¹Each had four faces and four wings, and under their wings were what looked like human hands. ²²Their faces looked exactly like the faces that I saw by the Chebar River. Each one went straight ahead.

Judgment on the Rulers of Israel

11 ¹Then the Spirit lifted me and took me to the east gate of the LORD's temple. (It's the gate that faces east.) Twenty-five men were at the entrance of the gate. I saw among them Azzur's son Jaazaniah and Benaiah's son Pelatiah. They were leaders of the people.

²Then the LORD said to me, "Son of man, these are the men who plan evil and give bad advice in this city. ³They say, 'It's almost time to rebuild homes. This city is a cooking pot, and we're the meat.' ⁴So prophesy against them. Prophesy, son of man."

⁵The LORD's Spirit came to me and told me to say, "This is what the LORD says: You are saying these things, nation of Israel. But I know what's going through your mind. ⁶You have killed many people in this city and have filled its streets with corpses.

⁷"So this is what the Almighty LORD says: The corpses that you put in the middle of the city are the meat, and the city is the cooking pot. I will force you out of the city. ⁸You are afraid of swords, so I will bring swords to attack you, declares the Almighty LORD. ⁹I will force you out of the city. I will hand you over to foreigners, and I will punish you. ¹⁰You will die in battle. I will judge you at Israel's borders. Then you will know that I am the LORD. ¹¹The city will not be your cooking pot, and you will not be the meat in it. I will judge you at Israel's borders. ¹²Then you will know that I am the LORD. You haven't lived by my laws, and you haven't obeyed my rules. You have followed the standards set by the nations around you."

¹³While I was prophesying, Benaiah's son Pelatiah died.

I immediately bowed down and cried out, "Almighty Lᴏʀᴅ, will you completely destroy all the remaining people in Israel?"

The Lᴏʀᴅ's Promise to Gather Israel from the Nations

¹⁴Then the Lᴏʀᴅ spoke his word to me. He said, ¹⁵"Son of man, the people who live in Jerusalem are talking about your own relatives and about the entire nation of Israel. The people who live in Jerusalem say, 'They are far away from the Lᴏʀᴅ. This land has been given to us as our own property.'

¹⁶"So tell them, 'This is what the Almighty Lᴏʀᴅ says: Although I sent them far away among the nations and scattered them among the countries, I have been their sanctuary for a little while among the countries where they've gone.'

¹⁷"So tell them, 'This is what the Almighty Lᴏʀᴅ says: I will bring them together from the nations and gather them from the countries where I've scattered them. I will give them the land of Israel. ¹⁸They will come and remove all the disgusting and detestable things that are there. ¹⁹I will give them a single purpose and put a new spirit in them. I will remove their stubborn hearts and give them obedient hearts. ²⁰Then they will live by my laws and obey my rules. They will be my people, and I will be their God. ²¹But as for those whose minds are set on following detestable and disgusting idols, I will pay them back for what they have done, declares the Almighty Lᴏʀᴅ.' "

The Glory of the Lᴏʀᴅ Leaves Jerusalem

²²Then the angels*ᵃ* raised their wings, with the wheels beside them. The glory of the God of Israel was above them. ²³The Lᴏʀᴅ's glory left the middle of the city and stopped above the mountain east of the city.

²⁴In this vision from God's Spirit, the Spirit lifted me and brought me to the exiles in Babylonia. Then the vision I saw left me.

²⁵I told the exiles everything the Lᴏʀᴅ had shown me.

Ezekiel Plays Out Israel's Exile

¹The Lᴏʀᴅ spoke his word to me. He said, ²"Son of man, you are living among rebellious people. They have eyes, but they can't see. They have ears, but they can't hear because they are rebellious people.

Good Morning, God
Ezekiel 11:19

Sometimes we do what we know is right. But other times we don't. Why are we like this? It's because we are all tempted by our disobedient hearts to do things we shouldn't. Every day we decide in our hearts if we will obey or disobey God. However, the Bible says God can replace our stubborn, disobedient hearts with brand new ones. Do you need a new heart? Ask God for one, today!

Lord, give me an obedient heart.

ᵃ11:22 Or "cherubim."

³"Son of man, pack your bags as if you were going into exile. Let the people see you leave in the daylight. March like a captive from your place to another place as they watch. Maybe they will understand, even though they are rebellious people. ⁴Let them see you in the daylight. Bring out your bags as if you were going into exile. In the evening let them see you leave like a captive going into exile. ⁵Dig a hole through the wall of your house, and leave through it. ⁶Let them see you put your bags on your shoulders and carry them out in the dark. Cover your face so that you won't see the land. I've made you a sign to warn the nation of Israel."

⁷I did what I was ordered to do. During the day I brought out bags as if I were going into exile. In the evening I dug a hole through the wall. I brought out my bags in the dark. I let the people see me as I carried my bags on my shoulders.

⁸The next morning the LORD spoke his word to me. He said, ⁹"Son of man, didn't the rebellious nation of Israel ask you what you were doing?

¹⁰"Tell them, 'This is what the Almighty LORD says: This is the divine revelation about the prince from Jerusalem and about all the people of Israel who live there.'

¹¹"Tell them, 'I am your warning sign. What I have done will happen to you. You will go into exile and into captivity. ¹²The prince who is among you will put his bags on his shoulders in the dark and leave. People will dig holes in the wall to go through. The prince will cover his face so that he cannot see the land. ¹³I will spread my net over him, and he will be caught in my net. I will bring him to Babylon, the land of the Babylonians, but he will not see it. And that's where he'll die. ¹⁴I will scatter in every direction all those who are around him—his staff and all his troops. I will pursue them with my sword. ¹⁵Then they will know that I am the LORD, because I will scatter them among the nations and force them into other countries. ¹⁶However, I will spare a few of them from wars, famines, and plagues. Wherever they go among the nations, they will realize that everything they did was disgusting. Then they will know that I am the LORD.' "

¹⁷The LORD spoke his word to me. He said, ¹⁸"Son of man, shake as you eat your food. Tremble and be worried as you drink your water.

¹⁹"Tell the people of this land, 'This is what the Almighty LORD says about the people who live in Jerusalem and in the land of Israel: They will be worried as they eat their food and terrified as they drink their water. Their country will be stripped of everything because everyone who lives there is violent. ²⁰The cities where people live will be destroyed, and the country will become a wasteland. Then they will know that I am the LORD.' "

²¹The LORD spoke his word to me. He said, ²²"Son of man, what is this proverb you have in Israel: 'Days go by, and every vision comes to nothing'?

²³"Tell the people, 'This is what the Almighty LORD says: I will put a stop to the use of this proverb. You will no longer quote it in Israel.' Instead, tell them, 'The time is near when every vision will come true. ²⁴There will no longer be any false visions or flattering fortunetelling to the people. ²⁵I, the LORD, will speak. Everything that I say will happen without any more delay. I will say something, and it will happen during your lifetime, you rebellious people, declares the Almighty LORD.' "

²⁶The LORD spoke his word to me. He said, ²⁷"Son of man, the people of Israel are saying, 'The vision that Ezekiel sees won't happen for a long time. What he prophesies will happen in the distant future.'

²⁸"Tell them, 'This is what the Almighty LORD says: Everything that I say will no longer be delayed. Whatever I say will happen, declares the Almighty LORD.' "

False Prophets Condemned

13 ¹The LORD spoke his word to me. He said, ²"Son of man, prophesy against the prophets of Israel. Tell those who make up their prophecies, 'Listen to the word of the LORD.

³" 'This is what the Almighty LORD says: How horrible it will be for the foolish prophets. They follow their own ideas, and they have seen nothing. ⁴Israel, your prophets are like foxes among the ruins ⌊of a city⌋. ⁵They haven't repaired the gaps in the wall or rebuilt the wall for the nation of Israel. So Israel will not be protected in battle on the day of the LORD. ⁶These foolish prophets see false visions, and their predictions don't come true. They say, "The LORD said this." But the LORD hasn't sent them. Then they hope that their message will come true. ⁷Prophets of Israel, haven't you seen false visions and predicted things that don't come true? Don't you say, "The LORD said this," even though I haven't said anything?

⁸" 'This is what the Almighty LORD says: Your predictions are false, and your visions are lies. That is why I'm against you, declares the Almighty LORD. ⁹I will use my power against the prophets who see false visions and predict things that don't come true. They will not help my people make decisions or be recorded in the records of the nation of Israel. They won't even enter Israel. Then you will know that I am the LORD.

¹⁰" 'They have deceived my people by saying that everything is alright, but it's not alright. When someone builds a flimsy wall, the prophets cover it up with paint. ¹¹Tell those who cover up the wall with paint that their wall will fall down. Rain will pour down, hailstones will fall on it, and stormy winds will break it to pieces. ¹²When the wall falls down, people will ask them, "Where's the paint that you used to cover the wall?"

¹³" 'This is what the Almighty LORD says: In my fury I'll cause a storm to break out. In my anger rain will pour down, and hailstones will destroy the wall. ¹⁴I will tear down the wall that the prophets covered up with paint. I will level it and expose its foundation. When the wall falls, they will be destroyed by it. Then you will know that I am the LORD. ¹⁵I will unleash my fury on the wall and on those who covered it up with paint.

" 'Then I will say to you, "The wall is gone, and so are those who painted it. ¹⁶The prophets of Israel who prophesied to Jerusalem are gone. Those who said that everything was alright, when it wasn't alright, are gone, declares the Almighty LORD.' "

¹⁷"Son of man, look at the women among your people who make up prophecies, and prophesy against them.

¹⁸"Tell them, 'This is what the Almighty LORD says: How horrible it will be for women who sew magic charms for people's wrists and make magic veils of every size for people's heads. You want to trap people. You want to control the lives of my people for your own profit. ¹⁹You dishonor me in front of my people for a few handfuls of barley and a few pieces of bread. You kill people who shouldn't die, and you spare the lives of people who shouldn't live. You lie to my people who are willing to listen.

²⁰" 'This is what the Almighty LORD says: I'm against the magic charms that you use to trap people like birds. I will tear them from your arms and free the people that you have trapped. ²¹I will tear off your magic veils and rescue my people from your power so that they will no longer be under your control. Then you will know that I am the LORD. ²²You have discouraged righteous people with your lies, even though I hadn't brought them any grief. You encouraged wicked people not to turn from their wicked ways to save their lives. ²³That is why you will no longer see false visions or

make predictions. I will rescue my people from your power. Then you will know that I am the LORD.' "

Idolaters Condemned

14 ¹Some of Israel's leaders came to me and sat down in front of me. ²Then the LORD spoke his word to me. He said, ³"Son of man, these people are devoted to their idols, and they are allowing themselves to fall into sin. Should they be allowed to ask me for help?

⁴"So speak to them. Tell them, 'This is what the LORD says: Suppose an Israelite is devoted to idols and allows himself to fall into sin. Suppose he goes to a prophet to ask for my help. I, the LORD, will give that Israelite an answer, the answer that his many idols deserve. ⁵I will do this to recapture the hearts of the nation of Israel. They have deserted me because of their disgusting idols.'

⁶"So tell the nation of Israel, 'This is what the Almighty LORD says: Change the way you think and act! Turn away from your idols, and don't return to any of your disgusting things. ⁷Suppose an Israelite or a foreigner who lives in Israel deserts me by devoting himself to idols and by allowing himself to fall into sin. If he goes to a prophet to ask for my help, I, the LORD, will give him an answer. ⁸I will reject him, and I will make an example of him. I will exclude him from my people. Then you will know that I am the LORD.

⁹" 'If a prophet is tricked into giving a prophecy, it is I, the LORD, who tricked the prophet. I will use my power against you and destroy you from among my people Israel. ¹⁰Both of you will suffer for your sins. The prophet will be as guilty as you are when you ask for his help. ¹¹Then the people of Israel will no longer wander away from me. They will no longer dishonor me with all their sins. Then they will be my people, and I will be their God, declares the Almighty LORD.' "

¹²The LORD spoke his word to me. He said, ¹³"Son of man, suppose a country sins against me by being unfaithful to me. I will use my power against it, cut off its food supply, send a famine to it, and destroy its people and animals. ¹⁴Even if these three men—Noah, Daniel, and Job—were in that country, they would, by their righteousness, rescue only themselves," declares the Almighty LORD.

¹⁵"Suppose I send wild animals through that country and they make it childless and turn it into such a wasteland that no one travels through it because of the animals. ¹⁶As I live, declares the Almighty LORD, not even Noah, Daniel, and Job could rescue their own sons or daughters. They could rescue only themselves. And the country would become a wasteland.

¹⁷"Suppose I bring a war against that country by saying, 'I will let a war go throughout this country.' Suppose I destroy the people and the animals in it. ¹⁸As I live, declares the Almighty LORD, not even Noah, Daniel, and Job could rescue their sons or daughters. They could rescue only themselves.

¹⁹"Suppose I send a plague into that country or pour out my fury on it by killing people and destroying animals. ²⁰As I live, declares the Almighty LORD, not even Noah, Daniel, and Job could, by their righteousness, rescue their sons or daughters. They could rescue only themselves.

²¹"This is what the Almighty LORD says: I will surely send four terrible punishments against Jerusalem. I will send wars, famines, wild animals, and plagues. They will destroy people and animals. ²²But some people will survive. Some of your sons and daughters will be brought out. When they come out to you, you will see how they live. Then you will be comforted after the disasters that I will bring on Jerusalem, after every disaster that I will bring against it. ²³You will be comforted when you see

how they live. Then you will know that everything I have done was done for a reason," declares the Almighty LORD.

Jerusalem Is Compared to Wood From a Wild Vine

15 ¹The LORD spoke his word to me. He said, ²"Son of man, what good is the wood from a vine? Is it better than the wood from a tree in the forest? ³Do people use it to make something? Do they make a peg from it to hang things on? ⁴No! It is only thrown into the fire as fuel. The fire burns up both its ends and chars its middle. Then can it be used to make anything? ⁵When the vine was in perfect condition, it couldn't be made into anything. How can it be used to make anything after the fire has burned and charred it?

⁶"So this is what the Almighty LORD says: As a vine is taken from among the trees in the forest to be used to feed the fire, so I will take the people who live in Jerusalem to punish them. ⁷I will turn against the people of Jerusalem. Even though they have escaped one fire, another fire will burn them. Then they will know that I am the LORD, because I will turn against them. ⁸I will turn the country into a wasteland because they have been unfaithful," declares the Almighty LORD.

A Description of Jerusalem's Sins

16 ¹The LORD spoke his word to me. He said, ²"Son of man, make known to the people of Jerusalem the disgusting things they have done. ³Tell them, 'This is what the Almighty LORD says to the people of Jerusalem: Your birthplace and your ancestors were in the land of the Canaanites. Your father was an Amorite, and your mother was a Hittite. ⁴When you were born, your umbilical cord wasn't cut. You weren't washed with water to make you clean. You weren't rubbed with salt or wrapped in cloth. ⁵No one who saw you felt sorry enough for you to do any of these things. But you were thrown into an open field. You were rejected when you were born.

⁶"'Then I went by you and saw you kicking around in your own blood. I said to you, "Live." ⁷I made you grow like a plant in the field. You grew up, matured, and became a young woman. Your breasts developed, and your hair grew. Yet, you were naked and bare.

⁸"'I went by you again and looked at you. You were old enough to make love to. So I spread my robe over you, and covered your naked body. I promised to love you, and I exchanged marriage vows with you. You became mine, declares the Almighty LORD.

⁹"'Then I bathed you with water, and I washed off your blood. I poured olive oil over you. ¹⁰I put an embroidered dress on you and fine leather sandals on your feet. I dressed you in fine linen and covered you with silk. ¹¹I gave you jewelry. I put bracelets on your wrists and a necklace around your neck. ¹²I put a ring in your nose, earrings on your ears, and a beautiful crown on your head. ¹³So you wore gold and silver jewelry. You were dressed in fine linen, silk, and embroidered clothes. Your food was flour, honey, and olive oil. You were very beautiful, and eventually you became a queen. ¹⁴You became famous in every nation because of your beauty. Your beauty was perfect because I gave you my glory, declares the Almighty LORD.

¹⁵"'But you trusted your beauty, and you used your fame to become a prostitute. You had sex with everyone who walked by. ¹⁶You took some of your clothes and made your worship sites colorful. This is where you acted like a prostitute. Such things shouldn't happen. They shouldn't occur. ¹⁷You took your beautiful gold and silver jewelry that I had given you and made male idols for yourself. Then you committed adultery with them. ¹⁸You took off your embroidered clothes and covered the idols with

them. You offered my olive oil and incense in their presence. ¹⁹You also offered them sweet and fragrant sacrifices. You gave flour, olive oil, and honey—all the food that I gave you to eat. This is what happened, declares the Almighty LORD.

²⁰" 'You took your sons and daughters, who belonged to me, and you sacrificed them as food to idols. Wasn't your prostitution enough? ²¹You slaughtered my children and presented them as burnt offerings to idols. ²²With all the disgusting things that you did and all your acts of prostitution, you didn't remember the time when you were young. You didn't remember when you were naked and bare, kicking around in your own blood.

²³" 'How horrible! How horrible it will be for you! declares the Almighty LORD. After all your wickedness, ²⁴you built yourself platforms and illegal worship sites in every city square. ²⁵You also built worship sites at the head of every street. You used your beauty to seduce people there. You offered your body to everyone who passed by. You increased your acts of prostitution. ²⁶You had sex with your lustful neighbors, the Egyptians. You used your prostitution to make me angry.

²⁷" 'So I used my power against you. I took away some of your land, and I handed you over to your greedy enemies, the Philistines, who were ashamed of what you had done.

²⁸" 'You had sex with the Assyrians because you weren't satisfied. You still weren't satisfied. ²⁹So you increased your acts of prostitution to include the land of the merchants, the Babylonians. Even after that, you weren't satisfied.

³⁰" 'You have no will power! declares the Almighty LORD. You do everything a shameless prostitute does. ³¹You build your platforms at the head of every street and place your illegal worship sites in every square. Yet, you aren't like other prostitutes, because you don't want to be paid. ³²You are an adulterous wife who prefers strangers to her husband. ³³All prostitutes get paid. But you give gifts to all your lovers and bribe them to come to you from all directions to have sex with you. ³⁴You are a different kind of prostitute. No one goes after you for favors. You are the opposite. You pay them, and you don't accept payment.

Jerusalem's Punishment

³⁵" 'Listen to the word of the LORD, you prostitute. ³⁶This is what the Almighty LORD says: You exposed yourself and uncovered your naked body when you gave yourself to your lovers and to all your disgusting idols. You also killed your children and sacrificed their blood to these idols. ³⁷That is why I will gather all your lovers with whom you found pleasure. I will have all those who love you and hate you gather around. I will uncover your body for them, and they will see you naked. ³⁸I will punish you the same way that those who are guilty of prostitution and murder are punished. I will give you the death penalty in my fury and burning anger. ³⁹I will hand you over to your lovers. They will destroy your platforms and tear down your illegal worship sites. They will tear off your clothes, take away your beautiful jewelry, and leave you naked and bare. ⁴⁰They will also bring a mob against you. They will stone you and cut you into pieces with their swords. ⁴¹They will burn your houses and punish you in the presence of many women. I will put an end to your prostitution, and you will no longer pay others. ⁴²Then I will rest from my fury against you, and I will stop being angry. I will be at peace. I will no longer be angry.

⁴³" 'You didn't remember the time when you were young, and you made me very angry with all these things. So I will pay you back for what you have done, declares the Almighty LORD. Didn't you make wicked plans in addition to all your disgusting practices?

⁴⁴" 'Everyone who uses proverbs will speak the following saying against you: Like

mother, like daughter. ⁴⁵You are your mother's daughter. She rejected her husband and her children. You are exactly like your sisters. They rejected their husbands and their children. Your mother was a Hittite, and your father was an Amorite.

⁴⁶" 'Your older sister was Samaria. She and her daughters lived north of you. Your younger sister is Sodom. She lives south of you with her daughters. ⁴⁷You didn't follow their ways. You didn't do the same disgusting things that they did. It only took you a little time to be more corrupt than they ever were. ⁴⁸As I live, declares the Almighty Lᴏʀᴅ, your sister Sodom and her daughters never did what you and your daughters have done. ⁴⁹This is what your sister Sodom has done wrong. She and her daughters were proud that they had plenty of food and had peace and security. They didn't help the poor and the needy. ⁵⁰They were arrogant and did disgusting things in front of me. So I did away with them when I saw this.

⁵¹" 'Samaria didn't commit half the sins you did. You have done many more disgusting things than they ever did. Because of all the disgusting things that you have done, you make your sisters look innocent. ⁵²You will have to suffer disgrace because you accused your sisters. Yet, your sins are more disgusting than theirs. They look like they are innocent compared to you. Be ashamed of yourself and suffer disgrace, because you have made your sisters look like they are innocent.

⁵³" 'I will restore the fortunes of Sodom and her daughters, and Samaria and her daughters. I will also restore your fortune along with theirs. ⁵⁴You will have to suffer disgrace and be ashamed of everything you have done, including comforting them. ⁵⁵When Sodom and her daughters and Samaria and her daughters return to what they once were, you and your daughters will return to what you once were. ⁵⁶You didn't mention your sister Sodom when you were arrogant. ⁵⁷You didn't mention her before your wickedness was revealed. Now the daughters of Aramᵃ and their neighbors despise you. The daughters of the Philistines also despise you. Those around you hate you. ⁵⁸You must suffer because of all the crude and disgusting things you have done, declares the Lᴏʀᴅ.

⁵⁹" 'This is what the Almighty Lᴏʀᴅ says: I will give you what you deserve. You despised your marriage vows and rejected my promise.ᵇ ⁶⁰I will remember the promise that I made with you when you were young, and I will make it a promise that will last forever. ⁶¹Then you will remember what you have done. You will be ashamed when I return your older and younger sisters to you. I will give them to you as daughters, but not because of my promise with you. ⁶²Then I will make my promise with you, and you will know that I am the Lᴏʀᴅ. ⁶³You will remember and be ashamed. You will never again open your mouth because of your disgrace when I forgive you for everything you did, declares the Almighty Lᴏʀᴅ.' "

Judah Is Compared to a Tree

17 ¹The Lᴏʀᴅ spoke his word to me. He said, ²"Son of man, tell this riddle. Give this illustration to the nation of Israel. ³Say, 'This is what the Almighty Lᴏʀᴅ says: A large eagle came to Lebanon. It had large wings with long, colorful feathers. It took hold of the top of a cedar tree. ⁴It broke off the highest twig and carried it to a country of merchants. It planted the twig in a city of merchants.

⁵" 'Then it took a seedling from that country and planted the seedling in fertile soil. The eagle planted the seedling like a willow where there was plenty of water. ⁶The plant sprouted and grew into a low vine that spread over the ground. Its branches turned upward toward the eagle, but its roots grew downward. So it became a vine, producing branches and growing shoots.

ᵃ16:57 Some Hebrew manuscripts; other Hebrew manuscripts, Syriac "Edom."   ᵇ16:59 Or "covenant."

⁷" 'There was another large eagle with large wings and many feathers. Now, the vine stretched its roots toward this eagle and sent its branches toward the eagle so that the eagle could water it. The vine turned away from the garden where it was planted. ⁸It was planted in good soil beside plenty of water so that it could grow branches, bear fruit, and become a wonderful vine.'

⁹"Tell the nation of Israel, 'This is what the Almighty Lord says: Will this vine live and grow? Won't the first eagle uproot it and tear off its fruit? Then it will wither. All the leaves on its branches will wither. It won't take much strength or many people to pull the vine up by its roots. ¹⁰It might be planted again, but will it live and grow? It will wither completely when the east wind blows on it. It will certainly wither in the garden where it is growing.' "

¹¹The Lord spoke his word to me. He said, ¹²"Ask these rebellious people, 'Don't you know what this means?' Tell them, 'The king of Babylon came to Jerusalem and captured its king and its leaders. He brought them home with him to Babylon. ¹³Then he took someone from the royal family, made a treaty with him, and made him promise to be loyal. He took away the leading citizens from Judah ¹⁴so that it would remain a humiliated country and be unable to regain its power. The country could only survive by keeping the treaty. ¹⁵But the king of Judah rebelled against the king of Babylon by sending his messengers to Egypt to get horses and many soldiers. Will the king of Judah succeed? Will anyone who does such things escape? He can't break a treaty and go unpunished.

¹⁶" 'As I live, declares the Almighty Lord, the king of Judah will die in Babylonia. He will die in the country of the king who appointed him king of Judah. The king of Judah broke his promise and his treaty with the king of Babylon. ¹⁷Even with a large army and many people, Pharaoh will not be able to help him in battle when the Babylonians put up dirt ramps and set up blockades to kill many people. ¹⁸The king of Judah broke the promise and the treaty that he pledged to keep. He did all these things, and he can't go unpunished.

¹⁹" 'So this is what the Almighty Lord says: As I live, I will certainly punish you for rejecting my promise and hating my treaty. ²⁰I will spread my net over you to catch you in my trap. I will take you to Babylon and judge you there for rebelling against me. ²¹The best of your troops will die in battle. Anyone who remains will be scattered in every direction that the wind blows. Then you will know that I, the Lord, have spoken.

²²" 'This is what the Almighty Lord says: I, too, will take hold of the top of a cedar tree. I will break off the highest twig and plant it on a high and lofty mountain. ²³I will plant it on a high mountain in Israel. It will grow branches and produce fruit. It will become a magnificent cedar tree. Every kind of bird will nest in it and find a home in the shelter of its branches. ²⁴Then all the trees in the field will know that I am the Lord. I cut down tall trees, and I make small trees grow tall. I dry up green trees, and I make dry trees grow. I, the Lord, have spoken, and I will do it.' "

Everyone Will Suffer for His Own Sins

18 ¹The Lord spoke his word to me. He said, ²"What do you mean when you use this proverb about the land of Israel: 'Fathers have eaten sour grapes, and their children's teeth are set on edge'? ³As I live, declares the Almighty Lord, you will no longer use this proverb in Israel. ⁴The life of every person belongs to me. Fathers and their children belong to me. The person who sins will die.

⁵"Suppose a righteous person does what is fair and right. ⁶He doesn't eat at the illegal mountain worship sites or look for help from the idols of the nation of Israel.

He doesn't dishonor his neighbor's wife or have sexual intercourse with a woman while she is having her period. ⁷He doesn't oppress anyone. He returns what a borrower gives him as security for a loan. He doesn't rob anyone. He gives food to people who are hungry, and he gives clothes to those who are naked. ⁸He doesn't lend money for interest or make an excessive profit. He refuses to do evil things, and he judges everyone fairly. ⁹He lives by my rules and obeys my laws faithfully. This person is righteous. He will certainly live," declares the Almighty LORD.

¹⁰"But suppose this person has a son who robs and murders. The son does all the things ¹¹that his father never did. He eats at the illegal mountain worship sites. He dishonors his neighbor's wife. ¹²He oppresses the poor and needy. He robs. He doesn't return the security for a loan. He looks to idols for help. He does disgusting things. ¹³He lends money for interest and makes excessive profits. Will this person live? He will not live. He has done all these disgusting things. So he must die, and he will be responsible for his own death.

¹⁴"But suppose this person has a son. The son sees all the sins that his father does. He is afraid, so he doesn't do such things.[a] ¹⁵He doesn't eat at the illegal mountain worship sites or look for help from the idols of the nation of Israel. He doesn't dishonor his neighbor's wife. ¹⁶He doesn't oppress anyone. He doesn't keep the security for a loan. He doesn't rob anyone. He gives food to people who are hungry, and he gives clothes to those who are naked. ¹⁷He refuses to hurt the poor. He doesn't charge interest or make excessive profits. He obeys my rules and lives by my laws. He won't die for his father's sins. He will certainly live. ¹⁸But his father has oppressed others, robbed his relative, and done what is wrong among his people. So the father will die because of his sin.

¹⁹"But you ask, 'Why isn't the son punished for his father's sin?' It is because the son has done what is fair and right. He obeyed my rules and followed them. He will certainly live. ²⁰The person who sins will die. A son will not be punished for his father's sins, and a father will not be punished for his son's sins. The righteousness of the righteous person will be his own, and the wickedness of the wicked person will be his own.

Forgiveness
Ezekiel 18:21-32

This chapter has a wonderful promise. You know that if you do right and love God, you will live with him. But this chapter promises that wicked people who turn away from their sins will also be forgiven by God. He doesn't want them to live without him. When you turn away from your sin, God will forgive you, too.

²¹"But suppose a wicked person turns away from all the sins that he has done. He obeys all my laws and does what is fair and right. He will certainly live. He will not die. ²²All the rebellious things that he did will not be remembered. He will live because

---

[a] 18:14 Many Hebrew manuscripts, Greek, Latin; other Hebrew manuscripts "Although he sees them, he doesn't do such things."

of the right things that he did. ²³I don't want wicked people to die." declares the Almighty LORD. "I want them to turn from their evil ways and live.

²⁴"But suppose a righteous person turns away from doing right and he does evil things. He does all the disgusting things that the wicked person did. Will he live? All the right things that he has done will not be remembered because of his unfaithfulness and because of his sin. He will die because of them.

²⁵"But you say, 'The Lord's way is unfair.' Listen, nation of Israel, isn't my way fair? Isn't it your ways that are unfair? ²⁶When a righteous person turns away from doing right and does evil things, he will die. He will die because of the evil things he has done. ²⁷When a wicked person turns away from the wicked things that he has done and does what is fair and right, he will live. ²⁸He realized what he was doing and turned away from all the rebellious things that he had done. He will certainly live. He will not die.

²⁹"But the nation of Israel says, 'The Lord's way is unfair.' Isn't my way fair, nation of Israel? Isn't it your ways that are unfair?

³⁰"That is why I will judge each of you by what you have done, people of Israel," declares the Almighty LORD. "Change the way you think and act. Turn away from all the rebellious things that you have done so that you will not fall into sin. ³¹Stop all the rebellious things that you are doing. Get yourselves new hearts and new spirits. Why do you want to die, nation of Israel? ³²I don't want anyone to die," declares the Almighty LORD. "Change the way you think and act!"

Funeral Songs for Israel's Princes

19 ¹Sing a funeral song for the princes of Israel. ²Say:

> Your mother was like a lioness.
>   She lay down among the lions.
>   She fed many cubs.
> ³ One of the cubs she raised became a young lion.
>   He learned to tear apart the animals he hunted.
>   He ate people.
> ⁴ The nations heard about him,
>   caught him in their pit,
>   and brought him with hooks to Egypt.
> ⁵ The lioness waited until she saw that there was no more hope.
>   Then she took another one of her cubs
>   and raised him into a young lion.
>
> ⁶ He became a young lion, and he prowled among the lions.
>   He learned to tear apart the animals he hunted.
>   He ate people.
> ⁷ He destroyed fortresses
>   and turned cities into wastelands.
>   The land and everyone living in it
>   were terrified by the sound of his roar.
> ⁸ The nations from every region came together against him.
>   They spread their net over him
>   and caught him in their pit.
> ⁹ With hooks they put him in a cage
>   and brought him to the king of Babylon.
>   They put him in prison

so that his roar wouldn't be heard anymore
    on the mountains of Israel.

¹⁰   Your mother was like a grapevine
        that was planted near water.
    It had a lot of fruit and many branches
        because there was plenty of water.
¹¹   Its branches were strong.
        They were used to make scepters for kings.
    It grew to be tall with many branches around it,
        and everyone saw it because of its many branches.
¹²   But in anger it was uprooted and thrown to the ground.
        The east wind dried up its fruit.
        Its strong branches broke off.
        They withered and were burned.
¹³   Now it is planted in the desert,
        in a dry and waterless land.
¹⁴   Fire has spread from the vine's main branch.
        Fire has destroyed its fruit.
    It no longer has any strong branches
        that could be used as a king's scepter.

This is a funeral song. It is to be used as a funeral song.

Israel's Past and Present Sins

20 ¹On the tenth day of the fifth month in the seventh year, some of the leaders of Israel came to ask for the Lord's help. They sat in front of me.

²Then the Lord spoke his word to me. He said, ³"Son of man, speak to the leaders of Israel. Tell them, 'This is what the Almighty Lord says: Are you coming to ask me for help? As I live, declares the Almighty Lord, you will not be allowed to ask me for help.'

⁴"Will you judge them? Will you judge them, son of man? Tell them about the disgusting things their ancestors did. ⁵Tell them, 'This is what the Almighty Lord says: When I chose Israel, I raised my hand and swore an oath to the descendants of Jacob's family. I made myself known to them in Egypt. I made a promise to them and said, "I am the Lord your God." ⁶At that time I promised to bring them out of Egypt to a land that I had chosen for them. This land is the most beautiful land, a land flowing with milk and honey. ⁷I said to them, "Get rid of the detestable idols that you look to for help. Don't dishonor yourselves with the disgusting idols of Egypt. I am the Lord your God."

⁸" 'But they rebelled against me and refused to listen to me. Not one of them got rid of the detestable idols that they looked to for help. They didn't abandon the disgusting idols of Egypt. So I was going to pour out my fury on them and unleash my anger on them in Egypt. ⁹But I acted so that my name would not be dishonored among the nations where they were living. While other nations were watching, I made myself known to them by bringing the Israelites out of Egypt.

¹⁰" 'So I brought the Israelites out of Egypt and led them into the desert. ¹¹I gave them my laws and made my rules known to them. If people obey them they will live. ¹²I also gave them certain days to worship me as a sign between us so that they would know that I, the Lord, made them holy.

¹³" 'But the people of Israel rebelled against me in the desert. They didn't live by

my laws, and they rejected my rules. If people obey them, they will live. They dishonored the days to worship me. So I was going to pour out my fury on them in the desert and completely wipe them out. ¹⁴But I acted so that my name would not be dishonored among the nations who had watched me bring the Israelites out of Egypt. ¹⁵I also swore an oath to them in the desert. I swore that I would not bring them into the land that I had promised to give them. This land is the most beautiful land, a land flowing with milk and honey. ¹⁶They rejected my rules, and they didn't live by my laws. They dishonored the days to worship me, because their hearts chased disgusting idols. ¹⁷But I had compassion on them. I didn't destroy them or completely wipe them out in the desert. ¹⁸I said to their children in the desert, "Don't live by the laws of your ancestors. Don't obey their rules or dishonor yourselves with their disgusting idols. ¹⁹I am the Lord your God. Live by my laws. Obey my rules and follow them. ²⁰Set apart certain holy days to worship me. This will be a sign between me and you so that you will know that I am the Lord your God."

²¹" 'But they rebelled against me. They didn't live by my laws, and they didn't obey my rules and follow them. If people obey them, they will live. They dishonored the days to worship me. So I was going to pour out my fury on them and unleash my anger on them in the desert. ²²But I didn't use my power so that my name would not be dishonored among the nations who had watched me bring the Israelites out of Egypt. ²³I raised my hand and swore an oath to them in the desert. I promised to scatter them among the nations and force them into other countries. ²⁴They didn't follow my rules, and they rejected my laws. They dishonored the days to worship me, and they looked to their ancestors' disgusting idols for help. ²⁵I also allowed them to follow laws that were no good and rules by which they could not live. ²⁶I let them dishonor themselves when they sacrificed all their firstborn sons as gifts to their false gods. I terrified them so that they would know that I am the Lord.'

²⁷"Speak to the nation of Israel, son of man. Tell them, 'This is what the Almighty Lord says: Your ancestors insulted me again because they were unfaithful to me. ²⁸I brought them to the land that I promised to give them. When they saw any high hill or any leafy tree, they made sacrifices and brought offerings there to make me angry. There they offered their sacrifices and poured out their wine offerings. ²⁹Then I asked them, "What is this worship site you're going to?' " (So it is still called 'worship site' today.)

³⁰"Tell the nation of Israel, 'This is what the Almighty Lord says: Will you dishonor yourselves the way your ancestors did? Will you chase their detestable idols like a prostitute? ³¹You offer your children as sacrifices by burning them alive. You dishonor yourselves with all your disgusting idols to this day. Should you be allowed to ask me for help, nation of Israel?

" 'As I live, declares the Almighty Lord, you won't be allowed to ask me for help. ³²What you have in mind will never happen. You think that you want to be like other nations, like the different people in other countries. You want to serve wood and stone.

³³" 'As I live, declares the Almighty Lord, I will rule you with a mighty hand and a powerful arm, and I will pour out my fury. ³⁴I will bring you out from the nations and gather you from the countries where I have scattered you with my mighty hand and powerful arm. I will pour out my fury. ³⁵I will bring you into the desert of the nations. There I will put you on trial face to face. ³⁶I will put you on trial as I put your ancestors on trial in the desert of Egypt, declares the Almighty Lord. ³⁷Then I will make you suffer punishment and make you keep the terms of the promise.ᵃ ³⁸I will get rid

---

ᵃ20:37 Or "covenant."

of rebels and those who do wrong against me. I will bring you out of the land where you are living. You will never enter Israel. Then you will know that I am the LORD.

Israel's Future

³⁹" 'Nation of Israel, this is what the Almighty LORD says: Serve your disgusting idols. But afterwards, you will listen to me. You will no longer dishonor my holy name with your gifts and your disgusting idols.

⁴⁰" 'The entire nation of Israel, everyone in the land, will worship me on my holy mountain, the high mountain of Israel, declares the Almighty LORD. There I will accept you. There I will look for your offerings, your best gifts, and all your holy gifts. ⁴¹When I bring you out from the nations and gather you from the countries where you have been scattered, I will accept you as if you were a pleasing sacrifice. Through you I will reveal myself as holy to the nations that are watching. ⁴²Then you will know that I am the LORD, because I will bring you to the land of Israel, the land that I promised to give your ancestors. ⁴³There you will remember the way you lived and everything you did to dishonor yourselves. You will be disgusted by every wrong thing that you did. ⁴⁴Then you will know that I am the LORD, because I will deal with you for the sake of my name. I will not deal with you based on the evil and corrupt things that you have done, nation of Israel, declares the Almighty LORD.' "ᵇ

The Burning Forest

⁴⁵The LORD spoke his word to me. He said, ⁴⁶"Son of man, turn to the south, preach against the south, and prophesy against the forest in the Negev. ⁴⁷Tell the forest in the Negev, 'Listen to the word of the LORD. This is what the Almighty LORD says: I am about to set fire to you to destroy all your green trees and all your dry trees. The blazing fire will not be put out. It will burn the whole land from the south to the north. ⁴⁸Then everyone will know that I, the LORD, started the fire. It will never beput out.' "

⁴⁹Then I said, "Oh no! Almighty LORD, no! The people already say that I'm only telling stories."

The Sword of the LORD

21 ᵃ¹The LORD spoke his word to me. He said, ²"Son of man, turn to Jerusalem, preach against the holy places. Prophesy against the land of Israel. ³Tell the land of Israel, 'This is what the LORD says: I am against you. I will take my sword out of its scabbard and kill the righteous people and the wicked people among you. ⁴I'm going to kill the righteous people and the wicked people among you. That is why my sword will come out of its scabbard to be used against everyone from the south to the north. ⁵Then everyone will know that I, the LORD, have taken my sword from its scabbard, and I will not put it back again.'

⁶"So, son of man, groan with a breaking heart and with bitter crying while the people watch you. ⁷When they ask you why you are groaning, say, 'News has come that will discourage everyone. People's hands will hang limp, their hearts will lose courage, and their knees will become as weak as water. It's coming! It will surely take place!' declares the Almighty LORD."

⁸The LORD spoke his word to me. He said, ⁹"Son of man, prophesy. Tell them, 'This is what the Lord says:

A sword, a sword is sharpened and polished,

10   It's sharpened to kill

ᵇ20:44 Ezekiel 20:45-49 in English Bibles is Ezekiel 21:1-5 in the Hebrew Bible.   ᵃ21:1 Ezekiel 21:1-32 in English Bibles is Ezekiel 21:6-37 in the Hebrew Bible.

and polished to flash like lightning.
How can we rejoice?
My son has refused to be disciplined or punished.[b]

11 The sword has been handed over to be polished,
to be placed in the hand.
The sword is being sharpened and polished
to be placed in the hands of killers.

12 " 'Cry and mourn, son of man,
because the sword will be used against my people
and against all the princes of Israel.
I will throw the princes and my people on the sword.
So beat your breast, and grieve.

13 Testing will surely come.
What if you refuse to be disciplined again?
Won't you be tested? declares the Almighty LORD.

14 So prophesy, son of man.
Clap your hands!
Let the sword strike again and again.
It's the sword for killing.
It's the sword for killing many people.
It's the sword that surrounds them.

15 I have appointed my sword to slaughter people at all their gates
so that their hearts will sink and many will die.
Yes! It's ready to flash like lightning.
It's polished to kill.

16 Sword, cut to the right.
Cut to the left
or wherever your blade is turned.

17 I will also clap my hands and rest from my fury.
I, the LORD, have spoken.' "

The Sword of the King of Babylon

18The LORD spoke his word to me. He said, 19"Son of man, mark two roads that the king of Babylon and his sword can take. Both of these roads should start from the same country. Make a sign, and put it where the roads start to fork toward the cities. 20Mark the road that the king and his sword can take to the Ammonite city of Rabbah, and mark the road that leads to Judah and the fortified city of Jerusalem. 21The king of Babylon will stop where the roads branch off, where there is a fork in the road. Then he will look for omens. He will shake some arrows, ask his household gods for help, and examine animal livers. 22The omens will indicate that he should go to the right, to Jerusalem. So he will set up his battering rams there, give the order to kill, raise a battle cry, aim the battering rams against the city gates, put up ramps, and set up blockades. 23The people won't believe this because they have made treaties with other nations. But the king of Babylon will remind them of their sins, and they will be captured.

24"This is what the Almighty LORD says: You make people remember how sinful you are because you openly do wrong. You show your sins in everything you do. So you will be taken captive.

---

[b]21:10 Hebrew meaning of this sentence uncertain.

²⁵"You dishonest and wicked prince of Israel, the time for your final punishment has come. ²⁶This is what the Almighty LORD says: Take off your turban and get rid of your crown. Things are going to change. Those who are unimportant will become important, and those who are important will become unimportant. ²⁷Ruins! Ruins! I will turn this place into ruins! It will not be restored until its rightful owner comes. Then I will give it to him.

²⁸"Son of man, prophesy. Tell them, 'This is what the Almighty LORD says about the Ammonites and their insults:

A sword, a sword is drawn ready to kill.
   It's polished to destroy and flash like lightning.
²⁹ People see false visions about you
   and prophesy lies about you.
The sword will be placed on the necks of dishonest, wicked people,
   for whom the time of final punishment has come.

³⁰ " 'Return your sword to its scabbard.
   In the place where you were created,
      in the land where you were born,
         there I will judge you.
³¹ I will pour out my fury on you
   and breathe on you with my fiery anger.
I will hand you over to cruel people who are skilled in destruction.
³² You will be fuel for the fire.
   You will die in the land.
      You will no longer be remembered.
I, the LORD, have spoken.' "

Jerusalem Is Judged Because of Its Murderous History

22 ¹The LORD spoke his word to me. He said, ²"Will you judge, son of man? Will you judge the city of murderers? Then tell it about all the disgusting things that it has done. ³Tell it, 'This is what the Almighty LORD says: Jerusalem, you are the city that murders people who live in you. Your time has come. You dishonor yourself with disgusting idols. ⁴You are guilty because of the people you have killed. You are dishonored because of the disgusting idols you have made. You have brought an end to your days, and you have come to the end of your years. That is why I will make you a disgrace to the nations and a joke in every land. ⁵Those near and those far away will mock you. Your name will be dishonored, and you will be filled with confusion.

⁶" 'See how all the princes of Israel who live in you have used their power to murder people. ⁷People in you hate their fathers and mothers. They oppress foreigners in you. They oppress orphans and widows in you. ⁸You have despised my holy things and dishonored the day to worship me. ⁹Some of your people slander. They want to kill people. People who live in you eat food sacrificed to idols at the worship sites on the hills, and they sin sexually. ¹⁰Men have sex with their father's wives. They have sex with women when the women are having their periods and are unclean.ᵃ ¹¹Men do disgusting things with their neighbors' wives. Some men sexually dishonor their daughters-in-law. Other men who live in you have sex with their sisters, their father's daughters. ¹²Other people take bribes to murder people. You collect interest and make excessive profits. You make profits by mistreating your neighbors. You have forgotten me, declares the Almighty LORD.

ᵃ22:10 "Unclean" refers to anything that Moses' Teachings say is not presentable to God.

¹³" 'I will use my power against you because of the excessive profits you have made and the murders you have committed. ¹⁴Will you still be brave? Will you remain strong when I deal with you? I, the LORD, have spoken, and I will do it. ¹⁵I will scatter you among the nations and force you into other countries. I will put an end to your uncleanness. ¹⁶You will be dishonored in the sight of the nations. Then you will know that I am the LORD.' "

¹⁷Then the LORD spoke his word to me. He said, ¹⁸"Son of man, the people of Israel have become worthless to me. All of them are like copper, tin, iron, and lead in a smelting furnace. They are like the impurities left from silver. ¹⁹This is what the Almighty LORD says: All of you have become worthless. That is why I'm going to gather you in Jerusalem. ²⁰People gather silver, copper, iron, lead, and tin together in a smelting furnace to melt them with a fiery blast. In the same way, in my anger and fury I will gather you and put you in the city. I will melt you there. ²¹Yes, I will gather you, breathe on you with my fiery anger, and melt you in the city. ²²You will be melted in the city like silver that is melted in a furnace. Then you will know that I, the LORD, have poured out my fury on you."

²³The LORD spoke his word to me. He said, ²⁴"Son of man, tell the city, 'You are an unclean land that has not had rain during the day of my anger. You have not been made clean.'ᵇ ²⁵Your princes are like roaring lions who tear their prey into pieces. They eat people and take their treasures and precious belongings. They turn many women into widows. ²⁶Your priests violate my teachings and dishonor my holy things. They don't distinguish between what is holy and what is unholy. They don't teach the difference between what is clean and what is unclean. They ignore the days to worship me. So I am dishonored among the people. ²⁷Your leaders are like wolves that tear their prey into pieces. They murder and destroy people to make excessive profits. ²⁸Your prophets cover up these things by seeing false visions and by prophesying lies. They say, "This is what the Almighty LORD says." Yet, the LORD hasn't spoken. ²⁹The common people oppress and rob others. They do wrong to humble people and to poor people. They oppress foreigners for no reason.

³⁰" 'I looked for someone among you who could build walls or stand in front of me by the gaps in the walls to defend the land and keep it from being destroyed. But I couldn't find anyone. ³¹So I will pour out my anger on you, and with my fiery anger I will consume you. This is because of all the things you have done,' " declares the Almighty LORD.

Samaria and Jerusalem Acted Like Prostitutes

²³ ¹The LORD spoke his word to me. He said, ²"Son of man, there were once two women, daughters of the same mother. ³They became prostitutes in Egypt when they were young. There men fondled and caressed their breasts.

⁴"The older girl was named Oholah, and the younger girl was named Oholibah. I married them, and they gave birth to sons and daughters. Oholah represents Samaria, and Oholibah represents Jerusalem. ⁵Oholah acted like a prostitute, although she was my wife. She lusted after her Assyrian lovers who lived nearby. ⁶They were governors and commanders clothed in purple. They were all handsome young men who rode on horses. ⁷She became a prostitute for all the important men in Assyria. She dishonored herself with the idols of all those with whom she fell in love. ⁸She continued the prostitution that she started in Egypt. When she was young, men went to bed with her, caressed her breasts, and treated her like a prostitute.

ᵇ22:24 "Clean" refers to anything that Moses' Teachings say is presentable to God.

⁹"That is why I handed her over to her lovers, to the Assyrians whom she lusted after. ¹⁰They stripped her naked, took away her sons and daughters, and killed her with a sword. Women gossiped about how she was punished.

¹¹"Even though her younger sister Oholibah saw this, Oholibah lusted after men more than her sister did. Oholibah's prostitution became worse than her sister's prostitution. ¹²She lusted after the Assyrians who were nearby. They were governors and commanders in full dress. They were mounted horsemen, all of them desirable young men. ¹³I saw that she was dishonoring herself. Both sisters acted the same way. ¹⁴Yet, she carried her prostitution even further. She saw pictures of men carved on walls. They were figures of Babylonian men, painted in bright red. ¹⁵The men had belts around their waists and flowing turbans on their heads. All of them looked like Babylonian officers who were born in Babylon. ¹⁶She fell in love with them at first sight and sent messengers to them in Babylonia. ¹⁷So these men came from Babylon, went to bed with her, and dishonored her with their lust. After they had dishonored her, she turned away from them in disgust.

¹⁸"She carried out her prostitution openly, and she lay around naked. I turned away from her in disgust as I had turned away from her sister. ¹⁹She remembered how she had been a prostitute in Egypt when she was young. So she took part in even more prostitution. ²⁰She lusted after her lovers, whose genitals were like those of donkeys and whose semen was like that of horses. ²¹So she longed to do the sinful things she did when she was young in Egypt, when young men caressed and fondled her breasts.

²²"Oholibah, this is what the Almighty Lᴏʀᴅ says: I'm going to stir up your lovers against you. They are the lovers you turned away from in disgust. I will bring them against you from every side. ²³I will bring men from Babylon and from all Babylonia, men from Pekod, Shoa, and Koa, as well as all the Assyrians. They are desirable young men, governors and commanders, military officers and important men. All of them ride on horses. ²⁴They will attack you from the north,ᵃ with chariots and wagons and with a large number of troops. They will attack you from all around with small and large shields and with helmets. I have handed you over to them for punishment. They will punish you with their own kind of punishment. ²⁵I will direct my burning anger against you so that they will deal with you in anger. They will cut off your nose and ears and kill everyone who remains. They will take your sons and your daughters and burn down whatever is left. ²⁶They will rip off your clothes and take away your beautiful jewels. ²⁷I will put a stop to your sinning and to your prostitution, which you began in Egypt. You won't desire these things anymore or remember Egypt anymore.

²⁸"This is what the Almighty Lᴏʀᴅ says: I'm going to hand you over to those you hate and to those you turned away from in disgust. ²⁹They will treat you hatefully and take away everything that you have worked for. They will leave you naked and bare. The shame of your prostitution will be revealed. ³⁰Your sinning and your prostitution have done this to you, because you lusted after the nations and dishonored yourself with their idols. ³¹You've acted the same way as your sister. That is why I will put her cup in your hand. ³²This is what the Almighty Lᴏʀᴅ says:

> You will drink from your sister's cup,
>> a cup that is deep and wide.
> You will be scorned and mocked,
>> because this cup holds so much.
³³   The cup of your sister Samaria will be filled

---

with drunkenness and sorrow.
³⁴ You will drink from it and drain it.
You will break it into pieces
and tear your breasts off your body.
I have spoken, declares the Almighty Lord.

³⁵"This is what the Almighty Lord says: You have forgotten me and turned your back on me. So you will be punished for your sinning and prostitution."

³⁶The Lord said to me, "Son of man, will you judge Oholah and Oholibah and tell them about their disgusting practices? ³⁷They have committed adultery. Their hands are covered with blood. They commit adultery with their idols. They have sacrificed the children they gave birth to for me as burnt offerings to idols. ³⁸They have also done this to me: They have polluted my holy places when they do these things and dishonored the days to worship me. ³⁹When they sacrificed their children to their idols, they came into my holy place and dishonored it. That is what they've done in my temple.

⁴⁰"They even sent messengers to invite men to come from far away. When the men arrived, they washed themselves for the men, painted their eyes, and put on their jewels. ⁴¹They sat on their fine couches with tables in front of them. They put my incense and my olive oil on their tables.

⁴²"I heard the noise from a carefree crowd. A large number of people came from the desert, and they put bracelets on the women's wrists and beautiful crowns on their heads. ⁴³Then I said, 'She is worn out from her acts of adultery.' Yet, men continued to have sex with her. ⁴⁴Men slept with her. They slept with those sinful women, Oholah and Oholibah, just as they slept with a prostitute. ⁴⁵Righteous people will punish these women for adultery and for murder, because these women have committed adultery and their hands are covered with blood.

⁴⁶"This is what the Almighty Lord says: Bring together a mob against the people of Samaria and Jerusalem. Hand them over to terror and looting. ⁴⁷Then the mob will stone them and kill them with swords. The mob will kill their sons and daughters and burn their homes. ⁴⁸So I will put a stop to the sinning in the land, and all the women will be warned not to sin as they do. ⁴⁹They will be punished for their sins, and they will pay for their sin of idolatry. Then they will know that I am the Almighty Lord."

Judah Is Compared to a Boiling Pot

24 ¹On the tenth day of the tenth month in the ninth year, the Lord spoke his word to me. He said, ²"Son of man, write down today's date. The king of Babylon has surrounded Jerusalem this very day. ³Tell these rebellious people a story. Tell them, 'This is what the Almighty Lord says:

Put the pot on the fire; put it on.
Pour water in it.
⁴   Cut the meat into pieces,
all the best pieces, the thigh and shoulder.
Fill the pot with the meatiest bones
⁵   selected from the best sheep.
Pile wood under the pot.
Bring the mixture in the pot to a boil.
Cook the bones that are in it well.

⁶" 'This is what the Almighty Lord says:

> How horrible it will be for that city of murderers,
>> for that tarnished pot.
>> Its tarnish will not come off.
> Empty the meat out of it piece by piece
>> without choosing any particular piece.

7 Blood is still in that city.
>> The blood was poured on a bare rock.
>> It wasn't poured on the ground where dust would cover it.

8 In order to stir up my fury so that I would pay that city back,
>> I put the blood of its victims on a bare rock.
>> Now that blood can't be covered.

9" 'This is what the Almighty LORD says:

> How horrible it will be for that city of murderers.
>> I, too, will pile the wood high.

10 Pile it high, and light the fire.
> Cook the meat thoroughly, stir the mixture,
>> and let the bones burn.

11 Then set the empty pot on the coals
>> so that it gets hot and its copper glows.
>> Its impurities will melt away,
>> and its tarnish will burn off.

12 'I have worn myself out trying to clean this pot. Even the fire can't take away its thick tarnish. 13I tried to clean you of your filthy lust, but you wouldn't clean yourself from your filth. You will never be clean until I unleash my fury on you. 14I, the LORD, have spoken. It will happen, and I will do it. I will not ignore you, pity you, or change my plans. I will punish you because of the way you lived and because of everything you have done,' " declares the Almighty LORD.

Ezekiel's Silent Sorrow Over the Destruction of Jerusalem

15Then the LORD spoke his word to me. He said, 16"Son of man, with one blow I'm going to take away from you the person you love the most. But you must not mourn, cry, or let tears run down your face. 17Groan silently. Don't grieve for the person who dies. Tie on your turban, and put on your sandals. Don't cover your face or eat the food that mourners eat."

18So I spoke to the people in the morning, and in the evening my wife died. The next morning I did as I was ordered.

19The people asked me, "Tell us, what do these things that you are doing mean to us?"

20I told them, "The LORD spoke his word to me. He said, 21"Tell the nation of Israel, "This is what the Almighty LORD says: I'm going to dishonor my holy place. You brag that my holy place gives you strength. It's the thing you love the most. It's your hearts' desire. So the sons and daughters that you left behind will die in battle. 22Then you must do as I did. Don't cover your faces or eat the food that mourners eat. 23Leave your turbans on your heads and your sandals on your feet. Don't grieve or cry! You will waste away because of your guilt and groan to one another. 24Ezekiel is a sign to you. You will do everything he has done. Then you will know that I am the Almighty LORD." '

25"Son of man, on that day I will take their stronghold away from them. It makes them happy and proud. It is their hearts' desire and the thing they love the most. I will also take away their sons and daughters. ²⁶On that day a refugee will come to you to tell you the news. ²⁷On that very day your mouth will be opened, and you will talk to the refugee. You will speak and not be silent anymore. You will be a sign to them. Then they will know that I am the Lord."

Judgment on Ammon

¹The Lord spoke his word to me. He said, ²"Son of man, turn to the Ammonites and prophesy against them. ³Tell the Ammonites, 'Listen to the word of the Almighty Lord. This is what the Almighty Lord says: You were glad when my holy place was dishonored, when the land of Israel was ruined, and when the nation of Judah went into exile. ⁴That is why I'm going to hand you over to the people in the east. They will possess your land. They will set up their camps and pitch their tents among you. They will eat your crops and drink your milk. ⁵I will turn Rabbah into a pasture for camels, and I will turn Ammon into a resting place for sheep. Then you will know that I am the Lord.

⁶" 'This is what the Almighty Lord says: You clapped your hands and stomped your feet. You rejoiced and felt contempt for the land of Israel. ⁷That is why I will use my power against you and hand you over to the nations as loot. I will wipe you out from among the nations, make you disappear, and destroy you. Then you will know that I am the Lord.

Judgment on Moab

⁸" 'This is what the Almighty Lord says: Moab and Seir said, "The nation of Judah is like all the other nations." ⁹That is why I'm going to open up the cities that protect Moab's borders. They are the beautiful cities of Beth Jeshimoth, Baal Meon, and Kiriathaim. ¹⁰I will hand the Moabites and the Ammonites over to the people in the east. So the Ammonites will no longer be remembered among the nations. ¹¹I will punish Moab. Then they will know that I am the Lord.

Judgment on Edom

¹²" 'This is what the Almighty Lord says: Edom took revenge on the nation of Judah and became guilty because of it. ¹³So this is what the Almighty Lord says: I will use my power against Edom. I will wipe out people and animals. I will turn the land into ruins from Teman to Dedan. People will die in battle. ¹⁴I will use my people Israel to take revenge on Edom. My people will deal with Edom based on my anger and my fury. Then the Edomites will know my revenge, declares the Almighty Lord.

Judgment on the Philistines

¹⁵" 'This is what the Almighty Lord says: The Philistines have taken revenge with spiteful hearts. They have tried to destroy their long-time enemies. ¹⁶So this is what the Almighty Lord says: I'm going to use my power against the Philistines, cut off the Cherethites, and destroy the people that are left on the coast. ¹⁷I will take fierce revenge on them and punish them with fury. I will take revenge on them. Then they will know that I am the Lord.' "

Judgment on Tyre

¹On the first day of the month in the eleventh year, the Lord spoke his word to me. He said, ²"Son of man, Tyre said this about Jerusalem: 'The city that was the gateway for the nations is destroyed, and its doors are swung open to me. I'll

get rich now that it's ruined.' ³So this is what the Almighty LORD says: I am against you, Tyre. I will bring many nations against you as the waves on the sea rise. ⁴They will destroy the walls of Tyre and tear down its towers. Then I will sweep up the dust and turn Tyre into a bare rock. ⁵It will become a place by the sea where people spread their fishing nets. I have spoken, declares the Almighty LORD. It will become a prize for the nations. ⁶The people in the villages and on the mainland will die in battle. Then they will know that I am the LORD.

⁷"This is what the Almighty LORD says: From the north I'm going to bring King Nebuchadnezzar of Babylon against you, Tyre. He is the greatest king. He will bring horses, chariots, war horses, many people, and many troops. ⁸He will destroy the villages on your mainland. He will set up blockades, put up dirt ramps, and raise his shields against you. ⁹He will direct his battering rams against your walls, and he will cut down your towers with his axes. ¹⁰He will have so many horses that their dust will cover you. The noise from the war horses, wagon wheels, and chariots will shake your walls when he enters your gates. He will enter as people enter a conquered city. ¹¹With his horses' hoofs he will trample all your streets. He will kill your people in battle, and your strong pillars will fall to the ground. ¹²His troops will loot your riches and take your goods as prizes. They will destroy your walls and tear down your delightful homes. They will throw your stones, wood, and soil into the water.

¹³"I will put a stop to your noisy songs, and the music from your harps will no longer be heard. ¹⁴I will turn you into bare rock. You will become a place to spread fishing nets. You will never be rebuilt. I, the LORD, have spoken, declares the Almighty LORD.

¹⁵"This is what the Almighty LORD says to Tyre: The people who live on the coast will shake with fear when they hear about your defeat. They will groan when your people are wounded and slaughtered. ¹⁶Then the princes from the coast will come down from their thrones. They will remove their robes and take off their embroidered clothes. Dressed in terror, they will sit on the ground. They will tremble constantly and be shocked at you. ¹⁷Then they will sing this funeral song for you:

> Tyre, you famous city, you have been destroyed.
>   You have been shattered by the sea.
>   You and your people ruled the sea.
>   All your people terrified those who lived by the coast.
> ¹⁸   Your defeat will make the people who live by the coast tremble.
>   Your end will terrify the islands in the sea.

¹⁹"This is what the Almighty LORD says: I will turn your city into ruins like cities that have no one living in them. I will bring the deep ocean over you, and the Mediterranean Sea will cover you. ²⁰I will bring you down with those who descend to the grave to join the people of long ago. I will make you live below the earth among the ancient ruins with those who go down to the grave. You will never return or take your place in the land of the living. ²¹I will turn you into a terror, and you will no longer exist. People will look for you, but they will never see you again," declares the Almighty LORD.

A Funeral Song About Tyre

27 ¹The LORD spoke his word to me. He said, ²"Son of man, sing a funeral song about Tyre. ³Tyre is the city at the entrance to the sea. It is the merchant to the nations. Say to Tyre, 'This is what the Almighty LORD says:

> Tyre, you used to brag about your perfect beauty.
> ⁴   Your home is the sea.

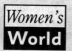

Dye / Ezekiel 27:16, 24

People in Bible times liked colorful clothing. Wool and linen threads were dyed a variety of colors. Red dye came from insects or roots, yellow and orange from various plants. Purple was the most expensive color to make because more than 10,000 Murex shellfish had to be collected by divers; the shellfish were then crushed and boiled in salt water to make less than an ounce of purple dye!

A successful businesswoman named Lydia, who sold purple dye, lived at Philippi. She became the first Christian convert in Europe and was friends with Paul, Silas, and Luke (Acts 16).

" 'Your builders made your beauty perfect.

5 Your builders made all your boards from pine trees on Mount Hermon.
 They took cedar trees from Lebanon to make a mast for you.
6 They made your oars from oaks in Bashan.
 They made your deck from pine trees on the shores of Cyprus.
  It had ivory set in it.
7 Your sails were made out of fine embroidered linen from Egypt.
 They were like your flags.
 Your awnings were violet and purple.
 They came from the coasts of Elishah.

8 " 'People from Sidon and Arvad used to row you.
 Your own skilled people were your sailors.
9 Master shipbuilders from Gebal went inside you to caulk your seams.
 All the ships on the sea and their sailors
  docked alongside you to trade with you.
10 People from Persia, Lud, and Put were soldiers in your army.
 They hung their shields and helmets inside you.
  Their victories made you look good.

11 " 'People from Arvad and Helech*were guards all around your walls. People from Gammad guarded your towers. They hung their shields all around your walls, making your beauty perfect.

12 " 'People from Tarshish traded with you because you were so very rich. They

*27:11 Or "Celicia."

exchanged silver, iron, tin, and lead for your merchandise. ¹³People from Greece, Tubal, and Meshech traded with you. They exchanged slaves and bronze items for your goods. ¹⁴People from Beth Togarmah exchanged horses, war horses, and mules for your merchandise. ¹⁵People from Dedan traded goods with you. You traded with many people on the coasts, and they brought you ivory and ebony as payment.

¹⁶" 'People from Syria traded with you because you had so many products. They exchanged emeralds, purple cloth, richly woven cloth, linen, coral, and rubies for your merchandise. ¹⁷Judah and Israel traded with you. They exchanged wheat from Minnith, baked goods, honey, olive oil, and balsam for your goods. ¹⁸People from Damascus traded with you because you had so many products. They exchanged wine from Helbon and wool from Sahar.

¹⁹" 'Danites and Greeks from Uzal traded for your merchandise. They exchanged wrought iron, cassia, and sugar cane for your goods. ²⁰Dedan traded saddle blankets with you. ²¹Arabia and all the officials of Kedar traded with you. They traded lambs, rams, and male goats. ²²The merchants from Sheba and Raamah traded with you. They traded the finest spices, precious stones, and gold for your merchandise. ²³Haran, Canneh, Eden, the merchants from Sheba, Assyria, and Kilmad traded with you. ²⁴In your marketplace they traded for beautiful clothes, purple robes, embroidered cloth, and many multicolored rugs with woven and twisted cords.

25   " 'Ships from Tarshish carried your goods.
       You were like a ship filled with heavy cargo in the sea.
26   Your rowers took you out to the high seas,
       and an east wind wrecked you in the sea.
27   Your wealth, your merchandise, and the goods you sell,
       your mariners and your sailors,
       your caulkers and your merchants,
       your soldiers and everyone else on board
         sank into the sea when your ship was wrecked.

28   " 'When your sailors cried out, people on the shore trembled.
29   All the rowers, the sailors,
       and all the mariners came down from their ships
         and stood on the shore.
30   They cried loudly and bitterly over you.
       They put dust on their heads and covered themselves with ashes.
31   They shaved their heads because of you and put on sackcloth.
       They cried over you with bitterness and with bitter mourning.
32   They sang a funeral song for you with loud crying:
       "Who is like Tyre, the city destroyed in the sea?"
33   Your merchandise was sent overseas.
       You filled many people with your great wealth and your goods.
       You made the kings of the earth rich.
34   Now you are wrecked in the sea, at the bottom of the sea.
       Your goods and your whole crew sank with you.
35   All those who live on the coasts are horrified because of you.
       Their kings are terribly afraid.
       Their faces show their fear.
36   The merchants among the nations laugh at you.
         You have come to a terrible end,
           and you will never exist again.' "

Judgment on the King of Tyre

28 ¹The LORD spoke his word to me. He said, ²"Son of man, tell the ruler of Tyre, 'This is what the Almighty LORD says:

In your arrogance you say,
　"I'm a god. I sit on God's throne in the sea."
　　But you're only human and not a god,
　　　although you think you are a god.
³　You think that you are wiser than Daniel
　　and that no secret can be hidden from you.
⁴　Because you are wise and understanding,
　　you've made yourself rich.
　　　You saved gold and silver in your treasuries.
⁵　Because of your great skill in trading,
　　you've made yourself very wealthy.
　　　You have become arrogant because of your wealth.

⁶" 'This is what the Almighty LORD says:

You think you are wise like God.
⁷　That is why I am going to bring foreigners against you,
　　the most ruthless foreigners among the nations.
　　They will draw their swords against your fine wisdom
　　　and dishonor your greatness.
⁸　They will throw you into a pit,
　　and you will die a violent death in the sea.
⁹　You will no longer say that you are a god
　　when you face those who kill you.
　　You will be a human, not a god, in the hands of those who kill you.
¹⁰　You will die at the hands of foreigners like a godless person.
　　I have spoken,' " declares the LORD.

¹¹The LORD spoke his word to me. He said, ¹²"Son of man, sing a funeral song for the ruler of Tyre. Tell him, 'This is what the Almighty LORD says:

You were the perfect example,
　　full of wisdom and perfect in beauty.
¹³　You were in Eden, God's garden.
　　You were covered with every kind of precious stone:

Good Morning, God
Ezekiel 28:14

We can learn many things about angels from the Bible. Angels often carry messages from God. They also fight against evil forces and help protect us. God appointed an angel to guard the King of Tyre. Thank God that he uses his angels to protect you and your family.

Thank you, God, for surrounding my family and me with your angels.

> red quartz, topaz, crystal,
> beryl, onyx, gray quartz, sapphire,
> turquoise, and emerald.
> Your settings and your sockets
> were made of gold when you were created.

14   I appointed an angel[a] to guard you.
> You were on God's holy mountain.
> You walked among fiery stones.

15   Your behavior was perfect from the time you were created,
> until evil was found in you.

16   You traded far and wide. You learned to be violent, and you sinned.
> So I threw you down from God's mountain in disgrace.
> The guardian angel forced you out from the fiery stones.

17   You became too proud because of your beauty.
> You wasted your wisdom because of your greatness.
> So I threw you to the ground
> and left you in front of the kings
> so that they could see you.

18   You dishonored your own holy places
> because of your many sins and dishonest trade.
> So I set fire to you to burn you up.
> I turned you into ashes on the ground
> in the presence of all who saw you.

19   All the nations who knew you are horrified because of you.
> You have come to a terrible end,
> and you will never exist again.' "

Judgment on Sidon Means Hope for Israel

20The Lord spoke his word to me. He said, 21"Son of man, turn to Sidon and prophesy against it. 22Tell it, 'This is what the Almighty Lord says:

> I'm against you, Sidon.
> I will show my greatness through you.
> Then people will know that I am the Lord,
> because I will punish you and show you how holy I am.

23   I will send a plague against you
> and make blood flow in your streets.
> Your people will fall dead.
> People with swords will attack you from every side.
> Then they will know that I am the Lord.

24   The nation of Israel will no longer be hurt
> by prickly thorns or sharp briars from everyone around them.
> Then they will know that I am the Almighty Lord.

25" 'This is what the Almighty Lord says: When I gather the people of Israel from the nations where they were scattered, I will show that I am holy as the nations watch. The people of Israel will live in their own land, the land I gave to my servant Jacob. 26They will live there in safety. They will build homes and plant vineyards. They will live in safety when I punish all the surrounding people who treat them with scorn. Then they will know that I am the Lord their God.' "

---

a 28:14 Or "one of the cherubim."

Judgment on Egypt

29 [1]On the twelfth day of the tenth month in the tenth year, the LORD spoke his word to me. He said, [2]"Son of man, turn to Pharaoh, king of Egypt, and prophesy against him and against all Egypt. [3]Tell him, 'This is what the Almighty LORD says:

I'm against you, Pharaoh, king of Egypt.
You are like a monster crocodile lying in the Nile River.
You say, "The Nile River is mine. I made it for myself."

[4]   " 'I will put hooks in your jaws
        and make the fish in the Nile River stick to your scales.
     I will pull you out of your river
        with all the fish in the Nile sticking to your scales.
[5]   I will leave you in the desert, you and all the fish from the Nile.
     You will fall in an open field.
        No one will pick you up or bury you.
     I will feed you to wild animals and birds.
[6]   Then all those living in Egypt will know that I am the LORD.
     Egypt, you have become like a ˌbrokenˌ walking stick
        to the nation of Israel.
[7]   When Israel grabbed you, you splintered and tore up their shoulders.
     When they leaned on you, you broke, and they wrenched their backs.

[8]" 'This is what the Almighty LORD says: I am going to attack you with a sword. I will kill people and animals. [9]Egypt will become a wasteland and a pile of rubble. Then you will know that I am the LORD. You said, "The Nile River is mine. I made it." [10]That is why I'm against you and the Nile River. I will turn Egypt into a pile of rubble. It will become a wasteland, from Migdol to Syene, all the way to the border of Sudan. [11]No human or animal will walk through it, and no one will live there for 40 years. [12]I will make Egypt the most desolate country in the world. For 40 years Egypt's cities will lie in ruins. They will be ruined more than any other city. I will scatter the Egyptians among the nations and force them into other countries.

[13]" 'This is what the Almighty LORD says: After 40 years I will gather the Egyptians from the nations where they have been scattered. [14]I will bring back the Egyptian captives and return them to Pathros,ª the land they came from. There they will be a weak kingdom. [15]They will be the weakest kingdom, and they will never rule the nations again. I will make them so weak that they will never rule the nations again. [16]The nation of Israel will never trust Egypt again. The people of Israel will remember how wrong they were whenever they turned to Egypt ˌfor helpˌ. Then they will know that I am the Almighty LORD.' "

[17]On the first day of the first month in the twenty-seventh year, the LORD spoke his word to me. He said, [18]"Son of man, King Nebuchadnezzar of Babylon made his army fight hard against Tyre. Every soldier's head was worn bald, and every soldier's shoulder was rubbed raw. Yet, he and his army got no reward for their hard-fought battle against Tyre. [19]This is what the Almighty LORD says: I'm going to give Egypt to King Nebuchadnezzar of Babylon. He will carry off its wealth, take its prized possessions, and loot it. That will be the pay for his army. [20]I have given him Egypt as pay for what he has done. Nebuchadnezzar and his army worked for me, declares the Almighty LORD.

ª29:14 Or "southern Egypt."

²¹"On that day I will make the people of Israel strong again, and I will give you, Ezekiel, something to say among them. Then they will know that I am the Lord."

Nebuchadnezzar Will Conquer Egypt

30 ¹The Lord spoke his word to me. He said, ²"Son of man, prophesy. Say, 'This is what the Almighty Lord says:

Cry for that day!
3   The day is near. The day of the Lord is near.
     It will be a gloomy day, a time of trouble for the nations.
4   There will be war in Egypt and anguish in Ethiopia.
     Many Egyptians will fall dead.
     People will take away Egypt's wealth,
         and its foundations will be torn down.
5   Sudan, Put, Lud, all the Arabs, the Libyans,
         and people from the promised land will die in battle.

⁶" 'This is what the Lord says:

All Egypt's allies will die.
     Egypt's strength will disappear.
         People will die in war from Migdol to Syene,
             declares the Almighty Lord.

⁷" 'Egypt will become the most desolate country in the world, and Egypt's cities will lie in ruins. They will be ruined more than other cities. ⁸Then they will know that I am the Lord, because I will set fire to Egypt and all her defenders will be killed. ⁹On that day I will send messengers in ships to terrify those who live in safety in Sudan. The people of Sudan will be in anguish when Egypt is in trouble. That day is coming!

¹⁰" 'This is what the Almighty Lord says: I will use King Nebuchadnezzar of Babylon to bring an end to Egypt. ¹¹He and his troops, the most ruthless troops among the nations, will be brought to destroy the land. They will draw their swords to attack Egypt and fill the land with dead bodies. ¹²I will dry up the Nile River and sell the land to wicked people. I will have foreigners destroy the land and everything in it. I, the Lord, have spoken.

¹³" 'This is what the Almighty Lord says: I will destroy the statues and put an end to the idols in Memphis. A prince will never rise again in Egypt. I will spread fear throughout Egypt. ¹⁴I will destroy Pathros, set fire to Zoan, and bring punishment on Thebes. ¹⁵I will pour out my fury on Sin, Egypt's fortress, and I will kill many people in Thebes. ¹⁶I will set fire to Egypt. Sin will be in much pain. Thebes will be broken into pieces, and Memphis will be in trouble every day. ¹⁷The young men from Heliopolis and Bubastis will die in battle, and people from these cities will go into exile. ¹⁸At Tahpanhes the day will turn dark when I break Egypt's power. Egypt's strong army will be defeated. Clouds will cover Egypt, and people from its villages will go into exile. ¹⁹Then they will know that I am the Lord, because I will bring punishment on Egypt.' "

²⁰On the seventh day of the first month in the eleventh year, the Lord spoke his word to me. He said, ²¹"Son of man, I have broken the arm of Pharaoh, king of Egypt. His arm isn't bandaged, so it can't heal and be strong enough to hold a sword.

²²"This is what the Almighty Lord says: I'm against Pharaoh, king of Egypt. I will break both his arms, the healthy one and the broken one. I will make the sword fall

from his hand. ²³I will scatter the Egyptians among the nations and force them into other countries. ²⁴I will make the arms of the king of Babylon strong. I will put my sword in his hand, but I will break Pharaoh's arms. Pharaoh will groan like a person who is dying. ²⁵I will strengthen the arms of the king of Babylon, but Pharaoh's arms will fall. Then they will know that I am the LORD, because I will put my sword in the hand of the king of Babylon. He will strike Egypt with it. ²⁶I will scatter the Egyptians among the nations and force them into other countries. Then they will know that I am the LORD."

Egypt Will Be Conquered as Assyria Was Conquered

¹On the first day of the third month in the eleventh year, the LORD spoke his word to me. He said, ²"Son of man, say to Pharaoh, king of Egypt, and his many people,

'Was there ever anyone as great as you?
3   What about Assyria?
       It was a cedar in Lebanon
          with fine branches that shaded the forest.
       It was very tall.
       Its top was among the clouds.
4   Water made the tree grow,
             and underground springs made it tall.
          Rivers flowed around the place where the tree was planted.
          Streams ran beside all the other trees around it.
5   That is why it grew taller than all the other trees in the field.
       Its branches became large and long because of so much water.
6   All the birds made their nests in its branches.
          All the wild animals gave birth to their young under it.
          All the powerful nations lived in its shade.
7   So the tree was big and beautiful with its long branches.
       Its roots reached down to many sources of water.
8   The cedar trees in God's garden couldn't compare to it.
     The pine trees couldn't equal its branches.
     The plane trees couldn't measure up to its branches.
       All the trees in God's garden couldn't match its beauty.
9   I was the one who made it beautiful with its many branches.
       This tree was the envy of all the trees in Eden, in God's garden.

¹⁰" 'This is what the Almighty LORD says: The tree grew very tall, and its top reached the clouds. It became arrogant because it was so tall. ¹¹So I handed it over to a mighty ruler among the nations, and he surely dealt with it. I forced it out because of its wickedness. ¹²Foreigners from the most ruthless nation cut it down and threw it away. Its branches fell on the mountains and in every valley. Its broken branches fell in every ravine in the land. All the nations in the world came out from under its shade and left. ¹³All the birds perched on the fallen tree, and all the wild animals lived in its branches. ¹⁴Then all the other trees growing by the water were kept from becoming arrogant because of their height, and their tops were no longer allowed to reach the clouds. So no tree, even if it is well-watered, will ever stand that tall. Every tree is going to die and go below the earth to join those who have died and gone down to the pit.

¹⁵" 'This is what the Almighty LORD says: When the tree went down to the grave,

I made people mourn. I covered the underground springs and held back the rivers. The many water sources stopped flowing. I made Lebanon mourn for the tree, and all the trees in the field fainted as they grieved over it. ¹⁶I made the nations tremble in fear at the sound of the tree's crash. I brought the tree down to the grave to join those who had gone down to the pit. Then all the trees in Eden, the choicest and best trees of Lebanon, and all the trees that were well-watered were comforted below the earth. ¹⁷They had gone down with the tree in the grave to join others killed in battle. All who lived in its shadow were scattered among the nations.

¹⁸" 'This tree is you, Pharaoh, and all your many people. No tree in Eden has ever been as honorable and as great as you. But you will be brought down below the earth with the trees of Eden. You will lie among the godless people who were killed in battle, declares the Almighty Lord.' "

A Funeral Song About Pharaoh

32 ¹On the first day of the twelfth month in the twelfth year, the Lord spoke his word to me. He said, ²"Son of man, sing a funeral song for Pharaoh, king of Egypt. Tell him,

'You think you are like a lion among the nations.
   Instead, you are like a crocodile in the water.
   You splash around in the water.
   You stir up the water with your feet.
   You make the streams muddy.

³" 'This is what the Almighty Lord says: When many nations gather together, I will spread my net over you, and they will haul you up in a net. ⁴I will throw you on the ground and toss you into an open field. I will make birds perch on you, and wild animals from all over the earth will feed on you. ⁵I will scatter your flesh on the hills and fill the valleys with your rotting corpse. ⁶I will drench the earth with your flowing blood all the way to the mountains. Ravines will be filled with your dead body.

⁷" 'When I put out your light, I will cover the sky and darken the stars. I will cover the sun with clouds, and the moon won't shine anymore. ⁸I will darken all the lights shining in the sky above you. I will bring darkness over your land, declares the Almighty Lord.

⁹" 'I will make many people troubled when I spread the news of your destruction among the nations to countries that you haven't heard of. ¹⁰Many people will be shocked by what I will do to you. Their kings will shudder when I swing my sword in their faces. When you die, all of them will tremble in fear for their own lives.

¹¹" 'This is what the Almighty Lord says: The sword of the king of Babylon will attack you. ¹²I will cut down your people with the swords of warriors. All of them will be the most ruthless warriors among the nations. They will shatter the pride of Egypt and destroy its many people. ¹³I will also destroy all the animals beside its many water sources. The feet of humans and the hoofs of animals won't stir up the water anymore. ¹⁴Then I will make its water clear and make its streams flow like oil, declares the Almighty Lord. ¹⁵I will turn Egypt into a wasteland. I will take everything in the land, and I will kill all the people who live there. Then they will know that I am the Lord.'

¹⁶"This is a funeral song. The people from the nations will sing this song. They will sing it as they mourn for Egypt and its many people," declares the Almighty Lord.

The Egyptians Will Join the Other Nations in the Grave

¹⁷On the fifteenth day of the month in the twelfth year, the LORD spoke his word to me. He said, ¹⁸"Son of man, cry for the many people of Egypt. Bring them down along with the other mighty nations. Send them down below the earth to be with those who have gone down to the pit.

¹⁹"Tell them, 'Are you more beautiful than anyone else? Go down and join the godless people.'

²⁰"The Egyptians will lie among those who were killed in battle. A sword has been drawn. Drag Egypt and all its people away. ²¹The mightiest warriors will say to Pharaoh from the grave, 'You and your defenders have come down, and you now lie with the godless people who were killed in battle.'

²²"Assyria is there with its whole army, and the graves of its soldiers are all around it. All of its soldiers are dead. They have been killed in battle. ²³Their graves are in the deepest parts of the pit. Assyria's army lies around its grave. All of its soldiers are dead. They have been killed in battle. They once terrified people in the land of the living.

²⁴"Elam is there with all its soldiers, and the graves of its soldiers are all around it. All of its soldiers are dead. They have been killed in battle. They went down below the earth as godless people. They once terrified people in the land of the living. Now they suffer disgrace with those who have gone down to the pit. ²⁵A bed has been made for Elam among the dead. The graves of its soldiers are all around it. The soldiers were godless people. They were killed in battle because they terrified others in the land of the living. Now they suffer disgrace with those who have gone down to the pit. They lie among the dead.

²⁶"Meshech and Tubal are there with all their soldiers, and the graves of their soldiers are all around them. Their soldiers were all godless people. They were killed in battle because they terrified others in the land of the living. ²⁷They don't lie with the godless warriors who died and went down to the grave with their weapons of war. Their swords were placed under their heads. Their shields were placed on their bones because they terrified others in the land of the living.

²⁸"You Egyptians will be crushed with the godless people, and you will lie with those who were killed in battle.

²⁹"Edom is there with its kings and its princes. They used to be powerful, but now they lie with those who were killed in battle. They lie there with the godless people and with those who have gone down to the pit.

³⁰"All the rulers from the north and all the people from Sidon are there. They, too, went down with the dead. They are disgraced because they terrified people with their power. They were godless people. Now they lie with those who were killed in battle. They suffer disgrace with those who went down to the pit.

³¹"Pharaoh and his army will see these things and be comforted over all the soldiers who have been killed in battle, declares the Almighty LORD. ³²I terrified people in the land of the living. Pharaoh and all his soldiers will be laid among the godless people who were killed in battle," declares the Almighty LORD.

Ezekiel Is Called to Be a Watchman

33 ¹The LORD spoke his word to me. He said, ²"Son of man, speak to your people. Tell them, 'Suppose I bring war on this country, and the people of this country choose one of their men and make him their watchman. ³If he sees the enemy coming to attack the country, he will blow his horn to warn the people. ⁴If the people hear the horn and ignore the warning and the enemy comes and takes them, they will be responsible for their own deaths. ⁵They heard the sound of the horn but ignored its warning. So they are responsible for their own deaths. If they had taken the warning, they would have saved themselves.

⁶" 'But if the watchman sees the enemy coming and doesn't blow his horn to warn the people and the enemy comes and kills someone, that watchman must die because of his sin. I will hold him responsible for their deaths.'

⁷"Son of man, I have appointed you as a watchman for the people of Israel. Listen to what I say, and warn them for me. ⁸Suppose I say to a wicked person, 'You wicked person, you will certainly die,' and you say nothing to warn him to change his ways. That wicked person will die because of his sin, and I will hold you responsible for his death. ⁹But if you warn a wicked person to turn from his ways and he doesn't turn from them, then he will die because of his sin. However, you will save yourself.

¹⁰"Son of man, say to the people of Israel, 'You have said this, "Our wickedness and our sins weigh us down, and we are rotting away because of them. How can we live?" '

¹¹"Tell them, 'As I live, declares the Almighty Lᴏʀᴅ, I don't want wicked people to die. Rather, I want them to turn from their ways and live. Change the way you think and act! Turn from your wicked ways! Do you want to die, people of Israel?'

¹²"Son of man, say to your people, 'The right things that a righteous person has done will not save him when he rebels. The wicked things that a wicked person has done will not make him stumble when he turns from his wickedness. The righteous person will not live when he sins.' ¹³I may promise the righteous person that he will certainly live. But if he trusts in the right things that he has done and he does evil, none of the right things that he has done will be remembered. He will die because of the evil things he has done. ¹⁴I may warn the wicked person that he will certainly die. But suppose he turns from his sin and does what is fair and right. ¹⁵He returns the security for a loan, pays back everything he stole, lives by the rules of life, and does nothing evil. Then he will certainly live. He will not die. ¹⁶None of the sins that he has done will be remembered. He has done what is fair and right. He will certainly live.

¹⁷"But your people say, 'The Lord's way is unfair.' Yet, their ways are unfair. ¹⁸If the righteous person turns from the right things that he has done and does evil, he will die because of it. ¹⁹If the wicked person turns from his wickedness and does what is fair and right, he will live because of it. ²⁰Yet, the people of Israel say, 'The Lord's way is unfair.' I will judge each of you by your own ways, people of Israel."

²¹On the fifth day of the tenth month in the twelfth year of our captivity, a refugee from Jerusalem came to me. He said, "The city has been captured." ²²The evening before the refugee arrived, the power of the Lᴏʀᴅ came over me. On the morning the refugee arrived, the Lᴏʀᴅ made me speak. So I spoke, and I was no longer quiet.

²³The Lᴏʀᴅ spoke his word to me. He said, ²⁴"Son of man, those who live in the ruined cities in Israel are saying, 'Abraham was only one person, and he was given the land. But we are many. Certainly the land has been given to us.' ²⁵So tell them, 'This is what the Almighty Lᴏʀᴅ says: You eat meat with blood in it. You look to your idols for help. You murder people. Should the land be given to you? ²⁶You rely on your swords. You do disgusting things. You dishonor your neighbor's wife. Should the land be given to you?'

²⁷"Tell them, 'This is what the Almighty Lᴏʀᴅ says: As I live, whoever is in the ruined cities will be killed in battle. Whoever is in the open field will become food for wild animals. Whoever is in fortified places and caves will die from plagues. ²⁸I will turn the land into a barren wasteland. People will no longer brag about its power. The mountains of Israel will become so ruined that no one will travel through them. ²⁹Then

people will know that I am the LORD, when I make the land a barren wasteland because of all the disgusting things that they have done.'

³⁰"Son of man, your people are talking about you by the walls and in the doorways of their homes. They are saying to each other, 'Let's go and hear the word that has come from the LORD.' ³¹Then they come to you, as if they are still my people, and they sit down in front of you. They listen to what you say, but they don't do it. They say that they love me, but in their hearts they chase dishonest profits. ³²To them you are nothing more than a singer with a beautiful voice who sings love songs or a musician who plays an instrument. They listen to your words, but they don't do them. ³³When all your words come true—and they certainly will come true—these people will know that a prophet has been among them."

The Promise of a New Shepherd for the LORD's Sheep

34 ¹The LORD spoke his word to me. He said, ²"Son of man, prophesy against the shepherds of Israel. Prophesy to these shepherds. Tell them, 'This is what the Almighty LORD says: How horrible it will be for the shepherds of Israel who have been taking care of only themselves. Shouldn't shepherds take care of the sheep? ³You eat the best parts of the sheep, dress in the wool, and butcher the finest sheep. Yet, you don't take care of the sheep. ⁴You have not strengthened those that were weak, healed those that were sick, or bandaged those that were injured. You have not brought back those that strayed away or looked for those that were lost. You have ruled them harshly and violently. ⁵So they were scattered because there was no shepherd. When they were scattered, they became food for every wild animal. ⁶My sheep wandered over all the mountains and on every high hill. They were scattered throughout the whole earth. No one searched or looked for them.

⁷" 'So, you shepherds, listen to the word of the LORD. ⁸As I live, declares the Almighty LORD, because there is no shepherd, my sheep have become prey. My sheep have become food for every wild animal. My shepherds haven't searched for my sheep. They have taken care of only themselves, not my sheep. ⁹So, you shepherds, listen to the word of the LORD. ¹⁰This is what the Almighty LORD says: I am against the shepherds. I will demand that they hand over my sheep. I won't let them take care of my sheep anymore, and they will no longer take care of only themselves. I will rescue my sheep from their mouths, and my sheep will no longer be their food.

¹¹" 'This is what the Almighty LORD says: I will search for my sheep myself, and I will look after them. ¹²As a shepherd looks after his flock when he is with his scattered sheep, so I will look after my sheep. I will rescue them on a cloudy and gloomy day from every place where they have been scattered. ¹³I will bring them out from the nations, gather them from the countries, and bring them to their own land. I will take care of them on the mountains of Israel, by the streams, and in all the inhabited places of the land. ¹⁴I will feed them in good pasture, and they will graze on the mountains of Israel. They will rest on the good land where they graze, and they will feed on the best pastures in the mountains of Israel. ¹⁵I will take care of my sheep and lead them to rest, declares the Almighty LORD. ¹⁶I will look for those that are lost, bring back those that have strayed away, bandage those that are injured, and strengthen those that are sick. I will destroy those that are fat and strong. I will take care of my sheep fairly.

¹⁷" 'As for you, my sheep, this is what the Almighty LORD says: I will judge disputes between one sheep and another, between rams and male goats. ¹⁸Isn't it enough for you to feed on the good pasture? Must you trample the rest of the pasture with your feet? You drink clean water. Must you muddy the rest of the water with your

feet? ¹⁹Must my sheep eat what your feet have trampled and drink what your feet have muddied?

²⁰" 'So this is what the Almighty LORD says to them: I will judge disputes between the fat sheep and the skinny sheep. ²¹You fat sheep push the skinny sheep with your sides and shoulders, and you knock down all the sick sheep with your horns. You have scattered them all over. ²²So I will rescue my sheep, and they will no longer be prey. I will judge between one sheep and another. ²³Then I will place one shepherd over them, my servant David, and he will take care of them. He will take care of them and be their shepherd. ²⁴I, the LORD, will be their God, and my servant David will be their prince. I, the LORD, have spoken.

²⁵" 'I will promise them peace. I will remove the wild animals from the land so that my sheep can live safely in the wilderness and sleep in the woods. ²⁶I will bless them and the places around my hill. I will send rain at the right time. These showers will be a blessing to them. ²⁷Then the trees in the field will produce fruit, the land will yield crops, and my sheep will live safely in their land. Then they will know that I am the LORD, because I will break off the bars on their yokes*ᵃ* and rescue them from the people who made them slaves. ²⁸They will no longer be prey to the nations, and the wild animals will no longer eat them. They will live safely, and no one will frighten them. ²⁹I will give them a place that is known for its good crops. They will no longer experience hunger in the land, and they will no longer suffer the insults of other nations. ³⁰Then they will know that I, the LORD their God, am with them and that they, the people of Israel, are my people, declares the Almighty LORD. ³¹You, my sheep, are the sheep in my pasture. You are mortal, and I am your God, declares the Almighty LORD.' "

Judgment on Edom

35 ¹The LORD spoke his word to me. He said, ²"Son of man, turn to Mount Seir, and prophesy against it. ³Tell it, 'This is what the Almighty LORD says:

I'm against you, Mount Seir.
　　I will use my power against you,
　　　　and you will become a wasteland.
⁴　　I will turn your cities into ruins,
　　　　and you will become a wasteland.
　　　　　　Then you will know that I am the LORD.

⁵　　" 'You have always been an enemy of Israel.
　　　　You deserted the people of Israel in battle
　　　　　　when they were in trouble during their final punishment.
⁶　　That is why, as I live, declares the Almighty LORD,
　　　　I will let you be murdered.
　　　　　　Murderers will pursue you.
　　Since you don't hate murdering people, murder will pursue you.
⁷　　I will turn Mount Seir into a barren wasteland,
　　　　and I will destroy everyone who comes or goes from there.
⁸　　I will fill your mountains with those who have been killed.
　　　　Those killed in battle will fall on your hills
　　　　　　and in your valleys and ravines.
⁹　　I will turn you into a permanent wasteland.

ᵃ34:27 A yoke is a wooden bar placed over the necks of work animals so that they can pull plows or carts.

Your cities will not be lived in.
Then you will know that I am the Lord.

¹⁰" 'You said, "These two nations, Israel and Judah, along with their land, belong to us. We will take possession of them." But the Lord was there. ¹¹That is why, as I live, declares the Almighty Lord, I will do to you what you did to them. When you were angry and jealous, you acted hatefully toward them. ¹²Then you will know that I, the Lord, heard all the insults that you spoke about the mountains of Israel. You said, "They have been deserted and handed over to us to use up." ¹³You bragged and continually talked against me. I heard you.

¹⁴" 'This is what the Almighty Lord says: The whole earth will be glad when I turn you into a wasteland. ¹⁵You were happy when the land of Israel became a wasteland. I will do the same thing to you. You will become a wasteland, Mount Seir, and so will all of Edom. Then you will know that I am the Lord.' "

Blessings for the Mountains of Israel

36 ¹The Lord said, "Son of man, prophesy to the mountains of Israel. Tell them, 'Mountains of Israel, listen to the word of the Lord. ²This is what the Almighty Lord says: Your enemies said this about you, "Aha! The ancient worship sites now belong to us." '

³"So prophesy. Say, 'This is what the Almighty Lord says: Your enemies turned you into ruins and crushed you from every side. You became the possession of the rest of the nations, and people began to talk and gossip about you.

⁴" 'Mountains of Israel, listen to the word of the Almighty Lord. This is what the Almighty Lord says to the mountains and hills, to the ravines and valleys, and to the empty ruins and abandoned cities that have become prey and are mocked by the rest of the surrounding nations: ⁵In my fiery anger I have spoken against the rest of the nations and against all of Edom. The Edomites have taken possession of my land with wholehearted joy and with complete scorn. They forced out the people and took their land.'

⁶"So prophesy about Israel. Tell the mountains and hills and the ravines and valleys, 'This is what the Almighty Lord says: I am speaking in my anger and fury because you have been insulted by the nations. ⁷So this is what the Almighty Lord says: I raise my hand and swear that the nations which surround you will be insulted.

⁸" 'But you, mountains of Israel, will grow branches and bear fruit for my people Israel. My people will come home soon. ⁹I am for you. I will turn to you, and you will be plowed and planted. ¹⁰I will increase the number of people who live on you. All the people of Israel, all of them, will live on you. The cities will be inhabited, and the ruins will be rebuilt. ¹¹I will increase the number of people and animals that live on you. They will grow and become many. I will let people live on you as in the past, and I will make you better off than ever before. Then you will know that I am the Lord. ¹²I will bring people, my people Israel, to you. They will take possession of you, and you will be their inheritance. You will no longer take their children away from them.

¹³" 'This is what the Almighty Lord says: People say that you devour your people and take the children away from your nation. ¹⁴So you will no longer devour your people or take the children away from your nation, declares the Almighty Lord. ¹⁵I will no longer let you hear the insults from the nations. You will no longer suffer the disgrace of the people. You will never again take the children away from your own nation, declares the Almighty Lord.' "

¹⁶The Lord spoke his word to me. He said, ¹⁷"Son of man, when the people of Israel

lived in their land, they dishonored it by the way they lived and by everything they did. Their ways were as unclean*ᵃ* as a woman's menstrual period. ¹⁸So I poured out my fury on them because they poured out blood on the land and they dishonored the land with their idols. ¹⁹I forced them into other nations, and they became scattered among the nations. I judged them based on the way that they lived and based on everything that they had done. ²⁰But wherever they went among the nations, they dishonored my holy name. People said about them, 'These are the Lᴏʀᴅ's people, yet they had to leave his land.' ²¹I became concerned about my holy name because my people dishonored it among the nations wherever they went.

²²"So tell the people of Israel, 'This is what the Almighty Lᴏʀᴅ says: I am about to do something, people of Israel. I will not do this for your sake but for the sake of my holy name, which you have dishonored among the nations wherever you have gone. ²³I will reveal the holiness of my great name, which has been dishonored by the nations, the name that you have dishonored among them. Then the nations will know that I am the Lᴏʀᴅ, because I will reveal my holiness among you as they watch, declares the Almighty Lᴏʀᴅ.

²⁴" 'I will take you from the nations and gather you from every country. I will bring you back to your own land. ²⁵I will sprinkle clean water on you and make you clean*ᵇ* instead of unclean. Then I will cleanse you from all your idols. ²⁶I will give you a new heart and put a new spirit in you. I will remove your stubborn hearts and give you obedient hearts. ²⁷I will put my Spirit in you. I will enable you to live by my laws, and you will obey my rules. ²⁸Then you will live in the land that I gave your ancestors. You will be my people, and I will be your God. ²⁹I will rescue you from all your uncleanness. I will make the grain grow so that you will never again have famines. ³⁰I will make fruit grow on the trees and crops grow in the fields so that you will no longer suffer disgrace among the nations because of famines. ³¹Then you will remember your evil ways and the bad things that you did, and you will hate yourselves for all these wicked and disgusting things. ³²I want you to know that I'm not doing this for your sake, declares the Almighty Lᴏʀᴅ. Be ashamed and disgraced because of your ways, people of Israel.

³³" 'This is what the Almighty Lᴏʀᴅ says: On the day that I cleanse you from all your wickedness, I will cause your cities to be lived in again, and your ruins will be rebuilt. ³⁴The wasteland will be plowed. It will no longer remain empty for everyone passing by to see. ³⁵People will say, "This wasteland has become like the garden of Eden. The cities were destroyed. They were empty and ruined, but now they are fortified and have people living in them." ³⁶The surrounding nations that are left will know that I, the Lᴏʀᴅ, have rebuilt the ruined places and planted crops in the land that was empty. I, the Lᴏʀᴅ, have spoken, and I will do it.'

³⁷"This is what the Almighty Lᴏʀᴅ says: I will also let the people of Israel ask me to make them as numerous as sheep. ³⁸They will be like the sheep for sacrifices, like the sheep in Jerusalem during the appointed festivals. Their ruined cities will be filled with flocks of people. Then they will know that I am the Lᴏʀᴅ."

The Valley of Dry Bones

37 ¹The power of the Lᴏʀᴅ came over me. The Lᴏʀᴅ brought me out by his Spirit and put me down in the middle of a valley. The valley was filled with bones. ²He led me all around them. I saw that there were very many bones at the bottom of the valley, and they were very dry.

ᵃ36:17 "Unclean" refers to anything that Moses' Teachings say is not presentable to God.   ᵇ36:25 "Clean" refers to anything that Moses' Teachings say is presentable to God.

³Then he asked me, "Son of man, can these bones live?"

I answered, "Only you know, Almighty LORD."

⁴Then he said to me, "Prophesy to these bones. Tell them, 'Dry bones, listen to the word of the LORD. ⁵This is what the Almighty LORD says to these bones: I will cause breath to enter you, and you will live. ⁶I will put ligaments on you, place muscles on you, and cover you with skin. I will put breath in you, and you will live. Then you will know that I am the LORD.' "

⁷So I prophesied as I was commanded. While I was prophesying, suddenly there was a rattling noise, and the bones came together, one bone attaching itself to another. ⁸As I looked, I saw that ligaments were on them, muscles were on them, and skin covered them. Yet, there was no breath in them.

⁹Then the LORD said to me, "Prophesy to the breath!ᵃ Prophesy, son of man. Tell the breath, 'This is what the Almighty LORD says: Come from the four winds, Breath, and breathe on these people who were killed so that they will live.' "

¹⁰So I prophesied as he commanded me, and the breath entered them. Then they came to life and stood on their feet. There were enough of them to form a very large army.

¹¹The LORD also said to me, "Son of man, all the people of Israel are like these bones. The people say, 'Our bones are dry, and our hope has vanished. We are completely destroyed.' ¹²So prophesy. Tell them, 'This is what the Almighty LORD says: My people, I will open your graves and take you out of them. I will bring you to Israel. ¹³Then, my people, you will know that I am the LORD, because I will open your graves and bring you out of your graves. ¹⁴I will put my Spirit in you, and you will live. I will place you in your own land. Then you will know that I, the LORD, have spoken, and I have done it, declares the LORD.' "

¹⁵The LORD spoke his word to me again. He said, ¹⁶"Son of man, take a stick and write on it: 'For Judah and for the Israelites who are associated with it.' Then take another stick and write on it, 'The stick of Ephraim, for Joseph and for all the people of Israel associated with it.' ¹⁷Then join both sticks together so that they will be one in your hand. Your people will say to you, ¹⁸'Tell us what you mean by this.' ¹⁹Then say to them, 'This is what the Almighty LORD says: I will take Joseph's stick, which is in Ephraim's hand, and the tribes of Israel associated with it, and I will put them with Judah's stick. I will make them into one stick. They will be one in my hand.' ²⁰When you hold the sticks in your hand, let the people see them.

²¹"Then tell them, 'This is what the Almighty LORD says: I will take the Israelites out of the nations where they've gone. I will gather them from everywhere and bring them to their own land. ²²I will form them into one nation in the land on the mountains of Israel. One king will rule all of them. They will no longer be two nations or be divided into two kingdoms. ²³They will no longer dishonor themselves with their idols, with their detestable things, or with their rebellious acts. I will forgive them for all the times they turned away from me and sinned. I will cleanse them so that they will be my people, and I will be their God.

²⁴ 'My servant David will be their king, and all of them will have one shepherd. They will live by my rules, and they will obey my laws. ²⁵They will live in the land that I gave my servant Jacob, the land where their ancestors lived. They, their children, and their grandchildren will live in it permanently. My servant David will always be their prince. ²⁶I will promise them peace. This promiseᵇ will last forever. I will establish them, make them increase in number, and put my holy place among them

---

ᵃ37:9 Or "Spirit." ᵇ37:26 Or "covenant."

permanently. ²⁷My dwelling place will be with them. I will be their God, and they will be my people. ²⁸Then the nations will know that I, the LORD, have set Israel apart as holy, because my holy place will be among them permanently.' "

The Destruction of Gog and Its Army

38 ¹The LORD spoke his word to me. He said, ²"Son of man, turn to Gog from the land of Magog. He is the chief prince of the nations of Meshech and Tubal. Prophesy against him. ³Tell him, 'This is what the Almighty LORD says: I am against you, Gog, chief prince of Meshech and Tubal. ⁴I will turn you around and put hooks in your jaws. I will lead you out with all your military forces, with horses and riders. Your soldiers will be fully armed. They will carry large and small shields and be able to use swords. ⁵Persia, Sudan, and Put will be with you. They, too, will have shields and helmets. ⁶Gomer will come with all its troops and with the nation of Togarmah from the far north. There will be many armies with you.

⁷" 'Be prepared! Be prepared, you and all the soldiers assembled around you. You will be their leader. ⁸After a long time you will be called to service. In the years to come, you will attack a land that has been rebuilt after a war. Its people have been gathered from many nations and brought to the mountains of Israel, mountains that have been ruined for a long time. These people were brought there from the nations, and all of them live there safely. ⁹You will attack like a storm and cover the land like a cloud. Your troops and the many armies will be with you.

¹⁰" 'This is what the Almighty LORD says: At that time ideas will enter your head, and you will make wicked plans. ¹¹You will say, "I'll attack a land with unwalled villages. I will attack peaceful people who live safely. All of them live without walls, locks, or gates. ¹²I will come to rob them and loot them. I will use my power against the ruins that people are living in again. I will use it against the people who were gathered from the nations. These people have cattle and property, and they live in the world."

¹³" 'Sheba, Dedan, the merchants from Tarshish, and all their villages will ask you, "Did you come to rob these people of their possessions? Did you assemble all these soldiers to carry away large amounts of silver and gold and to take cattle and property?" '

¹⁴"So prophesy, son of man. Tell Gog, 'This is what the Almighty LORD says: At that time my people Israel will live safely, and you will know it. ¹⁵You will come from your place in the far north and many armies will be with you. All of you will ride on horses. You will be a large crowd and a mighty army. ¹⁶You will attack my people Israel like a cloud that covers the land. In the days to come, I will let you attack my land so that nations will know me. I will use you for my holy purpose as they watch.

¹⁷" 'This is what the Almighty LORD says: You are the one I spoke about long ago through my servants the prophets of Israel. They prophesied in those days that I would bring you to attack them. ¹⁸On the day that Gog attacks the land of Israel, I will be filled with burning anger, declares the Almighty LORD. ¹⁹In my fiery anger I tell you this. On that day there will be a large earthquake in the land of Israel. ²⁰Fish, birds, wild animals, everything that crawls on the ground, and every person on earth will tremble in my presence. The mountains will be torn down, the cliffs will crumble, and every wall will fall to the ground. ²¹I will declare war against Gog on all my mountains, declares the Almighty LORD. Each person will use his sword against his relative. ²²I will punish Gog with plagues and death. I will send rainstorms, large hailstones, fire, and burning sulfur on his troops and on the many armies with him. ²³I will show my greatness and my holiness. I will reveal myself to many nations. Then they will know that I am the LORD.' "

39 [1]The Lord said, "Son of man, prophesy against Gog. Tell it, 'This is what the Almighty Lord says: I am against you, Gog, the chief prince of Meshech and Tubal. [2]I will turn you around and lead you. I will bring you from the far north and have you attack the mountains of Israel. [3]Then I will knock the bow out of your left hand and make you drop the arrows in your right hand. [4]You will die on the mountains of Israel with your troops and the armies that are with you. I will let you become food for every bird of prey and for every wild animal. [5]You will die in the open field because I said so, declares the Almighty Lord. [6]I will send fire on Magog and on those who live safely on the coasts. Then they will know that I am the Lord. [7]I will make my holy name known among my people Israel, and I will never let them dishonor my holy name again. Then the nations will know that I am the Lord, the Holy One in Israel.

[8]" 'It's coming! It will happen! declares the Almighty Lord. This is the day I have spoken about. [9]Those living in the cities of Israel will go out. They will set fire to weapons and burn them. They will burn small and large shields, bows and arrows, and war clubs and spears. They will burn them for seven years. [10]They will not need to get wood from the field or cut down trees in the woods. They will make fires with the weapons. They will loot those who looted them, and they will grab things back from those who grabbed their things, declares the Almighty Lord.

[11]" 'When that day comes, I will give Gog a burial place in Israel. It will be in Travelers Valley, east of the Dead Sea. It will block those who travel through the valley. Gog and his whole army will be buried there. So it will be called the valley of Gog's troops. [12]The people of Israel will be burying them there for seven months to make the land clean.[a] [13]All the common people will be burying them. The people of Israel will be honored on the day of my victory, declares the Almighty Lord.

[14]" 'People will be chosen to go through the land and make it clean. With the help of others they will bury the dead soldiers that are still on the ground. At the end of seven months they will begin their search. [15]Whenever they go through the land and see a human bone, they will set up a marker beside it until the grave diggers have buried that bone in the valley of Gog's troops. [16](A city named Hamonah[b] will also be there.) In this way they will cleanse the land.'

[17]"Son of man, this is what the Almighty Lord says: Tell every kind of bird and every wild animal, 'Assemble, and come together from all around for the sacrifice that I'm preparing for you. It will be a huge feast on the mountains of Israel. You can eat meat and drink blood there. [18]You can eat the meat of warriors and drink the blood of the princes of the earth. All of them will be killed like rams, lambs, goats, bulls and all the best animals of Bashan. [19]You can eat the best meat until you are full and drink blood until you are drunk at the sacrifice that I am preparing for you. [20]At my table you will be filled with horses and riders, warriors, and soldiers of every kind, declares the Almighty Lord.'

[21]"I will show my greatness among the nations. All the nations will see how I will turn my power against them to punish them. [22]From that day on, the people of Israel will know that I am the Lord their God. [23]Then the nations will know that the people of Israel went into captivity because they did wrong and rebelled against me. So I hid my face from them and handed them over to their enemies. They were killed in battle. [24]I paid them back for their uncleanness and their sins, and I hid my face from them.

[25]"So this is what the Almighty Lord says: Now I will bring back Jacob's captives and have compassion for the whole nation of Israel. I will stand up for my holy name.

---

[a]39:12 "Clean" refers to anything that Moses' Teachings say is presentable to God. [b]39:16 There is a play on words here between Hebrew *hamon* (troops) and Hamonah.

²⁶When they live safely in a land where no one will frighten them, they will forget their shame and all the unfaithful things they have done against me. ²⁷I will bring them back from the other nations and gather them from the countries of their enemies. Many nations will see that I am holy. ²⁸Then my people will know that I am the Lord their God. I sent them into captivity among the nations, and I brought them back again to their land. I left none of them behind. ²⁹I will no longer hide my face from them, because I will pour out my Spirit on the nation of Israel, declares the Almighty Lord."

The New Temple of God

40 ¹It was the tenth day of the month in the beginning of the twenty-fifth year of our captivity and fourteen years after Jerusalem was captured. At that time the Lord's power came over me, and he brought me to Jerusalem. ²In visions, God brought me to Israel and set me down on a very high mountain. On the south side of the mountain were some buildings that looked like those in a city. ³He brought me closer. I saw a man who looked like he was covered with bronze. The man was holding a linen tape measure and a measuring stick, and he stood in a gateway. ⁴He said to me, "Son of man, look with your eyes, and listen with your ears. Pay close attention to everything I'm going to show you. You were brought here to be shown these things. Tell the nation of Israel everything that you see."

The East Gateway

⁵I saw a wall that surrounded the temple. The man had a measuring stick that was 10½ feet long. He measured the wall. It was 10½ feet thick and 10½ feet high.

⁶Then the man went to the gateway that faced east. He went up its steps and measured the entrance to the gateway. It was 10½ feet wide. ⁷There were also guardrooms. Each guardroom was 10½ feet long and 10½ feet wide. The space between the guardrooms was 9 feet thick. And the entrance to the gateway by the entrance hall of the temple was 10½ feet wide. ⁸He also measured the entrance hall of the gateway. ⁹It extended 14 feet from the temple. Its recessed walls were 3½ feet thick. The gateway's entrance hall faced the temple.

¹⁰Now, there were three guardrooms on each side of the eastern gateway. All three rooms on each side were the same size, and the recessed walls on each side were the same size.

¹¹Then the man measured the width of the entrance to the gateway. It was 17½ feet wide, and the gateway was 23 feet long. ¹²There was a barrier about 21 inches in front of each guardroom. The guardrooms were 10½ feet square.

¹³He measured the gateway from the top of one guardroom to the top of the opposite guardroom. It was 44 feet wide from one door to the opposite door. ¹⁴He also measured the entrance hall. It was 35 feet wide. In front of the entrance hall to the gateway was a courtyard on all sides.

¹⁵The total length of the gateway from the front of the outer part to the front of the inner part of the entrance hall was 87½ feet.

¹⁶The guardrooms and recessed walls inside the gateway had small windows all around. The entrance hall also had windows all around on the inside. Pictures of palm trees were carved on the recessed walls.

The Outer Courtyard

¹⁷Then the man brought me into the outer courtyard. I saw rooms there and pavement all around the courtyard. There were 30 rooms along the edge of the pavement. ¹⁸The pavement in the lower courtyard ran alongside the gateways. It was as wide as

it was long. ¹⁹The man measured the distance from the inside of the lower gateway to the outside of the inner courtyard. It was 175 feet from east to north.

The North Gateway

²⁰Then the man measured the length and width of the gateway, leading to the outer courtyard. This was the gateway that faced north. ²¹Its three guardrooms, its recessed walls, and its entrance hall were the same size as those in the east gateway. The gateway was 87½ feet long and 44 feet wide. ²²Its windows, recessed walls, and palm tree pictures were the same size as those in the east gateway. Seven steps went up to it and led to its entrance hall. ²³The inner courtyard had a gateway opposite the north gate just like the east gateway. The man measured the distance from one gate to the other gate. It was 175 feet.

The South Gateway

²⁴Then the man led me to the south side, and I saw a gateway that faced south. He measured its recessed walls and its entrance hall. They were the same size as those of the other gateways. ²⁵The gateway and its entrance hall had windows on all sides like the windows in the other gateways. It was 87½ feet long and 44 feet wide. ²⁶Seven steps went up to it and led to its entrance hall. Pictures of palm trees were carved on the recessed walls, one picture on each side. ²⁷The inner courtyard had a gateway facing south. The man measured the distance from the gateway on the south side to its opposite gateway. It was 175 feet.

The Inner Courtyard

²⁸Then the man brought me to the inner courtyard through the south gateway. He measured the south gateway. It was the same size as the others. ²⁹Its guardrooms, recessed walls, and entrance hall were the same size as the other gateways. The guardrooms and the entrance hall had windows all around. The gateway was 87½ feet long and 44 feet wide. ³⁰There were entrance halls all around the inner courtyard. They were all 44 feet long and 9 feet wide. ³¹The entrance halls faced the outer courtyard. Pictures of palm trees were carved on the recessed walls, and eight steps led up to each gateway.

³²Then the man brought me to the east side of the inner courtyard. He measured the gateway. It was the same size as the others. ³³Its guardrooms, recessed walls, and entrance halls were the same size as those of the other gateways. Its guardrooms and entrance hall had windows all around. The gateway was 87½ feet long and 44 feet wide. ³⁴Its entrance hall faced the outer courtyard. Pictures of palm trees were carved on the recessed walls, and eight steps led up to the gateway.

³⁵Then the man brought me to the north gateway. He measured it. It was the same size as the others. ³⁶Its guardrooms, recessed walls, and entrance hall had windows all around. The gateway was 87½ feet long and 44 feet wide. ³⁷Its recessed walls faced the outer courtyard. Pictures of palm trees were carved on the recessed walls, and eight steps led up to the gateway.

Special Rooms

³⁸There was a room with a door that opened toward the entrance hall of the gateway. This is the room where the priests washed the animals for the burnt offerings. ³⁹In the entrance hall of the gateway there were two tables on each side of the room. On these tables the animals were slaughtered for burnt offerings, offerings for sin, and guilt offerings. ⁴⁰On each side of the entrance to the north gateway there were

two tables, and on the other side of the entrance hall of the gateway there were two tables. ⁴¹So there were four tables on each side of the gateway, eight tables in all, on which they slaughtered animals. ⁴²There were four tables made of cut stone for burnt offerings. They were 3 feet long, 3 feet wide, and 21 inches high. On these tables the priests laid the utensils that were used to slaughter animals for burnt offerings and sacrifices. ⁴³Double-pronged hooks, three inches long, were attached to the wall all around the room, and the tables were for the meat of the animals. ⁴⁴Outside the gateways to the inner courtyard were the rooms for the singers in the inner courtyards. One room was at the side of the north gateway. It faced south. The other room was at the side of the south gateway. It faced north. ⁴⁵The man said to me, "This room that faces south is for the priests who serve in the temple. ⁴⁶The room that faces north is for the priests who serve at the altar. These priests are Zadok's descendants. They are the only Levites who are able to come near the Lord and serve him." ⁴⁷The man measured the courtyard. It was a perfect square—175 feet long and 175 feet wide. And the altar was in front of the temple.

⁴⁸Then the man brought me to the entrance hall of the temple and measured its recessed walls. They were 9 feet on each side. The gateway was 24½ feet wide, and the walls on each side were 5 feet wide. ⁴⁹The entrance hall was 35 feet long and 21 feet wide. Steps led up to it. Pillars stood by the recessed walls, one on each side of the entrance hall.

The Holy Place in the Temple

41 ¹Then the man brought me into the holy place in the temple and measured the recessed walls. They were 10½ feet wide on each side. ²The entrance was 17½ feet wide, and on each side of the entrance the walls were 9 feet wide. Then he measured the length of the holy place. It was 70 feet long and 35 feet wide.

³Then the man went inside and measured the passageway. It was 3½ feet thick. The entrance was 10½ feet high and 12 feet wide. ⁴Then he measured the room at the end of the holy place. It was 35 feet long and 35 feet wide. The man said to me, "This is the most holy place."

⁵Next, the man measured the temple wall. It was 10½ feet wide. The width of each side room around the temple was 7 feet. ⁶The rooms were arranged on three different stories. There were 30 rooms on each story. These rooms had supports all the way around the temple wall, but these supports were not fastened to the temple wall. ⁷The side rooms grew wider all the way around as they went up, story after story. The surrounding structure went from story to story all around the temple. The structure grew wider as it went higher. A stairway went from the first story through the second story to the third story.

⁸I also saw a raised base all around the temple. This base was the foundation for the side rooms. It measured the full length of the measuring rod, 10½ feet. ⁹The outer wall of the side rooms was 9 feet thick. There was an open area between the side rooms connected to the temple ¹⁰and the priests' rooms. It was 35 feet wide and went all around the temple. ¹¹The doors in the side rooms were entrances into the open area. There was one door to the north and another to the south. The base of the open area was 9 feet wide all the way around.

¹²At the far end of the open area, on the west side of the temple, was a building 122½ feet wide. The wall of the building was 9 feet thick all the way around, and it was 157½ feet long.

¹³Then the man measured the temple. It was 175 feet long. This included the open area with the building and its walls. All together it was 175 feet long. ¹⁴The eastern

side of the temple, including the open area, was also 175 feet wide. ¹⁵He also measured the length of the building facing the courtyard on the west side along with its corridors on both sides. It was 175 feet long.

The holy place and the most holy place were paneled. ¹⁶The doorposts, the small windows, and the corridors of all three stories were paneled. The walls, from the floor up to the windows, were paneled. ¹⁷In the space above the door to the most holy place and on the walls all around it, ¹⁸there were pictures of angels*ᵃ* and palm trees. Palm trees were positioned between each of the angels, and each angel had two faces: ¹⁹the face of a man, which was turned toward a palm tree on one side, and the face of a lion, which was turned toward a palm tree on the other side. These pictures were carved all around the temple. ²⁰Pictures of angels and palm trees were carved on the walls from the floor to the space above the door.

²¹The doorframes in the holy place were square. In front of the most holy place was something similar. ²²There was a wooden altar, 5 feet high and 3½ feet wide. Its corners, its base, and its sides were made of wood. Then the man told me, "This is the table that is in the presence of the Lord."

²³The holy place and the most holy place had two doors. ²⁴Each of the doors were double doors that swung open. ²⁵Pictures of angels and palm trees were carved on the doors of the holy place as on the walls. There was a wooden roof hanging over the outer entrance hall. ²⁶There were small windows and palm trees on both sides of the entrance hall, on the side rooms of the temple, and on the roofs.

The Courtyards of the LORD's New Temple

¹Then the man led me out toward the north to the outer courtyard. He brought me to the side rooms opposite both the open area and the northern building. ²The building that faced north was 175 feet long and 87½ feet wide. ³Opposite the inner courtyard was an area that was 35 feet wide, and opposite the pavement of the outer courtyard were corridors facing corridors on all three stories. ⁴In front of the side rooms was a walkway, 17½ feet wide and 175 feet long. The doors of these side rooms faced north.

⁵The side rooms on the third story were narrower than those on the first or second stories of the building because the corridors took space away from them. ⁶The rooms were in three stories. They didn't have pillars like the pillars in the courtyards. That is why the rooms on the third story were set farther back than those on the first and second stories. ⁷There was a wall which ran parallel to the side rooms and the outer courtyard. It ran alongside the side rooms for 87½ feet. ⁸The row of rooms in the outer courtyard was 87½ feet long. The rooms that faced the temple were 175 feet long. ⁹These lower side rooms had an entrance on the east side. A person was able to enter the outer courtyard through them.

¹⁰There were side rooms parallel to the wall of the courtyard on the south side.*ᵃ* They faced the open area and the building. ¹¹There was a walkway in front of them like the one that was in front of the side rooms on the north side. These side rooms were as long and as wide as the northern rooms. They had the same exits, dimensions, and doors. ¹²The doors to the south rooms were the same as the doors to the north rooms. There was a doorway at the other end of the walkway that was parallel to the corresponding wall that ran eastward. People entered through that doorway.

¹³Then the man said to me, "The northern and southern side rooms that face the open area are holy rooms. These rooms are where the priests who come near the

---

*ᵃ*41:18 Or "cherubim." *ᵃ*42:10 Greek; Masoretic Text "east side."

LORD eat the holiest offerings. Because these rooms are holy, the priests keep the holiest offerings there: the grain offerings, the offerings for sin, and the guilt offerings. ¹⁴Once the priests enter the holy place, they must not go out of the holy place into the outer courtyard until they leave behind the clothes that they wore as they served. These clothes are holy. The priests must put on other clothes. Then they can go into the area that is for the people."

¹⁵When the man had finished measuring the inner part of the temple area, he led me out through the east gate. Then he measured all the way around the outer area. ¹⁶He measured the east side with a measuring stick. It was 875 feet long according to the measuring stick. ¹⁷He measured the north side. It was 875 feet long according to the measuring stick. ¹⁸He measured the south side. It was 875 feet long according to the measuring stick. ¹⁹He came around to the west side and measured it. It was 875 feet long according to the measuring stick. ²⁰So he measured all four sides. There was a wall all around it. The wall was 875 feet long and 875 feet wide. It separated what was holy from what was unholy.

The Glory of the LORD Fills the New Temple

43 ¹Then the man took me to the east gate. ²I saw the glory of the God of Israel coming from the east. His voice was like the sound of rushing water, and the earth was shining because of his glory. ³This vision was like the one I saw when he came*ᵃ* to destroy Jerusalem and like the one I saw by the Chebar River. I immediately bowed down. ⁴The LORD's glory came into the temple through the east gate.

⁵The Spirit lifted me and brought me into the inner courtyard. I saw the LORD's glory fill the temple. ⁶I heard someone speaking to me from inside the temple while the man was standing beside me. ⁷The voice said to me, "Son of man, this is the place where my throne is and the place where my feet rest. This is where I will live among the Israelites forever. Then the people of Israel and their kings will no longer dishonor my holy name by acting like prostitutes, nor will they dishonor it with the dead bodies of their kings. ⁸They put their doorway by my doorway and their doorposts by my doorposts. Only a wall separated me from them. They dishonored my holy name because of the disgusting things that they have done. So I destroyed them in my anger. ⁹Now they must stop acting like prostitutes and take the dead bodies of their kings far away from me. Then I will live among them forever.

¹⁰"Son of man, describe this temple to the people of Israel. Then they will be ashamed because of their sins. Let them study the plans. ¹¹Suppose they are ashamed of everything that they have done. Then show them the design of the temple, its arrangements, its exits and entrances—its entire design. Tell them about all its rules and regulations. Then write these things down for them so that they can remember its design and follow all its rules.

¹²"This is a regulation of the temple: The whole area all the way around the top of the mountain is most holy. Yes, this is a regulation of the temple."

The Altar in the New Temple

¹³These are the measurements of the altar, using royal measurements. (The royal measuring stick was 21 inches long.) The base of the altar was 21 inches high and 21 inches wide. All around the edge of the altar was a rim measuring 9 inches wide. This was the height of the altar: ¹⁴From the base on the ground to the lower ledge it was 3½ feet high, and from the lower ledge to the upper ledge it was 7 feet high and 21

ᵃ 43:3 Some Hebrew manuscripts, Greek, Latin; other Hebrew manuscripts "When I came."

inches wide. [15]The place where the sacrifices were burned was 7 feet high. There were four horns above it. [16]It was square, 21 feet wide and 21 feet long. [17]The upper ledge was also square. It was 24½ feet long and 24½ feet wide. It had a rim all the way around that was 10½ inches wide. Its base was 21 inches. The steps to the altar faced east.

[18]Then the man said to me, "Son of man, this is what the Almighty LORD says: These are the rules for sacrificing burnt offerings and for sprinkling blood on the altar after the altar is built. [19]Give a young bull to the priests as an offering for sin. These priests are Zadok's descendants, men from the tribe of Levi, who can come near me and serve me. [20]Take some of the bull's blood, and put it on the altar's four horns, on the four corners of the ledge, and on the rim all the way around the altar. When you do this, you will remove sin from the altar and make peace with the LORD. [21]Then take a young bull as an offering for sin, and burn it in the place appointed near the temple, outside the holy place.

[22]"On the second day bring a male goat that has no defects as an offering for sin. Remove sin from the altar as you did with the young bull. [23]When you finish removing sin, offer a young bull and a ram that have no defects. [24]Offer them to the LORD. The priests must throw salt on them and offer them as burnt offerings to the LORD. [25]Every day for seven days you must sacrifice a goat, a young bull, and a ram from the flock as an offering for sin. They must be animals that have no defects. [26]For seven days the priests should make peace with the LORD at the altar, purify it, and consecrate it. [27]When those days are over, on the eighth day, the priests must sacrifice burnt offerings and fellowship offerings on the altar. Then I will accept them, declares the Almighty LORD."

The East Gate Is Sealed Shut

44 [1]Then the man took me back to the outer east gate of the holy place, and the gate was shut. [2]The LORD said to me, "This gate will stay shut and will not be opened. No one may enter through it because the LORD God of Israel entered through it. It must be kept shut. [3]Only the prince may sit there and eat food in the presence of the LORD. He will enter through the entrance hall of the gateway and leave the same way."

[4]The man brought me through the north gate in front of the temple. When I looked, I saw the LORD's glory fill the LORD's temple. I immediately bowed down.

The People Serving in the New Temple

[5]The LORD said to me, "Son of man, pay close attention. Look, and listen to everything I'm going to tell you. Listen to all the rules and regulations for the LORD's temple. Pay close attention to everyone who enters the temple and leaves from the holy place. [6]Tell the rebellious people of Israel, 'This is what the Almighty LORD says: I've had enough of all the disgusting things that you have done, people of Israel. [7]You brought godless foreigners[a] into my holy place. You dishonored my temple when you offered fat and blood to me. You rejected my promise so that you could do all your disgusting things. [8]You didn't take care of my holy things. You put foreigners in charge of my temple. [9]So this is what the Almighty LORD says: Any godless foreigner who lives among the Israelites may not enter my holy place.

[10]" 'Some Levites went far away from me when Israel wandered off to follow their idols. They must be punished for their sins. [11]They could have served in my holy place.

---

[a] 44:7 Or "foreigners whose hearts and bodies are uncircumcised."

They could have guarded the gates of the temple. They could have served in the temple by slaughtering the animals for the burnt offerings and the sacrifices for the people. They could have stood in front of the people and served them. ¹²But they served the people by standing in front of their idols and by making Israel fall into sin. So I raised my hand and swore that they would be punished for their sins, declares the Lᴏʀᴅ. ¹³They must not come near me and serve me as priests. They must not come near any of my holy things or my most holy things. They must suffer disgrace because of the disgusting things that they have done. ¹⁴I will assign them all of the less important work in the temple.

¹⁵" 'But the priests who are Levites and descendants of Zadok took care of my holy place when the Israelites wandered away from me. They may come near me and serve me, and they may stand in my presence. They may bring fat and blood to me, declares the Almighty Lᴏʀᴅ. ¹⁶They may enter my holy place, come near my table to serve me, and take care of everything I gave them. ¹⁷When they enter the gateways to the inner courtyard, they must wear linen clothes. They must have no wool on them while they serve in the gateways to the inner courtyard and in the temple. ¹⁸They must wear linen turbans on their heads and linen undergarments. They must not wear anything that makes them sweat. ¹⁹When they go out among the people in the outer courtyard, they must take off the clothes that they wore as they served. They must leave their clothes in the side rooms of the holy place and put on other clothes so that they do not transfer the holiness from their clothes to the people.

²⁰" 'They must not shave their heads or let their hair grow long. They must keep the hair on their heads trimmed. ²¹None of the priests may drink wine when they enter the inner courtyard. ²²They must not marry widows or women who have been divorced. They may marry only virgins from the nation of Israel or widows of priests. ²³They must teach my people the difference between what is holy and what is unholy. They must show the people how to tell the difference between what is clean and what is unclean.*ᵇ* ²⁴In all disputes the priests must act as judges and make decisions based on my laws. They must obey my rules and my regulations at all my festivals. They must observe holy days to worship me.

²⁵" 'A priest must not make himself unclean by going near a dead body. But a priest may become unclean if the dead person is his father, mother, son, daughter, brother, or unmarried sister. ²⁶After a priest is made clean, he must wait seven days. ²⁷When he enters the inner courtyard of the holy place to serve in the holy place, he must bring his offering for sin, declares the Almighty Lᴏʀᴅ.

²⁸" 'The priests will have no inheritance. I am their inheritance. Don't give them any possessions in Israel. The priests belong to me. ²⁹They will eat grain offerings, offerings for sin, and guilt offerings. Everything in Israel that is devoted to the Lᴏʀᴅ will belong to them. ³⁰The priests should have the best of all the first ripened fruits. The best of every gift from all your contributions must go to the priests. The best of your dough must go to the priests. This will cause a blessing to rest on your home. ³¹The priests must never eat any bird or animal that has died naturally or was killed by other wild animals.

Land for the Priests, Levites, and the Prince

45 ¹" 'Divide the land by drawing lots for the property you will inherit. Set aside an area 43,750 feet long and 35,000 feet wide for the Lᴏʀᴅ. The entire area will be holy. ²An area of 875 feet square will be for the holy place with an open area

---

ᵇ44:23 "Clean" refers to anything that Moses' Teachings say is presentable to God. "Unclean" refers to anything that Moses' Teachings say is not presentable to God.

87½ feet wide. ³Measure off an area 43,750 feet long and 17,500 feet wide. The holy place, that is, the most holy place, will be in this area. ⁴This holy part of the land will belong to the priests who serve in the holy place, the priests who come near to serve the LORD. They will use this place for their homes, and it will be the location for the holy place. ⁵An area 43,750 feet long and 17,500 feet wide will belong to the Levites who serve in the temple. It will be given to them so that they have cities to live in.

⁶" 'You must designate an area 8,750 feet wide and 43,750 feet long as the city's property. It will be located alongside the holy area. It will belong to all the people of Israel.

⁷" 'The prince will have all the land on both sides of the holy area and on both sides of the property belonging to the city. From the western boundary of the holy area, his land will extend to the Mediterranean Sea. From the eastern boundary of the holy area, his land will extend to the eastern border of the country. His territory will be as large as the territory of one of the tribes. ⁸This land will belong to the prince in Israel. Then my princes will no longer oppress my people. They will give land to each tribe of the nation of Israel.

Honest Weights and Measures for the LORD's People

⁹" 'This is what the Almighty LORD says: I've had enough of you, you princes of Israel. Stop your violence and looting, and do what is fair and right. Stop evicting my people, declares the Almighty LORD. ¹⁰You must have honest scales and honest dry and liquid measures. ¹¹The dry and liquid measures must always be the same: The ephah and the bath should hold the same as one-tenth of a homer. The homer must be the standard measure.ᵃ ¹²One shekel must weigh 20 gerahs. One mina must weigh 60 shekels.ᵇ

Rules for Worship

¹³" 'This is the contribution you must give to the LORD: seventeen percent of your wheat and seventeen percent of your barley. ¹⁴You must give one percent of your olive oil using the standard measure. ¹⁵You must take one sheep out of every 200 from the well-watered pastures of Israel. You must sacrifice them with grain offerings, burnt offerings, and fellowship offerings to make peace with the LORD, declares the Almighty LORD. ¹⁶All the common people must give this contribution to the prince in Israel. ¹⁷Then the prince is responsible to provide burnt offerings, grain offerings, and wine

Be Fair
Ezekiel 45:9-12

Do you have a toy you don't want anymore? It's okay to sell it to a friend or to trade for something else. Just make sure that the price you charge is fair. Don't sell a broken toy as if it were as good as new. Don't buy a necklace you know is worth a lot of money from someone who thinks it's only worth a little. God wants you to be honest in all you do.

be all you can be

ᵃ45:11 A homer was about 60 gallons as a liquid measure or 6 bushels as a dry measure. ᵇ45:12 A shekel was about four-tenths of an ounce.

offerings at the annual festivals, the New Moon Festivals, the weekly days of worship, and all the other appointed festivals of the nation of Israel. He must prepare offerings for sin, grain offerings, burnt offerings, and fellowship offerings to make peace with the LORD for the nation of Israel.

¹⁸" 'This is what the Almighty LORD says: On the first day of the first month, take a young bull that has no defects and remove sin from the holy place. ¹⁹The priest must take some blood from the offering for sin and put it on the doorposts of the temple, on the four corners of the ledge of the altar, and on the doorposts of the gateways of the inner courtyard. ²⁰You must do the same on the seventh day of the month for everyone who unintentionally does something wrong and is unaware of it. So you must make peace with the LORD for the temple.

²¹" 'On the fourteenth day of the first month, you will celebrate the Passover, a festival lasting seven days when unleavened bread is eaten. ²²At that time the prince must prepare for himself and for all the common people a young bull as an offering for sin. ²³Every day during the seven days of the festival, he must prepare burnt offerings for the LORD: seven young bulls that have no defects, seven rams that have no defects, and one male goat as an offering for sin. ²⁴He must also give as a grain offering a half-bushel for each young bull and a half-bushel for each ram. He must also give one gallon of olive oil for every half-bushel of grain. ²⁵On the fifteenth day of the seventh month, at the Festival of Booths, he must do the same as on those seven days. He must prepare the same offerings for sin, burnt offerings, grain offerings, and olive oil.

46 ¹" 'This is what the Almighty LORD says: The east gate of the inner courtyard must be closed during the six working days, but it must be opened on the weekly day of worship. It must also be opened on the New Moon Festival. ²The prince must enter from the outside through the entrance hall of the gateway. He must stand by the doorposts of the gateway. Then the priests must prepare the prince's burnt offerings and fellowship offerings. He must worship at the entrance of the gateway and then leave. The gate must not be closed until evening. ³The common people must worship at the door of the gateway in the presence of the LORD on the weekly days of worship and on New Moon Festivals. ⁴The prince must offer to the LORD six lambs that have no defects and one ram that has no defects as a burnt offering on the day of worship. ⁵The grain offering that is to be brought with the ram must be a half-bushel, and the grain offering that is to be brought with the lambs must be whatever the prince can bring. One gallon of olive oil must be brought with each half-bushel of grain. ⁶On the first day of the month, the burnt offering must be one young bull, six lambs, and one ram—all animals that have no defects. ⁷With each young bull and each ram the offering must include a half-bushel of grain, and with each lamb the offering must be whatever the prince wants to bring. One gallon of olive oil must be offered with each half-bushel of grain. ⁸When the prince enters, he must enter through the entrance hall of the gateway. He must enter and leave the same way.

⁹" 'The people will enter the LORD's presence at the time of the appointed festivals. Those entering through the north gate to worship must leave through the south gate. Those entering through the south gate must leave through the north gate. They must not leave through the same gate they entered. They must leave through the opposite gate. ¹⁰The prince must be among them. When they enter, he must enter. When they leave, he must leave.

¹¹" 'On festival days and at appointed festivals, a grain offering of a half-bushel must be brought with each young bull, and a half-bushel must be brought with each ram. But with the lambs, the prince may bring whatever he wants to bring. One gallon of

olive oil must be brought with each half-bushel of grain. ¹²When the prince prepares a freewill burnt offering, either a burnt offering or a fellowship offering to the LORD, the east gate must be opened for him. He must sacrifice burnt offerings and fellowship offerings as he does on the day of worship. When he leaves, the gate must be shut after him.

¹³" 'Prepare a year-old lamb that has no defects every day as a burnt offering to the LORD. Do this every morning. ¹⁴Also, prepare a grain offering with it every morning: three-and-a-third quarts of grain and one-and-a-third quarts of olive oil to moisten the flour. It will be a grain offering dedicated to the LORD. These rules are to be followed always. ¹⁵Prepare the lamb, the grain offering, and the olive oil every morning as a daily burnt offering.

¹⁶" 'This is what the Almighty LORD says: Suppose the prince offers one of his sons a gift from his property. The gift will belong to his descendants because it is their inheritance. ¹⁷But suppose the prince offers a gift from his property to one of his servants. The gift will belong to the servant only until the year of freedom. Then the gift will go back to the prince. Only his sons can inherit his property. ¹⁸The prince must not take any of the people's property. He must not force them to give up their property. He must give his own property as an inheritance to his sons so that none of my people will be separated from their property.' "

¹⁹The man brought me through a passage beside the gateway to the side rooms that faced north. These rooms were reserved for the priests. He showed me a place on the west side of the rooms. ²⁰He said to me, "This is the place where the priests must boil the meat for the guilt offering and the offering for sin. This is the place where they must bake grain offerings so that they don't have to bring the offerings into the outer courtyard. This way they won't transfer holiness to the people."

²¹Then the man led me to the outer courtyard and took me past the four corners of the courtyard. I saw that in each corner of the courtyard there was a smaller courtyard. ²²The smaller courtyards that were in each of the four corners of the courtyard were 60 feet long and 45 feet wide. All four of the smaller courtyards in the corners of the courtyard were the same size. ²³Around each of the four courtyards were stone walls, and these walls were equipped with fireplaces.

²⁴Then the man said to me, "These are the kitchens where the temple servants must boil the people's sacrifices."

Water Flowing From the Temple

47 ¹Then the man took me back to the door of the temple. I saw water flowing from under the entrance of the temple toward the east. (The temple faced east.) The water was flowing under the south side of the temple, south of the altar. ²Then he led me through the north gate and around to the outer east gate. The water was flowing down the south side of the gate.

³With a measuring line in his hand, the man went eastward. He measured off 1,500 feet and led me through the water. The water came up to my ankles. ⁴Then he measured off another 1,500 feet and led me through the water. The water came up to my knees. He measured off another 1,500 feet and led me through the water. The water came up to my waist. ⁵Then he measured another 1,500 feet. But the water had risen so much that it became a river which I couldn't cross. The river was too deep to cross except by swimming. ⁶Then he asked me, "Son of man, do you see this?"

⁷Then the man led me back along the bank of the river. As I went back, I saw many trees on both sides of the river. ⁸Then the man said to me, "This water flows through the land to the east, down into the Jordan Valley, and into the Dead Sea. When the

water flows into the Dead Sea, it will replace the salt water there with fresh water. [9]Wherever the river flows, there will be many fish and animals. The river will make the water in the Dead Sea fresh. Wherever the river flows, it will bring life. [10]From En Gedi to En Eglaim people will be standing on the shore of the sea with their fishing nets spread out. As many kinds of fish will be there as there are in the Mediterranean Sea. [11]But the water in the swamps and marshes won't become fresh. It will remain salty. [12]All kinds of fruit trees will grow on both sides of the river. Their leaves won't wither, and they won't fail to produce fruit. Each month they will produce fresh fruit because this water flows from the holy place. The fruit will be good food, and the leaves will be used for healing."

Dividing the Land for the LORD's People

[13]This is what the Almighty LORD says: These are the borders of the land that is to be divided among the 12 tribes of Israel. Joseph gets two parts. [14]Divide the land equally. I raised my hand and swore that I would give the land to your ancestors. So this land will be your inheritance.

[15]This is the northern border for the land: On the north side the border will run from the Mediterranean Sea all the way to Hethlon and Hamath Pass. It will run through the city of Zedad and through [16]Berothah and Sibraim, which are between the borders of Damascus and Hamath. It will run to Hazer Hatticon, which is on the border of Hauran. [17]So the border will run from the Mediterranean Sea to Hazar Enon on the border of Damascus. The border of Hamath will lie to the north. This is the north side.

[18]On the east side the border will run between Hauran and Damascus. The Jordan River will serve as the border between Gilead and the land of Israel. The border will continue from the Dead Sea down to Tamar. This is the east side.

[19]On the south side the border will run from Tamar to the oasis at Meribah in Kadesh along the ravine to the Mediterranean Sea. This is the southern border.

[20]On the west side the Mediterranean Sea is the border up to a point opposite Hamath Pass. This is the west side.

[21]Divide this land among yourselves for each of the tribes of Israel. [22]Divide it by drawing lots. This land will be for you. It will also be for the foreign residents who live among you and have given birth to children while they lived with you. Think of them as Israelites. They will draw lots with you for their inheritance among the tribes of Israel. [23]Foreign residents will receive their share of the inheritance with the people of the tribe among whom they are living, declares the Almighty LORD.

[1]These are the names of the tribes. Beginning at the northern border, **Dan** will have one part of the land. It will extend from the road to Hethlon to Hamath Pass and Hazar Enon, on the northern border of Damascus near Hamath, from the eastern border to the western border.

[2]**Asher** will have one part of the land and border Dan on the south. It will extend from the eastern border to the western border.

[3]**Naphtali** will have one part of the land and border Asher on the south. It will extend from the eastern border to the western border.

[4]**Manasseh** will have one part of the land and border Naphtali on the south. It will extend from the eastern border to the western border.

[5]**Ephraim** will have one part of the land and border Manasseh on the south. It will extend from the eastern border to the western border.

[6]**Reuben** will have one part of the land and border Ephraim on the south. It will extend from the eastern border to the western border.

⁷**Judah** will have one part of the land and border Reuben on the south. It will extend from the eastern border to the western border.

⁸The land that you set aside as a special gift for the Lord will border Judah on the south. It will be 43,750 feet wide, and it will be as long as one of the sections of the tribes. It will extend from the eastern border to the western border, and the holy place will be in the middle of it.

⁹This special land that you set aside for the Lord will be 43,750 feet long and 17,500 feet wide. ¹⁰This holy area will belong to the priests. On the north side it will be 43,750 feet long. On the west side it will be 17,500 feet wide. On the east side it will be 17,500 feet wide. On the south side it will be 43,750 feet long. The Lord's holy place will be in the middle of it. ¹¹This land that has been set apart will belong to the priests who are descendants of Zadok. They took care of my holy place. They didn't wander away with the Israelites as the Levites did. ¹²So they will have a special portion from the land. It will be the holiest part of land, next to the land belonging to the Levites.

¹³Alongside the land belonging to the priests will be the land belonging to the Levites. It will be 43,750 feet long and 17,500 feet wide. ¹⁴They must not sell any of it or trade any of it. They must not let others have the best part of the land, because the land is the Lord's and it is holy.

¹⁵A strip of land, 8,750 feet wide by 43,750 feet long, will be left for cities, homes, and pastures. The city will be in the middle of it. ¹⁶These will be the measurements for the city: On the north side it will be 7,875 feet long. On the south side it will be 7,875 feet long. On the east side it will be 7,875 feet wide. And on the west side it will be 7,875 feet wide. ¹⁷The city's pastureland will be 4,375 feet on the north, 4,375 feet on the south, 4,375 feet on the east, and 4,375 feet on the west. ¹⁸The rest of the land borders the holy area and runs lengthwise. This land will be 17,500 feet on its east side and 17,500 feet on its west side. It will be used to provide food for the city workers. ¹⁹City workers from all the tribes in Israel will farm it. ²⁰The whole area will be 43,750 feet square. You must give this land as a special gift to the Lord along with the city property.

²¹Whatever is left on the east side and west side of the holy area and the city property will belong to the prince. This land will extend eastward from the holy area to the eastern border, and it will extend westward to the western border. Both of these areas are as long as one of the sections of the tribes. These areas belong to the prince, and the holy area with the holy place of the temple will be between them. ²²So the Levites' property and the city's property will be between the prince's part of the land. What is between Judah's and Benjamin's boundaries will belong to the prince.

²³This is what the rest of the tribes will receive: **Benjamin** will have one part of the land. It will extend from the eastern border to the western border.

²⁴**Simeon** will have one part of the land and border Benjamin on the south. It will extend from the eastern border to the western border.

²⁵**Issachar** will have one part of the land and border Simeon on the south. It will extend from the eastern border to the western border.

²⁶**Zebulun** will have one part of the land and border Issachar on the south. It will extend from the eastern border to the western border.

²⁷**Gad** will have one part of the land and border Zebulun on the south. It will extend from the eastern border to the western border.

²⁸The southern border of Gad will run south from Tamar to the oasis at Meribah in Kadesh, and it will run along the Brook of Egypt to the Mediterranean Sea. ²⁹This is the land you will divide as your inheritance among the tribes of Israel, and these are their areas, declares the Almighty Lord.

The New City of God

³⁰These will be the exits for the city: The north side will be 7,875 feet long. ³¹The gates of the city will be named after the tribes of Israel. The three gates on the north side will be Reuben Gate, Judah Gate, and Levi Gate.

³²The east side will be 7,875 feet long. The three gates on the east side will be Joseph Gate, Benjamin Gate, and Dan Gate.

³³The south side will be 7,875 feet long. The three gates on the south side will be Simeon Gate, Issachar Gate, and Zebulun Gate.

³⁴The west side will be 7,875 feet long. The three gates on the west side will be Gad Gate, Asher Gate, and Naphtali Gate.

³⁵The city will measure about 31,500 feet all the way around. From then on the city's name will be: The Lord Is There.

Daniel

As a teenager, Daniel was taken as a captive to Babylon. The king of Babylon, Nebuchadnezzar, had Daniel and some of his friends trained to serve the king.

Even though Daniel lived in a pagan land, he chose to remain loyal to God.

God protected Daniel from harm and gave him a position of great importance in Babylon and, later, in Persia. Through visions, God also revealed to Daniel many things that would happen in the future.

Headlines

Daniel Likes His Veggies
Daniel 1, page 1193

**Mystery Man
Saves Three**
Daniel 3, page 1196

**Prophet Keeps
Cats Company**
Daniel 6, page 1201

**Special Delivery
for Daniel**
Daniel 10, page 1207

"Who is the fourth figure, and where did he come from?" See Daniel 3.

Solve These Puzzles

LdIaOnNi'S DeEiN

Answer: Daniel in the lion's den.

Morning	Ba
Afternoon	by
Evening	lo
Nighttime	n - - - - -> Persia

Answer: Babylon falls to Persia in a day.

What's In It For Me?

Remaining true to my convictions . . .

PLEASES GOD.

EARNS THE RESPECT OF OTHERS.

SHOWS MY FAITH IN GOD.

MAKES ME A GOOD EXAMPLE TO PEOPLE WHO DON'T KNOW GOD.

WILL BE REWARDED BY GOD.

Can a Christian Be in Politics?

Sometimes people wonder if a Christian should be in politics. Daniel was an important person in the government of Babylon and, later, of Persia. Daniel did what pleased God. He was honest and didn't take bribes. He always told rulers the truth, even when he thought they might not like what he said.

It may be hard for people in politics to be honest and to always tell the truth. But don't you think it would be good for our country to have a lot of Christians in high offices?

Perhaps you can become a Christian mayor, senator, or even president! If you put God first in your life as Daniel did, you could serve the Lord in government, too.

Angels at War

Daniel 10 gives us a rare look into the world of angels. Here are some of the things we discover about angels in the book of Daniel:

- God's angels and Satan's angels are at war.
- Satan's angels try to harm or interfere with God's people.
- Angel commanders are assigned to nations.
- Angels have ranks, like soldiers. Daniel's angel was stopped by a higher-ranking enemy angel until chief commander Michael, an archangel, arrived.

Daniel

Daniel and His Friends Remain Faithful to God

1 ¹In the third year of the reign of King Jehoiakim of Judah, King Nebuchadnezzar of Babylon came to Jerusalem and attacked it. ²The Lord handed King Jehoiakim of Judah and some utensils from God's temple over to Nebuchadnezzar. Nebuchadnezzar took the utensils to the temple of his god in Babylonia and put them in the temple treasury.

³The king told Ashpenaz, the chief-of-staff, to bring some of the Israelites, the royal family, and the nobility. ⁴They were to be young men who were healthy, good-looking, knowledgeable in all subjects, well-informed, intelligent, and able to serve in the king's palace. They were to be taught the language and literature of the Babylonians.

⁵The king arranged for them to get a daily allowance of the king's rich food and wine. They were to be trained for three years. After that, they were to serve the king. ⁶Among these young men were some Judeans: Daniel, Hananiah, Mishael, and Azariah. ⁷The chief-of-staff gave them ⌊Babylonian⌋ names: To Daniel he gave the name Belteshazzar. To Hananiah he gave the name Shadrach. To Mishael he gave the name Meshach. And to Azariah he gave the name Abednego.

⁸Daniel made up his mind not to harm himself by eating the king's rich food and drinking the king's wine. So he asked the chief-of-staff for permission not to harm himself in this way.

⁹God made the chief-of-staff kind and compassionate toward Daniel. ¹⁰The chief-of-staff told Daniel, "I'm afraid of my master, the king. The king determined what you should eat and drink. If he sees that you look worse than the other young men your age, he would have my head cut off."

¹¹The chief-of-staff put a supervisor in charge of Daniel, Hananiah, Mishael, and Azariah. Daniel said to the supervisor, ¹²"Please test us for ten days. Give us only vegetables to eat and water to drink. ¹³Then compare us to the young men who are eating the king's rich food. Decide how to treat us on the basis of how we look."

¹⁴The supervisor listened to them about this matter and tested them for ten days. ¹⁵After ten days they looked healthier and stronger than the young men who had been

Respect

Daniel didn't want to eat food that God told him not to eat. But when the king's food was placed before him, Daniel didn't stamp his foot and shout, "I won't!" When Daniel talked to the chief-of-staff at his school, he showed respect. It's right to show respect to any adult. When you show respect, adults are more likely to listen to you, too.

be
all you
can be

eating the king's rich food. [16]So the supervisor took away the king's rich food and wine and gave them vegetables.

[17]God gave these four men knowledge, wisdom, and the ability to understand all kinds of literature. Daniel could also understand all kinds of visions and dreams.

[18]At the end of the three-year training period, the chief-of-staff brought all the young men to Nebuchadnezzar. [19]The king talked to them and found no one like Daniel, Hananiah, Mishael, and Azariah among all of them. So these four men served the king. [20]Whenever the king asked them about things that required wisdom and insight, he found that they knew ten times more than all the magicians and psychics in his whole kingdom.

[21]Daniel served the royal palace until the first year of King Cyrus of Persia.

Nebuchadnezzar's Dream About a Statue Made of Four Metals

[1]During the second year of Nebuchadnezzar's reign, he had some dreams. He was troubled, but he stayed asleep. [2]The king sent for the magicians, psychics, sorcerers, and astrologers so that they could tell him what he had dreamed. So they came to the king.

[3]The king said to them, "I had a dream, and I'm troubled by it. I want to know what the dream was."

[4]The astrologers spoke to the king in Aramaic, "Your Majesty, may you live forever! Tell us the dream, and we'll interpret it for you."

[5]The king answered the astrologers, "I meant what I said! If you don't tell me the dream and its meaning, you will be torn limb from limb, and your houses will be turned into piles of rubble. [6]But if you tell me the dream and its meaning, I will give you gifts, awards, and high honors. Now tell me the dream and its meaning."

[7]Once more they said, "Your Majesty, tell us the dream, and we'll tell you its meaning."

[8]The king replied, "I'm sure you're trying to buy some time because you know that I meant what I said. [9]If you don't tell me the dream, you'll all receive the same punishment. You have agreed among yourselves to make up a phony explanation to give me, hoping that things will change. So tell me the dream. Then I'll know that you can explain its meaning to me."

[10]The astrologers answered the king, "No one on earth can tell the king what he asks. No other king, no matter how great and powerful, has ever asked such a thing of any magician, psychic, or astrologer. [11]What you ask is difficult, Your Majesty. No one can tell what you dreamed except the gods, and they don't live with humans."

[12]This made the king so angry and furious that he gave an order to destroy all the wise advisers in Babylon. [13]So a decree was issued that the wise advisers were to be killed, and some men were sent to find Daniel and his friends and kill them.

[14]While Arioch, the captain of the royal guard, was leaving to kill the wise advisers in Babylon, Daniel spoke to him using shrewd judgment. [15]He asked Arioch, the royal official, "Why is the king's decree so harsh?" So Arioch explained everything to Daniel.

[16]Daniel went and asked the king to give him some time so that he could explain the dream's meaning. [17]Then Daniel went home and told his friends Hananiah, Mishael, and Azariah about this matter. [18]He told them to ask the God of heaven to be merciful and to explain this secret to them so that they would not be destroyed with the rest of the wise advisers in Babylon.

¹⁹The secret was revealed to Daniel in a vision during the night. So Daniel praised the God of heaven. ²⁰He said,

> "Praise God's name from everlasting to everlasting
>   because he is wise and powerful.
> 21 He changes times and periods of history.
>   He removes kings and establishes them.
>   He gives wisdom to those who are wise
>   and knowledge to those who have insight.
> 22 He reveals deeply hidden things.
>   He knows what is in the dark,
>   and light lives with him.
> 23 God of my ancestors, I thank and praise you.
>   You gave me wisdom and power.
>   You told me the answer to our question.
>   You told us what the king wants to know."

²⁴Then Daniel went to Arioch, whom the king had appointed to destroy Babylon's wise advisers. Daniel told him, "Don't destroy Babylon's wise advisers. Take me to the king, and I'll explain the dream's meaning to him."

²⁵Arioch immediately took Daniel to the king. He told the king, "I've found one of the captives from Judah who can explain the dream's meaning to you, Your Majesty."

²⁶The king asked Daniel (who had been renamed Belteshazzar), "Can you tell me the dream I had and its meaning?"

²⁷Daniel answered the king, "No wise adviser, psychic, magician, or fortuneteller can tell the king this secret. ²⁸But there is a God in heaven who reveals secrets. He will tell King Nebuchadnezzar what is going to happen in the days to come. This is your dream, the vision you had while you were asleep: ²⁹Your Majesty, while you were lying in bed, thoughts about what would happen in the future came to you. The one who reveals secrets told you what is going to happen. ³⁰This secret wasn't revealed to me because I'm wiser than anyone else. It was revealed so that you could be told the meaning and so that you would know your innermost thoughts.

³¹"Your Majesty, you had a vision. You saw a large statue. This statue was very bright. It stood in front of you, and it looked terrifying. ³²The head of this statue was made of fine gold. Its chest and arms were made of silver. Its stomach and hips were made of bronze. ³³Its legs were made of iron. Its feet were made partly of iron and partly of clay. ³⁴While you were watching, a stone was cut out, but not by humans. It struck the statue's iron-and-clay feet and smashed them. ³⁵Then all at once, the iron, clay, bronze, silver, and gold were smashed. They became like husks on a threshing floor*ᵃ* in summer. The wind carried them away, and not a trace of them could be found. But the stone that struck the statue became a large mountain which filled the whole world. ³⁶This is the dream. Now we'll tell you its meaning.

³⁷"Your Majesty, you are the greatest king. The God of heaven has given you a kingdom. He has given you power, strength, and honor. ³⁸He has given you control over people, wild animals, and birds, wherever they live. He has made you ruler of them all. You are the head of gold. ³⁹Another kingdom, inferior to yours, will rise to power after you. Then there will be a third kingdom, a kingdom of bronze, that will rule the whole world. ⁴⁰There will also be a fourth kingdom. It will be as strong as iron. (Iron smashes and shatters everything.) As iron crushes things, this fourth kingdom will smash and crush all the other kingdoms. ⁴¹You also saw the feet and toes.

ᵃ2:35 A threshing floor is an outdoor area where grain is separated from its husks.

They were partly potters' clay and partly iron. This means that there will be a divided kingdom which has some of the firmness of iron. As you saw, iron was mixed with clay. ⁴²The toes were partly iron and partly clay. Part of the kingdom will be strong, and part will be brittle. ⁴³As you saw, iron was mixed with clay. So the two parts of the kingdom will mix by intermarrying, but they will not hold together any more than iron can mix with clay.

⁴⁴"At the time of those kings, the God of heaven will establish a kingdom that will never be destroyed. No other people will be permitted to rule it. It will smash all the other kingdoms and put an end to them. But it will be established forever. ⁴⁵This is the stone that you saw cut out from a mountain, but not by humans. It smashed the iron, bronze, clay, silver, and gold. The great God has told you what will happen in the future, Your Majesty. The dream is true, and you can trust that this is its meaning."

⁴⁶King Nebuchadnezzar immediately bowed down on the ground in front of Daniel. He ordered that gifts and offerings be given to Daniel. ⁴⁷The king said to Daniel, "Your God is truly the greatest of gods, the Lord over kings. He can reveal secrets because you were able to reveal this secret."

⁴⁸Then the king promoted Daniel and gave him many wonderful gifts. Nebuchadnezzar made Daniel governor of the whole province of Babylon and head of all Babylon's wise advisers. ⁴⁹With the king's permission, Daniel appointed Shadrach, Meshach, and Abednego to govern the province of Babylon. But Daniel stayed at the king's court.

Shadrach, Meshach, and Abednego Refuse to Worship an Idol

¹King Nebuchadnezzar made a gold statue 90 feet high and 9 feet wide. He set it up in a recessed area in the wall*ᵃ* in the province of Babylon. ²King Nebuchadnezzar sent messengers to assemble the satraps, governors, mayors, military advisers, treasurers, judges, officers, and all the other provincial officials to dedicate the statue he had set up. ³Then the satraps, governors, mayors, military advisers, treasurers, judges, officers, and all the other provincial officials assembled to dedicate the statue King Nebuchadnezzar had set up. They stood in front of the statue.

⁴The herald called out loudly, "People of every province, nation, and language! ⁵When you hear the sound of rams' horns, flutes, lyres, harps, and three-stringed harps playing at the same time with all other kinds of instruments, bow down and worship the gold statue that King Nebuchadnezzar has set up. ⁶Whoever doesn't bow down and worship will immediately be thrown into a blazing furnace." ⁷As soon as they heard the sound of rams' horns, flutes, lyres, harps, and three-stringed harps with all other kinds of instruments, all the people from every province, nation, and language bowed down and worshiped the gold statue King Nebuchadnezzar had set up.

⁸After that happened, some astrologers came forward and brought charges against the Jews. ⁹They addressed King Nebuchadnezzar, "Your Majesty, may you live forever! ¹⁰Your Majesty, you gave an order that everyone who hears the sound of rams' horns, flutes, lyres, harps, and three-stringed harps playing at the same time with all other kinds of instruments should bow down and worship the gold statue. ¹¹Your order said that whoever doesn't bow down and worship will be thrown into a blazing furnace. ¹²There are certain Jews whom you appointed to govern the province of Babylon: Shadrach, Meshach, and Abednego. These men didn't obey your order, Your Majesty. They don't honor your gods or worship the statue that you set up."

¹³Then, in a fit of rage and anger, Nebuchadnezzar summoned Shadrach, Meshach,

---

ᵃ3:1 Or "in the plain of Dura."

and Abednego. Immediately, they were brought to the king. [14]Nebuchadnezzar asked them, "Shadrach, Meshach, and Abednego, is it true that you don't honor my gods or worship the gold statue that I set up? [15]When you hear the sound of the rams' horns, flutes, lyres, harps, and three-stringed harps playing at the same time with all other kinds of instruments, will you bow down and worship the gold statue I made? If you don't worship it, you will immediately be thrown into a blazing furnace. What god can save you from my power then?"

[16]Shadrach, Meshach, and Abednego answered King Nebuchadnezzar, "We don't need to answer your last question. [17]If our God, whom we honor, can save us from a blazing furnace and from your power, he will, Your Majesty. [18]But if he doesn't, you should know, Your Majesty, we'll never honor your gods or worship the gold statue that you set up."

[19]Nebuchadnezzar was so filled with anger toward Shadrach, Meshach, and Abednego that his face turned red. He ordered that the furnace should be heated seven times hotter than normal. [20]He told some soldiers from his army to tie up Shadrach, Meshach, and Abednego so that they could be thrown into the blazing furnace. [21]Then the three men were thrown into the blazing furnace. They were wearing their clothes, hats, and other clothing. [22]The king's order was so urgent and the furnace was so extremely hot that the men who carried Shadrach, Meshach, and Abednego were killed by the flames from the fire. [23]So these three men—Shadrach, Meshach, and Abednego—fell into the blazing furnace. They were still tied up.

[24]Then Nebuchadnezzar was startled. He sprang to his feet. He asked his advisers, "Didn't we throw three men into the fire?"

"That's true, Your Majesty," they answered.

[25]The king replied, "But look, I see four men. They're untied, walking in the middle of the fire, and unharmed. The fourth one looks like a son of the gods."

[26]Then Nebuchadnezzar went to the door of the blazing furnace and said, "Shadrach, Meshach, and Abednego—servants of the Most High God—come out here."

Shadrach, Meshach, and Abednego came out of the fire. [27]The king's satraps, governors, mayors, and advisers gathered around the three men. They saw that the fire had not harmed their bodies. The hair on their heads wasn't singed, their clothes weren't burned, and they didn't smell of smoke.

[28]Nebuchadnezzar said, "Praise the God of Shadrach, Meshach, and Abednego. He sent his angel and saved his servants, who trusted him. They disobeyed the king and risked their lives so that they would not have to honor or worship any god except their own God. [29]So I order that people from every province, nation, or language who say anything slanderous about the God of Shadrach, Meshach, and Abednego will be torn limb from limb. Their houses will be turned into piles of rubble. No other god can rescue like this."

[30]Then the king promoted Shadrach, Meshach, and Abednego to higher positions in the province of Babylon.

A Letter From Nebuchadnezzar About His Insanity

[a1]From King Nebuchadnezzar.

To the people of every province, nation, and language in the world.

I wish you peace and prosperity.

[2]I am pleased to write to you about the miraculous signs and amazing things the Most High God did for me.

---

[a]4:1 Daniel 4:1-37 in English Bibles is Daniel 3:31–4:34 in the Hebrew Bible.

³   His miraculous signs are impressive.
He uses his power to do amazing things.
His kingdom is an eternal kingdom.
His power lasts from one generation to the next.

⁴I, Nebuchadnezzar, was living comfortably at home. I was prosperous while living in my palace. ⁵I had a dream that terrified me. The visions I had while I was asleep frightened me. ⁶So I ordered all the wise advisers in Babylon to be brought to me to tell me the dream's meaning. ⁷The magicians, psychics, astrologers, and fortunetellers came to me. I told them the dream, but they couldn't tell me its meaning. ⁸Finally, Daniel came to me. (He had been renamed Belteshazzar after my god ˌBelˌ.) The spirit of the holy gods is in him.

I told him the dream: ⁹"Belteshazzar, head of the magicians, I know the spirit of the holy gods is in you. No secret is too hard for you ˌto uncoverˌ. Tell me the meaning of the visions I had in my dream. ¹⁰These are the visions I had while I was asleep: I was looking, and I saw an oak tree in the middle of the earth. It was very tall. ¹¹The tree grew, and it became strong enough and tall enough to reach the sky. It could be seen everywhere on earth. ¹²It had beautiful leaves and plenty of fruit, enough to feed everyone. Wild animals found shade under it. Birds came to live in its branches. It fed every living creature.

¹³"I was seeing these visions as I was asleep. I saw a guardian, a holy being, come down from heaven. ¹⁴He shouted loudly, 'Cut down the oak tree! Cut off its branches! Strip off its leaves! Scatter its fruit! Make the animals under it run away, and make the birds fly from its branches. ¹⁵But leave the stump and its roots in the ground. Secure it with an iron and bronze chain in the grass in the field. Let it get wet with the dew from the sky. And let it get its share of the plants on the ground with the animals. ¹⁶Let its human mind be changed, and give it the mind of an animal. Let it remain like this for seven time periods. ¹⁷The guardians have announced this decision. The holy ones have announced this so that every living creature will know that the Most High has power over human kingdoms. He gives them to whomever he wishes. He can place the lowest of people in charge of them.' "

¹⁸ˌI said,ˌ "This is the dream I, King Nebuchadnezzar, had. Now you, Belteshazzar, tell me its meaning because the wise advisers in my kingdom can't tell it to me. However, you can, because the spirit of the holy gods is in you."

¹⁹Then Daniel (who had been renamed Belteshazzar) was momentarily stunned. What he was thinking frightened him. I told him, "Belteshazzar, don't let the dream and its meaning frighten you."

Belteshazzar answered, "Sir, I wish that the dream were about those who hate you and its meaning were about your enemies. ²⁰You saw an oak tree grow and become strong enough and tall enough to reach the sky. It could be seen everywhere on earth. ²¹It had beautiful leaves and plenty of fruit, enough to feed everyone. Wild animals lived under it, and birds made their homes in its branches. ²²You are that tree, Your Majesty. You grew and became strong and mighty until you reached the sky. Your power reaches the most distant part of the world. ²³You saw a guardian, a holy being, come down from heaven. He said, 'Cut down the oak tree! Destroy it! But leave the stump and its roots in the ground. Secure it with an iron and bronze chain in the grass in the field. Let it get wet with the dew from the sky. Let it get its share of the plants on the ground with the wild animals for seven time periods.'

²⁴"This is the meaning, Your Majesty. The Most High has decided to apply it to you, Your Majesty. ²⁵You will be forced away from people and live with the wild animals.

You will eat grass like cattle. The dew from the sky will make you wet. And seven time periods will pass until you realize that the Most High has power over human kingdoms and that he gives them to whomever he wishes. ²⁶Since I said that the stump and the tree's roots were to be left, your kingdom will be restored to you as soon as you realize that heaven rules.

²⁷"That is why, Your Majesty, my best advice is that you stop sinning, and do what is right. Stop committing the same errors, and have pity on the poor. Maybe you can prolong your prosperity."

²⁸All this happened to King Nebuchadnezzar. ²⁹Twelve months later, he was walking around the royal palace in Babylon. ³⁰The king thought, "Look how great Babylon is! I built the royal palace by my own impressive power and for my glorious honor." ³¹Before the words came out of his mouth, a voice said from heaven, "King Nebuchadnezzar, listen to this: The kingdom has been taken from you. ³²You will be forced away from people and live with the wild animals. You will eat grass like cattle. And seven time periods will pass until you realize that the Most High has power over human kingdoms and that he gives them to whomever he wishes." ³³Just then the prediction about Nebuchadnezzar came true. He was forced away from people and ate grass like cattle. Dew from the sky made his body wet until his hair grew as long as eagles' feathers and his nails grew as long as birds' claws.

³⁴At the end of the seven time periods, I, Nebuchadnezzar, looked up to heaven, and my mind came back to me. I thanked the Most High, and I praised and honored the one who lives forever, because his power lasts forever and his kingdom lasts from one generation to the next. ³⁵Everyone who lives on earth is nothing compared to him. He does whatever he wishes with the army of heaven and with those who live on earth. There is no one who can oppose him or ask him, "What are you doing?"

³⁶Just then my mind came back to me. My royal honor and glory were also given back to me. My advisers and nobles wanted to meet with me ⌊again⌋. I was given back my kingdom and made extraordinarily great. ³⁷Now I, Nebuchadnezzar, will praise, honor, and give glory to the King of Heaven. Everything he does is true, his ways are right, and he can humiliate those who act arrogantly.

Good Morning, God

Daniel 4:31-33

God gave King Nebuchadnezzar two great gifts: wealth and power. But soon the king began to take the credit for his greatness. He was so proud of himself! He wondered, *Who needs God?* These verses show that the king learned a lesson about pride the hard way. You may have special talents or abilities. Whenever you are tempted to be proud about who you are or what you have done, remember the king's story. Give God the credit that he deserves for making you special.

Lord, help me never to forget that my talents and gifts are from you.

The Handwriting on the Wall

5 [1]King Belshazzar threw a large banquet for 1,000 nobles and drank wine with them. [2]As they were tasting the wine, Belshazzar ordered that the gold and silver utensils which his grandfather Nebuchadnezzar had taken from the temple in Jerusalem be brought to him. He wanted to drink from them with his nobles, his wives, and his concubines.*

[3]So the servants brought the gold utensils that had been taken from God's temple in Jerusalem. The king, his nobles, wives, and concubines drank from them. [4]They drank the wine and praised their gods made of gold, silver, bronze, iron, wood, or stone.

[5]Suddenly, the fingers of a person's hand appeared and wrote on the plaster wall opposite the lamp stand of the royal palace. The king watched as the hand wrote. [6]Then the king turned pale, and his thoughts frightened him. His hip joints became loose, and his knees knocked against each other.

[7]The king screamed for the psychics, astrologers, and fortunetellers to be brought to him. He told these wise advisers of Babylon, "Whoever reads this writing and tells me its meaning will be dressed in purple, wear a gold chain on his neck, and become the third-highest ruler in the kingdom." [8]All the king's wise advisers came, but they couldn't read the writing or tell the king its meaning. [9]King Belshazzar was terrified, and his face turned pale. His nobles didn't know what to do.

[10]The discussion between the king and his nobles brought the queen herself into the banquet hall. The queen said, "Your Majesty, may you live forever! Don't let your thoughts frighten you, and don't turn pale. [11]There's a man in your kingdom who has the spirit of the holy gods. In the days of your grandfather, he was found to have insight, good judgment, and wisdom like the wisdom of the gods. Your grandfather, King Nebuchadnezzar, made him head of the magicians, psychics, astrologers, and fortunetellers. [12]This Daniel (who had been renamed Belteshazzar) was found to have knowledge, judgment, and an extraordinary spirit. He has the ability to interpret dreams, solve riddles, and untangle problems. Now, call Daniel, and he will tell you what it means."

[13]So Daniel was taken to the king. The king asked him, "Are you Daniel, one of the captives that my grandfather brought from Judah? [14]I've heard that you have the spirit of the gods and that you have insight, good judgment, and extraordinary wisdom. [15]The wise advisers and the psychics were brought to me to read this writing and tell me its meaning. But they couldn't tell me its meaning. [16]I have heard that you can interpret such things and untangle problems. If you can read the writing and tell me its meaning, you will be dressed in purple, wear a gold chain on your neck, and become the third-highest ruler in the kingdom."

[17]Daniel told the king, "Keep your gifts. Give your gifts and awards to someone else. I'll still read the writing for you and tell you its meaning.

[18]"Your Majesty, the Most High God gave your grandfather Nebuchadnezzar a kingdom, might, honor, and glory. [19]People from every province, nation, and language trembled and were terrified by him, because God gave him power. Nebuchadnezzar killed whomever he wanted to kill, and he kept alive whomever he wanted to keep alive. He promoted whomever he wanted to promote, and he demoted whomever he wanted to demote. [20]But when he became so arrogant and conceited that he became overconfident, he was removed from the royal throne. His honor was taken away from him. [21]He was chased away from people, and his mind was changed into an animal's mind. He lived with wild donkeys, ate grass like cattle, and his body became wet with

---

a 5:2 A concubine is considered a wife except she has fewer rights under the law.

dew from the sky. This happened until he realized that the Most High God has power over human kingdoms. God puts whomever he wishes in charge of them.

²²"Belshazzar, you are one of Nebuchadnezzar's successors. You didn't remain humble, even though you knew all this. ²³But you made yourself greater than the Lord of heaven. You had the utensils from his temple brought to you. You, your nobles, wives, and concubines drank wine from them. You praised your gods made of silver, gold, bronze, iron, wood, or stone. These gods can't see, hear, or know anything. You didn't honor God, who has power over your life and everything you do. ²⁴So he sent the hand to write this inscription. ²⁵This is what has been written: Numbered, Numbered, Weighed, and Divided. ²⁶This is its meaning: Numbered—God has numbered the days of your kingdom and will bring it to an end. ²⁷Weighed—you have been weighed on a scale and found to be too light. ²⁸Divided—your kingdom will be divided and given to the Medes and Persians."[b]

²⁹Then Belshazzar ordered that Daniel be dressed in purple and wear a gold chain on his neck. He made Daniel the third-highest ruler in the kingdom. ³⁰That night King Belshazzar of Babylon was killed.[c] ³¹Darius the Mede took over the kingdom. He was 62 years old.

Daniel in the Lions' Den

6 [a]¹Darius decided it would be good to appoint 120 satraps to rule throughout the kingdom. ²Over these satraps were three officials. Daniel was one of these officials. The satraps were to report to these three officials so that the king wouldn't be cheated.

³This man, Daniel, distinguished himself among the other officials and satraps because there was an extraordinary spirit in him. The king thought about putting him in charge of the whole kingdom. ⁴So the other officials and satraps tried to find something to accuse Daniel of in his duties for the kingdom. But they couldn't find anything wrong because he was trustworthy. No error or fault could be found. ⁵These men said, "We won't find anything to accuse this man, Daniel, unless we find it in his religious practices."

⁶So these officials and satraps went to the king as a group. They said to him, "May King Darius live forever! ⁷All the officials, governors, satraps, advisers, and mayors agree that the king should make a statute and enforce a decree. The decree should state that for the next 30 days whoever asks for anything from any god or person except you, Your Majesty, will be thrown into a lions' den. ⁸Your Majesty, issue this decree, and sign it. According to the law of the Medes and Persians no one could change it or repeal it." ⁹So Darius signed the written decree.

¹⁰When Daniel learned that the document had been signed, he went to his house. An upper room in his house had windows that opened in the direction of Jerusalem. Three times each day he got down on his knees and prayed to his God. He had always praised God this way.

¹¹One of those times the men came in as a group and found Daniel praying and pleading to his God. ¹²Then they went and spoke to the king about his decree. They asked, "Didn't you sign a decree which stated that for 30 days whoever asks for anything from any god or person except you, Your Majesty, will be thrown into a lions' den?"

The king answered, "That's true. According to the law of the Medes and Persians the decree can't be repealed."

---

^b5:28 There is a play on words here between Aramaic *peres* (divided) and *paras* (Persians). ^c5:30 Daniel 5:31 in English Bibles is Daniel 6:1 in the Hebrew Bible. ^a6:1 Daniel 6:1-28 in English Bibles is Daniel 6:2-29 in the Hebrew Bible.

¹³They replied, "Your Majesty, Daniel, one of the captives from Judah, refuses to obey your order or the decree that you signed. He prays three times each day."

¹⁴The king was very displeased when he heard this. He tried every way he could think of to save Daniel. Until sundown he did everything he could to rescue him.

¹⁵Then Daniel's accusers gathered in front of the king. They said to him, "Remember, Your Majesty, the Medes and Persians have a law that no decree or statute the king makes can be changed."

¹⁶So the king gave the order, and Daniel was brought to him and thrown into the lions' den. The king told Daniel, "May your God, whom you always worship, save you!"

¹⁷A stone was brought and placed over the opening of the den. The king put his seal on the stone, using his ring and the rings of his nobles, so that Daniel's situation could not be changed.

¹⁸Then the king went to his palace and spent the night without food or company. He couldn't get to sleep. ¹⁹At dawn, as soon as it was light, the king got up and quickly went to the lions' den. ²⁰As he came near the den where Daniel was, the king called to Daniel with anguish in his voice, "Daniel, servant of the living God! Was God, whom you always worship, able to save you from the lions?"

²¹Daniel said to the king, "Your Majesty, may you live forever! ²²My God sent his angel and shut the lions' mouths so that they couldn't hurt me. He did this because he considered me innocent. Your Majesty, I haven't committed any crime."

²³The king was overjoyed and had Daniel taken out of the den. When Daniel was taken out of the den, people saw that he was completely unharmed because he trusted his God.

²⁴The king ordered those men who had brought charges against Daniel to be brought to him. They, their wives, and their children were thrown into the lions' den. Before they reached the bottom of the den, the lions attacked them and crushed all their bones.

²⁵Then King Darius wrote to the people of every province, nation, and language all over the world:

I wish you peace and prosperity.

²⁶I decree that in every part of my kingdom people should tremble with terror in front of Daniel's God, the living God who continues forever. His kingdom will never be destroyed. His power lasts to the end of time. ²⁷He

Good Morning, God
Daniel 6:23

Daniel was arrested for praying and was thrown into the lions' den to be eaten! To everyone's surprise, Daniel was still alive the next morning after spending the night with the ferocious felines. God had sent an angel to shut the mouths of the lions so Daniel was protected. If God can protect Daniel, what do you think he can do for you? If you need God's protection, just ask him. And watch him work in your life.

God, I know I can trust you to help me because of what you did for Daniel.

saves, rescues, and does miraculous signs and amazing things in heaven and on earth. He saved Daniel from the lions.

²⁸This man, Daniel, prospered during the reign of Darius and the reign of Cyrus the Persian.

Daniel's Vision About Four Animals

¹In Belshazzar's first year as king of Babylon, Daniel had a dream. He saw a vision while he was asleep. He wrote down the main parts of the dream.

²In my visions at night I, Daniel, saw the four winds of heaven stirring up the Mediterranean Sea. ³Four large animals, each one different from the others, came out of the sea.

⁴The first animal was like a lion, but it had wings like an eagle. I watched until its wings were plucked off and it was lifted off the ground. It was made to stand on two feet like a human and was given a human mind.

⁵I saw a second animal. It looked like a bear. It was raised on one side and had three ribs in its mouth between its teeth. It was told, "Get up, and eat as much meat as you want."

⁶After this, I saw another animal. It looked like a leopard. On its back it had four wings, like the wings of a bird. The animal also had four heads. It was given power to rule.

⁷After this, I saw a fourth animal in my vision during the night. It was terrifying, dreadful, extraordinarily strong, and had large iron teeth. It devoured and crushed its victims and trampled whatever was left. It acted differently from all the other animals that I had seen before. It had ten horns. ⁸While I was thinking about the horns, another horn, a little horn, came up among them. It uprooted three of the other horns. This horn had eyes like human eyes and a mouth that spoke impressive things.

9 I watched until thrones were set up
   and the Ancient One, who has lived for endless years, sat down.
     His clothes were as white as snow
       and the hair on his head was like pure wool.
     His throne was fiery flames,
       and its wheels were burning fire.
10   A river of fire flowed.
       It came from him.
     Thousands and thousands served him.
     Ten thousand times ten thousand were stationed in front of him.
   The court convened,
     and the books were opened.

¹¹I continued to watch because of the impressive words that the horn was speaking. I watched until the animal was killed. Its body was destroyed and put into a raging fire. ¹²The power of the rest of the animals was taken away, but they were allowed to live for a period of time.

¹³In my visions during the night, I saw among the clouds in heaven someone like the Son of Man.ᵃ He came to the Ancient One, who has lived for endless years, and was presented to him. ¹⁴He was given power, honor, and a kingdom. People from every province, nation, and language were to serve him. His power is an eternal power that will not be taken away. His kingdom will never be destroyed.

ᵃ7:13 Or "like a human."

¹⁵I, Daniel, was deeply troubled, and my visions frightened me. ¹⁶I went to someone who was standing there and asked him to tell me the truth about all this. So he told me what all this meant. ¹⁷He said, "These four large animals are four kingdoms that will rise to power on the earth. ¹⁸But the holy people of the Most High will take possession of the kingdom and keep it forever and ever."

¹⁹Then I wanted to know the truth about the fourth animal, which was so different from all the others. It was very terrifying and had iron teeth and bronze claws. It devoured and crushed its victims, and trampled whatever was left. ²⁰I also wanted to know about the ten horns on its head and about the other horn that had come up and made three of the horns fall out. That horn had eyes and a mouth that spoke impressive things. It appeared to be bigger than the others. ²¹I saw that horn making war against the holy people and defeating them. ²²It did this until the Ancient One, who has lived for endless years, came and judged in favor of the holy people of the Most High. The time came when the holy people took possession of the kingdom.

²³He said, "The fourth animal will be the fourth of these kingdoms on earth. It will be different from all other kingdoms. It will devour, trample, and crush the whole world. ²⁴The ten horns are ten kings that will rise to power from that kingdom. Another king will rise to power after them. He will be different from the kings who came before him, and he will humble three kings. ²⁵He will speak against the Most High God, oppress the holy people of the Most High, and plan to change the appointed times and laws. The holy people will be handed over to him for a time, times, and half of a time. ²⁶But judgment will be handed down, his power will be taken away, and he will be completely and permanently destroyed. ²⁷The kingdom, along with the power and greatness of all the kingdoms under heaven, will be given to the holy people of the Most High. Their kingdom is eternal. All other powers will serve and obey them."

²⁸Here is the end of the matter. I, Daniel, was terrified by my thoughts, and I turned pale. I kept this to myself.

Daniel's Vision About the Ram and the Goat

8 ¹In Belshazzar's third year as king, I, Daniel, saw a vision. This vision came after the one I saw earlier. ²In my vision I saw myself in the fortress of Susa in the province of Elam. In my vision I saw myself at Ulai Gate. ³I looked up and saw a single ram standing beside the gate. The ram had two long horns, one longer than the other, though the longer one had grown up later. ⁴I saw the ram charging west, north, and south. No other animal could stand in front of it, and no one could escape from its power. It did anything it pleased and continued to grow.

⁵As I was watching closely, I saw a male goat coming from the west. It crossed the whole earth without touching it. This goat had a prominent horn between its eyes. ⁶The goat was coming toward the two-horned ram that I had seen standing beside the gate. It furiously ran at the ram. ⁷I saw it come closer to the ram. The goat was extremely angry with the ram, so it attacked the ram. It broke both of the ram's horns. The ram didn't have the strength to stand up against the goat. So the ram was thrown down on the ground and trampled. No one could rescue the ram from the goat's power.

⁸The male goat became very important. But when the goat became powerful, his large horn broke off. In its place grew four horns. They corresponded to the four winds of heaven. ⁹Out of one of the horns came a small horn. It gained power over the south, the east, and the beautiful land. ¹⁰It continued to gain power until it reached the army of heaven. It threw some of the army of heaven, the stars, down on the ground and trampled them. ¹¹Then it attacked the commander of the army so that it took the daily burnt offering from him and wrecked his holy place. ¹²In its rebelliousness it was given

an army to put a stop to the daily burnt offering. It threw truth on the ground. The horn was successful in everything it did.*

¹³Then I heard a holy one speaking. Another holy one said to the one who was speaking, "How long will the things in this vision—the daily burnt offering, the destructive rebellion, the surrender of the holy place, and the trampling of the army—take place?"

¹⁴He told me, "For 2,300 evenings and mornings. Then the holy place will be made acceptable to God."

¹⁵Now as I, Daniel, watched the vision and tried to understand it, I saw someone who looked like a man standing in front of me. ¹⁶I heard a man in Ulai Gate call loudly, "Gabriel, explain the vision to this man."

¹⁷Gabriel came up beside me, and when he came, I was terrified and immediately knelt down.

He said to me, "Son of man, understand that the vision is about the end times." ¹⁸As he spoke to me, I fainted facedown on the ground, but he touched me and made me stand up. ¹⁹He said, "I will tell you what will happen in the last days, the time of God's anger, because the end time has been determined.

²⁰"The two-horned ram that you saw represents the kingdoms of Media and Persia. ²¹The hairy male goat is the kingdom of Greece, and the large horn between its eyes is its first king. ²²The horn broke off, and four horns replaced it. Four kingdoms will come out of that nation, but they won't be as strong as the first king was.

²³"In the last days of those kingdoms, when rebellions are finished, a stern-looking king who understands mysterious things will rise to power. ²⁴He will become very strong, but not by his own strength. He will cause astounding destruction and will be successful in everything he does. He will destroy those who are powerful along with some holy people. ²⁵He will cleverly use his power to deceive others successfully. He will consider himself to be great and destroy many people when they don't expect it. He will oppose the Commander of Commanders, but he will be defeated, though not by any human power. ²⁶The vision about the 2,300 evenings and mornings that was explained to you is true. Seal the vision, because it is about things that will happen in the distant future."

²⁷I, Daniel, was exhausted and sick for days. Then I got up and worked for the king. The vision horrified me because I couldn't understand it.

Daniel's Prayer About Jerusalem Is Answered

9 ¹Xerxes' son Darius, who was a Mede by birth, was made ruler of the kingdom of Babylon. ²In the first year of his reign, I, Daniel, learned from the Scriptures the number of years that Jerusalem would remain in ruins. The Lord had told the prophet Jeremiah that Jerusalem would remain in ruins for 70 years. ³So I turned to the Lord God and looked to him for help. I prayed, pleaded, and fasted in sackcloth and ashes.

⁴I prayed to the Lord my God. I confessed and said, "Lord, you are great and deserve respect as the only God. You keep your promise* and show mercy to those who love you and obey your commandments. ⁵We have sinned, done wrong, acted wickedly, rebelled, and turned away from your commandments and laws. ⁶We haven't listened to your servants the prophets, who spoke in your name to our kings, leaders, ancestors, and all the common people. ⁷You, Lord, are righteous. But we—the men of Judah, the citizens of Jerusalem, and all the Israelites whom you scattered in countries near and far—are still ashamed because we have been unfaithful to you.

---

*8:12 Hebrew meaning of this verse uncertain. *9:4 Or "covenant."

⁸We, our kings, leaders, and ancestors are ashamed because we have sinned against you, Lᴏʀᴅ.

⁹"But you, Lord our God, are compassionate and forgiving, although we have rebelled against you. ¹⁰We never listened to you or lived by the teachings you gave us through your servants the prophets. ¹¹All Israel has ignored your teachings and refused to listen to you. So you brought on us the curses you swore in an oath, the curses written in the Teachings of your servant Moses. We sinned against you. ¹²So you did what you said you would do to us and our rulers by bringing a great disaster on us. Nowhere in the world has anything ever happened like what has happened to Jerusalem. ¹³This entire disaster happened to us, exactly as it was written in Moses' Teachings. Lᴏʀᴅ our God, we never tried to gain your favor by turning from our wrongs and dedicating ourselves to your truth. ¹⁴So you were prepared to bring this disaster on us. Lᴏʀᴅ our God, you are righteous in everything you do. But we never listened to you.

¹⁵"Lord our God, you brought your people out of Egypt with your strong hand and made yourself famous even today. We have sinned and done evil things. ¹⁶Lord, since you are very righteous, turn your anger and fury away from your city, Jerusalem, your holy mountain. Jerusalem and your people are insulted by everyone around us because of our sins and the wicked things our ancestors did.

¹⁷"Our God, listen to my prayer and request. For your own sake, Lord, look favorably on your holy place, which is lying in ruins. ¹⁸Open your ears and listen, my God. Open your eyes and look at our ruins and at the city called by your name. We are not requesting this from you because we are righteous, but because you are very compassionate. ¹⁹Listen to us, Lord. Forgive us, Lord. Pay attention, and act. Don't delay! Do this for your sake, my God, because your city and your people are called by your name."

²⁰I continued to pray, confessing my sins and the sins of my people Israel. I humbly placed my request about my God's holy mountain in front of the Lᴏʀᴅ my God. ²¹While I was praying, the man Gabriel, whom I had seen in the first vision, came to me about the time of the evening sacrifice. He was exhausted. ²²He informed me, "Daniel, this time I have come to give you insight. ²³As soon as you began to make

Prayer
Daniel 9:4-23

Daniel 9 includes one of Daniel's prayers. In this prayer Daniel tells us why he knew that God would answer him. Find the reasons and underline them. Then think about your own prayers. Can you write down a prayer of your own? What would you say? Try writing a prayer that includes some of Daniel's reasons for trusting God.

be all you can be

your request, a reply was sent. I have come to give you the reply because you are highly respected. So study the message, and understand the vision.

²⁴"Seventy sets of seven time periods have been assigned for your people and your holy city. These time periods will serve to bring an end to rebellion, to stop sin, to forgive wrongs, to usher in everlasting righteousness, to put a seal on a prophet's vision, and to anoint the Most Holy One. ²⁵Learn, then, and understand that from the time the command is given to restore and rebuild Jerusalem until the anointed prince comes, seven sets of seven time periods and sixty-two sets of seven time periods will pass. Jerusalem will be restored and rebuilt with a city square and a moat during the troubles of those times. ²⁶But after the sixty-two sets of seven time periods, the Anointed One*b* will be cut off and have nothing. The city and the holy place will be destroyed with the prince who is to come.*c* His end will come with a flood until the end of the destructive war that has been determined. ²⁷He will confirm his promise with many for one set of seven time periods. In the middle of the seven time periods, he will stop the sacrifices and food offerings. This will happen along with disgusting things that cause destruction until those time periods come to an end. It has been determined that this will happen to those who destroy the city."

An Angel Comes to Daniel With a Message

10 ¹In Cyrus' third year as king of Persia, a message was revealed to Daniel (who had been renamed Belteshazzar). The message was true. It was about a great war. Daniel understood the message because he was given insight during the vision.

²During those days I, Daniel, mourned for three whole weeks. ³I didn't eat any good-tasting food. No meat or wine entered my mouth. I didn't wash myself until the entire three weeks were over.

⁴On the twenty-fourth day of the first month, I was by the great Tigris River. ⁵When I looked up, I saw a man dressed in linen, and he had a belt made of gold from Uphaz around his waist. ⁶His body was like beryl. His face looked like lightning. His eyes were like flaming torches. His arms and legs looked like polished bronze. When he spoke, his voice sounded like the roar of a crowd. ⁷I, Daniel, was the only one who saw the vision. The men with me didn't see the vision. Yet, they started to tremble violently, and they quickly hid themselves. ⁸So I was left alone to see this grand vision. I had no strength left in me. My face turned deathly pale, and I was helpless. ⁹I heard the man speak, and as I listened to his words, I fainted facedown on the ground.

¹⁰Then a hand touched me and made my hands and knees shake. ¹¹The man said to me, "Daniel, you are highly respected. Pay attention to my words. Stand up, because I've been sent to you." When he said this to me, I stood up, trembling. ¹²He told me, "Don't be afraid, Daniel. God has heard everything that you said ever since the first day you decided to humble yourself in front of your God so that you could learn to understand things. I have come in response to your prayer. ¹³The commander of the Persian kingdom opposed me for 21 days. But then Michael, one of the chief commanders, came to help me because I was left alone with the kings of Persia. ¹⁴I have come to explain to you what will happen to your people in the last days, because the vision is about times still to come."

¹⁵When he said this to me, I bowed down with my face touching the ground and was silent. ¹⁶Then someone who looked like a human touched my lips. I opened my mouth and began to talk. I said to the person standing in front of me, "Sir, because of this vision, pain has overwhelmed me, and I'm helpless. ¹⁷How can I talk to you, sir?

---

b 9:26 Or "Messiah." *c* 9:26 Or "The people of the prince who is to come will destroy the city and the holy place."

I have no strength left, and the wind has been knocked out of me."

¹⁸Again, the person who looked like a human touched me, and I became stronger. ¹⁹He said, "Don't be afraid. You are highly respected. Everything is alright! Be strong! Be strong!"

As he talked to me, I became stronger. I said, "Sir, tell me what you came to say. You have strengthened me."

²⁰He asked, "Do you know why I have come to you? Now I will return to fight the commander of Persia. When I go, the commander of Greece will come. ²¹However, I will tell you what is inscribed in the true writings. No one will support me when I fight these commanders except your commander, Michael. ¹During Darius the Mede's first year as king, I strengthened and defended Michael."

Greece Will Conquer Persia

²The person who looked like a human continued, "What I am about to tell you is the truth. Three more kings will rule Persia. Then there will be a fourth, who will become much richer than all the others. As he becomes strong through his wealth, he will turn everyone against the kingdom of Greece.

³"Then a warrior-king will come. He will rule a vast empire and do as he pleases. ⁴But as soon as he is established, his kingdom will be broken into pieces and divided in the directions of the four winds of heaven. The empire will not be given to his descendants. It will no longer be like his empire, since it will be uprooted and given to others.

The Northern and Southern Kings

⁵"The southern king will be strong, but one of his officers will become stronger than he is and rule a vast empire. ⁶After a few years the southern and northern kings will make an alliance. The southern king's daughter will go to the northern king to make peace. She won't hold on to her power, and the alliance won't last. She, those who came with her, and the one who fathered*ᵈ* and protected her will be given away.

⁷"At that time a shoot will grow from her roots to replace her father. He will attack the northern army, enter the stronghold of the northern king, fight against them, and be victorious. ⁸He will take the metal statues of their gods and their precious utensils of silver and gold back to Egypt. He will rule for more years than the northern king. ⁹He will invade the southern kingdom and return to his own country.

¹⁰"Then his sons will prepare for war. They will assemble a large number of forces so that they can overwhelm the enemy and pass through its land. They will return and wage war all the way to the stronghold. ¹¹The southern king will be outraged. He will go to fight the northern king, who will raise a large army that will fall into the southern king's hands. ¹²When that army is captured, the southern king will become conceited. Although he will dominate tens of thousands of people, he will not always be strong.

¹³"The northern king will return and raise an army larger than the first one. After a few years he will invade with a large army and a lot of equipment. ¹⁴In those times many people will rebel against the southern king, and violent men from your own people will rebel in keeping with this vision, but they will be defeated. ¹⁵Then the northern king will come, build dirt attack ramps, and capture a fortified city. The southern forces will not be able to withstand him. Even their best troops will not be strong enough. ¹⁶The invader will do as he pleases, and no one will be able to withstand

---

ᵃ 11:6 Most Hebrew manuscripts; one Hebrew manuscript, some Greek manuscripts "her son."

his attack. He will rise to power in the beautiful land and it will be completely under his control.

¹⁷"Then the northern king will decide to invade with the power of his entire kingdom, and some decent men will invade with him. He will give the southern king his daughter as a wife in order to destroy the southern kingdom. But this will not succeed or help him. ¹⁸Then he will turn his attention to the coastlands and capture many of them. But a commander will silence the insults that the northern king makes and even insult him.[b] ¹⁹He will turn back toward the fortresses in his own country, but he will stumble, fall, and disappear.

²⁰"Another king will take his place. He will have a cruel official go out in royal splendor. But in a few days the king will be destroyed, although not in anger or war.

²¹"A contemptible person will take his place. He will not be given royal splendor. He will invade when people are feeling secure, and he will seize the kingdom using false promises. ²²He will overwhelm large forces and defeat them, including the prince of the promise.[c] ²³After an alliance has been made with him, he will act deceitfully and rise to power with only a few people. ²⁴When people feel secure, he will invade the richest parts of the provinces and do something that none of his predecessors ever did. He will distribute loot and wealth to his followers. He will invent new ways of attacking fortifications. But this will last only for a little while.

²⁵"With a large army he will summon his power and courage against the southern king, who will prepare for war with a large, strong army. But the southern king won't be able to withstand him because of the schemes devised against him. ²⁶People who eat the king's rich food will ruin him. His army will be overwhelmed, and many will die in battle. ²⁷The two kings will both plan to do evil. They will sit at the same table and tell lies. But they will not succeed, because the end must wait until the appointed time. ²⁸The northern king will return to his country with a lot of wealth. He will be determined to fight against the holy promise. He will take action and return to his own country.

²⁹"At the appointed time he will again invade the south, but this time will be different from the first. ³⁰Ships will come from the west to attack him, and he will be discouraged and turn back. Angry at the holy promise, he will return, take action, and favor those who abandon the holy promise. ³¹His forces will dishonor the holy place (the fortress), take away the daily burnt offering, and set up the disgusting thing that causes destruction. ³²With flattery he will corrupt those who abandon the promise. But the people who know their God will be strong and take action.

³³"People who are wise will help many to understand. But for some time they will be defeated by swords and flames. They will be captured and looted. ³⁴As they are being defeated, they will get a little help, but many who are not sincere will join them. ³⁵Some of the wise people will be defeated in order to refine, purify, and make them white until the end times. But the appointed time is still to come.

³⁶"The king will do as he pleases. He will highly honor himself above every god. He will say amazing things against the God of gods. He will succeed until God's anger is over, because what has been decided must be done. ³⁷He will have no interest in the gods of his ancestors or desire for women. He will have no interest in any god, because he will make himself greater than anyone else. ³⁸Instead, he will honor the god of fortresses. With gold, silver, precious stones, and other expensive things he will honor a god his ancestors never heard of. ³⁹With the help of a foreign god, he will

---

[b]11:18 Hebrew meaning of this sentence uncertain.   [c]11:22 Or "covenant."

deal with strong fortresses. He will give high honors to those who acknowledge him, make them rulers over many people, and distribute land for a price.

[40]"In the end times the southern king will attack him. The northern king will rush at him like a storm with chariots, horses, and many ships. He will invade countries, overwhelm them, and pass through their land. [41]He will invade the beautiful land, and tens of thousands will be defeated. But Edom, Moab, and the leaders of the Ammonites will escape from his power. [42]He will use his power against many countries. Even Egypt will not escape. [43]He will control gold and silver treasures and all Egypt's treasuries. Libya and Sudan will surrender to him. [44]But news from the east and the north will frighten him. He will leave very angry to destroy and exterminate many. [45]He will pitch his royal tents between the seas at a beautiful holy mountain. When he comes to his end, there will be no one to help him."

[1]The person who looked like a human continued, "At that time Michael, the great commander, will stand up on behalf of the descendants of your people. It will be a time of trouble unlike any that has existed from the time there have been nations until that time. But at that time your people, everyone written in the book, will be rescued. [2]Many sleeping in the ground will wake up. Some will wake up to live forever, but others will wake up to be ashamed and disgraced forever. [3]Those who are wise will shine like the brightness on the horizon. Those who lead many people to righteousness will shine like the stars forever and ever.

[4]"But you, Daniel, keep these words secret, and seal the book until the end times. Many will travel everywhere, and knowledge will grow."

The Words Are Sealed Up

[5]When I, Daniel, looked up, I saw two men standing there. One man stood on one side of the river, and the other one stood on the other side. [6]One of them asked the man dressed in linen clothes who was above the river, "How long will it be until these miracles are over?" [7]I heard the man dressed in linen clothes who was above the river. He raised his right hand and left hand to heaven and swore an oath by the one who lives forever. He said, "It will be for a time, times, and half of a time. When the power of the holy people has been completely shattered, then all these things will be finished."

[8]I heard him, but I did not understand. So I asked him, "Sir, how will these things end?"

[9]He replied, "Go, Daniel. These words are to be kept secret and sealed until the end times. [10]Many will be purified, made white, and refined. But wicked people will do wicked things, and none of them will understand. Only wise people will understand. [11]From the time the daily burnt offering is taken away and the disgusting thing that causes destruction is set up, there will be 1,290 days. [12]Blessed are those who wait until they reach 1,335 days. [13]But go on until the end. You will rest, and you will rise for your inheritance at the end of time."

AN INTRODUCTION TO
Hosea

The prophet Hosea married a woman named Gomer. But she was unfaithful to him. Gomer ended up a slave.

In this book, Hosea's unfaithful wife was an example of how Israel had been unfaithful to God. God told Hosea to forgive his wife and bring her back home. In the same way, God will forgive his unfaithful people and bring them back to their home with him. God never stops loving those who are his children.

Why the happy ending?
See Hosea 3.

What's In It For Me?

Sin is unfaithfulness to God. . . .

GOD WILL PUNISH UNFAITHFULNESS.

GOD STILL LOVES THOSE WHO SIN.

GOD FORGIVES THOSE WHO RETURN TO HIM.

AFTER A PERSON IS SORRY FOR SINNING, GOD WILL BLESS THAT PERSON.

Headlines

Marriage Made in Heaven?
Hosea 1, page 1212

Can't Feed Bullheaded Sheep
Hosea 4:16, page 1215

Just Plain Rotten?
Hosea 10, page 1221

God Has the Cure
Hosea 14, page 1225

Hosea

The Prophet Hosea

1 ¹The LORD spoke his word to Hosea, son of Beeri, when Uzziah, Jotham, Ahaz, and Hezekiah were kings of Judah and when Jeroboam, son of Joash, was king of Israel.

Hosea Marries a Prostitute

²When the LORD first spoke to Hosea, the LORD told him, "Marry a prostitute, and have children with that prostitute. The people in this land have acted like prostitutes and abandoned the LORD." ³So Hosea married Gomer, daughter of Diblaim. She became pregnant and had a son.

⁴The LORD told Hosea, "Name him Jezreel. In a little while I will punish Jehu's family for the people they slaughtered at Jezreel. Then I will put an end to the kingdom of Israel. ⁵On that day I will break Israel's bows and arrows in the valley of Jezreel."

⁶Gomer became pregnant again and had a daughter. The LORD told Hosea, "Name her Lo Ruhamah [Unloved]. I will no longer love the nation of Israel. I will no longer forgive them. ⁷Yet, I will love the descendants of Judah. I will rescue them because I am the LORD their God. I won't use bows, swords, wars, horses, or horsemen to rescue them."

⁸After Gomer had weaned Lo Ruhamah, she became pregnant again and had a son. ⁹The LORD said, "Name him Lo Ammi [Not My People]. You are no longer my people, and I am no longer your God.ᵃ,ᵇ

¹⁰"Yet, the Israelites will become as numerous as the grains of sand on the seashore. No one will be able to measure them or count them. Wherever they were told, 'You are not my people,' they will be told, 'You are the children of the living God.' ¹¹The people of Judah and Israel will be gathered together. They will appoint one leader for themselves, and they will grow in the land. The day of Jezreel will be a great day.

Israel Is the LORD's Unfaithful Wife

2 ᵃ¹ "So call your brothers Ammi [My People],
and call your sisters Ruhamah [Loved].

² "Plead with your mother; plead with her.
She no longer acts like my wife.
She no longer treats me like her husband.
Tell her to stop acting like a prostitute.
Tell her to remove the lovers from between her breasts.
³ If she refuses, I will strip her.
I will leave her as naked as the day she was born.
I will turn her into a dry and barren land,
and she will die of thirst.
⁴ I won't love her children,
because they are children of a prostitute.

ᵃ1:9 Or "I am no longer I Am to you." (See Exodus 3:14.)   ᵇ1:9 Hosea 1:10-11 in English Bibles is Hosea 2:1-2 in the Hebrew Bible.   ᵃ2:1 Hosea 2:1-23 in English Bibles is Hosea 2:3-25 in the Hebrew Bible.

5   Their mother acted like a prostitute.
    The woman who became pregnant with them did shameful things.
        She said, 'I'll chase after my lovers.
        They will give me food and water,
            wool and linen, olive oil and wine.'

6   "That is why I will block her way with thornbushes
        and build a wall so that she can't get through.
7   She will run after her lovers, but she won't catch them.
    She will search for them, but she won't find them.
        Then she will say, 'I'll go back to my first husband.
        Things were better for me than they are now.'

8   "She doesn't believe that I gave her grain, new wine, and olive oil.
        I gave her plenty of silver and gold,
            but she used it to make statues of Baal.
9   That is why I will take back my grain when it has ripened
        and my new wine when it's in season.
    I will take away the wool and the linen
        that I gave her to cover her naked body.
10 I will show her naked body to her lovers,
        and no one will rescue her from my power.
11 I will put an end to all her celebrations:
        her annual festivals, her New Moon Festivals,
        her weekly worship days—all her appointed festivals.
12 I will destroy her grapevines and fig trees.
        She said that they were gifts from her lovers.
    I will turn her vineyards into a forest, and wild animals will devour them.
13 I will punish her for all the times she burned incense
        as an offering to other gods—the Baals.
        She put on her rings and jewelry,
            and she chased after her lovers.
        She forgot me," declares the LORD.

The LORD Continues to Love Israel

14 "That is why I'm going to win her back.
        I will lead her into the desert.
        I will speak tenderly to her.
15 I will give her vineyards there.
        I will make the valley of Achor [Disaster] a door of hope.
        Then she will respond as she did when she was young,
            as she did when she came out of Egypt.

16 "On that day she will call me her husband," declares the LORD.
        "She will no longer call me her master.[b]
17 I won't allow her to say the names of other gods called Baal.
        She will never again call out their names.

18 "On that day I will make an arrangement with the wild animals,
        the birds, and the animals that crawl on the ground.

---

[b] 2:16 Or "her Baal."

I will destroy all the bows, swords, and weapons of war,
so people can live safely.
19 "Israel, I will make you my wife forever.
I will be honest and faithful to you.
I will show you my love and compassion.
20 I will be true to you, my wife.
Then you will know the LORD.
21 "On that day I will answer your ⌞prayers⌟," declares the LORD.
"I will speak to the sky,
it will speak to the earth,
22 and the earth will produce grain, new wine, and olive oil.
You will produce many crops, Jezreel.
23 I will plant my people in the land.
Those who are not loved I will call my loved ones.
Those who are not my people I will call my people.
Then they will say, 'You are our God!' "

Hosea's Adulterous Wife

3 ¹Then the LORD told me, "Love your wife again, even though she is loved by others and has committed adultery. Love her as I, the LORD, love the Israelites, even though they have turned to other gods and love to eat raisin cakes."

²So I bought her for 23 ounces of silver and 10 bushels of barley. ³Then I told her, "You must wait for me a long time. Don't be a prostitute or offer yourself to any man. I will wait for you."

⁴In the same way, the Israelites will wait a long time without kings or officials, without sacrifices or sacred stones, and without ephods*a* or family idols. ⁵After that, the Israelites will turn and look to the LORD their God and David their king. They will come trembling to the LORD for his blessings in the last days.

The LORD's Legal Case Against Israel

4 ¹Listen to the word of the LORD, you Israelites. The LORD has brought these charges against those who live in the land:

"There is no faith, no love, and no knowledge of God in the land.
2 There is cursing, lying, murdering, stealing, and adultery.
People break ⌞my laws⌟, and there is one murder after another.
3 That is why the land is drying up,
and everyone who lives in it is passing away.
Wild animals, birds, and fish are dying.

4 "No one should accuse other people or bring charges against them.
My case is against you priests.
5 During the day you stumble,
and during the night the prophets stumble with you.
So I will destroy your mother, ⌞the nation of Israel⌟.
6 I will destroy my people because they are ignorant.
You have refused to learn,
so I will refuse to let you be my priests.

---

*a*3:4 *Ephod* is a technical term for part of the priest's clothes. Its exact usage and shape are unknown.

You have forgotten the teachings of your God,
  so I will forget your children.
7 The more priests there are,
  the more they sin against me.
  So I will turn their glory into shame.
8 They feed on the sins of my people,
  and they want them to do wicked things.
9   So the priests will be punished like the people.
  I will punish them for their wicked ways
  and pay them back for what they have done.

10 "They will eat, but they'll never be full.
  They will have sex with prostitutes, but they'll never have children.
  They have abandoned the LORD.
11 Prostitutes, old wine, and new wine have robbed them of their senses.
12   My people ask their wooden idols for help.
  A piece of wood tells them what to do.
  A spirit of prostitution leads them astray.
    They commit adultery
      by giving themselves to other gods.
13 They offer sacrifices on mountaintops,
  and they burn incense on the hills
    under oaks, poplars, and other trees.
    They think that these trees provide good shade.

"That is why your daughters become prostitutes,
  and your daughters-in-law commit adultery.
14 Yet, I will not punish your daughters when they become prostitutes
  or your daughters-in-law when they commit adultery.
    The men go to prostitutes
      and offer sacrifices with temple prostitutes.
      These foolish people will be trampled.

15 "Israel, you act like a prostitute.
  Don't let Judah become guilty too.
    Don't go to Gilgal.
    Don't go to Beth Aven.
    Don't take the oath, 'As the LORD lives. . . .'

16 "The people of Israel are as stubborn as a bull.
  How can the LORD feed them like lambs in an open pasture?
17 The people of Ephraim have chosen to worship idols.
  Leave them alone!
18 When they're done drinking their wine,
    they continue to have sex with the prostitutes.
    Their rulers dearly love to act shamefully.
19   The wind will carry them away in its wings,
      and their sacrifices will bring them shame.

The LORD Announces the Verdict Against Israel

5 1 "Listen to this, you priests!
  Pay attention, nation of Israel!

Open your ears, royal family!
    This is my decision about you.
You set traps at Mizpah
    and spread out nets on Mount Tabor.
2 You are deeply involved in sin.
    So I will punish all of you.*ᵃ*
3 I know Ephraim,
    and Israel isn't a stranger to me.
Now, Ephraim, you are acting like a prostitute,
    and Israel is unclean.*ᵇ*

4 "The wicked things that the people have done
    keep them from returning to their God.
      They have a spirit of prostitution,
        and they don't know the LORD.
5 The people of Israel's arrogance testifies against them.
Israel and Ephraim stumble because of their sins,
    and Judah stumbles with them.
6 They go with their sheep and their cattle to search for the LORD,
    but they can't find him.
      He has left them.
7 They have been unfaithful to the LORD,
    because their children do not belong to him.
Now their New Moon ˻Festivals˼ will devour them and their fields.

8 "Blow the ram's horn in Gibeah.
Blow the trumpet in Ramah.
Sound the alarm at Beth Aven, you descendants of Benjamin.
9   Ephraim will become a wasteland
      when the time for punishment comes.
        I will make the truth known among the tribes of Israel.
10 The leaders of Judah are like those who move boundary markers.
    I will pour my fury on them like water.
11 Ephraim is oppressed—crushed by punishment,
    because its people are determined to chase idols.*ᶜ*
12 I will destroy Ephraim as a moth destroys clothing.
I will destroy the nation of Judah as rot destroys wood.

13 "When Ephraim saw that he was sick
    and when Judah saw his own wounds,
      Ephraim went to Assyria to ask the great king for help.*ᵈ*
      But the king couldn't cure them or heal their wounds.
14 I will be like a lion to Ephraim
    and like a young lion to the nation of Judah.
I will carry ˻them˼ off, and no one will rescue ˻them˼.
15 I will go back to my place until they admit that they are guilty.
    Then they will search for me.
      In their distress they will eagerly look for me."

ᵃ5:2 Hebrew meaning of this verse uncertain.   *ᵇ5:3 "Unclean" refers to anything that Moses' Teachings say is not presentable to God.*   *ᶜ5:11 Greek, Syriac, Targum; Masoretic Text "to chase commands."*   *ᵈ5:13 Or "to ask King Jareb for help."*

Israel Rejected the LORD's Promise

6 ¹ Let's return to the LORD.
Even though he has torn us to pieces,
    he will heal us.
Even though he has wounded us,
    he will bandage our wounds.
² After two days he will revive us.
On the third day he will raise us
    so that we may live in his presence.
³ Let's learn about the LORD.
Let's get to know the LORD.
He will come to us as sure as the morning comes.
He will come to us like the autumn rains and the spring rains
    that water the ground.

⁴ "What should I do with you, Ephraim?
What should I do with you, Judah?
    Your love is like fog in the morning.
    It disappears as quickly as the morning dew.
⁵ That is why I cut you down by sending the prophets.
    I killed you with the words from my mouth.
    My judgments shined on you like light.
⁶ I want your loyalty, not your sacrifices.
I want you to know me, not to give me burnt offerings.

⁷ "Like Adam, you rejected the promise.ᵃ
    You were unfaithful to me.
⁸ Gilead is a city filled with troublemakers.
    It is stained with bloody footprints.
⁹ The priests are like gangs of robbers who lie in ambush for a person.
    They murder on the road to Shechem.
        Certainly, they have committed a crime.

¹⁰ "I have seen horrible things in the nation of Israel.
    Ephraim is acting like a prostitute,
        and Israel is unclean.ᵇ

¹¹ "Yet, Judah, I have set a harvest time for you
    when I bring my people back from captivity.

7 ¹ "Whenever I want to heal Israel,
    all I can see is Ephraim's sin and Samaria's wickedness.
        People cheat each other.
        They break into houses and steal.
        They rob people in the streets.
² They don't realize that I remember
    all the evil things they've done.
        Now their sins surround them.
        Their sins are in my presence.

ᵃ6:7 Or "You have walked all over my promise as if it were dirt."   ᵇ6:10 "Unclean" refers to anything that Moses'
Teachings say is not presentable to God.

3   "They make kings happy with the wicked things they do.
    They make officials happy with the lies they tell.
4   They all commit adultery.
        They are like a heated oven,
            an oven so hot that a baker doesn't have to fan its flames
                when he makes bread.
5   On the day of the king's celebration,
        the officials become drunk from wine,
            and the king joins mockers.
6   They become hot like an oven while they lie in ambush.
        All night long their anger smolders,
            but in the morning it burns like a raging fire.
7   They are all as hot as an oven.
        They consume their judges like a fire.
            All their kings die in battle, and none of them calls to me.

Israel Turns to Other Nations for Help

8   "Ephraim mixes with other nations.
    Ephraim, you are like a half-baked loaf of bread.
9   Foreigners are using up your strength, but you don't realize it.
        You have become a gray-haired, old man, but you don't realize it.
10 Israel, your arrogance testifies against you,
        but even after all this, you don't turn to the LORD your God
            or look to him for help.
11 Ephraim, you are like a silly, senseless dove.
        You call for Egypt and run to Assyria for help.
12   When you go, I will spread my net over you.
            I will snatch you out of the air like a bird.
            I will punish you for all the evil things you have done.

13 "How horrible it will be for these people.
        They have run away from me.
        They must be destroyed because they've rebelled against me.
            I want to reclaim them, but they tell lies about me.
14   They don't pray to me sincerely,
            even though they cry in their beds
                and make cuts on their bodies
                    while praying for grain and new wine.
        They have turned against me.
15   I trained them and made them strong.
            Yet, they plan evil against me.
16   They don't return to the Most High.
            They are like a defective bow.
                Their officials will die in battle
                    because they curse.
                        The people in Egypt will ridicule them for this.

The LORD Will Punish Israel for Its Rebellion

8   1   "Sound the alarm on the ram's horn.
        The enemy swoops down on the LORD's temple like an eagle.
            The people of Israel have rejected my promise

and rebelled against my teachings.
2 They cry out to me, 'We acknowledge you as our God.'
3 However, they have rejected what is good.
The enemy will persecute them.

4 "They chose their own kings, kings I didn't approve.
They chose their own princes, princes I didn't know.
They chose to make idols with their own silver and gold.
Because of this, they will be destroyed.
5 Get rid of your calf-shaped idol, Samaria.
My anger burns against these people.
How long will they remain unclean?[a]
6 Samaria's calf-shaped idol was made in Israel.
Skilled workers made it.
It is not a god.
It will be smashed to pieces.

7 "The people of Israel plant the wind, but they harvest a storm.
A field of grain that doesn't ripen will never produce any grain.
Even if it did produce grain, foreigners would eat it all.
8 Israel will be swallowed up.
It has already mixed in with the other nations.
It has become worthless.

9 "The people of Israel went to Assyria.
They were like wild donkeys wandering off alone.
The people of Ephraim sold themselves to their lovers.
10 Even though they sold themselves among the nations,
I will gather them now.
They will suffer for a while under the burdens of kings and princes.

11 "The more altars that the people of Ephraim build
to make offerings to pay for their sins,
the more places they have for sinning.
12 I have written many things for them in my teachings,
but they consider these things strange and foreign.
13 They offer sacrifices to me and eat the meat of sacrifices,
but I, the LORD, do not accept these sacrifices.
Now I will remember their wickedness
and punish them because of their sins.
They will go back to Egypt.
14 The people of Israel have built palaces,
and they have forgotten their maker.
The people of Judah have built many fortified cities.
I will send a fire on their cities and burn down their palaces."

9 1 Israel, don't rejoice.
Don't celebrate as other nations do.
You have been unfaithful to your God.
You have sold sex on every threshing floor.[a]

---

[a]8:5 "Unclean" refers to anything that Moses' Teachings say is not presentable to God.   [a]9:1 a threshing floor is an outdoor area where grain is separated from its husks.

2   There won't be enough grain to feed people.
    There won't be enough wine to go around.

3   The people of Ephraim won't stay in the LORD's land.
        They will return to Egypt,
            and they will eat unclean[b] food in Assyria.

4   They won't pour wine offerings to the LORD,
        and their sacrifices won't please him.
    Their sacrifices will be like the food that mourners eat.
    All who eat this food will be unclean.
    Their food will only satisfy their hunger.
    It will not be brought ⌞as an offering⌟ to the LORD's temple.

5   What will they do on the day of an appointed festival
        or on the LORD's festival days?

6   Even if they escape without being destroyed,
        Egypt will capture them
            and Memphis will bury them.
                Weeds will grow over their silver treasures.
                Thorns will grow over their tents.

7   The time for them to be punished will come.
    The time for them to pay for their sins will come.
    ⌞When this happens,⌟ Israel will know it.
    ⌞They think that⌟ prophets are fools
        and that spiritual people are crazy.
            They have sinned a lot, and they are very hostile.

8   Prophets are God's watchmen over Ephraim.
        Yet, traps are set on every prophet's path,
            and people are hostile in the temple of their God.

9   People have deeply corrupted themselves as they once did at Gibeah.
        God will remember their wickedness
            and punish them because of their sins.

Israel Is Like Rotten Grapes or Rotten Figs

10 ⌞The LORD said,⌟ "When I found Israel,
        it was like finding grapes in the desert.
    When I saw your ancestors,
        it was like seeing the first figs of the harvest.
            But they went to Baal Peor and worshiped shameful idols.
                They became as disgusting as the things they worshiped.

11 "Ephraim's glory will fly away like a bird.
        There will be no more pregnancies, births, or babies.

12 Even if they bring up children,
        I will take those children away before they grow up.
    Yes, how horrible it will be for them when I leave them.

13 I have seen Ephraim, like Tyre, planted in a pleasant place.
        But the people of Ephraim will bring out their children
            to be killed."

---

b 9:3 "Unclean" refers to anything that Moses' Teachings say is not presentable to God.

14 LORD, give them what they deserve.
　　Make the women miscarry,
　　　　or else make them unable to nurse their babies.

15 "All Ephraim's wickedness began in Gilgal; I hated the people there.
　　I will force them out of my temple because of their wickedness,
　　　　and I won't love them anymore.
All their officials are rebellious.

16 "The people of Ephraim are like sick plants.
　　Their roots are dried up.
　　They have no fruit.
　　　　Even if they were to have children,
　　　　　　I would kill their dear children."

17 My God will reject them
　　because they refused to listen to him.
　　　　They will wander among the nations.

Israel Is Like a Rotten Vine

10 1 The people of Israel are like vines that used to produce fruit.
　　The more fruit they produced,
　　　　the more altars they built.
　　The more their land produced,
　　　　the more stone markers they set up to honor other gods.

2 They are hypocrites. Now they must take their punishment.
　　God will tear down their altars and destroy their stone markers.
3 So they'll say,
　　　　"We have no king because we didn't fear the LORD.
　　　　Even if we had a king, he couldn't do anything for us."
4 They say many things. They lie when they take oaths,
　　and they make promises they don't intend to keep.
　　　　That's why lawsuits spring up
　　　　　　like poisonous weeds in the furrows of a field.

5 Those who live in Samaria fear the calf-shaped idol at Beth Aven.
　　The people will mourn over it.
　　The priests will cry loudly
　　　　because its glory will be taken away into captivity.
6 The thing itself will be carried to Assyria
　　as a present to the great king.*
　　　　Ephraim will be disgraced.
　　　　Israel will be ashamed because of its plans.
7 The king of Samaria will be carried away
　　like a piece of wood on water.
8 The illegal worship sites of Aven will be destroyed.
　　Israel sins there.
　　　　Thorns and weeds will grow over those altars.
　　　　　　People will say to the mountains, "Cover us!"
　　　　　　　　and to the hills, "Fall on us!"

---

*10:6 Or "to King Jareb."

9   Israel, you have sinned ever since the incident at Gibeah.
> You never change.
>> War will overtake the wicked people in Gibeah.

10   "I will punish them when I'm ready.
> Armies will gather to attack them.
>> They will be punished for their many sins.

Israel Is Like a Cow That Threshed Grain

11   "Ephraim is like a trained calf that loves to thresh[b] grain.
> I will put a yoke[c] on its beautiful neck.
> I will harness Ephraim.
>> Judah must plow.
>> Jacob must break up the ground.

12   "Break new ground.
> Plant righteousness,
>> and harvest the fruit that your loyalty will produce for me."

> It's time to seek the LORD!
>> When he comes, he will rain righteousness on you.

13   You have planted wickedness and harvested evil.
> You have eaten the fruit that your lies produced.
> You have trusted your own power and your many warriors.

14   So your army will hear the noise of battle.
> All your fortresses will be destroyed
>> like the time Shalman destroyed Beth Arbel in battle.
>> Mothers and their children were smashed to death.

15   This is what will happen to you, Bethel,
> because you have done many wicked things.
>> At daybreak, the king of Israel will be completely destroyed.

Israel Is Like a Bad Son

11

1   "When Israel was a child, I loved him,
> and I called my son out of Egypt.

2   The more I called them,[a] the farther they went away.
> They sacrificed to other gods—the Baals,
>> and they burned incense to idols.

3   I was the one who taught the people of Ephraim to walk.[b]
> I took them by the hand.
>> But they didn't realize that I had healed them.

4   I led them with cords of human kindness, with ropes of love.
> I removed the yokes[c] from their necks.
>> I bent down and fed them.

5   "They will not return to Egypt.
> Instead, Assyria will rule them
>> because they have refused to return to me.

6   War will sweep through their cities,

---

[b]10:11 Threshing is the process of beating stalks to separate them from the grain.   [c]10:11 A yoke is a wooden bar placed over the necks of work animals so that they can pull plows or carts.   [a]11:2 Greek; Masoretic Text "The more they called them."   [b]11:3 Or "I was the one who guided Ephraim."   [c]11:4 A yoke is a wooden bar placed over the necks of work animals so that they can pull plows or carts.

demolish their city gates,
    and put an end to their plans.
7 My people are determined to turn away from me.
    Even if they call to the Most High,
        he will not pardon them.

8 "How can I give you up, Ephraim?
How can I hand you over, Israel?
How can I make you like Admah?
How can I treat you like Zeboim?
    I have changed my mind.
        I am deeply moved.
9 I will not act on my burning anger.
I will not destroy Ephraim again.
    I am God, not a human.
    I am the Holy One among you,
        and I will not come to you in anger.

10 "My people will follow me when I roar like a lion.
    When I roar, my children will come trembling from the west.
11   They will come trembling like birds from Egypt
    and like doves from Assyria.
        I will settle them in their own homes,"
        declares the LORD.*d*

12 "Ephraim surrounds me with lies.
The nation of Israel surrounds me with deceit."
    Judah rebels against God, against the Holy One who is faithful.

The People of Israel Ignored What the LORD Had Done for Them

12 *a*1 The people of Ephraim try to catch the wind
    and try to chase the east wind all day.
They are very violent and destructive.
They make treaties with Assyria and take olive oil to Egypt.

2 The LORD brings charges against Judah and punishes Jacob
    because of the way their people act.
He will pay them back for what they have done.
3 Their ancestor Jacob held on to his brother's heel
    while the two of them were in their mother's womb.
When Jacob became a man, he struggled with God.
4   He struggled with the Messenger and won.
    Jacob cried and pleaded with him.
    Jacob found him at Bethel,
        and he talked with him there.
5 The LORD is the God of Armies.
    The LORD is the name by which he is remembered.
6   Return to your God.
    Be loyal and fair, and always wait with hope for your God.

---

*d*11:11 Hosea 11:12 in English Bibles is Hosea 12:1 in the Hebrew Bible. *a*12:1 Hosea 12:1-14 in English Bibles is Hosea 12:2-15 in the Hebrew Bible.

7   The Lord says, "The merchants use dishonest scales.
        They love to cheat people.
8   The people of Ephraim say, 'We're rich. We've made a fortune.
        With all this wealth, no one will find us guilty of any sin.'
9   I am the Lord your God.
    I brought you out of Egypt.
    I will make you live in tents again
        as you did during your appointed festivals.
10 I spoke to the prophets and gave them many visions.
    I taught lessons through the prophets."[b]

11 The people of Gilead are evil.
        They are worthless.
        They sacrifice bulls in Gilgal.
            But their altars will become like piles of rubble
                beside a plowed field.
12 Jacob fled to the country of Syria.
        Israel worked to get a wife; he took care of sheep to pay for her.
13 The Lord used a prophet to bring the people of Israel out of Egypt.
        He used a prophet to take care of them.

14 The people of Ephraim made the Lord bitter.
        He will hold them guilty of murder.
        The Lord will pay them back for their insults.

The People of Israel Will Be Punished for Their Idolatry

13 1   When the tribe of Ephraim spoke, people trembled.
            The people of Ephraim were important in Israel.
                Then they became guilty of worshiping Baal,
                    so they must die.
2   They keep on sinning more and more.
        They make idols from silver for themselves.
        These idols are skillfully made.
            All of them are the work of craftsmen.
    People say this about the Israelites: "They offer human sacrifices
        and kiss calf-shaped idols."
3   That is why they will be like fog in the morning
        and like morning dew that disappears quickly.
            They will be like straw blown away from threshing floors.[a]
            They will be like smoke rising from chimneys.

4   "I am the Lord your God. I brought you out of Egypt.
        You have known no god besides me.
        There is no savior except me.
5   I took care of you[b] in the desert, in a dry land.
6   When I fed you, you were full.
        When you were full, you became arrogant.
            That is why you forgot me.
7   So I will be like a lion.

---

[b] 12:10 Or "I brought destruction through the prophets."   [a] 13:3 A threshing floor is an outdoor area where grain is separated from its husks.   [b] 13:5 Greek; Masoretic Text "I knew you."

8 Like a leopard I will wait by the road to ambush you.
Like a bear that has lost her cubs, I will attack you.
I will rip you open.
Like a lion I will devour you.
Like a wild animal I will tear you apart.

9 You are destroying yourself, Israel.
You are against me, your helper.

10 "Where, now, is your king, the one who is supposed to save you?
Where in all your cities are your judges?
You said, 'Give us kings and officials!'

11 I gave you a king when I was angry,
and I took him away when I was furious.

12 "Ephraim's wickedness is on record.
The record of the people's sins is safely stored away.

13 They have the opportunity to live again,
but they are not smart enough to take it.
They are like a baby who is about to be born
but won't come out of its mother's womb.

14 "I want to free them from the power of the grave.
I want to reclaim them from death.
Death, I want to be a plague to you.
Grave, I want to destroy you.[c]
I won't even think of changing my plans."

15 The people of Ephraim have become important among their relatives.
However, the LORD's scorching wind will come from the east.
It will blow out of the desert.
Then their springs will run dry,
and their wells will dry up.
The wind will destroy every precious thing in their storehouses.[d]

16 The people of Samaria are guilty as charged
because they rebelled against their God.
They will be killed in war,
their children will be smashed to death,
and their pregnant women will be ripped open.

The LORD Offers to Forgive Israel

[a]1 Israel, return to the LORD your God.
You have stumbled because of your sins.

2 Return to the LORD, and say these things to him:
"Forgive all our sins, and kindly receive us.
Then we'll praise you with our lips.

3 Assyria cannot save us.
We won't ride on horses anymore.
We will never again say
that the things our hands have made are our gods.
You love orphans."

---

[c]13:14 Or "Death, where is your plague? Grave, where is your destruction?"   [d]13:15 Hosea 13:16 in English Bibles
is Hosea 14:1 in the Hebrew Bible.   [a]14:1 Hosea 14:1-9 in English Bibles is Hosea 14:2-10 in the Hebrew Bible.

4 ⌊The LORD says,⌋ "I will cure them of their unfaithfulness.
I will love them freely.
I will no longer be angry with them.
5 I will be like dew to the people of Israel.
They will blossom like flowers.
They will be firmly rooted like cedars from Lebanon.
6 They will be like growing branches.
They will be beautiful like olive trees.
They will be fragrant like cedars from Lebanon.
7 They will live again in God's shadow.
They will grow like grain.
They will blossom like grapevines.
They will be as famous as the wines from Lebanon.

8 "The people of Ephraim will have nothing more to do with idols.
I will answer them and take care of them.
I am like a growing pine tree.
Their fruit comes from me."

9 Wise people will understand these things.
A person with insight will recognize them.
The LORD's ways are right.
Righteous people live by them.
Rebellious people stumble over them.

Joel

In Joel's time, a terrible cloud of locusts swept into Israel. They destroyed all the crops. The prophet Joel said that the insect plague was a warning from God so the people would turn back to their Lord.

Then Joel had a vision of a future time when an army of men would invade Israel. The invasions described in the book of Joel warn that God will judge sins. But God will also forgive sins and bless those who turn to him.

Why is this woman sad? See Joel 1.

What's In It For Me?

Gems from the book of Joel . . .

TROUBLES COME WHEN WE TURN FROM GOD.

WHEN WE ASK THE LORD FOR HELP, WE WILL BE SAVED.

GOD'S SPIRIT USES BOTH MEN AND WOMEN.

GREAT BLESSINGS WILL COME TO ALL OF GOD'S PEOPLE.

Headlines

God Plagues Israel
Joel 1, page 1228

Daughters Speak Out!
Joel 2:28, page 1232

Tired of Tyre
Joel 3, page 1232

Joel

The Prophet Joel

¹This is what the LORD said to Joel, son of Pethuel.

Judah Is Plagued With Locusts and Famine

2 Listen to this, you leaders!
Open your ears, all inhabitants of this land!
  Nothing like this has ever happened in your lifetime
  or in your ancestors' lifetime.
3 Tell your children about it.
Have your children tell their children.
Have your grandchildren tell their children.
4   What young locusts leave, mature locusts will eat.
  What mature locusts leave, adult locusts will eat.
  What adult locusts leave, grasshoppers will eat.

5 Wake up and cry, you drunks!
Cry loudly, you wine drinkers!
  New wine has been taken away from you.
6 A strong nation attacked my land.
  It has too many soldiers to count.
    They have teeth like lions.
    They have fangs like grown lions.
7   They destroyed my grapevines.
    They ruined my fig trees.
      They stripped off what they could eat,
        threw the rest away,
          and left the branches bare.

8 Cry loudly like a young woman who is dressed in sackcloth,
  mourning for the man she was going to marry.
9 Grain offerings and wine offerings
  are no longer brought to the LORD's temple.
    The priests, the LORD's servants, mourn.
10 Israel's fields are ruined, and the ground is dried up.
  The grain has been destroyed.
  The new wine has dried up.
  The olive oil has run out.
11   Be sad, you farmers!
  Cry loudly, you grape growers!
    Mourn for the wheat and the barley.
      The harvest is destroyed in the field.
12 The grapevines are dried up.
  The fig trees are withered.
  The pomegranate, palm, and apricot trees,
    as well as all the trees in the orchards, have died.
      Yes, the joy of these people has died too.

¹³ Put on your sackcloth and mourn, you priests.
   Cry loudly, you servants of the altar.
   Spend the night in sackcloth, you servants of my God.
      Grain offerings and wine offerings
         are withheld from your God's temple.
¹⁴ Schedule a time to fast!
   Call for an assembly!
      Gather the leaders and everyone who lives in the land.
      Bring them to the temple of the L<small>ORD</small> your God,
         and cry to the L<small>ORD</small> for help.

¹⁵ This will be a terrible day!
      The day of the L<small>ORD</small> is near,
         and it will come like destruction from the Almighty.
¹⁶ Food disappears right before our eyes.
   Happiness and rejoicing disappear from our God's temple.
¹⁷   Seeds shrivel up in their shells.ª
      Storehouses are destroyed.
         Barns are ruined.
            The grain has dried up.
¹⁸ The animals groan.
      Herds of cattle wander around confused.
         There's no pasture for them.
            Even flocks of sheep are suffering.

¹⁹ O L<small>ORD</small>, I cry to you for help!
      Fire has burned up the open pastures.
         Flames have burned up all the trees in the orchards.
²⁰   Even wild animals long for you.
            Streams run dry.
      Fire has burned up the open pastures.

The Day of the L<small>ORD</small>

¹ Blow the ram's horn in Zion.
Sound the alarm on my holy mountain.
   Everyone who lives in the land should tremble,
      because the day of the L<small>ORD</small> is coming.
Certainly, it is near.
²   It is a day of darkness and gloom,
      a day of clouds and overcast skies.
         A large and mighty army
            will spread over the mountains like the dawn.ª
Nothing like this has ever happened.
Nothing like this will ever happen again.

³ In front of this army a fire burns.
      Behind it flames are blazing.
In front of it the land is like the garden of Eden.
      Behind it the land is like a barren desert.
         Nothing escapes it!

---

^ª1:17 Hebrew meaning of this line uncertain.   ^ª2:2 Or "like darkness."

4 The soldiers look like horses.
      They run like war horses.
5 As they leap on mountaintops,
      they sound like rattling chariots,
         like crackling fire burning up straw,
            and like a mighty army prepared for battle.

6 People are terrified in their presence.
      Every face turns pale.

7 They run like warriors.
   They climb walls like soldiers.
   They march straight ahead.
   They do not leave their places.
8 They do not crowd one another.
   They keep in their own lines.
      Even when they break through the defenses,
         they do not break their ranks.
9   They rush into the city.
          They run along the wall.
          They climb into houses.
          They enter through windows like thieves.

10 The earth quakes in their presence,
      and the sky shakes.
         The sun and the moon turn dark,
            and the stars no longer shine.
11 The Lord shouts out orders to his army.
      His forces are very large.
         The troops that carry out his commands are mighty.
   The day of the Lord is extremely terrifying.
      Who can endure it?

The LORD Invites the People to Return to Him

12 "But even now," declares the Lord,
      "return to me with all your heart—
         with fasting, crying, and mourning."

13 Tear your hearts, not your clothes.
      Return to the Lord your God.
         He is merciful and compassionate,
            patient, and always ready to forgive
               and to change his plans about disaster.
14 Who knows?
      He may reconsider and change his plan
         and leave a blessing for you.
            Then you could give grain offerings and wine offerings
               to the Lord your God.

15 Blow the ram's horn in Zion.
      Schedule a time to fast.
         Call for an assembly.

16   Gather the people.
          Prepare them for a holy meeting.
          Assemble the leaders.
          Gather the children, even the nursing infants.

     Grooms leave their rooms.
     Brides leave their chambers.
17   The priests who serve the LORD cry
          between the altar and the entrance to the temple.
     They say,
          "Spare your people, O LORD.
          Don't let the people who belong to you become a disgrace.
          Don't let the nations ridicule them.
     Why should people ask, 'Where is their God?' "

The LORD Will Give Earthly Blessings to His People

18   Then the LORD became concerned about his land,
          and he had pity on his people.
19   The LORD said to his people,
          "I am going to send grain, new wine, and olive oil to you.
          You will be satisfied with them.
          I will no longer make you a disgrace among the nations.

20   "I will keep the northern army far from you,
          and I will force it into a dry and barren land.
          The soldiers in front will be forced into the eastern sea.
          The soldiers in back will be forced into the western sea.
          A foul odor will rise from the dead bodies.
          They will stink."

     He has done great things!
21   Land, do not be afraid.
          Be glad and rejoice.
     The LORD has done great things!
22   Wild animals, do not be afraid.
          The pastures in the wilderness have turned green.

Good Morning, God

Joel 2:13

Have you ever been "too late"? It's like losing the last slice of your favorite pizza to the lightning-fast grasp of a little brother. It's like tuning in to a great TV show just in time to see the credits rolling. Too late. Joel's message tells us that it is never too late with God. When we sin, we feel far away from God. But it's never too late to come back to him. If you don't feel close to God, remember Joel's message. It's not too late. God is only a prayer away.

I praise you, Lord, for your mercy and forgiveness.

The trees have produced their fruit.
There are plenty of figs and grapes.
23 People of Zion, be glad and find joy in the Lord your God.
The Lord has given you the Teacher of Righteousness.[b]
He has sent the autumn rain and the spring rain as before.
24 The threshing floors[c] will be filled with grain.
The vats will overflow with new wine and olive oil.

25 "Then I will repay you for the years
that the mature locusts, the adult locusts,
the grasshoppers, and the young locusts ate your crops.
(They are the large army that I sent against you.)
26 You will have plenty to eat, and you will be full.
You will praise the name of the Lord your God,
who has performed miracles for you.
My people will never be ashamed again.
27 You will know that I am in Israel.
I am the Lord your God, and there is no other.
My people will never be ashamed again.[d]

The Lord Will Pour His Spirit on All People

28 "After this, I will pour my Spirit on everyone.
Your sons and daughters will prophesy.
Your old men will dream dreams.
Your young men will see visions.
29 In those days I will pour my Spirit on servants,
on both men and women.
30 I will work miracles in the sky and on the earth:
blood, fire, and clouds of smoke.
31 The sun will become dark,
and the moon will become as red as blood
before the terrifying day of the Lord comes."

32 Then whoever calls on the name of the Lord will be saved.
Those who escape will be on Mount Zion and in Jerusalem.
Among the survivors will be those whom the Lord calls,
as the Lord has promised.

The Lord Will Rescue His People

3 1 "In those days and at that time,
I will bring back the captives of Judah and Jerusalem.
2 I will gather all the nations.
I will bring them down to the valley of Jehoshaphat.[b]
I will judge them there.
They scattered the Israelites, the people who belong to me,
among the nations.
They divided my land.
3 They threw dice for my people.

---

[b]2:23 Or "The Lord has given you plenty of autumn rain." [c]2:24 A threshing floor is an outdoor area where grain is separated from its husks. [d]2:27 Joel 2:28-32 in English Bibles is Joel 3:1-5 in the Hebrew Bible. [a]3:1 Joel 3:1-21 in English Bibles is Joel 4:1-21 in the Hebrew Bible. [b]3:2 Or "the valley where the Lord judges."

They traded boys for prostitutes.
They sold girls so that they could buy wine to drink.

4 "Now what do you have against me, Tyre and Sidon
   and all the regions of Philistia?
   Are you paying me back for something I have done?
      If you are paying me back,
      I will quickly pay you back for what you have done.
5 You took my silver and my gold.
   You brought my finest treasures to your temples.
6 You sold the people of Judah and Jerusalem to the Greeks.
   That way you could send them far away from their land.
7 I am going to make them leave the place where you sold them.
   I will pay you back for what you have done.
8 I will sell your sons and daughters to the people of Judah.
   They will sell them to the people of Sheba,
      a nation that is far away."
   The LORD has spoken.

9 Announce this among the nations:
   Prepare yourselves for war.
      Wake up the warriors.
         Have all the warriors come near and attack.
10 Hammer your plowblades into swords
   and your pruning shears into spears.
      Weaklings should say that they are warriors.

11 Hurry from every direction, and gather there, all you nations.
   O LORD, bring your soldiers.
12 Wake up, you nations.
   Come to the valley of Jehoshaphat.
      There I will sit to judge all the surrounding nations.

13 Cut them down like grain.
   The harvest is ripe.
   Stomp on them as you would stomp on grapes.
      The winepress is full.
      The vats overflow.
         The nations are very wicked.
14 There are many, many people in the valley of decision.
   The day of the LORD is near in the valley of decision.
15 The sun and the moon will turn dark.
   The stars will no longer shine.
16 The LORD will roar from Zion,
      and his voice will thunder from Jerusalem.
         The sky and the earth will shake.
   The LORD will be a refuge for his people.
   He will be a stronghold for the people of Israel.

17 "You will know that I am the LORD your God.
   I live on my holy mountain, Zion.
      Jerusalem will be holy.

Foreigners will never invade it again.
18 On that day new wine will cover the mountains.
Milk will flow on the hills.
Water will flow in all the brooks of Judah.
A spring will flow from the LORD's temple.
It will water the valley of Shittim.
19 Egypt will become a wasteland.
Edom will become a barren desert.
This is because the nations were cruel to Judah.
They murdered innocent people in their land.
20 People will always live in Judah.
People will live in Jerusalem from now on.
21 I will punish those who murder."*c*
The LORD lives in Zion!

---

*c*3:21 Hebrew meaning of this line uncertain.

The Fish Spitting Jonah Out onto Shore

Jonah's Prayer Inside the Fish

Jonah 2:5–10

5 "Water surrounded me, threatening my life.
  The deep ˪sea˩ covered me completely.
    Seaweed was wrapped around my head.
6 I sank to the foot of the mountains.
  I sank to the bottom,
    where bars held me forever.
  But you brought me back from the pit, O Lord, my God.

7 "As my life was slipping away, I remembered the Lord.
  My prayer came to you in your holy temple.
8 Those who hold on to worthless idols abandon their loyalty ˪to you˩.
9   But I will sacrifice to you with songs of thanksgiving.
  I will keep my vow.
    Victory belongs to the Lord!"
10 Then the Lord spoke to the fish, and it spit Jonah out onto the shore.

AN INTRODUCTION TO

Amos

The prophet Amos was a sheep rancher who lived in Judah. God sent him to warn the rich people of Israel that God was angry because the Israelites had turned away from the Lord and were cruel to the poor.

Amos' message shows us how much God cares for those in need. And because God cares, we should, too!

Headlines

Countries' Crimes Condemned
Amos 1, page 1237

Rich Samaritans Are Called Names
Amos 4:1, page 1240

Women Faint From Thirst
Amos 8, page 1246

You Can't Hide From God!
Amos 9:1-4, page 1247

Who thought people were less important than a pair of new shoes? See Amos 2:6.

Be Concerned About Others

The selfish people in Amos' time just didn't care about the poor. They were more interested in cheating the poor than in helping them (see Amos 8:4-6). That way the selfish rich people could buy more for themselves!

God doesn't want us to be like that! People are more important than possessions. Since God cares about poor people, we should, too.

The Day of the LORD

When Old Testament prophets spoke of "the day of the LORD," they meant a time when God would act to change history. Often, the phrase refers to the end of history. Amos warned the people of Israel that the day of the LORD would bring judgment to their sinful nation.

How should a person get ready for the day of the LORD? The message of Amos was that sinners should beware. But those who love God and do right can look forward to blessings.

What's In It For Me?

God cares about people in need. . . .

GOD WANTS FAIR TREATMENT FOR EVERYONE.

GOD WILL PUNISH THOSE WHO ARE UNFAIR.

GOD WANTS PEOPLE TO CARE FOR THE POOR.

GOD WANTS ME TO CARE FOR OTHERS, TOO.

Fair to the Poor?

Is it fair for some people to be wealthy and other people to be poor? Some people say we should take money away from the rich and give it to the poor.

It's wrong to be selfish and not care about people who have needs. But it's also wrong for people who can work and take care of themselves to be lazy. How did God solve this problem?

In Old Testament law, God told the wealthy to be generous to the poor. Wealthy people were to let the poor pick up any grain or fruit left in the fields. The wealthy people were also to give or loan money to people who had no food. The wealthy also could "buy" a poor person. For seven years the poor person would work for the wealthy person and learn a trade. After seven years the wealthy person would give the poor person money to get a fresh start.

Did the poor people work to help themselves? Yes. Poor people went out in the fields to pick up the leftover grain and fruit. People didn't sit at home and expect wealthy people to bring them food. When people "sold" themselves to a wealthy person, they worked hard for those seven years to learn a new trade.

God's way is to care about the poor and to try to help them. But poor people are supposed to help themselves, too.

Amos

¹These are the words of Amos, one of the sheep farmers from Tekoa. He saw ⌞a vision⌟ about Israel during the reigns of Judah's King Uzziah and Israel's King Jeroboam, son of Joash. This happened two years before the earthquake.
²He said:

> The LORD roars from Zion,
>   and his voice thunders from Jerusalem.
> The pastures of the shepherds are turning brown,
>   and the top of ⌞Mount⌟ Carmel is dried up.

Damascus Will Be Judged for Its Crimes

³This is what the LORD says:

> Because Damascus has committed three crimes, and now a fourth crime,
>   I will not change my plans.
>   The Arameans have crushed ⌞the people of⌟ Gilead
>   with iron-spiked threshing*ᵃ* sledges.
> 4   I will send a fire on the house of Hazael
>   and burn down the palaces of Ben Hadad.
> 5   I will break the bars ⌞on the gates⌟ of Damascus.
>   I will cut off those living in Aven Valley
>   and the one who holds the scepter in Beth Eden.
> The people of Aram will go into captivity at Kir.

The LORD has said this.

Gaza Will Be Judged for Its Crimes

⁶This is what the LORD says:

> Because Gaza has committed three crimes, and now a fourth crime,
>   I will not change my plans.
>   The Philistines have taken all the people captive
>   in order to hand them over to the Edomites.
> 7   I will send a fire on the walls of Gaza
>   and burn down its palaces.
> 8   I will cut off those living in Ashdod
>   and the one who holds the scepter in Ashkelon.
>   I will turn my power against Ekron.
> The rest of the Philistines will die.

The Almighty LORD has said this.

Tyre Will Be Judged for Its Crimes

⁹This is what the LORD says:

> Because Tyre has committed three crimes, and now a fourth crime,
>   I will not change my plans.

ᵃ 1:3 Threshing is the process of beating stalks to separate them from the grain.

The Tyrians have handed all the people over to the Edomites.
The Tyrians didn't remember their treaty with their relatives.
¹⁰   I will send a fire on the walls of Tyre
and burn down its palaces.

Edom Will Be Judged for Its Crimes

¹¹This is what the LORD says:

Because Edom has committed three crimes, and now a fourth crime,
I will not change my plans.
The Edomites pursued their relatives with swords.
They refused to show any compassion to them.
Their anger was unstoppable.
They refused to control their fury.
¹²   I will send a fire on Teman
and burn down the palaces of Bozrah.

Ammon Will Be Judged for Its Crimes

¹³This is what the LORD says:

Because Ammon has committed three crimes, and now a fourth crime,
I will not change my plans.
The Ammonites enlarged their territory
by ripping open pregnant women in Gilead.
¹⁴   I will set fire to the walls of Rabbah
and burn down its palaces
while troops are shouting on the day of battle
and winds are howling on the day of the storm.
¹⁵   Their king will go into captivity along with his officials.

The LORD has said this.

Moab Will Be Judged for Its Crimes

2 ¹This is what the LORD says:

Because Moab has committed three crimes, and now a fourth crime,
I will not change my plans.
The Moabites have cremated Edom's king.
²   I will send a fire on Moab
and burn down the palaces of Kerioth.
Moab will die during the noise of battle
while troops are shouting and rams' horns are blowing.
³   I will take their judges away from them.
I will kill all their officials at the same time.

The LORD has said this.

Judah Will Be Judged for Its Crimes

⁴This is what the LORD says:

Because Judah has committed three crimes, and now a fourth crime,
I will not change my plans.
The people of Judah have rejected the LORD's Teachings

and haven't kept his laws.
They have been led astray by false teachings,
the same ones their ancestors followed.

5 I will send a fire on Judah
and burn down the palaces of Jerusalem.

Israel Will Be Judged for Its Crimes

6This is what the LORD says:

Because Israel has committed three crimes, and now a fourth crime,
I will not change my plans.
The people of Israel sell the righteous for money
and the needy for a pair of sandals.

7 They stomp the heads of the poor into the dust.
They push the humble out of the way.
Father and son sleep with the same woman.
They dishonor my holy name.

8 Beside every altar, they spread themselves out on clothes
taken as security.
In the temples of their gods, they drink the wine
that they bought with fines.

9 I destroyed the Amorites in front of them,
although the Amorites were as tall as cedars and as strong as oaks.
I destroyed their fruit above the ground and their roots below it.

10 I brought you out of Egypt.
I led you through the desert for 40 years
so that you could take possession of the land of the Amorites.

11 I also sent you prophets from among your children
and Nazirites from among your youths.
Isn't that so, people of Israel?

The LORD has declared this.

12 You made the Nazirites drink wine.
You commanded the prophets to stop prophesying.

13 I am going to crush you as an overloaded wagon crushes a person.

14 Runners will not be able to escape.
Strong men will find that their strength is useless.
Soldiers will not be able to save themselves.

15 Archers will not stand their ground.
Fast runners will not be able to escape.
Horsemen will not be able to save themselves.

16 Brave soldiers will run away naked that day.

The LORD has declared this.

The LORD Will Punish Israel for Its Immoral Behavior

3 1Listen to this message which I, the LORD, have spoken against you Israelites,
against your whole family that I brought out of Egypt.

2   Out of all the families on earth, I have known no one else but you.
      That is why I am going to punish you for all your sins.

3   Do two people ever walk together without meeting first?
4   Does a lion roar in the forest if it has no prey?
      Does a young lion growl in its den unless it has caught something?
5   Does a bird land in a trap on the ground if there's no bait in it?
      Does a trap spring up from the ground unless it has caught something?
6   If a ram's horn sounds an alarm in a city, won't the people be alarmed?
      If there is a disaster in a city, hasn't the Lord done it?
7   Certainly, the Almighty Lord doesn't do anything
        unless he ˻first˼ reveals his secret to his servants the prophets.
8   The lion has roared. Who isn't afraid?
        The Almighty Lord has spoken. Who can keep from prophesying?

9   Announce in the palaces of Ashdod and in the palaces of Egypt,
      "Gather together on the mountains of Samaria.
        See the widespread confusion and oppression in Samaria."
10   Those who collect profits in their palaces
      through violent and destructive acts
        don't know how to do what is right, declares the Lord.

11This is what the Almighty Lord says:

    An enemy will surround your land,
      strip you of your defenses,
        and loot your palaces.

12This is what the Lord says:

    As a shepherd rescues two legs or a piece of an ear out of a lion's mouth,
      so the Israelites living in Samaria will be rescued,
        ˻having only˼ a corner of a bed or a piece of a couch.ᵃ

13   Listen, and testify against the descendants of Jacob,
      declares the Almighty Lord, the God of Armies.
14   On the day I punish Israel for its disobedience,
      I will also destroy the altars at Bethel.
        The horns of the altar will be cut off and will fall to the ground.
15   I will tear down winter houses as well as summer houses.
      Houses ˻decorated˼ with ivory will be destroyed.
      Mansions will be demolished, declares the Lord.

The Lord Will Punish the Women of Samaria

4   1   Listen to this message, you cows of Bashan who live on Mount Samaria.
      You women oppress the poor and abuse the needy.
      You say to your husbands, "Get some wine! Let's drink!"

2The Almighty Lord has taken an oath on his holiness:
    Surely, the time is going to come
      when you will be taken away on hooks,
        and the rest of you on fishhooks.
3   Each of you will leave ˻the city˼

ᵃ3:12 Or "a couch of Damascus."

through breaks in the wall, one woman ahead of another.
You will be thrown into a garbage dump.

The LORD declares this.

4 Go to Bethel and sin.
Go to Gilgal and sin even more.
Bring your sacrifices every morning.
Bring a tenth of your income every three days.
5 Burn bread as a thank offering.
Brag and boast about your freewill offerings.
This is what you people of Israel love to do.

The Almighty LORD declares this.

6 I left you with nothing to eat in any of your cities.
I left you with no food in your entire land.
And you still didn't return to me, declares the LORD.

7 I stopped the rain from falling
three months before the harvest.
I sent rain on one city and not on another.
One field had rain.
Another field had none and dried up.
8 So people from two or three cities staggered
as they walked to another city in order to get a drink of water.
But they couldn't get enough.
And you still didn't return to me, declares the LORD.

9 I struck your ⸢crops⸣ with blight and mildew.
Locusts repeatedly devoured your gardens, vineyards,
fig trees, and olive trees.
And you still didn't return to me, declares the LORD.

10 I sent plagues on you as I did to Egypt.
With swords I killed your best young men along with your captured horses.
I made the stench from your camps fill your noses.
And you still didn't return to me, declares the LORD.

11 I destroyed some of you as I destroyed Sodom and Gomorrah.
You were like a burning log snatched from a fire.
And you still didn't return to me, declares the LORD.

12 This is what I will do to you, Israel.
Prepare to meet your God.
This is what I will do to you, Israel!

13 God forms the mountains and creates the wind.
He reveals his thoughts to humans.
He makes dawn and dusk ⸢appear⸣.
He walks on the high places of the earth.
His name is the LORD God of Armies.

A Funeral Song About Israel

5 ¹Listen to this message, this funeral song that I sing about you, nation of Israel:

² The people of Israel have fallen,
     never to rise again.
They lie abandoned in their own land.
     There is no one to help them.

³This is what the Almighty LORD says:

The city that sends 1,000 troops off to war
     will have ˻only˼ 100 left.
The one that sends 100 troops off to war
     will have ˻only˼ 10 left for the nation of Israel.

A Threefold Call to Turn Away From Sin

⁴This is what the LORD says to the nation of Israel:

Search for me and live!
⁵   But don't search ˻for me˼
       at Bethel.
       Don't go to Gilgal.
         Don't travel to Beersheba.
       Gilgal will certainly go
         into exile.
       Bethel will come to nothing.
⁶   Search for the LORD and live!
       If you don't, he will spread
         like a fire through the house
         of Joseph
       and burn it down.
         Bethel will have no one
         to put it out.

⁷ You, Israel, turn justice
     into poison
and throw righteousness
     on the ground.

⁸ God made the ˻constellations˼
     Pleiades and Orion.
He turns deep darkness
     into dawn.
He turns day into night.
He calls for water
     from the sea
       to pour it over the face
       of the earth.
His name is the LORD.
⁹   He destroys strongholds and ruins fortresses.

¹⁰ Israel, you hate anyone who speaks out against injustice.
     You are disgusted by anyone who speaks the truth.

Giving
Amos 5:10-13

It's easy to forget that others don't have as much as we do. It's not wrong for us to have nice things. But it is wrong not to care about others. Maybe you can pack up a box of books for a church library or give some of your toys or clothes to others who don't have as much as you do. Talk with your parents and find out what your family can do to help others.

be all you can be

11 You trample on the poor
   and take their wheat from them for taxes.
      That is why you build houses from hand-cut stones,
         but you will not live in them.
      You plant beautiful vineyards,
         but you will not drink their wine.
12 I know that your crimes are numerous and your sins are many.
   You oppress the righteous by taking bribes.
   You deny the needy access to the courts.
13   That is why a wise person remains silent at such times,
            because those times are so evil.

14 Search for good instead of evil so that you may live.
   Then the LORD God of Armies will be with you, as you have said.
15 Hate evil and love good.
      Then you will be able to have justice in your courts.
      Maybe the LORD God of Armies
         will have pity on the faithful few of Joseph.

16 This is what the LORD, the Almighty God of Armies, says:

   There will be loud crying in every city square,
      and people will say in every street, "Oh, no!"
   They will call on farmers to mourn
      and on professional mourners to cry loudly.
17 There will be loud crying in every vineyard,
      because I will pass through your land with death.

   The LORD has said this.

The Terrifying Day of the LORD

18 How horrible it will be for those who long for the day of the LORD!
      Why do you long for that day?
   The day of the LORD is one of darkness and not light.
19   It is like a person who flees from a lion
         only to be attacked by a bear.
      It is like a person who goes home and puts his hand on the wall
         only to be bitten by a snake.
20 The day of the LORD brings darkness and not light.
      It is pitch black, with no light.

The LORD Rejects Israel's Worship

21 I hate your festivals; I despise them.
   I'm not pleased with your religious assemblies.
22 Even though you bring me burnt offerings and grain offerings,
      I won't accept them.
      I won't even look at the fellowship offerings of your choicest animals.
23 Spare me the sound of your songs.
      I won't listen to the music of your harps.
24   But let justice flow like a river
            and righteousness like an ever-flowing stream.

²⁵ Did you bring me sacrifices and grain offerings
    in the desert for 40 years, nation of Israel?
²⁶ You carried along the statues of the god, Sikkuth as your king
    and the star Kiyyun,
        the gods you made for yourselves.

²⁷ I will send you into exile beyond Damascus,
    says the LORD, whose name is the God of Armies.

The Fall of Samaria

6 ¹ How horrible it will be for those who are at ease in Zion,
    for those who feel secure on the mountain of Samaria,
        and for the heads of the leading nations,
            to whom the nation of Israel comes.

²   Go to Calneh and look.
    Go from there to the great city of Hamath.
        Then go to Gath, the city of the Philistines.
    Are you better than these kingdoms?
    Is their territory larger than yours?

³ How horrible it will be for those who think that a day of disaster is far away.
    They bring the reign of violence closer.
⁴ How horrible it will be for those who sleep on ivory beds.
    They sprawl out on their couches
        and eat lambs from their flocks and calves from their stalls.
⁵ How horrible it will be for those who make up songs as they strum a harp.
    Like David, they write all kinds of songs for themselves.
⁶ How horrible it will be for those who drink wine by the jugful.
    They rub the finest oils all over themselves
        and are not sorry for the ruin of the descendants of Joseph.

⁷ That is why they will now be the first to go into exile.
    The celebrating of those sprawled around the banquet table will stop.

⁸ The Almighty LORD has sworn an oath on himself.
The LORD God of Armies declares:
    I am disgusted with Jacob's pride,
        and I hate his palaces.
            So I will hand over the city and everything in it.
⁹ If ten people are left in one house, they will die.
¹⁰ If a relative or a mortician
    comes to take the dead bodies out of the house
        and asks someone who is inside the house,
        "Is there anyone else with you?"
          that person will answer, "No."
        "Hush," he will add.
          "We shouldn't mention the name of the LORD!"
¹¹ The LORD is going to give the command
    to level big houses and flatten little houses.

¹² Do horses run on rocks?
Does a farmer plow the sea with oxen?

> Yet, you have turned justice into something deadly
> and what is righteous into poison.
13 How horrible it will be for those who rejoice over Lo Debar
> and who say, "We were strong enough to capture Karnaim by ourselves."

14 I am going to lead a nation to attack you, nation of Israel,
> declares the LORD God of the Armies of the Nations.
> They will oppress you from the border of Hamath to the valley of Arabah.

The LORD Threatens to Bring a Famine by Locusts

¹This is what the Almighty LORD showed me: He was preparing swarms of locusts when the second crop was being harvested. It was the harvest that followed the harvest for the king. ²When the locusts had finished eating every plant in the land, I said, "Almighty LORD, please forgive us! How can the descendants of Jacob survive? There are so few of them."

³The LORD changed his plans about this. "This won't happen," the LORD said.

The LORD Threatens to Bring a Drought by Fire

⁴This is what the Almighty LORD showed me: The Almighty LORD was calling for judgment by fire. The fire dried up the ocean and burned up the land. ⁵Then I said, "Almighty LORD, please stop! How can the descendants of Jacob survive? There are so few of them."

⁶The LORD changed his plans about this. "This won't happen either," the Almighty LORD said.

The LORD Refuses to Overlook Israel's Sin

⁷This is what he showed me: The Lord was standing by a wall built with the use of a plumb line, and he had a plumb line in his hand. ⁸He asked me, "What do you see, Amos?"

I answered, "A plumb line."

Then the Lord said, "I'm going to hold a plumb line in the middle of my people Israel. I will no longer overlook what they have done. ⁹The worship sites of Isaac will be destroyed, and the holy places of Israel will be in ruins. I will attack Jeroboam's heirs with my sword."

Amaziah Opposes Amos

¹⁰Then Amaziah, the priest at Bethel, sent a message to King Jeroboam of Israel. It read, "Amos is plotting against you among the people of Israel. The country isn't able to endure everything he is saying. ¹¹Amos says that Jeroboam will be killed with a sword and that Israel cannot avoid being taken from its land into exile."

¹²Then Amaziah said to Amos, "You seer,ᵃ run away to Judah! Eat there, and prophesy there! ¹³But don't ever prophesy again in Bethel, because this is the king's holy place and the king's palace."

¹⁴Amos responded, "I'm not a prophet, and I'm not a disciple of the prophets. I am a rancher and a grower of figs. ¹⁵But the LORD took me away from herding the flock and said to me, 'Prophesy to my people Israel.'

¹⁶"Now listen to the word of the LORD: You said, 'Stop prophesying against Israel, and stop preaching against the descendants of Isaac.'

ᵃ7:12 A seer is a prophet.

¹⁷"However, this is what the Lord says: Your wife will become a prostitute in the city, and your sons and daughters will be killed with swords. Your land will be surveyed and divided up, and you will die in an unclean[b] land. Israel cannot avoid being taken from its land into exile."

The End Has Come for Israel

8 ¹This is what the Almighty Lord showed me: a basket of ripe summer fruit. ²He asked, "What do you see, Amos?"

"A basket of ripe summer fruit," I answered.

Then the Lord said to me, "My people Israel are now ripe. I will no longer overlook what they have done. ³On that day the songs of the temple will become loud cries," declares the Almighty Lord. "There will be dead bodies scattered everywhere. Hush!"

4   Listen to this, those who trample on the needy
         and ruin those who are oppressed in the world.

5   You say to yourselves,
      "When will the New Moon Festival be over
         so that we can sell more grain?
      When will the day of worship be over
         so that we can sell more wheat?
      We can shrink the size of the bushel baskets,
         increase the cost,
            and cheat with dishonest scales.

6   We can buy the poor with money
         and the needy for a pair of sandals.
      We can sell the husks mixed in with the wheat."

7   The Lord has sworn an oath by Jacob's pride:
      "I will never forget anything that they have done."

8   The land will tremble because of this.
      Everyone who lives in it will mourn.
      The entire land will rise like the Nile,
         be tossed about, and then sink like Egypt's river.

9   On that day, declares the Almighty Lord,
      I will make the sun go down at noon
         and darken the earth in broad daylight.

10   I will turn your festivals into funerals
         and all your songs into funeral songs.
      I will put sackcloth around everyone's waist
         and shave everyone's head.
      I will make that day seem like a funeral for an only child,
         and its end will be bitter.

11   The days are going to come, declares the Almighty Lord,
         when I will send a famine throughout the land.
      It won't be an ordinary famine or drought.
         Instead, there will be a famine of hearing the words of the Lord.

---

[b]7:17 "Unclean" refers to anything that Moses' Teachings say is not presentable to God.

12 People will wander from sea to sea
and roam from the north to the east,
searching for the word of the Lord.
But they won't find it.

13 On that day beautiful young women and strong young men
will faint because of their thirst.

14 ⸢How horrible it will be for⸣ those who swear by Ashimah,ᵃ
the idol of Samaria, and say,
"I solemnly swear, Dan, as your god lives. . . ."
"I solemnly swear as long as there is a road to Beersheba. . . ."
Those who say this will fall and never get up again.

The Lord Will Sift Israel out of All the Nations

9 ¹I saw the Lord standing by the altar, and he said:

Strike the tops of the pillars so that the foundations shake.
Cut off everyone's head.
I will kill with a sword all who are left.
None of them will be able to get away.
None of them will be able to escape.

2 Even if they dig their way into Sheol,
my hand will take them from there.
Even if they go up to heaven,
I will bring them down from there.

3 Even if they hide on top of Mount Carmel,
I will look for them and take them from there.
Even if they hide from me at the bottom of the sea,
I will command a sea snake to bite them.

4 Even if they go into exile ahead of their enemies,
I will command a sword to kill them.
I will keep my eyes on them
so that I can bring disaster on them and not help them.

5 The Almighty Lord of Armies touches the earth.
It quakes, and all who live on it mourn.
All of it rises like the Nile
and sinks like Egypt's river.

6 The one who builds stairs up to heaven
and sets their foundation on the earth,
the one who calls for the water in the sea
and pours it over the face of the earth—
His name is the Lord.

7 You people of Israel are like the people from Sudan, says the Lord.
Didn't I bring Israel from Egypt?
Didn't I bring the Philistines from Crete and the Arameans from Kir?

8 I, the Almighty Lord, have my eyes on this sinful kingdom.
I will wipe it off the face of the earth.

ᵃ8:14 Hebrew meaning uncertain.

But I won't totally destroy the descendants of Jacob, declares the LORD.

9 I'm going to give the order.
I will sift the nation of Israel out of all the nations
   as if I were using a sieve.
Not one pebble will fall to the ground.

10 All the sinners among my people are thinking,
   "Destruction will not catch up to us or run into us."
   In spite of this, they will be killed with swords.

The LORD Will Restore His People

11 On that day I will set up David's fallen tent.
   I will repair the holes in it.
   I will restore its ruined places.
   I will rebuild them as they were a long time ago.

12 They will capture the few survivors of Edom
   and all the other nations that were under my authority,
      declares the LORD, who will do these things.

13 The days are going to come, declares the LORD,
   when the one who plows will catch up to the one who harvests,
      and the one who stomps on grapes will catch up to the one who plants.
   New wine will drip from the mountains
      and flow from all the hills.

14 I will restore my people Israel.
   They will rebuild the ruined cities and live in them.
   They will plant vineyards and drink the wine from them.
   They will plant gardens and eat their fruit.

15 I will plant the people of Israel in their land,
   and they won't be uprooted again from the land that I gave them,
      says the LORD your God.

Obadiah

The prophet Obadiah spoke out against the Edomites. The Edomites helped Judah's enemies who attacked and stole from the people of Jerusalem. The Edomites were glad when the people of Judah suffered. Obadiah said that Edom would be punished and would cease to exist as a nation. This book teaches us that it's dangerous to take sides against God.

What's In It For Me?

Be on the LORD's side . . .

AND GOD WILL BE ON YOUR SIDE.

BE KIND, NOT UNCARING.

BE HUMBLE, NOT PROUD.

BE LIKE CHRIST, NOT GODLESS.

Headlines

What a Lousy Relative!
Obadiah 1:10-12, page 1250

Edom's Lost, but Israel Will Last
Obadiah 1:15-18, page 1251

Obadiah

Edom's Fall—
Jeremiah 49:14-16, 9

¹This is the vision of Obadiah.

This is what the Almighty LORD says about Edom:

> We have heard a message from the LORD.
> > A messenger was sent among the nations to say,
> > > "Get ready! Let's go to war against Edom."

² "Edom, I will make you the smallest of nations.
> Others will despise you.

³ > Your arrogance has deceived you.
> > You live on rocky cliffs.
> > You make your home up high.
> > You say to yourself,
> > > 'No one can bring me down to earth.'

⁴ Even though you fly high like an eagle
> and build your nest among the stars,
> > I will bring you down from there," declares the LORD.

⁵ "If thieves or looters come to you during the night,
> won't they steal only until they've had enough?
> > You will be ruined!
> If people come to pick your grapes,
> won't they leave a few grapes behind?

⁶ > But you, Esau,ᵃ will lose everything.
> > Even your hidden treasures will be looted.

⁷ All your allies will force you to leave your land.
> The people who are at peace with you will deceive you.
> > Those who eat food with you will set traps for you,
> > and you won't even know about it.

⁸ "On that day I will destroy the wise people in Edom
> and take wisdom away from Esau's mountain," declares the LORD.

⁹ "Teman, your warriors will be terrified.
> Everyone on Esau's mountain will be slaughtered.

Why Edom Will Be Destroyed

¹⁰ "Because of the violence you did to Jacob, your relative,
> you will be covered with shame.
> You will be destroyed forever.

¹¹ While you stood there doing nothing,
> strangers carried off Jacob's wealth.
> > Foreigners entered his gates and threw dice for Jerusalem.

ᵃ6 Esau was the son of Isaac and the ancestor of the people of Edom.

You acted like one of them.
12 Don't gloat over your relative's misfortune
or be happy when the people of Judah are destroyed.
Don't brag so much when they're in distress.
13 Don't march through the gates of my people when disaster strikes
or gloat over their misery when disaster strikes.
Don't take their wealth when disaster strikes.
14 Don't stand at the crossroads to kill their refugees.
Don't hand over their survivors when they're in distress.

The Day of the LORD

15 "The day of the LORD is near for all nations.
Edom, you will be treated as you have treated others.
You will get back what you have given.
16 As you, Israel, drank on my holy mountain,
so all nations will drink in turn.
They will drink and guzzle down everything in it.
They will be like those who have never existed.

17 "But refugees will live on Mount Zion.
It will be holy.
The descendants of Jacob will get back their possessions.
18 The descendants of Jacob will be like a fire.
The descendants of Joseph will be like a flame.
But the descendants of Esau will be like straw.
They will be burned and destroyed.
There will be no one left among the descendants of Esau."
The LORD has spoken.

19 "People from the Negev will take possession of Esau's mountain.
People from the foothills will take possession of Philistia.
They will take possession of the lands of Ephraim and Samaria,
and the descendants of Benjamin will take possession of Gilead.
20 Exiles from Israel will take possession of Canaan.
They will possess land as far as Zarephath.
Exiles from Jerusalem who are in Sepharad
will take possession of the cities in the Negev.
21 Those who are victorious will come from Mount Zion
to rule Esau's mountain.
The kingdom will belong to the LORD."

Jonah

When God instructed Jonah to go to Nineveh and preach to Israel's enemies, Jonah headed in the opposite direction. But Jonah ended up truly sorry that he had disobeyed when he found himself in the belly of a big fish! Then God gave him a second chance. We can all be grateful that we serve such a gracious God.

Headlines

Fish Throws Man Back
Jonah 2, page 1254

**Nineveh Makes
Right Turn**
Jonah 3, page 1255

**Lost Vine Makes
Prophet Whine**
Jonah 4, page 1256

Why is Jonah running?
See Jonah 1.

The Patriotic Prophet

Some people say a person's first duty is to "God and country." But God and country are two different things. Jonah found that out when God told him to preach to the Ninevites, Israel's enemy. Jonah was a patriot and loved his country. So he chose to run away rather than help his nation's enemy.

It's good to be patriotic, but a Christian's first duty is to God. No nation is perfect, and some are very bad. But God is perfect and God is good. Choose to serve God first, and you will never go wrong.

What's In It For Me?

If I try to run from God . . .

GOD WILL ALWAYS FIND ME.

GOD WILL WORK TO BRING ME BACK.

GOD WILL HEAR WHEN I AM IN TROUBLE.

WHEN I TURN TO HIM, GOD WILL FORGIVE ME.

You Can't Run Away From God

If you wanted to run away from God, where would you go? Jonah ran to Tarshish, the farthest place he knew in the opposite direction from Nineveh. But God had no trouble tracking down the fleeing prophet.

You can run to Mount Everest or the South Pole, but you can't get away from God. It's a good thing, too! Like Jonah, we sometimes make foolish choices. But when we are in trouble, we can turn to God, and he will always be there for us. There's just no getting away! God has promised that "nothing can ever separate us from God's love" (Romans 8:38-39).

JONAH'S A-MAZE-ING JOURNEY!

QUESTION: Why did the fish let Jonah go?

ANSWER: The big one always gets away.

Jonah

Jonah Tries to Run Away From the LORD

1 ¹The LORD spoke his word to Jonah, son of Amittai. He said, ²"Leave at once for the important city, Nineveh. Announce to the people that I can no longer overlook the wicked things they have done."

³Jonah immediately tried to run away from the LORD by going to Tarshish. He went to Joppa and found a ship going to Tarshish. He paid for the trip and went on board. He wanted to go to Tarshish to get away from the LORD.

⁴The LORD sent a violent wind over the sea. The storm was so powerful that the ship was in danger of breaking up. ⁵The sailors were afraid, and they cried to their gods for help. They began to throw the cargo overboard to lighten the ship's load.

Now, Jonah had gone below deck and was lying there sound asleep. ⁶The captain of the ship went to him and asked, "How can you sleep? Get up, and pray to your God. Maybe he will notice us, and we won't die."

⁷Then the sailors said to each other, "Let's throw dice to find out who is responsible for bringing this disaster on us." So they threw dice, and the dice indicated that Jonah was responsible.

⁸They asked him, "Tell us, why has this disaster happened to us? What do you do for a living? Where do you come from? What country are you from? What nationality are you?"

⁹Jonah answered them, "I'm a Hebrew. I worship the LORD, the God of heaven. He is the God who made the sea and the land."

¹⁰Then the men were terrified. They knew that he was running away from the LORD, because he had told them. They asked Jonah, "Why have you done this?"

¹¹The storm was getting worse. So they asked Jonah, "What should we do with you to calm the sea?"

¹²He told them, "Throw me overboard. Then the sea will become calm. I know that I'm responsible for this violent storm."

¹³Instead, the men tried to row harder to get the ship back to shore, but they couldn't do it. The storm was getting worse.

¹⁴So they cried to the LORD for help: "Please, LORD, don't let us die for taking this man's life. Don't hold us responsible for the death of an innocent man, because you, LORD, do whatever you want." ¹⁵Then they took Jonah and threw him overboard, and the sea became calm. ¹⁶The men were terrified of the LORD. They offered sacrifices and made vows to the LORD.*

¹⁷The LORD sent a big fish to swallow Jonah. Jonah was inside the fish for three days and three nights.

Jonah's Prayer Inside the Fish

2 *¹From inside the fish Jonah prayed to the LORD his God.

²Jonah prayed:

> "I called to the LORD in my distress,
>   and he answered me.

---

*1:16 Jonah 1:17 in English Bibles is Jonah 2:1 in the Hebrew Bible. *2:1 Jonah 2:1-10 in English Bibles is Jonah 2:2-11 in the Hebrew Bible.

From the depths of my ⸢watery⸣ grave I cried for help,
   and you heard my cry.
3   You threw me into the deep, into the depths of the sea,
   and water surrounded me.
      All the whitecaps on your waves have swept over me.

4   "Then I thought,
   'I have been banished from your sight.
      Will I ever see your holy temple again?'

5   "Water surrounded me, threatening my life.
   The deep ⸢sea⸣ covered me completely.
      Seaweed was wrapped around my head.
6   I sank to the foot of the mountains.
   I sank to the bottom,
      where bars held me forever.
   But you brought me back from the pit, O LORD, my God.

7   "As my life was slipping away, I remembered the LORD.
   My prayer came to you
      in your holy temple.
8   Those who hold on
      to worthless idols abandon
      their loyalty ⸢to you⸣.
9   But I will sacrifice to you
      with songs
         of thanksgiving.
   I will keep my vow.
      Victory belongs
         to the LORD!"

¹⁰Then the LORD spoke to the fish, and it spit Jonah out onto the shore.

Nineveh Turns From Its Wicked Ways

3 ¹Then the LORD spoke his word to Jonah a second time. He said, ²"Leave at once for the important city, Nineveh. Announce to the people the message I have given you."

³Jonah immediately went to Nineveh as the LORD told him. Nineveh was a very large city. It took three days to walk through* it. ⁴Jonah entered the city and walked for about a day. Then he said, "In forty days Nineveh will be destroyed."

⁵The people of Nineveh believed God. They decided to fast, and everyone, from the most important to the least important, dressed in sackcloth.

Work
Jonah 3:1-5

In the opening chapters of Jonah, the reluctant prophet runs away when God tells him to go to Nineveh. When God gave Jonah a second chance, Jonah went "immediately." Whenever you're given a job, it's a good idea to do it right away. Then you won't have to be sorry for not obeying.

be you can be

---

*3:3 Or "around."

⁶When the news reached the king of Nineveh, he got up from his throne, took off his robe, put on sackcloth, and sat in ashes. ⁷Then he made this announcement and sent it throughout the city:

"This is an order from the king and his nobles: No one is to eat or drink anything. This includes all people, animals, cattle, and sheep. ⁸Every person and animal must put on sackcloth. Cry loudly to God for help. Turn from your wicked ways and your acts of violence. ⁹Who knows? God may reconsider his plans and turn from his burning anger so that we won't die."

¹⁰God saw what they did. He saw that they turned from their wicked ways. So God reconsidered his threat to destroy them, and he didn't do it.

The LORD Has to Remind Jonah About His Mercy

4 ¹Jonah was very upset about this, and he became angry. ²So he prayed to the LORD, "LORD, isn't this what I said would happen when I was still in my own country? That's why I tried to run to Tarshish in the first place. I knew that you are a merciful and compassionate God, patient, and always ready to forgive and to reconsider your threats of destruction. ³So now, LORD, take my life. I'd rather be dead than alive."

⁴The LORD asked, "What right do you have to be angry?"

⁵Jonah left the city and sat down east of it. He made himself a shelter there. He sat in its shade and waited to see what would happen to the city. ⁶The LORD God made a plant grow up beside Jonah to give him shade and make him more comfortable. Jonah was very happy with the plant.

⁷At dawn the next day, God sent a worm to attack the plant so that it withered. ⁸When the sun rose, God made a hot east wind blow. The sun beat down on Jonah's head so that he was about to faint. He wanted to die. So he said, "I'd rather be dead than alive."

⁹Then God asked Jonah, "What right do you have to be angry over this plant?"

Jonah answered, "I have every right to be angry—so angry that I want to die."

¹⁰The LORD replied, "This plant grew up overnight and died overnight. You didn't plant it or make it grow. Yet, you feel sorry for this plant. ¹¹Shouldn't I feel sorry for this important city, Nineveh? It has more than 120,000 people in it as well as many animals. These people couldn't tell their right hand from their left."

Micah

Micah spread God's news in Judah during the time of Isaiah and Amos. Micah spoke out against powerful people in both Israel and Judah. These people made plans to gain wealth but ignored God's laws. Because they were unfair to so many people, God made his own plans to punish these people and their nations. But God's plans also included forgiveness for his stubborn people.

Who's really in trouble here? See Micah 2:8-10.

What's In It For Me?

God's plans . . .

SHOW HIS CONCERN FOR JUSTICE.

INCLUDE PUNISHING THE WICKED.

OFFER HOPE TO THE WEAK.

PROMISE COMPASSION ON THOSE HE LOVES.

WILL ALWAYS COME TRUE.

Headlines

Women Forced Out of Homes!
Micah 2:9, page 1259

Best Place to Be Born
Micah 5:2, page 1262

Daughter Rebels Against Mother
Micah 7:6, page 1265

Micah Asks for Miracles
Micah 7:15, page 1265

Micah

The Prophet Micah

¹The LORD spoke his word to Micah, who was from Moresheth, when Jotham, Ahaz, and Hezekiah were kings of Judah. This is the vision that Micah saw about Samaria and Jerusalem.

The Capital Cities of Israel and Judah Destroyed

2 Listen, all you people!
Pay attention, earth and all who are on it.
  The Almighty LORD will be a witness against you.
  The Lord will be a witness from his holy temple.
3 The LORD is going to come from his place.
He is going to come down and step on the worship places of the earth.
4   Mountains will melt under him like wax near a fire.
  Valleys will split apart like water pouring down a steep hill.
5 All this is because of Jacob's crime and Israel's sin.
  What is Jacob's crime? Isn't it Samaria?
  What is Judah's worship place? Isn't it Jerusalem?

6 So I will turn Samaria into a pile of rubble,
  a place for planting vineyards.
I will roll its stones down into a valley and expose its foundations.
7   All its idols will be smashed to pieces.
  All its wages for being a prostitute will be burned.
  All its statues will be turned into a pile of rubble.
    Samaria collected its wages for being a prostitute.
    That money will again pay for prostitutes.

8 I will mourn and cry because of this.
I will walk around barefoot and naked.
I will cry like a jackal and mourn like an ostrich.
9   Samaria's wounds are incurable.
    The news about Samaria will come to Judah.
  It will reach the gates of my people in Jerusalem.
10   Don't report it in Gath. Don't cry there.
  Roll in the dust of Beth Leaphrah.ᵃ
11 Pass by, naked and ashamed, inhabitants of Shaphir.
Don't come out, inhabitants of Zaanan.
  Beth Ezel is in mourning.
    It will take its support away from you.
12 Wait anxiously for good, inhabitants of Maroth.
  From the LORD disaster will come on the gates of Jerusalem.
13 Harness the horses to the chariots, inhabitants of Lachish.
  You were the first to lead the people of Zion into sin.
  The rebellious acts of Israel are found in you.

ᵃ 1:10 Or "I rolled in the dust of Beth Leaphrah."

14 　That is why you will give farewell gifts to Moresheth Gath.
　　　The town of Achzib will betray the kings of Israel.
15 I will again bring a conqueror against the inhabitants of Mareshah.
　　　The glory of Israel will come to Adullam.
16 Shave your head in mourning for the children you love.
　　　Make yourselves as bald as vultures
　　　　　because your children will be taken from you into exile.

Israel's Sins Are Condemned

1 How horrible it will be for those who invent trouble
　　　and work out plans for disaster while in bed.
　　　When the morning dawns, they carry out their plans
　　　　because they are able to.
2 They desire ˌother people's˒ fields, so they seize them.
　　　They desire ˌpeople's˒ houses, so they take them.
　　　They cheat a man and his family,
　　　　a man and his inheritance.

³So this is what the Lord says:

　　　I'm planning a disaster to punish your family.
　　　You won't be able to rescue yourselves.
　　　You will no longer be able to walk proudly.
　　　　This will be a time of disaster.
4 When that day comes, people will make fun of you.
　　　They will sing this sad song about you:
　　　"We are completely ruined.
　　　　The Lord gives our people's possessions ˌto others˒.
　　　　He takes them from us.
　　　　He divides our fields among our captors."
5 That is why none of you in the Lord's assembly will draw lots
　　　to divide your property.

6 Your prophets say, "Don't prophesy!
　　　Don't prophesy such things!
　　　　Disgrace will never overtake us."
7 Should the descendants of Jacob be asked:
　　　Has the Spirit of the Lord become impatient with you?
　　　　Has he done these things?
　　　　Are his words good for those who live honestly?

8 Recently, my people have turned into enemies.
　　　You take coats from those who pass by without a care
　　　　as they return from war.
9 You force the women among my people out of their pleasant homes
　　　and take my glory away from their children forever.
10 Get up, and go away!
　　　This is not a place to rest!
　　　　It will be destroyed, completely destroyed,
　　　　　because it offends me.
11 Liars and frauds may go around and say,

"We will preach to you about wine and liquor."
They would be just the type of preacher you want.

Israel Will Be Gathered Again by the LORD

12 I will surely gather all of you, Jacob.
I will surely bring together the few people left in Israel.
I will gather them together like sheep in a pen,
like a flock in its pasture.
They will make a lot of noise
because there will be so many people.
13 The LORD will open the way and lead them.
They will break out, go through the gate, and leave.
Their king will travel in front of them.
The LORD will lead the people.

Israel's Sinful Leaders—Rulers, Prophets, and Priests

3 ¹Then I said:

Listen, you leaders of Jacob, you rulers of the nation of Israel.
You should know justice.
2 You hate good and love evil.
You strip the skin off my people and the flesh off their bones.
3 You eat my people's flesh.
You strip off their skin.
You break their bones to pieces.
You chop them up like meat for a pot, like stew meat for a kettle.
4 Then you will cry to the LORD,
but he will not answer you.
He will hide his face from you at that time
because you have done evil things.

⁵This is what the LORD says about the prophets who mislead my people:

When they have something to eat, they say, "All is well!"
But they declare a holy war against those who don't feed them.
6 That is why you will have nights without visions.
You will have darkness without revelations.
The sun will set on the prophets,
and the day will turn dark for them.
7 Seers* will be put to shame.
Those who practice witchcraft will be disgraced.
All of them will cover their faces, because God won't answer them.

8 But I am filled with the power of the LORD's Spirit,
with justice, and with strength.
So I will tell the descendants of Jacob about their crimes
and the nation of Israel about its sins.
9 Listen to this, you leaders of the descendants of Jacob,
you rulers of the nation of Israel.

---

*3:7 A seer is a prophet.

You despise justice and pervert everything that is right.

10 You build Zion on bloodshed and Jerusalem on wickedness.

11   Your leaders exchange justice for bribes.

Your priests teach for a price.

Your prophets tell the future for money.

But they rely on the LORD when they say,

"After all, the LORD is with us.

Nothing bad will happen to us."

12 Because of you,

Zion will be plowed like a field,

Jerusalem will become a pile of rubble,

and the temple mountain will become a worship site

covered with trees.

The LORD Will Teach the Nations—
Isaiah 2:2-4

4   1 In the last days the mountain of the LORD's house

will be established as the highest of the mountains

and raised above the hills.

People will stream to it.

2 Then many nations will come and say,

"Let's go to the mountain of the LORD,

to the house of the God of Jacob.

He will teach us his ways so that we may live by them."

The teachings will go out from Zion.

The word of the LORD will go out from Jerusalem.

3   Then he will judge disputes between many people

and settle arguments between many nations far and wide.

They will hammer their swords into plowblades

and their spears into pruning shears.

Nations will never fight against each other,

and they will never train for war again.

4 They will sit under their grapevines and their fig trees,

and no one will make them afraid.

The LORD of Armies has spoken.

5 All the nations live by the names of their gods,

but we will live by the name of the LORD our God forever.

6 "When that day comes," declares the LORD,

"I will gather those who are lame.

I will bring together those who are scattered

and those whom I have injured.

7 I will change those who are lame into a faithful people.

I will change those who are forced away into a strong nation."

The LORD will rule them on Mount Zion now and forever.

8 You, Jerusalem, watchtower of the flock,

stronghold of the people of Zion,

your former government will come back to you.

The kingdom will return to the people of Jerusalem.

9 Now why are you crying so loudly?
　　Don't you have a king?
　　　Has your counselor died?
　　Pain grips you like a woman in labor.
10 Daughter of Zion, writhe in pain and groan like a woman in labor.
　　Now you will leave the city,
　　　live in the open fields,
　　　　and go to Babylon.
　　　　　There you will be rescued.
　　　　　There the LORD will reclaim you from your enemies.

11 But now many nations gather against you.
　　They say, "Let's dishonor Zion and gloat over it."
12 They don't know the thoughts of the LORD or understand his plan.
　　He will bring them together
　　　like cut grain on the threshing floor.*
13 Get up and thresh,* people of Zion.
　　I will make your horns as hard as iron
　　　and your hoofs as hard as bronze.
　　You will smash many nations into small pieces.
　　You will claim their loot for the LORD,
　　　their wealth for the Lord of the whole earth.

5 *1 Now, gather your troops, you city of troops.
　　We are under attack.
　　Enemies will strike the judge of Israel on the cheek with a stick.

The LORD's Leader for Israel

2 You, Bethlehem Ephrathah,
　　are too small to be included among Judah's cities.
　　　Yet, from you Israel's future ruler will come for me.
　　　　His origins go back to the distant past, to days long ago.
3 That is why the LORD will abandon Israel
　　until the time a mother has a child.
　　Then the rest of the LORD's people will return to the people of Israel.
4 The child will become the shepherd of his flock.
　　He will lead them, with the strength of the LORD,
　　　with the majestic name of the LORD his God.
　　They will live in safety
　　　because his greatness will reach the ends of the earth.
5 　　This man will be their peace.

When the Assyrians invade our land and trample our palaces,
　　we will attack them with seven shepherds and eight leaders.
6 　　They will rule Assyria with their swords
　　　and the country of Nimrod with drawn swords.
　　They will rescue us from the Assyrians
　　　when they come into our land

---

*4:12 A threshing floor is an outdoor area where grain is separated from its husks. *4:13 Threshing is the process of beating stalks to separate them from the grain. *5:1 Micah 5:1-15 in English Bibles is Micah 4:14–5:14 in the Hebrew Bible.

and walk within our territory.
⁷ Then the few people left from Jacob will be among many people
like dew from the Lord, like showers on the grass.
They do not put their hope in humans or wait for mortals.
⁸ The few people left from Jacob will be among the nations,
among many people.

They will be like a lion among animals in the forest,
like a young lion among flocks of sheep.
When a lion hunts,
it tramples ⸢its victims⸣ and tears ⸢them⸣ to pieces,
and there is no one to rescue them.
⁹ You will use your power against your opponents,
and all your enemies will be destroyed.

¹⁰ "When that day comes," declares the Lord,
"I will destroy your horses
and demolish your chariots.
¹¹ I will destroy the cities in your land
and tear down all your fortresses.
¹² I will destroy your sorcerers,
and you will have no more fortunetellers.
¹³ I will destroy your idols and your sacred monuments.
You will no longer worship what your hands have made.
¹⁴ I will pull out your poles dedicated to the goddess Asherah.
I will wipe out your cities.
¹⁵ I will take revenge with great anger
on the nations that do not obey me."

The LORD's Lawsuit Against His People

6 ¹ Now listen to what the Lord is saying,
"Stand up! Plead your case in front of the mountains,
and let the hills listen to your request.
² Listen to the Lord's lawsuit, you mountains.
Listen, you strong foundations of the earth.
The Lord has filed a lawsuit against his people.
He is arguing his case against Israel.

³ "My people, what have I done to you?
How have I tried your patience? Answer me!
⁴ I brought you out of Egypt and freed you from slavery.
I sent Moses, Aaron, and Miriam to lead you.
⁵ My people, remember what King Balak of Moab planned ⸢to do to you⸣
and how Balaam, son of Beor, responded to him.
Remember ⸢your journey⸣ from Shittim to Gilgal*
so that you may know the victories of the Lord."

⁶ What should I bring when I come into the Lord's presence,
when I bow in front of the God of heaven?
Should I bring him year-old calves as burnt offerings?
⁷ Will the Lord be pleased with thousands of rams

---

*6:5 Hebrew meaning of this line uncertain.

or with endless streams of olive oil?
Should I give him my firstborn child because of my rebellious acts?
Should I give him my young child for my sin?

8 You mortals, the LORD has told you what is good.
 This is what the LORD requires from you:
  to do what is right,
   to love mercy,
    and to live humbly with your God.

9 The voice of the LORD calls out to the city.
  (The fear of your name is wisdom.)
  "Listen, you tribe assembled in the city.*b*

10 I have cursed all the wicked people who use their money for evil
  and use inaccurate weights and measures.

11 I cannot tolerate dishonest scales
  and bags filled with inaccurate weights.

12 The rich people in the city are violent.
  Those who live in the city speak lies,
   and their tongues speak deceitfully.

13 I have begun to strike you with heavy blows
  and to ruin you because of your sins.

14 You will eat, but you won't be full.
  So you will always be hungry.
  You will put things away, but you won't save them.
  Anything you save I will destroy.

15 You will plant, but you won't harvest.
  You will crush olives, but you won't rub the oil on your skin.
  You will make new wine, but you won't drink it.

16 You have kept Omri's laws
  and all the practices of the descendants of Ahab,
   and you have followed their advice.
  That is why I will ruin you.
   Your people will be ridiculed.
    You will bear the disgrace of my people."

The LORD's People Confess Their Sin

7 1 Poor me!
  I am like those gathering summer fruit,
   like those picking grapes.
    But there aren't any grapes to eat
     or any ripened figs that I crave.

2 Faithful people are gone from the earth,
  and no one is decent.
  All people lie in ambush to commit murder.
   They trap each other with nets.

3   Their hands are skilled in doing evil.
    Officials ask for gifts.
    Judges accept bribes.
    Powerful people dictate what they want.

---

*b*6:9 Greek; Masoretic Text "Listen to the stick and the one who appointed it."

So they scheme together.[a]

4 The best of them is like a briar.
The most decent person is sharper than thornbushes.
   The day you thought you would be punished has come.
   Now is the time you will be confused.
5 Don't trust your neighbors.
Don't have confidence in ˌyourˌ friends.
   Keep your mouth shut even when a woman is lying in your arms.
6 A son treats his father with contempt.
A daughter rebels against her mother.
A daughter-in-law rebels against her mother-in-law.
   People's enemies are the members of their own families.

7 I will look to the LORD.
I will wait for God to save me.
I will wait for my God to listen to me.

8 Don't laugh at me, my enemies.
   Although I've fallen, I will get up.
   Although I sit in the dark, the LORD is my light.
9 I have sinned against the LORD.
   So I will endure his fury
      until he takes up my cause and wins my case.
      He will bring me into the light,
         and I will see his victory.
10 Then my enemies will see this, and they will be covered with shame,
   because they asked me, "Where is the LORD your God?"
      Now I look at them.
      They are trampled like mud in the streets.

11 The day for rebuilding your walls
   and extending your borders is coming.
12 When that day comes, your people will come to you
   from Assyria and the cities of Egypt,
   from Egypt to the Euphrates River,
   from sea to sea, and from mountain to mountain.
13 The earth will become a wasteland for those who live on it
   because of what the people living there have done.

14 With your shepherd's staff, take care of your people,
   the sheep that belong to you.
      They live alone in the woods, in fertile pastures.
         Let them feed in Bashan and Gilead like before.
15 Let us see miracles
   like the time you came out of Egypt.
16 Nations will see this and be ashamed in spite of all their strength.
   They will put their hands over their mouths.
   Their ears will become deaf.
17 They will lick dust like snakes,
   like animals that crawl on the ground.

---

[a] 7:3 Hebrew meaning of this line uncertain.

They will come out of their hiding places trembling.
They will turn away from your presence in fear, O LORD our God.
They will be afraid of you.

18 Who is a God like you?
You forgive sin
and overlook the rebellion of your faithful people.
You will not be angry forever,
because you would rather show mercy.

19 You will again have compassion on us.
You will overcome our wrongdoing.
You will throw all our sins into the deep sea.

20 You will be faithful to Jacob.
You will have mercy on Abraham
as you swore by an oath to our ancestors long ago.

Nahum

For decades the cruel Assyrians bullied other nations, including Israel and Judah. But Nahum had good news for God's suffering people: The Lord was on his way to Nineveh, capital of Assyria, to punish those who were hurting the people of God.

How many warriors did it take to conquer Nineveh? See Nahum 1:9.

What's In It For Me?

God's ways . . .

GOD IS A HOLY JUDGE.

GOD IS FAIR AND SLOW TO GET ANGRY.

GOD IS A FRIEND TO THE INNOCENT.

GOD WILL AVENGE TERRIBLE WRONGDOING.

GOD WILL FREE THE OPPRESSED.

Headlines

Nineveh All Washed Up
Nahum 1, page 1268

Nineveh Will Lose Friends!
Nahum 3:6-7, page 1270

Nahum

Nahum's Vision

¹This is a revelation from the Lord about Nineveh. This book contains the vision of Nahum from Elkosh.

Who Can Withstand the LORD's Anger?

2   God does not tolerate rivals. The Lord takes revenge.
    The Lord takes revenge and is full of anger.
    The Lord takes revenge against his enemies
        and holds a grudge against his foes.
3   The Lord is patient and has great strength.
    The Lord will never let the guilty go unpunished.
    Raging winds and storms mark his path,
        and clouds are the dust from his feet.
4   He yells at the sea and makes it dry.
    He dries up all the rivers.
        Bashan and Carmel wither.
        The flowers of Lebanon wither.
5   The mountains quake because of him.
        The hills melt.
            The earth draws back in his presence.
                The world and all who live in it draw back as well.
6   Who can stand in the presence of his rage?
    Who can oppose his burning anger?
    He pours out his rage like fire
        and smashes the rocky cliffs.

Why Does Nineveh Oppose the LORD?

7   The Lord is good.
        He is, a fortress in the day of trouble.
        He knows those who seek shelter in him.
8   He will put an end to Nineveh
            with a devastating flood.
        He will pursue his enemies with darkness.
9   What do you think about the Lord?
        He is the one who will bring Nineveh to an end.
        This trouble will never happen again.
10   The people of Nineveh will be, like tangled thorns
            and like people drunk on their own drink.
                They will be completely burned up like very dry straw.
11 From you, Nineveh, a person who plans evil against the Lord sets out.
        His advice is wicked.

Nineveh Will Fall

12 This is what the Lord says:
        Though the people of Nineveh are physically fit and many in number,
            they will be cut down and die.
        Though I have humbled you, Judah,
            I will not humble you again.

13 But now I will break Nineveh's yoke*a* off of you
and tear its chains from you.

14 The LORD has given this command about you, Nineveh:
You will no longer have descendants to carry on your name.
I will remove the wooden and metal idols from the temple of your gods.
I will prepare your grave because you are worthless.*b*

An Army Will Conquer Nineveh

15 There on the mountains are the feet of a messenger
who announces the good news: "All is well!"
Celebrate your festivals, Judah! Keep your vows!
This wickedness will never pass your way again.
It will be completely removed.

2 *a*1 The one who will scatter you is coming to attack you.
Guard your fortress!
Keep a lookout on the road!
Prepare for battle!
Be very courageous!

2 The LORD will restore Jacob's glory like Israel's glory,
although enemies have looted it
and have destroyed its vines.

3 The shields of his warriors are painted red.
His soldiers have red uniforms.
The metal on his chariots flashes fiery red,
so do the spears when they are waved
on the day he prepares for battle.

4 Chariots are racing madly through the streets,
rushing this way and that in the city squares.
They look like torches, like lightning, as they dart about.

5 He remembers his best fighting men.
They stumble over themselves as they march.
They hurry to Nineveh's wall.
The shield has been set up for the battering ram.

6 The gates of the rivers are opened, and the palace melts away.

Nineveh's Treasures Will Be Taken

7 The LORD has determined:
"It will be stripped.
It will be carried away.
Its young women will be mourning like doves
as they beat their breasts."

8 Nineveh was like a pool of water from its first day on.
But now its people are fleeing.
"Stop! Stop!"
But no one turns around.

9 Steal the silver! Steal the gold!

---

a 1:13 A yoke is a wooden bar placed over the necks of work animals so that they can pull plows or carts.
b 1:14 Nahum 1:15 in English Bibles is Nahum 2:1 in the Hebrew Bible.   *a* 2:1 Nahum 2:1-13 in English Bibles is Nahum 2:2-14 in the Hebrew Bible.

There is no end to what is stored here—
everything a person could ever want.
10 Nineveh is destroyed, deserted, demolished.
Hearts are melting.
Knees are knocking.
Every stomach becomes upset.
Every face turns pale.

Nineveh Will Be Destroyed

11 Where is the lions' den,
that feeding place for young lions?
Where are the lion, the lioness, and the lion cub who moved about
with no one to terrify them?
12 The lion tore its prey to pieces to feed its cubs.
It strangled the prey for its mates.
It used to fill its caves with torn carcasses
and its dens with torn flesh.

13 "I am against you, Nineveh," declares the Lord of Armies.
"I will send your chariots up in smoke,
and a sword will kill your young lions.
I will remove your prey from the earth,
and no one will ever hear the voice of your messengers again."

Nineveh's Punishment for Sin

3
1 How horrible it will be for that city of bloody violence!
It is completely full of lies and stolen goods—never without victims.
2 The sound of the whip!
The sound of rattling wheels!
Horses gallop!
Chariots bounce along!
3 Horses charge!
Swords flash!
Spears glitter!
Many are killed!
Dead bodies pile up!
There is no end to the corpses!
People trip over corpses
4 because of Nineveh's constant prostitution,
this very charming mistress of evil magic.
She used to sell
nations her prostitution
and people her evil magic."

5 "I am against you, Nineveh," declares the Lord of Armies.
"I will lift up your dress over your face.
I will show nations your naked body and kingdoms your disgrace.
6 I will throw filth on you.
I will make you look like a fool.
I will make you a sight to be seen.
7 Everyone who sees you will run from you, saying,

'Nineveh has been violently destroyed!
Who will feel sorry for her?'
Where can I find anyone to comfort you?"

Nineveh Will Not Escape Punishment

8 Are you better than No-amon,[a] which sits by the streams of the Nile
with water surrounding her?
The sea was ˌherˌ defense.
The water was her wall.
9 Sudan and Egypt were her endless strength.
Put and the Lybians were her help.
10 Even she went into captivity and was exiled.
Even her little children were smashed to death at every street corner.
Soldiers tossed dice for her important men,
and all her best men were bound in chains.
11 Even you, Nineveh, will stagger like a drunk.
You will disappear.
Even you will look for a fortress ˌto escapeˌ from the enemy.
12 All your defenses will be like fig trees with the earliest figs.
When shaken, the figs fall into the mouth of the eater.
13 Look at your soldiers; they're women!
The gates of your country are wide open to your enemies.
Fire has destroyed the bars of your gates.

Nineveh's Strength Will Not Save Her

14 Store water for the siege!
Strengthen your defenses!
Step into the claypits and trample the clay!
Grab the brick mold!
15 Fire will consume you there.
A sword will cut you down.
It will consume you like locusts.
Multiply like locusts!
Multiply like hungry locusts!
16 You have produced more businessmen than there are stars in the sky.
ˌThey areˌ like locusts that attack and then fly away.
17 Your officers are like locusts,
and your scribes are like swarms of locusts
that settle on the fences when it is cold.
The sun rises, and they scatter in every direction.
No one knows where they've gone.
18 Your shepherds, king of Assyria, have fallen into a deep sleep.
Your best fighting men are at rest.
Your people are scattered on the mountains,
and there is no one to gather them.
19 There is no relief for your collapse.
Your wound is fatal.
All who hear the news about you will clap their hands.
Who hasn't suffered from your endless evil?

---

[a] 3:8 The city No-amon, also called Thebes, was the capital of southern Egypt.

Habakkuk

Sometimes life just seems unfair! Troublemakers get away with everything, and innocent people suffer. Habakkuk wanted to know why evil people don't get what they deserve. And God had an answer for him. It only looks like sinners have success. The truth is that they are never satisfied. And they will be punished. Only those who love God will be truly happy.

**Did she say, "Wake up"?
See Habakkuk 2:18-19.**

What's In It For Me?

God will right the world's wrongs. . . .

EVIL PEOPLE DON'T "GET AWAY" WITH SIN.

THE GREEDY ARE NEVER SATISFIED.

TRUSTING GOD HELPS ME FEEL SAFE IN TIMES OF TROUBLE.

Headlines

Don't Watch Violence!
Habakkuk 1, page 1273

Deer Feet
Habakkuk 3:19, page 1277

" 'How horrible it will be for the one who makes himself rich
with what is not his own
and makes himself wealthy on loans.
How long will this go on?'

7 Won't your creditors suddenly rise up
and those who are going to shake you wake up?
Then you will become their prize.

8 You have looted many nations.
All the rest of the people will loot you
because of the slaughter and violence done
to lands, cities, and all their inhabitants.

9 " 'How horrible it will be for the one who uses violence
to get things for his own household
in order to set his nest up high
and save himself from disaster.'

10 You have planned disgrace for your household
by cutting off many people and forfeiting your own life.

11 A stone in the wall will cry out.
A beam in the roof will answer it.

12 " 'How horrible it will be for the one who builds a city by slaughter
and founds a town by crime.'

13 Isn't it from the Lord of Armies
that people grow tired only to feed the flames
and nations exhaust themselves for nothing?

14 But the earth will be filled with the knowledge of the Lord's glory
like the water covers the sea.

15 " 'How horrible it will be for the one who makes his neighbor drink
from the bowl of God's rage,
making him drunk in order to stare at his nakedness.'

16 You are filled with disgrace rather than glory.
Drink! Yes you! And expose yourself as godless.
The cup in the Lord's right hand will come around to you,
and disgrace will cover your glory.

17 The violence done to Lebanon will overwhelm you,
and the destruction done to the animals will terrify you
because of the slaughter and violence done
to lands, cities, and all their inhabitants.

18 "What benefit is there in a carved idol
when its maker has carved it?
What benefit is there in a molded statue, a teacher of lies,
when its maker has molded it?
The one who formed it trusts himself
to make worthless idols that cannot speak.

19 'How horrible it will be for the one
who says to a piece of wood, "Wake up!"
and to a stone that cannot talk, "Get up!" "
Can that thing teach anyone?
Just look at it!

It's covered with gold and silver,
    but there's absolutely no life in it."

20 The Lord is in his holy temple.
    All the earth should be silent in his presence.

A Psalm

¹A prayer of the prophet Habakkuk; according to *shigionoth.*ᵃ

2 Lord, I have heard the report about you.
    Lord, I fear your work.
        In the course of the years, renew it.
        In the course of the years, reveal it.
        In all this chaos, remember to be merciful.

3 God comes from Teman.
    The Holy One comes from Mount Paran.   *Selah*
        His splendor covers the heavens.
        His praise fills the earth.
4   His brightness is like the sunlight.
            Rays of light ˻stream˼ from his hand.
            That is where his power is hidden.
5   Diseases go ahead of him.
        Plagues follow after him.
6 He stands and shakes the earth.
    He casts a glance and startles the nations.
        The oldest mountains break apart.
        The ancient hills sink.
        The ancient paths belong to him.
7 I see trouble in the tents of Cushan.
    I see trembling in the tents of Midian.

8 The Lord is not angry with the rivers, is he?
        If you are angry with the rivers,
        if you are furious with the sea,
            ˻why˼ do you ride your horses,
                your chariots of salvation?
9 You get your bow ready for action,
        for the arrows ˻you˼ promised.   *Selah*
    You split the land with rivers.
10 The mountains look at you. They writhe in pain.
    Floodwaters pass by.
        The deep ocean roars. Its waves rise up high.
11 The sun and the moon stand still.
        They scatter at the light of your arrows,
            at the bright lightning of your spear.

12 You march through the earth with fury.
    You trample the nations in anger.
13 You go out to save your people,
        to save your anointed.ᵇ

ᵃ3:1 Unknown musical term.   ᵇ3:13 Or "to save with your anointed."

You crush the leader of the wicked household,
   stripping him bare from head to toe.

Selah

14 You pierce the leader of his gang with his own arrows.
   His soldiers come like a violent storm to scatter me.
   They are arrogant like those who secretly eat up the poor.

15 You march with your horses into the sea,
   into the mighty raging waters.

16 I have heard, so there's trembling within me.
At the report my lips quivered.
A rotten feeling has entered me.
   I tremble where I stand.
   I wait for the day of trouble
      to come to the people who will attack us.

17 Even if the fig tree does not bloom
   and the vines have no grapes,
even if the olive tree fails to produce
   and the fields yield no food,
even if the sheep pen is empty
   and the stalls have no cattle—

18 even then,
   I will be happy with the Lord.
   I will truly find joy in God, who saves me.

19 The Lord Almighty is my strength.
He makes my feet like those of a deer.
   He makes me walk on the mountains.

For the choir director; on stringed instruments.

AN INTRODUCTION TO
Zephaniah

Zephaniah wrote during the reign of the good king Josiah. During this time, many prophets had warned the people of approaching judgment. But the people thought, *God won't do anything.* Zephaniah's message for these doubters was "God will act!" When the time is right, God will judge all the nations of the world.

What's In It For Me?

To be safe when God judges . . .

REMEMBER THAT **GOD** WILL ACT.

BE HUMBLE, NOT PROUD.

DO WHAT IS RIGHT.

SEEK THE **LORD**; **GOD** WILL SHELTER YOU.

Who lives in Nineveh now? See Zephaniah 2:13-15.

Headlines

Foreign Clothes, Bad Fashion
Zephaniah 1, page 1279

Listen and Learn!
Zephaniah 2:14, page 1281

Zephaniah

Zephaniah's Prophecy

1 ¹This is the word that the LORD spoke to Zephaniah, who was the son of Cushi, the grandson of Gedaliah, and the great-grandson of Amariah, son of Hezekiah. The LORD spoke his word in the days of Judah's King Josiah, son of Amon.

The LORD Will Judge the Earth

² "I will gather everything on the face of the earth
    and put an end to it," declares the LORD.
³ "I will put an end to humans and animals.
I will put an end to
    the birds in the sky,
    the fish in the sea,
      and the sins that make people fall, together with the sinners.
I will remove all people from the face of the earth," declares the LORD.

The LORD Will Judge Judah

⁴ "I will use my power against Judah
    and against those who live in Jerusalem.
I will remove the faithful few of Baal from this place
    and the names of the pagan priests along with my priests.
⁵ I will remove those who worship all the stars in the sky on their rooftops
    and those who worship by swearing loyalty to the LORD
      while also swearing loyalty to the god Milcom.ᵃ
⁶ I will remove those who have turned away from following the LORD
    and those who no longer seek the LORD or ask him for help."

⁷ Be silent in the presence of the Almighty LORD,
    because the day of the LORD is near.
The LORD has prepared a sacrifice.
    He has invited his special guests.

⁸ "On the day of the LORD's sacrifice I will punish the officials,
    the king's sons, and all who dress in foreign clothing.ᵇ
⁹ On that day I will punish all who jump over the doorway
    and all who fill their master's house with violence and deception.
¹⁰ On that day a loud cry will come from Fish Gate,
    a howling from the Second Part of the city,
      and a loud crashing sound from the hills," declares the LORD.
¹¹   "Howl, inhabitants of the Mortar,ᶜ
      because all the merchants will be destroyed
      and all who handle money will be killed.

¹² "At that time I will search Jerusalem with lamps and punish those
    who are satisfied with their hardened lifestyle,

ᵃ1:5 Or "to their king." ᵇ1:8 Wearing foreign clothing was a sign of worshiping foreign gods. ᶜ1:10-11 The Mortar was in the northern part of Jerusalem, the Second Part of the city, which could be entered through the Fish Gate.

who think that the Lord won't do anything—good or bad.
13   Their wealth will be looted.
   Their homes will be demolished.
   They will build houses, but they won't live in them.
   They will plant vineyards, but they won't drink their wine."

The Day of the LORD

14   The frightening day of the Lord is near.
   It is near and coming very quickly.
Listen! Warriors will cry out bitterly on the day of the Lord.
15   That day will be a day of overflowing fury,
   a day of trouble and distress,
   a day of devastation and desolation,
   a day of darkness and gloom,
   a day of clouds and overcast skies,
16   a day of rams' horns and battle cries
      against the fortified cities
         and against the high corner towers.
17   "I will bring such distress on humans that they will walk like they are blind,
   because they have sinned against the Lord."
   Their blood will be poured out like dust
      and their intestines like manure.
18   Their silver and their gold will not be able to rescue them
      on the day of the Lord's overflowing fury.
   The whole earth will be consumed by his fiery anger,
      because he will put an end, a frightening end,
         to those who live on earth.

A Call for Judah to Turn Away From Sin

2 1 Gather yourselves together!
Yes, gather together, you shameless nation,
2   before the decree is carried out
      ˛and˛ the day passes like windblown husks,
   before the Lord's burning anger comes to you,
   before the day of the Lord's anger comes to you.
3   Search for the Lord, all you humble people in the land
      who carry out his justice.
   Search for what is right.
   Search for humility.
      Maybe you will find shelter on the day of the Lord's anger.

The LORD Will Judge His People's Enemies

4   Gaza will be deserted,
      and Ashkelon will be destroyed.
   Ashdod will be driven out at noon,
      and Ekron will be torn out by the roots.
5   How horrible it will be for those who live on the seacoast,
      for the nation from Crete.
   The word of the Lord is against you, Canaan, the land of the Philistines:
      "I will destroy you so that no one will be living there."

⁶ The seacoast will become pastureland
   with meadows for shepherds
      and fenced-off places for sheep.
⁷ The coast will belong to the faithful few from the nation of Judah.
   There they will graze their sheep.
   In the evening they will lie down in the houses of Ashkelon.
   The LORD their God will take care of them
      and will restore their fortunes.

⁸ "I have heard the insults from Moab and the mockery from Ammon.
   They insulted my people and bragged about their territory.
⁹ Therefore, I solemnly swear, as I live,"
      declares the LORD of Armies, the God of Israel,
   "Moab will become like Sodom, and Ammon will become like Gomorrah:
      a place of weeds, salt pits, and ruins forever.
   The faithful few of my people will loot them,
      and those who are left in my nation will take possession of them."

¹⁰ This is what they will get for their sinful pride,
      because they insulted the people who belong to the LORD of Armies
         and made themselves greater than them.
¹¹ The LORD will terrify them,
      because he will make all the gods of the earth waste away.
   So every person from every coast and nation will bow to him.

¹² "Even you, the people from Sudan,
      you will also die by my sword."

¹³ The LORD will use his power against the north and destroy Assyria.
      He will turn Nineveh into a deserted ruin,
         a dried up wasteland like the desert.
¹⁴ Flocks will lie down in it along with animals of every kind.
   Even pelicans and herons will nest on top of its columns.
   Listen! A bird will sing in a window.
   The doorway will be in ruins,
      because the LORD will expose the cedar beams.
¹⁵ Is this the arrogant city?
   Is this the city that used to live securely,
      the city that used to think to itself,
         "I'm the only one, and no one else exists but me"?
   What a wasteland it is now, a resting place for wild animals!
   All who pass by it will hiss and make an obscene gesture.

Jerusalem Will Be Destroyed

3 ¹ How horrible it will be for that rebellious
      and corrupt place, the city of violence.
² It obeys no one.
   It does not accept correction.
   It does not trust the LORD.
   It does not draw close to its God.
³ Its officials are ⸢like⸣ roaring lions.
   Its judges are ⸢like⸣ wolves in the evening.

They leave nothing to gnaw on for the morning.

4   Its prophets are reckless and unfaithful.
    Its priests contaminate what is holy.
       They violate the teachings.

5   The righteous LORD is in that city.
       He does no wrong.
       He brings his judgment to light every morning.
       He does not fail.
         But those who are perverted are shameless.

6   "I will cut off the nations.
       Their towers will be destroyed.
       I will demolish their streets.
         No one will walk through them.
       Their cities will be completely destroyed.
         Not a single person will be left.
         No one will be living there.

7   I said to my people,
       'You will fear me.
       You will accept correction!'
    Then their homeland would not be wiped out
       even though I have punished them.
         Still, they continued to be corrupt in everything they did."

8   The LORD declares, "Just wait!
       One day I will stand up as a witness.
    I have decided to gather nations,
       to bring kingdoms together,
         and to pour my rage, my burning anger, on them.
    The whole land will be consumed by my fiery fury.

Israel Will Turn Away From Sin

9   "Then I will give all people pure lips
       to worship the LORD
         and to serve him with one purpose.

10   From beyond the rivers of Sudan
       my worshipers, my scattered people, will bring my offering.

11   On that day you will no longer be ashamed
       of all your rebellious acts against me.
    Then I will remove your arrogance
       and never again will you act proud on my holy mountain.

12   So with you I will leave a faithful few, a humble and poor people.
       They will seek refuge in the name of the LORD.

13   The faithful few in Israel will not do wrong, tell lies,
       or use their tongues to deceive others.
    They will graze their sheep and lie down,
       and there will be no one to terrify them."

Israel's Joyful Song

14   Sing happily, people of Zion!
       Shout loudly, Israel!

Celebrate and rejoice with all your heart, people of Jerusalem.
15   The LORD has reversed the judgments against you.
        He has forced out your enemies.
      The king of Israel, the LORD, is with you.
        You will never fear disaster again.
16   On that day Jerusalem will be told,
        "Do not be afraid, Zion!
        Do not lose courage!"
17   The LORD your God is with you.
        He is a hero who saves you.
          He happily rejoices over you,
            renews you with his love,
              and celebrates over you with shouts of joy.

Israel Will Return Home

18   "I will gather those among you who are troubled because of the festivals.
        They bear a burden of disgrace.
19   At that time
        I will deal with all who have overpowered you.
        I will rescue those who are lame.
        I will gather those who have been scattered.
        I will make them praised and famous in all the world,
          though they had been ashamed.
20   At that time I will bring you ˏhomeˏ.
        Yes, at that time I will gather you together.
      I will make you famous and praised among all the people of the earth
        when I restore your fortunes right before your eyes," says the LORD.

AN INTRODUCTION TO

Haggai

Haggai spread the news of God to the exiles who had returned to Judah from Babylon. When the exiled Israelites got back to Jerusalem, they started rebuilding the temple. But then they stopped. Haggai urged them, "Don't give up! Get to work!"

The people obeyed. And because they put the Lord first, God promised to richly bless them.

Who's foolish enough to put money in a purse with holes? See Haggai 1:1-6.

What's In It For Me?

I will receive God's blessing when I . . .

TRY TO DO WHAT GOD WANTS.

MAKE TIME TO **SERVE** THE **LORD**.

TRUST GOD TO CARE FOR MY NEEDS.

PUT GOD FIRST.

Headlines

God's Housework
Haggai 1:12-15, page 1285

God Blesses His People
Haggai 2:10-19, page 1286

AN INTRODUCTION TO
Zechariah

Zechariah was a prophet to the exiles who returned to Judah from Babylon. He encouraged the people to commit themselves to God and to finish rebuilding the temple. The first half of this book reports Zechariah's visions which contained many strange symbols. The second half contains many prophecies about Jesus Christ, the Messiah.

Who's the woman in the flying basket? See Zechariah 5:5-11.

What's In It For Me?

Why I have hope . . .

GOD WILL FORGIVE ALL MY FAILURES.

GOD WASHES AWAY MY SIN.

GOD SENT JESUS TO SAVE ME.

JESUS WILL RETURN TO RULE THE WORLD.

Headlines

Angels Patrol the Earth
Zechariah 1, page 1288

Scroll Flies Away
Zechariah 5, page 1290

King Takes a Donkey Ride
Zechariah 9:9-17, page 1294

Holy Cooking Pots!
Zechariah 14, page 1299

Zechariah

Turn From Your Evil Ways

1 ¹In the eighth month of Darius' second year as king, the LORD spoke his word to the prophet Zechariah, who was the son of Berechiah and the grandson of Iddo. He said, ²"The LORD was very angry with your ancestors. ³Tell the people, 'This is what the LORD of Armies says: Return to me, declares the LORD of Armies, and I will return to you, says the LORD of Armies.' ⁴Don't be like your ancestors, who heard the earlier prophets preach to them, 'This is what the LORD of Armies says: Turn from your evil ways and your evil deeds.' But they didn't listen or pay attention to me, declares the LORD. ⁵Your ancestors—where are they now? And the prophets—are they still alive? ⁶Didn't my warnings and my laws, which I've commanded my servants the prophets to preach, finally catch up with your ancestors? Then your ancestors turned away from their sins and said, 'The LORD of Armies has done to us what he had planned to do. He has dealt with us as our ways and deeds deserve.' "

The LORD Will Comfort Zion

⁷On the twenty-fourth day of the eleventh month (the month of Shebat) in Darius' second year as king, the LORD spoke his word to the prophet Zechariah, who was the son of Berechiah and the grandson of Iddo.

⁸During that night I saw a man riding on a red horse. He was standing among the myrtle trees in a ravine. Behind him were red, chestnut, and white horses.

⁹"What do these horses mean, sir?" I asked.

The angel who was speaking with me answered, "I will show you what they mean."

¹⁰The man standing among the myrtle trees explained, "They're the horses the LORD has sent to patrol the earth." ¹¹Then they reported to the Messenger of the LORD standing among the myrtle trees, "We have patrolled the earth. The whole world is at rest and in peace."

¹²Then the Messenger of the LORD said, "LORD of Armies, how much longer until you show compassion to Jerusalem and the cities of Judah? You've been angry with them for 70 years." ¹³The LORD responded to the angel who was speaking with me, using kind and comforting words.

¹⁴The angel who was speaking with me said, "Announce: This is what the LORD of Armies says: I'm very jealous about Jerusalem and Zion, ¹⁵and I'm very angry with the nations who think they are at ease. I was only a little angry, but they made things worse. ¹⁶This is what the LORD of Armies says: I have returned to Jerusalem with compassion. My house will be rebuilt in it, declares the LORD of Armies. A measuring line will be used to rebuild Jerusalem.

¹⁷"Announce again: This is what the LORD of Armies says: My cities will overflow with prosperity once more. The LORD will again comfort Zion and will again choose Jerusalem." [a]

---

[a] 1:17 Zechariah 1:18-21 in English Bibles is Zechariah 2:1-4 in the Hebrew Bible.

Punishment for the Nations That Scattered Judah

[18]I looked up and saw four animal horns. [19]So I asked the angel who was speaking with me, "What do these horns mean?"

He said to me, "These are the horns of the nations that scattered Judah, Israel, and Jerusalem."

[20]Then the LORD showed me four craftsmen. [21]I asked, "What are they going to do?"

He answered, "Those horns scattered Judah so widely that no one could lift up his head. But the craftsmen have come to terrify them, to throw down the horns of the nations. The nations raised their horns to scatter the land of Judah."

The LORD Will Choose Jerusalem

[a][1]I looked up and saw a man with a measuring line in his hand. [2]I asked him, "Where are you going?"

He answered, "I am going to measure Jerusalem to see how wide and how long it is."

[3]Then the angel who was speaking with me left. Another angel came out to meet him [4]and said to him, "Run, and say to that young man, 'Jerusalem will be inhabited like an unwalled village because it will have so many people and animals in it. [5]I will be a wall of fire around it, declares the LORD. I will be the glory within it.'

[6]"Hurry, hurry! Flee from the land of the north, declares the LORD. I've scattered you to the four winds of heaven. [7]Hurry, Zion! Escape, you inhabitants of Babylon! [8]This is what the LORD of Armies says: Afterwards, the Glory sent me to the nations who looted you. Whoever touches you touches the apple of his eye. [9]I'm going to shake my fist at the nations, and their own slaves will loot them. Then you will know that the LORD of Armies has sent me. [10]Sing for joy and rejoice, people of Zion. I'm going to come and live among you, declares the LORD. [11]On that day many nations will join the LORD and become my people. I will live among you. Then you will know that the LORD of Armies has sent me to you. [12]The LORD will claim Judah as his own in the holy land and will again choose Jerusalem.

[13]"Everyone be silent in the presence of the LORD. He is waking up and setting out from his holy dwelling place."

The LORD Will Send His Servant, the Branch

[1]Then he showed me Joshua, the chief priest, standing in front of the Messenger of the LORD. Satan the Accuser was standing at Joshua's right side to accuse him. [2]The LORD said to Satan, "I, the LORD, silence you, Satan! I, the LORD, who has chosen Jerusalem, silence you! Isn't this man like a burning log snatched from a fire?"

[3]Joshua was wearing filthy clothes and was standing in front of the Messenger. [4]The Messenger said to those who were standing in front of him, "Remove Joshua's filthy clothes." Then he said to Joshua, "See, I have taken your sin away from you, and I will dress you in fine clothing."

[5]So I said, "Put a clean turban on his head." They put a clean turban on his head and dressed him while the Messenger of the LORD was standing there.

[6]The Messenger of the LORD advised Joshua, [7]"This is what the LORD of Armies says: If you live according to my ways and follow my requirements, you will govern my temple and watch over my courtyards. Then I will give you free access to walk among those standing here.

---

[a]2:1 Zechariah 2:1-13 in English Bibles is Zechariah 2:5-17 in the Hebrew Bible.

⁸"Listen, Chief Priest Joshua and your friends sitting with you. These men are a sign of things to come: I'm going to bring my servant, the Branch. ⁹"Look at the stone I have set in front of Joshua. That one stone has seven eyes.ᵃ I am engraving an inscription on it," declares the LORD of Armies. "I will remove this land's sin in a single day. ¹⁰On that day," declares the LORD of Armies, "each of you will invite your neighbor to sit under your vine and fig tree."

The LORD's House Will Be Rebuilt

¹The angel who was speaking with me returned and woke me up as one might wake up someone who is sleeping. ²He asked me, "What do you see?"

I answered, "I see a solid gold lamp stand with a bowl on top and seven lamps on it. There are seven spouts for each lamp that is on top of it. ³There are also two olive trees beside it, one on the right of the bowl and the other on its left."

⁴I asked the angel who was speaking with me, "What do these things mean, sir?"

⁵Then the angel asked me, "Don't you know what they mean?"

"No, sir," I answered.

⁶Then he replied, "This is the word the LORD spoke to Zerubbabel: You won't succeed by might or by power, but by my Spirit, says the LORD of Armies. ⁷What a high mountain you are! In front of Zerubbabel you will become a plain. He will bring out the topmost stone with shouts of 'Blessings, blessings on it!' "

⁸Then the LORD spoke his word to me. He said, ⁹"Zerubbabel's hands have laid the foundation of this house, and his hands will finish it. Then you will know that the LORD of Armies has sent me to you. ¹⁰Who despised the day when little things began to happen? They will be delighted when they see the plumb line in Zerubbabel's hand. (These seven eyes of the LORD roam over all the earth.)"

¹¹I asked the angel, "What do these two olive trees at the right and the left of the lamp stand mean?" ¹²Again I asked him, "What is the meaning of the two branches from the olive trees next to the two golden pipes that are pouring out gold?"

¹³He asked me, "Don't you know what these things mean?"

"No, sir," I answered.

¹⁴So he said, "These are the two anointed ones who are standing beside the Lord of the whole earth."

Sinners Will Be Separated From the LORD's People

¹I looked up again and saw a flying scroll.

²The angel asked me, "What do you see?"

"I see a flying scroll," I answered. "It's 30 feet long and 15 feet wide."

³Then he said to me, "This is a curse that will go out all over the earth. The one side of the scroll says that every thief will be forced away. The other side of the scroll says that everyone who takes an oath will be forced away. ⁴I will send out a curse, declares the LORD of Armies, and it will enter the houses of thieves and the houses of those who take oaths in my name. It will stay in their houses and destroy the timber and stone."

Wickedness Will Be Removed From the Land

⁵The angel who was speaking with me came forward. He said, "Look up, and see what's coming."

⁶"What is it?" I asked.

ᵃ3:9 Or "facets."

"A basket is coming," he said. Then he added, "This is what the people's sins look like all over the earth."ᵃ ⁷A lead cover ₍on the basket₎ was raised, and a woman was sitting in the basket. ⁸The angel said, "This is wickedness," and he pushed her back into the basket and forced the lead cover down on top of it.

⁹I looked up and saw two women coming forward with wind in their wings. They had wings like those of a stork. They carried the basket into the sky.

¹⁰I asked the angel who was speaking with me, "Where are they taking the basket?"

¹¹He answered me, "They are going to build a house for it in Shinar [Babylonia]. When the house is ready, they will set the basket there on a stand."

The LORD's Victory Throughout the Earth

¹I looked up again and saw four chariots going out from between the two mountains. They were mountains of bronze. ²The first chariot had red horses. The second had black horses. ³The third had white horses. And the fourth had strong, spotted horses. ⁴I asked the angel who was speaking with me, "What do these horses mean, sir?"

⁵The angel answered, "They are the four spirits of heaven. They are going out after standing in the presence of the Lord of the whole earth. ⁶The chariot with the black horses is going toward the north, and the white horses are following them. The spotted ones are going toward the south."

⁷When these strong horses went out, they were eager to patrol the earth.

He said, "Go, patrol the earth!" And they patrolled the earth.

⁸Then he called out to me, "Look! Those who went to the north have made my Spirit rest in the north."

Priest and King

⁹The LORD spoke his word to me. He said, ¹⁰"Take an offering from the exiles Heldai, Tobijah, and Jedaiah, who have arrived from Babylon. This same day go to the house of Josiah, son of Zephaniah. ¹¹Take the silver and gold, make a crown, and put it on the head of Chief Priest Joshua, son of Jehozadak. ¹²Then say to him, 'This is what the LORD of Armies says: Here is the man whose name is Branch. He will branch out from where he is, and he will rebuild the LORD's temple. ¹³He will rebuild the LORD's temple and receive royal honor. He will sit and rule from his throne. He will be a priest on his throne. There will be a peaceful understanding between them. ¹⁴The crown will be a reminder to Helem, Tobijah, Jedaiah, and Hen (son of Zephaniah) in the LORD's temple. ¹⁵Those who are far away will come and rebuild the LORD's temple. Then you will know the LORD of Armies has sent me to you. This will happen if you obey the LORD your God completely.' "

You Should Have Obeyed the LORD's Prophets

¹On the fourth day of the ninth month (the month of Chislev) in Darius' fourth year as king, the LORD spoke his word to Zechariah. ²Now, ₍the people from₎ Bethel sent Sharezer and Regem Melech with their menᵃ to ask the LORD for a blessing. ³They asked the priests from the house of the LORD of Armies as well as the prophets, "Should we mourn and fast in the fifth month as we have done for so many years?"

⁴Then the LORD of Armies spoke his word to me. He said, ⁵"Tell all the people of the land and the priests, 'When you fasted and mourned in the fifth and seventh months

---

ᵃ5:6 One Hebrew manuscript, Greek, Syriac; other Hebrew manuscripts "This is their eye all over the earth."
ᵃ7:2 Or "Bethel Sharezer sent Regem Melech with his men."

these past 70 years, did you really do it for me? ⁶When you ate and drank, didn't you do it to benefit yourselves? ⁷Aren't these the same words that the Lᴏʀᴅ announced through the earlier prophets, when Jerusalem and its surrounding cities were inhabited and undisturbed and the Negev and the foothills were still inhabited?' "

⁸Then the Lᴏʀᴅ spoke his word to Zechariah. He said, ⁹"This is what the Lᴏʀᴅ of Armies says: Administer real justice, and be compassionate and kind to each other. ¹⁰Don't oppress widows, orphans, foreigners, and poor people. And don't even think of doing evil to each other.

¹¹"But people refused to pay attention. They shrugged their shoulders at me and shut their ears so that they couldn't hear. ¹²They made their hearts as hard as flint so that they couldn't hear the Lᴏʀᴅ's teachings, the words that the Lᴏʀᴅ of Armies had sent by his Spirit through the earlier prophets. So the Lᴏʀᴅ of Armies became very angry.

¹³"When I called, they wouldn't listen. So now when they call, I won't listen, says the Lᴏʀᴅ of Armies. ¹⁴I used a windstorm to scatter them among all the nations, nations they hadn't even heard of. They left behind a land so ruined that no one is able to travel through it. They have turned a pleasant land into a wasteland."

What the Lᴏʀᴅ Will Do for Zion

8 ¹The Lᴏʀᴅ of Armies spoke his word.

²This is what the Lᴏʀᴅ of Armies says:

> I am very jealous about Zion.
> I am fiercely possessive of it.

³This is what the Lᴏʀᴅ says:

> I will return to Zion and live in Jerusalem.
> Jerusalem will be called the City of Truth.
> The mountain of the Lᴏʀᴅ of Armies will be called the holy mountain.

⁴This is what the Lᴏʀᴅ of Armies says:

> Old men and old women will again sit in the streets of Jerusalem.
> Each will have a cane in hand because of old age.
> ⁵ The city will be filled with boys and girls playing in the streets.

⁶This is what the Lᴏʀᴅ of Armies says:

> It may seem impossible to the few remaining people in those days,
> but will it seem impossible to me? declares the Lᴏʀᴅ of Armies.

⁷This is what the Lᴏʀᴅ of Armies says:

> I am going to save my people
> from the land where the sun rises
> and from the land where the sun sets.
> ⁸ I will bring them back, and they will live in Jerusalem.
> They will be my people, and I will be their God, who is faithful and just.

⁹This is what the Lᴏʀᴅ of Armies says:

> Be strong so that the temple might be rebuilt,
> you people who are presently listening
> to the words from the mouths of the prophets

who spoke when the foundation
for the house of the Lord of Armies was laid.

10 Before that time there was no money to hire any person or animal.
No one who traveled was safe from the enemy.
I turned every person against his neighbor.

11 But now I won't deal with the few remaining people
as I did in earlier times, declares the Lord of Armies.

12 Seeds will thrive in peacetime.
Vines will produce their grapes.
The land will yield its crops.
The sky will produce its dew.
I will give the few remaining people
all these things as an inheritance.

13 Just as you, people of Judah and people of Israel,
have been a curse among the nations,
so I will now save you,
and you will become a blessing.
Don't be afraid. Let your hands work hard.

14 This is what the Lord of Armies says:

When your ancestors made me angry,
I made plans to destroy you, declares the Lord of Armies,
and I didn't change my plans.

15 So now I have again made plans, but this time to do good
to Jerusalem and the people of Judah.
Don't be afraid.

16 You must do these things:
Speak the truth to each other.
Give correct and fair verdicts for peace in your courts.

17 Don't even think of doing evil to each other.
Don't enjoy false testimony.
I hate all these things, declares the Lord.

Many Nations Will Come to the LORD's People

18 The Lord of Armies spoke his word to me again.

19 This is what the Lord of Armies says:

The fast in the fourth month, the fast in the fifth month,
the fast in the seventh month, and the fast in the tenth month
will become joyful and glad occasions
as well as happy festivals for the nation of Judah.
So love truth and peace.

20 This is what the Lord of Armies says:

People and citizens from many cities are going to come.

21 The citizens of one city will come to another city, saying,
"Let's make a habit of going to ask the Lord for a blessing
and to seek the Lord of Armies.
I'm also going."

22 Many people and powerful nations will come

to seek the LORD of Armies in Jerusalem
and to ask the LORD for a blessing.

23This is what the LORD of Armies says:

In those days ten people from every language found among the nations
will take hold of the clothes of a Jew. They will say,
"Let us go with you
because we have heard that God is with you."

The LORD Protects His House

9 ¹This is the divine revelation.

The word of the LORD is against the land of Hadrach
and will rest on Damascus
2   and also Hamath, which borders on it,
and Tyre and Sidon, though they are very wise.
(The eyes of humanity and of all the tribes of Israel
are on the LORD.)ᵃ

3   Tyre built itself a fortress.
It piled up silver like dust
and gold like mud in the streets.
4   The Lord will take away its possessions.
He will throw its wealth into the sea
and burn the city down.
5   Ashkelon will see ˌthisˌ and be afraid.
Gaza will also be in great pain,
also Ekron, because its hope will fade.
Gaza will lose its king.
Ashkelon will no longer be lived in.
6   A mixed race will live in Ashdod,
and I will cut off the Philistines' arrogance.
7   I will remove the blood from their mouths
and the disgusting things from between their teeth.
Then only a few of them will be left for our God
like a tribe in Judah,
and Ekron will be like a Jebusite.
8   I will camp in front of my house
as a guard against those who come and go.
No oppressors will pass through them,
because I have seen it with my own eyes.ᵇ

The LORD Sends His King

9   Rejoice with all your heart, people of Zion!
Shout in triumph, people of Jerusalem!
Look! Your King is coming to you:
He is righteous and victorious.
He is humble and rides on a donkey,
on a colt, a young pack animal.

ᵃ9:2 This sentence has been moved from verse 1 to express the complex Hebrew paragraph structure more clearly in English.   ᵇ9:8 Hebrew meaning of verses 7-8 uncertain.

10 He[c] will make sure there are no chariots in Ephraim
     or war horses in Jerusalem.
       There will be no battle bows.
     He will announce peace to the nations.
     He will rule from sea to sea
       and from the ˌEuphratesˌ River to the ends of the earth.

11 I will set your captives free from the waterless pit
     because of the blood that sealed my promise[d] to you.

12 Return to your fortress, you captives who have hope.
     Today I tell you that I will return to you double ˌblessingsˌ.

13 I will bend Judah as my bow
     and draw my bow with Ephraim ˌas its arrowˌ.
    I will stir up your people, Zion, against your people, Greece,
     and I will use you like a warrior's sword.

14 The Lord will appear over them,
     and his arrow will go out like lightning.
    The Almighty Lord will blow the ram's horn
     and will march in the storms from the south.

15 The Lord of Armies will defend them.
     They will destroy and trample the stones used in slings.
     They will drink and shout as if they were drunk.
     They will be filled like a sacrificial bowl
      ˌused for sprinklingˌ the corners of the altar.

16 On that day the Lord their God will rescue them
     as the flock of his people.
     They will certainly sparkle in his land like jewels in a crown.

17   They will be beautiful and lovely.[e]
      Young men will prosper on grain,
       and young women will prosper on new wine.

The Lord's People Will Be Victorious

10 1 Ask the Lord for rain in the springtime.
     The Lord makes thunderstorms.
     He gives everyone rain showers for the plants in the field.

2 The idols speak lies.
     The fortunetellers see false visions.
     They speak about false dreams.
      They give useless comfort.
   That is why people wander around like sheep.
    They are troubled because there is no shepherd.

3 "My burning anger is directed against the shepherds.
     I will punish the male goats.
      The Lord of Armies takes care of his flock, the people of Judah.
     He makes them like his splendid war horse."

4 From them will come a cornerstone,
    from them a tent peg,
     from them a battle bow,

---

[c]9:10 Greek, Syriac; Masoretic Text "I."   [d]9:11 Or "covenant."   [e]9:17 Or "He will be beautiful and lovely."

from them every leader.

5 Together they will be like warriors
    who trample the enemy in the mud on the streets.
They will fight because the LORD is with them.
They will put to shame those who ride on horses.

6 "I will strengthen the people of Judah.
I will rescue Joseph's people.
I will bring them back, because I have compassion for them.
    It will be as though I had never rejected them,
        because I am the LORD their God, and I will answer them.

7 The people of Ephraim will be like mighty warriors.
    Their hearts will be glad as if they had some wine to drink.
    Their sons will see it and be glad.
    Their hearts will find joy in the LORD.

8 I will signal them with a whistle
    and gather them because I have reclaimed them.
        They will be as numerous as they have ever been.

9 Although I have scattered them among the nations,
    they will remember me even in faraway places.
        They will live with their children and then return.

10 I will bring them back from Egypt.
I will gather them from Assyria.
I will bring them to Gilead and to Lebanon,
    and there won't be enough room for them."

11 The LORD will pass through a sea of distress,
    strike the waves in the sea,
        and dry up all the deep places of the Nile River.
The pride of Assyria will be humiliated,
    and the scepter of Egypt will depart.

12 "I will strengthen them in the LORD.
    They will live in his name," declares the LORD.

Zechariah Is Told to Take Care of the Sheep

1 Open your doors, Lebanon,
    so that fire will be able to burn down your cedars.

2 Cry, cypress trees,
    because the cedars have fallen
        and the stately trees have been destroyed.
Cry, oak trees of Bashan,
    because your dense forest has fallen down.

3 Listen! The shepherds are crying,
    because their rich pastures are destroyed.
Listen! The young lions are roaring,
    because the lush banks of the Jordan are destroyed.

4 This is what the LORD my God says: Take care of the sheep that are about to be slaughtered. 5 Those who buy them will kill them and go unpunished. Those who sell them will say, "Praise the LORD! I've become rich!" Even their own shepherds will have no pity on them.

⁶The Lord declares, "I will no longer have pity on those who live in the land. I am going to hand the people over to their neighbors and their king, who will crush the land. And I won't rescue any of them from their power."

⁷So I became the shepherd of the sheep that were to be slaughtered and also of the oppressed sheep. I took two shepherd staffs and named one Favor and the other Unity. And I took care of the sheep. ⁸I got rid of three shepherds in one month. I became impatient with the sheep, and they also became disgusted with me. ⁹So I said, "I won't be your shepherd. Let those that are dying die. Let those that are missing stay missing. And let those that are left devour each other."

¹⁰Then I took my staff called Favor and broke it in pieces, to break the promise*ᵃ* that I had made to all the nations. ¹¹So it was broken on that day, and the oppressed among the sheep who were watching me realized that it was the word of the Lord.

¹²Then I said to them, "If it's alright with you, pay me my wages. But if it's not, don't." And they paid me my wages—30 pieces of silver.

¹³The Lord told me, "Give it to the potter." So I took the 30 pieces of silver. Such a magnificent price was set by them! I gave the pieces of silver to the potter at the house of the Lord.

¹⁴Then I broke my second staff, called Unity, in pieces, to break off the brotherhood between Judah and Israel.

¹⁵Then the Lord said to me, "Use the equipment of a foolish shepherd again. ¹⁶I'm about to place a shepherd in the land. He will not take care of those that are dying. He will not search for the young. He will not heal those that have broken their legs or support those that can still stand. But he will eat the meat of the fat animals and tear off their hoofs.

¹⁷   "How horrible it will be for the foolish shepherd who abandoned the sheep.
       A sword will strike his arm and his right eye.
       His arm will be completely withered.
       His right eye will be completely blind."

The Lord Will Save Jerusalem

12 ¹This is the prophetic revelation, the word of the Lord about Israel. The Lord— who spread out the heavens, laid the foundation of the earth, and forms the spirit in a person—says, ²"I'm going to make Jerusalem like a cup of wine that makes all the surrounding people stagger. They will attack Judah along with Jerusalem. ³On that day I will make Jerusalem a stone too heavy for all the nations to lift. All who try to lift it will be severely injured. All the nations in the world will gather to fight against Jerusalem."

⁴The Lord declares, "On that day I will strike every horse with panic and every rider with madness. I will watch over the people of Judah, but I will strike all the horses of the nations blind. ⁵Then the leaders of Judah will think to themselves, 'The people who live in Jerusalem are strong because of the Lord of Armies, their God.'

⁶"On that day I will make the leaders of Judah like a fire on a pile of wood and like a burning torch among freshly cut straw. They will burn up all the surrounding nations to the right and to the left. But the people of Jerusalem will remain safe in Jerusalem.

⁷"The Lord will save Judah's tents first so that the honor of David's family and the honor of those who live in Jerusalem will not be greater than the honor of Judah. ⁸On that day the Lord will defend those who live in Jerusalem so that even those who

ᵃ 11:10 Or "covenant."

stumble will be like David, and David's family will be like God, like the Messenger of the Lord ahead of them.

⁹"On that day I will seek to destroy all the nations who attack Jerusalem.

The People of Jerusalem Will Look at the One They Stabbed

¹⁰"I will pour out the Spirit of blessing and mercy on David's family and on those who live in Jerusalem. They will look at me, whom they have stabbed. Then they will mourn for him as one mourns for an only son, and they will cry bitterly for him as one cries for a firstborn son. ¹¹On that day the mourning in Jerusalem will be as intense as the mourning at Hadad Rimmon in the plain of Megiddo. ¹²The land will mourn, each family by itself: the family of David by itself, and the wives by themselves; the family of Nathan by itself, and the wives by themselves; ¹³the family of Levi by itself, and the wives by themselves; the family of Shimei by itself, and the wives by themselves. ¹⁴All the families that are left will mourn, each by itself, and the wives by themselves."

13 ¹The Lord declares, "On that day a fountain will be opened for David's family and for those who live in Jerusalem to wash away their sin and stain.

False Prophets Will Be Judged

²"On that day," declares the Lord of Armies, "I will wipe away the names of the idols from the land. They will no longer be remembered. I will also remove the false prophets and the unclean*ᵃ* spirit from the land.

³"If a man still prophesies, his father and his mother, who gave birth to him, will say, 'You don't deserve to live because you speak lies in the name of the Lord.' Then his father and his mother, who gave birth to him, will stab him when he prophesies.

⁴"On that day every prophet will be ashamed of his vision when he prophesies. He won't deceive people by dressing like a prophet in a coat made of hair. ⁵He will say, 'I am not a prophet. I'm a farmer. I've owned this land since I was a child.'

⁶"When someone asks him, 'What are these scars on your chest?' he will answer, 'I was hurt at my friend's house.'

Good Morning, God ·······

Zechariah 13:9

Gold doesn't come out of the ground looking like it does in a jewelry store. It has to be tested. This is done by heating the metal until it becomes liquid. As a result, the impurities are burned away. When the metal cools, it becomes solid again. Only the pure, beautiful metal remains. The Bible says that people go through a similar process. God allows us to experience hard times to test us. But he uses our trials to make us into more beautiful people.

Thank you, Lord, for treating me like precious gold.

ᵃ 13:2 "Unclean" refers to anything that Moses' Teachings say is not presentable to God.

The Shepherd Struck, the Sheep Scattered

7 "Arise, sword, against my shepherd,
    against the man who is my friend," declares the LORD of Armies.
"Strike the shepherd, and the sheep will be scattered.
    Then I will turn my hand against the little ones."

8 The LORD declares,

"Throughout the land two-thirds will be cut off and die.
    Yet, one-third will be left in it.
9 I will bring this third of the people through the fire.
I will refine them as silver is refined.
I will test them as gold is tested.
    They will call on me, and I will answer them.
        I will say, 'They are my people.'
            They will reply, 'The LORD is our God.' "

The LORD Will Fight the Nations

14 ¹A day is going to come for the LORD when the loot you have taken will be divided among you. ²I will gather all the nations to Jerusalem for battle. The city will be captured, the houses looted, and the women raped. Half of the people in the city will go into exile, but the rest of the people won't be taken from the city.

³Then the LORD will go out and fight against those nations as he does when he fights a battle. ⁴On that day his feet will stand on the Mount of Olives, just east of Jerusalem. The Mount of Olives will be split in two, forming a very large valley from east to west. Half of the mountain will move toward the north, and the other half will move toward the south. ⁵Then you will flee to the valley of my mountains, because this valley between the mountains will go as far as Azel.ᵃ You will flee as you did from the earthquake at the time of King Uzziah of Judah. The LORD my God will come, and all the holy ones will be with him.

⁶On that day there will be neither heat nor freezing cold.ᵇ ⁷There will be one day—a day known to the LORD—with no difference between day and night. It will be light even in the evening.

Living Water From Jerusalem

⁸On that day living water will flow out from Jerusalem, half of it to the Dead Sea and the other half to the Mediterranean Sea. It will continue in summer and in winter.

⁹The LORD will be king over all the earth. On that day the LORD will be the only Lord and his name the only name.

¹⁰The whole earth will become like the plains from Geba to Rimmon, south of Jerusalem. Jerusalem will rise and remain on its site, from Benjamin Gate to the place of First Gate, Corner Gate, and from the Tower of Hananel to the king's winepresses. ¹¹People will live there, and it will never be threatened with destruction. Jerusalem will live securely.

¹²This will be the plague the LORD will use to strike all the people from the nations that have gone to war against Jerusalem. Their flesh will rot while they are standing on their feet. Their eyes will rot in their sockets, and their tongues will rot in their mouths.

¹³On that day a large-scale panic from the LORD will spread among them. One person

---

ᵃ 14:5 Hebrew meaning uncertain.   ᵇ 14:6 Hebrew meaning uncertain.

will grab the hand of another, and one will attack the other. ¹⁴Judah will also fight in Jerusalem. The wealth of all the surrounding nations will be collected, a very large amount of gold, silver, and clothes. ¹⁵A similar plague will also affect horses, mules, camels, donkeys, and all other animals in those camps.

¹⁶Everyone who is left from all the nations that attacked Jerusalem will come every year to worship the king, the Lord of Armies, and to celebrate the Festival of Booths. ¹⁷If any of the families on the earth won't go to Jerusalem to worship the king, the Lord of Armies, then rain won't fall on them. ¹⁸If the people of Egypt won't go or enter Jerusalem, then rain won't fall on them. The plague the Lord uses to strike the nations will affect those who won't come to celebrate the Festival of Booths. ¹⁹This will be the punishment for Egypt's sin and for the sin of all the nations that won't go to celebrate the Festival of Booths.

²⁰On that day "Holy to the Lord" will be written on the bells of the horses. And the cooking pots in the house of the Lord will be like the bowls in front of the altar. ²¹Yes, every pot in Jerusalem and in Judah will be holy to the Lord of Armies. All who come to sacrifice will take some of them and cook in them. On that day there will no longer be any Canaanite^c in the house of the Lord of Armies.

---

^c14:21 Or "merchant."

Malachi

This book contains a list of questions asked by Malachi, followed by God's answers. The book of Malachi shows that God's people had once again drifted away from God. They needed to return to God and remain committed to him. Great rewards were in store for those who did.

What's In It For Me?

God will . . .

HEAR THOSE WHO HONOR HIM.

BLESS THOSE WHO GIVE TO HIM.

SHOW FAVOR TO THOSE WHO SERVE HIM.

EXPECT FAITHFULNESS IN MARRIAGE.

BRING PARENTS AND CHILDREN TOGETHER.

What does God think of men who are unfaithful to their wives? To find out, see Malachi 2:13-16.

Headlines

Can You Trust Teachers?
Malachi 2:1-9, page 1302

A Wife Is for Life
Malachi 2:10-17, page 1303

New Attitudes for Parents and Kids
Malachi 4, page 1305

Malachi

"I Loved Jacob, but Esau I Hated"

¹This is a divine revelation. The Lord spoke his word to Israel through Malachi.
²"I loved you," says the Lord.

"But you ask, 'How did you love us?'

"Wasn't Esau Jacob's brother?" declares the Lord. "I loved Jacob, ³but Esau I hated. I turned his mountains into a wasteland and left his inheritance to the jackals in the desert.

⁴"The descendants of Esau may say, 'We have been beaten down, but we will rebuild the ruins.'

"Yet, this is what the Lord of Armies says: They may rebuild, but I will tear it down. They will be called 'the Wicked Land' and 'the people with whom the Lord is always angry.' ⁵You will see these things with your own eyes and say, 'Even outside the borders of Israel the Lord is great.'

The Priests Offer Unacceptable Sacrifices to the LORD

⁶"This is what the Lord of Armies says: A son honors his father, and a servant honors his master. So if I am a father, where is my honor? If I am a master, where is my respect? You priests despise my name.

"But you ask, 'How have we despised your name?'

⁷"You offer contaminated food on my altar.

"But you ask, 'Then how have we contaminated you?'

"When you say that the Lord's table may be despised. ⁸When you bring a blind animal to sacrifice, isn't that wrong? When you bring a lame or a sick animal, isn't that wrong? Try offering it to your governor. Would he accept it from you? Would he welcome you?" asks the Lord of Armies.

⁹"Now try asking God to be kind to you. This is what you are doing! Will he welcome you?" asks the Lord of Armies.

¹⁰"I wish one of you would shut the doors to my house so that you could not light fires on my altar for no reason. I'm not pleased with you," says the Lord of Armies, "and I won't accept your offerings.

¹¹"From the nations where the sun rises to the nations where the sun sets, my name will be great. Incense and pure offerings will be offered everywhere in my name, because my name will be great among the nations," says the Lord of Armies. ¹²"But you dishonor it when you say that the Lord's table may be contaminated and that its food may be despised.

¹³"You say, 'Oh what a nuisance it is,' and you sniff at it in disgust," says the Lord of Armies. "You bring stolen, lame, and sick animals. When you bring such offerings, should I accept them from you?" asks the Lord.

¹⁴"Cheaters are under a curse. They have male animals in their flocks that they vow to give as a sacrifice. But they sacrifice second-rate ones to the Lord instead. I am a great king," says the Lord of Armies. "Among the nations my name is respected.

The Priests Do Not Teach the LORD's Word Correctly

¹"And now, you priests, this warning is for you. ²If you won't listen and if you won't consider giving honor to my name," says the Lord of Armies, "then I'll send a

curse on you, and I'll curse the blessings you give. Yes, I've already cursed them because you don't carefully consider this.

³"I'm going to punish your descendants. I'm going to spread excrement on your faces, the excrement from your festival sacrifices. You will be discarded with it. ⁴Then you will know that I sent you this warning so that my promise*ᵃ*to Levi will continue," says the LORD of Armies. ⁵"I promised Levi life and peace. I gave them to him so that he would respect me. He respected me and stood in awe of my name. ⁶The teaching that came from his mouth was true. Nothing unjust was found on his lips. He lived with me in peace and honesty and turned many people away from sin.

⁷"A priest's lips should preserve knowledge. Then, because he is the messenger for the LORD of Armies, people will seek instruction from his mouth.

⁸"But you have turned from the ‚correct‚ path and caused many to stumble over my teachings. You have corrupted the promise made to Levi," says the LORD of Armies. ⁹"So I have made you disgusting, and I have humiliated you in front of all the people, because you have not followed my ways. You have been unfair when ‚applying‚ my teachings."

The People Break Their Marriage Vows

¹⁰Don't all of us have the same father? Hasn't the same God created us? Why are we unfaithful to each other? And why do we dishonor the promise given to our ancestors? ¹¹Judah has been unfaithful! A disgusting thing has been done in Israel and Jerusalem. Judah has dishonored the holy place that the LORD loves and has married a woman who worships a foreign god. ¹²May the LORD exclude anyone who does this, whoever he may be. May he exclude them from Jacob's tents and from bringing offerings to the LORD of Armies.

¹³Here is another thing you do: You cover the LORD's altar with tears. You moan and groan because he no longer pays attention to your offerings or accepts them from you.

¹⁴But you ask, "Why ‚aren't‚ our offerings accepted‚?" It is because the LORD is a witness between you and the wife of your youth, to whom you have been unfaithful. Yet, she is your companion, the wife of your marriage vows. ¹⁵Didn't ‚God‚ make you one? Your flesh and spirit belong to him. And what does the same ‚God‚ look for but godly descendants? So be careful not to be unfaithful to the wife of your youth.*ᵇ*

¹⁶"I hate divorce," says the LORD God of Israel. "I hate the person who covers himself with violence," says the LORD of Armies. "Be careful not to be unfaithful."

¹⁷You have tried the patience of the LORD with your words.

But you ask, "How have we tried his patience?"

When you say, "Everyone who does evil is considered good by the LORD. He is pleased with them," or "Where is the God of justice?"

The Coming of the Messenger of the Promise

¹"I'm going to send my messenger, and he will clear the way ahead of me. Then the Lord you are looking for will suddenly come to his temple. The messenger of the promise*ᵃ* will come. He is the one you want," says the LORD of Armies.

²But who will be able to endure the day he comes? Who will be able to survive on the day he appears? He is like a purifying fire and like a cleansing soap. ³He will act like a refiner and a purifier of silver. He will purify Levi's sons and refine them like gold and silver. Then they will bring acceptable offerings to the LORD. ⁴The offerings

---

ᵃ2:4 Or "covenant."   ᵇ2:15 Hebrew meaning of this verse uncertain.   ᵃ3:1 Or "covenant."

from Judah and Jerusalem will be pleasing to the Lord as in the past, as in years long ago.

⁵"I will come to judge you. I will be quick to testify against sorcerers, adulterers, lying witnesses, and those who cheat workers out of their wages and oppress widows and orphans. I will also testify against those who deprive foreigners of their rights. None of them fear me," says the Lord of Armies.

The People Are Cheating God

⁶"I, the Lord, never change. That is why you descendants of Jacob haven't been destroyed yet. ⁷Since the time of your ancestors you have turned away from my laws and have not followed them. Return to me, and I will return to you," says the Lord of Armies.

"But you ask, 'How can we return?'

⁸"Can a person cheat God? Yet, you are cheating me!

"But you ask, 'How are we cheating you?'

"When ⌐you don't bring⌐ a tenth of your income and other contributions. ⁹So a curse is on you because the whole nation is cheating me!

¹⁰"Bring one-tenth of your income into the storehouse so that there may be food in my house. Test me in this way," says the Lord of Armies. "See if I won't open the windows of heaven for you and flood you with blessings. ¹¹Then, for your sake, I will stop insects from eating ⌐your crops⌐. They will not destroy the produce of your land. The vines in your fields will not lose their unripened grapes," says the Lord of Armies. ¹²"All nations will call you blessed because you will be a delightful land," says the Lord of Armies.

¹³"You have used harsh words against me," says the Lord.

"You ask, 'How have we spoken against you?'

¹⁴"You have said, 'It's pointless to serve God. What do we gain if we meet his standards or if we walk around feeling sorry for what we've done? ¹⁵So now we call arrogant people blessed. Not only are evildoers encouraged, they even test God and get away with it.' "

¹⁶Then those who feared the Lord spoke to one another, and the Lord paid attention and listened. A book was written in his presence to be a reminder to those who feared the Lord and respected his name.

¹⁷"They will be mine," says the Lord of Armies. "On that day I will make them

Good Morning, God
Malachi 3:16-18

What makes you afraid? Being alone? Sitting through a scary movie? When the Bible says to "fear God," it doesn't mean to be afraid of him like some kids are afraid of the dark. He simply wants us to respect who he is. The Bible promises that we will be rewarded for honoring God and serving him. What are some creative ways you can you show God you respect him?

God, thank you that I do not have to be afraid of you. Show me how I can be respectful instead.

my special possession. I will spare them as a man spares his own son who serves him. ¹⁸Then you will again see the difference between righteous people and wicked people, between the one who serves God and the one who doesn't serve him.

The Day of the LORD Brings Judgment

4 [a]¹"Certainly the day is coming! It will burn like a furnace. All arrogant people and all evildoers will be ⌐like⌐ straw. The day that is coming will burn them up completely," says the LORD of Armies. "It won't leave a single root or branch.

²"The Sun of Righteousness will rise with healing in his wings for you people who fear my name. You will go out and leap like calves let out of a stall. ³You will trample on wicked people, because on the day I act they will be ashes under the soles of your feet," says the LORD of Armies.

Remember What God Has Done and Will Do

⁴"Remember the teachings of my servant Moses, the rules and regulations that I gave to him at Horeb for all Israel.

⁵"I'm going to send you the prophet Elijah before that very terrifying day of the LORD comes. ⁶He will change parents' attitudes toward their children and children's attitudes toward their parents. If not, I will come and reclaim my land by destroying you."

---

[a] 4:1 Malachi 4:1-6 in English Bibles is Malachi 3:19-24 in the Hebrew Bible.

New Testament

Matthew

Matthew tells the story of Jesus, the Savior predicted by Old Testament prophets. Jesus didn't act the way the Jewish people expected. Instead of being a conqueror, Jesus was a teacher. Instead of punishing sinners, he died to pay for people's sins and to bring salvation to anyone who believed in him. Matthew, one of Jesus' disciples, wrote this book about Jesus, so even today we can know that Jesus offers salvation to anyone who will believe in him.

Women were the first to know! What did they discover? See Matthew 28:1-10.

Headlines

Wise Men Throw Baby Shower
Matthew 2, page 1311

Jesus Hires People-Catchers
Matthew 4, page 1313

Peter's Mom Gets Cooled Off
Matthew 8, page 1320

Dead Daughter Just Sleeping!
Matthew 9, page 1321

Canaanite Woman Dogs Jesus
Matthew 15, page 1332

Mom Asks a Favor
Matthew 20, page 1341

Who's Ready for the Wedding?
Matthew 22, page 1345

Women Make Amazing Discovery!
Matthew 28, page 1358

The Messiah

Messiah means "anointed one." The Old Testament prophets wrote about a man anointed by God who would come to Earth to save the Jewish people. When Jesus came to Earth, he fulfilled the Old Testament prophecies about the Messiah. But many Jews did not believe that Jesus was the Messiah. They expected a military leader to save them from the Romans. Jesus came instead to save people from something far worse—sin.

Prophecy about Messiah	Old Testament	New Testament
Born of a virgin	Isaiah 7:14	Matthew 1:18-23
Born in Bethlehem	Micah 5:2	Matthew 2:1
Preceded by a messenger	Malachi 3:1	Matthew 3:1-3
Tortured and crucified	Psalm 22:1-18	Matthew 27:27-50
Raised from the dead	Psalm 16:9-10	Matthew 28:5-6

What's In It For Me?

Jesus is . . .

THE MESSIAH PROMISED IN THE OLD TESTAMENT.

GOD'S SERVANT.

MY TEACHER.

MY SAVIOR.

THE SON OF GOD.

THE RISEN LORD.

The Pharisees

The Pharisees carefully followed special rules that they believed kept them from breaking Moses' law. They thought if they kept all the rules, they would please God. Jesus described what the Pharisees were really like in Matthew 23.

Like blind guides (Matthew 23:16). They led people away from true righteousness to false righteousness.

Like dirty cups and dishes (Matthew 23:25). They looked good outside, but inside they were sinners.

Like whitewashed graves (Matthew 23:27). The Pharisees tried to look good but were dead inside.

Like poisonous snakes (Matthew 23:33). The Pharisees who opposed Jesus would kill the apostles Jesus sent.

Everybody needs to be saved from sin and given new life by Jesus—even people like the Pharisees who look good to other people.

Matthew

The Family Line of Jesus Christ

1 ¹This is the list of ancestors of Jesus Christ, descendant of David and Abraham.

² **Abraham** was the father of Isaac,
Isaac the father of Jacob,
Jacob the father of Judah and his brothers.

³ **Judah** and **Tamar** were the father and mother of Perez and Zerah.
Perez was the father of Hezron,
Hezron the father of Ram,

⁴ **Ram** the father of Amminadab,
Amminadab the father of Nahshon,
Nahshon the father of Salmon.

⁵ **Salmon** and **Rahab** were the father and mother of Boaz.
Boaz and **Ruth** were the father and mother of Obed.
Obed was the father of Jesse,

⁶ **Jesse** the father of King David.
David and **Uriah's wife** Bathsheba, were the father and mother of Solomon.

⁷ **Solomon** was the father of Rehoboam,
Rehoboam the father of Abijah,
Abijah the father of Asa,

⁸ **Asa** the father of Jehoshaphat,
Jehoshaphat the father of Joram,
Joram the father of Uzziah,

⁹ **Uzziah** the father of Jotham,
Jotham the father of Ahaz,
Ahaz the father of Hezekiah,

¹⁰ **Hezekiah** the father of Manasseh,
Manasseh the father of Amon,
Amon the father of Josiah.

¹¹ **Josiah** was the father of **Jechoniah** and his brothers.
They lived at the time when the people were exiled to Babylon.

¹²After the exile to Babylon,

Jechoniah became the father of Shealtiel.
Shealtiel was the father of Zerubbabel,

¹³ **Zerubbabel** the father of Abiud,
Abiud the father of Eliakim,
Eliakim the father of Azor,

¹⁴ **Azor** the father of Zadok,
Zadok the father of Achim,
Achim the father of Eliud,

¹⁵ **Eliud** the father of Eleazar,
Eleazar the father of Matthan,
Matthan the father of Jacob.

¹⁶ **Jacob** was the father of **Joseph**, who was the husband of Mary.
Mary was the mother of **Jesus**, who is called Christ.

¹⁷So there were

14 generations from Abraham to David,
14 generations from David until the exile to Babylon,
14 generations from the exile until the Messiah.

The Virgin Birth of Jesus

¹⁸The birth of Jesus Christ took place in this way. His mother Mary had been promised to Joseph in marriage. But before they were married, Mary realized that she was pregnant by the Holy Spirit. ¹⁹Her husband Joseph was an honorable man and did not want to disgrace her publicly. So he decided to break the marriage agreement with her secretly.

²⁰Joseph had this in mind when an angel of the Lord appeared to him in a dream. The angel said to him, "Joseph, descendant of David, don't be afraid to take Mary as your wife. She is pregnant by the Holy Spirit. ²¹She will give birth to a son, and you will name him Jesus [He Saves], because he will save his people from their sins." ²²All this happened so that what the Lord had spoken through the prophet came true: ²³"The virgin will become pregnant and give birth to a son, and they will name him Immanuel," which means "God is with us."

²⁴When Joseph woke up, he did what the angel of the Lord had commanded him to do. He took Mary to be his wife. ²⁵He did not have marital relations with her before she gave birth to a son. Joseph named the child Jesus.

The Wise Men Visit

¹Jesus was born in Bethlehem in Judea when Herod was king. After Jesus' birth wise men*ᵃ* from the east arrived in Jerusalem. ²They asked, "Where is the one who was born to be the king of the Jews? We saw his star rising and have come to worship him."

³When King Herod and all Jerusalem heard about this, they became disturbed. ⁴He called together all the chief priests and scribes and tried to find out from them where the Messiah was supposed to be born.

⁵They told him, "In Bethlehem in Judea. The prophet wrote about this:

⁶ Bethlehem in the land of Judah,
    you are by no means least among the leaders of Judah.
    A leader will come from you.
    He will shepherd my people Israel."

⁷Then Herod secretly called the wise men and found out from them exactly when the star had appeared. ⁸As he sent them to Bethlehem, he said, "Go and search carefully for the child. When you have found him, report to me so that I may go and worship him too."

⁹After they had heard the king, they started out. The star they had seen rising led them until it stopped over the place where the child was. ¹⁰They were overwhelmed with joy to see the star. ¹¹When they entered the house, they saw the child with his mother Mary. So they bowed down and worshiped him. Then they opened their treasure chests and offered him gifts of gold, frankincense, and myrrh.*ᵇ*

¹²God warned them in a dream not to go back to Herod. So they left for their country by another road.

---

*ᵃ*2:1 Or "astrologers."   *ᵇ*2:11 Myrrh is a fragrant resin used for perfumes, embalming, and deodorizers.

The Escape to Egypt

¹³After they had left, an angel of the Lord appeared to Joseph in a dream. The angel said to him, "Get up, take the child and his mother, and flee to Egypt. Stay there until I tell you, because Herod intends to search for the child and kill him."

¹⁴Joseph got up, took the child and his mother, and left for Egypt that night. ¹⁵He stayed there until Herod died. What the Lord had spoken through the prophet came true: "I have called my son out of Egypt."

¹⁶When Herod saw that the wise men had tricked him, he became furious. He sent soldiers to kill all the boys two years old and younger in or near Bethlehem. This matched the exact time he had learned from the wise men. ¹⁷Then the words spoken through the prophet Jeremiah came true:

¹⁸   "A sound was heard in Ramah,
        the sound of crying in bitter grief.
     Rachel was crying for her children.
     She refused to be comforted
        because they were dead."

From Egypt to Nazareth

¹⁹After Herod was dead, an angel of the Lord appeared in a dream to Joseph in Egypt. ²⁰The angel said to him, "Get up, take the child and his mother, and go to Israel. Those who tried to kill the child are dead."

²¹Joseph got up, took the child and his mother, and went to Israel. ²²But when he heard that Archelaus had succeeded his father Herod as king of Judea, Joseph was afraid to go there. Warned in a dream, he left for Galilee ²³and made his home in a city called Nazareth. So what the prophets had said came true: "He will be called a Nazarene."

John Prepares the Way—
Mark 1:1-8; Luke 3:1-18; John 1:19-28

¹Later, John the Baptizer appeared in the desert of Judea. His message was, ²"Turn to God and change the way you think and act, because the kingdom of heaven is near." ³Isaiah the prophet spoke about this man when he said,

     "A voice cries out in the desert:
       'Prepare the way for the Lord!
       Make his paths straight!' "

⁴John wore clothes made from camel's hair and had a leather belt around his waist. His diet consisted of locusts and wild honey.

⁵Jerusalem, all Judea, and the whole Jordan Valley went to him. ⁶As they confessed their sins, he baptized them in the Jordan River.

⁷But when he saw many Pharisees and Sadducees coming to be baptized, he said to them, "You poisonous snakes! Who showed you how to flee from God's coming anger? ⁸Do those things that prove you have turned to God and have changed the way you think and act. ⁹Don't think you can say, 'Abraham is our ancestor.' I can guarantee that God can raise up descendants for Abraham from these stones. ¹⁰The ax is now ready to cut the roots of the trees. Any tree that doesn't produce good fruit will be cut down and thrown into a fire. ¹¹I baptize you with water so that you will change the way you think and act. But the one who comes after me is more powerful than I. I am not worthy to remove his sandals. He will baptize you with the Holy Spirit and

fire. [12]His winnowing[a] shovel is in his hand, and he will clean up his threshing floor.[b] He will gather his wheat into a barn, but he will burn the husks in a fire that can never be put out."

John Baptizes Jesus—
Mark 1:9-11; Luke 3:21-22

[13]Then Jesus appeared. He came from Galilee to the Jordan River to be baptized by John. [14]But John tried to stop him and said, "I need to be baptized by you. Why are you coming to me?"

[15]Jesus answered him, "This is the way it has to be now. This is the proper way to do everything that God requires of us."

Then John gave in to him. [16]After Jesus was baptized, he immediately came up from the water. Suddenly, the heavens were opened, and he saw the Spirit of God coming down as a dove to him. [17]Then a voice from heaven said, "This is my Son, whom I love—my Son with whom I am pleased."

The Temptation of Jesus—
Mark 1:12-13; Luke 4:1-13

[1]Then the Spirit led Jesus into the desert to be tempted by the devil. [2]Jesus did not eat anything for 40 days and 40 nights. At the end of that time, he was hungry.

[3]The tempter came to him and said, "If you are the Son of God, tell these stones to become loaves of bread."

[4]Jesus answered, "Scripture says, 'A person cannot live on bread alone but on every word that God speaks.'"

[5]Then the devil took him into the holy city and had him stand on the highest part of the temple. [6]He said to Jesus, "If you are the Son of God, jump! Scripture says, 'He will put his angels in charge of you. They will carry you in their hands so that you never hit your foot against a rock.'"

[7]Jesus said to him, "Again, Scripture says, 'Never tempt the Lord your God.'"[a]

[8]Once more the devil took him to a very high mountain and showed him all the kingdoms in the world and their glory. [9]The devil said to him, "I will give you all this if you will bow down and worship me."

[10]Jesus said to him, "Go away, Satan! Scripture says, 'Worship the Lord your God and serve only him.'"

[11]Then the devil left him, and angels came to take care of him.

A Light Has Risen

[12]When Jesus heard that John had been put in prison, he went back to Galilee. [13]He left Nazareth and made his home in Capernaum on the shores of the Sea of Galilee. This was in the region of Zebulun and Naphtali. [14]So what the prophet Isaiah had said came true:

[15]   "Land of Zebulun and land of Naphtali,
             on the way to the sea,
                 across the Jordan River,
                     Galilee, where foreigners live!
[16]   The people who lived in darkness
             have seen a bright light.

---

[a]3:12 Winnowing is the process of separating husks from grain.   [b]3:12 A threshing floor is an outdoor area where grain is separated from its husks.   [a]4:7 Or "Never put the Lord your God to any test."

A light has risen
    for those who live in a land overshadowed by death."

¹⁷From then on, Jesus began to tell people, "Turn to God and change the way you think and act, because the kingdom of heaven is near!"

Calling of the First Disciples—
Mark 1:16-20; Luke 5:1-11

¹⁸As he was walking along the Sea of Galilee, he saw two brothers, Simon (called Peter) and Andrew. They were throwing a net into the sea because they were fishermen. ¹⁹Jesus said to them, "Come, follow me! I will teach you how to catch people instead of fish." ²⁰They immediately left their nets and followed him.

²¹As Jesus went on, he saw two other brothers, James and John, the sons of Zebedee. They were in a boat with their father Zebedee preparing their nets to go fishing. He called them, ²²and they immediately left the boat and their father and followed Jesus.

Spreading the Good News in Galilee—
Mark 1:35-39; Luke 4:42-44

²³Jesus went all over Galilee. He taught in the synagogues and spread the Good News of the kingdom. He also cured every disease and sickness among the people.

²⁴The news about Jesus spread throughout Syria. People brought him everyone who was sick, those who suffered from any kind of disease or pain. They also brought epileptics, those who were paralyzed, and people possessed by demons, and he cured them all. ²⁵Large crowds followed him. They came from Galilee, the Ten Cities,ᵇ Jerusalem, Judea, and from across the Jordan River.

The Sermon on a Mountain:
The Beatitudes

5 ¹When Jesus saw the crowds, he went up a mountain and sat down. His disciples came to him, ²and he began to teach them:

³   "Blessed are those who recognize they are spiritually helpless.
        The kingdom of heaven belongs to them.
⁴   Blessed are those who mourn.
        They will be comforted.
⁵   Blessed are those who are gentle.
        They will inherit the earth.
⁶   Blessed are those who hunger and thirst for God's approval.
        They will be satisfied.
⁷   Blessed are those who show mercy.
        They will be treated mercifully.
⁸   Blessed are those whose thoughts are pure.
        They will see God.
⁹   Blessed are those who make peace.
        They will be called God's children.
¹⁰   Blessed are those who are persecuted for doing what God approves of.
        The kingdom of heaven belongs to them.

ᵇ 4:25 A federation of ten Greek city states east and west of the Jordan River.

[11] "Blessed are you when people insult you,
persecute you,
lie, and say all kinds of evil things about you because of me.
[12] Rejoice and be glad because you have a great reward in heaven!
The prophets who lived before you were persecuted in these ways.

God's People Make a Difference in the World—
Mark 4:21-23; Luke 11:33

[13]"You are salt for the earth. But if salt loses its taste, how will it be made salty again? It is no longer good for anything except to be thrown out and trampled on by people. [14]"You are light for the world. A city cannot be hidden when it is located on a hill. [15]No one lights a lamp and puts it under a basket. Instead, everyone who lights a lamp puts it on a lamp stand. Then its light shines on everyone in the house. [16]In the same way let your light shine in front of people. Then they will see the good that you do and praise your Father in heaven.

Jesus Fulfills the Old Testament Scriptures

[17]"Don't ever think that I came to set aside Moses' Teachings or the Prophets. I didn't come to set them aside but to make them come true. [18]I can guarantee this truth: Until the earth and the heavens disappear, neither a period nor a comma will disappear from Moses' Teachings before everything has come true. [19]So whoever sets aside any command that seems unimportant and teaches others to do the same will be unimportant in the kingdom of heaven. But whoever does and teaches what the commands say will be called great in the kingdom of heaven. [20]I can guarantee that unless you live a life that has God's approval and do it more faithfully than the scribes and Pharisees, you will never enter the kingdom of heaven.

Jesus Talks About Anger

[21]"You have heard that it was said to your ancestors, 'Never murder. Whoever murders will answer for it in court.' [22]But I can guarantee that whoever is angry with another believer[a] will answer for it in court. Whoever calls another believer an insulting name will answer for it in the highest court. Whoever calls another believer a fool will answer for it in hellfire.

Good Morning, God
Matthew 5:1-10

People who are not Christians often see things differently than Jesus did. Some people think that by bullying others they will appear strong. But Jesus says those who are gentle are special. Some folks don't care about the pain of others. Jesus says those who are sad will be comforted. If you follow Jesus, you will be different from many others around you. But that difference is what makes you special.

Lord, help me have the unique qualities Jesus talked about.

---

[a] 5:22 Some manuscripts and translations add "without a cause."

²³"So if you are offering your gift at the altar and remember there that another believer has something against you, ²⁴leave your gift at the altar. First go away and make peace with that person. Then come back and offer your gift.

²⁵"Make peace quickly with your opponent while you are on the way to court with him. Otherwise, he will hand you over to the judge. Then the judge will hand you over to an officer, who will throw you into prison. ²⁶I can guarantee this truth: You will never get out until you pay every penny of your fine.

About Sexual Sin

²⁷"You have heard that it was said, 'Never commit adultery.' ²⁸But I can guarantee that whoever looks with lust at a woman has already committed adultery in his heart.

²⁹"So if your right eye causes you to sin, tear it out and throw it away. It is better for you to lose a part of your body than to have all of it thrown into hell. ³⁰And if your right hand leads you to sin, cut it off and throw it away. It is better for you to lose a part of your body than to have all of it go into hell.

³¹"It has also been said, 'Whoever divorces his wife must give her a written notice.' ³²But I can guarantee that any man who divorces his wife for any reason other than unfaithfulness makes her look as though she has committed adultery. Whoever marries a woman divorced in this way makes himself look as though he has committed adultery.

About Oaths

³³"You have heard that it was said to your ancestors, 'Never break your oath, but give to the Lord what you swore in an oath to give him.' ³⁴But I tell you don't swear an oath at all. Don't swear an oath by heaven, which is God's throne, ³⁵or by the earth, which is his footstool, or by Jerusalem, which is the city of the great King. ³⁶And don't swear an oath by your head. After all, you cannot make one hair black or white. ³⁷Simply say yes or no. Anything more than that comes from the evil one.

Love Your Enemies—
Luke 6:27-36

³⁸"You have heard that it was said, 'An eye for an eye and a tooth for a tooth.' ³⁹But I tell you not to oppose an evil person. If someone slaps you on your right cheek, turn your other cheek to him as well. ⁴⁰If someone wants to sue you in order to take your shirt, let him have your coat too. ⁴¹If someone forces you to go one mile, go two miles with him. ⁴²Give to everyone who asks you for something. Don't turn anyone away who wants to borrow something from you.

⁴³"You have heard that it was said, 'Love your neighbor, and hate your enemy.' ⁴⁴But I tell you this: Love your enemies, and pray for those who persecute you. ⁴⁵In this way you show that you are children of your Father in heaven. He makes his sun rise on people whether they are good or evil. He lets rain fall on them whether they are just or unjust. ⁴⁶If you love those who love you, do you deserve a reward? Even the tax collectors do that! ⁴⁷Are you doing anything remarkable if you welcome only your friends? Everyone does that! ⁴⁸That is why you must be perfect as your Father in heaven is perfect.

The Sermon on a Mountain Continues:
Don't Do Good Works to Be Praised by People

6 ¹"Be careful not to do your good works in public in order to attract attention. If you do, your Father in heaven will not reward you. ²So when you give to the poor, don't announce it with trumpet fanfare. This is what hypocrites do in the synagogues and on the streets in order to be praised by people. I can guarantee this truth: That will be their only reward. [3]When you give to the poor, don't let your left hand know what your right hand is doing. [4]Give your contributions privately. Your Father sees what you do in private. He will reward you.

The Lord's Prayer—
Luke 11:1-4

[5]"When you pray, don't be like hypocrites. They like to stand in synagogues and on street corners to pray so that everyone can see them. I can guarantee this truth: That will be their only reward. [6]When you pray, go to your room and close the door. Pray privately to your Father who is with you. Your Father sees what you do in private. He will reward you.

[7]"When you pray, don't ramble like heathens who think they'll be heard if they talk a lot. [8]Don't be like them. Your Father knows what you need before you ask him.

[9]"This is how you should pray:

> Our Father in heaven,
> let your name be kept holy.
[10]   Let your kingdom come.
> Let your will be done on earth
> as it is done in heaven.
[11]   Give us our daily bread today.
[12]   Forgive us as we forgive others.
[13]   Don't allow us to be tempted.
> Instead, rescue us from the evil one.[a]

[14]"If you forgive the failures of others, your heavenly Father will also forgive you. [15]But if you don't forgive others, your Father will not forgive your failures.

Fasting

[16]"When you fast, stop looking sad like hypocrites. They put on sad faces to make it obvious that they're fasting. I can guarantee this truth: That will be their only reward. [17]When you fast, wash your face and comb your hair. [18]Then your fasting won't be obvious. Instead, it will be obvious to your Father who is with you in private. Your Father sees what you do in private. He will reward you.

True Riches

[19]"Stop storing up treasures for yourselves on earth, where moths and rust destroy and thieves break in and steal. [20]Instead, store up treasures for yourselves in heaven, where moths and rust don't destroy and thieves don't break in and steal. [21]Your heart will be where your treasure is.

[22]"The eye is the lamp of the body. So if your eye is unclouded, your whole body will be full of light. [23]But if your eye is evil, your whole body will be full of darkness. If the light in you is darkness, how dark it will be!

[24]"No one can serve two masters. He will hate the first master and love the second, or he will be devoted to the first and despise the second. You cannot serve God and wealth.

---

[a] 6:13 Or "rescue us from evil."

Stop Worrying—
Luke 12:22-34

²⁵"So I tell you to stop worrying about what you will eat, drink, or wear. Isn't life more than food and the body more than clothes?

²⁶"Look at the birds. They don't plant, harvest, or gather the harvest into barns. Yet, your heavenly Father feeds them. Aren't you worth more than they?

²⁷"Can any of you add a single hour to your life by worrying?

²⁸"And why worry about clothes? Notice how the flowers grow in the field. They never work or spin yarn for clothes. ²⁹But I say that not even Solomon in all his majesty was dressed like one of these flowers. ³⁰That's the way God clothes the grass in the field. Today it's alive, and tomorrow it's thrown into an incinerator. So how much more will he clothe you people who have so little faith?

³¹"Don't ever worry and say, 'What are we going to eat?' or 'What are we going to drink?' or 'What are we going to wear?' ³²Everyone is concerned about these things, and your heavenly Father certainly knows you need all of them. ³³But first, be concerned about his kingdom and what has his approval. Then all these things will be provided for you.

³⁴"So don't ever worry about tomorrow. After all, tomorrow will worry about itself. Each day has enough trouble of its own.

The Sermon on a Mountain Continues:
Stop Judging—
Luke 6:37-42

7 ¹"Stop judging so that you will not be judged. ²Otherwise, you will be judged by the same standard you use to judge others. The standards you use for others will be applied to you. ³So why do you see the piece of sawdust in another believer's eye and not notice the wooden beam in your own eye? ⁴How can you say to another believer, 'Let me take the piece of sawdust out of your eye,' when you have a beam in your own eye? ⁵You hypocrite! First remove the beam from your own eye. Then you will see clearly to remove the piece of sawdust from another believer's eye.

Don't Throw Pearls to Pigs

⁶"Don't give what is holy to dogs or throw your pearls to pigs. Otherwise, they will trample them and then tear you to pieces.

Your Heavenly Father
Matthew 6:25-34

Not every girl has a loving and responsible dad. But God is our heavenly Father. He loves you and is always there for you. When you realize how much God loves you, you won't worry about what you don't have. Trust your heavenly Father to take care of you.

be you all can be

The Power of Prayer—
Luke 11:5-13

[7]"Ask, and you will receive. Search, and you will find. Knock, and the door will be opened for you. [8]Everyone who asks will receive. The one who searches will find, and for the one who knocks, the door will be opened.

[9]"If your child asks you for bread, would any of you give him a stone? [10]Or if your child asks for a fish, would you give him a snake? [11]Even though you're evil, you know how to give good gifts to your children. So how much more will your Father in heaven give good things to those who ask him?

The Golden Rule—
Luke 6:31

[12]"Always do for other people everything you want them to do for you. That is the meaning of Moses' Teachings and the Prophets.

The Narrow Gate

[13]"Enter through the narrow gate because the gate and road that lead to destruction are wide. Many enter through the wide gate. [14]But the narrow gate and the road that lead to life are full of trouble. Only a few people find the narrow gate.

False Prophets—
Luke 6:43-45

[15]"Beware of false prophets. They come to you disguised as sheep, but in their hearts they are vicious wolves. [16]You will know them by what they produce.

"People don't pick grapes from thornbushes or figs from thistles, do they? [17]In the same way every good tree produces good fruit, but a rotten tree produces bad fruit. [18]A good tree cannot produce bad fruit, and a rotten tree cannot produce good fruit. [19]Any tree that fails to produce good fruit is cut down and thrown into a fire. [20]So you will know them by what they produce.

[21]"Not everyone who says to me, 'Lord, Lord!' will enter the kingdom of heaven, but only the person who does what my Father in heaven wants. [22]Many will say to me on that day, 'Lord, Lord, didn't we prophesy in your name? Didn't we force out demons and do many miracles by the power and authority of your name?' [23]Then I will tell them publicly, 'I've never known you. Get away from me, you evil people.'

Build on the Rock—
Luke 6:47-49

[24]"Therefore, everyone who hears what I say and obeys it will be like a wise person who built a house on rock. [25]Rain poured, and floods came. Winds blew and beat against that house. But it did not collapse, because its foundation was on rock.

[26]"Everyone who hears what I say but doesn't obey it will be like a foolish person who built a house on sand. [27]Rain poured, and floods came. Winds blew and struck that house. It collapsed, and the result was a total disaster."

[28]When Jesus finished this speech, the crowds were amazed at his teachings. [29]Unlike their scribes, he taught them with authority.

Jesus Cures a Man With a Skin Disease—
Mark 1:40-45; Luke 5:12-16

8 ¹When Jesus came down from the mountain, large crowds followed him. ²A man with a serious skin disease came and bowed down in front of him. The man said to Jesus, "Sir, if you're willing, you can make me clean."ᵃ

³Jesus reached out, touched him, and said, "I'm willing. So be clean!" Immediately, his skin disease went away, and he was clean.

⁴Jesus said to him, "Don't tell anyone about this! Instead, show yourself to the priest. Then offer the sacrifice Moses commanded as proof to people that you are clean."

A Believing Army Officer—
Luke 7:1-10

⁵When Jesus went to Capernaum, a Roman army officer came to beg him for help. ⁶The officer said, "Sir, my servant is lying at home paralyzed and in terrible pain."

⁷Jesus said to him, "I'll come to heal him."

⁸The officer responded, "Sir, I don't deserve to have you come into my house. But just give a command, and my servant will be healed. ⁹As you know, I'm in a chain of command and have soldiers at my command. I tell one of them, 'Go!' and he goes, and another, 'Come!' and he comes. I tell my servant, 'Do this!' and he does it."

¹⁰Jesus was amazed when he heard this. He said to those who were following him, "I can guarantee this truth: I haven't found faith as great as this in anyone in Israel. ¹¹I can guarantee that many will come from all over the world. They will eat with Abraham, Isaac, and Jacob in the kingdom of heaven. ¹²The citizens of that kingdom will be thrown outside into the darkness. People will cry and be in extreme pain there."

¹³Jesus told the officer, "Go! What you believed will be done for you." And at that moment the servant was healed.

Jesus Cures Peter's Mother-in-Law and Many Others—
Mark 1:29-34; Luke 4:38-41

¹⁴When Jesus went to Peter's house, he saw Peter's mother-in-law in bed with a fever. ¹⁵Jesus touched her hand, and the fever went away. So she got up and prepared a meal for him.

¹⁶In the evening the people brought him many who were possessed by demons. He forced the ˌevilˌ spirits out of people with a command and cured everyone who was sick. ¹⁷So what the prophet Isaiah had said came true: "He took away our weaknesses and removed our diseases."

¹⁸Now, when Jesus saw a crowd around him, he ordered ˌhis disciplesˌ to cross to the other side of the Sea of Galilee.

What It Takes to Be a Disciple—
Luke 9:57-62

¹⁹A scribe came to him and said, "Teacher, I'll follow you wherever you go."

²⁰Jesus told him, "Foxes have holes, and birds have nests, but the Son of Man has nowhere to sleep."

²¹Another disciple said to him, "Sir, first let me go to bury my father."

²²But Jesus told him, "Follow me, and let the dead bury their own dead."

ᵃ8:2 "Clean" refers to anything that Moses' Teachings say is presentable to God.

Jesus Calms the Sea—
Mark 4:35-41; Luke 8:22-25

23Jesus' disciples went with him as he left in a boat. 24Suddenly, a severe storm came across the sea. The waves were covering the boat. Yet, Jesus was sleeping.

25So they woke him up, saying, "Lord! Save us! We're going to die!"

26Jesus said to them, "Why do you cowards have so little faith?" Then he got up, gave an order to the wind and the sea, and the sea became very calm.

27The men were amazed and asked, "What kind of man is this? Even the wind and the sea obey him!"

Jesus Cures Two Demon-Possessed Men—
Mark 5:1-20; Luke 8:26-39

28When he arrived in the territory of the Gadarenes on the other side of the Sea of Galilee, two men met him. They were possessed by demons and had come out of the tombs. No one could travel along that road because the men were so dangerous.

29They shouted, "Why are you bothering us now, Son of God? Did you come here to torture us before it is time?"

30A large herd of pigs was feeding in the distance. 31The demons begged Jesus, "If you're going to force us out, send us into that herd of pigs."

32Jesus said to them, "Go!" The demons came out and went into the pigs. Suddenly, the whole herd rushed down the cliff into the sea and died in the water. 33Those who took care of the pigs ran into the city. There they reported everything, especially about the men possessed by demons.

34Everyone from the city went to meet Jesus. When they saw him, they begged him to leave their territory.

Jesus Forgives Sins—
Mark 2:1-12; Luke 5:17-26

1Jesus got into a boat, crossed the sea, and came to his own city. 2Some people brought him a paralyzed man on a stretcher.

When Jesus saw their faith, he said to the man, "Cheer up, friend! Your sins are forgiven."

3Then some of the scribes thought, "He's dishonoring God."

4Jesus knew what they were thinking. He asked them, "Why are you thinking evil things? 5Is it easier to say, 'Your sins are forgiven,' or to say, 'Get up and walk'? 6I want you to know that the Son of Man has authority on earth to forgive sins." Then he said to the paralyzed man, "Get up, pick up your stretcher, and go home."

7So the man got up and went home. 8When the crowd saw this, they were filled with awe and praised God for giving such authority to humans.

Jesus Chooses Matthew to Be a Disciple—
Mark 2:13-17; Luke 5:27-32

9When Jesus was leaving that place, he saw a man sitting in a tax office. The man's name was Matthew. Jesus said to him, "Follow me!" So Matthew got up and followed him.

10Later Jesus was having dinner at Matthew's house. Many tax collectors and sinners came to eat with Jesus and his disciples. 11The Pharisees saw this and asked his disciples, "Why does your teacher eat with tax collectors and sinners?"

12When Jesus heard that, he said, "Healthy people don't need a doctor; those who are sick do. ¹³Learn what this means: 'I want mercy, not sacrifices.' I've come to call sinners, not people who think they have God's approval."

Jesus Is Questioned About Fasting—
Mark 2:18-22; Luke 5:33-39

¹⁴Then John's disciples came to Jesus. They said, "Why do we and the Pharisees fast often but your disciples never do?"

¹⁵Jesus replied, "Can wedding guests be sad while the groom is still with them? The time will come when the groom will be taken away from them. Then they will fast.

¹⁶"No one patches an old coat with a new piece of cloth that will shrink. When the patch shrinks, it will rip away from the coat, and the tear will become worse. ¹⁷Nor do people pour new wine into old wineskins. If they do, the skins burst, the wine runs out, and the skins are ruined. Rather, people pour new wine into fresh skins, and both are saved."

A Synagogue Leader's Daughter and the Woman With Chronic Bleeding—
Mark 5:21-43; Luke 8:40-56

¹⁸A synagogue leader came to Jesus while he was talking to John's disciples. He bowed down in front of Jesus and said, "My daughter just died. Come, lay your hand on her, and she will live."

¹⁹Jesus and his disciples got up and followed the man.

²⁰Then a woman came up behind Jesus and touched the edge of his clothes. She had been suffering from chronic bleeding for twelve years. ²¹She thought, "If I only touch his clothes, I'll get well."

²²When Jesus turned and saw her he said, "Cheer up, daughter! Your faith has made you well." At that very moment the woman became well.

²³Jesus came to the synagogue leader's house. He saw flute players and a noisy crowd. ²⁴He said to them, "Leave! The girl is not dead. She's sleeping." But they laughed at him.

²⁵When the crowd had been put outside, Jesus went in, took her hand, and the girl came back to life.

²⁶The news about this spread throughout that region.

Good Morning, God
Matthew 9:12

Some people said bad things about Jesus because he ate and talked with sinful people. When Jesus heard these comments, he compared himself to a doctor. Healthy people don't need a doctor—but sick people do. In the same way, those who seem to behave the worst are the ones who need Jesus the most. Are you a friend and a good witness to all kinds of people?

Lord, thank you that you are a friend to all people.

Jesus Heals Two Blind Men

²⁷When Jesus left that place, two blind men followed him. They shouted, "Have mercy on us, Son of David."

²⁸Jesus went into a house, and the blind men followed him. He said to them, "Do you believe that I can do this?"

"Yes, Lord," they answered.

²⁹He touched their eyes and said, "What you have believed will be done for you!" ³⁰Then they could see.

He warned them, "Don't let anyone know about this!" ³¹But they went out and spread the news about him throughout that region.

Jesus Forces a Demon out of a Man Who Couldn't Talk

³²As they were leaving, some people brought a man to Jesus. The man was unable to talk because he was possessed by a demon. ³³But as soon as the demon was forced out, the man began to speak.

The crowds were amazed and said, "We have never seen anything like this in Israel!"

³⁴But the Pharisees said, "He forces demons out of people with the help of the ruler of demons."

Jesus' Compassion for People

³⁵Jesus went to all the towns and villages. He taught in the synagogues and spread the Good News of the kingdom. He also cured every disease and sickness.

³⁶When he saw the crowds, he felt sorry for them. They were troubled and helpless like sheep without a shepherd. ³⁷Then he said to his disciples, "The harvest is large, but the workers are few. ³⁸So ask the Lord who gives this harvest to send workers to harvest his crops."

Jesus Appoints Twelve Apostles—
Mark 3:13-19; Luke 6:12-16

10 ¹Jesus called his twelve disciples and gave them authority to force evil spirits out of people and to cure every disease and sickness.

²These are the names of the twelve apostles: first and foremost, Simon (who is called Peter) and his brother Andrew; James and his brother John, the sons of Zebedee; ³Philip and Bartholomew; Thomas and Matthew the tax collector; James (son of Alphaeus), and Thaddaeus; ⁴Simon the Zealot and Judas Iscariot, who later betrayed Jesus.

Jesus Sends Out the Twelve—
Mark 6:7-13; Luke 9:1-6

⁵Jesus sent these twelve out with the following instructions: "Don't go among people who are not Jewish or into any Samaritan city. ⁶Instead, go to the lost sheep of the nation of Israel. ⁷As you go, spread this message: 'The kingdom of heaven is near.' ⁸Cure the sick, bring the dead back to life, cleanse those with skin diseases, and force demons out of people. Give these things without charging, since you received them without paying.

⁹"Don't take any gold, silver, or even copper coins in your pockets. ¹⁰Don't take a traveling bag for the trip, a change of clothes, sandals, or a walking stick. After all, the worker deserves to have his needs met.

¹¹"When you go into a city or village, look for people who will listen to you there.

Stay with them until you leave that place. [12]When you go into a house, greet the family. [13]If it is a family that listens to you, allow your greeting to stand. But if it is not receptive, take back your greeting. [14]If anyone doesn't welcome you or listen to what you say, leave that house or city, and shake its dust off your feet. [15]I can guarantee this truth: Judgment day will be better for Sodom and Gomorrah than for that city.

[16]"I'm sending you out like sheep among wolves. So be as cunning as snakes but as innocent as doves. [17]Watch out for people who will hand you over to the Jewish courts and whip you in their synagogues. [18]Because of me you will even be brought in front of governors and kings to testify to them and to everyone in the world. [19]When they hand you over to the authorities, don't worry about what to say or how to say it. When the time comes, you will be given what to say. [20]Indeed, you're not the ones who will be speaking. The Spirit of your Father will be speaking through you.

[21]"Brother will hand over brother to death; a father will hand over his child. Children will rebel against their parents and kill them. [22]Everyone will hate you because you are committed to me. But the person who patiently endures to the end will be saved. [23]So when they persecute you in one city, flee to another. I can guarantee this truth: Before you have gone through every city in Israel, the Son of Man will come.

[24]"A student is not better than his teacher. Nor is a slave better than his owner. [25]It is enough for a student to become like his teacher and a slave like his owner. If they have called the owner of the house Beelzebul,[a] they will certainly call the family members the same name. [26]So don't be afraid of them. Nothing has been covered that will not be exposed. Whatever is secret will be made known. [27]Tell in the daylight what I say to you in the dark. Shout from the housetops what you hear whispered. [28]Don't be afraid of those who kill the body but cannot kill the soul. Instead, fear the one who can destroy both body and soul in hell.

[29]"Aren't two sparrows sold for a penny? Not one of them will fall to the ground without your Father's permission. [30]Every hair on your head has been counted. [31]Don't be afraid! You are worth more than many sparrows.

[32]"So I will acknowledge in front of my Father in heaven that person who acknowledges me in front of others. [33]But I will tell my Father in heaven that I don't know the person who tells others that he doesn't know me.

[34]"Don't think that I came to bring peace to earth. I didn't come to bring peace but conflict. [35]I came to turn a man against his father, a daughter against her mother, a daughter-in-law against her mother-in-law. [36]A person's enemies will be the members of his own family.

[37]"The person who loves his father or mother more than me does not deserve to be my disciple. The person who loves a son or daughter more than me does not deserve to be my disciple. [38]Whoever doesn't take up his cross and follow me doesn't deserve to be my disciple. [39]The person who tries to preserve his life will lose it, but the person who loses his life for me will preserve it.

[40]"The person who welcomes you welcomes me, and the person who welcomes me welcomes the one who sent me. [41]The person who welcomes a prophet as a prophet will receive a prophet's reward. The person who welcomes a righteous person as a righteous person will receive a righteous person's reward. [42]I can guarantee this truth: Whoever gives any of my humble followers a cup of cold water because that person is my disciple will certainly never lose his reward."

[1]After Jesus finished giving his twelve disciples these instructions, he moved on from there to teach his message in their cities.

---

[a] 10:25 *Beelzebul* is another name for the devil. See Matthew 12:24.

John Sends Two Disciples—
Luke 7:18-23

²When John was in prison, he heard about the things Christ had done. So he sent his disciples ³to ask Jesus, "Are you the one who is coming, or should we look for someone else?"

⁴Jesus answered John's disciples, "Go back, and tell John what you hear and see: ⁵Blind people see again, lame people are walking, those with skin diseases are made clean, deaf people hear again, dead people are brought back to life, and poor people hear the Good News. ⁶Whoever doesn't lose his faith in me is indeed blessed."

Jesus Speaks About John—
Luke 7:24-35

⁷As they were leaving, Jesus spoke to the crowds about John. "What did you go into the desert to see? Tall grass swaying in the wind? ⁸Really, what did you go to see? A man dressed in fine clothes? Those who wear fine clothes are in royal palaces. ⁹"Really, what did you go to see? A prophet? Let me tell you that he is far more than a prophet. ¹⁰John is the one about whom Scripture says,

'I'm sending my messenger ahead of you
to prepare the way in front of you.'

¹¹"I can guarantee this truth: Of all the people ever born, no one is greater than John the Baptizer. Yet, the least important person in the kingdom of heaven is greater than John. ¹²From the time of John the Baptizer until now, the kingdom of heaven has been forcefully advancing, and forceful people have been seizing it. ¹³All the Prophets and Moses' Teachings prophesied up to the time of John. ¹⁴If you are willing to accept their message, John is the Elijah who was to come. ¹⁵Let the person who has ears listen!

¹⁶"How can I describe the people who are living now? They are like children who sit in the marketplaces and shout to other children,

¹⁷ 'We played music for you,
but you didn't dance.
We sang a funeral song,
but you didn't show any sadness.'

¹⁸"John came neither eating nor drinking, and people say, 'There's a demon in him!' ¹⁹The Son of Man came eating and drinking, and people say, 'Look at him! He's a glutton and a drunk, a friend of tax collectors and sinners!'

"Yet, wisdom is proved right by its actions."

Jesus Warns Chorazin, Bethsaida, and Capernaum

²⁰Then Jesus denounced the cities where he had worked most of his miracles because they had not changed the way they thought and acted. ²¹"How horrible it will be for you, Chorazin! How horrible it will be for you, Bethsaida! If the miracles worked in you had been worked in Tyre and Sidon, they would have changed the way they thought and acted long ago in sackcloth and ashes. ²²I can guarantee that judgment day will be better for Tyre and Sidon than for you. ²³And you, Capernaum, will you be lifted to heaven? No, you will go down to hell! If the miracles that had been worked in you had been worked in Sodom, it would still be there today. ²⁴I can guarantee that judgment day will be better for Sodom than for you."

Jesus Praises the Father and Invites Disciples to Come to Him

²⁵At that time Jesus said, "I praise you, Father, Lord of heaven and earth, for hiding these things from wise and intelligent people and revealing them to little children. ²⁶Yes, Father, this is what pleased you.

²⁷"My Father has turned everything over to me. Only the Father knows the Son. And no one knows the Father except the Son and those to whom the Son is willing to reveal him.

²⁸"Come to me, all who are tired from carrying heavy loads, and I will give you rest. ²⁹Place my yoke*ᵃ* over your shoulders, and learn from me, because I am gentle and humble. Then you will find rest for yourselves ³⁰because my yoke is easy and my burden is light."

Jesus Has Authority Over the Day of Worship—
Mark 2:23-28; Luke 6:1-5

12 ¹Then on a day of worship Jesus walked through the grainfields. His disciples were hungry and began to pick the heads of grain to eat.

²When the Pharisees saw this, they said to him, "Look! Your disciples are doing something that is not right to do on the day of worship."

³Jesus asked them, "Haven't you read what David did when he and his men were hungry? ⁴Haven't you read how he went into the house of God and ate*ᵃ* the bread of the presence? He and his men had no right to eat those loaves. Only the priests have that right. ⁵Or haven't you read in Moses' Teachings that on the day of worship the priests in the temple do things they shouldn't on the day of worship yet remain innocent? ⁶I can guarantee that something*ᵇ* greater than the temple is here. ⁷If you had known what 'I want mercy, not sacrifices' means, you would not have condemned innocent people.

⁸"The Son of Man has authority over the day of worship."

Jesus Heals on the Day of Worship—
Mark 3:1-6; Luke 6:6-11

⁹Jesus moved on from there and went into a synagogue. ¹⁰A man with a paralyzed hand was there. The people asked Jesus whether it was right to heal on a day of worship so that they could accuse him of doing something wrong.

¹¹Jesus said to them, "Suppose one of you has a sheep. If it falls into a pit on a day of worship, wouldn't you take hold of it and lift it out? ¹²Certainly, a human is more valuable than a sheep! So it is right to do good on the day of worship."

¹³Then he said to the man, "Hold out your hand." The man held it out, and it became normal again, as healthy as the other.

¹⁴The Pharisees left and plotted to kill Jesus. ¹⁵He knew about this, so he left that place.

Jesus Is God's Servant

Many people followed him, and he cured all of them. ¹⁶He also ordered them not to tell people who he was. ¹⁷So what the prophet Isaiah had said came true:

ᵃ11:29 A yoke is a wooden bar placed over the necks of work animals so that they can pull plows or carts.
ᵃ12:4 Some manuscripts and translations read "they ate." ᵇ12:6 Some manuscripts and translations read "someone."

18 "Here is my servant
      whom I have chosen,
      whom I love,
        and in whom I delight.
    I will put my Spirit on him,
      and he will announce justice to the nations.
19 He will not quarrel or shout,
      and no one will hear his voice in the streets.
20 He will not break off a damaged cattail.
    He will not even put out a smoking wick
      until he has made justice victorious.
21 The nations will have hope because of him."

Jesus Is Accused of Working With Beelzebul—
Mark 3:20-30; Luke 11:14-23

22Then some people brought Jesus a man possessed by a demon. The demon made the man blind and unable to talk. Jesus cured him so that he could talk and see.

23The crowds were all amazed and said, "Can this man be the Son of David?" 24When the Pharisees heard this, they said, "This man can force demons out of people only with the help of Beelzebul, the ruler of demons."

25Since Jesus knew what they were thinking, he said to them, "Every kingdom divided against itself is ruined. And every city or household divided against itself will not last. 26If Satan forces Satan out, he is divided against himself. How, then, can his kingdom last? 27If I force demons out of people with the help of Beelzebul, who helps your followers force them out? That's why they will be your judges. 28But if I force demons out with the help of God's Spirit, then the kingdom of God has come to you. 29How can anyone go into a strong man's house and steal his property? First he must tie up the strong man. Then he can go through his house and steal his property.

30"Whoever isn't with me is against me. Whoever doesn't gather with me scatters. 31So I can guarantee that people will be forgiven for any sin or cursing. However, cursing the Spirit will not be forgiven. 32Whoever speaks a word against the Son of Man will be forgiven. But whoever speaks against the Holy Spirit will not be forgiven in this world or the next.

33"Make a tree good, and then its fruit will be good. Or make a tree rotten, and then its fruit will be rotten. A person can recognize a tree by its fruit. 34You poisonous snakes! How can you evil people say anything good? Your mouth says what comes from inside you. 35Good people do the good things that are in them. But evil people do the evil things that are in them.

36"I can guarantee that on judgment day people will have to give an account of every careless word they say. 37By your words you will be declared innocent, or by your words you will be declared guilty."

The Sign of Jonah—
Luke 11:29-32, 24-26

38Then some scribes and Pharisees said, "Teacher, we want you to show us a miraculous sign."

39He responded, "The people of an evil and unfaithful era look for a miraculous sign. But the only sign they will get is the sign of the prophet Jonah. 40Just as Jonah was in the belly of a huge fish for three days and three nights, so the Son of Man will be in the heart of the earth for three days and three nights. 41The men of Nineveh will stand up with you at the time of judgment and will condemn you, because they turned to God and changed the way they thought and acted when Jonah spoke his message. But look, someone greater than Jonah is here! ⁴²The queen from the south will stand up at the time of judgment with you. She will condemn you, because she came from the ends of the earth to hear Solomon's wisdom. But look, someone greater than Solomon is here!

⁴³"When an evil spirit comes out of a person, it goes through dry places looking for a place to rest. But it doesn't find any. ⁴⁴Then it says, 'I'll go back to the home I left.' When it arrives, it finds the house unoccupied, swept clean, and in order. ⁴⁵Then it goes and brings along seven other spirits more evil than itself. They enter and take up permanent residence there. In the end the condition of that person is worse than it was before. That is what will happen to the evil people of this day."

The True Family of Jesus—
Mark 3:31-35; Luke 8:19-21

⁴⁶While Jesus was still talking to the crowds, his mother and brothers were standing outside. They wanted to talk to him. ⁴⁷Someone told him, "Your mother and your brothers are standing outside. They want to talk to you."

⁴⁸He replied to the man speaking to him, "Who is my mother, and who are my brothers?" ⁴⁹Pointing with his hand at his disciples, he said, "Look, here are my mother and my brothers. ⁵⁰Whoever does what my Father in heaven wants is my brother and sister and mother."

A Story About a Farmer—
Mark 4:1-20; Luke 8:4-15

¹That same day Jesus left the house and sat down by the Sea of Galilee. ²The crowd that gathered around him was so large that he got into a boat. He sat in the boat while the entire crowd stood on the shore. ³Then he used stories as illustrations to tell them many things.

He said, "Listen! A farmer went to plant seed. ⁴Some seeds were planted along the road, and birds came and devoured them. ⁵Other seeds were planted on rocky ground, where there was little soil. The plants sprouted quickly because the soil wasn't deep. ⁶But when the sun came up, they were scorched. They withered because their roots weren't deep enough. ⁷Other seeds were planted among thornbushes, and the thornbushes grew up and choked them. ⁸But other seeds were planted on good ground and produced grain. They produced one hundred, sixty, or thirty times as much as was planted. ⁹Let the person who has ears listen!"

¹⁰The disciples asked him, "Why do you use stories as illustrations when you speak to people?"

¹¹Jesus answered, "Knowledge about the mysteries of the kingdom of heaven has been given to you. But it has not been given to the crowd. ¹²Those who understand these mysteries will be given more knowledge, and they will excel in understanding them. However, some people don't understand these mysteries. Even what they understand will be taken away from them. ¹³This is why I speak to them this way. They see, but they're blind. They hear, but they don't listen. They don't even try to understand. ¹⁴So they make Isaiah's prophecy come true:

'You will hear clearly but never understand.
You will see clearly but never comprehend.
¹⁵   These people have become close-minded

and hard of hearing.
They have shut their eyes
so that their eyes never see.
Their ears never hear.
Their minds never understand.
And they never return to me for healing!'

¹⁶"Blessed are your eyes because they see and your ears because they hear. ¹⁷I can guarantee this truth: Many prophets and many of God's people longed to see what you see but didn't see it, to hear what you hear but didn't hear it.

¹⁸"Listen to what the story about the farmer means. ¹⁹Someone hears the word about the kingdom but doesn't understand it. The evil one comes at once and snatches away what was planted in him. This is what the seed planted along the road illustrates. ²⁰The seed planted on rocky ground ˌis the person whoˌ hears the word and accepts it at once with joy. ²¹Since he doesn't have any root, he lasts only a little while. When suffering or persecution comes along because of the word, he immediately falls ˌfrom faithˌ. ²²The seed planted among thornbushes ˌis another person whoˌ hears the word. But the worries of life and the deceitful pleasures of riches choke the word so that it can't produce anything. ²³But the seed planted on good ground ˌis the person whoˌ hears and understands the word. This type produces crops. They produce one hundred, sixty, or thirty times as much as was planted."

A Story About Weeds in the Wheat

²⁴Jesus used another illustration. He said, "The kingdom of heaven is like a man who planted good seed in his field. ²⁵But while people were asleep, his enemy planted weeds in the wheat field and went away. ²⁶When the wheat came up and formed kernels, weeds appeared.

²⁷"The owner's workers came to him and asked, 'Sir, didn't you plant good seed in your field? Where did the weeds come from?'

²⁸"He told them, 'An enemy did this.'

"His workers asked him, 'Do you want us to pull out the weeds?'

²⁹"He replied, 'No. If you pull out the weeds, you may pull out the wheat with them. ³⁰Let both grow together until the harvest. When the grain is cut, I will tell the workers to gather the weeds first and tie them in bundles to be burned. But I'll have them bring the wheat into my barn.' "

Good Morning, God
Matthew 13:31-32

Jesus said the kingdom of heaven is like a mustard seed. This kind of seed is very small, but it grows to be a very big plant. Some people expected God's kingdom to begin in a big way, with a powerful king. Instead, the kingdom of God began in a humble way, with Jesus' birth in a stable. Since then, this kingdom has grown greater and greater each day. Aren't you glad to be a part of the growing kingdom?

Jesus, thank you for being a great king.

Stories About a Mustard Seed and Yeast—
Mark 4:30-34; Luke 13:18-21

³¹Jesus used another illustration. He said, "The kingdom of heaven is like a mustard seed that someone planted in a field. ³²It's one of the smallest seeds. However, when it has grown, it is taller than the garden plants. It becomes a tree that is large enough for birds to nest in its branches."

³³He used another illustration. "The kingdom of heaven is like yeast that a woman mixed into a large amount of flour until the yeast worked its way through all the dough."

³⁴Jesus used illustrations to tell the crowds all these things. He did not tell them anything without illustrating it with a story. ³⁵So what the prophet had said came true:

"I will open my mouth to illustrate points.
I will tell what has been hidden since the world was made."

The Meaning of the Weeds in the Wheat

³⁶When Jesus had sent the people away, he went into the house. His disciples came to him and said, "Explain what the illustration of the weeds in the field means."

³⁷He answered, "The one who plants the good seeds is the Son of Man. ³⁸The field is the world. The good seeds are those who belong to the kingdom. The weeds are those who belong to the evil one. ³⁹The enemy who planted them is the devil. The harvest is the end of the world. The workers are angels. ⁴⁰Just as weeds are gathered and burned, so it will be at the end of time. ⁴¹The Son of Man will send his angels. They will gather everything in his kingdom that causes people to sin and everyone who does evil. ⁴²The angels will throw them into a blazing furnace. People will cry and be in extreme pain there. ⁴³Then the people who have God's approval will shine like the sun in their Father's kingdom. Let the person who has ears listen!

Stories About a Treasure, a Merchant, and a Net

⁴⁴"The kingdom of heaven is like a treasure buried in a field. When a man discovered it, he buried it again. He was so delighted with it that he went away, sold everything he had, and bought that field.

⁴⁵"Also, the kingdom of heaven is like a merchant who was searching for fine pearls. ⁴⁶When he found a valuable pearl, he went away, sold everything he had, and bought it.

⁴⁷"Also, the kingdom of heaven is like a net that was thrown into the sea. It gathered all kinds of fish. ⁴⁸When it was full, they pulled it to the shore. Then they sat down, gathered the good fish into containers, and threw the bad ones away. ⁴⁹The same thing will happen at the end of time. The angels will go out and separate the evil people from people who have God's approval. ⁵⁰Then the angels will throw the evil people into a blazing furnace. They will cry and be in extreme pain there.

⁵¹"Have you understood all of this?"

"Yes," they answered.

⁵²So Jesus said to them, "That is why every scribe who has become a disciple of the kingdom of heaven is like a home owner. He brings new and old things out of his treasure chest."

⁵³When Jesus had finished these illustrations, he left that place.

Nazareth Rejects Jesus—
Mark 6:1-6; Luke 4:14-30

⁵⁴Jesus went to his hometown and taught the people in the synagogue in a way that amazed them. People were asking, "Where did this man get this wisdom and the

power to do these miracles? ⁵⁵Isn't this the carpenter's son? Isn't his mother's name Mary? Aren't his brothers' names James, Joseph, Simon, and Judas? ⁵⁶And aren't all his sisters here with us? Where, then, did this man get all this?" ⁵⁷So they took offense at him.

But Jesus said to them, "The only place a prophet isn't honored is in his hometown and in his own house."

⁵⁸He didn't work many miracles there because of their lack of faith.

Recalling John's Death—
Mark 6:14-29; Luke 9:7-9

¹At that time Herod, ruler of Galilee, heard the news about Jesus. ²He said to his officials, "This is John the Baptizer! He has come back to life. That's why he has the power to perform these miracles."

³Herod had arrested John, tied him up, and put him in prison. Herod did this for Herodias, the wife of his brother Philip. ⁴John had been telling Herod, "It's not right for you to be married to her." ⁵So Herod wanted to kill John. However, he was afraid of the people because they thought John was a prophet.

⁶When Herod celebrated his birthday, Herodias' daughter danced for his guests. Herod was so delighted with her that ⁷he swore he would give her anything she wanted.

⁸Urged by her mother, she said, "Give me the head of John the Baptizer on a platter."

⁹The king regretted his promise. But because of his oath and his guests, he ordered that her wish be granted. ¹⁰He had John's head cut off in prison. ¹¹So the head was brought on a platter and given to the girl, who took it to her mother.

¹²John's disciples came for the body and buried it. Then they went to tell Jesus.

Jesus Feeds More Than Five Thousand—
Mark 6:30-44; Luke 9:10-17; John 6:1-14

¹³When Jesus heard about John, he left in a boat and went to a place where he could be alone. The crowds heard about this and followed him on foot from the cities. ¹⁴When Jesus got out of the boat, he saw a large crowd. He felt sorry for them and cured their sick people.

¹⁵In the evening the disciples came to him. They said, "No one lives around here, and it's already late. Send the crowds to the villages to buy food for themselves."

¹⁶Jesus said to them, "They don't need to go away. You give them something to eat."

¹⁷They told him, "All we have here are five loaves of bread and two fish."

¹⁸Jesus said, "Bring them to me."

¹⁹Then he ordered the people to sit down on the grass. After he took the five loaves and the two fish, he looked up to heaven and blessed the food. He broke the loaves apart, gave them to the disciples, and they gave them to the people. ²⁰All of them ate as much as they wanted. When they picked up the leftover pieces, they filled twelve baskets.

²¹About five thousand men had eaten. (This number does not include the women and children who had eaten.)

Jesus Walks on the Sea—
Mark 6:45-56; John 6:15-21

²²Jesus quickly made his disciples get into a boat and cross to the other side ahead of him while he sent the people away. ²³After sending the people away, he went up a mountain to pray by himself. When evening came, he was there alone.

²⁴The boat, now hundreds of yards from shore, was being thrown around by the waves because it was going against the wind.

²⁵Between three and six o'clock in the morning, he came to them. He was walking on the sea. ²⁶When the disciples saw him walking on the sea, they were terrified. They said, "It's a ghost!" and began to scream because they were afraid.

²⁷Immediately, Jesus said, "Calm down! It's me. Don't be afraid!"

²⁸Peter answered, "Lord, if it is you, order me to come to you on the water."

²⁹Jesus said, "Come!" So Peter got out of the boat and walked on the water toward Jesus. ³⁰But when he noticed how strong the wind was, he became afraid and started to sink. He shouted, "Lord, save me!"

³¹Immediately, Jesus reached out, caught hold of him, and said, "You have so little faith! Why did you doubt?"

³²When they got into the boat, the wind stopped blowing. ³³The men in the boat bowed down in front of Jesus and said, "You are truly the Son of God."

³⁴They crossed the sea and landed at Gennesaret. ³⁵The men there recognized Jesus and sent messengers all around the countryside. The people brought him everyone who was sick. ³⁶They begged him to let them touch just the edge of his clothes. Everyone who touched his clothes was made well.

Jesus Challenges the Pharisees' Traditions—
Mark 7:1-23

15 ¹Then some Pharisees and scribes came from Jerusalem to Jesus. They asked, ²"Why do your disciples break the traditions of our ancestors? They do not wash their hands before they eat."

³He answered them, "Why do you break the commandment of God because of your traditions? ⁴For example, God said, 'Honor your father and your mother' and 'Whoever curses father or mother must be put to death.' ⁵But you say that whoever tells his father or mother, 'I have given to God whatever support you might have received from me,' ⁶does not have to honor his father. Because of your traditions you have destroyed the authority of God's word. ⁷You hypocrites! Isaiah was right when he prophesied about you:

⁸   'These people honor me with their lips,
        but their hearts are far from me.
⁹   Their worship of me is pointless,
        because their teachings are rules made by humans.' "

¹⁰Then he called the crowd and said to them, "Listen and try to understand! ¹¹What goes into a person's mouth doesn't make him unclean.ᵃ It's what comes out of the mouth that makes a person unclean."

¹²Then the disciples came and said to him, "Do you realize that when the Pharisees heard your statement they were offended?"

¹³He answered, "Any plant that my heavenly Father did not plant will be uprooted.

ᵃ15:11 "Unclean" refers to anything that Moses' Teachings say is not presentable to God.

¹⁴Leave them alone! They are blind leaders. When one blind person leads another, both will fall into the same pit."

¹⁵Peter said to him, "Explain this illustration to us."

¹⁶Jesus said, "Don't you understand yet? ¹⁷Don't you know that whatever goes into the mouth goes into the stomach and then into a toilet? ¹⁸But whatever goes out of the mouth comes from within, and that's what makes a person unclean. ¹⁹Evil thoughts, murder, adultery, ⌊other⌋ sexual sins, stealing, lying, and cursing come from within. ²⁰These are the things that make a person unclean. But eating without washing one's hands doesn't make a person unclean."

The Faith of a Canaanite Woman—
Mark 7:24-30

²¹Jesus left that place and went to the region of Tyre and Sidon.

²²A Canaanite woman from that territory came ⌊to him⌋ and began to shout, "Have mercy on me, Lord, Son of David! My daughter is tormented by a demon."

²³But he did not answer her at all. Then his disciples came to him and urged him, "Send her away. She keeps shouting behind us."

²⁴Jesus responded, "I was sent only to the lost sheep of the nation of Israel."

²⁵She came to him, bowed down, and said, "Lord, help me!"

²⁶Jesus replied, "It's not right to take the children's food and throw it to the dogs."

²⁷She said, "You're right, Lord. But even the dogs eat scraps that fall from their masters' tables."

²⁸Then Jesus answered her, "Woman, you have strong faith! What you wanted will be done for you." At that moment her daughter was cured.

²⁹Jesus moved on from there and went along the Sea of Galilee. Then he went up a mountain and sat there.

³⁰A large crowd came to him, bringing with them the lame, blind, disabled, those unable to talk, and many others. They laid them at his feet, and he cured them. ³¹The crowd was amazed to see mute people talking, the disabled cured, the lame walking, and the blind seeing. So they praised the God of Israel.

Jesus Feeds More Than Four Thousand—
Mark 8:1-10

³²Jesus called his disciples and said, "I feel sorry for the people. They have been with me three days now and have nothing to eat. I don't want to send them away hungry, or they may become exhausted on their way home."

³³His disciples asked him, "Where could we get enough bread to feed such a crowd in this place where no one lives?"

³⁴Jesus asked them, "How many loaves of bread do you have?"

They answered, "Seven, and a few small fish."

³⁵He ordered the crowd to sit down on the ground. ³⁶He took the seven loaves and the fish and gave thanks to God. Then he broke the bread and gave it to the disciples, and they gave the bread and fish to the people.

³⁷All of them ate as much as they wanted. The disciples picked up the leftover pieces and filled seven large baskets. ³⁸Four thousand men had eaten. (This number does not include the women and children who had eaten.)

³⁹After he sent the people on their way, Jesus stepped into the boat and came to the territory of Magadan.

Peter

Peter left his fishing business to follow Jesus.

Peter had a successful fishing business. Then Jesus said, "Follow me."
Peter left his nets and his boats. He traveled everywhere with Jesus.

Peter heard Jesus teach. He saw Jesus perform miracles. He watched as
Jesus talked with people. After being with Jesus for many months, Peter knew
who Jesus was. When Jesus asked who the disciples thought he was, Peter
said, "You are the Messiah, the Son of the living God."

After Jesus died and came back to life, Peter preached the first sermon to
the Jews. He told them Jesus had died for their sins. Many people believed in
Jesus because Peter preached to them.

When Peter healed a lame man, a crowd gathered to hear him tell about Jesus. (See Acts 3:1-16.)

Peter had been a fisherman.

Peter became a disciple of Jesus.

Peter is named first on every list of the twelve apostles.

Getting to Know Peter

✹ Peter was a successful businessman. Why would he leave his job to follow Jesus?

✹ Do you think Peter liked traveling with Jesus? Why?

✹ How do you think Peter felt when he told people about Jesus, and they became Christians?

✹ Have you ever told anyone that Jesus died for his or her sins?

Peter was jailed for telling others about Jesus. God's angel set Peter free. (See Acts 12:1-19.)

The Pharisees Ask For a Sign From Heaven—
Mark 8:11-13a

16 ¹The Pharisees and Sadducees came to test Jesus. So they asked him to show them a miraculous sign from heaven.

²He responded to them, "In the evening you say that the weather will be fine because the sky is red. ³And in the morning you say that there will be a storm today because the sky is red and overcast. You can forecast the weather by judging the appearance of the sky, but you cannot interpret the signs of the times.

⁴"Evil and unfaithful people look for a miraculous sign. But the only sign they will be given is that of Jonah."

Then he left them standing there and went away.

The Yeast of the Pharisees—
Mark 8:13b-21

⁵The disciples had forgotten to take any bread along when they went to the other side of the Sea of Galilee.

⁶Jesus said to them, "Be careful! Watch out for the yeast of the Pharisees and Sadducees!"

⁷The disciples had been discussing among themselves that they had not taken any bread along.

⁸Jesus knew about their conversation and asked, "Why are you discussing among yourselves that you don't have any bread? You have so little faith! ⁹Don't you understand yet? Don't you remember the five loaves for the five thousand and how many baskets you filled? ¹⁰Don't you remember the seven loaves for the four thousand and how many large baskets you filled? ¹¹Why don't you understand that I wasn't talking to you about bread? Watch out for the yeast of the Pharisees and Sadducees!"

¹²Then they understood that he didn't say to watch out for the yeast in bread, but to watch out for the teachings of the Pharisees and Sadducees.

Peter Declares His Belief About Jesus—
Mark 8:27-30; Luke 9:18-21

¹³When Jesus came to the region of Caesarea Philippi, he asked his disciples, "Who do people say the Son of Man is?"

¹⁴They answered, "Some say you are John the Baptizer, others Elijah, still others Jeremiah or one of the prophets."

¹⁵He asked them, "But who do you say I am?"

¹⁶Simon Peter answered, "You are the Messiah, the Son of the living God!"

¹⁷Jesus replied, "Simon, son of Jonah, you are blessed! No human revealed this to you, but my Father in heaven revealed it to you. ¹⁸You are Peter, and I can guarantee that on this rock[a] I will build my church. And the gates of hell will not overpower it. ¹⁹I will give you the keys of the kingdom of heaven. Whatever you imprison, God will imprison. And whatever you set free, God will set free."

²⁰Then he strictly ordered the disciples not to tell anyone that he was the Messiah.

Jesus Foretells That He Will Die and Come Back to Life—
Mark 8:31-33; Luke 9:22

²¹From that time on Jesus began to inform his disciples that he had to go to Jerusalem. There he would have to suffer a lot because of the leaders, chief priests, and scribes. He would be killed, but on the third day he would be brought back to life.

---

[a] 16:18 In Greek there is a play on words between *petros* (Peter or pebble) and *petra* (rock).

²²Peter took him aside and objected to this. He said, "Heaven forbid, Lord! This must never happen to you!"

²³But Jesus turned and said to Peter, "Get out of my way, Satan! You are tempting me to sin. You aren't thinking the way God thinks but the way humans think."

What It Means to Follow Jesus—
Mark 8:34–9:1; Luke 9:23-27

²⁴Then Jesus said to his disciples, "Those who want to come with me must say no to the things they want, pick up their crosses, and follow me. ²⁵Those who want to save their lives will lose them. But those who lose their lives for me will find them. ²⁶What good will it do for people to win the whole world and lose their lives? Or what will a person give in exchange for life? ²⁷The Son of Man will come with his angels in his Father's glory. Then he will pay back each person based on what that person has done. ²⁸I can guarantee this truth: Some people who are standing here will not die until they see the Son of Man coming in his kingdom."

Moses and Elijah Appear With Jesus—
Mark 9:2-13; Luke 9:28-36

¹After six days Jesus took Peter, James, and John (the brother of James) and led them up a high mountain where they could be alone.

²Jesus' appearance changed in front of them. His face became as bright as the sun and his clothes as white as light. ³Suddenly, Moses and Elijah appeared to them and were talking with Jesus.

⁴Peter said to Jesus, "Lord, it's good that we're here. If you want, I'll put up three tents here—one for you, one for Moses, and one for Elijah."

⁵He was still speaking when a bright cloud overshadowed them. Then a voice came out of the cloud and said, "This is my Son, whom I love and with whom I am pleased. Listen to him!"

⁶The disciples were terrified when they heard this and fell facedown on the ground. ⁷But Jesus touched them and said, "Get up, and don't be afraid!" ⁸As they raised their heads, they saw no one but Jesus.

⁹On their way down the mountain, Jesus ordered them, "Don't tell anyone what you have seen. Wait until the Son of Man has been brought back to life."

¹⁰So the disciples asked him, "Why do the scribes say that Elijah must come first?"

¹¹Jesus answered, "Elijah is coming and will put everything in order again. ¹²Actually, I can guarantee that Elijah has already come. Yet, people treated him as they pleased because they didn't recognize him. In the same way they're going to make the Son of Man suffer."

¹³Then the disciples understood that he was talking about John the Baptizer.

Jesus Cures a Demon-Possessed Boy—
Mark 9:14-29; Luke 9:37-43a

¹⁴When they came to a crowd, a man came up to Jesus, knelt in front of him, ¹⁵and said, "Sir, have mercy on my son. He suffers from seizures. Often he falls into fire or water. ¹⁶I brought him to your disciples, but they couldn't cure him."

¹⁷Jesus replied, "You unbelieving and corrupt generation! How long must I be with you? How long must I put up with you? Bring him here to me!"

¹⁸Jesus ordered the demon to come out of the boy. At that moment the boy was cured.

¹⁹Then the disciples came to Jesus privately and asked, "Why couldn't we force the demon out of the boy?"

²⁰He told them, "Because you have so little faith. I can guarantee this truth: If your faith is the size of a mustard seed, you can say to this mountain, 'Move from here to there,' and it will move. Nothing will be impossible for you."[a]

Jesus Again Foretells That He Will Die and Come Back to Life—
Mark 9:30-32; Luke 9:43b-45

²²While they were traveling together in Galilee, Jesus told them, "The Son of Man will be betrayed and handed over to people. ²³They will kill him, but on the third day he will be brought back to life." Then the disciples became very sad.

Paying the Temple Tax

²⁴When they came to Capernaum, the collectors of the temple tax came to Peter. They asked him, "Doesn't your teacher pay the temple tax?"

²⁵"Certainly," he answered.

Peter went into the house. Before he could speak, Jesus asked him, "What do you think, Simon? From whom do the kings of the world collect fees or taxes? Is it from their family members or from other people?"

²⁶"From other people," Peter answered.

Jesus said to him, "Then the family members are exempt. ²⁷However, so that we don't create a scandal, go to the sea and throw in a hook. Take the first fish that you catch. Open its mouth, and you will find a coin. Give that coin to them for you and me."

Greatness in the Kingdom—
Mark 9:33-37; Luke 9:46-48

¹At that time the disciples came to Jesus and asked, "Who is greatest in the kingdom of heaven?"

²He called a little child and had him stand among them. ³Then he said to them, "I can guarantee this truth: Unless you change and become like little children, you will never enter the kingdom of heaven. ⁴Whoever becomes like this little child is the greatest in the kingdom of heaven. ⁵And whoever welcomes a child like this in my name welcomes me.

Causing Others to Lose Faith—
Mark 9:42-50; Luke 17:1-4

⁶"These little ones believe in me. It would be best for the person who causes one of them to lose faith to be drowned in the sea with a large stone hung around his neck. ⁷How horrible it will be for the world because it causes people to lose their faith. Situations that cause people to lose their faith will arise. How horrible it will be for the person who causes someone to lose his faith!

⁸"If your hand or your foot causes you to lose your faith, cut it off and throw it away. It is better for you to enter life disabled or injured than to have two hands or two feet and be thrown into everlasting fire. ⁹If your eye causes you to lose your faith, tear it out and throw it away. It is better for you to enter life with one eye than to have two eyes and be thrown into hellfire.

---

[a] 17:20 Some manuscripts and translations add verse 21: "However, this kind ⸤of demon⸥ goes away only by prayer and fasting."

¹⁰"Be careful not to despise these little ones. I can guarantee that their angels in heaven always see the face of my Father, who is in heaven.ᵃ

The Lost Sheep—
Luke 15:1-7

¹²"What do you think? Suppose a man has 100 sheep and one of them strays. Won't he leave the 99 sheep in the hills to look for the one that has strayed? ¹³I can guarantee this truth: If he finds it, he is happier about it than about the 99 that have not strayed. ¹⁴In the same way, your Father in heaven does not want one of these little ones to be lost.

Dealing With Believers When They Do Wrong

¹⁵"If a believer does something wrong,ᵇ go, confront him when the two of you are alone. If he listens to you, you have won back that believer. ¹⁶But if he does not listen, take one or two others with you so that every accusation may be verified by two or three witnesses. ¹⁷If he ignores these witnesses, tell it to the community of believers. If he also ignores the community, deal with him as you would a heathen or a tax collector. ¹⁸I can guarantee this truth: Whatever you imprison, God will imprison. And whatever you set free, God will set free.

¹⁹"I can guarantee again that if two of you agree on anything here on earth, my Father in heaven will accept it. ²⁰Where two or three have come together in my name, I am there among them."

Personally Forgiving Others

²¹Then Peter came to Jesus and asked him, "Lord, how often do I have to forgive a believer who wrongs me? Seven times?"

²²Jesus answered him, "I tell you, not just seven times, but seventy times seven. ²³"That is why the kingdom of heaven is like a king who wanted to settle accounts with his servants. ²⁴When he began to do this, a servant who owed him millions of dollars was brought to him. ²⁵Because he could not pay off the debt, the master ordered him, his wife, his children, and all that he had to be sold to pay off the account. ²⁶Then the servant fell at his master's feet and said, 'Be patient with me, and I will repay everything!'

²⁷"The master felt sorry for his servant, freed him, and canceled his debt. ²⁸But when that servant went away, he found a servant who owed him hundreds of dollars. He grabbed the servant he found and began to choke him. 'Pay what you owe!' he said.

²⁹"Then that other servant fell at his feet and begged him, 'Be patient with me, and I will repay you.' ³⁰But he refused. Instead, he turned away and had that servant put into prison until he would repay what he owed.

³¹"The other servants who worked with him saw what had happened and felt very sad. They told their master the whole story.

³²"Then his master sent for him and said to him, 'You evil servant! I canceled your entire debt, because you begged me. ³³Shouldn't you have treated the other servant as mercifully as I treated you?'

³⁴"His master was so angry that he handed him over to the torturers until he would repay everything that he owed. ³⁵That is what my Father in heaven will do to you if each of you does not sincerely forgive other believers."

ᵃ18:10 Some manuscripts and translations add verse 11: "The Son of Man came to save the lost."   ᵇ18:15 Some manuscripts and translations add "against you."

A Discussion About Divorce and Celibacy—
Mark 10:1-12

19 ¹When Jesus finished speaking, he left Galilee and traveled along the other side of the Jordan River to the territory of Judea. ²Large crowds followed him, and he healed them there.

³Some Pharisees came to test him. They asked, "Can a man divorce his wife for any reason?"

⁴Jesus answered, "Haven't you read that the Creator made them male and female in the beginning ⁵and that he said, 'That's why a man will leave his father and mother and will remain united with his wife, and the two will be one'? ⁶So they are no longer two but one. Therefore, don't let anyone separate what God has joined together."

⁷The Pharisees asked him, "Why, then, did Moses order a man to give his wife a written notice to divorce her?"

⁸Jesus answered them, "Moses allowed you to divorce your wives because you're heartless. It was never this way in the beginning. ⁹I can guarantee that whoever divorces his wife for any reason other than her unfaithfulness is committing adultery if he marries another woman."

¹⁰The disciples said to him, "If that is the only reason a man can use to divorce his wife, it's better not to get married."

¹¹He answered them, "Not everyone can do what you suggest. Only those who have that gift can. ¹²For example, some men are celibate because they were born that way. Others are celibate because they were castrated. Still others have decided to be celibate because of the kingdom of heaven. If anyone can do what you've suggested, then he should do it."

Jesus Blesses Children—
Mark 10:13-16; Luke 18:15-17

Divorce
Matthew 19:1-8

When parents divorce, everyone feels bad. Sometimes children even feel it's their fault. But it's not the fault of children. Some married people just hurt each other more and more. Remember it's not your fault if your parents divorce, and it's okay to keep loving both of them.

be
all you
can be

¹³Then some people brought little children to Jesus to have him bless them and pray for them. But the disciples told the people not to do that.

¹⁴Jesus said, "Don't stop children from coming to me! Children like these are part of the kingdom of God." ¹⁵After Jesus blessed them, he went away from there.

Eternal Life in the Kingdom—
Mark 10:17-31; Luke 18:18-30

¹⁶Then a man came to Jesus and said, "Teacher, what good deed should I do to gain eternal life?"

¹⁷Jesus said to him, "Why do you ask me about what is good? There is only one who is good. If you want to enter into life, obey the commandments."

¹⁸"Which commandments?" the man asked.

Jesus said, "Never murder. Never commit adultery. Never steal. Never give false testimony. ¹⁹Honor your father and mother. Love your neighbor as you love yourself."

²⁰The young man replied, "I have obeyed all these commandments. What else do I need to do?"

²¹Jesus said to him, "If you want to be perfect, sell what you own. Give the money to the poor, and you will have treasure in heaven. Then follow me!"

²²When the young man heard this, he went away sad because he owned a lot of property.

²³Jesus said to his disciples, "I can guarantee this truth: It will be hard for a rich person to enter the kingdom of heaven. ²⁴I can guarantee again that it is easier for a camel to go through the eye of a needle than for a rich person to enter the kingdom of God."

²⁵He amazed his disciples more than ever when they heard this. "Then who can be saved?" they asked.

²⁶Jesus looked at them and said, "It is impossible for people to save themselves, but everything is possible for God."

²⁷Then Peter replied to him, "Look, we've given up everything to follow you. What will we get out of it?"

²⁸Jesus said to them, "I can guarantee this truth: When the Son of Man sits on his glorious throne in the world to come, you, my followers, will also sit on twelve thrones, judging the twelve tribes of Israel. ²⁹And everyone who gave up homes, brothers or sisters, father, mother, children, or fields because of my name will receive a hundred times more and will inherit eternal life. ³⁰However, many who are first will be last, and many who are last will be first.

A Story About Vineyard Workers

20 ¹"The kingdom of heaven is like a landowner who went out at daybreak to hire workers for his vineyard. ²After agreeing to pay the workers the usual day's wages, he sent them to work in his vineyard.

³About 9 a.m. he saw others standing in the marketplace without work. ⁴He said to them, 'Work in my vineyard, and I'll give you whatever is right.' So they went.

⁵He went out again about noon and 3 p.m. and did the same thing. ⁶About 5 p.m. he went out and found some others standing around. He said to them, 'Why are you standing here all day long without work?'

⁷"'No one has hired us,' they answered him.

"He said to them, 'Work in my vineyard.'

⁸"When evening came, the owner of the vineyard told the supervisor, 'Call the workers, and give them their wages. Start with the last, and end with the first.'

⁹"Those who started working about 5 p.m. came, and each received a day's wages. ¹⁰When those who had been hired first came, they expected to receive more. But each of them received a day's wages. ¹¹Although they took it, they began to protest to the owner. ¹²They said, 'These last workers have worked only one hour. Yet, you've treated us all the same, even though we worked hard all day under a blazing sun.'

¹³"The owner said to one of them, 'Friend, I'm not treating you unfairly. Didn't you agree with me on a day's wages? ¹⁴Take your money and go! I want to give this last worker as much as I gave you. ¹⁵Can't I do what I want with my own money? Or do you resent my generosity towards others?'

¹⁶"In this way the last will be first, and the first will be last."

For the Third Time Jesus Foretells That He Will Die and Come Back to Life—
Mark 10:32-34; Luke 18:31-34

¹⁷When Jesus was on his way to Jerusalem, he took the twelve apostles aside and said to them privately, ¹⁸"We're going to Jerusalem. There the Son of Man will be betrayed to the chief priests and scribes. They will condemn him to death ¹⁹and hand him over to foreigners. They will make fun of him, whip him, and crucify him. But on the third day he will be brought back to life."

A Mother Makes a Request—
Mark 10:35-45

²⁰Then the mother of Zebedee's sons came to Jesus with her two sons. She bowed down in front of him to ask him for a favor.

²¹"What do you want?" he asked her.

She said to him, "Promise that one of my sons will sit at your right and the other at your left in your kingdom."

²²Jesus replied, "You don't realize what you're asking. Can you drink the cup that I'm going to drink?"

"We can," they told him.

²³Jesus said to them, "You will drink my cup. But I don't have the authority to grant you a seat at my right or left. My Father has already prepared these positions for certain people."

²⁴When the other ten apostles heard about this, they were irritated with the two brothers. ²⁵Jesus called the apostles and said, "You know that the rulers of nations have absolute power over people and their officials have absolute authority over people. ²⁶But that's not the way it's going to be among you. Whoever wants to become great among you will be your servant. ²⁷Whoever wants to be most important among you will be your slave. ²⁸It's the same way with the Son of Man. He didn't come so that others could serve him. He came to serve and to give his life as a ransom for many people."

Jesus Gives Two Blind Men Their Sight—
Mark 10:46-52; Luke 18:35-43

²⁹As they were leaving Jericho, a large crowd followed Jesus. ³⁰Two blind men were sitting by the road. When they heard that Jesus was passing by, they shouted, "Lord, Son of David, have mercy on us!"

³¹The crowd told them to be quiet. But they shouted even louder, "Lord, Son of David, have mercy on us!"

³²Jesus stopped and called them. "What do you want me to do for you?" he asked.

³³They told him, "Lord, we want you to give us our eyesight back."

³⁴Jesus felt sorry for them, so he touched their eyes. Their sight was restored at once, and they followed him.

The King Comes to Jerusalem—
Mark 11:1-11; Luke 19:29-44; John 12:12-19

21 ¹When they came near Jerusalem and had reached Bethphage on the Mount of Olives, Jesus sent two disciples ahead of him. ²He said to them, "Go into the village ahead of you. You will find a donkey tied there and a colt with it. Untie them, and bring them to me. ³If anyone says anything to you, tell him that the Lord needs them. That person will send them at once."

⁴This happened so that what the prophet had said came true:

5   "Tell the people of Zion,
      'Your king is coming to you.
      He's gentle,
         riding on a donkey,
            on a colt, a young pack animal.' "

⁶The disciples did as Jesus had directed them. ⁷They brought the donkey and the colt and put their coats on them for Jesus to sit on. ⁸Most of the people spread their coats on the road. Others cut branches from the trees and spread them on the road. ⁹The crowd that went ahead of him and that followed him was shouting,

"Hosanna to the Son of David!
Blessed is the one who comes in the name of the Lord!
Hosanna in the highest heaven!"

¹⁰When Jesus came into Jerusalem, the whole city was in an uproar. People were asking, "Who is this?"

¹¹The crowd answered, "This is the prophet Jesus from Nazareth in Galilee."

Jesus Throws Out the Moneychangers—
Mark 11:15-19; Luke 19:45-48

¹²Jesus went into the temple courtyard and threw out everyone who was buying and selling there. He overturned the moneychangers' tables and the chairs of those who sold pigeons. ¹³He told them, "Scripture says, 'My house will be called a house of prayer,' but you're turning it into a gathering place for thieves!"

¹⁴Blind and lame people came to him in the temple courtyard, and he healed them.

¹⁵When the chief priests and the scribes saw the amazing miracles he performed and the children shouting in the temple courtyard, "Hosanna to the Son of David!" they were irritated. ¹⁶They said to him, "Do you hear what these children are saying?"

Jesus replied, "Yes, I do. Have you never read, 'From the mouths of little children and infants, you have created praise'?"

¹⁷He left them and went out of the city to Bethany and spent the night there.

Jesus Curses the Fig Tree—
Mark 11:12-14, 20-25

¹⁸In the morning, as Jesus returned to the city, he became hungry. ¹⁹When he saw a fig tree by the road, he went up to the tree and found nothing on it but leaves. He said to the tree, "May fruit never grow on you again!" At once the fig tree dried up.

²⁰The disciples were surprised to see this. They asked, "How did the fig tree dry up so quickly?"

²¹Jesus answered them, "I can guarantee this truth: If you have faith and do not doubt, you will be able to do what I did to the fig tree. You could also say to this

mountain, 'Be uprooted and thrown into the sea,' and it will happen. ²²Have faith that you will receive whatever you ask for in prayer."

Jesus' Authority Challenged—
Mark 11:27-33; Luke 20:1-8

²³Then Jesus went into the temple courtyard and began to teach. The chief priests and the leaders of the people came to him. They asked, "What gives you the right to do these things? Who told you that you could do this?"

²⁴Jesus answered them, "I, too, have a question for you. If you answer it for me, I'll tell you why I have the right to do these things. ²⁵Did John's right to baptize come from heaven or from humans?"

They discussed this among themselves. They said, "If we say, 'from heaven,' he will ask us, 'Then why didn't you believe him?' ²⁶But if we say, 'from humans,' we're afraid of what the crowd might do. All those people think of John as a prophet." ²⁷So they answered Jesus, "We don't know."

Jesus told them, "Then I won't tell you why I have the right to do these things.

A Story About Two Sons

²⁸"What do you think about this? A man had two sons. He went to the first and said, 'Son, go to work in the vineyard today.'

²⁹"His son replied, 'I don't want to!' But later he changed his mind and went.

³⁰"The father went to the other son and told him the same thing. He replied, 'I will, sir,' but he didn't go.

³¹"Which of the two sons did what the father wanted?"

"The first," they answered.

Jesus said to them, "I can guarantee this truth: Tax collectors and prostitutes are going into the kingdom of God ahead of you. ³²John came to you and showed you the way that God wants you to live, but you didn't believe him. The tax collectors and prostitutes believed him. But even after you had seen that, you didn't change your minds and believe him.

A Story About a Vineyard—
Mark 12:1-12; Luke 20:9-19

³³"Listen to another illustration. A landowner planted a vineyard. He put a wall around it, made a winepress, and built a watchtower. Then he leased it to vineyard workers and went on a trip.

³⁴"When the grapes were getting ripe, he sent his servants to the workers to collect his share of the produce. ³⁵The workers took his servants and beat one, killed another, and stoned a third to death. ³⁶So the landowner sent more servants. But the workers treated them the same way.

³⁷"Finally, he sent his son to them. He thought, 'They will respect my son.'

³⁸"When the workers saw his son, they said to one another, 'This is the heir. Let's kill him and get his inheritance.' ³⁹So they grabbed him, threw him out of the vineyard, and killed him.

⁴⁰"Now, when the owner of the vineyard comes, what will he do to those workers?"

⁴¹They answered, "He will destroy those evil people. Then he will lease the vineyard to other workers who will give him his share of the produce when it is ready."

⁴²Jesus asked them, "Have you never read in the Scriptures:

'The stone that the builders rejected
has become the cornerstone.
The Lord is responsible for this,
and it is amazing for us to see'?

⁴³That is why I can guarantee that the kingdom of God will be taken away from you and given to a people who will produce what God wants. ⁴⁴Anyone who falls on this stone will be broken. If the stone falls on anyone, it will crush that person."ᵃ

⁴⁵When the chief priests and the Pharisees heard his illustrations, they knew that he was talking about them. ⁴⁶They wanted to arrest him but were afraid of the crowds, who thought he was a prophet.

A Story About a Wedding Reception

22 ¹Again Jesus used stories as illustrations when he spoke to them. He said, ²"The kingdom of heaven is like a king who planned a wedding for his son. ³He sent his servants to those who had been invited to the wedding, but they refused to come. ⁴He sent other servants to tell the people who had been invited, 'I've prepared dinner. My bulls and fattened calves have been butchered. Everything is ready. Come to the wedding!'

⁵"But they paid no attention and went away. Some went to work in their own fields, and others went to their businesses. ⁶The rest grabbed the king's servants, mistreated them, and then killed them.

⁷"The king became angry. He sent his soldiers, killed those murderers, and burned their city.

⁸"Then the king said to his servants, 'The wedding is ready, but those who were invited don't deserve the honor. ⁹Go where the roads leave the city. Invite everyone you find to the wedding.' ¹⁰The servants went into the streets and brought in all the good people and all the evil people they found. And the wedding hall was filled with guests.

¹¹"When the king came to see the guests, he saw a person who was not dressed in the wedding clothes ⌊provided for the guests⌋. ¹²He said to him, 'Friend, how did you get in here without proper wedding clothes?'

"The man had nothing to say. ¹³Then the king told his servants, 'Tie his hands and feet, and throw him outside into the darkness. People will cry and be in extreme pain there.'

¹⁴"Therefore, many are invited, but few of those are chosen to stay."

A Question About Taxes—
Mark 12:13-17; Luke 20:20-26

¹⁵Then the Pharisees went away and planned to trap Jesus into saying the wrong thing. ¹⁶They sent their disciples to him along with Herod's followers. They said to him, "Teacher, we know that you tell the truth and that you teach the truth about the way of God. You don't favor individuals because of who they are. ¹⁷So tell us what you think. Is it right to pay taxes to the emperor or not?"

¹⁸Jesus recognized their evil plan, so he asked, "Why do you test me, you hypocrites? ¹⁹Show me a coin used to pay taxes."

They brought him a coin. ²⁰He said to them, "Whose face and name is this?"

²¹They replied, "The emperor's."

ᵃ21:44 Some manuscripts and translations omit this verse.

Then he said to them, "Very well, give the emperor what belongs to the emperor, and give God what belongs to God."

²²They were surprised to hear this. Then they left him alone and went away.

The Dead Come Back to Life—
Mark 12:18-27; Luke 20:27-40

²³On that day some Sadducees, who say that people will never come back to life, came to Jesus. They asked him, ²⁴"Teacher, Moses said, 'If a man dies childless, his brother should marry his widow and have children for his brother.' ²⁵There were seven brothers among us. The first married and died. Since he had no children, he left his widow to his brother. ²⁶The second brother also died, as well as the third, and the rest of the seven brothers. ²⁷At last the woman died. ²⁸Now, when the dead come back to life, whose wife will she be? All seven brothers had been married to her."

²⁹Jesus answered, "You're mistaken because you don't know the Scriptures or God's power. ³⁰When people come back to life, they don't marry. Rather, they are like the angels in heaven. ³¹Haven't you read what God told you about the dead coming back to life? He said, ³²'I am the God of Abraham, Isaac, and Jacob.' He's not the God of the dead but of the living."

³³He amazed the crowds who heard his teaching.

Love God and Your Neighbor—
Mark 12:28-34

³⁴When the Pharisees heard that Jesus had silenced the Sadducees, they gathered together. ³⁵One of them, an expert in Moses' Teachings, tested Jesus by asking, ³⁶"Teacher, which commandment is the greatest in Moses' Teachings?"

³⁷Jesus answered him, " 'Love the Lord your God with all your heart, with all your soul, and with all your mind.' ³⁸This is the greatest and most important commandment. ³⁹The second is like it: 'Love your neighbor as you love yourself.' ⁴⁰All of Moses' Teachings and the Prophets depend on these two commandments."

How Can David's Son Be David's Lord?—
Mark 12:35-37a; Luke 20:41-44

⁴¹While the Pharisees were still gathered, Jesus asked them, ⁴²"What do you think about the Messiah? Whose son is he?"

They answered him, "David's."

Good Morning, God
Matthew 22:41-46

The Pharisees couldn't understand how Jesus could be both a descendant of David and God's own Son. So they accused Jesus of being a fraud. Many people doubt the Bible because they don't understand it. That's where faith comes in. We have to believe what God says, even when we don't understand. How can you show people your faith in the Bible?

Dear Lord, help me to trust your word, even when I don't understand it.

⁴³He said to them, "Then how can David, guided by the Spirit, call him Lord? David says,

⁴⁴ 'The Lord said to my Lord,
    "Take the highest position in heaven
        until I put your enemies under your control." '

⁴⁵If David calls him Lord, how can he be his son?"

⁴⁶No one could answer him, and from that time on no one dared to ask him another question.

Jesus Disapproves of the Example Set By Scribes and Pharisees—
Mark 12:37b-40; Luke 20:45-47

¹Then Jesus said to the crowds and to his disciples, ²"The scribes and the Pharisees teach with Moses' authority. ³So be careful to do everything they tell you. But don't follow their example, because they don't practice what they preach. ⁴They make loads that are hard to carry and lay them on the shoulders of the people. However, they are not willing to lift a finger to move them.

⁵"They do everything to attract people's attention. They make their headbands large and the tassels on their shawls long. ⁶They love the place of honor at dinners and the front seats in synagogues. ⁷They love to be greeted in the marketplaces and to have people call them Rabbi. ⁸But don't make others call you Rabbi, because you have only one teacher, and you are all followers. ⁹And don't call anyone on earth your father, because you have only one Father, and he is in heaven. ¹⁰Don't make others call you a leader, because you have only one leader, the Messiah. ¹¹The person who is greatest among you will be your servant. ¹²Whoever honors himself will be humbled, and whoever humbles himself will be honored.

The Hypocrisy of the Scribes and Pharisees

¹³"How horrible it will be for you, scribes and Pharisees! You hypocrites! You lock people out of the kingdom of heaven. You don't enter it yourselves, and you don't permit others to enter when they try.ª

¹⁵"How horrible it will be for you, scribes and Pharisees! You hypocrites! You cross land and sea to recruit a single follower, and when you do, you make that person twice as fit for hell as you are.

¹⁶"How horrible it will be for you, you blind guides! You say, 'To swear an oath by the temple doesn't mean a thing. But to swear an oath by the gold in the temple means a person must keep his oath.' ¹⁷You blind fools! What is more important, the gold or the temple that made the gold holy? ¹⁸Again you say, 'To swear an oath by the altar doesn't mean a thing. But to swear an oath by the gift on the altar means a person must keep his oath.' ¹⁹You blind men! What is more important, the gift or the altar that makes the gift holy? ²⁰To swear an oath by the altar is to swear by it and by everything on it. ²¹To swear an oath by the temple is to swear by it and by the one who lives there. ²²And to swear an oath by heaven is to swear by God's throne and the one who sits on it.

²³"How horrible it will be for you, scribes and Pharisees! You hypocrites! You give God one-tenth of your mint, dill, and cumin. But you have neglected justice, mercy,

---

ª23:13 Some manuscripts and translations add verse 14: "How horrible it will be for you, scribes and Pharisees! You hypocrites! You rob widows by taking their houses and then say long prayers to make yourselves look good. You will receive a most severe punishment." (See Mark 12:40 and Luke 20:47.)

and faithfulness. These are the most important things in Moses' Teachings. You should have done these things without neglecting the others. [24]You blind guides! You strain gnats out of your wine, but you swallow camels.

[25]"How horrible it will be for you, scribes and Pharisees! You hypocrites! You clean the outside of cups and dishes. But inside they are full of greed and uncontrolled desires. [26]You blind Pharisees! First clean the inside of the cups and dishes so that the outside may also be clean.

[27]"How horrible it will be for you, scribes and Pharisees! You hypocrites! You are like whitewashed graves that look beautiful on the outside but inside are full of dead people's bones and every kind of impurity. [28]So on the outside you look as though you have God's approval, but inside you are full of hypocrisy and lawlessness.

[29]"How horrible it will be for you, scribes and Pharisees! You hypocrites! You build tombs for the prophets and decorate the monuments of those who had God's approval. [30]Then you say, 'If we had lived at the time of our ancestors, we would not have helped to murder the prophets.' [31]So you testify against yourselves that you are the descendants of those who murdered the prophets. [32]Go ahead, finish what your ancestors started!

[33]"You snakes! You poisonous snakes! How can you escape being condemned to hell? [34]I'm sending you prophets, wise men, and teachers of the Scriptures. You will kill and crucify some of them. Others you will whip in your synagogues and persecute from city to city. [35]As a result, you will be held accountable for all the innocent blood of those murdered on earth, from the murder of righteous Abel to that of Zechariah, son of Barachiah, whom you murdered between the temple and the altar. [36]I can guarantee this truth: The people living now will be held accountable for all these things.

[37]"Jerusalem, Jerusalem, you kill the prophets and stone to death those sent to you! How often I wanted to gather your children together the way a hen gathers her chicks under her wings! But you were not willing! [38]Your house will be abandoned, deserted. [39]I can guarantee that you will not see me again until you say, 'Blessed is the one who comes in the name of the Lord!' "

Jesus Teaches His Disciples on the Mount of Olives—
Mark 13:1-31; Luke 21:5-33

24 [1]As Jesus left the temple courtyard and was walking away, his disciples came to him. They proudly pointed out to him the temple buildings. [2]Jesus said to them, "You see all these buildings, don't you? I can guarantee this truth: Not one of these stones will be left on top of another. Each one will be torn down."

[3]As Jesus was sitting on the Mount of Olives, his disciples came to him privately and said, "Tell us, when will this happen? What will be the sign that you are coming again, and when will the world come to an end?"

[4]Jesus answered them, "Be careful not to let anyone deceive you. [5]Many will come using my name. They will say, 'I am the Messiah,' and they will deceive many people.

[6]"You will hear of wars and rumors of wars. Don't be alarmed! These things must happen, but they don't mean that the end has come. [7]Nation will fight against nation and kingdom against kingdom. There will be famines and earthquakes in various places. [8]All of these are only the beginning pains of the end.

[9]"Then they will hand you over to those who will torture and kill you. All nations will hate you because you are committed to me. [10]Then many will lose faith. They will betray and hate each other. [11]Many false prophets will appear and deceive many people. [12]And because there will be more and more lawlessness, most people's love will grow cold. [13]But the person who endures to the end will be saved.

Millstones / *Matthew 24:41*

Millstones were used to grind grain into flour. Women moved one rounded stone back and forth on top of a heavier, anchored stone to grind different types of grain into a coarse flour. Usually each home had its own set of millstones. Grinding grain was a daily task for women throughout Bible times.

¹⁴"This Good News about the kingdom will be spread throughout the world as a testimony to all nations. Then the end will come.

¹⁵"The prophet Daniel said that the disgusting thing that will cause destruction will stand in the holy place. When you see this (let the reader take note), ¹⁶those of you in Judea should flee to the mountains. ¹⁷Those who are on the roof should not come down to get anything out of their houses. ¹⁸Those who are in the field should not turn back to get their coats.

¹⁹"How horrible it will be for the women who are pregnant or who are nursing babies in those days. ²⁰Pray that it will not be winter or a day of worship when you flee. ²¹There will be a lot of misery at that time, a kind of misery that has not happened from the beginning of the world until now and will certainly never happen again. ²²If God does not reduce the number of those days, no one will be saved. But those days will be reduced because of those whom God has chosen.

²³"At that time don't believe anyone who tells you, 'Here is the Messiah!' or 'There he is!' ²⁴False messiahs and false prophets will appear. They will work spectacular, miraculous signs and do wonderful things to deceive, if possible, even those whom God has chosen. ²⁵Listen! I've told you this before it happens. ²⁶So if someone tells you, 'He's in the desert!' don't go out looking for him . And don't believe anyone who says, 'He's in a secret place!' ²⁷The Son of Man will come again just as lightning flashes from east to west. ²⁸Vultures will gather wherever there is a dead body.

²⁹"Immediately after the misery of those days, the sun will turn dark, the moon will not give light, the stars will fall from the sky, and the powers of the universe will be shaken.

³⁰"Then the sign of the Son of Man will appear in the sky. All the people on earth will cry in agony when they see the Son of Man coming on the clouds in the sky with power and great glory. ³¹He will send out his angels with a loud trumpet call, and from every direction under the sky, they will gather those whom God has chosen.

³²"Learn from the story of the fig tree. When its branch becomes tender and it sprouts leaves, you know that summer is near. ³³In the same way, when you see all these things, you know that he is near, at the door.

³⁴"I can guarantee this truth: This generation will not disappear until all these

things take place. ³⁵The earth and the heavens will disappear, but my words will never disappear.

No One Knows When the Son of Man Will Return

³⁶"No one knows when that day or hour will come. Even the angels in heaven and the Son don't know. Only the Father knows.

³⁷"When the Son of Man comes again, it will be exactly like the days of Noah. ³⁸In the days before the flood, people were eating, drinking, and getting married until the day that Noah went into the ship. ³⁹They were not aware of what was happening until the flood came and swept all of them away. That is how it will be when the Son of Man comes again.

⁴⁰"At that time two men will be working in the field. One will be taken, and the other one will be left. ⁴¹Two women will be working at a mill. One will be taken, and the other one will be left.

⁴²"Therefore, be alert, because you don't know on what day your Lord will return. ⁴³You realize that if a homeowner had known at what time of the night a thief was coming, he would have stayed awake. He would not have let the thief break into his house. ⁴⁴Therefore, you, too, must be ready because the Son of Man will return when you least expect him.

⁴⁵"Who, then, is the faithful and wise servant? The master will put that person in charge of giving the other servants their food at the right time. ⁴⁶That servant will be blessed if his master finds him doing this job when he comes. ⁴⁷I can guarantee this truth: He will put that servant in charge of all his property. ⁴⁸On the other hand, that servant, if he is wicked, may think that it will be a long time before his master comes. ⁴⁹The servant may begin to beat the other servants and eat and drink with the drunks. ⁵⁰His master will return unexpectedly. ⁵¹Then his master will severely punish him and assign him a place with the hypocrites. People will cry and be in extreme pain there.

A Story About Ten Bridesmaids

¹"When the end comes, the kingdom of heaven will be like ten bridesmaids. They took their oil lamps and went to meet the groom. ²Five of them were foolish, and five were wise. ³The foolish bridesmaids took their lamps, but they didn't take any extra oil. ⁴The wise bridesmaids, however, took along extra oil for their lamps. ⁵Since the groom was late, all the bridesmaids became drowsy and fell asleep.

⁶"At midnight someone shouted, 'The groom is here! Come to meet him!' ⁷Then all the bridesmaids woke up and got their lamps ready.

⁸"The foolish ones said to the wise ones, 'Give us some of your oil. Our lamps are going out.'

⁹"But the wise bridesmaids replied, 'We can't do that. There won't be enough for both of us. Go! Find someone to sell you some oil.'

¹⁰"While they were buying oil, the groom arrived. The bridesmaids who were ready went with him into the wedding hall, and the door was shut.

¹¹"Later the other bridesmaids arrived and said, 'Sir, sir, open the door for us!'

¹²"But he answered them, 'I don't even know who you are!'

¹³"So stay awake, because you don't know the day or the hour.

A Story About Three Servants

¹⁴"The kingdom of heaven is like a man going on a trip. He called his servants and entrusted some money to them. ¹⁵He gave one man ten thousand dollars, another

four thousand dollars, and another two thousand dollars. Each was given money based on his ability. Then the man went on his trip.

[16]"The one who received ten thousand dollars invested the money at once and doubled his money. [17]The one who had four thousand dollars did the same and also doubled his money. [18]But the one who received two thousand dollars went off, dug a hole in the ground, and hid his master's money.

[19]"After a long time the master of those servants returned and settled accounts with them. [20]The one who received ten thousand dollars brought the additional ten thousand. He said, 'Sir, you gave me ten thousand dollars. I've doubled the amount.'

[21]"His master replied, 'Good job! You're a good and faithful servant! You proved that you could be trusted with a small amount. I will put you in charge of a large amount. Come and share your master's happiness.'

[22]"The one who received four thousand dollars came and said, 'Sir, you gave me four thousand dollars. I've doubled the amount.'

[23]"His master replied, 'Good job! You're a good and faithful servant! You proved that you could be trusted with a small amount. I will put you in charge of a large amount. Come and share your master's happiness.'

[24]"Then the one who received two thousand dollars came and said, 'Sir, I knew that you are a hard person to please. You harvest where you haven't planted and gather where you haven't scattered any seeds. [25]I was afraid. So I hid your two thousand dollars in the ground. Here's your money!'

[26]"His master responded, 'You evil and lazy servant! If you knew that I harvest where I haven't planted and gather where I haven't scattered, [27]then you should have invested my money with the bankers. When I returned, I would have received my money back with interest. [28]Take the two thousand dollars away from him! Give it to the one who has the ten thousand! [29]To all who have, more will be given, and they will have more than enough. But everything will be taken away from those who don't have much. [30]Throw this useless servant outside into the darkness. People will cry and be in extreme pain there.'

Use Your Gifts
Matthew 25:14-23

When you exercise your muscles regularly, they get stronger. It's the same with being friendly and courteous or doing good. The more you practice, the better you get. When you practice using the gifts God gives you, God will praise you. And he'll give you more and better gifts.

Jesus Will Judge the World

[31]"When the Son of Man comes in his glory and all his angels are with him, he will sit on his glorious throne. [32]The people of every nation will be gathered in front of him. He will separate them as a shepherd separates the sheep from the goats. [33]He will put the sheep on his right but the goats on his left.

³⁴"Then the king will say to those on his right, 'Come, my Father has blessed you! Inherit the kingdom prepared for you from the creation of the world. ³⁵I was hungry, and you gave me something to eat. I was thirsty, and you gave me something to drink. I was a stranger, and you took me into your home. ³⁶I needed clothes, and you gave me something to wear. I was sick, and you took care of me. I was in prison, and you visited me.'

³⁷"Then the people who have God's approval will reply to him, 'Lord, when did we see you hungry and feed you or see you thirsty and give you something to drink? ³⁸When did we see you as a stranger and take you into our homes or see you in need of clothes and give you something to wear? ³⁹When did we see you sick or in prison and visit you?'

⁴⁰"The king will answer them, 'I can guarantee this truth: Whatever you did for one of my brothers or sisters, no matter how unimportant ˌthey seemedˌ, you did for me.'

⁴¹"Then the king will say to those on his left, 'Get away from me! God has cursed you! Go into everlasting fire that was prepared for the devil and his angels! ⁴²I was hungry, and you gave me nothing to eat. I was thirsty, and you gave me nothing to drink. ⁴³I was a stranger, and you didn't take me into your homes. I needed clothes, and you didn't give me anything to wear. I was sick and in prison, and you didn't take care of me.'

⁴⁴"They, too, will ask, 'Lord, when did we see you hungry or thirsty or as a stranger or in need of clothes or sick or in prison and didn't help you?'

⁴⁵"He will answer them, 'I can guarantee this truth: Whatever you failed to do for one of my brothers or sisters, no matter how unimportant ˌthey seemedˌ, you failed to do for me.'

⁴⁶"These people will go away into eternal punishment, but those with God's approval will go into eternal life."

The Plot to Kill Jesus—
Mark 14:1-2; Luke 22:1-6; John 11:45-57

26 ¹When Jesus finished saying all these things, he told his disciples, ²"You know that the Passover will take place in two days. At that time the Son of Man will be handed over to be crucified."

³Then the chief priests and the leaders of the people gathered in the palace of the chief priest Caiaphas. ⁴They made plans to arrest Jesus in an underhanded way and to kill him. ⁵But they said, "We shouldn't arrest him during the festival, or else there may be a riot among the people."

A Woman Prepares Jesus' Body for the Tomb—
Mark 14:3-9; John 12:1-8

⁶Jesus was in Bethany in the home of Simon, a man who had suffered from a skin disease. ⁷While Jesus was sitting there, a woman went to him with a bottle of very expensive perfume and poured it on his head.

⁸The disciples were irritated when they saw this. They asked, "Why did she waste it like this? ⁹It could have been sold for a high price, and the money could have been given to the poor."

¹⁰Since Jesus knew what was going on, he said to them, "Why are you bothering this woman? She has done a beautiful thing for me. ¹¹You will always have the poor with you, but you will not always have me with you. ¹²She poured this perfume on my body before it is placed in a tomb. ¹³I can guarantee this truth: Wherever this Good News is spoken in the world, what she has done will also be told in memory of her."

Judas Plans to Betray Jesus—
Mark 14:10-11; Luke 22:3-6

¹⁴Then one of the twelve apostles, the one named Judas Iscariot, went to the chief priests. ¹⁵He asked, "What will you pay me if I hand him over to you?"

They offered him 30 silver coins. ¹⁶From then on, he looked for a chance to betray Jesus.

Preparations for the Passover—
Mark 14:12-17; Luke 22:7-17

¹⁷On the first day of the Festival of Unleavened Bread, the disciples went to Jesus. They asked, "Where do you want us to prepare the Passover meal for you?"

¹⁸He said, "Go to a certain man in the city, and tell him that the teacher says, 'My time is near. I will celebrate the Passover with my disciples at your house.' "

¹⁹The disciples did as Jesus had directed them and prepared the Passover.

²⁰When evening came, Jesus was at the table with the twelve apostles.

Jesus Knows Who Will Betray Him—
Mark 14:18-2ı; Luke 22:21-23; John 13:21-30

²¹While they were eating, he said, "I can guarantee this truth: One of you is going to betray me."

²²Feeling deeply hurt, they asked him one by one, "You don't mean me, do you, Lord?"

²³Jesus answered, "Someone who has dipped his hand into the bowl with me will betray me. ²⁴The Son of Man is going to die as the Scriptures say he will. But how horrible it will be for that person who betrays the Son of Man. It would have been better for that person if he had never been born."

²⁵Then Judas, who betrayed him, asked, "You don't mean me, do you, Rabbi?"

"Yes, I do," Jesus replied.

The Lord's Supper—
Mark 14:22-26; Luke 22:19-20

²⁶While they were eating, Jesus took bread and blessed it. He broke the bread, gave it to his disciples, and said, "Take this, and eat it. This is my body."

²⁷Then he took a cup and spoke a prayer of thanksgiving. He gave it to them and

Good Morning, God
Matthew 26:7-13

Some of the disciples were angry when a woman poured expensive perfume on Jesus' head. They thought, *What a waste!* But Jesus knew the woman had given him a special gift of love, and he graciously accepted her gift. When someone gives you a gift, it means that person cares about you.

You show others you care about them, too, when you kindly accept their gifts. What's the best gift anyone ever gave to you? What's the best gift you ever gave to someone?

Lord, help me to be a generous giver and a gracious receiver.

said, "Drink from it, all of you. ²⁸This is my blood, the blood of the promise.ᵃ It is poured out for many people so that sins are forgiven.

²⁹"I can guarantee that I won't drink this wine again until that day when I drink new wine with you in my Father's kingdom."

³⁰After they sang a hymn, they went to the Mount of Olives.

Jesus Predicts Peter's Denial—
Mark 14:27-31; Luke 22:31-34; John 13:36-38

³¹Then Jesus said to them, "All of you will abandon me tonight. Scripture says,

'I will strike the shepherd,
and the sheep in the flock will be scattered.'

³²"But after I am brought back to life, I will go to Galilee ahead of you."

³³Peter said to him, "Even if everyone else abandons you, I never will."

³⁴Jesus replied to Peter, "I can guarantee this truth: Before a rooster crows tonight, you will say three times that you don't know me."

³⁵Peter told him, "Even if I have to die with you, I'll never say that I don't know you!" All the other disciples said the same thing.

Jesus Prays in the Garden of Gethsemane—
Mark 14:32-42; Luke 22:39-46

³⁶Then Jesus went with the disciples to a place called Gethsemane. He said to them, "Stay here while I go over there and pray."

³⁷He took Peter and Zebedee's two sons with him. He was beginning to feel deep anguish. ³⁸Then he said to them, "My anguish is so great that I feel as if I'm dying. Wait here, and stay awake with me."

³⁹After walking a little farther, he quickly bowed with his face to the ground and prayed, "Father, if it's possible, let this cup of suffering be taken away from me. But let your will be done rather than mine."

⁴⁰When he went back to the disciples, he found them asleep. He said to Peter, "Couldn't you stay awake with me for one hour? ⁴¹Stay awake, and pray that you won't be tempted. You want to do what's right, but you're weak."

⁴²Then he went away a second time and prayed, "Father, if this cup cannot be taken away unless I drink it, let your will be done."

⁴³He found them asleep again because they couldn't keep their eyes open.

⁴⁴After leaving them again, he went away and prayed the same prayer a third time. ⁴⁵Then he came back to the disciples and said to them, "You might as well sleep now. The time is near for the Son of Man to be handed over to sinners. ⁴⁶Get up! Let's go! The one who is betraying me is near."

Jesus Is Arrested—
Mark 14:43-52; Luke 22:47-54a; John 18:1-14

⁴⁷Just then, while Jesus was still speaking, Judas, one of the twelve apostles, arrived. A large crowd carrying swords and clubs was with him. They were from the chief priests and leaders of the people. ⁴⁸Now, the traitor had given them a signal. He said, "The one I kiss is the man you want. Arrest him!"

⁴⁹Then Judas quickly stepped up to Jesus and said, "Hello, Rabbi!" and kissed him. ⁵⁰Jesus said to him, "Friend, why are you here?"

ᵃ26:28 Or "testament," or "covenant."

Then some men came forward, took hold of Jesus, and arrested him. ⁵¹Suddenly, one of the men with Jesus pulled out his sword and cut off the ear of the chief priest's servant. ⁵²Then Jesus said to him, "Put your sword away! All who use a sword will be killed by a sword. ⁵³Don't you think that I could call on my Father to send more than twelve legions of angels to help me now? ⁵⁴How, then, are the Scriptures to be fulfilled that say this must happen?"

⁵⁵At that time Jesus said to the crowd, "Have you come out with swords and clubs to arrest me as if I were a criminal? I used to sit teaching in the temple courtyard every day. But you didn't arrest me then. ⁵⁶All of this has happened so that what the prophets have written would come true."

Then all the disciples abandoned him and ran away.

The Trial in Front of the Jewish Council—
Mark 14:53-65; Luke 22:63-71

⁵⁷Those who had arrested Jesus took him to Caiaphas, the chief priest, where the scribes and the leaders had gathered together. ⁵⁸Peter followed at a distance until he came to the chief priest's courtyard. He went inside and sat with the guards to see how this would turn out.

⁵⁹The chief priests and the whole council were searching for false testimony to use against Jesus in order to execute him. ⁶⁰But they did not find any, although many came forward with false testimony. At last two men came forward. ⁶¹They stated, "This man said, 'I can tear down God's temple and rebuild it in three days.' "

⁶²The chief priest stood up and said to Jesus, "Don't you have any answer to what these men testify against you?"

⁶³But Jesus was silent.

Then the chief priest said to him, "Swear an oath in front of the living God and tell us, are you the Messiah, the Son of God?"

⁶⁴Jesus answered him, "Yes, I am. But I can guarantee that from now on you will see the Son of Man in the highest position in heaven. He will be coming on the clouds of heaven."

⁶⁵Then the chief priest tore his robes in horror and said, "He has dishonored God! Why do we need any more witnesses? You've just heard him dishonor God! ⁶⁶What's your verdict?"

They answered, "He deserves the death penalty!"

⁶⁷Then they spit in his face, hit him with their fists, and some of them slapped him. ⁶⁸They said, "You Christ, if you're a prophet, tell us who hit you."

Peter Denies Jesus—
Mark 14:66-72; Luke 22:54b-62; John 18:15-18, 25-27

⁶⁹Peter was sitting in the courtyard. A female servant came to him and said, "You, too, were with Jesus the Galilean."

⁷⁰But Peter denied it in front of them all by saying, "I don't know what you're talking about."

⁷¹As he went to the entrance, another female servant saw him. She told those who were there, "This man was with Jesus from Nazareth."

⁷²Again Peter denied it and swore with an oath, "I don't know the man!"

⁷³After a little while the men standing there approached Peter and said, "It's obvious you're also one of them. Your accent gives you away!"

⁷⁴Then Peter began to curse and swear with an oath, "I don't know the man!" Just then a rooster crowed. ⁷⁵Peter remembered what Jesus had said: "Before a rooster

crows, you will say three times that you don't know me." Then Peter went outside and cried bitterly.

The Death of Judas

¹Early in the morning all the chief priests and the leaders of the people decided to execute Jesus. ²They tied him up, led him away, and handed him over to Pilate, the governor.

³Then Judas, who had betrayed Jesus, regretted what had happened when he saw that Jesus was condemned. He brought the 30 silver coins back to the chief priests and leaders. ⁴He said, "I've sinned by betraying an innocent man."

They replied, "What do we care? That's your problem."

⁵So he threw the money into the temple, went away, and hanged himself.

⁶The chief priests took the money and said, "It's not right to put it into the temple treasury, because it's blood money." ⁷So they decided to use it to buy a potter's field for the burial of strangers. ⁸That's why that field has been called the Field of Blood ever since. ⁹Then what the prophet Jeremiah had said came true, "They took the 30 silver coins, the price the people of Israel had placed on him, ¹⁰and used the coins to buy a potter's field, as the Lord had directed me."

Pilate Questions Jesus—
Mark 15:1-5; Luke 23:1-4; John 18:28-38

¹¹Jesus stood in front of the governor, Pilate. The governor asked him, "Are you the king of the Jews?"

"Yes, I am," Jesus answered.

¹²While the chief priests and leaders were accusing him, he said nothing. ¹³Then Pilate asked him, "Don't you hear how many charges they're bringing against you?"

¹⁴But Jesus said absolutely nothing to him in reply, so the governor was very surprised.

The Crowd Rejects Jesus—
Mark 15:6-15; Luke 23:18-25; John 18:39, 40

¹⁵At every Passover festival the governor would free one prisoner whom the crowd wanted. ¹⁶At that time there was a well-known prisoner by the name of Barabbas. ¹⁷So when the people gathered, Pilate asked them, "Which man do you want me to free for you? Do you want me to free Barabbas or Jesus, who is called Christ?" ¹⁸Pilate knew that they had handed Jesus over to him because they were jealous.

¹⁹While Pilate was judging the case, his wife sent him a message. It said, "Leave that innocent man alone. I've been very upset today because of a dream I had about him."

²⁰But the chief priests and leaders persuaded the crowd to ask for the release of Barabbas and the execution of Jesus.

²¹The governor asked them, "Which of the two do you want me to free for you?"

They said, "Barabbas."

²²Pilate asked them, "Then what should I do with Jesus, who is called Christ?"

"He should be crucified!" they all said.

²³Pilate asked, "Why? What has he done wrong?"

But they began to shout loudly, "He should be crucified!"

²⁴Pilate saw that he was not getting anywhere. Instead, a riot was breaking out. So Pilate took some water and washed his hands in front of the crowd. He said, "I won't be guilty of killing this man. Do what you want!"

[25]All the people answered, "The responsibility for killing him will rest on us and our children."

[26]Then Pilate freed Barabbas for the people. But he had Jesus whipped and handed over to be crucified.

The Soldiers Make Fun of Jesus—
Mark 15:16-19; John 19:1-3

[27]Then the governor's soldiers took Jesus into the palace and gathered the whole troop around him. [28]They took off his clothes and put a bright red cape on him. [29]They twisted some thorns into a crown, placed it on his head, and put a stick in his right hand. They knelt in front of him and made fun of him by saying, "Long live the king of the Jews!" [30]After they had spit on him, they took the stick and kept hitting him on the head with it.

The Crucifixion—
Mark 15:20-32; Luke 23:33-38; John 19:16b-24

[31]After the soldiers finished making fun of Jesus, they took off the cape and put his own clothes back on him. Then they led him away to crucify him.

[32]On the way they found a man named Simon. He was from the city of Cyrene. The soldiers forced him to carry Jesus' cross.

[33]They came to a place called Golgotha (which means "the place of the skull"). [34]They gave him a drink of wine mixed with a drug called gall. When he tasted it, he refused to drink it. [35]After they had crucified him, they divided his clothes among themselves by throwing dice. [36]Then they sat there and kept watch over him. [37]They placed a written accusation above his head. It read, "This is Jesus, the king of the Jews."

[38]At that time they crucified two criminals with him, one on his right and the other on his left.

[39]Those who passed by insulted him. They shook their heads [40]and said, "You were going to tear down God's temple and build it again in three days. Save yourself! If you're the Son of God, come down from the cross." [41]The chief priests together with the scribes and the leaders made fun of him in the same way. They said, [42]"He saved others, but he can't save himself. So he's Israel's king! Let him come down from the cross now, and we'll believe him. [43]He trusted God. Let God rescue him now if he wants. After all, this man said, 'I am the Son of God.' " [44]Even the criminals crucified with him were insulting him the same way.

Jesus Dies on the Cross—
Mark 15:33-41; Luke 23:44-49; John 19:28-30

[45]At noon darkness came over the whole land until three in the afternoon. [46]About three o'clock Jesus cried out in a loud voice, "Eli, Eli, lema sabachthani?" which means, "My God, my God, why have you abandoned me?" [47]When some of the people standing there heard him say that, they said, "He's calling Elijah." [48]One of the men ran at once, took a sponge, and soaked it in some vinegar. Then he put it on a stick and offered Jesus a drink. [49]The others said, "Leave him alone! Let's see if Elijah comes to save him."

[50]Then Jesus loudly cried out once again and gave up his life.

[51]Suddenly, the curtain in the temple was split in two from top to bottom. The earth shook, and the rocks were split open. [52]The tombs were opened, and the bodies of many holy people who had died came back to life. [53]They came out of the tombs after

he had come back to life, and they went into the holy city where they appeared to many people.

[54]An army officer and those watching Jesus with him saw the earthquake and the other things happening. They were terrified and said, "Certainly, this was the Son of God!"

[55]Many women were there watching from a distance. They had followed Jesus from Galilee and had always supported him. [56]Among them were Mary from Magdala, Mary (the mother of James and Joseph), and the mother of Zebedee's sons.

Jesus Is Buried—
Mark 15:42-47; Luke 23:50-56; John 19:38-42

[57]In the evening a rich man named Joseph arrived. He was from the city of Arimathea and had become a disciple of Jesus. [58]He went to Pilate and asked for the body of Jesus. Pilate ordered that it be given to him.

[59]Joseph took the body and wrapped it in a clean linen cloth. [60]Then he laid it in his own new tomb, which had been cut in a rock. After rolling a large stone against the door of the tomb, he went away. [61]Mary from Magdala and the other Mary were sitting there, facing the tomb.

The Chief Priests and Pharisees Secure Jesus' Tomb

[62]The next day, which was the day of worship, the chief priests and Pharisees gathered together and went to Pilate. [63]They said, "Sir, we remember how that deceiver said while he was still alive, 'After three days I will be brought back to life.' [64]Therefore, give the order to make the tomb secure until the third day. Otherwise, his disciples may steal him and say to the people, 'He has been brought back to life.' Then the last deception will be worse than the first."

[65]Pilate told them, "You have the soldiers you want for guard duty. Go and make the tomb as secure as you know how."

[66]So they went to secure the tomb. They placed a seal on the stone and posted the soldiers on guard duty.

Jesus Comes Back to Life—
Mark 16:1-8; Luke 24:1-12; John 20:1-10

28 [1]After the day of worship, as the sun rose Sunday morning, Mary from Magdala and the other Mary went to look at the tomb.

Good Morning, God
Matthew 27:51-54

When Jesus was dying on the cross, the sky became black for three hours. The earth quaked and the huge, thick curtain in the temple tore apart on its own. Many dead people came back to life and wandered into town. Some people who witnessed these things realized Jesus was the Son of God. It takes a lot for some people to believe. What can you share about Jesus that might convince someone to believe in him?

Thank you, Lord, that I can show others that you are real.

²Suddenly, there was a powerful earthquake. An angel of the Lord had come down from heaven, rolled the stone away, and was sitting on it. ³He was as bright as lightning, and his clothes were as white as snow. ⁴The guards were so deathly afraid of him that they shook.

⁵The angel said to the women, "Don't be afraid! I know you're looking for Jesus, who was crucified. ⁶He's not here. He has been brought back to life as he said. Come, see the place where he was lying. ⁷Then go quickly, and tell his disciples that he has been brought back to life. He's going ahead of them into Galilee. There they will see him. Take note that I have told you."

⁸They hurried away from the tomb with fear and great joy and ran to tell his disciples.

⁹Suddenly, Jesus met them and greeted them. They went up to him, bowed down to worship him, and took hold of his feet.

¹⁰Then Jesus said to them, "Don't be afraid! Go, tell my followers to go to Galilee. There they will see me."

The Guards Report to the Chief Priests

¹¹While the women were on their way, some of the guards went into the city. They told the chief priests everything that had happened.

¹²The chief priests gathered together with the leaders and agreed on a plan. They gave the soldiers a large amount of money ¹³and told them to say that Jesus' disciples had come at night and had stolen his body while they were sleeping. ¹⁴They added, "If the governor hears about it, we'll take care of it, and you'll have nothing to worry about."

¹⁵The soldiers took the money and did as they were told. Their story has been spread among the Jewish people to this day.

Jesus Gives Instructions to the Disciples

¹⁶The eleven disciples went to the mountain in Galilee where Jesus had told them to go. ¹⁷When they saw him, they bowed down in worship, though some had doubts.

¹⁸When Jesus came near, he spoke to them. He said, "All authority in heaven and on earth has been given to me. ¹⁹So wherever you go, make disciples of all nations: Baptize them in the name of the Father, and of the Son, and of the Holy Spirit. ²⁰Teach them to do everything I have commanded you.

"And remember that I am always with you until the end of time."

Mark

This book was written by John Mark, a young man who wrote down the stories Peter told him about Jesus. John Mark described events from Jesus' life to the people of the Roman Empire. He wanted to show them what Jesus was like. Mark shows us that Jesus was a man of strength and courage who was also gentle and loving. Jesus is our Lord.

Headlines

This woman did something that will be remembered forever. See Mark 14:3-9.

Heart of a Healer

Jesus was no ordinary religious teacher. His miracles showed he was truly the Son of God. But Jesus' miracles showed more than his power. By healing so many sick and needy people, Jesus showed how much God cares about people.

Some, like the diseased man in Mark 1:40-45, were people no one would even touch! Jesus did more than feel sorry for such people. Jesus reached out and touched them to let them know he cared.

We may not be able to do miracles like Jesus did. But like Jesus, we can show that we care. We can pray for the sick. We can comfort the lonely or hurting. By reaching out to others, we show what Jesus is like.

Children Are Important

Adults sometimes treat children as if they don't matter. Mark 10:13-16 tells about a time when some people brought their little children to see Jesus. The disciples tried to send the children away. They thought Jesus was too busy and too important to be bothered with little kids. But to Jesus, children are just as important as anybody else. He called the children back and blessed them one by one.

When you feel that no one pays attention to you, try praying to Jesus. He always has time for you.

What's In It For Me?

What did Jesus do? . . .

JESUS, GOD'S SON, BECAME A HUMAN BEING FOR ME.

JESUS BROUGHT ME THE GOOD NEWS OF SALVATION.

JESUS HAS OFFERED TO FORGIVE MY SINS.

JESUS SUFFERED PAIN AND INSULTS FOR ME.

JESUS GAVE HIS LIFE FOR ME.

JESUS ROSE AGAIN TO GIVE ME ETERNAL LIFE.

JESUS WILL COME AGAIN TO TAKE ME TO HEAVEN.

HUMOR

Why did Jesus calm the storm?

He didn't want to rock the boat. (See Mark 4:35-41.)

How did Jesus feed five thousand?

He knew how to stretch a meal. (See Mark 6:30-44.)

Mark

John Prepares the Way—
Matthew 3:1-12; Luke 3:1-18

¹This is the beginning of the Good News about Jesus Christ, the Son of God. ²The prophet Isaiah wrote,

> "I am sending my messenger ahead of you
> to prepare the way for you."
> ³ "A voice cries out in the desert:
> 'Prepare the way for the Lord!
> Make his paths straight!' "

⁴John the Baptizer was in the desert telling people about a baptism of repentance[a] for the forgiveness of sins. ⁵All Judea and all the people of Jerusalem went to him. As they confessed their sins, he baptized them in the Jordan River.

⁶John was dressed in clothes made from camel's hair. He wore a leather belt around his waist and ate locusts and wild honey.

⁷He announced, "The one who comes after me is more powerful than I. I am not worthy to bend down and untie his sandal straps. ⁸I have baptized you with water, but he will baptize you with the Holy Spirit."

John Baptizes Jesus—
Matthew 3:13-17; Luke 3:21-22

⁹At that time Jesus came from Nazareth in Galilee and was baptized by John in the Jordan River. ¹⁰As Jesus came out of the water, he saw heaven split open and the Spirit coming down to him as a dove. ¹¹A voice from heaven said, "You are my Son, whom I love. I am pleased with you."

Satan Tempts Jesus—
Matthew 4:1-11; Luke 4:1-13

¹²At once the Spirit brought him into the desert, ¹³where he was tempted by Satan for 40 days. He was there with the wild animals, and the angels took care of him.

Calling of the First Disciples—
Matthew 4:18-22; Luke 5:1-11

¹⁴After John had been put in prison, Jesus went to Galilee and told people the Good News of God. ¹⁵He said, "The time has come, and the kingdom of God is near. Change the way you think and act, and believe the Good News."

¹⁶As he was going along the Sea of Galilee, he saw Simon and his brother Andrew. They were throwing a net into the sea because they were fishermen. ¹⁷Jesus said to them, "Come, follow me! I will teach you how to catch people instead of fish." ¹⁸They immediately left their nets and followed him.

¹⁹As Jesus went on a little farther, he saw James and John, the sons of Zebedee. They were in a boat preparing their nets ˌto go fishingˌ. ²⁰He immediately called them, and they left their father Zebedee and the hired men in the boat and followed Jesus.

ᵃ1:4 "Repentance" is turning to God with a complete change in the way a person thinks and acts.

Jesus Forces an Evil Spirit out of a Man—
Luke 4:31-37

²¹Then they went to Capernaum. On the next day of worship, Jesus went into the synagogue and began to teach. ²²The people were amazed at his teachings. Unlike their scribes, he taught them with authority.

²³At that time there was a man in the synagogue who was controlled by an evil spirit. He shouted, ²⁴"What do you want with us, Jesus from Nazareth? Have you come to destroy us? I know who you are—the Holy One of God!"

²⁵Jesus ordered the spirit, "Keep quiet, and come out of him!" ²⁶The evil spirit threw the man into convulsions and came out of him with a loud shriek.

²⁷Everyone was stunned. They said to each other, "What is this? This is a new teaching that has authority behind it! He gives orders to evil spirits, and they obey him."

²⁸The news about him spread quickly throughout the surrounding region of Galilee.

Jesus Cures Simon's Mother-in-Law and Many Others—
Matthew 8:14-18; Luke 4:38-41

²⁹After they left the synagogue, they went directly to the house of Simon and Andrew. James and John went with them. ³⁰Simon's mother-in-law was in bed with a fever. The first thing they did was to tell Jesus about her. ³¹Jesus went to her, took her hand, and helped her get up. The fever went away, and she prepared a meal for them.

³²In the evening, when the sun had set, people brought to him everyone who was sick and those possessed by demons. ³³The whole city had gathered at his door. ³⁴He cured many who were sick with various diseases and forced many demons out of people. However, he would not allow the demons to speak. After all, they knew who he was.

Spreading the Good News in Galilee—
Matthew 4:23-25; Luke 4:42-44

³⁵In the morning, long before sunrise, Jesus went to a place where he could be alone to pray. ³⁶Simon and his friends searched for him. ³⁷When they found him, they told him, "Everyone is looking for you."

³⁸Jesus said to them, "Let's go somewhere else, to the small towns that are nearby. I have to spread the Good News in them also. This is why I have come."

³⁹So he went to spread the Good News in the synagogues all over Galilee, and he forced demons out of people.

Jesus Cures a Man With a Skin Disease—
Matthew 8:1-4; Luke 5:12-14

⁴⁰Then a man with a serious skin disease came to him. The man fell to his knees and begged Jesus, "If you're willing, you can make me clean."ᵇ

⁴¹Jesus felt sorry for him, reached out, touched him, and said, "I'm willing. So be clean!"

⁴²Immediately, his skin disease went away, and he was clean.

⁴³Jesus sent him away at once and warned him, ⁴⁴"Don't tell anyone about this! Instead, show yourself to the priest. Then offer the sacrifices which Moses commanded as proof to people that you are clean."

⁴⁵When the man left, he began to talk freely. He spread his story so widely that

---

ᵇ 1:40 "Clean" refers to anything that Moses' Teachings say is presentable to God.

Jesus could no longer enter any city openly. Instead, he stayed in places where he could be alone. But people still kept coming to him from everywhere.

Jesus Forgives Sins—
Matthew 9:1-8; Luke 5:17-26

¹Several days later Jesus came back to Capernaum. The report went out that he was home. ²Many people had gathered. There was no room left, even in front of the door. Jesus was speaking God's word to them.

³Four men came to him carrying a paralyzed man. ⁴Since they could not bring him to Jesus because of the crowd, they made an opening in the roof over the place where Jesus was. Then they lowered the cot on which the paralyzed man was lying.

⁵When Jesus saw their faith, he said to the man, "Friend, your sins are forgiven."

⁶Some scribes were sitting there. They thought, ⁷"Why does he talk this way? He's dishonoring God. Who besides God can forgive sins?"

⁸At once, Jesus knew inwardly what they were thinking. He asked them, "Why do you have these thoughts? ⁹Is it easier to say to this paralyzed man, 'Your sins are forgiven,' or to say, 'Get up, pick up your cot, and walk'? ¹⁰I want you to know that the Son of Man has authority on earth to forgive sins." Then he said to the paralyzed man, ¹¹"I'm telling you to get up, pick up your cot, and go home!"

¹²The man got up, immediately picked up his cot, and walked away while everyone watched. Everyone was amazed and praised God, saying, "We have never seen anything like this."

Jesus Chooses Levi [Matthew] to Be a Disciple—
Matthew 9:9-13; Luke 5:27-32

¹³Jesus went to the seashore again. Large crowds came to him, and he taught them.

¹⁴When Jesus was leaving, he saw Levi, son of Alphaeus, sitting in a tax office. Jesus said to him, "Follow me!" So Levi got up and followed him.

¹⁵Later Jesus was having dinner at Levi's house. Many tax collectors and sinners who were followers of Jesus were eating with him and his disciples. ¹⁶When the scribes who were Pharisees saw him eating with sinners and tax collectors, they asked his disciples, "Why does he eat with tax collectors and sinners?"

¹⁷When Jesus heard that, he said to them, "Healthy people don't need a doctor; those who are sick do. I've come to call sinners, not people who think they have God's approval."

Good Morning, God
Mark 2:1-5

Four men lowered their paralyzed friend through the roof of a house where Jesus was teaching, so Jesus could heal him. Because of the great faith of the man's friends, Jesus healed the man. The four friends took a great risk to bring their friend to Jesus. When was a time you took a risk, big or small, to share Christ with a friend in need? Ask Jesus for the courage to take risks for him.

God, give me the courage to tell others about you.

Jesus Is Questioned About Fasting—
Matthew 9:14-17; Luke 5:33-39

¹⁸John's disciples and the Pharisees were fasting. Some people came to Jesus and said to him, "Why do John's disciples and the Pharisees' disciples fast, but your disciples don't?"

¹⁹Jesus replied, "Can wedding guests fast while the groom is still with them? As long as they have the groom with them, they cannot fast. ²⁰But the time will come when the groom will be taken away from them. Then they will fast.

²¹"No one patches an old coat with a new piece of cloth that will shrink. Otherwise, the new patch will shrink and rip away some of the old cloth, and the tear will become worse. ²²People don't pour new wine into old wineskins. If they do, the wine will make the skins burst, and both the wine and the skins will be ruined. Rather, new wine is to be poured into fresh skins."

Jesus Has Authority Over the Day of Worship—
Matthew 12:1-8; Luke 6:1-5

²³Once on a day of worship Jesus was going through the grainfields. As the disciples walked along, they began to pick the heads of grain.

²⁴The Pharisees asked him, "Look! Why are your disciples doing something that is not permitted on the day of worship?"

²⁵Jesus asked them, "Haven't you ever read what David did when he and his men were in need and were hungry? ²⁶Haven't you ever read how he went into the house of God when Abiathar was chief priest and ate the bread of the presence? He had no right to eat those loaves. Only the priests have that right. Haven't you ever read how he also gave some of it to his men?"

²⁷Then he added, "The day of worship was made for people, not people for the day of worship. ²⁸For this reason the Son of Man has authority over the day of worship."

Jesus Heals on the Day of Worship—
Matthew 12:9-15a; Luke 6:6-11

¹Jesus went into a synagogue again. A man who had a paralyzed hand was there. ²The people were watching Jesus closely. They wanted to see whether he would heal the man on the day of worship so that they could accuse him of doing something wrong.

³So he told the man with the paralyzed hand, "Stand in the center of the synagogue." ⁴Then he asked them, "Is it right to do good or to do evil on the day of worship, to give a person back his health or to let him die?"

But they were silent. ⁵Jesus was angry as he looked around at them. He was deeply hurt because their minds were closed. Then he told the man, "Hold out your hand." The man held it out, and his hand became normal again.

⁶The Pharisees left, and with Herod's followers they immediately plotted to kill Jesus.

Many People Are Cured—
Luke 6:17-19

⁷Jesus left with his disciples for the Sea of Galilee. A large crowd from Galilee, Judea, ⁸Jerusalem, Idumea, and from across the Jordan River, and from around Tyre and Sidon followed him. They came to him because they had heard about everything he was doing. ⁹Jesus told his disciples to have a boat ready so that the crowd would not crush him. ¹⁰He had cured so many that everyone with a disease rushed up to

him in order to touch him. ¹¹Whenever people with evil spirits saw him, they would fall down in front of him and shout, "You are the Son of God!" ¹²He gave them orders not to tell people who he was.

Jesus Appoints Twelve Apostles—
Matthew 10:1-4; Luke 6:13-16

¹³Jesus went up a mountain, called those whom he wanted, and they came to him. ¹⁴He appointed twelve whom he called apostles.ᵃ They were to accompany him and to be sent out by him to spread the Good News. ¹⁵They also had the authority to force demons out of people.

¹⁶He appointed these twelve: Simon (whom Jesus named Peter), ¹⁷James and his brother John (Zebedee's sons whom Jesus named Boanerges, which means "Thunderbolts"), ¹⁸Andrew, Philip, Bartholomew, Matthew, Thomas, James (son of Alphaeus), Thaddaeus, Simon the Zealot, ¹⁹and Judas Iscariot (who later betrayed Jesus).

Jesus Is Accused of Working With Beelzebul—
Matthew 12:22-32; Luke 11:14-23

²⁰Then Jesus went home. Another crowd gathered so that Jesus and his disciples could not even eat. ²¹When his family heard about it, they went to get him. They said, "He's out of his mind!"

²²The scribes who had come from Jerusalem said, "Beelzebul is in him," and "He forces demons out of people with the help of the ruler of demons."

²³Jesus called them together and used this illustration: "How can Satan force out Satan? ²⁴If a kingdom is divided against itself, that kingdom cannot last. ²⁵And if a household is divided against itself, that household will not last. ²⁶So if Satan rebels against himself and is divided, he cannot last. That will be the end of him.

²⁷"No one can go into a strong man's house and steal his property. First he must tie up the strong man. Then he can go through the strong man's house and steal his property.

²⁸"I can guarantee this truth: People will be forgiven for any sin or curse. ²⁹But whoever curses the Holy Spirit will never be forgiven. He is guilty of an everlasting sin." ³⁰Jesus said this because the scribes had said that he had an evil spirit.

The True Family of Jesus—
Matthew 12:46-50; Luke 8:19-21

³¹Then his mother and his brothers arrived. They stood outside and sent someone to ask him to come out. ³²The crowd sitting around Jesus told him, "Your mother and your brothers are outside looking for you."

³³He replied to them, "Who is my mother, and who are my brothers?" ³⁴Then looking at those who sat in a circle around him, he said, "Look, here are my mother and my brothers. ³⁵Whoever does what God wants is my brother and sister and mother."

A Story About a Farmer—
Matthew 13:1-23; Luke 8:4-15

¹Jesus began to teach again by the Sea of Galilee. A very large crowd gathered around him, so he got into a boat and sat in it. The boat was in the water while the entire crowd lined the shore. ²He used stories as illustrations to teach them many things.

ᵃ3:14 Some manuscripts and translations omit "whom he called apostles."

While he was teaching them, he said, ³"Listen! A farmer went to plant seed. ⁴Some seeds were planted along the road, and birds came and devoured them. ⁵Other seeds were planted on rocky ground, where there wasn't much soil. The plants sprouted quickly because the soil wasn't deep. ⁶When the sun came up, they were scorched. They didn't have any roots, so they withered. ⁷Other seeds were planted among thornbushes. The thornbushes grew up and choked them, and they didn't produce anything. ⁸But other seeds were planted on good ground, sprouted, and produced thirty, sixty, or one hundred times as much as was planted." ⁹He added, "Let the person who has ears listen!"

¹⁰When he was alone with his followers and the twelve apostles, they asked him about the stories.

¹¹Jesus replied to them, "The mystery about the kingdom of God has been given directly to you. To those on the outside, it is given in stories:

¹² 'They see clearly but don't perceive.
They hear clearly but don't understand.
They never return to me
    and are never forgiven.' "

¹³Jesus asked them, "Don't you understand this story? How, then, will you understand any of the stories I use as illustrations? ¹⁴"The farmer plants the word. ¹⁵Some people are like seeds that were planted along the road. Whenever they hear the word, Satan comes at once and takes away the word that was planted in them. ¹⁶Other people are like seeds that were planted on rocky ground. Whenever they hear the word, they accept it at once with joy. ¹⁷But they don't develop any roots. They last for a short time. When suffering or persecution comes along because of the word, they immediately fall from faith. ¹⁸Other people are like seeds planted among thornbushes. They hear the word, ¹⁹but the worries of life, the deceitful pleasures of riches, and the desires for other things take over. They choke the word so that it can't produce anything. ²⁰Others are like seeds planted on good ground. They hear the word, accept it, and produce crops—thirty, sixty, or one hundred times as much as was planted."

A Story About a Lamp

²¹Jesus said to them, "Does anyone bring a lamp into a room to put it under a basket or under a bed? Isn't it put on a lamp stand? ²²There is nothing hidden that will not be revealed. There is nothing kept secret that will not come to light. ²³Let the person who has ears listen!"

²⁴He went on to say, "Pay attention to what you're listening to! Knowledge will be measured out to you by the measure of attention you give. This is the way knowledge increases. ²⁵Those who understand these mysteries will be given more knowledge. However, some people don't understand these mysteries. Even what they understand will be taken away from them."

A Story About Seeds That Grow

²⁶Jesus said, "The kingdom of God is like a man who scatters seeds on the ground. ²⁷He sleeps at night and is awake during the day. The seeds sprout and grow, although the man doesn't know how. ²⁸The ground produces grain by itself. First the green blade appears, then the head, then the head full of grain. ²⁹As soon as the grain is ready, he cuts it with a sickle, because harvest time has come."

A Story About a Mustard Seed—
Matthew 13:31-32; Luke 13:18-19

³⁰Jesus asked, "How can we show what the kingdom of God is like? To what can we compare it? ³¹It's like a mustard seed planted in the ground. The mustard seed is one of the smallest seeds on earth. ³²However, when planted, it comes up and becomes taller than all the garden plants. It grows such large branches that birds can nest in its shade."

³³Jesus spoke God's word to them using many illustrations like these. In this way people could understand what he taught. ³⁴He did not speak to them without using an illustration. But when he was alone with his disciples, he explained everything to them.

Jesus Calms the Sea—
Matthew 8:23-27; Luke 8:22-25

³⁵That evening, Jesus said to his disciples, "Let's cross to the other side."

³⁶Leaving the crowd, they took Jesus along in a boat just as he was. Other boats were with him.

³⁷A violent windstorm came up. The waves were breaking into the boat so that it was quickly filling up. ³⁸But he was sleeping on a cushion in the back of the boat.

So they woke him up and said to him, "Teacher, don't you care that we're going to die?"

³⁹Then he got up, ordered the wind to stop, and said to the sea, "Be still, absolutely still!" The wind stopped blowing, and the sea became very calm.

⁴⁰He asked them, "Why are you such cowards? Don't you have any faith yet?"

⁴¹They were overcome with fear and asked each other, "Who is this man? Even the wind and the sea obey him!"

Jesus Cures a Demon-Possessed Man—
Matthew 8:28-34; Luke 8:26-39

5¹They arrived in the territory of the Gerasenes on the other side of the Sea of Galilee. ²As Jesus stepped out of the boat, a man came out of the tombs and met him. The man was controlled by an evil spirit ³and lived among the tombs. No one could restrain him any longer, not even with a chain. ⁴He had often been chained hand and foot. However, he snapped the chains off his hands and broke the chains from his feet. No one could control him. ⁵Night and day he was among the tombs and on the mountainsides screaming and cutting himself with stones.

⁶The man saw Jesus at a distance. So he ran to Jesus, bowed down in front of him, ⁷and shouted, "Why are you bothering me now, Jesus, Son of the Most High God? Swear to God that you won't torture me." ⁸He shouted this because Jesus said, "You evil spirit, come out of the man."

⁹Jesus asked him, "What is your name?"

He told Jesus, "My name is Legion [Six Thousand], because there are many of us." ¹⁰He begged Jesus not to send them out of the territory.

¹¹A large herd of pigs was feeding on a mountainside nearby. ¹²The demons begged him, "Send us into the pigs! Let us enter them!"

¹³Jesus let them do this. The evil spirits came out of the man and went into the pigs. The herd of about two thousand pigs rushed down the cliff into the sea and drowned.

¹⁴Those who took care of the pigs ran away. In the city and countryside they reported everything that had happened. So the people came to see what had happened.

¹⁵They came to Jesus and saw the man who had been possessed by the legion of demons. The man was sitting there dressed and in his right mind. The people were frightened. ¹⁶Those who saw this told what had happened to the demon-possessed man and the pigs. ¹⁷Then the people began to beg Jesus to leave their territory.

¹⁸As Jesus stepped into the boat, the man who had been demon-possessed begged him, "Let me stay with you." ¹⁹But Jesus would not allow it. Instead, he told the man, "Go home to your family, and tell them how much the Lord has done for you and how merciful he has been to you."

²⁰So the man left. He began to tell how much Jesus had done for him in the Ten Cities.ᵃ Everyone was amazed.

Jairus' Daughter and a Woman With Chronic Bleeding—
Matthew 9:18-26; Luke 8:40-56

²¹Jesus again crossed to the other side of the Sea of Galilee in a boat. A large crowd gathered around him by the seashore.

²²A synagogue leader named Jairus also arrived. When he saw Jesus, he quickly bowed down in front of him. ²³He begged Jesus, "My little daughter is dying. Come, lay your hands on her so that she may get well and live."

²⁴Jesus went with the man. A huge crowd followed Jesus and pressed him on every side.

²⁵In the crowd was a woman who had been suffering from chronic bleeding for twelve years. ²⁶Although she had been under the care of many doctors and had spent all her money, she had not been helped at all. Actually, she had become worse. ²⁷Since she had heard about Jesus, she came from behind in the crowd and touched his clothes. ²⁸She said, "If I can just touch his clothes, I'll get well." ²⁹Her bleeding stopped immediately. She felt cured from her illness.

³⁰At that moment Jesus felt power had gone out of him. He turned around in the crowd and asked, "Who touched my clothes?"

³¹His disciples said to him, "How can you ask, 'Who touched me,' when you see the crowd pressing you on all sides?"

³²But he kept looking around to see the woman who had done this. ³³The woman trembled with fear. She knew what had happened to her. So she quickly bowed in front of him and told him the whole truth.

³⁴Jesus told her, "Daughter, your faith has made you well. Go in peace! Be cured from your illness."

³⁵While Jesus was still speaking to her, some people came from the synagogue leader's home. They told the synagogue leader, "Your daughter has died. Why bother the teacher anymore?"

³⁶When Jesus overheard what they said, he told the synagogue leader, "Don't be afraid! Just believe."

³⁷Jesus allowed no one to go with him except Peter and the two brothers James and John. ³⁸When they came to the home of the synagogue leader, Jesus saw a noisy crowd there. People were crying and sobbing loudly. ³⁹When he came into the house, he asked them, "Why are you making so much noise and crying? The child isn't dead. She's just sleeping."

⁴⁰They laughed at him. So he made all of them go outside. Then he took the child's father, mother, and his three disciples and went to the child. ⁴¹Jesus took the child's hand and said to her, "Talitha, koum!" which means, "Little girl, I'm telling you to get up!"

ᵃ5:20 A federation of ten Greek city states east and west of the Jordan River.

⁴²The girl got up at once and started to walk. (She was twelve years old.) They were astonished.

⁴³Jesus ordered them not to let anyone know about this. He also told them to give the little girl something to eat.

Nazareth Rejects Jesus—
Matthew 13:54-58; Luke 4:14-30

¹Jesus left that place and went to his hometown. His disciples followed him. ²When the day of worship came, he began to teach in the synagogue. He amazed many who heard him. They asked, "Where did this man get these ideas? Who gave him this kind of wisdom and the ability to do such great miracles? ³Isn't this the carpenter, the son of Mary, and the brother of James, Joseph, Judas, and Simon? Aren't his sisters here with us?" So they took offense at him.

⁴But Jesus told them, "The only place a prophet isn't honored is in his hometown, among his relatives, and in his own house." ⁵He couldn't work any miracles there except to lay his hands on a few sick people and cure them. ⁶Their unbelief amazed him.

Jesus Sends Out the Twelve—
Matthew 10:5-42; Luke 9:1-6

Then Jesus went around to the villages and taught.

⁷He called the twelve apostles, sent them out two by two, and gave them authority over evil spirits. ⁸He instructed them to take nothing along on the trip except a walking stick. They were not to take any food, a traveling bag, or money in their pockets. ⁹They could wear sandals but could not take along a change of clothes.

¹⁰He told them, "Whenever you go into a home, stay there until you're ready to leave that place. ¹¹Wherever people don't welcome you or listen to you, leave and shake the dust from your feet as a warning to them."

¹²So the apostles went and told people that they should turn to God and change the way they think and act. ¹³They also forced many demons out of people and poured oil on many who were sick to cure them.

Recalling John's Death—
Matthew 14:1-12; Luke 9:7-9

¹⁴King Herod heard about Jesus, because Jesus' name had become well-known. Some people were saying, "John the Baptizer has come back to life. That's why he has the power to perform these miracles." ¹⁵Others said, "He is Elijah." Still others said, "He is a prophet like one of the other prophets." ¹⁶But when Herod heard about it, he said, "I had John's head cut off, and he has come back to life!"

¹⁷Herod had sent men who had arrested John, tied him up, and put him in prison. Herod did that for Herodias, whom he had married. (She used to be his brother Philip's wife.) ¹⁸John had been telling Herod, "It's not right for you to be married to your brother's wife."

¹⁹So Herodias held a grudge against John and wanted to kill him. But she wasn't allowed to do it ²⁰because Herod was afraid of John. Herod knew that John was a fair and holy man, so he protected him. When he listened to John, he would become very disturbed, and yet he liked to listen to him.

²¹An opportunity finally came on Herod's birthday. Herod gave a dinner for his top officials, army officers, and the most important people of Galilee. ²²His daughter, that is, Herodias' daughter, came in and danced. Herod and his guests were delighted with

her. The king told the girl, "Ask me for anything you want, and I'll give it to you." ²³He swore an oath to her: "I'll give you anything you ask for, up to half of my kingdom."

²⁴So she went out and asked her mother, "What should I ask for?"

Her mother said, "Ask for the head of John the Baptizer."

²⁵So the girl hurried back to the king with her request. She said, "I want you to give me the head of John the Baptizer on a platter at once."

²⁶The king deeply regretted his promise. But because of his oath and his guests, he didn't want to refuse her. ²⁷Immediately, the king sent a guard and ordered him to bring John's head. The guard cut off John's head in prison. ²⁸Then he brought the head on a platter and gave it to the girl, and the girl gave it to her mother.

²⁹When John's disciples heard about this, they came for his body and laid it in a tomb.

Jesus Feeds Five Thousand—
Matthew 14:13-21; Luke 9:10-17; John 6:1-14

³⁰The apostles gathered around Jesus. They reported to him everything they had done and taught. ³¹So he said to them, "Let's go to a place where we can be alone to rest for a while." Many people were coming and going, and Jesus and the apostles didn't even have a chance to eat.

³²So they went away in a boat to a place where they could be alone. ³³But many people saw them leave and recognized them. The people ran from all the cities and arrived ahead of them. ³⁴When Jesus got out of the boat, he saw a large crowd and felt sorry for them. They were like sheep without a shepherd. So he spent a lot of time teaching them.

³⁵When it was late, his disciples came to him. They said, "No one lives around here, and it's already late. ³⁶Send the people to the closest farms and villages to buy themselves something to eat."

³⁷Jesus replied, "You give them something to eat."

They said to him, "Should we go and spend about a year's wages on bread to feed them?"

³⁸He said to them, "How many loaves do you have? Go and see."

When they found out, they told him, "Five loaves of bread and two fish."

³⁹Then he ordered all of them to sit down in groups on the green grass. ⁴⁰They sat down in groups of hundreds and fifties.

⁴¹After he took the five loaves and the two fish, he looked up to heaven and blessed the food. He broke the loaves apart and kept giving them to the disciples to give to the people. He also gave pieces of the two fish to everyone. ⁴²All of them ate as much as they wanted. ⁴³When they picked up the leftover pieces, they filled twelve baskets with bread and fish. ⁴⁴There were 5,000 men who had eaten the bread.

Jesus Walks on the Sea—
Matthew 14:22-36; John 6:15-21

⁴⁵Jesus quickly made his disciples get into a boat and cross to Bethsaida ahead of him while he sent the people away. ⁴⁶After saying goodbye to them, he went up a mountain to pray. ⁴⁷When evening came, the boat was in the middle of the sea, and he was alone on the land.

⁴⁸Jesus saw that they were in a lot of trouble as they rowed, because they were going against the wind. Between three and six o'clock in the morning, he came to them. He was walking on the sea. He wanted to pass by them. ⁴⁹When they saw him

walking on the sea, they thought, "It's a ghost!" and they began to scream. ⁵⁰All of them saw him and were terrified.

Immediately, he said, "Calm down! It's me. Don't be afraid!" ⁵¹He got into the boat with them, and the wind stopped blowing. The disciples were astounded. ⁵²(They didn't understand what had happened with the loaves of bread. Instead, their minds were closed.)

⁵³They crossed the sea, came to shore at Gennesaret, and anchored there.

⁵⁴As soon as they stepped out of the boat, the people recognized Jesus. ⁵⁵They ran all over the countryside and began to carry the sick on cots to any place where they heard he was. ⁵⁶Whenever he would go into villages, cities, or farms, people would put their sick in the marketplaces. They begged him to let them touch the edge of his clothes. Everyone who touched his clothes was made well.

Jesus Challenges the Pharisees' Traditions—
Matthew 15:1-20

7 ¹The Pharisees and some scribes who had come from Jerusalem gathered around Jesus. ²They saw that some of his disciples were unclean*ᵃ* because they ate without washing their hands.

³(The Pharisees, like all other Jewish people, don't eat unless they have properly washed their hands. They follow the traditions of their ancestors. ⁴When they come from the marketplace, they don't eat unless they have washed first. They have been taught to follow many other rules. For example, they must also wash their cups, jars, brass pots, and dinner tables*ᵇ*.)

⁵The Pharisees and the scribes asked Jesus, "Why don't your disciples follow the traditions taught by our ancestors? They are unclean because they don't wash their hands before they eat!"

⁶Jesus told them, "Isaiah was right when he prophesied about you hypocrites in Scripture:

'These people honor me with their lips,
   but their hearts are far from me.
7 Their worship of me is pointless,
   because their teachings are rules made by humans.'

⁸"You abandon the commandments of God to follow human traditions." ⁹He added, "You have no trouble rejecting the commandments of God in order to keep your own traditions! ¹⁰For example, Moses said, 'Honor your father and your mother' and 'Whoever curses father or mother must be put to death.' ¹¹But you say, 'If a person tells his father or mother that whatever he might have used to help them is *corban* (that is, an offering to God), ¹²he no longer has to do anything for his father or mother.' ¹³Because of your traditions you have destroyed the authority of God's word. And you do many other things like that."

¹⁴Then he called the crowd again and said to them, "Listen to me, all of you, and try to understand! ¹⁵Nothing that goes into a person from the outside can make him unclean. It's what comes out of a person that makes him unclean. ¹⁶Let the person who has ears listen!"*ᶜ*

¹⁷When he had left the people and gone home, his disciples asked him about this illustration.

¹⁸Jesus said to them, "Don't you understand? Don't you know that whatever goes

---

*ᵃ7:2 "Unclean" refers to anything that Moses' Teachings say is not presentable to God. *ᵇ7:4 Some manuscripts and translations omit "and dinner tables." *ᶜ7:16 Some manuscripts and translations omit this verse.

Women's World

Demons / Mark 7:24-30

The Bible says demons, or "evil spirits," are real. They are angels who followed Satan when he rebelled against God (Matthew 25:41). Demons like to make people suffer. When Jesus found people oppressed by demons, he sent the demons away. Jesus is more powerful than evil spirits; he can protect Christians from them.

Demons have long been associated with the worship of false gods and goddesses. Today, people involved with the occult are often confused by demons. That's why Christians should stay away from things like Ouija boards and psychics. Christians should have nothing to do with evil spirits or with people who may be involved with them.

into a person from the outside can't make him unclean? [19]It doesn't go into his thoughts but into his stomach and then into a toilet." (By saying this, Jesus declared all foods acceptable.) [20]He continued, "It's what comes out of a person that makes him unclean. [21]Evil thoughts, sexual sins, stealing, murder, [22]adultery, greed, wickedness, cheating, shameless lust, envy, cursing, arrogance, and foolishness come from within a person. [23]All these evils come from within and make a person unclean."

The Faith of a Greek Woman—
Matthew 15:21-31

[24]Jesus left that place and went to the territory of Tyre. He didn't want anyone to know that he was staying in a house there. However, it couldn't be kept a secret.

[25]A woman whose little daughter had an evil spirit heard about Jesus. She went to him and bowed down. [26]The woman happened to be Greek, born in Phoenicia in Syria. She asked him to force the demon out of her daughter.

[27]Jesus said to her, "First, let the children eat all they want. It's not right to take the children's food and throw it to the dogs."

[28]She answered him, "Lord, even the dogs under the table eat some of the children's scraps."

[29]Jesus said to her, "Because you have said this, go! The demon has left your daughter."

[30]The woman went home and found the little child lying on her bed, and the demon was gone.

Jesus Cures a Deaf Man

[31]Jesus then left the neighborhood of Tyre. He went through Sidon and the territory of the Ten Cities[d] to the Sea of Galilee.

[32]Some people brought to him a man who was deaf and who also had a speech defect. They begged Jesus to lay his hand on him. [33]Jesus took him away from the crowd to be alone with him. He put his fingers into the man's ears, and after spitting, he touched the man's tongue. [34]Then he looked up to heaven, sighed, and said to the man, "Ephphatha!" which means, "Be opened!" [35]At once the man could hear and talk normally.

[36]Jesus ordered the people not to tell anyone. But the more he ordered them, the more they spread the news. [37]Jesus completely amazed the people. They said, "He has done everything well. He makes the deaf hear and the mute talk."

Jesus Feeds Four Thousand—
Matthew 15:32-39

8 [1]About that time there was once again a large crowd with nothing to eat. Jesus called his disciples and said to them, [2]"I feel sorry for the people. They have been with me three days now and have nothing to eat. [3]If I send them home before they've eaten, they will become exhausted on the road. Some of them have come a long distance."

[4]His disciples asked him, "Where could anyone get enough bread to feed these people in this place where no one lives?"

[5]Jesus asked them, "How many loaves of bread do you have?"

They answered, "Seven."

[6]He ordered the crowd to sit down on the ground. He took the seven loaves and gave thanks to God. Then he broke the bread and gave it to his disciples to serve to the people. [7]They also had a few small fish. He blessed them and said that the fish should also be served to the people. [8]The people ate as much as they wanted. The disciples picked up the leftover pieces and filled seven large baskets. [9]About four thousand people were there. Then he sent the people on their way.

[10]After that, Jesus and his disciples got into a boat and went into the region of Dalmanutha.

The Pharisees Ask For a Sign From Heaven—
Matthew 16:1-4

[11]The Pharisees went to Jesus and began to argue with him. They tested him by demanding that he perform a miraculous sign from heaven.

[12]With a deep sigh he asked, "Why do these people demand a sign? I can guarantee this truth: If these people are given a sign, it will be far different than what they want!"

[13]Then he left them there.

The Yeast of the Pharisees—
Matthew 16:5-12

He got into a boat again and crossed to the other side of the Sea of Galilee. [14]The disciples had forgotten to take any bread along and had only one loaf with them in the boat.

---

[d]7:31 A federation of ten Greek city states east and west of the Jordan River.

¹⁵Jesus warned them, "Be careful! Watch out for the yeast of the Pharisees and the yeast of Herod!"

¹⁶They had been discussing with one another that they didn't have any bread.

¹⁷Jesus knew what they were saying and asked them, "Why are you discussing the fact that you don't have any bread? Don't you understand yet? Don't you catch on? Are your minds closed? ¹⁸Are you blind and deaf? Don't you remember? ¹⁹When I broke the five loaves for the five thousand, how many baskets did you fill with left-over pieces?"

They told him, "Twelve."

²⁰"When I broke the seven loaves for the four thousand, how many large baskets did you fill with leftover pieces?"

They answered him, "Seven."

²¹He asked them, "Don't you catch on yet?"

Jesus Gives Sight to a Blind Man

²²As they came to Bethsaida, some people brought a blind man to Jesus. They begged Jesus to touch him. ²³Jesus took the blind man's hand and led him out of the village. He spit into the man's eyes and placed his hands on him. Jesus asked him, "Can you see anything?"

²⁴The man looked up and said, "I see people. They look like trees walking around."

²⁵Then Jesus placed his hands on the man's eyes a second time, and the man saw clearly. His sight was normal again. He could see everything clearly even at a distance. ²⁶Jesus told him when he sent him home, "Don't go into the village."

Peter Declares His Belief About Jesus—
Matthew 16:13-20; Luke 9:18-21

²⁷Then Jesus and his disciples went to the villages around Caesarea Philippi. On the way he asked his disciples, "Who do people say I am?"

²⁸They answered him, "Some say you are John the Baptizer, others Elijah, still others one of the prophets."

²⁹He asked them, "But who do you say I am?"

Peter answered him, "You are the Messiah!"

³⁰He ordered them not to tell anyone about him.

Jesus Foretells That He Will Die and Come Back to Life—
Matthew 16:21-23; Luke 9:22

³¹Then he began to teach them that the Son of Man would have to suffer a lot. He taught them that he would be rejected by the leaders, the chief priests, and the scribes. He would be killed, but after three days he would come back to life. ³²He told them very clearly what he meant.

Peter took him aside and objected to this. ³³Jesus turned, looked at his disciples, and objected to what Peter said. Jesus said, "Get out of my way, Satan! You aren't thinking the way God thinks but the way humans think."

What It Means to Follow Jesus—
Matthew 16:24-28; Luke 9:23-27

³⁴Then Jesus called the crowd to himself along with his disciples. He said to them, "Those who want to follow me must say no to the things they want, pick up their crosses, and follow me. ³⁵Those who want to save their lives will lose them. But those who lose their lives for me and for the Good News will save them. ³⁶What good does

it do for people to win the whole world yet lose their lives? ³⁷Or what should a person give in exchange for life? ³⁸If people are ashamed of me and what I say in this unfaithful and sinful generation, the Son of Man will be ashamed of those people when he comes with the holy angels in his Father's glory."

9 ¹He said to them, "I can guarantee this truth: Some people who are standing here will not die until they see the kingdom of God arrive with power."

Moses and Elijah Appear With Jesus—
Matthew 17:1-8; Luke 9:28-36

²After six days Jesus took only Peter, James, and John and led them up a high mountain where they could be alone.

Jesus' appearance changed in front of them. ³His clothes became dazzling white, whiter than anyone on earth could bleach them. ⁴Then Elijah and Moses appeared to them and were talking with Jesus.

⁵Peter said to Jesus, "Rabbi, it's good that we're here. Let's put up three tents—one for you, one for Moses, and one for Elijah." ⁶(Peter didn't know how to respond. He and the others were terrified.)

⁷Then a cloud overshadowed them. A voice came out of the cloud and said, "This is my Son, whom I love. Listen to him!"

⁸Suddenly, as they looked around, they saw no one with them but Jesus.

⁹On their way down the mountain, Jesus ordered them not to tell anyone what they had seen. They were to wait until the Son of Man had come back to life. ¹⁰They kept in mind what he said but argued among themselves what he meant by "come back to life." ¹¹So they asked him, "Don't the scribes say that Elijah must come first?"

¹²Jesus said to them, "Elijah is coming first and will put everything in order again. But in what sense was it written that the Son of Man must suffer a lot and be treated shamefully? ¹³Indeed, I can guarantee that Elijah has come. Yet, people treated him as they pleased, as Scripture says about him."

Jesus Cures a Demon-Possessed Boy—
Matthew 17:14-20; Luke 9:37-43a

¹⁴When they came to the other disciples, they saw a large crowd around them. Some scribes were arguing with them. ¹⁵All the people were very surprised to see Jesus and ran to welcome him.

¹⁶Jesus asked the scribes, "What are you arguing about with them?"

¹⁷A man in the crowd answered, "Teacher, I brought you my son. He is possessed by a spirit that won't let him talk. ¹⁸Whenever the spirit brings on a seizure, it throws him to the ground. Then he foams at the mouth, grinds his teeth, and becomes exhausted. I asked your disciples to force the spirit out, but they didn't have the power to do it."

¹⁹Jesus said to them, "You unbelieving generation! How long must I be with you? How long must I put up with you? Bring him to me!"

²⁰They brought the boy to him. As soon as the spirit saw Jesus, it threw the boy into convulsions. He fell on the ground, rolled around, and foamed at the mouth.

²¹Jesus asked his father, "How long has he been like this?"

The father replied, "He has been this way since he was a child. ²²The demon has often thrown him into fire or into water to destroy him. If it's possible for you, put yourself in our place, and help us!"